Constitutional Development
and
National Movement of India

Freedom Movement, Acts and Indian Constitution

For Students of B.A., B.A. (Honours) and Aspirants of various Competitive Examinations like IAS, PCS etc.

R. C. AGARWAL
M.A. (Pol. Science & Hist.) LL.B, H.E.S.(I)
Principal (Retd.) Government College
Naraingarh, Haryana

***Revised by*:**
Dr. MAHESH BHATNAGAR

S.CHAND
PUBLISHING

S Chand And Company Limited
(ISO 9001 Certified Company)

S Chand And Company Limited
(ISO 9001 Certified Company)
Head Office: D-92, Sector–2, Noida – 201301, U.P. (India), Ph. 91-120-4682700
Registered Office: A-27, 2nd Floor, Mohan Co-operative Industrial Estate,
New Delhi – 110 044, Phone: 011-49731800
www.**schandpublishing.com**; e-mail: **info@schandpublishing.com**

Marketing Offices:

Chennai	:	Ph: 23632120; chennai@schandpublishing.com
Guwahati	:	Ph: 2738811, 2735640; guwahati@schandpublishing.com
Hyderabad	:	Ph: 40186018; hyderabad@schandpublishing.com
Jalandhar	:	Ph: 4645630; jalandhar@schandpublishing.com
Kolkata	:	Ph: 23357458, 23353914; kolkata@schandpublishing.com
Lucknow	:	Ph: 4003633; lucknow@schandpublishing.com
Mumbai	:	Ph: 25000297; mumbai@schandpublishing.com
Patna	:	Ph: 4011400; patna@schandpublishing.com

First Edition 1994
Subsequent Editions and Reprints 1996, 97, 98, 2000, 2002, 2005, 2007, 2009, 2010, 2013, 2014, 2016, 2021, 2022 (Twice), 2023

Reprint 2026

ISBN: 978-81-219-0565-7 **Product Code:** H5CNS41PLSC10ENAO0XO

PRINTED IN INDIA

By Shri Shyamlal Printing Press Private Limited, Plot 20/4, Site-IV, Industrial Area Sahibabad, Ghaziabad–201 010 and Published by S Chand And Company Limited, A-27, 2nd Floor, Mohan Co-operative Industrial Estate, New Delhi – 110 044.

PREFACE TO THE FIFTEENTH REVISED EDITION

The present edition of the book has been extensively revised with the addition of new chapters and incorporation of up-to-date changes and developments that have taken place in the constitutional development.

Multiple choice questions have been added at the end of each chapter in order to make the book more useful for those who are studying in Graduation Courses and appearing in different competitive examinations.

We hope that the book in its new format with all the improvements will enhance its utility.

Suggestions for improvements are welcome.

Dr. MAHESH BHATNAGAR

PREFACE TO THE FIRST EDITION

This book consists of three parts clearly. While the Charter Acts have been again included by many universities, the author had little option but to include them. Therefore these "Charter Acts" have been given in Part I, which had been excluded by the author formerly.

Part II includes 'Constitutional Development and National Movement'. In this part, I have tried to show the march of British imperialism and the resistance by the Indians. Before Warren Hastings arrived, there was a severe famine in Bengal in 1970. Therefore, Swami Shivanand made a heroic struggle against the British rule. It has been mentioned in '*Ushakal*' by Hari Narain Apte and Shri Bankim Chandra Chatterji's very famous book '*Anand Matha*'. It goes to the credit of Tipu Sultan that he resisted the attempts of the British imperialists tooth and nail. Had the Marathas or Nizam of Hyderabad sided with him, he would have won. While the Nizam of Hyderabad (Deccan) was a friend of the British, the Marathas led by Nana Hananis waited for the outcome, so Tipu Sultan was alone in resisting the British imperialists.

The British imperialists defeated Tipu Sultan. The Marathas resisted the British imperialists tooth and nail very heroically but they were defeated ultimately by the British. Last resistance was offered by the Sikhs after the death of Maharaja Ranjit Singh in 1845. Though the command was divided, yet the Sikhs offered gallant resistance. By 1849 the British had conquered the whole of India. While the Marathas had fought four wars to resist the British imperialists, the Sikhs fought two wars to resist the British imperialists.

Then there was the Ist War of Independence in 1857. The war was fought violently under the leadership of Bahadurshah Zafar. Though he was already 85, yet he assumed the command when the soldiers from Meerut insisted. But after sometime the Ist War of Independence met its doom.

The birth of the Indian National Congress in 1885 at first was welcomed by the Viceroy but with the passage of Russian menace, did not welcome it. The third President of the Indian National Congress was Badruddin Tayybji. He invited Sir Sayyad Ahmad Khan to join the Indian National Congress but he declined the invitation. Then Shri Lokmanya Bal Gangadhar Tilak clamoured for Swadeshi. He began the festival of Shivaji, the harbinger of Swaraj and the Ganesh festival. He used both the festivals to bring political conciousness or awakening among the masses. He often use to say, "*If Swaraj was possible in the time of Shivaji, why not now ?* Therefore he gave the famous slogan of *Swaraj* to the people. He often said, "*Swaraj is our birth-right and we will have it.*"

It must be noted that Lokmanya Tilak was pro-Hindu but not anti-Muslim because he brought about Lucknow pact between the Muslim League and the Congress in 1916. Jinnah served him in one case against the British as early as in 1908. Maulana Abul Kalam Azad, Mohd. Ali and Shaukat Ali, the leading Muslim leaders of their time were convinced about the bonafide of Lokmanya Tilak.

It goes to the credit of Gandhiji that he combined the methods of Tilak and Gokhale both. Alas ! Tilak died a pre-mature death on Ist August, 1920. Had he lived, he would have supported the Non-co-operation Movement of Gandhiji but Mohd. Ali and Shaukat Ali supported Gandhiji in his objective and toured the whole country in order to arouse the masses from their political slumber as hinted by Tilak to Gandhiji during his illness before his death. Gandhiji started the Civil Disobedience Movement in 1930 and Quit India Movement in 1942. He won the *Swaraj* in 1947.

I have given in the 1st Appendix that Gandhiji had to agree to the partition of the country because Jawaharlal Nehru and Sardar Vallabh Bhai Patel supported it. When Khan Abdul Ghaffar Khan objected to it, Mahatma Gandhi hinted that both Nehru and Patel supported it. He said in the meeting of the Congress Working Committee that both Nehru and Patel were tried leaders and if the Congress Working Committee does not support them, they will have to change the leaders. So only Maulana Azad, Khan Abdul Ghaffar Khan and Purshottam Tandon voted against the partition, others supported it. So the resolution was carried by majority.

In the IInd Appendix, I have explained that Gandhiji undertook the fast for a cause. Indira Gandhi used to say that *Satyagrah* and Non-violence are as ancient in this country as the hills but before him, these two were being used for religious purposes. It goes to the credit of Gandhiji that he converted Non-violence into a political weapon because Gandhiji, Nehru and Patel were convinced that India could get independence only by non-violent means. So was convinced Khan Abdul Ghaffar Khan who converted the Pathans into non-violence and started their Khudai Khidmatgar movement.

I am deeply indebted to the eminent authors whose work I had the privilege to quote. I am also grateful to Mr. Mukesh Kumar who has typed the sheets without delay. In the end I am grateful to the publishers, proof-reader and the press for bringing out the book as early as possible without mistakes.

If any reader gives some useful suggestions for improving the book further, I assure him that these would be incorporated in the next edition.

R.C. Agarwal
Principal (Retd.)

Arun Bhawan
New Railway Road
(Opposite Union Bank of India)
Gurgaon-122001 (Haryana)

CONTENTS

PART I
CONSTITUTIONAL DEVELOPMENT OF INDIA

PART II
NATIONAL MOVEMENT
(STRUGGLE FOR FREEDOM AGAINST FOREIGN RULE)

PART III

MODERN INDIAN CONSTITUTION

(GREATEST INSTRUMENT OF LEGAL POLITICAL SYSTEM)

PART – I

CONSTITUTIONAL DEVELOPMENT OF INDIA

1. Regulating Act
2. Pitt's India Act
3. Charter Act of 1793
4. Charter Act of 1813
5. Constitutional Development Upto 1853
6. Charter Act of 1853

1

CHAPTER

Regulating Act

> *"Lord North's reforms were one-sided and were limited to the administrative machinery of the company in London."*
> **— A. C. Bannerjee**

The Regulating Act, 1773 is of great constitutional importance. It was passed by Lord North's Government. It is an Act which definitely recognised the political functions of the Company. It asserted for the first time the rights of the Parliament to dictate the form of Government which was considered till then the private possession of the company. It was the first of a long series of Parliamentary statutes that altered the form of Government in India. The Act provided the basis of the Anglo-India constitution.

CIRCUMSTANCES FOR THE ENACTMENT OF THE ACT OR CAUSES WHICH NECESSITATED THE PASSING OF THE ACT

Many factors or circumstances or causes were responsible for the enactment of the Regulating Act, 1773. Here we are discussing some of the important causes which necessitated the passing of the Regulating Act by the British Parliament. Some of the causes were as follows –

1. Agitation for Parliamentary control over Indian affairs. Whatever rights the Company had acquired till 1694 were granted by the Crown through Royal Charters. It enjoyed the exclusive right of trading with India. The monopolistic rights of the Company gave rise to jealousy and public resentment in England. The demand for free-trade became so strong that the Parliament by an Act, decided to revoke the monopoly and allow every British subject to trade in the East till prohibited by a Parliamentary law. The Company, however, averted the danger by obliging British Government with enormous loans. The move for free trade was shelved for some time not without making it clear that the independence of the Company was subordinate to the supremacy of the Parliament. Three British merchants continued to demand Parliament's intervention in the affairs of the Company. The active and direct control of the British Parliament over Indian affairs began from 1773 with the enactment of the Regulating Act.

2. Constitutional Difficulties. The battles of Plassey and Buxar fought in 1757 and 1764 respectively, established the supremacy of the Company over Bengal, Bihar and Orissa. A big chunk of Indian territory came under the Company's possession. The Company acquired the Diwani (the right to collect revenue) and the Nizamat (the right to administer criminal justice) and became a territorial power. Its quasi-sovereign position created a constitutional difficulty. The English Constitution did not permit anybody to possess territory except in the name of the Crown. Hence, the British public insisted on the taking over of Company's territories by the Crown. But such a proposition gave rise to another knotty problem. While the Company could continue to act in the capacity of the Dewan of the Mughal Emperor, the Crown could not take that subordinate role upon himself. Secondly, direct control of the Crown over the Provinces of Bengal, Bihar and Orissa was likely to displease the Mughal Emperor, the Marathas and other native 'Rajas'. Thirdly, right to property was considered to be legitimate and sacred in England in the 18th century; and Indian territories were in no way different from the private property of the Company. Hence, State control over the Indian territories was considered repugnant to the principle of private property. Yet leaving the Company free of State control was also not advisable because Company's misrule in India was likely to bring a bad name to Great Britain. Keeping the aforesaid difficulties in view, the Parliament decided to let the Company keep its territorial gains but to act as an agent of the British Government.

3. Bribe, private trade and gifts to the Company's servants. The British goods were either totally exempted from paying local taxes or were charged only token excise duties. The servants of the Company began to abuse their privileges. They earned a fortune for themselves by allowing the goods of Indian traders to pass without paying any tax whatsover. They also began to accept presents from Indian businessmen and other civilians in return for favours done to them. They filled their pockets with ill-gotten wealth. When they returned to England with their booty, they lived luxuriously like 'Indian Nawabs'. Their fat purse enabled them to capture parliamentary seats and to exert their influence on the policies of the British Government. According to Macaulay: "*The human mind was horror struck at the way in which they had got the money, and at the way they spent it.*" Naturally everybody in England grew jealous of them and began to agitate for immediate State control over Company's affairs.

4. The pitiable condition of the people of Bengal. The system of Double Government in Bengal led to a reign of corruption and oppression in the Province. Nobody cared for the welfare of the people. If an aggrieved person approached the officers of the Nawab with the complaint, he was told that the Nawab was helpless and that the real power was vested in the Company. If the same person appealed to the good offices of the Company, he was put off with the excuse that the administrative power lay with the Nawab and that the Company was nowhere in the picture. According to Mr. Lyall, "*In the Double Government the magistracy, the police, the revenue officials being diverse bodies working upon different systems with conflicting interests under no common head, vied with each other in misgovernment; there was no positive law and there was very little justice in the country.*" As told above the administration of the 'English Nawabs' was badly corrupt. The sufferings of the people were aggravated by the famine that broke out in 1770. The famine reduced the population of Bengal by one-fifth. The starving people migrated to other Provinces, which meant a huge loss of revenue to the Company. The Company in its turn followed the most cruel policy of raising the prices of the daily necessities and enhancing the taxes. The piteous cry of famine-stricken Bengal reached the British people and roused their sympathies. The public opinion in England swung in favour of a thorough investigation into the causes of the famine.

5. Defeat of the Company. In 1769, the Company suffered an inglorious defeat at the hands of Haider Ali, the Sultan of Mysore who also compelled the Madras Government to sign a treaty on his own terms. When this news reached England, the British Government as well as the public was greatly shocked. England took this defeat as a severe below to her prestige.

6. Apprehensions about the failure of the Company. When in 1765 the Company acquired the Diwani of Bengal, Bihar and Orissa, the joy of the Directors knew no bounds. Clive speculated that Company's gross income from the land alone would touch the figure of £ 5,000,000 while its net profit would not be less than £ 1,650,000. Encouraged by Clive's report, the Directors raised the dividends from 6% to 10% and soon after to $12^1/_2$%. The demand for Company's shares went up suddenly, but as soon as the rumour went round that it was all a michievous deception and that the Company was heading towards bankruptcy, the shareholders in sheer fright began to demand quick action by the 'Parliament to safeguard their interests.'

7. Evils of Dual System. The dual control on the three Provinces of Bengal, Bihar and Orissa wrecked the economic life of the people. The unnatural division of the administration into two halves produced confusion, chaos and corruption. The servants of the Company behaved in the most irresponsible manner. "*The divided and complicated authority of Dual Government,*" *wrote Verelst,* "*gave rise to oppression and intrigues unknown in any other period.*" Mr. Richard Brecher wrote: "It must give pain to Englishmen that since the accession of the Dewani to the Company, the condition of the people of the country had been worse than it was before." *Sir Lewis said*: "*No civilised Government ever existed on the face of this earth which was more corrupt, more perfidious and more rapacious than the Government of East India Company from 1765 to 1772.*" The pathetic condition of the Indians under the Company's rule naturally drew the attention of the British public and provoked the Parliament to mend the Company's affairs through legislation.

8. Non-payment of an annuity of £ 40 lakhs as tribute by the East India Company to the British Exchequer. Since the day the Company acquired the Diwani of three Provinces in India, the British Statesmen had been anxious to share the huge profits of the Company. The Parliament by an Act passed in 1767 required the Company to pay an annual sum of £ 400,000 for its monopolistic privileges. The Company continued to pay this huge sum till 1772, after which it failed to pay because of its weak financial position. Non-payment of this annual sum gave an excuse to the Parliament to intervene in the affairs of the Company.

9. Company's request for a loan. When the Company was driven to a financial crisis, it approached the British Government for a loan. The British Government was already on the look out for such an excuse to probe into the Company's affairs. Thus, the Company's application for a loan of one million led to the Parliamentary intervention.

THE PREAMBLE OF THE ACT

'Whereas the several powers and authorities granted by Charters of the United Company of Merchants of England trading to the East India have been found by experience, not to have sufficient force and efficacy to prevent various abuses which have prevailed in the government and administration of the affairs of the said United Company, as well of home as in India, to the manifest injury of the public credit, and of the commercial interests of the said Company; and it has therefore become highly expedient that certain further regulations, better adopted to present circumstances and condition, should be provided and established. And whereas the electing and choosing of Directors of the said United Company every year, in such a manner as at present prescribed by Charter, has not answered the good purposes intended thereby, but on the contrary, by limiting the duration of their office to so short a time, evidently tends so weaken the authority of the court directors .... May it, therefore, please be enacted.'

MAIN PROVISIONS OF THE REGULATING ACT

The following are its main provisions :—

1. Subordination of Bombay and Madras to Bengal. Prior to the enactment of 1773, the three Governments of the Presidencies of Madras, Bombay and Bengal were separate from and independent of one another. Each acted on its own in matters of making war and peace. The Company was put to much inconvenience because of their unregulated actions. There was no uniform policy or co-ordination of work. The Governor of each Presidency had direct dealings with the Court of Directors. The Regulating Act declared that the Governors of Madras and Bombay would be subordinate to the Governor-General of Bengal.

The Governor-General was authorised to superintend and control the Governments of Bombay and Madras. The Presidency Governments were instructed not to declare war or make peace or conclude treaties with Indian powers without the previous sanction of the Governor-General of Bengal or the Company's Directors in England unless compelling circumstances demanded an immediate action. *This provision laid the foundation of a unitary type of government in British India.* The Governor-General was also given the power to suspend the Presidency Governors and their councils, if need be.

2. Establishment of the Council of Governor-General. The Act made provision for the Council of four members to assist the Governor-General. Three councillors were to hold office for five years and could be removed only by the British king on the recommendation of the Directors. All important matters were to be decided by the majority opinion of the Council. The Governor-General was bound to accept the majority decision of the Council. He did not possess any overriding powers. In case of equality of votes in the Council, he exercised his casting vote. The names of the Governor-General and his four Councillors, as given in the Act, were : Warren Hastings (Governor-General), General Clavering, Richard Barwell, Col. Monson and Phillip Francis.

3. Right to make laws. The Governor-General-in-Council was authorised to make laws and issue ordinances for the good government of Company's settlements and other territories subordinate to it. Such laws and ordinances were to be just, reasonable and consistent with the British laws. These could be repealed or superseded only by the Crown.

4. Establishment of a Supreme Court at Fort William. The Regulating Act provided for the establishment of a Supreme Court at Fort William. It consisted of one Chief Justice and three other judges. It enjoyed full civil, criminal and ecclesiastical jurisdiction which extended to all British subjects in India and the persons in the services of the Company. In the event of a dispute between an Indian and an Englishman, the Supreme Court was empowered to hear and decide the case if the Indian was willing to abide by its decision and the subject matter did not exceed ₹ 500 in value. Its criminal jurisdiction did not extend to the Governor-General or any member of his Council except in cases of treason or felony. Similarly the Governor-General, members of the Council and the Judges of the Supreme Court were immune from arrest or imprisonment in any action, suit or proceeding in the Supreme Court. This immunity was, however, limited to civil cases only. Moreover, the Governor-General, members of his Council and the Judges of the Supreme Court were empowered to act as Justices of Peace for the settlement of Fort William and factories subordinate thereto. The cases of the British residing in Calcutta were to be tried with the help of jury by the Supreme Court. The British could also appeal to the King-in-Council against the decisions of the Supreme Court.

5. Prohibition of accepting presents and bribe. Since the Governor-General, his Councillors and the Judges of the Supreme Court drew handsome salaries, the Act warned them strictly not to run any private trade and also not to accept presents or bribe from the natives.

6. Rights of the shareholders. Prior to the enactment of 1773, all those persons whose investment in the Company's capital amounted to £ 500 were entitled to elect the Directors. The new Act restricted this right only to those who owned shares worth £ 1,000.

7. Tenure of the Directors. In order to ensure stability and continuity in the policy of the Company's executive, the tenure of the Directors was extended from one year to four years with one-forth of their number retiring every year.

8. Extension of the State control over the Company. The Act required the Directors to lay before the Treasury all papers from India dealing with the revenues; and all correspondence dealing with the civil and military administration of the Company, before the Secretary concerned.

9. Salaries of Governor-General, the Members of his Council and the Judges. The salary of the Governor-General under the new Act was fixed as £ 25,000 per annum, of each Councillor as £ 10,000, of the Chief Justice as £ 8,000 and of other Judges as £ 6,000 per annum.

10. Special arrangements in England for the punishment of offences committed in India. The Act provided for the hearing of the cases and the awarding of punishment in England for offences committed by Governor-General, his Councillors, any Judge of the Supreme Court or any other servant of the Company in India.

11. Clauses dealing with other evils. The Act stated expressly that no British subject in India was to charge interest at a rate higher than 12%.

12. Control of the Supreme Court. One other significant provision of the Regulating Act was that no rule, ordinance or regulation made by the Governor-General and his Council was to be valid or effective unless approved by the Supreme Court.

13. Provision for trying the British in Great Britain for offences committed in India. A provision was made in the Act for trying the servants of the Company who defrauded the Company or committed some breach of public trust or embezzled public money. Similarly, any servant of the Company, Governor, Governor-General or any member of the Council or Judge of the Supreme Court who committed any offence against this Act or proved guilty of any crime, misdemeanour or offence against any British subject or inhabitant of India, could be tried and punished by the court of the King's Bench Division in England.

MERITS OF THE REGULATING ACT

The most striking merits of the Regulating Act, 1773 were –

1. Solid, clear and decisive establishment. Commenting on the merits of the Act, *Lord North* has remarked, "*Every article in it is framed with a view to placing the affairs of the Company on a solid, clear and decisive establishment.*" Uptill now the East India Company was functioning in a haphazard way. The Regulating Act of 1773 gave it a clear and solid footing. It was the first time that an attempt was made to set up a written constitution in place of an ordinary rule of the company for the British possessions in India. The Act provided the framework of all constitutional enactments which later on were to be made.

2. Better Home Government. Another important thing to be noted is that the Act introduced certain welcome changes in the Home Government. The chaotic state of affairs in the Court of Proprietors was sought to be removed. The qualifications of the voters were raised and the number of court of Proprietors was reduced to such an extent that the real power came into a few interested and better experienced hands. *Punniah* is of the opinion," *The long tenure and partial renewal provided by the Act to the Directors brought security and continuity in their policy.* When the Directors were elected only for one year, the first half of the year was spent in discharging the obligations of their supporters and the other half was spent in convassing for the coming elections. The extension of term of the office of Directors from one year to four years greatly removed this evil.

3. Control of Parliament over company. Uptil now the control of the parliament over the affairs of the East India Company was very little. The Regulating Act required the company to submit their regular report on the revenues of India to the British treasury. This was the first step towards subordinating the commercial interests of the Company to the political interest of Britain in India.

4. Company Recognised. The East India Company started its carreer in India as a purely commercial concern but by its acquisition of territories, the right of Diwani etc; its character had changed. It also started to handle political power for which it had no recognition from the British Government. This act corrected this confusing position and recognised the Company as really it had become.

5. Company's Patronage Curtailed. The Regulating Act of 1773 curtailed some of the powers hiter to enjoyed by the Company. By this Act, the first Governor-General and members of his council, the first Chief Justice and his colleagues were appointed. For the appointment of these officials, the Company was bound to secure the prior approval of the Crown. Consequently, the Crown developed its control over the affairs of the Company.

6. Introduction to Collegiate system. The Regulating Act of 1773 established a short of Collegiate system in order to prevent the Governor-General from collecting autocratic powers in England. It was the first step by which the European Government assumed the responsibility of governing the territories acquired by it outside the Europe and inherited by civilized people.

7. Control of British Parliament over Company's Administrative Activities. Uptill now the Company's territorial acquisition in India were considered to be its private concern but this Act provided for the right of British Parliament to control over the administrative activities of East India Company. It was a bold-step at securing good Government in the Company's territories in India, without the Crown's directly assuming the responsibility for the same.

8. Check on the Corruption. The British Parliament tried to check the Corruption of the official of the East India Company by the Regulating Act of 1773. Uptill now the official of the Company were collecting huge wealth by way of the private business and gifts. The highest officials like the Governor-General and the member of his Council were forbidden by this Act from entering into any private commercial transactions in India. It was also resolved that no European would lend money to the Indians at more than a 12 per cent interest. All these provisions of the Act checked the corruptions upto a great extent.

9. Centralisation of Administrative Machinery. The Regulating Act of 1773 is significant from the view that an attempt was made to centralise the administrative machinery in India which was a step towards the right direction. The vast territories acquired by the East India Company in India were required to be consolidated. The three Presidencies in India had some conflicting interests which were against the British interest. This Act clearly provided that the Governor-General and his council were to control and direct the Presidencies in their relations with the Indian powers. By this Act, an attempt was made to set up a supreme authority for all the dominions of the Company in India.

DEFECTS OF THE REGULATING ACT
OR
THE PRINCIPAL DEFECTS OF THE REGULATING ACT OF 1773

Various observations have been made on the Regulating Act, 1773.

According to Mr. Bouton Rouse, "The object of the Regulating Act was good but the system that it established was faulty and imperfect". The Act intended to regulate the affairs of the Company, to check its autocratic powers and to secure a good Government in India. *According to Lord North's own words: "Every article in it is framed with a view to the placing of the affairs of the Company on a solid, clear and decisive establishment."* But the Act clearly failed in its purpose. It had many drawbacks and inefficiencies in it.

Mr. A. C. Bannerjee holds the view that Lord North's reforms were one-sided and were limited to the administrative machinery of the Company in London. In other words through Regulating Act, Lord North sought to make changes in the Constitution of the Company but made no attempt to improve the lot of Indians. Lord North did not care to realise that the basic cause of the sufferings of the people of Bengal was the foreign rule itself. Some critics are of the opinion that instead of organising the Government of Company's territories in India on better lines, the Act set up various centres of conflict. It made the Governor-General powerless before the Councillors. Such a restriction on the head of the State led to occasional disputes between him and his colleagues. In the second place, the provisions relating to the jurisdiction and powers of the Supreme Court were so vague and confusing that it led to serious disputes between the Court and the Council and also between the Supreme Court and the Subordicate Courts. Another defect in the Act was that it allowed the Governments of Madras and Bombay to make war and peace independently during emergency periods. On the pretext of urgency, the Presidency Governments began to abuse their power and flout the superintending authority of the Governor-General. The Regulating Act, in short, suffered from the following defects:—

1. Conflict between the Governor -General and the Supreme Court. The Governor-General and the Supreme Court were mostly at loggerheads. The ostensible reason was that the jurisdiction of the Supreme Court was not defined clearly. In Kasijora case the breach between the Governor-General's Council and the Supreme Court became wider and more serious. The Court issued a writ against the Rajah of Kasijora, a Zamindar of the Company. But the Council advised the Rajah to avoid the service of the writ as he, not being a servant of the Company, was outside the jurisdiction of the Court. The situation worsened further when the Company's sepoys arrested Sheriff's officers and created a deadlock. In this way the conflict between the Government and the Court prolonged. Since the powers of the Company were derived from the Mughal Subedars, the Parliament also could not define them properly and rigidly. Such an anomaly in the Act led to conflicts which could not be resolved easily.

2. Vagueness of the provisions relating to the jurisdiction of the Supreme Court. The Act did not explain precisely as to who were the British subjects within the meaning of the Charter of the Supreme Court. In one sense all the people living in Company's territories could be called British subjects and in another sense only those persons came under this head who were English citizens by birth. The Supreme Court claimed to have the right to judge all cases brought to it by any person living in the territories of the Company. The Government of the East India Company's territories refuted it and said that the Court had original or appellate jurisdiction only in those cases in which the Englishmen or any employee of the Company was involved. The Council said that the case relating to the people of Bengal could be brought before the Court only when they agreed to accept the decision of the Court.

3. Conflict between the Supreme Court and the Provincial Courts. Since the jurisdiction of the Supreme Court was not clearly defined, it came in conflict with the Provincial Court's which were subordinate to Governor-General and his Council. The Supreme Court which derived its authority directly from the Crown refused to recognise the exclusive jurisdiction of the Provincial Courts in cases relating to the people of Bengal.

4. Conflict between the Governor-General and his Council. The Act made it obligatory for the Governor-General to consult his Councillors and stand by the opinion of the majority in the Council. This provision made the position of the Governor-General deplorable. In most cases three of the four Councillors opposed him and voted down his suggestions. Warren Hastings who was sick of the non-co-operating attitude of the Council once wrote. "My situation is truly painful and mortifying, deprived of powers with which I have been invested by a solemn Act of legislation, denied the respect which is due to my station and character and condemned to bear my share in the responsibility of measures which I do not approve." "The entire dependence of the Governor-General on the notes of his Council," observes Lyall, "reduced him to a cipher, threw all his foreign policy out of gear and gave birth to a six years' struggle between Hastings and his Councillors." This violent and long-drawn struggle in the highest executive had injurious effect on affairs of the Company.

5. Inadequate control of the Governor-General over the Presidencies of Bombay and Madras. The Act made the mistake of providing an exception to the general rule that the Presidency Governors were not to declare war against or make peace with any native power without the previous permission of the Governor-General. Under this exception, the Presidency Governors of Bombay and Madras were, during emergency, authorised to make any alliance or war without waiting for the permission of the Governor-General. The Governors of Bombay and Madras abused this power and at times put the Company to great loss of men and money. Inadequate control of the Calcutta Government over the Subordinate Presidencies amounted to a serious defect in the Act.

6. Inexperience of the members of the Council. One unfortunate feature of the Regulating Act was that the persons nominated to the Council of Warren Hastings possessed no experience of Indian affairs. Moreover their relations with Warren Hastings were not cordial. They had preconceived notions that Company's administration was corrupt with the result that they made it their aim to oppose the Governor-General and hit the Government right and left.

7. Defective changes in the Constitution of the Home Government of the Company. The Regulating Act failed in its object of weeding out the influence of the retired Company's servants on the Home Government of the Company. By altering the voting qualification of the General Court from £ 500 to £ 1,000 the purpose was not solved. According to G. N. Singh, "the alteration in the voting qualification in the General Court did not improve the existing state of affairs because the laudable object of preventing the retired Company's servants from gaining an excessive influence in the Councils of the Company was not realised. On the other hand, the Court of Directors was transformed into a more or less permanent obligarchy."

8. Inadequancy of the Parliamentary control over the Company. Although the Act made it necessary for the Directors to forward the copies of all civil and military dispatches from India to one of the Secretaries of State for scrutiny, in practice this measure bore no effective results. The Parliament had no expert on Indian affairs to study those papers and suggest necessary actions. Hence, it could not exert any effective control over the Company's affairs.

9. According to Burke, *"the Regulating Act was an infringement of national right, national faith and national justice."*

10. According to P.E. Roberts, "Regulating Act was a half-measure and disastrously vague on many points. The titular authority of the Nawab of Bengal was left by implication intact and no assertion was made of the sovereignty of the Crown or the Company in India."

11. According to the Report on Indian Constitutional Reforms of 1918, the Regulating Act sought to create the post of such a Governor-General as was powerless before his Council. The Council itself was powerless before the Supreme Court. The Supreme Court shouldered no responsibility for the welfare of the people. Still if such a queer machinery could work in India, it was because of the tolerance and personal stature of one man alone, that is the Governor-General.

In short, Regulating Act had established a system which was full of defects but this system served the purpose of that time. The author of the Cambridge History, Volume V, truly remarked. "It had neither given the State a definite control over the Company not the Directors a definite control over their servants, nor the Governor-General over his council nor the Calcutta Presidency a definite control over Bombay and Madras."

Note : In order to remove the defects inherent in the Regulating Act, the British Parliament had to pass Bengal Judicature Act in 1781 and Pitt's India Act in 1784. The Bengal Judicature Act defined the powers of the Supreme Court and Pitt's India Act empowered the Governor-General to ignore the majority decisions of the Council in special circumstances.

IMPORTANCE OR SIGNIFICANCE OF THE REGULATING ACT

Inspite of the above mentioned short-comings and obscurities of the Regulating Act, it was of great constitutional significance in the constitutional History of India. It was undoubtedly a landmark in the constitutional development of India. This Act, for the first time in the history of the Trading Company, recognised its political and administrative functions. Through this Act the Parliament made a bold attempt to establish Parliamentary control over the Comapny. So *Mr. G. N. Singh* remarks, "*The Act of 1773 is of great constitutional importance because it definitely recognised the political functions of the Company, because it asserted for the first time the right of the Parliament to dictate the form of Government in what were considered till then the private possessions of the Company and because it is the first of a long series of Parliament statutes that altered the form of Government of India. The sole right of Parliament to impose whatever constitution it may deem fit or necessary on the people of India was finally and emphatically asserted in the Preamble of the Government of India Act, 1919.*"

According to Principal Sri Ram Sharma, "The Regulating Act made a bold attempt at securing good Government in the Company's territory in India without the Crown's directly assuming the responsibility for the same. It was the first measure by which a European Government assumed the responsibility for governing territories acquired by it outside Europe and inhabited by civilised people. No other European nation had so far made sure of its kind." According to *Mr. Lyall*, "*The system of administration set up by the Act of 1773 embodied the first attempt at giving some definite and recognizable form to the vague and arbitrary rulership that had developed upon the Company. From that time forward, the outline of the Anglo-Indian Government was gradually filled in.*"

This Act constituted the first serious effort to cleanse the Company's administration of the evils of private trade and corruption. It also marked the beginning of Parliamentary control over the affairs of the Company. This Act drastically curbed the arbitary powers of the Company. The Supreme Court began to act as Crown's Representative to superintend and control the Company's affairs and to bring the Company's servants to trial for their questionable deeds. Company's power to make nominations to the posts of Governor-General and his councillors, the Chief Justice and his colleagues was also curtailed and subordinated to the approval of the Crown. One redeeming feature of the Act was that it sought to establish a supreme authority for the whole of the Company's territories which laid the foundation of a unitary system in the country. The Act also marked the beginning of the written constitution of India. It was also the first of the long series of Acts which shaped and moulded the structure of the Government of India from time to time.

In short, we can say that it is landmark from where the constitutional History really starts, because

- It introduces the sovereignty of the British Parliament over Indian territory for the first time.
- It gave a new executive for the Government of the Presidency of Bengal.
- It provided a new relationship between the Presidency of Bengal and those of Madras and Bombay.
- It established a Supreme Court at Calcutta.
- It made reforms in Civil Service and provided a new process for the formation of the Regulation.
- A close study of the act shows that it relied considerably on the theory of separation of Powers.
- This Act also put into effect a system of checks and balances though it did not work properly.

Thus, this act has a very important place in the constitutional History of India.

EXERCISES

Long Answer Type Questions

1. "Instead of organising Government the Regulation Act organised centres of conflict." Discuss this statement in brief.
2. "The object of the Regulating Act was good but the system that it established was imperfect." Elucidate.
3. What were the circumstances for the enactment of the Regulating Act?
4. What were the provisions of the Regulating Act 1773?
5. Discuss in brief the merits of the Regulating Act.
6. What were the defects of the Regulating Act of 1773?
7. Write a brief note on the significance of Regulating Act.

Short Answer Type Questions

1. There were many responsible factors for the inactment of the Regulating Act. Write any two factors.
2. What were the constitutional difficulties before Lord North's Government for the enactment of Regulating Act.?
3. Write a brief note on 'The Preamble of the Regulating Act'.
4. What were the evils of Dual System? Write in brief.
5. Write any two provisions of the Regulating Act.
6. Write any two merits of Regulating Act.
7. Write any two defects of Regulating Act.
8. What was the conflict between the Governor-General and the Supreme Court?
9. Write a very brief note on conflict between the Supreme Court and the Provincial Courts.
10. What was the importance of Regulating Act? Write in brief.

Objective Type Questions

Choose the correct answer

1. A Bill known as Regulating Act was moved in the Parliament on 18th May, 1773 aimed at extending state control over the affairs of the Company. It was moved by

   (*a*) Lord North (*b*) Lord William Bentinck

   (*c*) Lord Macaulay (*d*) Sir Richard Bacher

2. The Regulating Act of 1773 made provision for a Council to assist the Governor-General and Members of the Council as given is the Act were

   (*a*) Richard Barwell and General Clavering

   (*b*) Philip Francis, Col. Monson, Richard Barwell and General Clavering

   (*c*) Richard Barwell and Col. Monson

   (*d*) Philip Francis and General Clavering

3. An important fall-out of the Regulating Act of 1773 was that

(*a*) It served the economic link between the Court of Directors and Proprietors of the Company.

(*b*) It concentrated the executive powers in the hands of the servants of the Company.

(*c*) It laid the foundation of a unitary type of Government in British India.

(*d*) None of the above.

4. The Regulating Act of 1773 fixed the annual salaries of the Governor-General and the Chief Justice respectively at

(*a*) £ 2,000 and £ 1,000 per annum.

(*b*) £ 20,000 and £ 10,000 per annum

(*c*) £ 2,500 and £ 800 per annum

(*d*) £ 25,000 and £ 8,000 per annum

5. The active and direct control of the British Parliament over Indian affairs began from

(*a*) 1773 (*b*) 1774

(*c*) 1775 (*d*) 1776

ANSWERS

1. (*a*) 2. (*b*) 3. (*c*) 4. (*d*) 5. (*a*)

2

CHAPTER

Pitt's India Act

> *"The Act enunciated a system with which its cumberous and dilatory procedure and its elaborate system of checks and counter-checks, though modified in details, remained substantially in force uptill 1858."*
>
> **— Sir C. Ilbert**

For seven years after passing the Regulating Act of 1773, the British Parliament could not pay attention to the Company's affairs. The system of Government set up by the Act was not functioning properly. So in 1781 two committees were appointed to enquire into the Company's administration. The findings of these two committees disclosed the wrongs in the administration of the Company. These were against the Governor-General.

There was great opposition of Fox's Indian Bill of 1783. The Bill though passed by the House of Commons was thrown out in the house of Lords. Consequently the Fox-North Ministry was dismissed by the king. In 1784, a new Bill was introduced and the same year it was passed by the two Houses. It is known as Pitt's India Act.

Pitt's India Act was necessiated by the increasing need of control of the Parliament over the East India Company. To safeguard the British economic interest it was felt necessary that the Parliament of British should have direct control over East India Company.

CIRCUMSTANCES FOR THE ENACTMENT OF PITT'S INDIA ACT

Many circumstances were responsible for the enactment of the Pitt's India Act. Here we are discussing some of the important circumstances which necessitated the passing of the Pitt's India Act by the British Parliament. Some of the circumstances were as follows —

1. Defects of the Regulating Act. As stated in the preceding chapter, the Regulating Act had many flaws. The working of the Act brought into light the seriousness of the defects because Warren Hastings who had to work with his team of non-co-operative councillors had a painful story to tell. He had adequate control neither on the Council nor on the subordinate Governments of Bombay and Madras. Because of the vague character of the jurisdiction of the Supreme Court, he had his conflicts with the Court also. The Bengal Judicature Act no doubt ascertained clearly the powers and functions of the Supreme Court but it left other defects in the Regulating Act unamended. The British Statesmen felt the need of another Act to deal squarely with other defects of the Regulating Act.

2. Ineffective control of the British Government over the Company. The misdeeds of Warrren Hastings and the sufferings of the people under the corrupt administration of the Company, stirred the conscience of the British Public. The situation required a definite State control over the Company. With this end in view, the House of Commons adopted a resolution in May, 1782, for recalling Hastings and Hornby. The Court of Proprietors defined the resolution and retained both the persons in their offices. The Parliament took a serious view of the defiant attitude of the Company.

3. Wrong foreign policy of the Company. The British subjects of the Crown in India continued to disregard the Provisions of the Regulating Act. They still entered into war and peace with the Indian powers not on behalf of the Crown but in the name of Company. The Presidencies led the Company into expensive wars, e.g., the Rohilla War, the First Anglo-Maratha war and the two Anglo-Mysore Wars. They waged the wars without the previous approval of the British Government, hence, it decided to curb the Company's irregularities by establishing effective control over Indian affairs.

4. Economic causes. The English trade in India suffered a great setback due to maladministration of the Company. America had already thrown off British yoke, and dealt thereby a severe blow to the British trade. The loss of American colonies increased the commercial importance of India to Great Britain. India promised to provide a good market for the English goods. So the British Statesmen began to realise the need of increasing more and more effective control over the Company's territories in India.

5. Ill-gotton wealth of the Company's officers. Although the Regulating Act had strictly forbidden the acceptance of presents and amassing of fortune by the Company's officers through unlawful means, yet the greedy Englishmen did not change their ways. They returned home with fat purpose and lived like 'Nawabs'. They also began to buy seats in Parliament and influence the policy of the country. Such an unhealthy influence of the 'English Nawabs' impelled the Parliament to bring the Company soon under its control.

6. The Welfare of India. The authors of the Act were moved by humanitarian considerations also when they demanded Parliamentary control over Company's administration. They also realised that corrupt administration of the Company would make the English rule in India unpopular and unstable. And in the interest of their trade and commerce, they were determined to perpetuate the British rule on India. Mr. Pitt, as such, wanted to introduce reforms in Indian administration so as to win the gratitude and loyalty of the natives.

7. The Dunda's Bill and Fox's Bill. Dunda and Fox had also introduced Bills in the Parliament, only a couple of months before Pitt's India Act, to correct the defects of the Regulating Act and to let the State Ministry assume the rulership of British territories in India. The Bills, although they failed, paved the way for Pitt's India Act. Only *two months* after the failure of Fox's Bill, Pitt introduced his Bill. It had to pass through stiff opposition for several months but ultimately found a place on the Statute Book in August 1784.

MAIN PROVISIONS OF PITT'S INDIA ACT

The Pitt's India Act of 1784 completely changed the administrative set up of the East India Company, which wanted the control of the British in the conduct of public affairs.

The object of the Act was the better Government and security of the territorial possession in this Kingdom in the East Indies. The main provisions of the Act may be discussed as under —

1. Set-up and composition of Board of Control. "The Act empowered the Crown to create a Board of six commissioners for the affairs of India." All the six commissioners were to be drawn from the Privy Council. The Board was to consist of a Secretary of State, a Chancellor of Exchequer and four other members of the Privy Council. It was to be the supreme governing body with Company's Directors and Proprietors subordinate to it.

2. Powers of the Board of Control. The Act empowered the Board to superintend, direct and control all acts, operations and concerns which in any way related to the civil, military Government or revenues of the British possessions in the East Indies. It had access to all the papers, documents and correspondence of the Company. The Directors were bound to supply any information which the Board might require. The Board ordinarily issued orders and instructions through the Court of Directors but, if it liked, it could get its secret orders despatched to India directly. In short, the Board was armed with full powers over the Company's affairs. The quorum necessary for a meeting of the Board was fixed at three. The meeting was to be presided by the Chancellor and in his absence by the Secretary of State. But both these persons were too busy to spare time for the meeting of the Board of Control. Naturally, the seniormost person of the remaining four members acted as the President of the Board. In due course the other three members also became inactive because they had no urge to attend the meetings. The President of the Board, eventually, began to discharge all the functions of the Board of Control single-handed. *Keith observes* : *"The President was virtually the Secretary of State for India, and Indian affairs became a matter for the Cabinet in the same manner as those colonial issues which dealt with by a Secretary of State".*

3. Double Government in England. The system, thus evolved, came to be known as Dual or Double Government. The Indian affairs in England came to be managed by two independent authorities—the Board of Control and the Court of Directors. The Directors who, under the Act, had been given an inferior position, still retained direct control over commercial activities of the Company and the appointment of Company's servants. The Board of Control on the other hand was there to revise and exercise control over the doings of the Directors.

4. Appointment of the Committee of Secrecy. The Act provided for a Secrecy Committee consisting of three out of twenty-four Directors of the Company. Ordinarily the Board of Control sent all its orders and instructions to India through the Directors but if it intended to communicate directly to the officers of the Company in India, it could send its secret orders to the Secrecy Committee which was to send them to India without disclosing the contents to other Directors.

5. Reduction in the strength of the Council of the Governor-General. The Governor-General's Council formely consisted of four members whose majority opinion was binding on the Governor-General. The Act reduced the number of members to three, so that even if the Governor-General had the support of one member of the Council, he might, with the use of his casting vote, impose his will on the Council and execute his policies effectively. The Act also laid down that only senior servants of the Company were to be appointed to the Council. The practice of sending new men from England was discontinued.

6. Governor-General's control over the Presidencies made real. Although the Governments of Madras and Bombay were required, under the Regulating Act, to seek the previous permission of the Bengal Government for entering into any alliance or war with any native state, they on the plea of emergency had been disregarding or sidetracking the authority of the Governor-General. Pitt's India Act made the control of the Governor-General over the Presidency Governments more real and decisive.

7. Establishment of Governor's Council in Madras and Bombay. The Act provided for the setting up of a Council in each Presidency to assist the Governor with Commander-in-Chief as one of its three members. The members of the Governor's Councils were to be appointed by the Directors but could be recalled or removed by the Crown.

8. Company was forbidden to pursue new conquests. The Company's territories in India were for the first time called 'the British possessions in India.' The Company was directed to put her house in order and to retrench the surplus staff. It was also asked to desist from pursuing schemes of conquest and extension of dominion in India.

9. Establishment of special Courts to try the offences committed by Britishers in India. The Act of 1784 further declared that acceptance of gifts and presents amounted to extortion and was punishable offence. The Act made it compulsory for every servant to the Company on his return to England to declare on oath the amount of property he brought from India. Provision was made for the setting up of a special court for the trial of offences committed by the servants of the Company in India. This court, however, was never set up.

10. The Court of Directors was freed from the undesirable control of the Court of Proprietors. The resolutions of the Directors, if approved by the Board of Control, could no more be rejected or suspended by the Proprietors.

11. The Act curtailed the powers of the Court of Directors with regard to the appointment of the Governor-General and made it obligatory for them to seek the final approval of the Crown.

12. Procedure of the Board of Control. The members of the Board of Control held office during the pleasure of the King. The Secretary of State acted as the Chairman of the Board and he was entitled to a casting vote if the members were divided equally on any issue. The Board had no initiating power. Under the Act all the appointments were to be made by the Court of Directors.

13. Powers of the Directors. The Directors continued to exercise the power of making appointments of Company's servants and also to look after the commercial interests of the Company. The Act, however, empowered the Crown to recall any officer of the Company from India. It also recognised the right of the Directors to appeal to the King-in-Council against any encroachment by the Board on Company's commercial privileges.

IMPACT OF PITT'S INDIA ACT

Commenting on the Act **Prof. Keith** observed that 'Special powers were given to Governor-General and Governors to authorise the arrest of persons suspected of carrying on illicit correspondence with persons in authority, whether in native states or European settlements but this power seems to have been allowed to remain unused.

By this Act the commercial, political and administrative affairs of the Company were divided into different parts. Now the political functions of the Company were under the control and supervision of the Board of Control and other matters, *i.e.*, commercial functions of the Company were left to the Directors of the Company to deal with.

Thus, a deal Government was established. In practice it has two authorities to deal with the Indian problems. The Crown and the Company. It was 'Compromise' according to Prof. Keith. The powers of the Board of Control were more than the Court of Directors. Therefore, it had a supremacy over the Court of Directors. In case of emergency, the Board of Control could order the Directors to prepare a despatch on a particular subject immediately. If they refused to comply with the order the Board was empowered to prepare the despatch itself and send it to the Directors. By the enforcement of this Act the Court of Directors became not powerless, still it had much importance. It had a great influence over civil servant of the Company. The whole routine of the Company was in the hands of Directors because the Board of Control was very busy in foreign and political affairs. Consequently the Board was quite unable to conduct day-to-day affairs of the Company. In this way, there were the Directors who controlled indirectly the whole routine work of the Company.

Pitt's India Act was lone of the wisest steps taken by the British Parliament to control the Indian affairs. It was almost the same in its essentials as the Bill of Fox. It aimed at putting the control as the conduct of public affairs by the Company in the hands of the British Government. The Pitt's India Act also could not decide the Company's right to territorial possessions. Pitt's India Act did not introduce any sweeping change in the Company's constitution and left the Indian patronage almost entirely in the Company's hands. Thus, in the words of Keith it embodied essentially a compromise.

IMPORTANCE OF PITT'S INDIA ACT

Pitt's India Act was measure of great constitutional significance. It proposed vital changes in the composition of the councils and in the relations of the Presidency Governments with the Governor-General. The reduction in the strength of the Councils enabled the Governor-General and the Governors to act freely. The complete subordination of the Presidency Governments to the Government of Bengal paved way for the co-ordination of policy of all the three Presidency Governments. One notable feature of the Act was that it, for the first time, called the Company's territories as the 'British possessions in India'. Company's territories became a part of the British Empire, with a Board of Control to superintend and control its administration. The Act made certain changes in the administrative set-up of the Company in England. The Court of Proprietors was deprived of its hold on the Court of Directors. The latter began to receive orders directly from the Board of Control instead of from the Proprietors. The Committee of Secrecy led to the diminution of the powers of the Directors also.

The greatest achievement of Pitt's India Act was that it firmly established Crown's control over all the civil, political and military affairs of India. Thus, the so far indirect and ineffective control of the Parliament over Company's affairs became direct and real. According to Principal *Sri Ram Sharma*, *"The Pitt's India Act altered the foundation of the direction of Indian affairs in England. The Court of Proprietors lost its political power. The Directors now played second fiddle to the British Government who possessed almost unlimited powers of issuing orders which the Directors were bound to obey."* *Mr. Lyall points out*, *"the immediate effect of the Pitt's India Act was a great and manifest improvement in the mechanism of Indian Government, removing most of the ill-contrived checks and hindrances which had brought Warren Hastings into collision with his Council and subordinate Governments, abolishing the defects that he had pointed out and applying the remedies that he had proposed."* Another welcome feature of the Act was that it proposed for the setting up of a Special Court in England to try servants of the Company of the offences committed by them in India.

The Act also enunciated clearly a marked change in the foreign policy of Great Britain. It clearly laid down that *"to pursue schemes of conquest and extension of dominion in India were measures repugnant to the wish, the policy and honour of the nation"*. The British policy of non-intervention marked the beginning of a new era in Indian politics. In pursuance of this policy the British help was denied to the Nizam of Hyderabad with the result that he was defeated by the Marathas in the Battle of Kharda. This attitude of the Company was considered as gross betrayal by the Nizam. He was so much annoyed that he dismissed all the English officers in his service.

According to Sir C. Ilbert : "The Act enunciated a system which with its cumberous and dilatory procedure and its elaborate system of checks and counter-checks, though modified in details, remained substantially in force uptill 1858."

Veto power to Lord Cornwallis. In 1786 when the Directors requested Lord Cornwallis to assume the office of the Governor-General of India, he made two demands, first that he would be the Commander-in-Chief also and secondly that he should be given power to overrule his Council whenever he deemed it necessary. By an Act passed in 1786, the British Government agreed to both the demands of Cornwallis.

EXERCISES

Long Answer Type Questions

1. Discuss the circumstance that led to the enactment of Pitt's India Act, 1784.
2. Discuss the main provisions of Pitt's India Act, 1784. Also discuss its impact.
3. "We must not conclude, however, that the supremacy of the Board of Control left the Directors with no real control." Discuss the effect of the Pitt's India Act of 1784 on the powers and position of the Court of Directors.
4. "Pitt's India Act of 1784 embodied essentially a compromise." Discuss this statement and explain the importance of the Pitt's India Act.
5. Discuss the importance of Pitt's India Act 1784.

Short Answer Type Questions

1. Write any two provisions of Pitt's India Act.
2. Write a very brief note on 'Double Government in England'.
3. Write any two circumstances for the enactment of Pitt's India Act.
4. Write a very brief note on the Dunda's Bill and Fox's Bill.

Objective Type Questions

Choose the correct answer

1. It was established by the Pitt's India Act. It consisted of six commissioners, all drawn from the Privy Council. It was to be the Supreme Governing Body with Company's Directors and Proprietors subordinate to it. It was called
   (*a*) Governor-General's Council (*b*) Board of Control
   (*c*) Council of Commissioners (*d*) None of the above
2. The Pitt's India Act of 1784 set up a system which came to be known as Dual Government, because
   (*a*) The Indian affairs in England came to be managed by two independent authorities–the Board of Control and the Court of Directors.
   (*b*) The Government of India was henceforth came to be headed by two authorities–The Governor General and the Secretary of India.
   (*c*) The political set-up in India was given a federal complexion and both Central and Provincial Governments exercised control over their respective subjects.
   (*d*) All the above.
3. The Pitt's India Act provided for a Secrecy Committee. It consisted of
   (*a*) 10 out of 24 Directors (*b*) 16 out of 24 Directors
   (*c*) 8 out of 24 Directors (*d*) 3 out of 24 Directors
4. The Pitt's India Act reduced the number of members of Governor-General's Council to three so that
   (*a*) The functioning of the Council did not become unmanageable.
   (*b*) Even if the Governor-General had the supports of one member of the Council, he might with the use of his casting vote impose his will on the Council and execute his policies effectively.

(*c*) The three member could individually and independently oversee the administration of the three Presidencies–Bengal, Bihar and Orissa.

(*d*) All of the above.

5. Which among the following for the first time called the East India Company's territories in India as 'British Possession in India'?

(*a*) Regulating Act of 1773

(*b*) Government of India Act, 1888

(*c*) Pitt's India Act of 1784

(*d*) None of the above.

6. Consider the following in connection with the Pitt's India Act of 1784.

1. The Act provided for setting up of a Council in each Presidency to assist the Governor with Commander-in-chief as one of its three members.
2. The Act curtailed the Powers of the Court of Directors with regard to the appointment of the Governor-General and make it obligatory for them to seek the final approval of the Crown.
3. The Director continued to exercise the power of making appointments of Company's servants and also to look after the commercial interests of the Company.
4. The Company was directed to put her house in order and to retrench the surplus staff.

Which of the above stand valid in connection with the Act?

Select the correct answer from the following :

(*a*) 1 and 2 (*b*) 2 and 3

(*c*) 2, 3 and 4 (*d*) 1, 2, 3 and 4

ANSWERS

1. (*b*) **2.** (*a*) **3.** (*d*) **4.** (*b*) **5.** (*c*) **6.** (*d*)

CHAPTER 3

Charter Act of 1793

> *"With this Act started the unfortunate practice which continued till the coming into force of the Government of India Act, 1919 with undesirable effects."* — *G. N. Singh*

British Government was not satisfied even by the enforcement of Parliamentary control over the Company's Indian administration. The Parliament always tried to extend its control over the Company's affairs day-by-day. On April 23, 1793, another Charter Act was passed without much noise. While introducing this Bill in the House of Commons, Dundas, Chairman of the Board of Control said, "Had I found that so many able men......had agreed in opinion on a system of Indian Government under the Crown, it would have been an inducement to build a system upon them, but from their difference of opinion I can only draw this conclusion that it is safer to restore the present system".

The Bill was passed with unusual quiteness in Parliament. By this Charter Act, Company's monopoly and power was renewed for 20 years with minor changes. Keith has observed. "It was essentially a consolidating measure and its alteration struck at points of detail". Dr. Bannerjee has also remarked. "No great constitutional change was introduced by this statute of consolidation".

There were two reasons for its smooth passage. The first was the influence of the Ministers who sided with the Company and the second was the critical situation the country was confronted with. England was apprehending an invasion by the revolutionary regime of France. British statesmen were too deeply occupied with their national problem to pay any serious attention to Company's Charter. The finances of the Company were also intolerably satisfactory condition. Hence, after a mild opposition, the Charter was renewed by the Parliament without any important alteration.

PROVISIONS OF THE ACT OF 1793

Following were the main provisions of the Act of 1793—

1. The charter Act of 1793 extended the commercial monopoly of the Company for another term of 20 years without prejudice to the claim of the public. The Private individuals were allowed to trade to the extent of three thousand tons of shipping, but this right was restricted to a large extent.

2. The Act provided that the members of the Board of Control and their staff were, henceforth, to be paid out of the Indian revenues.
3. The Act gave the Governor-General full powers over the civil and military Governments of the Presidencies of Bombay and Madras. It also empowered him to superintend, direct and control the Presidency Governments in all cases relating to war and peace with the Indian States and the employment of forces.
4. The Act further underlined the power of the Governer-General and the Governors to override the majority decision of their Councils in matters relating to maintenance of law and order, internal security and interests of the British possessions in India.
5. The Act contributed to the growth of a strong Central power in India. The Governor -General even before the enactment of 1793 was vested with the power to superintend and control the Governments of Bombay and Madras. The new Act increased his powers and authorised him to issue orders to the servants of the Company in the Presidencies and during his visit to Bombay or Madras, and preside over the meeting of the Presidency Councils. He was allowed to nominate a Vice-President of his Council to officiate during his absence.
6. The Act laid down that the Governor-General or the Governor or the Commander-in-Chief was not to go out of India on leave during his tenure of office.
7. The Commander-in-Chief ceased to be a member of the Bengal Council unless so appointed by the Directors.
8. The Act of 1793 reiterated that the Crown did not approve of further conquests and extension of dominion of India.
9. The administrative jurisdiction of the Supreme Court was extended to High Seas.
10. The Act reduced the number of the members of the Councils to three and said that only those persons were eligible for appointment who had complete 12 years of services in India at the time of appointment.
11. Receiving of gifts and presents by the Company's servants was strictly prohibited again.
12. The Governor-General-in-Council was empowered to appoint Justices of Peace in any Presidency.
13. The Act authorised the Local Governments to appoint scavengers for the Presidency town and to levy a sanitation tax to meet the cost.
14. The local bodies were also authorised to grant licences for the sale of spirituous liquors.
15. The Act reduced the strength of the Board of Control from 6 to 5. The junior members who were now to be three only, were not rquired to be Privy Councillors.
16. The Act besides renewing the company's monopoly of Eastern trade, also allowed the private individuals to trade to the extent of 3,000 tons of shipping.
17. The Act laid down that out of the anticipated annual profits of the Company, 5 lakhs were to be set apart for repaying the debts and the rest to be distributed as dividend among the share-holders.
18. An annual statement about the affairs of the Company both in India and England was required to be placed before the Parliament.
19. The Act reiterated that—"To pursue schemes of conquests and extension of Dominion in India are measures repugnant to the wish, honour and policy of the nation."

But according to G. N. Singh— "The force of circumstances and ambition of the man on the spot led to the adoption of just the opposite policy in actual practice".

Thus, we see that the Act of 1793, though a long one was not of much constitutional importance and was merely of a consolidating nature for the establishment of British administration in Bengal.

IMPORTANCE OF CHARTER ACT OF 1793

The Act of 1793, according to Keith, was essentially a consolidating measure. It simply emphasised the implementation of the provisions of the Pitt's India Act. It repeated the other previous Acts and tried to clarify and extend their application. One significant feature of the Act was that it provided for the expenses of the Board of Control to be met from the Indian revenue. *According to Mr. G. N. Singh, "With this Act started the unfortunate practice (aforesaid) which continued till the coming into force of the Government of India Act, 1919, with undesirable effects."* (Though the Board of Control was abolished in 1858 but it was substituted by the Secretary of State for India and his Council. The salary of the Secretary of State for India and his establishment also continued to be paid out of the Indian revenues till 1919.)

EXERCISES

Long Answer Type Questions

1. Prepare a detailed note on Charter Act of 1793.
2. What were the circumstances leading to the enactment of the Charter Act of 1793? Discuss its chief provisions and throw light on the importance of the Act.
3. Discuss the main provisions of the Charter Act, 1793.

Short Answer Type Questions

1. Write any three main provisions of Charter Act, 1793.
2. Discuss in very brief the circumstance leading to the enactment of the Charter Act of 1793.
3. Write in very brief the importance of Charter Act, 1793.

Objective Type Questions

Choose the correct answer

1. In which year the East India Company's monopoly of Eastern trade granted by the Charter of 1773 expired?

   (*a*) 1803 (*b*) 1783
   (*c*) 1793 (*d*) 1813

2. Which of the following Acts provided that the members of the Board of Control and their staff were henceforth to be paid out of the Indian revenues?

   (*a*) Government of India Act, 1935 (*b*) Charter Act of 1793
   (*c*) Regulating Act of 1773 (*d*) None of the above

3. The Charter Act of 1793 extended the commercial monopoly of the Company for another term of

   (*a*) 20 years (*b*) 21 years
   (*c*) 15 years (*d*) 50 years

ANSWERS

1. (*c*) **2.** (*b*) **3.** (*a*)

4

CHAPTER

Charter Act of 1813

> *"The Act of 1813, therefore, continued the Company in the enjoyment of its territorial possessions and revenues, over which the sovereignty of the Crown was now expressly proclaimed for 20 years."*
>
> — *Prof. Keith*

The Charter Act of 1793 was followed by the Charter Act of 1813. The East India Company was granted monopoly of trade in 1793 for twenty years. This period of monopoly expired in 1813. It was but natural for the Directors to apply for its renewal. In addition to the renewal of the Charter of 1793, some other considerations also led the Parliament to enact this constitutional measures. At the time of renewal of the Charter of 1793 the people cried against the commercial monopoly of the Company and demanded a share in the trade with India.

According to **Prof. Keith,** "*The Act of 1813, therefore, continued the Company in the enjoyment of its territorial possessions and revenues, over which the sovereignty of the Crown was now expressly proclaimed for 20 years.*"

The Parliamentarians subjected the Charter to thorough investigation. The Company's financial condition was causing concern. Its public debts had increased considerably. It petitioned to the British Government for a loan. Before granting relief, the Parliament appointed an enquiry committee to report on Company's state of affairs in India. The report was published in 1812. Thus, when the Charter came up for discussion in 1813 the Parliament had the report of the enquiry committee before it.

The Parliament had to take into consideration two other questions during its discussions on the Charter of 1793. The British merchants, manufacturers and shipowners had sent petitions not to renew the Company's monopoly. They argued that trade with India and China should be thrown open to all the British subjects. Closely related with this question was the demand of the missionaries who wanted to be allowed to go to India for the propagation of Christianity. The supporters of the Company objected to this demand on the ground that it would amount to interference with the religion of the people likely to make the English rule unpopular. The ceaseless agitation of the people for the abolition of Company's monopoly, however, called for immediate Parliamentary action. The public petitions and agitations thus constituted the basis of the Charter Act of 1813.

MAIN PROVISIONS OF CHARTER ACT OF 1813

Following were the main provisions of the Charter Act of 1813—

1. Termination of Company's monopoly of Indian trade. The new Act threw open the Indian trade to all the British subjects. The system of granting licences and permits was, however, introduced lest the unscrupulous English merchants should, by harassing Indians, bring discredit to the Crown. The British authorities were required by the Act to issue permits after a thorough check up. Though the Act abolished the Company's monopoly of trade with India, it renewed its monopoly of Chinese trade for a further period of twenty years.

2. Concession to Missionaries. The Act made it obligatory on the Company to form a regular ecclesiastical department. The missionaries were allowed to proceed to India under permits to enlighten the people. It was thus the first step taken by the Government to popularise the religion of Christ and western education in India. In justification of its evil designs, the Government said that its intention was simply to give perfect religious freedom to every Indian.

3. Spread of western education. The Act provided for setting apart a sum of one lakh for the 'revival and improvement of literature and the encouragement of the learned natives of India and for the introduction and promotion of knowledge of the sciences among the inhabitants of the British territories in India'.

4. Regulation of the finances of the Company. The Act required the Company to maintain its territorial and commercial accounts separately. It laid down that the payments were to be made in order of priority. The maintenance of the armed forces was to be the first charge, the payment of the interest being the second and the maintenance of the civil and commercial establishments the third, on the Company's revenues.

5. Provisions relating to the powers of the Board of Control. The Act provided for the ultimate and overall control of the Crown over the Company but it allowed the Company to retain its hold on the details of administration and Indian revenues. The Act further defined the powers of the Board of Control and enlarged its right to superintend Company's affairs and issue instructions to India directly. It gave the Board the right to supervise and control the two institutions set up in England for training the officers, selected by the Directors for administrative services in India.

6. Approval of the Board of Control in regard to big appointments. The Act restricted the powers of the Directors in regard to appointments of the Governor-General, the Governors and the Commander-in-Chief. The approval of the Crown became necessary for the appointment of the dignitaries mentioned above. The Company also required the approval of the Board of Control for the appointment of the members of the Councils of the Governor-General and the Governors.

7. Provisions for the training of the civil and military personnel of the Company. The Act made special provisions for the training of the civil and military officers of the Company. It asked the Board of Control to run and supervise a college at Haileybury for training civil officers and another school at Adiscombe to produce personnel for training army officers. The Board was also authorised to look after the two training colleges at Madras and Calcutta.

8. Powers of Local Governments enhanced. The Act empowered the Local Governments in India to impose taxes on the people and to punish the offenders for non-payment.

9. Provisions relating to administration of justice. The Act made special provisions for the hearing of cases in which both the British and Indians were involved. It fixed special penalties for the offences like theft, foregery and unlawful minting of coins.

10. Limiting the number of British troops. Since Company's territories in India had become a part of the British Empire, the Act empowered the British Government to station 20,000 Royal troops in India at the cost of the Company. These troops were to be paid out of Indian revenues. The

Company was, however, authorised to make rules and regulations for the Indian troops and also to hold Court martials to punish the offenders.

11. Appointment of Bishop and Archdeacons. Provision was made for the appointment of a Bishop and three Archdeacons under him at Calcutta for the benefit of the Europeans in India. This marked the beginning of a regular church establishment in India.

SIGNIFICANCE OF THE CHARTER ACT OF 1813

Through the Charter Act, 1813 retained the old constitution without any modification, yet it was significant on account of the following reasons —

1. Abolition of Company's Monopoly of Indian Trade. It meant the triumph of the theory of free trade. The Act scrapped the Company's monopolistic right of trade with India and allowed all His Majesty's subjects to compete for Indian trade. The Act also marked the victory of the public opinion and defeat of the defenders of Company's privileges. The policy of free trade heralded the ruin of Indian textile industry. The country-made coarse cloth could not compete with the fine mill-made cloth of Lancashire. With the decline of textile industry, India's economy became purely agricultural. In short, free trade proved a boom for British trade.

2. Provisions made for the Welfare of the people of the Country. Provision for the promotion of western education in India proved a blessing in disguise for the British Government. Promotion of the study of English enabled the rulers to get cheap clerks. The Indians educated in English schools began to hate their own culture and admire everything that came from the west. The considerable amount was sanctioned for the education. Though the money was not utilized for the next 20 years but this sanction opened a new chapter in the advancement of Indian education.

3. Merchants and Missionaries were permitted to settle in India. The British merchants and missionaries were given permission to settle in India. The territories of India were considered as a property of Britain.

4. Influence of British Missionaries. The coming of British missionaries to India for propagating their religion had also far-reaching effects. They built churches and ran hospitals and missionary schools. Their activities in due course spread such an infection among ignorant Indians that many of them embraced Christianity. Swami Dayanand and Swami Vivekanand in later years took a serious view of this growing danger and they did glorious work to check the expansion of Christianity in the country.

5. Influence of British Capital and Enterprise. With the mass migration of Britishers in India, the English Capital and enterprise began to flow in India and this led to an era of exploitation. It was practically difficult for the Indian merchants to compete with the Britishers. The Indian industries also ruined and agriculture became the sole occupation of Indians. **Dr. Ishwari Prasad** has rightly remarked, *"From this date approximately begins the ruin of Indian industries the growing dependence upon agriculture and the consequent poverty of our people."*

EXERCISES

Long Answer Type Questions

1. Explain the main provisions of the Charter Act, 1813.
2. Discuss the importance of the Charter Act, 1813.

Short Answer Type Questions

1. Write any two provisions of the Charter Act, 1813.
2. Write any two reasons of importance of Charter Act, 1813.

Objective Type Questions

Choose the correct answer

1. Which Act among the following terminated the East India Company's monopoly of Indian trade and threw open the Indian trade to all the British subjects ?

   (*a*) Charter Act of 1793 (*b*) Government of India Act, 1858

   (*c*) Charter Act of 1813 (*d*) None of the above

2. Which Act among the following made the provision for the promotion of Western Education in India ?

   (*a*) Charter Act of 1793 (*b*) Government of India Act, 1858

   (*c*) Charter Act of 1813 (*d*) None of the above

ANSWERS

1. (*c*) **2.** (*c*)

5

CHAPTER

Constitutional Development upto 1853

> *"I do not look upon the Legislative Council, as some of the Indians do, as the nucleus and beginning of a constitutional Parliament in India."*
>
> ***— Sir Charles Wood, President of the Board of Control***

ACT OF 1833

The Act of 1813 conferred upon the Company the exclusive right of trade with China for a period of twenty years. At the expiry of this period when the Charter was brought before the Parliament for renewal, Adam Smith's theory of *laissez-faire* or free trade had become quite popular. So the Act of 1833 terminated the monopoly of Company's trade with China and allowed all the British subjects to try their luck in the East. The British statesmen were even inclined to give representative institutions to Indians but such a move failed because of Macaulay who stood strongly for the continuation of Company's rule in India. The Act was finally passed on August 28, 1833, and put into force on 22nd April, 1834.

MAIN PROVISIONS OF THE ACT OF 1833

Following were the main provisions of the Act of 1833 —

1. End of the commercial functions of the Company. The Act stated in very clear words that the Company, henceforth shall have no commercial functions; it was to run the administration of India in trust for His Majesty. The Company was asked to wind up its business and was promised to get nearly 90 million pounds as compensation for the loss of its commercial privileges, from the revenues of India. Although Mr. Buckingham and other members of the Parliament strongly opposed the preposterous move of leaving the political Government of India in the hands of a joint stock company, the British Government allowed the Company to retain its political and administrative powers over its Indian territories.

2. Restriction of European immigrants removed. The Act removed all restrictions on the immigration of British subjects to India for trade, missionary work or any other lawful purpose. It also permitted Britishers to buy land and settle down permanently in India. The Act also empowered the Governor-General-in-Council to make laws and ordinances for ensuring protection to Indians from insults to their person or religion by the British subjects.

3. Increase in the powers of the Governor-General. The Act further strengthened the hands of the Central Government over the Presidency Governments. The designation of the Governor-General of Bengal was changed to Governor-General of India. The reason behind such a change was that the whole of country leaving the Punjab had by that time come under the heels of the Company. Need was being felt for a centralised administration of India. So the authors of the Act invested the Governor-General with full power and authority to control civil and military administration of the Presidency Governments. The Act made it binding on the Governors to obey in all cases the instructions received from the Governor-General. They were to raise and spend the revenues only under the authority of the Governor-General. In short only one budget was prepared for the whole of India by the Governor-General-in-Council.

The new Act confirmed the power of the Governor-General, granted by the Act of 1784, to suspend any member of the Presidency Governments for disobedience. Even the entire Provincial Government could be suspended by the Governor-General with the consent of his Council on the charge of failing to carry out his instructions. Such provisions tended to centralise the authority in the hands of the Governor-General.

4. Legislative powers vested in the Central Government. The Act of 1833 also established the centralisation of Legislative powers in India. Prior to this enactment, Provincial Governments enjoyed a large measure of freedom in matters of making laws for their territories. There was no uniformity of legislation. There existed in fact five bodies of statute laws in India—they were Charter Acts, Parliamentary Laws, the Orders of the Governor-General-in-Council, Presidency Laws and Supreme Court's orders. Sometimes a Presidency Law conflicted with a Central Law resulting in confusion for the people and inefficiency in administration. So, in order to secure uniformity of legislation, the Act of 1833 empowered the Governor-General to make laws for 'all persons whether British or native, foreigners or others; and for all Courts of justice; and for all places of the Indian territories, as well as for all the servants of the Company'. The Presidency Governments could, henceforth, submit drafts of any law they considered necessary to the Governor-General who permitted or disallowed them as the deemed fit.

5. The veto power of Governor-General and the Governors over their Councils was well defined. The Governor-General and the Governors had been empowered by the Act of 1793 to disregard or override the decision of their respective Councils. This Act further defined the veto powers of the Governor-General and the Governors. In case of the exercise of veto powers, they had to explain the reason of their doing so. The Act advised them to exercise their veto power sparingly.

6. Laws to improve the condition of Indians. The Act empowered the Governor-General to make laws and regulations for the welfare of Indians. Armed with this power, the Governor-General went ahead with a measure for the abolition of slavery in India.

7. Addition of Law member to the Council of the Governor General. Provision was made for the addition of a Law member to Governor-General's Council. He was to be appointed by the Directors to advise the Governor-General on law-matters. He had no right to vote except on matters pertaining to making laws and regulations. He was not be a person in the service of the Company. He was to act as a substitute for the approval of the Supreme Court. Macaulay was the first Law Member appointed under the Act. The Governor-General was also advised under the Act to appoint a Law Commission to codify all the laws.

8. All discrimination against Indians abolished. The Act laid down that "No native of India nor any natural born subject of His Majesty, would be disabled from holding any place, office or employment only by reason of his religion, place of birth, descent or colour". Fitness was henceforth to be the criterion of eligibility for any Government job.

9. Appointment of other Bishops. The Act suggested the number of Bishopries to be increased from one to three. It made the Bishop of Calcutta, henceforth, the Metropolitan Bishop of India.

10. Establishment of Central control over the forces of the Presidencies. The Governments of the Bombay and Madras were allowed to retain separate military force under their respective Commander-in-Chief, but their overall and ultimate control was vested in the Governor-General.

11. The Act reduced the strength of each Presidency Council from three to two.

12. Payment of the loan for the Company. The Act deprived the Company of its monopolistic trade rights with India and China but allowed it to retain its political and administrative powers. Since the Company had ceased to be a trading concern, provision was made for the repayment of debts that it owed to others. All the debts and liabilities of the Company were to be paid out of Indian Revenues and the Shareholders were promised $10^1/_2$% as dividend annually for a period of fifty years. As a compensation for the loss suffered, the Company was offered a lumpsum of 90 million pound sterlings.

13. The President of the Board of Control to be Minister for Indian affairs. The Act changed the constitution of the Board of Control. The President became a Minister for Indian affairs. He was to have two Assistant Commissioners and a Secretary. The importance of the secretary can be guaged from the fact that while the President answered the questions on Indian affairs in the House of Lords, the Secretary represented him in the House of Commons. This provision prepared the background for the significant role that the Secretary of State for India was to play in later years. The Directors of the Company were stripped of all their powers and made to act as advisers to the President of Board of Control.

14. Patronage of the Directors restricted. The Act directed the Directors to nominate as many persons as were double the number of existing vacancies in Indian services. The candidates received instruction in the Haileybury College. The merit list of the candidates was supplied to the Directors for appointment to various vacancies in Indian services. The Directors opposed the provision strongly. Hence by another Act of 1834 they were allowed their patronage for another twenty years.

15. The Act made provision for the creation of Agra Presidency by splitting up the Presidency of Bengal into two divisions. But before the provision could be given effect to, it was suspended by an Act passed in 1835.

IMPORTANCE OF THE ACT

The Act of 1833, as observed by Lord Morely, was the most important Act passed by the Parliament till 1909. The first thing that the Act accomplished was a strong centralised Government for the whole of British India. With Legislative centralisation, it ensured uniformity of laws in the country. Above all, it ensured a fair and impartial treatment to Indians in matter of selection for State service. No other Act passed in the 19th century contained such lofty principles as this one. It accorded the subject race equality of status with the ruling community. Section 87 of the Act by its implication meant that there would be no governing caste in British India and that race and religion will not qualify or disqualify a person in matters of higher services and employments. Macaulay called this provision as the most 'wise, benevolent and noble clause of the Act.'

According to Dr. Ishwari Prasad, *"the Charter Act of 1833 was also significant in so far as it made certain important provisions regarding the governance of India and marked the beginning of Indian Legislature"* The Act empowered the Governor-General to legislate for the whole of British India. In the discharge of his new onerous responsibility, he was to be assisted by a Law member. For the first time all variations and complexities in legal system from Province to Province were removed. All the rules and regulations were codified. The Indian Penal Code and the Code of Civil and Criminal Procedure came into existence.The Act promoted the unification of the country both politically and emotionally.

The Act also changed the shape of the Company from a joint stock company into a ruling body. This step brought about a substantial and far-reaching change in the outlook of the Company. It ceased to be dominated by profit-motives and began to pay greater attention to the welfare of the people. The purely political character of the Company paved way for increasing measure of His Majesty's control over the administration of India. This process culminated in the elimination of the Company and annexation of India to the British Empire in 1858.

EXERCISES

Long Answer Type Questions

1. Write a note on the Act of 1833.
2. What were the main provisions of the Act of 1833? Discuss in brief the importance of the Act.

Short Answer Type Questions

1. Write any three provisions of the Act of 1833.
2. How the Act of 1833 increase in the powers of the Governor-General?
3. Write in brief the importance of the Act of 1833.

Objective Type Questions

Choose the correct answer

1. The Act of 1833 was finally passed on August 20.
   (*a*) 1833 (*b*) 1834
   (*c*) 1835 (*d*) 1836
2. The Act of 1833 put into force on 22nd April,
   (*a*) 1833 (*b*) 1834
   (*b*) 1835 (*d*) 1836
3. Which section of the Act makes provision that there would be no governing caste in British India ?
   (*a*) Section 85 (*b*) Section 86
   (*c*) Section 87 (*d*) Section 88

ANSWERS

1. (*a*) **2.** (*b*) **3.** (*c*)

6

CHAPTER

Charter Act of 1853

This was the last of the series of Charter Acts passed by the British Parliament between 1793 and 1853. The Act of 1853 extended the rule of the Company over India for another term of twenty years. When the time came for the renewal of the Charter in 1853, opposition ensued both from British public and the residents of the three Presidencies of Bengal, Bombay and Madras. The people of Madras in their petition urged the need of construction public works and providing more facilities for the education of the people. The people of Bombay demanded the setting up of an Indian Council in place of Board of Control and Board of Directors. The Petition submitted on behalf of the people of Bengal prayed that in place of dual system of Government in England, there should be one Secretary of State assisted by a Council of India. The petition also protested against failure of the Company to appoint Indians to higher posts. It further demanded a partly representative legislative body in India, largely free from the pressure of the executive organ of the Government. The British Parliament then appointed a committee to look into the demands of the people of India. The report of this committee formed the basis of the Act of 1853.

MAIN PROVISIONS OF THE ACT OF 1853

The principal provisions of this Act were as follows —

1. Empowered to give the administration of India to the British Crown. The Act allowed the Company to govern its territories in India on behalf of Her Majesty until the Parliament should otherwise direct. Thus, the Parliament reserved its right to relieve the Company of its political functions at any time it liked.

2. Influence of the Directors further curtailed. The Act reduced further the patronage of the Directors. Their number was reduced from 24 to 18, six out of which were to be the nominees of the Crown. The quorum was also reduced from 13 to 10, so that the nominees of the Crown may form a majority in a thinly attended meeting of Directors.

3. Indian Civil Service opened for all. The Act took away from the Directors their privilege to nominate persons for Civil Services in India. The competition was thrown open to all the British subjects irrespective of race, caste or religion. Recruitment to Indian Civil Service through competitive examinations lessened the possibility of personal consideration governing the Directors in making appointments.

4. Governor-General's Legislative Council enlarged. The Act of 1833 had provided for the addition of a Law member of Governor-General's Council. His function was confined to advising the Governor-General in matters relating to making laws and regulations. He was naturally denied the experience of other departments of the Government. The new Act brought him on a footing of equality with the three ordinary members of the Governor-General's Council. He was given the right to sit and vote like other members at all the executive meetings. The Act also enlarged the Council of the Governor-General by the addition of the Chief Justice of Bengal, one other Judge of the Supreme Court and one representative each of the Government of Bombay, Madras, Bengal and North West Frontier Province (Agra division). Thus, the expanded Council for legislative purpose was henceforth to consist of twelve members.

5. Codification of Indian laws. Macaulay had already done a lot of spadework regarding the compilation of laws but his labour had not been given a final shape and approval. The new Act provided for the appointment of a body of English Commissioners to give a final legal form to the Codes prepared by the Indian Law Commission appointed under the Act of 1833 and headed by Macaulay.

6. Separate Governors for Bengal and the Punjab. The Act in order to relieve the Governor-General of some administrative burden, provided for a separate Governor for Bengal and a Lieutenant-Governor for the Punjab.

7. Creation of new Provinces. The Act vested the Governor-General-in-Council with the authority to alter or readjust the boundaries of the existing Provinces or to create a new Province. But all such measures required the approval of the Directors and the Board of Control. In the exercise of the power conferred by this Act, the Governor-General-in-Council gave shape to new Provinces of Assam, Central Provinces, North West Frontier Province, Burma, British Baluchistan and Delhi.

8. Fixed the salary of each member. The new Act fixed the salary of each member of the Governor-General's Council at £ 500 per year. The presence of at least seven of the total number of 12 members was made essential for any lawful meeting of the Legislative Council of Governor-General.

9. Procedure of the Legislative Council. The Governor-General's Legislative Council put the British Parliament procedure as a model for purposes of making laws. Every Bill was sent to a select committee for expert opinion. The Legislative Council could also discuss freely the policy matters of the central executive.

10. Consent of the Governor-General. The Legislative Council under the new Act was not to be a sovereign law-making body. Any Bill passed by it could not go into the Statute Book unless assented to by the Governor-General. Any Bill passed by it could be vetoed by the Governor-General-in-Council.

IMPORTANCE OF THE ACT

This Act was a step forward in the constitutional development of India. The most welcome feature of this Act was the enlargement of the Governor-General's Executive Council for legislative purposes. The legislative wing began to function as a Parliament in miniature and adopted the same business procedure as practised in the British Parliament. Every Bill before being given the stamp of finality, passed through three readings and scrutiny by an expert committee. The Legislative Council also showed inclination to inquire into executive business and criticize the Government for its acts of omission and commission.

Another radical feature of the Act was that it did not fix any definite period for which the Company was to retain its powers. The Charter said that the Company was allowed to hold and govern its possessions in India in trust for Her Majesty, her heirs and successors until Parliament should otherwise direct. This was a clear indication that the Company's privileges could be withdrawn and the trust terminated at any time the Parliament liked. And we find that only five years after this Charter, the Crown relieved the Company of all its powers and assumed the rulership of India.

The Act gave another kick to the already dwindling powers of the Directors. It reduced their number from 24 to 18 out of which six were to be nominated by the Crown from amongst those persons who had served in India for at least ten years. Another six of the remaining twelve members were also required to possess long experience of Indian affairs. Thus, the Court of Directors became an expert council of advice on Indian affairs. The Act also deprived the Directors of their power to make nominations for Indian services. The candidates henceforth were to be selected through competitive examinations, open to all British subjects. The Act also relieved the Governor-General of much of his burden. With the appointment of a separate Governor for Bengal, the Governor-General could now devote more time to problems of all-India nature. This provision accounted for greater efficiency in the Company's administration of its territories.

The Act is also significant for giving representation to the Presidencies in the Central Legislative Council. Although Sir Charles Wood stressed on the nomination of only Civil servants of ten years standing, it had one good effect. At least the door was opened for the inclusion of provincial representatives in the Central Legislative. It served as a base for the nationalists to demand that the official nominees be replaced by popularly elected representatives. The British Law Commission, constituted under the Act, also did some creditable work to give a shape and form to Civil and Penal Codes, already prepared by Macaulay and his colleagues.

The most noteworthy aspect of the new Act was that it threw open the Civil Service to competitions. This step marked the end of the patronage and arbitrary powers of the Directors in regard to appointments for Indian services. It also gave equality of opportunity to ambitious and outstanding Indian students to compete with the British candidates for senior jobs. Although open competition did not prove of any great benefit to Indian candidates because of lower age limit and the holding of tests in London, yet this gave an incentive to the nationalists to demand the Indianisation of services and holding of a simultaneous test for I.C.S. in India.

In short, we can say that this Act was important only in two respects. One, the Crown could take up the governance of India in its own hand at any time. Second, a miniature though ineffective Legislative Council was at least established at the centre. Contrary to the intention of the framers of the Act, it became 'An Anglo-Indian House of Commons' which started questioning the Executive Council and refused to submit to the wishes of the Governor-General concerning legislation.

DEFECTS OF THE ACT

The Act of 1853 was not an unmixed blessing. The improvements contemplated in the Act were half hearted and piecemeal. The Act took no step to remove the chief defect of administration namely the Double Government. The Court of Directors and Board of Control continued to function as affective authorities over Indian affairs. Conflicts among them created confusion for the Indian Government. Secondly, the authors of the Act brushed aside the popular demand for representative institutions in India with cold indifference. They did not care to consider the petitions submitted by the three Presidencies. Thirdly, the formation of the Legislative Council failed utterly to satisfy the Indian aspirations. There was no elected person in the Council to act as the spokesmen of the people. For the aforesaid reason, the Act was a great disappointment to the people.

EXERCISES

Long Answer Type Questions

1. Write a brief note on the 'Charter Act of 1853'.
2. What were the main provisions of 'Charter Act of 1853'?
3. Discuss in brief the importance of the Act of 1853.

Short Answer Type Questions

1. Write any three main provisions of 'Charter Act of 1853'.
2. Discuss the importance of the 'Charter Act of 1853'.

Objective Type Questions

Choose the correct answer

1. The Act of 1853 extended the rule of the Company over India for another term of
   (*a*) 20 years (*b*) 25 years
   (*c*) 30 years (*d*) 35 years
2. The Act of 1853 reduced the number of the Directors from 24 to
   (*a*) 17 (*b*) 18
   (*c*) 19 (*d*) 20
3. A separate Lieutenant-Governor was appointed for the administration of
   (*a*) Bengal (*b*) Punjab
   (*c*) Both *a* and *b* (*d*) None of the above

ANSWERS

1. (*a*) **2.** (*b*) **3.** (*c*)

PART – II

NATIONAL MOVEMENT

(STRUGGLE FOR FREEDOM AGAINST FOREIGN RULE)

1. March of British Imperialism
2. Disastrous effects of British Imperialism
3. First Armed Struggle for Freedom, 1857 and Act of 1858
4. Act of 1861
5. Rise of Nationalism in India
6. Birth of Indian National Congress and National Movement
7. The Indian Council Act of 1892
8. Moderate and Extremist Programme of Congress
9. Revolutionary Movement in India and Abroad
10. Rise and Growth of Commuhalism
11. Morley-Minto Reforms (Act of 1909)
12. The Impact of First world war and the Home Rule Movement
13. Government of India Act, 1919
14. Nature and Working of Dyarchy in the Provinces
15. Non-Co-Operation Movement and Swaraj Party
16. Civil Disobedience Movement
17. Socialist and Communist Trends in National Movement
18. Central Government (Act of 1935)
19. Provincial Governments (Act of 1935)
20. Working of the Provincial Autonomy
21. Quit India Movement and Dawn of Independence
22. Some Prominent Leaders of Freedom Struggle

■ Appendix : Heroic Struggle for Freedom in Assam

1

CHAPTER

March of British Imperialism
(Toughest Resistance Offered by the Indians)

> *"No civilized Government ever existed on the face of this earth which was more corrupt, more perfidious and more rapacious than the Government of East India Company from* 1765 *to* 1772".
> — ***Sir Lewis***

Before we understand the march of British imperialism in this country, it is most essential to understand the meaning and motives of the British colonialists and imperialists because colonialism ultimately takes the shape of imperialism. According to **Prof. Shuman**– "Imperialism is to control national states by means of force." There is absolutely no doubt that an imperialist country looks after its own interests only and it exploits the countries under it. **Shuman** has made it amply clear by saying that "It is no more the purpose of the imperialism to confer benefits upon home country." **Parker Moon** also says —"The reason why the British entered in India and the primary reason why they remained there was not to benefit India but to benefit Great Britain." It is, therefore, clear that the white races may say that God has deputed them to make the black races civilised and for this purpose, they conquered the countries of Asia and Africa but their talk of charity is only to deceive others.

India had trade relations with Europe from times immemorial. There were three main trade routes along which all Indo-European trade passed—the Northern by way of the Oxus, the Caspian and the Black seas, the middle through Syria to the Mediterranean and the Southern by sea to Egypt and thence to Europe. Principalities of Venice and Genoa, owed all their prosperity to the Indian trade, as it passed through them to Central and Western Europe.

Portuguese reach India. The Turks conquered Constantinople (the capital of Bezantine Empire ruled by Christians, in 1453 and it enabled them to capture northern and middle route and they looted European traders who belonged to Christianity. The Ottoman Empire of Turks became a naval power in 1470 and they captured Egypt in 1516-17. Thus they blocked all the trade routes of Europe to India. Consequently, people of Europe had to face great hardships because the spices had to be imported from South India, which made their dishes tasty. Therefore, the Portuguese tried their best to explore a new route. The credit of exploring a new route to India belongs solely to Vasco da Gama who reached Calicut in 1498 by way of Cape of Good Hope, after making a round of Africa. He concluded a treaty of friendship with Zamorin of Calicut. The rich cargo that he carried with him tempted many other rich merchants of his country. They too entered upon their Indian enterprises in a big way. For a century they remained the masters of trade with the Asian countries.

Coming of the other European Traders to India. The fabulous wealth of India attracted a host of European traders to this country. On December 31, 1600—Queen Elizabeth of England was prevailed upon to grant a charter and the English East India Company was formed. The objective of the Company at the time of formation was not to establish colonies but simply to make money by trading with India and other Far-Eastern countries but these objectives were not followed later on strictly and factories were established at Surat, Ahmedabad and Broach following the embassy of Sir Thomas Roe (1615–19) at the court of Jehangir. Later on the factories were established at Madras, Bombay and Calcutta.

The Dutch East India Company came into existence in 1602. It was followed by the French East India Company in 1664. The first French factory was established at Surat in 1667 and the second at Masaulipattam in 1669. Later on factories were established in Mahi, Chandranagar and Yenam.

Changes in the policy of the English Company. The sack of Surat in 1664 and in 1670 by Shivaji under the very eyes of the Mughal Governor made it evident that the Company could no longer depend on Mughal protection but must defend or be wiped out. The year 1681 saw the election of Sir Joshua to the Governorship of the Company and he completely dominated the affairs of the Company till his death in 1699. To him the Mughal Empire was dead because Aurangzeb had miserably failed to subdue the Marathas even after the death of Shivaji in 1680. Therefore, the policy that Sir Joshua evolved was to build up a power on the Indian coastline sufficiently strong to enforce respect and repel attacks. Factories were to be fortified, forts were to be constructed and a standing army to be maintained, the cost of all to be met by increased rents, custom dues and municipal taxation. Accordingly, Bombay, Madras and other places on the coast were to be fortified and provided with a strong military and naval support. *This final declaration of policy which aimed at transforming the English from traders into a nation in India clearly marks a transition from the policy of peaceful trade to that of territorial aggrandisement.*

Conflict amongst European Traders to Monopolise Indian Trade. Rivalries between European traders became deeper and more pronounced day by day. Serious competition for monopolising Indian trade led inevitably to violent hostilities and wars. The Portuguese Company received a great setback when Spain annexed Portugal in 1580. Another reason of its downfall was the deep-rooted enmity to the Muslims. The Portuguese crusaders against Islam displeased the Mughal Emperor Shah Jahan so much that he adopted a stern attitude towards them. The final and fatal blow was given to the Portuguese Company by the British traders.

After the exit of the Portuguese from the field, the English turned to deal with the Dutch traders. The commercial rivalry between the Dutch and English cultimated in the massacre of the latter at Amboyna in February, 1623. Cromwell, however, avenged the massacre by defeating Holland in 1654 and recovering £ 85,000 from the Dutch as compensation. The defeat of Holland in Europe further weakened their power in India also.

Now the only formidable rival of British trade interests in India was the French Company. Dupleix, who came to India in 1742, as the Governor of Pondicherry, conceived the idea of establishing a French dominion in this country. With that end in view, he began to intervene in disputes among the native princes.

The year 1744 witnessed a war between England and France in Europe. It had its repercussions in India. Dupleix, the French Governor, attacked and captured Madras. But as soon as the two countries concluded peace in Europe, hostilities between the French and the English ceased in India also. Again in 1748 the two nations went on war which lasted for six years. The cause this time was the issue of Subedarship of the Deccan. After the death of Asafjah Nizamul Mulk in 1748, a quarrel for the throne ensued between Nasir Jung and Muzaffar Jung. Dupleix supported Muzaffar

Jung whereas the British extended help to Nasir Jung. The same thing happened in Carnatic where the French backed Chanda Sahib against Muhammed Ali who received aid from the English camp. Luck favoured the French for the time being and the nominees of Dupleix were put to the thrones of Hyderabad and Carnatic. But soon the tables were turned in favour of the English and their own stooges acquired dominance. Dupleix failed because his resources and destiny failed him. He was recalled by his Government in 1754 . Mr. Godheau succeeded Dupleix in India. He signed a peace treaty with the English and thus the hostilities between the two came to an end.

The peace treaty negotiated by Godheau proved short-lived. The French and the English were locked in a grim struggle again as soon as the 'Seven Years' War' broke out in 1756. The English forces inflicted a crushing defeat on the French in the battle of Wandewash on 22nd January, 1760. The French dream of establishing a dominion in India was, thus, shattered for ever. Their hold was restricted to Chandranagar, Pondicherry, Yenam and Mahi. The English after defeating the French became the supreme European power in India.

CONQUEST OF BENGAL BY BRITISHERS BY TREACHEROUS MEANS: ERA OF IMPERIALISM STARTS

The last great Mughal emperor Aurangzeb died on 3rd March, 1707. His death marked the end of strong empire of Mughal history. Intrigues and rifts raised their ugly heads. The situation became so acute that no king could rule over Delhi for a reasonably long time. The Mughal Empire began to disintegrate and chaotic conditions prevailed everywhere. Bengal became independent under Alivardi Khan. The English exploited the situations for expanding their territory. They set about fortifying their settlement and abusing their trade privileges obtained from the Mughal Emperor Farukh Siyyar. Besides it, they began to conspire for putting their puppet on the throne of Bengal. With this end in view, the English signed a treaty with Mir Jafar.

Siraj-ud-dowlah (son of the daughter of Alivardi Khan) who came to the throne after the death of Alivardi Khan in April, 1756 foresaw the danger. He forbade both the English and the French from building forts. While the French obeyed, the English refused to desist from fortifying their settlements. The hostilities led to the **Battle of Plassey** on 23rd June, 1757 in which Nawab lost because of betrayal by Mir Jafar (his son-in-law) and Rai Durlabh who commanded large portions of the Nawab's army. Siraj-ud-dowlah was caught and beheaded by Mir Jafar's son.The battle of Plassey, which the English won by treachery, proved one of the few decisive battles of history. It made the English the supreme masters of Bengal. Mir Jafar was made to pay a heavy price for his Nawabship. He resented the bullying tactics of the English. This led to his deposition and installation of Mir Qasim in his place as the Nawab of Bengal.

Battle of Buxar. Mir Qasim, too, could not tolerate any interference in his affairs by the Company. Matters came to a head. The combined forces of Mir Qasim, the Nawab Wazir Shuja-ud-dowlah of Oudh and the Emperor Shah Alam met the English forces at Buxar on 22nd October, 1764. But luck favoured British once again. Mir Qasim fled towards Delhi where he died in 1777. In 1765, the English concluded a treaty with Shah Alam who needed British help to recover the throne of his forefathers. According to this treaty, the Company agreed to cede Allahabad and Kara and also to pay Shah Alam a sum of ₹ 26 lakhs annually, and in turn obtained from him the grant of *Diwani of Bengal, Bihar and Orissa.* According to Dr. Ishwari Prasad : "The importance of the grant of Dewani (Right of collection of revenue) lay in the fact that Shah Alam was theoretically and legally the Emperor and this gave a colour to the Company's transaction."

Before Warren Hastings arrived, there was a severe famine in Bengal in 1770, so Shivanand made a heroic attempt to liberate Bengal from the yoke of British imperialists.

The battles of Plassey and Buxar are the two important events of Indian History. These had far-reaching effects. Firstly, the English became the virtual masters of the three provinces—Bengal,

Bihar and Orissa. Secondly, the fugitive Shah Alam became a pensioner of the Company. Success in these battles made the Company dream of rounding off their conquests for which the three provinces mentioned above served as strong bases.

Double Government or the Dual System in Bengal. As narrated above, the Company's victory in the battle of Plassey and Buxar made it the virtual master of three provinces of Bengal, Bihar and Orissa. The administrative machinery in their hands became loose and corrupt. The Company acquired the Diwani, *i.e.* —the right to collect revenue and organise civil justice but the Nizamat-executive power, the police and criminal justice was carried on by the Nawab who received a fixed amount from the Company to run the administrative show. The Company reinstated Mir Jafar as Nawab of Bengal on conditions favourable to them, but incidently he died in February 1765. He was succeeded by his son Najib-ud-dowlah from whom the Company secured the **Nizamat** (The right of administration and criminal justice) also. The transfer of power from the Nawab into the British hands was thus made complete and final. The suzerainty of the company became unchallenged. Lord Clive, however, in view of some practical difficulties, did not consider it advisable for the company to assume the rulership of the three provinces directly.

He made a treaty with Najib-ud-dowlah in 1765 and promised to pay him a fixed amount of ₹ 53 lakhs annually for running the administration. This arrangement enabled the company to deal with the purse without shouldering any responsibility. This system came to be called the Dual System or Double Government in Bengal.

Consequences of the Dual System. The dual system introduced by Lord Clive worked from 1765 to 1772. Between the departure of Lord Clive and arrival of Warren Hastings, the reins of office were held by Verelst (1766–69) and Cartier (1769–72). Both these persons were men of mediocre abilities. People suffered much under the weak and irresponsible rule of the Company. Commenting on the effects of British policy and methods, during the Double System of Government in Bengal, Mr. Goram D. Sanderson writes : "*British Imperialism exhibited its true colours when engaged in the collection of revenue in a conquered district. Let us follow British imperialism to Bengal. The Province of Bengal , until the advent of the British, was undoubtedly the richest land in the world. No famine was ever recorded by history to have entered the rich and populous area. For millennia, Bengal has been famous for its continuous and abundant prosperity. British imperialism needed only thirteen years to bring destruction, death and famine to the Province of Bengal.*" Available records tell us while the revenue collected by the Mughal rulers never exceeded the figure of £ 817,533 yearly, the English began to exact as much as £ 2,680,000 from the Province of Bengal.

The division of authority, as envisaged by the Dual System, presented a host of difficulties for the Nawab in running the administration. He was saddled with power without having any hold over the purse. His power was only shadowy and nominal. The Company collected the revenue without discharging its duties towards the tax payers. The Nawab was always in need of money to meet the expenses of the administration. **Kaye** rightly observes that the divorce of power from responsibility "made confusion more confounded and corrupt more corrupt."

The abuses of private trade under the Dual system reached an unprecedented height. The Company's servants entered into private trade in defiance of native authority. The officers of Nawab were corrupt. The Company's servants tried recklessly to fill their pockets with ill-gotten wealth. The result was a confusion in which the people suffered heavily. Corrupt administration and private trade by the Company's servants affected the interests of the Company also. Its income from land fell considerably. *Another consequence of Company's misrule was that the native industries were completely ruined.* The silk weavers were forced to work in the Company's factories and were prohibited from working in their own homes. Defiance of the native laws by the employees of the Company infected the minds even of the subjects of the Nawab who eventually lost their regard for judiciary. All these evils were remedied by the Home Government by the Regulating Act, 1773.

Exploitation by Warren Hastings

Clive was the chief architect of the British dominion in Bengal. After him Warren Hastings, Governor-General of Bengal (1772–1785 A.D.) followed in his footsteps. He extended the British control over Oudh by various undesirable means. He extracted ₹ 76 lakhs from the Begums of Oudh by adopting various illegal and obnoxious methods. The British historian **Sir Alfred Lyall** writes,

"The employment of personal severities, under the superintendence of British Officers in order to extract money from women and eunuchs is an ignoble kind of undertaking .... to push the Nawab on and actively assisting in measures of coercion against women and eunuchs was conduct unworthy and indefensible."

Another British historian **P. Roberts** also writes, "Making every allowance for difficulties of Hastings, it is impossible not to regret and condemn this proceeding."

His equally condemnable act was the invasion of Rohilkhand on 17th April, 1772 on collusion with Nawab Wazir of Oudh, in which the ruler of Rohilkhand, Hafiz Rahmat was killed along with his 2,000 soldiers. After this 20,000 Rohillas were driven out from the country. It is noteworthy that Hastings's policy in connection with the Rohilla War has been severely condemned by Burke, Macaulay and the older schools of historians like Mill and others who hold that "*Hastings deliberately sold the lives and liberties of a free people and condoned horrible atrocities on the part of the armies of the Nawab of Oudh.*"

The British historian **Sir Alfred Lyall** writes, "*The expedition against the Rohillas was wrong in principle, for they had not provoked us and the Wazir could only be relied upon to abuse his advantages.*" It is to be admitted that Hastings chief motive was mercenary.[1]

Warren Hastings extracted ₹ 1,50,000 from Muny Begum, the widow of Mir Jafar for appointing her guardian to the young prince. So, P. Roberts writes, "*it was really a monstrous abuse that when the Governor of Bengal, whose salary and allowances amounted to between* £ 20,000 *and* £ 30,000, *visited Murshidabad, he should receive from the Nawab an allowance amounting to* £ 225 *a day.*"

Warren Hastings was the first Governor-General who had to work under the Regulation Act of 1773. He had to face numerous difficulties under the Act, mainly because the majority of the members of his Executive Council were against him. Warren Hastings resigned in 1784 when Pitts India Act was passed. He went to England where he was tried for his misdeeds but was acquitted later on.

BRITISH IMPERIALISM MARCHES AHEAD: STRONGEST RESISTANCE BY TIPU SULTAN AND THE MARATHAS

Subsidiary Alliance. The next Governor-General who extended the British dominions in India was Lord Wellesly. He invented the system of Subsidiary Alliances. It implies that "the native powers were to make no wars and to carry on no negotiations with any other State, whatsoever without the knowledge and consent of the British Government. The greater principalities were each to maintain a native force commanded by British officers for the preservation of the public peace, and they were each to cede certain territories in full sovereignty to meet the yearly charges of this force. The lesser principalities were to pay a tribute to the paramount power. In return, the British Government was to protect them, one and all, against foreign enemies of every sort or kind".[2] So in other words, it was an attempt to subordinate the Indian States and make the East India Company as supreme power in India.

Nizam of Hyderabad accepts subsidiary alliance and loses independence. The Nizam of Hyderabad was the first to accept it in 1798 because after his crushing defeat by the Marathas in March, 1795 at the battle of Kharda, (fifty-six miles South East of Ahmednagar), he was facing constant threat of fresh invasion on one side from the Marathas and on another side from Tipu

1. Strachey, *Hastings and the Rohilla war*, p.55.
2. Wheeler, *History of India*, pp. 426–427.

Sultan of Mysore. After this the British disarmed the French contingent which had been employed by the Nizam and stationed their own army to protect the Nizam whose cost was to be borne by him.

Fall of Tipu Sultan, the leading power of Deccan. Tipu Sultan of Mysore was the greatest adversary of the British in India. He was corresponding with Napoleon Bonaparte to enlist the help of the French. He was seeking the help of Zaman Shah, the ruler of Afghanistan to expel the British, but all his efforts in this direction, did not materialise. Unfortunately he was not having good relations with the Marathas and the Nizam, so the British taking advantage of this fact, invaded Mysore on 5th March, 1799 in collusion with the forces of the Nizam. After being defeated twice in March, he retired to Seringapattam, his capital. The British forces besieged it in April and it was taken by assault on 4th May, 1799. Tipu died bravely in the defence of his metropolis : his son surrendered to the English. For several days British troops plundered Seringapattam, meeting with no resistance at all. After this the British partitioned Mysore, giving some territories to the Nizam, keeping major territory with themselves and from the rest of the territory carved out a new vassal state of Mysore, which was given to one of the descendants of the old Hindu Raja from whom Hyder Ali had snatched power 33 years ago. The new Raja was compelled to accept subsidiary system enunciated by Wellesly and other humiliating terms beneficial to the British.

Views of Karl Marx about the fall of Mysore. The fall of Mysore resulted in the complete subjugation of the Deccan except the Maratha territory. For 30 years the people of Mysore had upheld the independence and resisted the onslaughts of British imperialism. In 1770 Hyder Ali was the first to realise that British represented the main enemy of the Indian princely states and that any agreements with them were out of question. Karl Marx writes, *"Hyder Ali and his son Tipu Sahib swore on the Qoran everlasting hate for the English and to crush them."*[1] The struggle of the people of Mysore against British colonialists had been truly heroic, but the final victory of the capitalist Britain over feudal Mysore was inevitable. However, the long years of resolute resistance from the people of Mysore had obliged the British colonialists to have large military forces constantly at the ready.[2] The fall of Mysore greatly augmented the sources of the British and it became easier for them now to face the formidable strength of the Marathas.

The death of Nana Phadnavis, leading statesman of Asia, enables the British Imperialists to conquer Maratha lands. The British were already in search of an opportunity to divide the Maratha rulers (Scindia, Holkar, Bhonsle and Gaekwad). This opportunity came when the great statesman, Nana Phadnavis died on 13th March, 1800 and "with him", remarked Colonel Palmer, the British resident at Poona, *"departed all the wisdom and moderation of the Maratha Government."* He had controlled Maratha politics for 38 long years and had rendered great service to the Marathas by consolidating their strength and keeping the British away from interfering in their affairs. Indirectly by his acts he had safeguarded the freedom of the greater part of India from the onslaughts of British imperialism because the Marathas were the greatest bulwark against the British. There was no other power in India except the Marathas who could safeguard the freedom of India against the expansionist policy of Lord Wellesly.

Peshwa, the Head of Maratha Confederacy accepts the humiliating terms of the Subsidiary Alliance

Chhatrapati Shivaji had founded the mighty Maratha kingdom in 1674 to fight the foreigners and establish Swaraj in the whole of India. That kingdom continued to struggle against the Mughal Empire till it was shattered to pieces and instead Maratha Empire was established but the last of the Peshwa, Baji Rao II was not a capable ruler, so he could not keep the Maratha Empire intact. The death of Nana Phadnavis, the wisest Stateman of Asia, gave the British golden opportunity to

1. Karl Marx, *Notes on Indian History, Moscow*, 1960, p.95.
2. K. Antenova, G. Bongare–Zexin, G. Kotosky—*A History of India.*

control the Maratha land because after him there was no body to control the Maratha Sardars and dissensions soon broke but amongst them, Daulat Rao Scindia of Gwalior and Jaswant Rao Holkar of Indore fought with each other unfortunately instead of fighting against the British imperialists and thus weakened each other and fecilitated the task of the Company.

The British were already fanning these hostilities. In 1802 in the Battle of Poona, Holkar's army completely routed the combined forces of Scindia and Peshwa Baji Rao II (1796–1818). Baji Rao fled to take refuge with the British at Bassein and in December, 1802 he signed the *subsidiary alliance,* under which he agreed to maintain in Maharashtra no less than 6,000 British troops. He would be required to spend an annual amount of ₹ 2,600,000 on them. In addition, he undertook to conduct his country's foreign affairs under strict supervision of the British authorities. The British restored Peshwa to the gaddi of Poona. *Thus, the Peshwa had sacrificed the independence of Maharashtra and made Maharashtra a protectorate of British Empire.* All the Maratha chiefs saw in the treaty of Bassein the entire annihilation of their national independence and they tried to forget their mutual rivalries and to organise a confederacy against the British. Daulat Rao Scindia of Gwalior and Raghu Ji Bhonsle II of Nagpur at once joined together. They also invited Jaswant Rao Holkar (1797–1811) of Indore and Gaekwad of Baroda. It is deplorable that even in these moments of national peril, they could not sink their mutual jealousies. Holkar came late in war against the British and Gaekwad remained neutral.

Second and Third Maratha Wars to keep away the British influence and control. Second Maratha war against the British broke out in August, 1803 to preserve the independence of the territory ruled by the Marathas and to keep away the foreign control.The Maratha army was defeated at Ahmadnagar, Assaye, Arragaon and Gwaligarh. In 1803 Bhonsle signed the treaty of Deogaon under which the principality of Nagpur lost its independence and the province of Cuttack (Orissa) that lay between the territories of Bengal and Madras presidencies was handed over to the British.

The British forces also defeated the forces of Scindia at a number of places and snatched from him Aligarh, Agra and Delhi. All his lands north of the river Chambal were occupied by the British. Thus on December 30, 1803 Scindia was obliged to sign the treaty of Suráji Arjungaon by which he agreed to cede the territories between the Jamuna and the Ganges and all those situated to the northward of the Rajput principalities of Jaipur, Jodhpur and Gohad. He also surrendered to the British, Ahmadnagar and Broach and his possession between Ajanta and Godavari. He, like Raghu Ji Bhonsle, renounced all claims over the Peshwa and the Nizam and Shah Alam II, Emperor of Delhi. The British installed Shah Alam II, now aged 83, on the throne of Delhi. He had been blinded by the Rohillas and had absolutely no political backing. Both the Maratha Rajas also promised that they would not keep any foreigner in their services.

Third Maratha War to keep away the influence of the Imperialists. In April, 1804, war against Holkar was declared by the British when he plundered the territories of Raja of Jaipur who had helped the British against the Marathas in the Second Maratha War. He defeated Col. Monson in the Mukund-dara pass (30 miles south of Kota). He also besieged Delhi but his invasion was repulsed by the British. A part of his armies was defeated at Deag (near Bharatpur) on 13th November and another commanded by Holkar himself was defeated by General Lake at Farrukhabad on 17th November, 1804. General Lake was also defeated near Bharatpur but the Jat Raja of Bharatpur soon made peace with the English and deserted Holkar when he was defeated by the British.

In the meanwhile Lord Wellesly was recalled by the British Government. The Company's debt had increased from 17 millions in 1797 to 31 millions in 1806 due to the forward policy of Lord Wellesly; so the directors did not approve of his policy. Pitt remarked that Lord Wellesly "had acted most imprudently and illegally and he could not be suffered to remain in the Government." So Wellesly was replaced by Lord Cornwallis and reached Calcutta on 30th July, 1805 but he died in October, 1805. So after him George Barlow, a senior member of the Council looked to the affairs of East India Company from 1805 to 1807.

Jaswant Rao Holkar had fled to Amritsar in the hope of getting some help from Maharaja Ranjit Singh but the latter refused any help against the British because Lord Lake was pursuing Holkar. Therefore, he had to open peace negotiations with the British. George Barlow was not in favour of continuing the war, so he gave some favourable terms to Holkar. The Holkar gave up all claims to places north of Chambal. He renounced all claims upon Poona, Bundelkhand and on the English and their allies and also engaged not to admit any Europeans in his service. On the other hand, the English also agreed not to interfere with his territories south of the Chambal and to give back his territories in the Deccan. George Barlow also agreed to withdraw his protection from the Rajput states which had helped the British against the Marathas. Thus the Rajput states were again left to the mercy of Scindia and Holkar.

4th Maratha War to end the control of the British Imperialists and to regain the cherished lost independence. After George Barlow, Lord Minto became the Governor-General who continued the policy of non-interference enunciated by his predecessor. After him Lord Hastings, popularly known as Marquis of Hastings, succeeded him. He reversed the policy of non-interference and resolved to extend the British Empire in India. Lord Hastings remained the Governor-General of India from 1813 to 1823. During ten years of rule he fought wars against Nepal, Marathas and the Pindaris successfully. He humbled Nepal and vanquished the Marathas and brought to knees the Pindaris.

Lord Hastings compelled Peshwa Baji Rao II to conclude the treaty of Poona with the English on 13th June, 1817 on rigorous terms. According to this treaty, he renounced his claims as head of the Maratha Empire and engaged not to have any negotiations with other powers, except through the British Resident. His claims on Gaekwad were commuted to an annual payment of four lacs of rupees and he promised to make no further demands on the Gaekwad. He had to cede some important portions of his territories to the English. A separate treaty was concluded by the English with Gaekwad on 6th November, 1817 by which the latter agreed to discharge a part of his irregular army and to cede certain territories to the British.

The British also compelled Raja Bhonsle of Nagpur to accept the Subsidiary Alliance on 27th May, 1816. Thus these two treaties—the treaty of Poona and the treaty of Nagpur—immensely increased the influence of the English and severely affected the Marathas. Besides that, Lord Hastings also compelled Daulat Rao Scindia to conclude the treaty of Gwalior on 5th November, 1817. By this treaty the latter engaged to assist the English against the Pindaris and the British Government got full liberty to enter into engagements with the states of Udaipur, Jodhpur, Kotah, Bundi and other states on the left bank of the Chambal. Scindia also agreed not to interfere in any shape in the affairs of Rajput states.[1]

The Peshwa could not brook these humiliating terms. So was the case with other Maratha leaders. Therefore, 4th Maratha War against the English broke out in November, 1817. Appa Sahib, the ruler of Nagpur and Malhar Rao (II) Holkar, son of Jaswant Rao Holkar and the ruler of Indore rose in revolt against the British but they were defeated at a number of places and had to submit to very humiliating terms and renounce all claims upon Rajput states. They had to come under British Sovereignty and had to submit their external relations to the company for arbitration. It was also provided that the Peshwa or his descendants would not exercise any sovereignty over Holkar and his descendants. Scindia was also reduced to a state of dependence upon the British Government.

The fate of Peshwa, the Head of Maratha confederacy was worst because he had burnt the British residency at Kirki (near Poona). He fought many desperate battles against the British but the British this time had mustered the largest ever collected force *i.e.* 1,20,000 men of whom 13,000 were British and 300 canons: So the Peshwa was defeated in a number of battles. He was chased from place to place. At last he surrendered in the camp of Sir John Malcolm on 3rd June, 1818. *Lord Hastings decided to abolish Peshwaship forever, so that no symbol of Maratha unity may remain.* He was of

1. Malcolom, *Memories of Central India*, Vol. II, Appendix A.

the opinion that even if this symbol was kept in decayed form, the Maratha chiefs would again rally. So the Peshwaship was ended and Baji Rao II was allowed to live at a place called Bithur, 42 miles north-west of Kanpur, under the guard of British agent and on a pension of eight lacs a year. After this, to appease the sentiments of the Marathas a small state of Satara was carved out of the dominions of the Peshwa and Pratap Singh, a lineal descendant of Shivaji was installed on the throne.

Most Disastrous effects of the defeat of the Marathas for the whole of India

After this the whole of Maharashtra was annexed to the Bombay Presidency, except Satara and Kolhapur which were given to the descendants of Shivaji. *Thus ended all the attempts of Marathas to preserve the independence of the greater part of India* (under their control) against the rapid advance of mighty British imperialism. They had fought continually for a quarter of century to check the advance of British imperialism but due to a number of reasons, their efforts were not crowned with success. The results of the defeat of the Marathas were disastrous for the whole of India. Except the Punjab and Sind, no territory of India remained independent. The Rajput states which had acknowledged the suzerainty of the Marathas, now came directly under the suzerainty of the Company, they accepted subsidiary alliance or subordinate positions.

After this Company became very powerful because all the sources of India except the Punjab and Sind were at its disposal. Henceforth it remained only a question of time when to undertake the conquest of the remaining territories.

FINAL CONQUEST OF INDIA BY THE BRITISH IMPERIALISTS – TOUGH RESISTANCE BY THE SIKHS

Ranjit Singh establishes a mighty Sikh Empire which ultimately checked the British imperialists. In the 2nd half of the eighteenth century the Punjab remained unaffected by the course of events that were shaping the destiny of India. The Punjab was being governed at that time, by the Sikh Misls or association of Sikh warriors in the Punjab who had been fighting against the Mughals and Afghan invaders. Each Misl was a separate principality in its own right but the common religion bound them altogether. The Sardars ruled independently and united only for joint campaigns after discussing them in advance at the Council of their leaders. Between 1765 and 1799 a fierce struggle took place among the different Sardars for supremacy while Zaman Shah of Kabul was invading the Punjab for establishing his own supremacy. From this long conflict at last the leader of Sukarchakia Misl, Ranjit Singh emerged supreme in 1799. He assumed the title of Maharaja in 1799 when he occupied Lahore and made it his capital. By 1821 he had established a strong Sikh State after conquering the territories of most of the Misls: Kasur (Ferozepur), Jammu, Kangra, Attock, Multan, Kashmir, Dera Gazi Khan, Dera Ismael Khan etc. He wrested Peshawar from the Afghans in 1833. The conquest of Multan, Kashmir and Peshawar are the most famous that extended his empire, augmented its resources and added lustre to it. In 1835 Ranjit Singh conquered Laddakh. So before his death in 1839 he had established a mighty empire extending upto Afghan border on one hand, and Sind on the other hand. The Sutlej formed the boundary between the British Empire and Sikh Empire. This proved a bulwark against the expansion of mighty British Imperialism.

Maharaja Ranjit Singh had established a very good administration of his vast and mighty empire. *He did not discriminate amongst the Hindus, Sikhs and the Muslims and appointed the high officers of all the communities, even he appointed Muslims as his Ministers. Faqir Azizuddin was his foreign minister. He distributed alms amongst all sects.* He also trained his army on modern lines with the help of French officers.

During his life time Maharaja Ranjit Singh avoided all conflicts with the British and established friendly relations with them. The Maharaja also concluded two treaties with the British, Treaty of Amritsar (1809) and Triparti Treaty (1838).

Death of Ranjit Singh opens the flood-gates of the Punjab for the surging tide of British Imperialism. Maharaja Ranjit was one of the most arresting personalities in Indian history. He breathed his last on 27th June, 1839 leaving his vast and mighty empire for his own weak successors. So soon intrigues and counter-intrigues plagued the Sikh politics. One after another, Prince and Prime Minister was the victim of conspiracy. Ranjit Singh's son, Kharak Singh died on 5th November, 1840 and his able son Nau Nihal Singh also died after a few days by the fall of a gate when he was returning after performing the funeral rites of his father. He was the victim of a plot. After this Sher Singh, the illegitimate son of Maharaja Ranjit Singh, managed to get the throne with the help of the army and intrigues of Raja Dhyan Singh, Prime Minister. Due to his conspiracy the widow of Kharak Singh, Rani Chand Kaur, was killed mercilessly who had assumed the reins of Government after the death of Nau Nihal Singh. This aroused the wrath of her brother Ajit Singh, one of the Sandhanwalla Chiefs and he assassinated Sher Singh on 15th September, 1843. He also got murdered Raja Dhyan Singh who had conspired to get the throne for Sher Singh. After this Dalip Singh, a minor son of Maharaja Ranjit Singh, was raised to the throne and her mother Rani Jindan became his Regent.

Hira Singh, son of Raja Dhyan Singh, was beside with rage when he heard of his father's murder. He took his troops and did not take any food or drink until he had found and cut the Sadhanwalias to pieces after a most stubborn resistance by them. After this the reign of terror began. Hira Singh became the Prime Minister but he was soon killed. After this Jawahar Singh was selected by the Army as Prime Minister who was the maternal uncle of Maharaja Dalip Singh. Now the army had became all in all and it became uncontrollable. Soon sharp differences arose between the Prime Minister and the army and endless demands were made by the army which the Prime Minister could not satisfy. Secondly, Peshawar Singh, son of Maharaja Ranjit Singh, had rebelled against Dalip Singh and attacked Attock due to the instigation of Gulab Singh, ruler of Kashmir. Jawahar Singh had put down the rebellion but got Kashmira Singh (his brother) killed. Lal Singh and Gulab Singh instigated the army on this point. The army Panchayats called him, declared him guilty and shot him dead on September 21, 1845 before the very eyes of Rani Jindan, his sister and Queen of Maharaja Ranjit Singh. When the Rani began to weep, the murderers poured ridicule on her and hurled insult on the Queen, "Why are you raising your loud wails for your wretched brother? He was no king's son. You should reward us with liberal gifts as you cannot rule without our help."

The Queen made up her mind there and then to get destroyed the Sikh army. She made Lal Singh, the Prime Minister and her paramour agreed to the proposal because the army had became totally uncontrollable. The only way to get the Sikh army destroyed was to instigate it to attack the British. As the British were collecting huge army at Ferozepur and their activities could be watched from the other bank of Sutlej, therefore, it was easy for Lal Singh to convince the army that the British wanted to attack Lahore. On the other hand, Rani Jindan sent secret emissaries to the British and assured them all help if they destroyed Sikh army. Teja Singh, the Commander-in-Chief of the Sikh army also agreed secretly to the proposals of Rani Jindan and Lal Singh, because the Lahore Durbar and Commander-in-Chief did not consider themselves safe when the army had become uncontrollable.

First heroic battle of the people of the Punjab against the Imperialists (Sikhs lose first War due to treachery). The Sikh army crossed the Sutlej unopposed on 11th December, 1845 because of the misconceptions and negligence of Major Broadfoot, the British Commander at Ferozepur and reached within a few miles of Ferozepur. The Governor-General Lord Hardinge (1844 – 48) issued his declaration of war on 13th December, 1845. The first battle was fought at Mudki, 20 miles to the south-east of Ferozepur on 18th December, 1845 between the Sikh and British forces. Huge Gough was the Commander-in-Chief of the British forces and Teja Singh was the Commander-in-Chief of the Sikh forces. The engagement at Mudki was very bloody and sharp. The British soldiers first receded before the Khalsa battalions; but Teja Singh treacherously left the field at a critical moment "leaving the Sikhs to fight as their valour might prompt." They were at last defeated with the loss of seventeen guns; but for the English "the victory was dearly purchased and by it the British learnt the true character of their foe." On their side 657 men were wounded and 215 were killed, including

Major-General Sir Robert Sale, known for his gallant defence of Jalalabad and Major-General Sir John M'Caskill.

The second battle between the Sikh and the British forces was fought on 21st December two days after the battle of Mudki. At the beginning of the contest, the Sikhs fought stubbornly and with terrific force; "the position of the English was one of real danger and great perplexity." The Commander-in-Chief Sir Huge Gough himself expressed the view: "*During night of horrors, we were in a critical and perilous state.*" The treachery of Sikh generals ultimately helped the English cause and the Sikh entrenchments were finally captured on 22nd December. But for the failure of Sikh leadership the result of the battle might have been otherwise. However, heavy losses were caused on both sides.

Sardar Sham Singh Attariwala offers heroic resistance to the British Imperialists. The Sikhs were badly defeated in the third battle which was fought at Aliwal on 28th January, 1846. The Sikhs fled across the Sutlej, many of them being drowned in the river. The final battle was fought on 10th February, 1846 at Sobraon where the Sikhs had constructed entrenchments. "Sobraon" remarks Mr. J. Talloy's Wheeler, "*proved to be the hardest fought battle in the history of British India.*" Sikh soldiers unlike their treacherous Commander Teja Singh were prepared to conquer or die for the glory of the Khalsa. But while the soldiers did everything, the Sikh commanders with the honourable exception of Sham Singh Attariwala, remained inactive or proved traitors. *Sardar Sham Singh Attariwala showed great feats of valour and his name deserves to be written in the letters of gold.* As Cunningham has observed: "*Hearts to dare and hands to execute were numerous, but there was no mind to guide and animate the whole.*" Though the Sikhs fought with greatest valour, yet they were defeated because of the treachery of their own commanders. The losses on both sides were heavy. *On 13th February, 1846, the whole British army crossed the Sutlej and on 20th occupied Lahore.*

Humiliating Treaty of Lahore. A treaty was concluded on 9th March, 1846, the terms of which were dictated by the English to the vanquished Sikhs in the old capital of Ranjit Singh. Many humiliating terms were imposed upon the Sikh Maharaja Dalip Singh. The Sikh forces were disbanded and limited only to 25 battalions of infantry and 12,000 cavalry and 34 guns which had been captured at the battle of Sabraon were surrendered to the English. A war indemnity of one and half crore was imposed on Lahore Durbar. As Lahore had not the sufficient money to pay, so the provinces of Kashmir and Hazara had to be handed over in perpetual sovereignty. *The foreign policy of the Lahore Durbar was completely subordinated to the British Government's approval.* Kashmir and the hill states from the Beas to the Indus were cut off from the Punjab and by a separate treaty concluded on 16th March, 1846 with Gulab Singh, a sardar serving the Lahore Durbar, these were transferred to him for one million sterling.[1]

SIKHS RALLY AGAIN FOR THE LIBERATION OF THE PUNJAB AND EXPULSION OF IMPERIALISTS (Second Sikh War, 1849)

The treaty of Lahore had sowed the seeds of another war because it was very humiliating and the self-respecting Sikhs could never tolerate it. The Sikhs were feeling that they had been defeated because of the treachery of their own leaders. The Queen-mother Rani Jindan was accused of hostile plot against the British Resident and she was removed from Lahore and interned in Sheikhupura. This added to the bitterness of Sikh feelings and their discontent against British ascendency which waited only for a suitable opportunity for a gigantic outburst. The Sikh nationalists who had given a proof of their strong determination and bravery and had a tradition of brilliant achievements behind them were not likely to submit without another attempt. In fact, the Second Sikh War was inevitable. The next Governor-General, Lord Dalhousie (1848–1856) was to see the Punjab aflame with rebellion within three months of his arrival. "It needed but an event of sufficient general interest to excite a national rising and that event was supplied by the city of Multan, a long storm centre".

1. Cunningham, *History of the Sikhs.*

Dewan Mulraj, the Governor of Multan rebelled against the British rule on 20th April, 1848 and asked everybody to join his standard. He was soon joined by Chatar Singh, the Governor of Hazara (N.W.F.P.). His son, Sher Singh, who was sent by the Lahore Durbar to quell the rebellion, also joined his father. Soon due to the efforts of Rani Jindan all the old Sikh leaders joined Sher Singh and called for a war.

All these things strengthened the belief of Lord Dalhousie (1848–1856) that another war would have to be fought. Lord Dalhousie declared war against the Sikhs on 10th October, 1848 and wrote to the directors: "*Unwarranted by precedents, uninfluenced by example, the Sikh nation has called for war and on my word, Sirs, they shall have it with a vengeance.*"[1]

On 16th November, 1848, Lord Gough, the Commander-in-Chief of the British forces, crossed the Ravi and on 22nd November, he fought an undecisive battle with Sher Singh at Ram Nagar on the Chenab. The Sikhs then entrenched themselves at Chillianwala, where a bloody but indecisive battle was fought on 13th January, 1849. In this battle the losses of the English were far greater than the Sikhs. Therefore, there was a very strong criticism of Lord Gough and the Directors of the East India Company ordered Sir Charles Napier to supersede Gough and take the command from him. But before Sir Charles Napier could take the command, Lord Gough whose army had swelled now to 2,50,000 men with 100 guns, defeated the Sikhs badly on 21st February, 1849 in the battle of Gujarat, a town situated on the bank of the Chenab. The Governor-General remarked that the action at Gujarat, "*must ever be regarded as one of the most memorable in the annals of the British warfare in India; a memorable alike from the greatness of the occasion, and from the brilliant and decisive issue of the encounter.*"

The Sikh Sardars laid down their arms on 13th March, 1849. The complete defeat of the Sikhs at the hands of the British sealed the fate of their kingdom. The prospects of maintaining independence disappeared and on 29th March, 1849 Lord Dalhousie on his own responsibility issued a proclamation announcing "*that the kingdom of the Punjab is at an end and that all the territories of the Maharaja Dalip Singh are now, and henceforth, a portion of the British Empire in India.*" He said to the Chief-Commissioner of Punjab, "I firmly believe that we shall not succeed in establishing a friendly Sikh power."

Annexation of the Punjab marks the completion of the conquest of India by Imperialists and enslavement of the whole of India

Sind had already been conquered by the Imperialists in 1843. The British rounded off their conquest in 1849 by the annexation of Punjab. The Punjab was the last State of India to come in the British fold. The Sikhs had fought bravely against the Mughal tyranny and liberated Punjab from foreign yoke. Then they fought ceaselessly against Afghan invaders (Ahmad Shah Abdali and others). After this they had stood as a great bulwark against the British for nearly half a century. *With the loss of the freedom of the Punjab, no part of India remained free and the whole of India was enslaved.* Thus the British colonialists and imperialists who had started the process of building an empire in India with the conquest of Plassey in 1757, completed it with the annexation of the Punjab in 1849.

The annexation of the Punjab was wholly unjust and uncalled for. According to the treaty of Bhairowal, 16th December, 1846 it was the responsibility of the British Government to maintain peace in the Punjab as the Maharaja was minor but the British Government allowed the revolt of Mulraj of Multan into an open national rebellion, so that it might get an excuse to annex the Punjab. In this connection Major Evans Bell, the British historian has observed :

"Lord Dalhousie violated treaties, about a sacred trust, threw away the grandest opportunity ever offered to the British Government of planting solid and vital reforms upto the northern limits of India; and by an acquisition as unjust as it was imprudent, weakened one frontier, scattered our military strength and entailed a heavy financial burden upon the empire. That I believe will be the verdict of posterity and history upon the transactions which have just passed under our review."[2]

1. Lord Dalhousie's Despatch to the Secret Committee, London.
2. Evans Bell: *Annexation of the Punjab,* p.88.

Dr. R.C. Majumdar writes: "Whatever views one might entertain about the cause of the war, there can hardly be two opinions on the injustice of the annexation of the Punjab. The Punjab, it should be remembered, was at that time under the absolute control of British and the administration carried on by the Resident on behalf of the minor Dalip Singh. If there were local rebellions, the Government had undoubted right to punish the rebels. But it passes one's comprehension how the penalty can be visited upon the unoffending boy-ruler. He evidently forfeited his throne for failing to check the revolt; in other words for not doing what he had no power or authority to do under the terms of a treaty imposed by the British themselves. By what logic, one might ask, was Dalip Singh deprived of the power, position and privileges which the British had granted to him by one treaty and undertaken to protect by another. The only logic which could be invoked was the logic of the strong towards the weak, which has been corner-stone of British imperialism in India."

After the annexation of the Punjab, colonial rule of East India Company was established. A Board of three persons consisting of Sir Henry Lawrence (Chief), John Lawrence and Robert Montegomery was formed to run the administration. The Sikh army was disbanded. Instead of that a new army of loyalist Jagirdars and other soldiers was created. Sikh Aristocracy was destroyed. After the resignation of Sir Lawrence in December, 1852, his younger brother John Lawrence ruled the Punjab with an iron hand, at the best as a benevolent despot and openly offered the challenge to the people. "*Will you be governed by the pen or by the sword? Choose.*" This line, which characterised the British rule in the Punjab after its annexation, was inscribed on the statue of John Lawrence, and was a rude reminder, for three quarters of a century, of the transfer of the last independent kingdom in India to the British dominions."[1]

EXERCISES

Long Answer Type Questions

1. What is meant by imperialism? Discuss in brief March of British Imperialism in India.
2. Discuss conquest of Bengal by Britishers by treacherous means.
3. What do you know about Dual System in Bengal? Discuss its Consequences.
4. Discuss the struggle of Tipu Sultan and the Marathas against British Imperialism.
5. Discuss the struggle of Sikhs against British Imperialism.

Short Answer Type Questions

1. Write a brief note on conflict amongst European traders to monopolise Indian Trade.
2. Write a brief note on Dual System in Bengal.
3. What do you know about Battle of Buxar? Discuss in brief.
4. What was subsidiary alliance?
5. Write a brief note on fall of Tipu Sultan.
6. What was the views of Karl Marx about the fall of Mysore?
7. What do you know about Second and Third Maratha Wars?
8. What do you know about Third Maratha War?
9. Write a short note on Fourth Maratha War.
10. Write a short note on treaty of Lahore.

1. Dr. R.C. Majumdar and others, "*British Paramountcy and India Renaissance* Vol. I, p. 289 (1963). Bhartia Vidya Bhawan, Bombay.

Objective Type Questions

Choose the correct answer

1. In which year the Turks conquered Constantinople ?
   (*a*) 1453 (*b*) 1454
   (*c*) 1455 (*d*) 1456
2. In which year the Ottoman Empire of Turks became a naval power ?
   (*a*) 1469 (*b*) 1470
   (*c*) 1471 (*d*) 1472
3. In which year the Ottoman Empire of Turks Captured Egypt ?
   (*a*) 1514-15 (*b*) 1515-16
   (*c*) 1516-17 (*d*) 1517-18
4. In which year Vasco da Gama reached Calicut ?
   (*a*) 1495 (*b*) 1496
   (*c*) 1497 (*d*) 1498
5. In which year English East India Company was formed ?
   (*a*) 1600 (*b*) 1601
   (*c*) 1602 (*d*) 1603
6. The Dutch East India Company came into existence in
   (*a*) 1601 (*b*) 1602
   (*c*) 1603 (*d*) 1604
7. The French East India Company was established in
   (*a*) 1662 (*b*) 1663
   (*c*) 1664 (*d*) 1665
8. At which place the first French factory was established ?
   (*a*) Bombay (*b*) Madras
   (*c*) Calcutta (*d*) Surat
9. In which year the first French factory was established ?
   (*a*) 1667 (*b*) 1668
   (*c*) 1669 (*d*) 1670
10. Seven year was broke out in
    (*a*) 1755 (*b*) 1756
    (*c*) 1757 (*d*) 1758

ANSWERS

1. (*a*)	2. (*b*)	3. (*c*)	4. (*d*)	5. (*a*)
6. (*b*)	7. (*c*)	8. (*d*)	9. (*a*)	10. (*b*)

CHAPTER 2

Disastrous Effects of British Imperialism

(Armed Uprisings Against it Before 1857)

While summing up the political and administrative impact of the colonial rule in India, Dr. R.C. Majumdar observes:

"All the while the Indians were mere passive onlookers-they had no place or power in the administration of their own country. The curse of slavery with all its attendant evils, so pithily described by Munro, was exercising a ruinous and degenerating influence upon the character of the people at large."

The colonial rule of the British East India Company lasted in India for nearly a century. It started with the conquest of Bengal and then it extended slowly and gradually over the whole of India. The story of its expansion has already been told in the previous chapter. There were far reaching consequences–political, social and economic of this foreign rule in India, which generated powerful forces for the liberation of the country.

(A) POLITICAL IMPACT OF THE COLONIAL RULE

Following is the political impact of the British colonial rule in India:

1. *Grave Resentment due to the Loss of Political Independence and enslavement of the people of whole of India.* For the first time European Foreign Rule had been established in India. It led to the loss of the independence of the entire country and enslavement of the whole people. This caused utmost bitterness, not only in the minds of the Rajas and Maharajas whose territories had been seized by superior military force and treachery, but also by the common people, who deeply mourned the loss of political freedom and gravely resented the despotic rule of the East India Company. In this regard the great historian of our country *Dr. R.C. Majumdar* observes:

"It was almost inevitable that the expansion of British dominions would leave behind a blazing trail of discontent and disaffection through out India. This was by no means confined to the ruling chiefs and royal families of the countries conquered by the British or annexed by them on other grounds, and not even grounds, to the immediate encourage and dependants of those royal courts. British rule during the period under review, was not favourably looked upon even by the people at large in any region where it was newly introduced, far less joyously welcome, as many of the British administrators and writers would have us believe. Discontent and disaffection were particularly strong in those regions like Burma, Assam, Coorg, Sind, the Punjab, Avadh, which were unjustly annexed at least according to their people. The arbitrary deposition of the ruler of Satara, the despotic coercion of the Scindia and similar other tyrannical acts generated a feeling of hatred and hostility against the British rule which was generally but not always confined to the upper starta of society."

2. *Disastrous Effects of Doctrine of Lapse*. Lord Dalhousie in order to annex more and more Indian territories applied the Doctrine of Lapse with the greatest possible rigour, which before him had been enunciated by the Directors but not applied by any Governor-General. According to this doctrine, if a Raja was without a son or a daughter to succeed to the throne, he could adopt the son only with the permission of the East India Company and if the permission was not granted, then his state would lapse and it would be annexed to the British territory. According to this doctrine famous Indian States like Satara, Nagpur, Jhansi, Jaitpur and Sambhalpur (Orissa) etc. were annexed. The other Indian Rulers were alarmed at this doctrine that sooner or later, their states would also be annexed on one pretext or the other.

Commenting on the policy of annexations followed by Lord Dalhousie, Governor-General of India (1848–1856 A.D.), *Dr. R.C. Majumdar* observed:

"But the policy of wholesale annexations, which found its most successful exponent in Lord Dalhousie and culminated in the map of India being all red, if not in theory at least in practice, did not unnerve the native rulers alone but affected the people as well. The fall of the old and renowned royal Houses like those of Peshwa, Bhonsle, Avadh, Jhansi, Punjab and Satara and the precarious existence of the rest, on mere sufferance of the British, not only gave a rude shock to the sentiments of the people, but cast a drift in the world, hopeless and helpless a large body of people, both high and low, who had hitherto earned their livelihood by service, both civil and military, in those defunct States."[1]

3. *Defective Administration.* The people of India had a strong dislike of the Foreign Rule and the administration established by British Colonialists purely to further their ends and fully exploit the people was bound to generate the feelings of animosity and hatred. It was totally against all the canons of ancient law-givers and political thinkers who had laid down this basic principle of governance. "Whatever pleases the ruler, he shall not consider as good but whatever pleases his subjects, he shall consider as good."

First, the people of India found it very difficult to adjust themselves according to the colonial administration which was radically different from the one to which they were accustomed for centuries. Secondly, it affected the interests of those people very much who had profited by the old system. For example, the old Rajas and Maharajas used to maintain the splendour of the court and large army. Many courtiers, officials, soldiers and the common people were benefited by them. Thirdly, many pious men, poets and religious institutions flourished under the patronage of the native rulers. Rent-free grants were also given to them but all vanished with the advent of the colonial rule. So the Rajas, Maharajas, Aristocrats and the common people alike began to groan under the misery of the foreign rule and administration.

4. *British officials not accessible to the common people.* The English officers were not accessible to the people because they possessed superiority complex. Therefore, the people could not lay their grievances directly before the officers. So, the difficulties of the people remained and it made the administration quite unpopular.

5. *The British system of administration lacked personal touch in the administration.* The British administration lacked personal touch altogether. Neither the Governor-General nor his officers came into contact not only with the masses but also leading citizens of India.

---

1. Dr. R.C. Majumdar and others, *British Paramountacy and indian Renaissance*, p.408.

6. *English laws were quite strange and* unintelligible to the Indians. The Indian people were habituated to the Hindu laws. Later on they were also acquainted with the Muslim laws but were quite unfamiliar with the British laws which were in English language: The masses did not understand English language at all. The substitution of English as the court language in place of Persian was highly disliked specially by the Muslims.

7. *Indians were deprived of all high posts in the administration.* The policy of the East India Company was not to give high posts to the Indians. This policy was particularly followed by Lord Cornwallis (1786–1793). More and more Indians began to be deprived of higher offices as the boundaries of the East India company began to expand rapidly. Those Indians who had been enjoying high offices during the regimes of the old Rajas and Maharajas began to be looked with suspicion and were deprived of all posts. So it resulted in great discontent.

It had been laid down by Section 57 of the Charter Act of 1833 that no Indian "*shall by reason only of his religion, place of birth, descent, colour, or any of them, be disabled from holding any place, office or employment under the East India Company." But it is deplorable that in spite of this Charter Act, the East India company continued the policy of discrimination.*

Urged by the same motive, and impressed by the ability of Raja Ram, Hobbeshouse proposed to nominate Raja Ram a writer (Corresponding to I.C.S. of later days) in the service of East India Company. This was the practical application of the Charter Act of 1833. Nevertheless, when the news of the proposed appointment began to appear in the Press, then many objections were raised by the British people and Bureaucracy that the convenated civil service, hitherto reserved for Europeans, was to be opened to an Indian. Therefore, Carnac, the President of the Court of Directors revised his opinion and said that the appointment would never pass. The Governor-General Lord Auckland also did not favour the appointment, so the appointment was not made.

8. *Arrogance of the British Officers*. The above genuine grievance of the Indians was aggravated by the undisguised contempt with which as a general rule, the British officials treated the Indians. Sir Syed Ahmed Khan, himself an official Pro-British to a remarkable degree, observes about the British officials that "*their pride and arrogance led them to consider the natives of India as undeserving the name of human beings.*[1] *Such* ill-treatment, he observes, was "more offensive to Muslims who for centuries past have received special honour and enjoyed special immunities in Hindustan."[2]

9. *Denial of Political Rights to the Indians.* The English educated class at first hoped that they would soon get higher posts in the highest Civil Service of the East India Company and improve their position but they were soon disillusioned when they were not given any high posts in any branch of the administration. Even the post of Superintendent of Police was reserved for the British. Similarly no post higher than the post of Sergeant was given to the Indians. Similar was the case with other Departments. *Besides that, the Indians were not given any political rights.* This gradually alienated the sympathy of the intellectual class, and discontent prevailed among certain sections who refused to hope against hope in the ultimate triumph of the sense of justice and political liberalism of the great English people.

10. *Corrupt Administration.* It is noteworthy that the administration of the East India Company was corrupt. In this regard Lewis observes "No civilised Government, ever existed on the face of the earth which was more corrupt, more perfidious and more rapacious than the government of East India Company from the year 1765 to 1774." Lord Clive's and Warren Hasting's conduct was not above board. Regarding Lord Clive, Dr. Ishwari Prasad observes:

"His lust for gold amounted to a mania which proved contagious and Bengal was rifled of its treasures by a set of rapacious adventurers whom none could control."

1. Syed Ahmed Khan, *An Essay on the Causes of the Indian Revolt.* Translated by Captain W.N. Less, Calcutta, 1860, p.42.
2. *Ibid.*, p.43.

This is corroborated by the evidence of *Richard Becher,* a servant of the Company who felt constrained to write in his letter to the Select committee in May, 1769. "*It must give pain to every Englishman to have reason to think that since the accession of the Company to the Diwani, the condition of the people of the country has been worse than it was before and yet I am afraid the fact is undoubted.... This fine country which flourished under the most despotic and arbitrary governments is verging towards ruin*". Similarly, Warren Hastings' conduct in regard to Rohilla War, Raja Chet Singh and Begums of Oudh was wholly immoral.

11. *Bad Police Administration.* Lord Cornwallis had organised the police administration on such lines which may suit the interests of the East India Company. Therefore, the main function of the police was to maintain law and order and to quell the disturbances or the revolts of the freedom-loving people who might raise their voice against the colonial rule from time to time. Therefore, the police made frequent lathi-charges or resorted to shootings whenever there was storm of protest against the British rule. In other words, the police showed all possible strictness against the freedom-loving people. The Parliamentary Committee submitted in its report in 1813, "*The police committed depredations on the peacable inhabitants of the same nature as those practised by the dacoits whom they were employed to suppress*". The inefficiency and corruption of the police have been vividly described in the Calcutta Gazette of April 30, 1827 and repeated in the same periodical of 10 June, 1830.

12. *Evils of the British Legal System.* The legal system established by the British Rulers in India was highly defective. It was extremely expensive because the plaintiff had to engage the lawyer who demanded a high fee. Similarly, the defendant had to engage lawyer to defend himself. He had also to pay heavy fees because if he did not engage a good lawyer, he would lose the case. Besides that, the plaintiff had to pay high stamp fee in advance for filing a case. Secondly, the procedure of the courts was highly complicated and much delay occurred. Therefore, thousands of persons were ruined by litigation. Thirdly, the laws were quite unintelligible to the masses because the laws were in English language and were very complex.

Dr. R.C. Majumdar observed, "There was security against foreign aggression but not against theft, robbery, and crimes and oppressions of other kind. The law-courts had not yet become efficient instruments of impartial justice, while the Police served as agencies of oppression rather than protection. The prison house was as wretched as it could be and the District Magistrate was determined that the prison should be a distinctly uncomfortable place, while the Medical Officer made an equally determined but unsuccessful effort to keep down the terrible death rate in jails."

13. *No amenities of life.* So far as the amenities of life were concerned, they are summed up in two sentences by Sir John Strachey while describing the condition of Bengal in 1854, *i.e.* after a continuous British Rule for nearly a century: "*There were almost no roads or bridges or schools and there was no protection to life or property. The police was worthless, and the robberies and violent crimes by gangs of armed men, which were unheard of in other provinces were common not far from Calcutta.*"

14. *Discontent and disaffection.* While summing up the political and administrative impact of the colonial rule in India., Dr. R.C. Majumdar observes:

"*All the while the Indians were mere passive onlookers,–they had no place or power in the administration of their own country. The curse of slavery with all the attendant evils, so pithily described by Munro, was exercising a ruinous and degenerating influence upon the character of the people at large. The early dreams and enthusiastic hopes of the small band of English-educated Indians were giving place to disillusion and despair, while the common people, full of discentent and disaffection, bided their time in sullen resentment marked by occasional outburst of violence. By the time British completed the first hundred years of their rule, they gained the whole of India but lost hold upon the heart of the Indians.*"[1]

1. Dr. R.C. Majumdar, *British Paramountacy and Indian Renaissance,* Vol. I, p.401.

(B) ECONOMIC IMPACT OF THE COLONIAL RULE (Disastrous Consequences)

The economic impact of the British Rule was most disastrous for the country. The few economic disastrous consequences of the colonial rule, are as under :

1. *Land-revenue system was wholly based on utmost exploitation.* Land revenue formed the backbone of the British Colonial Rule in India. Different systems of land revenue were introduced into different parts of India due to various reasons but all of them intended to bring the highest possible revenue to the British East India company. Lord Cornwallis had introduced the Permanent Settlement System in Bengal. While the British Government realised its fixed share from the Zamindars, it imposed no restrictions upon the Zamindars who exploited the poor peasants fully. So Raja Ram Mohan Roy observed in 1831 in a communication to the Board of Control, "While the Zamindars or land-holders had been greatly benefited by the Permanent Settlement System of Bengal of 1793, while their wealth and the wealth of the community had generally increased, the poor cultivator was no better of." According to him, the land revenue during the thirty-five years form 1792-93 to 1827-1828 had been raised above 100 per cent (101.07). Therefore, he suggested, in the first place, the prohibition of any further rise in rent, and secondly–rents now so exorbitantly high as to leave the ryot in a state of extreme misery,–a reduction in the revenue demanded from the Zamindar so as to ensure a reduction in the ryot's rent. The decrease in revenue should be met by increasing taxes upon luxuries or by employing as Collectors low salaried Indians instead of high salaried Europeans.[1]

According to Dr. R.C. Majumdar, "The Ryotwari System reduced the cultivators to a state of wretched misery which differed in degree, but not in kind, in different parts of India."[2]

2. *Resumption of rent-free tenures of land or Inam lands.* Another wrong policy followed by the colonialists in India was the resumption of rent-free tenures of land, sometimes even of entire villages, granted in perpetuity by the Hindu and Muslim rulers in the past, either to an individual as a reward for public service or distinguished talents, or for the maintenance of religious or charitable institutions and pious learned Brahmans or Muslim Saints. The British Government was always anxious to resume these rent-free grants of land and increase its income. Consequently, the British government issued Regulations from time to time to tighten their grip over such lands. Therefore, the various commissioners were appointed from time to time to inquire into the validity of the titles of these grants. Finally, an Inam Commission was appointed in Bombay in 1852 to resume those rent-free grants whose holders were unable to produce the valid certificates. As these grants of land were made centuries ago, therefore, most of the holders had lost their original documents in support of the grant, though these grants had remained with the holders for centuries according to the usage of the country. The Inam Commission rejected the claims of all such persons who could not produce the original documents and ordered that their rent-free lands should be resumed by the Government. In all 21,000 land-free grants were resumed. This caused grave discontent amongst the affected people and led frequently to violence, armed resistance and widespread disturbances. This became one of the potent cause of the rebellion of 1857 or more popularly known as First War of Independence.

3. *Constant Drain of Indian Wealth.* The most important feature of the colonial financial administration in India was the constant drain of the wealth. The debt of India was constantly increasing during the imperialist wars and conquests undertaken by the colonial company. The Maratha Wars, the Burma War, the Afgan War and Sikh Wars all helped to increase the deficit of the British Government. The following table shows the steady increase of both expenditure and revenue of the colonial regime of East India company.

While the total debt of India, bearing interest was over £ 7 millions in 1792, it stood

1. *Rammohan Ray,* p.84 Complied and Edited by Amal Home and published under the auspices of the Rammohan Ray Centenary Committee, Calcutta, 1933.
2. Dr. R.C. Majumdar, *British Paramountcy and Indian Renaissance* Vol. I. I. p.373.

as £ 26,947,437 on 30th April, 1836. The subsequent increase in public debt is shown in the following table:[1]

1837-38	£ 33,772,718
1847-48	£ 48,757,213
1857-58	£ 69,473,484

Dr. R.C.Majumdar remarks:

"The growth of Indian debt was also partly due to the British policy of expansion in India. In other words, India had to pay the expenses of her conquest by England"[2]

The inequity of making Indian Exchequer pay the cost of the foreign wars was exposed in the British House of Commons by liberal minded politicians like *John Bright* who said:

"Last year I referred to the enormous expense of the Afghan War–about 15 million sterling–the whole of which ought to have been thrown on the taxation of the people of England, because it was a war commended by the English Cabinet for objects supposed to be English."[3]

Even the East India Company registered emphatic protest against paying the expenses of the Afghan War. It is interesting to note that while the East India Company received no payment for the service of Indian troops outside India (China, Afghanistan), they had to bear the expenses of British troops sent out from England to suppress the mutiny.[4]

Besides this the entire cost of the Colonial Office or Home Government and military defence of India had to be borne out by the Indian Government. Major Wingate has forcefully expressed this point of view and fully exposed the British Government.[5]

Another Englishman *Montgomery Martin* wrote in 1838:

"The annual drain of £ 30,00,000 on British India amounted in thirty years, at 12 per cent (the usual Indian rate) compound interest to the enormous sum of £723,997,917 sterling or at a low rate, as £ 20,000,000 for fifty years, to £ 84,000,000,000 sterling! So constant and accumulating a drain even on England would soon impoverish her, whatever may be its effects on India, where the wages of labourer is from two pence to three pence a day. For half a century we have gone on draining from two to three and sometimes four million pounds sterling a year from India, which has been remitted to Great Britain...... I do not think it possible for human ingenuity to avert entirely the evil effects of a continued drain of three or four million pounds a year from a distant country like India and which is never returned to it in any shape."[6]

4. *Deliberate ruin of Indian Trade by colonialists.* The rule of the Mercantile Company ruined the trade and commerce of India. Armed with political authority the British Rulers before 1857 deliberately fostered the growth of British trade and commerce at the cost of India. As this combined with the deliberate impoverishment of the cultivators, so India, which was considered as one of the richest countries of the world at the advent of the British Rule, was brought down to the level of the poorest. The Board of Directors adopted this policy of ruining the trade of Bengal as early as 1769. In the early 19th century the duty on Muslin and Calico was, respectively more than 27 and 71 per cent. Even then unable to compete with Indian manufacturers, Britain prohibited the import of Calico cloths. Heavy protective duties in England, 70 or 80 per cent respectively–on Indian silk and cotton goods ruined those industries while British goods were imported into India at a nominal duty. The British Historian of India, *Wilson* observes:

1. Dr. R.C. Majumdar and others, *British Paramountay and Indian Renaissance,* Vol.I, p.357.
2. *Ibid.*
3. *Ibid.*
4. *Ibid.*
5. *Ibid.*, p.385. also Major Wingate, *Our Financial Relations with India,* quoted in Ramesh Dutt, *Economic History of India in the Victorian Age,* Vol. II, p.213.
6. Montgomery Martin, *Eastern India,* Introduction (Dutt–I, pp. 409-410).

"It was stated in evidence (in 1813) that the cotton and silk goods of India up to the period could be sold for a profit in the British markets at a price from 50 to 60 per cent lower than those fabricated in England. It consequently became necessary to protect the latter by duties of 70 and 80 per cent on their value, or by positive prohibition. Had this not been the case, had not such prohibitory duties and decrees existed , the mills of Paisley and Manchester would have been stopped in their outset and could scarcely have been again set in motion, even by the power of steam. They were created by the sacrifice of the Indian manufacturer."[1]

In 1832 *R.M. Martin* observed:

"By increase of export of cotton goods to India from Britain many millions of Indo-British subjects have been totally ruined."[2]

This process continued throughout the period under review. In the Parliamentary enquiry of 1840 it was reported that "while British cotton and silk goods imported into India paid a duty of $3\frac{1}{2}$ per cent and woollen goods 2 per cent, Indian cotton goods imported into Britain paid 10 per cent, silk goods 20 per cent and woollen goods 30 per cent."[3] The result was that by the middle of the nineteenth century Indian export of cotton and silk goods practically ceased.

In this connection, Karl Marx writes:

From 1818 to 1836 the export of twist from Great Britain to India rose in the proportion of 1 to 5,200. In 1824 the export of British muslin to India hardly amounted to 60,00,000 yards, while in 1937 it surpassed 64,000,000 yards. But at the same time the population of Decca decreased from 1,50,000 inhabitants to 20,000. This decline of Indian towns celebrated for their fabrics was by no means the worst consequence. British steam and science uprooted, over the whole surface of Hindustan, the union between agricultural and manufacturing industry."[4]

5. *Total ruin of Indian Industries.* In India very fine cloth especially the Muslin was made and since ancient times there had been a great demand of it in the European markets. Dr. Tara Chand observes, *"The English people developed a preference for light cotton garments in place of the coarse woollens that they had worn for centuries."*

First of all the East India Company earned a huge profit by importing the Indian cloth and selling it at a higher price. Later on the British Industrialists pressurised their government to levy heavy import duty on Indian cloth, so that indigenous cloth might sell. Consequently, a law was passed in 1760 according to which the import of Indian coloured cloth was prohibited in Britain. After some time 70 to 80 per cent import duty was levied on the Indian cloth. The agents of East India Company purchased the raw cotton from Indian growers at a very cheap price against their will and then exported it to Britain where it was converted into fine cloth by British mills and then again sent to India to sell at a very high price. In this way British industrialist earned crores of rupees every year by exploiting the poor Indian cotton growers and the masses. We have already quoted Mr. Wilson who shrewdly observed that if this had not been done, then the mills of Paisley and Manchester would have been closed and not be set in motion again even by the power of steam. So India was converted into a British market for selling its manufactured goods at a very high price and earn huge profit. Therefore, R.M. Martin observed in 1832, *"By increase of export of cotton goods to India from Britain many millions of Indo-British subjects have been totally ruined."*

Griffiths, the famous British Historian also remarked *"Free trade and refusal to levy protective duties against machine-made goods of Britain ruined Indian manufacturers."*[5]

---

1. Quoted by Dr. R.C. Majumdar in his *British Paramountacy and Indian Renaissance,* Part I, p.413(1963)
2. *Ibid.*
3. Rajni Palme Dutt-*India Today,* P. 101 (Bombay, 1947).
4. Karl Marx, in New York, in *New Work Daily Tribune,* June 10, 1853, quoted by Rajni Palme Dutt, *India Today,* pp.77-78.
5. Griffiths Percival, *The British Impact on India,* p. 391 (1952).

The results of this policy of the British Government were disastrous for Indian industries. Montgomery Martin's Report to the Parliamentary Inquiry Committee in 1840 rightly observed:

"The decay and distribution of Surat, Dacca (Dhaka), of Murshidabad and other places where native manufactures have been carried on is too painful a fact to dwell upon. I do not consider that it has been in the fair course of trade. I think it has been the power of the stronger exercised over the weaker."[1]

The Governor-General Lord William Bentinck reported in 1834-35, *"The misery hardly finds a parallel in the history of commerce. The bones of the cotton-weavers are bleaching the plains of India."*[2]

6. *India was deliberately converted into a poorest country by the colonialists.*

This is corroborated by the statement of *Karl Marx* who wrote on June 24, 1853 that

"During whole course of the 18th century, the Treasures transported from India to England were gained much less by comparatively insignificant commerce than by direct exploitation of that country, and by the colossal fortunes there exorted and transmitted to England. "The total value of British exports during 1780 was £ 1,26,48,616 so that Indian trade amounted to only 1/32 of the entire foreign trade. In 1850, the total exports to India from Great Britain and England were £ 80,24,000 of which cotton goods alone amounted to £ 52,20,000 so that it reached more than $\frac{1}{8}$ of the whole export, and more than $\frac{1}{4}$ of the foreign cotton trade.

"There exists now national debt of 50 million pounds, a continual decrease in the resources of the revenue and the corresponding increase in the expenditure dubiously balanced by the gambling income of the opium tax, now threatened with extinction by the Chinese beginning themselves to cultivate the poppy and aggravated by the expenses to be anticipated from the senseless Burmese War."[3]

7. *Destruction of Village Economy by the colonialists.* The basis of the village economy in India was the union of agriculture and cottage or small-scale industries. The basis had not been disturbed by the various conquests during the Hindu and Muslim rule but it was unfortunately disturbed by the British colonialists. *Rajni Palnme Dutt* observes in this regard:

"The ruin of Indian industry and commerce was followed by another disastrous result. It was not only the manufacturing towns and centres that were laid waste, and their population driven to crowded and over crowd the villages, it was above all the basis of the old village economy, the union of agriculture and domestic industry, that received its mortal blow. The millions of ruined artisans and craftsmen, spinners, weavers, potters, tanners, smelters, smiths, alike from the towns and from the villages had no alternative save to crowd into agriculture. In this way India was forcibly transformed from being a country of combined agriculture and manufactures, into an agricultural colony of British manufacturing capitalism."[4]

8. *Appalling Famines.* In this regard Indian Historian Dr. R.C. Majumdar adds: "It would thus appear that the zamindars or landed nobility, the middle class, the peasants, artisans, traders and industrialists—in short all classes of people were hard hit by the new economic policy introduced by the British and large number was reduced to abject poverty. It is hardly any wonder, therefore, that grave discontent and disaffection, prevailed all over India and this was kept alive, rather than underlined, by the most visible sign of the wretched condition of the people, namely periodical recurrence of famine. There were no less than seven famines in the first half of the nineteenth century with an estimated total of one and a half million deaths."[5]

1. Montgomery Martin's Report to the Parliamentary Inquiry Committee in 1840 quoted by Dr. R.C. Majumdar, *History and Culture of the Indian People,* p.414, Vol. IX.
2. Quoted by Rajni Palme Dutt in his book, *India Today,* p.78; also Karl Marx, *Das Capital,* Vol. I, Chapter XV, Section 5.
3. Written by Karl Marx on June 24, 1853, published in the *New York Daily Tribune,* No. 3816 of July 11, 1853.
4. Rajni Palme Dutt, *India Today.,* p.103.
5. Dr. R.C. Majumdar, *History and Culture of the Indian People,* Vol. IX, p.417.

(C) SOCIAL AND RELIGIOUS IMPACT OF COLONIAL RULE

The following were the social and religious consequences of the colonial rule in India.

1. *Destruction of old educational system based on moral values.* The educational system in ancient India was highly beneficial and it attracted the praise of even foreign scholars like Hieun-Tsang and Al-Beruni. The Turk, Pathan and Moghul rulers tried their best to supplant this system by their own system of education but even then the old system continued with its vigour especially in villages. In those days in every village there was a Sanskrit School where education was imparted free of charge. Consequently, illiteracy was nominal and it was also admitted by early British Historians. The British uprooted the old system and instead introduced a new system of education on English lines. Very few schools and colleges were opened by the government and mostly the educational institutions were run by the Christian Missionaries. The new system of education was highly expensive, therefore, the few people benefited by it. Consequently, mass illiteracy began to prevail in India. Moreover, the new educational system was completely divorced of high ancient ideals, history and culture, Sanskrit literature, learning, knowledge and traditions. It taught only Western literature, history, traditions and science. Consequently, the English educated people forgot their glorious history, traditions and culture and began to take pride in everything that was Western. This retarded the growth of Indian nationalism for some time.

2. *Discrimination in jobs.* The Charter Act of 1813 provided for setting apart a sum of rupees one lakh annually for the revival and improvement of literature and the encouragement of the learned natives of India and for the introduction and promotion knowledge of the sciences among the inhabitants of the British territories in India. The East India Company needed the cheap clerks to run its administration. Therefore, to teach English to the Indians became the urgent need of the hour as the British clerks demanded a high salary for serving in India. The English educated people began to aspire soon for the higher jobs but they were soon disillusioned to find that they were solely reserved for the lower jobs. In this way discrimination on racial basis in the services continued which caused great discontent amongst the local educated persons. It also became one of the causes of the popular upsurge of 1857. Later on they began to demand the democratic institutions on the line of British parliamentary institutions.

3. *Decline in the moral standard of the Indians due to poverty.* When the British arrived in this country, India was considered a rich and prosperous country but the British colonialists fully drained the wealth of the country and converted India into one of the poorest countries of the world. Naturally owing to mass poverty, the moral standard of the people of our country declined.

4. *Degrading influence of the Western Civilisation.* The Western civilisation had a degrading effect on the Indians because English educated persons began to ape British manners and customs. Not only that they began to correspond also with each other in English language, some persons also went to England to get higher English education and obtained either the Bar-at-law degree or any other degree. They were also much influenced by the Western literature, science, learning and knowledge. They began to demand higher jobs in the Company's service according to the Charter Act of 1833 but they were soon disillusioned when they found the discriminatory treatment against them. So it gave rise to lot of discontent which ultimately exploded in the First war of Independence, 1857.

5. *Insulting behaviour of the British Officers.* The British officers considered themselves superior to the Indians and treated them badly. The insulting behaviour of the British officers was not only visible in the sphere of administration but also in the army. They did not entertain any complaint of the common man. The net result was the ever widening gulf between the rulers and the ruled.

6. *Propagation of Christianity.* The East India Company after perfecting its hold on the Indian territories thought of converting the whole of India into Christianity. Revered Kennedy said, "Our chief work is the propagation of Christianity in the land. Until Hindustan from Cape Comorin to the Himalayas, embraces the religion of Christ and until it condemns the Hindu and Muslim religions, our efforts must continue persistently."[1]

1. Rev. Kennedy, *Indian Freedom Struggle*–Centenary Souvenir, p.39.

7. *Reorganisation of the Indian army on discriminatory basis.* The East India Company kept three aims in view while reorganising the army–(1) Conquest of the Indian territories ruled by the Rajas and Maharajas: (2) Defence of the British territories from foreign aggression; (3) Protection of British territories from internal revolt. While the British soldiers demanded a very high salary, the Indian soldiers were available at a comparative small salary. Therefore, the East India Company adopted the policy of recruiting the Indian soldiers in large number but they were to be manned by British officers. Besides that some British regiments were maintained in order to quell the rebellion of the Indian soldiers.

8. *Changes in Hindu Inheritance Law Favouring Christianity.* Another impact of the British Colonial Rule in India was the decline of Hindu Joint Family System. Lord William Bentinck changed the Hindu Inheritance Law in 1832 and allowed the converts to Christianity to inherit land in the property of the father. This caused grave discontentment against the British Rule amongst the Hindus and unleashed the forces of nationalism. Besides that the British also allowed legally to mortgage or divide or sell the landed property. Therefore, after death of the father, the sons began to quarrel and divide the land. In this way the fields were divided amongst the sons frequently. The result was a lot of litigation and the division of the land into petty fields.

9. *The emergence of Zamindar and Indian Middle Class.* New laws regarding land tenure were enacted during the British rule as a result of which the Zamindary System came into existence which was based on the total exploitation of the farmers. Hence, it was the worst.

Therefore, the Zamindars came into existence. Besides that a new middle class consisting of lawyers, traders, teachers and clerks also emerged. This class produced many able persons. At first they had full faith in the justice and fair play of the colonial government but they were soon disillusioned when they were discriminated and did not get anything from the British. Consequently, they became arch nationlaists and threw themselves in the struggle against the colonial rule.

10. *Encouragement to communalism.* The colonialists in order to prolong their rule sowed the seeds of dissension between the Hindus and Muslims and they encouraged communalism. They played one community against the other. Similarly, they set one state against the other.

(D) DISAFFECTION AND DISCONTENT AGAINST THE FOREIGN RULE AND UPRISINGS AGAINST IT (DURING COMPANY'S RULE)

The utmost exploitation made by the British Imperialists mentioned in the previous chapter and this chapter led to frequent uprisings against the English East India Company but they were crushed ruthlessly (mercilessly) by its superior military might. Besides that they were isolated. Now a mention of each is made briefly because they failed to oust the British.

1. *Sanyasi Andolan.* It was the first uprising against the alien rule because it broke out in Bengal as early as 1770. Its main cause was the devastating (destructive) famine and the sheer exploitation of the farmers (It has been described in detail by Bankim Chandra Chatterji in his famous novel 'Anand Math'). The Sanyasis were moved by the sad plight of the farmers. So they took to arms and fought many battles against the British but they ultimately lost them because of the superior might of the imperialists. Anyhow the attention of the Home Government was attracted towards the mismanagement of the company and they regulated its affairs by the Regulating Act, 1773.

Note. The first armed struggle for freedom waged by the former Rajas, Maharajas and the Nawabs against the Foreign Rule will be related in the next chapter. Here the revolts of the feudal landlords, peasants, tribesmen and the sepoys are being mentioned.

2. *Uprisings of the feudal landlords.* It is noteworthy that during the whole of the first half of the 19th century various parts of India were the scene of uninterrupted disturbances of dispossessed

landlords, peasantry, tribesmen and the sepoys. The feudal landlords;–*padayakers* in the Northern Sarkars (Madras Presidency) had been staunchly resisting British domination since the beginning of the 19th century and in the period 1801-1805 a whole series of punitive expeditions was sent to the area. An uprising broke out again in 1813-14 and again in 1831. Several years were required for the suppression of the later uprisings.

Other noteworthy uprisings of the landlords against the British imperialists were the following:

(1) Revolt of Vijay Raj of Vijay Nagram (1794); (2) Revolt of Payarsi Raja of Kerala (1799-1805 (3) Revolt of Ali Khan, Nawab-wazir of Oudh (1799); (4) Armed struggle of zamindars of Ganjam district; (5) Freedom movement of Travancore under the leadership of Velupanthi (1808-1809); (6) Revolt of Taluqdar or Raja Dayaram of Hathras (U.P.); (7) Revolt of Kitoor (Mysore) under the leadership of Rani Chennamma; (8) Revolt of Coorg (1833-34); (9) Revolt of Surendra Sai in Sambhalpur (Moradabad); (10) Revolt of Madhukar Shyam Bundela in Bundelkhand (1812); (11) Revolt of Assam under the leadership of Gomdhar Konwar, son of Phena Konwar (1828). He was the first torch bearer of revolution after the treaty of Yandbu of 1826; (12) Another great rebellion in Assam took place under the leadership of Peali Berphukkam, Jenuram Daulia Borua, Roop Chand Konwar, Deoram Dishingia Deka, Bom Singhpho and Hurnath. They were convicted of treason and sentenced to death but fire of nationalism in Assam was not extinguished till India achieved independence; (13) Revolt of the landlords of Kutch; (14) Revolt of the Kolis of Gujarat (1825-50) with intermittent uprisings here and there (15) Revolt of the Zamindars of Kolhapur (Maharashtra) (1844)

3. Revolts of the peasants. (1) Revolt in Gorakhpur (1778-1781); (2) Revolt of Rangpur (Eastern Bengal) (1783); (3) Revolt in Sambadia or Bakar district of East Bengal (now Bangladesh) (1792); (4) Revolt of the Ryot of Mysore (1830-31); (5) Fraji revolt in Faridpur district (East Bengal) (1834-37); (6) Revolt in connection with the survey of Maharashtra.

4. Revolts of Tribesmen. The famous revolts of the tribesmen were the following: (1) Revolt in Bankura and Midnapur districts of West Bengal (1798-99); (2) Revolts of Bhils of Western Ghat (1818-1831); (3) Revolt in Singhbhum district of Bihar (1820-21); (4) Revolt in Garo district of Assam (1825-1833), (1846-66); (5) Kol's tribes revolt in the district of Chhotanagpur of Bihar; (6) Geed tribes revolt in Sambhalpur (1833), (7) Gwad revolt in Orissa; (8) Naga revolt (1848-1900); (9) Santhal revolt (1855-56). The Santhal revolt was the most famous.

Revolts of Sepoys. There was also a great discontent amongst the sepoys due to many reasons. First, the sepoys got comparatively a smaller salary than the British soldiers, thus they were openly discriminated. Secondly, the higher ranks were only given to the British officers and no Indian soldier, however capable, was promoted to the higher rank. The Indian sepoys were always commanded by the British officers. Thirdly, the Indian sepoys were asked to go to Burma in 1824 in connection with the Burmese War which was very unpopular. Fourthly, the Indian soldiers demanded double allowance when they went to a foreign country which was sometimes denied. Hence the discontent arose amongst them and erupted on several occasions, Bellore revolt of 1806 and Barrackpur revolt 1824, are the most famous.

Revolt at Barrackpur (Calcutta). On October 30, 1824 the 47th Native Infantry of Barrackpur (Bengal) refused to proceed to Rangoon in connection with the Burmese War unless they were given double *bhatta* (additional or special allowance). On November 2, the sepoys showed open defiance and burst into acts of open violence. The same mutinous spirit also affected the other regiments stationed at Barrackpur. The commander-in-Chief, therefore, brought in European troops from Calcutta and in the next parade, when the sepoys refused to comply with the order "to ground arms", the European soldiers fired against from a battery in their rear. A Calcutta letter dated 3 November, 1825 published in the *Glasgow Herald,* gives a graphic description of what followed:

"About 410 held out..........Sir Edward Paget gave orders to fire. In a moment after, grapeshot and cannon bullets played upon the poor fellows from all quarters; then they threw down their guns and ran; some escaped by running into Hooghly—some were taken prisoners—upwards of 60 lay dead upon the field and this afternoon about a dozen or two are either to be hanged or shot".[1]

But whatever might have been the causes, the mutiny at Barrackpur in November, 1824, made a deep impression upon the sepoys, and the memory of the martyrs for the cause of religion was long cherished by them with reverence by setting up memorials. This was brought to light in the issue of the *Englishman* of Calcutta, dated May 30, 1857. Such memories and memorials were undoubtedly important factors in the outbreak of the mutiny in 1857.[2]

Grenadier Company's Revolt in Assam. On the morning of 14 October, 1825 disturbances broke out in the Grenadier Company of Assam. The Court Martial sentenced all the ring leaders to death.[3]

Mutiny in Sholapur and other Regiments. On November 24, 1838 occurred the first mutiny in the native Sholapur Regiment owing to the non-payment of the full *bhatta* (additional or special allowance). At first the negative regiment did not join the parade but later turned out when the Infantry and Horse Artillery marched towards them. One man in each ten was punished–they were discharged after suffering imprisonment for two years. The non-payment of the *bhatta* led to mutiny of sepoys in Secunderabad, Hyderabad, Kotah and Malligaun in the Sagar Division in 1842. Some of the regiments were disbanded and the rest were pardoned.

Mutinous spirit at the time of Afghan War. The Afghan war broke out in 1839. The Hindu soldiers were unwilling to go beyond the Indus because they thought that it was forbidden by their religion and will have to forgo their daily bath and take bread from the Muslims and to wear jackets made of sheep-skin. The Muslim soldiers were unwilling because they thought that they would have to fight against their co-religionists. But they had to march against their will on the assurance of the payment of full special allowance but none escaped and all of them were killed.[4]

Mutiny of 34th N.I. and three other Regiments. The 34th N.I. and three other regiments also refused to proceed to Sind in 1844 unless the *old bhatta* (Full or special allowance) was restored. As Sindh had been annexed in 1843, therefore the British Government refused to give *bhatta* to the sepoys. The sepoys were taken to Meerut and in the presence of other troops, their arms and other things were taken away and they were disbanded. After this example, the other sepoys marched to Sind unconditionally.

Mutiny in the occupation army of the Punjab. The Punjab had been annexed to the British Empire in 1849 but there was a lot of discontent in the army of occupation due to various reasons. Sir Charles Napier collected "evidence which, in his judgement, proved that twenty-four regiments were waiting only for their opportunity to rise." A mutiny broke out in the native troops at Wazeerabad and Gobindgarh in February, 1850. The European army suddenly attacked then and order was restored. Ninetyfive sepoys were sentenced to various terms of imprisonment and the whole regiment to Gobindgarh was disbanded.

Conclusion. Thus, it is clear from the above account that grave discontent prevailed among all sections of the Indian society before 1857. The people and the sepoys were highly dissatisfied and utterly disgusted. They were waiting only for a suitable opportunity and that opportunity came in 1857 when the discontent burst into First Armed Struggle for Freedom which will be fully dealt with in the next chapter.

---

1. Dr. R.C. Majumdar, *British Paramountacy and Indian Renaissance*, part I, p.429.
2. *Ibid, p*.430
3. *Ibid.*
4. *Ibid, p.* 432.

(E) GRAVEST DISCONTENT AGAINST THE IMPERIALIST
EXPLOITATION UNLEASHES MIGHTY FORCES OF NATIONALISM

The full exploitation of our countrymen by the imperialists did not go unchallenged and resulted in unleashing the mighty forces of nationalism which ultimately shattered the British Rule to pieces. Henceforth violent or non-violent struggle against the imperialism continued in one form or the other till India achieved independence. The British witnessed first of all a *large-scale armed struggle* against their rule in 1857. Then the congress since its inception in 1885 uptill 1947 continued its non-violent heroic struggle against the alien rule. Besides that the revolutionaries made no small sacrifices for the freedom of the country and made a unique contribution. The result was that due to unparalleled sacrifices of our countrymen, the imperialists had to leave the country bag and baggage in 1947 and award independence. Therefore in the subsequent chapters this saga of matchless sacrifices has been described briefly in order to give a glimpse to the readers of that struggle which was waged relentlessly against the imperialists, due to which we are living as freemen and not slaves.

EXERCISES

Long Answer Type Questions

1. Discuss the political impact of the colonial rule on India.
2. What was the impact of colonial rule on India? Discuss in brief.
3. Write a detailed note on social and religious impact of colonial rule on India.

Short Answer Type Questions

1. Write a short note on Doctrine of Lapse. What was its disastrous effect?
2. What were the evils of the British Legal System? Discuss in brief.
3. "Land revenue system of British Government was wholly based on utmost exploitation." Discuss this statement in very brief.
4. What is meant by constant drain of Indian Wealth?
5. "The British Government uprooted the old system of education and instead introduced a new system of education on English lines." What is your opinion about this statement? Discuss in brief.
6. What was Sanyasi Andolan?

Objective Type Questions

Choose the correct answer

1. Which was the first uprising against British Rule in India ?
   (*a*) Sanyasi Andolan (*b*) Revolt of Gorakhpur
   (*c*) Revolt of Rangpur (*d*) Revolt of Vijay Nagram
2. Sanyasi Andolan broke out in
   (*a*) Madras (*b*) Bengal
   (*c*) Bombay (*d*) Central Province
3. Which revolt broke out on October 30, 1824 ?
   (*a*) Revolt of Bankura (*b*) Revolt of Bhils
   (*c*) Revolt of Barrackpur (*d*) The Santhal Revolt
4. The Santhal Revolt was the most famous. In which year it was broke out ?
   (*a*) 1798-99 (*b*) 1818-1831
   (*c*) 1825-1833 (*d*) 1855-56

ANSWERS

1. (*a*) 2. (*b*) 3. (*c*) 4. (*d*)

CHAPTER 3

First Armed Struggle for Freedom, 1857 and Act of 1858

"The upheaval of 1857 was India's first war of independence"

—Dr. Pattabhi Sitaramayya.

CAUSES OR CIRCUMSTANCES LEADING TO THE FIRST INDIAN ARMED STRUGGLE FOR INDEPENDENCE

The first major armed attempt to overthrow the alien rule in India in 1857 might have been styled as a mutiny or a sepoy rebellion by the British Historians but we have no hesitation in calling it India's first glorious struggle for independence. There was the force of militant patriotism and studied planning behind the bloody, upsurge of people's wrath against the British rule. It was a national and holy war waged with the object of securing freedom from English bondage. It was not just a sudden outburst as some English Historians tell us. The incident of greased cartridge was but the chance spark which set the mine ablaze. Give it any name and attribute any reason for its outbreak, the significance of the great upsurge of 1857 cannot be undermined. Let us first discuss the causes responsible for this revolt.

Political Causes

The political causes which contributed towards the rise and growth of Revolt of 1857 were as follows—

1. *Doctrine of Lapse.* This doctrine was based on the presumption that the East India Company was the Supreme Power in India and that all native States were subordinate to it. The Doctrine of Lapse made it obligatory on the issueless rulers of native States to get the sanction of the Company before adopting sons to inherit the rulership of their respective States. The Court of Directors stated it clearly that such sanction was to be granted only as a special favour and not as a rule. They asserted their right to withhold the sanction if they liked. This principle was implemented by no other Governor-General so rigidly as by Lord Dalhousie. He asserted, "I hold that on all occasions where heirs natural shall fail, the territory should be made lapse and adoption should not be permitted, excepting in those cases in which some strong political reason may render it expedient to depart from the general rule."

There were, however, several who opposed these annexations on the ground of expendiency. **Sir George Clerk** and **Colonel Low** opposed Dalhousie's policy in the Council. They contended that the dependent states were useful, in as much as they afforded employment by us and who would sink into the 'dead level' of the population under our rule; that absorption of native states would therefore create discontent among a large body of men; that the rulers of other native states would be alarmed by these annexations, fearing the application of the same doctrines to their own successions; a childless ruler would feel no interest in the future well-being of his state and might even be tempted to extort as much as possible from his subjects during his life-time; that our territory was already large enough, and that natives prefer their own rulers to the British Government.

Sleeman was strongly against annexations and warned Lord Dalhousie in writing that the annexation of Oudh would cost the British power more than the value of ten such kingdoms and would inevitably lead to a mutiny of the sepoys, a prediction he died just too soon to see fulfilled. He held as others of his thinking did that the native states were breakwaters and when they are all swept away, native army, which may not be always sufficiently under control. **Lord Stanley** also unequivocally condemned the annexation policy. **Sir Henry Russel, Malcom** and **Elphinisten** expressed respectively, the following views on the subject : "I consider the extinction of a Native State as a nail driven into our coffin." "Tranquillity, not to say security, of our power will be hazarded in proportion as the territories of native princes and chiefs fall under our direct rule". "The period of our downfall in India will probably by hastened by every increase of our territory and subjects."[1]

He employed it to extend the bounds of British Empire by annexing the native States and Principalities. He availed himself of every opportunity to decline the sanction and deprive the rulers of their palace, power and prestige. In 1853 when Raghoji Bhonsle, the Raja of Nagpur, died without a legitimate heir, Lord Dalhousie annexed the state in the ensuing year. On the same plea the states of Jhansi, Udaipur (a small State under the ruler of Sarguja and not Mewar) Baghat (Punjab hill state) Jaitpur (Gujarat) and Sambalpur (Orissa) and Satara (Maharashtra) were merged with British India. The ceremony of adoption was time-honoured practice, and also permitted by the Hindu Law. The Doctrine of Lapse, as such, hurt the religious sentiments of the people. Besides it, the other rulers of Indian States feared that sooner or later their territories would be confiscated by the British Government.

Sir Charles Napier, once the Commander-in-Chief of British forces wrote: "Were I the emperor of India for 12 years, no Indian Prince could exist. The Nizam should be no more heard of .... Nepal would be ours."

2. *Annexation of Oudh (Avadh).* Nawab Wazid Ali Shah was the ruler of Oudh with Lucknow as its capital. The Nawab of Oudh from 1765 onwards had been very loyal and faithful to the British rule. The State which was quite rich in resources and fertility of soil had always served as a wet nurse to feed the Government with money. But this State could not escape the greedy and imperialistic designs of the Company. When no other valid reason could be discovered for its absorption, Lord Dalhousie alleged that the administration of Oudh was weak and inefficient. On this same plea, he abrogated the treaty of 1801 and by a proclamation dated 13th February 1856, annexed the State of Oudh. A large number of soldiers in the army of Bengal belonged to Oudh. They were shocked to hear the news. The treacherous role of the British Government also antagonised other Indian rulers and they ceased to trust its promises. **Mr. Malleson** observed. *"The annexation of Oudh alienated the territorial aristocracy who were stripped of their estates by the action of the newly introduced system, the Mohammedan aristocracy, the military classes, the British sepoys and the peasantry which converted into a hotbed discount." Commenting on the annexation of Indian States, Ludlow writes* : *"Surely the natives of India must be less than men if their feelings could not be moved under such circumstances in favour of the victims of the annexation and against the annexure. Surely there was*

1. Bell, Major E. *"The Empire India" Madras,* 1935, II, 14.

not a woman whom annexation did not tend to make our enemy, not a child whom they did not tend to train upon hatred to the Feringhee rule."

3. *Ill-treatment meted out to Mughal Emperor Bahadur Shah II or Zafar.* The Company in the beginning received many favours from the Mughal Emperors. Even the coins of the Company bore the name of the Mughal King. Later on the English became ungrateful and stopped offering presents to Bahadur Shah. They even removed his name from their currency. They resolved to extinguish the myth of Mughal Government. The Company became a rival of the Emperor. The disregard of the Mughal Emperor profoundly shocked the people who were still loyal to the throne. Lord Dalhousie went a step further and refused to accept Bahadur Shah's eldest son, Jawan-Bakht, as Crown-prince because of his anti-British feelings. He installed the younger son of Bahadur Shah Zafar as heir to the Mughal Throne on the condition that the would vacate the Red Fort of Delhi and secondly that he would be contented with only ₹ 15,000 instead of one lakh per month. When the prince accepted the conditions, Lord Dalhousie ordered Bahadur Shah to shift from Red Fort to Qutab. The Emperor was rudely shocked and he became the sworn enemy of the British Government.

4. *Injustice with Nana Sahib.* The fourth cause of the upheaval of 1857 was the injustice done to Nana Sahib. He was the adopted son of Baji Rao II, the ex-Peshwa. After the Maratha wars Baji Rao was granted annual pension of ₹ 8 lakhs and the estate of Bithur near Kanpur. After Baji Rao's death, Lord Dalhousie refused to accept Nana Sahib as heir to Baji Rao. This was not all. Nana Sahib was directed to vacate his estate of Bithur as and when asked by the Governor-General. This embittered Nana so strongly that he, too, became an arch enemy of the British Government.

5. *Effects of Crimean and Afghan Wars*—The reverses suffered by the English in Afghanistan in the year 1841-42 shattered the state of discipline in Company's forces. The Indian soldiers were convinced that Britishers were not indomitable. Azim ullah Khan, the leader of the rebellion, drew the inference from the British reverses in Crimea that it was not all difficult to rout the English forces.

6. *Most inhuman means employed for the conquest of India.*

William Howitt writes:

"The mode by which the East India Company has possessed itself of Hindustan, is the most revolting and unchristian that can possibly be conceived—if there was one system more Machiavellian, more appropriate of the show of justice where the basest injustice was attempted, more cold, cruel, haughty and unrelenting than another, it is the system by which the government of the different states of India had been wrested from the hands of their respective princes and collected into grasp of the British power.

Whenever we talk of other nations of British faith and integrity, they may well point to India in derisive scorn. The system which for more than a century was steadily at work to strip the native princes of the dominions and that too, under the most sacred pleas of right and expendiency, is a system of torture more. exquisite than legal or spiritual tyranny ever before discovered, such as the world has nothing similar to show."[1]

7. *Fervent desire of the Indians to liberate themselves.* Love of freedom is deeply rooted in every heart. Indians are no exception to this rule. Indians living in whatever part of the country even before 1857 had unity of outlook both in social and religious fields. All of them were imbued alike with the desire to secure freedom from English bondage. This common desire for freedom was given a spur and strength by the reckless attitude of the Government. Soldiers and civilians alike fretted with rage and hatred against the rulers. They were taken aback to see how a trading company which began its career as the agent of the Mughal Empire rounded off its adventures by robbing the Mughal Emperor of all its powers. The Company displeased not one but everyone. There was another factor,

1. William Howitt "*The English in India–System of Territorial Acquisition.*

equally responsible for the outbreak of mass uprising in 1857. There was a current belief that the Company's rule was destined to end exactly hundred years after the Battle of Plassy, 1757. So the common man made common cause with the rebelled soldiers and blew the bugle of a rebellion all over the country.

Social and Religious Causes

The social and religious causes were as follows —

1. The English committed a serious blunder by disrupting the social and religious systems of the Hindus. They stopped "Sati System" by law. The measure which appears to us so just and reasonable today, was then considered by Hindus as outrageous and insulting to their sacred religion.

2. The Company antagonised the people introducing changes in their laws of inheritance and succession. By the law, the Government entitled a Hindu even after embracing Christianity to claim his share in his ancestral property. This was greatly resented by the people.

3. The English played havoc with educational system prevailing in those days. It was their sustained effort to keep the people backward and illiterate, because education, they knew, fosters independent thinking.

4. The snobbish British officers who ruled with arrogance had no sympathies with the coloured people of India. They looked upon Indians as pariahs. *Mr. Malcolm Lewin in his book 'Indian Revolt' writes : "We (the English and Indians) are ignorant of each other, as members of society, the bond of union has been that of Spartan and Helot. Grasping everything that could render life desirable, we have denied to the people of the country all that could elevate them as men; we have insulted their caste ; we have abrogated their laws of inheritance ; we have changed their marriage institutions ; we have delivered up their temple property to confiscation ; we have branded them in official records as heathens ; we have seized the possessions of their native princes and confiscated the estate of their nobles; we have unsettled the country by our exactions and collected the revenue by means of torture; we have sought to uproot the most ancient artistocracy of the world and to degrade it to the condition of pariahs."*

5. *Karl Marx writes, "All the civil wars, invasions, revolutions, conquests, famines, strangely complex, rapid and destructive as the successive actions in Hindustan may appear, did not go deeper than its surface. England has broken down entire framework of Indian society, without any symptoms of reconstruction yet appearing. This loss of his old world, with no gain of a new one, imparts a particular kind of melancholy to the present misery of the Hindus, and separates Hindustan, ruled by Britain, from all its ancient traditions, and from the whole of its past history.*[1]

6. *Efforts to convert Indians into Christianity.* Another reason that served as fuel to the resentment of the people against the British rule was the activities of the missionaries to convert the natives into Christianity. The British authorities encouraged the missionaries with a sinister political design. They thought that Christianisation of India would stabilize and perpetuate their political domination over the country. Their design of religious expansion was the same as had been adopted by the Spanish colonialists in the South America. *Mr. Mangles, Chairman of the Board of Directors of the East India Company, said in the House of Commons on one occasion, "Providence has entrusted the extensive empire of Hindustan to England in order that the banner of Christ should wave triumphant from one end of India to the other. Everyone must exert all his strength that there may be no dilatoriness on any account in continuing in the country this grand work of making all India Christian.*

1. Karl Marx and F. Engel—The First War of Independence (1857-1859) p. 15-16.

The English religious policy in India was two -fold—(*i*) to stop giving any type of material aid to Indian institutions and in the name of the secularism even refused to impart religious instructions in the State schools; (*ii*) to encourage the missionaries to preach the tenets of Christ and persuade the people to embrace Christian religion. Army provided the most suitable field for the dirty activities of the missionaries. The army was infiltrated by 'missionary colonels' and 'Padri Lieutenants'. They began to denounce openly both Hindustan and Islam. This hurt severely the religious sentiments of the docile soldiers. Those who embraced the religion of Christ were offered easy and quick promotions. In the beginning they (missionaries) were tolerated sometimes with disgust and sometimes with indifference but as their activities increased, the soldiers felt alarmed. The British attempts at religious expansion simultaneously with territorial expansion, simply accelerated the causes of rebellion."

Economic Causes

The economic causes were as follows —

1. *Drain of Wealth.* During the British Rule, Indian wealth began to flow out of the country. Secondly, the industrial revolution gave a historic turn to the economic policy of English. The British merchants began to hunger for Asian markets to consume the British-made goods. British policy in India was so adjusted as to meet the needs of industrialised England. The native industries were given a calculated death blow. India was turned into a British colony which exported raw materials and imported finished goods. It led to the impoverishment of the country. The British Government compelled Indian weavers to work in English factories. The British economic policy thus created unrest in the whole country. The situation was further worsened by a famine that broke out in Purnea district of Bengal in 1770. The famine reduced the population of that district by one-third. The Company in order to make up the loss of land revenue increased rent in land holding and resorted to the practice of auctioning the land if a farmer failed to pay enhanced rents. From 1850 to 1875 nearly five million people in Bengal alone died of starvation. In Bombay the Company forfeited nearly 21,000 zamindaries in 1852. Oudh had the same story to tell. The profounded discontent in Oudh ultimately found an outlet in armed revolt in 1857.

2. *Views of Karl Marx on the Economic Exploitation of India by the British East India Company (Decline of Agriculture).* Karl Marx writes, "There have been in Asia, generally from immemorial times but three departments of Government; that of Finance, or the plunder of the interior; that of War, or the plunder of the exterior; and finally the department of Public Works....... Now the British in East India accepted from their predecessors the department of finance and of war, but they have neglected entirely that of public works. Hence the deterioration of an agriculture which is not capable of being conducted on the British principle of free competition of *laissez faires and laissez.*"[1]

3. *Marx on the decline of Indian Industries.* Karl Marx further observes about the decline industries in this country :

"It was the British intruder who broke up the Indian handloom and destroyed the spinning wheel. England began with driving the Indian cottons from the European market; it then introduced twist into Hindustan and in the end inundated the very mother country of cotton with cottons. From 1818 to 1836, the export of twist from Great Britain to India rose in proportion of 1 to 5,200. In 1824 the export of British muslins to India hardly amounted to 100,000 yards while in 1837 it surpassed 64,000,000 yards. But at the same time the population of Dacca decreased from 1,50,000 inhabitants to 20,000. The decline of Indian towns celebrated for their fabrics was by no means the worst consequence. British steam and science uprooted, over the whole surface of Hindustan, the union between agriculture and manufacturing industry."[2]

1. *Ibid,* p.16.
2. *Ibid,* p.18

4. *Marx on the decline of Indian Trade.* About the decline of Indian trade Marx observed, "During the whole course of the 18th century the treasures transported from India to England were gained much less by comparatively insignificant commerce, than by the direct exploitation of that country, and by the colossal fortunes there extorted and transmitted to England. After the opening of the trade in 1813 the commerce with India more than trebled in a very short time. But this was not all. The whole character of the trade was changed. Till 1813 India had been chiefly an exporting country, while it now became an importing one; and in such a quick progression, that already in 1823 the rate of exchange, which had generally been 2/6 per rupe, sank down to 2 per rupee. India the great workshop of cotton manufacture for the world, from immemorial times, became now inundated with English twists and common stuffs. After its own produce had been excluded from England or only admitted on the most cruel terms, British manufactures were poured into it at a small and merely nominal duty, to the ruin of the native cotton fabrics once so celebrated. *In* 1780 *the value of British produce and manufactures amounted only to* £ 386,152, *the bullion exported during the same year to* £ 15,041, *the total value of exports during* 1780 *being* £ 12,648,616, *so that the Indian trade amounted to only* 1/32 *of the entire foreign trade. In* 1850 *the total exports to India from Great Britain and Ireland were* £ 8,024, 000 *of which cotton goods alone amounted to* £ 5,220,000 *so that it reached more than* 1/8 *of the whole export, and more than* 1/4 *of the foreign trade. But the cotton manufacture also employed now* 1/8 *of the whole population of Britain, and contributed* 1/12 *of the whole national revenue.*[1]

Since 1784 *Indian finances have got involved more and more deeply into difficulty. There exists now a national debt of* 50 *million pounds, a continual decrease in the resources of the revenue, and a corresponding increase in the expenditure; dubiously balanced by the gambling income of the opium tax, now threatened with extinction by the Chinese beginning themselves to cultivate the poppy, and aggravated by the expenses to be anticipated from the senseless Burmese war.*" (*Written by Karl Marx on June* 24, 1853. *Published in the New York Daily Tribune, No.*3816, *of July* 11, 1853).[2]

Military Causes

The Military causes which contributed towards the rise and growth of Revolt of 1857 were as follows —

1. *Greased Cartridges.* The arrogant English dug their grave by displeasing the Indian soldiers enlisted in the British army. Indian Soldiers were denied equality of status with the English soldiers. Their loyalties grew weak. British reverses in the Afghan wars also strengthened their belief that their white masters were not the chosen sons of God. The soldiers of the Bengal troops, who hailed mostly from Oudh, were already annoyed with the British over the annexation of their home-province. The other measures of Lord Canning roused further discontentment. He issued a general order which made it compulsory for the new recruits to serve overseas. Such an order was distasteful to the soldiers whose religion forbade them to go across the seas. When the discontent was already mounting, the greased cartridges served as a match to haystock. The new cartridges were greased with beef and cow fat and required biting before they could be used. That the cartridges contained fat is beyond doubt. *The English historian Sir Kaye writes, "There is no question that beef fat was not in the composition of this tallow."* A factory for manufacturing the cartridges was set up near Dum Dum (Calcutta). Company's records tell us that a contractor undertook to supply cow's fat at the rate of annas four a seer. ***Lord Roberts*** *who was in India in* 1885 *wrote* : "*The recent researches of Mr. Forest in the records of the Government of India prove that the lubricating mixture used in preparing the cartridges was actually composed of objectionable ingredients—cow's fat and lard; and that incredible disregard of the soldiers' religious prejudices was displayed in the manufacture of these cartridges.*"[3]

1. *Ibid*, p.30
2. *Ibid*, p 31.
3. Lord Roberts, *forty Years in India*, p.43.

2. The famous Indian Historian Dr. R.C Majumdar observed, "The sepoys fully shared the general apprehension and suspicion that it was the deliberate object of the government to convert the Indians into Christianity by subtle means, fair or foul. The danger was specially brought home to them by missionary propaganda within military cantonments, Col. Wheeler, the commanding officer of a sepoy regiment at Barrackpur, used to distribute religious tracts among the sepoys and openly addressed them with a view to proselytise............. The name of another military missionary Major Mackenzie may be referred to in this connection."

Dr. R.C. Majumdar further observes, "The facts and circumstances that created in the minds of the people a vague and dread of mass conversion to Christianity, strengthened by the letters of Edmond and activities of Wheeler, brought home to the mind of the sepoy the grave and imminent peril which threatened their religion. And this feeling worked upon minds thoroughly disaffected against the British for many years past. A discerning eye could see that the mine was loaded and the train prepared, and spark might be easily furnished by any inflammable passion. The story of the greased cartridge supplied the spark and caused an explosion which shook the British Empire in India to its very foundations."[1]

3. No doubt the issuing of greased cartridges was a deliberate attempt to hurt the religious sentiments and prejudices of both Hindus and Muslims; but it was not the only reason for the outbreak of violence in the whole country. In the words of Justice Mc Carthy : "*The fact was that throughout the greater part of the northern and north-western Provinces of the Indian peninsula, there was rebellion of the native races against the English power......... The quarrel about the greased cartridges was but the chance spark flung in among all the combustible material .... a national and religious war.*"[2] *Another historian* Mr. Medley says, "*But in fact, the greased cartridge was merely the match that exploded the mine which had owing to a variety of causes been for a long time preparing.*"

4. Our contention is also corroborated by the writing of Marx who observed, "*The alleged cause of the dissatisfaction which began to spread four months ago in the Bengal army was the apprehension on the part of the natives lest the Government should interfere with their religion. The serving out of cartridges, the paper of which was said to have been greased with the fat of bullocks and pigs, and of the compulsory biting of which was therefore, considered by the natives as an infringement of their religious prescriptions, gave the signal for local disturbances.*" (Written by Karl Marx on June 30, 1857, Published in the New York *Daily Tribune* No. 5065, of July 15, 1857, as a leading article, "The Revolt In The Indian Army)."

Administrative causes

The Indians disliked and distrusted the administration of the British. The British System had abolished several intermediaries like Jaagirdar, Taluqdars etc. with whom the people had direct contacts and they drew certain advantages as well. Therefore, the system had not only created a section of dissatisfied people who wielded influence on the masses but also had created dissatisfaction among a large segment of the people themselves. The British system lacked the personal touch to which the Indians were habituated from the past centuries. The Judicial system of the British was costly, mechanical and involved much time. The poor could draw no advantage from it. The rich disliked it because they could be brought to trial even by the appeals of the common men who had been subservient to them for centuries. The police system of the British was not effective by that time and the people always felt insecure with respect to their property, life and honour. The most affected part of administration was revenue under the peasants and the zamindars were deprived of their special privileges. The British excluded the Indians from all high civil and military jobs. In the army, the highest post which an Indian could get was that of a Subedar while the highest post in the

1. Dr. R.C. Majumdar and others, History and Culture of the Indian People, Vol. IX *British Paramountacy and Indian Renaissance*, pp, 629-630.
2. Justice McCarthy, *History of Our Times*, Vol. III.

Civil Services for which an Indian could qualify was that of a Sardar Amin. It dissatisfied the educated Indians who expected to get gainful employment in the service of the company.

EVENTS

31st May, 1857, was the date, originally fixed, for the outbreak of revolt on a courtrywide scale. Unfortunately it fixed up earlier because of the mistake of a Brahmin sepoy Mangal Pandey, in Barrackpore. He received a big shock when he learnt that he would have to bite greased cartridges containing cow's fat. He reported the news to his fellow soldiers. The news spread like wild fire. The English officers vainly tried to prove that the news was unfounded. 'Revenge' became the watchword of the soldiers. Mangal Pandey had to lose his life for supplying the news to other soldiers. The heroic sacrifice of the first martyr of Indian struggle for independence had its desired effect. The whole country took up arms to uproot the British power.

Beginning of armed struggle for freedom in Meerut. On 6th May 1857, the new cartridges were issued to 90 Indian soldiers in Meerut, 85 of them refused to bite it with their teeth. They were court-martialled and sentenced to 10 years' rigorous imprisonment. They were disarmed and handcuffed and brought on a parade. In the presence of the entire Indian garrison they were stripped of their uniforms and taken to the prison. The effect of such a dramatic scene was just the reverse of what was intended. It was done on the morning of 9th May, 1857. The same afternoon when the Indian troops were strolling in the streets of Meerut, they were hooted and looked at by the ladies of the town for their cowardice. Their remarks were penetrating. It became difficult for the soldiers to wait till 31st May. The spark was struck and the revolution was on its way. The troops and the civilians raided the jails and set the fellow convicts free. The sky was rent with the deafening shouts of "Maro Farranghi ko." On the 10th night, the Indian troops joined by thousands of able-bodied men of the town marched on to Delhi.

Entry into Delhi. The hastiness of Indian troops in Meerut in fact saved the British Raj from its impending ruin, as planned by Nana Sahib and his associates. Maleson, White and Wilson—the three noted historians—agree to the fact that such a premature uprising proved fortunate for the British and fatal for the planners. Had it started simultaneously throughout the country on a fixed day, the results would have been different from what they were. Not a single Englishman would have escaped alive.

The Indian cavalry comprising two thousand soldiers entered Delhi on 11th May, 1857. The English Colonel Ripley tried to thwart the advancing rebels with the support of Indian troops under his command but the attempt proved abortive. His soldiers walked over to the side of the rebels and put Col. Ripley to death. Within a couple of days Delhi was freed from English hands. The rebels declared Bahadur Shah as the Emperor of India who was 82 years old and rallied under the Mughal banner to cross swords with the British authority in India.

Spread of the Movement. The news of the fall of Delhi into hands of rebels spread like wild fire all over the Northern India. By the 24th May, 1857, the neighbouring districts of Delhi including Aligarh, Etawah and Manipuri declared themselves free. The fire spread to Rohilkhand where Khan Bahadur Khan also joined the revolutionaries. The Englishmen were massacred and their houses burnt. It was a unique instance of Hindu-Muslim unity and co-operation in the common cause of driving Britishers out of their land. The stimulating news of the revolt soon spread to Kanpur, Lucknow, Bihar and Central Provinces (now Madhya Pradesh). The reaction was immediate.

Siege of Delhi by Britishers. Lord Canning, the then Governor-General of India, showed presence of mind at this critical hour. He ordered all the Indian troops to be disarmed speedily. He also employed diplomatic tactics to break the union of Hindus and Muslims. He frightened the Muslims by telling them about the designs of the Hindus to establish Maratha rule. He told the Hindus to beware of the Muslims who were planning to establish Muslim Raj again. Lord Canning succeeded in procuring help from the State of Patiala, Nabha, Jind, Hyderabad, Gwalior and Rajutana. Nepal and Punjab provided excellent recruits to the British ranks. The British circulated in the Punjab a false *Firman* in the name of the Mughal Emperor which said that after the success of the revolt every Sikh would be put to death. Bahadur Shah tried his best to remove the misunderstanding but did not get much success. The Sikhs joined the British ranks in large number and became instrumental in suppressing the revolt. Had the Punjab sided with revolutionaries events might have taken a different turn.

Capture of Delhi. Lord Canning instructed Anson, the Commander-in-Chief then at Simla, to proceed towards Delhi and General Neil to march with his well-equipped forces to recapture Benares, Allahabad and other districts. The Englilsh Commander-in-Chief and Brigadier Wilson laid the siege of Delhi. They alongwith their forces stuck to the outer walls of Delhi notwithstanding the attacks by Bahadur Shah's forces. The siege continued for several months. Circumstances both in the Capital and other parts of the country turned in favour of the British. The British troops blocked all the supply lines and caused scarcity of food and war material in the capital. Moreover, Indian troops in Delhi did not have a strong leader to inspire them to a joint action except Bakht Khan (Subedar) who was appointed commander-in-chief of Delhi. Emperor Bahadur Shah was too old (82 years old) to lead his army. His orders were not obeyed by many anti-social elements and sepoys.

Haryana. It is highly regrettable that historians have not taken any pains to depict the freedom struggle in Haryana which has always been in the forefront from the time immemorial either in checking the foreign invasions or to regain the lost independence. For this purpose Haryana has made unparalleled sacrifices during the past ages. On 20th May, 1995 this state comprised the districts of Gurgaon, Faridabad, Rohtak, Karnal, Panipat, Sonepat, Bhiwani, Kurukshetra, Sirsa, Rewari, Mahendragarh, Kaithal, Ambala, Yamuna Nagar, Jind and Hissar.

The first planned resistance of a wider scale against the foreign rule was mooted in Ambala Cantt., but the plan leaked out, so it came to nothing. However when Bahadur Shah joined the freedom struggle after the arrival of Meerut sepoys, the native rulers also raised the standard of revolt. *Hence Rewari under the able leadership of Rao Tula Ram and his cousin brother Rao Gopal Krishan (also the Kotwal of Meerut) Jhajjar under the leadership of Nawab Abdul Rahman, Farrukhnagar under the leadership of Ahmad Ali Khan, Ballabhgarh under Raja Nahar singh, Jharsa Pargana under the valiant Chowdhry Bakhtawar Singh became the strong centre of resistance. Besides that there was a revolt in Rohtak, the premier city of Haryana.. Here the standard of revolt was first raised by Ranghars (Rajputs) but later on joined by all. Ali Hasan Khan and his father-in-law Samad Khan led the freedom struggle in Mewat (Distt. Gurgaon.) Hansi (Tehsil of Hissar district), Hissar and many villages like Bilaspur, Murthal, Kundli, Alipore, Hamidpur and Sarai etc. also joined the fray.* The freedom fighters offered toughest resistance to the British commanders from May to September 1857 and did not allow the conquest of an inch of land by the various British Commanders but after the fall of Delhi on September 20, 1857 all changed. The British army relieved to a great extent was sent to conquer the various parts of Haryana. The freedom fighters fought many pitched battles against the British forces at Sirsa, Hazimpur (a village near Hansi) and Mangla village (Hissar district) but they were defeated because the British possessed better weapons and their number far exceeded the forces of freedom fighters. At least 400 freedom fighters lost their lives in the battles of Mangla village alone. The Indian forces were being led by Prince Muhammad Azim. Though he was defeated and his wife was captured by the British forces, yet he did not lose the heart and marched towards Narnaul to join the other freedom fighters of Haryana because the whole of Hissar district had been occupied by the British forces.

Brigadier-General Shevars left Delhi on October 2, 1857 with 1500 soldiers and with some tanks in order to quell the disturbances in various parts of Haryana. First of all he made a plan to invade Rewari. When Rao Tula Ram heard about the arrival of Brigadier-General Shevars, he thought it useless to face the enemy at Rampura Palace of Rewari because a stronger Red Fort of Delhi had already fallen. Therefore he left his palace for Narnaul. Thus Rewari fell without resistance. After that Shevars attacked Jhajjar. The Nawab of Jhajjar left at once for Chhuchhakwas, (a village of then Jhajjar State) where he handed himself gladly over to the British commander. He was at once imprisoned and sent to Delhi. Similarly Nawab Ahmad Ali Khan of Farrukhnagar and Raja Nahar Singh of Ballabhgarh were imprisoned and sent to Delhi. After this all the rest of the freedom fighters of Haryana including Prince Muhammed Azim and Samad Khan got together at Narnaul. The hardest fought battle of Haryana against the British imperialists was at Nasibpura (two miles away from Narnaul). In this battle Rao Kishen Singh, commander of the Indian forces as well as British Commander Jerard were killed. Besides that the talented leader of the freedom fighters like Rao Ram Lal, Prince Muhammad Azim and the son of the Samad Khan fell in the battlefield while fighting very heroically. After the fall of these leaders the Indian army lost heart. Meanwhile the sun had also set in, so the Indian army ran away. *After this horrible atrocities were committed by the British forces on the poor people of Haryana, thousands of people were either imprisoned or hanged, many villages were burnt and property of hundreds of people was confiscated.*

Chowdhry Bakhtawar Singh of Jharsa pargana, Raja Nahar of Ballabgarh, Nawab Ahmad Ali of Farrukhnagar and Abdul Rahman of Jhajjar were hanged in Delhi. The Quanugo of Hansi was hanged before his own house and so thousands of people of Haryana were hanged at different places. After this Rao Tula Ram joined Tatya Tope who sent him to Afghanistan for help but he died there of dysentery. Thus ended the 1st armed struggle for freedom in Haryana where there was no lack of courage, unity, enthusiasm or bravery on the part of the people but the British won the various battles due to treachery, superiority of generalship and weapons and extra-ordinary help received from the States of Bikaner, Jaipur, Nabha, Patiala and Jind.

Fall of Delhi. Above all espionage and bribery also helped the cause of the English. They got the military secrets from Mirza Ilahi Bakhsha, a close relative of the Emperor. Lord Canning reinforced the British troops round Delhi. More troops from Kashmir and the Sikh States of Punjab swelled their sides. On 14th September, 1857, the British forces, divided into five divisions, started their onward march. Fierce battle raged on all sides. The stars of the British being in the ascendant, they broke through the outer walls and captured the city completely on 24th September. Because of the treachery of Ilahi Bakhsha, Bahadur Shah fell into the British hands. General Hudson ordered the two sons of Bahadur Shah to be stripped of their clothes and be shot dead. Not satisfied with his cruelty, he severed their heads from their bodies and sent them to Bahadur Shah. The Emperor was deported to Rangoon where he died on Nov. 7, 1862. The fall of Delhi was followed by massacre and loot of the people by the British troops. Every house was ransacked and every conceivable method of torture was employed to get information about the underground wealth. Within a couple of days thousands of people were killed or mangled. The imperial city became the favorite haunt of vultures and jackals. *Lord Elphinston writes : "After the siege was over, the outrage committed by our army are simply heart-rending. A wholesale vengeance is being taken without distinction of friend and foe. As regards the looting, we have indeed surpassed Nadir Shah.' General Chaplain also admitted: "A general massacre of the inhabitants of Delhi, a large number of whom were known to wish our success, was openly proclaimed.*

Punjab. The Punjab was the only Province in Northern India which remained quiet. Emperor Bahadur Shah did make efforts to get the support of Sikh leaders and Sikh States but all his attempts were foiled by the machinations of Sir John Lawrence. Whenever the Indian troops in the British ranks showed signs of unrest, they were speedily disarmed. In spite of all the precautions taken by Sir Lawrence, the native troops at Peshawar, Ferozpore, Lahore and Jullundur turned their guns against the white Generals but soon they were suppressed. Those who fled for life were pursued, arrested and shot dead.

Jhansi, Oudh and Bihar. The revolt in Cawnpore (Kanpur) was led by Nana Sahib and Tatya Tope who received enthusiastic support from every civilian and soldier. Bareily and the whole of Rohilkhand were also astir with brisk activities. The fire of revolt in Oudh was enkindled by Begum

Hazrat Mahal and Wazir Ali Naki Khan. Rani Laxmi Bai became the spearhead of revolt in Jhansi and the whole Central India. In Bihar Raja Kunwar Singh and Amar Singh of Jagdishpur joined the forces of revolt. They showed exemplary valour. Kunwar Singh was an old man. But the stray attempts by Indian rulers failed to get much success for want of one leadership and concerted action. Laxmi Bai, the Joan of Arc of the Revolt, mounted her horse and moved up and down her forces, encouraging and inspiring her soldiers. She died on 18th June, 1858 near Gwalior, but her valour (name and fame) has become immortal. Tatya Tope was betrayed by one of his friends Man Singh and was hanged on 18th April, 1859. Maulvi Ahmed Shah was also murdered by the brother of Raja Jagannath Singh of Pawan. Nana Sahib, Begum Hazrat Mahal and Amar Singh of Jagdishpur fled towards Nepal and nobody knows what happened to them there. Thus the great struggle which began in 1857 boiled down completely by April, 1859.

Part played by the South India. There is a wrong notion prevalent among the people of our country that the South did not play any role in the Great Liberation Movement and the First War of Independence was mainly confirmed to the North India. Shri V.D. Divekar in his learned research work '*South India in 1857*' has proved it wrong. J.S. Tilak, Chairman of Lokmanya Tilak Smarak Trust writes, "The official brochure brought out by Andaman administration lists about 25 freedom fighters who were transported to the Andaman in 1857. The Research of Tilak Smarak Trust, Pune, has now uncovered more than 800 such names who were sent there from different regions in India and who belonged to different communities for taking part in 1857 War of Independence."

"The resolution of the Government of Madras in the Judicial Department dated 3rd September, 1857 may be mentioned here. It says, "On the 28th July, 1857 a conspiracy was discovered the ramifications of which extended from Belgaum, Karnool and Madras generally. In the middle of June 1857 bands of armed Rohillas who proclaimed that they were the servants of Nana Sahib Peshwa crossed from the Nizam's country, into the Karnool and Cuddapah Districts with a *deeper object*. They were apparently connected with the party who made the attack on the Hyderabad Residency (on the 17th July). In Mysore about the middle of July 1857, it was found necessary to despatch some European infantry and guns etc. to overawe the Mohammadans near Seringapatam and Mysore."

"In Masaulipatam a green flag and a proclamation, urging the slaughter of the English were seized on the 10th July and it was reported on the 15th August that prayers for the success of the King of Delhi were offered in mosques. In Bellary, seditious rumours unfavourable to our Government began to spread abroad in June and fires of gun attacks along the frontier were reported on 10th June (1857)."

"In Madras itself the state of feelings in Triplicate ..... became so suspicious that on the 29th June, military posts were established in different parts of the town and other precautions taken. Among other signs of disaffection, proclamations and seditious letters were seized urging the Nizam and his Ministers to begin a holy war in which they were ready to join. Both in Madras and in the surrounding provinces much seditious language and correspondence was going on. *The approaching downfall of power was openly talked of.* In Chinglepet some seditious plotting was discovered."

Similar situation prevailed in Mysore State. **Sir Mark Gibbon** the British Commissioner in charge of Mysore in his reply to the Governor General's circular letter dated 26th Feb., 1858 regarding a report on the conduct of parties in Mysore during the Mutiny observed : "The Brahamancial caste were discontented and hostile, the great sowcars, the petty poetigar and heads of villages are *all against our rule and disaffected towards British Government.*

There was, among the classes above named a spirit exceedingly hostile to the British Government evinced in carrying on correspondence with the malcontent in the north, in favourable reception of emissaries of from that quarter and in the convening of treasonable meetings at their own houses, for the purpose of plotting the subversion of our power".

"Moving to the region of Pune-Satara-Kolhapur, it would be helpful to understand the situation by referring to the report to the Bombay Government by Major General *Le Grand Jacob,* in charge of the command of the area, submitted on 21st March, 1858. Jacob's conclusions were : (1) "That there was communication and planning between the Native Infantry at Kolhapur (No. 27th), Belgaum (No. 29th) and Dharwar (No. 28th); (2) That, *Chimansahib*, the younger brother of Raja of Kolhapur was moving spirit behind the organisation, (3) That, Chimansaheb had contacts with Nana Sahib whose emessary had brought a gilded sword for him; (4) That, Chimansaheb had contacts with Gwalior leaders from where a deputation had visited Kolhapur under some pretext and negotiations with Chimansaheb; (5) That, Chimensaheb also had assured the Satara emissaries, in June 1857, that Kolhapur sepoys and also some chiefs were ready for action and that they were waiting for a signal from Satara." We also know that there was a link between Kolhapur and the Puna School of Musketry and that, one of the emissaries from south, coming from Mysore, and he had secured by then the co-operation of forty different regiments of the British army."

The above observation made confidentially by the Chief commander of the area give an idea of the efforts made by the leaders of the War of Independence to make it a truly national war against the foreign rule. As for reference to Bhadur Shah, the King of Delhi or Nana Sahib's emissaries, letters, contacts and influences in other ways in the south, we find them distributed in as distant areas as Khandesh, Nasik, Kohlapur, Rajahmundry, Madras, Coimbatore etc.

It is remarkable that at Stara the call to rise came not from a Maratha noble, but from a Hindustani Chaprasi **Musai Singh.** For one thing we should know that in 1857 Indians had forgotten regional, religious, caste or social boundaries in fighting the British uprisings. The part played by the **Rango Bauji Gupte** in organising the uprising is worth remembering. He was the principal and foremost leader.

"Such views that war of independence was confined to North India that it lacked total planning or that it was merely a Sepoy Mutiny etc. appear to be too ficile. For example, Lowe in his work, *Central India During the Rebellion of 1857* (London, 1860, p. 24) poses the question,"Why did the discovery of a plan to destroy all Europeans at Nagpur synchronies with Mutiny at Aurangabad?" Mr. H. Russel in his work, *My Diary in the year 1858-1859* (London, 1860 Vol. 2 p. 259) wondered that if it was only a Sepoy Mutiny, why was it deemed necessary to punish the country people and citizens by fines and hanging, for complicity in acts with which they of their own accord had nothing to do? That the people of all communities involved in the war or were mostly sympathetic to it is no wonder." As it has happened in the histories of the revolutionaries and freedom struggles everywhere in the world, there is no doubt, sections of the people who were loyalists to the foreign rule or rather the Establishment and many were sitting on the fence. But that does affect the basic character of the war. Similar was the situation in other countries during the days of; say, French Revolution, American War of Independence etc[1].

Prominent persons to be hanged were Abdul Rahim Khan Rohilla, Aladuddin Maulvi Syed, Arjun Krishan Patel, Arjun, Awachit etc. Besides that leading Maratha citizens were either killed in battle or were blown off by cannons or shot dead or hanged.

Causes of the Failure of the First Great Armed Struggle for Freedom. There were three main causes of the failure of India's first armed struggle of great magnitude. These were: lack of simultaneous action, lack of resources, and lack of common ideal after the arrest of Bahadur Shah and lack of discipline. One great handicap of the rebel forces was that they were very poorly equipped. Some of the rebel armies had only the swords to fight with against the British guns. Secondly, the rebels were short of men and money. They had no such territories as Nepal wherefrom to recruit soldiers. Moreover, the British forces far outnumbered the rebel armies. The worst of all was that the native states by their prolific help to the British ensured and hastened the doom of the revolt. Disunity amongst the Indians themselves and the limited character of the uprising which did not spread in the Punjab and beyond Narmada, proved fatal to the cause. *"Yet it must be admitted,"*

1. V.D. Divekar; *South India in 1857*, p.VIII, IX.

writes Sir. W. Russell in 'My Diary in India'. "That with all their courage, they (the English) would have been quite exterminated, if the natives had been, all and altogether hostile to them..... .. Our siege of Delhi would have been quite impossible if the Rajahs of Patiala and Jind had not been our friends and if the Sikhs had not got recruited in our battalions and remained quiet in the Punjab. The Sikhs at Lucknow did good service and in all cases our garrisons were helped, fed and served by the natives, as our armies were attended and strengthened by them in the field".

Lack of discipline in Delhi and other places of revolt. There is on record a petition from Chand Khan and Gulab Khan of the Pharganj area of Delhi that " the sepoys forcibly took away goods from shops without payment and entered houses of poor people and took away beds, woods, vessels etc. But on 27th June, long before Delhi fell and Bahadur Shah was still hopeful of victory, he wrote a letter to his Commander-in-Chief to the following effect : "Not a day had elapsed since the arrival of the army and its taking up quarters in the city, that petitions from towns people have not been submitted, representing the excesses committed by numerous infantry sepoys." Bahadur Shah alleged in his written statement during his trial that sepoys paid no respects to him or acknowledged his authority ; they threatened to depose him, kill his queen and other officials and one day even went to the house of Queen Zinat Mahal, intending to plunder it but did not succeed in breaking open the door. Bahadur Shah said he was virtually the prisoner of the sepoys, who had set up a council of their own in which all matters were discussed and line of action decided upon. But there was no order or discipline among them. "Thus", continues Bahadur Shah, "without my knowledge or order, they plunged not only many individuals, but several entire streets, plundering robbing, killing and imprisoning all they chose; and forcibly extorting, whatever sums of money they thought fit from the merchants and other respectable residents of the city and appropriating such exactions to their own private purpose. I did whatever they required, otherwise they would immediately have killed me. This is a universally known fact."

But the climax of indiscipline was reached when the sepoys refused to serve under Bakht Khan as Commander-in-Chief and actually sent a petition to the King to this effect. When an army assumes the power and responsibility of making and unmaking the king and exercises a veto upon appointment of their Commander-in-Chief and when the officers openly plead inability to control the soldiers and save the civil population from their plunder ; its chances of gaining success in the prolonged and sustained struggle may be rendered as negligible. Military history has shown again and again that valour, courage, heroism and self-sacrifice of individual soldiers cannot make up for the lack of discipline of the army as a whole. Bareily, Farrukhabad and Bijnor also witnessed the same scenes of indiscipline.

Another cause that marred the chances of success of armed struggle was the lack of experienced generals. The British forces were commanded by the most trained and experienced persons while amongst the rebel there were no outstanding leaders except Tatya Tope and Laxmi Bai and a few others. The rebels forces suffered from want of quick means of communications and transportation. The British forces had all the facilities of Post, Telegraph and Railways at their disposal. Lastly, the premature patriotic outburst of Mangal Pandey was also partly responsible for the failure of the grand designs of Nana Sahib and others. Since the outbreak was not simultaneous in different parts, the government got the warning and time to consolidate its forces.

Atrocities. Mr Gurumukh Nihal Singh writes, "In restoring order, however, the British committed great atrocities, the memory of which rankled in Indian mind long after the rising was suppressed and produced consequences whose significance escaped recognition till only recently. The English killed their prisoners without trial and in a manner held by all Indians to be the height of barbarity. They also massacred thousands of civilian population not only in Delhi but also in the countryside. General Neil gave orders to his lieutenants that certain villages were marked out for destruction and all the men inhabiting them were slaughtered and the indiscriminate burning of their inhabitants occurred wherever English armies moved."

Martin R. Montgomery writes : "After the occupation of Delhi by British troops all the city people found within the walls were bayoneted and the number was considerable as you may suppose, when I tell you that in some houses forty or fifty persons were hiding. These were not mutineers but residents of the city who trusted to our well-known mild rule for pardon. I am glad to say they were disappointed. I have given up walking about the back streets of Delhi, as yesterday an officer and myself had taken a party of twenty men out to the patrolling, and we found fifteen women with their throats cut from ear to ear by their own husbands and laid out in their shawls. We caught a man there who said he saw them killed, for fear they should fell into our hands; and showed us their husbands, who had done the best thing they could do afterwards and killed themselves."[1]

The Bombay Correspondent of the **Times** wrote : "No such scene had been witnessed in the city of Shah Jehan since the day that Nadirshah seated in the little mosque in Chandni Chowk directed and superintended the massacre of its inhabitants."[2]

Kaye Observes, "Many who had never struck a blow against us–who had tried to follow their peaceful pursuits–and who had been plundered and buffered by their own armed countrymen, were pierced by our bayonets or cloven by our sabres or brained by our muskets or rifles."

Dr. Ishwari Prasad writes : "Benares had never passed out of English hands. With the arrival of General Neill it became the headquarters of the English for the reconquest of the upper provinces. Terror with Neill was a part of his strategy. Whole arrests were ordered, villages were burnt and men and women were shot dead or hanged from the branches of trees. The corpses were left rotting or hanging as the case might be an example of British butchery."

NATURE OF THE MOVEMENT OF 1857

The suppression of the Revolt of 1857 marked the end of one phase of India's struggle for Freedom. A question is often raised whether it was a 'War of Independence' or a 'Sepoy-revolt'. Most of the western historians have called it a sudden outburst of discontent among the sepoy of the Company. This view was borrowed and repeated by a few Indian historians also. But now it is admitted by the majority of the historians with little controversy that the aim of the uprising was to secure freedom from the foreign yoke. No matter it was not well planned or not organised properly, it was an outburst of patriotic fervour. It might have begun as a mutiny of the sepoys but later on it assumed the dimensions of a national struggle.

Planning in the Movement. It would also be wrong to suppose that there was no planning behind the War of Independence. Dr. Ishwari Prasad remarks, "for long this rising was being planned, its organisation being perfected, its threads being spread to the remotest corners of the land by a band of selfless patriots who had nothing dearer to them than the *freedom* of their country." "From the available evidence I am quite convinced," writes J. C. Wilson, the Judge of *Moradabad in those times, "that the 31st May, 1857 had been decided as the date for the simultaneous rising." "For months, for years, indeed." writes Kaye, "they (agents of Nana Sahib) had been spreading their network intrigue all over the country. From one native court to another, from one extremity to another of the great continent of India, the agents of Nana Sahib had passed with overtures and invitations, discretely, perhaps mysteriously worded, to princes and chiefs of different races and religions.*" Kaye further writes that at the call of Ali Naqi Khan, the Hindu and Muslim sepoys swore by the Ganges and the Quran that they would lay down their lives to drive the English out of the land. The agents of Ali Naqi disguised as Sadhus and Faqirs , starting from Calcutta, visited every cantonment of Northern India spreading the fire of rebellion. *"But is is difficult to describe", writes Sir Grand Jacob in his book 'Western India', "the wonderful secrecy with which the whole conspiracy was conducted and forethought supplying the schemes and caution with with each group of conspirators worked apart, conciliating the connecting links, and instructing them with just sufficient information for the purpose*

1. Martin R. Montgomery, *The Indian Empire* II, 449.
2. *Ibid*, 450.

in view. And all this was equalled only by the fidelity with which they adhered to each other." All evidence supports the view that there was years of planning behind such a tremendous preparedness ad simultaneous outbreak of violence in the whole of Northern India. How could otherwise the revolt have got the support of every person—the high and low, the old and young and the men and women.

Object of the Movement: Proclamation of Bahadur Shah Zafar. That the object of this uprising was to secure freedom from the alien rule is further proved by the Proclamation of War issued by Nana Sahib on behalf of the Mughal Emperor, Bahadur Shah. In it he solicited the co-operation of all the princes and jagirdars to join in the jihad or 'holy war' declared against the British. Nana Sahib said : "The English who are *Kaffirs (heathens) came to the country under the pretence of carrying on trade. Afterwards by practising treachery, they seized all the Hindu and Muhammedan kingdoms.*"

"The *Kaffirs* upon the strength of their acquisition of the Empire have turned very arrogant, and keeping up outward appearance of justice, have most unjustly destroyed life and acquired wealth and property. They have been endeavoring to delude and convert the population of this country by inducing them to abandon their own religion and caste; but having failed by mild means to do this, they were out to use force."

"Ye Heroes ! this is the best time for you to avenge the wrongs and wickedness perpetrated by the *Kaffir* English, on our grandfathers and your Kings! By allowing such an opportunity to escape, do not suffer the stain of being effeminate and foolish to attach to the people of the south."

Bahadur Shah Zafar, the last Mughal Emperor of Delhi, had also issued a letter to Indian Princes asking them to co-operate in the 'Grand Struggle for Independence.' The letter read as follows: *"This is my heartfelt wish that whatever be the cost and means employed, the Firranghis must be driven out of the country and Hindustan may acquire the independence. After the expulsion of the English 'Kaffirs' I have no intention to lord over the country myself... If all the rulers and princes of India are willing to pool their resources and forces to be used against the 'Firranghis', I am also. prepared to surrender my authority to a body of persons, agreeable to all, to take over the reins of administration."*

From Dhondo Pant-Nana Peshwa, Pant Prudhan to all the Surunjamdars, Jageerdars, Deshmookhs, Deshpandeys and other Zameendars, Patels, Coolkernees, Naikwads, Shetsundes and the whole of the population of the Deccan and the Carnatic, "It is ordered to be proclaimed that —

The English who are "Kaffirs" came to this country under pretence of carrying on trade. Afterwards instigating sedition among our Surunjamdar and practising treachery they seized all the Hindu and Mahomedan Kingdoms imprisoning some of the descendants of the former Kings and driving others to beggary, they themselves enjoy the country. This is well known to the whole of you.

Tyranny, wickedness and injustice having been much practised by the "*Kaffir*" English on the faithful and sinfearing. I have been commissioned by God to punish the "*Kaffirs*" by annihilating them and to re-establish the Hindu and Mahommedan Kingdoms as formerly and to protect our country and I have conquered the country north of the Narmada river.

To submit to an live under such wicked "Kaffirs" is very disgrassceful, so immediately on the perusal of this Proclamation you are bravely to take up your swords and without mercy destroy the "Kaffirs". By this you will gain merit and show your manliness and your courage will be proved."

Views of Mr. V.D. Savarkar. In his proclamation of the establishment of Swaraj, Bhahadur Shah II, Emperor of Delhi, further said : "Oh, you sons of Hindustan, if we make up our mind, we can destroy the enemy in no time ! *We shall destroy the enemy and will release from dread our religion and our country, dearer to us than life itself.*"[1] **Shri V.D. Savarkar** observed, "What is holier in this world than such a Revolutionary War, a war for the noble principles propounded in this sentence, release from dread our religion and our country, dearer to us than life itself? The seed of the Revolution of 1857 is in this holy and inspiring idea, clear and explicit, propounded from the throne of Delhi, the Protection of Religion and Country."[2] In the Proclamation issued at Bareilly Emperor Bahadur

1. Lecky's *Fiction Exposed* and Urdu Works.
2. V.D. *Savarkar, The Indian War of Independence*, 1857, p.8.

Shah II of Delhi further says: "Hindus and Muhammedans of India ! Arise ! Brethren arise ! *Of all the gifts of God, the most gracious is that of Swaraj*. Will the oppressive demon who has robbed us of it by deceit be able to keep it aways from us for ever ? Can such an act against the will of God stand for ever? No, no. The English have committed so many atrocities that the cup of their sins is already full. To add to it, they have got now the wicked desire to destroy our holy religion ? Are you going to remain idle even now ? God does not wish that you should remain so; for He has inspired in the hearts of Hindus and Muhammedans the desire to turn the English out of our country. *And by the grace of God and your valour they will so completely be defeated that in this our Hindustan, there will not remain even the least trac of them*."[1]

Views of Justice McCarthy. About the nature of the Revolt of 1857, Mr. Justice McCarthy says, "The fact was it was not alone the sepoy who rose in revolt — it was not by any means a merely a military mutiny. *It was a combination of military grievance, national hatred and religious fanaticism against the English occupation of India.* The native princes and the native soldiers were in it. Muhammendans and the Hindus forgot their old antipathies to join against the Christians. Hatred and panic were the stimulants of that great rebellious movement... The Meerut sepoys found in a moment a leader, a flag and a cause and the *mutiny was transformed into a revolutionary war*. When they reached the Jumna, glittering in the morning light, they had all unconsciously seized one of the great critical moments of history and converted a military mutiny *into a national and religious war*."[2]

Mr. Charles Ball writes : "At length the torment overflowed the banks and saturated the normal soil of India. It was then expected that those waves would overwhelm and destroy the entire European element and that while the torrent of rebellion should again confine itself within bounds, partriotic India, freed from its alien rulers would bow only to independent sceptre of a native prince. The movement now assumed a more important aspect. *It became the rebellion of a whole people incited* to outrage by resentment, by imaginary wrongs and sustained in their delusions by hatred and fanaticism."[3]

Views of Mr. S.N. Sen : Mr. S.N. Sen observes, "The Mutiny was inevitable. No independent nation can ever reconcile itself to foreign domination. A despotic government must ultimately rule by the sword though it might be sheathed in velvet. In India the sword was apparently in the custody of the Sepoy Army. Between the sepoy and his foreign master, there was no common tie of race, language and religion.

The author does not agree with the views of those who say that there was no nationalism in 1857. We should never forget that we had feudal India in 1857 and some landlords were selfish but at the same time some others who were inspired by the lofty ideal of protecting their religion and culture. At least all the freedom fighters had one common goal that is the expulsion of the *Feringhis* (the British) and liberation of the holy land from the rule of foreigners. Therefore at least some top leaders had one common goal whatever their individual grievance.

Thus the uprising of 1857 was essentially a mighty effort on an extensive scale to shake off the religious and political domination of an alien race. The truth of this statement is further borne out by the following extract from *William Horward Russel's ' My Dairy in India in the year 1858-59'*: "*... We had a war of religion, a war of race and a war of revenge, of hope, of national determination to shake off the yoke of a stranger and re-establish the full power of native chief and the full sway of native religions*." Judge the outbreak of 1857 from whatever angle, we cannot deviate from the general conviction that the mass uprising of 1857 was an epic struggle of a subject nation for political independence. Whether it was joined by few or many, that is immaterial because the revolutions are joined by few only.

1. *Ibid*
2. McCarthy, *History of Our Times*, Vol. III.
3. Charles Ball, *Indian Mutiny*, Vol. 1, p.644.

Consequences of the Movement of 1857. The First War of Independence is so to say the most significant event of Indian history. It marked the end of an epoch of Indian history — epoch of British intrigues and diplomatic tactics for the expansion of British Empire. The events of 1857 brought the Company rule to an end. As remarked by Bright, "the conscience of the nation had been touched upon the question and it came by leap — and it were by an irrepressible instinct — to conclusion that the East India Company must be abolished". Nana Sahib, Begum Hazrat Mahal and their followers had to run for safety to Nepal.

Secondly, it roused and increased racial ill-will between the British and the natives. The snobbish Englishmen withdrew themselves to their shell of vanity and stopped having much association with the coloured natives. The relations between the two races became that of the master and the slave.

Thirdly, the Englishmen lost their faith in the Indian subjects. Their trust in the loyalty of Indian troops was also shaken. They were so greatly frightened that they decided not to offer key posts in the administration to Indians. They practised this policy for a pretty long time.

Fourthly, the bitter experiences of the events of 1857 made the British government realise that the rule of the sword simply would not be sufficient. For the stability of the British rule, the hearts of the subject race should also be changed. In pursuance of this aim strong efforts were made to popularise the learning of English language so that the Indians may start appreciating the British laws and system of justice. In short, the end of 'Mutiny' marked the beginning of systematised attempts to anglicise the people.

Fifthly, the British government set about the reorganization of Indian troops. The number of British officers was increased and the battalions and regiments were reconstituted on the basis of religion, province and caste. The motive behind it was to foster narrow mindedness and discord between one caste and the other. Besides it, the charge of heavy guns and cannons was given exclusively to European officers.

Sixthly, the Government realised the mistake of antagonising the rulers of Indian Sates. It decided thenceforth to befriend them. The Queen in her Proclamation assured the natives princes that all the treaties made with them by the Company shall be honoured and no attempt will be made to deprive them of their States or titles. The Queen also promised to the Princes to protect their States from any sort of aggression or encroachment. This Proclamation was received by the Princes quite warmly. They became the allies of the British Government in crushing the national forces and stemming the rise of patrotic sentiments in the masses.

THE ACT OF 1858

End of the Colonial Rule of East India Company: India comes directly under the British Crown

England went to the polls in 1857 and voted Lord Palmerston to the office of the Prime Minister. While introducing the Bill in the House of Commons on February 12, 1858, he said, "The principle of our political system is that all administrative functions should be accompanied by ministerial responsibility—responsibility to the Crown; but in this case the chief functions in the Government of India are committed to a body not responsible to Parliament, not appointed by the Crown, but elected by persons who have no more connection with India than consists in the simple possession of so much stock."

Lord Palmerston during his Premiership introduced a Bill which proposed the transfer of Government of India to the Crown, the liquidation of the Court of Directors and Proprietors and setting up of an Executive Council headed by a Cabinet Minister to conduct the affairs of India on behalf of the Crown.

The Bill first introduced by Palmerston and then by Derby and Disraeli in a modified form was passed by the Parliament in 1858.

Main Provisions of the Act of 1858

The main provisions of the Act were as follows :

1. *Taking over the Indian administration by the British Crown.* The Act provided that India henceforth was to be governed by and in the name of *Her Majesty*. It changed the designation of the Governor-General to "The Viceroy of India". (Governor-General and Viceroy was the same person. When he dealt with the British Provinces, he was known as Governor-General but when he dealt with Indian States, he was called Viceroy because he acted as Crown's representative in that capacity). It also provided for the transfer of military and naval forces of the Company to the Crown.

2. *Appointments.* The Act empowered the Crown to appoint the Viceroy of India and Government of Presidencies. It vested in the Viceroy the power to appoint Lieutenant-Governors with the approval of Her Majesty. The power of appointing the Members of Council both at the Centre and the Provinces was given to the Secretary of State-in-Council.

3. *Secretary of State for India and his Council.* The Act provided that the powers and duties relating to the Government and revenues of India, which till then used to be exercised by the Court of Directors and Board of Control, were to be exercised by the Secretary of State for India. The Secretary of State was to be a member of the British Cabinet and responsible to the British Parliament. He was to be assisted by a Council of fifteen members, eight of them to be nominated by the Crown and the remaining to be elected by the Directors. In order to make the Council an expert body on Indian affairs, the Act laid down that at least nine out of the fifteen members were to be selected from persons who had served or resided in India for at least ten years and had not left the country more than ten years before their appointment. The members could be removed from office by the Crown on representation being made by both Houses of Parliament.

4. *Role of the Council.* The Council of India was to be an advisory body and its concurrence was not to be obligatory for the Secretary of State. All the meetings of the Council were presided over by the Secretary of State. Each member of the Council was entitled to a salary of £ 1,200 to be paid out of Indian revenues. The Council was to meet once every week in which the Secretary of State was to place all his orders to be sent to Indians. The quorum of the meeting was five.

5. *Powers of Secretary of State for India.* The Secretary of State for India, who presided over the Council meeting, was also empowered to override the view of the majority. But whenever he did so, he had to record in writing the reasons for overriding the majority decision of the Council. He also possessed a casting vote to be exercised in the event of equal division in the Council on any issue. He was, however, bound by the decisions of the Council in matters like (*i*) appropriation of revenues and property. (*ii*) issuing of securities of money, and (*iii*) sale or mortgage of property, contracts, etc.

6. The Secretary of State for India could even send his secret orders, concerning the making of war, peace, or negotiations, to Government of India without taking the Council into confidence.

7. Secretary of State for India was also given power to frame rules and regulations for recruitment to Indian Civil Service.

8. *Control of British Parliament over the Secretary of State for India.* The Act required the Secretary of State for India to lay annually before Parliament a financial statement of expenditure and revenues of India. The Parliament could also ask him questions relating to India, criticise him on the charge of inefficiency.

9. *Appointments to the Councils of Governor-General and Governors.* The India Council was empowered to make appointments to the Councils of the Governor-General and the Governors. It should also exercise control over the civil and military servants of the Crown.
10. *Rules regarding the guidance of the Indian Government.* The Secretary of State for India and his Council were empowered to frame certain rules regarding the guidance of Indian Government in all its dealings with the British Crown and Government. The Secretary of State for India, henceforth, was to control all the legislative and financial measures, various projects concerning the railways and construction of the public works; creation of new jobs and policy matters of the Indian Government.

Defects of the Act of 1858

Indians were not benefited from the transfer of the Government and revenues of India from the Company of the Crown. The keenness of the British Parliament to know about India was greater during Company's rule, but it subsided with the appointment of the Secretary of State to run the administration of India. The Parliament "had full faith in the Secretary for India and the Viceroy of India." It began to approve and justify all their actions. The provision regarding the payment of the salary of the Secretary of State for India and his establishment out of the Indian revenues was solely in the British interest, so it was greatly resented by the Indians.

Significance of the Act of 1858

According to Shri G.N. Singh one great significance of the Act was that it "closed one great period of Indian history and ushered in another great era—the direct rule of the Crown. It rang the death-knell of the trading Company which was born in 1600 *A.D." Mr. Marshman observes, "It (Company) transferred to the Crown on relinquishing its functions, an Empire more magnificent than that of Rome."* The abolition of Double Government in England, *i.e.*, the Court of Directors and Parliamentary Board of Control had also some salutary effect. The Governor-General was now to obey the orders of only the Secretary of State. The centralisation of authority did away with all sorts of confusion, red-tapism and uncertainty in Company's hold over the Indian Government. The post of the Secretary of State for India became more dignified and responsible. The establishment of India Council was a unique measure because it provided the Secretary of State with expert advice.

PROCLAMATION OF QUEEN VICTORIA

In order to celebrate the occasion of the taking over of the Government of India by the Crown, a Darbar was held at Allahabad where Lord Canning read out the Queen's Proclamation to the Princes and People of India. It declared, "We have resolved to take upon ourselves the Government of the territories in India hitherto administered in trust for us by the Honorable East India Company." It assured the Princes that "all treaties and engagements made with them by or under the authority of the Honorable East India Company are by us accepted and will be scrupulously maintained: and we look for the like observance on their part....... We shall respect the rights, dignity and honour of Native Princes as our own....... We *desire no extension of our present territorial possession,* and while we will permit no aggression upon our dominions or our rights to be attempted with impunity, we shall sanction no encroachment on those of others."

The Proclamation assured the people of India that "We declare it to be our royal will and pleasure that none be anywise favoured, none molested or disqualified by reason of their religious faith and observances, but that all shall alike enjoy the equal and impartial protection of the law...... and it is our further will that so far as may be, our subjects of whatever race or creed, be freely and impartially admitted to offices in our service, the duties of which they may be qualified by their education, ability and integrity duly to discharge."

"We know and respect the feeling of attachment with which the Natives of India regard the land inherited by them from their ancestors and we desire to protect them in all rights connected therewith subject to the equitable demands of the State and we will (wish) that generally in framing and administering the law due regard be paid to the ancient rights, usages and customs of India."

The proclamation went on to declare unconditional pardon, amnesty and oblivion for the late offernces and ended by declaring that "When by blessing of Providence internal tranquillity shall be restored, it is our earnest desire to stimulate the peaceful industry, to promote works of public utility and improvement and to administer its government for the benefit of all our subjects resident therein. In their prosperity will be our strength, in their contentment our security, and in their gratitude our best reward."

Importance of the Proclamation. The Proclamation was important in many respects because it laid the foundation of a new policy in India. The right of adoption was given to the Indian Princes and the policy of the annexation of their States was ended. Thus they were assured of the territorial integrity of their states. Regarding other effects of the Proclamation, Dr. Ishwari Prasad observes : *"To the people of the India the Proclamation brought a new heaven on earth. It promised them peace and the prosperity, protection of their religion, equality of treatment with other subjects of the Queen and above all promised to them a share in the highest service of the State, if so qualified,"* As general amnesty had been declared, so the Proclamation went a long way in pacifying the people and it became easier for Canning to restore law and order.

EXERCISES

Long Answer Type Questions

1. Discuss the causes and nature of the Revolt of 1857.
2. How far is it correct to say that the Revolt of 1857 was the First war of Indian Independence?
3. "The Revolt of 1857 was anything but a war of Independence." Discuss.
4. "The Revolt of 1857 harmed the interests of both the English and the Indian." Discuss in view of the effects of the revolt on British policies and it contribution towards national movement.
5. "The great Revolt of 1857 makes an epoch in British Indian History." Discuss.
6. Discuss the results of the upheavel of 1857.
7. Discuss the political causes of Revolt of 1857.
8. What were the social and religious causes of Revolt of 1857 ?

Short Answer Type Questions

1. Discuss in brief the Political Causes of the Revolt of 1857.
2. Write a short note on Administrative Causes of the Revolt of 1857.
3. Write the economic causes of the Revolt of 1857.
4. What were the social and religious causes of the Revolt of 1857 ?
5. Write a very brief note on military causes of the Revolt of 1857.
6. Discuss the nature of the Revolt of 1857.

Objective Type Questions

Choose the correct answer

1. William Bentinck prohibited the practice of Sati in

(*a*) 1829 (*b*) 1830

(*c*) 1831 (*d*) 1832

2. Who prohibited the practice of Sati in 1829?

(*a*) Hastings (*b*) William Bentinack

(*c*) Lord clive (*d*) Wellisaly

3. In which year the laws were passed concerning succession of property?

(*a*) 1856 (*b*) 1829

(*c*) 1832 and 1850 (*d*) 1830

4. The Religious Disabilities Act passed in

(*a*) 1853 (*b*) 1854

(*c*) 1855 (*d*) 1856

5. Which Act passed in 1856

(*a*) Widow Remarriage Act (*b*) Education Act

(*c*) Poverty Act (*d*) None of the above

ANSWERS

1. (*a*) **2.** (*b*) **3.** (*c*) **4.** (*d*) **5.** (*a*)

CHAPTER

4

Act of 1861

> *"The addition of the native element (to the Councils) has, I think become necessary, unless one is prepared for the perilous experiment of continuing to legislate for millions of people with few means of knowing, except by a rebellion, whatever the laws suit them or not."*
>
> **—Sir Bartle Frere**

BEGINNING OF THE POLICY OF ASSOCIATION

The Indian Council Act of 1861 has an important place in the Constitutional History of India. Under this Act, Indians were first nominated as the members of the Executive Council. It means, it was for the first time when Indians were associated with the administration of the Government. This policy of 'Benevolent Despotism' is a landmark in the Constitutional History of India. By the Act of 1861, the foundations of an Indian Legislature were made broader. Besides, the Act provided a frame work of Government which continued till the British Rule in India.

Circumstances leading to the Act of 1861

It would be interesting to have a short account of the circumstances under which the measure was enacted. These were as under.

1. *Need of associating Indians.* The great uprising of 1857 served as an eye-opener to the British Government. It brought to British statemen that no Government can be secure in its seat by antagonising the people. They felt the necessity of seeking the cooperation of the Indians in the administration of their country. The British Government realised it for certain that the only cause responsible for the revolt was hundred years' misrule of the Company. Sir Syed Ahmed Khan stressed the same point when he said, " Had there been a native of Hindustan in the same Legislative Council, the people would never have fallen into such errors."

2. *Defective system of Law-making in India.* The urgency of a new constitutional measure was felt in view of the people's demand that some representative element should be introduced in the Government of India. The Legislative Council of the Governor General did not work satisfactorily. It observed all the formalities of a Parliamentary procedure, hence caused delay in the enactment of laws. Moreover, it had no representative of the people on it. It consisted of only official members who had no sympathies with the people.

3. *Difficulties in making laws for the Provinces.* The Act of 1833 had brought about the centralisation of legislative powers. It was done with a view of securing uniformity of laws in the whole country but this system proved defective. Although it had one representative each of the four Provinces, it failed to make laws which could suit the local conditions of Province. Hence the need was felt for allowing the presidencies to frame rule for themselves.

4. *Question of defining the powers of the Legislative Council.* The Legislative Council of the Governor-General in due course widened its scope of work and began to work as a Parliament in miniature. It sometimes embarrassed the Governor–General by asking him to supply all information and correspondence with the Secretary of State. At time it refused to comply with the wishes of the Home Government. Sir Charles Wood, the President of the Board of Control, told the Council to contain its activities but to no purpose. The independent attitude of the Council created difficulties both for the Governor-General and the Board of Control.

5. *Despatch of the Governor-General.* Lord Canning, the Governor-General of India, forwarded some suggestions to the Secretary of State for setting things right. The new proposals made by the Government of India in their Despatch of January 1861 were: the establishment of the Councils for Bengal, North-Western Provinces and the Punjab; the exclusion of Judges from the Councils; an increase in the number of non-official Members from three to five in the Presidency Councils of Bombay and Madras; addition to the Supreme Council of Members, not exceeding twelve of whom half were to be non-officials. Members were to be appointed for a period not longer than two years; the holding of meetings of the Supreme Councils at places other than Calcutta;. and legislative business to be transacted as done in a committee or commission and not done in the form of set parliamentary debates."[1] These recommendations of Lord Canning formed the basis of a Bill which Sir Charles Wood moved in the House of Commons on June 6, 1861. It received royal assent on August 1, 1861. It came into force at the close of the year.

In short we can say that the cumulative results of all the above mentioned causes was the act of 1861.

Main Provisions of the Act

The Indian Councils Act 1861 introduced changes in the Central as well as the Provincial Governments. For the sake of convenience its provisions may be studied under the following points:

Preamble. The Preamble to the Act declared, "Whereas it is expedient that the provisions of the former Acts of Parliament respecting the constitution and functions of the Council of the Governor-General of India should be consolidated and in certain respects amended and that power should be given to the Governors-in-Council of the Presidencies of Fort Saint George and Bombay to make laws and regulation for the government of the said Presidencies, and that provision should be made for constituting the like authority in other parts of Her Majesty's Indian Dominions."

Other Clauses of this Act were as follows:

1. *Addition of fifth member of the Executive Council of Viceroy.* The Act provided for the enlargement of Viceroy's Council by adding one ordinary member to it. The fifth member was to be a financial expert.

2. The Viceroy was empowered to make *rules and regulations* for the convenient transaction of business.

3. *Powers of the Legislative Council were curtailed.* The Act defined clearly the functions of the Legislative Council. It empowered Council to legislate on all subjects concerning all persons and courts in British India. But every Bill passed by it required the assent of the Viceroy to become

1. Despatch to the Secretary of State for India, No. 2A, Home Deptt., January 15, 1861.

an Act. The Act armed the Viceroy with the power to withhold his assent to exercise his veto power if he felt that the Bill affected the safety, peace and interest of British India. Besides that, all laws were communicated to the Secretary of State for India who could disallow them with the assent of the Crown.

4. *Right of making new Provinces.* The Viceroy was empowered to alter, modify or adjust the limits of the Provinces or create a new province for administrative convenience.

5. *Extension of the Legislative Council.* The Act suggested reorganisation of the Legislative Council on a new basis. In place of the representatives of the Provincial governments, provision was made for an addition of 6 to 12 members to the Central Executive for legislative purpose. At least half of the additional members were to be non-officials. These members were to be nominated by the Viceroy for a period of two years.

6. *Provincial Councils were again empowered to make laws.* The Act provided for the enlargement of the Executive Councils of Madras and Bombay by the addition of one Advocate-General and 4 to 8 members for legislative purposes. The Provincial Legislative Council could make laws for the good government of the province. Army, customs, currency and coinage, post and telegraph, foreign and political relations were, however, outside its scope of legislation. The Governor was to be the sanctioning authority of all Bills passed by it. Besides that the Governor-General's assent was also necessary. The Secretary of State-in-Council could also disallow it with the approval of the Crown.

7. *Right to issue Ordinances.* The sad bitter experiences of the Governor-General to cope with the situation created by the revolt in 1857 necessitated the strengthening of the hands of the Viceroy. Under the new Act the Viceroy was empowered to issue Ordinances during an emergency. The life of such an Ordinance was six months. It could be suspended even earlier by the Secretary of State-in-Council.

8. *Previous sanction of the Governor-General in certain matters.* It was laid down that the previous sanction of the Governor-General would be necessary for the introduction of the Bills concerning vital matters like Public Debt, the Army, the Coinage, and Currency, the Foreign and Political Relation, Posts and Telegraphs, etc.

9. *Alternation in the Provincial boundaries.* The Governor-General was authorised to alter the boundaries of the Province if he deemed it necessary.

10. *Establishment of the Councils for Smaller Provinces.* The Act authorised the Governor-General to create Council for North Western Provinces and the Punjab. In this matter, the Governor-General could act in his own discretion.

11. *Enlargement of the Presidency of Council and their Powers.* The Governor of each Presidency (Bombay, Madras and Bengal) was empowered to nominate not less than four and not more than eight additional members besides the Advocate-General for legislative purpose. Not less that half of these nominated members were to be non-officials. The term of the additional members was kept two years. The Provincial Legislative Councils could make laws for the betterment of the Provinces subject to the overall control and restrictions of the Centre. If any Bill affected such vital matters as the Public Revenue, Public Debt, Foreign and Political Relations, sanction of the Governor was essential.

Importance of the Act

The Act of 1861, it was one of the important Constitutional measure of the time of Lord Canning. In order to evaluate of the Act, it would be interesting to have a short account of the following facts.

1. *Non-officials Associated:* Commenting on the Act of 1861, **Mr. G.N. Singh** observes: "The Indian Councils Act, 1861 is important in the constitutional history of India for two chief reasons,

first, because it enabled the Governor-General to associate the people of the land with the work of legislation, and secondly, by restoring legislative powers of the Governments of Bombay and Madras and by making provision for the institution of similar Legislative Councils in other Provinces. It laid the foundation of the policy of legislative devotion which resulted in the grant of almost complete internal autonomy to the province in 1937."

2. *Portfolios Introduced:* The Act laid also the foundation of some good principles of Indian administration. For example, it introduced a portfolio system, the ordinance power and Legislative system with non-officials which constitute uptill now the cardinal features of Indian Administration.

3. *Governor-General Strong:* This Act made the Governor-General, 'Omnipotent', brought the whole of India under his control, vested powers of emergency in the Governor-General, put restrictions on the right of the people regarding free discussion and introduction of motions other than those of Legislation, and tried to unify India by bringing both the Regulation and Non-Regulation Provinces under the supreme control of the Governor-General who himself was to abide by the Crown, the authority of Parliament and its enactments, Thus, the Act modified the Constitution of the Governor-General's Executive and remodelled the Indian Legislatures.

4. *Opportunities for the British Rulers to know the feelings of the Indians:* Thus, we notice that this Act provided opportunities for the British Rulers to acquaint themselves with the feeling of the Indians in regard to their administration. This Act helped to Lessen the feelings of distrust and antagonism, which was prevailing in India since Mutiny. **Coupland** has rightly remarked, "Since most of the non-officials members thus chosen were Indians, the Act of 1861 may be said to have introduced the representative principle into the Indian Constitution."

5. *Restored Legislative Authority of the Presidency Councils:* The Act has also its significance as it restored the Legislative Authority of the Presidency Councils. Provisions were also there for the institution of Legislative Council in some more Provinces, Thus, it was the beginning of the policy of Legislative decentralisation. **Professor Coupland** has said, "In admitting to Indians to the Council and in restoring powers to the provinces a dual process of 'Indian Nation' and "Decentralisation' has been been started, which was to lend stage by stage, to **Indian** self-Government."

6. *Furnished a frame work of the Government.* **Mr. M.V. Pylee** has rightly remarked, "It was the primary charter of the Indian Legislatures of the 20th century." The Act furnished a complete frame-work of the Government.

Criticism of the Act or Drawbacks of the Act

In spite of all the important changes introduced by the Act of 1861, it was not much satisfying to the national aspirations. It fell far short of the public demands. It was criticised for the following reasons:

1. The Indian Councils Act, 1861 did not establish Legislative Councils in the real sense of the term. While introducing the Indian Council Bill, 1861 in the House of Commons, *Sir Charles Wood* candidly declared that the establishment of representative council, was simply and utterly impossible under the prevailing circumstances of the country. He also complained in the House of Commons that contrary to the intentions of its founders, the Council had become a sort of debating society or Parliament.[1] The scope of the Councils was, therefore, restricted to legislation alone.

2. **Sir Charles Wood** clearly declared in British Parliament that he had no intention to make the Council a debating society. The Act of 1861 unequivocally provided that the Legislative Councils, both at the Centre and in the Provinces, were not to transact any business other than the consideration and enactment of measures introduced in them for the purpose of enactment. The establishment of Parliamentary institutions in India even in their most rudimentary form was not liked by British politicians and philosophers of the mid-nineteenth century.

1. Report on the Indian Constitutional Reforms (1918), p. 39/2, Clause 38 and 99 of the Act of the 1861.

3. For two decades the non-official members who were nominated to the Governor-General's Council for legislative purpose were either ruling Princes or their Dewans, big Zamindars or retired officials. The ruling Princes or their Dewans did not show any interest in the legislation for the British India as it did not affect them.

4. The Legislative Councils provided by this Act were mere phantoms of which they should have been. They were mere committees to assist the executive in making laws. *According to Mr. Cowell, the laws exacted by them were nothing but the orders of the Government.* They were not empowered to exercise any check on the Government, nor could they call for any information they required. The laws passed by them were in the nature of the advice rendered to the executive. They had no right to remove any member of the Viceroy's Executive Council by a vote of no-confidence.

5. The Act by investing the Governor-General with veto power took away whatever few rights it had conferred on Councils in theory. This power armed him with the discretionary power to override the Council easily. His power of issuing ordinances made him an absolute despot.

6. The Act made no progress towards giving representative government to India. It showed no difference to the political and national sentiments of people. The question of giving representation to Indians was discussed at length by Sir Charles Wood, the Secretary of State for India, in his opening speech in Parliament but it was regarded as simply and utterly impossible.

EXERCISES

Long Answer Type Questions

1. Examine the circumstances which led to passing of the Indian Council Act of 1861.
2. Discuss the main provisions of the Indian Councils Act 1861.
3. Discuss the importance of the Indian Councils Act 1861. What were its drawbacks?

Short Answer Type Questions

1. Write any three circumstances leading to the Act of 1861.
2. Discuss any three provisions of the Indian Council Act of 1861.
3. Write a short note on the importance of the Indian Council Act of 1861.
4. Write any three drawbacks of the Indian Council Act of 1861.

Objective Type Questions

Choose the correct answer

1. Under which Act, Indians were first nominated as the members of the Executive Council ?
   (*a*) The Indian Council Act 1861 (*b*) The Act of 1858
   (*c*) The Charter Act of 1853 (*d*) The Charter Act of 1833
2. Under which Act Indians were associated with the administration of the Government for the first time ?
   (*a*) The Regulating Act of 1773 (*b*) The Indian Council Act of 1861
   (*c*) The Charter Act of 1853 (*d*) The Charter Act of 1833

ANSWERS

1. (*a*) 2. (*b*)

5

CHAPTER

Rise of Nationalism in India

> *"Indian Nationalism is a modern phenomenon. It came into being during the British period as a result of the action and inter-action of numerous subjective and objective forces and factors which developed within the Indian society under the conditions of British Rule and impact of World forces."*
> *— A.R. Desai*

Nationalism is a great unifying force. It is a sort of spiritual bond which brings together persons having unity of language, religion, race, literature, history, customs. It is further strengthened by common economic and political interests and also geographical unity. A nationalist's sole care is the freedom and advancement of his country. He hates slavery. He loves his country and stakes all his possessions so that his country may live. It is incorrect to say that national awakening in India was the product of 19th century. Our holy scriptures like Vedas, Ramayana and Mahabharata abound in hymns which breathe of patriotic sentiments. Our history is a glorious saga of heroic struggles and great sacrifices. The rise of Rajputs, Marathas and Sikhs added glorious chapters to the annals of India. There cannot be a better instance of our love for freedom than exhibited by our patritots in 1857. Another phase of our struggle this time was of a unique order and it shook the mighty soul of India from its short slumber.

CAUSES OF THE BIRTH AND RAPID GROWTH OF NATIONALISM IN THE 19TH CENTURY

Two opposite views have been expressed about the rise of Nationalism in India. According to one view the "Indian Nationalism is a modern phenomenon. It came into being during the British period as a result of the actions and inter-actions of numerous subjective and objective forces and factors which developed within the Indian Society under the conditions of British Rule and impact of World forces.[1] This view holds that the very existence of the foreign rule in India helped the development of national sentiments in the country. As the Britishers tried to carry on the administration of India primarily with a view to promote their own interests and completely ignored the interests of the people, this naturally gave rise to bitterness against the foreign rule and promoted the feeling of nationalism among all classes of the Indian population. In short, this view gives the credit for the rise of nationalism in India to the British Rule which for the first time in Indian History bound the various parts into a single unit.

1. A.R. Desai – Social Background of Indian Nationalism

On the other hand **Prof. Hans Kohn** is not inclined to share the above view. He maintains that "a truer basis of unity than modern national sentiments was to be found in a common intellectual heritage persisting through an unbroken tradition and wielding and permeating India's whole social life to the minutest detail, and in the peculiar contemplative piety which lies at the root of the various forms of Hinduism.[1]

Prof. S.L. Sikri while giving due credit to the British Rule for the rise of nationalism is not willing to concede that the Indian Nationalism was the outcome of the British Rule in India alone. On the other hand, he argues it was the result of a combination of factors. He says, "Some of these factors sowed its seed, some nurtured its growth; some moulded its forms; and some influenced its ideology and technique. Hence the causes responsible for the origin, growth and rapid development of the Indian National Movement were various and manifold."[2]

The Main causes which contributed to the rise and development of Nationalism in India were as follows–

1. Effects of the first War of Indian Independence against the Imperial rule: Though opinions might differ on the character of the movement of 1857, yet the bulk of the Indian intelligentsia have now come to regard it as an organised struggle for national independence in the light of latest facts. It should not be forgotten that the people of our country waged war against the imperialist rule at a time when it had established itself firmly from the Himalaya to the cape of Comorin and Brahmaputra Valley to the Indus. Though the British Historians, who were imperialist to the core, have dubbed it as the Sepoy Mutiny but the unparalleled sacrifices, and heroism of the people of our country could not go in vain and the posterity always took inspiration from the martyrs of 1857 for the future freedom struggle of the country.

Famous Indian Historian

Dr. R.C. Majumdar beautifully summed up his conclusions on this subject in the following words :

"The outbreak of 1857 would surely go down in history as the first and direct challenge to the British rule in india, on an extensive scale. As such inspired the national movement for the freedom of India from British yoke, which started half a century later. The memory of 1857-58 sustained the later movement, infused courage into the hearts of its fighters, furnished a historical basis for the grim struggle, and gave it a moral stimulus, the value of which it is impossible to exaggerate. The memory of the revolt of 1857 distorted but hallowed with sanctity, perhaps did more damage to the cause of the British rule than the revolt itself."[3]

"The national uprising though subdued, left a great effect on the mind of the people. Their common sufferings during the upsurge broadened their vision which supported the growth of the conception of India as a common "motherland". People from every part of the country started becoming acquainted with each other. As the war spread from Nepal to the territories of the Nizam, the participants came in close contact with the people of various provinces and principalities. The growth of this conception paved the way for the rise of new type of political leadership. It inspired the struggle for independence in the years to come. Therefore, the later half of the nineteenth century following the First War of National Independence of 1857 was characterised by the rapid development of national consciousness."[4]

2. Social and Religious Movements. India owes a great deal to socio-religious movements led by Raja Ram Mohan Roy, Swami Dayanand Saraswati, Ram Krishna Paramhansa and Swami

1. Hans Kohn – A History of Nationalism in the East, Page 349
2. Sikri - Rise and fulfilment of Indian National Movement Page 2.
3. Dr. R.C. Majumdar, *The Sepoy Mutiny and Revolt of 1857* (Calcutta, 1958), p. 278.
4. Dr. Sukhbir Chowdhry, *Growth of Nationalism in India,* Vol. I, p.57.

Vivekananda for its resurgence and national awakening in the 19th century. They played leading roles not only in combating with the eradicating social evils but also in reviving pride in our ancient culture and heritage. The wave of cultural revivalism was a reaction against the great challenge thrown by the western culture and civilisation which was politically dominant and economically powerful. Indians realised the urgency of grappling with not only the missionaries but also the ruling party which backed the spreading of Christianity. Thus, the movements, which were essentially religious in character, affected the political thinking of the nation.

(*i*) *Raja Ram Mohan Roy* (1774-1833) and *Brahmo Samaj*. One of the greatest forces in making of renascent India was the Brahmo Samaj. It was formally founded by Raja Ram Mohan Roy on January 23, 1830. Ram Mohan was a great scholar of all the living religions. He was a great social reformer and his mission was to cleanse the society of all its social evils and impurities. He had no prejudices against any religion nor was he reluctant to borrow what was good in European culture.

Raja Ram Mohan Roy

Ram Mohan was in fact an exponent of world's conscience and a passionate champion of humanitarianism. He had a catholic approach to religious truths. He led a crusade against *Sati Pratha*. He was opposed to polygamy and in the favour of remarriage of widows. It was on his instance that Lord Bentinack, the then Governor-General of India, banned the inhuman practice of *Sati*. He condemned and discouraged idol worship. He believed in God who was shapeless, timeless and deathless. He believed in the fundamental truth and unity of all religions. Fraternity for him was the essence of all religions. *He urged the necessity of personal freedom and administrative reforms and stood for the freedom of Press, political rights of the people and western education system with emphasis on the study of science subjects.* Many a time he submitted petitions to the British Government, praying for the granting of certain privileges to the people.

He drew the attention of the people to their glorious past and how it could be revived. This led to political awakening in the country. He defended Hinduism from impact of Christianity. He tried to purge it of all evils and make it a strong and living faith. It would not be too much to say that he was a great force in the social and political resurgence of India. So he has been rightly described as the Father of Indian Renaissance and the Prophet of Indian Nationalism.

Raja Ram Mohan Roy wanted to reform Hindu society and rejuvenate it. Therefore, he opposed caste system with its attendant evils of untouchability. He once said, "I regret to say that the system adhered to by the Hindus is not well calculated to promote their political interests. The distinction of castes, introducing divisions and subdivisions among them, had entirely deprived them of political feelings, multitude of religious rites and ceremonies and the laws of purification have totally disqualified them from undertaking any difficult enterprise. It is, I think, necessary that some change should take place in their religion at least for the sake of their political advantage and social comfort." So Raja Ram Mohan Roy has been rightly called, "the herald of a new age." *According to Monier Williams, the Raja was perhaps the first earnest-minded investigator of the science of comparative religions that the world has produced. According to Rabindra Nath Tagore, Raja Ram Mohan Roy "inaugurated the modern age in India."* According to **Mr. Brijendra Nath Seal,** the Raja was "the harbinger of the idea of universal humanism, the humanist, pure and simple, watching from his conning tower the procession of universal history. "According to **Miss Coelt**, "Ram Mohan Roy stands in history as the living bridge over which India marches from her unmeasured past to her incalculable future." So we say that Raja Ram Mohan Roy was a great champion of the liberties of the people, an agitator for the construction, social, legal and administrative reforms and ardent supporter of the rights of the tenants.

(*ii*) *Swami Dayanand Saraswati* (1824-1883 A.D.) *And Arya Samaj.* Another powerful religious and social movement that was started in the 19th century was Arya Samaj. The founder of Arya Samaj was Dayanand Saraswati, a renowned scholar of the Vedas. He once said, "The world is fettered by the chain forged by superstition and ignorance. I have come to snap as under that chain and set slaves at liberty." He was an arch-rebel, a rebel against orthodoxy, against dominant Christianity and against all that was alien to the vedic spirit of India. He was a master dialectician and a profound Vedic Scholar. Like Raja Ram Mohan Roy, he too had faith in the abstract, ageless and deathless God.

Swamiji's social philosophy was of a revolutionary character. He condemned the territorial notion of superiority conferred by birth. He said that the caste of a person was to be determined by his psychology and occupation. He gave a death blow to untouchability, child marriage and animal sacrifice practised in the name of religion. He travelled widely across the country and propagated his enlightened philosophy. He accepted the growing challenge of Islam and Christianity boldly. He strongly refuted the false and mischievous propaganda being carried on by other religionists in order to discredit Hindu religion. After making a comparative study of several religions, he enunciated his philosophy in his monumental work entitled *Satyartha Prakash*. He also did commendable work for cow-protection in India.

Dayanandji was a staunch nationalist and he made a unique contribution in the political field. It was his belief that Vedic idealism has been the saviour of India in some of her great trials. Hence he pleaded for the revival of Vedic idealism. His creed of cultural revivalism had its implications in the political field also. He preached the lesson of fearlessness and freedom–both in the spiritual and political sense. He had ardent love for India, which he used to call *Aryavarta*. He regarded it as the land of the philosophers and gold. He wrote in his book : "*Foreign government, perfectly free from religious prejudices, impartial towards all the natives and the foreigners–kind, beneficent and just though it be–can never render the people perfectly happy.*" There is a good deal of truth in the remark of Vanetine Chirol ".... the whole drift of Dayanand's teaching is far less to reform Hindustan than to range it into active resistance to the alien influences which threatened, in his opinion, to denationalise it."

Swami Dayanand

Besides inspiring love for Swarajya in every heart, Swamiji also helped the rise of Indian nationalism by popularising Hindi. He wrote his commentaries on the Vedas in Hindi and also preached through the medium of Hindi. The bond of common language proved quite strong and lasting. The masses of Northern India sank their narrow differences and developed a feeling of oneness. Mrs. Annie Besant rightly declared: *"It was Dayanand Saraswati who first proclaimed that India was for the Indians." The Arya Samaj did a great service to foster Indian nationalism especially in the Punjab and produced great patriots like Lala Lajpat Rai. It infused a new militant spirit among Hindus. In the field of education Mahatma Hansraj and Swami Shardhanand did commendable work by founding D.A.V. College, Lahore, and Gurukul Kangri. Work done by the chain of Anglo-Vedic Institutions in the nation cannot be underrated. These colleges breathed the new life into the nation and youngmen, who came out of the portals of D.A.V. Colleges, carried the sacred torch of patriotism towards the temple of freedom.*

Dayanand was the first Indian to preach the gospel of *Swadeshi.* He emphatically declared that good government by a foreign ruler was no substitute for the self-government. He was greatly attached to his mother-land and sincerely believed in its regeneration. He was a democrat in this sense that he introduced the system of election for the first time into his organisation–Arya Samaj. He revived the theory of Vedic Swaraj. Dr. Kashi Prasad Jayaswal says, " The Sanyasi gave freedom to the soul of the

Hindu, as Luther did unto the European. And he forged that freedom from inside, that is, from Hindu literature itself.........Dayanand was only the greatest Indian of the Nineteenth century..........In the nineteenth century there was nowhere else such a powerful teacher of monotheism, such a preacher of the unity of man, such a successful crusader against capitalism in spirituality."[1] *Shri Rabindra Nath Tagore says*: "*With a clear sighted vision of truth and courage of determination, Dayanand preached and worked for our self-respect and vigorous awakenment of mind that could strive for a harmonious adjustment with the progressive spirit of the modern age and at the same time keep in perfect touch with that glorious past of India when it revealed its personality in freedom of thought and action, in an unclouded radiance of spiritual realisation.*"

(*iii*) *Ram Krishna Mission.* Ram Krishna Mission also made a notable contribution in the religious and national regeneration of India. This mission was founded in memory of Shri Ram Krishna who was great devotee of goddess 'Kali'. He was a man of enlightened and liberal outlook. He saw no sense in being fanatic or slandering other religions. Indian culture, he said, was definitely superior to western culture which was purely materialistic. The assertion of the cultural superiority of Hindus had wholesome effect on the budding youths who grew out of the rut of inferiority complex. His teachings gave a stunning blow to the awe and temptation of western culture on Indian minds.

After the death of Shri Ram Krishna in 1886, his work was taken by his foremost disciple Vivekananda. He started a movement to make Hindus feel proud of their ancient heritage. He carried the message of his Master to all the four corners of India, and even beyond its geographical boundaries. He urged the people to arise, awake and invade the world with their spirituality. Strength combined with fearlessness was the political testament of Vivekananda to the Indian nation. His gospel of fearlessness to a politically prostrate nation was of great political significance. He stressed the need of building the foundation of national character on the formulas of Vedanta. He attended the Chicago Conference in 1893 as the arch priest of Vedantism. When he interpreted it to the western philosophers in their own medium, they were taken aback.

Swami Vivekananda was a Hero-Prophet; a Patriot-saint of India. Mr. M.N. Roy in *'India in Transition'* writes: Vivekananda's nationalism was a spiritual imperialism. He called on young India to believe in the spiritual mission of India. His philosophy, on which was subsequently built the orthodox nationalism of the declassed young intellectuals, organised into secret societies advocating violence and terrorism for the overthrow of British rule. He was a strong critic of social westernization. He wrote: "We must grow according to our nature. Vain is to attempt the lines of action that foreign societies have grafted upon us; it is impossible..... Suppose you can imitate the westerners, that moment you will die, you will have no more life in you." He gave an inspiring call to Indians: "Thou brave one, be bold, take courage, be proud that thou art an Indian, and proudly proclaim. 'Iam an Indian, every Indian is my brother." The teachings of Vivekanand had profound effect both on the intelligentia and the masses. The great saint inspired the people to action for the attainment of freedom.

(*iv*) *Prarthana Samaj.* Inspired by the ideals of Brahmo Samaj Prarthana Samaj was founded in 1857 in Maharashtra. It came into existence only three years after Keshav Chandra Sen's tour of Bombay State. The three stalwarts of this movement were Justice Ranade, Sri Bhandarkar and Sri Narayana Chandrawarkar. Its membership was not wide, still this society did creditable work for social reforms. Through educational institutions run by it, the Samaj infused new consciousness and vitality in the languid society of Maharashtra. It gave a spur to the wave of nationalism. In its religious philosophy, it was akin to Brahmo Samaj. It also opposed untouchability, casteism and idol worship. It advocated widow-marriage and women education.

(*v*) *Theosophical Society.* Theosophical Society was founded in 1875 in New York by a Russian Lady Madame Blavatsky and Olcott. At the invitation of Swami Dayanand, both the founders of the

1. K.P. Jayaswal, *Artical in Dayanand Commemoration Volume*, pp. 162-68

Society visited India in 1879. Col. Olcott spole highly of Hindu religion and established its excellence. He argued for the removal of evils that had crept into it. He also warned against the growing menace of Christianity. The Hindus were quite stunned to hear a foreigner admiring their religion. It led to strengthening of their faith in the superiority of their religion.

On May 10, 1889, Mrs. Annie Besant became a member of the Theosophical Society. Mrs. Annie Besant was an Irish lady. She evinced keen interest in Vedic religion and declared her faith in the Vedas and Upanishads. She dedicated herself to popularising Hindu religion and culture. She had burning enthusiasm for Hinduism and admitted without any reservation that it was distinctly superior to all the religious faiths of the West. She led a strong propaganda against early marriage. She wrote several books on education, theosophy and politics. In the field of politics she is credited with two major works *'India, a nation' and 'How India Wrought Her Freedom'*. She went to jail for the cause of Indian people and also started Home Rule Movement. She was made the President of the Indian National Congress in 1917 at Calcutta. One good effect of her teachings was that she shook the people out of their age-long sleep and made them realise the excellence of their ancient cultural heritage. We perfectly agree with the observation of Sarkar and Dutta : "*The religious and social reformers of 19th century of India like Ram Mohan Roy, Rabindra Nath Tagore, Keshav Chandra Sen, Pratap Chandra Majumdar, Pyarey Charan Sarkar, Ishwarchandra Vidyasagar, Dayanand Saraswati, Ram Krishna Paramahansa, and his great disciple Vivekanand impressed on the minds of the people the greatness and universality of much of the ancient thought of the country and this served to awaken in them a keen desire for national regeneration on the basis of the best in the past.*"

3. Effects of the British Rule. Renaissance in the field of religion was aided by other factors, equally powerful, in the growth of nationalism in our country. The alien rule which was indifferent to the sentiments of the people, also contributed to intensify the forces of freedom. The arrogant Britishers paid no heed to the traditions of the Indian ruling classes, who still enjoyed the esteem of the people, just like commoners. All of them irrespective of their class or status were crushed ruthlessly. The British policy of blood and iron filled every heart with rage and indignation against the ruling race.

Although Queen victoria in her Proclamation had made high sounding promises that Indians would be given better treatment and would not be discriminated against, yet nothing was given effect to in practice. The English continued to get preference over the Indians and hold all the key posts. Christian missionaries still indulged in their nasty practice of denouncing Hinduism and converting the people to Christianity. No attention was paid to national education, agriculture, industries, irrigation and sanitation. No opportunity was missed to humiliate the national leaders and their followers. Indians were kept out of all offices and administrative machinery. Naturally the people began to agitate against their heartless masters. The British Rule for all the harm it did to us, proved a bessing in one respect. The network of Railways and Telegraphs, which had been laid to facilitate the movement of troops to beat down the popular agitators, aroused and fostered feeling of oneness in the country. It made inter-provincial inter-course and exchange of thoughts possible. The political leaders through lectures and correspondence began to have wide publicity and larger audience.

4. Western Education. Another factor which played a significant role in the growth of national awakening was the spread of Western education. Whereas Vedic idealism and revival of Hinduism instilled a sense of self-confidence in the people, English education brougut the people in touch with the philosophies of Western thinkers with their accent on nationalism and democracy. The Indians who had received English education studied the political systems of the Western nations and were moved by the aspirations for self-government and for representative institutions.

The history of Western education in India dates back to the Act of 1813 which provided for the setting apart of ₹ one lakh every year for the promotion of education of the natives. Macaulay during the time of Lord Bentinack sought the permission of the Crown to introduce the Western system of education. It proved both a boon and a curse. Its poisonous effect was seen on the minds of those educated Indians who drifted away from their own moorings and bore the stamp of English culture and civilisation. On the other hand the study of English language and literature brought Indians under the impact of Milton, Burke, Mill and Herbert Spencer. The political theories of the Western Philosophers intensified the urge of the people for dominion status. Macaulay had already foreseen the consequences of the study of English by the natives. In 1833 A.D. he said, "It would be the proudest day in English history, when having become instructed in European knowledge, the Indians shall demand European institutions." Whatever might have been the motives of Macaulay in introducing Western education, the inevitable result was that young intellectuals of India began to press for freedom. Their visits to foreign countries filled them with a remorse for their fellow countrymen who lived a wretched life as compared to an average Westerner.

5. Social Changes. English education also enlightened the people and gave them a scientific outlook. The educated Indians lost faith in superstitions and outmoded customs. University education created a new class consisting of pleaders, doctors, professors and clerks. And when the educated Indians were denied admission in Government offices, they began to nurse a grudge against the ruling class. Sri Surendra Nath Bannerjee, for instance, qualified for I.C.S. in 1869; still the prejudiced Government of India on one plea or other refused to provide him an administrative job. Aurobindo Ghose was another victim of racial hatred. He proved his merit by passing the I.C.S. test in 1877 but was rejected on the trivial excuse that he was not good at riding.

Later on the age limit for the candidates preparing for I.C.S. was lowered from 21 to 19. Such a move was distinctly directed against the Indian candidates for whom it became humanly impossible to compete for the Civil Services. The reactionary attitude of the rulers gave occasion for a nationwide agitation. Mr. S.N. Bannerjee toured the country and addressed crowded meetings to register his protest against the decision of the Secretary of State for India. Analysing the significance of the movement he said, "The agitation (against the lowering of the maximum age limit) was the means, the raising of the maximum limit of age for the open competitive examinations and the holding of simultaneous examinations were among the ends; but the underlying conception and the true aim and purpose of the Civil Service agitation was the awakening of a spirit of unity and solidarity among the people of India."

6. Economic exploitation of India. A great deal of anti-British feeling was created by the economic policy pursed by the Government of India. The English in a systematic way managed to ruin Indian trade and native industries. The Dacca muslin which had been a good export item was given a death blow by the Company so as to create market for English textiles manufactured in Lancashire and Liverpool. Import duty on English made cloth was removed in order to keep the wheels of English textile mills running. Indian wealth began to flow to the West resulting in the abject poverty of the people. The selfish commercial Company paid no heed to improving the lot of the cultivators. India became poorer day by day. *Mr Garret also pointed out, "the interest of the educated class in nationalism has always been partly economic and partly religious and it is an undeniable fact that the deteriorating economic position of the country and the anti-national economic policy followed by the Government together with the policy of excluding Indians from the higher ranks of the services were responsible to no small extent for arousing anti-British feeling and the national spirit among the people in India."* Moreover, the expenses of the Company's administrative setup in England had to be borne by the tax payers of India. This heavy and recurring drain on poor Indian pockets further increased discontentment in the country.

In the middle of the 19th century India began to be used as a sphere of investment for British capital. The first major outlet for British investment in India was that provided by the railways. The exploitation of India as a source of raw materials and as a market demanded modern methods of communication and transport. In the 1860-1890s there was an increase in the length of railways from 1300 kilometres to 25,600 kilometres. The arrangement of the railways network, which fanned out into the interior from the main ports and linked together the main British strongholds in India, was dictated above all by military and strategic considerations. The building of the railways was designed in such a way as to facilitate the enslavement and exploitation of the country by British colonialists.

View of Marx. The British imperialists making use of all the methods of colonial exploitation–taxation, import of manufactured goods, export of materials–were draining this enslaved country of enormous colonial "tribute" which amounted to close on a hundred million pounds a year. In 1881 Marx made the following comment on the situation in India:

"What the English take from them annually in the form of rent, dividends for railways useless to the Hindus; pensions for military and civil servicemen, for Afghanistan and other wars etc. What they take from them without *any equivalent* and quite apart from what they appropriate to themselves annually within India, speaking only the value of commodities the Indian have *gratuitously* and annually to *send over* to England it amounts to *more than the total sum* of income of the 60 million of agricultural and industrial labourers of India: This is bleeding process with a vengeance: The famine years are pressing each other and in *dimensions* till now yet suspected in Europe".[1]

7. Oppressive Agrarian System. Dr. R.C. Majumdar writes, "the new and changing agrarian system and exorbitant (high) land revenue impoverished peasantry to such an extent that they never had the minimum requirement for food and clothing."[2]

8. Severe famines. Dr. R.C. Majumdar observes, "In the first half of ninteenth century there were seven famines, with an estimated total of one million deaths from famine. In the second half of the nineteenth century there were twenty-four (six between 1851 and 1875 and eighteen between 1876 and 1900), with an estimated total, according to official records, of over 20 million deaths.[3] "Stated roughly, famines and scarcities have been four times as numerous during the last thirty years of nineteenth century as they were one hundred years earlier, four times more widespread."[4]

9. Universal Poverty of India. Dr. R.C.Majumdar observes. "The first fifty years of British rule in India witnessed the ruin of her trade and industry, driving an increasingly large portion of her people to the lands. The next fifty years of British rule brought the cultivators as a class, forming nearly fourth-fifths of the population, to the brink of ruin and destruction. Ninety per cent of them never had two square meals a day or decent cloth and house fit for human beings. Thus was laid the foundation of that abject and universal poverty of india, which forms the chief characteristic feature of the first century of British rule in India."[5]

10. The role of the Press. A Munroe writes, "A free press and the dominion of strangers are things which are quite incompatible and cannot long exist together." The history of the Indian-owned Press also supports this statement. In the beginning there were only English newspapers, owned and edited by Englishmen. They were anti-nationalist and pro-government. In due course newspapers in Indian languages came into existence and began to criticise the policies and doings of the Government of India. The Government felt annoyed with hostile attitude of the Vernacular Press and it imposed restrictions on the Press in 1878 by an Act known as the Vernacular Press Act. The Act provoked a lot of resentment both in India and England and hence was revoked after four years. But soon other measures were adopted by the government to deny freedom of thought and speech to the people. Such highhandedness of the Government of India also intensified anti-British campaign by the national leaders.

1. Marx, Engles, *Selected Correspondence,* Moscow, 1975, p-317.
2. Dr. R.C.Majumdar, *History & Culture of The Indian People,* Vol. IX (British Paramouontacy and Renaissance, p.416.
3. Dr. R.C.Majumdar, *History & Culture of The Indian People,* p.837.
4. Rajni Palme Dutt, *'India Today'* p.106, see also Mrs. Dibgy, *Prosperous British India.*
5. Dr. R.C. Majumdar, *History & Culture of the Indian People,* Vol. IX. p. 373.

11. Repressive measures of Lord Lytton. There were many other factors which made the British rule unpopular in India. People blamed the rulers for the famine that broke out in the south in 1876 and which took away a toll of thousands of lives. The callous indifference shown by the rulers filled every heart with bitterness and hatred against the alien rule. While people were starving in millions, Lord Lytton held a Durbar at Delhi in 1877 to announce that Queen Victoria had assumed the title of the Empress of India. The vain show cost millions to the Indian treasury. It was the case of Nero fiddling when the rome was burning. The motive of holding the Durbar was also fulfilled. Instead of winning the loyalty of the people, the Government drew bitter public criticism, Sharply stung by the criticism from leading persons and the newspapers. Lord Lytton passed the nasty Vernacular Press Act in 1878 which added fuel to fire.

The notorious regime of Lord Lytton was also responsible for some other incidents which strained the relations between the rulers and the ruled. When the ruler of Afghanistan concluded an alliance with the Czar of Russia, the Viceroy of India felt alarmed. He feared Russian invasion of India via Afghanistan. Hence in order to establish a scientific boundary, he drove the country into Second Afghan war. His foolish venture proved a failure. The country suffered an enormous loss in the form of men and money. It was during the tenure of Lord Lytton that Arms Act also came into force. Keeping or bearing arms without licence was made a punishable offence and heavy penalties were imposed on those who violated the law. What pained the people most was that the Europeans were exempted from this law. The natives of India took it as a great national insult.

12. Ilbert Bill Controversy. Under the existing law an European could be tried only by an European Judge. In order to do away with the racial discrimination, Mr. Ripon, the Law Member of the Viceroy's Executive Council, moved a Bill in 1883. The Bill was designed to empower the Indian magistrate to judge the European offenders also. Indians welcomed the move, but the Europeans organised such a stiff opposition to the Bill that it had to be withdrawn. The educated Indians learnt two lessons from this incident; (a) first, that it was hoping against hope that the rulers would forego their privileges or be just to Indians; (b) secondly, that a strong agitation was always effective and fruitful. The leading public men of India, ever since, made up their minds to create public opinion on political and economic matters. It was for protesting against the Government's policy of racial discrimination that Sri Surendra Nath Banerjee called a National Conference in Calcutta in 1883. By the time Lord Lytton completed his term as Viceroy of India, the country was bordering on revolution.

13. Impact of Foreign events. Certain events beyond the borders of India also exercised tremendous influence on the Indians and helped in the promotion of Nationalism in India. The Indians were particularly inspired by the political events in Germany, Italy and France and encouraged them to work for the liberation of their country. The American Civil War and the various reform acts passed in Britain also had a profound influence on the thinking of the Indian people and strengthened their conviction to establish a free government in the country.

It is thus clear from the above discussion that the rise and growth of Nationalism in India was the result of a combination of number of factors. No doubt the British imperialism was one of the important factor in the process of development of Nationalism in India. As **Prof Ishwari Prasad** has observed, "The consciousness of the French that their troubles were due to Bourbons led to the French Revolution, of the English that their troubles were due to the unrestrained prerogatives of the crown led to the Civil War, and of the Indians that their troubles were due to British Rule led to the formation of the Indian National Congress in 1885 whose object was to secure India's liberation." But the other factors played no less significant role.

EXERCISES

Long Answer Type Questions

1. Discuss the causes of the birth and rapid growth of Nationalism in India.
2. Discuss the role of Social and religious movements in growth of Nationalism in India.

Short Answer Type Questions

1. Discuss in brief the effect of the First war of Indian Independence against the imperial rule.
2. Discuss the contribution of Raja Ram Mohan Roy and Brahma Samaj in growth of Nationalism in India.
3. "Dayanand Saraswati was a staunch nationalist and he made a unique contribution in growth of Nationalism in India." Discuss this statement in brief.
4. Write a short note on Ram Krishna Mission.
5. What do you know about Prarthana Samaj? Discuss in brief.
6. What do you know about Theosophical Society?

Objective Type Questions

Choose the correct answer

1. In which year Theosophical Society was founded ?
   (*a*) 1875 (*b*) 1876
   (*c*) 1877 (*d*) 1878
2. In which city Theosophical Society was founded ?
   (*a*) Washington (*b*) New York
   (*c*) Salisbury (*d*) Rome
3. Who was the founder of Theosophical Society ?
   (*a*) Raja Ram Mohan Roy (*b*) Dayanand Saraswati
   (*c*) Madame Blavatsky and Olcott (*d*) Annie Besant.
4. In which year both the founders of Theosophical Society visited India ?
   (*a*) 1876 (*b*) 1877
   (*c*) 1878 (*d*) 1879
5. In which year Mrs. Annie Besant became a member of the Theosophical Society ?
   (*a*) 1889 (*b*) 1890
   (*c*) 1891 (*d*) 1892
6. In which year Prarthana Samaj was founded ?
   (*a*) 1856 (*b*) 1857
   (*c*) 1858 (*d*) 1859
7. Who was the founder of Arya Samaj ?
   (*a*) Raja Ram Mohan Roy (*b*) Swami Vivekanand
   (*c*) Swami Dayanand Saraswati (*d*) None of the above

ANSWERS

1. (*a*) 2. (*b*) 3. (*c*) 4. (*d*) 5. (*a*) 6. (*b*) 7. (*c*)

CHAPTER 6

Birth of Indian National Congress and National Movement

> *"There was no sudden emergence of the Indian National Congress and there was nothing novel either in its ideas or methods, for the National Conference held in Calcutta in 1883 forestolled it in all essential aspects."* —R.C. Majumdar

BIRTH OF INDIAN NATIONAL CONGRESS

The National Movement of India assumed an institutionalised form in the Indian National Congress set up in 1885. The circumstances which led to the founding of the Indian National Congress are shrouded in mystery and different views have been expressed. According to the most popular view the Indian National Congress was set up by A.O. Hume, a retired Indian Civil Servant under direction from Lord Dufferin, the then Governor General of India. The main purpose for the creation of this organisation was to provide a 'safety-valve' to the anticipated or actual discontent of the Indian intelligentsia and to form a quasi-constitutional party on the pattern of Her Majesty's Opposition in England. **Prof. Sundar Ram,** who was one of the seventy-two participants in the first session of the Indian National Congress gives a slight different version. He says that Hume wanted to form an Organisation in England to rouse the conscience of the English people through persistent agitation. But Lord Dufferin prevailed upon him to confine his activities to India for the time being and help the Indian public men all over the country to form a national organisation, and provide sympathetic and courageous leadership to the organisation.

According to yet another theory Hume took initiative to form the Indian National Congress because he came to know through secret reports about the plans of the impending rebellion of the peasants, and he took this step to avoid the impending calamity.

Womesh Chandra Bannerjee, the first President of the Indian National Congress, says that Hume wanted to create a national forum where the leading Indian politicians could be brought together to discuss the social problems facing the country. He did not want this organisation to take up political issues because a number of political bodies already existed in different parts of India.

However, certain scholars have challenged the theory that the Indian National Congress was formed as a result of agreement between Lord Dufferin and A.O. Hume. On the basis of a survey of correspondence of Lord Dufferin they do not find any proof to show that Lord Dufferin took any initiative in suggesting to A.O. Hume about the formation of Indian National Congress and that Hume acted as the spokesman of Lord Dufferin. On the contrary they assert that the documents show that Dufferin was a severe critic of the indian National Congress. Further he was quite unhappy with Hume and criticised him for arousing the suspicions of the people of India about Lord Dufferin's policies. He is said to have sent a complaint about the conduct of Hume to Lord Northbrook, the Secretary of State for India. In view of this it is difficult to see how they could have acted together.

The theory that Lord Dufferin persuaded Hume to set up Indian National Congress is further disproved by the following views expressed by Lord Dufferin in his minutes which he wrote before leaving India. "The fact is that the Congress is the product of that infinitesimal section of Indian community to whom I have already referred as having been tinctured either directly or indirectly with an infusion of European education....They neither represent the aristocratic sympathy with great masses of the population, they do not understand their wants or necessities, if indeed they are indifferent or even opposed to them–as evidenced by the strenuous resistance of the important Native Associations to our recent Land Legislation–and they are very imperfectly fitted to grasp any of the larger questions which affect the stability or safety of the Empire as a whole".

According to yet another theory the idea of bringing men from different parts of India at a common platform was mooted by the Theosophical Society of India at a meeting held at the residence of Raghunath Rao at Madras in December 1884 and Hume stole the thunder by taking a public initiative. But this theory does not seem to be plausible on two counts. First, the idea of holding annual conferences of representatives from different parts of the country was current even before the founding of the Theosophical Society in 1879. Further, the organisation of the Indian National Congress was quite different from the one agreed upon by the Theosophical Society at its meeting at Madras.

Another theory attributes the birth of the Indian National Congress to the spontaneous reaction against measures like Vernacular Press Act, the Arms Act, the reduction of the age limit for entrance to the Indian Civil Service and the Ilbert Bill controversy. Initially this reaction appeared in the shape of separate political associations in different parts of the country but subsequently they joined hand to create this all India organisation. Prof. Majumdar says the emergence of the Indian National Congress was not sudden and "the National Conference held in Calcutta in 1884 forestalled it in all essential aspects." Even before the creation of the Indian National Congress a number of organisations and public bodies had been formed in different parts of the country. The prominent amongst these organisations were the British Indian Association (founded in Bengal in 1843); India League (founded in 1875); Indian Association (founded in 1876), Bombay Association (founded in early fifties of ninteenth century) Poona Sarvajanik Sabha (founded in 1867); the National Conference (founded in 1883). Almost all these organisations were formed with a view to stimulate sense of patriotism and nationalism among the people of India, although they operated within limited area. Out of these organisations only one body viz. National Conference could claim to be a national organisation while all others were regional and sectional organisations.

The lead in setting up the Indian National Congress was taken by A.O. Hume on 1 March 1885 when he addressed an open letter to the graduates of the Calcutta University and appealed to them to form an association for the moral, social and political regeneration of the Indians. He said "Constituting as you do a large body of the most highly educated Indians, you should in the natural order of things, constitute also the most important source of all mental, moral, social and political progress in India. Whether in the individual or in the nation, all vital progress must spring from within and it is to you, her most cultured, enlightened minds, her most favoured sons that your country must look for initiative. In vain, many aliens like myself love India and her children, as well as the most loving of these; in vain may they, for her and their good, give time and trouble, money and thought, in vain may they struggle and sacrifice; they may assist with advice and suggestions; they may place their experience, abilities and knowledge at the disposal of the workers, but they lack the essential of nationality, and the real work must ever be done by the people of the country themselves." He further said "As I said before, you are the salt of the land. And if amongst even you, the elite, fifty men cannot be found with sufficient power of self-sacrifice, sufficient love for and pride in their country, sufficient genuine and unselfish heart-felt patriotism to take the initiative, and if need be, devote the rest of their lives to the cause, then there is no hope for India. Her sons must and will remain more humble and helpless instruments in the hands of foreign rulers for they would be free, themselves must strike the blow. And if even the leaders of thought are all either such poor creatures, or so selfishly wedded to personal concerns, that they dare not or will not strike a blow for their country's sake, then justly and rightly are they kept down and trampled on, for they deserve nothing better. Every nation secures precisely as good a government as it merits. If you, the picked men, the most highly educated of the nation, cannot, scorning personal ease and selfish objects, make a resolute struggle to secure greater freedom for yourselves and your country, a more impartial administration, a larger share in the management of your own affairs, then we, your friends are wrong.' The letter ended with the assertion whether in the case of individuals or nations, self-sacrifice and unselfishness are the only unfailing guides to freedom and happiness."

The appeal of A.O. Hume evoked a very favourable response from the educated Indians. Hume after establishing a contact with leaders of public opinion in the country decided to hold a meeting of the representatives from all the parts of India in December, 1885. However, in the intervening period Hume paid a visit to Britain and obtained support from liberal politicians like Lord Ripon, John Bright etc.

The first session of the Indian National Congress was held at Bombay which was Presided over by W.C. Bannerjee, while A.O. Hume acted as its Secretary. In all about 100 persons attended the meeting of the Indian National Congress, the largest contingent of thirty-eight persons being from the Presidency of Bombay. Twenty-one representatives came from the Madras Presidency. Bengal sent only three representatives. Similarly three representatives came from Punjab. Thus the first meeting of the Indian National Congress was attended by people representing all the parts of India. They represented the cross sections of the Indian society and included Barristers, solicitors, pleaders, merchants, land-holders, bankers, medical men, journalists and proprietors, principals and professors of independent colleges, headmasters of schools, reformers etc. There were Hindus, Muslims, Christians as well as Europeans.

Objects of Indian National Congress

The objects of the Indian National Congress were spelt out by **W.C. Bannerjee** during the course of his presidential address. He listed the following as the objectives of the Indian National Congress.

1. The promotion of personal intimacy and friendship among all the more earnest workers in our country's cause in various parts of the Empire.
2. The eradication by direct friendly intercourse of all possible race, creed or provincial prejudices amongst all lovers of the country and the fuller development and consolidation of those sentiments of national unity that took their origin in our beloved Lord Ripon's ever memorable reign.
3. The authoritative record of the mature opinions of the educated classes in India on some of the more important and pressing of the social questions of the day.
4. The determination of the methods by which during the next twelve months it is desirable for native politicians to labour in public interest. However, these objects of Congress underwent changes according to exigencies of time. Whereas initially the Congress demanded only piecemeal reforms but subsequently it broadened its object to include self-government. Ultimately it revised its goal as complete independence. Likewise the methods for the attainment of these objects were also not static and were modified according to the demand of the situation. In the initial years the Congress believed in petitions, resolutions and deputations but subsequently it resorted to direct methods like non-co-operation and civil disobedience.

The formation of the Indian National Congress was lauded by the Press and was described as an important chapter in the history of British rule in India. *Indu Prakash* wrote "It (session of the Congress) marks the beginning of a new life and whatever traducers may say, it will greatly help in creating a national feeling and binding together distant people by common sympathies and common ends.... The very fact that such a conference has met and fairly promises to be a success belies the supposition that we are not a nation. It must be conceded that we are wanting in many qualities which make a nation. We are divided by a variety of languages, religions and social customs, separated from each other by long distances and are wanting in homogeneity of race and feeling. Nevertheless, it is undeniable that we are at present politically one nation or at least have the makings of one."

The famous historian **Dr. Tara Chand** has brought out the importance of the formation of the Indian National Congress thus: "The birth of the Indian National Congress was an unprecedented phenomenon in the political history of India. It proclaimed the advent of a new era, the era of political unity, not imposed from above but the expression of the deliberate will of the people. The Congress was the central organ of the new society which had evolved as a result of economic, social and cultural changes taking place during the hundred years since Plassey. It marked the consummation of a process which affected all Indians, individually and collectively".

Reaction of Indians to the founding of Indian National Congress

The founding of the Indian National Congress by and large received favourable response from the Indians. Realising that the government would not look with kindly eyes on any move on the part of the Indians to form an organisation which could fight for reforms in administration and greater share for the Indians in administration, they welcomed the call of A.O. Hume and extended full support to the idea of the formation of Indian National Congress. **Gopal Krishan Gokhale** expressed the feelings of the people when he observed: "No Indian could have started the Indian National Congress. Apart from the fact that any one putting his hand to such a gigantic task had need to have Mr. Hume's commanding personality, even if an Indian had possessed such a personality and had come forward to start such a movement embracing all india, the officials would not have allowed it to come into existence. If the founder of the Congress had not been a great Englishman and distinguished ex-official, such was the distrust of political agitation in those days that the authorities would have at once found some way or the other of suppressing the movement." *The Indian Mirror* writing about the first session of the Indian National Congress wrote "The first National Congress at Bombay forms an important chapter in the history of the British rule in India. The day on which it opened, namely the 28th December, 1885, will form a red-letter day in the annals of the national progress of the Native races. It is the nucleus of future parliament for our country and will lead to good of inconceivable magnitude for our countrymen. If we were asked what was the proudest day in our life, we should unhesitatingly say it was the day on which we, for the first time, met all our brothers of Madras, Bombay, the North-Western Provinces and the Punjab under the roof of the Gokul Das Tejpal Sanskrit College for the purpose of the National Congress. From the date of this Congress we may well count the more rapid development of national progress in India in future".

Reaction of the Government

The initial reaction of the British Government towards the formation of the Indian National Congress was quite favourable. When Hume informed Lord Dufferin about the move to form such an organisation he declared, "that he found the greatest difficulty in ascertaining the zeal, wishes of the people and that it would be a public benefit if there existed some responsible organization through which the government might be kept informed regarding the best Indian public opinion." When the first session of the Congress was held he encouraged the Anglo-Indian officials and non-officials to attend the meetings and even take part in its deliberation. During the next two sessions of the Congress held at Calcutta and Madras the members of Congress were invited to garden parties at

Government House. However, this attitude of friendliness was only short-lived. Soon the Congress started a vigorous campaign of agitation for the attainment of its programme which greatly perturbed the Government. In 1888 at a dinner at Calcutta Lord Dufferin bitterly criticised the Congress. He said "How could any reasonable man imagine that the British Government would be content to allow this microscopic minority to control the administration of that majestic and multiform empire for whose safety and welfare, they are responsible in the eyes of God and before the face of civilization? It appears to me a groundless contention that it represents the people of India. It is not evident that large sections of the community are already become alarmed at the thought of such self-constituted bodies, interposing between themselves and the august impartiality of English rule." Two years later the Government debarred the government officials from attending the meetings of the Congress through an official notification. Thus within a short span of five years of its founding the Congress, instead of being treated as a friendly consultative body, developed into an opposition to the Government which challenged the status and the authority of the British Government.

Character of the Congress. The character of the Indian National Congress has also been a subject of debate among scholars. Broadly speaking two views have been expressed. According to one view the Indian National Congress was merely a sectional body which represented a small section of the indian society viz., those who had acquired western education, and did not in any way represent the aspirations of the general people. Further even the landed classes, ruling chiefs and the Muslims were not associated with this body.

The second view holds that the Congress from its very inception was a national body and contained representatives of all the classes and communities. While its founder was a Christian, two of its most prominent supporters–Dadabhai Naoroji and Pherozeshah Mehta---were Parsis. Enlightened Muslim like Badrud-din Tyabji were also associated with it.

The National character of the Indian National Congress has been challenged by the scholars on the plea that majority of its members were Hindus. This was inevitable in a country with a preponderance of Hindu population. It is true that Muslims like Sir Sayeed Ahmad Khan did not join the Congress, but the blame for this rests with concerned persons rather than the Congress. The Congress at no stage shut its door to any section of the Indian society. Again, the critics have challenged the national character of Congress on the ground that it did not associate the princes of the Indian State and the landed classes with it. In fact the members of these two classes shun the membership of the Congress due to the unsympathetic attitude of the Government towards the new organisation.

But Congress certainly tried to protect the interests of the Indian princes and passed a resolution in 1896 demanding that no prince should be deposed on the ground of mal-administration or misconduct unless the charge was fully established through public tribunals consisting of persons enjoying confidence of the government as well as the princes. Similarly, it supported the permanent settlement with a view to protect the interests of the landed classes. The common masses could not be associated with the Congress due to lack of proper medias of contact with the masses and indifferent attitude of the people due to lack of education. In course of time when the membership of the Congress increased people from all the sections of society came in its fold and it turned into a mass organisation in the strict sense of the term. Emphasising the national character of the indian National Congress Mahatma Gandhi said "The Congress is the oldest political organisation we have in India. It is what it means–national. It represents no particular community, no particular interest. It claims to represent all Indian interests and all classes. From the very commencement the Congress had Musalmans, Christians, Anglo-Indians...all religious sects, creeds represented upon it more or less fully".

PHASES OF NATIONAL MOVEMENT IN INDIA

Historians have divided the national movement in India into three phases–Moderate Nationalism, Extremist Nationalism and Nationalism of the Gandhian Phase. Since National movement during these three phases possessed different features, it is desirable to study them in details.

1. Phase of Moderate Nationalists (1885-1905). This phase of Indian nationalist movement lasted from 1885 to 1905. During this period the Indian National Congress was mainly dominated by the educated middle class intelligentsia. Most of the leaders came from liberal professions like law, teaching, medicine, engineering and journalism. Some of the prominent leaders of this phase of nationalism were Dadabhai Naoroji, Surendranath Banerji, Pherozeshah Mehta, Gopal Krishna Gokhale, M.G. Ranade, M.M. Malviya etc. As these people hailed mainly from the cities the Congress was mainly an urban organisation which did not have any contact with the general masses of India. The nationalist leaders during this period placed the blame for country's miseries on the social and economic backwardness of the people, and not the British rule. On the other hand they held faith in the British sense of fair play and justice and asserted that once the Indian leaders were able to present a fool-proof case of their cause to the British authorities they would immediately concede their genuine demands. In short their attitude towards the British Government was quite friendly. They considered the stability of the British rule as *sine qua non* of India's progress. Gopal Krishna Gokhale, a prominent Moderate Leader paid tributes to the contributions of British Rule in these words "The blessings of peace, the establishment of law and order, the introduction of western education, freedom of speech and appreciation of liberal institutions, which have followed in its wake–all these are things, which stand to the credit of the British rule." The leaders of Indian national movement during this phase realised that it was not possible for them to throw off the British yoke with the help of force. Therefore they insisted on peaceful and constitutional methods. They carried on propaganda in favour of their demands through press, platform and periodical representations. In addition they also carried on propaganda through annual sessions of the Congress. In the words of Prof. Hira Lal Singh, "Among the various methods of Congress propaganda, the holding of annual sessions was by far the most important. It was at these meetings that the Congress leaders discussed their demands in an authoritative manner, and it was then that the Congress machinery was in full swing. Besides, the annual sessions not only attracted the attention of the educated classes but also of the Government".

The demands of the nationalist leaders during this period were of a very moderate nature. In view of the moderate nature of these demands the leaders of this phase came to be described as Moderates. The moderate leaders pleaded for gradual reforms. They did not pitch their demands very high which could arouse the suspicion of the British. Throughout this period the Congress never raised the demand for introduction of representative institutions for the masses. It merely demanded the association of the educated community with the institutions of administration. It also laid emphasis on the need of adopting other liberal principles in existence in England *viz.* Separation of judiciary and executive at the district level, curtailment of military expenses, introduction of simultaneous examinations for recruitment to Indian Civil Services in India. In short, the moderate nationalist leaders, says Dr. R.G. Pradhan, "were practical reformers imbued with the spirit, principles and methods of mid-Victorian Liberalism and bent on winning freedom by gradual stages, broadening from step to step."[1]

The policy and the methods of the moderate nationalist leaders were severely criticised by the Indian Youth and was branded as "a policy of political mendicacy." But if we analyse things in the right perspective we find that under the prevailing circumstances no other policy was possible. If the Indian national leaders had pitched their demands very high and adopted aggressive policies, the nationalist movement in India would have died a pre-mature death. It was chiefly due to the restraint

1. R.G. Pradhan, *India's Struggle for Swaraj,* p. 24.

exercised by the moderate leaders that the Indian National Congress succeeded in taking deep roots into the Indian soil and ultimately attained independence for India. **Dr. Ishwari Prasad** says, "With all the ridicule to which their methods had been subjected none can withhold the need of praise from its early leaders (Moderates)–men of high intellectual attainments, character and patriotism–for doing pioneer work in the way of India's regeneration and championing the cause of the people against a powerful, alien bureaucracy strongly entrenched in its own citadel of obstinacy and prejudice."[1] Dr. Pattabhi Sittaramayya, the official historian of the Indian National Congress also says, "We cannot blame them for the attitude they adopted as pioneers of Indian political reform any more than we can blame the brick and mortar that is buried six feet deep in the foundation and plinth of a modern edifice. They have made possible the super-structure story by story, by colonial self-government, Home Rule within the Empire, *Swaraj* and on the top of all, complete independence".

K.M. Munshi has also paid high compliments to the contributions of the moderate nationalist leaders to the Indian national movement. He says if there had not been an all-India organisation functioning for more than thirty years, none of the great movements led by Gandhiji would have any chance of success, nor would it have reached its highest efficiency as a political machine under the dexterous guidance of Sardar Patel.[2]

Gopal Krishna Gokhale highlighted the contributions of moderates to the Indian national movement thus : "The minds of the people have been familiarised with the idea of a united India working for her salvation; a national public opinion has been created; close bonds of sympathy now kit together the different provinces; castes and creeds hamper less and less the pursuit of common aims; the dignity of a consciousness of national existence has spread over the whole land..... Above all, there is a general perception now of the goal towards which we have to strive and a wide recognition of the arduous character to the struggle and the immense sacrifices it requires".

2. Phase of Extremist Nationalists (1905-1919). In 1905 the Indian National Movement entered the second phase of its career, and is popularly known as phase of extremist nationalism. This phase lasted upto 1919 when Gandhi assumed the leadership of the nationalist movement. During this phase the leadership of Congress passed into the hands of persons who did not have any faith in the British sense of justice or the constitutional methods for the attainment of their objective. They believed in the principle of self-reliance and wanted to attain Swaraj through direct action. A section of the new leaders also believed in terrorist methods and wanted to strike a terror in the minds of the Britishers with a view to compel them to run away from India.

The main factors which contributed to the growth of extremist nationalism in India were as follows—

1. Firstly, most of the young Indians were greatly disillusioned with the achievements of the Moderate leaders. In spite of their constant resolutions, demonstrations, petitions etc, the Congress failed to gain any substantial political concessions for the people. The unsatisfactory attitude of the British Government towards the demands of the Congress leaders further convinced them that they could not attain their objectives through constitutional and peaceful methods, which was interpreted by the British as a sign of their weakness, and a change in methods was called for. Bal Gangadhar Tilak said "Political rights will have to be fought for. The Moderates think that these can be won by purusuasion. We think that they can only be obtained by strong pressure."

2. Secondly, as a result of the socio-religious movements of the late nineteenth century a number of young Indians developed a sense of pride in the ancient culture and rich heritage. They were so much fired by the sense of patriotism that they did not want the western institutions to be introduced in the country. They also held the British rule responsible for all the ills of the country and argued that Swaraj alone could get the people rid of these evils.

1. Ishwari Prasad, *History of Modern India,* p.315.
2. K.M. Munshi, *Advent of Independence* p.viii.

3. Thirdly, the sufferings caused by natural calamities like famine, bubonic plague etc. which broke out towards the closing years of the nineteenth century, also greatly agitated the minds of Indians. They were not satisfied with the arrangements made by the Government to deal with these calamities. They argued that if there had been a national government the miseries of the people would have been considerably reduced. They attributed the famine to the anti-Indian economic policies of the British Government. Some of the Moderate Leaders like Dadabhai Naoroji, Ranade were also disillusioned with the British sense of justice and highlighted the evil effects of the British economic policy. In this atmosphere of growing resentment towards the British Government the people murdered the Plague Commissioner (Mr. Rand). This invited repression from the British Government. A number of nationalist leaders were imprisoned. This aroused the sympathy of the people for the extremists and greatly swelled the ranks of their followers.

4. Fourthly, the growing unemployment among the educated Indians towards the closing years of the nineteenth century (which was the result of expansion of education in the seventies and eighties of the nineteenth century) and the miserable plight of the people due to a sagging economy also greatly contributed to the growth of extremist national movement in India. According to A.R. Desai "Political discontent born of the economic suffering due to unemployment among the educated middle class was an important factor in the growth of the political current of militant nationalism of which Bal, Lal and Pal were the principal leaders."[1]

5. Fifthly, the inhuman treatment meted out to the Indians in foreign countries, specially in South Africa, where the Indians were treated as slaves and denied all human rights gave rise to anti-British feelings, and contributed towards the growth of extremist nationalism.

6. Sixthly, the repressive policies of Lord Curzon during the period 1899-1905 also provided a fillip to the extremist movement. Curzon, a staunch advocate of an efficient administration, was strongly opposed to the idea of associating the Indians with administration because he had no faith in the capacity of the Indians to rule themselves. He enacted a number of measures for this purpose *viz.* Calcutta Corporation Act, Official Secrets Act, Indian Universities Act etc. These measures were strongly resented by the Indians and went a long way in strengthening the anti-British feelings. Surendra Nath Banerjee highlighted the contributions of Lord Curzon to the national movement thus "He (Curzon) has built better than he knew he had laid, broad and deep foundations of our national life; he has stimulated those forces which contribute to the upbuilding of nations, he has made us a nation, and the most reactionary of Indian viceroys, will go down to the posterity as the architect of Indian life".

7. Seventhly, the partition of Bengal carried out by Lord Curzon in 1905 in the teeth of a unanimous opposition, also greatly contributed to the growth of extremist movement. Though Lord Curzon ostensibly took this step with a view to improve the efficiency of administration of the province, his real objective was to draw a wedge between the Hindus and the Muslims and thus check the growing wave of nationalism. This was greatly resented by the Indians in general and the Bengalis in particular. A strong agitation was launched for the annulment of the partition. It has been argued by scholars that the rise of extremism and terrorism in India was chiefly due to the partition of Bengal.

8. Eighthly, the study of the western literature and history showed the Indians that even in western countries resort to force was made to gain or preserve democracy. The unification of Germany and Italy was achieved through violent methods. Similarly the independence of U.S.A. and the French Revolution were also accomplished through violent means. Even in Britain people beheaded Charles I to preserve the freedom and liberty of the people. The Indians, who had received western education, were convinced that similar methods could also be used for the attainment of independence in India. This feeling greatly strengthened the extremist movement in India.

1. A.R.Desai, *Social Background of Indian Nationalism*, p.182.

9. Ninthly, certain events in foreign countries towards the closing years of nineteenth century and the beginning of the twentieth century also exercised profound influence on the Indian nationalist movement and strengthened the extremist elements. The victory of Abyssinia over Italy in 1896 and the victory of Japan, a tiny island country, over Russia, one of the largest states in 1905, convinced the Indians that they could do the same thing to the British rulers. The nationalist movements in Egypt, Turkey and Persia also provided a new vigour to the nationalist movement in India. Prof. H.N. Mukerjee has brought out the impact of these events on the Indian national movement thus: "Interpretation of contemporary events and a reverent resurrection of vanished glory combined to intensify a wide-spread desire to seek escape from foreign domination that had bound India, body and soul."

EXERCISES

Long Answer Type Questions

1. Discuss the circumstances which led to the founding of the Indian National Congress.
2. What were the objects of Indian National Congress?
3. Discuss the reaction of Indians and the Government to the founding of Indian National Congress.
4. Discuss the different phases of National Movement in India.

Short Answer Type Questions

1. Write a short note on the character of the Congress.
2. What do you know about the phase of moderate nationalists?
3. Write a brief note on the phase of Extremists Nationalists.
4. Write any four objects of Indian National Congress.

Objective Type Questions

Choose the correct answer

1. The Indian National Congress set up in
   (*a*) 1885 (*b*) 1886
   (*c*) 1887 (*d*) 1888
2. Who was the founder of Indian National Congress ?
   (*a*) Mahatma Gandhi (*b*) A.O. Hume
   (*c*) Motilal Nehru (*d*) J.L. Nehru.
3. Who was A.O. Hume ?
   (*a*) A Businessman (*b*) A Politician
   (*c*) Retired Indian Civil Servant (*d*) Governor General of India.
4. At which place the first session of the Indian National Congress was held ?
   (*a*) Calcutta (*b*) Madras
   (*c*) Allahabad (*d*) Bombay
5. Who Presided the first session of the Indian National Congress ?
   (*a*) W.C. Banerji (*b*) A.O. Hume
   (*c*) Motilal Nehru (*d*) Gopal Krishna Gokhale

ANSWERS

1. (*a*) 2. (*b*) 3. (*c*) 4. (*d*) 5. (*a*)

7

CHAPTER

The Indian Councils Act of 1892

> *"I will not say that they (Rules) have been deliberately so framed as to defeat the object of the Act of 1892, but I will say that if the officer who drafted them had been asked to sit down with deliberate purpose of framing a scheme to defeat that purpose, he could not have done better."*
>
> —*Gopal Krishna Gokhale*

The Indian Councils Act of 1892 constituted the second instalment of reforms. It marked a decisive step and in advance. According to **Heera Lal Singh,** "The Act of 1892 was the revised and enlarged edition of the Indian Councils Act of 1861".[1]

Circumstances Leading to the Act

The circumstances favouring the enactment of the Councils Act of 1892 were as follows—

We have discussed at length in preceding chapter the various factors which stimulated political consciousness and national awakening in the country. A few important factors that contributed to the growth of nationalism were religious movements, Western education, economic exploitation of India by the British traders and the policy of repression adopted by the Government of India. The foolish doings of Lord Lytton including his Vernacular Press Act and Afghan wars embittered the people against the British rule. The possibilities of a countrywide revolution had fairly increased before the birth of Indian National Congress. Every Indian heart was red with a new aspiration.

Mr. Hume founds Congress. The fear of the imminent revolution in India and the anxiety to save the British Empire from disruption induced the retired civil servant, Mr. Hume, to lay the foundation of Indian National Congress.

Demand of Indian National Congress for representative institutions. The national awakening of the 19th century had given fillip to demand of representative institutions. First of all Madras Mahajan Sabha gave a lead in this connection and demanded representative institutions in December 1885. It made a fervent plea to the government that the selection of members of the Council should be made by an electorate consisting of local bodies, the Universities and the Chambers of Commerce. Indian National Congress followed the suit. **W.C. Bannerjee,** President of the first session of the Indian National Congress, demanded that elected members should be included in the Councils, budget should

1. Heera Lal Singh — *Problems and Policies of the British Rule in India.*-page 118.

be presented to them for discussion and members should have right to ask questions. In a resolution in 1885 the Indian Congress prayed that the supreme (Central) and existing local Councils (Provincial Councils) should be expanded through the admission of a considerable proportion of elected members, the creation of similar Councils for the North-Western Provinces and Oudh and also for the Punjab, that all budgets should be referred to these councils, that the right of interpellations be granted, and that "a Standing committee of the House of Commons should be constituted to receive and consider any formal protests that might be recorded by majorities of such Councils against the exercise by the Executive of the power which would be vested in it, of overruling the decisions of such majorities."[1] *Dr. Pattabhi Sitramayya observes, "the object of the Indian National Congress in 1885 was to ensure a Parliamentary safeguard against bureaucratic actions, such as have been lately witnessed in profusion in the Assembly in respect of the rejection or vetoing of popular demands accepted by a majority, and certification of Government demands* rejected by the people's representatives."[2]

Dadabhai Naoroji in his presidential address to the second session of the Congress again emphasised *"the need of introducing elective element in the Councils. If this representation is introduced, the greatest benefit will be conferred upon the Government itself, because at present whatever Acts they pass do not quite please us."* He held the existing constitution of the councils as most unsatisfactory and maintained, "It is true that we have some of our people in Councils. But we have no right to demand any explanation even from them; they are not our representatives, and the Government cannot relieve themselves from the dissatisfaction we may feel against any law we do not like. If our own representatives make a mistake and get a law passed which we do not want, the Government at any rate will escape the greater portion of the consequent unpopularity."[3]

Lord Dufferin's Suggestions. In 1888 he set up a Committee to suggest the reforms in the composition of the Councils. On the basis of the Committee's report, he sent a Despatch to the Home Government in England. He suggested that the Councils should be expanded into petty Parliaments. Two-fifths of the non-official members should be elected members. "The main object," he said, "was to give a still wider share in the administration of public affairs to such Indian gentlemen as are fit to assist with their counsel the responsible rulers of the country." He made it very clear in his Despatch that Indians were not to be entrusted with the reins of administration. He further wrote that Indian destinies have been confined to the guidance of an alien rule and hence the enlarged legislative councils were to act merely as consultative bodies to help Government with advice and suggestions. The British Government even after receiving Viceroy's proposals moved slowly and passed an Act in 1890. It became an Act of Parliament on June 20,1892.

Main Provisions of the Act of 1892

The Act of 1892 was only an amending Act, therefore, basically the structure of the Government of India remained the same as envisaged in the Act of 1891.

In other words, we can say that the Indian Councils Act 1892 was designed on the pattern of the Act of 1861. Its important provisions were as under :

1. *Enlargement of Central and Provincial Councils.* The Act made provision for an increase in the number of additional members in the councils. In the Central Council the minimum number of additional members for legislative functions was raised from 8 to 10 and the maximum limit from 12 to 16. In the case of Madras and Bombay, the increased strength was to be not less than eight and not more than twenty. The maximum for Bengal was fixed at twenty and for U.P. only fifteen. The increase was very 'paltry and miserable.' Of the sixteen additional members in the Central Council ten were to be non-officials of whom four were to be nominated on the recommendations of the non-official members of the Provincial legislatures, one on the recommendation of the Calcutta Chamber

1. Dr. Pattabhi Sitaramayya, *History of the National Congress,* Vol. I, p.24.
2. Ibid.
3. Banerjee, A.C., *Indian Constitutional Documents,* Vol. II, pp.85-86

of Commerce and the remaining to represent the landlords and other interests in the country. Thus there was practically no directly elected member in the Central Legislature.

2. *Rules.* The Act empowered the Governor-General-in Council to make rules regarding the nomination of members . But the Governor-General was required to seek the approval of the Secretary of State-in-council in exercising his right.

3. *More rights were given to the members of the Councils.* The Act proposed an appreciable increase in powers of the legislatures. The members could ask questions on domestic matters. A prior notice of six days was to be given to the President for asking a question. The members were also authorised to discuss the Budget but without the right to vote on it or demand a division of the House on any issue. The Act further said that the questions on public interest could be asked "subject to such conditions and rules as prescribed in rules made by Governor-General or the Governors."

As the rules did not specify the subjects to which the questions were limited, the President of the Council could disallow any question without assigning any reason, or an answer to a question could be refused on the ground of its inconsistency with public interest. In the Provincial Councils, Members were not allowed to put questions regarding administration except the local administration. Regarding those matters in which there was controversy between Local Government and the Governor-General-in-Council or the Secondary of State for India, the questions were allowed. No questions could be asked except as to matters of fact, and the answer was to be confined to a statement of facts. No discussion was allowed on any answer given to a question. Therefore the right to ask the questions mainly depended on the sweet will of the Government.

4. *Governor-General, Governors and Lieutenant-Governors empowered to fill vacancies.* Technically all the members were to be nominated by the Governor-General, Governor or the Lieutenant-Governor. If a member failed to attend the sitting of the Legislature for two months, or resigned his membership or died, his seat was declared vacant. Such vacancies were to be filled by the Governor-General in the case of Central Legislature and by the Governor in the case of a Provincial Legislature.

5. *Provincial Legislatures empowered to repeal or amend laws.* The functions of the Provincial Legislative Councils were further enlarged. They were empowered to make new laws or repeal the old ones with the prior permission of the Governor-General. This power, however, did not affect the powers of the Governor-General-in-Council at meetings for the purpose of making laws and regulations.

6. As a result of the pressure brought by the Indian National Congress, the Government agreed to introduce elective element in the Councils. The elected members could take their seats only after being nominated by the head of the Government. In the case of the Imperial Legislature, the Chamber of Commerce was asked to submit a panel of names having been chosen by election, and the Governor-General approved one name for the membership of the Central Legislature. Same was the case in the Provinces where the Municipal Committees, District Boards, Zamindars and University Senates recommended the person to the Governor who made his selection for the legislature from the list submitted.

Importance of the Act of 1892

The Act of 1892 has its own importance in the Constitutional History of India. In other words we can say that the Act of 1892 may be called a landmark in the constitutional development of India. It made definite advance on the Act of 1861. For the first time the elective principle was accepted and introduced by the Act. Persons of Indian origin got an opportunity to sit with the Viceroy and share privilege of law-making for their country. It was a sort of an "attempt at compromise between the official view of the Councils as pocket Legislatures and the educated Indian view of them as embryo Parliaments." The Act is significant for making provision for elected members in the legislatures although only through restricted and indirect elections. The Act also authorised the members to discuss the Budget. The right of the members to discuss and criticise the financial policies of the Executive, laid, as it were, the foundation of Parliamentary Government. The new Act gave effect to the official policy stated in the Act of 1861, of giving Indians a large share in the administration of the affairs of their country.

The Indian Councils Bill of 1892 was an amending measure and consequently it was not expected, as Gladstone said, to produce "large and imposing results."[1] Curzon's own estimate of the Bill was precisely the same. "The Bill", he said, "is not, perhaps, a great, or heroic measure but at the same time, it does mark a decisive step and a step in advance." Lord Lansdowne remarked that though the proposals would disappoint those who had expected radical changes, yet they marked substantial steps in advance."[2]

Its important features were as under :

1. Introduction of the elective principle. The achievements of the Act, though they appear to be very meagre but the Act did lay down the foundations of the Representative Government in India. Before this Act, no prominent Indian enjoyed the privilege of being a member of the Council but by this Act, eminent Indians like G.K. Gokhale, Ashutosh Mukherjee were allowed to sit with with Viceroy and his Councillors. Though it is true that Indians were unable to override the official majority in the Council, because their number was too small, yet their opinions and views were listened to with some attention.

2. Indians Associated. According to this Act certain non-official members were to be nominated by Head of the Government, no the recommendation of certain bodies. Speaking on this Bill, **Gladstone** said: "the great question we have before us that the question of Ireland profound interest in the question of the introduction of the elective element in the Government of India, while the language of Bill cannot be said to embody the elective principle, it is intended to pave the way for the adoption of the principle." Out of 16 non-official members of the Central Legislative Councils, five were to be elected. In the Provincial Councils, too, the same procedure was adopted. In fact the principle of election was conceded in an indirect way.

3. Expansion of the Legislative Councils. The Act of 1892 enlarged the number of members of the Legislative Councils and also their powers. Lord Curzon strongly defended the ideal of increasing the number on the plea "that the efficiency of a deliberative loby does not necessarily, commensurate with its numerical strength.......over large bodies.......do not promote economic administration but are apt to diffuse their force in vogue and rapid talk." The Act also increased the powers of members of the Legislative Councils. The members were given the right to discuss the final policy of the government. The non-official members thus got the opportunity to criticize the financial policy of the Government.

4. Powers of Legislative Councils enlarged. The Act also empowered the members of Council to put interpellation on matters of public interest. They were also authorised to ask supplementary questions. Restrictions in this connection were in no way more comprehensive than those prescribed for the House of Commons in England. No doubt, it was a great thing. The Report on Constitutional Reforms nicely described the advance made by the Act of 1892 on that of 1861: "Whereas in 1861 men had said, we had better hear, what a few Indians of our choosing have to say about our laws"; they said in 1892, "our laws have positively benefited by Indian advice and criticism; let us have more of it."

5. An attempt to compromise between official view and the Indian view. In fact, the gains appear very meagre but their significance be minimised. **Puniah** has rightly remarked: "It was an attempt at compromise between the official view of the Councils as pocket Legislatures and the Educated Indian view of them as embroy Parliament while no efforts were made to enlarge the boundries of the educated class to provide them any training in responsible Government are no lay

1. Parliamentary debates, Commons, March 28, 1892 col 98-99
2. *Ibid.*

the foundations of a future electorate to control them the Act deliberate by attempted to delay with the elective idea."

It is true to say that the Act did not mark the beginning of Parliamentary Government in India but at least it was a step in this direction.

Criticism of the Act of 1892

First, the Act of 1892, although a great stride forward, failed to arouse much enthusiasm. It fell far short of the national demands. The disappointment of the people was due to the fact that this Act did not give anything substantial. According to Dr. Pattabhi Sitaramayya, "We must not omit to mention that the reforms of 1892 did not provide for the election of the representatives to the Legislative Council. The so-called right to election to the legislatures enjoyed by local bodies and by other electorate amounted merely to nominations by those bodies, but it was up to the Government to accept them or reject them." The persons who got into the legislatures through indirect elections did not represent the people in the real sense of the word.

Secondly, Gopal Krishna Gokhale expressed his great disappointment with the Act in these words: "*I will not say that they (Rules) have been deliberately so framed as to defeat the object of the Act of 1892, but I will say that if the officer who drafted them had been asked to sit down with deliberate purpose of framing a scheme to defeat that purpose, he could not have done better.*"

Thirdly, Keith observes, "the newly granted powers were not very important.[1] "The Government of India themselves remarked in a Despatch in 1908 that" the facilities of debate were limited and the nature of discussion was, therefore, of a desultory nature."[2] The right of discussion on the annual financial statement was allowed but the Members could not move any resolution and demand voting there-upon. While explaining the effect of this provision, Pandit Madan Mohan Malaviya said, "*The Act still left Indians without any real voice in the administration of the country. They found that the administration was not being conducted in the best interests of the people of the country but it continued to be conducted on extravagantly costly lines. They found that the level of the taxation was maintained much higher than was necessary for the purpose of good administration; that the military expenditure of the Government was beyond the capacity of the country to bear; that an excessively large portion of the revenue for the people was being spent on what we may call imperial purpose.*"

Fourthly, the control of the Secretary of the State over the Government of India was not relaxed. With regard to the legislation itself, the Secretary of State emphasised in his Despatch that the Indian Government being subordinate was bound to obey all directions issued by the Home Government."[3] All the non-official Bills intended to be introduced in the Central Legislative Council had to first seek the approval of the Secretary of State. Similarly, no non-official Bill could be moved in the Provincial Councils without the prior approval of the Governor-General. The official members of the Councils (Central and Provincial) voted en bloc according to the instructions of the higher authority (Governor-General or Governor). Therefore, the measures introduced by the non-official members had only slim chance of success.

Fifthly, the voice of the elected members was not all effective. The official members being in majority had little difficulty in imposing their will on the House. The functions of the Legislative Councils were also very limited. The members were not to ask supplementary questions and no discussion was permitted in respect of an answer given to a question. According to Smith, "The budget could be discussed but not until after the estimates had already been settled by the executive."

1. Keith, A.E., *A Constitutional History of India*, p.177.
2. Public Despatch No.21, October 1, 1908, to the Secretary of State for India.
3. Legislative Despatch No.15, June 30, 1892, from the Secretary of State for India.

Sixthly, the distribution of seats to different communities for representation in the legislature was most unsatisfactory. While certain classes were over-represented, others did not find any representation at all.

Summing up the implications of the changes introduced by the Act of 1892, Dadabhai Naoroji said that, *"By this Act no member shall have the power to submit or propose any resolution or divide the Council in respect of any financial discussion or in answer to any question asked under the authority of this Act or the rules made under this Act. Such is the poor character of the extent of the concessions made to discuss finances or to put questions. Rules made under this Act shall not be subjected to alternation or amendment at meetings for the purpose of making laws and regulations. Thus we are, to all intents and purposes, under an arbitrary rule."*[1]

EXERCISES

Long Answer Type Questions

1. Examine the circumstances which were responsible for the passage of the Indian Councils Act, 1892. In what respects the Act is an improvement upon the Act of 1861?
2. Discuss the main provisions of the Indian Councils Act, 1892.
3. Critically assess the importance of the Indian Councils Act, 1892. What were its defects?

Short Answer Type Questions

1. Write any two circumstances which were responsible for the passage of the Indian Councils Act, 1892.
2. What was the role of Lord Dufferin for the enactment of the Indian Councils Act, 1892?
3. Discuss any three provisions of the Act of 1892.
4. Write any three features of the Act of 1892.

Objective Type Questions

Choose the correct answer

1. Which instalment of reforms was the Indian Councils Act of 1892 ?
   (*a*) Second (*b*) third
   (*c*) fourth (*d*) fifth
2. The Act of 1892 was the revised and enlarged edition of the
   (*a*) Government of India Act 1858 (*b*) Indian Councils Act of 1861
   (*c*) The Charter Act of 1853 (*d*) The Charter Act of 1833

Answers

1. (*a*) **2.** (*b*)

1. Dadabhai Naoroji, *Presidential Address* to the Congress, 1893.

CHAPTER 8

Moderate and Extremist Programme of Congress

"Swaraj is not the colonial form of Government nor any form of Government. It means the fulfilment of our national life. That is what we seek, that is why god has sent us into the world to fulfil Him by fulfilling ourselves in our individual life, in the family, in the community, in the nation, in humanity."

—Arvind Ghosh.

CONSTITUTIONAL MOVEMENT OR MOVEMENT OF MODERATES (1885-1907)

The History of the Constitutional Movements for regaining freedom commences from 1885, the year of the birth of Indian National Congress. For three years after its beginning, it remained in the good books of British Government so much so that the delegates to Congress Sessions were extended garden parties at the Government House. The meeting of the Congress in 1885 was proposed to be held at Poona but the venue was soon changed to Bombay. Speaking from the Presidential Chair, Mr. **W.C. Bannerjee** laid down the following objects of the Congress:

1. "The promotion of personal intimacy and friendship amongst all the more earnest workers in our country's cause in the various parts of the Empire."
2. "The eradication by direct friendly personal intercourse of all possible race, creed or provincial prejudices amongst all lovers of the country and fuller development and consolidation of those sentiments of national unity that took their origin in our beloved Lord Ripon's ever memorable reign."
3. "The authoritative record of the matured opinion of the educated classes in India on some of the more important and pressing of the social questions of the day."
4. "The determination of the methods by which during the next twelve months it is desirable for native politicians to labour in public interest."

The Congress was, from the very start, a National Organisation. It represented all sections and classes of the society. Its object was to secure more political reforms and more representative element in the enlarged Legislative Councils. It also demanded more powers for the legislatures. **Dadabhai Naoroji** in his Presidential Address in 1886 said, "It is true that we have some of our own people in Council. But we have no right to demand any explanations, even from them;

they are not our representatives.......If our own representatives make a mistake and get a law passed, which we do not want, the Government at any rate will escape the greater portion of the consequent unpopularity."

For the period of two decades the leadership of the Congress was held by the Moderates who had a firm faith in the British sense of justice and righteousness. They were mighty sure that the Government would sooner or later accept all their reasonable demands. They had leaning towards the West and faith in the fact that the British Rule was in the interest of the people. In order to mobilise the opinion of the British Press and public in favour of India's national urge for reforms, the Congress sent a deputation to England. The deputation included Mr. Hume, Ferozeshah Mehta, Man Mohan Ghosh and S.N. Bannerjee. The leaders tried to plead the case of India before the British public through their stirring speeches. One outcome of their mission to England was the setting up of a Parliamentary Committee to look into their demands. Till 1905 the political goal of the Congress was not independence but only greater share in the administration of the country and expansion of Representative Institutions. Unfurling the tricolour flag at the third annual session of the Congress, Surendra Nath Bannerjee repeated that 'Representative Institutions' was the goal of the Congress. When the Reforms Act of 1892 was passed, it was discovered that the Act did not give the right of election to members of Councils but allowed the Viceroy to make rules subject to the approval of the Secretary of State. Gopal Krishna Gokhale said, "I will not say that they have been deliberately so framed as to defeat the object of the Act of 1892, but I will say this that if the officer who drafted them had been asked to sit down with the deliberate purpose of framing a scheme to defeat that object, he could not have done better."

Programme of Indian National Congress from 1885 *to* 1905. From 1885 to 1905 the Congress held its Annual Sessions at various places in India and passed resolutions demanding: (1) That the Viceroy's and Governor's Executive Council should be enlarged and made to have more Indians and representative element in them; (2) that the defence budget should be reduced and English officers be replaced by Indian officers; (3) that the Secretary of State for India and his India Council be done away with; (4) that the local bodies may be given more powers and a degree of autonomy in local affairs; (5) reduction of salt-tax; (6) that Indian textile industry may be revived and new industries may be set up so as to create more jobs for unemployed Indian youth; (7) that the judiciary may be freed from the pressure of the executive; (8) that the interests of the Indian living abroad may also be safeguarded; (9) that the competitive examination for recruitment to Civil Services may also be held in India; (10) that the peasant's may be protected from exploitation by the landlords; (11) that the burden of tax and rent on land be reduced; (12) that the Press may be guaranteed freedom of expression; (13) that rural banks may be set up to offer loans to the agriculturists at a low rate of interest; (14) that Indians may not be excluded from higher ranks of services; (15) that the economic condition of the people be improved; (16) that facilities may be provided for more technical and industrial education in India; and (17) that more colleges for military training be set up in the country.

Resolution of Dominion Status in 1906. The British Government gave a cold reception to Congress demands. When the Congress Leaders had no more patience left, they proposed a change in their programme. **Dadabhai Naoroji** in his Presidential Address at the Calcutta Session of the Congress in 1906 declared that *Dominion Status or Swaraj for India was the goal of Congress activities.* The following resolutions were adopted by the Congress in 1906 :

1. *Boycott Movement.* "Resolved that having regard to the fact that the people of this country have little or no voice in the administration and that their representations to the Government do not receive due consideration, the Congress is of opinion that the Boycott Movement inaugurated in Bengal, by way of protest against the partition of the Province, was, and is, legitimate."

2. *Self-Government (or Dominion Status).* Resolved that this Congress is of opinion that the system of Government obtaining in the Self-Governing British Colonies should be extended

to India and that, as steps leading to it urge that the following reforms should be immediately carried out:–

(*a*) All examinations held in England only should be simultaneously held in India and in England and that all higher appointments which are made in India should be competitive examinations only.

(*b*) The adequate representation of Indians in the Councils of the Governor of Madras and Bombay.

(*c*) The expansion of the Supreme and Provincial Legislative Councils, allowing a larger and truly effective representation of the peoples and a large control over the financial and executive administration of the country.

(*d*) The powers of local and municipal bodies should be extended and official control over them should not be more than what is exercised by the Local Government Board in England over similar bodies.

3. *Swadeshi.* Resolved that this Congress accords its most cordial support to the Swadeshi Movement and calls upon the people of the country to labour for its success, by making earnest and sustained efforts to promote the growth of indigenous industries and to stimulate the production of indigenous articles by giving them preference over imported commodities, even at some sacrifice.

4. *National Education.* Resolved that in the opinion of this Congress the time has arrived for the people all over the country earnestly to take up the question of national education for both boys and girls and organise a system of education, literary, scientific and technical, suited to the requirements of the country on National lines and under National control.

The Congress, henceforth, began to demand better status for Indians in foreign lands, more political rights to the people, assurance of production to native industries, reduction in land tax and more irrigational facilities.

PRINCIPLES OF MODERATES

The Congress remained completely in the hands of the Moderates from 1885 to 1906. At that time its important leaders were Dadabhai Naoroji, Sir Feroze Shah Mehta, Gopal Krishna Gokhale and Surendra Nath Bannerjee. They believed in the following principles:

1. British rule is a blessing. Before the advent of the British Rule Anarchy prevailed in India due to a number of reasons. Gokhale was of the opinion that one might criticise and abuse the British but there could not be two opinions on the subject that the British Rulers had at least restored law and order. He held the view that in our country it was not at all difficult to spread disorder. That had been the bane of this country for centuries. As the British had established law and order and without law and order, there could not be any progress of the civilization and culture, so it would be difficult to find an alternative to the British Rule.

Gokhale considered the British Rule as a divine gift because in his opinion it was preparing the Indians for self-government. He held the conviction that the main aim of the British Rule in India should be the moral and material progress of the people.

2. Swadeshi. Speaking of the Swadeshi Movement Gokhale in his Presidential Address on 27th December, 1905 at Varanasi (Banaras) said :

"The devotion to Motherland, which is enshrined in the highest *swadeshi,* is an influence so profound and so passionate that its very thought, thrills and its actual touch lifts one out of oneself. India needs to-day above everything else that the gospel of this devotion should be preached to high and low, to prince and to peasant, in town and in hamlet, till the service of Motherland becomes with us overmastering a passion as it is in Japan."

3. Attitude towards Partition of Bengal. Welcoming the Prince of Wales and New Viceroy Lord Minto, Gokhale made a survey of the regime of Lord Curzon. He compared the rule of Lord Curzon to the rule of Aurangzeb at Banaras. Both regimes were excessively centralised and intensely personal. Lord Curson made tremendous efforts to strengthen British Rule in India and treated Indians as dumb-driven cattle. Gokhale said that if people were to be humiliated and were to be rendered helpless, then all he could say was, "Good-bye to all hope of co-operating in any way with the bureaucracy in the interests of the people."

4. Belief in Dominion Status. The Moderates believed in self-government and not complete independence. They considered it as the only practical ideal under the then prevailing circumstances. After 1906 the Moderates began to believe in *Dominion Status* because Dada Bhai Naoroji, Grand Old Man of India (then 82), had fixed that goal of the Congress.

5. The Moderates believed in Constitutional Means. Gopal Krishna Gokhale and others believed in the constitutional methods and not agitational methods. They believed in petitions and prayers which the extremists called the policy of mendicancy.

Gokhale believed in the policy of constructive criticism. He also believed in peaceful processions and was ready to co-operate with the British to maintain peace. He tried his best to convince the higher authorities (Viceroy and Secretary of State for India) about the excesses and atrocities of British Bureaucracy.

6. Spiritualisation of Politics. Gokhale also believed in the spiritualisation of politics. He did not believe in immoral means and was never ready to align himself against his foes to achieve his ends. He always believed that there should be good means to achieve good end. He did not believe in spreading hatred against the foreign rule. He always advised the Members of the Servants of India Society to follow always the Policy of Truth and Non-violence in Politics which was later on followed strictly by his disciple Mahatma Gandhi.

7. The Moderates had abiding faith in Western Education.

8. The Moderates had firm faith in Hindu-Muslim unity.

9. The Moderates had unflinching faith in the service of their country. Therefore, Gokhale had founded the "*Servants of India Society*" in 1905 and shunned the knighthood and membership of the Council of the Secretary of State for India which was offered to him by the British because that would have proved an obstacle in the path of service of the nation.

10. Gokhale believed in the freedom of speech and press. Therefore, he fully opposed the repressive British Laws.

ACHIEVEMENTS OF MODERATES

Following are the achievements of the Moderates :

1. They followed a realist policy in Politics. The Congress had not become strong enough to oppose the British Government upto 1905. The British had crushed armed resistance in 1857 and before it. If the Congress had followed a policy of fighting the British Government upto 1905, it would have been crushed because the Congress had not become a mass organisation and its membership was limited only to English-speaking people. Therefore, they followed a policy of demanding more rights for the Indians in every sphere of administration.

2. Exploitation by the British rule fully exposed. Dadabhai Naoroji was the first to expose the exploitation of the British Rule. In his famous book, *Poverty and Un-British Rule in India,* he expounded his well-known Drain Theory. He wrote that 'England was eating India's resources at the rate of some £ 30,000,000 to £ 40,000,000 a year.' He further wrote, "It is at India's cost and blood that this British Empire has been formed and maintained upto this day. It is in consequence of the tremendous cost of these wars and because of the millions and millions you draw from us year by year that India is so completely exhaust and bled. It is no wonder that the time has come when India is bleeding to death. You have brought India to this condition by the constant drain upon the wealth of that country."

Similarly, Gokhale in his various budget speeches has fully highlighted the utmost exploitation of the British Government. This proves that the Moderates were not less patriots but they did not adopt the programme of the extremists because that did not suit their policy.

3. Political Education of the People. Congress was joined first of all by the English-educated people. After being influenced by Western Literature, History, culture and democratic institutions, they also demanded local self-government, reforms in the revenue-system and the conferment of higher ranks in the army. The newspapers published the speeches and resolutions passed in the Congress Sessions and public functions. Besides that they took special note of the illuminating speeches delivered by the Congress Leaders in the Imperial Legislative Council on the occasion of the presentation of budget (because at no other time they could do so). That imparted great political education to the people.

Dr. Ishwari Prasad also observes :

"The Congress resolutions and the speeches there-on printed in the press, were circulated throughout the country, moulding public opinion and drawing larger numbers within its fold. True enough, by and by, its moderation and constitutionalism made it the subject of ridicule among the younger generation, but none can withhold the deed of praise from its early leaders–men of high intellectual attainments, character and patriotism for doing pioneer work in the way of India's regeneration and championing the cause of the people against powerful alien bureaucracy strongly entrenched in its own citadel of obstinacy and prejudice."[1]

4. The Early Congress Programme helped the awakening of the masses. The British had thoroughly crushed the First Indian War of Independence (1857). After that they continued to frame the repressive laws. Lord Curzon had ventured to partition Bengal in spite of loud protests of the people. Under these circumstances, it was boldness on the part of the Congress Leaders to demand more and more rights in every sphere, representative institutions and even the Dominion Status. Therefore, Prof. Gurmukh Nihal Singh truly observes: "*With all its professions of loyalty, studied moderation and appealing, nay begging tone, the early Congress did in these days a great amount of spadework in national awakening, political education and uniting Indians and in creating in them the consciousness of common nationality.*"

5. Prepared the basis for the freedom struggle. There is no denying the fact that the early Congress leaders prepared a strong base for the future freedom struggles. The Speeches of Gokhale delivered in the Imperial Legislative Council and other leaders on various occasions especially the annual sessions, were printed in the newspapers and they aroused the literate persons, at least, from political slumber. It should be noted that the Partition of Bengal had generated feeling of oneness amongst the Indians.

6. Boycott of foreign cloth. The Congress under the Presidentship of Gokhale passed the following resolution at Banaras Session in 1905. "That the Congress records its earnest and emphatic protest against the repressive measures which have been adopted by the authorities in Bengal after the people there had been compelled to resort to the boycott of foreign foods as a last resort and perhaps the only constitutional and effective means left to them of drawing the attention of the British public to the action of the Government of India in persisting in their determination to partition Bengal, in utter disregard of the universal prayers and protests of the people."

According to **Gopal Krishna Gokhale,** boycott was a political weapon which should be reserved for extreme occasions. It was useful in drawing the attention of the ruling class to the grievances of

1. Dr. Ishwari Prasad, *History of Modern India,* p. 315.

the ruled. He admitted that it was a legitimate weapon. Before using it there ought to be a recognition of common danger all round, and all personal differences must be sunk.

7. The Acts of 1892 and 1909. Due to strenuous efforts of the Moderates, the Act of 1892 was framed which was far ahead of the Act of 1861 but the Congress was not satisfied by that. Due to the herculean efforts of Gopal Krishna Gokhale, however, the Act of 1909 was framed which was, though far ahead of the Act of 1892, yet failed to meet the aspirations of the people due to a number of reasons. However, that was the greatest achievement of the Moderates.

"Every year the Congress by means of resolutions and occasional deputations to England focussed the attention of the people on the grievances under which they were labouring, impressed upon them the efficiency of the united action and called upon them to sacrifice personal or sectarian interests for the good of the country: Its resolutions and the speeches there-on, printed in the press were circulated throughout the country, moulding public opinion and drawing larger numbers within its fold. True enough, by and by, its moderation and constitutionalism made it the subject of ridicule among the younger generation, but none can withhold the need of praise from its early leaders–men of high intellectual attainments, character and patriotism for doing pioneer work in the way of India's regeneration and championing the cause of the people against a powerful alien bureaucracy strongly entrenched in its own citadel of obstinacy and prejudice."

So it will not be proper to treat the attempts of the Moderates for achieving more rights for the Indians in every branch of administration as useless. They emphasised more and more the bureaucratic character of the administration and demanded first of all representative institutions and later on Dominion Status like all other dominions. Though they were not able to get all that they wanted but they were able to get something at least (Achievement of the Act of 1909).

BIRTH OF EXTREMIST MOVEMENT

The Congress from 1885 to 1906 submitted petitions and led deputations without getting much success. The Government showed no inclination to relent. Lokmanya Tilak, Bipin Chandra Pal and Lajpat Rai lost their patience with the Moderates and their method of work. Bal Gangadhar Tilak suggested a militant course to obtain self-government. His aggressive nationalism found favour with the masses and he became a national hero. The trio, Lal, Bal, and Pal provided dynamic leadership to the people and stirred them to life. But the liberals like Gokhale, Pt. Madan Mohan Malaviya, Ras Behari Bose, Dada Bhai Naoroji, S.N. Bannerjee and Ramesh Chandra Dutt had still a hold on the Congress. Consequently, Bal Gangadhar Tilak and his associates could not come to power.

Principles of the Extremists. They believed in the following principles:

(1)The Extremists or Militant Nationalists, as they were also known were in favour of not piecemeal but *complete independence*. Tilak, the leading man of this movement, gave the country the slogan of 'Excelsior', the *Mantra* that freedom was their birthright and they must have it. He simply laughed at the Moderates' request for constitutional reforms and addition of elected representatives to the Legislative Councils. (2) He was against the policy of political begging. The alternative method that he suggested was to *boycott foreign goods*. The Extremists were frank and unsparing in denouncing the economic exploitation of India and the official attempt to impose social reforms on Hindu society. (3) Tilak had unflinching faith in the superiority of Vedic culture, literature, language and civilisation. He stood for driving out the rulers rather than entreating them for favour. The method that he suggested to accomplish this end was, however, not terrorism but constitutional struggle. He wanted the struggle to be waged with courage and fearlessness, no matter if British were displaced. Aurobindo Ghosh was also a leader of the Extremist camp. He declared, *"Independence in all our movements is the goal of life and Hinduism can fulfil this aspiration of ours."*

DIFFERENCES BETWEEN EXTREMISTS AND MODERATES

The following were the differences between the 'Extremists and Moderates':

1. Extremists were in favour of complete independence, while the Moderates favoured only self-government within the British Empire. However, they adopted Dominion Status as their goal in 1906 but nothing was done to achieve that goal till 1919. While Bal Gangadhar Tilak gave a new slogan to our people, *"Freedom is our birth right and we shall have it."*

2. While Moderates considered the British rule as the greatest blessing as it restored law and order and imparted the knowledge of science and Western literature through English education, the Extremists laughed over loudly upon such conjectures. They believed that the ancient system of education was far superior to the present system of education. They were not ready to accept the idea at all that the alien (foreign) rule was blessing in any shape or form as it was fully based on exploitation. Even if it was good, it could not get the place of swaraj because swaraj (self-rule) was far better than the foreign rule. Tilak used to say frequently that if swaraj was possible in the time of Shivaji, why not now? Therefore, for the inspiration of youth, he asked them to celebrate every year the birthday of Shivaji who did not differentiate between the Hindus and Mohammedans and liberated the Motherland from foreign yoke.

3. The Moderates believed in constitutional means (petitions and prayers) to achieve their ends. Their end was self-government or more rights in administration and councils. The Extremists on the other hand believed in the passive resistance, demonstration, national education, Swadeshi and boycott of foreign goods as the most potent weapon to achieve their sublime goal. It has already been said that Moderates did not believe in national education, Swadeshi and boycott and they had adopted this programme most reluctantly in 1905 and 1906, and excluded the same in 1907 which led to the split of the Congress at Surat.

4. Tilak firmly believed in national education, Swadeshi, Self-Government or Swaraj and boycott while the Moderates did not believe in them at all but as a compromise they had to adopt it in 1906. In 1907 they excluded all these things from the Congress Programme which lead to the split at Surat.

Lala Lajpat Rai and B.C.Pal too were the strong pillars of the aggressive nationalism. Sri Pal on his return from England started *Vande Matram.* In Boycott, the Extremists found an effective weapon for injuring British interests. Lala Lajpat Rai gave expression to his temper in the following words: "Indians should no longer be content to be beggars, whinning for favours; for if they really cared for their country, they would have to strike a blow for themselves."

Difference between Bal Gangadhar Tilak and Gopal Krishna Gokhale. Gokhale, the true disciple of Mahadeo Gobind Ranade, was a staunch Moderate. From his guru, he had learnt the principle of toleration and forbearance both in thoughts and actions. He and his colleagues were never weary of eulogising the benefits conferred upon India by the British Rule. He believed that political dogmatism and hasty action were not the ways to reconstruct India. It was in the interest of India to grow gradually for self-government by making the bonds between India and England deeper and durable. He explained his point of view in the following words: "Our old public life was based on frank and loyal acceptance of British Rule due to a recognition of the fact that it alone could secure to the country the peace and order which were necessary for slowly evolving a nation out of the heterogeneous elements of which India was composed and for ensuring to it a steady advance in different directions. The new teaching condemns all faith in the British Government as childish and all hope of real progress under it as rash."

Pointing out the differences between Bal Gangadhar Tilak and Gopal Krishna Gokhale, Dr. Pattabhi Sitaramayya writes: *"Both Gokhale and Tilak were the patriots of the first order but their temperaments were widely different from each other. Gokhale was moderate and Tilak was an ex-*

tremist. Gokhale's plan was to improve existing constitution, Tilak's was to reconstruct it. Gokhale had necessarily to work with the bureaucracy, Tilak had necessarily to fight it. Gokhale stood for co-operation wherever possible and opposition wherever necessary. Tilak inclined towards a policy of obstruction. Gokhale's ideal was love and service, Tilak's was service and suffering. Gokhale's method sought to win the foreigner, Tilak's to replace him. Gokhale's objective was self government for which the people have to fit themselves by answering the tests prescribed by English. Tilak's objective was Swaraj which is birth-right of every Indian and which he shall have without let or hindrance from the foreigner. Gokhale was on the level of his age, Tilak was in advance of his time."

The Moderates in spite of their faith in British generosity were neither loyalists nor were their activities unavailing. Both moderates and extremists were equally patriotic and their methods, although radically different, did some real good to the country. Before passing any judgement on the attitude of the old leadership, one must care to learn that in the then-existing conditions, co-operation with the Government was the only sensible approach to political questions. The Congress could not have survived without its creed of non-violence. Freedom was a far cry and any such demand was likely to offend the rulers. Securing Council reforms itself was an uphill task and hence the Moderates planned to proceed step by step without displeasing the white masters. But much more can be said in favour of the triple leadership of Lal-Bal-Pal. Their approach to political affairs was manly and militant. Going with a begging bowl was not in their line. They stressed the need of constitutional agitations to rouse political consciousness and together all forces under one banner. In the context of the hostile attitude of the Government, it was a perilous project. As a natural sequel, the Extremists came into clash with the Government and they were put to much suffering. It was in order to suppress the extremist movement that the British Government adopted the policy of appeasing the harmless old leadership of the Congress. The reforms of 1909 were a direct outcome of the changed attitude of the British Government.

CAUSES OF THE BIRTH OF EXTREMIST MOVEMENT

Following were the causes of the birth of extremist movement :

1. Misrule of the Tory Government. The rise of Extremism in India can directly be traced to the misrule of Tory (Conservative) Party Government. From 1888 to 1902, Lord Salisbury headed the British Government except during the brief intervals when Liberals were in power. **Mr. R.C. Dutt** observes, "although not an imperialist himself, Salisbury had the capacity to yield and to drift with the tide when he could not oppose it."[1] Lord Hamilton who presided over the India Office from 1895 to 1903, was very unsympathetic to India. He wrote to Curzon on September 20, 1899:

"I think that the real danger to our rule in India, not now but 50 years hence, is the gradual adoption and extension of Western ideas of agitation and organisation and if we could break the educated Hindu Party into two sections holding widely different views, we should by such a division, strengthen our position against the subtle and continuous attack which the spread of education must make upon our present system of Government."

During the time when Hamilton was in the office, unparalleled calamities of war, famine and pestilences visited India but he remained indifferent to the distress of the Indians. This aroused great indignation against the British rule in India.

2. Discontent over the Reforms of 1892. Several factors were responsible for the birth of militant nationalism in India. One of the reasons was dissatisfaction with the working of the Act of 1892. The rights conferred by the Act were quite inadequate and disappointing. The Council were still ridden with official nominees with the result that the Government faced with no opposition in making laws. Even the elected members did not represent the voice of the people. They were elected

1. Dutt, R.C., *India in the Victorian Age*, p.422.

in an indirect manner by the universities, municipalities and chamber of commerce. Besides it, they were ineffective in preventing the Government from doing what it had set mind on. Much against the wish of the people, the Government of India imposed excise duty on cotton goods produced in India to help the British trade interests. The Government paid no heed to Congress demands of the Indianisation of services, reduction of military expenditure or lowering of taxes on the people. Disillusionment was so great that the people began to question the utility of the method of passive resistance. A few Congress Leaders began to feel that a more revolutionary method would yield quicker and greater results. Tilak, Bipin Chandra Pal and Aurobindo Ghosh suggested the methods of constitutional agitation and boycott of foreign goods as a means to achieve their goal of freedom for India.

3. Revivalism of Hinduism. The Moderate group in the Congress (led by Pt. Madan Mohan Malaviya, Gopal Krishna Gokhale, and Surendra Nath Bannerjee) had abiding faith in the British sense of justice and fairplay. They wanted to acquire self-government within the fold of British Commonwealth. They felt grateful to the British rule for the numerous benefits it had conferred on India and hence they were against any cut and dried demand for complete independence. A few of them were so great devotees of European culture and civilisation that they considered the British rule as a boon to India. According to **Sri Surendra Nath Bannerjee:** "England is our political guide and our moral preceptor in the exalted sphere of political duty." In the words of **Sri Pattabhi Sitaramayya:** "*His (Bannerjee's) ideal was to work with unwavering loyalty to the British connections, for the object was not the suppression of the British rule in India but the broadening of its basis, the liberalising of its spirit, the ennobling of its character and placing it on the unchangeable foundations of a nation's affections.*" The Extremists, namely, Lal-Bal-Pal used to laugh at the absurdity of Sri Surendra Nath Bannerjee's philosophy. Bal Gangadhar Tilak, Swamy Dayanand Saraswati, Swamy Vivekanand and Mrs. Annie Besant reminded the people of their glorious past and the superiority of Vedic culture. They also suggested the methods how that could be revived. Their teachings nursed the spirit of virile nationalism in the country. Sri Aurobindo Ghosh declared that *"nationalism is a religion that comes from God"*. He also stated, "Independence in all our movements is the goal of life and Hinduism alone can fulfill this aspirations of ours." In Bengal, the worship of Kali and Durga was revived so as to inspire the people to take to arms against the usurpers of India's birthright of freedom. The Extremist leaders also revived the memories of Maharana Pratap and Shivaji, of Laxmibai and the leaders of 1857. Bankim Chandra's novel *Anandamath* gave the people the inspiring song of *Vande Matram.*

4. Economic exploitation of India. The economic exploitation of India by the European traders and growing poverty of the people also helped the rise of extremism in Indian politics. Unemployement became so acute and disastrous that people lost their faith in moderate and constitutional methods for redressing their grievances. The leaders like Dadabhai Naoroji, Ramesh Chandra Dutta and others through books and speeches came out with their criticism of the cruel economic policy of the Government.

5. Famine. A great famine broke out in India in 1896-97. It affected about 20 million people and seventy thousand square miles in different regions. The Government did nothing to provide relief to the starving millions. The gross indifference of the Government piqued the people so severely that they began to rebuke and curse the rulers openly.

6. Plague. The wounds of famine were still fresh when bubonic plague broke out in Poona. The officials mishandled the situation. Mr. Rand was the Plague Commissioner of Poona. He was criticised strongly by the people, particularly by Sri Bal Gangadhar Tilak in the *Kesari* edited by him. The popular resentment became so strong that Damodar Hari Chapekar shot dead Mr. Rand and his associate. The youngman was hanged and many suspects were brutally punished. Tilak was also arrested and sentenced to 18 months' rigorous imprisonment. The doings of the Bombay Government hurt the people of other parts of India also. Not content with it, Government took recourse to more severe methods of taking revenge. Special police was stationed at Poona to punish the innocent people. Mr Surendra Nath Bannerjee condemed the imprisonment of Bal Gangadhar Tilak and said, *"We regard the quartering of the Punitive Police of Poona as a mistake. We regard the imprisonment of Tilak and the Poona editors as a still greater mistake. A nation is in tears. We are resolved by every constitutional means that may be available to us to assert under the Providence of God, our rights as British subjects, not the least important of which is the inestimable right of personal liberty."*

7. Repressive Policy of Lord Curzon and other Viceroys. During the regime of Lord Lansdowne (1888-94) and Elgin (1894-98) several unpopular measures were enacted to harass the people. While Lord Elgin was the Viceroy of India, a grèat famine broke out. Instead of helping the people, the treasury was emptied in expanding the forces and on holding a splendid Durbar in Delhi. Mr. Lal Mohan Ghosh while delivering the Presidential Address of Indian National congress at Madras in 1903 said, "It cannot be denied that if even half of the vast sum spent in connection with the Delhi Durbar had been made over for the purposes of famine relief, it might have been the means of saving millions of men, women and children from death by starvation. Do you think that any administration in England or France or the United States would have ventured to waste vast sums of money on an empty pageant when famine and pestilence were stalking over the land and Angel of Death was flapping his wings almost within hearing of the light-hearted revelers?"

The events which occurred during the Viceroyalty of Lord Curzon added insult to injury. He was the arch-priest of British imperialilsm. According to him, "The highest ranks of civil employment must, as a rule, be held by Englishmen." In pursuance of his policy, he passed the famous Calcutta Corporation Act, the Official Secrets Act and the Indian Universities Act. By his misdoings he inflamed the public opinion against the British rule. His Frontier Policy and mission to Lhasa also embittered the people. According to him it was God's wish that Englishmen should rule over India, hence he did not care a fig for the sentiments and reactions of the people. In February 1905, Lord Curzon while delivering the Convocation Address of Calcutta University remarked, *"The higher ideal of truth, to a large extent, is a Western conception and that truth took a higher place in the moral codes of the West, before it had been similarly honoured in the East, where craftiness and diplomatic vile have been held in high esteem."* Such an unwarranted remark infuriated the people. When an Indian delegation waited upon the Viceroy to give him a correct picture of Indian character, the latter refused to meet it. The Congress sent a delegation to England to plead the case of India before the British public and statesmen, but to no purpose.

8. Partition of Bengal and Swadeshi Movement. Lord Curzon committed the greatest mistake of his life when he partitioned the Province of Bengal on July 20, 1905. Bengal was a big Province including the whole of Bihar, Orissa and Chhota Nagpur. For the convenience of administration, Partition was quite urgent and useful too. But when Lord Curzon set about partitioning Bengal, he had the sinister motive of creating a Muslim-majority Province and thereby creating a rift between the Hindus and the Muslims.

This is abundantly clear from the speech of Lord Curzon at Dacca on 18th February, 1904, from which the following extract is quoted:

"Will any one here pretend that Dacca is anything but a shadow of its former self? The proposed scheme of partition would make Dacca the Centre and possibly the capital of a new and self-sufficing province which must give to the people of these districts by reason of their numerical strength and their superior culture the prepondering voice in the province so created, which would invest the Mohammadans in Eastern Bengal with a unity which they have not enjoyed since the days of the old Musalman Viceroys and Kings and which would go far to revive the traditions which the historical students assure us once attached to the Kingdom of Eastern Bengal."

There was also the motive of placating the Muhammadans and creating a solid Muhammadan bloc against the Hindus in respect of political view. This is proved by the following extract of a letter from Herbert Risely, dated 13th September, 1904.

"The boundary suggested would bring within the Eastern Province the bulk of the characteristic Muhammadans of Bengal who form 78 per cent of the population in Rajshahi, 50 per cent in Dinajpur, and 48 per cent in Malda. Not only would it give Dacca a central position in relation to the rest of the new Province, but it would tend, in course of time, to confer on that city the special character of provincial capital where Muhammadan interests would be strongly represented it not predominant."[1]

Strongest possible reaction against Partition. The people of Bengal considered partition as an "attack on the growing solidarity of Bengali nationalism" and felt that they had been "humiliated, insulted and tricked." More than two thousand public meetings attended by both Hindus and Muslims, varying in number from 500 to 5,000 and occasionally even 50,000 were held in different parts of Bengal, protesting against the partition. The Indian Press, both in Bengal, and other Provinces, were unanimous in their condemnation of the measure, and even a large section of Anglo-Indian Press, some of which were recognised as semi-official organs, joined in the protest. It is, indeed, difficult to conceive of a more unanimous and persistent opposition to a government measure; there is certainly no precedent in the previous history of British rule in India."[2] The partition was also strongly condemned by some British newspapers.[3] The movement soon spread to other parts of India and was joined by Tilak and other national leaders.

On 16th October, 1905, when the partition was given effect to, Bengal plunged into grief. *"The partition announcement fell like a bombshell," writes Sir Surendra Nath Bannerjee. "We felt that we had been insulted, humiliated and tricked. We felt that it was a deliberate blow aimed at the growing solidarity and self-consciousness of the Bengali-speaking population."*

Ambika Charan Majumdar very justly observed in the Congress in 1908: "If the partition is a settled fact, the unrest in India is also a settled fact, and it is for Lord Morley and the Government of India to decide which should be unsettled to settle the question."[4]

Importance of the Partition of Bengal. It awakened into activity the dormant political consciousness of the people at large and gave a new and definite shape to the spirit of nationalism which had been gathering strength for some time past, but had not yet assumed any clearly recognised form and engaged as a force to reckon with in Indian politics. A great national impulse suddenly brought to the fore what was hitherto hidden and latent, and gave cohesion and vitality to vague and scattered forces. The giant was asleep, and nothing but a rude and violent shake could awaken him. The partition gave that shock to Bengal and whole political life of Bengal was revolutionised, almost over night.[5]

That Bengal's heroic fight made a deep impress upon Indian politics and changed its character was acknowledged by Gokhale in the following eloquent words:

"The tremendous upheaval of popular feeling which has taken place in Bengal in consequence of the partition, will constitute a landmark in the history of our national progress. For the first time since British rule began all sections of the Indian community, without distinction of caste or creed, have been moved, by a common impulse and without the stimulus of external pressure, to act together in offering resistance to a common wrong. A wave of true national consciousness has swept over the Province and at its touch, old barriers have, for the time at any rate, been thrown down, personal

1. Blue Book, Cd 2746 p.203, quoted by C.J. O'Donnel, *The Causes of Discontent in India,* Ch. VI, pp.68ff.
2. Dr. R.C. Majumdar, *History of the Freedom Movement in India,* II, Ch.I.
3. The Times, Manchester Guardian, London Daily News.
4. Similar views were expressed by Mrs. Annie Besant and Surendra Nath Bannerjee in very strong terms. The Congress also passed resolution for the annulment of the partition of Bengal from 1905-1910.
5. Dr. R.C. Majumdar and others, *'Struggle for Freedom'*, History and Culture of Indian People, vol. XI, pp. 59-60.

jealousies have vanished, other controversies have been hushed. Bengal's heroic stand against the oppression of a harsh and uncontrolled bureaucracy has astonished and gratified all India, and her sufferings have not been endured in vain, when they have helped to draw closer all parts of the country in sympathy and in aspiration.....*The most astounding fact of the situation is that the public life of this country has received an accession of strength of great importance, and for this all India owes a deep debt of gratitude to Bengal*"

Lala Lajpat Rai also echoed the same sentiment on the same occasion. "We are", he said, "perfectly justified in.....trying to obtain freedom. I think the people of Bengal ought to be congratulated on being leaders of the march in the way on progress. And if the people of India will just learn that lesson from the people of Bengal, I think the struggle is not hopeless."

The agitators held public meetings and took out processions reciting *Vande Matram*. The Bengal government restored to repressive measures. The people decided to boycott the foreign goods and use *Swadeshi*. The boycott movement was a tremendous success. Bonfire of imported textiles was organised at many places. The police used batons and bullets to suppress it. Sri Gopal Krishna Gokhale went to London and requested the Secretary of State of India to revoke the partition of Bengal. His entreaties, however, fell on the deaf ears of Lord Morley. The policy of the Moderate group in the Congress had failed. Indians lost their faith in the constitutional methods. *Gokhale admitted that, "youngmen are beginning to ask what was the good of the constitutional method, if it was only to end in the Partition of Bengal."* He ultimately changed his attitude and said goodbye to his policy of co-operation with the Government. At Benarus session of the Congress in 1905, he agreed to the cult of *Swadeshi* and boycott of British goods. The prolonged indifference of the Government in regard to Indian public opinion paved way for the growth of extremism and terrorism.

9. Foreign events. Several events that occurred in Europe in later part of the 19th century also inspired the youths of India to work for emancipation of India. The defeat of Italy at the hands of the Abyssinian forces in 1896 and of Russia by the Japanese forces in 1905 also gave a stimulus to Indian nationalism. The victory of the Afro-Asian forces over the Western Powers proved for certain that Britian was not invincible. The new consciousness helped the rise of extremism in India.

10. Split in Surat Congress. The factors mentioned above gave birth to the left wing in the Congress party. There appeared a marked change in the outlook of the moderate group also. Gokhale in his Presidential Address at Benares Session in 1905 condemned the Partition of Bengal and supported Swadeshi movement. Next year the extremist group in the Congress proposed the name of Tilak for Presidentship. The Moderates opposed the move strongly. Ultimately Dadabhai Naoroji was elected to the chair. Under his President, the Extremists succeeded in passing resolution on Swadeshi, boycott of foreign-made goods and promotion of education having a national bias. Calcutta session marked the victory of the Extremist group. Dadabhai Naoroji stated clearly that the objective of the Congress, henceforth, was to acquire Dominion Status on the lines granted to other British Dominions like Canada and New Zealand.

Although the Congress had ratified the extremist proposals at Calcutta session, the Moderates were still not prepared to execute them. Since the talks with the British Government regarding further constitutional reforms were in progress, the Moderates were opposed to any movement whatsoever. When the next Congress met at Surat in 1907, both groups vied with each other to capture the Congress. Tilak made all possible attempts to avoid open conflict by evolving some compromise but he failed. The new constitution of the Congress drafted by Gokhale showed a clear change in the objective of the Congress from what it had accepted the previous year. Tilak was opposed to any sliding back of the Congress. He also agreed to a joint committee to settle the dispute but the moderates adopted uncompromising attitude. When the Congress met on 27th December, 1907, the Moderates proposed the name of Ras Behari Ghosh for the presidentship while the extremists proposed the name of Lala

Lajpat Rai. Lalaji had lately been released from jail. By electing him the President of the Congress, Tilak wanted to demonstrate to the Government the confidence and esteem of the nation enjoyed by Lalaji. Lalaji, however, withdrew his name. The Extremists then pressed for open election but to no effect. The next day Ras Behari Bose occupied the chair. When he got up to deliver his Address, Sri Bal Gangadhar Tilak ascended the platform and demanded that he should be allowed to speak. The request was rejected but Bal Gangadhar Tilak refused to submit to the ruling of the chair. It led to clashes between the two groups and the meeting was adjourned. Pandemonium prevailed on the next day also. The delegates came to blows. The police interfered and the session had to be suspended.

Thus the Surat session ended in a complete rupture between the two wings of the Congress. The Moderates held a separate convention and drafted a new constitution. The Nationalists who were not prepared to go back from the position taken at the Calcutta Congress, were left out completely. Bal Gangadhar Tilak was abused and called a traitor. The Moderate Press wrote: "Tilak had been feeding the flames which have burnt the Congress to ashes. He is not a patriot but a traitor to the country, and has blackened himself. May God save us from such patriots." The Surat fiasco thus divided Congress into two camps–one led by Bal Gangadhar Tilak and the other by Gopal Krishna Gokhale. The new constitution drafted by the Moderates stated that the objective of the Congress was to attain Dominion Status for India in stages by peaceful and constitutional means.

The Government was less afraid of the Moderates than the Extremists. Hence with a vengeance it began to crush the extremist movement. It rendered indirect help to the Moderates by arresting most of the Extremist leaders. *Earlier in 1907 the Government had already arrested Lala Lajpat Rai and Ajit Singh and deported them to Mandalay jail.* In 1908 it passed the Newspapers' Incitement to Offences Act. The new enactment gagged the press. Lokmanya Bal Gangadhar Tilak was sentenced to six years' rigorous imprisonment on the charge of writing inflammatory articles against the Government in his paper *Kesari*. Several leaders and paper-editors of Bengal were also clapped in jail without trial. The Seditious Meetings Act of 1907 gave arbitrary powers to the police to prevent the holding of public meetings. In view of the above-mentioned consequences, Mrs. Annie Besant wrote that Surat split was the most unfortunate in the history of the Congress. One direct outcome of the repressive measures of the Government was the increase in terrorist activities. The exasperated Indian youth turned to violent methods, feeling that 'an ounce of lead can work more wonders than a ton of argument and moral persuasion.' Secret organisations were formed and bomb factories started.

The arrest of Tilak and the trial which followed (July 13-22, 1908) led to mass demonstration and protest meetings throughout the Bombay province. Tilak's supporters started preparing for protest strike in the Bombay factories.

Tilak turned his 21 hours' magnificent speech for his defence into a fiery condemnation of British imperialist policy in India. Tilak's speech had wide-scale repercussion within India and his fame spread beyond the country's borders.

Strong reaction against the imprisonment of Tilak–Growth of the mass struggle, political strike in Bombay. After the sentence against Tilak had been announced, the extremists appealed to the people of Bombay to organise a six-day general strike in protest–one day for each of the years of hard labour to which Tilak had been sentenced. On July 23, 1908 a general political strike began. Workers from all Bombay's factories went on strike, all shops were closed and educational establishments shut their doors. Patriotic slogans were raised and portraits of Tilak sprang everywhere.

Lenin condemns Imprisonment Sentence against Tilak. In his assessment of the historic significance of these events in Bombay, Lenin wrote:

"The infamous sentence pronounced by the British jackals on the Indian democrat Tilak, he was sentenced to a long term of exile, the question in the British House of Commons the other day revealing that the Indian jurors had declared for acquittal and *that the verdict had been passed by the* *vote of the British Jurors......*this revenge against a democrat by the lackeys of the money-bags, evoked street demonstrations and a strike in Bombay. In India too, the proletariat has already developed to conscious political mass struggle–and that being the case, the Russian-style British regime in India is doomed."[1]

The Bombay strike marked the climax of the revolutionary upsurge in the years 1905-1908.

IMPORTANCE OF SWADESHI MOVEMENT

As Swadeshi Movement and boycott of foreign goods had been the main plank of the extremist leaders and later on this programme was also adopted by Mahatma Gandhi and they created mass awakening and prepared the people for future struggle, so it is being given in detail here.

Birth of the Swadeshi Movement. The twin ideas of *Swadeshi* and Boycott, the first spontaneous fruits of the great upsurge of outraged popular feelings in 1905–were largely supplementary, as one could not succeed without the other. The boycott of foreign goods required that their supply should be met by those produced in the country. The *Swadeshi* or promotion of indigenous industry could not succeed when Indian industry was at its nascent stage, unless people deliberately eschewed foreign and purchased native goods even at pecuniary loss and sacrifice of comfort.

Transformation of the Swadeshi into a great national movement: *"The silent* transformation of the Swadeshi movement into a great national movement, which later merged itself into the successful struggle for freedom constituted the first great landmark in the history of India's fight for freedom in the first half of the twentieth century."

"The Swadeshi movement gave a great impetus to nationalism through the nationalist cum patriotic literature which it brought into being. The literacy talents of Arbinda Ghosh blazed forth day after day in the articles in the *Vande Matram.* He not only expounded the religious and philosophical basis of nationalism but also present it as a sublime sentiment in human life. "Love has a place in politics", said he, "but it is the love of one's country."

"If Arbinda was the highest priest, Ravidranath Tagore was the great poet of the Swadeshi Movement. What Arbinda achieved in the real of thought by his fearless writings, Ravindranath conveyed to the masses by his songs, incomparable in diction and imitable in the melody of its time."[2]

The idea which inspired Bankim Chandra to write the *Vande Matram* hymn, was expressed through charming poems and songs by Rabindranath Tagore. He sang the glories of ancient India and its culture and held vividly before the people, the portrait of Shivaji and Guru Govind Singh as nation builders, and of Band a as a symbol of the stoic heroism and spirit of sacrifice displayed by the Sikhs. Many of his ballads touch upon the patriotism, chivalry and heroism of the Rajputs and struggle of the Marathas and Sikhs for freedom. How profoundly they stirred the blood of the young Bengalis in the hectic days of the Swadeshi and prepared them for the great struggle that lay ahead–no words can adequately convey. But Arbinda and Rabindranath proved that the pen is mightier than the sword. To them is mainly due the credit for the fact that the mighty British power failed to subdue the national spirit of the Bengalis.[3]

Importance. It would be hardly an exaggeration to say that the whole atmosphere of Bengal was surcharge by a new literary current which galvanised the whole country. It gave a new meaning to Swadeshi and a formidable impetus to the newly awakened national consciousness of the people. Indeed it may be said without hesitation that such a powerful impact of a great popular movement on contemporary literature and vice-versa is unprecedented in the annals of India, and nothing like this was even seen when Civil Disobedience Movement initiated by Mahatma Gandhi reached its highest

1. V.I. Lenin, *Collected Works,* Vol. 15, p.184.
2. Dr. R.C. Majumdar and others, *Struggle for Freedom',* p.65 (1969).
3. *Ibid.,* p.66

point. Much of this literature has become a permanent asset and will remain standing testimony to the new spirit that convulsed Bengal from one end to the other.[1]

Reference may also be made to remarkable pronouncement by a foreigner on the part that Swadeshi movement of Bengal played in transforming the nationalism of India and making it richer and more comprehensive. Mr.J. Ramasay McDonald who later became the Prime Minister of Britain, wrote in the *Daily Chronicle*:

"The Bengalee inspires the Indian Nationalist movement......but Bengal is perhaps doing better than political agitation. It is idealising India. It is translating nationalism into religion, into music and poetry, into painting and literature...From Bengal gush innumerable freshhets of religion, all flowing to revive and invigorate the nationalist spirit. A literary revival makes for the same end.[2]

According to Mahatma Gandhi, "The Swadeshi movement taught the people to challenge and defy the authority of the Government openly in the public and took away from the minds of even ordinary men the dread of police assault and prison as well as the sense of ignomy which hitherto attached to them. To go to prison or get *lathi*-blows from the police become a badge of honour, and not, as hitherto, a brand of infamy."

Even still more important that the people's readiness to suffer was the public sympathy, openly displayed for the sufferers in the cause of the country. Several public meetings were held to honour the political sufferers.[3]

EXERCISES

Long Answer Type Questions

1. What were the Principles of Moderates?
2. Discuss the achievements of Moderates.
3. Write a brief note on Birth of Extremists Movement. Discuss also the principles of Extremists.
4. What were the differences between Extremists and Moderates?
5. What were the causes of the birth of Extremist Movement?
6. Write a note on Swadeshi Movement. Discuss its importance also.

Short Answer Type Questions

1. Write a brief note on the programme of Indian National Congress from 1885 to 1905.
2. Write a note on the resolutions adopted by the Congress in 1906.
3. What were the Principles of Extremists?
4. Discuss in very brief the differences between Extremists and Moderates.
5. Discuss the difference between Bal Gangadhar Tilak and Gopal Krishna Gokhale.
6. What was the discontent over the reforms of 1892 ?
7. Discuss Revivalism of Hinduism.
8. Write a short note on Partition of Bengal and Swadeshi Movement.
9. What was the importance of the Partition of Bengal?
10. Write a short note on split of Surat Congress.

1. *Ibid.*
2. Modern Review, VIII, pp. 458 ff.
3. Dr. R.C. Majumdar and others, *Freedom Struggle*, p.64, (1969).

Objective Type Questions

Choose the correct answer

1. The Meeting of the Congress in 1885 was proposed to be held firstly at
   (*a*) Poona (*b*) Bombay
   (*c*) Calcutta (*d*) Lahore
2. Who presided the Calcutta Session of the Congress in 1906 ?
   (*a*) Surendra Nath Banerjee (*b*) Dadabhai Naorojee
   (*c*) Lala Lajpat Rai (*d*) Bal Gangadhar Tilak
3. In which year Congress passed the Resolution of Dominion Status ?
   (*a*) 1904 (*b*) 1905
   (*c*) 1906 (*d*) 1907
4. Who was Grand Old Man of India ?
   (*a*) Bal Gangadhar Tilak (*b*) Gopal Krishna Gokhale
   (*c*) Ras Behari Bose (*d*) Dada Bhai Naorojee
5. Who was the President in Varanasi Session of Congress ?
   (*a*) Gopal Krishna Gokhale (*b*) Dada Bhai Naorjee
   (*c*) Bal Gangadhar Tilak (*d*) Ras Behari Bose
6. In which year Benarus Session of Congress was held ?
   (*a*) 1904 (*b*) 1905
   (*c*) 1906 (*d*) 1907
7. Who was leading Leader of Extremist Movement ?
   (*a*) Lala Lajpat Rai (*b*) Bipin Chandra Pal
   (*c*) Bal Gangadhar Tilak (*d*) Pt. Madan Mohan Malviya
8. Who gave the slogan "Freedom is our birth right and we shall have it ?"
   (*a*) Bipin Chandra Pal (*b*) Lala Lajpat Rai
   (*c*) Pt. Madan Mohan Malviya (*d*) Bal Gangadhar Tilak

ANSWERS

1. (*a*) 2. (*b*) 3. (*c*) 4. (*d*) 5. (*a*) 6. (*b*) 7. (*c*) 8. (*d*)

9

CHAPTER

Revolutionary Movement in India and Abroad

> *"The opponents of revolution mistakenly believe that revolution means violence with arms, weapons and such other means. But revolution is not confined to this process. It may be that these are used as instruments but it should not be forgotten that behind them, it is the solid strength and spirit of the revolution and that strength is the will, the aspiration of the people to demand and get a change, a revolution in the current economic structure, the shape and form of Political Government of the nation. Our idea of the revolution has never been simply the bloodshed of some individuals. It is to end the present regime of exploitation of man by man and to secure to our nation absolute right of self-determination. That is the ultimate objective of our idea of revolution."*
>
> *–Sardar Bhagat Singh.*

CAUSES OF THE BIRTH OF REVOLUTIONARY MOVEMENT

We have discussed at length in the preceding chapter how the aggrieved Indians resisted the high handedness of the ruthless rulers through constitutional methods, through petitions and prayers. Surendra Nath Banerjee, Pt. Madan Mohan Malaviya, Gopal Krishna Gokhale, Dadabhai Naoroji and others adopted this course with great optimism but were ultimately disappointed. The Partition of Bengal and famine and plague that raged unchecked in Maharashtra fostered anti-British feelings. Leaders like Bal Gangadhar Tilak, Lala Lajpat Rai and Bipin Chandra Pal were convinced that resolutions alone unless backed by force will not bring India an inch nearer to her goal of freedom. They began to doubt the efficacy of peaceful methods and stressed the need of forceful constitutional agitations. Lala Lajpat Rai and Sardar Ajit Singh launched Peasants' Movement in the Punjab in 1906-07. Bal Gangadhar Tilak revived the memories of Vedic past and persuaded the people to celebrate Shivaji festival and Ganesh festival. In one of his meetings he said:

"We are at present clamouring for *Swaraj* and therefore Shivaji festival is the most fitting one for us to celebrate. If Shivaji was able to establish *Swaraj* two centuries ago, we too may expect to achieve it some day. *Swaraj belongs to us by birth right.... We* are masters of our fortunes and can govern them if we only make up our minds to do so. *Swarajya* is not far off from us. It will come to us the moment we learn to stand on our own legs."

Bal Gangadhar Tilak also sponsored the *Swadeshi* Movement. When the Partition of Bengal took place, the whole country registered her protest. Meetings were organised and processions taken out.

The Government instead of considering the legitimate demands of the people resorted to the policy of blood and iron. It trod under foot the aspirations of the people. Repressive laws were passed and patriots subjected to bestial treatment. The young blood of India, imbued with patriotic sentiments, was left with no alternative but to take recourse to violent methods. 'No freedom without an armed fight' echoed in the mind of every young man.

The Revolutionaries held secret meetings, awakened militant nationalism through personal contacts and organised the fiery young men who preferred death to slavery. They also tried to make in roads into the military camps and to sow seeds of hatred against the British bureaucracy. No sacrifice was too great for them if it helped them in breaking the chain of bondage. Their goal was not to murder the English officers but to end the alien rule by force. They planned to kill an Englishman only when his removal became unavoidable in the interest of the nation. For instance, Mr. Saunders who had rained fatal lathi blows on Lala Rajpat Rai became the target of the Revolutionaries. In the same way Sardar Udham Singh hounded Sir Michael O'Dwyer to England and made him pay the price of Jallianwalah Bagh tragedy by his life. Thus, the Revolutionaries had no intention to create lawlessness in the society but they certainly meant to terrorise and teach the English Officers that they would earn death by resorting to repression. But for the fear of the terrorists, the ruthlessness of the English Officers would have exceeded all limits and the Congress Movement would have been nipped long ago with brute force. The difference between the methods of the Congress Leaders and the Revolutionaries was that whereas the former let their scars fester for long, the latter tried to heal their wounds by throwing bombs on the wrongdoer. Eventually the Government felt the urgency of appeasing the Congress by giving concessions and to isolate the terrorists to be hanged without a word in their defence from the nationalist leaders. These concessions were couched in the Act of 1909.

AIM OF THE REVOLUTIONARY MOVEMENT

The British Authorities and Historians dubbed the Revolutionaries as saboteurs, murderers and bandits. They were justified in their own way because the Goal of the Revolutionaries was to uproot the British Rule. The Revolutionaries no doubt adopted the path of bloodshed but their goal was noble. *They had faith in democracy. Their ideal was to set up the rule of the farmers and workers and to remove all social and economic disparities.* In fact they were neither marauders nor highwaymen but the disbursers of poetic justice to tyrant British Officers. Believe it or not but their activities did serve as eye-openers to the British Imperialilsts. The Revolutionaries retaliated only when their national pride was hurt or when the ladies were insulted. Their plan of action was to infuse patriotic sentiments through articles and inspiring literature, and to instigate the soldiers for an armed revolt. We call them Revolutionaries because their object was to bring about a political and economic revolution in the country. *Their goal was to reconstruct a society based on equality and justice.* They embarked on more perilous course than that adopted by the Moderates or the Extremists. They knew well the penalties for their activities yet they were undaunted and cheerful. They organised guerilla raids on army bases to procure arms and ammunition. Sometimes they smuggled the arms in India from neighboring countries. In doing so they had often to pay the price by their lives. It is the moral duty of free India to pay glorious tributes to her martyrs and there can be no better way of showing our gratitude to them than by recognising their valuable contribution to country's freedom struggle and also to draw inspiration from their dedicated lives. Failing to do so tantamounts to ingratitude on our part and an insult to those fighters who sacrificed their lives like moths of freedom. In the following pages we would recall their heroic deeds one by one.

FREEDOM MOVEMENT OF THE NAMDHARI SIKHS OR THE KOOKAS IN THE PUNJAB

The land of the five rivers where the ancient Aryan sages had evolved the Hindu philosophy of life, and where Guru Nanak preached spiritualism and sacrifice and where Guru Gobind Singh and Banda Bahadur once enkindled the fire of freedom and undaunted heroism was ultimately annexed to the British Empire in 1849 by treachery. The Punjab then fell on evil days. The fall of the native rule brought slavery and sufferings for the freedom-loving sturdy Punjabis. Guru Ram Singh refused to serve the white race and returned to his village Bhaini Sahib near Ludhiana. Inspired by the teachings of Guru Balakji, he founded a new sect with the object of reforming the structure of the society. His followers were called Namdhari Sikhs or Kookas. In due course the religious sect changed in form and character to a political revolutionary organisation. Guru Ram Singh's disciples came to be called Kookas because they raised their kook or voice against the British Rule. Guru Ram Singh advised his followers:–

(1) to abstain from taking meat, drinking wine, committing thefts, telling lies or lending money on interest;

(2) to refrain from killing one's daughters or trading on them or preventing the remarriage of widows;

(3) to say prayers every morning and evening, to protect the cows, to be hospitable to guests and to perform *yajna*; and

(4) to boycott Government job, English dress, courts of law and postal facilities.

He encouraged the use of *Swadeshi* and *Panchayat* system. He ordered his followers to employ letter-carriers and to defy the laws which were unjust. In short, he injected the minds of the people with hatred of the British rule.

Ram Singh set up a sort of parallel administration in the Punjab. He divided the province into twenty-one divisions and appointed a *Panth* officer for every division. Through the divisional officers, he injected the minds of the people with hatred of the British rule. The anti-British propaganda carried on by the Namdharis caused panic in the official circle. The Government waited for an excuse to suppress the movement. With a lifting of ban on cow-slaughter, many slaughter-houses were set up in Amritsar and other towns of the Punjab. It was a severe blow to the religious sentiments of the Hindus. One day in 1869 while some Kookas were proceeding to Amritsar, some butchers crossed them. It led to communal riot. The hasty action of the Kookas provided the much-awaited opportunity to the Government to harass the respectable and innocent people. Ram singh called the guilty followers and advised them to surrender. The guilty persons did accordingly and thus saved others from police atrocities. In 1871 the Kookas were provoked again when one of them was ill-treated and killed by a Muslim. A band of fire brand Kookas raided a slaughter-house in front of Golden Temple, Amritsar on 14th and 15th June, 1871. Many butchers were killed and the cows set free. At the instance of Guru Ram Singh ten persons confessed their guilt. Four of them were hanged, three were sentenced to life imprisonment and three others declared as outlaws. On 15th September, 1871, the four Namdhari Sikhs embraced death cheerfully.

Many Namdharis blown off by the cannons. The persecution of Namdharis at Amritsar, instead of demoralising them, added to their enthusiasm. On January 13, 1872 another band of Namdharis without seeking the permission of Guru Ram Singh stormed the fort of Malodh near Ludhiana and captured a good stock of war materials and horses. The rebels then reached Malerkotla (near Ludhiana) to attack a slaughter-house of the cows. The native Muslim ruler of the state rallied his forces and faced them. The rebels faced the state forces bravely but were unnerved when a British regiment headed by Mr. Caven, Deputy Commissioner of Ludhiana, came to the rescue of the state forces. They were besieged while resting in village Sherpur. Sixty eight Namdharis were captured and dragged like dead cattle to Malerkotla. They were tried by a military court and awarded death punishment. In defiance of the instructions of the Commissioner, the Deputy Commissioner of Ludhiana, Mr. Caven procured troops cannons from the State of Nabha, Patiala and Jind and fastened the prisoners to the cannons. With the thunder of cannon balls, all of them were blown off. It is notable that instead of standing with their backs towards the cannon mouth, they preferred to face death boldly. Thousands of spectators who had been purposely invited to the scene were struck dumb to see the spectacle. In one of the batches was a twelve year old boy. Mr. Caven promised to pardon him if he declared that he was not a follower of Ram Singh. The boy uttered an emphatic 'No' and preferred to share the lot of other convicts. The flesh and bones of so tender a human flower were also torn to pieces. The barbaric act of Mr. Caven was enjoyed by other Englishmen present there as a light comedy but it is such acts that inspired the youth of India to pine and endeavour for freedom.

Thus, the first revolt of the Namdharis was cruelly supressed. All the followers of that sect were declared as outlaws. In 1878 the British Government apprehended that the Kookas were carrying on negotiations with the Czar of Russia and conspiring against the British rule. Guru Ram Singh was arrested and deported to Burma where this great leader of the Punjab expired with a broken heart in 1885. The Government of India put into action its steamroller of oppression. It did all that it could to liquidate the Namdharis but failed. Ideas never die. The Namdharis remained true to the teachings of their Guru. Till the dawn of independence they never ran after Government jobs, nor did they take disputes to law courts. Dr. Rajendra Prasad paid a befitting tribute to the Namdhari patriots in an article. He wrote:" Guru *Ram Singh considered political emancipation as an integral part of religion. Namdhari organisation was quite forceful in its time. In fact Guru Ram Singh by launching non-co-operation movement 'anticipated Gandhiji nearly half a century ago."*

FREEDOM MOVEMENT OF CHAPEKAR BANDHU IN MAHARASHTRA AND SRI SHYAMJI KRISHNA VERMA IN EUROPE

About the year 1894 Chapekar brothers formed a society for the protection of Hinduism. Damodar Chapekar came of a respectable family of priests and preachers. Damodar in the beginning took up his family profession of 'Kirtan' but he was essentially a soldier. He could not get into the army because Brahmins were ineligible for recruitment. His rejection on caste basis pained Damodar so much that he began to nurse hatred against the English administration.

Once on the occasion of Shivaji festival he said: "*Mere recalling the mighty deeds of Shivaji will not deliver the goods. If we want freedom, we shall have to plunge into action like our ideal heroes, Shivaji and Baji Rao. My young friends! The time has come to sharpen our swords in order to behead the enemies. Let us take a pledge to fight till the last breath and die bravely but not without tainting the earth red with English blood. Be not idle, be not a lifeless burden on the country. Be up and doing; be a hero in the strife. Is it not shameful that we call our country Hindustan (the land of Hindus) but let it be ruled over by the Englishmen?"* The speech quoted above indicates the feelings that were seething in his heart.

June 22, 1897 was celebrated all over India as the Diamond Jubilee Day of Queen Victoria's coronations. Grand preparations were afoot in Poona also. These were the days when plague was raging in the city. Mr. Rand, the notorious 'Sultan' as he was called, took over the charge of Poona on 17th February, 1897. He was armed with autocratic powers to deal both with plague and the political workers of the city. Preventive squads were formed to remove the dead, the dying and the diseased from every house in the city. But activities of the Plague Commissioner did not stop here. He ordered the removal of all the plague-affected persons to segregation camps which were "little hells". The preventive measures adopted by Rand and his associate Mr. Ayerest became hot subjects of bitter criticism. On the Diamond Jubilee Day when Rand and associates were returning from the Government house in separate carriages, they were shot dead by Damodar Chapekar. Chapekar along with a few others was sent to gallows.

Before being hanged Damodar in a statement admitted that there was a plot on foot to overthrow the alien rule and to kill the maximum number of Englishmen. The Government suspected the hand of Sri Shyamji Krishna Verma in the death of Mr. Rand. Shyamji was a great Sanskrit scholar. He had also been the Dewan of Udaipur and Junagarh States. He was a staunch protagonist of Hindu culture and civilization. He was so much harassed by the Government of India that he sailed out to England. He delivered a few lectures at Oxford University and impressed by his profound learning even scholars like Monier Williams. Shyamji Verma in England took to business and earned fortune. He was a staunch nationalist. He began to spend his money lavishly in helping the cause of his country's freedom. He offered scholarships to Indian students to proceed to England and carry on revolutionary activities. He laid the foundation of India House which in course of time became the meeting place of Indian revolutionaries. It was at India House where revolutionaries like Veer Savarkar, Madan Lal Dhingra, Sardar Singh Rana and others, used to assemble and formulate plans. Shyamji Verma was the brain behind all the revolutionary activities in London. In a way Shyamji Verma was the first man to initiate and fight India's war of independence from outside India. In January,1905, he started a journal *'Sociologist'* to propagate his views. His articles published in the *'Sociologist'* used to be stimulating and challenging. His anti-British propaganda could not escape the vigilant eyes of the British Government. When his stay in England became insecure, Shyamji Verma slunk off to Paris. Before his departure he handed over the charge of India House to Veer Savarkar. In 1909, he made arrangements for bringing out *Bande Mataram* with the co-operation of Lala Har Dayal. When Savarkar was arrested in London, he made all possible efforts to help him in escaping from police custody. During the First World War (1914-18) when the French authorities began to harass him, he left Paris for Geneva where he died on March 30, 1930. The meritorious services of Vermaji in enkindling the fire of patriotism in the hearts of Indians, settled in Western Countries can never be belittled or forgotten.

VINAYAK DAMODAR SAVARKAR'S FREEDOM STRUGGLE IN INDIA AND LONDON

Vinayak Savarkar, the first champion of Hindu nationhood in modern times, was born in 1883. His elder brother Ganesh was four years elder to him, while Narayan was five years younger than he. All the three brothers underwent hair-raising hardships for their country's sake. Vinayak Damodar Savarkar was a young boy when Chapekar was hanged. The thrilling episode of Chapekar's martyrdom impressed him so profoundly that he swore before his family deity: *"I will raise the banner of an armed revolution to achieve the freedom of my Motherland till i die fighting the enemy. I will spare no breath in performing this sacred pledge."* And truly he kept his word. Two persons had their share in shaping his character and ideology–one was his father and the other his National Guru Lokmanya Bal Gangadhar Tilak. In 1900 he started an association which was called *'Mitra-mela'*. The members of this group were those fire-band youngmen who were prepared to dedicate their lives for the sake of their Motherland. In 1904 he changed the name of his Friends' Club into *Abhinava-Bharat.* This students' organisation enabled him to carry his message of revolution to a chain of educational institutions. The pledge that every member of Abhinava Bharat had to take was: *"In the sacred name of Chhatrapati Shivaji, in the name of my sacred religion, for the sake of my beloved country, involving my forefathers, I swear that my nation will be prosperous only after freedom, full freedom is achieved. Convinced of this, I dedicate all my health, wealth and talents for the freedom of my country and for her total uplift. I will not spare myself or slacken in this mission. I will never disclose anything about the organisation."* Savarkar maintained strict secrecy about the activities of his organisation. This society celebrated Shivaji anniversaries and Ganesh festivals and organised study circles and lectures to infuse the spirit of patriotism in young hearts.

The partition of Bengal in 1905 gave birth to the double movement of Swadeshi and boycott. The movement had the blessings of Sri Tilak, Savarkar being an ardent admirer of Tilak, also staged a bonfire of English clothes in Poona. The *Holi* of English clothes set ablaze the popular discontentment with the British administration. Bonfire of foreign goods in public places created commotion in the country. The attention of the authorities was drawn to the activities of Savarkar who had played a leading role in conducting *Swadeshi* Movement in Maharashtra. The Bombay University debarred him from taking university examination for one year.

With the recommendation of Bal Gangadhar Tilak, Veer Savarkar secured the Shivaji scholarship sponsored by Shyamji Verma and he proceeded to England for the study of law. Before leaving the shores of India, he addressed the meeting of *Abhinava-Bharat* and said: "My sphere of work till now has been Ferguson College, Poona, and only limited circle of Maharashtra youth. During my stay in England, I shall communicate my views to intelligent and rich Indian students prosecuting their studies there. I shall awaken their conscience and I am sure that on their return to India as Barristers, they would bring about a revolution in the country. I hope to measure swords with my enemy in his den. From Russian revolutionaries I shall learn how to make bombs and pistols. And then freedom will dawn over our country before long."

Veer Sarvarkar in London. Sarvarkar on his arrival in London was received by Shyamji Verma. Shyamji Verma bestowed his affection on him as a father. Veer Savarkar stayed in India House and began to inject revolutionary feelings in the minds of other boarders. India House soon turned into a stronghold of revolutionary activities. Other Indian students who were given to pleasures and times were attracted towards Savarkar by his magnetic personality and penetrating intellect. It was at this time that Lala Hardayal came in contact with Savarkar. He was a Punjabi youth who had gone to England for higher studies. But his meeting with Savarkar revolutionaised his thoughts and way of living. He gave up English education and abandoned English dress too. Shri Balshastri Hardas observes: "Savarkar and Hardayal, the twin angles of revolution, created a spirtied atmosphere in the Indian circles in England. India House became a busy cell of revolutionary activity. The tunes of *Vande Matram* began to resound in the city of London and annoy the British Government." By the end of 1906, Savarkar completed his book '*Joseph Mazzini–Biography and Politics.*' It was published in India and had a quick response.

In 1907 the British Government decided to celebrate the 50th year of suppression of uprising in 1857. As a protest against it, Veer Savarkar planned to arrange a grand festival in commemoration of the 50th anniversary of the First War of Indian Independence on May 8, 1908, at India House. On this sacred occasion he revealed the true nature of the great uprising of 1857 which hitherto was abused as Sepoy Mutiny. He also wrote a book in this connection entitled "*Indian War of Independence.*" The book was originally written in Marathi and translated into English later on. When the British Government got the scent of this book, it made no delay in proscribing it. Savarkar was confronted with the uphill task of how to get it published. He strove hard without success to arrange for its publication in any other European country. Ultimately the book was published in Holland but was soon forfeited by the British Government. *Abhinava Bharat,* the organisation started by Savarkar in India, did admirable work in Europe. Lala Hardayal, Shyamji Verma and others went to France and Russia as the emissaries of India's freedom. This organisation also published a paper *"Vande Matram"* from Paris to air India's demand for freedom.

While Veer Savarkar was enthusing Indian hearts in Europe, his elder brother Ganesh was doing the same in India. He wrote several poems exhorting the fire of patriotism. At the instignation of Sir Curzon Willie, Mr. Jackson, the Collector of Nasik, arrested Ganesh on the hollow excuse of possessing seditious poems and spreading hatred against the British rule. For this petty and ungrounded suspicion, Ganesh was sentenced to life imprisonment and transportation on June 8, 1908. When Savarkar received this news in London, he resolved to take revenge. The members of *Abhinava Bharat* took a unanimous decision to murder Mr. Jackson and Curzon Willie.

Madan Lal Dhingra hanged. The young man who took upon himself the dangerous task of killing Curzon Willie was Madan Lal Dhingra. A chit recovered from his pocket when he was arrested, stated the reason why he agreed to do it. Its first paragraph was as follows: "I attempted to shed English blood intentionally and with purpose as an humble protest against the inhuman transportation and hangings of Indian youths."

Curzon Willie was the person who dictated the British policies concerning India. He had also laid a ring of spies round the India House to watch the activities of Indian students. He had a hand in the deportation of Ganesh Savarkar. So at the instance of Savarkar, Sir Curzon Willie was shot dead on July 1, 1909, by Madan Lal Dhingra. Dhingra was presented before the court on July 20, 1909. He refused to engage defence counsel. He requested that the statement recovered by police from his pocket should be read out in the court. But when the authorities refused to produce that statement, he made another statement which reads as follows:

"I admit, the other day I attempted to shed English blood as an humble revenge for the inhuman happenings and deportations of the Indian patriotic youths. And his I have consulted with none but by own conscience. I have conspired with none but with my own duty. I believe that a nation held in bondage with the help of bayonets, is in a state of perpetual war and since the guns are denied to me, I drew forth my pistol and attacked by surprise. What could a son poor in wealth and intellect like me offer to the Motherland except my own blood! My only prayer to god is that I may again return to the same Mother and die in the same cause till the Motherland is freed for the service of humanity and glory of God. *Vande Mataram.*"

Madan Lal was sentenced to death and hanged on August 16, 1909. Even after his death, his face betrayed no sign of regret or grief.

Nasik Conspiracy Case. The unjustifiable punishment meted out to Ganesh Savarkar was avenged in London by the murder of Curzon Willie. It had its effect on India also. Jackson, the Collector of Nasik, was fully responsible for the conviction and transportation of Shri Ganesh Savarkar. *'Abhinava-Bharat'* after serious deliberations planned to take revenge on Jackson. The work was entrusted to a handsome art student, Anant Laxman Kanhere. While Jackson was proceeding to take his chair in a function, Kanhere came before him and fired seven rounds at him. Jackson died on the spot. Kanhere was arrested and brought to trial. In his statement he confessed: "I have performed my part. Ganesh Damodar Savarkar is being sentenced to transportation for life in your administration whereas your Executive Engineer, Mr. Williams, who caused the death of an Indian cartman, is being rewarded with life. It is for this that I have killed Jackson. I have no desire to run away."

Unfortunately the Nasik Branch of *Abhinava Bharat* had a traitor in it. One of its members Ganu Vaidya divulged the plan behind the murder to the police. The Government was bent on hanging all the revolutionaries. Acting on the information supplied by Vaidya, the police rounded up 37 youths. Three of them were hanged and the rest sentenced to varying terms of imprisonment. The whole affair was given the name of 'Nasik Conspiracy Case'.

Arrest and conviction of Veer Savarkar. Savarkar received, while he was in Paris, the shocking news of the hangings and imprisonment of his friends. Since the murder of Curzon Willie, he was being apprehended by London police. For the sake of his security, he had to migrate to Paris. The news stunned him and he became restless to return to London and resume his work. Shyamji Verma, Lala Hardayal and Madame Cama–all dissuaded him from taking risk. They argued that he being the soul of the organisation should act more cautiously and not let himself fall into the hands of Scotland Yard. Savarkar, however, had no rest. He cursed himself for strolling in Paris-gardens-when many of his friends and brothers were rotting in prisons. He said: "It is a different matter whether I am a leader or not–that has yet to be established! But when my friends are undergoing such hardships, how can I rest and lag behind. I must also share in their miseries–then only our mission will be accomplished. I must go where my friends and relatives are being tortured–I must join them." Driven by his lofty sentiments he went to London where he was arrested on 13th March, 1910.

Veer Savarkar, apprehending his death to be near, wrote in a letter to his brother's wife: *"We had taken a solemn pedge to free our country from political slavery. We are proud to lay down our lives one by one to attain our goal. It is a great day for me–the day of the fruition of all my aspirations. I am extremely glad that I have done my bit to free my Motherland from the shackles of bondage. Oh my Motherland! I have already offered at your feet my brother and sister. Here I am ready to offer my body. Thanked be they who have dedicated their lives to the service of the nation. Dear sister-in-law, entertain such thoughts and hold on to your pledge and add lustrè to the fair name of the family."*

The Government implicated Savarkar in Nasik Conspiracy Case. Orders were issued for his removal to India. His friends made last minute efforts to get him out of jail but failed. Even the legal question whether a person can be officially taken to India for an offence committed in England was also not admitted. Savarkar, under heavy guards, boarded a ship bound for India. When the ship touched the port of Marseilles, Savarkar through the pothole in the lavatory, leapt out in the ocean. The guards broke open the door and were startled to find that the bird had flown out of the cage. The British officers opened fire on the swimming lion but failed to hit him. Savarkar ran into the french harbour town with the British officers chasing him. He handed himself over to the charge of a French policeman and requested to produce him before a Magistrate. The English officers also reached there. They silenced the Policeman with gold coins and dragged Savarkar back to the ship. In fact arresting a person on French soil was in contravention of International Law. Shyamji Verma on this point moved the International Court at Hague but the Judges in mockery of justice gave decision in favour of the British Government. At Nasik Savarkar was produced before the Sessions Court. *On 22nd March, 1911, he was sentenced to 50 years' imprisonment and transportation. He was sent to Andamans at the age of 28 and there was little hope of his returning safely after completion his term of fifty years.* When the jailor feeling exclaimed, "O God! fifty years," Savarkar replied in a cool and confident tone: "Why worry! Fifty years! Is the British rule going to survive these fifty years."

In his prison cell in Andamans, Savarkar was subjected to inhuman tortures. Bhai Parmanand after his release from Andamans in 1920 returned to Lahore. Incidentally a British M.P. was staying with Lala Lajpat Rai in those days. Parmanand requested the honourable member of the British Parliament to use his good offices for the release of Savarkar. As a result of the latter's efforts, both Savarkar and his brother Ganesh were allowed to enjoy each other's company. Ganesh was sent to Alipur jail and Savarkar to Ratnagiri jail. In 1937 when the Congress Ministry was formed in Bombay, it secured Savarkar's release. Words fail to express what he felt on receiving his release orders after a period of 26 years in British jail. In 1937 Hindu Mahasabha honoured him by electing him its President at Ahmedabad session. Even after his release Savarkar's political activities did not abate. Nation is certainly proud of this great hero, the prophet of freedom who served his country most excellently till his death on February 28, 1966. His dedicated life will continue to be a souce of greatest inspiration to the budding youths of this country for ever.

SARDAR SINGH RANA AND MADAME CAMA'S REVOLUTIONARY ACTIVITIES IN EUROPE

Shyamji Verma in his paper '*Sociologist*' wrote in 1907: "When Natu Brothers were arrested in 1897 and Lokmanya Bal Gangadhar Tilak was also convicted, I was convinced that there is no such thing as freedom of the individuals or the Press in British India. The British pretension of justice is a mere hoax. In my opinion no political organisation in India can work openly. It is bound to carry on its activities secretly. The only course open for the overthrow of the British yoke is to adopt the ways of Russian Nihilists. No one can say for certain what methods we may have to adopt under changing circumstances. That will be determined by the exigency of the situation." Such were the reasons which compelled Indian revolutionaries to take to the cult of bombs. While Shyamji was spreading his views among Indian students in London, a young man Sardar Singh Rana was introduced to him. Rana and one Madame Cama proved great helping hands to Shyamji in producing revolutonary literature.

Sardar Singh Rana had been closely associated with the editing of papers like *Vande Matram, Talwar and Indian Freedom.* He also supplied the money when the revolutionaries sent Sri Hem Chandra to Russia to learn the technique of making bombs. In 1920 he smuggled twenty automic shining pistols and bullets into India. One of these bullets was used in killing Jackson. During the First Great War he was transported to a remote island from where he was released at the end of war.

Madame Cama was also a force to reckon with in the revolutionary set-up in Europe. For thirty years she devoted her energies to carrying message of revolution to Indian youths in England and France. Both Rana and Madame Cama attended the International Socialist Conference held in Germany in 1907, as Indian representatives. Madame Cama unfurled the national flag of India and in a resolution urged all the freedom-loving nations of the world to lend their help to Indian patriots in their glorious effort to overthrow the foreign yoke. She told the delegates that the continuance of British rule in India was certainly injurious and harmful to the supreme interest of India. In a conference of Indian nationalists held in Caxton Hall, London, on December 20, 1908, and attended by Lala Lajpat Rai and Bipin Chandra Pal, she was arrested and deported to an island for four years. She returned to India in 1934 and died two years later. Another name which must also be mentioned alongwith Vermaji, Rana and Madame Cama was Virendra Chattopadhyaya, the brother of Sarojini Naidu. He had also been an active enthusiastic member of Vermaji's group.

REVOLUTIONARY MOVEMENT IN BENGAL (ARVIND GHOSH VIRENDRA KUMAR GHOSH, UPENDRA, ETC.)

We have already described how Lord Curzon by his Universities Act, outrageous Convocation address of Calcutta University and Partition of Bengal had roused the indignation of not only the Bengali-speaking section but all the people of India. The people of Bengal through demonstrations and public meetings ventilated their injured feelings. Tilak, Gokhale and Lala Lajpat Rai also shared and sympathised with the feelings of the agitators. The leaders of this movement in Bengal were Surendra Nath Banerjee, Bipin Chandra Pal, Arvind Ghosh, Upendra Nath and Virendra Ghosh. for Yogi Arvind to achieve independence of India was the commandment of the Lord. Virendra also lived the life of a sannyasi with a passion for freedom of his country. In 1906 Virendra and Bhupendra Dutta, the younger brother of Vivekanand, brought out and edited a paper '*Yugantar*'. The paper served as a powerful vehicle of revolutionary propoganda. The number of its subscribers was over 20,000. In addition to *'Yugantar'*, there were *'Vande Matram'*, *'Sandhya'*, *'Nav-shakti'*, *'New India'* which also fanned the flames of revolution. '*Vande Matram*' was edited by Arvind Ghosh, and *'New India'* by Bipin Chandra Pal. Virendra who had founded *'Yugantar'* called upon the youths of Bengal to resist the repressive policy of the British administration and to offer their blood as price for freedom. He also organised a revolutionary party *'Anushilan Samiti'*, *'Abhinava Bharat'* with 500 branches all over the Province. One of his friends Hem Chandra Das as a member of *'Anushilan Samiti'* went to Russia to get the formula of and practical lessons in the manufacture of bombs.

The Government of Bengal resolved to nip the new organisation *'Anushilan Samiti'* in its early stages. The Samiti then could not but become a secret organisation. When the British officers began to harass the revolutionaries, the latter decided to punish them. They made an attempt to blow off the special train carrying the Governor of Bengal. On December 6, 1907, the bomb exploded on the rail tracks and the train was derailed but the Governor escaped narrowly. On 23rd December, 1907, a Magistrate of Dacca was shot dead at Faridpur station. The next target of public fury was Mr. Kingsford. As a Magistrate posted in Calcutta he had earned notoriety for awarding long-term sentences to the revolutionaries. He got the wind that his life was unsafe in Calcutta. He managed for his transfer to Muzaffarpur (Bihar). The Samiti deputed Khudiram Bose and Prafulla Chaki to deal with him. The daring youths threw a bomb on a carriage which they thought belonged to Kingsford. Unfortunately the occupants of the carriage were two English ladies who died on the spot. Prafull Chandra Chaki killed himself with his own revolver. But Khudiram Bose, barely fifteen at the time, was arrested and hanged on 11th August, 1908.

ALIPUR CONSPIRACY CASE

Many revolutionaries of Bengal convicted. The revolutionaries ran a bomb factory in Calcutta. The police got the clue of it. It raided the factory and recovered several live bombs, explosive materials and certain letters. This was called Alipur Conspiracy Case. Virendra Ghosh, Ulhas Dutta, Hem Chandra Das, Upendra Banerji and several others were implicated and convicted in this case. Virendra in his statement before the Magistrate said: "My aim all through had been to work like a missionary to expand and strengthen India's efforts for freedom. I visited almost all the districts of Bengal and organised *'Akharas'*. My personal observation told me that purely political awakening will not be sufficient. Peoples need some spiritual training also to be able to brave the dangers boldly. By the time this realisation came to me, Swadeshi movement was already in full swing. Hence I started the '*Yugantar*' and began to organise the youths. I and my colleagues have never had any doubts that revolution was inevitable and so we set about collecting arms and ammunition. Ulhas Dutta and Hemchandra enabled us to manufacture bombs. We knew it for certain that political murders here and there will not procure freedom for us, but we restored to shed British blood now and then to keep the spirit of freedom alive."

BOMB THROWN ON LORD HARDINGE BY RASH BEHARI BOSE

The activities of the revolutionaries all over India and particularly in Bengal terrorised the British administration. The atmosphere of Bengal was replete with tension and insecurity for the British officers. In spite of the repressive measures used by the Government, the activities of the revolutionaries did not slacken. The annulment of the Partition of Bengal by His Majesty George V in the Durbar held on December 12, 1911 also failed to cool down the fire raging all over the country. So Lord Hardinge soon after taking over the charge of the Viceroy of India, decided to shift the capital of country from Calcutta to Delhi. when the viceroy triumphantly entered the historic city of Delhi, a huge ceremonial procession was taken out to impress the Indian subjects. Lord Hardinge sat proudly on an elephant. As the procession pased through the crowded bazar of Chandni chowk on December 23, 1912, suddenly a bomb exploded as if to crack the shell of Viceroy's vanity. The bomb missed the target narrowly. It not only injured the Viceroy but killed his A.D.C. The bomb had been thrown by a great patriot and revolutionary leader Rash Behari Bose. In the commotion and panic created by the explosion, Rash Behari slipped away quietly. Shri Manmatha Nath observes in his monumental work "*History of Revolutionary Movement*" that with the daring feat of Rash Behari, the frustrated Indians once again regained the confidence that their motherland was not devoid of valiant souls.

The Government resolved to trace every link in the conspiracy.The Central Intelligence spared no pains to round up the conspirators. But the bomb affair had been planned so well that not the slightest clue could be discovered. A reward of ₹ 7,500 was announced for the arrest of Rash Behari Bose. The C.I.D. chased Rash Behari from place to place but every time he escaped. In 1915 he chalked out a grand plan for staging an armed revolution in India but unfortunately his scheme failed because of betrayal by a blacksheep Kripal singh. The revolutionary organisation then requested him to proceed to Japan wherefrom to direct the revolutionary activities in India. Under fictious name he went away with Ravindra Nath Tagore to Japan and organised Indian Independence League and became adviser to Subhas Bose regarding I.N.A. This great captain of Indian revolution died on 21 January, 1945, with his soul still pining for the freedom of his country.

DELHI CONSPIRACY CASE

Master Amir Chand and others were hanged. The capital police strained every nerve to unearth the conspiracy behind the incident of bomb explosion aimed at killing Lord Hardinge. The police arrested thirteen persons in this connection including Master Amir Chand, his adopted son Sultan Chand, Dinanath, Avadhbehari, Bhai Balmukand, Basant Kumar, Hanumant Sahai, Vasant Kumar Biswas and Balraj Bhalla. Bhalla and Hanumant Sahai were sentenced to seven years' term.

Four of them were sentenced to be hanged. The police appllied third-class methods to get a confession from Dinanath. Dinanath succumbed to police tortures and turned an approver. In the course of the trial held in March 1914, the police produced in the court a letter written by Amir Chand. It said: "*Constitutional struggle and agitations have borne no fruit. The only effective and unfailing means to liberate our country is that of armed revolution. History testifies to the fact that the rulers never offer independence on a silver platter, they surrender it to the threat of sword.* Master Amir Chand was a school teacher. He was a pillar of courage and national pride. He created a cell of revolutionary youths from amongst his pupils. Avadhbehari was his student and younger to him by twenty years. Bhai Balmukand was a distant relative of Bhai Parmanad. Both were the descendants of Bhai Mati Ram who during the reign of Aurangzeb had courted death for refusing to embrace Islam. A little before Avadhbehari was to be hanged, an Englishman asked him to tell his last wish. "The end of the British rule," came the quick reply from him. The Englishman advised him to die peacefully whereupon Avadhbehari snapped : "Peace? I wish that a conflagration may break out in the country gutting the British rule, the band of revolutionaries and also our abject servility. Let my country emerge out of this fire like pure gold."

REVOLUTIONARY ACTIVITIES DURING FIRST GREAT WAR

First Great War broke out in Europe on 4th August, 1914. While the British Government was already preoccupied and vexed with the German aggression in Europe, the revolutionaries decided to capitalise the occasion in their own interest. They had been well grounded in the principle that England's difficulty was India's opportunity. Hundreds of persons with the burning zeal for their country, returned to India from abroad. Rash Behari Bose, Schindra Sanyal, Ganesh Pingale and *Bagi* Kartar Singh prepared a master plan to stage a countrywide revolution on February 21, 1915. Bomb factories were opened in Amritsar, Ludhiana, Zabewal, etc. It was arranged to infiltrate and sprinkle revolutionaries in almost all the military camps and bases, particularly those at Lahore, Meerut and Benares. Understanding was reached with the Indian troops. Villages of Punjab were also willing to join in the uprising. The organisation fell short of finances. A batch of 15 revolutionaries raided the treasury of Moga sub-division in the Punjab. In a serious encounter with the police, two revolutionaries were killed and seven arrested. All the seven were hanged on the gallows. Still there was not to be any alteration in the original plan of opening '*Gadar*' in India from Lahore to Dacca on the appointed day. 21st February, 1915 was fixed for an organised mutiny in line with that of 1857.

The scheme worked well. There was no flaw anywhere. But the destiny willed it otherwise. One Kripal Singh who had got into the organisation as a British agent, passed on the secrets to the Punjab police. His treachery toppled down the whole scheme. All was lost. The police raided several houses and recovered bombs and many secret papers. All the revolutionary leaders of Punjab fell into the hands of the police. Warning signals were sent to all the military bases to resist any eventuality or uprising. Several platons were disbanded on suspicion of being in league with the revolutionaries. Rash Behari, Ganesh Pingle and Kartar Singh, however, escaped the police swoop. Rash Behari returned to Benares, Pingale despite the leader's advice got down at Meerut and Kartar Singh also slipped out of Punjab.

Vishu Ganesh Pingle was a promising young man. While the police was combing the country for the arrest of all the suspects, Pingle at Meerut stayed with a Muslim Inspector. The Inspector was a British agent who feigned to be a revolutionary. He duped Pingale and got him arrested. November 16, 1915 was the day fixed for his execution. When asked about his last wish he only desired to say his last prayer. With his hands folded, he said, "O God! May the task left incomplete by me be executed by You. *My only wish is that my country may be free.*" After saying his prayer, he let the nose fall round his neck and tighten till his soul left his mortal cage.

Kartar Singh Saraba and his companions were brought to dock by the Punjab police. The case was named First Lahore Conspiracy Case. Twenty four persons including Kartar Singh, Jagat Singh, Bhai Parmanand, Man Singh and Udham Singh were awarded death punishment, while many others were transported for life. The judgement was pronounced on 13th December, 1916. The death sentence of Bhai Parmanand was later on commuted to life imprisonment. The Chief Justice was inclined to commute the death sentence in the case of Kartar Singh also to life imprisonment but Kartar Singh deposed, *"I prefer gallows to life sentence. I wish I were born again to unfetter my Motherland. I shall be glad to be hanged every time I am reborn till my country achieves independence."*

Bhai Parmanand, referred to above, also figured prominently in Lahore Conspiracy Case. He too was a prophet of revolution. The British Government considered him to be the most dangerous of the leaders who directed the movement. His reservedness was more baffling to the Government than the talkativeness of Hardayal. For some time he had been on the Staff of D.A.V. College, Lahore. He then went to Africa as a missionary to propagate the ideology of Arya Samaj and came in contact with Mahatma Gandhi. On his visit to London, he came under the spell of Shyamji Krishna Verma. When in 1908 Lala Lajpat Rai and Sardar Ajit Singh were deported to Burma, Bhai Parmanand addressed several protest meetings in London. He sailed back to India and associated himself with the revolutionary activities. He gave shelter to Sardar Ajit Singh and Kishan Singh (uncle and father of Sardar Bhagat Singh) when the police were after them. The police raided his house and seized many relevant papers. Bhai Parmanand was also taken into custody but was soon released for want of evidence against him. In 1915 he was implicated in Lahore Conspiracy Case. The prosecution alleged him to be member of the Gadar Party formed by Lala Hardayal in America. He was also considered to be the leader of Delhi and Lahore conspiracy cases. He was deported to Andaman where alongwith Veer Savarkar he was subjected to monstrous tortures. He was released in 1924. Since his release up to his death (shortly after the partition of India), he dedicated himself to constructive work for attaining freedom.

INDIAN FREEDOM MOVEMENT IN FOREIGN COUNTRIES – KOMAGATA MARU AND GADAR PARTY

Indians living abroad also made no mean contribution to the cause of India's independence. In the foregoing pages we have already reviewed the activities of Shyamji Krishna Verma and other members of '*Abhinava Bharat*' in England, France, Germany and Switzerland. Bhai Parmanand held aloft the torch of revolution in America and England. Lala Hardayal, another veteran revolutionary, blazed new fire in Indian hearts in the American continent. He was a profound philosopher and a powerful orator. On 10th May, 1913, he called a big rally of revolutionary workers in a town in California. By his eloquence he moved the hearts of the audience to action and filled them with indomitable desire to fight. He started an independent Press and brought out a paper named *Gadar.* It was published in English, Hindi, Urdu, Bengali, Marathi and Gurumukhi. English edition which was of course the most significant one was edited by Lala Hardayal himself. The paper unreservedly exposed the misdoings of the British bureaucracy and also explained the object of the Gadar Movement. The paper was known for its exciting articles. He was sent to all the countries where Indians lived. Demand for this paper was fairly high in China, Japan, Singapore, Germany and Canada. Rash Behari at this time was carrying on his activities in Japan.

Now we will relate the incident of Komagata Maru and the plight of Indian occupants of this ship. In 1913 there lived nearly 4,000 Indians in a colony in Canada. Majority of them were Sikhs. The Canadian Government was unhappy with the increasing number of Indian settlers in Canada. It harassed the immigrants and planned to shift all of them to Hondurus Inland which was known for its unhealthy climate. There being no burning ghats, the Indians were made to bury the dead, instead of consecrating them to the holy fire according to Hindu rites. In order to arrest the inflow of Indians, the Canadian Government passed an Immigration Act which permitted only those Indians to land in Canada who were direct passengers from Calcutta. Unfortunately no passenger ship in those days sailed directly for Canada from any Indian port. Indians had-to board a Canada-bound ship either from Hong Kong or Shanghai.

The new Act put Indian passengers to much inconvenience. Baba Gurdut Singh, a man of affluent means and a contractor of repute, came to the rescue of Indians stranded in Hong Kong. In 1910 he floated a shipping company under the name of Guru Nanak Navigation Company and hired a Japanese ship *Komagata Maru.* The ship reached Calcutta and accommodated nearly five hundred passengers. It reached the Port of Vancouver on 22nd May, 1914. These people did not come under the restraints of the Canadian Act. But in violation of their own Act, the authorities neither allowed the ship to go to the harbour nor allowed the passengers to land on the shore. The ship was not allowed even to unload the goods which were meant for the port. Telegrams were sent to Government of India, George V, Maharaja of Patiala and other important personalities to use their good offices to resolve the matter but all was to no purpose. When Baba Gurdut Singh insisted on taking his ship to the harbour, the Canadian police came upon to punish him. The passengers were in a miserable plight. They had neither food nor water. Many of them were sick and needed immediate medical attention. Canadian Government, instead of giving them any medical aid, ordered the police force to throw boiling water on the hungry and afflicted passengers. The desperate occupants of the ship got up in self-defence and repelled the police attack by hurling live coal on them. The Canadian Government then sent two warships to sink the vessel. There was no alternative left except to turn and sail back to India.

Komagata Maru after two months of stay in Canadian water started on its return voyage on 23rd July. Its miseries were, however, not over. It was not allowed to touch any British port, which meant that it could neither disembark the passengers nor procure food and water for them. The British Government, it was obvious, had so conspired that the passengers of the ship might either be drowned in the sea or die of starvation and diseases. Hong Kong and Singapore–both were British colonies–but at none of the two was the ship offered any berth or facilities to refuel and procure provisions. The ship at last reached Budge Budge harbour about 17 miles from Calcutta, on 26th September, 1914. The Government had already got the smell to the revolutionary leanings of the occupants of the ship. The authorities knew well that Baba Gurdut Singh, a revolutionary himself had supplied the copies of *'Gadar'* to the passengers. A special train was kept waiting to carry the persons under heavy police guards. When passengers refused to get into the train, they were forcibly dragged out and pushed into the train. It led to an armed resistence by the passengers who used American revolvers. 18 Sikhs fell down dead and many were wounded. Baba Gurdut Singh also received injuries but he escaped and went underground. The authorities even announced a reward for his arrest but got no clue about him.

When the Indians in Canada received the news of the harassment and tragic end of many of their kith and kin, they wer rudely shocked and distressed. Bhai Bhag Singh and Bhai Vatan Singh led an agitation against the unjust act of the Canadian government. The Sikh settlers in Canada sought the help of Gadar Party to rouse public sentiments against the Government. The Chief of the immigration section of Canada was one Mr. Hopkins. He employed a Sikh Bela Singh to shoot down treacherouosly both Bhag Singh and Vatan Singh. The insult could not be brooked by the compatriots of the victims. One Sri Mewa Singh killed Hopkins in the open court and thus wreaked revenge.

The incident of Komagata Maru brought the British Government into bad reputation. Discontentment and public anger rose high against it. The Gadar Party increased its activities and decided to provide an outflow to mounting indignation into violent agitations against British Administration in India. The Party, through its numerous branches in various countries, had already recruited thousands of Indians who were willig to 'do and die' for their country's honour. In the issue of 18th August , 1914 the *Gadar'* gave the following instructions to its subscribers:

> 'Spread the literature of revolution;
> Help and encourage all resistance, armed and pasive;
> Destroy the railways lines;
> Withdraw all your funds from British banks;
> Inspire the Indian Army to strike at every point against the Firangis.'

Scheme of the revolutionaries during First Great War. The First World War was already in progress. Most of the Indian armies had been deployed on European war-fields. The Gadar Party considered it as a fit hour to summon its followers to action and to take advantage of the weakness of the British administration in India. Lala Hardayal proceeded to Germany to negotiate with the German Emperor Kaiser II. Those were the days when Raja Mahendra Pratap on inspiration from Hardayal set up a Provincial Government in Kabul. It was agreed upon that the Mussalmans of Iran, Arabia, Iraq and Afghanistan might, with the military aid of Germany and Turkey, take up arms against the British, and the Sikhs in Punjab might raise a banner of revolt simultaneously in India. Lala Hardayal in pursuance of his plan sent thousands of recruits and much explosive material to India. As narrated earlier, 21st February, 1915 was fixed as the day for Gadar to break out under the leadership of Rash Behari Bose, Kartar Singh, Pingale and Sachindra Sanyal. Unfortunately the scheme fizzled out because of betrayal of Kripal Singh. Had the plan been executed, India would have regained her freedom much earlier. Just because of traitor Kripal Singh, hundreds of persons were arrested and many of them hanged in connection with the first Lahore Conspiracy Case.

REVOLUTIONARY MOVEMENT OF RAM PRASAD BISMIL, ASHFAQ ULLAH AND OTHERS (KAKORI CASE)

Before relating this incident, it is worthwhile to review background of Indian politics. The Rowlatt Act which came into force in 1918 gagged the Indian Press and curbed freedom of expression. Mahatma Gandhi and other nationalists expressed their resentment through speeches and articles. In a meeting held at Amritsar, General Dyer under the instructions of the Punjab Governor Sir Michael O'Dwyer, ordered reckless firing on the innocent and unarmed people. The venue of this barbaric act was Jallianwallah Bagh. It is said that nearly 1,000 people were killed and twice the number injured. Gandhiji condemned the brutal action of the British officer and made it an issue for his Non-Cooperation Movement in 1920. The Movement continued for two years but without any tangible or satisfying results.

Indian Republican Association founded. Mahatma Gandhi at the time of launching the Movement and even after that laid much stress on *Ahimsa* or non-violence. The revolutionaries suspended their activities temporarily to wait and watch the outcome of the experiment of passive resistance. They were much disillusinoed when the *Ahimsa* bore no fruit. Then they set about organising themselves vigorously once again to test the efficacy of violent methods. On 20th February, 1920, general amnesty was granted to all political prisoners, Sachindra Nath Sanyal also came out of jail. He knit up all the revolutionary units working in different Provinces of India and formed an association called *Indian Republican Association.* It was later termed Hindustan Socialist Republican Army. In 1922 all the revolutionaries of the country took a pledge to continue the work more intensively. The Government, on the other hand, resolved to sweep the country clean of all the revolutionary elements. It arrested the chief leader of the revolutionaries, Sri Gopi Mohan Sah, and passed the Bengal Ordinance Act on October 25, 1924.

The Revolutionaries were, however, not to be cowed down by the repressive measures of the Government. They procured arms and ammunition for an armed uprising. The organisation needed money urgently to pay for the materials it had purchased. It did not have money at all. The penniless soldiers of freedom had no other alternative but to commit dacoities in order to lick up a sizeable fortune. At a party meeting Ram Prasad Bismil suggested that the postal treasures being taken by railway trains should be looted. His resolution was carried by a majority vote. It was decided to halt the train by pulling its alarm chain near the Kakori Station and carry away the postal bags containing the treasury. Kakori is a wayside station on the Lucknow-Shah Jehanpur. On 9th August, 1925, the ten lancers boarded the train. They were equipped with revolvers and sufficient number of catridges. When the train had left Kakori Station and gathered high speed, on of the revolutionaries pulled the alarm chain. The train stopped. It was just dusk time. The guard was made to lie down quietly.

The Revolutionaries entered the compartment which contained the iron chests. It was well high difficult to smash the iron box. Ashfaq who was one of the riders, showered hammer blows on the box and broke it open. All the money was collected in bundles. No passenger dared come out of the compartment because of pistol shots booming outside. The Revolutionaries decamped safely and successfully with their spoils which amounted to ₹ 5,000. The daring hold-up of the train shook the rulers in their shoes from Delhi to London.

The police and intelligence department set about collecting clues and rounding up the suspects. Nearly 40 persons were entrapped and brought to trial. The case was known as Kakori Case. The trial which lasted for a long time and inwhich the Government produced 250 witnesses and wasted ten lakhs of rupees, at last concluded on 6th April, 1927. It was in fact the farce of a trial. The accused were defended by eminent lawyers. *Pt. Ram Prasad Bismil, Roshan Singh and Rajendra Lahiri were awarded death punishment,* Manmatha Nath Gupta to fourteen years' term and many others were sentenced to various other types of sentences. Of the two arrested later, *Ashfaq Ullah Khan, was given hanging and Sachindra Nath Bakshi was given transportaion for life.*

Two persons of the accused group–Pt. Ram Prasad Bismil and Ashfaq Ullah Khan were widely known for their indomitable courage and leadership. Ram Prasad was born in about the year 1897 in the Gwalior State. He had participated in the Mainpuri Conspiracy also. He was a born patriot and an arch revolutionary. He was a poet too and he wrote in Hindi under the pen-name of Bismil. He was hanged in Gorakhpur jail on 19th December, 1927. When his mother came to see him for the last time, tears came up in his eyes. Seeing her son weeping the mother said, "I wonder how a boy like you who always cared for country is shedding tears for my sake. This is cowardice. Now I wish, I should see you welcoming this heroic death smilingly. I am greatly proud of having given birth to a soldier of freedom who laid this life at the feet of his motherland. Your country has greater claim on you than I have. You have fallen for a noble cause and I see no reason to feel sorry." Bismil replied, "Dear mother, death is not a terror for me. But as butter must melt if brought near the fire, so also I could not help my tears when I saw you. I assure you that I shall die cheerfully."

A few days before his death, Bismil wrote in a letter to his friend. "I am fully prepared for what is to come on the 19th instant. What is there to be afraid of Death? Isn't like slipping out of one body into another? Iam sure my restless soul will come back to work with greater fire and enthusiasm for people and my motherland." A little before being hanged Ashfaq Ullah Khan also left an inspiring message for his countrymen: *"We have played our role on the political stage of our country. Right or wrong all our actions were motivated by the lofty object of securing independence.....I know my actions will elicit praise from some quarters and criticism from the other but as a true revolutionary, I am indifferent to such remarks. One thing I beg to clarify before I die. It never had been our object to create terror in the country. Our trial has lasted for such a long time but tell me if ever we tried to shoot down any approver or a prosecution witness. That is not in our line. My only wish is that my countrymen may irrespective of thei religion or creed unite like a solid bloc to smash the citadel of British rule. The British are the common enemies of all the religious section of our country. It is the moral duty of every Indian to dig the grave of the British bureaucracy. I am far from being a murderer as has been established by the prosecution. I am rather proud of being the first Musalman to lay down my life at the altar of india's freedom."*

Sachindra Sanyal died in 1940 and till his death he continued his work.

GREAT REVOLUTIONARY MOVEMENT OF SARDAR BHAGAT SINGH

Lala Lajpat Rai faces baton-charges at the time of boycott of Simon Commission and leaves the world for heavenly abode. When India was a hot bed of revolutionary movement and constitutional agitation was being carried on by the Congress and the Swarajist Party, the British Government realised the gravity of the situation and sent Simon Commission to suggest constitutional reforms.

Mr. Simon was a reputed barrister of England. When he came to India with an all-British team to study the demands of the Indian subjects, he was greeted with black flags. The chief reason behind it was the grievance of the people that no Indian was considered eligible for the membership of the Commission. So all the leading organisations of India, particularly the Congress, decided to boycott it and expressed their resentment through black flags, demonstrations and anti-Commission slogans. On 20th October, 1928, the Congress Party took out a huge procession as a demonstration of protest against the Commission. At the head of the swarming people was Lala Lajpat Rai, the most respected leader of the Punjab. The authorities wanted the mob to disperse. The protesters were, however, adamant. When persuasion and threats had no effect on the mob, the police resorted to lathi-charge. Mr. Saunders with a baton in his hand showered blows on the head and chest of Lalaji and caused grievous injuries on his person. The same evening Lalaji addressing a mammoth gathering declared: *"The Government which attacks its own innocent subjects has no claim to be called civilised government. Bear in mind such Government does not survive long. I declare that the blows struck at me will be the last nails in the coffin of the British rule in India."* The blows which Saunders had rained upon Lalaji proved fatal and he breathed his last on November 17, 1928.

The death of Lalaji plunged the country into gloom and despair. The nation took the incident a serious affront. The discontent of the people reached an explosive pitch against the barbaric British officers. How significant and provocative were the following words of Srimati Basanti Debi (the wife of Sri. C.R. Das) which she said in a public meeting–*"My blood boils with rage to think that Lalaji, who had been so aged, and so dear to his countrymen, has been baten to death by the brute English police officer. It is a challenge to the youth and manliness of three hundred million Indians. On behalf of the women of India I want a reply to my question whether Indian youths are dead or alive. Is there anybody from the young generation of India to step forward and respond to my question?"*

Strong reaction amongst the revolutionaries at the death of Lala Lajpat Rai. When Sardar Bhagat Singh and his friends heard a lady questioning their manliness and patriotic fervour, they were touched to the quick. Bhagat Singh had even otherwise been an eyewitness to that heartrending scene when Lalaji was being subjected to baton charge by Mr. Saunders. He was a leader of the Hindustan Socialist Republican Association. In a party meeting he put forward a resolution for the revenge of Lalaji's murder, the resolution was wholly and unanimously approved and it was decided to kill both Mr. Scott who ordered lathi-charge and Saunders who killed Lalaji. Details were worked out by Azad, Bhagat Singh, Sukhdeo, Rajguru and Jai Gopal. On 17th December, 1928, when Saunders on his bicycle was approaching the police gate, Shivaram Rajguru fired the first shot followed by Bhagat Singh who emptied his pistol shots on Saunders' head and tore it to pieces. All the revolutionaries took refuge in D.A.V. College, Lahore. The police did its utmost to arrest them but failed. They slipped away in disguise to Shimla. Within five days of the incident, the people of the town read the posters issued by the Party and displayed on the city walls justifying the murder of Saunders.

Only a few months after the murder of Saunders there occurred another incident on April 8, 1929. The Government of India introduced two Bills in the Central Legislative Council in Delhi. One was Public Safety Bill and the other Traders Dispute Bill. Both the Bills were intended to serve as instruments of suppression. The twin measures were likely to give a death blow to all efforts for freedom. All the elected members in the Legislature opposed these Bills vehemently but their protests fell on deaf ears. The revolutionaries decided to throw a big bomb on the day on which the Safety Bill rejected by the elected members, was to be given a stamp of approval by Government. The revolutionaries by the proposed explosion wanted to warn the government against proceeding with a legislation in defiance of public opinion. The task was entrusted to Sardar Bhagat Singh and Batukeshwar Datta. The central body of the Republican Party proposed that the person after throwing bomb should make good his escape. Bhagat Singh disagreed with the proposal. He pleaded that bold surrender would serve two purposes. Such a bold display of their patriotism would dispel all doubts from the people's mind that the revolutionaries were given to violence and terrorism. Secondly, the persons would get an opportunity to make a statement in the court and thus broadcast ideology of their party. It was a foregone conclusion that the arrest of Bhagat Singh and Datta would mean hangings but the risk was considered worth taking for the vindication of the party's aims and objects.

On 8th April, 1929 when the question-hour was over, Bhagat Singh threw a bomb on the wall, which exploded with a thundering boom. He then fired two bullets to frighten the Speaker of the House. When the cloud of smoke had cleared, he threw leaflets into the Hall which read: *"Bombs are needed to let the deaf hear."* Had he wanted so, he could have safely run away in the confusion created by the explosion. But he abided by the Party's decision and courted arrest. The police strove hard to track down the conspiracy behind the incident and arrested several persons on mere suspicion. On 4th June, 1929, the accused made lengthy statement before the Sessions Judge. According to plan Bhagat Singh and Batukeshwar Datta in their statement explained at length the aim and objective of Republican Army. It is to be noted that through such a statement alone could the party publicise and communicate its message to the public at large, since the party could not otherwise launch anti-British propaganda openly. They knew well that their statement made in the court would be published in the papers and thus remove all misunderstanding about the revolutionaries.

Joint statement of Bhagat Singh and Batukeshwar Datta on June 4, 1929, before the Sessions Judge throwing light on the aims of the revolutionaries

"The resolutions and Bills passed so seriously by this House have been trampled under foot on the floor of the very House which is called the Indian Parliament. The laws meant to end all oppression and autocracy have been treated with utter contempt whereas the Bills which have been rejected by the elected representatives of the people are enacted by a single stroke of pen. In short the present system of administration is built upon the plunder of wealth extorted from the sweating millions of the Indian people."

Sardar Bhagat Singh and Datta further said, "We have failed to discover even after a long search and study of the situation a single reason justifying its existence. We have not been able to understand the psychology and attitude of our leaders who indulge in thoughtless squandering of the public money and precious time in the unashamed exhibition of the helpless serfdom of our Indian people. We were since long deliberating upon the whole situation and the unlawful arrests of leaders of the labour movements when the news of the Trades Disputes Bill came to our ears. We visited the Assembly House to witness the progress of the Bill. The nature of the discussion in the House drove us to a firm conclusion that it was futile for the Indian workers to hope to get anything from the state which is a cursed symbol of the strangling power which knows only the exploitation and pillaging of the enslaved Indians including the working classes. We saw how the humiliation of the barbaric and beastly enactment was inflicted on the head of the elected representatives of the country. We noticed how with that autocratic measure, millions of struggling and starving people were deprived of their fundamental right and the only course open to them to improve their economic conditions. No one who feels as we do, for the helpless working classes, can bear to see their plight without passions being aroused."

Sardar Bhagat Singh continued, "Can there be a person whose heart feels the agony of the tortures inflicted by the State and bleeds for the suffering and starving humanity, which has sacrificed its very life for the economic well-being and personal pleasures of the exploiters, that can step forward to silence our lamentations and assuage the heart-rendering grief? It had become necessary to wake up England from her dream only with bombs. We threw the bombs in the House (with a clear recollection in our minds of what late Sri. S.R. Das, once a law-member in the Executive Council of the Viceroy, had said in a letter addressed to his son) on behalf of all those who had no other means to give vent to their heart-rending afflictions in order to express their feelings."

"Our sole object was to warn the listless and wake up the deaf. Many others are thinking just like us. The bombs which were thrown were intentionally so manufactured as to cause insignificant damage, and they were thrown also in such a clear place as to produce the least injury to anybody. Under the apparent calm on the surface of the Indian mind there is a ceaseless terrible seething discontent on the point of bursing into a storm. Our action is mere a danger-signal to those who are rushing ahead thoughtlessly without caring for the serious consequences before them. We have, as if, heralded the end of the era of non-violence, the idealist dream, about whose utter failure the young generation is now doubtlessly convinced. We have adopted this course of striking a warning purely out of our love and goodwill for humanity to ward off, the unheard of harassments and hardships. The new spirit, notice of whose dawn has been just given by us, is really inspired by the idealism of Guru Govind Singh, Shivaji, Mustafa Kamal Pasha, Raza Khan, Washington, Garibaldi, Lafayat and Lenin. It was because the Government and the Indian leaders had closed their eyes and ears that we had to sound that warning to attract their attention."

Sardar Bhagat Singh and Datta finally said, *"The opponents of revolution mistakingly believe that revolution means violence with arms, weapons and such other means. But revolution is not confined to this process. It may be that these are used as instruments but it should not be forgotten that behind them, it is the solid strength and spirit of the revolution and that strength is the will, the aspiration of the people to demand and get a change, revolution in the current economic structure, the shape and form of Political Government of the nation. Our idea of revolution has never been simply the bloodshed of some individuals. It is to end the present regime of exploitation of man by man and to secure for our nation absolute right of self-determination.* That is the ultimate objective of our idea of revolution. Freedom is birth-right of man. We welcome any amount of suffering and sacrifice that might fall to our lot for this idealism and devotion to it. Long live that Revolution."[1]

TRIAL AND CONVICTION OF SARDAR BHAGAT SINGH AND OTHERS

The police not contented with prosecuting Bhagat Singh alone, involved several other persons in the case. All of them were accorded inhuman treatment in jail. As a protest against it, Yatindranath Das and others observed a fast unto death. It created a stir in the country. Even the Congress was persuaded to express positive sympathy for the persons observing fast. The Government, however, refused to give them rights of regular prisoners. The condition of Yatindranath became serious day by day. All his limbs became inactive. On the 62nd day of his historic fast, Yatindranath left for his heavenly ablode. The tribunal delivered its judgment on October 7, 1930. *Sardar Bhagat Singh, Shiva Ram Rajguru and Sukhdeva were hanged on the gallows on 23rd March, 1931.* The Government instead off handing over the dead bodies to their relatives, decided to dispose them of secretly. Under the cover of darkness the dead bodies of three stalwarts of revolution were taken to Ferozepur and given over to holy fire on the bank of river. But the people got the scent of the crooked design of the authorities. They ran after the police van carrying the deceased patriots. When they reached the river, bank, the corpses were already in flames and only the ashes could be collected by them. The sacred spot where three leaders were burnt became a place of pilgrimage for years to come. A memorial has been built there.

REVOLUTIONARY MOVEMENT OF CHANDRA SHEKHAR AZAD, BHAGWATI CHARAN BOHRA AND YASHPAL

Chandra Shekhar Azad was a man of sterling character and indomitable courage. He was also a military genius worthy of a commander on the battlefield. He had a leading hand in the romantic and daring hold-up of train better known as Kakori Case but luckily he evaded arrest and absconded. After the hanging of Ram Prasad Bismil, he assumed the leadership of the organisation. He assisted

1. Balshastri Hardas, *Armed Struggle for Freedom.*

Bhagat Singh in doing away with Saunders. He made every conceivable attempt to get Bhagat singh out of jail but all his attempts proved abortive. After Bhagat Singh's execution, Chandra Shekhar Azad deputed Yashpal and Bhagwati Charan Bohra to organise the firebrand youths in the Punjab. Shrimati Durga Devi, wife of Bohra, also joined the organisation. Other lady workers in the organisation were Mrs. Sushila Devi, Mrs. Premwati and Mrs. Prakashwati Kapoor.

In spite of the requests made by Gandhiji and the people of country, the British Government refused to condone the death sentence passed on Bhagat Singh and his companions. It was a brazen defiance of and a blow to public sentiments. Lord Irwin, the Viceroy of India, was an arch imperialist whose plan was to crush the Congress also. The revolutionaries decided to wreak vengeance on the Viceroy. Azad and Yashpal chalked out a perfect plan to explode the train, carrying the Viceroy. Lord Irwin was scheduled to return to Delhi from his visit to Kolhapur State on 23rd December, 1929 and meet Mahatma Gandhi in connection with the Congress demands for constitutional reforms. The revolutionaries had lost all faith in the Congress policy of appeasement and reconciliation. They wanted this secure game to end soon and be replaced by open conflict. So they decided to register the opposition to the proposed constitutional talks by exploding the bomb just on the eve of Gandhi-Irwin meeting.

The bombs were duly deposited at the appointed spot near Nizamuddin Station on Delhi-Mathura line. An electric wire connected the bomb with a battery switch 300 yards away. As soon as the train carrying the Viceroy left Nizamuddin Station, the switch was pressed and the bomb exploded with a bang as loud as that of a cannon-shot. The train got derailed. The dining car was shattered into pieces but by a stroke of luck the Viceroy escaped unhurt. Exactly a year later, on 23rd December, 1930, an attempt was made on the life of the Governor of Punjab while he had gone to read the Convocation Address of the Punjab University. Mr. Hari Krishan fired a shot at him. The Governor was struck but not fatally. He tried to escape in the adjoining room. Hari Krishnan chased him but was overpowered and ultimately hanged on 9th June 1931.

The Hindustan Socialist Republican Army suffered heavy casualties over a period of a few years. Most of its pledged workers and leaders fell into the hands of the police. Its future appeared to be dark and dismal. But Azad and Yashpal were still steady without losing hopes. On 27th February, 1931, Azad, Yashpal and Surendra Pandey assembled in Allahabad to finalise plans for procuring help from Russia so as to continue their relentless struggle for freedom. Yashpal and Pandey left Azad in Alfred Park to meet another revolutionary Sukhdeo Raj. While the two were engrossed in conversation some informant recognised them and informed the police. Immediately the park was besieged and armed police posted at the exit gates of the park. Azad had no idea of the danger. He realised the situation only when the Police Superintendent shouted at him. He got ready to fight the last battle of his life with revolvers in both hands. He asked Sukhdeo to run away. The great Commander of the Republican Army fought his battle alone and with surprising distinction. He was a sure shot. A number of bullets coming from different directions punctured the body of the hero. He exhausted all the bullets in fighting his enemies who outnumbered him by a wide margin. The last bullet he used on himself and thus died a glorious death. The whole of the country felt bereaved with death of Azad. The void caused in the ranks of the organisation could never be made up. The plan of sending Yashpal to Russia was shelved for ever. He was elected by the party as its new Commander-in-Chief. The Government announced big rewards for information leading to his arrest. Yashpal organised the Revolutionary Army again and made a declaration of general revolt. On 23rd janauary, 1932, while he was proceeding to Allahabad, he was spotted by the C.I.D. In Allahabad while he was asleep in Savitri Devi's house, he was surrounded by a strong police force. When the revolver he held in his hand did not work, he surrendered. He was arrested and sentenced to 14 years imprisonment. Fortunately for him the Congress formed its Ministry in U.P. in 1937 and he was released unconditionally on 2nd March, 1938. He died in free India a few years ago.

SUBHAS BOSE AND AZAD HIND FAUJ

(The last great revolutionary struggle to liberate India from the clutches of the imperialists during Second World War)

Subhas Bose holds a distinguished place amongst the revolutionary leaders of India. He was a political disciple of Sri. C.R. Das who had a big hand in bringing him on the stage of Indian politics. Subhas was born on 23rd January, 1897 in Cuttack. His father, Sri Janakinath Bose, was a successful lawyer. Subhas was an exceptional child who showed the signs of a genius even from his school days. He qualified for Civil Services in 1920 but refused to serve as agent of the British Government. Those were the days of Non-Co-operation Movement. Subhas refrained from plunging into agitation, because he did not agree with Gandhiji's philosophy and his method of work. He belonged to the School of Tilak and Arvind whose idols were mighty Hindu heroes of History–namely, Rana Pratap and Shivaji. He once said, "A day will dawn when the Indians will have to follow the Maharashtrian way for the regaining of freedom. They will have to copy the example of Great Shivaji." Sri Das in those days was bringing out a paper and also running a national college so as to give a prop to national awakening. He entrusted Subhas with the work of editing the paper and spreading his views in every nook and corner of the country. Subhas sponsored an organised demonstration in the city of Calcutta to protest against the visit of the Prince of Wales. He was arrested and awarded six months' imprisonment for having led the boycott movement. This was his first confinement in the British prison. He became an active member and ardent supporter of the Swarjist Party.

When C.R. Das became the Mayor of Calcutta Corporation in 1923, he appointed Subhas as the Chief Executive Officer on remuneration of ₹ 1,500 per month. Because of his association with the revolutonaries, he became a thorn in the eyes of the Government. On 24th October, 1924, the Government arrested him under Special Ordinance and sent him to Mandalay Jail (Burma). He was, therefrom, set free in 1927 on the grounds of ill health. With renewed vigour he began to devote himself to public work. He contested for an Assembly Seat in 1927, organised Independence League and boycotted Simon Commission. When Yatindra Nath, a member of Bhagat Singh's group, expired after a prolonged fast in jail in 1929, his dead body was brought to Calcutta. A huge funeral procession was taken out which exhibited the resentment of the people. Subhas delivered a fiery and stirring speech on this occasion for which he had to go to jail for six months. He visited jail again in 1931 for six months. On his release, he addressed a Youth Conference in Mathura and lashed at the British hypocrisy so vehemently that he was clapped behind the bars again. In 1938 he was offered the Presidential Chair at Haripura Congress. He raised the slogan of complete independence and suggested that a deadline be fixed and an ultimatum given to the British Government regarding the unconditional surrender of power. His extremist views did not find favour with Gandhiji. Hence when he filed his paper for the Presidentship of the Congress again next year, Gandhiji pitted Pattabhi Sitaramayya as a rival candidate. In the teeth of stiff opposition from the old leadership of the Congress, Subhas withdrew from the Congress and founded a new organisation–Forward Bloc. He toured the country and told the people to give an open fight to the Government if it did not concede complete freedom to India within six months.

The Second World War had already broken out. The triumphant march of Hitler over the continent of Europe unnerved the British Government. Britain was in a crisis. Subhas, as a student of political strategy, knew that the time was ripe for an armed revolt. During his stay in Europe for his treatment, he had already met Herr Hitler, Mussolini and D'Valera. It was at this time that Sardar Udham Singh shot down Sir Michael O'Dwyer in London in broad day light. O'Dwyer had been the Governor of Punjab when thousands of innocent citizens had been shot dead in the Jallianwalah Bagh, Amritsar. O'dwyer was the person responsible for that reckless butchery. Udham Singh who was a staunch revolutionary left for England in 1919 and waited for full twenty years to take revenge. On 13th March, 1940 he got the suitable opportunity. Sir Michel O'Dwyer was scheduled to attend a lecture in Caxton Hall, London. While he was leaving the hall, Udham Singh fired at him from point blank range. That human brute O'Dwyer fell dead with the second bullet. A few others also received injuries, Udham Singh was sentenced to death. In his statement he declared: "I have seen my starving countrymen being trampled under the jackboot of British Imperialism. I am not the least afraid of death. What after all is the use of prolonging life till dotage. There is bravery in dying young, in sacrificing life for the country!"[1]

The daring deed of Udham Singh blew the bugle for renewed struggle of India's freedom. Subhas toured the country to feel the pulse of the people. He met Veer Savarkar and told him about his plan to start an agitation for removing the British memorials from Calcutta. It was, he said, only the beginning of an all-India movement, Savarkar, the veteran revolutionary, said, " is there any sense when Britain is involved in the catastrophe of the world war that leader of your abilities and genius should remain in India and confine himself to petty agitations like the removal of British statues and in consequence rot into the British prison......Real politics lies in checkmating and imprisoning the enemy and not one's ownself...Like Rash Behari and other armed revolutionaries who tricked the British rulers and escaped to Germany and Japan, you should also dupe the British and get out successfully. Mobilise the Indian war prisoners fallen into the hands of Germany and Italy; and give a correct lead to them! As soon as Japan joins war, manage to invade India either through the Bay of Bengal or from the Indo-Burmese borders." Subhas promised to think over his suggestion seriously.

When Subhas returned to Calcutta, the authorities put him under detention. The thought-provoking advice of Savarkar weaved its grand design in his imagination but then there were the prison bars to deal with. The ideals of Shivaji and his magnificent escape were ready before him. To begin with he observed a fast. It was a routine trick of the revolutionaries to secure their release. The authorities natively set Subhas free. Subhas feigned illness and confined himself to his room. The Press began to publicise that his spiritual mood was overtaking him again. He avoided interviews, and grew a beard. Nobody saw him for days together. The authorities also were convinced that Subhas too was treading on the line of Arvind who after retirement from politics and become a recluse. On 16th January, 1941 at 8 P.M. Subhas hoodwinked the police and spirited away in the guise of a Pathan. He boarded a train forty miles from Calcutta and reached Peshwar. Under the fictitious name Zia-ud-din, he was taken to Kabul to his associate Bhagat Ram. From Kabul he went to Rome and then to Germany. Subhas found Germans to be quite helpful. Even Hitler addressed him as 'His Excellency'. He mobilised the Indians living in Germany and formed the 'Free Indian Army'. He then organised all the Indian war-prisoners and formed a 'Liberation Army' with its Headquarters at Dresden.

FORMATION OF I.N.A.

On 7th December, 1941 Japan entered war on the side of Germany and attacked Pearl Harbour, the mighty military base of the Allies. On 15th February 1942, Japan captured the so called British sea fortress of Singapore and then ran down Malaya and Burma. After the fall of Singapore on 15th February, 1942, Col. Hunt on behalf of the British Government handed over 40,000 Indian prisoners of war to Japanese Government, who in his turn handed them over to Captain Mohan Singh. *Giani Pritam Singh (a holy man) and Major Fuzihara induced Shri Mohan Singh, with great difficulty to work for the Independence of India.* Mohan Singh, now asked for volunteers from among the prisoners to join the Indian National Army (I.N.A.) or Azad Hind Fauz to be organised by him to fight along with the Japanese army against the British in order to drive the latter from India. Many of them joined the I.N.A. but many refused to do so.

Rash Behari Bose who had fled to Japan in June 1915 along with Shri Ravindra Nath Tagore, never ceased to work for his motherland and he called a conference of representatives of the Indians living in South East Asia at Tokyo from 28 to 30 March, 1942 for deliberating the means to bring

1. Balshastri Hardas, *Armed Struggle for Freedom.*

about independence. *The Tokyo conference passed a resolution to form an Indian National Army.* It was decided to hold a conference at Bangkok from 15 to 23rd June, 1942. It was attended by 100 delegates from Burma, Malaya, Thailand, Indo-China, Philippines, Japan, China, Borneo, Java, Sumatra, Hongkong and Andamans. Rash Behari Bose was elected the Chairman and Captain Mohan Singh, one of the four members took up the portfolio of the Commander-in-Chief of I.N.A. *On Ist September, 1942, the Indian National Army (I.N.A.) was formally established.* A programme of intensive training was launched for I.N.A. The lessons from national history were given to the soldiers. They were taught the living conditions of the Indians under the British rule. Subhas Bose was invited from Germany by the Bangkok conference. He accepted the invitation and reached Tokyo on 13th June, 1943 with great difficulty. After landing in Tokyo, he declared in his first Statement, *"The opportunity which this Great War has offered may not recur in a hundred years to come. It is our resolve to avail fully of this opportune moment for the liberation of Bharat. It is our duty to offer blood as the price for freedom. Those who have raised their arms against us deserve to be replied with arms, that is our duty."*

On 2nd July, 1943, Subhas Bose delivered his epoch-making speech in Singapore, *"Our fight is against all types of imperialism–whether it is English or Japanese. What we must guard ourselves against is the betrayal by the fifth-columnists among our own people. Comrades, let your one slogan be "Chalo Delhi" (March on to Delhi). Whatever befalls you in sunshine and dark hours, in grief or joy, in hardships or through triumphs, I assure you, will always remain with you. But today I cannot offer you anything except hunger, thirst, hardships, travails and death itself! It is no matter who of us lives or dies. Let us sacrifice everything and make India free, for in that achievement everything has been achieved.*

On 4th July, 1943, Rash Behari Bose handed over to him the leadership of both Indian Independence League and I.N.A. On July 5, 1943, Rash Behari conferred on Subhas Bose the Presidentship of the Indian Independence League and decided to act himself as an adviser. On 25th August Subhas also assumed the supreme command for the free Indian National army–the I.N.A. He then made a provisional Government of Free India and formed a Cabinet. He and his Ministers took the following oath when the Provisional Government was formed: *"In the name of God, I take this sacred oath that to liberate India and thirty-eight crores of my countrymen, I will continue the sacred war of freedom till the last breath of my life. I shall always remain a servant of India and to look after the welfare of the thirtyeight crores of Indian brothers and sisters shall be my highest duty. After winning freedom, I will always be prepared to shed even the last drop of my blood for the preservation of India's freedom."*

In this Proclamation of Provisional Government, Subhas Bose traced the history of India's subjection over two centuries and made a stirring emotional appeal to his countrymen living in all the countries of the East. The free Governments of Japan, Germany, Philippines, Korea, China and the Irish Republic accorded official recognition to the Provisional Government of free India. In 1943 the Japanese Government handed over the administration of Andaman and Nicobar Islands to Netaji Subhas. Netaji visited these islands and renamed them as 'Shahid Island' and 'Swarajya Island' respectively. The flag of Free India was hoisted on the island on 30th December, 1943. Subhas then celebrated the Independence Day in Rangoon and floated Free Indian Bank with the subscribed capital of over eight crores.

In 1944 Subhas Chandra Bose began his historic march from Rangoon to invade India. On 4th February the I.N.A. broke British defence on the Indo-Burmese borders and liberated Ramu, Kohima, Palel, Tiddim and Manipur. Even the British Generals had to admire the skill and bravery of the soldiers of I.N.A. It is said that the women platoons at one place fought for sixteen hours on end against the British force. One great mistake that the I.N.A. made was to begin its operations in February which is the month of heavy monsoon in Assam. The Siege of Imphal had to be suspended because of heavy rains. On 22nd September, 1944, the Army celebrated the Martyrs'

Day. Field Marshal Subhas Chandra Bose declared, *"Our Motherland is in search of freedom; she is in need of rebels who will drown the enemy in their pool of blood. Give me your blood–I will give you independence."*

World Politics suddenly took an unexpected turn. Germany laid down arms on 7th May, 1945. Japanese aggression also slackened. The allied forces increased their tempo of advance into the erstwhile conquered territories. On 13th August American Bombers dropped two atom bombs on the crowded Japanese towns of Hiroshima and Nagasaki. The tremendous loss of life and property shattered the confidence of the Japanese. Japan went on its knees and offered complete surrender. The news of the capitulation of Japan stunned and shattered the dream of Subhas.

Netaji Shubhash Chandra Bose left Bangkok with a single companion in a two-engined Japanese bomber carrying senior Japanese officers to Tokyo via Dairen in Manchuria. It arrived safely at Taipai (Taipoku) in Formosa at about 2 P.M. on 18th August. After lunch it left Taipai. What happened afterwards is uncertain. The Japanese official version issued at the time, was that almost immediately after the plane had taken off, it caught fire. Netaji badly burnt, somehow came out of the plane and was removed to hospital where he died that very night between 8 and 9 P.M. but this story was discredited in India from the very beginning. The Government of India, on the demand of the public appointed an Enquiry Committee. Though the majority of the members held that the official version was substantially correct but the elder brother of Netaji, Mr. Sarat Chandra Bose did not agree with the report and pointed out many flaws. The committee never visited the aerodrome and place of the accident. A few years later, Satya Narain Sinha, who was a Minister at that time, visited the site and met some officers who were on duty on 18th August, 1945. The result of this inquirty may be summed up as follows:

"Netaji Subhash Chandra Bose plane halted at Taipai for refuelling and took off for Dairen (Manchuria) at 14.30 hours on 18th August. He arrived safely at Dairen and stayed there in disguise even after it was occupied by the Russians. But his identity was discovered by the Russian officers. He was looked upon as a friend and partisan of the German Nazis and was transported to Siberia. No further information could be gathered by Sinha about Netaji's life behind the iron curtain. The truth story had not been challenged upto 15th January, 1991"

The life of Subhas Chandra Bose reads like a thrilling saga of most dramatic events. His rise was meteoric but miraculous at the same time. He was truly the greatest hero of India's struggle for freedom. Even though he failed to realise his cherished dream of free India, he roused by his example such a mighty wave of hatred for the British in the hearts of all three wings of Defence Forces as climaxed in the departure of the British from India. After the fall of Burma, most of the Soldiers and Generals of I.N.A. were captured and tried for treason. The Government was resolved to shoot them down. The most sensational trial of Major General Shah Nawaz, Sehgal and Dhillon was held in Red Fort, Delhi. Sri J.L. Nehru, Bhulabhai Desai and Tej Bahadur Sapru appeared as defence counsels. They presented most logical convincing arguments on the basis of International Law and justified the right of a country under subjection to fight for her independence. They pleaded for their acquittal and release of I.N.A. prisoners. Moreover, the defence forces were overwhelmingly in favour of the release of the freedom-fighters and hence the British Government did a wise thing in setting them free. The acquittal of persons who had violated the military law was a highly significant event. It was a sign of changing times and indication of the loosening grip of the British over the Indian army. The British Government took the growing discontent in the armed forces as a signal-alarm and so hastened to withdraw honourably from the Indian scene.

Role of I.N.A. Dr. R.C. Majumdar observes, "In spite of failure, the I.N.A. occupies an important place in the history of India's struggle for freedom. The formation of this force and its heroic exploits proved beyond doubt that the British could no longer rely upon the Indian sepoys to maintain their hold on India. The universal sympathy expressed all over India for the I.N.A.

officers, when they were tried for treason in the Red Fort, Delhi gave a rude shock to the British, in as much as it clearly demonstrated that Indians of all shades of opinion put a premium on the loyalty of the Indian troops to their foreign masters and looked upon it as a true and welcome sign of nationalism. The honour and esteem with which every Indian regarded the members of the I.N.A. offered a striking contrast to ill-conceived disgust and contempt for the sepoys who refused to join the I.N.A. and remained true to their salt. Incredible though it may seem, it is nonetheless true that even the stories of oppression and torture suffered by the latter for their loyalty evoked no sympathy for them in the hearts of the Indians who remained absolutely unmoved. *All these opened the eyes of the British to their perilous situation in India. They realised that they were sitting on the brink of the volcano which might erupt at any moment. This decision played an important role in their final decision to quit India. So the members of I.N.A. did not die or suffer in vain and their leader Netaji Subhas Chandra Bose, has secured a place of honour in the history of India's struggle for freedom."*

MUTINY IN THE NAVY AND AIR FORCE, 1946

(The last death-blow to the Imperial rule)

While the I.N.A. trials were being conducted in the historic Red Fort, there was mass agitation in public for the release of the three Generals. The tame surrender of the Government to the pressure of the public opinion and the lowering of the British prestige in the international field had its impact on the defence forces too. Discontent broke out and reached an all-time pitch in the Air Force. Only a spark was needed to set it ablaze. The strained relations between the English officers and Indian soldiers reached such a stage of conflict that personnel in the air Force in Karachi declared a strike on 20th January, 1946. The fire spread to the aerodromes at Bombay, Lahore and Delhi. Nearly 5,200 employees of the Air Wing struck work. The Naval forces followed suit. 5,000 personnel of the Navy went on strike on 19th February, 1946. They also displayed the badges of Azad Hind Fauj on their breasts. The general strike took the form of a revolt. The strikers attacked the English officers in Bombay. When they were treated to bullets, they also replied in the language of bullets and hand grenades. In other ports also the Navymen turned their guns towards their English bosses. All discipline was torn to shreds. The soldiers demonstrated in an unmistakable way that they were unwilling to accept the British authority any more. Had not Vallahbhai Patel mediated, there would have been an all-out revolution. The time had come for the English race of shopkeepers to wind up their business and sail back safely to their homes. The British Prime Minister, Mr. Attlee, read the writing on the wall and made an announcement to the effect that the British would before long quit India and let Indians rule themselves.

When the Indian Independence Act was moved in the British Parliament, Mr. Winston Churchill, the leader of the Opposition group, raised a great hue and cry. He charged the then British Prime Minister Attlee with liquidating the British Empire which, he said, had been build with their sweat and blood. The Labour leader, Mr. Attlee, made a very clean confession and said,"Britain is transferring power due to the fact that the Indian mercenary army is no longer loyal to Britain and Britain cannot afford to have a large British army to hold down India." The formalities of the transference of power were rapidly completed and on 15th of August, 1947, Lord Mountbatten lowered down the English flag, making for the Indian flag to go up. Thus the struggle for India's freedom which had begun in the year 1857 culminated in complete freedom, exactly ninety years later in 1947. It would be silliness on the part of any single party if it claims to have achieved freedom exclusively by its own sacrifices. The liberals and the extremists, constitutional agitators and the bomb-throwers–all have a share in the credit of winning freedom. But it will have to be admitted that the major credit goes to armed revolutionaries who made the meadows of India too precarious a place for the British to graze and exploit.

REVIEW AND EVALUATION OF THE ARMED STRUGGLE FOR FREEDOM

Armed and Non-armed Freedom struggle prove contributory to each other. It is very necessary to tell the readers that after 1857, two kinds of national movements started in our country, violent and non-violent. Though the aim of both was to achieve independence from foreign yoke, yet they differed widely in their methods. While the revolutionaries believed in violent methods, the Congressmen led by Gandhiji strictly believed in non-violence. Both had originated because of the the political circumstances prevalent at that time.

The partition of Bengal had taken place on 20th July, 1905 but it was given effect on 16th October of that year. It produced the gravest resentment in the public but Lord Curzon refused to meet any deputation for its annulment. When the People of Bengal launched a strong protest against it in the form of peaceful demonstrations, then the police lathicharged it and imprisoned several hundred persons. Therefore the movement went underground and gave birth to the revolutionary movement. The revolutionaries threw some bombs on various high officers including one on Lord Hardinge on 23rd December, 1912 and hatched conspiracy on 21st February, 1915 to bring down the downfall of the British Government during the First world War (1914-18) but nothing came out of it as the conspiracy leaked.

In the meanwhile the Moderates in order to earn some concessions in the form of Morley-Minto Reforms also did not care for the implementation of the Extremist Programme of Lokmanya Bal Gangadhar Tilak adopted in the Congress of 1906, so there was a split in the Surat congress. Bal Gangadhar Tilak was imprisoned on September 13, 1908 and sent to Rangoon where he was given 8 years of rigorous imprisonment for writing inflamtory articles in his newspapers. He was released on 16th June, 1914. He refused to extend all help to the British Government during First World War broke unconditionally, which broke out on 4th August, 1914. He had gained the sole control of the Congress after the death of Gopal Krishna Gokhale in February 1915 and that of Sir Ferozeshah Mehta in November 1915. He started the Home Rule Movement in 1916 and demanded the right of self-determination for India and submitted a memorandum to this effect to the Paris Peace Conference in 1919 but could achieve no success.

The Government of India, instead of feeling grateful and giving Swaraj to the people, gave them Rowlatt and Jallianwala Bagh (Amritsar) Massacre. Mahatma Gandhi started the Non-co-operation and Khilafat Movement in December 1920 to redress the wrongs of the Punjab, win Swaraj in one year and to get the Turkish question of Khilafat settled according to the will of the Mohammadans. (Tilak had already left for his heavenly abode on 1st August, 1920). The revolutionary experiment was suspended for two years but as Congress could not achieve anything, therefore the revolutionary movement had to be again reinvigorated and activised. In 1922 all the Revolutionaries of the country took a pledge to continue the work more intensively. The Government on the other hand resolved to sweep the country clean of all the revolutionary elements. It arrested the chief leader of the Revolutionaries, Shri Gopi Mohan Shah on 25 October, 1924. As the Revolutionaries were in dire need of money, therefore they decided to loot the postal money-bags from the train which was running from the side of Shah Jehanpur to Lucknow. On 9th August, 1925 the treasury was looted at the Kakori Railway Station. Some of the leading Revolutionaries like Pandit Ram Prasad Bismil and Ashfaq Ullah Khan were hanged in December 1927.

Afterwards Simon Commission landed at Bombay on February 7, 1928. The Congress decided to boycott it. Therefore the Simon Commission was greeted with black flags everywhere and asked to go back. When the Commission went to Lahore, then there was a huge procession taken against it under the leadership of Lala Lajpat Rai, the lion of the Punjab. A police officer namely, Mr. Saunders rained lathi blows upon Lala Lajpat Rai mercilessly as a result of which he breathed his last on 17th

November, 1928. Thereupon Basanti Devi, wife of Mr. C.R. Das asked the youth of the country to give a befitting reply. Consequently, the Revolutionary Party decided to avenge the death of Lala Lajpat Rai. Sardar Bhagat Singh, Shiv Ram Rajguru and Sukh Dev shot dead Saunders on 17th December, 1928. Chandra Shekhar Azad was also involved in it but all the four escaped from the dragnet of Lahore Police under the false guise and fake names.

The Government of India did not learn any lesson even from this incident. After few months, it introduced the Public Safety Bill and the Trades Dispute Bill in the Central Legislature. The sole aim of both the Bills was to curb the freedom of the people completely. The two Bills had been passed despite the objection of the elected representatives because the Government commanded a majority. Therefore upon the instructions of the Revolutionary Party, Sardar Bhagat Singh and Shri Batukeshwar Dutta threw the bomb on 4th June, 1929 in the Central Assembly at an open space to let the deaf hear. For this crime Sardar Bhagat Singh, Shiv Ram Rajguru and Sukhdev were hanged on the gallows on 23rd March, 1931.

Let us now look to the politics of Indian National Congress. Before passing the Independence Resolution, Mahatma Gandhi wanted to meet Viceroy, Lord Irwin in order to get an assurance for the Dominion Status. Therefore, he had arranged a meeting for 23rd December, 1929. The Viceroy had to reach Delhi on the morning of that day after his visit to Kolhapur. The Revolutionaries derailed the train so that Mahatma Gandhi may not be able to see the Viceroy and the nation may not feel insulted. Thereupon Mahatma Gandhi wrote an article on the '*Cult of Bomb*' and severely indicted the act of the Revolutionaries. The Revolutionaries on the other hand issued reply to it in their pamphlet '*Philosophy of Bomb*'. They threw light on the aims and objects of the Revolutionaries and further added, "The Congress had asked for many things from the British Government in 1928 but got nothing. On the other hand the Government insulted the nation. Therefore, in order to avenge the national insult and to prevent further insults by the meetings between the Viceroy and Mahatma Gandhi, the revolutionaries deliberately put the bomb under the rails. What is the use of the meeting of Mahatma Gandhi with him? *Home Rule, Dominion Status and Right of Self-determination demands etc. are the symbols of slavery. The Revolutionaries had declared their aims complete independence 25 years ago when the Congress has declared its aim as the complete independence only this year (1929).*

In this pamphlet namely *'Philosophy of the Bomb'* the Revolutionaries wrote further that Mahatma Gandhi had emphasised this fact that he wanted to change the mind of the foreign rulers and thereby fulfil all the national ambitions–but we may ask how many Britishers have been won by love? Whose mind has changed out of Sir Michael O'dwyer, General Dyer, Lord Reading, Lord Irwin? Who has become the friend of India? Therefore the expectation that the British race would be won by love is useless. Gandhiji again emphasises that national awakening has occurred due to the Non-Co-operation Movement but the hard fact is that it has occurred due to the long struggle against the British rule. Mahatma Gandhi's experiment in South Africa failed and the talk of winning Swaraj within one year also proved baseless. There is a basic difference between the approaches of the revolutionaries and the Congress. *Where the Congress wants to use only moral force for the attainment of freedom, the Revolutionaries want to use every means (violent and non-violent) because they believe that end justifies the means.* Terrorism is the only way to bring about the revolution because it creates a terror both in the minds of the unjust as well as tyrant rulers. At the same time it creates the power of resistance amongst the downtrodden. The lesson of other countries where revolution has occurred is always present before the revolutionaries. The history of the revolution teaches us the lesson that the revolution truly means that the just and ideal social system be established. Our ideal is to establish a classless society after ending the native as well as foreign exploitation where the people will get the best possible opportunities.

From this it seems clear that the Revolutionaries considered it essential to use force to expel the British exploiters. We give another example of the then prevailing situation. From Sabarmati Ashram Mahatma Gandhi wrote on 2nd April, 1930 a letter to Lord Irwin in which Mahatma Gandhi said, "British rule was the greatest curse for India. It has made the people extremely poor by sheer exploitation. It has made totally hollow the roots of our culture and made our condition worse from political point of view. We expected that the coming Round-Table Conference would solve Indian problem but you have declined to give the promise of Dominion Status for which the people are feeling thirsty. This is clear that the British Government has absolutely no intention to grant the dominion status. So many taxes have been imposed upon the people that their blood has been sucked. Heavy taxes have been imposed upon salt also which common man uses. It is my increasing belief that the organised violence of the British Government can be checked only by non-violence. I want to remove all these evils by means of Civil Disobedience Movement. If my letter does not exercise any effect, then I will start the Movement on 11th April, 1930 for violating the salt laws.[1]" The Viceroy sent a very rough reply to it. Therefore, Gandhiji wrote, "*On bended knees, I asked for bread and received a stone instead. The English nation responds only to force and I am not surprised by the Viceregal reply. The only place that Nation knows is the peace of the public prison. India is a vast prison house, I repudiate this British law and regard it as my sacred duty to break the mournful monotony of compulsory peace that is choking the heart of the Nation for want of free vent.*"

In spite of this Gandhiji clung to the belief strongly that armed revolution was not possible in the entire country and it could not succeed in achieving independence. Pandit Jawaharlal Nehru also repeated this view in Lahore Session of the Congress, 1929. The author agrees to this point of view.

Subhas Chandra Bose was the last great Revolutionary of India. The I.N.A. was led by him. With the defeat of Japan on 14th August, 1945, the three military officers of I.N.A. fell into the British hands. The Red Fort Trial took place in November, 1945. Jawaharlal Nehru, Bhulabhai Desai and Sir Tej Bahadur Sapru–pleaded their case. They were later on released by the orders of the Commander-in-Chief Lord Auchinlek.

Importance of I.N.A. Trial. Dr. R.C. Majumdar observes, "I.N.A. Trial, however justifiable from strict military point of view, was a fatal political blunder. *It convulsed the whole of India from one end to the other and gave a new turn for the worse to the political situation in India (from the British point of view). It may also be regarded as an indirect cause of the mutiny of the Naval Ratings in February, 1946 which gave blow to the prestige of the British.*"

Conclusion. There is no doubt that the sacrifices of the Revolutionaries are unparalleled but there is no denying the hard fact that the Congress made a unique contribution to the mass awakening through all its programmes and movements. Before the Revolutionaries, Lokmanya Bal Gangadhar Tilak had done his best to rouse the political consciousness of the people against the foreign rule by the following effective methods: (1) starting the celebration of the birthday of Shivaji, Ganapati festival and opening various educational institutions; (2) giving the nation a new slogan for the first time that freedom was his birth-right and he would have it; (3) insisting on the implementation of the programme of national education, Swadeshi, and boycott of British goods (4) writing exciting articles in his newspapers *Maratha and Kesari;* (5) making extremely impressive self-sacrifice of going to worst horrible Mandlay jail (1908-14) and bearing innumerable tortures; (6) awakening the masses against the war efforts by stirring speeches without caring for the consequences and starting of Home Rule Movement; (7) utmost defiance of the British might by every possible means.

Though it is a very significant contribution but the readers should not forget this fact also that this was the period of the nation-in-making. Therefore, the readers have forgotten the extremely important (notable) contribution of Lokmanya Bal Gangadhar Tilak.

After him Gandhiji gave a new weapon to the people and created mass awakening, imbided a national character and created a spirit of self-sacrifice of an unprecedented scale and let three movements (Non-co-operation, Civil disobedience and Quit India) before whom the British race which had not bowed before the German might during the two World Wars had to bow and leave the country bag and baggage.

1. Dr. Pattabhi Sitaramayya, *History of Congress*, p.631-47.

Thus the right conclusion would be that both the Revolutionaries and Non-Revolutionaries (Congressmen) have contributed their best in their own way for the regeneration of Bharat (India) and were able to oust the mightiest imperialism of the world and free the country from its clutches. It should not be forgotten also that the overthrow of imperialism in India broke its backbone and paved the way for the liberation of Lanka, Burma, Malaya, Indonesia, the whole of Africa and other parts of the world. Therefore the contribution of India for the elimination of imperialism from the world is unique and should never be forgotten.

EXERCISES

Long Answer Type Questions

1. Discuss the causes of the Birth of Revolutionary Movement.
2. Write a short note on the Aims of the Revolutionary Movement.
3. What do you know about the Freedom Movement of the Namdhari Sikhs?

   OR

   What do you know about Kookas Movement in Punjab?
4. Discuss the Freedom Movement of Chapekar Bandhu in Maharashtra.
5. What do you know about Vinayak Damodar Savarkar's freedom struggle in India and London?
6. Discuss Sardar Singh Rana and Madame Cama's Revolutionary Activities in Europe.
7. Write a short note on Revolutionary Movement in Bengal.
8. What do you know about Indian Freedom Movement in Foreign Countries?
9. What do you know about Revolutionary Movement of Ram Prasad Bismi and Ashfaq Ullah?
10. What do you know about Sardar Bhagat Singh? Discuss his contribution in Revolutionary Movement.
11. What do you know about Chandra Shekhar Azad? Discuss his contribution in Revolutionary Movement.
12. What do you know about Shubhash Chandra Bose?

Short Answer Type Questions

1. What do you know about Shyamji Krishna Verma? Discuss in brief his role in Revolutionary Movement.
2. Write a short note on Nasik Conspiracy case.
3. What do you know about Arvind Ghosh?
4. Discuss the role of Virendra Kumar Ghosh in Revolutionary Movement.
5. Write a short note on Upendra.
6. Write a short note on Alipur Conspiracy Case.
7. What was Delhi Conspiracy Case.?
8. What do you know about Komagata Maru?
9. Write a brief note on Gadar Party.
10. What do you know about Kakori Case?
11. What do you know about Bhagwati Charan Vohra?
12. Write a brief note on Yashpal's Contribution in Revolutionary Movement.

Objective Type Questions

Choose the correct answer

1. Who launched Peasants Movement ?
   (*a*) Lala Lajpat Rai (*b*) Sardar Ajit Singh
   (*c*) Both a and b (*d*) None of the above
2. Who persuaded the people to celebrate Shivaji Festival and Ganesh Festival ?
   (*a*) Bal Gangadhar Tilak (*b*) Lala Lajpat Rai
   (*c*) Veer Saavarkar (*d*) Bipin Chandra Pal
3. Who sponsored the Swadeshi Movement ?
   (*a*) Lala Lajpat Rai (*b*) Bal Gangadhar Tilak
   (*c*) Mahatma Gandhi (*d*) Bipin Chandra Pal
4. Whose followers were called Namdhari Sikhs ?
   (*a*) Guru Naanak (*b*) Banda Bahadur
   (*c*) Guru Ramsingh (*d*) Guru Baalakjee
5. Vinayak Damodar Savarkar was born in
   (*a*) 1880 (*b*) 1881
   (*c*) 1882 (*d*) 1883
6. Who was National Guru of Vinayak Damodar Savarkar ?
   (*a*) Bal Gangadhar Tilak (*b*) Gopal Krishna Gokhale
   (*c*) Chapekar Bandhu (*d*) Bipin Chandra Pal

ANSWERS

1. (*c*) **2.** (*a*) **3.** (*b*) **4.** (*c*) **5.** (*d*) **6.** (*a*)

10

CHAPTER

Rise and Growth of Communalism

(Muslim League Fights for Pakistan or Partition of the Country)

> *"Muslims are not in a minority and they are a nation by any definition. It is a dream that the Hindus and Muslims can ever evolve a common nationality. The Hindus and Mohammedans belong to two different religious philosophies, social customs and literature. They neither intermarry, nor interdine and indeed they belong to different civilizations which are based mainly on conflicting ideas and conceptions. They have different epics, their heroes are different and possess different episodes. Very often the hero of one is the foe of another and likewise their victories and defeats overlap. The only course open to us all is to allow the major nations separate homelands by dividing India into autonomous national states."* —*Jinnah*

Communalism in Indian Politics has been a great and formidable obstacle in our constitutional advance. The hatred between Hindus and Muslims was engendered by the British as a political device to perpetuate their rule. 'Divide and rule' has always been the corner-stone of the British Administration in India. Not only did the British statesmen prevent the welding of them into a single nation, but they also tried to foment ill-will between them so as to use their mutual difference as an excuse for withholding the transfer for power to Indian hands. During the first few decades of the present century both communities worked in a spirit of comradeship for the expulsion of the British. The British Statesmen realised the situation at a very early date and scented the danger in case they pooled their efforts to overthrow the foreign rule. The rulers knew that the numbered British officers in India would be no match to the overwhelming strength of the natives. Hence, they employed the practice of giving preferential treatment to one and indifference towards the others so as to sow discord amongst them. For a few decades after the Mutiny of 1857, the British Government nursed a grudge against the Muslims who, it knew, were largely responsible for the outbreak. The Muslims were crushed and debarred from occupying key posts both in the Civil Administration and in the Military. In 1871, out of a total of 2,141 persons employed by the Bengal Government, there were 711 Hindus, 1,338 Europeans and only 92 Muslims. The Muslims, too having been deprived of all their titles, privileges and position had bitter resentment against the British. This state of affairs continued till the advent of Sir Syed Ahmed Khan on the political scene.

The rise of strong nationalism amongst the Hindus for a number of years found favour with the Muslims who too were anti-British. The sentiments of unity stuck like a thorn in the sides of British

Government. It decided to create a division into two communities to make its own rule more lasting. This polity was given effect to in two ways. The first was the reorganisation of the Army which hitherto used to have all the communities mixed up in its ranks. In order to encourage separatist tendencies, regiments and battalions were created on the caste and religious distinctions. Secondly, the Government began to patronise the Muslims in order that may cease to join hands with the Congress. The British tacticians terrified the Muslims by telling them that they would be worse under the domination of the Hindus. They also encouraged the Muslims to demand separate electorate, even a separate Muslim Majority State. Partition of Bengal was the first step in that direction. And when it was annulled by Lord Hardinge, the bogey of Pakistan was raised to smash our territorial and national integrity. Thus, the communal problem in India was not merely religious in character as styled by the rulers, it was propped up for political gains. And it is an admitted fact that it was a deliberate creation of British imperialism for stabilising their rule over India.

WAHABI MOVEMENT

Wahabi Movement which started in Arabia towards the end of the 18th century for the revitalisation of Islam also fanned the flame of communalism in India. The religious movement was sponsored in India by Syed Ahmed Brelvi. The object of this movement was the glorification of Islam. Mr. Syed Ahmed Brelvi after his return from Mecca in 1820, preached for the eradication of all the evils and impurities that had crept into Islam. The followers of Mr. Syed Ahmed Brelvi became very fanatic and intolerant. They went to the extent of declaring a Holy War or crusade against the Sikhs and non Wahabis. The Government, however, dealt with them with an iron hand and suppressed it before the movement could take a dangerous form.

ALIGARH MOVEMENT OF SIR SYED AHMED KHAN (1817-1898)

The British Government for quite a long period looked upon the Muslims as untrustworthy and disloyal. It interpreted the Mutiny of 1857 as an attempt by the Muslims to revive the Mughal rule in India and hence, it continued to nurse a prejudice against them. The Muslims were deliberately kept out of Government jobs. Accounting to Mr. Norman, "The British people had decided that for the expansion of the new power and its continuance, the only course was to crush the Mussalmans and had deliberately adopted policies which had for their aim the economic ruin of Muslims and their intellectual stagnation and general degeneration." Another factor which accounted for the backwardness of the Muslims was their religious hatred for English education. The Hindus who received Western Education stole a clear march over the Muslims and occupied many important posts in the administration. Sir Syed Ahmed Khan (1817-1898) encouraged the Muslims to grow out of their prejudices and welcome Western Education as the gateway to material prosperity. In pursuance of his aim, he founded a Mohammedan Anglo-Oriental College at Aligarh which in course of time became the Muslim University, Aligarh. This university later on became a nursery of fanatic Muslims and a nucleus of all the anti-national activities.

Sir Syed Ahmed Khan was of the nationalist views in the beginning. On one occassion he had remarked : "*In the word 'Nation', I include both Hindus and Mohammedans because it is the only meaning attached to it. With me it is not worth considering what is their religious faith, because we do not see anything of it. What we see is that we inhabit the same land, are subject to the rule of the same Governors, the fountains of benefit for all are the same, and the pangs of famine also we suffer equally. These are the different grounds upon which I call both these races which inhabit India by one word, i.e., Hindus, meaning to say that they are inhabitants of Hindustan.*" But such tolerant views of Sir Syed Ahmed Khan soon changed into communal hatred. He became an arch-enemy of the Congress and the Nationalism. As a loyal friend of the British, he became the champion of Anglo-Muslim alliance. The change in his attitude is said to have been brought about by Mr. Beck, the Principal of M. A. O. College, Aligarh. Mr. Beck impressed upon him the need of cooperation with Britishers in the interest of his community. Mr. Syed Ahmed Khan thus, became a pawn in the British game of creating communal divisions in India. In an address presented to Lord Lytton in 1877 he said that, "*The chief object of founding the M. A. O. College was to reconcile Oriental learning with Western literature and science to make the Muslims of India worthy and useful subjects of the British Crown, to inspire in them that loyalty which springs not from servile submission to foreign rule but from a genuine appreciation of the blessings of good government.*"

In order to wash out from the face of the Muslims the blot of having been Mutineers, Sir Syed Ahmed Khan started a paper *Loyal Mohammedans* of India. He, through his articles and speeches, tried to convince the rulers that Indian Muslims had reconciled to the foreign rule and become loyal to them. He advised Muslims to shed their religious ill-will towards Christianity. In one of his books he tended to prove that Islam permitted its followers to share meals with a Christian or a Jew. "These writings of Sir Syed Ahmed Khan," remarks **Justice Shah Din,** "brought conviction home to many an official sceptic, and the ominous cloud that hung for a time over Muslim loyalty soon rolled away."

Sir Syed Ahmed Khan strove hard to bring about a rapprochement between Muslims and the Government. For this reason he directed all his energies towards keeping his community free from the influence of the Congress which was a nationalist and anti-Government organisation. He laid the foundation of the *Annual Muslim Educational Conference* in 1886 which by holding its sessions simultaneously with the Congress Session in the same town, tried to withhold the Muslims from attending the Congress session. The Congress which in its early years enjoyed the blessings of the Government fell out of its favour. Sir Syed Ahmed Khan went ahead with the set purpose of promoting among the Muslims loyalty to the British Government and hatred for the Congress. In 1888 he founded in league with Raja Shiva Prasad of Benares, the *Patriotic Association* to act as the rival of the Congress. It was a reactionary body and began to oppose the progressive views of the Congress in all possible ways. *In his memoirs Mr. Surendra Nath Bannerji writes, that soon after a few years the Congress began to be dubbed as a Hindu body, while we were straining every nerve to secure the co-operation of our Mohammedan fellow-countrymen in this great national work. We sometimes paid the fares of the Mohammedan delegates and offered them other facilities.*[1] Sir Syed Ahmed Khan at the instigation of the Government, also founded Mohammedan Anglo-Oriental Defence Association in 1893. The object of this body was to persuade the Muslims to give up their religious prejudices against Christianity and to strengthen the hands of government for protecting their political interests.

FUNDAMENTALIST MUSLIMS, DEMAND FOR COMMUNAL REPRESENTATION

The Partition of Bengal caused much heart burning and resentment among the Bengali-speaking people of that Province. The Government proceeded diplomatically and sowed discord between the Hindus and Muslims. It demarcated East Bengal as predominantly Muslim area and provoked and poisoned the minds of the Muslims against the Hindus who were in minority in that area. Despite this manoeuvering, when the fervour of nationalism did not subside, Lord Morley, the then Secretary of State, advised Lord Minto, the Viceroy of India, to appease the people by introducing constitutional reforms. Lord Minto was, however, in favour of widening the gulf between the Hindus and Muslims in order to strike a nail into nationalism of Bengal. Consequently, Mr. Smith, Private Secretary of the Viceroy, wrote to Mr. Archbold, the Principal of the Aligarh College, that the Viceroy would be glad to meet a deputation of the Muslims and try to meet the demands of the Muslim community. Mr. Archbold made no delay in passing on to Mohsin-ul-Mulk, the Secretary of the College, the contents of the letter he had received. He also advised the Secretary of the College to demand nomination or representation on communal basis. Mr. Archbold agreed to draft the address. Nawab Mohsin-ul-Mulk, the Secretary of Aligarh College, soon organised a representative body of the

1. Surendra Nath Bannerjee – *A nation in Making,* p.118.

Muslims headed by Sir Agha Khan to wait on the viceroy. The deputation on 1st October, 1906, put the following demands before the Viceroy :

(*i*) Separate electoral constituency for the Mohammedans; (*ii*) representation of the Muslims in the newly constituted legislative assemblies and other elected bodies not on the numerical strength of the community but on its political importance; (*iii*) reservation of seats in the State services for the Muslims; (*iv*) more state aid for the setting up new Muslim universities; and (*v*) preference to be given to Muslims in regard to nominations in the Governor-General's Council.

Lord Minto who was over-anxious to please the Muslims said, "*The pith of your Address, as I understand it, is a claim that in any system of representation, whether it affects a Municipality, a District Board or a Legislature in which it is proposed to introduce or to increase the electoral organisation, the Mohammedan Community should be represented as a body. You justly claimed that your position should be estimated nor merely on your numerical strength but in respect to the political importance of your community and the service that it has rendered to the Empire.*" One can easily smell from Lord Minto's statement that he himself was more inclined to introduce communal electorate than the Muslim themselves. Lord Morley personally was not in accord with Minto's policy but in the interest of the British Empire, he had to submit to the Viceroy's views. A paper like *Statesman* which had always been known for its pro-Government views also did not fail to criticise the principle of separate electorate. One sinister effect of this official policy on Indian politics was that the Muslims were driven farther from the Congress and the Hindus: and in order to acquire more political gains, they became thick with the British. The system of communal representation intensified hatred and religious animosity between the two communities which climaxed in the partition of the country in 1947.

COMMUNAL MOVEMENT OF THE MUSLIM LEAGUE

Birth of Muslim League. The success of the Muslim deputation that waited upon the Viceroy at Simla enthused the Muslims to start a separate political organisation of their own. The British officialdom was also interested in it so as to counterbalance the Congress. Consequently on 31st December, 1906 the Muslim League was formed at Dacca with a view to "support, whatever possible, all measures emanating from the Góvernment, and to protect the cause and advance the interest of our co-religionists throughout the country, to controvert the growing influence of the so-called Indian National Congress....and to enable our young men of education to join this organisation who for want of such an organisation have joined the Congress...." The object of the League was defined as follows :

(*a*) "To promote among the Mussalmans of India feeling of loyalty to the British Government and to remove any misconception that may arise as to the intention of the government with regard to any of its measures.

(*b*) To protect and advance the political rights and interests of the Mussalmans of India and to respectfully represent their needs and aspirations to the Government.

(*c*) To prevent the rise among the Mussalmans of India of any feelings of hostility towards other communities without prejudice to other aforementioned objects of the League."

Thus the Muslim League provided a political and nonetheless communal platform to the Muslim community. It was from the day of its birth an unpatriotic and anti-national organism with an avowed aim of promoting loyalty towards the British Government. The first conference of the All India Muslim was held at Amritsar under the Presidentship of Sir Syed Ali Imam. The League leaders at the conference demanded more weightage to the Muslims in the Legislative Councils and in the Civil Services. In Governor-General's Executive Council it demanded equality of representation with the majority community. These very demands were voiced again in the succeeding conferences held in 1909 and 1910.

Changes in the Policy of Muslim League. It is worth noting that the Muslim League then failed to enlist the support of the entire Muslim intelligentsia. Its communal character proved distasteful to the Nationalist Mohammedans. Even Mr. Jinnah for many years had been an opponent of the League and in the Allahabad Session of the Congress in 1910, he moved a resolution condemning the system of communal representation. His resolution was seconded by Maulana Mazhar-ul-Haq who advocated for greater friendship and understanding between the Hindus and Muslims. Since all the Muslims were extremely happy over the undue representation in the elected bodies given to them according to the Act of 1909, it was certainly an act of great courage for the Muslim leaders to decry the system of Separate Electorate and to make an appeal for Hindu-Muslim unity. Nawab Syed Muhammed Ali and Maulana Azad not only refused to have any dealing with the League but also attacked the communalism and loyalty of the League. Maulana Muhammad Ali started an English paper *Comrade* and an Urdu paper *Hamdard* to propagate his anti-League views. Maulana Azad also brought out a paper *Al Hilal* from Calcutta to serve as the mouthpiece of his nationalist views. Besides these, there were other progressive Muslim leaders like Syed Wazir Hussain, Hassan Iman and Hakim Ajmal·Khan who also did not see eye to eye with the League.

Under the pressure of eminent Muslim leaders mentioned above the League was compelled to modify its constitution and effect certain changes in its aims and objects. Besides it, Maulana Muhammad-ul-Hassan founded Jamiat-Ul-Ulema-i-Hind, League's rival in the political field. The national organisation vigorously opposed the communalism of League and did yeoman's service to bring the Muslims to the Congress fold. With the popularity of nationalist Muslim leaders growing, the influence of he League began to decline. Eventually the Muslim League gave up its dogmatism and drifted closer to the Congress creed. It amended its constitution and included the promotion of goodwill between the two major communities and the attainment of 'Swarajya' under the patronage of the British Crown in the Charter of its aims and objects. Several factors in the international field compelled the League to change its attitude from loyalty to the British to one of patriotism. There was a campaign going on in the south-east European countries to throw off the yoke of Turkey. Russia extended its support to the countries struggling against Turkey for their independence. And since Britain was friendly with Russia, the Indian Mussalmans began to distrust Britishers. Another reason responsible for the drift of League towards the Congress was that Turkey had joined hands with Germany and fought against the British during the First Great War. Indian Muslims who accepted the Emperor of Turkey as their Khalifa (Religious Guru) began to look upon the British as their enemies. Thus began a new chapter in the history of the League. Both the Congress and the League held their annual sessions at Lucknow. The League and the Congress leaders met in a cordial atmosphere and formulated a scheme for post-war reforms. The cloud of distrust and hostility melted so thoroughly that Mahatma Gandhi, Sarojini Naidu and Pt. Malaviya even attended the League Sessions in 1916 and 1917 and delivered speeches from its platform.

Muslim League's attitude towards Khilafat Movement. The First Great War ended in 1918. England and Turkey concluded a treaty. The British dethroned the Sultan of Turkey for his complicity with Germany during the war. Turkish Empire was also disintegrated and a large part of it was annexed to the British Empire. Indian Muslims expressed their resentment against the high handedness of the British Government and resolved to start an anti-British agitation. With this end in view they formed Khilafat Committee. There was heartburning and frustration in the Congress camp also because the British Government after the termination of hostilities in Europe not only refused to transfer power to Indians but also massacred the unarmed agitators in cold blood at Jallianwallah Bagh, Amritsar. Gandhiji, as such, launched the great Non-Co-operation Movement in 1920 to register nation's protest against the British brutalities in the Punjab and the Khilafat wrongs. The League, although did not decline to associate itself with the Congress, participated in the movement only half-heartedly. The active support came from the nationalist Muslims; hence the League became greatly unpopular.

Revival of Muslim League. The truce between the League and the Congress proved quite temporary. The communal accord which had begun with Lucknow Pact ended in 1922 with the calling off of the Non-Co-operation and Khilafat Movement by Gandhiji. For the next ten years the country passed through the fire of communal madness and riots. The communal disturbances were partly the creation of the British Government. The British bureaucracy in India not to speak of remaining indifferent to orgy of murders in the name of religion, rather shamelessly encouraged the Muslims to attack their Hindu neighbours. Arya Samaj then appeared as the saviour of Hinduism from the onslaughts of Islam. Hindu Mahasabha also intensified its activities to safeguard the Hindus. Mopla Muslims in Malabar subjected the Hindus of that area to loot and arson. The woeful tales of Malabar Hindus were so horrifying that leaders like Lala Lajpat Rai and Pt. Malaviya also could not remain passively indifferent to it. When the atmosphere was so highly charged with communal tension, the Muslim League exploited the situation for consolidating its hold on the community. Mr. M.A. Jinnah, who had already left the Congress a few years ago, assumed the leadership of the League. Maulana Mohammad Ali and Shaukat Ali also withdrew from the Congress and began to strengthen the Muslim League. Thus the Hindus-Muslim unity, which had appeared to be a probable proposition during the Khilafat agitation, went to winds.

Muslim League and Simon Commission. When the All-English Simon Commission came to India there appeared a rift in the League leadership. The Congress decided to boycott it vigorously. The Muslim League found itself in a fix. Its members were divided on the question of what attitude they should adopt towards the Commission. The League ranks were split into two sections. One section led by Mr. Jinnah stood for boycott; while the other section led by Sir Muhammad Shafi was in favour of co-operating with it. Both the sections held their sessions separately at Calcutta and Lahore to chalk out their future course of action.

Muslim League and Nehru Report. Pt. Motilal Nehru in his Report proposed joint electorate with reservation of seats for the Muslims. After the publication of Nehru Report, the Muslim League was divided into two groups. Mr. Mohammed Ali Jinnah' was opposed to the scheme from the very beginning. His famous Fourteen Points which are given in chapter XVI, were presented by the Muslim League, as an alternative to the Nehru Report. The ginger group led by Mohammad Shafi called a Muslim All Parties Conference to discuss the solution of Communal Problem chalked out in the Nehru Report. The Report was held to ridicule and criticism by Shafi group. They demanded separate electorate. The result was that the house of the League became divided into itself. Nationalist Muslims like Dr.Ansari., Hakim Ajmal Khan, Sir Wazir Hussain, Dr. Syed Muhammed, Asaf Ali, Dr. Kitchlew and Abdul Kalam Azad dissociated themselves from the League. Shafi group wielded greater influence than the nationalists on the Muslim middle class because it enjoyed the patronage of the Government. The British officialdom remained more kind and accommodating towards the League demand in order to win its support in crushing the wave of nationalism. The League members who were highly placed in the administration of the country succeeded better in benefiting the Muslim Community. Naturally League drew the Muslim intelligentsia towards itself day by day. Mention should also be made of another Muslim organisation called Ahrar Party in the Punjab and Krishak Praja Party in Bengal. The leader of Ahrar Party was Mr. Ataullah Shah Bukhari. It was a moderate group which although did not agree with the economic programmes of the Congress but was more akin to it than to the Muslim League in its political creed. It had large following amongst the Muslim peasants. After 1944, however, the Ahrar Party suffered an eclipse, paving the way clear for the Muslim League to lord over the Muslim masses of India.

League's Struggle for Pakistan. In due course Jinnah reconciled to communal politics of Muslim League. He negotiated with the Shafi group and struck out a Fourteen-Point Programme. It was a sort of irrevocable charter of Muslim demands for any compromise with the Congress. It contained such fantastic demands as the Congress with all its liberal outlook could not accept it. During the two Round Table Conferences in London, the Muslim Leagues stuck fast to its Fourteen-Point

Programme and foiled all the attempts made by the Congress to solve the communal problem. The British Government utilised the communal tangle in beating down the Congress demand. Gandhiji returned to India from the Second Round Table Conference much disappointed and empty-handed. Mr. Ramsay McDonald issued the Communal Award conceding the Muslims all they had asked for. A phase of Congress-League co-operation occurred again while the reforms of 1935 were in the making. Mr. Jinnah showed eagerness to collaborate with the Congress in opposing the Federal scheme as proposed in the Act of 1935. He sincerely believed than the proposed reforms were only a trick to put off the country's demands for self-government for an indefinite period. The Congress workers went to the extent of supporting the League candidates against non-League Muslim candidates in the elections to the Provincial legislatures in 1937. But this superficial unity was broken again and the two premier organisations drifted further apart never to reconcile again.

The idea of Pakistan which came from the League platform in 1940 at Lahore session had actually been conceived ten years ago by Muhammad Iqbal in 1930. At League's annual conference at Allahabad Mr. Iqbal had expressed his dream of 'a consolidated North-West Indian Muslim State'. People then had laughted it away as 'loud thinking' or a fantastic dream. It then came from Mr. Rahmat Ali, a Cambridge student, in a more precise and forceful way. Neither Mr. Jinnah nor Mr. Zafrullah Khan then considered it practicable. However, on March 23, 1940, the Muslim League passed a resolution at its Lahore session. The text of the resolution ran as under: "*Resolved that it is the considered view of this session of the All India Muslim League that no constitutional scheme would be workable in this country or acceptable to Muslims unless it is designed on the following basic principles, viz., that geographically contiguous units are demarcated into regions which should be constituted with such territorial readjustments as may be necessary, that the area in which the Muslims are numerically in majority should be grouped to constitute independent states.*" The League resolved that the British government before leaving India must effect the partition of the country into Indian Union and Pakistan. Pakistan was in fact the demand of a separate Muslim state, comprising the Muslim-majority Provinces of Bengal, Assam and Hyderabad. The basis of League's demand was its mischievous "Two-Nation theory" which first came from Sir Wazir Hussain in his presidential address at Bombay session of League in 1936. He said, "*The Hindus and Mussalmans inhabiting this vast continent are not two communities but should be considered two nations in many respects.*"

In 1942, when the Congress started 'Quit India' Movement, the Muslim League instead of supporting it, co-operated with the government to crush the national uprising. During the two years from 1942 to 1944 while all the top class leaders of the Congress were behind the bars, Jinnah got the field free for his nasty propaganda against the Congress, which he dubbed as a purely Hindu body wedded to the goal of establishing 'Hindu Raj' in India. The crooked designs of Jinnah had the desired effect. The idea of Pakistan went deep into the minds and hearts of the Mussalmans.

In the General Elections which took place in India in 1946, the League captured majority of Muslim seats. The phenomenal success of the League stunned every leader and student of political development in India. Only a few years ago in the elections for the provincial Assemblies in 1937, the League had fared poorly even in predominantly Muslim provinces like Sind and N.W.F.P., the Punjab and Bengal. It had suffered crushing defeats by Red Shirts Party of Khan Abdul Gaffar Khan in N.W.F.P., by Azad Muslim Party of Allah Bux in Sind, by the Unionist Party of Sikander Hyat Khan in the Punjab and by the Krishak Praja Party of Fazlul Huq in Bengal. The League had been able to claim some notable success only in Uttar Pradesh, Bihar, Madras, Bombay and Central Provinces. The gap of nine years made a world of difference in the strength and popularity of the League. At the polls in 1946 the tables were turned in favour of the League. It drove the other Muslim organisations out of the field and claimed nearly all the Muslim seats in every Province. The Congress could pocket Hindu seats only. The election results of 1946 established the fact once for ever that Congress and League–the two premier organisations of India–represented essentially the Hindus and the Muslims respectively.

Encouraged by its staggering at the polls, the Muslim League launched its campaign for the formation of Pakistan with redoubled energy. The demand pricked the balloon of the Congress claim that it was a national organisation having under its umbrella both the the Hindus and Muslims. It still dubbed the idea of Pakistan (in the words of Zafrullah Khan) as 'chimercial and impracticable'. The Jamait-ul-Ulema-i-Hind, Ahrars, the Khudai Khidmatgars and All-India Shia Conference denounced League's dream of Pakistan. The Cabinet Mission also hinted at the hollowness of such an idea and stated that without wholesale transfer of minority population from India to Pakistan and vice versa, the communal conflict would not subside. Partition, the Cabinet Mission said, was an inadequate solution of the communal problem. The Muslim League under Mr. Jinnah then decided to employ bullying and coercive methods to secure submission from the Congress. It launched 'Direct Action' in Muslim Majority Provinces. Once more the communal riots flared up in the country on a vast scale. The British officials who were interested in creating chaos in the country, let the Muslim good as take law into their hands. Hosts of hired goondas attacked Hindu homes, plundered the rich, and killed the people. The incalculable loss of life and property suffered by the Hindus in the Muslim majority Provinces shook the Congress leaders out of their complacent dream. Cracks appeared in their resolution of 'Undivided India'. In spite of the theoretical, economical, geographical unsoundness and absurdity of the idea of Pakistan, it became a hard painful reality. 14th August, 1947, was inasuspicious day when Pakistan came into existence. No doubt it was not exactly Pakistan of Mr. Jinnah's dreams, it was certainly a triumph of communalism over national solildarity, of sword over constitutionalism and of Two Nations' Theory over the historical fact of *Akhand Bharat.* The geographical oneness of our country was split up not in two but three units. The Muslims got the eastern parts while the heterogeneous group of the three hundred million souls got the truncated India. Thank God that the original plan of Pakistan was greatly pruned. Assam, Hyderabad, Kashmir and Parts of Bengal and Punjab were excluded from it.

East and West Pakistan could not live in unity any longer and East Pakistan separated itself after indo-Pak War in Dec. 1971. East Pakistan named herself Bangladesh and became a reality on December 16, 1971.

EXERCISES

Long Answer Type Questions

1. Discuss the factors which contributed to the formation of the Muslim League. Do you agree with the view that it was primarily a result of the British Policy of Divide and Rule?
2. Trace the role of the Muslim League in Indian Politics.
3. "Communalism in Indian Politics has been a great and formidable obstacle." Discuss this statement.
4. What do you know about Aligarh Movement of Sir Syed Ahmed Khan?

Short Answer Type Questions

1. What do you know about Wahabi Movement? Discuss in brief.
2. What do you know about Sir Syed Ahmed Khan?
3. Write a short note on the birth of Muslim League.
4. Write a short note on the objectives of Muslim League.
5. What was Muslim League's attitude towards Khilafat Movement?
6. Write a short note on 'Muslim League and Simon Commission'.
7. Write a short note on 'Muslim League and Nehru Report'.

Objective Type Questions

Choose the correct answer

1. Who was sponsored of Wahabi Movement in India ?
   (*a*) Syed Ahmed Brelvi (*b*) Sir Syed Ahmed Khan
   (*c*) Khan Abdul Gaffar Khan (*d*) None of the above
2. Sir Syed Ahmed Khan started a Newspaper. What was its name?
   (*a*) Muslim Nama (*b*) Loyal Mohammedans of India
   (*c*) Jung (*d*) None of the above
3. In which year Sir Syed Ahmed Khan laid the foundation of the "Annual Muslim Educational Conference" ?
   (*a*) 1884 (*b*) 1885
   (*c*) 1886 (*d*) 1887
4. In which year Sir Syed Ahmed Khan founded the 'Patriotic Association' ?
   (*a*) 1885 (*b*) 1886
   (*c*) 1887 (*d*) 1888
5. In which year Sir Syed Ahmed Khan founded 'Mohammedan Anglo-Oriental Defence Association'?
   (*a*) 1893 (*b*) 1894
   (*c*) 1895 (*d*) 1896
6. In which year Muslim League was formed ?
   (*a*) 1905 (*b*) 1906
   (*c*) 1907 (*d*) 1908

ANSWERS

1. (*a*) **2.** (*b*) **3.** (*c*) **4.** (*d*) **5.** (*a*) **6.** (*b*)

11

CHAPTER

Morley-Minto Reforms (Act of 1909)

"If I were attempted to set up a parliamentary system in India, or if it could be said that this chapter of reforms led directly or necessarily up to the establishment of a parliamentary system in India, I, for one would have nothing to do with it." —Mr. Morley, Secretary of State for India.

CIRCUMSTANCES LEADING TO THE ACT OF 1909

The Indian Councils Act, 1909, popularly known as 'Morley-Minto Reforms' has its own importance in the constitutional history of India. Mr. Morley was the then Secretary of State and Lord Minto was the Governor-General of India at that time. Many factors were responsible for Morley-Minto Reforms. Here we are discussing some of them in short :

1. Dissatisfaction with the Act of 1892– The Act of 1892 did not fulfill the aspirations of the people of India. The constitution and the functions of the Legislative Council disappointed the Indians. To a large extent, the rules framed by the Central and Provincial Governments had limited the rights given to the Members of the Councils. The Councils were no better than the debating societies. The Members of the Council could not ask any questions on the financial policy of the Government. The President of the Council had the right to disallow any question without assigning any reason. Moreover, the Act deliberately attempted to tally with the elective idea and the 'principle of election' was not conceded to them in a clear form. The increase of non-official element in the Council was also very meagre. The Indian National Congress was greatly agitated over the reforms and the members of the Congress clamoured for more reforms in the Council. The attitude of the authorities towards the demand of the Nationalists was not encouraging. The indifferents and evasive attitude of the British Government, greatly enhanced the discontent and it ultimately resulted into political agitation of great magnitude.

2. Uncommon sufferings of the Indians– Only four years after the passing of the Councils Act of 1892, India had to face many sufferings. Plague broke out in the country, and it was followed by the famine. The famine of 1896-97, as described by Frazer, was "The most intense and severe famine ever then known under the British Rule. By the Spring of 1897, over four million people were receiving relief, and mortality was extremely heavy." Famine was followed by bubonic Plague in the Bombay Presidency. According to the official figures, 1,730000 people died of epidemic in the year 1898. There was a severe famine again in the year 1899. The suffering millions became the cruel victims of British economic policy. The measures adopted by the Government were vigorous but the way in which they were implemented, was not appealing to the masses. Soldiers went into the homes of Indians and in the name of help, they exercised pressure and violence. '*Bal Gangadhar Tilak*' opposed the methods enforced by the Government. Riots broke out at many places. On 23rd June, 1897, Mr. Rand, the unpopular Plague Commissioner was shot dead, In this way, there was a great dissatisfaction against the Government amongst the Indian people.

3. Lord Curzon's unpopular measures (1899-1905)– *Punniah* has remarked, "the Viceroyalty of Lord Curzon (1898-1905) marked an important stage in the development of political unrest in our country." Curzon, in order to effect the development and efficiency in administration crushed the Indian people. His imperious nature, bureaucratic attitude and autocratic temperament were the main causes of the dissatisfaction amongst Indian. There was a stormy opposition to his measure, Calcutta Corporation Act of 1900, by which the size of the Corporation was considerably decreased from 75 to 50 by eliminating 25 elected members. The Indian Universities Act of 1904 also led to a good deal of controversy. It was regarded as an attempt to check the growth of higher education for political reasons.

In 1904 his budget speech–that the highest ranks in the civil service will be given to only Englishmen added fuel to the fire. The Partition of Bengal, to check the Indian nationalism was the main factor of Indian opposition. Curzon always tried that Indians should quarrel with each other. He tried to gain the sympathy of Muslims on the plea, that they were given a Province in the Eastern Bengal. In this connection *Mr. A.C. Majumdar* has written :

"Fully resolved to crush the new spirit by dividing the people against themselves, Lord Curzon proceeded to East Bengal and there at meetings of Mohammedans specially converted for the purpose, explained to them that his object in partitioning was not only to relieve Bengal Administration but also to create Mohammedan Province where Islam could be predominant and its followers in the ascendancy.

Mr. S.N. Bannerjee and B.C. Pal, the two revolutionary leaders, raised voice against the partition and partition have came to be observed as a national mourning day every year. Due to the Partition of Bengal, the Extremist block of the Congress became very popular. *'Vande Matram'* became the popular national song. In the words of *Gokhale*: "Many people are losing faith in English integrity and sense of justice. Our young men are beginning to ask what is good of constitutional agitation if it only result in insult and the partition of Bengal."

Curzon's policy on the whole, cause great resentment in the country. *Dr. Pattabhi Sitaramayya* has also described his policy in the following beautiful words:

"His curtailment of the powers of the Calcutta Corporation his Official, Secrets Act, his Officialisation of the Universities which made education costly and finally his Partition of Bengal broke the back of loyal India and roused a new spirit in the national. Even more galling to our sense of self-respect that this speech in Calcutta regarding out untruthfulness was his sweeping charge that we Indians were by environment, our heritage and our up bringing 'unequal to the responsibilities of high office under British Rule."

Lord Morley was also opposed to the Policy of *Curzon*. He wrote: "We were told by the leading moderates that even the general loyalty had been chilled by his (Lord curzen's) declared policy of centralization; by his whittling away...of liberal principle and promises of Queen Victoria's Proclamation of 1858, by the openly expressed contempt for Indian standards of morality and by measures like the Partition of Bengal carried out against the strong wishes of the people concerned."

4. Victory of Japan over Russia– Victory of Abyssinia over Italy in 1896, and of Japan over Russia in 1905, clearly indicated that the dawn of new era for the whole Asia was about to come. The national uplift of Egypt, Persia and Turkey influenced the minds of Indians. *Mr. G.N. Singh* has written :

"The influence exerted under the inspiring leadership of Mazzini, Garribaldi and Cavour was of special significance. The life and words of Mazzini, in particular, were written and translated in Indian languages and the national leaders in India used the Italian example to arouse patriotism in the minds of their countrymen."

The Victory of Japan over Russia gave impetus to Bengalees for fighting against foreign government. Amrit Bazar Patrika a Bengalee newspaper exhorted "what was the difference between the Japanese and the Bengalees, except that the former were armed whereas the latter had been deprived of their arms by high handed and suspicious foreign government."

5. Humiliation of Indians abroad– Indians in South Africa, Fizi and Canada were meted with the most humiliating treatment. Imposition of three pound Toll Tax on Indian Labourers in Natal if they overstayed and prohibitions on Indians in Transval to have lands in their own names, added fuel to the fire. In 1888, the Indians of Orange River Colony were expelled and were subjected to many intolerable discriminations. *Punniah* has rightly remarked :

"The cup of humiliation was filled to the brim, when in 1907, the Transvaal Government passed the Asiatic Registration Act requiring Indians to be registered by means of finger prints."

Gandhiji launched Satyagrah against the Act, in South Africa that Mr. Bal Gangadhar Tilak said at time, 'A good foreign Government was redesirable than an inferior national Government.' The whole atmosphere of India was filled with the opposition to the British Government.

6. Deterioration in economic condition– The Economic condition of the country further deteriorated in the beginning of 20th Century. With the raising of land revenue and irrigation rates, the farmers had to suffer a lot. "The growing poverty of India was not an opinion, it was a fact asserts Ahluwalia.....A country where taxes were collected in utmost disregard of people's capacity, and were spent with unutterable indifference and waste, was bound to be poor." There were famines, complete negligence of irrigation facilities, *etc.* The wages became very low. While the price were going up. There was no progress in the field of agriculture. The educated class of the country was disgusted with the Government policy. Middle class was the main sufferer. The government of India did not attach any importance to the difficulties of Indians with the more import of British goods in India, the industries of India failed miserably. The leader of the country criticised the government economic policy but it was all in vain.

7. Freedom of press and platform– Press and Platforms played an important role, in the development of the national movement, Daillies like *Kesari Kal Vaibao* and *Pratode* and *Yugantar* powerful slogans like *'Vandematram'* developed a national feeling amongst the Indians from the point of view of mass circulation papers like *Kesari, Yugantar,* had a top circulation. These papers had a strong hold on the people. The fiery speeches of Bal Gangadhar Tilak, Lala Lajpat Rai and Bipan Chandra Paul, denouncing to British government were widely circulated by these dailies and weeklies. Thus the native became conscious of the injustices done by the Britishers and cried far the responsible Government.

8. The Extremists porpoganda– The repressive policy of the government and the frustration among the Indians against the British imperialism gave birth to Extremist's group in the Congress. *Mr. B.C. Pal* said, "If the government were to come and tell me, take Swaraj, I would say 'thank you very much for the gift, but I will not have that which I cannot acquire by my own hand."

The trio of Bal, Pal and Lal did a wonderful job of awakening the Indian masses. Bal Ganga Dhar Tilak, who is called the father of Indian civil commotion by his patriotic song and speeches, inculcated the spirit of patriotism in the Indian masses. He said "it is possible to make administration deplorable difficult and to create conditions impossible for the British bureaucracy, by fighting for our rights with determination and tenacity and by boycott and strike". *Lala Lajpat Rai* said in 1905, "in our utterance, in our agitation and our fight and struggle for liberty, we ought to be more manly than we have been hereto fore." He inaugurated few religious functions such as Ganpati festival in 1893 and Shivaji festival in 1895.

B.C. Pal intensified the agitation in Bengal. Lala Lajpat Rai, the Lion of Punjab and his colleague Ajit Singh awakened the masses of Punjab. The year 1907 and 1908 opened and closed with deportations of Lajpat Rai, Ajit Singh, Tilak and several public men of Bengal. Tilak was deported for 6 years and 9 prominent leaders were deported from Bengal. In the words of *G.N. Singh* "The deportation of Lala Lajpat Rai caused a great concentration among the people in the various parts of the country and had the effect of stiffening the parks of young men, specially in Bengal and converting them into Extremists and even believers in violence and terrorism."

Thus, the violent crusade launched by the Extremist against the British Imperialism compelled the government to introduce substantial reforms.

9. The Terrorists Movement– The Extremists preached that the Constitutional method could never improve the lot of the Indians. The use of force was essential for the liberation of the country. With their propaganda, a new era of revolutionary activities ensued in the country. Crimes and murders became the features of the every day life. In 1907, Mr. Rand was shot dead. An attempt was made on 5th December, 1907, to blow up the Lieutenant Governor's train. Mr. Allen was shot in the back and two innocent English ladies Mrs. and Miss Kanedy were shot dead on their way. These revolutionaries were prosecuted and many of them were sentenced to death. But all these activities made the government nervous and the government seriously thought about the situation and introduced some reforms in the administration. Dr. Ahluwalia concludes that "whatever might be their own idea, at least this may be safely concluded that their efforts formed the most vital, and also inevitable and useful link in India's March towards freedom.....The nation experienced the heart throbs of patriotism. The urge for self-effacement among the millions, was invigorated."

10. The Expectations of the Congress– The Indian National Congress held its session in Benares in 1905 under the presidentship of Gopal Krishna Gokhale. Gokhale, who was a Moderate, but he also criticised the Partition of Bengal. He emphasised the Swadeshi movement and explained the goal of the Congress in the following words :–

"The goal of the Congress is that India should be governed in the interests of the Indian themselves, and that in course of time a form of government should be attained in this country similar to what exist in the self-governing Colonies of the British Empire. For better, for worse, our destinies are now linked with those of England and the Congress freely recognizes that whatever advance we seek must be within the Empire itself. That advance, moreover, can only be gradual, as at each stage of the progress it may be necessary for us to pass through a brief course of apprenticeship before we are enabled to go to the next one; for it is a reasonable proposition that the sense of responsibility, required for the proper exercise of the political institutions of the West can be acquired by an Eastern people through practical training and experiment only. It is liberty alone, says *Mr. Glandstone* in words of profound wisdom, which fits men for liberty."

11. The Rise and Growth of Muslim Communalism– Britishers not only tried to divide the Congress into groups, but they also tried their best to widen the gulf between Hindus and Muslim. *Lord Minto* inspired a section of Muslims to meet him in a deputation and demand the right of separate electorates. A deputation under the leadership of H.H. the *Agha Khan,* met the Viceroy and put the demands of Muslims for separate representation. The Viceroy was himself anxious for separate representation of Muslims and so he readily accepted their demand.

Lord Minto also supported this proposal in his correspondence with Mr. Morley. Mr. Morely was a man of liberal outlook and he was against the introduction of separate electorate. He wrote to Minto on 6th December, 1909 "I won't follow you again into our Mohammedan dispute. Only I respectfully remained you once again that it was your early speech about their extra claims that started the Muslim ban. I am convinced my decision was the best." But Morely did not asset effectively against the scheme. Muslim League was formed in 1906 and it again demanded for separate electorates in 1908 and 1909. Lord Minto, who was in favour of 'Divide and Rule' policy; although Lord Disraeli had earlier confessed in 1857, that "our Empire in India was, indeed, founded upon the old principle of *divide it impera,* but the principle was put into action by us not with any Machiavellian devices, but by merely taking advantage of the natural and spontaneous circumstances of the country in which we were acting a part". The Congress was opposed to Muslim communalism and passed the following resolutions; "This Congress strongly depreciate the extension or application of the principle of separate communal Electorates to Municipalities, District Boards, or other local bodies." But, later on it was realised that Muslim League did not remain an organisation of the supporters of Britishers but many nationalists persuaded the League to come in open fight with the Britishers.

12. The Advent of Liberal and Radical Ministry in England– In 1905, the Liberal Government was formed in England and Mr. Morley became the Secretary of State for India. This government was very liberal towards Indians. On June 6, 1906, *Morley* wrote to *Lord Minto*: "Fundamental difference between us really believe; there is none. Not one with more than you do, I think is desirable or possible or even conceivable to adopt English political institution to the nations, who inhabit India.... Everybody warns that a new spirit is growing and spreading over India..you cannot go on governing in the same spirit: you have got to deal with the Congress party and Congress principle, whatever you may think of them, be sure that before long the Mohammedands will throw in their lot with the Congress men against you."

From the above letter it is quite clear that Morley was fully aware of the political condition of India. He, in his private letter to Minto, on June 15, 1906, wrote to set the ball in motion. The result of this was that a committee under the presidentship of Sir Arudel was appointed. The committee was asked to formulate proposals far introducing the reforms.

The committee submitted its report in October and Viceroy-in-Council, held serious discussions on the report. On March 19, 1907, he sent a letter to the Secretary of State regarding the proposal of the committee. The Secretary of State authorised the government of India to consult local government on the proposals of the committee. The government invited the opinion of the local government but local government took about one year for this purpose. On October 1, 1908, the Government of India sent another letter regarding the revised proposals. The Council carefully discussed the proposals and a final scheme was drawn up by Lord Morley. The scheme was ratified by the British cabinet. On December 17, 1908, Lord Morley explained the proposals to the House of Lords. In February 1909, a Bill was introduced, in the House of Lords, and after the procedural formalities, it became an Act. Though this bill was passed in the year 1909, but the reforms of Act were implemented in the year 1910.

MAIN PROVISIONS OF THE INDIAN COUNCILS ACT OF 1909

The Act of 1909, has its own significance in the Constitutional History of India. By this Act, Indians were not only associated with the work of Legislation but they were allowed to participate in the administration of the country. The Act increased the strength of the Councils and also enhanced their powers. The Act by introducing a separate electorate, narrow franchise and indirect election heralded a new era in the Indian political life. The main provisions of the Act may be summarised as under :

1. Expansion of the Councils. The Act provided for the enlargement of the Councils both Central and Provincial. The number of additional members for legislative purposes in the Viceroy's Executive Council was raised from 16 to 60. The Legislative Councils of Madras, Bengal and Bombay were also increased to 50 members each. The Provincial Legislature of U.P. was to have 50, of Punjab, Assam and Burma 30 each. Changes in the Councils of other Provinces were made later in 1912 when readjustments in provincial territorial limits were affected.

2. Official majority in the Imperial Legislative Council retained. The Governor-General's Legislative Council consisted of four categories of members: (*a*) Ex-officio members, (*b*) Nominated officials, (*c*) Nominated non-officials, and (*d*) Elected members. The Governor-General and his councillors enjoyed the membership of the Central Legislature by virtue of their being the Members of the Highest Executive. They were called ex-officio members. The nominated officials were those civil servants who were nominated on the Legislature. The members belonging to the third category were men from public life nominated by the Government as Members of Legislature. Under the fourth category came those persons who were returned by the Chambers of Commerce, Municipalities, District Boards and Landlords.

The Act of 1909 retained the majority of official members so as to avert any form of difficulty arising in the passage of Government Bills. According to the Act of 1912 strength of the Central Legislature, had been raised to 69. Out of 69 members in the Central Legislature, 37 were officials, 5 nominated non-officials and 27 elected members. Of the 27 elected members, 5 were returned by the Muslims, 6 by Hindu Landlords, 1 by Muslim Zamindars, one each by Bengal Chamber of Commerce and Bombay Chamber of Commerce. The remaining 43 were sent by Provincial Legislative Councils. Every member held office for three years only.

3. Non-official Majority in the Provincial Legislative Council. The Act, dispensed with the official majority, in the Provincial Legislatures. It was certainly a welcome feature but it should not be assumed that the Legislatures began to have the majority of elected element. The combined strength of official and nominated non-official members still outnumbered the elected members. They formed a solid pro-Government bloc to support all the moves of the Government. Despite the official majority if ever there arose some difficulty in carrying a legislation, that was easily overcome by submitting the Bill to Central Legislature for enactment. Generally, the Provincial Government encountered no difficulties in the passage of any Bill. The nominated non-official members always voted in favour of official moves whereas the elected members could never unite as one.

4. Introduction of Communal Electorate. The most unfortunate feature of the new Act was the undue importance that it gave to communal interests. The Act favoured the Muslims by giving them representation disproportionate to their population. This was done on the excuse of the political importance of the Muslim community. Separate representation was also given to Presidency Corporations, Universities, Chambers of Commerce, and the Land-holders.

5. Enlargement of functions of the Legislative Councils. The Legislative Councils till the new enactment were only legislative or to be more precise only advisory bodies to assist the Executive in legislation. *The Act of 1892 gave the members of the Legislature the right to discuss the budget only after it had been approved and finalised by the Executive.* They had no right to propose an increase or cut in any item. The Act of 1909 empowered the members to discuss the budget and move resolutions before it was finally approved. They were also allowed to ask supplementary questions, to move resolutions on matters relating to loans to local bodies, additional grants and new taxes. The Act also extended to the members the right to discuss matters of public interest, adopt resolutions or divide the House on them. But the resolutions adopted by the House were not absolute and binding on the Government. The President of the House was authorised to drop any resolution or a part thereof in the name of public interest without stating any sound reason. Besides it, there were certain heads of revenue and expenditure which were not even open to discussion. In short, the Legislatures got the right to talk but not to influence the Government in any way.

6. Increase in the Size of Executive Council. Under this Act the number of members of the Executive Council of Bombay and Madras was increased to four. The Act empowered the Governor-General-in-Council to create with the approval of the Secretary of State, Executive Council for Bengal and for the Lieutenant-Governor's Provinces. Another significant feature of the Act was appointment of the Indians to the Executive Council (With a view to giving more representation to

Indians. Morley in 1907 had already appointed two Indians, viz. Mr. K.G. Gupta and Syed Hussain Bilgrammi to India Council) He, under this Act appointed Mr. S.P. Sinha, Law Member to the Governor-General's Executive Council.

7. System of Election. The Act of 1909 for the first time gave recognition to elective principle for the appointment of non-official members to the Councils. The Governor-General was empowered to make detailed regulations for giving effect to the proposal of elective principle. The system that he devised proved vicious and unscientific. He suggested a restricted and discriminatory franchise. *The electorate for returning the representatives were divided on the basis of class, community and interest. Moreover,* the voting qualification also differed from Province to Province. For the Central Legislature there were four kinds of electorate–General, Special, Class electorate, and Muslims while for the Provincial legislature the electorate were divided into first three categories.

How discriminatory the franchise was can be judged from the following facts and figures: For the Central Council only those Landowners from the Landowners' constituency were entitled to vote who had certain specified income which varied from Province to Province. In Madras the minimum fixed income was ₹ 15,000 a year or land revenue payments up to ₹ 10,000 a year. In Bengal persons holding the titles of Raja or Nawab and in C.P. persons holding honorary offices enjoyed the privilege to vote from the Landholders' constituency.

There was much disparity in voting qualification among the Muslim electorate in different Provinces. Not only that but the qualifications for voting right also varied between the Muslims and Non-Muslims considerably. The Muslim community which was like a dearer wife to the British Government was shown favour. Whereas a Muslim who paid income tax on an annual income of ₹ 3,000 was given the right of vote, a Parsi, a Hindu or a Christian, even if his taxable income was ₹ 3 lakhs, was denied the voting right. Again a Muslim graduate of five years' standing acquired the right to vote but a graduate of any other community could not claim it even twenty years after his graduation. So the Act did gross injustice to Non-Muslims. Besides that the Government could debar those persons from contesting the election, who participated in the agitations against the Government.

CRITICISM OF MORLEY-MINTO REFORMS OR CHIEF DEFECTS OF MORLEY-MINTO REFORMS

The Reforms of 1909 were in the nature of concessions to appease the Moderates so that by securing their sympathies the Government might crush the revolutionary movement. *In the words of Dr. Ishwari Prasad: "The design underlying the reforms was conciliation and division.* The former was attempted by the numerical expansion of the legislatures, the appointment of Indians to the Viceroy's Executive and increased powers of discussion. *The latter was sought by the vicious character of the system of representation that was devised."* Some defects of the Act of 1909 were as follows —

1. Strong criticism by the Congress–Even Moderates disillusioned. When the detailed rules and regulations were made under this Act by the Government, the liberal spirit of this Act was utterly destroyed. The Muslims were given the fight of plural voting and direct elections. Landlords too were given a preferential treatment. The Government of India wanted to crush the nationalists and destroy their oneness and solidarity and please the communal and reactionary elements, therefore, forsaking the spirit of justice and fairply, they had unduly favoured Mohammedans and the Landlords. So even the Moderates, who had expressed great jot over these reforms at the initial stage, were soon disillusioned. Pandit Madan Mohan Malviya in his Presidential Address to the Indian National Congress Session at Lahore in 1909 expressed his disappointment over these reforms in the following words: *"We find that the regulations have been vitiated by the disproportionate representation which* *they have secured to Mohammadans and to the landed classes, and the small room for representation which they have left for the educated classes, also by the fact that they have made an invidious and irritating distinction between Muslim and Non-Muslim subjects of His majesty, in the matter of the protection of minorities and franchise and lastly in that they have laid down unnecessarily narrow and arbitrary restrictions in the choice of the electors.*"[1] At the 1910 session, the Indian National Congress again urged the government in the name of justice and expediency to modify the regulations before another election comes on, so as to remove anomalous distinctions between different sections of His Majesty's subjects in the matter of the franchise and the qualifications of candidates seeking election to the Councils."[2] The actual working of the reform brought into limelight the evil consequences of communal representation in the Councils. *Sri S.N. Bannerjee declared that the Rules and Regulations formed for the implementation of the Reforms practically wrecked the Reform-Scheme and asked: "Is the bureaucracy having its revenge upon us for the part we have played in securing these concessions?"*

2. It did not establish parliamentary form of government. The Act of 1909 was in its true colours a subtle attempt to blend in one of the two elements of autocracy and constitutionalism, *i.e.*, to create a constitutional autocracy. The father of the Act, Mr. Morley, had no intention to give a representative government to India for he considered the conditions in the country highly unsuitable to parliamentary form of Government. At the time of introducing the Bill in the British House of Lords in 1908 he stated frankly, *"If I were attempting to set up a parliamentary system in India, or if it could be said that this chapter of reforms led directly or necessarily up to the establishment of a parliamentary system in India, I, for one, would have nothing to do with it."* This speech of his caused much disappointment to Indian people. Dr. Zacharias rightly observes, *"The reforms had given the people the shadow rather than substance." According to Mr. Roberts these reforms were only a halfway house. Mr. Majumdar condemned the reforms by saying that 'they were mere moonshine.' Since the motives of the authors of the Reforms were not considerate or clean, the Act failed to rouse the expected enthusiasm.*

3. The vicious system of communal electorate. Another ugly feature of the Act was its recognition of communal basis of representation. A fixed number of seats were reserved for the Muslims in the Councils as well as in public services. Separate constituencies of Muslim electorate were created to further widen the gulf between the Hindus and Muslims. Every Muslim candidate elected on communal basis tried to justify himself by helping his co-religionists and supporting the Government without whose favours he would have been nowhere. Thus the communal interests predominated the national interests. Since the Muslims had no more need to depend on Hindu votes for their election to the Councils, they adopted a very uncompromising attitude. The granting of separate representation to Muslims proved in fact the beginning of an era of gross communalism in Indian politics. It gave a clue to other minority communities *viz.*, Sikhs, Harijans, Anglo-Indians, Europeans and Indian Christians to claim for themselves similar privileges and they by proving their loyalty to the British Government did succeed in acquiring separate representation under the subsequent Acts of 1919 and 1935. The Act of 1909 as such may be said to have struck the first nail into the coffin of nationalism.

4. Congress denounces strongly the system of communal electorate. The poison of communal electorate injected by the Morley-Minto Reforms was deplored in the resolution of the Congress which read, *"The Congress while gratefully appreciating the earnest and arduous endeavours of Lord Morley and Lord Minto in extending to the people of this country a fairly liberal measure of constitutional reforms of* 1909, *deems its duty to place on record its strong sense of disapproval of the creation of separate electorate*". The Congress resolution also strongly criticised the unjust and humiliating distinctions made between the Non-Muslim (Hindus) and the Mohammadans in the matter for electorate, the franchise and qualifications of candidates. Later on Mahatma Gandhi said,

1. Bannerjee, A.C., *Indian Constiutional Documents,* Vol. II. pp. 269-70.
2. Annie Besant, *"How India Wrought for Freedom"* p. 568.

"The Minto-Morley Reforms have been our undoing. Had it not been for separate electorate then established, we (Hindus and Mohammadans) should have settled our differences by now." Jawaharlal criticised the communal electorate system in these words :

"A political barrier was created round them (Muslims) isolating them from the rest of India and reversing the unifying and amalgamating process which had been going on for centuries.......This barrier was a small one at first, for the electorate were very limited, but with every extension of the franchise, it grew and affected the whole structure of public and social life, like some canker which corrupted the entire system. It poisoned the municipal and local self-government, and ultimately it led to the fantastic divisions. Three came into existence separate Muslim Trade Unions and Students Organisation and merchant's chambers........these electorate first introduced among the Muslims spread to other minorities and groups till India became a mosaic of the separatist tendencies and finally the demand for the splitting up of India."[1]

Pandit Madan Mohan Malviya in his Presidential Address to the Congress at Lahore condemned the communal electorate in these words: *"It looks more like a case of allowing the majority to be driven to a corner by a minority. What makes the matter worse, however is that this advantages has been reserved only to the favoured minority of our Mohammedan fellow subjects. No such protection has been extended to the Hindu minorities in the Punjab and Eastern Bengal and Assam. The Hindu minorities in the said two Provinces have been left out severely in the cold."*[2]

5. Indirect elections. Another serious defect in the new Act was that a large number of the additional members for legislative purpose were to be returned on the basis of indirect elections. The goods which the elective principle was to deliver were set off by the practice of indirect elections. Secondly, the people at large got no right to send their representatives directly in the Central or in the Provincial legislatures and hence the Act failed to encourage any sense of responsibility. The franchise was so narrow and limited that only a fraction of adult population secured the right to vote. How funny it is that the number of voters for Central Legislature was only 650, while for a Provincial Legislature nearly 200.

6. Domination of pro-Government bloc in the Councils. The reform proposed by the Act of 1909 was mere eye-wash because there continued to be the preponderance of official majority in the Central Legislature and of the pro-Government bloc in the Provincial Councils. In the Imperial Legislature (Central Legislature) the elected members became ineffective against the strong band of nominated officials. Although in theory there was a majority of non-official members in the Provincial Legislature, they were reduced into a minority against combined strength of officials and nominated non-officials in practice. The European elected members, the Landlords, the Muslims–all vied with one another to earn the goodwill of the British masters. In the words of Dr. Ishwari Prasad: *"The Councils were transformed into a museum rather than Legislatures, representing the will of people. Elected, nominated non-officials and officials jostled with each other; some representing the will of the people, others representing none but themselves and looking to the hand that had brought them in for direction and support."*

7. Strictly limited powers of the Legislative Councils– With the increase in size of the Councils, the Act did not enlarge their functions and powers. The members were allowed to discuss the budget but could not make any substantial change in any item. They could ask questions but not insist on a reply from the Executive. Even the resolution that they were permitted to adopt on matters of public importance were not obligatory on the Government. The recommendations of the Legislative Councils could be rejected or vetoed by the Governor-General or the Governor as the case may be. Besides these, there were statutory restrictions on the powers of the legislaters. They had no direct

1. Jawaharlal Nehru, *Discovery of India*, pp.295-296.
2. Pandit Madan Mohan Malviya's *Presidential Address to the Lahore Congress*. Bannerjee, A.C., *Indian Constitutional Documents*, Vol.II, p. 268.

control over any head of revenue or expenditure. Certain items of the budget were not even open to discussion. Thus the responsibility for the administration of country remained undivided. The real powers continued to be centralised in the Executive. According to Mr. K.V. Punniah, *"the main function of the official bloc was to vote, to vote with the Government and to vote against the non-official opposition. However eloquent the non-official speakers might talk and however reasonable and weighty their arguments might be, when the time for voting came, the silent official phalanx stepped in and decided the matter against them."*

Principal Shri Ram Sharma remarks: *"The debates lacked life. The proceedings bore an air of unreality. What was still more irritating to the Indian members was the Government's usual policy of letting the non-official members speak and intervene in the debate at the end, though the members-in-charge exhibiting an unconcern for the views of the Indian members which left them smarting."* In 1910 Mr. Gokhale complained before the Imperial Legislature, *"That once the Government had made up their mind to adopt a particular course, nothing that the non-official members may say in the Councils is particularly of any avail in bringing about any change in that course."*

8. Curtailment of the rights of the Members. The rules and regulations governing the proceedings of the Legislative Councils, were so framed that the powers of its members were substantially restricted. The Morley-Minto reforms neither contemplated any transfer of power nor meant to make the Councils real law-making bodies. The function of the members was confined to heated deliberations without affecting the policies of the Government. *Mr. Coupland had justly remarked that the Legislative Councils looked more like Durbars than parliaments. To quote the Montagu Chelmsford Report, "To recur to Sir Bartle Frere's figure, the Government is still a monarch in durbar, but his councillors are uneasy, and not wholly content with his personal rule; and the administration in consequence has become slow and timid in operation..... We have in India neither the best of the old system, nor the best of the new. Responsibility is the savour of popular government and that savour the present councils wholly lack."*

IMPORTANCE AND UTILITY OF MORLEY-MINTO REFORMS

Despite all the drawbacks the Act of 1909 suffered from, it was a definite advance on the proceeding Act of 1892. It marked an important stage in the growth of representative institutions in India. For the first time recognition was given to elective principle as the basis of the composition of Legislative Councils. In spite of the disclaimer of Lord Morley, the Act did pave way for a parliamentary government although indirectly in the country. *According to Shri Ram Sharma, The constitutional autocracy that he (Morley) set up was bound to find its autocratic side challenged by its constitutionalism, and an answer had to be found for that challenge. Autocracy was likely to go overboard."* The elected Indians in the councils got a platform to ventilate their grievances.

W.H. Morris Jones observes about the Morley-Minto reforms, "The atmosphere may not have been wholly parliamentary but the change, as compared with the pre-1909 period, was marked enough."[1]

It was not less heartening a fact that an Indian was also included in Governor-General's Executive Council. The enlargement of the size of Legislatures and the presence of elected members in it, although by indirect elections, set the ball rolling of increasing demand for complete Indianisation of Legislatures. Another significant feature of the Act was the increase in the rights of the members. They were empowered to discuss the budget and divide the House on many of the items included in it. Thus the members got the opportunity to criticize the executive and make suggestions for better administration of the country. *To quote Mr. Ramsay Macdonald, "It (Act of 1909) was a compromise*

1. Morris Jones, W.H., *Parliament in India*, p.50.

between bureaucracy and democracy, inevitably a shortlived if, necessary, experiment." The reforms thus brought the country to a stage whence there was no going back, instead the only course open was further advancement towards self-government which was confirmed by Montagu's August Declaration of 1917.

CAUSES OF THE FAILURE OF MORLEY-MINTO REFORMS

Some causes of failure of the Act of 1909 were as follows :

1. The Act was no doubt an improvement upon the preceding Act but it fell far short of the national expectations. What disappointed the people most was the admixture of the two incompatible elements of constitutionalism and autocracy, of the nominative and elective principles. Supreme power continued to be vested in the Executive on the principle that the responsibility to rule over India had devolved exclusively on the British people. Indians were considered ill-fitted for higher posts in the administration. The local bodies continued to be officialised. The Councils established under the new Act remained 'gilded shams' and 'magnified nonentities where constituency was the Government House.'

2. Another cause of the failure of Reforms was the introduction of indirect elections for returning the members to the Legislative Councils.

3. The system of communal representation also proved a thorn in the sides of the discerning leaders.

4. On proper analysis they found it nothing better than a political game of the Government to inflame communal passions and crack national solidarity. The public opinion also objected to the excessive importance that the Act gave to vested interests by giving them special representation. According *to the Report on Indian Constitutional Reforms (1918): "It was opposed to the teaching of history. It perpetuated division by creeds and classes which meant the creation of political camps organised against each other and taught them to think as partisans and not citizens. It stereotyped existing relation and was a very serious hindrance to the development of the self-governing principle.*"

The exclusion of Indians from senior posts and from public services also pin-pricked the educated unemployed youths of India. Indians continued to be treated like 'pariah' by the arrogant British. Even the Secretary of State during his visit to India was taken aback to learn that the doors of British clubs were closed for his Indian friends. The inadequacy of the reforms as such gave a fillip to extremist movement in India.

EXERCISES

Long Answer Type Questions

1. Discuss the circumstances leading to the enactment of the Indian Councils Act, 1909.
2. Discuss the main provisions of the Indian Councils Act of 1909.
3. What were the salient provisions of the Minto-Morley Reforms?
4. "The Reforms of 1909 failed in their object." How far do you agree with this statement? Also give the significance of the Reforms.
5. Discuss the chief defects of the Indian Councils Act, 1909.
6. The Reforms of 1909 were only "the moonshine". Is this the true assessment of the Reforms?

Short Answer Type Questions

1. Write any three circumstances leading to the Act of 1909.
2. Write any three provisions of the Indian Councils Act of 1909.

3. Write any three defects of Morley-Minto Reforms.
4. Write a short note on importance of Morley-Minto Reforms.
5. What were the causes of the failure of Morley-Minto Reforms?

Objective Type Questions

Choose the correct answer

1. The Indian Councils Act of 1909 provided for the enlargement of the councils both central and provincial. In this regard which of the following are correct?
   (*a*) The number of additional members for legislative purposes in the Viceroy's Executive Council was raised from 16 to 60.
   (*b*) The legislative councils of Madras, Bengal and Bombay were also increased to 50 members each.
   (*c*) The Provincial Legislature of U.P. was to have 50, of Punjab, Assam and Burma 30 each.
   (*d*) All of the above.
2. Under the Act of 1909, the Governor-General's Legislative Council consisted of four categories of members. In this context match List I (Categories of members) with List II (Description) and select the correct answer from the codes given below the lists :

List I	List II
(*A*) Ex-officio members	1. They were men from public life nominated by the Government as members of legislature.
(*B*) Nominated officials	2. These were the Governor-General and his councillors who enjoyed the membership of the Central Legislature by virtue of their being the Members of Highest Executive
(*C*) Nominated non-officials	3. They were those civil servant who were nominated on the Legislature.
(*D*) Elected members	4. They were those persons who were returned by the Chambers of Commerce, Muncipalities, District Boards and Landlords.

Codes:	A	B	C	D
(*a*)	2	1	3	4
(*b*)	2	3	1	4
(*c*)	4	3	1	2
(*d*)	1	2	4	3

3. Though the Act of 1909 dispensed with official majority in the Provincial Legislatures, it cannot be assumed that the Act heralded the beginning of a democratic regime in the Provinces because :
   (*a*) The combined strength of official and nominated non-official members still outnumbered the elected members. They formed a *sold pro-Government bloc* to support all the moves of the Government.

(*b*) Despite the official majority if ever there arose any difficulty in carrying a legislation, that was easily overcome by submitting the Bill to Central Legislature for enactment.

(*c*) Generally the Provincial Governments encountered no difficulty in the passage of any Bill as the nominated non-official members always voted in favour of official moves whereas the elected members who represented different classes, communities and interests could never unite as one.

(*d*) All of the above.

4. The most unwelcome feature of the New Act was the undesirable importance that it gave to communal interests. The Act favoured the Muslims by giving them representation disproportionate to their population. This was done on the excuse of the political importance of the Muslim Community. Separate representation was also given to Presidency Corporations, Universities, Chambers of Commerce and the Landholders. The New Act was:

(*a*) Indian Councils Act, 1909 (*b*) Government of India Act, 1919

(*c*) Government of India Act, 1935 (*d*) All of the above

ANSWERS

1. (*d*) 2. (*b*) 3. (*d*) 4. (*a*)

CHAPTER 12

The Impact of First World War and Home Rule Movement

First World War broke out in Europe on 4th August, 1914. Its causes lay deeper and more remote than the immediate cause, the assassination of heir-apparent to the Austrian throne. This war had important bearing on the events in India and its constitutional development. The British Government declared that it was fighting against Germany and her allies to make the world safe for democracy, Mr. Wilson, the President of the U.S.A., also echoed the same thing later on. Many Moderate Leaders of the Indian National Congress thought that when Britain was fighting for saving democracy then naturally she could not deny the same to India which was her due. Lord Hardinge was the Governor-General when the war broke out. He had won the sympathy of the Indian people by his tactful handling of the situation. Therefore, Princes of Indian States and the people of this country extended all help to the British Government. The President of the Indian National Congress Session of 1914 declared that India and Britain were fighting a devastating war side by side for honour, liberty and justice. Lord Pentland, Governor of Madras, attended the open session of the Congress when the resolution of unswerving allegiance to Britain was passed. Supporting the resolution Surendra Nath Bannerjee emphasized that the Congress would not trade in its loyalty to England. Mohan Das Karam chand Gandhi who had done much for alleviating the sufferings of the Indians in South Africa was in London when the war broke out. He extended his full sympathy and support to British Government in that crisis. He rejected the opposite argument that it was the duty of the slave seeking to be free to make the master's need his opportunity! He remarked, "If we could improve our status through the help and co-operation of the British, it was also our duty to win their help by standing them in their hour of need."[1] Gandhiji and Surendra Nath Bannerjee went from one place to another to urge their countrymen to extend all help to the British in their hour of need and give maximum recruitment for the army. The keynote of the speeches of Surendra Nath Bannerjee was that self-government which was the goal of our political aspirations, connotated self-defence, and that, if we sought the privileges of Imperial citizenship, we must bear its burdens and responsibilities and the foremost among them was to fight for the defence of the empire."[2] Similarly, the Indian Princes lent their full support to the British Government and placed their resources at its disposal. The Maharajas of Bikaner, Jodhpur, Kishengarh and Patiala went into the field at the head of their State Forces. Besides that India sent over a million and a quarter men including those who served in the labour corps, to the different theatres of war and subscribed £ 30,000,000 annually to the British Government besides handsome donation to Red Cross and subscriptions to War loans amounting to £ 75,000,000.

1. Mohan Das Karamchand Gandhi, *The Story of My Experiments with Truth*, pp. 424-425.
2. Surendra Nath Bannerjee, *A Nation in Making*, p. 300.

Statesmen, political leaders of all parties and the people of England were highly impressed by India's significant contribution in all fields. They noted with great satisfaction that Indian people had exposed their cause. Mr. Aaquith, Prime Minister of Great Britain, observed, "We welcome with appreciation and affection their (Indians) preferred aid and in an empire which knows no distinctions of race or class. We all alike are subjects of the King-Emperor and are joint and equal custodians of our common interests and fortunes..."[1] Montague spoke of the common devotion of Great Britain and India to the ideal of freedom.

War had created a feeling of self-respect in India, **Sir Satyendra Sinha** expressed these sentiments in these words: "a feeling of profound pride that she has not fallen behind other portions of the British Empire but has stood shoulder to shoulder with them in the hour of their sorest trial." Indians were, therefore, to be given equal status with other Dominion countries in international conferences. The Supreme Legislative Council (Central Legislative Council) passed a resolution in 1915, demanding that India should be represented at the Imperial Conference along with other countries. The demand was conceded and India was represented in the Imperial War Cabinet and Conferences in 1917-18. The Representative India signed the Paris Peace Agreement in her own right and India became the original member of the League of Nations like the Dominions.

The war had generated a greater demand for self-government in India because it had created an awakening in India never witnessed before. First of all, the assurances of Mr. Asquith (British Prime Minister) that in future Indian questions would be viewed from a different angle of vision and the declaration later on of Mr. Lloyd George (British Prime Minister) that the principle of self-determination would be applied "in tropical countries also" raised new hopes and expectations amongst the Indians. They thought that they were fighting against despotism to preserve democracy and after the war in lieu of the services rendered to the British Empire, they would be given Dominion Status. The high-sounding words of President Wilson of the U.S.A. that after the war right of self-determination would be granted to small nations and nationalities had further heightened the spirit of freedom. *To quote Principal Shri Ram Sharma, "The affirmation of moral values in the war and the emergence of the doctrine of self-determination, deeply influenced Indian public opinion. If the war was being fought to make the world safe for democracy, it was hoped that it would at last put India on the road of self-government.*" The elaborate war preparations had telling effect even in the remotest village from Delhi. Extortion of money for war fund resulted in financial bankruptcy of our country and political awakening in the masses. The Indian soldiers and officers who fought on foreign soil witnessed for themselves the tremendous differences between the status of a slave and free citizen. They came back to their motherland at the end of war with mutilated bodies and injured feelings. Thus the country which had received from war wooden legs (mutilated soldiers), orphans, widows and bankruptcy naturally demanded substantial reward in the form of 'Dominion Status.' The British Government puffed up with their victory gave a cold shoulder to national aspirations which eventually led to increased activities of the revolutionaries and the Home Rule Movement of Annie Besant and Tilak.

Lokmanya Bal Gangadhar Tilak had been released a little after the mid-night of June 16, 1914 after six years' internment (imprisonment) at Mandalay. Britain had declared war against Germany on August 4, 1914. It is significant that Tilak's first reaction to the war betrayed no bargaining spirit. He chivalrously declared in a statement on August 27, 1914: "At such a crisis the duty of every Indian, be he great or small, rich or poor, is to support and assist His Majesty's Government to the best of his ability." He went further and added: "I have like other political workers my own differences with the Government as regards certain measures and, to certain extent, even the system of internal administration. But it is absurd on that account to speak of my attitude as in any way hostile to His Majesty's Government. I may state once and for all that we are trying in India as the Irish Home Rulers have been doing in Ireland for a reform of the system of administration and not for the overthrow of

1. As quoted in Annie Besant's *India : Bonded or Free*, p. 167

the Government. I have no hesitation in saying that the acts of violence which have been committed in different parts of India are not only repugnant to me, but have, in my opinion, only unfortunately retarded, to great extent, the pace of our political progress. Whether looked at from an individual or a public point of view they deserve to be equally condemned."[1]

This initial reaction of Lokmanya Bal Gangadhar Tilak soon changed. Bal Gangadhar Tilak soon foresaw that the British Government only wanted its own maximum help during the war crisis but was not ready to give any thing to the Indians. Therefore, Bal Gangadhar Tilak demanded from the British Government that it must promise the self-government to the Indians in lieu of the help that India has rendered to the British Empire. On 20th February, 1917, Bal Gangadhar Tilak wrote in *Kesari* that even before the enactment of Defense of India Force Bill our leaders like Mahatma Gandhi were encouraging the people to get themselves recruited in the army and for that purpose they were holding public meetings. The Viceroy should have no doubt on this point that the people would not listen to his appeal for the recruitment. The Indians still doubted whether the British Government would begin an era of liberal and just policy or even in such a crisis it would continue its policy of discrimination between the black and white. Whatever be the policy of the Government, we had decided our policy and action and our leaders like Mahatma Gandhi were giving the recruitment to the Government without any condition.

Bal Gangadhar Tilak further wrote that it had to be seen whether the Government accepted the various appeals made by the Indian leaders or not. What was the meaning of opening the recruitment of the Indians for the army? Its meaning was clear that the Government could not do well without the help of the Indians. Therefore, the facility granted to the Indians was not a liberal measure of the British Government, rather it was an utmost necessity of the British Government. He further wrote, "We want to ask the Government whether it is ready to do justice actually with India or it merely wants to make us soldiers for the fulfilment of its own ends. How far we listen to the call of Government for recruitment depends on the answer of the British Government to our query?"

The Home Rule League had been established on April 28, 1916 at Belgaum with the object of "attaining self-government within the British Empire by all constitutional means and to educate and organise public opinion in the country towards the attainment of the same." Bal Gangadhar Tilak made vigorous propaganda for the attainment of that goal. Everywhere he was received enthusiastically and thousands of people attended the League meetings. The British Government took serious notice of the utterances of Bal Gangadhar Tilak. The Government was in no mood to tolerate mass agitation in the midst of the war. On the basis of Bal Gangadhar Tilak's speeches at Belgaum and Ahmedabad, the District Magistrate of Poona served a notice to Bal Gangadhar Tilak on July 22, 1916, asking him to show cause why he should not be ordered to execute a bond for a sum of ₹ 20,000 with two sureties in a sum of ₹ 10,000 for his good behavior for a period of one year. On next day fell the sixtieth birthday of Tilak and thousands of his admirers decided to celebrate it with the presentation of an address and a purse of Rs. one lakh. Tilak and his admirers did not worry at all about the notice of the District Magistrate and the function was held with great enthusiasm. On the occasion Tilak said, *"The national task that faces us today is so great and so urgent that you must work together with zeal and courage greater than I might have been able to show. It is a task that cannot be put off. Our motherland tells every one of us to be up and doing. I do not think that her sons will disregard this call. God alone can help us in our efforts and if not by us, it is certain that the fruit will be gathered by the next generation."* Though the District Magistrate convicted Tilak but the Bombay High Court let him off. The Bombay High Court quashed the interpretation of sedition which had hounded Tilak since his conviction in 1897. In exonerating Tilak, Justice Lallubhai Shah of Bombay High Court observed that "reading his speeches as a whole it appeared that his object

1. N.C. Jog, *Lokmanya Bal Gangadhar Tilak.*

was only to make a demand for Indians getting Home Rule, educating public opinion in support of the demand and enlisting membership of the Home Rule League. Tilak had not advocated any unconstitutional or unlawful methods in pursuing his objective." This judgment was of paramount importance to the cause of free speech. Tilak's acquittal gave a fillip to the Home Rule Movement. Another effect of the war was that the Muslims of India came nearest to the Congress as Sultan of Turkey, Caliph of the entire Muslim world, was fighting against the British. Therefore, there was a Lucknow Pact between the Congress and the Muslim League in 1916 and both of them presented their joint demand to the British Government.

Revolutionaries and the First World War

Whereas the Moderates were extending all help to the British Government and the Extremists were ready to give help to the British on the condition of conferring self-government or Home rule upon the Indians, the Revolutionaries foresaw in the war a golden opportunity to free the country completely from the bondage. Therefore, Rash Behari Bose, who had thrown bomb upon Lord Hardinge in 1911, organised a great Revolutionary Movement in collusion with the Gadar Party which had been founded by Lala Hardayal in the U.S.A. While the British Government was preoccupied and vexed with the German aggression in Europe, the revolutionaries decided to capitalize the occasion in their own interest. They believed in this principle that England's difficulty was their best opportunity. A few hundred Indian Revolutionaries, who were ready to face death for the liberation of their country, came to India to help Rash Behari Bose. Rash Behari Bose, Bagi Kartar Singh (Kartar Singh Saraba), Sachindra Sanyal and Ganesh Pingale prepared a master plan to stage a countrywide revolution on February 21, 1915, but the Punjab police detected the scheme through one traitor, namely Kripal Singh. His treachery brought to naught the entire scheme of the Revolution. The police at several places arrested many revolutionaries, famous amongst whom were Bagi Kartar Singh, Vishnu Ganesh Pingale, Jagat Singh, Bhai Parmanand, Man Singh and Udham singh. However, Rash Behari Bose escaped. Twenty-four persons including Kartar Singh, Bhai Parmanand, Man Singh and Udham Singh were awarded death sentence, while many others were transported for life. This case was termed by the Government as Lahore Conspiracy Case of 1915 because the trial of the revolutionaries, who were caught, took place at Lahore. The death sentence of Bhai Parmanand later on was commuted to life sentence. The Chief Justice was also inclined to commute the death sentence of Bagi Kartar Singh to life imprisonment who was handsome youth and very learned one but he declined the offer. Bagi Kartar Singh (Saraba) said, "I prefer gallows to life sentences." *"I wish I were born again to unfetter my Motherland. I shall be glad to be hanged every time I am reborn till my country achieves independence."*

HOME RULE MOVEMENT

Home Rule Movement under the inspiring leadership of Mrs. Annie Besant gained momentum during the war because many Indians saw in it the best opportunity to snatch some concessions from Britishers. Mrs. Besant was an Irish lady by birth but an Indian by domicile and religious outlook. She had great regard for Indian culture and Vedic philosophy. She had a feeling heart for the ill-fated people of this country. She knew that the roots of their misery lay in political subjection, hence she advocated the case of India and demanded Home Rule or Dominion Status. She argued that a free India was likely to be a more dependable friend of Great Britain than a dependent one. Explaining her mission to her audience, she said, *"I am an Indian Tomtom, waking up all the sleeping sleepers so that they may wake and work for their motherland... This is my task."* Mrs. Besant was neither an arrogant imperialist nor an arch-enemy of the British Empire. She wanted compromise and enduring co-operation between the two countries. *Zacharias holds that 'her plan was to disentangle the nationalist extremists from their compromising alliance with the revolutionaries, to reconcile them to a position within the Empire and to bring them with the moderate into line in a united Congress.'*

During her visits to England between 1908 and 1913 as President of Theosophical Society, Mrs. Annie Besant was much impressed by Redmond's Home Rule Movement in favour of Ireland. She decided to start a similar movement in India. After working for twenty years for the revival of Hinduism, she joined the Congress in 1914. For propagating her views she started in English weekly *'Common Weal'* and then an English daily *'New India'*. She defined the goal in the first issue of *'Common Weal'* in the following words: *"in political reforms we aim at the building up of complete self-government from Village Councils, through District and Municipal Boards and Provincial Legislative Assemblies, to a National Parliament, equal in its powers to the Legislative bodies of the self-governing colonies, by whatever name they may be called, also at the direct representation of India in the Imperial Parliament when that body shall contain representatives of the self-governing States of the Empire."*

After joining the Congress in 1914, Mrs. Annie Besant put India's case of self-government in a way that was both forceful and compatible with the nation's dignity. She said, *"There had been talk of a reward due to India's loyalty; but India does not chaffer* (*bargain*) *with the blood of her sons and the proud tears of her daughters in exchange for so much liberty, so much right. India claims the right as a Nation, to justice among the peoples of the Empire. India asked for this before this war, but not as a reward but as a right does she ask for it. On this there must not be any mistake."* In a short time Mrs. Annie Besant came to the forefront in political field also. She impressed the people by her eloquence and passionate love for India's good. At Madras session of the Congress in 1914 she said, *"India was not prepared to be any longer a child in the nursery of the Empire, and that it was necessary to confer self-government on her."*

The beginning of war in Europe nearly coincided with the release of Bal Gangadhar Tilak from Mandalay Jail at the end of his six years' term. He was accorded a hero's reception by the nationalist elements. His presence gave a stimulus to patriotic fervour. Tilak and his Extremist group agreed to the policies and programmes of Mrs. Besant. But the Moderates were reluctant in their approval of Home Rule. So, Mrs. Besant for some time did not get much success in reuniting the Moderates and the Extremists under the banner of the Congress but with the death of Sri Gopal Krishna Gokhale in February, 1915, and of Sir Ferozeshah Mehta in November of the same year, the Moderate group became leaderless. Mrs. Besant utilised the opportunity for prevailing upon both the groups to work together again.

Mrs. Besant and Tilak gave inspiring lead to Home Rule Movement. Besant started the Home Rule League at Gokhale Hall, Madras, in September, 1916, and Tilak started the same Home Rule at Poona. The Home Rule League raised the slogan of Swadeshi, National Education and Home Rule for India. The movement gathered momentum with lightning speed. The Government had no patience with the agitators, particularly when it was involved in war on the fields of Euorpe. The Bombay Government imposed restrictions on the movement and activities of Tilak. Action was also taken by the Madras Government against Mrs. Besant. She was arrested along with two co-workers, Sri Aurobindo and Sri Wadia. The highhandedness of the authorities raised a storm of protests all over the country. Public fury compelled the Government to release Mrs. Besant. The Congress in recognition of her valuable services elected her as President in 1917.

Montague's visit to India. In order to enlist the firm support of the Indians in cause of war, Montague, Secretary of State for India, arrived in Bombay on 10th November, 1917. Tilak joined the large body to welcome him and garlanded him on behalf of the Home Rule League. After his arrival at Delhi, Montague received a series of deputations. A joint delegation representing the Indian National Congress and the Muslim League waited upon him on 26 November. Montague was fully conscious of the political importance of the delegation as would appear from the following entry in his diary: "We were face to face with the real giants of the Indian political world." Then followed the Home Rule Delegation, Montague writes, "And then Mrs. Besant and the great Tilak came with their Home Rule League and read us a more extreme and a bitter address but one which was undoubtedly interesting and good." Montague also interviewed Tilak separately and wrote the very next day, "Then after lunch, we saw Tilak, the politician, who probably has the greatest influence of any person in India and who is very extreme. His procession to Delhi to see me was a veritable triumphant one. He was really the author of the Congress-League scheme and although he did not impress me very much in argument, he is a scientific man of great erudition and training. It was quite obvious that he was not going to be satisfied with anything but what the Congress asks for. "We shall take whatever the Government gives us", he said, "*But it will not satisfy us unless it is at least what the Congress asks for*". He also received other delegations. His main purpose was to formulate the scheme of reforms in consultation with the Government of India and various political leaders and at the same time to divert the attention of the Indian politicians from war and think of nothing else but the mission of the Secretary of State. In his mission he admirably succeeded.

Congress session of 1917 demands Home Rule for India. The Congress session was held in Calcutta in 1917 with Mrs. Annie Besant as President. The Moderates in spite of their best efforts could not prevent the election of Mrs. Besant who was a nominee of Lokmanya Tilak. She said the following words in her Presidential address:

"Early in the war, I ventured to say that the war would not end until England recognised that autocracy and bureaucracy must perish in India as well as in Europe. The good Bishop of Calcutta with a courage worthy of his free race, lately declared that it would be hypocritic to pray for victory over autocracy in Europe and to maintain it in India."

I once said in England: "*The condition of India's loyalty is India's freedom.*" I now add, "The condition of India's usefulness to the Empire is India's freedom." India demands Home Rule for two reasons: one essential and vital, the less important but weighty. First because freedom is the birth right of every nation; secondly, because her most important interests are now made subservient to the interests of the British Empire without her consent and her resources are not utilised for her greatest needs. It is enough only to mention money spent on her army, not for local defence but for Imperial purposes, as compared with that spent on primary education."

Thank god that India's eye are opening; that myriads of her people realise that they are men, with a man's right to manage his own affairs. India is no longer on her knees for boons; she is on her feet for Rights. It is because I have taught this that the English in India misunderstand me and call me seditious. It is because I have taught this that I am the President of this Congress to-day.

The presidential address of Mrs. Besant offers a striking contrast to those delivered by Bhupendra Nath Basu in 1914 and by S.P. Sinha in 1916 when the Congress was being dominated by the Moderates. The Congress under the Presidentship of Mrs. Besant heard first of all such a critical address. Such critical sentiments were voiced only by the extremists during the Swadeshi movement. The resolution passed by the Indian National Congress in 1917 demanded immediate legislation for granting self-government to India within a prescribed period.

Moving appeal to the President of U.S.A. about Home Rule. The appeal of the Home Rule movement was not confined within the frontiers of India. Sir Subramanian Aiyer, K.C.I.E. retd. judge and Acting Chief Justice of the Madras High Court was the President of the Indian Home Rule League, Madras and in this capacity wrote a letter to President Wilson of the U.S.A. on 24th June, 1917. He described the intolerable condition of India under alien rule and made a moving appeal to the President to apply his war message of democracy and self-determination of nations to India. "At present, he said; we are a subject nation held in chains," but he added, "an immediate promise of Home Rule–an autonomy–for India would result in an offer from India of at least 5,000,000 men in three months for service at the front and of 5,000,000 more in another three months. The publication of this letter created a furore in the House of Lords and the House of Commons. Montagu described the letter as disgraceful and Aiyar, as a protest renounced his titles, K.C.I.E. and Diwan Bahadur.

Strong reaction in U.S.A. There was a strong reaction of the letter in U.S.A. A printed copy of the letter was placed on the desk of the senators and members of the House of Representatives. There was a great sensation and 1500 newspapers with 20,000,000 readers flashed the offer of ten million men. England was strongly criticised. The military men were strongly impressed. American labour at once demanded Home Rule for India as in Canada and Australia. An Indian Home Rule League was also established in New York. It started a newspaper known as *Young India* which supplied correct news to the American readers instead of false news which were supplied at the instance of Great Britain.

Home Rule League in London. A Home Rule League for India was also established in London. Mrs. Besant sent a stirring message to the British labourers concluding with the following words:

"Help us to become a free commonwealth under the British Crown and we will bring our manpower to secure world peace. Our people have died in your war for freedom. Will you consent that the children of our dead shall remain a subject race?"

Tilak also sent Lala Lajpat Rai with Shri N.S. Hardikar and K.D. Shastri to U.S.A. whose democratic ideas were greatly appreciated in India. A branch of the Home Rule League was established in California. The activities of London and California Home Rule Leagues bore fruit. Eminent American and Englishmen wrote and spoke for self-government in India. A committee of members of Parliament was formed in London for the purpose of pressing the claims of India to self-government. The Labour Party Conference at Nottingham early in 1918 unanimously passed a resolution in favour of Home Rule for India.

Tilak demands Home Rule from Paris Peace Conference. Tilak wrote to Mr. Clemenceau, President of the Paris Peace conference requesting him to solve the Indian problem so that India might "be a leading power in Asia" and "a powerful steward of the League of Nations in the East for maintaining the peace of the world,"[1] but Lloyed George, the British Prime Minister obstructed it. Consequently, India was not given the Home Rule in 1919. That situation continued till 1929 when the Congress had to pass the resolution of completely Independence.

Importance of the Home Rule Movement. The Home Rule Movement marked the beginning of a new phase in India's struggle for freedom. It placed before the country a concrete scheme of Self-Government, bereft of the verbiage with which the Congress led the Moderates, surrounded this political goal. It also emphasised the point that if the Congress really wanted to achieve the goal, it must cease to be a club of arm-chair politicians taking to public work only to the extent to which their leisure permitted them; instead it should be guided by leaders who were prepared to place their whole time and energy at the service of their country. This new ideal of a political leader soon commended itself to the whole country and developed a new standard of public life.

The Home Rule Movement of Lokmanya Tilak shines brilliantly during his noble political career. This great movement shows him at his best–*a sincere, fearless, unbending patriot,* who fought for his beloved country with a religious zeal without caring for the favour or frowns, either of the opposite people or of the Government. An intellectual aristocrat, he brought himself to the level of the common people, and initiated that mass movement in the political field which worked such a miracle in the hands of Mahatma Gandhi.

1. Ram Gopal, *Tilak* p. 422

LUCKNOW PACT AND THE CONGRESS-MUSLIM LEAGUE SCHEME, 1916

As soon as war broke out in Europe, the Indian Mussalmans became highly critical of the British Government. The authorities invoked the 'Seditious Meetings Act' and arrested the prominent Muslims for their outspoken nationalism. Their arrests brought the League closer to the Congress. As a step towards strengthening the ties of comradeship, both the parties held their sessions simultaneously at Bombay in 1915. Prominent Congress Leaders, namely : Mahatma Gandhi, Pt. Malviya and Sarojini Naidu, also spoke from the League platform. Agha Khan, the stooge of the British Government resigned the presidentship of Muslim League and turned to the more enjoyable hobby of horse race. The League appointed a committee to prepare a scheme for India in consultation with the Congress. The report of the committee was the basis of the Lucknow Pact ratified by both the parties in 1916 at Lucknow.

Features. The main features of the Lucknow Pact or the Congress League Scheme were as follows : —

1. That the existing structure of the Government needed radical changes in order to win the approval of the people. "India must cease to be a dependency and be raised to the status of a self-governing state as an equal partner with equal rights and responsibilities as an independent unit of the Empire."
2. The Pact laid down that the number of elected members in the Provincial Legislatures should be raised to four-fifths of the total strength. The membership of the Legislatures in big Provinces should be raised to 125 and in the smaller ones between 50 and 75. As far as possible all the members of the Legislatures should be elected on the basis of as broad a franchise as possible.
3. The minorities should be given adequate separate representation in the elected bodies. The Muslims may be entitled to a share in the seats to the extent of 50 per cent in the Punjab, 30 per cent in U.P., 40 per cent in Bengal, 25 per cent in Bihar, 15 per cent in C.P., 15 per cent in Madras and one-third in Bombay. The Muslims would be debarred from contesting the elective seats in excess of the number allotted to them.
4. That no Bill would be introduced by a non-official member, if it affected the interests of any other community, and such a Bill would not be passed if three-fourths of the members of that community opposed it.
5. The scheme suggested that every Bill passed by the Provincial Legislature should be given effect to unless vetoed by the Governor-in-council. And if the same was passed again by the Legislature within a year, it should be obligatory on the Government to enforce it.
6. Extensive powers of control over the money matters should be given to the Legislature. The members should be empowered to move any non-money Bill without seeking the permission of the Governor.
7. The scheme accepted the right of the Governor and the Governor-General to veto a bill or refuse to give assent.
8. It was demanded that at least half the members of the Executive Council of the Governor-General were to be Indians returned by only the elected members of the Central Legislature. The same procedure was to be adopted in the case of Provincial Executive Councils.
9. The Provinces should be given a large measure of autonomy in their sphere. The Central Government should confine itself to acts of general supervision over them.
10. The membership of the Central Legislature should be raised to 150, one-third of whose elected element was to be from Muslim community, elected only by Muslim electorate. In all other respects, in its constitution, proportion of elected and nominated members, powers of the House and the individual members, it was to resemble the Provincial Legislatures.

11. The scheme laid down that the Government of India should be independent of the control of the Secretary of State for India in legislative and administrative matters. The India Council of the Secretary of State should be abolished and replaced by two permanent Under-Secretaries out of which one should be an Indian. The salary of the Secretary should be paid out of the British revenues and not charged on Indian revenues.
12. Indians should be placed on a footing of equality in respect of status and right of citizenship with other subjects of His Majesty, the King Emperor throughout the Empire.
13. India should be given adequate and equal representation in any body that might be formed to decide any affair relating to the British Empire.
14. Indians should be declared eligible for all the military and naval services. Adequate provision be made for their selection and training in India.
15. Judicial powers should be taken away from the Executive officers. Lower courts in every Province should be made subordinate to the High Court.

The Congress-League scheme was regarded by the authors of the report on Indian Constitutional Reforms as "the latest, most complete and most authoritative presentation of the claims of the leading political organisations." But in fact the Congress in her bid to win Muslim support committed blunders. *According to Dr. Lal Bahadur, "A diplomatic blunder of high magnitude was committed in conceding the right of separate Muslim representation through members of the community themselves:.It was an evidence of the bankruptcy of the Congress leaders and their helpless lack of shrewdness. They ought to have understood that this concession to the Mussalmans would tear the nation for ever into two sharply divided communities and the breach shall be widened by the foreign ruling power."* Besides perpetuating the system of communal and separate electorate, it is surprising why the Congress agreed to give the Muslims unfair representation much in excess of their numerical strength. The compromise demanded more sacrifice on the part of Hindus and abject yielding to League's demands. According to many political thinkers the Lucknow Pact marked the beginning of the appeasement policy of the Congress towards the Muslim community. Acceptance of the basis of separate electorate led inevitably to the division of the country. The second defect of the Pact was that it did not advance its demand for self-government in an emphatic manner.

Mesopotamian Muddle

the campaign against Turkey in Mesopotamia during the war left completely, in the charge of the Government of India. It was handled so inefficiently that it proved a high misadventure. The Parliamentary Commission which was appointed to go into the question charged the Government of India of gross mishandling of the campaign. One of the members of the Commission reported that the only way to make the Indian Government competent was to give the Indians reasonable share in the administration of their country. The then Secretary of State for India, Mr. Austin Chamberlain, was made to resign on Mesopotamian issue. He was succeeded by Mr. Montagu who was known for liberal views.

MONTAGU'S DECLARATION, AUGUST 20, 1917

The growing unrest in India compelled the British statesmen to look at Indian affairs from a new angle. They wanted to give a political dose that might soothe the Indian unrest. Mr. Montagu, the new Secretary of State, had sympathetic attitude towards Indian aspirations. He had once declared in the Parliament, "The Government of India is too wooden, too iron, too inelastic, too antidiluvial, to be of any use for the modern purpose we have in view.....Unless you are prepared to remodel, in the light of modern experience, this century-old and cumbrous machine, then I verily believe, that you will lose your right to control the destinies of the Indian Empire." Soon after taking over the office of the Secretary of State in July 1917, he set about drafting a declaration to minimise unrest in India. On August 20, 1917, he made the following statement: "*The policy of his Majesty's Government, with which the Government of India are in complete accord, is that of the increasing association of Indians in every branch of the administration and gradual development of self-governing institutions with a view to the progressive realisation of responsible Government in India as an integral part of the British Empire. They have decided that substantial steps in this direction should be taken as soon as possible..I would add that progress in this policy can only be achieved by successive stages. The British Government and the Government of India, on whom the responsibility lies for the welfare and advancement of Indian people, must be judges of the time and measure of each advance, and they must be guided by the co-operation received from those upon whom new opportunities of service will be conferred and by the extent to which it is found that confidence can be reposed in their sense of responsibility.*"

The declaration was so to say a 'masterpiece of vagueness and ambiguity.' It was non-committal, true to the usual game of the British diplomacy. It was couched in a sweet language but words alone were not going to satisfy the Extremists. The Moderates welcomed it as the 'Magna Carta' of India. Even the Authors of Report on the Indian Constitutional Reforms regarded it as "the most momentous utterance ever made in India's chequered history." The sacred promises made in the Declaration were, the Extremists thought, meant to befool the nationalists. *To quote Sir Reginald Craddock, "Mr. Montagu announced the verdict first and commenced to hold the inquest afterwards. He began to build a tower before he had counted the cost.*" Mr. Montagu, however, came to India as the head of a mission to study the political situation personally. He stayed here for over five months and worked himself to exhaustion. Once he wrote, "I spend my whole time rocking my brains as to how I am going to get something which India will accept and the House of Commons will allow me to do without whittling it down." The Report prepared by him and agreed upon by the Viceroy of India was published in 1918. It served as the basis of the Government of India Act, 1919.

Significance of the Declaration

Montague declaration of 1917 has an important place in the constitutional history of India. The factors revealing its importance are as mentioned below:–

(1) Served as a basis of the British Policy towards India :– Since the transfer to India from the Company to the Crown, it was an important step for the benefit of Indians. This declaration served as a basis of the British Policy towards India in its independence. Mr. E.W.R. Lumby has written: "Here was the beginning of a policy, which British can claim credit for having followed consistently and faithfully right up to the eventual transfer of power." Sir Surendra Nath Banerjee, wrote: "The pages of Anglo-Indian history are strewn with the fragements of the broken promises but perhaps a new chapter was now to begin."

It was the only declaration, which only declared that there would be no difference between the British regarding India and other dominions of the British Commonwealth. Indian's would be treated as the subject of other dominions were treated. The self-government would be other ultimate goal of British Rule in India. No doubt this was the step which made a road for the independence of India.

(2) Responsible government to the Indians–The Declaration promised a responsible Government to the Indians. In 1908 Morley the Secretary of State for India had declared that it was not his intention to introduce Parliamentary Government in India; and in the year 1912 Lord Crew had emphatically announced that there was no future for India on the lines of colonial, self-government. But just after the five years in the years 1917 Montague through this declaration repudiated that the self-government would be the goal of British Rule in India. Thus, this declaration clearly indicated change of British Policy towards India.

(3)Moral Support to Indian National Congress :– The Declaration gave a moral of support to Indian National Congress. Before this declaration Indian National Congress never believed in Britishers, but after this declaration, the Congress thought that the British could go back from their commitment. The congress passed a resolution in 1917 in Calcutta that this Congress extends to the Rt. Hon.E.S. Montague, a most cordial welcome on the occasion of his visit to India. The Congress hopes that the visit will be crowned with success and that it will convince him of the supreme necessity for the establishment of responsible Government.

Though it is true to say that certain other factors were responsible for this declaration but the efforts of Indian National Congress and Muslim League was an important factor.

(4)Acceptance of India's right to Swaraj– According to Professor *Sri Ram Sharma* : "The declaration closed one chapter in the Constitutional History of India and opened another, Benevolent despotism was now dead and gone. It was out of date in Indian administration. The goal of British Government in India was defined to be responsible Government within the British Empire. This goal had to be reached by progressive stage.....India's right to Swaraj was admitted, and despotism was to give place to Constitutional Government. It was true that the peace of progress was to depend on the success of the step taken, yet the Indians had doubts in their minds about their capacity to work representative institutions. So, all if and buts were ignored and the announcement was welcomed by almost all political parties."

Demerits– No doubt the Declaration of 1917 was favourable to Indians but it was disappointing in many respects. Indians were not sure that when the final stage would be reached. The only thing that kept them quiet was the hope of formation of self-government in the near future.

Coupland was of the view that the declaration was based on the idea that 'Liberty alone fits men for liberty'. But the way in which this resolution was adopted would hardly justify the liberty for Indians. British Parliament had to judge the progress of Indians and it was quite possible that they might think that they did not deserve for the Liberty. There was no justification in prescribing the period and stages when Indians were to be made their own masters. There was no definite time limit for watching subsequent progress. The declaration in the view of Extremists was rather ambiguous. Though it promised self-government but it was vague and full of illustration.

EXERCISES

Long Answer Type Questions

1. Discuss the impact of First World War on the events of Indian National Movement and Constitutional Development.
2. What was the attitude of Mahatma Gandhi and Bal Gangadhar Tilak on participation of India in First World war?
3. Write a short note on 'Revolutionaries and First World War'.
4. What do you know about 'Home Rule Movement'?
5. Write an essay on 'Home Rule Movement'.
6. Write a note on Lucknow Pact and the Congress Muslim League Scheme 1916.
7. Discuss the features of Lucknow Pact.

Short Answer Type Questions

1. Write a short note on 'Importance of Home Rule Movement'.
2. What was Congress-League scheme? Write in brief.
3. What was Mesopotamian Muddle?
4. Write a short note on "Montague's Declaration' August 20, 1917.

Objective Type Questions

Choose the correct answer

1. In which year First World War broke out ?

(*a*) 1914 (*b*) 1915

(*c*) 1916 (*d*) 1917.

2. In which year's session the President of Indian National Congress declared that India and Britain were fighting a devastating war for honour, liberty and justice ?

(*a*) 1913 (*b*) 1914

(*c*) 1915 (*d*) 1916

3. In which year the Supreme Legislative Council passed a resolution demanding that India should be represented at the Imperial Conference along with other Countries ?

(*a*) 1913 (*b*) 1914

(*c*) 1915 (*d*) 1916

4. In which year Rash Behari Bose thrown Bomb upon Lord Hardinge ?

(*a*) 1908 (*b*) 1909

(*c*) 1910 (*d*) 1911

5. Rash Behari Bose, Bagi Kartar Singh, Sachindra Sanyal and Ganesh Pingle prepared a Master Plan to stage a countrywide revolution on February 21, 1915. This plan was termed by the Government as

(*a*) Lahore Conspiracy Case of 1915

(*b*) Delhi Conspiracy Case of 1915

(*c*) Karachi Conspiracy Case of 1915

(*d*) None of the above.

ANSWERS

1. (*a*) **2.** (*b*) **3.** (*c*) **4.** (*d*) **5.** (*a*)

13

CHAPTER

Government of India, Act, 1919

> *"If it could be said that this chapter of reforms led directly or necessarily up to the establishment of a Parliamentary system in India, I, for one, would have nothing to do with it."*
>
> *—Lord Morley.*

CIRCUMSTANCES LEADING TO THE ACT OF 1919

The Montague-Chelmsford Reforms came only a decade after the Morley Minto Reforms with a constitutional scheme of much greater importance. They caused the break in the old bureaucratic rule and made a beginning in Representative Government.

Following are the circumstances leading to the Act of 1919 :

1. Disappointment over the reforms of 1909. The reforms introduced by the Act of 1909 proved disappointing because they made no significant change in the autocratic character of the Government. Parliamentary usages were adopted and generally followed but the spirit of Parliamentary Government was missing. *In the words of Lionel Curtis: "The vital defect of Minto-Morley principle is that it leaves the whole responsibility of government on one set of men, while rapidly transferring power to another set of men.......It creates a situation eminently calculated to exasperate the executive and legislature with each other and, therefore, to throw the British Government and the Indian community at large into a posture of mutual antagonism."* The Act served the vicious design of the Government to see that "class was set against class, community against community, each to cancel out the effect of the other." *According to Zacharias, "These reforms introduced elective principle of democracy, yet at the same time added anti-democratic communal representation. The official majority was done away with but the elected members remained in a minority. The membership was considerably enlarged but an emphatic disclaimer was issued simultaneously that the new councils in no way meant the introduction of parliamentary system."* The system of communal representation was deemed as an ulcer in the body politic. The act was, in fact, so full of anti-democratic elements and fraught with much vicious consequences, that it drew criticism not only from the revolutionaries and Extremists but also from the Moderates.

2. Dual Policy of the Government. The first two decades of the present century were marked by the attitude of the Government sometimes to conciliate and sometimes to suppress the National Movement. Lord Curzon in his mad rush for reforms tended to gather all the strings of Government in the hands of the Central Authority. His reformative measures gave rise to political agitations which he dealt with sternly. People lost faith in the Government and began to suspect every official move. The officers also adopted the corresponding attitude of contemptuous indifference and ruthless repression. The reforms came only after violent agitations. The result was that the reforms, howsoever significant, did not rouse much popular enthusiasm because they came too late. Secondly, the agitators developed the notion that the Government was amenable only to violent agitations and not moral persuasion or beggary.

The Act of 1909 was received with unrelieved coldness. The Moderates despite their awareness of the shortcomings of the new Act, favoured co-operation with the Government in working out the reforms. The Extremists refused to accept the reforms. Thus, the split in the Congress ranks became more pronounced. Lord Hardinge followed a calculated policy of winning back the people in favour of the British Government, through repression and sympathy. Bal Gangadhar Tilak was deported to Mandalay Jail. The 'cult of bombs' in Bengal was crushed firmly, although temporarily. Shri Arvind Ghose, the spearhead of anti-partition agitation in Bengal, retired from politics and turned to meditation at Pondicherry. The Extremists, however, through Press and Platform remained active. Lord Hardinge proceeded with the Indian Press Act, 1910, followed by the Prevention of Seditions Meetings Act to stifle the Press and even the honest criticism of Government through public speeches. The Criminal Law Amendment Act of 1913 defined conspiracy and made it an independent offence. All the aforesaid measures armed the Executive with boundless powers to suppress militant nationalism. But Lord Hardinge was a shrewd administrator. He tempered his repression with sympathy for the aggrieved people of Bengal. With this end in view he wrote to the Government at home regarding the reunification of Bengal. His suggestion was accepted and the Partition was annulled on December 11,1911, on the occasion of the visit of Emperor George V. This gesture of British goodwill was much appreciated in the Congress ranks.

Besides the annulment of the Partition of Bengal, the Viceroy also decided to overawe the Indian subjects with the British might and splendour. He held an Imperial Durbar in December, 1911, to celebrate the visit of George V. The occasion was made memorable by the announcement of various 'boons' designed to impress the Indian public. The most notable 'boons' were the reversal of Partition and shifting of capital from Calcutta to Delhi.

(3)Change in the policy of Muslim League The Morley-Minto reform of 1909 created a great change in India. The Hindus and Muslims came at cross. The Muslim League welcomed the communal electorates and showed its faith in Anglo Muslim friendship. But only after two years policy changed. The partition of Bengal in 1911 (the annulment of the partition was accompanied by the separation of Bihar from Bengal) excited the Muslim of the country. They thought that it was a great favour to Hindus and so they lost faith in Britishers.

The happenings in other countries also made the Anglo Muslim relations more bitter. The British attitude towards Turkey in the Turko-Indian war (1911), the agreement between Russia and England regarding Persia, and the Balkan wars of October 1912, injured the sentiment of the Muslims, and aroused fears that independent Islamic powers were in danger.

The sympathies of the Congress for Turkey inspired the Muslim to see the activities of Congress. Maulana Abul Kalam Azad and Maulana Mohammad Ali tried for the Hindu-Muslim unity. The younger generations of Muslims was influenced by a nationalists movement. The constitution of the Muslim League was amended and the object of League became the attainment of 'self-government' through constitutional means. This change in the policy of Muslim League paved the way for the communal unity. Indian National Congress also appreciated the attitude of Muslim League, in this respect. The arrest of nationalists like Mohammad Ali and Shaukat Ali, Maulana Abul Kalam Azad and Hasrat Mohani, for their sympathy for the Sultan of Turkey, also directed the Muslims to leave the favour of government, and to favour the Congress. Thus at the time of first World War, Indian

National Congress and Muslim League were coming nearer and nearer. After the war, though Lucknow Pact, December 31, 1916, the Congress and League were united. Both of them, now raised their voice against the British Government.

(4)The re-union of Moderates and Extremists (1916)– The Congress organisation became most popular with the re-union of Moderates and Extemists. Since 1907, Moderates were dominating the Congress organisation and Extremists were not allowed to come into organisation. With the release of Tilak from jail, the hope of compromise became quite clear and with the efforts Mrs.Annie Besant, the two wings of the Congress were again united in the Lucknow Session of 1916. Naturally, with the united efforts of both the group the government was compelled to think for reforms.

(5)The Home Rule Movement– The Home Rule Movement of Mr. Tilak and Mrs. Annie Besant also helped a lot in compelling the government to pass the Government of India Act of 1909. She inaugurated the All India Home Rule League at Madras in September 1916. She wrote, thus in commonweal, "In political reform we aim at the building up of complete self-government from village councils, through District and Municipal Boards and Provincial Legislative Assemblies, to a national parliament, equal in its powers to the legislative bodies of the self-governing colonies, by whatever name they may be called ; also at the direct representation of India in the Imperial parliament when that body shall contain representatives of the self governing States of the Empire."

(6)Mesopotamian Commission Report– The report of Mesopotamian Commission 1917 was published at the time when the political agitation in India was at its peak. The commission was to decide existing system of government. Mr. Montague an Ex-under Secretary for State for India described the government of India as "too wooden, too iron and too inelastic and antedeluvian to subverse its purpose in modern times." He also recommended for the substantial reforms. He supported the demand of the Indians said:

"If you want to use loyalty (of the Indian people) you must give them that higher opportunity of controlling their own destinies, common merely by Councils, which cannot act, but by control by growing control of the Executive itself. Unless you are prepared to remodel this century old and cumbrous machine......you will loose your right to control the destinies of the Indian Empire."

The speech of Mr. Montague pushed forward the Home Rule Movement and Mr. Austin Chamberlain, the Secretary of State for India had to vacate the office.

(7)Announcement of Montague August 20, 1917– With the resignation of Mr. Chamerlain, the government of Britain thought once again about its old policies. Mr. Montague, the new Secretary for State of India, suggested for constitutional reforms. He was greatly honoured in India and was considered her best friend. On August 20, he declared the two new principles of his policy, *viz.* "The increasing association of Indians in every branches of administration and the gradual development of self-governing institutions with a view to progressive realisation of responsible government in India as an integral part of the British Empire. They have decided that substantial steps should be taken in this direction as soon as possible." He also said he would be visiting India very shortly to consult the Indian Government, and the Indian people.

(8)Montford Scheme– In November 1917, Mr. Montague came to India. He consulted the top ranking leaders of Congress and Muslim League, along with Lord Chelmsford. After this consultation he again consulted Viceroy and a small committee of five persons –Sir William duke, Earl of Donoughmore, Bhopendra Nath Basu and Charles Roberts was appointed. He published his report which is known as Montford Scheme.

(9) The disappointing declaration of Lord Crew. Lord Hardinge in his despatch of August 25, 1918, to the Secretary of State for India, Mr.Crew, stated, ".......Nevertheless it is certain that, in course of time, the just demands of Indians for a larger share in the Government of the country will have to be satisfied and the question will be how this devolution of power can be conceded, without impairing the supreme authority of the Governor-in-Council. The only possible solution of the difficulty would appear to be gradually to give to the Provinces a larger measure of self-government." The despatch of the Viceroy was interpreted by Congress leaders as a guarded promise to extend autonomy to the provinces and to subordinate the executive wing to the legislature of the province. The British Government had in fact no intention to grant self-government to the people. Discounting the baseless optimism in the minds of the nationalists, *Mr. Crew, the Secretary of the State, in a speech in the House of Lords in June 1912 said, "There is certain section in India, which looks forward to a measure of self-government approaching that which had been granted to Dominions. I see no future for India on these lines. The experiment of extending a measure of self-government practically free from parliamentary control to a race which is not our own, even though that race enjoys the services of the best men belonging to our race is one which cannot be tried."* This gave rise to a lot of discontent amongst the Indians and forces of nationalism grew stronger.

(10) The Outbreak of the First World War– At the outbreak of war in 1914, the British Government affirmed that it was entering the war to make world safe for democracy. The Indians took the promise on its face value and extended wholehearted support to the war efforts of the Government. At the end of hostilities the Indian public looked forward to a reward of their wartime services. But they were treated with bullets and martial laws. Shri Tilak and Mrs. Annie Besant began to demand Home Rule. The Muslim League sank its differences with the Congress and formulated a joint scheme known as Congress-League Scheme. At last Mr. Montague, the Secretary of State for India, made a declaration on behalf of the British Government in 1917. In his statement before the House of Commons he said that the British policy in India would thenceforth be directed towards securing the association of Indians in every branch of administration of progressive realisation of responsible Government in India. In pursuance of this policy, the Parliament passed an Act in 1919 entitled 'Government of India Act, 1919'.

MAIN PROVISIONS OF THE ACT OF 1919

Within six months of his arrival in India, Mr. Montague in consultation with the Viceroy, Mr. Chelmsford, and a committee of four members formulated his proposals. The report known as Mont-Ford Reforms, was simultaneously published in India and England in 1918. On the basis of the reforms scheme proposed by Mont-Ford Reforms, was introduced in British Parliament and passed in 1919. It received royal assent on December 23, 1919. The new Act had a Preamble prefixed to it which defined the underlying principles on which the Act had been prepared. The changes introduced by the Act were as follows —

1. Preamble

"Whereas it is the declared policy of the Parliament to provide for the increasing association of Indians in every branch of Indian administrations, and for the general development of self-governing institutions, with a view to the progressive realisation of responsible Government in British India as an integral part of the Empire;

"And whereas progress in giving effect to this policy can only be achieved by successive stages, it is expedient that substantial steps in this direction should now be taken;

"And whereas the line and manner of each advance can be determined only by Parliament upon whom responsibility lies for the welfare and advancement of the Indian people;

"And whereas the action of Parliament in such matters must be guided by the inspiration received from those on whom new opportunities of service will be conferred and by the extent to which it is found that confidence can be reposed in the sense of responsibility;

"And whereas concurrently with the gradual development of self-governing institutions in the Provinces of India it is expedient to give to the Provinces, in provincial matters the largest measure of independence of the Government of India, which is compatible with the due discharge by the latter of its own responsibilities;

"Be it therefore enacted...."

There are several points to note in the Preamble. The first is that India was to remain an integral part of the British Empire. Secondly, the Preamble suggested decentralisation of authority without loosening the supreme hold of the Central Government. Thirdly, the time and manner of gradual advance towards the distant goal of responsible Government was to be decided not by the Indians but the British Parliament which was an outside authority. This provision meant a vague indefiniteness about the intentions of the Government. The Congress leaders who were anxious to get the right of self-determination at the earliest and-a specified date, resented the doctrine of the discretion of the British Parliament. Fourthly, the Preamble proposed the conferment of partial responsibility in the Provinces and the largest measure of independence in their sphere. The Government of India was to remain responsible to the British Parliament but in order to seek the co-operation of the people, the size of the Central Legislature was to be enlarged. The preamble thus made no change in the character of the Central Government or the Home Administration of Indian affairs.

2. Home Government

Relaxation of the control of Secretary of State in regard to transferred subjects. Under the new Act the administrative subjects were divided under the heads of 'Central' and Provincial'. The Provincial subjects were further divided into 'Reserved' and 'Transferred'. The reserve subjects were to be administered by the Governor while the transferred subjects were placed in the charge of Indian Ministers. Since the Ministers were to be responsible to the legislature, it became necessary to restrict the powers of the Secretary of State in regard to the administration of subjects under 'Transferred' head. The Act, hence, empowered the Secretary of State to make rules and regulations to the extent it might be necessary to give effect to the Provincial part of the Act. The rules thus made by him restricted his control over the transferred subjects for the purposes of (*a*) safeguarding the interests of the Empire, (*b*) deciding controversial issues between Provinces, (*c*) safeguarding the due exercise of power and discharge of duties imposed upon the Governor-General-in-Council by the Act, (*d*) safeguarding the exercise his own powers relating to High Commissioner, public services and borrowing, and (*e*) safeguarding the administration of central subjects. So far as the subjects under the 'Reserved' head were concerned, there was no question of the relaxation of the overall authority and control of the Secretary of State for India.

3. Governor General and his Executive Council—Responsive Autocracy at the Centre

The Act of 1919 did not introduce any fundamental change in composition and powers of the Central Executive Council. The *unrestricted and despotic powers of the Governor-General were left untouched.* He continued to be responsible to the British Parliament through the Secretary of State. The Central Legislature got no effective control over him. As before, the superintendence, direction and control of entire administration–both civil and military–remained vested in him. Although he was required to take all decisions in his Executive Council, he was in no way afraid of his Council. In a way he constituted the whole of the Executive. His dominating position in the Council was due to various reasons. He enjoyed a unique position because of being Crown's representative in India. Secondly, he had a powerful say in the appointment and promotion of his Councillors and made rules and regulations regarding conduct of work. Above all he was not bound to act on the advice of his Council.

The Governor-General of India held the most responsible and distinguished office. He was appointed by the Crown on the recommendation of the British Prime Minister for a period of 5 years. He discharged his onerous duties with the help of his Executive and Legislative Councils. Since he was individually responsible to British Parliament for the good governance of India, he was armed with extensive discretionary powers. His salary was fixed at ₹ 2,56,000 a year in addition to the allowances to the tune of ₹ 172,000 annually. He was also provided with a free and well furnished Government House to live in.

The new Act empovered the Governor-General to have direct control over the *External Affairs Department and Political Department. Through the latter he exercised his power of supervision and control over the Indian States.*

4. Central Legislature

The Act of 1919 set up a bicameral legislature at the Centre instead of Imperial Legislative Council which consisted of one House only. The two Houses were known as Legislative Assembly and Council of State *having* 145 *members and* 60 *members respectively.* Thus the total membership under the new Act rose to 205 as against 68 under the Act of 1909. Both the chambers began to have a *majority of elected members.* Out of 145 members in the Assembly 41 were nominated members and the remaining elected members. The elective seats were distributed among the Provinces in accordance with their population. The seats fixed for a Province were further distributed between communities and classes. The elected members included 30 Muslims, 2 sikhs, 7 landholders, 4 representatives of Indian Commerce and 52 general. Of the nominated members 26 were to be officials and 15 non-officials. The tenure of the *Lower House was three years.* The method of their election was direct and not indirect as under the Act of 1909.

It had, however no right to change the constitution or enact any law derogatory to an Act of the Parliament. The limitations imposed on its legislative functions made it an ineffective body.

No Bill could be introduced in the legislature without the previous sanction of the Governor-General on matters relating to Defence, Foreign Relations, Ecclesiastical Affairs and the Public Debt.

Financial Powers of the Legislative Assembly. The financial powers of the Legislative Assembly were as much restricted as its law-making powers. The Act required the Budget to be framed by the Executive and presented first in the Assembly. The budget was to be divided into two parts, votable and non-votable. The difference between the two being that the members had the right to discuss and vote on the votable items while they could simply discuss and not vote on the non-votable items. The second non-votable part included (*a*) Interest and sinking fund charges, (*b*) Salaries and pension of persons appointed by or with thc approval of His Majesty or the Secretary of State for India, (*c*) expenditure on Defence, Political Department, Ecclesiastical Affairs (missionaries) and lastly (*d*) salary of Chief Commissioners. *Nearly 60 per cent of the budget was classed as 'non-votable, i.e.,* free from the control of the Legislature. On the remaining 40 per cent of the budget, the House could refuse or reduce the grants but had no right to increase the appropriated sum on any item. The powers of the House even in regard to votable part of the budget were shadowy. The Governor-General had the power to certify any expenditure refused by the House and also restore any grant reduced by it. The Central Legislature created by the Act of 1919 was not sovereign law-making body.

Composition of the Council of State. The Council of State or the Upper House of the Indian Legislature had 60 members–33 elected and 27 nominated ones. The 27 nominated members consisted of 17 officials and 10 non-officials. The 33 elected members included 16 non-Muslims, 11 Muslims, 1 Sikh, 2 non-communal and 3 Europeans. The life of the Upper House was five years.

Elections and Franchise: The Function of the Upper House was restricted to reconsider the Bills passed and forwarded to it by the Assembly. Since it had no originating functions, it was deliberately given a conservative character. It was a meeting place of the capitalists, business community and landlords. Its franchise was so restricted that there were only 17,000 voters for electing 33 elected members. Women were not eligible for becoming its members or voters. In Madras only those persons were entitled to vote, the rental value of whose property was ₹ 3,000 or their taxable income was ₹ 30,000 or who paid ₹ 3,000 as land revenue. Other qualifications for its voters were the past experience in a Legislative Council of India, membership of University Senate, the holding of certain offices in local bodies or holding of some specified titles. *The President of the Council was nominated by the Governor-General.*

Powers of the Council of State: Except in regard to financial matters, *the two House enjoyed equal and concurrent powers.* No Bill could go into the Statute Book unless passed by both the Houses in the same form. The budget was presented in both the Houses on the same day and date. All other Money Bills were first introduced in the Lower House and then were forwarded to the Council of State. Voting on grants could take place only in the Assembly and not in the Council. If a Finance Bill passed by the Assembly was rejected or returned with suggestions for amendment, not acceptable to the Assembly, it could not become an Act unless certified by the Governor-General. The members of the Council of State were also authorised to ask *questions and supplementary questions* from the members of the Executive Council.

Conflicts between the two Houses : In case of a conflict arising between the Council and the Assembly, the Act provided for three different modes of arriving at a compromise. They were *joint committees, joint conferences and joint sittings.* The first method was meant to avoid the possibility of a deadlock, the second was meant to solve the differences after they had arisen by agreeing to a conference of equal number of representatives of both Houses.

The third method was used as a last resort. Joint sitting of both Houses could be convened only by the Governor-General in the event of a Bill passed by one House but not approved by the other within six months. In the joint sitting the Bill was submitted to vote and thus was either adopted or dropped. In this case also the Lower House was always at an advantage because of its superior numerical strength.

5. Special powers of the Governor-General and defective organisation of the Central Legislature

It should be noted that the authors of the Act of 1919 had definitely no intention to model the Indian Legislature on the pattern of British Parliament. The Governor-General had the last word on any Bill or resolution passed by the legislature. Besides being the head of the Executive, the *Governor-General had unlimited powers in the legislative sphere. He also summoned and prorogued the legislature, dissolved the Legislative Assembly and also extended its life under special circumstances.* He also possessed the power to *prevent the consideration of a Bill* or a part thereof if in his opinion it affected peace and tranquillity of the country. He could disallow a question in the Legislature. He could also address either or both the Houses as and when he pleased. No Bill passed by the Legislature could become an Act unless assented to by the Governor-General who could even withhold his assent or return the same with his suggestion for reconsideration of the House. He was also empowered to disallow an adjournment motion or debate on any resolution. *The Central Legislature was not a sovereign law-making body.* He was authorised *to reserve any Bill duly passed by both the Houses for the consideration of the Crown.* He possessed law-making power also. *He could enact a law which he considered essential for the safety and tranquillity of the Empire even if the Legislature had refused to pass it.* The Princes Protection Act, 1923, and Finance Bill, 1925, were enacted by the Governor-General in the exercise of his special powers. Any Acts thus passed by him could be cancelled or repealed not by the Legislature but by the British Parliament and His Majesty-in-Council.

The Governor-General was also empowered to promulgate ordinances in cases of emergency while the Legislature was not in session. The life of such an *ordinance was normally six months* unless extended for six months again. The financial powers of the Governor-General were no less significant and extensive than his legislative powers. *He had the final say in the preparation of annual budget.* The Budget in the form of demands for grants was submitted to the vote of the Legislature only after receiving into votable and non-votable heads. Sanction of the Legislature was needed only in case of votable grants which covered only one-third of the total expenditure. Even in this sphere the *Governor-General was empowered to restore any grant refused or reduced by the Legislature.*

6. Changes in the Provincial Setup

The Act of 1919 reoriented the Provincial setup by introducing dyarchy. The word 'Dyarchy' is a compound of 'Di' which means *'two'* and *'Archia'*, meaning 'rule'. The word means rule by two authorities or double Government. The Provincial subjects were divided into Reserved and Transferred. The Reserved subjects were administered by the Governor of each Province with the help of his Executive Council whose members had no responsibility towards the Legislative Council. The Transferred subjects were administered by the Governor with the help of Indian Ministers who were responsible to the legislature. This dual arrangement in the Provincial Executive came to be known as Dyarchy.

Division of subjects into Central and Provincial. Before dealing with dyarchical system in detail, it is worthwhile to consider the underlying principles of the division of subjects between the Centre and Provinces. The matters which were of all-India interest and in regard to which uniformity in legislation was necessary for the whole of India, were regarded as Central subjects. *The central list contained* 47 *subjects,* chief among them being Defence, Foreign and Political Relations, Patents and Copyright, Currency and Coinage, Communications, Commerce and Shipping, Excise duties on cotton, salt, Income-tax and Public Debt in India. The subjects which were chiefly of local importance and interest were treated as Provincial subjects. The *Provincial list contained 50 subjects* including Local Self-Government, Public Health and Sanitation and Medical Administration, Education, Public Works, Water Supplies and Irrigation, Famine Relief, Forests, Co-operative Societies, Law and Order, etc. The Act also stated that if the Governor-General-in-Council declared any Central subject as of Provincial interest, then the Provincial legislature would be empowered to make laws pertaining to that subject. *Essentially the Centre continued to have a Unitary Government.*

Division of Reserved and Transferred Subjects in the Provinces. The subjects to be dealt with by the Provincial Governments were subdivided into two parts–Reserved and Transferred. In the words of Montford Report the principle underlying the division was "to include within transferred subjects those departments which afforded most opportunity for local knowledge and social service, those in which Indians had shown themselves to be keenly interested, those in which mistakes that may occur, though serious, would not be irremediable and those which stand most in need of development." The reserved list included Police, Land Revenue Administration, Justice, Irrigation and Canals, Famine Relief, Control of Newspapers, Borrowing, Forests, etc. The subjects included in the transferred list were Local Self-Government, Public Health, Sanitation and Medical Administration, Education, Public Works including roads, bridges and tramways, fisheries, excise, technical education, and agriculture, etc. The administration of reserved subjects was controlled by the Governor with the co-operation of his Councillors. For the good governance of reserved subjects the Governor was answerable not to the voters of the Province but to the British Parliament through the Governor-General and Secretary of State. As to dispute whether a particular subject was reserved or transferred the decision of the Governor was made final.

SOME OTHER FEATURES OF THE ACT OF 1919

Following were the other salient features of the Government of India Act, 1919 —

(1)System of Representation – The system of representation was the basic principle of the Act of 1919. This representation was to be secured either by nomination or by election. The principle of communal representation was also adopted. The constituencies for the various interest *viz.* Landholders, labourers, Universities *etc.,* were also envisaged under the Act.

(2)The Indian States: (*i*) The chamber of Princes– The princes of India represented their grievances to Mr. Montague and Lord Chelmsford when they were touring over the whole country. Rushbrook William has written that the princes asked for many changes. In this connection *Mr. G.N. Singh* has written :

"The felt that they had no voice in the determination of all India policy. Secondly they deplored the lack of any impartial tribunal to decide dispute arising between them and the British in Indian authority, for it seemed to them that in a number of cases, the Government of India was at once a party and a judge. Finally they believed that the Political Department............occasionally acted in this regard of the treaties and in general, exercised an authority, which if benevolent, was never the less in certain respects undeniably arbitrary."

The Princes of India also put forward a scheme to Mr. Chelmsford for calling assembly in which they could discuss the matters of their common interests. They also demanded the constitution of an impartial tribunal for settling their disputes. They also requested that there should be association of their committee with the political secretary, so that harmony between the sentiments of the Princes and Government might acquired.

The Montford report accepted the main proposals of the conference of the princes. The conference approved generally all the things in interests of the princes. The recommendation of the conference were submitted to the Secretary of the State. The Viceroy consulted the secretary of State and drafted a scheme for forming the Chamber of Princes. The scheme was approved in the year 1919.......Codification committee was appointed to help the Viceroy in framing the rules and regulations concerning Courts of Arbitration and Commission of Inquiry. The Chamber of Princes was inaugurated an February 8, 1921. In the Act of 1919 there was no provision for the creation of the new machinery for co-operation between the British India and the Indian State.

The Chamber of princes represented 108 States. The members of the States had the right to participate to the working of the Chamber. Other 127 States were given the right to elect 12 representatives of their own. In such a way there were 120 members in the Chamber. The members had to elect the Chancellor and Pre-Chancellor annually. The Viceroy was the Chairman of the Chamber of Princes. In this absence Chancellor used to preside over the functions. It was mentioned be the Viceroy that attendance and voting in the Chamber would be voluntary. He also made clear that the Chamber would not be an executive body but a consultative body. The Chamber was not supposed to debar any individual state whether represented in the Chamber or not. The Chamber was not allowed to discuss internal affairs of any State or action of any Indian Ruler. The Chamber used to meet yearly in its own hall of Debate which was known as Narendra Mandal. The Royal proclamation described the powers and limitation of the Chamber in the following manner : —

"My Viceroy will take its counsel freely in matters relating to the territories of Indian states generally and in matters which affects those territory jointly with Indian or with the affairs of the individual states or their Rules or with the relations of Indian State Government vide the existing system of the States and their freedom of action will be in no way prejudiced or impaired."

The Chamber had to elect Standing Committee of four or five members. The Princes of Rajputana, Central India, Bombay and Punjab must be represented in the Standing Committee.

(*ii*) Other provisions regarding State– In cases of dispute between two states or in a Local State and Government of India, the matter was finally to be referred to the Viceroy. This matter was to be referred to a report by a commission, consisting of one nominee each side and presided by judge. The Viceroy had the power to refer the same to the Secretary of State if findings in the reports were not acceptable to him.

(3)The Civil Services in India – Special provisions were made in part IV of the Act, to regularise the position of Civil Services in India. All existing Rules regarding the services were regarded as valid but the alterations could be made in future. The Secretary of State in Council was given the power to appoint a Public Service Commission. The numbers of the members of the Commission should not be more than 5 and they had to hold three or five years. The functions of the Public Service Commission were to be prescribed by the Secretary of the State in Council. The Secretary of State in Council had also the power to make special rules for the admission of Indians in Civil Services. The Secretary of State in Council was empowered to make rules regarding the classification of Civil Service in India, the methods of their recruitment, there conditions of service, pay and allowances, and discipline and conduct.

(4)The Statutory Commission– There was also a provision for the establishment of a commission to enquire into the working of the system of Government, the growth of education; and the development of representative institutions in British India. The commission so appointed after the expiry of 10 years, period would submit a report on responsible Government in India. The establishment of second chambers in India.

The commission was also expected to report about desirability for the responsible Government. The commission was asked to report that whether the second chambers of the Local Legislature was desirable or not? The Crown might also refer any matter to the commission regarding the British India and Provinces. This commission was to come into existence after ten years of the passage of the Act of 1919. Keith has remarked, "The structure contemplated was obviously to complex that the revision must be contemplated. It was thought fit to give breathing space of ten years from the passing of the Act."

DEFECTS OF THE ACT

Montford Report on the basis of which Act of 1919, was passed gave a rude shock to those Indians who were seeing the dreams of 'self government' embodying the 'right of self-determination'. Leaving the Anglo Indians and Moderates of the Congress all sections condemned the Report. *Mrs. Annie Besant* wrote that the scheme was, "ungenerous for England to offer and unworthy for India to accept. In fact, there were very few concessions extended to Indians but even those concessions were hedged with many limitations." The few glaring mistakes of the Act are given below: —

1. Central Executive Not a Representative body– Due to this Act, the central executive was not a representative body but it was the body of flatteres. The members of the Executive Council did not feel any responsibility to the Central Legislature as they could not be removed by this Legislature. Their responsibility to the Central Legislature was reduced to nothing because the Governor-General had all the Legislative, financial and Administrative powers. So the Indian members always preferred to assist the Governor-General in collecting requisite informations about the Indian affairs and appreciate his policies. The Indian members were always given unimportant departments, such as Law, Education. Health *etc.* and the significant departments were always kept under the jurisdiction of the Britishers.

2. Limited Franchise–The authority of the Central Legislature was limited and the Franchise was rather very narrow. No doubt a Bicameral Legislature was established at the Centre and the number of elected members was increased, yet there was no significance of the Central Legislature. In fact this Legislature was not given the powers of real Legislature. This Legislature had no control over the Executive and it could not direct the finance Sixty percent of the budget was non votable. The remaining 4% was also practised non-votable because the Governor was given the power to restore any demand refused or reduced by the Central Legislature. In emergency the Governor-General could do whatever he liked without consulting anyone in matters of finance. So it is true to say that nothing substantial was granted to the Central Legislative. Neither the Legislature could control the purse nor it had the also Legislative authority. Governor-General was given the power to veto any Bill passed by the Legislature and previous sanction of Governor-General was essential to introduce certain types of Bills. The Legislature was not a representative body in the real sense. The formation of second chamber was just to help the Government.

The Franchise for Legislative Council and Legislative Assembly was extremely restricted. Holding of high property qualification and academic titles, membership of the University Senate. Zamindari rights, were regarded as the proper qualifications for the membership of the Upper House. In the Assembly also this franchise was very defective. Separate electorates for the minor communities made the Assembly undemocratic in character. The partial representation and limited franchise clearly indicates that the formation of responsible Government at centre was merely a false dream.

3. No clear-cut Division of Subjects– The division of subjects between the Central and Provincial was not clear-cut or definite. There were many subjects on which both the Government–Central and Provincial had their say. For instance, (defence, foreign relations, customs, posts and telegraphs, currency and coinage, Railways Sale tax, Income tax belonged to the Centre) and Laws regarding property were in the Central list while Laws regarding Land revenue, and excise, Jails, *etc.,* were assigned to the provinces.

Provincial government was not fully authorised to deal with the subjects under their list, far the purposes of Legislation. Certain parts of them regarding which uniformity in Legislation was desirable, were subject to legislation by the Indian Legislature. The division of the subject was rather very flexible and not rigid. There was concurrent list, under the provisions the Act of 1919. In any matter of controversy, the Governor-General had to decide whether it was a provincial matter or not. The Central Government could interfere in any matter of Provincial Government and the Provincial Legislature, with the previous sanction of the Governor-General could legislate on any Central subject.

IMPORTANCE OF THE ACT

No doubt, the reforms of 1919 could not satisfy the Indians but their significance cannot be minimised. This Act was truly considered as a land-mark in the constitutional history of India. It was a step towards the self-government. In the words of Coupland: "The Government of India Act 1919 was by far the most important measure of Indian policy adopted by the British parliament since the process of constitutional development began in 1861, for it crossed the line between Legislative and Executive authority. Previous measures had enabled Indians increasingly to control their Legislatures but not their Governments Some Indians, it is true, had been members of both Governments, but they had been officially appointed and were responsible; and like their colleagues, to the Secretary of State and Parliament. Now Indians were to govern, so to speak, on their own. They were to take the charge of great departments of the Provincial administration, not as official nominees but as the leaders of the elected majorities in their Legislatures and responsible only to them" In brief, the following facts reveal the Importance of the Act of 1919:–

(1)Introduction of Dyarchy– The introduction of dyarchy affected a radical change in the conception of the provincial Government. It was the first time when a large number of people got the right to vote. In this connection *Punniah* has remarked, "Dyarchy was a unique experiment which was tried in 9 provinces for over a period of 16 years. Its main objects and purpose was to trend the people of India in the art of responsible self Government Its authors were no doubt aware of its defects and shortcomings, but thought that there was no better alternative to it under the circumstances".

(2)Indianisation in the Services– The presence of Indian Ministers as heads of the various departments increased the pace of Indianisation in the services. Now the Indian could be easily absorbed in the secret services. The Indian ministers could effect much needed reforms and eradicate evils, which the Britishers were reluctant to do on religious grounds. In this connection *Mr. Shri Ram Sharma* has rightly remarked:

".... unlike the foreign bureaucracy, Indian Ministers were not afraid of touching the pitch of social evils for fear it might defile them. Several creditable pieces of social Legislations were undertaken, which the foreign rules of the country had avoided in their reluctance to interfere with established customs and beliefs."

(3) Powers vested to Central Legislature–The work of Central Legislation were also very significant. It is true to say that the Executive was not responsible to the Central Legislature, but the Legislature was vested with large powers of influencing the Executive, The Legislature often used its powers for the benefit of the people.

According to *Prof. Percival Spear*: "The Montford Reforms were attacked on all sides. Right wing British opinion considered that they undermined the raj and gave authority to irresponsibility. Congressmen loudly proclaimed that they are a sham and not worth trying to work, and soon they were joined by some who had worked them for a time and again and acquired some grievance while so doing. Specially large targets were the reserved power of the Viceroy and Governors, the lack of any ministerial responsibility at the Centre, and the communal provisions. There is no doubt that the reforms were full of defects and difficulties. But now that they have passed into history we can see them in truer perspective. Time has dimmed many of the censures, while leaving others in sharper relief. The reserve powers, for example, are seen to have been perhaps only an excessive dose of a necessary medicine; many of them were retained by the critics themselves in the constitutions of 1949 on the plea of the necessity of a strong executive. Looking back after thirty years. We may pick out certain special points of weakness. One was the financial provision. The central finances were flexible, but the provincial ones were not, so that ministers often in fact found themselves without the means of carrying out their cherished measures such as the extension of education. They tended very naturally to suspect the reserved half who control the revenue of starving them of funds. Then, there was the question of responsibility.

The more closely the ministers were identified with the Governors and Councillors, the more they were liable to lose the confidence of there supporters. Yet such co-operation was necessary if anything was to be done. On the British side, every assertion of authority in the interest of law and order increased their unpopularity while any constructive measure went to the credit of the minister. It has further to be noticed that the provincial reforms were on the parliamentary plan of ministerial responsibility towards elected councils. This system presupposes a party system to provide the ministers, In India the major Congress party would not play. Only in Madras and Punjab were local parties where strong enough to take office, and, there the reforms worked better than anywhere else. Elsewhere there was a tendency for members to split into pressure and personal groups and for Governors to construct 'adhoc, coalitions which did nothing but dissolved into fresh patterns. The reforms certainly suffered from jack of Congress co-operation as well as from excessive restriction and division of authority.

(4)Inducement towards Self-Government– "When all this is said the fact remains that the reforms proved to be a solid and substantial achievement. They were an essential mile stone on the road to self-government. Without them Indian political progress would have been belated, erratic and probably revolutionary. They gave by and large, enough inducement to enough people to work them, and enough scope to provide experience and incentives for the future. Whenever there were determined leaders backed by coherent parties, solid results could be achieved. Thus the justice party of Madras was able to reform the administration of wealthy south Indian temples and the unionist party in Punjab, led by Sir Fazl-i-Husain and Chaudhari Chothu Ram, to extend education and protect the cultivator. Though tensions and frustrations could not be avoided, the new system went far enough and worked well enough to make further advance inevitable. This was its essential justification. It started the constitutional clock which would not stop. The present Indian Government is the heir of montague as well as Gandhi."

Thus, we conclude that though the Act was full of defects yet it paved way for the spread of democratic principles.

EXERCISES

Long Answer Type Questions

1. Discuss the causes which laid to the famous Declaration of British Policy towards India on August 20, 1917.
2. What were the main provisions of the Government of India Act, 1919?
3. What were the main defects of the Government of India Act 1919?
4. Estimate the importance of the Government of India Act 1919.

Short Answer Type Questions

1. Write any three important causes which were responsible for the enactment of the Government of India Act, 1919.
2. Which significant changes were made in the Central Legislature with the help of the Government of India Act, 1919?
3. What were the functions and powers of the Central Legislature according to the Government of India Act, 1919?

Objective Type Questions

Choose the correct answer

1. According to the Government of India Act, 1919 the life of Legislative Assembly was
   (*a*) four years (*b*) five years
   (*c*) six years (*d*) seven years.
2. According to the Government of India Act, 1919 the voter should not be less than
   (*a*) 24 years (*b*) 25 years
   (*c*) 26 years (*d*) 27 years

ANSWERS

1. (*a*) 2. (*b*)

14

CHAPTER

Nature and Working of Dyarchy in the Provinces

"Dyarchy failed in its primary purpose which its authors intended to serve. It did not provide a real training in responsible Government." —*Prof. Coupland*

The Government of India Act, 1919 introduced a new system of administration in some provinces, known as Dyarchy. This system of Government was introduced to meet the popular demand of responsible government in India.

Dyarchy has been derived from the Greek words 'di' meaning 'twice' and 'archie' meaning 'rule'. So it meant 'twice rule'. It was an experiment of double Government. In this system, the provincial subjects were divided into two parts – the 'Reserved' (which were to be disposed of by the Governor in Council) and the 'transferred, Jails, Police, Justice, Finance, Irrigation, comparatively more important subjects were the 'Reserved subjects' and they were to be governed by the governor and his executive Council. Education, Agriculture, Local self Government etc. the subjects of loss significance were transferred to the Indian Ministers under the control of the Governors.

Governor and His Ministers. The Act provided for the appointment of Ministers to help the Governor in dealing with the transferred subjects. The maximum number of Ministers to be appointed in various Provinces was fixed by the Act. Bombay, Calcutta and Madras had three Ministers each while the remaining Provinces had only two Ministers each. *The Ministers were selected by the Governor to hold office during his pleasure, from among the non-official members of the local legislature.* Membership of the Legislature was essential for becoming a Minister. If a person at the time of his appointment did not happen to be a member of the Legislature of that Province, he could not hold ministerial office for more than six months. The salaries of the Ministers were determined by the legislature which thus got power to oust a Minister from office by withholding his pay. The Legislature could also punish a defaulting Minister by proposing a reduction in his salary. The Bombay Legislative Council actually took a lead by reducing the annual salary of a Minister from ₹ 64,000 to ₹ 48,000.

The responsibility of the Ministers to the voters was further secured by another measure. Besides refusing to sanction the grant for the Ministers' salary, the Legislature was also empowered to secure a Minister's resignation by expressing its *lack of confidence in him.* Thus the Governor's choice of a Minister was restricted only to those persons who commanded the support of a sizable group in legislature. In U.P. When the Legislature censured a Minister, the Governor had to remove him from office despite his unwillingness. There was no discrimination between a Minister and a member of the Executive Council in so far as their status and salary were concerned, but as regards position and tenure of office, the Minister was at a great disadvantage. He had to please two masters–the Governor and the Legislature. The Governor was empowered to remove a Minister without assigning a reason, no less was the legislature empowered to do the same.

Normally in a Parliamentary Government the head of the State enjoys nominal rights. He has to work according to the advice of his team of Ministers. Judged in this light, the Provinces were far from getting full parliamentary or responsible Government. *The Governor continued to be the real and not constitutional head.*

To guide the Governor in his relation to the Ministers an instrument of instructions was issued to the Governors. The Government of India Bill, 1919, contained the provision, "In relation to transferred subjects, the Governor shall be guided by the advice of his Ministers, unless he sees sufficient cause to dissent from their opinion, in which case he may require action to be taken otherwise then in accordance with the advice." **The Joint Parliamentary Committee** observed, "The Committee is of the opinion that the Ministers selected by the Governor to advise him on the transferred subjects should be elected members of the Legislative Council, enjoying its confidence and capable of leading it. A Minister shall have the option of resigning if his advice is not accepted by the Governor; and the Governor will have the ordinary constitutional right of dismissing a Minister whose policy he believes to be seriously at fault or out of accord with the views of the Legislative Council. In the last resort the governor can always dissolve his Legislative Council and choose new Minister after a fresh election but if this course is adopted, the Committee hopes that the Governor will find himself able to accept such views as his new Ministers may press upon him regarding the issue which forced the dissolution." The Joint Parliamentary Committee, therefore, urged that the Ministers who enjoyed the confidence of a majority in the Legislative Council should be given the fullest opportunity of managing the Department entrusted to their charge. The Governor should accept their advice and promote their policy to the farthest extent possible. "It will be for him." Observed the Committee, "to help with sympathy and courage the popular side of his government in their new responsibilities. He should never hesitate to point out to his Ministers what he thinks is the right course or to warn them if he thinks that they are taking the wrong course. But, if, after hearing all the arguments, Ministers should decide not to adopt his advice then in the opinion of the Committee the Governor should ordinarily allow Ministers to have their way fixing the responsibility upon them, even if it may subsequently be necessary for him to veto any particular piece of legislation." The Committee was fully seized of the fact that Ministers in India, as in all other countries, would commit mistakes, acting with the approval of a majority of the Legislative Council but there is no way of learning except through experience and by the realisation of responsibility.

It is noteworthy that the Government of India Act, 1919 entrusted the Governor with many special responsibilities. Under the plea of discharging his special responsibilities, the Governor could disagree with his Minister on any significant matter and could do whatever he liked. In this way he neither violated the Act of 1919 or the Instrument of Instructions and could have his way also. According to the Indian Statutory Commission, the Governor combined in himself, "ordinary and extraordinary powers and duties. He is a part of the day-to day administration, but he is also the authority in reserve, who may have to override normal processes when he is convinced that the ordinary administration of the province needs his special intervention." History bears ample testimony to the fact that the intervention of the Governor was not confined only to the extraordinary circumstances but also to other ordinary circumstances.

So in practice the Ministers were far from being the real masters of their departments. They were not free agents. *They had to submit to the wishes of the Governor who could even ignore the advice of a Minister and act in his discretion* if he considered it necessary in the interest of minorities, the depressed classes, public services or for maintaining peace and tranquillity in the Province. Though the authors of the Act had expected the Governor to encourage the principle of joint responsibility amongst the Ministers, by deliberating with them in a body, no such thing was practised by the Governors. The Governors generally dealt with the Ministers individually and thus hampered the growth of team spirit amongst them. The Ministers were found criticising each other openly and looking up to the Governor for their nomination to the Executive Council at the end of their term. For want of a joint stand by the Ministers, the real powers remained concentrated in the hands of the Governors.

Governor and His Executive Councillors. The administration of reserved subjects was vested exclusively in the Governor-in-Council. *The membership of the Executive Councils of Calcutta, Bombay and Madras was four each while that of other Provinces only two each.* Although the Act said nothing about the inclusion of Indians in the Council, the Governors developed a convention of nominating Indians to the extent of 50 per cent of the total strength of the Council. The Indian Councillors were taken from outside the official group. Thus effect was given to the principle stated in August Declaration of Montagu of associating Indians in the administration of the country.

The members of the Governor's Executive Council were appointed by the Crown on the recommendation of the Governor. Evidently every Councillor owed his appointment to the Governor's good offices. The Secretary of State hardly ever overruled the recommendation of a Governor or the Governor-General in the selection of his team. *The salary and allowances of the Councillors were fixed by the Act and could not be changed by the Legislature.* They were the ex-officio members of the Legislative Council without being responsible to it for any act of omission or commission. Unlike the Ministers, *they were not removable by the legislature's motion of censure or non-confidence. Consequently* they had to be loyal to the Governor and through him to the Secretary of State and the British Parliament. The Governor on whom was the duty laid by the Instrument of Instructions of maintaining the safety and tranquillity in the State and also the standard of good administration, was given extensive powers to discharge his multiple duties. He acted as the head of the Council in which matters were decided by a majority vote. *But the Governor was given the power of overriding decisions of the Council if he considered such an action necessary for the safety, tranquillity or interest of his Province.*

Governor's control over the finance. The Finance portfolio was treated as a reserved subject. The fear in transferring it to the Minister was that the financial issue might be used as an indirect method of controlling the reserved heads. Finance being the key department, was largely controlled by the Governor. The Budget was prepared strictly under the supervision of the Governor. For the allocation of funds to the transferred and reserved heads, the Governor could summon a joint meeting of the Councillors and the Ministers. However, in cases of difference, he was given the power to make allocations of revenue and balances which were binding on both sides. *Nearly 70 per cent of total demands for grants was non-votable,* that is, the legislature could discuss those items but not vote upon them. The Governor was also given the power to restore any demand for grant relating to a reserved subject, reduced or rejected by the legislature, by certifying that the amount was essential for good administration of that department. In case of transferred subjects, the Governor was not given any power of resorting or sanctioning a grant reduced or rejected by the legislature. However, in case of emergency he could authorise such expenditure as might be necessary for the peace and tranquility of the Province or for the carrying on of any department. The Governors found ample opportunities to exercise their special powers in Bengal and C.P. While the Swarajists played their game of obstructing the passage of official Bills with a view to paralysing the Government in those Provinces.

Working of Dyarchy. The system of setting up two co-ordinate authorities in the Province was introduced in 1921 in nine Governors' Provinces, *viz.*, Madras, Bengal, Bombay, U.P., the Punjab, Bihar and Orissa, Central Provinces and Assam. Subsequently, Burma and N.W.F.P. were also included in the scheme. Elections took place in 1920-21 for implementing Dyarchy but the Congress not satisfied with the Reforms boycotted the elections. So from 1921 to 1923, the Liberals co-operated with the Government in working out the Constitution. They entered the Councils and the Executive. In 1924 the Swarajist Party contested the Council seats on behalf of the Congress. But since the Swarajists were pledged to a policy of wrecking the constitution from within, there occurred a temporary breakdown of dyarchy. They persisted in their demand for a revision of the Constitution so as to lead to the establishment of full responsible government in the Provinces. The outcome of their campaign was the appointment of a Reforms Enquiry Committee in 1924. The British members of the Muddiman Committee suggested some reforms for the fruitful working of the dyarchic system but the Indian members, namely, Mr. Jinnah and Sir Sapru, styled the scheme as fundamentally defective. The Simon Commission also pointed out the defects of Dyarchy.

INTERNAL CAUSES OF THE FAILURE OF DYARCHY

Many internal factors were responsible for the failure of dyarchy system but few important ones are given here.

The novel experiment of dyarchy worked with varying degrees of success in different Provinces. There were some grave and potent reasons which accounted for the failure of the scheme in practice.

1. Theoretically Wrong. The dyarchic scheme while it was in the making was condemned even by the Governor-General and Secretary of State. The former called it an admirable system while to the latter it was a kind of pedantic and hide-bound constitution. The system was badly conceived and half-heartedly implemented. Its opponents considered it unsound in principle and unworkable in practice. The Governor went to the extent of saying that 'dyarchy was a cumbrous, complex, confused system, having no logical basis and rooted in compromise.' To quote Lord Lytton, "My experience was that the Reserved half of Government was disliked but that it was respected, whereas the Transferred half of Government was not only disliked, but also despised." The word dyarchy became a term of abuse in common speech.

Secondly, the division of executive work under dyarchy into two halves was both unnatural and unscientific. The government too like human body is an organism which cannot be divided without killing it. Another odd thing was that two authorities–the Councillors and the Ministers–were divided in their loyalties. One set was responsible to a foreign government while the other to the Indian electorate. The two halves in their attempt to please different masters often clashed with each other.

2. Lack of Necessary Qualities in the Governors. Another cause responsible for the failure of dyarchy was the Governors' unwillingness to let the Ministers work freely. The Governors who were armed with extensive superseding powers were required to show tolerance and foresight in not offending the Ministers by frequent exercise of their special powers. They were expected to have due regard for the public sentiments and to extend co-operation to the Ministers in running their departments smoothly. But unfortunately most of the Governors showed deplorable lack of the above-mentioned qualities.

3. Unscientific Distribution of Provincial Subjects. The Ministers, in actual working of dyarchic system, faced a number of difficulties. Their general grievance was that they were not given full control over any subject whatsoever. Haphazard and illogical demarcation of subjects added to the inefficiency of administration. An ex-minister of Madras, Mr. K.V. Reddi, describing the plight of the Ministers told the Muddiman Committee: *"I was a Minister for Development without Forest, I was a Minister for Agriculture minus Irrigation. As Minister of Agriculture, I had nothing to do with the Madras Agriculturists' Loans Act.........Famine Relief, of course, could not be touched by* *the Minister for Agriculture."* Similar was the lot of the Minister for Industries who had no control over the Factories, Mines, Water, Power, etc. Education was a Transferred subject but the Minister for Education had nothing to do with the European and Anglo-Indian education which was looked after by a Councillor. The Ministers found themselves too much dependent on the reserved departments, particularly the Finance department.

4. Special Powers of the Governors. The practice of investing the Governor with unlimited powers was inconsistent with the Dyarchic scheme. The authors of the Act of 1919 had certainly no intention to curtail the powers of the imperial agent *i.e.,* the Governor. He was at best changed into a constitutional autocrat. The Instrument of Instructions required the Governor to accommodate the suggestion of the Ministers so far as they did not mean to undermine the imperial interests. For two years after the implementation of Montford Reforms, while the Congress had been conducting agitation against it, the Governors refrained from interfering much in the affairs of the liberal Ministers. But as soon as the movement was called off and Lord Montague ceased to be Secretary of State, the Governors began to poke their noses in the administration of Transferred subjects. They usurped all powers from the Ministers through three different ways. In the exercise of their power to make rules and regulations for securing the good administration of the Province, the Governor allowed the permanent secretaries of all departments to meet him once a week and place before him all matters of conflict with the Ministers. Thus the direct access of the secretaries of Transferred departments to the Governor resulted in considerable reduction in the powers of the Ministers. The secretaries became defiant and tale-carriers. They also began to poison the ears of the Governor against their departmental heads. The second trick which the Governor employed was to meet the Ministers separately and not jointly. This trick weakened the Ministerial group for when alone, none had the courage to take a bold stand against the Governor. Thirdly, some Governors with a view to demoralising the Ministers cooked up a new theory that the Ministers were mere advisers whose advice was not binding upon the head of the Executive.

5. Public Services. The position of the Minister was no better than that of puppet or at best a dignified secretary. He had no voice in formulating the Government policy. If he opposed the Councillors, besides creating a deadlock he feared losing his ministership; and if he seconded their policies, he displeased the elected majority in the legislature which could censure and remove him in no time.

6. Financial Stringency. A great economic depression occurred in India at the end of the First Great War. The transferred departments were badly hit with the shortage of funds. The defence expenditure went up from thirty crores in pre-war days to over eighty crores after the war. A major portion of Provincial revenue had to be given away every year to the Central Government according to Meston Award. The financial position of the Provinces became deplorable. The finance department which was a Reserved subject began to extend step-motherly treatment to Transferred departments. Another design of the Councillors was to starve the Transferred subjects financially and thus make the Ministers unpopular. According to Mr. Chintamani it had always been the attempt of the finance department, "to see that Reserved departments got all the money they required before the other departments got what they wanted......I am prepared to state this without any exaggeration that the Ministers had to contend with great difficulties when they went to Finance Department, that pretty frequently they had to go before the Governor, pretty frequently the Governor did not side with them and pretty frequently they would only gain their point in the end by placing their offices at the disposal of the Governor."

EXTERNAL CIRCUMSTANCES RESPONSIBLE FOR THE FAILURE OF DYARCHY

The external circumstances leading to the failure were as follows:—

1. Non-co-operation and Khilafat Movement. The Government of India Act, 1919, was a definite advance on the Morley-Minto Reforms because for the first time the British Government in principle agreed to train Indians in the technique of self-government and also, as a proof of their good intentions, introduced partially responsible government at the provincial level. But the reason why dyarchy in operation failed to satisfy national aspirations was that the conditions were unfavourable to it. The Act fell far short of the hopes raised by the solemn declarations made by the British Government during war-time. The spirit of nationalism was very much alert and stimulated in post-war India. Indians wanted a reward of their war services and the minimum that they expected to get was Dominion Status. And when they were offered bullets, it was but natural that they should begin not only to distrust the alien rulers but also resort to violent methods to achieve their goals. The massacre of unarmed people at Jallianwala Bagh, Amritsar, on 13th April, 1919, and the rule of the martial law in the Punjab embittered the people to the farthest degree. Despite people's demand for an enquiry into the Punjab-firing, the criminals responsible for the massacre were allowed to go scot free. The case of the Sultan of Turkey or the Khilafat issue weakened the affection of the Indian Muslims towards the British Government. At last, disgusted with the savagery of the British Government, Gandhiji moved a resolution at Calcutta session of the Congress to launch Non-co-operation Movement. The Non-violent Non-co-operation Movement meant surrendering of titles and boycott of law courts, legislatures and Government educational institutions. Gandhiji's resolution was adopted and the movement launched. It was carried on vigorously for two years. Gandhiji was arrested and imprisoned. All such unhappy developments naturally led to further estrangements and disaffection between the Indians and the British. It was silly in such atmosphere to expect any response for dyarchy which was commonly defined as a 'tricky deal'.

2. Activities of Swarajists. With the decline of Non-co-operation, the Congress ranks were split into two groups—one which stood for entering the councils and the other which supported no-change policy. The prochangers formed a council-entery party under the leadership of Mr. C.R. Das and Motilal Nehru. The congress after much hesitation approved the programme of the Swarajist Party on the condition that its members would enter the Legislature not to work but to wreck the Constitution. The Swarajists thus were pledged to a policy of wrecking the Constitution from within and disproving the claim of the Government that it had been carrying on the administration with the consent of the people. Dr. Appadorai remarked, "With this view the Swarajists intended to present an ultimatum to Government demanding the right of the Indian people to control their own destiny. In the event of the demand being refused, the party pledged itself to a policy of uniform, continuous obstruction with a view to make Government through the Councils impossible."

The Swarajist Party got notable success at the general elections in two Provinces. In C.P. It got absolute majority and in Bengal it formed a coalition with the independents. In pursuance of their aim of obstructing the working of dyarchy, the Swarajist members in Bengal refused to grant salaries to the Ministers and also rejected certain important demands for grants in the budget. It happened more than once and hence the transfer of subjects was suspended from August 28, 1924 to March 13, 1925, and again from March 26, 1925 to June 12, 1925. The same story was repeated in C.P. where the Swarajists refused to accept ministership and took recourse to defeating every move of the Government. They censured the Ministers and fixed their salaries at Rs. 2 annually. The Governor of C.P. had however to invoke his special powers to restore and certify the demands rejected or reduced by the legislature but he was constitutionally helpless in sanctioning the salaries of the Ministers. Since the Constitution did not permit a Minister to continue in office after losing the confidence of the elected House, the Governor removed the Ministers and took over the charge of the Transferred subjects. For many months the working of Dyarchy remained suspended in C.P. and this heralded the success of the Swarajists.

3. Civil Disobedience Movement. Towards the end of 1927 an Indian Statutory Commission was appointed to report on the working of Dyarchy in the Provinces. The Commission which consisted of only British element had to face sustained and stiff opposition from all quarters. On the basis of the Commission's report submitted in 1930 the British Government called the First Round Table Conference. The Nationalists boycotted the Conference for they knew it was not going to discuss the vital issues of giving Dominion Status or complete independence to India. Gandhiji launched Civil Disobedience Movement to use pressure on the Government to honour the national sentiments. As a result of talks between the Viceroy and Gandhiji, the movement was suspended for some time in 1931 but was restarted in 1932 after the talks failed. Thus we find that right from the inception of the reforms in 1919 till another enactment in 1935, the country had been in a turmoil. The reforms could not be given a serious and sympathetic trial and hence their failure was inevitable.

4. Indifference of Government towards Reforms. The strongest cause for the unsatisfactory working of the Act of 1919 was the attitude of the British Government itself. Instead of winning the affection and goodwill of Indians at the close of war, the Government put on the mask of a tyrant. People felt deceived and swindled. Their war services went unrecognised. Lathicharges, firing and martial law were all they got from their white masters. This breach of faith on the part of His Majesty's Government changed Gandhiji from a co-operator into a non-co-operator. The coming of Tory party to power in England further worsened the situation. Zacharias observes that "Instructions were issued from London that henceforth the Reforms were to be worked with a view not how much but how little, self-government for India they could be made to yield."

Achievements of Dyarchy. The novel experiment of Dyarchy in the Provinces remained in operation for nearly sixteen years to be replaced finally by Provincial autonomy in 1935. In spite of its serious drawbacks, it was not altogether barren of good results. Dyarchic systems, if nothing else, brought many Indians in touch with problems of administration and trained them in the art of self-government. It serviced as a bridge between autocracy and responsibility. It hastened the pace of the country towards autonomy. Besides its educative value, it gave the legislators an opportunity to look into the working of the Government and also criticize its antinational policies. The speeches by the Swarajist members, both within the House and without, focussed the attention of the people to unjust laws and wicked intentions of the ruling race. The fear of their criticism did have some salutary effect on the executive. Above all the steady opposition to dyarchic system kept alive our passion for freedom. The Swarjists warned the people not to lose sight of the flower of freedom in the weeds of so-called reforms.

Another gain of Dyarchy was that the Ministers got the opportunity to deal with the social evils without any fear of popular opposition. Two concrete steps taken to eradicate certain social evils were the passing of the Hindu Religious Endowment Act in Madras and Children's Act in Bengal The Ministers also did some good work in the field of education, sanitation and Local Government.

Dyarchy brought about a radical change in the outlook of the British bureaucracy. The permanent officials and civil servants who worked under the Ministers in the Transferred departments had to shed their vanity and feel the direction of the wind. With the introduction of partially responsible government in the provinces, a beginning was made towards the Indianisation of public services. In order to make the share of Indians in government real, Lord Sinha was made Governor of Bihar and Orissa. In the words of Dr. Keith: "The legislative assembly during this period showed its real importance and value as a critic of the Government; naturally its interests were focussed on the issues which had so often been dealt with by the National Congress, i.e. finance and army expenditure."

The system of joint responsibility worked in different ways and with varying degree of success in different Provinces. Practically there arose no trouble in U.P. and Madras for the first two years. The Ministers shared the Government with the Councillors and remained responsible to the legislature. Sri. S.N. Bannerjee who had been a Minister for Local Self-Government in Bengal writes in his autobiography that dyarchy did not fail in his Province, the reason being , "both Lord Ronaldshay and Lord Lytton, the Governors were statesmanlike in their attitude of sympathy and help, and stood by the Ministers with their generous support. They acted as constitutional sovereigns and made no distinction between Executive Councillors and Ministers."

EXERCISES

Long Answer Type Questions

1. Discuss the system of Dyarchy and the reasons for its failure.
2. "The system of Dyarchy was full of defects but it made the masses conscious of the blessings of the self-government." Discuss.
3. Discuss the internal causes of the failure of Dyarchy.
4. Discuss the external causes of the failure of Dyarchy.

Short Answer Type Questions

1. Discuss in brief the working Dyarchy.
2. What is meant by Dyarchy? Discuss in brief.
3. "The Dyarchic scheme was theoretically wrong." Discuss in very brief.
4. How Non-cooperation and Khilafat Movement were responsible for the failure of Dyarchy system?
5. Discuss the achievements of Dyarchy in brief.

Objective Type Questions

Choose the correct answer

1. The Act provided for the appointment of Ministers to help the Governor in dealing with the transferred subjects. Bombay, Calcutta and Madras had
   (*a*) Three Ministers (*b*) Four Ministers
   (*c*) Five Ministers (*d*) Six Ministers
2. The maximum number of Ministers to be appointed in various Provinces was fixed by the Act. Bombay, Calcutta and Madras had three ministers each while the remaining Provinces had only
   (*a*) One Minister each (*b*) Two Ministers each
   (*c*) Three Ministers each (*d*) None of the above
3. In 'Dyarchy' system the Provincial subjects were divided in
   (*a*) Four parts (*b*) Three parts
   (*c*) Two parts (*d*) None of the above.

ANSWERS

1. (*a*) 2. (*b*) 3. (*c*)

15

CHAPTER

Non-Co-operation Movement and Swaraj Party

"The year 1921 *undoubtedly gave the country a highly organised party organisation... Before that the Congress was a constitutional party and mainly a talking body. The Mahatma not only gave it a new constitution and a nationwide basis but what it is more important, converted it into a revolutionary organisation.... Uniform slogans were repeated everywhere and a uniform policy and ideology gained currency from one end of India to the other. The English language lost its importance and the Congress adopted Hindi as the lingua franca for the whole country. Khadi became official for all Congressmen. The most important event in Indian politics in* 1919 *is the emergence of Mohan Das Karamchand Gandhi, better known as Mahatma Gandhi as the political leader. He played the dominant role in the momentous events that led to the freedom of India from British control and he introduced the novel methods and the new spirit in Indian politics."*

—*Subhas Chandra Bose*

NEW ERA AND GANDHIJI'S ENTRY

In the year 1920, Gandhiji took up the leadership of the Indian National Movement and remained the chief architect of the Indian Politics till independence. Hence, the period from 1920 to 1947 is generally called the 'Gandhian Era'.

During the period (1920–1935), Gandhiji dominated the scene of Indian politics and awoke the Indian masses against the British Government. During his life time Indian National Congress was a fighting machine and a revolutionary organisation. Though it was non-violent in character but had tremendous inner strength. His call for the 'Satyagrah' galvanised the millions of people against the British imperialism. Due to this efforts alone. India attained her Independence in the year 1947.

The emergence of Gandhiji in the Indian politics was very opportune. Till the 1920, Indian National Movement was dominated by leaders like Gopal Krishna Gokhale, Bal Gangadhar Tilak and Lala Lajpat Rai. When Gandhiji took up the leadership of Congress, Indian National Movement was devoid of imaginative thought of leadership, Gopal Krishna Gokhale had died in 1915 and Bal Gangadhar Tilak also left this world in July 1920. Lala Lajpat Rai was essentially a Moderate and believer of the constitutional reforms. So, there was a need for a man who could change the course of National Movement. Gandhiji came back from South Africa in 1915 at the height of his power and brought with him a clear cut philosophy of life and political technique which had proved its efficacy.

MAHATMA GANDHI AS A CO-OPERATOR

We have already stated that Gandhiji was greatly influenced by Gokhale's political philosophy. Hence in his political views he became as Moderate as his Guru. He agreed to Gopal Krishna Gokhale's policy of co-operating with the Government in working out the constitutional reforms. He proceeded with full faith in British intentions which he declared were not against the interests of Indian people. He also helped the Government in its recruitment drive and also by serving those wounded in the war. In recognition of his services he was awarded a medal. But despite his all-out-co-operation, when the British Government refused to transfer power to Indians, nearly all the national leaders were so much disappointed that they lost the faith in British goodness. Gandhiji alone refused to change his views. He still remained as ardent a co-operator as before. While Deshbandhu, C.R. Das, B.C. Pal and others rejected the reforms proposed by the Act of 1919 on the grounds that they were inadequate and unsatisfactory, Gandhiji still favoured the idea of working the Montford Reforms. His views can be easily ascertained from what he wrote in *Young India*: "The Reforms Act coupled with the proclamation is an earnest expression of the intention of the British people to do justice to India and it ought to remove suspicion on that score......Our duty is not to subject the Reforms to bitter criticism but to settle down quietly to work so as to make them a success."

But the phase of Gandhiji's role as a co-operator proved a shortlived one. There were certain reasons which shook his faith in British fairness and justice. The events which changed Gandhiji from a co-operator into a staunch non-co-operator were as follows:

ROWLATT ACT AND JALLIANWALA BAGH MASSACRE

In the beginning of the 20th century, there was a spurt of revolutionary and terrorist activities in India. The factor chiefly responsible for the increase in violent activities was the arrogance and highhandedness of the British officers. The partition of Bengal, *the unpalatable land laws in the Punjab, and the famine and plague* that occurred in Maharashtra increased the discontent of the people. *The Revolutionary Organisations* began to work more vigorously during the First World War and assumed an alarming character. The Government by passing Defence of India Act armed itself with extensive powers to suppress this subversive activities. The Act was to expire at the end of war but the Government decided to keep it in force for a little longer. The First World War was over but new problems assailed the Government of India. Afghanistan turned into a trouble-spot. Besides the growing disorder in the country, the Government of India apprehended an attack by Tzarist Russia via Afghanistan. So it appointed a commitee under the chairmanship of Justice Rowlatt to study the problem of revolutionary activities and submit its report. The Government of India moved two Bills in the Central Legislature in February, 1919, to give effect to the recommendations of Rowlatt Committee. They came to be known as Rowlatt Bills or Black Bills. Under these Acts the Government of India armed itself with unrestricted powers to control the Press, to try the political offenders without the help of juries and to arrest and detain a person suspected of subversive activities for any length of time without holding a trial. Violent protests were directed at the "Black Rowlatt Bills". Since the war was over and there was hardly any revolutionary activity going on in the country, the continuance of Defence of India Rules was looked upon by the nationalists with grave suspicion. They feared that the Rowlatt Act would be employed to suppress even peaceful and legitimate agitations. Rowlatt Act was no doubt a measure to strangle the elementary rights of the people, hence, the whole country was stirred to action. Gandhiji came to the forefront with a solemn ultimatum to the Government that he would be called upon to lead an agitation if any attempt was made to rob the people of their personal freedom. The warning fell on deaf ears. In spite of strong opposition both within the Central Legislature and without, the Government passed an Act known as Anarchical and Revolutionary Crime Act, 1919.

On 6th April, 1919, *Gandhiji started a countrywide campaign against Rowlatt Act.* He called upon the people to observe total *hartal* and the country responded to his call admirably. Processions were taken out to express public resentment against the repressive legislation. *Swami Shradhananda* led one such procession in Delhi. Police force blocked the way and ordered the processionists to disperse. A few British soldiers threatened to shoot Swamiji who thereupon, uncovered his breast to receive the bullet. Overawed by his dauntlessness, the soldiers could not execute their threat. The clash between the people and the police occurred near the Delhi Railway Station. The police opened fire which resulted in the loss of eight lives. Such incidents occurred in Lahore and Calcutta also. Gandhiji left Bombay for Delhi on 8th April. On the way he was served with a notice banning his entry into Delhi and Punjab. On his refusal to abide by the notice, he was arrested at Palwal near Delhi and was sent back to Bombay.

The news of Gandhiji's arrest spread with amazing rapidity all over the country. It led to disturbances at various places particularly in Ahmedabad, Viramgaum and Nadiad. Such happenings took place in the Punjab districts of Gurjanwala, Lahore and Kassür. The Government arrested the two prominent leaders of the Punjab—Dr. Satya Pal and Dr. Kitchlew. The citizens of Amritsar were so much provoked by the arrest of their favourite leaders, that the formed a procession and marched towards the residence of the District Magistrate. The military contingent barred their way and opened fire on the mob, killing two and injuring many others. The people lifted the dead bodies on their shoulders and paraded along the main streets of Amrtisar. On the way they set fire to National Bank and killed the Bank Manager. In all five Europeans lost their lives and several buildings were burnt on that day. On the 10th April, 1919, martial law was imposed on the city.

On 13th April, 1919, the Baisakhi day, a public meeting was held in the *Jallianwala Bagh, Amritsar.* The place was enclosed on all sides by the back walls of the houses. It had only one entrance gate, that too so narrow that no carriage could pass through it. The martial law administrator Dyer allowed the people to assemble at the Bagh and when it was packed to capacity, he along with a contingent of 100 Indian and 50 British soldiers reached the venue of the meeting. The only passage leading into the Bagh was so narrow that the machine-gun could not be taken in. The peaceful gathering was being addressed by one Mr. Hansraj. The speakers one by one, demanded the release of the Punjab leaders as well as Gandhiji. Protests were being made against the Rowlatt Act when General Dyer, without even giving a warning to the crowd to disperse, opened fire. It is said that 1,650 rounds of 303 were fired. The firing stopped only when the ammunition was exhausted. Dyer later admitted himself that no doubt he asked the people to clear off but within three minutes of his orders, he opened fire. Commonsense says that 20,000 people could not disperse in three minutes. According to the official report nearly 400 people were killed and more than a thousand wounded as a result of firing. Actually the casualties must have been much more than the official figure. All precautions were taken not to let the news of firing trickle out of the Province. Dyer massacred the people with a spirit of revenge is above dispute. It was further confirmed from what Dyer himself stated before the Hunter Committee which had been set up to enquire into the unfortunate incident. In answer to a question by Justice Rankin, a member of the Hunter Committee who asked, "*Excuse me putting in this way, General, but was it not a form of frightfulness?* "*Dyer answered,* "*No, it was not. It was horrible duty I had to perform. I think it was a merciful thing; I thought that I should shoot well and shoot strong so that I or anybody else should not have to shoot again. I think it is quite possible that I could have dispersed the crowd without firing but they would have come back again and laughed and I should have made what I consider to be a fool of myself*". In approval of his action, Dyer got a telegram from the Punjab Governor, Sir Michael O'Dwyer : "Your action correct, Lieutenant-Governor approves."

Hunter Report. Since the news from the Punjab was strictly censored, the people in other parts of the country came to know about the atrocities of General Dyer pretty late. The Indian National Congress reacted sharply and speedily. It demanded a high level enquiry into incidents of firing in the Punjab. For having first-hand information it formed a committee of its own, consisting of Pt. Motilal Nehru, Gandhiji, Pt. Madan Mohan Malaiya and others. Rabindra Nath Tagore also was so acutely pained that he surrendered his knighthood. Sir Shankaran Nair resigned his membership of the Viceroy's Executive Council. The Government of India was ultimately compelled to set up a committee to investigate into and report on the sad happenings in the Punjab. *The Hunter Committee which was constituted in October,* 1919, *submitted its report in March,* 1920. In the meantime, the Government of India by passing Indemnity Act absolved all the officials of any trial or punishment in connection with the Punjab firing incident. The Hunter Committee in its report also tried to whitewash the conduct of the British officers. It gave a clean chit to all others except notorious Dyer for whom it suggested compulsory retirement. The only charge that the Committee made out against Dyer was that he exceeded the reasonable requirements of the case due to grave error of judgement." Worse still, the British Press and Parliament showered praise upon Dyer and hailed him as the savior of British rule. The British Government in recognition of his services presented him with a Sword of Honour and a purse of £ 2000. The news shocked Gandhiji as well as the whole country. The investigation committee appointed by the Congress reported that the number of the dead in Jallianwala Bagh tragedy was considerably large than the official figures. It condemned vehemently the reign of terror and anarchy that was imposed upon Punjab after the occurrence of Jallianwala Bagh tragedy. Sir Valentine Chirol and Sivaswamy have given us graphic details of the martial law administration in the Punjab. Chirol writes, "*Sir Michael O'Dwyer protested, it is true, against Dyer's monstrous crawling order and it was promptly disallowed. But what of many other 'orders' which were not disallowed? What of the promiscuous flogging and whippings, the indiscriminate arrests and confiscations, the so-called 'fancy punishments' designed not so much to punish individual rebels as to terrorise and humiliate? What of the whole judicial or quasi-judicial administration of martial law ?*" The Congress demanded adequate punishment to be awarded to the persons responsible for firing and also monetary compensation to be given to the dependants of the victims of firing. The Government gave a cold shoulder to these demands. The cruel indifference of the Government to public good was one of the reasons which made Gandhiji cross the floor to the side of non-co-operators. He lost all faith in British fairness and justice.

KHILAFAT QUESTION

The second reason which embittered Gandhiji was the Khilafat issue. The Sultan of Turkey was accepted by the Indian Mussalmans as their spiritual head. Turkey during the First World War joined hands with *Axis* Powers and fought against England. The Indian Muslims found themselves in a dilemma whether to support England or Turkey. They feared, and their fear was not unfounded too, that in the event of losing the battle, Turkey would be completely dismembered, *i.e.*, would be dispossessed of many parts of her big empire. In order to win the support of Indian Muslims the British Prime Minister, Mr. Lloyd George, declared: "Nor are we fighting to deprive Turkey of the rich and renowned lands of Asia Minor and Thrace which are preponderantly Turkish in race." Misled by the assurance the Muslims extended whole-hearted support to England in her war operations. But after the signing of armistice, the British Government refused to honour its promise. Thrace was presented to greece and the Asiatic portions of Turkish Empire were divided between England and France. Naturally the Muslims felt as if they had been cheated and befooled. Hence they adopted hostile attitude towards the British.

Mahatma Gandhi saw his chance of utilising the rupture between the British and the Muslims. He knew well that without Hindu-Muslim unity and a strong opposition, the English could not be driven out. So he set about wooing the Muslims and enlisting their support for a common front against the Government. He sympathised with the grievances of the Muslim community and convened a Khilafat Conference on November 14, 1919. He also occupied the presidential chair. He suggested a Muslim deputation to wait upon the Viceroy and see if he could do anything to redeem the British promise. The deputation, however, returned disappointed. A deputation led by Maulana Shaukat Ali and Mohammed Ali also met the British Prime Minister in March, 1920, and requested the latter to mete out better treatment to the Sultan of Turkey but to no avail. The Turkish Empire was disintegrated and distributed between the Allied Powers. A high Commission was appointed by the Allied Powers to rule over the country, with Sultan as nothing better than a prisoner. Indignation amongst the Muslims touched the peak point, Gandhiji put before them his non-co-operation programme and they accepted the scheme.

GANDHI AS A NON-CO-OPERATOR

Factors responsible. Thus the two main factors which led to a change in Gandhiji's attitude towards the British Government were failure of the Government to heal up the wounds of Punjab firings and secondly, non-ful-filment of the promise made by the British Prime Minister in regard to Khilafat issue. In a letter to Viceroy written in August, 1920, he wrote thus: "*Events that have happened during the past month have confirmed me in the opinion that the Imperial Government have acted in the Khilafat matter in an unscrupulous, immoral and unjust manner and have been moving from wrong to wrong in order to defend their immorality. I can retain neither respect nor affection for such a Government. Your Excellency's light-hearted treatment of official crime, your exoneration of Sir Michael O'Dwyer, Mr. Montagu's Despatch and above all the shameful ignorance of the Punjab events and the callous disregard of the feelings of Indians betrayed by the House of Lords, have filled me with the gravest misgivings as regards the future of the Empire, have estranged me completely from the present Government and have disabled me from rendering, as I have hitherto whole-heartedly rendered, my total co-operation.*" Mahatma Gandhi further said: "I consider that I would be less than truthful if I did not describe as Satanic a Government which has been guilty of fraud, murder and wanton cruelty and which still remains unrepentant and resorts to untruth to cover its guilts."

NON-CO-OPERATION MOVEMENT

When Gandhiji lost all hopes of getting any fair and equitable treatment at the hands of the British Government, he planned to wreck the administration of the country by withdrawing country's co-operation from the Government. In this project, he hoped to get the support of the Muslims who had become anti-British on Turkey-issue. He made a fervent appeal to the Hindus to support the cause of the Muslims. A committee which had been appointed to draw up the details suggested, to begin with, the boycott of schools, colleges and courts. Gandhiji and Ali Brothers toured the country and explained the meaning and significance of the movement. A special session of the Congress was convened at Calcutta in September, 1920, to approve the scheme. It was presided over by Lala Lajpat Rai. The delegates passed several resolutions, condemning the British Government for breaking its promise in connection with the Khilafat and the failure to protect innocent people of the Punjab from the atrocious behaviour of the officials. In one of the resolutions the Congress declared, "That there can be no contentment in India without redress of two aforementioned wrongs and that the only effectual means to vindicate national honour and to prevent a repetition of similar wrongs in future is the establishment of Swarajya." The resolution further said that "there is no course left open for the people of India but to approve and adopt the policy of progressive non-violent non-co-operation inaugurated by Mahatma Gandhi until the said wrongs are righted and Swarajya is established."

The resolution on Non-co-operation evoked a heated controversy. Pt. Motilal Nehru and Ali Brothers supported the resolution but Shri C.R. Das, Pt. Madan Mohan Malaviya and Mrs. Annie

Besant opposed it strongly. Even Lala Lajpat Rai, the President of the Calcutta Congress session, also did not react favourably towards the resolution. Lokmanya Bal Gangadhar Tilak had already died in August, 1920, who might have supported the movement if he had lived. 1,886 delegates voted for and 844 voted against the scheme of Non-Co-operation.

The resolution on Non-Co-operation was again repeated at the Nagpur Congress in December, 1920. This time it received greater support than it had received at Calcutta. The Congress changed its creed and defined its object as "The attainment of Swaraj by peaceful and legitimate means." Certain changes were made also on the organisational side of the Congress. Congress circles were reorganised on a linguistic basis. A working committee was formed to look after its day-to-day work. Formerly the two factions in the Congress—the Moderates and the Extremists—had no programme agreeable to both. The Moderates aimed at attaining self-government within the British Empire, while Extremists claimed complete independence without any relationship with the British Government. The Nagpur Session was momentous in the respect that it changed the constitution of the Congress in a way which satisfied both the sections. The word **'Swaraj'** was defined by each section in its own way. What Gandhiji meant by Swaraj was the attainment of self-government within British Empire with full liberty to secede at any time. The nature and scope of Congress activities to achieve its goals was also widened—from the constitutional means to all peaceful and legitimate means. Peaceful means included not only sending petitions but also the more effective and direct measure of refusal to pay taxes. Nagpur, thus, marked a new era in the history of freedom struggle. Mr. Jinnah, Mrs. Besant and B.C. Pal, who did not approve such a radical change in the technique of freedom struggle, left the Congress.

CIRCUMSTANCES FAVOURING THE NON-CO-OPERATION MOVEMENT

Following circumstances were favouring for the Non-co-operation Movement.

1. Criticism of the Act of 1919– There was great criticism of Montague-Chelmsford report. Leaving aside few Moderates, all the Nationalists bitterly criticised it. The public of India was thinking of Purna Swaraj since the first World War.

2. Rowlatt Bill and its consequences– Government of India appointed a Sedition Committee in 1918 with Justice Rowlatt to report on the seditious movements. On the recommendations of the committee, two Bills were passed. Now, the people could be arrested and imprisoned for seditious activities and being in possession of either published or unpublished pictures or documents of seditious nature. The Executive was given the power for preventive detention or enforced residence on all suspected political leaders. Dr. Ishwari Prasad has remarked: "The provisions of these Bills were a shabby device to place on the Statute Book, some of the most repressive measures like the Defence of India Act. Their wordings were so comprehensive and the powers bestowed on the Executive, so unrestricted that the Civil Liberty or the subject lost all its meaning."

All the sections in India opposed these Bills. "A wave of anger greeting them from all over India and even the moderates joined in this and opposed the measures with all their might. Indeed there was universal opposition on the part of Indian of all shades of opinion." In these Bills Indians saw the denial of self determination and popular liberty. The Act gave the Police and Executive the unlimited authority for suppressing civil liberty. Even the faith of Mahatma Gandhi in the good intention of the British, was shattered. He also became a non co-operator and called for Satyagrah against the notorious Rowlatt Act. March 30, 1919, was fixed for the suspension of all business for fasts and prayers. Later on, the date was changed to 6th April, 1919. Gandhiji's appeal for Hartal met with a wonderful success all over India. One noticeable feature of the general excitement was unprecedented fraternization between Hindus and Muslims.....Hindu Muslim unity was the watchword of processions indicated by cries and by banners." Unfortunately there were disorders and disturbances at certain places. He thus suspended the Satyagrah on 18th April. Mahatma Gandhi was arrested on

8th April, 1919 at Paliwal. Indian masses were greatly agitated at the arrest of Mahatma Gandhi and they intnesified an agitation particularly at Delhi, Ahmedabad and the Punjab. The arrest of Dr. Satyapal and Dr. Kitchlew created a storm in Punjab.

3. Jallianwala Bagh Massacre (April 13, 1919)—Dr. Kitchlew and Dr. Satyapal two prominent leaders of Punjab, were arrested on April 10. As the people of Punjab knew the incident, the bazars of the city were crowded. The inhabitants of Amritsar took out a procession and demanded the release of their leaders. On the way at the Hall Gate Bridge, they were stopped by a military force. Naturally, the people were agitated against this. This led to police firing on the non-violent mob, which was extremely excited. The crowd also became violent and 5 Europeans were killed and several buildings were set on fire. Town Hall and Indian Christian Church became the main victims of the crowd, General Dwyer officer commanding of the troops took up a very hasty step. Dr. Ishwari Prasad has written :

"General Dwyer believed that it was expected to him to distinguish himself Signal Act of Butchery as a means of putting an end of the disturbances." General Dwyer determined to teach Indians a lesson with the feelings of relation and revenge. The whole Amritsar became a post of Military Camp. An order was passed for banning all the public meetings but it was not properly published. A public meeting was announced on 13th April in the Jallianwala Bagh. The historians like Dr. Hari Ram Gupta was of the view that the meeting was deliberately organised by the Britishers. It was the 'Baisakhi day. A few traitors like Hansraj were hired for the publicity of the meeting. Thus, thousands of people assembled at Jallianwala Bagh and were waiting for the president of the meeting. In the meantime General Dwyer entered the place and without a warning to a peaceful mob, he opened fire at about 100 yards upon a dense crowd; 1,650 rounds were fired. The firing was heavy at the points where the crowd was thick. According to official report 379 persons were shot dead and 1,200 were wounded and left unattended. The casualty could have been heavier still if Dwyer had succeeded his cars with machine guns on the spot. As the passage was very narrow so he could not do that. *Mr. Thompson has written*: "The Amritsar tragedy was a turning point in Indo-British relations almost as important as the mutiny of 1857." This tragedy will go in annals of the Indian History, as a great slur on Britishers. Two days after Jalianwala Bagh, Martial law was declared and promulgated in 5 districts of Punjab.

The Jallianwala Bagh is a turning point in the History of Indian National Movement. *R.C. Majumdar* has written: "The lesson of Jallianwala Bagh was nothing short of this that while some English Officers had descended to a level for below that of humanity, the English people, by their active or passive support to his outrage on the humanity had lost all claim and prestige to rule over India. It thus became the paramount duty of the Indians to avenge at any cost, the rowns and insults inflicted by those who were short of all human instincts, and animated by nothing better higher than a nacked brutal force. This lesson was deeply implanted in the heart of every Indian particularly that of Gandhi, the greatest Indian of the day, and inspired him to launch a compaign against the British, which ultimately led to their final expulsion from India."

4. Lord Hunter Committee— The Government instead of punishing the wrong officers passed a Bill-shielding the guilty officers passed a Bill shielding the guilty officers. A Committee of six persons known as Lord Hunter Committee was appointed to wash off guilt of General Dwyer. The Committee reported that General's conduct was based on 'an honest but mistaken conception of duty.' General Dwyer was not punished severely but simply removed from the service. Even some of the British Parliamentarians commanded his service to the nation. He was handed over a purse of £20,000 and a sword of honour by his admirals. It was a matter of great shame. The Congress Enquiry Committee wrote, thus, "a cold-blooded, calculated masscare of innocent, unoffending, unarmed men and children, unparalleled for its heartlessness and a cowardly brutality in modern times". This all effected Gandhiji and his followers to turn into co-operation. Mr. Surendra Nath Bannerjee has rightly remarked that the Rowlatt-Act was the parent of non-co-operation.

5. The Khilafat Movement and National Unity— The sincerity of Britishers further exposed over the khilafat question. This issue was concerned with the Khilafat the highest religious office in the Islamic world. After the first World War the Ali decided to dismember the Ottoman Empire and to disband the office of Khilafat. Muslims in India became hostile at this decision. A deputation was sent in march 1920, to London to stop the disruption of Turkish Empire but it was all in vain. Muslims demanded, "The preservation of the Turkish Empire.......and they continued, existence of the Khilafat as a temporal not less than spiritual institution."

Maulana Mohd. Ali (Ali brothers) joined the Congress and decided to follow Mahatma Gandhi. Muslim theologians also supported to the Khilafat Movement and there was great excitement all over the country. A large section of hindus under the leadership of Mahatma Gandhi took part in the movement. It was an opportune time for uniting Hindus and Muslims and Mahatma Gandhi took the full advantage of it. Coupland writes: "Such an opportunity for uniting Hindus and Mohammadans as would not arise in a hundred years." The Khilafat Committee accepted the non-co-operations programme and a special session of Indian National Congress was held in Calcutta to launch the movement *Dr. Pattabhi Sitaramayya* writes: "The Triveni of Khilafat and Punjab wrong and the invisible flow of inadequate reforms, became full to the brim, and by their confluence enriched both in volume and content the stream of national discontent."

Non-Co-operation launched by Mahatma Gandhi

As we have already pointed out that after acceptance of Khailafat Committee, the non-co-operation programme became the main goal of the Congress. A special session of Congress under the presidentship of Lala Lajpat Rai was convened in September 1920 at Calcutta and a resolution for launching non-co-operation movement was accepted. A large number of Muslims were also present at the session. The resolution was moved by Mahatma Gandhi and supported by Pandit Motilal Nehru and Ali Brothers. Non-Co-operation become Congress policy though many senior Congressmen like C.R. Das, Mrs. Besant, Pt. Madan Mohan Malviya and B.C. Pal; opposed it. In the Congress session of December 1920, at Nagpur those who were against the non-co-operation movement were also non-over and the resolution was passed with an overwhelming majority of votes. Mr. Michael Brother has rightly remarked: "So persuasive was Gandhiji even among the older men that C.R. Das, who had gone to Nagpur with the avowed intention of undoing the Calcutta resolution, with hundreds of delegates at his own expense, succumbed after an all night discussion with the Mahatma."

Programme of the Non-Co-operation Movement. The policy and programme which the Congress adopted at Calcutta Session and reiterated at Nagpur Session was as follows:—

(1) *boycott of foreign goods and use of swadeshi.* (The Congress workers were also asked to spin yarn and thousands of weavers were encouraged to weave cloth).

(2) Surrender of *titles* and *honorary offices* and resignation of members occupying nominated seats in Local Bodies.

(3) Refusal to attend official Durbars.

(4) Gradual boycott of British courts by lawyers and litigants.

(5) Boycott of Government and State-aided schools.

(6) Boycott of elections to the new Councils and refusal by the voters to vote at the elections.

(7) Refusal by soldiers, clerks and working people to serve in Mesopotamia. In short the Non-co-operation scheme aimed at the boycott of colleges, courts, councils and government jobs. In short the Non-Co-operation scheme aimed at the boycott of colleges, courts, councils and Government jobs.

Besides the boycott measures, the Congress also adopted a constructive programme. It included the opening of national educational institutions, the setting up of Panchayats as a substitute of British courts, the popularisation of *Charkha* plying and yarnspinning, promotion of communal harmony and the removal of untouchability.

Progress of the Non-Co-operation Movement. The response to the Congress Programme of Non-co-operation was quite enthusiastic. Gandhiji and his stalwarts went round the country and mobilised public opinion in favour of the new movement. They persuaded the students to stay away from State institutions and seek admission to national schools. Thousands of students left their schools. For their benefit several national educational institutions came into existence—notable among them being Gujarat Vidyapeeth, Bihar Vidyapeeth, Kashi Vidyapeeth, Aligarh University, Jamia Milia, National College, Lahore, and others. Even lawyers of great standing and lucrative practice also gave up their profession and dedicated themselves to political work. C.R. Das, Pt. Motilal Nehru, Jawaharlal Nehru, Vithal Bhai Patel and Rajendra Prasad became whole time workers of the Congress. Seth Jamnalal Bajaj set apart a sum of Rs. one lakh to support those lawyers who had given up practice in favour of political work. Prominent Muslim leaders like Dr. Ansari, Maulana Abul Kalaam Azad, Shaukat Ali and Mohammad Ali also toured the country and called upon the Muslims to support the movement. Hindu and Muslim workers rubbed shoulders with each other without any malice or communal feeling.

Of all the boycotts enunciated in the Non-co-operation scheme, the most successful was the boycott of elections to the Reformed Councils. Thousands of voters stayed away from the polling booths and no Congress candidates contested the elections. The Congress being out of field, the Liberals, the opportunists and the loyalists fought the elections and entered the Legislative Councils. The Duke of Connaught who came to India to inaugurate the new reforms was also greeted with black flags and *hartals*. People organised bonfire of foreign cloth and garments. In order to make Non-co-operation a mass agitation, the Congress resolved to collect ₹ 1 crore for the Swarajya Fund, to enrol one crore members and to introduce 20 lakh *charkhas* in the country. Soon the fund was over subscribed by ₹ 15 lakhs. Hundreds of people willingly renounced their titles.

The Congress then decided to show country's temper to Prince of Wales. It issued an appeal to observe complete *hartal* on the day of the Prince's landing. The Government adopted a stern attitude towards the organisers and agitators. All the renowned leaders except Gandhiji were put behind the bars. The Congress was declared an unlawful organisation. Khilafat leaders set up their parallel government at various places. The movement could not remain a peaceful one. Acts of violence became frequent. On August 20, 1921, Moplahs in Malabar took law in their hands and killed not only Europeans but also thousands of Hindus. The Prince landed in Bombay on 17th November, 1921. A few loyalists who turned up to receive the Prince came in clash with the boycotters which resulted in brick-batting and outbreak of violence. Gandhiji looked upon violence with distaste, so he criticised the defaulters strongly.

The venue of the next session of the Congress was Ahmedabad. It was held in December, 1921. The party resolved to intensify and speed up the movement and invested Gandhiji with full authority to carry on Congress activities in the manner he thought fit. Gandhiji was also empowered to launch a Civil Disobedience Movement if he felt the need. On 1st February, 1922, Gandhiji gave an ultimatum to Lord Reading, the Viceroy of India, to withdraw all repressive laws and give proof of his changed attitude within seven days or face the consequences of another Satyagrah in the form of non-payment of taxes.

Suspension of the Movement. But before the expiry of seven days' notice, an unforeseen incident took place at Chauri Chaura in U.P. An excited mob attacked a police outpost on February 5, 1922, and killed a few constables. Gandhiji, apprehending similar troubles in other parts of the country, announced the suspension of the campaign relating to non-payment of taxes. The reaction to the withdrawal of movement by the unilateral action of Gandhiji was adverse. The policy of retreat was not liked by many leaders, *viz.,* C. Rajgopalachari, Nehru family, Ali Brothers and Lala Lajpat Rai. Gandhiji's popularity suffered a setback because of his arbitrary action. The Government availed itself of the opportunity and arrested Gandhiji. The "Great Trial" began on 18th March, 1922, in the court of Sessions Judge, Mr. Bloomfield. In his statement of historic importance, Gandhiji indicted the Government of doing 'satanic acts' which could convert a person from a loyal subject to a seditionist. The court sentenced him to six years' simple imprisonment. In this way the Non-co-operation Movement fizzled out but the flame of nationalism continued to burn brighter. Only the front was shifted from public places to well inside the Legislative Councils.

Defects of the Movement. That the Congress programme of the boycott of courts, colleges and councils or that of the surrender of titles would not get sweeping success, was a foregone conclusion. The chief reason was that the country was not prepared for such a mass agitation to go in a disciplined way. The Congress decision to keep away from the elections to new Councils only opened the field for the traitors to become legislators. Secondly, the sudden suspension of the movement was a blunder on the part of Gandhiji. Other Congress leaders resented Gandhiji's action. They felt further distressed when Gandhiji took upon himself the sole responsibility for the riots at Bombay, Madras and Chauri Chaura. It was true, they argued, that the movement took a violent turn because the people were not adequately trained to receive blows and bullets quietly but the Government itself was partly responsible for it. It provoked the mob to become violent by raining *lathis* on it. No flesh and blood can stand atrocities without registering a reaction. If the movement had continued for a little longer, the Government would certainly have agreed to negotiate with the Congress. Gandhiji's mistake, however, spoiled the chances of success. Since Gandhiji could neither redress the grievances of the Punjab nor fulfil his promise of securing Swaraj within a year of the launching of movement, the people were filled with a bitter sense of frustration. The several shock was received by those who had made great sacrifices at the call of Gandhiji. The faith of the people in the Congress programme and particularly Gandhiji was rudely shaken. Even the findings of the Civil Disobedience Enquiry Committee appointed by the congress also confirmed the general feeling that boycott programme was erroneous and the Congressmen should have been allowed to contest the elections to the Legislative Councils and to the Local Bodies.

Lastly, Gandhiji approach to Khilafat was quite unrealistic. He tried to be too idealistic in political matters. He espoused the Khilafat with a view to forging Hindu-Muslim unity but the results obtained were disappointing. The discord between the two communities became wider than it was ever before, resulting in communal riots at various places. The suspension of the movement gave an occasion to the Muslim League to discredit the Congress. The League launched a vicious propaganda that Congress had used the Muslims as tools during the Non-Co-operation Movement to achieve its selfish ends and that it had deceived the Muslims by calling off the movement abruptly. Another point that Gandhiji overlooked at the time of joining hands with the League over the Khilafat issue was that Khilafat was a religious issue in which not to speak of all non-Muslims, even the Mussalmans of Turkey, had no interest. As soon as Kemal Pasha came to power in Turkey, he called off the Khilafat movement and even turned the Khalifa out of Turkey. By confusing a religious issue with national struggle, Gandhiji earned nothing but dissatisfaction and criticism. His effort to promote Hindu-Muslim unity by appeasing the Muslims also bore bitter fruits in the years that followed.

ACHIEVEMENT OR CONTRIBUTION OF MOVEMENT TO THE NATIONAL STRUGGLE

The following were the achievements of Non-Co-operation Movement to the National struggle:

(1)There is no doubt that of all the movements launched by the Congress from the year of its inception to 1920, Non-Co-operation was of the greatest historical importance. It marked a change of great magnitude in the object and programme of the congress. It ushered in a new era in the political life of the country. *The Congress for the first time declared that its goal was the attainment of Swarajya, not petty reforms. It also changed the means to achieve its goal from petitions to direct action against the Government. It approved the policy of mass agitations with the result that every Indian was imbued with national feelings.* The fury of the people against the white rulers reached its peak point and they came out in thousands to lose all they had for the sake of dear freedom. *Thus the net gain of the Congress movement was that the torch of patriotism was carried and lighted in every cottage and castle. The struggle for freedom which hitherto used to be fought by the few educated politicians became a mass struggle to be fought by every peasant, worker and common man.*

(2) Another salutary effect of the Non-co-operation Movement was that the Indians learnt how to face the police and military atrocities boldly. Formerly, jails were a terror and criticising the Government a taboo. Under the dynamic leadership of Gandhiji, going to jail for the national cause became an act of patriotism and subjecting the Government to searching criticism in public meetings a popular fashion. The word Swarajya settled down on the tip of every tongue.

"The movement put a new life into Indian nationalism. The old feeling of oppression and fearfulness was completely gone," writes Jawaharlal Nehru.

(3) The weapon of passive resistance or satyagraha which the Congress employed for attaining independence proved unique and unparalleled. The Government had no effective reply to it. The language of *lathi* which the police used to deal with peaceful satyagrahis was too heinous and unsuitable. In fact the weapon of satyagraha paralysed the striking power of the authorities. Non-co-operation was the first step towards the great glorious struggle which delivered us our long-cherished freedom. If nothing else, the movement had its great educative value. It imparted necessary political training and foretaste of future hardships to the fighters for freedom.

(4) Another advantage of the movement was that for the time it continued, the Government remained eager to win the goodwill and co-operation of the Moderates in working the new Reforms. But as soon as the movement was called off, it assumed the same attitude of cold indifference towards the Reforms of 1919.

(5) The constructive side of the movement, that is the Khadi, *charkha* spinning, starting of national educational institutions and the cult of Swadeshi, also proved of great benefit to the country. The boycott of foreign goods gave a staggering blow to British tradc interest in India. The national schools and colleges became training fields for the patriots. The use of Swadeshi provided employment to thousand of weavers. The achievement of the movement may be summed up in the words of Subhas Chandra Bose: "*The year 1921 undoubtedly gave the country a highly organised party organisation............Before that the Congress was a constitutional party and mainly a talking body. The Mahatma not only gave it a new constitution and a nationwide basis but, what is more important, converted it into a revolutionary organisation.........Uniform slogans were repeated everywhere and a uniform policy and ideology gained currency from one end of India to the other. The English language lost its importance and the congress adopted Hindi as the lingua franca for the whole country......Khadi became the official uniform for all Congressmen.*" Lord Chelmsford was thoroughly wrong when he stated that the Non-Co-operation scheme was nothing but non-sensical.

An impartial observer cannot overlook the fact that Gandhiji's greatest contribution to the Indian Nationalist Movement lay in the point that he created a mass awakening of unprecedented scale for the first time. He was the father, pioneer of the first mass national libertion struggle of the Indian people after 1857. Again it was Gandhiji who exploded the illusion lovingly cherished by the Moderates that freedom could be obtained only with the assistance and co-operation of foreign "democracy". This was undoubtedly Gandhiji's progressive contribution to Indian nationalism. "The

Indian people, under his leadership, became." writes one of his formidable critics, "heroic, audacious fighters for national freedom, courters of jails and receivers of hail-storms of bullets of the imperialist enemy. *Gandhiji injected the people with deep hatred for the 'satanic' British government and with an unquenchable thirst for national freedom. Gandhi was the highest expression of nationalism.......... Subjectively he incarnated the very spirit of nationalism, its profound hatred of foreign enslavement and heroic will and determination to end that enslavement.*"[1]

Significance of the Non-Co-operation Movement. Though the Non-Co-operation Movement suddenly collapsed out it served a great purpose to inspire the Indians in new faith and new hope. It was the first time the congress Movement because the mass movement. The achievements of the Non-Co-operation Movement were great. The movement has shown the willingness of Indians to endure hardships and punishments for the cause of liberation. It made countrymen bold and patriotic. The Indians were no more afraid of imprisonment. According to Subhash Chandra Bose: "The year 1921 undoubtedly gave the country a highly organised party organisation. Before that the Congress was a constitutional party and mainly a talking body. The Mahatma not only gave it a constitution and a nation-wide basis, but what is more important covered it into a revolutionary organisation. Uniform slogans were repeated everywhere and uniform policy and ideology gained currency from one end of India to the other. The English language lost its importance and the Congress adopted Hindi as the 'Language France' for the whole country. Khadi became the official uniform for Congressmen."

In the words of *Mr. A.R. Desai,* "With a section of workers and peasants participating in it, the nationalists movement, which was restricted to the upper and middle classes till 1917, got a mass basis for the first time."

SWARAJ PARTY

Causes of the formation of Swaraj Party. The suspension of the Non-Co-operation Movement on the decision of Mahatma Gandhi was greatly cricised by his colleagues. Many of his colleagues were hurt and some were very angry. The leaders like Lala Lajpat Rai and Pandit Motilal Nehru wrote letters to Mahatma Gandhi from jail in the North India and N.C. Kelker in Deccan expressed resentment and dissatisfaction against Mahatma Gandhi. The removal of Gandhiji from the political scene left a gap in leadership of the Congress. There was no other person who commanded universal respect in the rank and file of the party. The failure of the Non-co-operation scheme left behind a bitter taste in every mouth. There was confusion and gloominess. The nation demanded a concrete programme and political guidance which were finally supplied by a set of leaders who had opposed Gandhi's boycott of Councils. The Congress was split into two sections, each pulling at different ends. There was a group of no-changers who disliked any change from lines laid down by Gandhiji before going to jail. The other group consisted of pro-changers who favoured Council entry programme as a means to wreck the Councils from within. The All India Congress Committee appointed a committee consisting of Pt. Motilal Nehru, Dr. Ansari, Rajagopalachari, Jamnalal Bajaj and others to tour the country and assess public opinion on civil disobedience question. In its findings the committee recommended that Non-co-operators should be allowed to enter the Local Bodies and Councils. But the recommendations of the committee became a subject of heated controversy between the forces loyal and opposed to Gandhi's way of thinking. The wrangle was solved by a message which Gandhiji sent from prison. He wrote to Congress President: "My views are well known, I expressed them before I went to jail and there has been no change in them since. I may assure you that if you choose to differ from me, it will not affect by one bit the sweetness of relations between you and me." The activities of the Congress were thus comparmentalised into constructive ones outside the Councils and the destructive ones inside the Councils.

1. C.G. Shah, *Marxcism, Gandhism, Stalinism* (Bombay, Popular Prakashan, 1963) pp. 291-292.

The Formation of the Swaraj Party. After their release from jail Sri. C.R. Das and Motilal Nehru put a new programme before the Congress. They were convinced that it was silly dissociate from the Legislative Councils and hence, they began to preach openly the gospel of capturing the Councils in order to end them or mend them. They argued that the Councils would provide them a platform to publicise their views and restore the waning trust of the people in the Congress ideology. Secondly, if the Congressmen contested the electioins, the opportunists, the liberals and the hirelings of the Government would be prevented from entering the Councils and doing mischief. Thirdly, the non-co-operators by entering the Councils would practise non-co-operation with the legislature and thus be able to put a check on the autorcracy of the Government. Fourthly, the criticism of the Government would keep up the enthusiasm of the people in political affairs. Fifthly, they would if returned in majority, be able to compel the Government to revise the Constitution by obstructing the working of Dyarchy in the Provinces. And lastly, they would be able to do useful legislation for the country besides keeping alive the country's demand for complete independence.

At Gaya Congress held under the Presidentship of Sri. C.R. Das in December 1922, Motilal Nehru and his followers tried hard to get their Council-entry programme approved but they failed in their attempt because of the opposition by Rajgopalachari, Dr. Ansari, Ranga and others. C.R. Das resigned the Presidentship of the Congress so as to organise the Swaraj Party and capture the organisation before the general elections due in 1923. He formed the Swaraj Party at Allahabad in March, 1923. The orthodox followers of Gandhiji headed by Rajgopalachari came to be known as 'no-changers'. The All India Congress Committee, however, did not accept the resignation of C.R. Das and persuaded both the 'no-changers' and the Swarajists to call a truce and stop carrying on any propoganda for their respective views. A special session of the Congress was convened in Delhi in September, 1923, to bring about a compromise. It was in this session that the Congress lifted the ban on Council entery and permitted the Congressmen to contest the electinos as independents. It was a triumph of the Swarajists. Mr. C.R. Das made it very clear that he was not at all opposed to constructive programme of the Congress He only wanted that capturing of Councils and Local Bodies may also be included in the programme of the Congress. When Gandhiji was released from jail on grounds of illness, Pt. Nehru and C.R. Das met him and placed their views before him. The talks were fruitful and Gandhiji gave his consent to the Swarajists to function not as an autonomous wing but as a part of the parent organisation.

Principles and Programmes of Swaraj Party. So far as the ultimate political aim was concerned, there was no controversy at all. Both Gandhiji and the Swarjists aimed at securing Swaraj or Dominion Status within the British Empire. The difference, however, arose on the methods to be adopted. Whereas the Gandhists put emphasis on the constructive programme of the Congress, the Swarajists preferred to make use of the Councils for displaying the popularity and strength of the organisation. They considered elections as an effective means to enthuse the people. their second motive was to eliminate the liberals and undesirable persons who after being elected helped the Government in suppressing national movement. The foremost consideration with them was either to secure necessary changes in the Act of 1919 or to make them completely unworkable. The Swarajists actually intended to fight their war of independence both by populatising constructive work and by discrediting the Government at the Council level. They had no hesitation in joining the Civil Disobedience Movement also if called upon to do so.

Success and Work of the Swarajists The results of the elections held in 1923 proved very encouraging and favourable for the Swarajist candidates. They were returned in large numbers. They secured clear majority in Central Assembly and the Legislative Council of Bengal and Central Province. In several other Provinces, although they failed to command a clear majority, they formed strong opposition groups. Under the leadership of astute parliamentarian Pt. Motilal Nehru, the Swarajist group consisted of 45 strong including a few Nationalists and Independents. In Bengal Assembly the group was led by Sri. C.R. Das. Thw Swarajists gained some notable success at the Centre.

Their prime achievement was the passing of a resolution on 8th February, 1924, which demanded: "That steps should be taken to have the Act of 1919 revised with a view to establish full responsible Government in India, and for that purpose to summon, at an early date, a representative Round Table Conference to recommend with due regard to the protection of the rights and interests of important minorities, a scheme for the constitution of India ; and after dissolving the Central Legislature to place it before the Newly Indian Legislature for its approval and to submit to the British Parliament to be embodied in a statute."

In January, 1924, Labour Party came to power in England with the help of Liberal Party and a Ministry was formed under Mr. Ramsay Macdonald. The Labour Party was well known for its sympathetic attitude towards Indian aspirations. So the hopes sprang high in India that the resolution passed by the Swaraj Party would be accepted by the British Parliament but they were disappointed. The British Government appreciated the feelings of the Swarajists but uttered not a word against the British bureaucracy. When the Swarajists were disillusioned, they stiffened their attitude towards the British Government. Acting on this principle they rejected several demands for grants and Financial Bills between 1924 and 1927. The governor-General had to exercise his special powers to restore those grants. Notwithstanding strong opposition from the side of the Government, the Swarajist Party by a resolution succeeded in condemning the repressive Acts of 1818. Some of the highlights of their victories in the Central Assembly were a demand for responsible self-government and a demand for the immediate release of political prisoners. The Swarajists abstained from attending official ceremonies and functions. The tactics of the Swarajists included attempts to throw out the budget, staging walk-outs and criticising the Government vehemently. In Bengal, Sri C.R. Das was invited by the Governor to form the ministry but he turned down the invitation and formed a formidable opposition with the co-operation of the Nationalists. Because of their obstructionist tactics the dyarchy had to be suspended in two Provinces–Bengal and Central Provinces (C.P., part of present M.P.).

Report of Muddiman Committee. The resolution passed by the Swarajists in Central Assembly in 1924 for immediate reforms yielded one good result. The Government appointed an enquiry committee under the Chairmanship of Home Member, Mr. Alexander Muddiman, to report on the working of Dyarchy. Pt. Motilal Nehru declined the membership of this committee. In the committee's opinion supported by the majority there was no fundamental flaw in the Dyarchial system. When the report came before the Central Assembly, Pt. Motilal Nehru raised a dissenting voice and dubbed Dyarchy as absurd and impracticable. He also moved against the committee's report a resolution which was passed by the House.

With the death of Sri Das in 1925, the Swarajist Party lost a pillar of strength. In Provinces where the party was not very strong, the policy of obstruction proved a fruitless exercise. The Party could not inflict many defeats on the Government. Even in Central Province and Bengal where the Swarajists acted as a strong group, they made it impossible for the Ministers to function but had no effect on the Governor's rule. In those Provinces the people were more harmed than benefited. In Central Assembly the Swarajists succeeded, no doubt, in inflicting defeats on the Government but, in view of the Governor-General's powers of certification and veto, they failed to create any deadlock. In short the results obtained were not very encouraging or substantial. This gave rise to disappointment and doubts in the ranks of the Party itself regarding the usefulness of their lines of work. Lala Lajpat Rai and Pt. Madan Mohan Malviya, the leaders of the Nationalist group in the Central Assembly, did not see any wisdom in harming the interests of the Hindu Community by their policy of offering 'uniform, continuous and consistent opposition' to the Government. The began to advocate for responsive co-operation. Thus, there appeared a split in the ranks of the Swarajists; Mahatma Gandhi and his band of followers had already no faith in the Swarajists' programme. Sri C. R. Das also a little before his death had begun to incline towards co-operation with the Government in working Dyarchy. The Government too was eager to secure the co-operation of the Swarajists. Hence, there was no course open for the Swarajists except to modify their methods. Mr. V. G. Patel, who was formerly a staunch Swarajist, took the first concrete step towards co-operation by accepting the office of the presiding officer of the Central Assembly. Pt. Motilal Nehru also accepted the membership of Ruskin Committee which had been appointed to report on the organisation of defence forces. The unfavourable results of the elections held in 1926 gave another jolt to the Swarajists. Since then the Party's attitude changed from one of consistent obstruction to that of responsible co-operation.

Evaluation of the work of Swarajists. The methodology of the Swarajists was disapproved and whipped by several leaders. Congressmen like B. C. Pal and an independent like Joseph Baptista expressed grave doubts in the soundness and practicability of the Swarajist programme.Surendarnath Bannerjee also called it futile and meaningless. According to Zacharias, "The Swarajists were in the position of the people who wanted to keep their cake and eat it at the same time. They considered it necessary, in order to retain their popularity, to talk extremism and yet were resolved to easy parliamentarianism. As a consequence, the Swarajists were driven to a course of quibbling, as to when Co-operation was Non-Co-operation." And there is certainly sound logic in the criticism that there was no meaning in joining the Councils if their purpose was merely to make its functioning impossible.

However, it cannot be denied that the Swarajists rendered some useful service. They emerged on the political horizon at a time when the abrupt suspension of the Non-Co-operation Movement had left behind much bitterness and frustration in every heart. The activities of the Swarajists infused new hope and enthusiasm in the masses. Through their fiery speeches, the prepared the country once again for Civil Disobedience and this enthusiasm was exhibited admirably when the Movement actually started a few years later. Through consistent criticism, they were able to discredit the Government in the eyes of the world. By making it impossible for the Ministers to work, they compelled the Government to contemplate the revision of the constitution on the reports of the Muddiman Committee and Simon Commission. They also exploded the false claim of the Government that the administration of the country was being run by the elected representatives of the people. The successive defeats suffered by the Government also served as eye-opener to the British Government. The work of the Swarajists within the legislatures drew the intelligentsia and all thinking people in the country closer to the Congress. No student of political history can underestimate the work done by Pt. Motilal Nehru and C. R. Das. Another highlight of their work was the passing of a resolution whereby they suggested the holding of a Round Table Conference to recommend a constitution of India based on the principle of full responsible Government. It was as a result of their efforts that the British Government finally agreed to end Dyarchy and grant full autonomy to the Provinces.

EXERCISES

Long Answer Type Questions

1. Briefly analyse the Circumstances favouring the commencement of the Non-Co-operation Movement. Also discuss its Programme and show how far was it a success ?
2. "He (Gandhi) had done what Lokmanya Bal Gangadhar Tilak had failed to do," Is it true in the context of the Non-Co-operation Movement launched by Mahatma Gandhi ?
3. Discuss the achievements and shortcomings of Non-Co-operation Movement.
4. Discuss the principles and programme of Swaraj Party. How Swarajists contributed in the National Movement ?

Short Answer Type Questions

1. Write a short note on significance of Non-Co-operation Movement.
2. Write a brief note on progress of Non-Co-operation Movement.
3. "The suspension of the Non-Co-operation Movement was Gandhiji's serious blunder," Are you agree with this opinion ? Discuss in very brief.

4. Discuss in brief the early formation of the Swarajist party.
5. Write a very brief note on the principles and progress of Swarajist party.

Objective Type Questions

Choose the correct answer

1. In which year Gandhiji took up the leadership of the Indian National Movement ?
   (*a*) 1920 (*b*) 1921
   (*c*) 1922 (*d*) 1923
2. Which period is generally called the Gandhian era ?
   (*a*) 1919-1934 (*b*) 1920-1935
   (*c*) 1921-1936 (*d*) 1922-1937
3. In which year Gopal Krishna Gokhale died ?
   (*a*) 1913 (*b*) 1914
   (*c*) 1915 (*d*) 1916
4. In July 1920 who was Moderate and believer of the constitutional reforms ?
   (*a*) Bal Gangadhar Tilak (*b*) Pt. Motilal Nehru
   (*c*) Gopal krishna Gokhale (*d*) Lala Lajpat Rai
5. In which year Gandhiji came back from South Africa ?
   (*a*) 1915 (*b*) 1916
   (*c*) 1917 (*d*) 1918
6. Gandhiji was greatly influenced by political philosophy of
   (*a*) Lokmanya Bal Gangadhar Tilak (*b*) Gopal Krishna Gokhale
   (*c*) Lala Lajpat Rai (*d*) Pt. Madan Mohan Malviya.
7. In which year Gandhiji started a countrywide compaign against Rowlatt Act ?
   (*a*) 1917 (*b*) 1918
   (*c*) 1919 (*d*) 1920
8. In which year on the date of 13th April a public meeting was held in the Jallianwala Bagh Amritsar ?
   (*a*) 1916 (*b*) 1917
   (*c*) 1918 (*d*) 1919
9. In which year Hunter committee was constituted ?
   (*a*) 1919 (*b*) 1920
   (*c*) 1921 (*d*) 1922
10. In which year Hunter committee submitted its report ?
    (*a*) 1919 (*b*) 1920
    (*c*) 1921 (*d*) 1922

ANSWERS

1. (*a*) **2.** (*b*) **3.** (*c*) **4.** (*d*) **5.** (*a*) **6.** (*b*) **7.** (*c*) **8.** (*d*) **9.** (*a*) **10.** (*b*)

16

CHAPTER

Civil Disobedience Movement

"We believe that it is the inalienable right of the Indian people as of any other people, to have freedom and to enjoy the fruits of their toil and have the nécessities of life so that they may have full opportunities of growth. We believe also that if any Government deprives the people of these rights and oppresses them, the people have a further right to alter or abolish it. The British Government in India has not only deprived the Indian people of their freedom but has ruined India economically, politically, culturally and spiritually. We believe therefore that India must sever the British connections and attain Purna Swaraj or complete independence".

—Independence Pledge, 26th January, 1930

The Non-co-operation Movement, which had been started in 1920, was suspended abruptly by Gandhiji in 1922.The waning popularity of Mahatma Gandhi emboldened the Government to arrest and detain him for a little over two years. Gandhiji, after his release from jail in February, 1924, engaged himself soley in constructive work, while the Swarajists took charge of the political front of the Congress. Thus, since the withdrawl of the Khilafat and Non-Co-operation Movement in 1922 till 1927 there was a period of lull. Only the Swarajists engaged themselves in some activity in the legislature. Another phase of movement begins after the appointment of Simon Commission but before we deal with the Commission, it is worthwhile to study the communal problem in India.

COMMUNAL PROBLEM

Communal Riots. The withdrawal of the Khilafat and Non-co-operation Movement came as a great shock to Indian Muslims. The semblance of communal harmony which appeared during the years 1920-22 disappeared for ever. The Muslim League revived its ignominious activities. Ali Brothers who at one time used to be called the two arms of Gandhiji began to preach the gospel of communalism. The wave of communal madness did maximum of damage in Malbar where Mopla Muslims raided Hindus homes and massacred Hindus in cold blood in 1922. In kohat (North West Frontier Province.) there was a serious riot also. For five years from 1922 to 1927 the country passed through the horrible phase of Hindu-Muslim riots. The Muslims had no dearth of excuses for playing with the lives and property of the Hindus. Muharram and Holi were the usual occasions for communal bloodbaths. The Muslim League expressed its fear that the Congress aimed at establishing Hindu Raj. It played into the hands of the British and thus foiled all the sincere attempts made by the Congress to form a united front against the British Rulers. The Government encouraged riots so as to disrupt national unity.

Foundation of Hindu Mahasabha, Rashtriya Swayamsewak Sangh. The growing menace of Muslim disturbing elements necessitated a strong Hindu or ganisation to protect the life and property of the Hindus. Congress was incapable of shielding the true nationals of India. Pt Madan Mohan Malaviya, Lala Lajpat Rai, Swami Shraddhanand, Dr. Moonje and others supported the cause of Hindulsm. The Hindu Mahasabha came into existence with a view to protecting the Hindu race from the attacks of Muslim fanatics. Swami Shraddhanand started *Shuddhi* movement to counteract the *Tablig* movement launched by Mohammed Ali. It was a concerted campaign to take back the Hindus who had accepted Islam. Swami Shraddhanand fell a martyr to his mission of *Shudhi* when he was stabbed to death by a Muslim fanatic. On Dussehra, 1925 Dr. K. B. Hedgewar founded another organisation known as *Rashtriya Swayamsewak Sangh* to unite Hindus for the regeneration of Bharat. However, it should be particularly noted that the Rashtriya Swayamsewak Sangh is not anti Muslim or anti-Christian in any way. It only wants to remove the defects of Hindu society in order to rejuvenate it.

Gandhiji's Fast and Unity Conference. The saintly heart of Gandhiji was deeply pained to see Hindus and Muslims shedding each other's blood foolishly. He observed 21 days, fast in 1924 to protest against the communal fury raging in all parts of the country. The leaders who were fanning the flames of communalism realised their mistake and formed a committee for reconciliation. The peace committee which was headed by Gandhiji had Hakin Ajmal Khan, Lala Lajpat Rai, Dr. S. K. Dutta, Master Sunder Singh and G. K. Narriman as its members. As a result of their efforts the tension subsided for a year only to restart with increased violence later on.

SIMON COMMISSION

Appointment of Simon Commission : According to the Government of India Act 1919 a statutory commission was to be appointed ten years after the introduction of the reforms to review the political situation in India. So the Commission was due in 1929. But Lord Irwin, the Viceroy of India, announced the appointment of a Royal Commission in 1927. It was to be headed by Sir John Simon, a member of the British Liberal Party. The other members of the commission were-Lord Burnham, Lord stratchcona, Mr. Gadogan Colonel Lane Fox, Mr. Attlee Several reasons were advanced for the setting up of the Commission a couple of years earlier. The British Parliament stated that the early appointment of the Commission was in response to Indians' demand of an early revision of the Constitution. But the Indians explained it in a different way. Their analysis was that the Conservative Party—the party in power in Great Britain—was afraid of being ousted by the Labour Party in the general elections to be held in 1929.

Aim of Simon Commission. The task assigned to the Commission was to inquire into the working of the then Constitution and to find out how successfully or otherwise the Dyarchy was working in the Provinces. It was also to report on the functioning of representative institution and whether it was desirable or not to make further progress towards a fully responsible Government. But few critics were of the opinion that the British Government was forced to appoint the Commission due to the agitations in India. However this reason does not appear to be very sound. Another reason for the appointment of commission might be to disintegrate the Swarajist Party.

Boycott of Simon Commission. Simon Commission consisted of British elements only. Lord Birkenhead, the Secretary of State, had already been sounded that a Commission consisting of only British members was likely to invite trouble but he paid no heed to this warning. His argument was that the Indians could not be included in the Commission which was to deal with a vital problem of suggesting constitutional reforms. He also tried to justify exclusion of Indians on the ground that it was difficult to give representation to all the political sections in India because in that case the size of the Commission would become to unwieldy. And if one party alone was represented, it would be represented by other groups. But at the bottom of these flimsy excuses was the distrust of Indian.

The exclusion of Indians from the Commission, which was to discuss Indian problems, was considered by the Indians as outrageous. Nearly all groups and sections of people in India's political life boycotted the Commission. On coming in Bombay on February 7, 1928, it was greeted with black flags in a wild demonstrations. The same was repeated at every place the commission visited during the course of its stay in India.

When the Commission reached Lahore, Lala Lajpat Rai led a huge Procession of demonstrators. A white police officer, Mr. Saunders, rained to blows on Lajpat Rai and inflicted grievous injuries resulting in the death of the great patriot. It was taken as a great insult to Indian nationhood. The revolutionary group of Bhagat Singh and his friends avenged the wrong by murdering Mr. Saunders. At Lucknow the demostrations against the Commission were organised and led by leaders like Govind Ballabh Pant and Pt. Motilal Nehru. They were also treated to stick-charge and firing. In view of disturbances all over the country, the Government made an announcement to the effect that committees elected by central as well as Provincial Legislature would also be associated with the Commission. But this assurance did not evoke any enthusiasm among the organised parties in the country. Only the loyalists came forward to form committees to assist the Commission in acquring essential information.

Report of Simon Commission. After two years of consistent work, the Commission prepared and published its report in May, 1930. Its recommendations were as follows :

1. *Abolition of Dyarchy and Introduction of Provincial Autonomy*: On a detailed and careful study of the Indian problem the Commission concluded that Dyarchy, the experiment in self-government, was unworkable because of certain inherent weaknesses in the scheme. It, therefore, recommended the introduction of Provincial Autonomy, in other words, the transference to and control of all the provincial subjects by popular Ministers.

2. *Special Powers of the Governors and the Governor-General* : The Commission suggested that the Governor-General and the Governors should remain 'in possession of full and simple powers to ensure a thoroughly efficient administrative system and to safeguard the interests of the minorities.' The Governor should also be allowed to include one or more non-elected experienced officials in his Council but such an official Minister should be responsible to the Legislative Council and not the Governor or the Governor-General.

3. *Extension of Franchise* : In the general election held in 1925 less than 3 percent of the total population enjoyed the right of vote. The Commission proposed the right of vote to be given to at least 10 per cent to 15 per cent of the people. It also suggested the retention of the communal electorate and special representation of minority communities and classes.

4. *Irresponsible Government at the Centre* : The Commission left the Centre untouched. It considered the introduction of Dyarchy at the Centre undesirable. It said that the Central Executive should be absolutely free from domination by the legislature. A strong Centre was of utmost importance for a few years. The Commission looked forward to the possibility of a federation including the States after which the issue of a responsible government at the Centre was to be reconsidered.

5. *India's Defence* : The Commission recognised the justness of the demand of Indianisation of the Army but recommended the retention of British forces till the country was adequately equipped to defend itself. It said that the responsibility of defending the country from external attack should remain with the British Government while India should raise forces sufficient enough to maintain law and order in the country.

6. *Reconstitution of Central Legislature* : The Commission suggested the desirability of the reconsititution of the Central Legislature on federal principle, having representatives from all the Provinces and those States only which consented to join the proposed federation. The method of election for both the Houses, the Commission said, should be indirect.

7. The Commission also recommended the separation of Burma from India and Sind from Bombay. It did not consider Notrh West Frontier Province as suitable for internal autonomy.

8. *Enlargement of Provincial Legislature* : The Commission recommended the enlargement of Provincial Legislatures. The more important Provinces should have not less than 200 and not more than 250 members. There should be no official bloc. Even the nominated non-officials should not exceed ten per cent of the total membership. The Muslims in Provinces where they were in minority should be given special and adequate representation.

9. *Home Government* : In regard to the Home Government, the Commission recommended the retention of India Council to advise Secretary of State but with reduced powers. It proposed no change in the rate of Indianisation of the services fixed on the basis of Lee Commission Report.

10. *New Constitution* : The Commission also proposed that the provision of appointing a Commission to review the constitutional progress after every ten years should be done away with. In its place the new constitution should be made flexible enough to admit changes whenever necessary.

Evaluation of Simon Report : The report published by the Commission did not evoke much enthusiasm because its recommendations fell far short of the national expectations. Not to speak of Dominion Status, it did not recommend even partial responsibility at the Centre. Defence of the country was kept under the charge of British Government. The army was made loyal to His Majesty's Government although its cost was to be borne by Indian tax-payers. Although the Commission had recommended Provincial Autonomy, the powers of the Ministers were greatly restricted by the special powers of the Governors and the Governor-General. There are two different views of critics about the Report. Some critics have strongly condemmed it and some have praised it. But Every national leader condemned the meagre reforms suggested by the Commission. According to Mr. Andrews, "its (Simon report) great demerit was that it failed to take note of the radical changes that had been brought about by the non-violent, Non-co-operation Movement, and of the aspirations generated by it. It dealt more with that old india which was nearly thirty years ago before the national movement had started; it showed little understanding of the young national movement which was rising on the tide of national upheaval" —

Sir Sivaswami Ayyar has remarked that the report should be placed on a scrap heap." A dispassionate appraisal of the report would reveal that it has no worsed than the provisions of 1935 Act. In the the words of **P. E. Roberts,** "It will always stand out as one of the greatest Indian state Papers."

According to **Richard B. Gregg,** "There are some distoration of emphasis amounting almost to omission of pertinent fact, but these were probably "international." **Professor Keith** has remarked, "It was probably foolish of Indian opinion to repudiate the report out and out if it had been accepted; the British Government would hardly have failed to work on it and responsible government in the provinces would have been achieved much earlier than it could be under any later scheme .....".

NEHRU REPORT

The All Parties Conference:

The Simmon Commission, though abused by the Indians had the good effect on Indian politics. It awoke the Indian leaders to formulate a scheme of Indian Constitution acceptable to all parties. Lord Bikenhead justified in an insolent mood the exclusion of Indians from the Simmon Commission and challenged the Indian leaders that they were unable to produce an agreed constitution for submission to the British Parliament. The Indian National Congress accepted the challenge and in February, 1928, All Parties Conference was held at Delhi. The Congress in a resolution said : "Having regard to the general desire of all political parties in the country to unite together in setting *Swaraj* Constitution, and having considered the various drafts submitted to it and the various suggestions received in reply to the working committee's circular this congress authorises the working committee which shall have power to co-opt, to confer with similar committees to be appointed by other organisations—political, Labour, Commercial and Communal in the country and draft a Swaraj Constitution on the basis of declaration of Rights and to place the same for consideration and approval before a special convention at Delhi." The conference appointed a Committee of Pt. Motilal Nehru, Sir Tej Bahadur Sapru, Sir Ali Imam. Sardar Mangal Singh, Shuaib Qureshi, M. S. Aney, G. K. Pradhan. S. C. Bose and J. L. Nehru. Pt. Motilal Nehru was the chairman of the committee and Pt. Jawaharlal Nehru acting as the Secretary. The committee worked hard to produce a memorable report, which in the words of Dr. Z. A. Charies was "a masterly and statesmen-like Report." This report was subsequently known as Nehru Report.

The following were the Recommendations of the Nehru Report :

1. *Dominion Status and Full Responsible Government—The majority opinion of the committee favoured Dominion Status. A minority section stood for complete independence. Hence, a compromise formula was evolved. Dominion Status was accepted not as the ultimate but the immediate goal. All the parties which present for complete independence were given liberty of action to pursue their goal. The Report also demanded a full responsible Government on the lines of self-governing Dominions.*
2. *Provincial Autonomy and Residuary Powers*— The committee envisaged a future federation in India. It emphasised the need of giving as much autonomy to the Provinces as was safely possible. The subjects should be divided into the Central and Provincial lists, the residuary powers to be exercised by the Centre. The Provinces were to have only one House each for making laws.
3. *Rejection of Communal Electorate*—The Report admitted that there was communal problem in India and expressed its faith that free India would be able to solve the problem satisfactorily. It held the British element in India as partly responsible for creating communal tension. The report further said that India was to be a secular State where there would be no State religion. It suggested cultural autonomy, safeguards and guarantees to be promised to minority communities but it rejected the system of communal electorate. In its place it offered the system of joint electorate with reservation of seats.
4. *Creating of New Provinces*— The sub-committee in its Report conceded the demand of the Muslims to create a separate Province of Sind and to give North West Frontier Province., a footing of equality with other Provinces although the motive behind such a demand was to have four Muslim-majority Provinces in India, *viz.*, Bengal, Punjab, Sind and North West Frontier Province.
5. *Fundamental Rights*—The Report said that sovereignty belonged to the people and it was to be exercised through their representatives in accordance with the Constitution. To ensure freedom to the individual, the Report mentioned nineteen Fundamental Rights to be included in the Constitution, notable amongst them were equality of men and women in regard to rights, and freedom of faith of every individual.
6. *Parliament*— According to the Report, India's Parliament should consist of the Crown, the Senate and the House of Representatives. The Senate should have 200 members elected by the members of the Provincial legislatures. Each Province was to be represented in the Senate in proportion to its population. The House of Representatives should have 500 members directly elected on the basis of adult franchise. The life of Lower House should be five years. In foreign matters the Indian Parliament was to have the same rights as exercised by the Parliaments of other Dominions.

7. *Indian States*—In regard to Indian States the Report said that the Indian Parliament should have the same rights and discharge the same obligations towards the Indian State as the then existing Government of India did. In case of a conflict between the State and Parliament, the Governor-General should have the power to refer the issue to the Supreme Court for arbitration.
8. *Central Executive*—The Report accepted the principle that the Crown was to remain the highest executive exercising his powers through his representative, *i.e.*, the Governor General of India. But the report said that the Governor-General should act perfectly in accordance with the Constitution and parliamentary laws. His executive should consist of one Prime Minister and six Ministers, collectively responsible to the Dominion Parliament of India.
9. *Supreme Court.*— The Report suggested the setting up of a Supreme Court in India charged with the duty of interpreting the constitution and deciding points of conflict between one Province and the other. It recommended that no appeal should therefrom lie to the Privy Council.
10. *Defence.*— The Report suggested that a defence committee should be formed comprising the Prime Minister, the Defence Minister, Commander-in-Chief, Chiefs of the Naval and Air Forces, Chief of the General Staff and two military experts; that the defence budget should be put to the House for approval; and that in emergency the Central Executive should have the right to sanction any sum it liked.
11. *Civil Services.*— All the civil Services should become offices of the commonwealth and a Public Service Commission should be appointed by the Governor-General.
12. *Provinces Respected*—The report recommended the preservations of the rights and the privileges of Rulers of the various States. They should also be warned that Indian Rulers would have to adopt the Membership of Federation, if it was constituted in the near future.
13. *North-West Provinces.*— The Report suggested that North West Frontiers Provinces should be brought to the level of Constitutional status as other Provinces had.

Reaction to the Report: There was All party conference to discuss the report.— According to Zacharias, Nehru Report was "a masterly and statesmanlike report. For the first time in India's history, all the political parties laid their heads together to discuss constitutional problems and their mutually agreeable solutions. No greater tribute can be paid to it than that it supplied the blueprint of the present Indian Constitution."

The Report was accepted unanimously by the All-Parties Conference at Lucknow but difficulties arose when it came up for scrutiny separately before all the parties which were represented at Lucknow Conference. They began to examine the report with a communal bias. Muslim League was divided on the issue. Maulana Abul Kalam Azad, Hakim Ajmal Khan, Dr. Ansari and other Nationalist Muslims were in favour of accepting the report in its original form. Mr. Mohammed Shafi stood for rejecting it. The third section was led by Mohammed Ali Jinnah who was prepared to accept it but only after certain vital changes, proposed by him.

In the National Convention at Calcutta he put forward his three suggestions : (*a*) The Muslim must have 1/3 representation in the Central Legislature. (b) There should be Muslim Representation in the Punjab and Bengal Legislatures on the population basis for ten years. (*c*) Residuary powers should not be vested in the centre but in the provinces.

The amendments were rejected in the convention and there were heated debates in the open session of the convention in December 1928. Mr. Mohammed Ali Jinnah left the convention and joined a more reactionary section of the Muslim led by Mr. Agha Khan. He also called a meeting of All India Muslim League at Delhi on December 1928, where he put forward his fourteen points formula as the pre-requisite to any political agreement. Not only Muslims, but forward his a large section of Sikhs, non-Brahmins and backward and Depressed Communities also did not like the Nehru Constitution. Christians of the country were also of the opinion that the Report did not safeguard the interest of minorities.

Congress Ultimatu, Calcutta, December, 1928.— The House of the Congress itself was divided in its support to the Report. The younger section led by Jawaharlal Nehru and Subhas Chandra Bose stood for nothing less than complete independence. The older group led by Pt. Motilal Nehru was in favour of accepting the Report as it was. Pt. Motilal Nehru it seemed doubtful, would be able to carry his resolution through the Calcutta Congress. Hence Gandhiji came to the rescue of Motilal Nehru and contended : "I am for complete independence—as complete as it can be—but I am not against full Dominion Status—as full as any dominion possesses it today, provided I get it before it loses all attraction".

No doubt, the Report was criticised by a large section of the country but it did not reflect that the report was not worthwhile. The Report was comprehensive document embodying the aspirations of partrotic Indians of that time. Even the present constitutions of Indians resembles with the Report to a large extent. *Dr. Zacharias* has rightly remarked : "The Nehru Report deserves to be read and studied in all its details as it sheds light on every subject it touches and displays a practical common sense which never losses itself in doctrinaire but which equally spurs to shelter itself behind the enunciation of mere platitudes."

MOHAMMED ALI JINNAH'S FOURTEEN POINTS TO COUNTER-ACT NEHRU REPORT

Mr. Mohammed Ali Jinnah who did not agree to Nehru Report put forward his Fourteen Points as the minimum demands of the muslims for any political settlement.

These points were presented before and ratified by the Muslim League. The substance of the Fourteen-Point formula was as follows:—

1. The form of any constitution to be drawn for free India should be federal with the residuary powers vested in the Provincial government.
2. Every province should enjoy a uniform measure of autonomy.
3. The Minorities should be adequately represented in all the Legislative Assemblies and Local Bodies. No attempt should be made to reduce their majority in any Province to a minority or even equality.
4. One-third of the total seats in the Central Asembly should be reserved for the Muslims.
5. Representation of all the communities should be on the basis of separate electorate. It should, however, be open to any group to abandon the system of separate electorate in favour of joint electorate.
6. Any territorial redistribution should not in any way affect the Muslim majority in the Punjab, Bengal and North-West Frontier Province.
7. Full religious liberty should be guaranteed to every individual.
8. No legislature or an elected body should adopt a Bill or resolution which was opposed by three-fourths of the members of that community in that body on the ground that it was injurious to the interest of that community.
9. Sind to be separated from Bombay Presidency.
10. North-West Frontier Province and Baluchistan should not be discriminated against in respect of reforms.

11. Adequate share for Mussalmans should be provided in the constitution of all services, subject to requirements of efficiency.
12. Adequate safeguards and State help should be given for the protection and promotion of Muslim culture, religion, language, education, laws and religious institutions.
13. At least one-third of total number of ministers in the Central and Provincial cabinets should be drawn from Muslim community.
14. No change in the Constitution should be made by Central Assembly except with the Concurrence of the units constituting the Indian federation.

LABOUR GOVERNMENT IN ENGLAND; LORD IRWIN'S PROCLAMATION, 31ST OCTOBER, 1929

The General Elections in England were completed in May, 1929. The Labour Government came into office with Mr. Ramsay Macdonald as the Prime Minister. The Labour Government has failed to obtain absolute majority in the House of Commons. With the help of the Liberals it, however, formed the Government. Soon after the polls, Mr. Macdonald declared at a conference of Commonwealth Labour Parties; "I hope that within a period of months rather than years, there will be another Dominion added to the Commonwealth of Nations, a Dominion of another race, a Dominion which will find respect as an equal within the Commonwealth. I refer to India." This declaration by the British Prime Minister revived hopes in Indian hearts. Mr. Ramsay Macdonald then invited Lord Irwin, the then Viceroy of India, to England for consultation.

Lord Irwin on his return to India on October 31, 1929, said : "I am authorized on behalf of His Majesty's Government to state clearly that in their judgement it is implicit in the Declaration of 1917 that the natural issue of India's constitutional progress, as then contemplated, is the attainment of Dominion Status".

Delhi Manifesto.— Lord Irwin's Proclamation was quite vague and disappointing because it did not mention the deadline for the grant of Dominion Status. Within 24 hours of the announcement the Congress leaders met in Delhi. They expressed hope that the object of the Round Table Conference probably was not only to fix the date on which Dominion Status was to be conferred but also to frame the Dominion-Constitution. This hope was expressed in a manifesto issued over the signatures of the leading politicians of India. Jawaharlal Nehru and Subhas Chandra Bose, however, did not share the exultation of the old guards in the Congress. To them the Proclamation was a mere bluff. They doubted the intentions of the British Government. And hence they, resigned from the Congress Working Committee.

Gandhi-Irwin Meeting. With a view to clearing the fog of doubts and ascertaining the intentions of the British Government regarding the future of India, Gandhiji called on the Viceroy on 23rd December, 1929. On the same day the Viceroy had narrow escape from a bomb-explosion on the rail track near Delhi. Gandhiji after congratulating the Viceroy enquired of him the purpose of holding the Round Table Conference. Pt. Motilal Nehru, Sir Tej Bahadur Sapru, Sardar Vallabh Bhai Patel and Mr. Mohammad Ali Jinnah were also present in this meeting. *The Viceroy clearly expressed his inability to assure a new constitution to India.* He was also not certain whether the conference to be held in England would consider the issue of conferring responsible Government. All the leaders left the Viceroy's residence empty-handed and much disillusioned.

Complete Independence Resolution at Lahore Congress. The next Congress Session was held at Lahore against this dismal background. There was frustration in every heart. All the leaders were now convinced that the British Imperialism would submit not to beggary but force only. There was no other alternative but to demand complete independence. It was a historic day (31st December, 1929) when at midnight the resolution was voted upon and adopted by a majority vote. The text of the resolution ran as follows:

"This Congress endorses the action of the Working Committee in connection with manifesto signed by party leaders, including Congressmen, on the Viceregal pronouncement of the 31st October, relating to Dominion Status and appreciates the efforts of the Viceroy towards a settlement of the National Movement for Swaraj. The Congress, however, having considered all that has since happened and the result of the meeting among Mahatma Gandhi, Pt. Motilal Nehru and other leaders and the Viceroy, is of the opinion that nothing is to be gained by the Congress being represented at the proposed Round Table Conference. This Congress, therefore, in pursuance of the resolution passed at its session at Calcutta last year, declares that the word, Swaraj, in Article I of the Congress Constitution shall mean Complete Independence and further declares the entire scheme of the Nehru Committee's Report to have lapsed and hopes that all Congressmen will henceforth devote their exclusive attention in the attainment of Complete Independence for India. As a preliminary step towards organising a campaign for Independence and in order to make the Congress only as consistent as possible with the change of the creed, the Congress calls upon Congressmen and others taking part in the National Movement to abstain from participation directly or indirectly in future elections and directs the present Congress members of the legislatures and committees to resign their seats. This Congress appeals to the Nation zealously to prosecute the constructive programme of the Congress and authorise the All India Congress Committee, whenever it deems fit, to launch a programme of Civil Disobedience including non-payment of taxes, whether in selected areas or otherwise and under such safeguards as it may consider necessary."

The Congress also issued a call to the country to celebrate 26th january as a "*Purna Swaraj Day*". A resolution drafted for adoption on that day was also issued. A pledge was drawn up to be taken by every Congressman. It said, "It is the inalienable right of the people of India to have freedom and to enjoy the fruits of their toil and have necessities of life, so that they might have full opportunities of growth. We believe also that if any government deprives the people of their rights and oppresses them, the people have further right to alter it or abolish it. The British Government in India has based itself on the exploitation of the masses and ruined India. We believe, therefore, that India must sever the British connection and attain Purna Swaraj or Complete Independence.

"We recognise that the most effective way of gaining freedom is not through violence."

This pledge was to be repeated year after year. It roused and inflamed the passion of the people for independence. In order to perpetuate the memory of 26th January, our New Constitution was also enforced on this day. The 26th January is still celebrated every year as the Republic Day.

CIVIL DISOBEDIENCE MOVEMENT (1930-31)

Circumstances Leading to Civil Disobedience. The patience of the Indian masses reached a breaking point. The intelligentsia of the country was convinced that the method of persuasion could not work effectively. They felt inclined to use the strong language of agitation to compel the British Government to listen to their demands. The adamant British Government had already rejected Nehru Report. Moreover, there was acute economic depression in the country which had telling effect on all the classes, especially the lower classes. Repression was going on as usual. Gandhiji before taking any extreme step, made another offer to the Government. It was an eleven-point demand. But once again there was no response. The Congress, therefore, was left with no alternative but to start a Civil Disobedience Movement. The peasants of Bardoli in 1928 had already offered satyagraha under the dynamic leadership of Sardar Vallabh Bhai Patel. Their no-tax campaign was a partial success. The Congress decided to use the same nonviolent weapon of satyagraha against the Government on a large scale.

The Communist workers in this hour of economic crisis assumed the leadership of the hardest-hit class of peasants and workers. The Government rounded up the leaders and tried them for seditious activities. The case called Meerut Conspiracy Case ran for four years.

The Communist leaders were kept as undertrial prisoners for four years against all canons of justice. Later on they were sentenced to varying terms of imprisonment. The incident caused much pain and resentment to every person. Gandhiji came to conclusion that the country was heading towards a violent revolution. He was unhappy with this trend. The ambition of his political career was to lead the country along the path of non-violence. With this end in view he wrote a letter to Lord Irwin on 2nd March, 1930. But his attempt to negotiate was responded with coldness on the part of Viceroy. He was thus compelled by the circumstances to launch a movement by breaking Salt Laws.

The Historic Dandi March. One striking quality of Gandhiji's method of work was that all his moves and actions were very well planned. After the Lahore Congress he selected a good number of his Ashram-mates to receive training in the technique of Satyagraha. The opportunity to make an experiment came soon when the Government enhanced the taxes on salt. Accompained by a band of 79 trained and disciplined workers, Gandhiji marched on foot from Sabarmati Ashram to the sea-shore on 12th March, 1930. The distance of 200 miles was travelled in 24 days. Sardar Vallabh Bhai patel set out a few days earlier to do the spadework. Thousands of admirers cheered the Mahatma Gandhi on the way. Gandhiji's tour generated a good deal of fervour and patriotic sentiment. On the 6th April, 1930, after the morning prayer the Mahatma Gandhi and his Satyagrahis started the Civil Disobedience Movement by picking salt lying on sea-shore.

Programme of the Civil Disobedience. The technical violation of the Salt Law was signal to the country to start mass movement. Gandhiji orders were faithfully obeyed. Salt Law was broken at hundreds of places all over the country. The programme of the movement included (1) the violation of Salt Law, (2) abstention from attending the educational institutions by the students and the offices by the public servants, (3) picketing of shops dealing in liquor, opium and foreign goods, (4) bonfire of cloth, and (5) non-payment of taxes.

Campaign in full Swing. The movement gathered momentum very soon. Thousands of ladies even from orthodox and aristocratic families fled out of their houses to picket the liquor shops. All of them were arrested and imprisoned. Boycott of foreign textiles was also started on an extensive scale. At Dharasana 2,500 Satyagrahis raided a salt depot. The police as usual resorted to merciless repression. Many people were badly wounded, some of them died also as a result of lathi-blows by the police.

The boycott of foreign cloth proved successful beyond all calculations. In 1930, the import of foreign cloth was reduced to one-fourth of the figures of the previous year. Sixteen English owned textile mills at Bombay had to be closed. It proved a blessing in disguise to Indian mills. The peasants also carried out no-tax campaign with great zeal.

The Attitude of the Muslims. In fact very few Muslims took part in the Civil Disobedience Movement. The followers of Mr. Mohammed Ali Jinnah did not associate with the movement at all. The argument of Mr. Mohammed Ali Jinnah was : "We refuse to join Mahatama Gandhi because his movement is not a movement for the Complete Independence of India but for making the seventy million of Indian Muslims dependents of the Hindu Mahasabha." Bulk of the Muslim leaders who had co-operated with Mahatama Gandhi on the Khilafat issue refused to have anything to do with this movement. Only the Pathans of North West Frontier Province under the leadership of Khan Abdul Ghaffar Khan carried out the Congress programme and braved the lathi-blows and bullets like other Congress workers.

Repression by the Government. The movement gained strength and volume quite steadily. It reached its peak point in June, 1930. The administrative machinery was paralysed at many places. The Government could not accept it lying down. The police force went into action and the public places turned red with thick and warm blood of the patriots. Pandit Jawaharlal Nehru, the Congress President, was arrested on 14th April. His arrest was followed by the arrest of other leaders also. Nearly 60,000 people went to jail. It was the first time that such a large number of people courted arrest. Whosoever wore Gandhi cap and *khaddar* was either arrested or beaten up. indiscriminate lathi-charge became the order of the day. An excited mob at Sholapur set fire to five police stations. The result was firing and deaths. The police were particularly hard upon the Red Shirts in Peshawar.

FIRST ROUND TABLE CONFERENCE

The Simmon Commission Report was published during the time when the civil disobedience was gaining momentum. In the words of Dr. Racharias, the Report, "betrayed a monstrous lack of understanding only equal by similar lack of sympathy." No political party appreciated the Report and nobody gave any importance to the recommendations of the Commission. Even the liberals were of the view that the Report should not be the basis of the discussion of the Round Table Conference.

Congress boycotted the conference— Here in India an energetic journalist George Solocombe interviewed Gandhiji and other National Leaders in the jail. He tried to abridge the gulf between the Government and Congress leaders and tried to prepare the leaders of the Congress to participate in the Round Table Conference. Gandhiji clearly told him that he was not prepared to call off the movement till he was not assured about independence. He also put four points for the suspension of the movement. Mr. Solocombe met Pt. Moti Lal Nehru and Jawahar Lal Nehru and drafted a statement, which in his opinion could be the basis of mutual negotiation between the Government and the Congress. In August, 1930 Dr. Jaykar and Sir Tej Bahadur also find out the way for the negotiations but they also failed. At last, the Round Table Conference was held at London at St. James Palace, on November 12,1930 without the representatives of the Indian National Congress.

Nationalist Muslim excluded— The conference was inaugurated by His Majesty, the King and Ramsay Macdonald, the Prime Minister of England Presided the Conference. 89 delegates of India and 16 delegates of Indian States attended the conference, 86 members from all the parties of British Parliament were also called to participate in the conference. The representatives from British India were nominated by Viceroy and representatives from states who were also the yesmen of the British Government were selected by the Viceroy. In this connection *Brailsford* has written : "In St. James Palace there did assemble, Princes and Untouchables, Sikhs, Muslisms, Hindus and Christians, Spokesmen of Landowners, Trade Unions and Chambers of Commerce but Mother India was not there."

Statement of Policy made by Ramsay Macdonald, Prime Minister of United Kingdom., at the conclusion of First Indian Round Table Conference january 19, 1931 was as follows :—

(1) Responsibility placed upon legislature— The view of His Majesty's Government is that responsibility for the Government of India should be placed upon Legislatures. Central and Provincial with such provisions as may be necessary to guarantee during a period of transition, the observance of certain obligations and to meet other special circumstances, and also with such guarantees as are required by Minorities to protect their political liberties and rights.

(2) Meeting the traditional needs— In such statutory safeguards as may be made for meeting the need of the transitional period, it will be a primary concern of His Majesty's Government to see that the reserved powers are so framed and exercied as not to prejudice the advance of India through the new constitution to full responsibility for her own Government.

(3) Further negotiations— His Majesty's Government, whilst making this declaration, is aware that some of the conditions which are essential to the working of such a constitution as is contemplated, have not been finally settled, but it believes that as the result of the work done here, they have been brought to a point which encourages the hope that further negotiations, after this declaration will be successful.

(4) Federal Government— His Majesty's Government has taken note of the fact that the deliberation of the conference have proceeded on the basis, accepted by all parties, that the Central

Government should be a federation of all India, embracing both the Indian States and British Indian a bicameral Legislature. The precise form and structure of the new Federal Government must be determined after further discussion with the Princes and representatives of British India. The rang of subjects to be committed to it will also require further discussion, because the Federal Government will have authority only in such matters concerning the states as will be ceded by their Rulers in agreements made by them on entering into federation. The connection of the States with the federation will remain subject to the basic principle that in regard to all matters not ceded by them to the Federation their relations will be with the Crown acting through the agency of the Vicerory. With a legislature constituted on a Federal basis. His Majesty's Government will be prepared to recognize the principle of the executive to the legislature.

(5) Defence and external affairs— Under existing condition the subjects of Defence and External Affair will be reserved to the Governor-General, and arrangment will be made to place in his hands the powers necessary for the administration of those subjects. Morever, as the Governor-General must, as a last resort be able in an emergency to maintain the tranquility of the State, and must similarly be responsible for the observance of the constitutional rights of minorities, he must be granted the necessary powers for these purposes.

(6) Financial responsibility—As regards Finance, the transfer of financial responsibility must necessarily be subject to such conditions as will ensure the fulfilment of the obligations incurred under the authority of the Secretary of State and the maintenance unimpaired of the financial stability and credit of India. The Report of the Federal Structure Sub-Committee indicates some ways of dealing with this subject including a Reserve Bank, the Service of Loans, and Exchange Policy, which, in the view of His Majesty's Government, will have to be provided for somehow in the new constitution. It is of vital interest to all parties in India to accept these provisions, to maintain financial confidence. Subject to these provisions Indian Government would have full financial responsibility for the methods of raising revenue and for the control of expenditure on non Reserved Services. This will mean that under existing conditions the Central Legislature and Executive will have some features of dualism which will have to be fitted into the constitutional structure.

(7) Reserved powers—The provision of reserved powers is necessary in the circumstances and some such reservation has indeed been incidental to the development of most free constitutions. But every care must be taken to prevent conditions arising which will necessitate their use. It is, for instance, undesirable that Ministers should trust to the special powers of the Governor-General as a means of avoiding responsibilities which are properly their own, thus defeating the development responsible Government by bringing into use powers meant to lie in reserve and in the background. Let there be no mistake about that.

(8) Provincial subject—The Governor's provinces will be constitued on a basis of full responsibility. Their Ministries will be taken from the Legislature and will be jointly responsible to it. The range of provincial subjects will be so defined as to given them the greatest possible measures of self-government. The authority of the Federal Government will be limited to provisions required to secure its administration of Federal subject, and so discharge its responsibility for subjects defined in the constitution as of all India concern.

These will be reserved t the Governor only that minimum of special powers which is required in order to secure, in exceptional circumstances, the preservation of tranquillity, and to guarantee the maintenance of rights provided by status for the public services and minorities.

(9) Responsible Government—Finally, His Majesty's Government considers that the institution in the provinces of responsible Government requires both that the Legislatures should enlarged, and that they should be based on a more liberal franchise.

(10) Framing the Constitution—In framing the constitution His Majesty's Government considers that it will be its duty to insert provisions guaranteeing to the various minorities, in addition to political representation, that differences of religion race, sect or caste, shall not themselves constitute civic disabilities.

(11) Duty of the Community—In the opinion of His Majesty's Government it is the duty of the communities to come to an agreement amongst themselves on the points raised by the minorities sub-committee but not settled there. During the continuing negotiations such an agreement ought to be reached and the Government will continue to render what good offices it can help to secure that end, as it is anxious not only that no delay should take place in putting the new constitution into operation, but that it should start with the goodwill and confidence of all the communities concerned.

(12) Sub-Committees—The various sub-committee which have been studying the more important principles of a constitution which would meet Indian conditions have surveyed a considerable part of the structure in detail and the still unsettled points have been advanced a good way to an agreement. His Majesty's Government, however, in view of the character of the conference and of the limited time at its disposal in London, has deemed it advisable to suspend its work at this point, so that Indian opinion may be consulted upon the work done, and expedients considered for overcoming the difficulties which have been raised. His Majesty's Government will consider, without delay a plan by which our co-operation may be continued so that the results of our completed work may be seen in a new Indian constitution. If, in the meantime, there is a response to the Viceroy's appeal from those engaged at present in civil disobedience, and others wish to co-operate on the general lines of this declaration, steps will be taken to enlist their services.

(13) Three principles—Prime Minister Macdonald suggested three principles as the basis of discussions. Firstly, a federation was proposed for India, secondly provinces were to be given full responsibility with necessary safeguards. Thirdly introduction of partial responsibility at the Centre with few limitations.

The federal principles was accepted without much discussion. Regarding the grant of provincial autonomy to the provinces, there was no difference regarding safeguards there was some discussion. All the representatives welcomed the idea of introducing partial responsibility of the Centre. Dr. Jaykar and Sir Tej Bahadur Sapru placed for the Dominion Status in India. *Dr. Jaykar* told, "If you give India Dominion Status today, the cry of independence will die out."

There were heated debates regarding the communal issues. Muslims representatives pleaded for the separate electorates. Mr. Mohammad Jinnah strongly supported his 4 Points Formula. Dr. Bhim Rao Ambedkar also insisted on the provision of separate electorates. Hindu delegets advocated for the Joint Electorates and thus the vital issue remained unsolved and the conference adjourned '*Sine die*' in January 1931. In fact nothing substantial came out the conference. The Nationalists like *Subhash Chandra Bose* has remarked that the Conference offered India, "two bitter pills Safeguards and Federation. To make the pills eatable, they were sugar-coated with responsibility." The Congress kept itself aloof from the first Round Table Conference.

THE GANDHI-IRWIN PACT AND SECOND ROUND TABLE CONFERENCE

The British Government knew it well that Congress was the premier political party of India and its co-operation was essential for solving the constitutional problem of the country. The Government realised the need of arriving at a settlement with the Congress. In pursuance of this policy and in order to create congenial atmosphere for negotiations, the Government lifted the ban on the Congress and released all the leaders including Mahatma Gandhi unconditionally on 17th February, 1931. It was followed by protracted correspondence between Gandhiji and Lord Irwin.

After few days of the release of Mahatma Gandhi, the India's delegation, to the First Round Table Conference, come factor. Dr. Jaykar and Sir Tej Bahadur Sapru played the role of intermedaries as peace makers and liberal leaders between Mahatma Gandhi and Victory. They along with Sri Niwas Shastri met the Congress leaders and asked them to attend the second session of Second Round Table Conference. They also emphasised the need of Gandhi Irwin meeting. On 4th February, 1931. Mahatma Gandhi wrote to Lord Irwin seeking an interview and the Viceroy agreed to it. Mahatma Gandhi and Irwin met six times and after the prolonged deleberations a Pact was signed on March 5, 1931 between the two.

Text of The Gandhi-Irwin Pact—The following is the text of Gandhi-Irwin Agreement on March 5, 1931—

1. Consequent on the conversations that have taken place between His Excellency the Viceroy and Mr. Gandhi, it has been arranged that the civil disobedience movement be discontinued, and that with the approval of His Majesty's Government of Indian and Local Governments.

2. As regards constitutional questions the scope of future discussion is stated, with the assent of His Majesty's Government, to be with the object of considering further the scheme for the constitutional Government of India discussed at the Round Table Conference. Of the scheme there outlined, Federation is essential Part, so also are Indian responsibility and reservations or safeguards in the interests of India, for such matters as, for instance, defence, external affairs, the position of minorities, the financial credit fo India, and the discharge of obligations.

3. In pursuance of the statement made by the Prime Minister in his announcement of 19th Jan. 1931, steps will be taken for the participation of the representatives of the Congress in the further discussion that are to take place on the scheme of constitutional reform.

4. The settlement relates to activities directly connected with the civil disobedience movement.

5. Civil disobedience will be effectively discontinued and reciprocal action will be taken by government. The effective discontinuance of the civil disobedience movement means the effective discontinuance of all activities in furtherance thereof, by whatever methods pursued and, in particular, the following:—

(*a*) The organised definance of the provision of any law;

(*b*) The movement for non-payment of land revenue and other legal dues;

(*c*) The publication of news-sheets in support of disobedience movement;

(*d*) Attempts to influence civil and militar servant or village officials against Government or to pursuade them to resign their posts.

6. As regards the boycott of foreign goods, there are two issues involed, firstly, the character of boycott and secondly, the methods employed in giving effect to it. The position of the government is as follows. They approve of the encouragement of Indian industries as part of the economic and industrial movement designed to improve the material conditions of India, and they have no desire to discourage methods of propaganda, persuasion or advertisement pursued with this objection in view, which do not interfere with the freedom of action of individuals, or are not prejudicial to the maintenance of law and order.................It is therefore, agreed that the discontinuance of civil disobedience movement connotes the definite discontinuance of employment of the boycott of British commodities as a political weapon and that in consequence, those who have given up, during a time of political excitement, the sale or purchase of British goods must be left free without any form of restrain to change their attitude if they so desire.

7. Mr. Gandhi has drawn the attention of Government to specific allegations against the conduct of the police and represented the desirability of a public enquiry into them. In present circumstances government see greatdifficulty in this course and feel that it must inevitably lead to charge and counter

charges, and so mitigate against the re-establishment of peace. Having regard to these considerations. Mr. Gandhi agreed not to press the matter.

In return Gandhiji agreed to stop Civil Disobedience Movement and to participate in the next Round Table Conference. He, however, made concession on the basic constitutional issue; he agreed that in the future scheme of Indian Government, "federation is an essential part; so also are responsibility and reservation of safeguard in the interest of India, for such matters as far as instance, defence, external affairs, the position of minorities, the financial credit of India, the discharge of obligation."

Reaction to Gandhi-Irwin Pact. The Pact concluded between Gandhi and Irwin got a mixed reception. The left-wing in the Congress did not feel satisfied. Sri Subhas and Jawaharlal Nehru argued that the safeguards agreed upon by the Congress were undesirable. These meant that on various matters of vital importance the ultimate power would rest not with the Indians but the Governor-General. Mr. K. M. Munshi hailed the Pact as an important landmark in the constitutional history of India. The Indian youths were also disgusted with Gandhiji who signed the Pact without securing pardon or at least the commutation of death sentence into life imprisonment in the case of Bhagat Singh. The next session of the Congress was held against this gloomy background at Karachi on 25th March, 1931, that is, only two days after the execution of Bhagat Singh and his comrades. Full-blooded youths of India, in the heat of disgust, greeted Gandhiji with black flags and slogans like "Down with Gandhi." Gandhiji had a hot time at the Karachi session in getting the Pact approved by the delegates.

Gloomy Karachi Session—Many persons in the country criticised the pact. Mr. Subhash Chandra Bose denounced it out rightly Even Pt. Jawaharlal Nehru was tremendously shocked to read the reservations and safeguards. The agreement was also condemned on the ground that Mahatma Gandhi could not have the execution of Sardar Bahgat Singh and his comrades. There was a black flag demonstration when Gandhiji went to attend to Karachi Session of Congress. He was greeted with slogans "Down with Gandhiji", "Gandhiji truce has sent Bhagat Singh to the gollows." In the Karachi Session on 25th March, 1931, many youths of the country openly criticised the pact before Gandhi. Gandhiji's tasteful and pathetic speech averted his defeat at the said session. His sentimental appeal induced the younger blood of the Congress to ratify the pact and thus paved way for the participation of the Congress in Second Round Table Conference which opened on September 7, 1931.

THE SECOND ROUND TABLE CONFERENCE (SEPTEMBER 7, 1931)

Change in political situation—Before the Second Round Table Conference, a significant change took place in the political scene of Britain. The Labour Government tumbled down. Macdonald remained the Prime Minister but he was the Head of the National Government, which was a coalition of Liberal and Conservative parties. Sir Samuel Hoare a firm Tory, became the Secretary of State and Viceroy Lord Irwin was replaced by Lord Willington as the Viceroy of India. This was a great shock to Indian leaders. Gandhiji sent his refusal to attend the Round Table Conference. Ultimately an interview was arranged between Viceroy and Gandhiji at Simla, which resulted in the agreement of Gandhiji to attend the conference. He sailed on 29th August, 1931 and reached London on 12th September.

Mahatma Gandhi in London. Gandhiji attended the Conference as the sole representative of the Congress. Other members of the delegation were Pt. Madan Mohan Malaviya, Sarojini Naidu, nominated by the Viceroy in their individual capacity. In fact Gandhiji wanted that the Viceroy should also nominate Dr. Ansari to join the Conference as Congress delegate. The Viceroy, however, refused to nominate a Muslim as Congress delegate simply because the Musims were not agreeable to it. Gandhiji in England was a picturesque figure. With *chappals*, *chaddar* and loin cloth, he attracted a big crowd around him.

Gandhiji's Stand—Gandhiji's opening speech created a great impression upon the delegates of the conference. He said, "If we are intent upon complete independence it is not from any sense of arrogance; it is not because we want to parade before the universe that we have now served all connection with the British people. Nothing of kind....I still aspire to be a citizen, not to be a citizen, not in the Empire, but in a commonwealth; in a partnership if possible government immediately. The delegates of minorities pleaded for the separate electorates but Gandhiji openly said that the question at framing a constitution should have precedence over the communal problem. The minorities claimed that it was the precondition of every thing else. This communal issue finally adjourned the conference and the Prime Minister closed the session of December 11, 1931.

In fact all the proceedings of the conference were rather empty. *Pt. Jawaharlal Nehru* in his autography has written : "The scales were terribly loaded against us to that conference..... we saw the pitiful and absurdly inadequate attempts to scrach the surface of national and economic problems, the pacts and intrigues and monocurves the joining of hands of some of our own countrymen with the most reactionary element of the British Conservative Party, the endless talk over petty issues, the deliberate shelving of all that really mattered, the continuous playing into the hands of the big vested interests and especially "British imperialism, the mutual squabbles, varied by feasting and natural administration. It was all jobbery. . . . different groups seemed to grown about like hungry wolves waiting for their petty—the spoils under the constitution. . . . No one thought in terms of independence. . . . of the solution of any of the vital and urgent economic problems facing the Indian people. . . . In that crowded and gilded Hall, Gandhiji sat. . . . with amazing patience. He carried on and made attempt after attempt to find some basis of agreement."

Gandhi was lonely voice and sole representative for the national interest but had to come back to India empty handed with great disgust. According to R. C. Majumdar, "Gandhiji's presence and lofty idealism created a great sensation, but his pious platitudes cut notice with this British people or Government. Certainly it is that his speeches personality and appeals did not influence the deliberation and decision of the Conference in the slightest degree."

Complicated Communal Problem—Gandhiji at the plenary session pressed his demand for complete independence in very clear words. He as the spokesman of the Congress and the Indian masses demanded full responsible Government at the Centre. He also demanded the undivided control of the Indians on the defence. The British Government, however, agreed to meet halfway by offering a partly responsible Government at the centre. The discussion was then stuck up on the communal problem. The delegates representing the minorities put forth their exaggerated demands for concessions and privileges. In fact the very composition of the delegation was such as made any agreement on communal problem nearly impossible. The British Government played off the Muslim League against the Congress. The unholy alliance between the Muslims and the ruling class served the designs of the Government to the bitter extreme. The natural result was that Gandhiji failed to evolve any point of agreement among the delegates. He returned to India empty-handed and much disappointed. The Conference closed on 1st December, 1931.

RESUMPTION OF CIVIL DISOBEDIENCE MOVEMENT (1932-34)

Several issues relating to structure of Federal juderal judiciary, composition of Federal legislature and the question of the Indian States joining the Federation were settled at the Conference. Only the communal problem of India was left unresolved. It was left as such to be decided by the British Prime Minister. Gandhiji returned to India with a bundle of complaints. Two issues had upset him most. The first was that the Harijan leaders treated the Harijans as a class separate from the Hindus. The second was the uncompromising attitude of the Muslims who played into the British hands.

Repressive Policy of Lord Willingdon—The political scene in India was in no way less acute and agitated than the failure of London talks. In the absence of Gandhiji, the Viceroy resorted to repression as a matter of policy. He believed not in settlement with but suppression of the Congress. He violated the Gandhi-Irwin Pact. The Conservative Party which was in office in England also favoured a stern attitude towards Indians and particularly the Congress. The Government held the Congress guilty of instigating the peasants of U. P. to refuse to pay land revenue and also inciting the Red Shirts to start Civil. Disobedience Movement under the leadership of Khan Abdul Ghaffar Khan. To this, the Congress replied with a countercharge. It said that the Government was violating the agreement concluded with Gandhiji.

Repression all over the country went in full swing. Pt. Jawaharlal Nehru was arrested for starting no-rent campaign in U.P. Khan Abdul Ghaffar Khan and his brother Khan Sahib were also arrested in North West Frontier Province. Bengal, U.P. and North West Frontier Province were brought under the heels of Ordinances. In Bengal the people were almost subjected to state of martial law. Gandhiji sought an interview with the Viceroy to apprise him of the public resentment against his 'rule by force' but the later curtly refused to meet him.

Civil Disobedience Campaign and Repression. When the Government showed no readliness to change its attitude, the Congress Working Committee decided to restart the movement. On 3rd January, 1932, Gandhiji called upon the Nation to be ready for another trial. He communicated his decision to the Viceroy also. The Government on the very next day issued four ordinances and assumed very wide powers to deal with the agitation. It was followed by the arrest of Mahatama Gandhi and Sardar Vallabh Bhai Patel, the President of the Congress. The Congress itself was declared unlawful. The police was authorised to arrest any person even on suspicion. All the Congress workers were put behind the bars. Even the sympathisers were not spared. Government confiscated the property of the Congressmen. The police also organised raids on Congress offices and seized all papers and documents. In short the Viceroy started on the mad and futile course of wiping out the Congress within six weeks.

The Congress this time was actually less prepared than on the former occasions. It was in a way compelled to start the movement because of regular pin-pricking and provocations by the Government. Moreover, mass arrrest of the leaders and workers left agitators without any guide. In spite of all the handicaps, the people gave a tough fight and foiled the attempt of the Viceroy to nip the Congress for ever. With waning intensity, the movement continued for six months. More than 1,20,000 persons went to jail.

On May 8, 1933, Gandhiji commenced his 21-day fast to atone for the sins of caste-Hindus against the untouchables. It was also a fight against the official attempt to dismember the Hindu community by treating the Harijans as a separate community. His fast had the desired effect. It suceeded in revolutionising the outlook of the people. A mass movement was started to win over the hearts of the Harijans. What induced Gandhiji to undertake the fast unto death was the 'Award' of Ramsay Macdonald whereby the untouchables were offered not-only separate electorate but also additional votes. This was a subtle mischief to widen the gulf between the caste Hindus and the untouchables.

Suspension of Movement—On 14th July, 1933, Mahatma Gandhi called off mass satyagraha but allowed the people to court arrest individually. The enthusiasm of the people was already waning and violence was on the increase. On wise considerations, Gandhiji withdrew the movement completely on 7th April 1934. Pt. Jawaharlal Nehru, Subhas Chandra Bose and B. G. Patel, however, did not approve this uncalled-for and arbitrary decision of Gandhiji.

COMMUNAL AWARD OF RAMSAY MCDONALD AND POONA PACT, (16TH AUGUST, 1932)

Mr. McDonald in his closing speech at the Conference had clearly stated that the British Government would be compelled to impose its own decision if the various communities failed to chalk out a formula, agreeable to all of them. Since the delegates at the London Conference could not offer a solution, Mr. McDonald announced his decision known as Communal Award on 16th August, 1932. Alongwith it he also declared that he would be glad to accept any other solution of the communal problem provided it satisfied all the communities.

Principal features of the Communal Award were the following:—

(1) The scope of the Award was confined to allocating seats to various communities in the Provincial Legislatures only. It said nothing about the seats in the Central Legislature.

(2) The Award accepted the demand of the Muslims, Sikhs, Indian Christians, Anglo-Indians and women for separate electorate.

(3) Labour, commerce, industry, landlords and universities were given separate constituencies and fixed seats. it also suggested the formation of general constituencies in which all persons other than Muslims, Sikhs, Anglo-Indians or Europeans were entitled to vote.

(4) Harijans were recognised as a minority, Separate seats were allotted to them. They exercised two votes each, one in the general constituency and the other in special contituencies as mentioned above. This was deliberately done to alienate Harijans from the Hindus.

(5) Hindus in Muslim-majority Provinces were not given the same concessions as were enjoyed by the Muslims in Hindu-Provinces. In Bengal and the Punjab, for instance, the Hindus were in minority. They were given rather fewer seats than their population warranted whereas Muslims in all the Provinces were given weighty representation.

(6) Sikhs in the Punjab and Europeans in Bengal were also given disproportionate representation in the legislature. This favour was shown to them at the expense of the Hindus.

Criticism of Communal Award—The Communal Award evoked a good deal of flutter and resentment in the country. It was criticised for the following reasons:—

(1) The Award was a mischievous attempt to divide and weaken the Hindus by separating the Harijans.

(2) The Award was unjust to the Hindus and partial to the Muslims.

(3) The underlying motive of the Award was to split the Indian people into small and mutually hostile sections. It was a direct hit on national solidarity. It not only retained communal electorate but also extended it. The Award made further divisions on the basis of religion, occupation and loyalty to the Government.

(4) Europeans who were only 0.1 per cent of the total population were given 10 per cent of the total seats.

(5) The award provided for separate representation even in the case of Indian Christians and women who had not made any demand of that nature.

(6) The Award was opposed to the spirit of democracy. It encouraged separation and religious ill-will. It gave birth to the idea of Pakistãn, the natural and painful result of which was the partition of the country.

(7) The Communal Award was an annachronism. It had no historical basis. In no country was the principle of separate electorate and representation eyer accepted on the basis of religion, sex or caste.

Gandhiji's Fast and Poona Pact, September, 1932—The Award of Mr. Macdonald came as a great shock to Gandhiji. His heart bled and revolted at the sight of Harijans gradually drifting away from the Hindu community. He communicated to Macdonald that he would begin his fast to death if the decision was not reversed. The Government slept over the ultimatum. Hence, on 20th September, 1932, Gandhiji began his fast. Dr. Bhim Rao Ambedkar called it Mahatma Gandhi's political stunt.

Others criticised Gandhiji for coercing the Government to come round to his viewpoint. The fast, however, had a salutary effect on the Hindu leaders who realised the necessity of earning the goodwill of untouchables. Secondly, it set the whole country in a flutter. Leaders both in India and England became active to prevent Gandiji from continuing that fateful fast. Pt. Madan Mohan Malaviya, Dr. Rajendra Prasad, Birla and Mrs.Sarojini Naidu initiated talks with MC. Raja and Dr. Bhim Rao Ambedkar, the leaders of the Depressed Classes. On the fifth day of the fast the leaders agreed on a formula. This settlement was called the Poona Pact and was signed by both parties on 26th September. The same day Gandhiji broke his fast. The fact was latter on ratified by Hindu Mahasabha and also accepted by the British Government.

Terms of Poona Pact—(1) Under the Poona Pact it was agreed upon by Gandhiji and Bhim Rao Ambedkar to retain joint electorate but the number of reserved seats for the scheduled classes as fixed by the Award in the Provincial Legislatures was doubled. As many as 148 seats were reserved for them against 71 allotted by the Award.

(2) All the members of the Depressed Classes registered in the general electoral roll in a constituency formed an electoral college. This small body was to elect a panel of four candidates for each of the reserved seats by the method of single transferable vote. One of these candidates was to be elected for the reserved seats by the joint electorate.

(3) Nearly 20 per cent of seats were reserved for the Harijans in the Central Legislature.

(4) Adequate representation was given to Harijans in Local Bodies and Public Services.

(5) Financial aid was promised to promote literacy among the Harijans.

THIRD ROUND TABLE CONFERENCE (17TH NOVEMBER TO 24TH DECEMBER, 1932)

Sir Samuel Hoare, the Secretary of State for India, was a perfect snob. He had deep-rooted contempt for Indians. The very idea of sitting along with Indian delegates for deliberation was revolting to him. His intention was to invite only a few Indians to put their case before a Committee of Parliament which was to draw the future constitution of India. With much reluctance, however, he agreed to call the Third R.T.C. which met from 17th November to 24th December, 1932. Only 46 delegates were invited this time as against 88 on the first occasion. The choice of Indian delegates was limited only to those persons who were loyal to the Government. Congress participation in the Conference was out of question. The Civil Disobedience Movement had been revived and the Government was busy in putting it down with an iron hand. Even the Hindu Mahasabha was not represented at the Conference. The British Labour Party also withdrew because its nominees were not acceptable to the British Government. Thus the Third R. T. C. was a body of only sycophants or 'yesmen' of the Government.

The Reports of various sub-committees appointed during the Second R. T. C. formed the basis of discussion. These problems received attention at the Conference. These were safeguards, the terms under which the States were to join the Federation and the distribution of residuary powers. Most of the recommendations, made by the Conference, were given place to in the Government of India Act, 1935. The Indian delegation at one stage suggested that the new Constitution might also include a Bill of Rights. But this suggestion was turned down by the British authorities.

White Paper, March, 1933—In March 1933, the British Government published a White Paper which indicated the lines on which the new Act of 1935 was to be made. This Paper was prepared on the basis of the discussions and decisions taken during the three Round Table Conferences. This Paper was so reactionary in character that the Congress and other progressive elements in India rejected in outright. It was most disappointing because it did not propose any curtailment in the powers of the Governor-General or the British Parliament over Indian affairs. In view of general discontentment, the Government submitted the proposals to a joint select committee of the Parliament to discuss it thoroughly. The committee met under Lord Linlithgow. It sat for eighteen months at the end of which it published its report on 11th November, 1934.

The Committee which had a clear majority of Conservative members of the Parliament made the White Paper still worse. Instead of being more lenient to and sympathetic with the Indian people, it withdrew what few concessions had been proposed in white Paper. Federal Assembly, for instance, as suggested in the White Paper was to have direct election. The joint committee rejected this democratic method and proposed the method of indirect election. Thus, the Report did more harm than good from Indian point of view, the net result of three Round Table Conference, White Paper and Joint Committee's report was the Government of India Act, 1935, which we shall discuss in the 18th chapter.

EXERCISES

Long Answer Type Questions

1. Give an account of the Civil Disobedience Movement (1930-31) and the historic Dandi March.
2. Describe the circumstances which led to the convention of the first and second round table conferences. Make a critical assessment of its achievement.
3. Discuss the circumstances which led to Civil Disobedience Movement.
4. Write a brief note on the Third Round Table Conference.

Short Answer Type Questions

1. Write Short notes on the following —
   (*a*) Simon Comission
   (*b*) Nehru Report
   (*c*) Mr. Mohammad Ali Jinnah's 14 points programme.
   (*d*) Irwin's Declaration
   (*e*) Declaration of Complete Independence.

Objective Type Questions

Choose the correct answer

1. Which act contained the Provision for the appointment of a statutory Commission ?
   (*a*) The Government of India Act, 1919
   (*b*) The Indian Councils Act, 1909
   (*c*) The Indian Councils Act, 1892
   (*d*) The Indian Councils Act, 1861
2. In which year Sir John Simmon Commission was appointed ?
   (*a*) 1926 (*b*) 1927
   (*c*) 1928 (*d*) 1929
3. Who was the President of the Satutory Commission ?
   (*a*) Lord Burnham (*b*) Mr. Attlee
   (*c*) Sir John Simmon (*d*) Lord Stratchcona

4. How many members were in the Commission ?

(*a*) 4 (*b*) 5

(*c*) 6 (*d*) 7

5. In which year the Simmon Commission came in India ?

(*a*) 1928 (*b*) 1929

(*c*) 1930 (*d*) 1931

6. In Bombay, on February 3, 1929 police fired on the Indians. In the same period Lahore saw the death of one of the greatest sons of motherland due to frutal lathi charge by the police. Who was that greatest son ?

(*a*) Bal Gangadhar Tilak (*b*) Lala Lajpat Rai

(*c*) Pt. Jawaharlal Nehru (*d*) Pt. Govind Ballabh Pant.

7. In which year Simmon Commission submitted its report ?

(*a*) 1928 (*b*) 1929

(*c*) 1930 (*d*) 1931

ANSWERS

1. (*a*) 2. (*b*) 3. (*c*) 4. (*d*) 5. (*a*) 6. (*b*) 7. (*c*)

CHAPTER 17

Socialist and Communist Trends in National Movement

G. Kotosky, a Russian historian writes :

"The intensive plunder of India during the First World War when Britain shifted most of the military expenditures on her principal colony, had dire consequences for the mass of the people.

"The decline of exports of jute, cotton, oil-bearing seed, and other technical crops due to the war-time dislocation of world economic relations, affected the interests of farmers. Landlords and the merchant class tried to cover their losses by intensifying the exploitation of peasants—the immediate producers. Between 1911 to 1925 the peasants' debt to money-lenders doubled, reaching an estimated total of 6,000 million rupees."[1]

The appearance on the labour market of hundreds of thousands of ruined craftsmen had a negative effect on the position of the industrial proletariat whose real wages sank in value as prices gradually rose.

The intensification of the National Liberation Struggle began with the new actions on the part of the working class. In 1918 a series of strikes on a fairly large scale for those times took place in Bombay, Madras, Kanpur and Ahmedabad. These were strikes of a spontaneous, economic character resulting to a large extent from mass dismissals of workers after war-time production was wound up. The first trade union was set up in Bombay and other industrial centres, including Ahmedabad, where in the same year the Ahmedabad Mill Mazdur Union was set up with the participation of Mohandas Karam chand Gandhi. The wave of revolutionary sentiments in the country gained new momentum from information concerning the revolution in Russia which was starting gradually to reach India.[2]

IMPACT OF THE RUSSIAN REVOLUTION

Socialist Revolution in Russia broke out on 7th November, 1917 (24th October according to the old defective calendar of Czar rulers of Russia) under the leadership of Lenin. Lenin adopted on November 15, 1917 famous Declaration of the Rights of the People of Russia and an appeal was also issued by the Council of People's Commissars (Council of Ministers) entitled *To All Muslim Toilers*

1. *A. History of India,* Vol. II, p. 153 (1979), Progress Publishers, Moscow.
2. *Ibid.*

in Russia and the East. Both the things were published in the Indian newspapers. The left wing of the National Movement saw the October Revolution as an epoch-making social change. One section of the Indian intelligentsia felt spell-bound by the Bolshevik Revolution which led to the fall of Czars of Russia. Many a Congressman saw in Lenin and other Bolshevik leaders great champions of freedom, who appeared to possess remarkable skill for organising and utilising the lower class masses for the seizure of political power to the benefit of all oppressed. Two most famous books of Lenin '*On Imperialism*' and '*State and Revolution*' exercised profound influence upon many Left wing leaders of the Congress. Lenin's very clear analysis of Imperialism gave them insight into the working of British Imperialism in India. Now they found Russian leader Lenin as naturally in their fight against British Imperialism. In the last analysis Lenin's proverbial saying that British Imperialism would meet its doom not on the banks of the Thames but on those of the Ganges and Yangtse—came out as thrilling declaration for the Left-wing Congress leaders.[1]

Moreover, another important communist leader Linoviev declared at the Congress of the Eastern People at Baku : WE ARE READY TO HELP ANY REVOLUTIONARY STRUGGLE AGAINST THE ENGLISH GOVERNMENT...OUR TASK IS TO KINDLE A REAL HOLY WAR AGAINST THE ENGLISH AND FRENCH CAPITALISTS."[2]

After listing Britain's misdeeds and cruelties the manifesto of the Eastern People at Baku gives a call to rise as one man for the holy war against the English conquerors Rise all of you against the common enemy, Imperialist England.[3]

Influence on Lala Lajpat Rai. Lala Lajpat Rai and other radical Congress leaders were much influenced by Soviet Russia's anti-imperialist policies. The Soviet Union thus became their hope. The fact came to light when Lala Lajpat Rai delivered his Presidential address to the First All-India Trade Union Congress in November, 1920. After referring to the fact that the truth in Europe was of two kinds : (*a*) Capitalistic and Govermmental truth represented by persons like Winston Churchill and the papers like the *London Times and the Morning Post;* (*b*) Socialistic and labour truth represented by the labour organs like the *Justice*, *Daily Herald* and *Soviet Russia*. Lala Lajpat Rai said :

"The Government of India wants us to swallow the first kind of truth without knowing the other side. Unfortunately for us truth is no longer truth. It is qualified by capitalism and imperialism on the one hand and socialism on the other...My own experience of Europe and America leads me to think that socialistic, even Bolshevik, truth is any day better, than the capitalistic and imperial truth.[4]

Influence on Pandit Jawaharlal Nehru. Above all Pandit Jawaharlal Nehru was much influenced by the achievements of Russia, though he had also some reservations about the Bolshevik ideal. Welcoming the Soviet Development even as late as 1946 in an article published in *Asia in the Americas*, the Russians were not a new people yet, "there has been a complete break from the old like that of death and they have been reincarnated."[5]

The Jallianwala Bagh Massacre and the non-fulfilment of the promise given by British Prime Minister Lloyd George to the Muslims regarding the Khilafat of Turkey and the worst treatment meted out to her, led to the Non-co-operation Movement in December, 1920. Refering to the unity

1. Referring to this gigantic struggle of human emancipation, Lenin had written on 2nd March, 1923 in *Pravada*: "In the last analysis, the outcome of the struggle will be determined by the fact that Russia, India and China etc. account for the overwhelming majority of the population of the globe. And it is precisely this majority that during the past few years, has been drawn into struggle for emancipation with extraordinary rapidity so that in this respect here cannot be the slightest shadow of doubt what the final outcome of the struggle will be." (V.I. Lenin, *The National Liberation Movement in the East* (Moscow, 1957, p 135).

2. Jane Degras, ed. by The Communist International, 1919-1943 : Documents (Oxford University Press, 1956), Vol. I, p. 105.

3. *Ibid.*

4. Lajpat Rai, *India's Will to Freedom* (Madras, 1936) pp. 76-77.

5. 'Remarks quoted by "*The Hidu*" (Madras), 5th February, 1946, p. 3, Col. 3.

of these two currents, Pandit Jawaharlal Nehru on the occasion of his first visit to the Soviet Union after independence, said :

"Nearly simultaneously with the October Revolution guided by the great Lenin, we in India entered a new stage of our struggle for freedom. Our people had been in the course of many years engrossed in this struggle and endured the grim oppression with courage and patience. Although under the leadership of Mahatma Gandhi we waged our struggle along different path, we admired Lenin and we were influenced by his example."[1]

Bal Gangadhar Tilak defends Lenin against the slanderous attacks on him in the British Press. Lokmanya Bal Gangadhar Tilak published an editorial in his newspaper *Kesari* (January 29, 1918) defending Lenin against the slanderous attacks on him in the British Press and pointing out that "Lenin's influence in the army and among the common people has increased as a result of the distribution of the lands of the nobility to the peasantry...."

Raja Mahendra Pratap and his associates meet Lenin on May 7, 1919 and narrate the British atrocities in Jallianwala Bagh. Lenin condemns them in an article in Amrit Bazar Patrika, Calcutta. After the October Revolution, 1917 the Indian underground revolutionaries began to establish direct contact with Soviet Russia as their natural ally against imperialism. After the end of 1917 at a meeting of the Muslim Nationalists in Delhi a message hailing the Russian Revolution was adopted and it was printed in some illegal Indian Publications. The Khairi Brothers—Sattar and Jabbar—were sent to Moscow to deliver the message of greeting to the Soviet Government.

In March 1918 the President of the Provincial Government of India (Kabul) Rajá Mahendra Pratap arrived in Petrograd. On this occasion a political meeting was presided over by Lunacharsky. The occasion was described as unforgettable and magnificent in the memoirs published by the Raja. On May 7, 1919 a delegation of Indian Revolutionaries led by Raja Mahendra Pratap Singh met Lenin in Moscow and narrated the horrifying tale of Jallianwala Bagh Massacre. Lenin was greatly moved and he wrote a very strong letter denouncing British Imperialism which was printed in *Amrit Bazar Patrika*, Calcutta and utmost sympathy was expressed for the families of the bereaved.[2] After this many meetings took place between Lenin and Indian Revolutionaries from time to time. Lenin took keen interest in the National Struggle of India which he regarded as an important component of the world's struggle against the imperialists.

Thus, the victory of the October Revolution promoted a considerable expansion of the international ties established by the Indian Liberation Movement and introduced in them a qualitatively new element—an alliance between the world's first socialist state and the National Liberation Struggle of the people of the East. Opening a session of the Indian National Congress in 1917, Annie Besant announced that the Russian Revolution and the probable rise of a Russian Republic in Europe and Asia, have all entirely changed the conditions existing before in India." The various organisations fighting for the liberation of the country drew this lession from Russian Revolution that to make the Liberation Struggle sucessful, the masses must be involved in it. So on the whole though many leaders welcomed the Russian Revolution but they did not approve of its socio-political programme.

Third International, Lenin and M.N. Roy. Third International was the leading international organisation of the world communist parties and movements. It had been organised by Lenin. Its first meeting was held in Moscow from 2nd March to 6th March, 1919. M.N. Roy, the greatest intellectual of the left movement in India had also been invited to this meeting by Lenin. He had written a book *India in Transition* at a time when Gandhiji's Non-Co-operation Movement was at its climax. This book was the first attempt to judge that movement in perspective of historical

1. "*Tributes to Lenin by leading Indians*" Anand Gupta, ed., India and Lenin, a collection of writings on and by Lenin (New Delhi, New Literature, 960), p. 50.
2. *Documents of the History of Communist Party of India,* Vol. I, People's Publishing House, New Delhi, 1971, p. 18.

materialism. Advancing his study fo socio-political development and particularly of the movement led by Gandhiji, Roy held that those who were genuinely interested in national emancipation, should not collaborate with the Movement of Non-co-operation because it served the interests of the national bourgeoisie.

Lenin and Stalin totally differed with M.N. Roy. Lenin believed that *bourgeoisie* nationalism of every oppressed nation had a general democratic content which was directed against oppression, and it was this content that the communists supported unconditionally.[1]

Similarly in his conversation with M.N. Roy at about this time, Stalin too stressed on the importance of the national movement. He held that as long as the natiionalist *bourgeoisie* led an anti-imperialist movement, they played an objectively revolutionary role, and therefore must be assisted. Not only the Nationalist bourgeoisie in less backward colonial counries like India and China, but even the feudal lords, ulemas and mullas in the Islamic countries must be helped. That was an elementary principle of world revolution.[2]

Lenin warmed him not to paint nationalism red.[3] He called him to think more about the ways and means to carry forward the masses under Gandhian leadership than to bother about Gandhiji's philosophy.

ESTABLISHMENT OF THE COMMUNIST PARTY OF INDIA

The Communist Party of India had been established for the first time in Tashkent (Russia) by Mr. M.N. Roy on 17th October, 1920 and Calcutta, Bombay, Madras and Lahore groups had been affiliated to it but technically the Communist Party of India was established on December 27, 1925 because Satyabhakt's Communist Party's name was changed to CPI (Communist Party of India). Mr. Amritpad Dange and Muzzaffar Ahmad were its important leaders.

Besides this Peasants' and Workers' Party was established on 1st November, 1925. Its main aim was to work with the C.P.I. for the overthrow of British Imperialism.

EMERGENCE OF SOCIALIST GROUP WITHIN THE CONGRESS

Jawaharlal Nehru along with his father Pandit Moti Lal Nehru visited Soviet Union in 1927 and was greatly impressed by her achievements. After sometime Pandit Motilal Nehru embarked on a wide scale work to set up branches of the League in India itself.

Madras session of Congress, 1927 declared the goal of the congress as Complete Independence. The Madras Session (1927) of the Congress was presided over by Dr. Ansari. This session was significant, as it not only reflected public opinion accurately and giving a vigorous lead to the country in connection with the unwanted Simon Commission but in variety of other ways. It was here that for the first time a definite shape was given to the national aspirations. The goal of the Congress was defined in a resolution to this effect. "This Congress declares the goal of the Indian people to be complete independence." To the formulation of this resolution, Pandit Jawaharlal Nehru's presence and advocacy gave an added impetus. Even Dr. Annie Beasant found nothing to object in it. Gandhi was absent at that time. He heard it later. What his reaction would have been if he had been present, it is hard to imagine.

It is also notable that Pandit Jawaharlal Nehru and Subhas Chandra Bose were also elected Congress Secretaries in that session. After the Madras Congress, during the year 1928, three events of outstanding importance occurred and have to be recorded, not merely because they have a chronological value but because their impact has a national significance. The first of them was the

1. V.I. Lenin, Selected Works (Moscow, Foreign Languages Publishing House, 1952) Pt. 2, p. 337
2. M.N. Roy's Memoirs (Allied Publishers, 1964) p. 527
3. *Ibid*

complete boycott of the Simon Commission, the second was the appointment of a committee by an All-Parties Conference under the chairmanship of Pandit Motilal Nehru for drafting a constitution for India, and the third was the Bardoli Satyagraha which was a triumph for the principles of Gandhiji.

The All Parties Conference held its meeting in Lucknow (Lakhnau) from 28th to 31st August, 1928. It recommended Dominion Status for India. The Congress had declared its goal as Complete Independence in Madras Session, so the younger section of the Congress led by Pandit Jawaharlal Nehru did not approve the report and organised an Independence League and carried on an active propaganda in favour of independence.

Calcutta Congress whittles down the resolution on independence, Nehru and Subhas resign. The next Annual Session of the Congress was held at Calcutta on 22nd December, 1928 under the Presidentship of Pandit Motilal Nehru. In it the Congress accepted again the Dominion Status as its goal because it represented the All Parties view on the condition that it would be accepted by the British Government on or before 31st December, 1929. This was a sort of compromise between the views of Gandhiji and strong national sentiment in favour of complete independence.

But even though Gandhiji declared that he would join the movement for independence in case the ultimatum given by the Congress was rejected, his proposal was vigorously opposed by the younger section led by Pandit Jawaharlal Nehru and Subhas Chandra Bose. An amendment was moved by the latter to that effect that the Congress would be content with nothing short of independence. The Amendment was lost by 973 votes to 1350, but the large number of votes cast in opposition to veteran leaders like Gandhiji and Pandit Motilal Nehru showed the rising strength of the left wing of the Congress. After this Pandit Jawahar lal Nehru and Subhas Chandra Bose resigned from Congress Secretaryship.

ACHIEVEMENT OF THE SOCIALIST FORUM

Pandit Jawaharlal Nehru presides over the Indian National Congress in 1929 and demands complete independence or severance of links from the British Empire. The Congress met at Lahore on 29th December, 1929 in a very tense atmosphere because the political workers were being arrested by the British Government indiscriminately. There was intense fervour throughout the country over the impending declaration of Independence. Pandit Jawaharlal Nehru, an embodiment of youthful ardour and indomitable enthusiasm was elected as President, so it lend a special glamour to the vast concourse assembled at the Congress pandal.

The Resolution of Complete Independence was passed on 31st December, 1929 at midnight (after 12 P.M) as that was the hour when the date and time of Congress ultimatum to the British Government for the acceptance of Dominion Status expired.

The Congress Resolution declared that the word 'Swaraj' in Article 1 of the Congress Constitution would mean *complete independence* and further declared the entire scheme of the Nehru Committee's report to have lapsed and hoped that all Congressmen would henceforth devote their exclusive attention to the attainment of complete Independence for India. The Congress also resolved upon complete boycott of the Central and Provincial Legislatures and Committees constituted by the Government and called upon the Congressmen and others taking part in the national movement to abstain from participating directly or indirectly in future elections, and directed the Congress members of the Legislatures and Committees to resign their seats. The Congress appealed to the nation zealously to prosecute the constructive programme of the Congress Committee whenever it deemed fit, to launch upon a programme of Civil Disobedience including non-payment of taxes, whether in selected areas or otherwise, and such safeguards as it might consider necessary.

Pandit Jawaharlal Nehru also declared that "Independence for us means complete freedom from British Dominion and *British Imperialism.* India could never be an equal member of the Commonwealth unless imperialism and all that it implies is discarded."

It was also decided that 26th of January should be observed all over India as the *Purna Swaraj* day (day of complete Independence). A declaration to that effect was prepared by Gandhiji which was to be read to the people in the villages and towns all over the country. The declaration began by emphasising the inalienable right of the Indians to enjoy freedom and then described "how the British Government has ruined India economically, politically, culturally and spiritually. Therefore, we solemnly resolve to carry out the Congress instructions issued from time to time for the purpose of establishing *Purna Swaraj*."

After this the Congress under the leadership of Mahatma Gandhi started Civil Disobedience Movement on 12th March, 1930 which has already been related.

MEERUT CONSPIRACY CASE : COMMUNIST LEADERS SENTENCED

The communists had organised strikes and demonstrations against the Simon Commission in 1928. Besides that they had demanded Complete Independence at the Congress Session in Madras (1927) and Calcutta (1928). Their avowed aim was to uproot the British empire from India.

There was a large number of strikes by the workers in 1928 which were organised by the communists. Over five lakh people took part in strikes. The first Trade Union, known as the *Girni Kamgar Union of Textile Workers of* Bombay was led by the President of the Communist Party, Amripad Dange. He was helped by Ben Bradley, a British Communist worker in India, who later became the core of the Left Trade Union Movement in the country.

The strike which began after a mass lockout at the Bombay Textile Factories lasted for a long period and involved all the textile workers of Bombay. Over 20 million working days were lost during six months (the strike lasted from April to October, 1928). This strike exerted considerable influence on the labour movement as a whole. At the conference of the All India Trade Union Congress in Jharia (Bengal) in 1928 resolutions were passed calling for the establishment of an independent socialist republic of India, in which land and industry would be nationalised. This move reflected the subtantial radicalisation of Trade Union Movement that had by this time taken place.

Repression and appointment of Wheatley Commission. In the meanwhile in Great Britain the Labour Party had formed the ministry with the help of Liberal Party. It adopted two fold policy of repression and reform. Thousands of workers had already been sacked. That policy was continued but at the same time it appointed Royal Commission under Wheatley to go into the question of strikes and make recommendation for workers' betterment so that they may be separated from the trade unionism of the communists. This commission could not do any thing as it was boycotted under the influence of the communists. Besides that, there was economic depression of 1929 which had started in 1928 and rendered thousands of workers jobless and discontent amongst them was fanned by the communists.

Under these circumstances the British Government in India decided to give a major blow at the left forces. The Government arrested 31 prominent leaders of the Communist Party on 20th March, 1929. They were brought to Meerut for trial, so the case was termed by the British as *Meerut Conspiracy Case.* The police searched many offices and hide-outs of the Communist Party and seized many secret documents which threw light on the plans, secret codes etc. of the communists. These, together with other evidences and testimony of the activity of the Communist Party in India.[1]

It should be noted that all the accused gained the sympathy of most of our countrymen due to their frank admission of anti-Imperialist designs and because the country was also yearing for the freedom. The team of lawyers which was constituted also included such prominent leaders as Pandit Jawaharlal Nehru and Kailash Nath Katju. Pandit JawaharLal Nehru looked upon the trial as "one phase of the offensive which the Government here has started against the Labour Movement." He added : "There is a lot of shouting about communists and communism in India, but it is equally certain

1. Massani, '*The Communist Party of India*', pp. 36 ff

that this way of communism is meant to cover a multitude of sins of the Government.[1] Mahatma Gandhi also visited the jail and offered encouragement to the prisoners.[2]

After a prolonged trial, 27 accused persons were found guilty and sentenced to various terms of imprisonment on 16th January, 1933. The High Court considerably reduced the sentences, and by 1935 all the accused were set free.

Effects of Meerut Conspiracy Case. The Meerut Conspiracy Case (named after the town in which the case was tried) which lasted for four years was made skilful use of by the communists as a tribune from which they denounced British colonial policy in India and also propagated the ideas of scientific socialism. Spratt, the British communist said: "On the whole the revelation of our secret methods caused people to admire us; we had done what most young men wanted to do...... We had our opportunity in the sessions court to make political statements, and these were widely published in the press. Several of them were long enough to make a short book and altogether no doubt most of what can be said in favour of communism was said.[3]

Saumyendra Nath Tagore observed that the Meerut Case "placed Communism on a sure footing in India."[4] Spratt agreed.[5]

SUBHAS CHANDRA BOSE AND SOCIALISM, CLASH WITH GANDHIJI

The fifty-first session of the Congress met at Vithalnagar, Haripur (Gujarat)on 12th February, 1938. The unanimous election of Subhas Bose, the leader of the radical party, as President of the Congress, was a distinct pointer to the growing influence of the younger section whose socialist creed was not in tune with the orthodox Congress views of which Gandhi was the most typical representative.

Cause of the rift between Subhas Chandra Bose and Mahatma Gandhi. Subhas Chandra Bose offers the following explanation of the breach between him and Mahatma Gandhi :

"As Congress President, the writer (Subhas Chandra Bose) did his best to stiffen the opposition of the Congress party to any compromise with Britain and this caused annoyance in Gandhian circles who were then looking forward to an understanding with the British Government. Later in the year 1938, he launched the National Planning Committee for drawing up a comprehensive plan of industrialization and of national development. This caused further annoyance to Mahatma Gandhi who was opposed to industrialisation.

"After the Munish Pact, in September 1938, the writer (Subhas Chandra Bose) began an open propaganda throughout India in order to prepare the Indian people for a national struggle, which should synchronise with the coming war in Europe. This move, though popular among the people in general was resented by the Gandhiites who did not want to be disturbed in their ministrial and parliamentary work and who at that time opposed to any national struggle.[6]

However, the fundamental difference between Subhas chandra Bose and Gandhi-Nehru group was in their attitude towards Britain. *Bose looked upon a war between Germany and Britain as a godsend which would enable India to exploit the situation to her advantage, for he followed the principle : England's necessity was India's opportunity.*

The already existing differences were widened by the insinuations of Subhas Chandra Bose that the members of Gandhiji's circle were not keen on carrying on the national struggle, and were looking forward to an understanding with the British Government presumably behind the back of the

1. G. D. Overstreet and Windmiller, *Communism in India*, p. 135
2. Lester Huchinson, *Conspiracy at Meerut*, p. 107 (Huchinson was one of the accused).
3. Spratt, *Blowing up India*, p. 53.
4. *Historical Documents of the Communist Movement in India*, p.21.
5. Overstreet and Windmiller, *Communism in India*, p. 137
6. Subhas Bose, *Indian Struggle*, pp. 331-332

declared policy of the Congress. Latter on, he particularly hinted that some leaders were hobnobbing with the British over the question of the Federation.[1] However, there is nothing to substantiate the charge. Gandhiji rightly complained that the allegations of Subhas regarding his colleagues were unjustified and unworthy.[2]

All these differences between the two leading personalities came to head over the election of the president for the next session of the Congress to be held at Tripuri (C.P.) between 10-12 March 1939. Gandhiji dissuaded Subhas from contesting the office but when he did not agree, then Gandhiji put up Pattabhi Sitaramayya, the official historian of the Congress and Gandhi put his whole weight in his nominee's favour during the contest. Nevertheless, Subhas Chandra Bose won by a margin of 95 votes which was attended by 2285 out 3319 delegates. Subhas Chandra Bose could not attend it due to illness. Subhas Chandra Bose after his election formed the Working Committee but later on 13 out of 15 members resigned and only Subhas Chandra Bose and his elder brother Sarat Chandra Bose remained on the Working Committee. They insisted that Subhas Chandra Bose might from the Working Committee according to the wishes of Gandhiji because he alone could lead the country to victory in the crisis that might develop. Subhas carried on the correspondence with Gandhiji but the latter did not give any name. Thereupon Subhas Chandra Bose resigned on 29th April, 1939 at the meeting of All India Congress Committee. Next day Dr. Rajendra Prasad was elected President of the Congress and he reappointed all the 12 members but Jawaharlal Nehru and Sarat Chandra Bose declined to serve on the committee.

After that Subhas Chandra Bose organised a new party of the Left Wing within the Congress known as Forward Bloc so that the entire left wing of the Congress might come under one banner.

Subhas Chandra Bose himself describes the genesis of the party : "In the absence of an organised and disciplined Left Wing, it was impossible for the writter (Subhas) to fight the Gandhi Wing. Consequently, India's primary political need in 1939 was an organised and disciplined Left Wing Party in the Congress.

Later on Subhas Chandra Bose carried on incessant struggle against the British which has been described in chapter IX. It resulted in the mutiny of navy, the end of British Imperialism and dawn of Independence.

So this great son of India who sacrificed everything for realising his cherished dream will always be remembered with the deepest gratitude by posterity as his contribution to the freedom struggle is unique.

EXERCISES

Long Answer Type Questions

1. Discuss the impact of Russian Revolution on National Movement.
2. What do you know about emergence of socialist group within the congress?
3. What were the achievements of the Socialist Forum? Discuss in brief.
4. What do you know about Meerut Conspiracy Case? Discuss its effect also.
5. What were the causes of the rift between Subhash Chandra Bose and Mahatma Gandhi? Discuss in brief.

Short Answer Type Questions

1. What was the influence of Russian Revolution ? Discuss in very brief on Lala Lajpat Rai.
2. What do you know about Third International? Discuss in very brief.

1. H.N. Das Gupta, *Subhash Chandra*, pp. 165 -166
2. Gandhiji's statement on 31st January, 1939

3. Write a very brief note on Madras Session of Congress, 1927.
4. Write a very brief note on effects of Meerut Conspiracy Case.

Objective Type Questions

Choose the correct answer

1. In which city the First Trade Union was setup ?
   (*a*) Bombay (*b*) Madras
   (*c*) Kanpur (*d*) Lucknow
2. Ahmedabad Mill Mazdoor Union was set up with the participation of
   (*a*) Bal Gangadhar Tilak (*b*) Mohandas Karamchand Gandhi
   (*c*) Lala Lajpat Rai (*d*) Mahendra Pratap
3. In which year Socialist Revolution broke out in Russia ?
   (*a*) 1915 (*b*) 1916
   (*c*) 1917 (*d*) 1918
4. Who was leader of Socialist Revolution in Russia ?
   (*a*) Breznev. (*b*) Czars of Russia
   (*c*) Lloyd George (*d*) Lenin
5. In which year a delegation of Indian Revolutionaries led by Raja Mahendra Pratap Singh met Lenin?
   (*a*) 1919 (*b*) 1920
   (*c*) 1921 (*d*) 1922

ANSWERS

1. (*a*) **2.** (*b*) **3.** (*c*) **4.** (*d*) **5.** (*a*)

18

CHAPTER

Central Government (Act of 1935)

"The Government of India Act, 1935, was a new charter of slavery."
—Jawaharlal Nehru

The Government of India Act, 1935, is regarded as the second milestone on the highway leading to full responsible government. This act was largely based on the recommendations of the Joint Parliamentary Select Committee which was appointed to examine the white Paper of March 1933. On the basis of these recommendations Sir Samuel Hoare, a Conservative Secretary of State for India drafted a Bill which was introduced in the House of Commons on 5 February, 1935.

The Bill faced Vehament criticism at the hands of the Labour Party and was finally possed by the House of Commons on 4 June, 1935. House of Lords passed the Bill in July 1935. The royal assent was accorded on 2 August, 1935.

SALIENT FEATURES OF THE ACT OF 1935

The Act of 1935 was quite a lengthy and detailed document. It consisted of 321 sections and 10 schedules. It partly came into operation in 1936 when the general elections in the country were held on the lines prescribed by it. It was fully enforced in April, 1937. The Act was largely disappointing because it did not hold out assurance about granting Dominion Status, nor did it consider sympathetically the feelings and urges of politically-conscious Indians. The new Constitution also said nothing regarding the fundamental rights of the people. It perpetuated the sovereignty of the British Parliament over India. In spite of the above mentioned drawbacks, the new Act had its own significance. It marked a second milestone on the road to full responsible Government, the first being the Act of 1919. The new glaring features of the Act were the suggestion to form a Federation consisting of the British India and the Indian States, autonomy in the Provinces and a partly responsible Government or Dyarchy at the Centre. We will now discuss the salient features of the Constitution in detail. The salient features of the Act of 1935 are as under —

1. Provincial Autonomy. One redeeming feature of the new Act was that it marked the beginning of the Provincial Autonomy. It was definitely an advance on the Act of 1919. The Provinces for the first time got a measure of Democratic Government. The system of Dyarchy or the division of subject into 'Transferred' and 'Reserved' was done away with. All the subjects were transferred to the charge of Ministers. The hold of the Centre over the Provincial subjects was also considerably reduced. This however, does not mean that the Act of 1935 established a full-fledged responsible Government in the Provinces. The Ministers were not absolutely free in the matter of running their departments. The Governors continued to possess a set of overriding powers although such powers were not exercised very often.

2. All-India Federation. The Act provided for an All-India Federation comprising the British Indian Provinces and the Indian States. The constituent units of the Federation were 11 Provinces, 6 Chief Commissioner's Provinces and all those States which agreed to join it. *The States were absolutely free to join or not to join the proposed Federation.* At the time of joining it, the ruler of that State was required to sign an Instrument of Accession, mentioning therein the extent to which it consented to surrender it authority to the Federal Government. The ruler was, however, authorised to extend the scope of Federal authority in respect of his State by executing another Instrument. Every unit enjoyed full autonomy in its internal affairs. The Act also provided for the setting up of a Federal Court to settle disputes between the Federal Government and units.

3. Dyarchy at the Centre. The Act of 1935 abolished Dyarchy at the provincial level and introduced it at the Centre. The Federal subjects were divided into two categories—the Reserved and the Transferred. The Reserved subject's list included *Defence, External affairs, Ecclesiastical affairs and Tribal areas.* These were to be administered by the Governor General with the help of three councillors to be appointed by him.

For the administration of Transferred subjects the Governor-General was to appoint a Council of Ministers whose number could not exceed ten. The Ministry was to consist of the persons who commanded the confidence of the legislature. By a Subsidiary Instrument of Instructions the Governor-General was also empowered to include in his Ministry the Representatives of the Indian States as well as the minority communities. The Ministry was collectively responsible to the Federal Legislature. *The Governor-General remained overall incharge of both the Reserved and Transferred subjects.* He was also responsible for the co-ordination of work between the two wings and for encouraging joint deliberation between the councillors and the Ministers.

4. Safeguards and Reservations. Another distinctive trait of the new Act was the *provision of elaborate safeguards and protective armours for the minorities.* The reason given for it was that the minorities needed protection from the dominance of the majority community. The nationalists, however, saw no sense in this argument. They knew that the so-called provisions in the Act relating to the safeguards were merely a trick to empower the Governor-General and the Governors to override the Ministers and Legislators. In fact the safeguards amounted to vital reduction in the powers of the Ministers.

5. Supremacy of the British Parliament. The Act of 1935 was a rigid one. No Indian Legislature whether Federal or Provincial was authorised to modify or amend it. The British Government alone was given the authority to make changes in it. The Indian Legislatures could at the most pray for a constitutional change by submitting a resolution to His Majesty's Government. Thus the new constitution was in no way an Indian constitution, it was an imposition on India by the British Parliament.

6. Federal Court. The Act also provided for the establishment of a Federal Court to settle disputes arising among the units themselves and also between a unit and the Federal Government. One of its functions was to interpret the controversial clauses of the Act. It was, however, not the final court of appeal. In certain circumstances, the appeals could be made to the Privy Council.

7. Increase in the Size of Legislatures and Extension of Franchise. Another highlight of the Act was the extension of franchise. Nearly 10 per cent of the total population got the right to vote. The Act not only retained communal electorate but also extended it. This was a calculated blow to the feeling of oneness in the country. The strength of the Council of State was increased to 260 and that of the Legislative Assembly to 375. The Federal Legislature and six out of eleven Provincial Legislatures became bicameral.

8. Division of Subjects. Under the Act of 1935, the subjects for administrative purposes were catalogued into three lists—the Federal list, the Provincial list and the Concurrent list. *The Federal list included* 59 *subjects, the Provincial list* 54 *and the Concurrent list* 36. The subjects which were of all-India interest and demanded uniform treatment were put in the Federal list. These subjects were Armed Forces, Currency and Coinage, Posts and Telegraphs, Railways, Central Services, External Affairs, Wireless, Customs, etc. Only the Federal Legislature could make laws on the Federal subjects.

Subjects mainly of local interest were placed in the Provincial list and were wholly within the jurisdiction of the Provincial Legislatures for the purpose of legislation. These subjects were *Public Order, Education, Local Self-Government, Public Health, Land Revenue, Forests, Mining and Fisheries and others.*

The third list known as the Concurrent list, and which contained 36 items, included subjects which were primarily of Provincial interest but at the same time required uniformity of treatment all over the country. Hence, the Act authorised both the Federal and Provincial Legislatures to pass laws on those subjects. *In the event of a conflict, the Federal law was to prevail.*

The authors of the Constitution had made the lists as exhaustive and complete as possible. But still there was the possibility of some powers left out. The Indian delegates at the conference could not decide whether the residuary powers were to be exercised by the Federal or the Provincial Legislature. In order to resolve this point of conflict, the Constitution authorised the Governor-General to allocate in his discretion the right to legislate on any subject, not included in the lists, to either the Centre or the Province.

9. Preamble. No new Preamble was affixed to the Act of 1935 because the new Constitution did not register any change in the British attitude towards India's sentiments. The Preamble of the Act of 1919 was, however, added to the new Act so as to appease the Indians that British Government still was committed to its promise of giving Dominion Status to India.

10. Abolition of India Council. The Indians had always been very critical of the India Council. The reasons for this bitterness were many. The new Act abolished India Council and provided for the appointment by the Secretary of State his team of *Advisers* whose number was *not to be less than* 3 *and not more than* 6. With the introduction of Provincial autonomy, the control of the Secretary of State over the Transferred subjects was greatly diminished. His control, however, remained intact over the discretionary powers of the Governor-General and the Governors.

11. Retention of Communal Electorate. Although the principle of communal electorate was not in the interests of the nation, yet in order to weaken the growing spirit of nationalism, the Act of 1935 not only retained communal electorate but also enlarged its scope. It granted this unholy concession to the Depressed Classes also. The *Muslims got* $33^1/_3$ *per cent of the seats in the Federal Legislature* although their number was much less than one-third of the total population of British India. Even the workers and women got separate representation although they had not asked for it.

12. Burma, Berzar and Aden. Another important feature of the new Constitution was that Burma ws separated from India and Aden was surrended to British Colonial Office. Berar, although it remained formally a part of Hyderabad State, was, for administrative purposes, merged with the Central Provinces.

CRITICISM OF THE GOVERNMENT OF INDIA ACT, 1935

Prof. Coupland described the Act of 1935 as "a great achievement of constructive political thought." In his opinion 'it made possible the transference of Indian destiny from British to Indian hands.' Indians, however, felt otherwise. Even the impartial British statesmen like Mr. Attlee admitted that the new keynote of the Act was mistrust. It was disappointing for it did not even make mention of Dominion Status. Every political party of India condemned the new draft for one reason or another.

Mr. Mohammad Ali Jinnah; the Leader of the Muslim League, described it as thoroughly rotten, fundamentally bad and totally unacceptable. According to C. Rajagopalachari, "The new Constitution is worse than Dyarchy." Pt. Madan Mohan Malaviya remarked, "The new Act has been thrust upon us. It has a somewhat democratic appearance outwardly, but is is absolutely hollow from inside." *Pt. Jawaharlal Nehru condemned it as "a new charter of slavery. It was a sort of machine with strong brakes and no engine."* Thus the Act was received with a chorus of condemnation from all sides. It was criticised on the following grounds :

1. Discretionary Powers of Governors and Governor-General. The new Act armed the Governors and the Governor-General with tremendous discretionary powers and thus reduced Provincial Autonomy to a farce. In a way the Act made the Governors so powerful that they could play the dictator if they liked. The only thing that can be said in favour of the Act is that it slightly enlarged the control of the Indian Legislatures over financial matters but on the whole the final powers remained vested in the hands of the Englishmen. The Governors and the Governor-General continued to have the last word in the preparation of budget and allocation of funds to various departments.

The Act also invested the Governors and Governor-General with a set of special responsibilities. These were in the nature of overriding powers. The Law portfolio was in the hands of a responsible Minister but prevention of any menace to peace and tranquality in the Province came under the special responsibility of the Governor. The excuse of special responsibilities was in fact a handy weapon to crush the revolutionary activities and Congress movements. Under this cover even the civil liberties could also be denied at any time. **Dr. Rajendra Prasad** in 1934 aptly remarked: "It would be mere camouflage and a fraud to declare that such and such subjects had been transferred when the responsibilities with regard to them were reserved with the British. The wide powers vested in the Governor, Governor-General and also in the Crown and the Parliament negatived the very essence of the Provincial Autonomy—the great prize awarded to the Indians."

2. Defective Federation. The proposed formation of the Federation was also fundamentally defective. Entry into the Federation was compulsory for the Provinces but voluntary for the Princely States. The Federation was thus going to be a jumble of dissimilar units. There was a world of difference in regard to population, area, political importance and status between the Provinces and the States. Whereas the British Provinces were partly autonomous units, the States were still under the autocratic rule of the Princes. Yoking together of such heterogeneous units under one Federation was highly absurd.

The second absurdity was that the States were to be Representative of the State subjects but by the nominees of the native rulers.

Thirdly, the wide range of powers vested in the Governor-General was a vital flaw in the proposed Federation. Such a thing is opposed to the spirit of a Federation.

3. Extension of Communal Electorate System. The Act of 1935 received a chorus of criticism for one or the other reason. It not only retained the system of Communal Electorate but also extended its application in the case of Harijans, labour and women. The sinister motive behind it was to separate the Harijans from the Hindu community and poison the political atmosphere with the evil of casteism and sectionalism.

4. Safeguards. The Act of 1935 armed the Governor-General and the Governor with far-reaching powers in the name of defending the minorities against the tyranny of the Hindus. The minorities naturally began to feel grateful to the rulers for the protection of their interests. They became their allies in arresting the growth of nationalism. The British diplomacy always used the Indian States, the minorities and the services as tools against the Congress.

5. Refusal to Grant Right of Self-Determination. Another flaw in the Constitution was its refusal to grant the right of self-determination to the Indians. The Indians had no say in the making or amendment of a Constitution for themselves. The new Constitution, it was but natural, could not get the approval and co-operation of Indians because it was not of their making. It was rather thrust upon them by the British Parliament which was also to be the judge of the eligibility or otherwise of the Indians for being given Dominion Status. The right to amend the Constitution was given not to the Indian Legislature but to the Crown. The Indians were simply given the toy of Provincial Autonomy to play with. They received nothing substantial to feel contented. The British Parliament and the Secretary of State for India continued to be the virtual rulers of the country till the year 1947. There was, as such, nothing surprising if the Act of 1935 was received with disgust and resentment.

PROPOSED ALL INDIA FEDERATION

The Act of 1935 proposed the formation of a Federation. The three distinctive and essential traits of any Federation are : (*a*) The precise division of powers between the Centre and units, (*b*) the supremacy of the Constitution, and (*c*) the special position of the Judiciary. The Act of 1935 contained all the three features. The subjects were clearly divided between the Centre and the units. The Constitution was also considered supreme, sacred and rigid. There was provision for the establishment of a Federal Court to interpret the Constitution. Apparently the proposed Indian Federation fulfilled all the three requirements. But still it was far from being an ideal or complete Federation. It was much different from other Federations of the world. Its distinctive features were as follows:—

1. Indian Federation did not consist of Independent States. A Federation may be called a Union of some independent States formed with a view to satisfying some common aims and interests. Such units delegate certain powers to the Federal Government beyond which the Central Government has no power in those States. Thus federalising is a process of uniting several independent States. Take for instance the U.S.A. There the 13 States and other colonies became first free from the domination of Great Britain. Later on in 1787 they made a constitution and established a Federal Government. The procedure adopted in India was just the reverse. Here the Act of 1935 proposed a federation by splitting up the unitary structure of the country. It was a federation of non-sovereign Provinces and States.

2. This Federation was not the Result of the Free Will of the People. A federation ordinarily comes into existence as a result of mutual agreement among the sovereign units to surrender a part of their sovereignty for matters of convenience and common benefit. The process was otherwise in India. Here the consent of the units was not obtained at all. It was imposed by a foreign Government with the mean motive of putting a check on the progressive elements by setting the reactionary nominees of the States against them. The Congress foresaw it clearly and hence opposed the move strongly.

3. Dissimilarity of Units. The units of a federation are generally similar in character. In India the bodies being brought under the federation were widely dissimilar. These units were of three types—the British Indian Provinces, the Chief Commissioners' Provinces and the Princely States. There was not a ghost of semblance in their political structure. The Provinces were almost autonomous units whereas the States were under autocratic rule. Hence the federation outlined by the Act of 1935 was likely to be a combination of conservative and progressive elements which normally cannot go together.

4. The authority of the Federal Government, under the new Act, was not to extend equally to all units. While joining the federation was imperative for the Provinces, it was matter of choice for the States. Only such States were to be members of the federation as cared to join it. Besides it, the authority of the Central Government was to extend to the States only to the extent mentioned in the Instrument of Accession. Thus, the range of federal powers which was uniform in the case of Provinces, differed from State to State. Such a complicated system was unprecedented in the history of the world.

5. No Legal Equality of Units and Weighted Representation to States. In every federation , all the big and small units are given a sort of legal equality by their equal representation in the Upper House. The authors of the Act of 1935 did not observe this rule. The Provinces were given representation in the Upper House in proportion to their population but the States were given weighty representation, that is, much more than they deserved according to the numerical strength of each of them. The population of the Indian States was only 23 per cent of the total population of the country but they were allotted 33 per cent of total seats in the Lower House and 40 per cent of total seats in the Upper House.

6. Nomination of the States' Representatives by the Rulers. Another absurdity in the federal scheme was that the Representatives of States, instead of beign elected by the people, were to be nominated by the rulers. It was done with a view to safeguarding the vested interests of the British Governrment. The game which the British Government intended to play was to outnumber the Congress Representatives at the Centre by the combined strength of zamindars, members representing the minorities and the State nominees.

7. Indirect Election to the Federal Assembly. The Lower House in every federation is directly elected. In Indian federation the Federal Assembly was to be indirectly elected while the Upper House was to have direct election. It was done to weaken the popular House. Besides indirect election, the Lower House was further weakened by the wide powers vested in the Governor-General and the British Parliament. The few powers that the Lower House commanded and could exercise were further made ineffective because of the mixed character of the House. The House was always divided against itself. The communal and class elements joined hands with the Government and foiled every attempt by the progressive forces to exercise their powers given to them by Constitution.

8. Special Powers of the Governor-General. In other federations, no outside authority possesses the power to interference in day-to-day working of the State. The glaring defect of Indian federation was that it was open to regular interference by the Governor-General and the Secretary of State. *The Governor-General could even abolish the federal structure and assume dictatorial powers by a mere Proclamation of Emergency.* He exercised some measure of control over the Provinces also. In the event of breakdown of the constitutional working in any Province, the Governor of that Province could take over the entire charge under Section 93 of the Act. And the Governor in the exercise of his discretionary powers or special responsibilities was always subordinate and answerable to the Governor-General. Besides it, the Governor-General could directly give directions to the Provinces relating to the maintenance of the law and order.

9. Residuary Powers. The powers, not included in any of the Federal State and Concurrent lists are called residuary powers. Such powers in other federations are either given over to the Federal Government as in Canada or to the State as in the U.S.A. But none of the two methods was adopted in the Act of 1935. The Muslim League insisted on leaving the residuary powers with the Provinces whereas the Congress wanted to strengthen the hands of the Centre. Since the two parties could not agree over this point, the *Act authorised the Governor-General to assign any subject*, not covered by any of the three lists, either to the Centre or to the units. In no other federation does the Governor-General enjoy such a privilege.

10. Amendment to the Constitution. The common practice in all federations is that the Federal Legislature has the power to amend the Constitution. But under the new Act the Indians had no right to amend the Constitution in any case. *It could be amended only by the British Parliament.*

The scheme of the federation with the Government of India Act, 1935 devised was, thus, a combination of the drawbacks of different systems. Professor Keith aptly remarked, "For the federal scheme it is difficult to feel any satisfaction. The units of which it is composed are too disparate to be joined suitably together and it is too obvious that on the British side, the scheme is favoured in order to provide an element of pure conservatism in order to combat any dangerous elements of democracy contributed by British India..... It is difficult to deny the justice of the contention in India that federation was largely evoked by the desire to evade the issue of extending responsible Government to the Central Government of British India. Moreover, the withholding of defence and external affairs from Federal control, inevitable as the course is, renders the alleged consession of responsibility all but meaningless. Whether a federation built on incoherent lines can operate successfully is wholly conjectural; if it does, it will probably be due to the virtual disappearance of responsibility and the assertion of the controlling power of the Governor-General backed by the conservative elements of the States and of British India."[1]

Rejection of the Federation. The long list of defects given above will convince anybody that the new Act was a complete failure from the viewpoint of Indians. The Federal Structure for India was so devised as to leave no opportunity for the elected representatives of the people to have any powerful say in the administration of India. Under the new Act the Federal Assembly was to be elected indirectly and the *States were given a privileged position*. These things were against the canons of democracy. The *endless chain of safeguards* and other protective devices were a serious check on the powers of the Ministers. The consensus of public opinion was against the *introduction of Dyarchy at the Centre*. Hence the Congress, Muslim League, Hindu Mahasabha and the Sikhs—all refused to accept the Federation. The Indian States were already reluctant to join it. When the British Government saw that the whole of India was hostile to their Federal Plan, it postponed its introduction. The Government decided to apply only that part of the Constitution which related to the Provinces. The Governor-General in his speech of 11th September, 1939, declared the suspension of the Federal Scheme.

SAFEGUARDS AND RESERVATIONS

Literally the word safeguards means protective devices to check certain unwanted activities. In the Constitution of the U.S.A. safeguards have been provided to check and curb revolutionary tendencies. In the new Constitution of 1935 these crafty devices were meant to safeguard the vested interest of the British Government. Indian nationalists had not an iota of doubt that safeguards were positively against the cannons of democracy. Their protests, however, fell on deaf ears. The British Parliament included them in the Act of 1935 in the interest of minorities, public services and British privileges.

The safeguards provided in the Act of 1935 were as under : —

1. Defence, External Affairs, Ecclesiastical Affairs and Tribal Affairs. In the proposal Federal scheme Defence, External Affairs, Ecclesiastical Affairs and Tribal Affairs were entrusted not to the responsible Ministers but to the Councillors of the Viceroy's Executive. The councillors were not answerable to the Legislature for any of their actions. They were directly and wholly under the Governor-General who was to administer the reserved departments in his discretion. He was not at all bound to consult the Ministers. Similar was the case regarding military affairs.

2. Finance. In financial matters also, not the Ministers and Legislature but the Governor-General could give the final word. Financial stability of the Federation was one of his special responsibilities. He also exercised real control over the currency and coinage through the Governor of the Reserve Bank, apointed by and responsible to him only. He could turn down or veto any suggestion given by the Finance Minister.

3. Special Responsibilities and Individual Judgment. The Act of 1935 contained a long list of the special responsibilities of the Governor-General and the Governors. In the discharge of these responsibilities they could easily interfere in the affairs of any Minister and his department. They were empowered to take any action in order to protect the interest of the *minorities, public services, princes and the British economic interests*. The Governor General could take any step, however drastic,

1. Keith, A.B., *A Constitutional History of India*, pp. 474-75

for the *defence* of the country. The Act of 1935 also made provision for direct British control over Indian affairs. The Governor-General in the exercise of his individual judgement was answerable to the Secretary of State for India. He had to obey all directions and instructions received from London office of the Secretary of State. The Governor in the exercise of individual judgement was subordinate both to the Governor-General and the Secretary of State for India.

4. The Governor-General and the Governors possessed such a wide range of legislative and executive powers as reduced the so-called responsible Government to a mere eye-wash.

5. Other Safeguards. The list of miscellaneous measures to safeguard the British interests was also fairly long. It included (*a*) indirect elections to the Federal Assembly, (*b*) extension of communal and special electorate to new groups, (*c*) more than proportionate seats given to minorities and special classes, (*d*) representation of the States by the nominees of the rulers, (*e*) keeping of the police and other higher services beyond the control of the Ministers, and (*f*) retention of the right to amend the Constitution by the British Parliament.

Critism of the Safeguards and Reservations. The safeguards and reservations evoked a good deal of criticism by the Indian leaders. The motive underlying them was, doubtlessly, to check the pace of progressive forces and rising nationalism in India. The British Government joined hands with the unpatriotic princes, minorities and public servants to prolong the duration of its rule over India. The princes and the Muslims also, in order to safeguard their sectional interests, agreed to play into the hands of the Government. Mr. Jawaharlal Nehru must have been thoroughly disgusted with these safeguards when he remarked that the new Act had 'all brakes and no engine.'

HOME GOVERNMENT

(Control of Secretary of State over the Indian Government)

The Secretary of State under the Act of 1919 possessed and exercised the power of superintendence, direction and control over the entire Indian administration. The Governor-General and the Governors had to pay due obedience to him. The Act of 1935, however, changed the position considerably. It suggested the introduction of Provincial autonomy—which meant partial control of the responsible Ministers over the administration of the Province. In the same way the suggestion to introduce Dyarchy at the Centre meant the transference of certain departments to the responsible Ministers. Both the Governor-General and the Governors, thus, had to run the administration to a large extent on the advice of Ministers. Naturally the powers of the Secretary of State for India had also be relaxed or reduced accordingly.

Control of Secretary of State for India on Reserved Departments. Through the servants of the Crown in India, the Secretary of State continued to administer all the vital departments of the administrative machinery of India. Besides his control over the Reserved subjects, he had *many powers with regard to the services.* He appointed officers belonging to the Indian Police, Irrigation Department and Civil Services. He also continued to be the Constitutional adviser of the Crown with regard to Indian affairs. All the Bills sent to His Majesty for consideration or even assented to by the Governor-General were actually handled by the Crown on the advice of the Secretary of State.

FEDERAL EXECUTIVE

(Governor-General and his Council)

The Executive Authority of the Indian Federation was to be exercised by the Governor-General on behalf of the Crown either directly in his discretion or with the help of his Councillors and Ministers. Thus the Federal Executive consisted of three parts : (*a*) The Governor-General; (*b*) the Councillor; and (*c*) the Council of Ministers.

(*a*) **Salaries, Allowances and Emoluments of Governor-General.** The status of the Governor-General in Indian Federation was unique and enviable. He was the chief executive of the Federation. He was appointed by the British Crown on the recommendation of the Prime Minister for a *period of 5 years*. He received a yearly salary of ₹ 2,51,800 out of Indian revenue. In addition to his salary he was entitled to other allowances and emoluments. Total expenditure on his office came to ₹18,00,000 per year.

Since the Governor-General was the key figure or pivot of the administration, the authors of the new Constitution conferred on him wide powers. These could be divided under three heads—(*i*) Discretionary Powers, (*ii*) Powers to be exercised in his individual judgement, (*iii*) Powers to be exercised on the advice of Ministers.

(*b*) **Discretionary Powers of the Governor-General.** The Act of 1935 mentioned a list of the subjects which were to be administered by the Governor-General in his discretion. His discretionary powers extended to all the vital subjects of Indian administration, classified in the Act as reserved departments. In dealing with Defence, Foreign Relations, Tribal Areas and Ecclesiastical Affairs, the Governor-General acted on his own. For the administration of these subjects he was responsible to the Secretary of State and not the Federal Legislature. It was not at all essential for him to consult the Ministers. The discretionary powers of the Governor-General thus were a big cut in the powers of the responsible Ministers.

The Governor-General was the real head of the Executive. Constitutionally, he had the power to appoint and dismiss his Ministers. He presided over the meetings of the Council of Ministers. He also nominated his Councillors, and appointed financial adviser and his staff, the Governor and Deputy Governor of the Reserve Bank. He determined their conditions of service, salaries and allowances. He could also remove any of them at will.

Governor-General's discretionary powers also included the *appointment of Chief Commissioner, the appointment of the Chairman and members of the Federal Public Service Commission; the appointment of 317 of the members of the Federal Railway Authority and the President thereof and also the President of the Railway Tribunal.* Besides appointing the members of the Public Service Commission, he also fixed their salary, tenure and conditions of service.

Apart from executive powers, the Governor-General was armed with vast legislative powers. He could summon, prorogue or dissolve the Federal Assembly. He made rules for the convenient transaction of Government business. He distributed work among the Ministers. He sent messages to the Legislature regarding any Bill. He could also hold the passage of a Bill or reject it altogether. Certain types of Bills required his previous consent for being moved in the Assembly. He could in his discretion reserve any Bill for the approval of the British Crown.

The Governor-General possessed and exercised extraordinary powers to make laws. The Acts made by him were called *Governor-General's Acts*. Such Acts were valid not withstanding the disapproval of the Federal Legislature. He could also send the draft of a Bill to the Assembly and invite its suggestions. In the exercise of his discretionary powers, he could issue *ordinances*. Such ordinance were of two types depending on whether the Federal Legislature was in session or not at the time of promulgation of the ordinance. An ordinance to meet some emergency at a time when the Legislature was not holding its session, could be issued by the Governor-General either on the advice of the Council of Ministers or in the exercise of his individual judgement. Such ordinances had the force of law but they had to be laid before the Assembly as soon as it reassembled. If such an ordinance failed to get the approval of both Houses within six weeks, it ceased to be effective. The second type of ordinances were those which the Governor-General could issue in emergency for the satisfactory discharge of his duties involving his discretion or individual judgement. Such an ordinance in the first instance was valid for six months and could be extend for further period of six months by another ordinance.

Under *Section* 45 of the Act, the Governor-General was given the power to issue a *Proclamation of Emergency if he was satisfied* that the Government of India could not be carried on in accordance with the provision of the Act. Such Proclamation meant the suspension of the Constitution. In that case the Governor-General assumed all the powers vested in the Federal Executive and the Legislature. His powers did not extend to the judicial field. Such a Proclamation was, however, required to be submitted to the Secretary of State who laid it before both the House of the Parliament. A Proclamation of Emergency could remain in effect for six months and, if approved by the Parliament, be extended for a further period of 12 months. In no case could it last for more than three years.

(*c*) **Governor-General's Special Responsibilities and Power of Individual Judgement.** The Act of 1935 which provided for the transfer of power to the people also laid down some special responsibilities of the Governor-General with a view to ensuring fair and good administration.

These were as follows :—

1. Prevention of any grave menace to the peace or tranquillity of India or any part thereof.
2. Protection of the legitimate interests of the *public services*.
3. Safeguarding of the interests of the *minorities*.
4. Safeguarding of the *financial stability* and credit of the federal government.
5. Prevention of discrimination against goods imported from England or Burma.
6. *Prevention of commercial discrimination* in the sphere of executive action.
7. Protection of the rights of *Indian States and Princes*.
8. Securing the due discharge of his functions with regard to matters in which he acted in his discretion or individual judgement.

The Governor-General was empowered to exercise his power of individual judgement with regard to his special responsibilities. He was required to consult his Ministers in these matters but was free to accept or reject their advice. Since the special responsibilities of the Governor-General meant a serious cut in the powers of the Minister, the Indian leaders criticised the Act in no uncertain terms. The field of special responsibility in a way covered the whole of administration. It made the transfer of political power to the people quite meaningless. The Governor-General virtually became the master of the whole federal show. According to K.T. Shah it removed 'the most considerable part of governmental routine from the hands of the responsible popular Ministers'.

(*d*) **Powers to be Exercised by Governor-General on the Advice of Ministers.** The Act of 1935 suggested the introduction of Dyarchy at the Centre. It divided the Central subjects into Reserved subjects and Transferred subjects. Defence, External Affairs, Tribal Areas and Ecclesiastical Affairs were treated as Reserved subjects while all the rest were transferred to responsible Ministers. In dealing with the Reserved subjects, the Governor-General acted his discretion. He controlled the Transferred subjects with the help of the Ministers, within the ministerial field also, the Governor-General was authorised to ignore the advice of Ministers in matters relating to his special responsibilities.

Councillors. In the Act of 1935 there was provision for an Executive Council to assist the Governor-General in running the administration of reserved subjects. The minimum number of Coucillors was three and maximum six. They were appointed by the Crown but were directly responsible to the Governor-General. They were ex-officio members of both the Houses of the Federal Legislature. *They could sit in both but vote in none.* Unlike the Ministers, they had no collective or individual responsibility to the legislature. *They were directly under the Governor-General. They had purely advisory functions.* The Federal Legislature, though incompetent to remove them, could ask them questions. Their salaries and conditions of service were fixed by His Majesty's Government.

Council of Ministers. For the administration of Transferred subjects, the Governor-General was assisted by a Council of Ministers. Constitutionally they were to be appointed and dismissed by the Governor-General. The Ministers whose number could not exceed 10 were to be responsible to the Federal Legislature. The Instrument of Instructions issued to the Governor-General advised him to appoint his Ministers on the advice of the leader of the majority party in the Assembly. Every Minister was required to be the member of one or the other House. If a Minister at the time of his appointment did not happen to be the member of any House, he was required to secure membership within six months or resign at the end of that period. The Instrument of Instructions also advised the Governor-General to encourage and foster the spirit of joint responsibility. He was to act as President of the Council. In case of difference of opinion, he had a casting vote. At the time of the nomination of his Ministers, he was advised to include in the Council the representatives of the minorities as well as the Indian States.

CRITICAL ESTIMATE OF THE POSITION OF THE GOVERNOR-GENERAL

The Act of 1935 was brought only partly into operation. Part I which concerned the Provinces was enforced and the Provinces received responsible Governments. But Part II or the federal part of the Act could not be introduced because of bitter criticism that it met within the country. The criticism was based on reasons quite sound and strong. In theory the Act proposed a partially responsible Government at the Centre but in effect it meant one-man's rule. *The Governor-General was armed with a host of discretionary powers* which took away whatever few powers had apparently been transferred to the *Ministers*. The reserved departments, for instance, Defence, Tribal Areas, External Affairs and Ecclesiastical Affairs were entirely under Governor-General's control *The Transferred subjects also were under his active supervision and guidance.* On the pretext of discharging his special responsibilities, he could interfere in the working of any department managed by the Ministers. Such powers of discretion and individual judgement were inconsistent with the conception of responsible Government.

The financial powers of the Govenor-General were equally vast. *Nearly* 80 *per cent of the budget was under his sway*. He was to decide what items were votable and what non-votable. He could *restore any cut made or grant rejected by the Legislature*. No proposal for the allocation of fund for any purpose could be made without his recommendations. He had large powers in the legislative field also. These included issuing of *ordinances and making of Governor-General's Acts.* Above all he could proclaim *emergency and suspend the working of the Constitution itself.* He was also the chief appointing authority. All the important posts including those of the financial adviser, Chief Commissioners, Governor and Deputy Governor of the Reserve Bank were filled by him. His position was thus deliberately designed by the authors of the Act to be very strong, rather supreme. Besides filling the key executive posts, he could veto any Bill passed by the Federal Legislature.

The Governer-General was all-powerful with regard to Rerserved subjects; he was equally powerful in influencing the working of Transferred subjects. Law and order, for instance, was a Transferred subject in the hands of a Minister, but it was a special responsibility of Governor-General to maintain peace and tranquility. By invoking this power he could bypass or override any Minister at any time. His discretionary powers and the powers of individual judgement reduced the responsible Government to a hollow vaunt, an empty dream.

PROPOSED FEDERAL LEGISLATURE

The Federal Legislature, consisted of two Houses—Council of States and Federal Assembly.

Council of States. The Council of States or the Upper House was to *consist of* 260 *members in all*, 156 *of them to be the representative of British India and* 104 *of the Indian States.* The conditional clause in the Act was that the Federation was to be formed only when as many States agreed to join in as could send 52 members in the Upper House. Whereas in other federations of the world, all the States are given equal representation in the Upper House, the Act of 1935 provided for uneven representation of the units. The number of seats allotted to an Indian State depended on their relative rank and importance. Hyderabad, for example, could send five nominees. Mysore, Gwalior, Kashmir and Baroda were given three seats each; and Travancore, Cochin and Udaipur two each. Another defective feature in the composition of Council of States was that the *States were to be represented not by the persons elected by the people but nominated by the rulers of the respective States.* This practice, it was feared, would lead to an alliance between the State nominees and the Government with the object of opposing the popular element in the House. This was the reason why the Indian public opinion vehemently opposed this provision of the Act.

Out of 156 representatives of British India, 150 were to be elected on communal basis. The remaining six were to be nominated by the Governor-General from amongst the women, minorities and Depressed Classes.

Federal Assembly. The Federal Assembly was to consist of 125 representatives of the States and 250 of the Provinces. We give a chart below showing the allocations of seats to different classes and communities.

Federal Assembly
Total Seats 375

- Representatives of Princely States 125
- Representatives of the Provinces 250
  - General seats (Including 9 Harijans) 105
  - Sikhs 6
  - Muslims 82
  - Anglo-Indians 4
  - Europeans 8
  - Indian Christians 8
  - Commerce and Industry 11
    - Zamindars 7
    - Labour 10
    - Women 9

As in the Council of States, the seats reserved for the Indian states were to be filled not by the representatives of the people but by the persons nominated by the rules. Secondly, the States got disproportionate number of seats in the Lower House. The Provinces remained under-represented. Thirdly, the number of seats allotted to each state was not determined on the population basis. Although the distribution of seats with regard to Provinces was determined on population-basis but further distribution of seats in each province among different communities was not fair or desirable. The Hindus, besides being the true nationals of the country, constituted 70 per cent of the total population. But they were given only 50 per cent of seats: *The minorities thus were given over representation* with the motive that they might always co-operate with the Government against the Hindus. The Act recommended indirect elections for the Federal Assembly when such a practice does not exist in any federation of the world. The Upper House which should have been indirectly elected was given direct election. The entire system as a matter of fact was so designed as to serve the British interests only.

The members of the Federal Assembly were to be elected by the members of the Lower Houses of Provincial legislatures. The electors were chiefly governed by communal or Provincial consideration in this choice. The duration of the Federal Assembly was five years if not dissolved earlier by the Governor-General.

POWERS OF THE FEDERAL LEGISLATURE

Legislative Powers. *The Federal Legislature could make laws on all subjects included in the Federal and Concurrent lists. It was also empowered to legislate on Provincial subjects in an emergency whereby the security of India was threatened and also when* two or more Provinces by mutual consent requested it to do so. Its authority over the Indian States extended to those subjects only which were mentioned in the Instrument of Accession. No Bill moved in either House could become an Act unless passed by both the Houses and approved by the Governor-General. In case of differences between the two Houses over any Bill, the Governor-General could summon a joint meeting and allow the decision to be taken by majority vote. In such joint sessions, the Lower House always had the advantage of its numerical strength.

Executive Power. The Assembly exercised more effective control over the Executive Council than the Upper House. It *alone commanded the responsibility of the Minister.* It means that only the Assembly or the Lower House could adopt a *vote of no-confidence* against the Council of Ministers and remove them from office. So far as Councillors were concerned they were beyond the control of both the Houses. The member of either House could ask a question pertaining to administration of the country; and the Minister or the Councillor to whom the question was addressed was required to supply the information to the House. Both the House were competent to move an adjournment motion. Bills could be moved in either House and sent to Governor-General for his assent. The Governor-General, however, was free to give his assent or withhold it. The Legislature was powerless in respect of those spheres in which the Governor-General could exercise his power of discretion or individual judgment.

Financial Power. He who controls the purse controls the administration, is a time-honoured saying. In order to judge the extent to which the political power has been transferred to the people, the best way is to see the extent of people's control over the country's purse. Let us now make an estimate of the financial powers of the Federal Legislature.

The Act gave nearly equal powers to both the Houses on money maters except that a Money Bill could be moved only in the Lower House. *The budget was prepared every year under the supervision of the Governor-General.* It was divided into two parts—(*i*) expenditure charged upon federal revenues, and (*ii*) sums required to meet all other heads of expenditure and included the salaries of the Governor-General, Ministers and Councillors, Judges of the High Courts and Federal Court, Advocate-General and other high-ranking State Officials. The Governor-General himself decided what items were to be placed in the first part of the Budget. *Thus* 80 *per cent of the budget fell outside the control of the Federal Legislature.* The remaining 20 per cent of the Budget was presented in the form of demands for grants. This money required the sanction of the Legislature which was authorised to reduce the amount or reject a demand for grant. But the power of the Legislature even in this limited sphere was not complete or absolute. The Governor-General was authorised to restore the reduction or sanction any amount rejected by the Legislature.

Note. Since the federal part of the Constitution could not be enforced because of the hostile attitude of the Indian public, the Central Legislature continued to work according to the Act of 1919. Hence unitary form of the Government continued to work at the Centre.

FEDERAL COURT

In a Federal system the scope of authority of the Centre as well as the federating units is clearly demarcated. As far as possible, the Constitution leaves no occasion for confusion. But there is always the possibility of a dispute arising out of the interpretation of a constitutional clause. It is possible that the Central or a Provincial Government may violate the provision of the Constitution. In order to meet such confusion and check the violate the provision of the Constitution. In order to meet such confusion and check the violation of the Constitution, every federal scheme provides for the establishment of a Federal Court. Till the coming into force of the new Act, India was treated as a unitary Government. Whatever powers the Provinces enjoyed were delegated by the Centre. And in the event of any dispute the decision of the Centre prevailed. But in a federal system, nothing is left to the whim of the Centre. Disputes are decided in the light of the dictates of the constitution. The new Act of 1935 was introduced in the Provinces from April 1, 1937, and hence the Federal Court was also established quite soon. It began to function from 1st October, 1937.

Constitution of the Federal Court. The Federal Court consisted of one *Chief Justice and not more than six other Judges*. To start with, only a Chief Justice and the two other Judges were appointed by His Majesty from amongst persons of eminence and high qualifications. Their salaries and allowances were fixed by His Majestry-in-Council and could not be changed to their disadvantage during their term of office. *Their salaries were charged upon the Indian revenue*. This was done with a view to ensure judicial independence.

The Act provided a number of safeguards for the judges of the Federal Court. *Their age of retirement was fixed at* 65. They could be dismissed even earlier on charges of misbehaviour or infirmity of mind or body by His Majesty on the recommendation of the Judicial Committee of the Privy Council. Thus the judges with regards to their appointments, salaries and dismissal were in no way subject to their authority of the Governor-General or the Federal Legislature.

Qualification of the Judges. A person was considered eligible for appointment as a Judge if he possessed the following qualifications :

Five years' standing as a Judge of a High Court in any Province/or federated State.

or

Two years' standing as a barrister of England or Northern Ireland .....

or

Ten years' standing as a member of the faculty of Advocates.

or

Ten years' standing as a High Court pleader.

The Chief Justice was required to have been an advocate or barrister of at least *fifteen years' standing at the time of appointment*. The Governor-General was authorised to appointment any Federal Judge to act as Chief Judice and other Judges were fixed by His Majesty-in-Council. *The Chief Justice was entitled to* ₹ 7,000 *per month and every other judge* ₹ 5,500 *per month.*

Original Jurisdiction of the Federal Court. *The original jurisdiction of the Federal Court extended to disputes arising out of the interpretation of any provision of the Constitution.* The conditions were that the case brought before it must involve legal rights and secondly, the parties to the dispute must be the Government and not the individuals.

Appellate Jurisdiction. *The Court's appellate jurisdiction included bearing of appeals against the decision of High Courts.* But it could allow an appeal only when it involved some constitutional right and the *High Court also granted a certificate to the effect that it was a fit case for appeal to the Federal Court.* The Federal Court was also competent to interpret any clause in the Instrument of Accession. If a dispute arose between the Federal Government and a federating State with regard to the extent of Federal control over the State, it was to be settled by the Federal Court.

Advisory Jurisdiction. The functions of the Federal Court included advisory functions also. The Governor-General could refer any point of law to the Court for information and legal guidance. Such an advice was given in the open court in the presence of the lawyers of all the parties concerned.

As a Court of Record. The Federal Court held its sittings in Delhi. The account of its proceedings was duly maintained and published. Its judgements and verdicts could also be referred to in Lower Courts.

The Federal Court, in fact, was not a Supreme Court. Appeals from its judgements could be taken to the Judicial Committee of the Privy Council even without obtaining a certificate from it. Such appeals could be made only in cases which (*i*) involved interpretation of any provision of the Act of 1935 or any Order-in-Council issued under it and where the court had heard the case under its original jurisdiction; (*ii*) related to extent of authority vested in the Federal Government by virtue of Instrument of Accession of a State; (*iii*) arose from the enforcement of a Federal law in any of the Federating States. Leaving the three types of appeals given above, no appeal of any other nature could be taken to the Privy Council without first obtaining leave of the Federal Court.

The Federal Court started functioning from 1st October, 1937. The record of its services, spread over a period of 13 years, was quite impressive and admirable. In 1950 when the new Constitution of free India came into force, it came to be known as Supreme Court of India. Its powers were also enlarged. Under the Act of 1935 the Federal Court did not have the right to hear appeals in civil or criminal cases. If the Federal Legislature wanted to empower the court to hear civil cases involving a sum of at least ₹ 50,000, it could do so with the previous permission of the Governor-General by passing an Act to that effect.

The Federal Court, as stated above did excellent work for over a dozen years. It defended *vigorously the civil liberties of the people* against the highhandedness of the Executive during the Second World War. Sir Maurice Gwyer, the first Chief Justice of the Federal Court, earnestly followed the principles which he stated at the inaugural function of the court. He said, "Independent of Government and parties, the court's primary duty is to interpret the Constitution........Its canons of Interpretation would not hamper of free evolution of those constitutional changes for which the law provided no sanction, but in which the political genius of a people can find its most fruitful expression."

N.B. The Federal Court was converted into the Supreme Court with few changes after independence.

EXERCISES

Long Answer Type Questions

1. Discuss the salient features of the Act of 1935.
2. Discuss critically the Government of India Act, 1935.
3. The Act of 1935 proposed the formation of a Fedration. What were the distinctive features of that Federation?
4. Discuss the safegurards provided in the Act of 1935.
5. Write a note on Federal Executive.
6. Discuss the form of Federal Legislature. Discuss its powers also.
7. Write a note on Federal Court.

Short Answer Type Questions

1. There was a provision of Provincial Autonomy in the Act of 1935. What was the meaning of Provincial Autonomy ?
2. The proposed formation of the Federation was fundamentally defective. What were the defects? Discuss in very brief.

3. Write a very brief note on proposed all India Federation.
4. What were the legislative, executive and financial powers of Federal Legislature ?

Objective Type Questions

Choose the correct answer :

1. In which year The Act of 1935 was fully enforced ?
   (*a*) 1937 (*b*) 1938
   (*c*) 1939 (*d*) 1940
2. How many sections there were in the Act of 1935 ?
   (*a*) 320 (*b*) 321
   (*c*) 322 (*d*) 323
3. How many schedules there were in the Act of 1935 ?
   (*a*) 8 (*b*) 9
   (*b*) 10 (*c*) 11
4. The Act of 1935 was definitely an advance on the act of
   (*a*) 1916 (*b*) 1917
   (*c*) 1918 (*d*) 1919
5. Under the Act of 1935, the Subjects for administrative purposes were catalogued into how many lists?
   (*a*) Three (*b*) Four
   (*c*) Five (*d*) Six

ANSWERS

1. (*a*) 2. (*b*) 3. (*c*) 4. (*d*) 5. (*a*)

19

CHAPTER

Provincial Governments (Act of 1935)

PROVINCIAL AUTONOMY

The Dyarchy was abolished in the Provinces and instead Provincial Autonomy was introduced.

Perhaps the only warming feature of the Act of 1935 was the new status that it accorded to the Provinces. It replaced Dyarchy by Autonomy. The division of Provincial Subjects into Reserved and Transferred as under the Act of 1919 was abolished. The new Act made no mention of Reserved Subjects or the Governor's Executive Council. The Provinces received a new constitutional status. Their scope of authority was clearly demarcated. The extent of Central control over the Provinces was considerably restricted. Under the Act of 1919 the Provinces were at the mercy of the Centre. They exercised only such powers as were delegated to them by the Central Government. The Provincial Governments were as such mere agents of the Central Authority. The Act of 1935 made a market advance from the Constitution. They got responsible Government also. Thus, their autonomy conveyed double sense. In the first case the Government of the Province got out of the absolute control of the Central Government and received a separate legal authority. Secondly, the Provinces got a responsible Government, i.e., the power to rule came into the hands of the popular Ministers. The joint Parliamentary Committee in its report explained the new status of the Provinces as units which have 'an executive and legislature having exclusive authority within the Provincial sphere broadly free from control by the Central Government and the Legislature'.

Distinctive Features

The distinctive features of the scheme of Provincial Autonomy were as follows :

1. As in the case of the Federation, the executive power of the Province was vested in and exercised by the Governor on behalf of the Crown. He was to discharge his functions with the help of a Council of Ministers. Since the Provinces had been given an autonomous character, the Governors were advised to act, as far as possible, according to the advice of the responsible Ministers. The Provincial Autonomy, however, did not mean full-fledged responsible Governments in the Provinces. The Governors were armed by the Act with a set of discretionary powers in which case they had no need to consult their Ministers. Beside it, in

the due discharge of their special responsibilities, they could act in their individual judgement by flouting the advice of their Ministers.

2. Excepting those spheres in which the Governors could act in their discretion or individual judgement, all other spheres were transferred to the Ministers. The Ministers for their actions and policies were made responsible to the Provincial Legislature.
3. The Act further extended the franchise with the liberalising of right of vote, the Legislatures became broadly representative in character. Six of the eleven Provinces got bicameral Legislature, i.e. two house each.
4. The Act made provision for the establishment of a High Court and Provincial Service Cadre in each Province.

Three Lists. The relations between the Centre and the Provinces were regulated by the Act of 1935 on Federal lines. The Act divided the administrative matters into three categories. *The Federal list contained 59 subjects* and the right to make laws on those subjects was given only to the Federal Legislature. The main items included in this list were—Defence, External Affairs, Income-tax, Salt, Post and Telegraph, Currency and Coinage, Customs, Broadcasting, etc. The subjects on which the Provincial Legislatures alone were constitutionally authorised to legislate were included in the Provincial list. The sphere of Provincial Authority included Law and Order, Forest, Local Self-Government, Jail, Education, Agriculture and Public Health. *The total number of provincial items were 54.* The third list known as *Concurrent list had 36 subjects,* including Industrial Disputes. Labour Welfare, Trade Welfare, Trade Union, Press, Civil and Criminal Law Procedure. Both the Centre and the Provinces were competent to legislate on subjects contained in Concurrent list but if on any subject both the authorities made a law which was inconsistent, then the federal law was to prevail.

RESTRICTION ON THE AUTONOMY OF THE PROVINCES

Under the Act of 1935, the first ever attempt was made to give the Provinces an autonomous status by freeing them from external interference. Theoretically the entire Executive and Legislative Authority was transferred to the people. But this autonomy was not absolute or unqualified. It was circumscribed both internally and externally. Externally, the Governor-General could interfere in the administration of the Province to the extent of seeing that it did not threaten the peace and tranquillity of India. Internally the Governor's power of discretion and individual judgement meant a drastic cut in the powers of the ministers.

1. Let us illustrate our point by a few example. In case of grave emergency, the Governor-General under Section 102 could issue a Proclamation of Emergency and empower the Federal Legislature to make laws on Provincial Subjects. He could also issue directions to the Governors to act in a manner that the peace and order of the country was not endangered. He could also direct any Governor to act as his agent in the Province in respect of Defence, Foreign Affairs, Ecclesiastical Affairs or Tribal Areas. The Provincial executive authority was to be exercised in such a manner as not to interfere with Federal Authority. Lastly, whenever the Governor of a Province acted in his discretion or individual judgement, he was responsible to the Governor-General.

2. In the legislative field also, the control of the Governor-General was a hard reality. Certain types of Bills and amendments could not be introduced in the Provincial Legislature without the previous sanction of the Governor-General. The Governor-General was also empowered to withhold his assent to those Provincial Bills sent to him by the Governor for consideration. He could also forward such Bills for the consideration of the Crown or return them to the Province for reconsideration.

3. The Governor-General had to shoulder certain special responsibilities in the name of which he could interfere in the working of any department in the Province. He could direct any Minister

to act in a way suggested by him. Thus, no subject transferred on paper to the Ministers was totally outside the control of the Governor-General. Dr. Rajendra Prasad rightly remarked regarding the subject of Law and Order : "It was nothing short of a camouflage and fraud to declare that Law and Order had been transferred when special responsibility in respect of them was reserved with the Governor-General and the Governor in wide and all-Pervasive terms."

4. The loud claim of autonomy proved a mere bluff and a farce because the *Governor instead of acting as a constitutional head acted as a real ruler.* No sphere of Provincial Administration was free from his influence. His legislative powers were also fairly extensive. He could return a Bill to the Legislature for reconsideration on the lines suggested by him. His position was modelled exactly on that of the Governor-General. He could withhold his assent or reserve a Bill for the consideration of the Governor-General and the king. The Provincial Legislature was no more than a silent spectator on many occasions. The Governor made considerable inroads into the Legislative functions. He could issue ordinances or Governor's Acts without consulting the Legislature or the Ministers. In financial sphere too he possessed large powers. The Budget of the Province was prepared under his supervision. He was the appointing authority of so-called responsible Ministers. He distributed work among the Ministers and summoned their meeting. No Minister could act against the wishes of the Governor. The secretaries of various departments, who happened to be part of permanent staff, were also allowed to see the Governor directly and keep him well informed about their departments. They rather acted as informers on the Ministers. The Governor also trusted the permanent secretaries more than the Ministers. Thus, the Ministers became powerless non-entities.

Thus, the Provincial Autonomy was introduced with heavy restrictions and safeguards. It could grow and work only to that extent which was allowed by the Governor. The discretionary powers of the Governor were not clearly defined and they were so wide and overwhelming that the Governors could interfere in the day-to-day working of the Ministers on the pretext of their discretionary powers. Dr. Shyama Prasad Mukherjee, Minister of Finance, Government of Bengal, in his letter of resignation dated November 16, 1942 complained to the Governor against his constant interference in the sphere of Ministers.

5. In this way Governor himself determined the scope of his interference because the discretionary powers of the Governor were kept deliberately vague and wide. Indicting the Governor, *Dr. Shyama Prasad Mukherjee* wrote :

"You will not allow Ministers to function and administers according to their own right and judgement. You and some of your officers will commit Government to policies and act which Ministers do not approve of and afterwards you expect them to stand up as obedient persons fully justifying the results of your mistaken policy. The brunt of the attack falls on the Ministers. The Legislature is even precluded from criticizing and commenting upon your conduct. You in your turn do not hesitate to take advantage of and sometimes even go beyond the spirit of, the provisions of the Government of India Act and the Instrument of Instructions thus reducing ministerial administration to a mockery ?"[1]

The dismissal of Allah Bukhsh, the Chief Minister of Sind, and forced resignation of Fazal-ul-Haq, Chief Minister of Bengal when they enjoyed the support of the Legislatures of their Provinces, proves the arbitrariness of the Governors. In non-Congress Provinces the Governors enjoyed unlimited powers. There was no strong and organised party to challenge or block their interference. For instance, when the Governor-General consulted Punjab Governor on the question of the release of political prisoners, the latter without even consulting the Chief Minister, Sir Sikandar Hayat Khan, wrote back that the Punjab Government was not going to release them. In Sind, Bengal, and North-Western Frontier Province; the Governors showed undue favour to the League and tried to keep it in power in spite of its poor strength in the Assembly. It was clearly unconstitutional.

1. *'India Unreconciled' (The Hindustan Times, New Delhi, 1944). pp. 100-107.*

6. All these things clearly prove that the assurances, given by the Governor-General were not adhered to at all. Lord Linlithgow had made it clear that the scope of a Government's potential interference was strictly defined in the Act, "and there is no foundation for any suggestion that Governor is free, or is entitled or would have the power, to interfere with the day-to-day administration of a Province outside the limited range of the responsibilities specially confined to him. Before taking a decision against the advice of his Ministers even within the limited range a Governor will spare no pains to make it clear to his Ministers the reasons which have weighed with him in thinking both that the decision is one which is incumbent on him to take, and that it is the right one. He will put them in possession of his mind. He will reach his decision with full understanding of those arguments and with a mind open to conviction."

7. Referring to the constitutional provision regarding the dismissal of the Ministry by the Governor, the Viceroy said, "The mere fact that the Government of India Act covers contingencies such as the dismissal of Ministers, the breakdown of the Constitution or the like, is not for one moment to be taken as involving an assumption or anyone, indeed, who is concerned for the constitutional progress and development of this great country, wishes to see those contingencies turned into realities. The design of Parliament and the object of those of us who are the servants of the Crown in India and to whom it falls to work the provision of this Act, must be and is to ensure the utmost degree practicable of harmonious co-operation with the elected representatives of the people ...; and to avoid in every way, consistent with the special responsibilities for minorities and the like which the Act imposes, any such lash of opinion as would be calculated unnecessarily to break down the machine of Government, or to result in severance, of that fruitful partnership between the Governor and his Ministers which is the basis of the Act." *But the working of the Provincial Autonomy proved beyond doubt that these solemn assurances of the Governor-General later on were clearly flouted.*

GOVERNOR

Position. The executive of the Province consisted of the *Governor and the Council of Ministers.* The Governor was the captain of the executive team. He acted as an agent of the King. The Governors of key towns—Bombay, Madras and Bengal—were appointed by the Crown on the advice of the Secretary of State for India. In appointing the Governors of the rest of Provinces, the King acted on the advice of the Governor-General. The new Act did not make any change in the emoluments, tenure and conditions of service of the Governor. The office of the Governor was offered to white men alone. Throughout the British period only one Indian held that August office in permanent vacancy.

A. Executive Powers of the Governor. The Governor was appointed usually for a term of 5 years. His executive powers resembled those of the Governor-General. He exercised them in three different capacities. First, he acted in his discretion. Secondly, he exercised certain powers in his individual judgement. Thirdly, he acted on the advice of the Council of Ministers.

Discretionary Powers of the Governor:—Unlike the Federal Government, there were no reserved departments in the Provinces. But armed with discretionary powers, the Governor became the dominating head of the executive. Prof. K.T. Shah has given a long list of occasions on which the Governor could act in his discretion. The most important of them being : —

(*a*) to decide whether a subject was or not one in which he was required to act in his discretion, (*b*) to take steps for safeguarding the interests of the *minorities,* (*c*) to secure the protection of the rights and prestige of *Indian Princes,* (*d*) to take steps to prevent any *attempt to overthrow the Government,* (*e*) *to summon, adjourn or dissolve the Lower House,* (*f*) to make *Governor's Acts, Ordinances and laws for the peace and good* Government of Excluded areas, (*g*) to appoint the chairman and members of the Provincial *Public Service Commission* and also determine their salaries and allowances, (*h*) to make rules for the efficient transaction of the business of the Government, (*i*) to make rules for securing that no members of the police force might reveal to unauthorised persons, the sources of their information relating to terrorists' activities, (*j*) to call the joint session of both House in order settle differences between them, (*k*) to appoint and dismiss the *Advocate-General and also to fix his salaries.*

The discretionary powers of the Governor in fact touched every sphere of administration. These were all-pervasive. The Governor for all his actions with regard to matters in which he used his discretionary powers was answerable to the Governor-General.

Special Responsibilities of the Governor. Besides his discretionary powers, the Governor was also authorised to act in his individual judgement. He exercised his individual judgement in the discharge of his special responsibilities. The only difference between the two types of powers was that while using his discretion, the Governor was not even required to consult his Ministers in the exercise of his individual judgement, it was essential for him to consult them, although he was not bound to accept and act upon their advice. His special responsibilities were as follows :

(*a*) The prevention of menace to the peace and tranquillity of the Province or any part thereof.

(*b*) The safeguarding of the legitimate interests of *minorities.*

(*c*) The safeguarding of the right of *civil servants,* past and present, and their dependants.

(*d*) The securing of *protection against discrimination.*

(*e*) The securing of the peace and good Government of partially *excluded areas.*

(*f*) The safeguarding of the rights of States and the *rights and dignity of any ruler.*

(*g*) The securing of the execution of orders issued to him by the Governor-General in his discretion.

Powers to be Exercised on the Advice of the Ministers. Matters on which the Governor was duty-bound to act on the advice of his Ministers were very few. After the introduction of the Provincial Autonomy, it was rightly hoped that the Governor would use his special powers to the minimum and not interfere much in the ministerial field. These hopes, however, did not materialise. The explanation lay in the motives of the authors of the Act. The intention of British Government was not to weaken the Governor and make him act as only a figurehead, but to arm him with real and comprehensive powers.

B. Legislative Powers of the Governor. We give below the exhaustive list of the powers of the Governor in the sphere of legislation : —

(1) The Governor was authorised to *summon, prorogue and* even *dissolve* the Legislature.

(2) He could call a *joint sitting* of the House to iron out all differences between them. He could also address both Houses either separately or jointly.

(3) His *assent* was necessary to every Bill before it became a Law. He could return a Bill to the Legislature for reconsideration or reserve it for approval of the King.

(4) He could, in consultation with the Speaker of the Lower House, *make rules* for the satisfactory transaction of business in the House.

(5) He could *stop any discussion* relating to any Federating State.

(6) He could *stop any discussion* in the Lower House pertaining to external affairs or the ruler and his dependants of any State.

(7) He could stop *the passage of any Bill* if, in his view, it threatened peace and tranquillity of the Provinces or any part thereof.

(8) Of all the Legislative powers of the Governor, the most significant was that of *making laws.* He was empowered to make Acts for the due discharge of his special responsibilities. He could prepare a Bill and send it to the Legislature for enactment. If the Legislature did not pass it within a month, the Governor after that period could exercise his special powers and give the Bill the final shape and effectiveness of an Act. Every such Act required to be submitted to the Governor-General before being enforced. A copy of the Act was then sent to the Secretary

of State who presented it before the Parliament. The rejection or approval by the Parliament was final and binding on the Governor.

(9) *Powers to Issue Ordinance.* The Governor was also empowered to issue Ordinances which were of two types. First, when the Legislature was not in session and the circumstances required immediate action, the Minister could advise the Governor to meet the situation by issuing an Ordinance. The Governor issued it by exercising his power of individual judgement. If necessary, he also obtained the previous consent of the Governor-General. Governor's Ordinance had the same force as an Act of the Legislature. One condition attached to it was that it cased to be effective at the *end of six weeks after the reassembly of the legislature* which could reject it even earlier. In that case the Ordinance lost its force even before the expiry of six weeks.

The second type of Ordinance could be issued even while the legislature of the Province was holding its session. The Governor issued such Ordinance when he felt the need of immediate action for the due discharge of his special responsibilities under powers of discretion and individual judgement. Such ordinance remained valid for six months in the first instance. These could be given another life of six months by a subsequent notification. Such an Ordinances was generally issued after obtaining the consent of the Governor-General. In emergency, the Governor could issue it on his own responsibility.

(10) *Power to Suspend the Constitution.* The Governor was armed with the power to suspend the working of the Constitution at any time. Under Section 93 of the Act, he could make a proclamation of emergency and assume to himself all or any of the powers exercised by any Provincial authority. The Governor resorted to this drastic step only when he was satisfied that the administration of the Province otherwise could not be carried on according to the provisions of the Act. He could by his proclamation disarm the executive and Legislature but not the Judiciary.

C. Financial Powers of the Governor. The hold of the Governor over the purse of the Provincial Government was as real and firm as that of the Governor-General on the Federal purse. The Governor got the annual statement of income and expending prepared under his supervision. *Without his consent not a penny could be sanctioned or spent on any head.* He alone decided in his discrction what items of expenditure were chargeable on the Provincial revenue and hence could not be voted upon in the Legislature. He could also restore in full or part any demand for grant or cut rejected by the Legislature.

Criticism. The executive, Legislative and financial powers of the Governor were so extensive that the scope of the responsible Government in the Provinces was considerably restricted. No sphere of administration was immune from his influence. The Governor was not a titular but real captain of the Provincial machinery. Every power of Governor meant an erosion in the powers of the Ministers. He alone commanded and exercised more powers than the sum total of the powers exercised by the whole body of Ministers. What the authors of the Act offered to the Provinces in theory and on paper, was taken away in essence and practice. The British Government was so distrustful of Indians that it could not take any risk. This is why it allowed the Governor to be the pivot of the administration of the Province.

COUNCIL OF MINISTERS

Appointment of the Ministers. Although the Governor was on paper and in essence the Chief executive authority, the Act of 1935 provided for a Council of Ministers. The function of this body was to aid and advise him on all matters excepting those which required the exercise of his discretion or individual judgement. The act said that the Governor was the appointing authority of the Ministers. But the Instrument of Instructions laid down that he was to *appoint the Ministers in consultation with* *the leader of the House.* In other words, *the person who commanded a stable majority in the Lower House was summoned to act as Chief Minister* and to select his team of Ministers. *The Ministers held office till they enjoyed the confidence of the Legislature.* The Governor, no doubt, had the power to dismiss any Minister in his discretion, but in practice he did not do so till the latter had a solid and sizable support in the Legislature.

Qualification and Salaries of the Ministers. The act did not specify any qualification for a ministerial job. It simply said that a Minister ought to be the member of either House. If a person did not happen to be the member of any House at the time of his appointment as a Minister, *he was required to secure membership within six months or vacate his office at the end of the period.* The Act did not fix the salaries of the Ministers. It was left for the Legislature of the Province to decide. *The salaries once fixed could not be changed or put to vote in the House.* The Council of Ministers functioned for a period of 5 years unless the Legislature showed its want of confidence in it or the Legislature itself was dissolved earlier.

Number of Ministers. The numerical strength of the ministers was not fixed by the Act. It varied from Province to Province. For instance, Orissa had three Ministers only whereas Bengal Cabinet consisted of 12 Ministers. Although the Act said nothing about the appointment of Parliamentary Secretaries, they were attached to every Minister to assist them in their work. The Provinces in which the Congress formed its ministries, the salary of a Parliamentary Secretary was fixed at ₹ 250.

Representation of Minorities in the Ministry. In the Instrument of Instructions issued to the Governors, it was said that the Ministries, as far as practicable, should include members of all the important minority communities. The Governor was also advised to foster a sense of joint responsibility among the Ministers and make them feel collectively responsible to the Legislature. In fact the inclusion of the representatives of minorities and promoting a sense of joint responsibility among the Ministers were quite contradictory things. It created later on cabinet crisis in U.P. where the Congress refused to accept Muslim League in the cabinet unless they joined the Congress.

The structure of Provincial Government as outlined in the Act of 1935 possessed several features of a responsible form of Government. But such half-baked trivialities alone could not satisfy the nation. The responsible Government in Provinces was incomplete and illusory. Although there were no reserved subjects as in the Centre, the Ministers were not the masters of their portfolios. Their powers were greatly restricted by the discretionary powers of the Governors. Communal element, both in the Legislature and the Cabinet, and the Governor's power to declare the breakdown of the Constitution were against the canons of a responsible Government.

PROVINCIAL LEGISLATURE

Under the Act of 1919, each province had *only one House.* The novel feature of the new Act was that it created second chambers in six Provinces, namely Assam, Bengal, Bihar, Bombay, Madras and U.P. The Lower House was called Legislative Assembly, and the Upper House as known as Legislative Council. The remaining five Provinces continued to have Unicameral Legislature. The public opinion resented the creation of second chambers because these were white elephants. Moreover, the Upper House were oligarchic and conservative in character. The general reaction was that they were, beside being an unnecessary burden on the Provincial purse, a calculated move of the British Government to safeguard its own interests.

Composition of the Provincial Legislature. The strength of the Upper and Lower House varied from Province to Province.

Every Legislative Assembly under the Act of 1919 had a powerful nominated bloc. The new Act abolished the system of nomination. *The Assemblies became truly democratic bodies consisting of elected members only.* The Upper Houses continued to have a few nominated members. *The*

Act suggested direct elections for both the Houses. The basis of the allotment of seats to various communities was the notorious Communal Award given by Mr. Ramsay Macdonald. According to the Poona Pact, some changes were made regarding the representation of the Depressed Classes. The Congress had agreed to reserve certain number of seats for them out of général seats. The Act not only retained the antinational scheme of *separate electorate* but also extended it. It created new classes of woman and labour and accorded them separate representation. The new Act in this sense was vicious for it tended to split the nation in ever-increasing number of camps. The Communal Award given by the British Prime Minister in 1932 and modified by the Poona Pact, created seventeen different electorate. The seats in the Provincial Legislature were filled in by the communities and classes according to the scheme enunciated in the Award. The basic principle of the scheme was that the seats reserved for a community were to be contested only by persons belonging to that community and they were to be elected by the members of that community alone. The Muslim seats were filled by Muslim candidates elected by Muslim electorate. The seventeen different electorate were as follows: (1) General electorate consisting of Hindus and Parsies; (2) Seats reserved for the Scheduled Castes in accordance with the Poona Pact. These were, however, out of general seats; (3) Muslims; (4) Europeans; (5) Anglo-Indians; (6) Indian Christians; (7) Landlords; (8) Registered graduates of Indian Universities; (9) Sikhs in the Punjab and N.W.F.P.; (10) Labour; (11) Industrialists; (12) Electorate for Backward areas and tribes; (13) Sikh women in the Punjab; (14) Muslim women; (15) Anglo-Indian women in Bengal; (16) Christian women in Madras; and (17) Women general.

Tenure and Officers of the Provincial Legislature. The *tenure of the Legislative Council was 9 years. One-third of its members retired after every three years were to be replaced by new members.* Thus at the end of three terms the Council had altogether new faces. Its permanent character was in line with Federal Council of State. *The member of a Legislative Assembly held office for 5 years* unless the House was dissolved earlier by the Governor. During the Second World War the Governor was also empowered to extend the life of the Assembly during a period of emergency when it was difficult to hold fresh elections. The *Legislative Assembly had the right of electing its Speaker and Deputy Speaker. Similarly the Legislative Council elected its President and Deputy President.* These officers could be removed by the respective Houses by a vote of no-confidence. The Presiding Officer usually did not exercise his right of vote except when the House was equally divided. In such a situation he could exercise casting vote to clinch the issue. All the Ministers and the Advocate-General had the right to attend the meetings of both the Houses. Whereas the Advocate General had no right to vote, *the Minister had this right; of course,* in the House of which he happened to be member.

Voting Qualifications and Constituencies. Whereas about 3 per cent of the adult population exercised the right of vote for the assemblies under the Act of 1919, the *new Act raised the percentage to 14. The voting qualifications varied from Province to Province.* Generally all those adults acquired the right of vote who were literate, or who paid income tax, municipal tax or vehicle tax. Women were not debarred from suffrage provided they possessed the minimum qualifications.

In the case of Councils, the voters were *moneyed persons* and title holders like Rai Bahadurs. Besides these, men belonging to respectable class, i.e., ex-members of Legislature, Executive Councillors, Ministers, Members of University Senates, High Court judges, Chairmen of Municipalities and Local Boards and Presidents of Co-operative Banks also acquired the voting right. Thus, the second chambers were dominated by the upper and propertied class of the society.

The scheme of communal electorate, as mentioned earlier, was extended to new classes. *The Act recognised women and labour as new classes for matter of separate representation.* Moreover, the unjust and provocative practice of giving over-representation to certain communities, e.g., Muslims and Europeans, was also retained. It is interesting to note that Muslims in Madras and U.P. constituted only 7.1 per cent and 14.8 per cent of the population respectively. They were, nevertheless, given 13 per cent and 27 per cent of the total seats in the respective assemblies. Europeans enjoyed maximum favour. They numbered even less than 1 per cent of the population of India but they got 3 per cent of total seats in the Provinces and 5 $^{1}/_{2}$ per cent of seats in the proposed Federal Assembly. Notwithstanding the defects pointed out above, the one redeeming feature of the new Act was that it extended voting rights to greater number of people. Nearly three crores and a half people including 60 lakh women were registered as voters. The electorate thus formed 14 per cent of the population as against 3 per cent undet the Act of 1919.

POWERS OF THE PROVINCIAL LEGISLATURE

The powers of the Provincial Legislature were essentially similar to those of the Federal Legislature. These can be studied under three heads : Legislative, Executive and Financial.

(*a*) **Legislative Powers.** *The Provincial Legislature was empowered to make laws both on Provincial and Concurrent subjects.* Its power to make laws for the whole Province or any part there of on matters included in the Provincial List was exclusive and complete. But on Concurrent subjects it was restricted and shared with the Federal Legislature. Federal Legislature was also competent to Legislate on Concurrent subjects. A Provincial law on a Concurrent subject held good in so far as it did not go against a Federal law on the same subject. In the case of a conflict, the Federal law was to prevail. A provincial law could remain valid in all circumstances if it had been made with the previous sanction of the Governor-General.

The following were the limitations imposed on the competence of the Provincial Legislature:

1. No Bill or amendment which intended to repeal or amend an Act of the British Parliament extending to India could be introduced without the previous sanction of the Governor-General.
2. No Bill to repeal or amend a Governor-General's Act or Governor's Act and Ordinances issued by him in his discretion could be introduced without the Governor-General's consent.
3. No Bill affecting the matters in which the Governor-General was required to act in discretion could be introduced without the Governor-General' consent.
4. No Bill or amendment which affected the procedure for criminal proceedings applicable in the case of European British subjects, could be introduced without the Governor-General's previous sanction.

The powers of the Provincial Legislature were further curtailed by the Governor's powers of discretion and individual judgement.

(*b*) **Executive Powers of the Provincial Legislature.** The Provincial Legislature enjoyed only nominal powers over the executive of the Province. The members of both the Houses could ask questions and supplementary questions from the Ministers. Adjournment motions could also be moved in both the Houses in order to draw the attention of the Government to matters of urgent public importance. The *Legislative Assembly could also remove the Ministers severally or collectively by expressing its want of confidence in them.* The way how it showed its lack of confidence in a Minister was by refusing to sanction a large part of demands for grants in the Budget. In such cases the Minister had to resign.

(*c*) **Financial Powers.** The Lower House being more democratic in its composition enjoyed certain privileges in money matters. Money Bills could be moved only in the Lower House. The budget of the Provinces was divided into two parts—non-votable items and votable items. The first part covered nearly 30 per cent of the total expenditure. The non-votable items were : (1) The salary and allowances of the Governor; (2) Debt charges; (3) The salaries and allowances of the Ministers, the Advocate-General and Judges of the High Court; (4) Expenditure for excluded areas and others. The expenditure under non-votable head was called a charge on the provincial revenues. It could be discussed and criticised in the Legislature but not reduced or rejected. It could not be voted upon in any House.

The remaining 70 per cent of the budget was presented in the form of demands for grants which were votable items. The House could both reduce or reject any grant but the decision of the House was not final. The Governor was empowered to restore any reduced or rejected grant if he considered it necessary for efficient administration of the Province. Besides it, no Bill relating to imposition of new taxes or an increases in the existing tax could be moved in the House without the previous sanction of the Governor. Thus the Provincial Legislature was a non-entity in the financial sphere. The Governor could nullify its decisions even in the case of votable items of the budget.

Evaluation of the Provincial Legislature : The act of 1935 was not without some redeeming features. It was disappointing in view of the great expectations raised in Indian minds—before its enactment. But otherwise it did make a marked advance towards responsible Government in the Provinces. It increased the number of members in the Legislature. For the first time the Provincial Assembly became purely elected House. The practice of nominating members was completely given up in case of Assemblies although the Councils continued to have a small element of nominated members. The Provincial Legislature for the first time acquired the right to remove the Ministers by vote of no-confidence. The Act also abolished Dyarchy. All the spheres of Provincial administration were given over to the Ministers.

But this does not mean that the Provincial Autonomy was absolute and complete. It was cramped by various limitations. The ordinary and extraordinary powers of the Governor reduced the powers of both the Ministers and the Legislature to the minimum. Then there was the interference by the Governor-General. The assemblies, too, did not happen to be truly representative of national will. The presence of communal elements and the representatives of various classes and interests always stood against national interests. The warring camps within the Legislature weakened the progressive forces working for independence. There could not be formed any group in the Assembly strong enough to question and check the waywardness of the Government. The number of voters who elected the Assemblies was also kept so low that only 14 per cent of the total adult population got the right of vote. The introduction of second chambers was also something which merited criticism. It was, so to say, thrust upon the Provinces much against the wishes of the people. The Upper Houses served no useful purpose. They continued to be strong holds of reactionary elements and vested interests.

EXERCISES

Long Answer Type Questions

1. What is meant by Provincial Autonomy? Discuss its distinctive features.
2. What were the restrictions on the Autonomy of the Provinces? Discuss in brief.
3. Write a note on Governor. Discuss their Executive, Legislative and Financial powers.
4. Write a note on council of Ministers.
5. Write a note on Provincial Legislature.
6. What were the powers of the Provincial Legislature?

Short Answer Type Questions

1. Write any three distinctive features of Provincial Autonomy.
2. Write any three restrictions on the Autonomy of the Provinces.
3. Discuss the executive powers of the Governor.
4. What were the special responsibilities of the Governor?

5. Discuss the legislative powers of the Governor.
6. Write a note on power to issue ordinances.
7. Write a very brief note on the financial powers of the Governor.
8. Write a note on Council of Ministers.
9. Discuss the composition of the Provincial Legislature.
10. Discuss the tenure and officers of the Provincial Legislature.
11. Write a very brief note on the Legislative Powers of the Provincial Legislature.
12. What were the limitations on the competence of the Provincial Legislature?
13. Write a very brief note on evaluation of the Provincial Legislature.

Objective Type Questions

Choose the correct answer

1. From which Act the division of Provincial Subjects into Reserved and Transferred was abolished ?
   (*a*) Act of 1919 (*b*) Act of 1935
   (*c*) Act of 1833 (*d*) Act of 1774
2. From which Act the Provinces were at the mercy of the centre ?
   (*a*) Act of 1833 (*b*) Act of 1919
   (*c*) Act of 1935 (*d*) Act of 1774
3. From which Act the relations between the centre and the Provinces were regulated on Federal lines?
   (*a*) Act of 1784 (*b*) Act of 1853
   (*c*) Act of 1935 (*d*) Act of 1858

ANSWERS

1. (*a*) 2. (*b*) 3. (*c*)

20

CHAPTER

Working of the Provincial Autonomy

"The position of the Federal Ministers, under the new constitution, was ornamental without being useful, onerous without being helpful to the people they were supposed to represent, responsibility without power, position without authority, name without any real influence."

—Prof. K.T. Shah

Before commenting upon the introduction and working of provincial Autonomy it would be better to mention that Provincial Autonomy was mere farce and far from leading reality. It was not the desire of Britishers to give Indians the Autonomy in the working of the administration of their country. Their main aim was just to befool them. The following two views will reveal this fact :—

According to *Lord Zet land,* who was the then Secretary of State for India in 1937 : "The parliament or this country reserved to itself a potential measure of control in a certain limited and clearly defined sphere—the special responsibilities of the Governor. Since the Governors when acting in respect of special responsibilities were responsible both for acts of commission and omission, to the parliament of this country, he would naturally be prepared to answer any question bearing upon the discharge by the Governors of their duties within their spheres."

According to Joint Select Committee, Provincial Autonomy is a scheme "Whereby each of the Governor's Provinces will possess a Executive and a Legislature .... broadly free from control by the Central Government of Legislature. This we conceive to be the essence of Provincial Autonomy, though no doubt there is room for wide differences of opinion with regard to the manner in which that exclusive authority is to be exercised ... the Central Government and Legislature would, generally speaking, cease to possess in the Governor's Provinces any legal power or authority or respect to any matter failing within the exclusive provincial sphere, though, as we shall explain later, the Governor's authority to secure compliance in certain respects with directions, which he may find it necessary to give."

Thus, the Provincial Autonomy according to the Government of India Act was merely as sham.

BRIEF INTRODUCTION OF PROVINCIAL AUTONOMY

The Government of India Act was widely denounced. The Indian National Congress dobbed it "a prodigy of imperialist statesmanship." Pt. Nehru condemned that as "a new Charter of bondage." All the Indian leaders were bitterly against the federal scheme but the second part of the Act regarding the provincial government, was however accepted by them. The Indian National Congress decided to go into the Legislatures but not to co-operate with the government but to seek the end of it. Congress fought the election and its victory at the poles was very striking. The Congress gained overwhelming majority in Bombay, Madras, Bihar, Uttar Pradesh, Central Province and Orissa.

Now, the immediate task before the Congress was to accept the office. Though many prominent Congressmen including Pt. Jawaharlal Nehru were against the accepting of the Offices but the majority of the Congressmen were in favour of forming the government, At last with the efforts of Mahatma Gandhi a compromise came in. The Congress agreed to form the Ministry in those provinces where the party leaders would publicly announce that they would work on the advice of the Ministers and the Governor would not exercise his powers in day-to-day administration. The Governors of the Provinces refused to give this assurance and the Congress refused to form the ministry. Governors did their best to form the interim Ministry of non-congress elements.

After three months, the Viceroy Lord Linlithgow issued a statement for the co-operation between the Governors and the Ministers. This statement provided a ground for reapproachment. Ultimately the interim ministers resigned and the Congress formed governments in six provinces in October 1937. This was a historic decision for till now Congress has followed a negative policy and refused to undertaken the responsibility of office. Now, for the first time, congress adopted a positive attitude towards administration and agreed to take up the bending government." In three provinces *viz.,* the Punjab, the Bengal and Sindh coalition Ministries were formed.

Elections of February, 1937. As narrated already in the preceding chapter, the federal part of the Act of 1935 could not come into force because of the hostile attitude of all the political parties and the reluctance of the Indian rules. Only the other part of the Act which relates to the Provinces came into force in 1937. Consequently elections were held for the Provincial Legislatures in February, 1937. Although the Congress was vehemently opposed to many provisions of the Act, it decided to fight the elections not to work it but to wreck it from within. In other words the object of the Congress was to make the working of Provincial autonomy impossible by refusing to co- operate with the Government. The Muslim League and the Liberals also agreed to fight the elections in order to judge the merits of the Act.

The elections yielded significant results. The Congress obtained clear majorities in Madras, Bihar, Uttar Pradesh., Bombay, Central Provinces and Orissa, the Provinces which claimed two-thirds of the Indian population. In Assam the Congress emerged as the single largest party by capturing 35 out of 108 seats. In North-West Frontier Provinces also it gained 19 out of 50 seats. The Muslim League fared badly at the polls. It could secure only 51 of the total of 482 seats reserved for the Muslims in Provincial assemblies. Nationalist Muslims contested 58 seats on Congress tickets and captured 26. The League could not show its strength even in Muslim majority Provinces of Punjab, Bengal and North-West Frontier Provinces. It rather notable gains in Hindu majority Provinces of Uttar Pradesh, Central Provinces, Bombay and others, Since Muslim League was a purely communal organisation, there was not the remotest chance of its capturing any general seat. It became very evident from the election results that the Muslim League had a very lean and doubtful hold even over the Muslims. It was more active in Hindu Provinces where it could gain strength by inflaming communal passions and enlist goondas as its supporters. In the Punjab the Unionist party, which was coalition of all the communities, emerged as the strongest party. In Bengal the Praja Party and the Independents captured two-thirds of the total seats.

There raged for a time acute controversy in the Congress circles over the question of the formation of ministries in the Congress- dominated Provinces. The issue was decided in favour of office- acceptance. And in July, 1937, the Congress formed its ministries in six Provinces of U.P., Bihar, Madras, Bombay, Orissa and Central Provinces. In North West Frontier Provinces and Assam it agreed to form Coalition Ministries with the co-operation of other political parties. In Provinces where it had gained clear majority, it refused to give any concession to League in the Cabinet. It adopted this course on some sound reasons. It feared rightly that a set of Ministers divided in loyalties would not be able to work in a team spirit. The Muslim League Ministers in the Cabinet were also likely to obstruct the passage of land reform schemes. The non-inclusion of League members in the Cabinet, however, proved harmful. It strained the relations between the Hindus and Muslims. Muhammad Ali Jinnah levelled several charges against Congress.

That the League's charges were unfounded was proved conclusively by the statement of Sir Haig who was the Governor of U.P. at that time. He gave a clean chit to the Congress when he said in 1939 that 'in dealing with communal issues, the (Congress) Ministers had normally acted with impartiality and a desire to do what was fair'. Prof. Coupland who happened to be one of Cripps' team, also made similar observation in 1940.

WORKING OF THE PROVINCIAL AUTONOMY

The Ministries formed in 1937 in eleven Provinces of India had different stories to tell. They could not function smoothly. In Bengal, Sind and Punjab the new setup worked for ten years. In other Provinces the so-called responsible governments remained in saddle just for two years. In October, 1939, the Congress Ministries in eight Provinces tendered their resignations on war issue. The Governors in those Provinces by issuing a Proclamation of Emergency assumed all the executive and legislative powers to themselves. The Governors' rule lasted till 1946 when fresh elections were held and responsible governments once again set up in the Provinces.

(*a*) **Role of Governors in Congress Provinces.** In Congress dominated Provinces the Governors usually behaved decently. They did not interfere much with the work of the Ministers. Instances when the Governors exercised their special powers were also few. They extended their co-operation to the ministries by giving their assent to nearly all the Acts passed by the legislatures. Hence the initial fear that the Governors by invoking their special responsibilities would obstruct and undo the work of the ministers, proved untrue. No doubt a few deadlocks and crises did occur in Congress Provincial but they were soon resolved.

(*i*) **Khare Controversy in Central Province.** A crisis arose in Central Province when Dr. N.B. Khare, the Chief Minister, demanded *en bloc* resignation of his ministers so as to enable him to reconstitute the ministry. Two ministers refused to resign on the plea that they had received no direction from the Congress High Command to do so. Thereupon Dr. Khare laid down his own office. The Governor of Central Province came to his rescue. He removed the insubordinate ministers and called Khare to form the Cabinet again. The Congress protested against the role played by the Governor. It took disciplinary action against Khare also and replaced him by Shri Ravishankar Shukla as Chief Minister.

(*ii*) **Constitutional Crisis in Orissa.** The British Government decided to let the Chief Secretary of Orissa Government officiate during the absences of the Governor who was proceeding on leave. The Congress ministry in power refused to work under one of its subordinates. It threatened to resign. A deadlock was created. The Congress High Command also felt likewise that it was highly unjust to allow a secretary to act as the Governor of the Province. The Governor, however, saved the situation and averted the crisis by withdrawing his application for leave.

(*iii*) **Questions of Political Prisoners in Uttar Pradesh and Bihar.** The Congress Ministries in Uttar Pradesh and Bihar decided to release all the political prisoners in February, 1938. The Governors of both the Provinces opposed this move on the excuse that such a step would disturb the peace and tranquility of the Provinces. The Governor-General under Section 126 of the Act directed the Governors to refuse the release of prisoners by invoking their special responsibility. The ministries made it a prestige issue and resigned. It seemed for the time being that even the Provincial part of the Act was also not going to work well. The British Government ultimately relented its attitude. Negotiations started between Governor-General and the Congress and it was decided that the political prisoners would be released gradually after examining each individual case thoroughly.

Alleged Congress Persecution of Muslims in Uttar Pradesh. The Congress decision not to join hands with any communal organisation had severe repercussions. When the Congress left out the League in selecting the team of Ministers, the League began to raise the bogey of Hindu tyranny over the Muslims. It alleged that Congress was essentially a Hindu organisation and was committing atrocities on the poor Muslims. According to Maulana Azad, "The Congress refusal to offer two ministerial posts to the Leaguers who offered to form coalition on his condition was unfortunate because it gave the League a new lease of life. It was from Uttar Pradesh that the League was reorganised. Mr. Jinnah took full advantage of the situation and started an offensive which ultimately led to Pakistan." In fact we don't agree with Maulana's views. Even if the Congress had conceded two posts to the Leaguers, the situation could not have improved much. The solution lay not in appeasement by the Congress but in the change of hearts on the part of Muslims. A coalition cabinet could not have worked for a long time. True to its creed, the Muslim League would have persisted in defying and obstructing the Congress programmes. Its demands might have multiplied endlessly. The Congress had many a time in the past also tried to please the League but no good came out of it. Maulana's line of argument is fallacious. Pt. Jawaharlal Nehru also did not agree with him on this point.

The Congress rebutted League's charges and demanded a judicial inquiry into the allegations made by Jinnah. The Viceroy, however, cancelled the proposal of inquiry, because he himself was satisfied with the fair and secular conduct of the Congress. The Governor-General and the Governors refused to interfere with the working of Congress Ministries in the name of safeguarding the interests of minorities. Mr. Jinnah was sorely disappointed. Thus the working of the Provincial Autonomy till 1939 remained quite unsatisfactory. The Governors remained true to the assurance given by the Governor-General before the acceptance of office by the Congress. They acted as constitutional heads. After the resignation of Congress ministries in 1939, they once again became the real heads of the Provinces.

Part Played by Governors in Non-Congress Provinces. In non-Congress Provinces, the Governors enjoyed unlimited powers. There was no strong and organised party to challenge or block their interference. For instance, when the Governor-General consulted Punjab Governor on the question of the release of political prisoners, the latter without even consulting the Chief Minister, Sir Sikandar Hayat Khan, wrote back that the Punjab Government was not going to release them.

In October, 1942, Allah Bukhsh, the Chief Minister of Sind, was dismissed by the Governor arbitrarily. The reason was that the Chief Minister had expressed doubts in the claim of the British Government that it was fighting the Second Great War in the interest of the people. When Allah Bukhsh gave up his title of Khan Bahadur, the Governor dismissed him immediately although he enjoyed the solid support of the legislature. *In Sind, Bengal and North West Frontier Provinces, the governors showed undue favour to the League* and tried to keep it in power in spite of its poor strength in the Assembly. It was clearly unconstitutional. Shri Shyama Prasad Mukherjee was constrained to say that the Governor of Bengal, in view of his pro-Muslim leaning, ought to have been on the Muslim League benches.

Working of the Ministries. The responsible governments in the Provinces functioned quite freely for two years. As a matter of convention the leader of the majority party in the Assembly was invited to form the ministry. Every ministry held its office till it enjoyed the confidence of the Assembly. The allocation of portfolios which was constitutionally to be done by the Governors was in practice done on the advice of the leader of the majority party. The ministries worked also on the principle of joint responsibility. The members of Legislative Assembly could put questions to the Ministers and demand information. The Assembly could also obtain the resignation of the Ministry by passing a vote of no confidence. The Congress Chief Ministers nearly in all the Provinces made it a point to include Muslims in the cabinet. In Orissa the Congress refused to do so because there was no eminent Muslim to be given a ministerial post. The Muslims started an agitation against it and waited on the Governor. The Governor told the Muslims that although he could not interfere, he could assure them that their interests would not suffer in the least.

According to the Act, the cabinet meetings were to be presided over by the Governor. The Congress deemed it asinconsistent with the concept of a responsible form of Government. Since the amendment of the Constitution was out of question, the Congress ministries began to hold informal meetings without inviting the Governor. In formal meetings presided over by the Governor, the ministries did not discuss matters of serious importance. In non-Congress Provinces the presence of Governors was rather gaily welcomed. Sir Sikandar Hayat Khan, the Chief Minister of Punjab, once stated that the Governor with his mature administrative experience was always helpful in cabinet meetings.

Even after the resignation of Congress ministries, the British Government made a few vain attempts to observe the rules of responsible government. In Orissa and Assam the Governors called the leaders of minority groups to form the cabinets. Orissa chief ministership was offered to a person who had the support of only 14 in a House of 60 members. Similarly, Chief Minister of Assam was retained in his office even after being defeated at the polls. On the other hand, the Chief Ministers of Sind and Bengal were dismissed although they had the solid backing of a stable majority in the legislature. Another funny thing about it was that the removal of a Minister did not lead to the resignation of all Ministers. Such a practice was highly repugnant to the canons of a responsible form of Government. This broke the time-honoured convention of collective responsibility and its natural upshot was that the cabinets became ridden with rivalries and intrigues. The ministries became unstable. From 1937 to 1948 in Sind alone, five times the ministries were formed and dissolved.

Part Played by Public Service. When the part of the Act, which related to Provinces came into force, the high officials belonging to the Public Services feared that they would be harassed by the Congress Ministers. Some of them retired on the eve of the introduction of Provincial Autonomy. Others stayed on either with a desire to adjust themselves or to play mischief. Since the Public Services served as the backbone of the British rule in India, the British Government provided some additional safeguards for them in the Act itself. For their appointment and conditions of service, the civil services were put directly under the control of the Secretary of State. The Congress Ministers apprehend that the public services being directly under the control of British Government, would not co-operate with them but their experience proved that their distrust and fear were unfounded. Only once did a crisis arise because of the overbearing nature of a civil servant. The Chief Secretary of Uttar Pradesh issued a circular to all his sub-ordinate officials that they should not execute any order from any Minister unless it was countersigned by him. Pt. Govind Vallabh Pant who then was the Chief Minister of the Province naturally objected to such a circular and demanded explanation from the Chief Secretary. He called the circular an act of either insubordination or incompetency. The circular had to be withdrawn. This incident had a wholesome effect on all other civil servants in the country.

Influence of Congress-High Command on the Congress Ministries. The Congress in March, 1937, set up a Parliamentary Sub-Committee which came to be known as Congress High Command. The Committee had Dr. Rajendra Prasad, Maulana Abul Kalam Azad and Sardar Ballabh Bhai Patel as its members. It reviewed and supervised the work of the Congress Ministers and Legislators. It imposed discipline on the Ministers and saw to it that Congress election manifesto was earnestly worked out. All the Ministers abided by the instructions received from the High Command. Those who disregarded it were penalised as happened in Central Province, when Dr. N.B. Khare dared defy the High Command's directive, he was removed and replaced by Pt. Ravi Shanker Shukla.

Achievement of the Ministers. The Congress did laudable work during its term of office in various Provinces. The Congress Ministers busied themselves with constructive work. Soon after assuming office, they set about tackling the question of elementary education, industrial wages, cottage industries and uplift of Harijans. They provided relief to the agriculturists from indebtedness. Efforts were made to abolish the evil of drinking and to benefit the farmers by passing tenancy laws. The political prisoners were released and their properties restored. Reviewing the work of Congress Ministries, Prof. Coupland remarks, "The Congress ministries proved themselves capable and hardworking men with a high sense of public duty and responsibility ..... The Legislatures were well conducted, hardworking and, except for an increasing tendency to ask unnecessary questions, business-like..."

The working of Provincial Autonomy yielded beneficial results in other ways too. It served as a good training ground in public administration. The Ministers gained confidence to shoulder the responsibilities of similar nature after independence. The short period of Congress rule gave a taste of self-government to the people whose desire for full independence became stronger day by day in the succeeding years.

EXERCISES

Long Answer Type Questions

1. Write a note on the working of Provincial Autonomy.
2. Write a note on the working of the Ministries.
3. Discuss influence of Congress High Command on the Congress Ministries.
4. "Provincial Autonomy was mere farce and for from leading reality" Discuss this statement in brief.

Short Answer Type Questions

1. Give a brief introduction of Provincial Autonomy.
2. What was the role of Governors in Congress Provinces ?
3. Write a very brief note on Dr. N.B. Khare Controversy.
4. What do you know about Constitutional Crisis in Orissa? Write in very brief.
5. What was the question of Political prisoners in Uttar Pradesh and Bihar?
6. Discuss part played by Governors in Non-Congress Provinces.
7. Write a note on working of the ministries.
8. Discuss part played by public services.
9. Discuss influence of Congress High Command on the Congress Ministries.
10. What were the achievements of the minister ?

Objective Type Questions

Choose the correct answer

1. In which year the Act which relates to the Provinces came in to force ?

   (*a*) 1937 (*b*) 1938

   (*c*) 1939 (*d*) 1940

2. In which year elections were held for the Provincial Legislatures ?

(*a*) 1936 (*b*) 1937

(*c*) 1938 (*d*) 1939

3. In which Provinces the Congress obtained clear majorities ?

(*a*) Madras, Bihar

(*b*) Madras, Uttar Pradesh

(*c*) Madras, Bihar, Uttar Pradesh, Bombay, Central Provinces and Orissa

(*d*) Bihar, Bombay.

4. In which State Congress emerged as the Single Largest Party by capturing 35 out of 108 seats ?

(*a*) Madras (*b*) Bombay

(*c*) Bihar (*d*) Assam

5. In which year the Congress Ministries in eight Provinces tendered their resignations on War issue.

(*a*) 1939 (*b*) 1940

(*c*) 1941 (*d*) 1942

ANSWERS

1. (*a*) **2.** (*b*) **3.** (*c*) **4.** (*d*) **5.** (*a*)

21

CHAPTER

Quit India Movement and Dawn of Independence

(TRIUMPH OF NATIONALISM OVER IMPERIALISM, IMPERIALISTS QUIT, PAKISTAN ESTABLISHED)

"It was the compulsion of events and feeling that we could not get out of the deadlock or morass by pursuing the way we had done. So we accepted the Partition." —*Jawaharlal Nehru.*

WORLD WAR II AND CONSTITUTIONAL DEADLOCK

On 1st September, 1939, Germany triumphantly marched into Poland. Britain, foreseeing the danger to the free world, declared war on Germany on 3rd September, 1939. The Second World War broke out in Europe on September 3, 1939. Britain could not remain aloof from the war. The reason advanced by the British Government was that it wanted to make world safe for democracy. On the same day Lord Linlithgow, the Governor-General of India, also declared that India was at war with Germany. It was a unilateral decision taken by the Viceroy, without seeking or ascertaining the views of Indian leaders. Soon he set about getting into touch with political leaders of India. His object was to explore the ways how best to secure their co-operation in war efforts. The Leaders of the Congress greatly criticised the action of the Viceroy. *Maulana Abul Kalam Azad* has written : "We are asked to fight not because we choose to fight but because England wants her to fight. Co-operation must be between equals by mutual consent for a cause which both consider to be worthy. India cannot associate herself in a war said to be for democratic freedom, when the very freedom is denied to her and such limited freedom as she possessed taken away from her."

Congress Reaction. The Congress Working Committee met on 10th October, 1939. It passed a lengthy resolution expressing its sympathy with the free world and condemning Germany's aggression. But it declared that it could not associate herself in war unless the British Government publicly stated that India would be granted political independence at the end of war. The Congress also demanded immediate transfer of maximum of control over country's administration to Indians. The Congress was not making war a bargaining-counter but it earnestly felt that without immediate transfer of power, willing help from the public might not be forthcoming. Pt. Jawaharlal Nehru openly declared that "in a conflict between democracy and freedom on the one side and fascism and aggression on the other, our sympathies must inevitably lie on the side of democracy."

Viceroy's Declaration of October 17, 1939. The Viceroy in reply to Congress demand for responsible Government at the Centre, invited 50 representatives of different political groups and after discussing with them issued a statement on October 17, 1939. He said that Britain had plunged into war not in order to secure any personal gain but to guarantee lasting peace and better political institutions to the free nations of the world. He also gave an undertaking to India that at the end of war the government would be prepared to modify the Act of 1935 in the light of Indian wishes.

The Viceroy's reply to the demands of Congress did not convince the leaders of the Congress, to help Britain in such a crucial phase. They demanded that India must be declared an Independent Nation and then only they would help Britain in the war. The Viceroy again sent a reply to the Congress on October 17, 1939 in which he wrote that the Congress's immediate demand for substantial powers impracticable, and after the war, the Government could think over the entire constitutional scheme. This reply was strongly criticised by the Indian Leaders.

Resignation of the Congress Ministries. The Working Committee of the Congress condemned the statement as a repetition of the same old imperialistic policy. Mahatma Gandhi said that "the old policy of divide and rule is to continue. The Congress has asked for bread and it got stone." The Congress resolution said: "The Viceroy's statement is in every way unfortunate." The High Command issued instruction to Congress Ministeries to resign immediately. In eight provinces the Congress Ministries resigned forthwith. In all these Provinces the Viceroy declared the breakdown of the Constitution and authorised the Governors to assume all powers hitherto vested in and exercised by the Ministers and the Legislature. Thus, whatever semblance of responsible Government had been given to Provinces by the Act of 1935, was finished and the chapter of autocratic rule of the Governors began once again.

Attitude of the Muslim League Or Communal Role of Mr. Mohammad Ali Jinnah. In the preceding paragraphs we have already discussed the attitude of Congress to British war efforts. Now we will try to analyse the stand of the Muslim League. A candid no from the Congress regarding war help made the Viceroy lean more and more on the support of Muslim League. By a resolution passed on September 18, 1939, the League had already showed its sympathy with the British Government and promised to associate actively with war efforts provided the interest of the Muslims were safeguarded in Congress-dominated Provinces and secondly, that no constitution would be enacted by His Majesty's Government without consulting the League. Thus, Mr. Mohammad Ali Jinnah adopted the policy of sitting on the fence. He neither accepted Viceroy's statement of October 17, 1939 nor rejected it openly. On 5th November, 1939 Mr. Mohammad Ali Jinnah addressed a letter to Lord, Linlithgow asking for assurances on four points. The reply that he received was also conciliatory.

The resignations of Congress Ministries came as a boon to Muslim League. Mr. Mohammad Ali Jinnah decided to capitalise the opportunity. He called on Muslims throughout India to mark and observe 22nd December, 1939 as a day of deliverance from the 'tyranny, oppression and injustice' of the Congress regime in the Provinces. Mahatma Gandhi's advice to Mohammad Ali Jinnah against celebrating the Day of Deliverance fell on deaf ears. Pt. Jawaharlal Nehru expressed his annoyance to Mahadev Desai in the following words: "You must have seen Mr. Mohammad Ali Jinnah's new statement. There is a limit to political falsehood and indecency but all limits have passed away. I do not see how I can even meet Mr. Mohammad Ali Jinnah now." After this the Muslim League passed a resolution of Pakistan on 23rd March, 1940 (Its details have been given in Chapter X.).

Congress offers Constitutional Co-operation to the Government. The war situation in Europe was changing fast. It became grave by the middle of 1940. Denmark, Czechoslovakia, Poland, Norway, Holland, Belgium and France—all had gone down before Germany by this time. England too stood in great and immediate danger. It was going to nuts with the recurring air raids by German bombers. Hitler's sphere of influence was expanding day by day. The Nazism of Hitler posed a serious threat to the very existence of democracy. In view of all these Mahatma Gandhi revised and toned down his stand and declared that India would not seek her independence out of Britain's ruin. He felt that a change in Congress attitude was imperative. The Working Committee of the Congress met at Poona and by a resolution offered help to the British Government on two conditions–the first was that the British Government should recognise India's right to complete independence after war; and secondly, that it should agree to set up a National Government composed of all the parties immediately.

Churchill Comes to Power. In the meantime significant political changes took place in England. Mr. Churchill a rank conservative succeeded Mr. Chamberlain as Prime Minister and Amery took over from Zetland the office of the Secretary of State for India on 10th May, 1940, as Hitler was advancing triumphantly in Europe. The Conservatives who came to power in England were not at all sympathetic to Indian wishes. But the deteriorating war situation in Europe compelled the Conservatives to pacify Indians by conceding some of their demands. The Viceroy invited the leaders of public opinion and after consultations issued on August 8, 1940.

OFFER OF AUGUST 8, 1940

A statement consisting of new proposals was issued on August 8, 1940 and hence it has been called 'The August offer' of the Viceroy.

The few significant features of the offer were as follows:

(*a*) It was the definite objective of the British Government to *grant Dominion Status* to India.

(*b*) The British Government was in sympathy with the strong insistence by the Indians that they should be allowed to make a constitution for themselves. After the war a body representative of all the principal elements in India's national life would be set up to work out the Constitution.

(*c*) The Governor-General's Council would be expanded to include a certain number of representatives of all political parties.

(*d*) The Governor-General would also establish a War Advisory Council consisting of the representatives of all political parties an all other interest in the national life of India.

(*e*) That the Government would not transfer its responsibilities for peace and welfare of India to any party whose authority was not acceptable to any major group in India's national life.

(*f*) The full weight would be given to the views of minorities in the constitution.

(*g*) A new constitutional scheme would be built with in the British Commonwealth of Nations.

An Appraisal—August offer registered an advance of the first rate importance in the method of handling the Constitutional Problem. It was the first time that Indians were made primarily responsible for making the new constitution for India. It was also declared that the goal of British Government was to establish the Dominion status in India.

To quote Mr. Amery : "The Status of Dominion or of this country for that matter for our status in the Commonwealth although not perhaps our status in the same as theirs — is one not inferior to that of nations that perforce stand alone, but superior ... there is no higher status in the world."

Congress Rejects the Offer. The Congress rejected the offer for the following reasons :

1. The Congress had demanded the setting up of a Provincial National Government immediately with full control over the Defence. The Viceroy's offer was non-committal in this respect. It simply promised to include Indians in the Executive Council without assuring that Defence would also be transferred to some Indian Members of the Council.
2. The second sinister element in the offer was its promise to the League that no change in the existing set-up would be made without its consent which meant that the League would have

a veto over the future constitutional progress of India. This assurance to the League breathed the foulness of usual British game of 'divide and rule'. The Hindus were left at the mercy of the Muslims. Such a step was anti-national and highly provocative. It was this assurance that encouraged the League to press for Pakistan.

Muslim League Rejects August Offer. The Working Committee of the Muslim League met in New Delhi on 28th September, 1940 and by a resolution declared that it was unable to accept the offer. It demanded that the League and the Congress should be given nothing less than equal representation in the Executive Council. Secondly, the League Representatives should be appointed as non-official advisers to the Governors in the Provinces administered by them Section 93.

Criticism : Some critics of the August Offer have said that the British Government missed the last chance of bringing the Congress into the war. The Congress Working Committee showed it willingness to help Britishers in the war but the attitude of the Britishers was not favourable to them. Mahatma Gandhi was in their favour but the President of the Congress Maulana Abul Kalam Azad rejected the August Offer, Mahatma Gandhi himself was of the opinion that 'August Offer' widened the gulf between the Congress and England. The Muslim League welcomed the August Offer. According to them; the offer met the League's demand for a clear assurance to the effect that no further constitution interim or final should be adopted by the British Government without their approval and consent. The League declared that the partition of India was the only solution of the most difficult problem of Indian's future constitution but it was very surprising that the Muslim League neither accepted nor rejected the offer.

The August offer failed to achieve its object. It was a direct encouragement and incitement to civil discard and strife. It could neither satisfy the people nor did it succeed in gaining the Indian's cooperation for war. It further widened the gulf not only in Congress and Britishers but in Congress and Muslim League also.

INDIVIDUAL SATYAGRAHA, OCTOBER, 1940

The rejection of the Congress demands by the British Government once again disappointed the Congress as well as Mahatma Gandhi. On 13th October, 1940 the Congress Working Committee met in Wardha where Mahatma Gandhi unfolded his plan of Individual Civil Disobedience. England was facing the most critical hour of her life. For a person like Subhas Chandra Bose this was the most opportune time to strike the last and the hardest blow to the tottering skeleton of British Authority. But Mahatma Gandhi even while he was in a mood to fight, could not come out of his shell of gentlemanliness. By starting a mass movement, he did not like to embarrass the Government. So he decided to offer individual Satyagraha simply with a view to register his mild protest against the uncompromising attitude of the Government.

Mahatma Gandhi selected his disciple Vinoba Bhave to inaugurate the movement. He started delivering anti-war speeches and was arrested after four days. Pt. Jawaharlal Nehru was arrested next. The satyagrahis in their speeches appealed to the people not to extend war help to the Government. By May, 1941, nearly 14,000 satyagrahis courted arrest.

Expansion of the Viceroy's Executive Council. Regardless of the Congress satyagraha and its demands, the Viceroy decided that he could no longer follow the policy of wait and see. He issued a communique on 21st July, 1941, to enlarge the Executive Council. He raised the strength of the Executive from 7 to 12. The number of Indian members in it was also increased from 3 to 8, all of them to be chosen from outside the Congress and the League fold. The Indians thus became in majority in the Executive. The Viceroy threw up and played upon this fact to prove that the Indians were being given major share in the administration of India. It was a mere make-believe. *The vital departments like Defence, Home and Finance remained in the charge of British members.* It was a clear proof of British distrust of Indians. Moreover, since the new additions made to the Executive were not made from the ranks of the Congress or the League, people had no confidence in them. All the new members were so to say the 'yesman' of the Viceroy and most faithful servants of the Crown. Under the cover of democratic expansion of the Executive, *the Viceroy continued to be* the real head of the State, possessing dictatorial powers. The broadbasing or the expansion of the Executive made, as such, no radical change in its character.

Suspension of Individual Satyagraha. As a concession to public opinion, the Viceroy on 3rd December, 1941 announced the release of all the satyagrahis. He did so perhaps to celebrate the occasion of the appointment of new members in his Executive or may be to restore public's confidence in them. Mahatma Gandhi did not feel much happy with this step of the Viceroy. He, in a press interview, said that the releases 'cannot evoke a single responsive or appreciative chord in me'. He wished the civil disobedience to continue. But he advised the released Congressmen not to offer Satyagraha again until they received clear instructions from the Congress Working Committee.

Hitler had violated the Non-Aggression Pact concluded with Russia on 23rd August, 1939 and attacked it on 22nd June, 1941. In the meantime war situation in Europe became more critical. Hitler's armies were marching triumphantly through Russia. On 7th December, 1941 Japan struck at Pearl Harbour and started war in the Pacific. Next day Japan overran Shanghai and Siam without much resistance. Singapore, Malaya, Indo-China and Indonesia fell to the Japanese forces which kept on advancing towards Burma. The deteriorating war situation demanded reappraisal of Congress programme. The leaders were convinced that Britain was a lesser evil than Nazi Germany or Japan. The Congress, therefore, called off the movement for the time being. At his own request Mahatma Gandhi was relieved of the responsibility to lead the Congress. It was also felt that National Defence Corps should be organised to meet the emergency of war which approaching the threshold of India.

THE CRIPP'S MISSION

Cripp's Proposals (March 1942) to end the Deadlock

In 1942, the British Government realised that it was difficult to remain indifferent towards the Indian problem any longer. The war situation became worst. Calcutta was threatended by Japanese invasion but still the attitude of Indian National Congress did not change. The Congress was not prepared to help Britishers against anybody. This caused Mr. Winston Churchill to announce on March 11, 1942 that war cabinet had come to unanimous decision of Indian Policy and that in order to explain it and "to satisfy himself upon the spot by personal consultation that the conclusions upon which we all agreed and which we believe represent a just and final solution, will achieve their purpose. Sir Stafford Cripps, the Leader of the House of Commons would as the Emissary of British Government proceed as soon as possible to India." He also declared that "the crisis in the affairs of India arising out of the Japanese advance has made Britain wish to rallying all the forces of Indian life to guard their land from the menace of the invader."

Japan's spectacular success in conquering one country after another disturbed the complacency of the British statesmen. Both England and the U.S.A. began to feel the necessity of revising and softening of their attitude towards India. On 22nd March, 1942, the British Government sent Sir Stafford Cripps to negotiate with Indian political parties and secure their co-operation in the prosecution of war. The choice of Cripps was a significant one. He was a member of the British War Cabinet and leader in the House of Commons. Above all he was said to be a personal friend of Pt. Jawaharlal Nehru. He had lately returned from Russia after completing his mission successfully. Hence there could be no better person than he to come to India as a negotiator.

Causes Leading to the Cripps Mission in India. In Churchill's own words, 'the decision to send Cripps out to India was taken because the crisis in the affairs of India arising out of the Japanese

advance has made us wish to rally all the forces of Indian life guard their land from the menace of the invader.' The causes for the Cripps Mission were the following :

1. **The Congress although it condemned Fascism, Nazism and Japanese militarism, refused to give active co-operation to the Government and insisted on the fulfilment of her demands. The Individual Civil Disobedience Movement launched by Gandhi also had disturbing effect on war efforts. The British public began to realise that Indians must be given some definite and substantial assurance as a price for winning their help against advancing Japanese forces.**
2. **Pressure of Chiang Kai-shek.** The visit to India by Marshal Chiang Kai-shek and his wife in February, 1942, also underlined the need of semi-agreement between British Government and the Indian Leaders. Mr. Chiang Kai-shek during his stay conferred with the Government of India and several prominent leaders including Mahatma Gandhi and Mohammad Ali Jinnah. In his farewell speech he made an appeal to the Indians for help in war. He also expressed hope that Britain would as early as possible concede real political power to the Indian People.
3. **Pressure of Roosevelt.** President Roosevelt of America also had a soft corner for the national aspirations of India. He also felt that British imperialistic interests were the main hurdle in arriving at a mutually honourable settlement between England and India. He did not like Winston Churchill's announcement in September, 1941, that Atlantic Charter would not be applicable in the case of India. The gist of the Charter was that every country would have the right of self-determination at the end of war. Roosevelt knew well that the Indian support in war efforts was not forthcoming only because Britain was disagreeable to promise Dominion Status to India even after the war was over. He took up India's case with Winston Churchill and the latter announced that provisions of Atlantic Charter would be applicable to all the countries without any exception.
4. Pressure on Winston Churchill to negotiate with the Indian politicians came from Australia also. Australian Foreign Minister, Mr. Evatt, expressed his wish in the Australian Parliament that India should be given self-government so as to enable her to extend war help effectively.
5. **Immediate Danger of Japan.** Japan's successes in Singapore (Malaya), Indonesia and Andamans alarmed the Allies. Japanese Men-of-War had started patrolling the Bay of Bengal. On March 8, 1942, Rangoon also fell. The fall of Burma frightened the British Government. Mr. Winston Churchill later on in his autobiography admitted that he and all his friends felt that if India was to be defended against the invader, the political deadlock in India had to be resolved speedily by all possible means. Only three days after the fall of Rangoon, Mr. Winston Churchill declared that the British War Cabinet had decided to send Cripps to India with a new plan.

   Sir Cripps arrived in Delhi on March 22, 1942, with the draft declaration on the basis of which he was to conduct negotiations with the leaders of Indian Political Parties.

The Terms of Cripps' Proposal

The following were the terms of Cripps' Proposal :

1. **Establishment of Dominion.** The British Government in view of the political unrest and doubts in Indian minds about the fulfilment of any promise made on behalf of the Crown, stated in very clear words that their object was the creation of Indian Union which would constitute a Dominion, equal in every respect to other Dominions and in no way subordinate to any foreign power in its domestic and external affairs.
2. **Establishment of a Constitutional Assembly.** The British Government would see to it that an elected body was set up soon after the end of war to frame a new constitution for India.
3. Provision would be made for the participation of Indian States in the constitution-making body.

4. **Right of the Provinces to Make Separate Constitutions.** The Provinces would have the option to accept the new constitution or retain their existing constitutional position. Doors would be open for them to join the Indian Union at any stage later on. The willing Provinces would have the right to frame a constitution of their own and enjoy the same status as the Indian Union.

5. **Treaty.** A treaty would be negotiated between and signed by the British Government and the Constitution-making body of India. Such a treaty would cover all the *matters arising out of the complete transfer of responsibility* from British to Indian hands. The Constituent Assembly would be bound to honour the assurance given to the *racial and religious minorities* regarding protection of their interests. The treaty would, however, not impose any restriction on the power of Indian Union to revise its relations with other states.

6. Whether or not an Indian State agreed to accept the new Constitution, it would be binding on it to get its former treaty revised in accordance with the New Constitution.

7. **Composition of the Constituent Assembly.** The Constituent Assembly would be composed as follows, unless the leaders of Indian opinion agreed upon some other form before the end of war.

Immediately upon the end of hostilities, Provinces would go to polls. The entire membership of the Lower House of Provincial Legislature would form a single electoral college and proceed to elect the Constituent Assembly on the basis of proportional representation. The new body would, in number, be *about one - tenth of the electoral college.*

Indian States shall be invited to appoint representatives in the same proportion to their total population as in the case of representatives of British India as a whole and with the same powers as members of British Provinces.

Cripps' Proposals Relating to Interim Settlement

The draft further said —

"During the critical period which now faces India and until the new constitution can be framed His Majesty's Government must inevitably bear the responsibility for, and retain the control and direction of the defence of India as part of their world war effort; but the task of organising to the full the military, moral and material resources of India must be the responsibility of the Government of India with the co-operation of the people of India. His Majesty's Government desire, and invite, the immediate and effective participation of the leaders of the principal sections of the Indian people in the counsels of the country of the Commonwealth and of the United Nations. Thus they will be enabled to give their active and constructive help to the discharge of a task which is vital and essential for the future freedom of India."

Rejection of Cripps' Proposals by the Congress

Indians could not be satisfied by the Cripps' Proposals. There was a lot of frustration in the country against the proposal Mr. Cripps were rejected by every section of the Indian Community. The Congress also rejected the proposals brought by Cripps for the following reasons :

1. **The People of the States were not given the right to send their representatives.** The Congress in principle could not accept that the States in the Constituent Assembly may be represented by the nominees of the rulers and not by the elected representatives of the people. The Congress feared that the State nominees would form a reactionary bloc and in league with other groups would obstruct all progressive legislation.

2. **Right of the Indian States and the Provinces to keep out of the Indian Union.** The Congress stood for undivided India. It was deadly opposed to the creation of Pakistan. The provision

in the Cripps' scheme regarding the right of the Provinces to keep out of the Indian Union was a clear hint and encouragement to the Muslims to stick to their demand for Pakistan. The Congress resented the subtle attempt made by the British Government to break up the country into several independent States. The same sort of mischief was being played with regard to States. The Indian States were also given the choice to accept or reject the new Constitution. According to Sir Tej Bahadur Sapru and M.R. Jayakar, "*The creation of more than one Union, howsoever consistent in theory with the principle of self-determination, will be disastrous to the lasting interests of the country and its integrity and security.*" Jawaharlal commenting on it said : "The states as well as the Provinces would all join in the Constitution-making, would influence the Constitution, and then would walk out of it...... Reactionary elements differing from each other in many ways would unite to frustrate the evolution of a strong, progressive, unified national state." The Congress deplored the incentive which the proposals gave to separatism. Although the Congress was resolved not to compel any Province or State to remain in the Indian Union, still it intended to preserve the territorial integrity of the country unimpaired. Had the Congress accepted Cripps' proposals, the communal problem would have become more complicated and tense than ever before. Besides it, the country would have also been split into several sovereign States.

3. **Indians were not given control over Defence.** The British Government flatly rejected the Congress demand for Indian control over the Defence department. The proposals said that during the critical war-period and until the new Constitution was framed, the Defence was to remain in the hands of an Englishman. The Congress in a resolution passed on 2nd April, 1942 said: " British War Cabinet's proposals are vague and altogether incomplete and there appears to be no vital change in the present structure. At any time Defence is a vital subject ... to take away Defence from the sphere of responsibility at this stage is to reduce that responsibility to a farce and nullity." Congress demanded full freedom as a condition precedent to Indian co-operation in War effort. It stated clearly that a slave country cannot have inspiration to shoulder any responsibility in the prosecution of war.

4. **Refused of Cripps to make Viceroy as the Constitutional head and establish National Government.** The Congress in view of the grave war position, insisted on setting up of a national Government and making Viceroy a titular head. The Congress was worried not about the 'post-dated cheque' so much as about the interim arrangement. It wanted the Executive Council of the Governor-General to work as a cabinet. It believed in the principle of having one bird in hand rather than two in the bush. It worked on the criterion laid down in its resolution that 'the real test of any declaration is its application to the present.' It is wrong to say that Gandhiji was responsible for the rejection of Cripps' Proposals. In fact he alone was favouring it while other members of the Congress Working Comm0ittee were unanimous in their denunciation of the scheme. Gandhiji described the proposal as a 'post-dated cheque'; someone added 'on a failing bank.'

Rejection of Cripps' Proposals by Muslim League

The Muslim League also rejected the proposals brought by Cripps'. The Muslim League in a resolution passed on 11th April, 1942, stated the following reasons for rejecting the proposals:

(1) The proposals had not clearly accepted the League's demand for Pakistan. Notwithstanding the giving of right to the Provinces to retain their independence, the proposals appeared to lay stress on the formation of a single Union of India.

(2) The proposals *did not provide for another Constituent Assembly* compromising only *Muslim members.*

(3) The proposals had failed to *provide for separate electorate* system for the Constituent Assembly. It was likely to have Hindu majority in it.

(4) The proposals were regarding the protection of the interests of racial and religious minorities. It also did not make clear what the wording and contents of the treaty would be and who would be the enforcing authority to secure its compliance.

(5) The proposals had not made it compulsory for the States to join the Constituent Assembly, which the League considered unjust.

(6) No date for the proposed interim arrangement had been fixed in Cripps' scheme.

(7) The representation of the Muslims in Provincial Assembly was inadequate.

CAUSES OF THE FAILURE OF CRIPPS' MISSION

Sir Cripps who came to India in a sanguine mood failed miserably in his mission in spite of the fact that he was an eminent diplomat as well as a personal friend of Pt. Jawaharlal Nehru. Causes of his failure were as follows :

1. Inadequacy of the Proposals. The principal reason of the failure of Cripps' mission was that the proposals were quite inadequate in substance to pacify the Indian leaders. They fell far short of the demands of the Congress and the League. According to Dr. A.K. Ghosal, the method of forming the Constitution-making body was defective based to sectionalism and communalism. The Provinces were considered as units to send representatives to the Constituent Assembly.

2. Nominated Members of the States. Another serious defect in the composition of the Constituent Assembly was the presence of the nominated members of the States. It was feared that the State nominees, in conjunction with other reactionary forces, would form a powerful group to oppose the Congress. Another shocking suggestion in Cripps' scheme was right of a Province to form an independent government and to frame a separate constitution. This provision was calculated to give the hardest and most fatal blow to the unity of the country. In that case there would have been not two but half a dozen Pakistans in India. The Congress was concerned more with the immediate gain than a deferred one. Its minimum demand was the setting up of a responsible government at the Centre with Indian control over the Defence Department. Since the British Government did not agree to it, the Congress could not but reject the scheme.

3. Selfish and Uncompromising attitude of British Authority. It was an admitted fact that the British Government was unwilling to confer independence on India. The British statesmen were planning to tide over, the war crisis with Indian help secured by befooling them. They were not sincere and firm even in regard to post-dated promises that they made. If the British were going to part with total power at the end of war, observes Michael Brecher, " a limited transfer could take place during the conflict, including the creation of a substantive Indian-controlled Defence Ministry, one of the technical bones of contention."

Laski remarked, " It seems that His Majesty's Government presided over by Mr. Churchill did not send Sir Stafford Cripps to India with an honest and earnest desire to solve the deadlock, the real thought was less the achievement of Indian freedom than of a *coup de main* in the propaqandist art among our allies who contrasted American relations with the Philippines against British relations with India." A Calcutta paper the *Statesman* wrote: "So long as the India Office and the Government of India drafted the proposals, no emissary can succeed and no effort will be made to cope with hourly increasing danger to this country. The blame lies with India Office and the official section of the Government of India."

4. Lord Halifax's Speech, April 7, 1942. Another reason which accounted for the sudden breakdown of the negotiations between Cripps and the Congress was the speech of the British ambassador in the U.S.A., Lord Halifax. While the atmosphere in India was alight with a fair degree of optimism, Lord Halifax criticised the Congress and predicted the failure of negotiations in India. He said, "If our best efforts fail, the British Government would find itself obliged to do its own duty without the assistance or co-operation of the larger organised Indian parties. We have had no co-operation from the Indian National Congress, the largest and best organised political party in India." He also added that the claim of the Congress to speak for the whole of India was also not true or tenable. His speech had an unhealthy effect on the attitude of Cripps. Only three days after Halifax's speech, Cripps wrote a sharp letter to the Congress President accusing the Congress of trying to lord over the minorities. Such a baseless accusation pained the leaders of the Congress which thereafter adopted a more stiff and uncompromising attitude than it was before.

5. Lack of Confidence in the Motives of the British. There was acute distrust of the British intensions in Indian minds. The bitter memories of the British attitude after the First Great War were still fresh. Indians being once burnt felt twice shy to attach any credence to British promises. Their misgivings were further confirmed by Churchill's statement in 1941 that he had assumed the office of British Prime Minister not with the purpose of disintegrating the British Empire. He had also stated that the principle of self-determination as mentioned in the Atlantic Charter would not apply in the case of India and Burma. Hence the Congress and all other major parties were resolved to secure something substantial and immediate before agreeing to extend war help to the British Government.

6. Wrong Notions of Cripps and His Tactless Handling of the Situation. Cripps, in fact, was labouring under many wrong notions. He had too inflated a notion about his diplomatic skill. He believed that his scheme was the best for solving the deadlock in Indian politics. Secondly, he proceeded with the wrong presumption that Pt. Jawaharlal Nehru could always carry the Congress with him. Pt. Jawaharlal Nehru himself explained his position in a letter to one of his friends : "Cripps could not understand that there were limits beyond which I could not carry the Congress and there were limits beyond which the Congress could not carry the people."

Cripps himself was partly responsible for the breakdown of negotiations. He tackled the situation clumsily. At first he agreed to set up a national and responsible government at the Centre but later on under the pressure of British Prime Minister and Indian Viceroy he changed his mind. By doing so he lost the trust reposed in him by Indian leaders. He committed another mistake by writing a strongly worded letter to the Congress President. For these two reasons the Congress refused to take his proposals seriously.

7. Firm Principles of the Congress. The Congress firmly adhered to its demand for complete independence. Nothing less than that was acceptable to it. Maulana Abul Kalam Azad writes in his book '*India Wins Freedom*' that he told Pt. Jawaharlal Nehru : *"If we accept Cripps' offer, we might have cause to rue it in future. In case the British went back on their word, we should not even have the justification for launching a fresh struggle. War had given India an opportunity for achieving her freedom. We must not lose it by depending upon a mere promise.*" Still the doors were open for an honourable settlement on the principle of 'give and take'. The atmosphere was quite congenial. Pt. Jawaharlal Nehru is said to have declared after Cripps' departure : "We are not going to surrender to Japanese invaders. In spite of all that had happened we are not going to embarrass British war effort in India." The Congress was earnest in its desire for a solution. The British authorities alone were responsible for undoing the work of Cripps and prolonging the constitutional crisis in India.

8. Question of Defence and the Veto of Viceroy. The Congress demanded cash, not a deferred payment for its war help. It cared more for immediate gain. At a time when the Japanese forces were at the threshold of India, the Congress was not going to be pacified by the inclusion of a few Indians in the Viceroy's Executive Council. It demanded a national government at the Centre with Viceroy acting as a nominal head. Neither Sir Cripps nor the British Government agreed to immediate transference of power. The second point which sealed the fate of Cripps' offer was disagreement over the control of Defence Department. The Congress claimed full control of the Defence in Indian hands while Cripps agreed to give only partial control. He consented to the appointment of a Defence Minister who might look after trivial matter of defence while all the important decisions were to be taken by the Commander-in-Chief. Talks failed because the Congress was disinclined to have a lukewarm control over the vital department of defence.

ANALYSIS OF THE CRIPPS' PROPOSALS

Pt. Jawaharlal Nehru's critical analysis of these proposals is worth quoting. He remarks,

"The more one thought of these proposals, the more fantastic they grew. India became a chequer-board containing scores of nominally independent or semi-independent States, many of them relaying on Britain for military protection of autocratic rule. There was to be neither political nor economic unity and Britain might will continue to exercise dominating power both physically and economically, through the many petty states she controlled."[1]

Mahatma Gandhi thought these proposals as inadequate and treated them as post-dated cheque. He opposed these proposals from the very begining. He is stated to have told to Cripps frankly: "*Why did you come if this is what you have to offer? If this is your entire proposal to India, I would advise you to take the next plane home.*" Dr. Pattabhi Sitaramayya observed, "Cripps' proposals embodied different items palatable to different tastes. To the Congress there was the Preamble which spoke of Dominion Status... and above all the Constituent Assembly and its right of secession even at the outset. To the Muslim League there was highly comforting provision of any Province having the right to secede from the Indian Union. The Princes were not only left free to join or not to join but were given the sole right to send representatives to the Constituent Assembly... There was no intention to part with power in them."[2]

Withdrawal of Cripps' Proposals. Owing to the unwillingness of all the political parties to accept the proposals, Sir Cripps withdrew his offer. On 12 April, 1942,he left for England.

QUIT INDIA MOVEMENT OF 1942 (LAST GREAT STRUGGLE OF THE CONGRESS TO OUST THE IMPERIALISTS)

Circumstances leading to Quit India Movement — On April 11, 1942, suddenly the Cripps proposals were withdrawn and the whole drama of Cripps Mission to India Proved to be cnly a propaganda without any intention of acceding to the demands of the Indians. Before the outside world, Britishers painted a dark picture of India as a divided house unfit for the immediate freedom, but in India there was utter frustration and disgust. The Congress efforts to re-organise India for an effective fight against the Japanese menance received a severe jolt and the general masses in India were bitterly against the Britishers. *Maulana Abul Kalam Azad* writes : " There was great bitterness against the British which at that time was so intence that they did not think of the consequences of the Japanese conquest of India." In the meanwhile, Japanese danger to India greatly increased and their attack on Bengal seemed imminent. However Mahatma Gandhi was of the opinion that if the British immediately left India there would be no reason left for Japan to attack this country. It was, therefore, proposed that 'Quit India' resolution should immediately be passed. The demand was for an immediate transfer of power to Indian failing which the Congress would, launch a non-violent movement against the British, Mahatma Gandhi was perhaps of the opinion that at the time when Japan was knocking at the very doors of India, the British Government in India would not take drastic steps against the movement and try to come to terms with the Congress.

(1) Cripps negotiations broke down because of the British obstinacy regarding term arrangement. Cripps offered a long-term plan whereas the Congress stuck to its demand of a Cabinet Government at the Centre immediately. All the parties rejected the offer for one or the other reason. Cripps in his frustration threw the entire responsibility for the failure of his mission on the Congress. In his speeches

1. Nehru, J. L., *Discovery of India*, p. 467.
2. Dr. Pattabhi Sitaramayya, *The History of the Congress*, p. 399

in London he raised an accusing finger at the Congress. This led to worsening of political situation in the country. Moreover, the abrupt announcement regarding the breakdown of negotiations and his swift departure from India convinced Indians that Cripps had deceived them in the interests of British propaganda in America. Some said that Cripps had no mission to fulfil except that of showing to the free world that the British were earnest in transferring power in Indian hands but Indians were a fool to decline the offer. Then there was vile propaganda going on in British Press that the Congress did not represent all sections of Indian people and that the British did not know whom to hand over the reins of the Indian administration. Such silly talks by the British statesmen caused much pain and despair in Indian hearts. People in exasperation began to feel that freedom could not be won by peaceful methods.

(2) The threat of Japanese invasion of India was becoming a grave reality. The long line of Indian refugees from Burma was pouring into India with their tales of woe and misery. Mr. Aney, who as a member of Viceroy's Executive Council and incharge of welfare of Overseas Indians, flew to Burma to see for himself the plight of Indians. He was accompanied by Pt. Hridaya Nath Kunzru and Mr. Dam. On return they issued a statement which said that Indian refugees were being treated in a manner as though they were 'pariahs' or untouchables.

(3) Mahatma Gandhi wrote in *Harijan* on May 10, 1942, "The admitted inequality of treatment of Indian and European evacuees and the manifestly over-bearing behaviour of troops are adding to the distrust of British intentions and declarations."

(4) Another factor which drove the people to the end of their tether was the reign of terror in East Bengal. The Government had acquired a vast land for military purposes. Thousands of farmers were thrown out of their ancestral fields. It created a good deal of unrest and agitation in every heart. It was not all. The Government added to the miseries of the people by destroying thousands of country-made boats which were the principal means of livelihood for lakhs of people. The prices of essential commodities also went up. Indians lost faith in paper currency.

(5) The national leaders were convinced that the English were too weak to defend India. This belief was strengthened by British reverses in Singapore, Malaya and Burma. They also felt that the Japanese had a grudge only with the British and if they left India immediately, the Japanese might give up the idea of invading India. Inspired by this belief, Mahatma Gandhi told the British to quit India lock, stock and barrel. On 5th July, 1942, he wrote in *Harijan* : "Don't leave India to Japan but leave India to Indians in an orderly manner." The menace of Japan had become so imminent that the Government had plans to evacuate Eastern India. This was the most opportune time, thought the Congress, for the orderly and timely withdrawal of the British from India.

'Quit India' Resolution, August 8, 1942. The country as one man was feeling desperate with the slow pace of events at the higher level. Japanese were advancing at terrific speed while the Government was not making any headway towards resolving the deadlock. Mahatma Gandhi felt that some quick and strong action was needed to meet the challenge of Japan. And that step could not be taken unless the Indians were made masters of their destiny. He wrote a number of articles in *Harijan* exhorting the people to be active. It was intolerable for him to see people accepting things lying down. He favoured the plan of some direct action even if it meant hampering the war efforts. In order to give shape to Mahatma Gandhi's views, the Congress Working Committee met on July 14, 1942, at Wardha and adopted the famous 'Quit India' Resolution. This resolution was accepted with some modification by All India Congress Committee when it met in Bombay on 7th and 8th August, 1942. The resolution ran on the following lines :

"That the immediate ending of the British rule in India is an urgent necessity both for the sake of India and for the success of the United Nations. The continuation of that rule is degrading and enfeebling India and making her progressively less capable of defending herself and of contributing to the cause of world freedom...(If India became free) a provisional Government will be formed and free

India will become an ally of the United Nations... It will be a composite Government representative of all important sections of the people of India. Its primary function must be to defend India and resist aggression with all the armed as well as non-violent forces at its command."

The resolution said :

"The Committee, therefore, resolves to sanction for the vindication of India's inalienable right to freedom and independence, the starting of a mass struggle on non-violent lines on the widest possible scale, so that the country might utilise all the non-violent strength it has gathered during the last 22 years of peaceful struggle... They (the people) must remember that non-violence is the basis of the movement..."

Repression of the Quit India Movement by the Government. The Congress Resolution of 8th August, 1942 was not in the nature of an immediate ultimatum or challenge to the British Government. It was a sort of policy-statement. Mahatma Gandhi did not mean to take any hasty step. He had written a letter to the Viceroy and was awaiting the reply. In his letters to President Roosevelt and Marshal Chiang Kai-shek, he had expressed hope that they would mediate and persuade the British Government to see reason and to grant independence to India. The Government, however, adopted its usual course.

On the 9th August, 1942 morning, following the adoption of Quit India Resolution, Mahatma Gandhi along with all other members of the Congress Working Committee was arrested under Section 26 of D.I.R. They were lodged in Agha Khan Palace in Poona and Ahmedanagar Fort. The whereabouts of the leaders were kept a secret from the public for a long time. The Congress Organisation was banned and party funds were forfeited. The police raided its offices and used severest measures to suppress the movement.

Character of the Movement. The news of sudden arrest of all Congress leaders took the people by surprise. The leaderless masses did not know what course to follow. No clear instructions had been issued by the Congress. Mahatma Gandhi had stated simply this much: "It will be a movement which will be felt by the whole world. It may not interfere with the movement of British troops, but it is sure to engage British attention. He had called upon the people to 'do or die'; and further said, "We shall either free India or die in the attempt." But at the same he had categorically stated that he was opposed to 'open rebellion.' It was to be mass movement of a 'strictly non-violent character.'

In this hour of confusion the remaining leaders of the Congress issued a booklet on behalf of the Party. This booklet contained 12-point programme as to how the movement was to be carried on. It included such items as peaceful *hartals* (strikes) throughout the country, manufacture of salt, nonpayment of land revenue, etc. Later on the point of strike by the workers and Government servants was also included in the booklet of instructions. There was specific instruction that the means of communications were not to be dislocated at all. The people were asked to put police stations, *tehsils* and district headquarters out of action through non-violence. The term nonviolence being vague, Shri K.C. Mashruwala clarified the scope of Ahimsa on August 23, 1942. He wrote : "In my opinion looting or burning of offices, banks, granaries, etc. is not permissible. Dislocation of traffic communications is permissible in a non-violent manner without endangering life." But after the arrest of leaders, the leadership of the movement passed into the hands of such men as did not care to take ample precaution to safeguard life. Hence the movement took a violent turn.

Phase of the 'Quit India' Movement. Roughly speaking, the movement passed through four phases. The first phase began from the day of Mahatma Gandhi's arrest, *i.e.*, 9th August, 1942. It lasted for three to four days. This period was marked by strikes (hartals), demonstrations, processions and meetings. The greatest enthusiasm was shown by labourers in mills and factories. The textile mills particularly those in Ahmedabad and Madras had to be closed. This imposed war efforts because the mills could not supply khaki cloth to the military. The Tata Iron and Steel Mills were also affected. The workers of Aircraft Factory, Bangalore, and Imperial Tobacco Company, Saharanpur, joined their fellow strikers at other places. The workers employed in big factories and mills returned to their villages and carried the flame of revolution with them. The Government resorted to repressive measures in order to suppress the movement. In Bombay alone the police opened fire as many as 13 times till 2.30 p.m. in a single day on 11th August, 1942. The casualties include women and children. This indiscriminate firing changed the character of movement which henceforth turned into a riot. Had the Government acted prudently and allowed the demonstrations to take place peacefully, the movement would have subsided automatically.

In the second phase of the movement, the people raided municipal and other Government buildings. Railway stations, police stations and post offices were also attacked and many of them set on fire. Wires were cut and rails were removed. In several Provinces the infuriated mob also attempted to capture the court buildings. Maximum damage was done to railway departments in Madras, Eastern Uttar Pradesh and Bihar where even the train service had to be suspended for a few days. In some parts this mob tried to burn the records and loot the Government treasury. In Ballia and some other parts of Eastern Uttar Pradesh, even provincial governments and courts were set up. Troops were called into terrorise the mob by firing and other atrocious measures.

The movement entered its third phase in September, 1942. In sheer desperation the mob resorted to armed attacks as happened in Madras and Bengal. In Bombay, Uttar Pradesh and Madhya Pradesh, the mob is said to have thrown bombs on the police. In its fourth phase, the movement became mild again as in its first phase. It continued till Mahatma Gandhi's release in May, 1944, in the form of demonstrations and processions on certain days of the month. Bal Gangadhar Tilak Anniversary and Independence Day were observed by taking out processions. Shri Jaya Prakash Narain and Shrimati Aruna Asaf Ali took leading part in this revolt. The contribution of students, peasants and workers was also commendable. The Muslims generally kept aloof. The landlords, rich merchants and princes also did not lend any support to the movement.

Importance of Movement. The revolt of 1942 is a memorable event of our national movement. It cannot be brushed aside as a trivial attempt for freedom. It was, we may say, the last formidable mass movement for securing freedom. According to data collected from varied sources, the police and the military had to open fire on 538 occasions. The official figure of the persons dead as a result of firing is 1,028, although unofficial estimates vary from 10,000 to 40,000. 60,229 persons were arrested. The immediate goal of the great uprising of 1942 was to secure freedom which it, no doubt, failed to realise. *The movement, however, succeeded very well in awakening and emboldening the masses. It removed from Indian hearts the fear of bullets. The movement in fact prepared the ground for the transfer of power.* The slogan of 'do or die' entered the souls of the people. This fury of unarmed people shook the roots of British rule in India. Even the Englishmen had to admit and prophesy that if the British failed to find soon a way of handing over power smoothly, there was likelihood of a greater revolution to drive them out. One unfortunate result of the movement was that the British and the Muslims in their common hatred for the Congress, came closer to each other. Mr. Mohammad Ali Jinnah acted as a staunch ally of the Government. He tapped all his resources to help the British war effort. He also told the Muslims to keep away from the Congress Movement of 1942. The Government, at a time when Japan was knocking at the door, badly needed. Mohammad Ali Jinnah's faithfulness to the Crown, that the British Government obliged him by granting his demand for Pakistan.

Some Reactions Abroad. One important gain of the revolt of 1942 was that it drew the attention of many nations to India's demand for Independence. The moral pressure of American public opinion became so strong that the British Government willy-nilly had to hand over independence to India. Marshal Chiang kai-shek also wrote to American President, Mr. Roosevelt, in July, 1942, that it was in British interest to expedite the transfer of real political power to Indians. Mr. Chiang kai-shek then wrote to Btitish Prime Minister also in the same tone.

Attitude of Muslim League and Communist Party Towards this Upheaval. The attitude of Indian Communist Party towards the Second World War was governed by the instructions received from Moscow. At the outbreak of war, the party called it an imperialistic war. But this stand changed completely as soon as Germany invaded Russia and Russia signed a defence pact with England and France. The Indian Communists began to call it Peoples' war to extend helping hand to the Government. The Communists naturally boycotted the Quit India Movement of 1942. For this betrayal, the Congress expelled all Communists from its fold.

The Congress did not get much active support from the Indian Muslims, except the Nationalist Muslims like Maulana Abul Kalam Azad, Rafi Ahmad Kidwai and Khan Abdul Gaffar Khan. Mr. Mohammad Ali Jinnah in order to earn the goodwill of the Government, denounced the movement and directed his followers not to have anything to do with it. The Muslim League endorsed the stand taken by Mohammad Ali Jinnah in a resolution adopted on August 20, 1942, the League declared that: "The Muslim were not a whit less insistent than the Congress on the attainment of independence, but the purpose of the Congress was not to secure freedom for all constituent elements in the life of India but to bring the establishment of a Hindu Raj and to deal a death-blow to the Muslim goal of Pakistan." The League also warned the revolutionaries that if they attempted to interfere in the normal life of the Muslims, they would meet with stiff resistance.

Causes of the Failure of 1942 Movement. The revolt of 1942 lasted for three months only. Broadly speaking, it failed in its attempt to paralyse the Government machinery in order to seize power. According to Dr. Amba Prasad, there were three main causes of its failure : "(1) Tactical mistakes of organisation and planning; (2) loyalty of the services; and (3) superior physical strength of the Government."

Dr. Amba Prasad writes : "Since it was a mass movement and involved a programme of action much wider in scope than that of any of the earlier movements, it required a different technique from the one Mahatma Gandhi was used to in his satyagraha campaigns. It was necessary that leaders should know the entire strategy and go underground before the Government clapped them into jails. As we have seen no one knew what course of action had to be taken. Mahatma Gandhi was proceeding on two assumptions : firstly, that the British would be willing to negotiate if threatened with a mass movement at that moment of crisis, since he credited them with a high sense of realism; secondly, he had hoped that he would not be arrested as was the case in 1930." Pt. Jawaharlal Nehru also felt likewise. He wrote that : "Mahatma Gandhi, to our surprise, still clung to the belief that a settlement with the British Government was possible, and he said he would try his utmost to achieve it. And so, though he talked a great deal about action, he did not define it or indicate what he indended to do." According to Jai Prakash Narain, "the lack of organisation was so considerable that even important Congressmen were not aware of the progress of the revolt and, till late in the course of the uprising, it remained a matter of debate in many Congress quarters whether what the people were doing was really in accordance with the Congress programme."

The second factor that accounted for the failure of the movement was the unflinching loyalty of the Government servants and officials. The military, the police, the State rulers and the big businessmen—all helped the Government in crushing the revolt. The Government offices in spite of such a mass uprising continued to work smoothly. Thirdly, it was not a child's play to measure swords with the Government which had ample resources at its disposal to run the engine of repression. The satyagrahis and demonstrators had no intelligence department to communicate with their fellowmen in other towns under cover of secrecy. Their financial position was also immensely weak. Despite the failure and weakness of revolt, it created mass awakening never witnessed before.

Results. The heroism and courage shown by the people did not go waste. The sacrifice of the patriots brought the country nearer its goal of independence and within five years of this uprising, the country got her freedom. All the national leaders after their release from jail stated very clearly that they were proud of the doings of the people. Pt. Jawaharlal Nehru declared : "I am very proud of what happened in 1942 ... I make it plain that I cannot condemn those who took part in the 1942 movement." Sardar Ballabh Bhai Patel's strong words were : *Never before had such widespread uprising happened in India in the history of British Raj; as they did during the last three years. We are proud of the spirit in which the people reached.*" Mahatma Gandhi told Sir Reginald Maxwell in unequivocal terms : "I cannot cancel the Congress rebellion which is of a purely non-violent character. I am proud of it. I have no reparations to make, for I have no consciousness of guilt." According to Dr. Ishwari Prasad, "*All talk of Dominion Status was consumed in the fires of the revolt. India could have nothing short of independence. 'Quit India' had come to stay. It was a terrific blow to the imperial India.*"

Gandhiji's Fast and Release from Jail. The Government threw the entire responsibility of widespread violence on Gandhiji. It claimed to be in possession of ample documentary evidence to prove that he Congress kept a double face. It talked of peace and non-violence in one breath but encouraged armed rebellion in the other. Gandhiji rebutted such baseless charges and decided to observe 21 days' fast to prove his innocence before God. The fast began on 19th February, 1943. He grew weaker day by day. His condition became critical after 13 days. There was countrywide agitation for his release. But the Viceroy refused to set him free. In protest, the three Indian members of the Viceroy's Executive Council—H.P. Modi, N.R. Sarkar and M.S. Aney—laid down their offices. Even the physicians attending on Gandhiji doubted if Gandhi would outlive the fast. But despite his old age and worsening condition, Gandhi survived his fast. Kasturba Gandhi died while Gandhi was in detention. In April, 1944, Mahatma Gandhi fell seriously ill again. Lord Wavell, who had taken over as the Viceroy of India, in October, 1943, released him on 6th May, 1944.

WAVELL PLAN AND SIMLA CONFERENCE (JUNE, 1945)

The war in Europe had ended but it was raging in Asia. Japan was still unbeaten. World attention was now focussed on the Eastern front. India was to be the base of military operations against Japan. The British now more than ever before needed the moral and material support of the Indian people. It was the one reason why the British Government made a new offer for settlement. The other two reasons were the pressure from the Russian Government and the accusation by the Labour Party that Churchill was incapable of handling the constitutional crisis in India. Lord Linlithgow completed his term in October, 1943, and Lord Wavell became the new incumbent of the office of Viceroy of India. Soon after his appointment Wavell announced that he was carrying bagful of presents for the Indian people. But after taking over the charge, he did nothing except releasing Mahatma Gandhi from jail in May, 1944.

Wavell flew to London on 21st March, 1945 to consult His Majesty's Government on Indian affairs for about a month and a half. During this period, the hostilities in Europe had ended and the entire attention of Allies was diverted towards Japan. This necessitated the return of Mr. Wavell to India and Mr. Amery, The secretary of state for India and Lord Wavell simultaneously issued a statement which is known as Amery–Wavell Plan of Simply Wavell Plan. Wavell came back on 4th June, 1945. On 4th June, 1945 he published his new plan known as Wavell Plan.

Main Provisions of Wavell Plan

This plan was mainly related to Viceroy's Executive Council and the following provisions were proposed :

(1) Lord Wavell's Plan was a sort of interim arrangement till a new Constitution for India was framed and agreed to by Indians themselves. The highlight of the Plan was the reconstitution of Viceroy's Executive Council. It was to be largely Indian in character and composition, and more representative of the organised political opinion in the country. It was to have only two

Englishmen—the Viceroy acting as its President and the Commander-in-Chief holding war portfolio. The Executive was to include equal number of Caste Hindus and the Muslims.

(2) The proposals, as Wavell said in his broadcast, were designed to ease the political situation and to advance India towards her goal of full self-government.

(3) Leaving the border arrangement and tribal affairs, all other affairs were to be looked after by the Indians themselves.

(4) The new Executive Council was to work under the Act of 1935. Lord Wavell, however, assured that he would not exercise his overriding powers unreasonably. He also promised that if at all the Secretary of State interfered, it would be not in British interests but in the interests of India.

(5) Since the Viceroy had to perform the dual role of the representative of the Crown and Head of the Indian Executive, the Wavell Plan proposed to appoint a High Commissioner to look after Great Britain's commercial interests in India.

(6) The Executive Council was to work like a Provisional National Government.

(7) The formation of the Interim Government was in no way to prejudice the framing of a New Constitution at some later stage by the the Indians themselves.

(8) The Provinces, which were being administered by the Governors under Section 93, were to have ministries again formed on coalition basis.

(9) All these changes will be introduced without making any change in the existing statute law except for one amendment to the 9th schedule to the Act of 1935 requiring that not less than three members of the Council must have atleast 10 years service under Crown in India.

Simla Conference and its Failure

With most of the political leaders in jail, political life of the country was practically at a standstill. In order to enable the Congress leaders to participate in the conference and also make the atmosphere congenial for a settlement, Lord Wavell ordered the release of all the members of the Congress Working Committee. He sent invitations to 21 leaders including the former Chief Ministers of Provincial Governments, the leaders of the Congress and the League in the Council of State, Gandhiji and Jinnah and one representative each of the Sikhs and the Scheduled Castes. The political conference began its deliberations in Simla on 29th June, 1945.

The question of parity of Caste Hindus and Muslims in the Viceroy's Executive also created some problem. The Congress, although quite unwillingly, agreed to equal representation of Hidus and Muslims in the Cabinet, it was certainly not prepared to forgo its right of appointing nationalist Muslims. Mohammad Ali Jinnah, however, stuck to the point that only the League was competent to send Muslim Representatives in the Executive. *Dawn*, the official organ of the Muslim League, on 15th June, 1945 said 'that with regard to Muslim Society, the Mussalmans will tolerate no infiltration of non-League stooges to humour any party.' Had the Congress submitted to this unreasonable demand of the League, then it would have lost its national character and Mohammad Ali Jinnah would have characterised the Congress as a purely Hindu organisation. The Congress President Maulana Abul Kalam Azad and the Punjab Chief Minister Khizr Hayat Khan Tiwana, strongly protested against League's exclusive claim of sending Muslims to the reconstituted Cabinet. Mr. Tiwana was intending to send one Muslim to represent the Unionist Party in the Cabinet. The Congress too had in nind to offer a couple of seats to the Nationalist Muslims. Mr. Mohammad Ali Jinnah refused to budge from the stand he had taken. He could not agree to the appointment in Executive Council of Muslims who did not belong to the league. The talks crashed on the rock of communalism. Lord Wavell announced the failure of conference on 14th July, 1945.

After the failure of talks, Maulana Abul Kalam Azad issued a statement at Simla. He declared that the Viceroy had assured him "In his first interview that no party to the conference would be allowed to obstruct settlement out of wilfulness. Everyone knew what Mr. Mohammad Ali Jinnah would do and everyone believed that against that possibility the Viceroy had armed himself with authority to deal with him appropriately. Yet Wavell's hand was stayed at the last moment even as Cripps' was."

Mr. Mohammad Ali Jinnah had his own explanation regarding the failure of Simla Conference. At a Press Conference on 14th July, 1945, he remarked : "On a final examination and analysis of the Wavell Plan, we found that it was a snare. There was the combination consisting of Gandhi-Hindu Congress, who stood for India's Hindu National Unity, Lord Wavell, and Glancy-Khizr, who were bent upon creating disruption among the Mussalmans in Punjab, and we were sought to be pushed into this arrangement, by which, if we had agreed to, as proposed by Lord Wavell, we would have signed our death warrant."

"On the top of this came the last straw on the camel's back, that even about the five members of the Muslim Bloc, which were allotted to us community-wise, which is the essence of the Wavell proposals, we were told that the Muslim League was not entitled to nominate all the Muslim Representatives as our chosen spokesmen and there were two claimants—the Congress which claimed two, and Glancy-khizr on behalf of the Punjab claimed one. This move on the part of these two went at the very root and the very existence of the Muslim League regarding its position, character and status. But finally we broke as Lord Wavell insisted upon his having one non-Leaguer, a Nominee of Malik Khizr Hayat Khan, representing the Punjab Muslims."

I.N.A. TRIAL, NOVEMBER, 1945

Wavell's Plan was a sincere attempt to lead the country to the goal of independence. The failure of Simla Conference plunged the country into despair once again. Nevertheless, it led to the release of all the members of the Congress Working Committee. Pt. Jawaharlal Nehru and Sardar Ballabh Bhai Patel after their release heartily praised the doings of the people and also paid homage to the martyrs of the revolt of 1942 and thus removed the gloom of despair. Moreover, the trial of I.N.A. personnel and their magnificent defence by our leaders further enthused the people. The trial was staged in the Red Fort, Delhi. Three officers who stood in the dock were Dhillon, Sehgal and Shah Nawaz. They were convicted for defection from the British forces and joining the Indian National Army of Netaji Subhas Chandra Bose. The three Generals — one a Hindu, other a Sikh and the third a Muslim—fell into British hands after the fall of Japan on 14th August, 1945. In order to defend the brave sons of soil, Pt. Jawaharlal Nehru appeared in the court donned as a barrister. Sir Tej Bahadur Sapru and Bhulabhai Desai also acted as defence counsels. In spite of their best efforts, the judges found the accused guilty and awarded death sentences. All the three were, however, released by the orders of the Commander-in-Chief, Sir Claude Auchinlek.

The release of the three I.N.A. accused meant another political victory of the Congress. The inspiring arguments of the defence counsels roused a wave of patriotism in every part of the country. Mr. Bhulabhai Desai in the course of his arguments asserted that it was the birthright of a slave people to take up arms against the foreign rulers. Another good outcome of the trial was that it dispelled the fear of British imperialism from Indian hearts. Thirdly, it had its stimulating effect on the Indian army. The Government was convinced that it would be foolish to expect faithfulness and loyalty from the Indian forces. The Naval Mutiny in February, 1946, further impressed on the British overlords the desirability of leaving India to Indians themselves.

BROADCASTS BY LORD WAVELL AND ATTLEE

Labour Party comes to power in Great Britain. On 10th July, 1945, Labour Party in England came to power. Mr. Attlee replaced Churchill as Prime Minister and Mr. Pethick Lawrence became the

Secretary of State in place of Mr. Amery. Both Attlee and Lawrence were in sympathy with India's demand for self-government. The change in British Cabinet was a good augury for India.

In August, 1945, Lord Wavell summoned all the Governors of the Provinces for consultations. It was decided to hold elections. On 25th August, 1945 the Viceroy flew to London and after conferring with Labour Leaders returned to India on 18th September, 1945. Next day he declared that the elections which had been postponed owing to the outbreak of war, would be held in coming winter. The British King in his address to the British Parliament declared that in accordance with the promises already made to my Indian people, my Government will do their utmost to promote to conjunction with the leaders of Indian opinion, early realisation of full self-government in India. The Viceroy also declared on behalf of the Crown that a constitution-making body would be set up soon after discussing the matter with the State Representatives. He expressed his hope that not before long the Provinces would again have responsible governments.

Results of the Election in India. During the winter months of the year 1945, elections were conducted in all the Provinces. The Congress made the famous 'Quit India' resolution as the central issue in its election manifesto and gained spectacular success. It swept the polls in general constituencies. It, however, could not gain much in Muslim Constituencies. The Muslim League captured 446 Muslim seats out of 495. Even the Unionist Party in the Punjab had a bad luck and it lost most of the seats to the League. The Congress succeeded in forming ministries in seven out of eleven Provinces. In North West Frontier Province, the Red Shirts formed the Ministry heated by Dr. Khan Sahib, who was a Congressman. The Muslim League seized power in Sind and Bengal. In the Punjab, a coalition Ministry was formed by Khizr Hayat Khan with the support of the Congress and the Sikhs led by Akali Party.

NAVAL MUTINY (FEBRUARY, 1946)

Before we proceed further, we must mention another incident which has serious bearing on the subject we are discussing. On the 19th of February, 1946, some personnel of Royal Indian Navy mutinied against the British officers. Some 3,000 ratings of the Signal School in Bombay held demonstration and went on hungerstrike in protest against 'untold hardships regarding pay and food, racial discrimination and against their commander's derogatory references to their national character.' Batches of ratings roamed the city in trucks and lorries. In the next two days the strike and trouble spread to other ports of Karachi, Calcutta and Madras. Congress, Communist and League flags were hoisted on lorries. The demonstrators attacked the British officers. When the British troops opened fire, the ratings retaliated with hand-grenades. By 22nd the mutineers got control of 20 naval vessels with guns mounted on them to open fire. At last Sardar Ballabh Bhai Patel intervened and persuaded the mutineers on 23rd February, 1946 to surrender. In the meantime disturbances broke out in Bombay city. The police opened fire several times. As a result of the civil and naval turmoil, over 200 persons were killed and more than 1,000 injured.

"The mutiny opened the eyes of the British to the fact that Indian nationalism could no longer be contained in the ring drawn with armed forces as Indian personnel in the forces were beginning to succumb to the attraction of nationalism and there was not enough British personnel to go to the full round."[1]

Mr. V.P.Menon, Constitutional Adviser to the Governor-General, has written, "The Viceroy (Lord Wavell) was confident that in a conflict with the Congress, he could count generally on the support of the officials, the police and the army. At the same time, it would be unwise to try the Indian Army too highly in the suppression of their own people and as time went on the loyalty of even the Indian officials, the Indian Army and the police might become problematical. A large number of British

1. From an article of Sri V.K.Menon. General Secretary, Indian Ex-Services Association.

Officials would probably take the first opportunity to retire, so that the British Government in India would be placed in a quite untenable position unless it found a very early solution and this it should do at any cost. The chief problem was to find some kind of bridge between the Hindu and Muslim."[1]

Lord Attlee's announcement, 15 March, 1946. The British Labour Party on the eve of elections in Great Britain had repeatedly assured the Indians that it would take up the case of India's Independence most sympathetically. After coming to office, despite the threat of Japan, it began to take interest in Indian Affairs. When the deliberations were being held in India, the Labour Government sent a parliamentary elections consisting of the representatives of all the British political parties to gather first-hand information about India. On the basis of the delegation's report, Mr. Attlee announced in the House of Commons on 15th March, 1946 that the tide of nationalism was surging very fast in India and that it was in the British interest to take a positive action. He further said that the Cabinet Mission was visiting India with the intention of helping her to attain independence as speedily as possible. The Indians themselves were to decide what form of government would suit them although he hoped that they would elect to remain in the Commonwealth. Concluding his speech, he said, "*we are mindful of the rights of minorities and the minorities should be able to live free from fear. On other hand, we cannot allow a minority to place their veto on the advance of the majority.*" This significant and historic announcement was a severe blow to the fantastic and silly demands of the League.

CABINET MISSION PLAN (16TH MAY, 1946)

The cabinet Mission which consisted of three British Cabinet Ministers—Lord Pethick-Lawrence, Secretary of state for India, Sir Stafford Cripps President of the Board of Trade and Mr. A.V. Alexander First Lord of Admiralty—arrived in New Delhi on 24th March, 1946. Just after arrival, the leader of the Commission said, "We are convinced that India is on the threshold of a great future." The members of the Mission contacted and discussed with the leaders of Indian opinion one by one. In the round of talks they gathered that the outstanding issue of communal deadlock was a United India versus Pakistan. Excepting the League, all other parties were in favour of a United India. The Mission studied various alternative schemes with a view to finding out some formula agreeable to the Congress as well as the League. The Commission started its work and presented a plan, which was known 'Cabinet Mission Plan' of 1946.

1. The Mission closely and partially examined League's demand for Pakistan. It felt that such a proposition was not likely to solve the communal minority problem. Moreover, the members of the delegation could see no justification for including Hindu-Majority areas of the Punjab, Assam and Bengal in the proposed scheme of Pakistan. They said that the partition of India would in no case be acceptable to the Hindus including Sikhs. There were other weighty considerations also against the creation of a separate sovereign State. The New State according to delegation would be sound neither economically nor militarily. "Lord Pethick-Lawrence and Sir Stafford Cripps", writes Maulana Abul Kalam Azad, "said repeatedly that they could not see how a State like the Pakistan envisaged by the Muslim League could be viable and stable." **The Cabinet Mission, hence, made the following proposals: —**

(*a*) *Union of India.* There should be a Union of India embodying both British India and the States. It should deal with foreign affairs, defence and communications, and should have the power, to raise finances necessary for these subjects.

(*b*) The Union should have an executive and a Legislature constituted from British India and States' Representatives.

(*c*) *Communal Questions.* Any question raising a major communal issue in the Legislature should require for its decision a majority of the representatives present and voting of each of two major communities as well as a majority of all the members present and voting.

1. Mr. V.P. Menon, *The Transfer of Power*, p. 232.

(*d*) All subjects other than the Union subjects and all residuary powers should vest in the Provinces.

(*e*) The States should retain all subjects and powers other than those ceded to the Union.

(*f*) *Groups of the Provinces.* Provinces should be free to form groups and each group should determine the Provincial subjects to be taken in common. The first group embodied Madras, Bombay, Uttar Pradesh, Central Province and Orissa. The Second group consisted of the Punjab, NorthWest Frontier Province and Sind whereas the third included Bengal and Assam.

(*g*) *Reconsideration of the terms of the Constitution.* The Constitution of the Union and of the groups should contain a provision whereby any province could by a majority vote of its Legislative Assembly call for a reconsideration of the terms of the Constitution after an initial period of ten years and at every ten-years interval thereafter.

2. Composition of the Constituent Assembly. The Mission also felt the need of suggesting the broad basis of future Constitution because without doing so, there was hardly any hope of persuading the Hindus and Muslims to join hands in the setting up of the constitution-making body.

(*a*) The Mission proposed the formation of a Constituent Assembly consisting of 389 members—93 States' Representatives; 4 from the Chief Commissioner's Provinces; and the remaining 292 from the British Indian Provinces.

(*b*) The Seats allotted to the Provinces should be further allocated to the main communities in proportion to their numerical strength. Every Province should send as many representatives to the Constituent Assembly as were proportionate to its population in the ratio of one to a million.

(*c*) The Representatives allocated to each community in a Province should be elected by members of that community in its Legislative Assembly.

(*d*) The Mission discarded the practice of giving over-representation to the minorities. It recognised only three categories of electorate—General, Muslim and Sikhs. Hindus, Parsees and Anglo-Indians were placed in the first group.

(*e*) The Representatives of the States not exceeding 93 should be distributed among the States on the basis of the population of each State. To begin with, the mode of their selection was to be decided by mutual talks between the Negotiating Committee of British Indian Provinces and a committee set up for that purpose by the Indian States

(*f*) After the elections, the Constituent Assembly should meet at New Delhi as one body and elect a chairman. The Representative of the Provincial Legislatures then should break up into three sections, as follows:—

Secton A—Madras, Bombay, Uttar Pradesh, Bihar, Central Province and Orissa.

Section B—Punjab, North West Frontier Province and Sind.

Section C—Bengal and Assam.

The Representatives of each group should confer separately and decide the constitutions for the Provinces within their group and also what Provincial subjects they deal with commonly, leaving the rest to be handled by the Legislature of each Province.

(*g*) The Provinces should have the power to withdraw from one group and join another, by a decision of their new Legislature after the new Union Constitution had come into force.

(*h*) If the Constituent Assembly proposed to make any change in recommendations of the Mission regarding the form of constitution or the raising of any communal issue, it could not do so without obtaining the approval of the majority of the representatives of both the Hindus and the Muslims.

(*i*) The new Constituent Assembly was not to be a sovereign body. There were some limitations placed on its powers, Besides observing the pattern given in the Mission Plan, it was to safeguard the interests of the minorities also.

3. Interim Government. The Mission Plan stated that until the new constitution was framed, the administration should be run by an interim Government having the support of all major political parties. All the portfolios including that of War Minister should be held by Indian leaders enjoying the full confidence of the people. The British Government promised to give the fullest co-operation to the Interim Government in the smooth administration of India and also in accomplishing the transfer of power at some early date.

Treaty. The Cabinet Mission also provided for the negotiation of a treaty between the Constituent Assembly and Great Britain to cover all matters arising out of the transfer of power. The Mission declared that after the transition, it would not be possible for the Crown to retain paramountcy over the States. That paramountcy could also not be transferred to the Indian Union. (*Implicitly it meant that the States would be free to become sovereign States after the withdrawal of the British*). The Mission hoped that India would not break off with the Commonwealth although she would be legally free to do so.

MERITS OF THE CABINET MISSION PLAN

The merits of the Cabinet Mission Plan were as follows —

1. Preservation of Indian Unity and Rejection of Pakistan. The first redeeming feature of the Mission Plan was that it ruled out League's demand for Pakistan and recommended an undivided India. The Congress and the League were already at daggers drawn over the issue of Pakistan. The Mission had tough job to suggest a plan agreeable to both the parties. The scheme that they offered went a long way to accommodate both the Congress and League. It pleased the Congress because it preserved the basic unity of India. It brushed aside the demand for Pakistan on the consideration that such a State would not be a viable unit. Moreover, Pakistan was no solution of minority problem. The Plan sought to satisfy the Sikhs by preserving the unity of the Punjab, their homeland. The Plan tried to please the Muslims also by weakening the Centre and allowing maximum freedom in many subjects to the Provinces. The grouping of the Provinces was a subtle way to allow the Muslims to direct their religion, culture, education, in their own way. Groups B and C of the Provinces virtually meant East and West Pakistan within the Union of India.

2. Democratic Basis of Constituent Assembly. The other point to the credit of the Plan was that it proposed the formation of a Constituent Assembly on democratic principle of population. It discarded the usual practice of weighty representation to the minorities. It did not show any undue favour to the States with regard to representation.

3. No Official Representatives. The Plan made no provision for the representation of the British interests and the Europeans in the Constituent Assembly which was to consist of purely Indian element.

4. Communal Representation Restricted. Another merit of Mission scheme was that it made communal representation quite restricted. Unlike the Acts of 1919 and 1935 wherein there was provision for separate representation of Europeans, Indian Christians, Anglo-Indians, Labour, Harijans and Women, the new scheme restricted this privilege only to Muslims in Hindu Majority Provinces and Sikhs in the Punjab.

5. Recognition of the Rights and Claims of the People of Indian States. That the Mission made an honest attempt to solve Indian problem, is further proved by the fact it did not leave scope for the coming in of reactionary elements in the Constituent Assembly. If it did not admit expressly the right of the people of the States to elect their representatives in the Assembly, it did not clearly state as well that the State Representatives would be nominated by the rulers.

6. Interim Government. Another highlight of the scheme was that all the members of the Interim Cabinet were to be Indians. They were to hold all the portfolios including that of War Minister. There was to be little interference by the Viceroy in day-to-day administration.

7. Sovereignty of the Constituent Assembly. The proposed Constituent Assembly was given full freedom to make a constitution within the framework of the Mission Plan. Mission also declared on behalf of the British Government that the New Constitution would be accepted by the Crown Provided due protection was given to minority interests and a treaty was signed between the framers of the constitution and the Crown to cover all the cases arising out of the transfer of power. Thus, for the first time an honest effort was made to let the Indians frame a Constitution for themselves.

8. The Plan also recognised the right of India to secede from the Commonwealth.

DEMERITS OF THE CABINET MISSION PLAN

In spite of the above mentioned good points of the Cabinet Mission Plan, there were certain bad points also. They were as follows :

1. Weak Centre. The Cabinet Mission scheme was not without some drawbacks. It was a mixed gift. The first defect of the Plan was that it proposed a weak Federal Government. It suggested the transfer of only three subjects—Defence, Communication and External Affairs—to the Union, leaving all other subjects to be administered by the Provinces. A weak Centre meant a weak nation.

2. Substance of Pakistan Demand Conceded. Though apparently the Plan discarded the partition of India, indirectly it granted the League's demand for Pakistan. The provisions regarding compulsory grouping of the Provinces into A, B and C categories and the right given to each group to enjoy perfect autonomy in all matters excepting the three Union subjects, was a clear proof of the Mission's motive to split the country into three parts. The Provinces were tagged with the others in each group without taking into account the wishes of the people. North West Frontier Province, in spite of being Congress majority Province, had to accept the decisions of the group. It was simply absurd to divide the Constituent Assembly first into three groups and then letting each group frame a constitution for itself before the final constitution for the Union was drafted.

3. Illegitimate Rights of the Indian State. The Mission Scheme was a sort of snake in the grass. It had sinister implications if accepted without any change. The Plan said that after the drafting of the new constitution the British Government could neither keep the paramountacy over the Indian States to itself nor transfer it to the Union Government. The motives of the Mission were certainly unclean and doubtful. In a way the scheme gave the option to the States to join the Union or remain independent.

4. Unscientific Grouping of the Provinces. The grouping of the Provinces was highly unscientific. Assam was predominantly a Hindu Majority Province but it was grouped with Bengal which had Muslim Majority. North West Frontier Province which had a Congress Majority was placed in Group B. In short the communal basis of making groups was highly detrimental to national interests.

5. Limitations on the Powers of the Constituent Assembly. The proposed Constituent Assembly was not to be a sovereign body. It could not go, at the time of constitution making, against the lines laid down by the Mission. Moreover, the constitution made by it had to satisfy certain conditions. It had to honour the British obligations towards the minorities and States. Above all, the Constituent Assembly was not to draft a constitution for the whole of India. The groups of the Provinces were authorised to make separate constitutions for themselves. The Federal Scheme suggested by the Mission was also mischievous. Nowhere has a federation been formed by yoking together the Autocratic States and Democratic Provinces, as proposed in Mission's Schemes.

6. Some Vague Provisions. The provisions relating to the Provinces were so vague that they yielded doubtful meanings. The Congress and the League interpreted them in different ways according as they suited their own interest. The powers of the Interim Government were also not clearly detailed.

7. Like Cripps' Proposals, Mission's Plan was also unalterable. It had either to be accepted in original or rejected completely. Its part acceptance was out of question.

Attitude of the Various Political Parties to the Plan. The reaction of various political groups to the Plan was favourable in the beginning. The Muslim League accepted it on 6th June, 1946 and the Congress on 25th June, 1946. The Sikhs at first refused to send their representatives to the Constituent Assembly but they changed their policy on the assurance given by the Congress and the Secretary of State. The Hindu Mahasabha denounced the compulsory grouping of Provinces in three sections. The Communist Party objected to the restrictions imposed on the powers of the constitution making body. The Congress decided to join the Constituent Assembly 'with a view to framing the constitution of a free, united and democratic India.' The League saw its dream of Pakistan inherent in the Plan. Both fell out on the point whether the grouping of Provinces was voluntary or compulsory.

Elections to the Constituent Assembly. Election to the Constituent Assembly were held in July, 1946. Out of 210 general seats allotted to the British Indian Provinces, the Congress captured 199. Out of the remaining 11 seats, Unionist Party of the Punjab got 2, Communists 1, Scheduled Caste Federation 2 and Independents 6. Out of 78 Muslim seats, the League got 73, Congress-Muslims 3, the Punjab Unionist Party and the Praja Party of Bengal one each. It meant that in a House of 296 members the Congress enjoyed the support of 212 members whereas the League commanded a group of 73 members. The remaining 11 members were uncertain in their loyalties.

Rejection of the Plan by Muslim League. The thumping majority of the Congress in the Constituent Assembly both disappointed and irritated the Muslim League. Its bitterness also sprang from the Viceroy's refusal to form an interim Government with League's help when the Congress was unwilling to join. Mr. Mohammad Ali Jinnah was further hurt when Lord Pethick Lawrence and Sir Stafford Cripps in a statement questioned and rejected League's sole right of nominating Muslim members in the Interim Cabinet. According to Maulana Abul Kalam Azad: Pt. Jawaharlal Nehru (the Congress President at that time) told the press representatives at Bombay that Congress had agreed only to participate in the Constituent Assembly and regarded itself free to change or modify the Cabinet Mission Plan. This statement of the Congress President was his greatest mistake. Mohammad Ali Jinnah exploited this statement in his favour and withdrew the acceptance of League. Pt. Jawaharlal Nehru further said that he was hopeful that there would be no grouping of Provinces. Mohammad Ali Jinnah reacted promptly. He accused the Congress of running down the scheme of Interim Government. He feared that the Congress would exercise its brute majority to bypass the interests of the Muslims. He intimated the Government of League's decision to boycott the plan and launch direct action to realise his goal of Pakistan.

DIRECT ACTION BY THE MUSLIM LEAGUE AND ESTABLISHMENT OF THE INTERIM GOVERNMENT

Since the Congress had ultimately accepted both the long-term and short-term plans of the Cabinet Mission, both of which had been rejected by the League completely, Lord Wavell, the Viceroy of India, Invited Pt. Jawaharlal Nehru on 12th August, 1946, to form the Interim Government. Pt. Jawaharlal Nehru agreed to do so. The Viceroy and Pt. Jawaharlal Nehru both made fresh efforts to bring round the League to agree to forming a coalition Government. Mohammad Ali Jinnah remained obstinate. He decided to bid good-bye to constitutional methods. He called upon his followers to observe 16th August, 1946 as direct action day. The Bengal and Sind ministries declared the 16th August, 1946 a public holiday. The Muslims took out processions and held meetings in all the big towns Suhrawardy, the Chief Minister of Bengal, went to the extent of saying that in case the Congress were put into power, the result would be 'the declaration of complete independence by

Bengal and the setting up of a parallel Government.' The Result was lawlessness and bloodshed on an unprecedented scale in Calcutta. Suhrawardy encouraged the Muslims to kill Hindus and pillage their property. According to rough official estimate nearly 5,000 Hindus lost their lives and over 15,000 were injured in Calcutta alone. Maulana Abul Kalam Azad who happened to be in Calcutta on that day writes in '*India Wins Freedom*': *The 16th August,* 1946 *was a black day in the History of India. Unprecedented mob violence plunged the great city into an orgy of bloodshed, murder and terror. Hundreds of lives were lost. Thousands were injured and property worth crores of rupees was destroyed. The city was in the grip of goondas.*

The Interim Government assumed office on September 2, 1946. The Viceroy renewed his efforts to induce the League to join the Cabinet and take part in the Constituent Assembly. The League agreed to enter the Executive Council but rejected the other part of the Plan. Mr. Mohammad Ali Jinnah in his letter of 13th October, 1946 to the Viceroy wrote; 'but since, according to your decision, we have a right to nominate five members of the Executive Council on behalf of the Muslim League, my committee have, for *various* reasons, come to the conclusion to join the Interim Government.' Thus, the League's decision was not guided by the spirit of co-operation but to keep a check on the position of the Congress. It was hoping against hope that the two parties work together. The League continued its campaign of 'direct action.'

In October, 1946, there was a large-scale outbreak of lawlessness, loot and arson in Noakhali and Tipperah Districts of East Bengal. In fact, it was not hooliganism by goondas but an organised attack planned by the Muslim League with the connivance of the executive officials. The Hindus suffered enormously both in person and property. The happenings of Noakhali sparked off communal trouble in Bihar, Garh Mukteshwar and Ahmedabad. The Muslim League then incited the Muslims in Punjab and North-West Frontier Province to raid Hindu houses and kill the inmates.

Attlee's Declaration to Leave India. When the country was in grip of communal frenzy and riots; when everything was in a state of flux; when law was in the hands of wolves (and all of British creation) the British Government decided to Quit India by a fixed date. Mr. Attlee made an announcement in the House of Commons on February 20, 1947 :

"His Majesty's Government desires to hand over responsibility to authorities established by a Constitution approved by all parties in India. But unfortunately there was at present no clear prospect that such a constitution and such authorities would emerge. If it should appear that an agreed constitution would not have been worked out by June, 1948, it should transfer the powers of the Central Government, whether as a whole to some form of Central Government for British India, or in some areas to the existing Provincial Governments, or in such other ways as may seem most reasonable and in the best interests of the Indian People."

It was also announced that Lord Wavell would be succeeded by Mountbatten as the last incumbent to the Viceregal office.

CIRCUMSTANCES LEADING TO THE PARTITION OF THE COUNTRY (PAKISTAN)

The statement of Mr. Attlee aroused mixed feelings of joy and tears. The Congress welcomed the first part of it which contained the desire of the British Government to Quit India soon, but the leaders felt nervous and panicky to learn that should India fail to draft constitution agreeable to all the parties, the Government would be free to leave India to any party it liked. The Constituent Assembly met on 9th December, 1946, with League benches lying unoccupied. The Congress set about wooing the League again but without any response from the other side. The League in Attlee's statement saw the implied acceptance of Pakistan.

As a result of League's 'direct action', gap between the standpoints of the League and Congress appeared to be unbridgeable. One stood for partition while the other for undivided India. The country was in the teeth of anarchy. Law and order had been thrown to the winds. Lord Mountbatten was called upon to take a quick and final course of action. He held discussions with the Congress high-ups and tried to explain the inevitability of partition. He did not approach Mahatma Gandhi to whom the very thought of the division of India was chilling and revolting. Mahatma Gandhi had once said, "Even if the whole of India is in flames, it will not bring Pakistan." In another context he had said that Pakistan would be made on his dead body. In view of Mahatma Gandhi's rigid unrelenting attitudes, Lord Mountbatten argued with Sardar Ballabh Bhai Patel and Pt. Jawaharlal Nehru. Both reviewed the past and foresaw the dark shadow of communal riots hanging over the country. Quite unwillingly, they gave their consent. The following are some of the reasons which induced them to submit to Pakistan scheme :

1. Communal Riots. As a result of League's 'direct action', several parts of India witnessed the worst form of communal riots. Thousands of lives were lost in the flames of communalism. The League engineered organised raids on Hindu localities and caravans of refugees. The police and British Officers stood away as silent spectators. Although defence had been entrusted to Sardar Baldev Singh in the Interim Cabinet, the British were still the masters of the whole machinery. Had the British wanted, they could easily have restored law and order in the country. But instead of remaining neutral, they played the partisan role. They encouraged the riots so as to compel the Congress to accept 'Two Nation Theory'. The British Government as well as the British Officers in India played up and supported the demand of Pakistan, for they hoped to get more concessions in the Muslim State.

Mr. V.P. Menon, the Constitutional Adviser to the Viceroy, in his talks with Sardar Ballabh Bhai Patel pressed the point of Dominion Status. He said the Congress by consenting to accept Dominion Status for the time being, would gain three advantages—a peaceful transfer of power, the goodwill of Britain and thirdly the smooth future administration of the country including the taking over of top posts by Indian Officers. Sardar Ballabh Bhai Patel accepted Menon's plan even though the Constituent Assembly had adopted a resolution to declare India a Sovereign Democratic Republic soon after the departure of the British. He in his forthright fashion declared that the British Policy of remaining neutral but holding on to power was a subtle way to promote civil war. There would be peace in the country within a week if power was transferred to the Central Government. In the absence of interference by a third party to whom either side could appeal, the Congress and Muslim League would settle their differences at once. If there still arose conflict in the Cabinet over any question, the majority would rule.

So the question which was uppermost in the minds of Congress Leaders at the time was somehow to get rid of the British Elements in India at any cost. The British Officers neither governed themselves nor let others govern. The law and order situation consequently deteriorated at such a rate that, in a speech before the London Royal Empire Society, Lord Ismay made this admission that whereas before coming to India he had felt that the deadline of June, 1948, for the completion of British evacuation of India was "far too early", upon his arrival in India he began to feel that it was almost "too late". The machinery of administration was cracking and communal bitterness was more intense both at headquarters in Delhi and in the Provinces than anything I could have imagined."[1]

The Congress was although determined not to partition the country, yet the circumstances seemed to conspire against it. The Congress Leadership, as Pt. Jawaharlal Nehru said, became at last willing "to cut off the head in order to get rid of the headache". The Congress High Command feared that if the matters were allowed to drift, the country would soon be overwhelmed by the wild forces of communalism, by riots and murders. The intention of the British Government was to hold on to power still. Lord Mountbatten once declared also that the British Power could agree to continue its rule at the request of the Indian Political Parties. The very presence of the British on top of Indian scene was the bane of Indian Politics. Mahatma Gandhi was constrained to say, "*It would be a good thing if the British were to go today—thirteen months means mischief to India...the thirteen months'*

1. Pyarelal – '*Mahatma Gandhi— The Last Phase*', p. 152

stay of British power and British arms is really a hindrance rather than a help". Pt. Jawaharlal Nehru too was afraid of the growing lawlessness in the country and the intransigent attitude of the League. In short, every Congress Leader began to feel that the only alternative of communal riots and civil war was the acceptance of the demand of Pakistan.

2. Intrigues of the British Officers. The disturbances in India on the eve of independence were largely the creation of the British Bureaucracy. The British Officers sided with League. It was so managed that the Muslims who were pro-League came to occupy all the key positions in police, information and defence. A League nominee was also holding in the Interim Government the key portfolio of Finance. 'Brisk, illegal traffic in arms was going on not without the connivance and sometimes active co-operation of British and Indian Military Officers. It had grown into an open scandal. Later, the Congress High Command had documentary evidence of the complicity of the Political Department; how in league with certain princes it was busy hatching a conspiracy to break in India's unity."[1] Referring to the way in which the Political Department was behaving, *Sardar Ballabh Bhai Patel gave expression to his feelings in the following words— "It was then that I was made fully conscious of the extent to which our interests were being prejudiced in every way by the machinations of the Political Department and came to the conclusion that the best course was to hasten the departure of these foreigners even at the cost of the partition of the country. It was also then that I felt that there was one way to make the country safe and strong that was the unification of the rest of India."*[2] On 25th November, 1948, Sardar Ballabh Bhai Patel again referred to this issue in the course of another speech at the Benaras Hindu University: "I felt that if we did not accept partition, India would be split into many bits and would lead us to disaster. We would not then have one Pakistan but several. There would have been Pakistan cells in every office"[3].

In November, 1949, speaking in the Constituent Assembly, Sardar Ballabh Bhai Patel gave further details which showed how effectively the two trump cards which the British had kept up their sleeves, till the very last, were played to force the hands of the Indian Leaders to bartar their cherished ideal of Indian unity for an early transfer of power. Of these the first was the reserve powers and control over the Services, the second was paramountacy in relation to the Indian States. "You have seen what was happening in the Punjab. In the five districts, where havoc was being wrought, five British Officers were in power and nothing could be done. I tried to get the District Magistrate of Gurgaon transferred. I could not succeed. I agreed to partition as a last resort, when we had reached a stage we would have lost all." "*We had five or six members of Muslim League in the Government—they had already established themselves as Members who had come to partition the country. At that stage we agreed to partition. We decided that partition could be agreed upon the terms that the Punjab should be partitioned—that Bengal should be partitioned. Mr. Jinnah did not want a truncated Pakistan but he had to swallow it.*"

3. Encouragement of the British to Muslim League. It had been the most calculated and sustained policy of the British to create rift between the Hindus and Muslims. They patronised the League and both directly and indirectly supported its demand for Pakistan. It was the usual British game to divide the country into warring camps and to hold on to power with a support of one of them. This is evidenced from the increasing communal elements in the Legislatures under the three Acts of 1909, 1919 and 1935. There were two motives of the British Appeasement of the Muslims—the first to weaken the Congress and the national demand for freedom; and secondly, to secure the loyalties of the Muslim Members in the Government. With this end in view, efforts were not wanting on the part of Cripps' Cabinet Mission and Attlee's announcement to please the League to the farthest extent. Lord Wavell too approached Mohammad Ali Jinnah time and again with his revised offers. The pro-Muslim attitude of the British Government was one reason why Mr. Mohammad Ali Jinnah remained so adamant on his demand for Pakistan.

1. *Ibid.*, p. 136
2. *Ibid.*
3. *Ibid.*

4. Policy of the Congress. The Congress, too, had to own a part of responsibility for the partition of India. It pursued the policy of giving a long rope to Muslim League by meeting its unreasonable demands one after another. Without caring to understand the Muslim League's policy of isolation and aggression, the Congress lived on the false hope that the League would see reason. Moreover, its effort to negotiate with League raised the stature of the League disproportionately. The initial mistake was made by the Congress in 1916 when under Lucknow Pact it agreed to separate electorate and separate Sind from Bombay. C.R. formula went too far to the extent of accepting the demand of Pakistan in substance. In their utterances, Pt. Jawaharlal Nehru and Sardar Ballabh Bhai Patel also admitted publicly that they would not compel any Province to remain in the Union of India. Mohammad Ali Jinnah was, thus, strengthened in his belief that a little pressure would bring round off Congress to concede Pakistan.

5. Congress Desire to Make India Strong. Another consideration which brought a change in Congress attitude; was the desire to end riots and bloodsheds. The attitude of the League had been non-co-operative and outrageous both in the Interim Government and in the public field. It was very clear to the Congress Leaders that if they insisted on unified India, there would be Pakistan cells in every office and the whole administrative machinery would begin to reek with communalism. The League Members in the Interim Government were openly talking of carving out a Pakistan. The Congress felt that the partition of the country would at least enable to make the partitioned Hindustan a strong and prosperous country. Then there would be no Muslim League to hinder its efforts.

6. Mohammad Ali Jinnah's Defiant Attitude. The greatest credit of founding the sovereign Muslim State of Pakistan goes to Mr. Mohammad Ali Jinnah who proved too good a match for the leaders of the Congress camp. The Nationalists of India mistakenly believed that their only enemy was the British Government and not the dragon of communalism. They sought Mohammad Ali Jinnah's friendship in driving out the British Rulers. Shrewd Mohammad Ali Jinnah exploited the situation and continued multiplying his demands. His stubborn attitude led to the failure of the two Round Table Conference besides the Simla Conference. His clear cut stand was that the Congress represented the Hindus while the League represented the Muslims. In spite of his anti-national ideas and doings, Mahatma Gandhi met him time and again to discuss the communal deadlock. The results were, however, just the reverse. Such negotiations simply raised the political stature of Mr. Mohammad Ali Jinnah and his arrogance and obstinacy increased after every meeting he had with Mahatma Gandhi. He drifted apart day by day. The weakened policy of the Congress emboldened him so much that he launched 'direct action' against Hindus. He frightened the Congress Leaders and terrorised the Hindus by massacre and loot. The Congress ultimately had to listen to his language of force and grant him Pakistan.

7. Failure of the Interim Government. The difficult functioning of the Interim Government also convinced the Congress that Coalition Government was not the solution of communal problem. League's Representatives in the Cabinet, particularly Mr. Liaquat Ali Khan who held the Finance, punctured all the plans of the Congress. No department could work smoothly for want of finance which Liaquat Ali refused to release. In these circumstances Sardar Ballabh Bhai Patel said, "If one limb is poisoned, it must be removed quickly lest the entire organisation should suffer irreparably". He showed his preparedness to allow the League to have a part of India if only such a step meant the end of League's mischief.

8. Influence of Lord Mountbatten. The loss of Hindu lives and property in Calcutta and other parts of India created a situation that made Sardar Ballabh Bhai Patel declare that Pakistan was better than the murder of innocent citizens. Lord Mountbatten also impressed upon Pt. Jawaharlal Nehru the desirability of getting rid of League by allowing it to have its Pakistan, so that the Congress might devote its energies to strengthening Hindu India. The British Government changed its date of departure from June, 1948 to 15th August, 1947. The Congress as such, had to choose between two evils—the

Partition of India and Civil War. Naturally it opted for Pakistan which was relatively a lesser evil. Pt. Jawaharlal Nehru, nine years after partition, stated, "A feeling that even if we got freedom for India with the background, it would be very weak India, that is, a Federal India with far too much power in the federating units. A larger India would have constant troubles, constant disintegrating pulls.... So we accepted and said, let us build a strong India. And if others do not want to be in it, well how can we and why should we force them to be in it." Pt. Jawaharlal Nehru further said, "It was the compulsion of events and the feeling that we could not get out of the deadlock morass by pursuing the way we had done. So we accepted the partition."

MOUNTBATTEN PLAN (3rd JUNE, 1947)
(Creation of Pakistan)

Lord Mountbatten even before being sent to India had been briefed by the British Government to arrange for the transfer of power in as smooth and quick a way as possible. He set himself to this task by holding talks with the leaders of both — the Congress and the League. He settled the details with the Congress and League Leaders. He left for England to discuss finally with Home Government and returned on June 2, with certain definite proposals. Next day he published his Plan. The salient features of Mountbatten Plan were as follows :

1. Mountbatten's Plan set down the partition of India as a settled fact. It proposed the division of India into two Dominions and the transference of power to take place on 15th August, 1947, instead of June, 1948, as declared earlier.

2. Contrary to League's demand for a Pakistan including the whole of Bengal and Assam in the East and the Punjab in the West, the plan excluded Assam completely and also suggested the partition of Bengal and the Punjab. The Provincial Legislatures of Bengal and Punjab were to meet separately in two parts each one representing the Muslim majority districts and the other Hindu majority districts. The members of the two parts of each Legislature were empowered to vote whether or not the Provinces should be partitioned.

3. Referendum in Sylhet and N.W.F.P. The Muslim majority district of Sylhet was to decide by a referendum whether it was to join East Bengal or remain in Assam. In the case of North-West Frontier Province., there was to be a referendum to ascertain whether the people wanted to be in Pakistan or India. The need arose because of the fact that North-West Frontier Province had a Congress Ministry.

Acceptance of Plan. The Representatives of the Hindu Majority Districts of the Punjab led by Dr. Gopichand Bhargava and Bengal led by Dr. Shyama Prasad Mukherjee in their respective Assemblies voted in favour of the partition of the provinces. Sylhet mainly chose to merge in East Bengal. The followers of Khan Abdul Ghaffar Khan in North-West Frontier Province boycotted referendum. The remaining Muslim population opted for Pakistan. Mr. Mohammad Ali Jinnah refused to accept mutilated Pakistan but ultimately had to submit to the pressure of Mountbatten and Churchil. The Working Committee of the Congress met at Delhi on 14th June, 1947, to discuss the draft plan of the Viceroy. Abdul Ghaffar Khan, Maulana Abul Kalam Azad and Nationalist Muslims, the Hindu Members representing Pakistan districts and Sri Purushottam Das Tandon opposed the Plan but Govind Ballabh Pant, Pt. Jawaharlal Nehru, Sardar Ballabh Bhai Patel, Acharya Kripalani and Mahatma Gandhi accepted it in view of the conditions prevailing in the country. Govind Ballabh Pant moving the resolution of acceptance said that "acceptance of June 3rd Plan was the only way to achieve freedom and liberty for the country. It would assure an Indian Union with a strong Centre which could ensure progress.... The choice today was between accepting the Plan or committing suicide."[1] Master Tara Singh opposed the partition of the Punjab tooth and nail.

1. Mr. V.P. Menon, *The Transfer of Power in India*, pp. 384-385.

Netaji Subhas Chandra Bose's Victory over 2nd World War could have averted Partition. The three surviving veterans of Indian National Army (I.N.A.) said in Singapore on 16th December, 1995, "India would not have been partitioned, had their Leader Subhas Chandra Bose been victorious."

As the three, Colonel G.S.Dhillon, Captain Lakshmi Sehgal and Captain S.S. Yadav prepare to reenact their famous march from here to India after 50 years they look back at their native land and see a world gone wrong. But the trio insisted, however, that despite the post-Independence decline and the INA's own defeat after Japan's fall, they did not feel their efforts were wasted and would repeat the struggle if they had to do it all over again.

They all believe that had Subhas Chandra Bose lived and the INA been victorious, India would not have been partitioned. Also, that politics in free India would not have the deep taints of caste and community it now displays.

"*India would have been more secular, disciplined as well as socialistic, religion would have been respected but it would have been an individual show, not a communal one,*" Col. G.S. Dhillon, who led the INA commando wing that bottled up the Royal Army's General Willian Slim on the banks of Burma's Irawaddy river for a critical six days in 1945, said.

In order to give effect to the scheme given by Mountbatten and agreed upon both by the Congress and the League the British Parliament passed the Indian Independence Act on July 5, 1947 and it received Royal assent on July 18, to become operative on August 15, 1947.

INDIAN INDEPENDENCE ACT, 1947 (END OF BRITISH IMPERIALISM)

The provisions of the Act were as given below :—

1. Clause 1 of the Act provided for the creation of two independent Dominions, India and Pakistan, from 15th August, 1947.

"The word independent emphasised", as Earl Listowel, Secretary of State for India, said in the House of Lords on the second reading of the Bill, "the absence of any external restraint. Independence in this sense is a universal attribute of Dominion Status, a fact that is often misunderstood by the outside world. It is also in accordance with the famous definition of the British Empire in the Report of the Imperial conference of 1926."[1]

2. Clause 2 of the Independence Act defined the territories of the two Dominions adjustable after the Award of the Boundary Commission (for that purpose two Boundary Commissions, one for the Punjab and another for Bengal had been set up both under the chairmanship of Sir Cyril Radcliff. In each Boundary Commission two representatives of Hindus and two representatives of Muslims had been taken). Clauses 3 and 4 provided for the partition of Bengal and the Punjab and secession of Sylhet from Assam after the wishes of the people have been known and also for the fixation of the final boundaries of India and Pakistan after the award of the Boundary Commission. When the Dominion of Pakistan was born on August 14, 1947 after the Partition of India, it consisted of two wings, Eastern and Western Pakistan. The Eastern Pakistan consisted of East Bengal and Sylhet. Sylhet was the Muslim majority district of Assam which had opted for East Pakistan in a referendum. The Western Wing of Pakistan consisted of West Punjab, Sind, North-West Frontier Province, Bahawalpur, Khairpur, Baluchistan and eight other relatively minor States in Baluchistan.

3. Both the Dominions were to have Governor-Generals appointed by British King for the purpose. The Act also provided for one common Governor-General if both the Dominions so agreed.

4. The Constituent Assemblies of both the Dominions got the power to draft a new constitution according to their wishes in addition to the right to withdraw from the British Commonwealth.

1. July 16, 1947, Parliamentary Debates: 1946-47, Vol. 150, pp. 802-18

5. For the time being till the new constitutions were framed each of the Dominion and all the Provinces were to be governed in accordance with the Act of 1935. Each Dominion was, however, authorised to modify the Act of 1935 as it pleased. In the case of each of the Dominions, the powers of the Legislature of the Dominions would be exercisable in the first instance by the Constituent Assembly of that Dominion. If any other provision is not made by the Constituent Assembly, then both the Dominions will be governed according to the Act of 1935 with such modifications, omisions or additions as may be done by the Governor-General-in-Council. The provisions regarding the Discretionary and Individual Judgement's powers will not remain effective after independence.

6. The British Government no longer possessed any control over the Dominions, Provinces or any part of the Dominions after 15th August, 1947.

7. The Legislature of each Dominion was empowered to frame the laws for the governance of that Dominion. No law made by that Dominion will be treated as null and void on this ground that it conflicted with any law of England or the provisions of the Indian Independence Act, 1947 or any rules regulation made thereunder.

8. The King of Great Britain ceased to be Emperor of India. The British King will no longer possess the power of disallowing any law made by the Dominion Legislature. The Governor-Generals became the constitutional heads. They were empowered to give assent to any ordinary Bill on behalf of the Crown.

9. No Provincial Bill was to be reserved for the assent of His Majesty in future. The Governor-General was, however, invested with adequate powers until March, 1948 to issue orders for the effective implementation of the provisions of the Indian Independence Act, 1947 and the division of the assets between the two Dominions and to make suitable changes in the Government of India Act, 1935 to remove any difficulty that might arise in the transitional period.

10. The office of Secretary of State for India and his advisers was abolished and affairs relating to the Dominions of India and Pakistan were to be conducted in future by Secretary of the Commonwealth Relation's Department.

11. Those persons who had been appointed by the Secretary of State or Secretary of State-in-Council to a civil service under the Crown in India before August 15, 1947 would continue in that service after Independence and enjoy the same privileges and rights in respect of leave, remuneration and pension, disciplinary matters and tenure of office which had been enjoyed by them before Independence.

12. After the establishment of two independent Dominions, the British Government would have absolutely no responsibility in regard to any territory which was included in British India. The paramountcy of His Majesty's Government over the Indian States lapsed and with it all treaties and agreements between the British Government and Indian Rulers which were in force at the time of the passing of the Indian Independence Act also lapsed. All obligation, jurisdiction and functions of His Majesty arising out of the various treaties, grants, usage, sufferance, or otherwise were also to lapse and the Indian States would become independent in their political relations with the Governments of the new Dominions. In other words, the British Government would have absolutely no relation of any kind with the Indian States and they will be free either to join India or Pakistan or remain independent.

13. The British Government would exercise no authority in future over the tribal areas and any treaty or agreement in force at the time of the passing of the Indian Independence Act between His Majesty and any tribal authority would also lapse.

14. Pakistan was henceforth to negotiate with the tribes of North Western Frontier Province.

THE DAWN OF INDEPENDENCE

India got out of the British Domination and became an independent State on 15th August, 1947. It was a historic day indeed. The chapter of India's slavery which had its beginning in 1757 with bad luck in the battle of Plassey, finally closed in 1947. After a long-drawn struggle our dream took a concrete shape. We owe the deepest gratitude to those countless heroes of our national struggle, who had to pay price for it through their precious blood or numerous other sacrifices. India will always remember her great sons with thankfulness and pride. Let us now review the helping factors which led India to her goal. Dr. Rajendra Prasad in his thanks-giving speech in the Constituent Assembly said, "While our achievement is in no small measure due to our own sufferings and sacrifices it is also the result of world forces and events and last though not least, it is the consummation and fulfilment of the historic tradition and the democratic ideals of the British race."

FACTORS RESPONSIBLE FOR THE INDEPENDENCE OF THE COUNTRY

A country usually gets freedom not by begging but by force. Freedom is never got on a silver platter, it is wrested from the unwilling hands. It is a unique event in the history of the world that an Imperialist country like England agreed to surrender power without much of bloodshed. History cannot cite any other example when a country got her independence through non-violent methods in such a short time though with a lot of sacrifice. The factors responsible for the transfer of power were as follows :

1. The spirit of nationalism and the strength of national movement—extremist, revolutionary and constitutional.
2. The growing consciousness in the whole of Asia that the people of the East were being exploited by the Colonial Nations of the West.
3. Weakening of England at the end of Second World War.
4. The alarm in the minds of the British Officers that the Indian armed forces were becoming disloyal and rebellious.
5. The coming of Labour Party to power—a party which had always been inclined to confer Independence on India.
6. Growing realisation in England that holding India in subjection was not at all profitable for war-torn England.
7. *The acceptance of Mohammad Ali Jinnah's demand of Pakistan by the Congress.* Had the Congress not accepted the League's demand, and the British Government might have postponed the issue of our freedom for an indefinite period.
8. *The pressure of world opinion.* England feared that she may not be able to save her face if she liquidated the German and Japanese possessions and not her own.
9. Last but not least was the pressure of the Governments of the U.S.A., the U.S.S.R. and China, who championed the cause of India.

Thus we learn that factors no. 1, 4, 5 and 7 were most potent in bringing Independence to India and drove the British beyond Indian shores by non-violent methods, many more potent factors compelled the British Government to hasten their withdrawal from the Indian scene. After achieving independence, the Constituent Assembly of India pushed on with the work of constitution-making. In the meantime India had to handle another problem of great magnitude, namely the rehabilitation of lakhs of Hindus who migrated to India in the wake of disturbances in Pakistan. Then the Government applied itself to reconstruction work, for which it launched Five-year Plans and community projects (now rural integrated programme) and construction of various dams. Sardar Ballabh Bhai Patel accomplished the miracle of securing the merger of all the petty and big Indian States in the Indian Union. A new India, cheerful and prosperous is emerging out of the rut of backwardness and poverty. It is hoped that soon we will catch up with the highly advanced nations of the West.

EXERCISES

Long Answer Type Questions

1. Discuss the circumstances for the August offer. What were its proposals?
2. Critically discuss the Cripp's proposals. What was the attitude of Indian National Congress towards the proposals?
3. What were the circumstances for the arrival of the Cripp's Mission? Give the text of the Cripps proposals and also comment on them.
4. Give an account of the Quit India Movement and discuss its importance in the Independence Movement of India.
5. Write a note on Wavell Plan.
6. What were the circumstances that led to the arrival of Cabinet Mission in India? What were its chief recommendations? Give an appraisal of the Mission?
7. "The Cabinet Mission proposals are supposed to be an honest effort of the British to solve the trangled political problem of India. These proposals sought to give the trangled political problem of different elements without sacrificing the essential principles of nationhood." Is this the correct appraisal of the Cabinet Mission? Discuss.
8. Give an account of the Mountbatten Plan.
9. Briefly discuss the history of Muslim Communalism.

Short Answer Type Questions

1. Write a brief note on 'War and India belligerent'.
2. What was Congress reaction to help Britain in War?
3. Write a very brief note on 'The August Offer'.
4. What were the causes leading to the Cripps Mission in India?
5. Write a very brief note on Quit India Resolution.
6. What was Wavell Plan?
7. Write a very brief note on 'Simla Conference and its failure'.
8. Write a short note on I.N.A. Trials.
9. What do you know about Naval Mutiny ?
10. What were the demerits of the Cabinet Mission Plan ?
11. "The Indian Independence Act of 1947 was thrust upon the Britishers." How far do you agree with this statement.?
12. Why the British left India?
13. Write a short note on 'Demand of Communal Representation'.
14. Write a short note on 'Foundation of Muslim League'.

Objective Type Questions

Choose the correct answer

1. In which year The Second World War broke out in Europe ?
(*a*) 1939 (*b*) 1940
(*c*) 1941 (*d*) 1942

2. In which year Indian Muslims celebrate the resigning day of Congress Ministers as a day of deliverance ?
(*a*) 1938 (*b*) 1939
(*c*) 1940 (*d*) 1941

3. Who replaced Mr. Chamberlain as the Prime Minister of Britain ?
(*a*) Mr. Amery (*b*) Lord Zetland
(*c*) Mr. Churchill (*d*) Lord Linlithgow

4. Who replaced Lord Zetland as the Secretary of State for India at the time of 'August Offer'?
(*a*) Mr. Cripps. (*b*) Mr. Wavell
(*c*) Mr. Hobbson (*d*) Lord Amery

5. In which year a statement consisting of new proposals was issued and hence it has been called 'The August Offer' ?
(*a*) 1940 (*b*) 1941
(*c*) 1942 (*d*) 1943

6. In which year Japan entered the war on the side of Axis powers ?
(*a*) 1940 (*b*) 1941
(*c*) 1942 (*d*) 1943

7. In which year Mr. Cripps arrived in India ?
(*a*) 1940 (*b*) 1941
(*c*) 1942 (*d*) 1943

8. In which year The Congress working Committee passed the 'Quit India Resolution' ?
(*a*) 1939 (*b*) 1940
(*c*) 1941 (*d*) 1942

9. At the time of 'Quit India Movement' who was the President of Congress ?
(*a*) Maulana Abul Kalam Azad (*b*) Mahatma Gandhi
(*c*) Pt. Jawaharlal Nehru (*d*) Pt. Motilal Nehru

10. In which year Mahatma Gandhi wrote a letter to Viceroy from the jail that he would undertake a fast for 21 days for his self-purification ?
(*a*) 1942 (*b*) 1943
(*c*) 1944 (*d*) 1945

ANSWERS

1. (*a*) **2.** (*b*) **3.** (*c*) **4.** (*d*) **5.** (*a*) **6.** (*b*) **7.** (*c*) **8.** (*d*) **9.** (*a*) **10.** (*b*)

CHAPTER 22

Some Prominent Leaders of Freedom Struggle

ALLAN OCTAVIAN HUME (1829-1912)

Mr. A. O. Hume is said to be the father of the Indian National Congress. He was a member of the Indian Civil Service. He held the post of Secretary to the Government of India from 1870 to 1879. He served India in various capacities. He was a zealous social reformer. He was one of those few Englishmen who did not have any prejudice against Indians. He always stood for an enlightened policy towards the Indians. Because of his critical opinion of the British policy in India, he was forced to resign in 1882. Three years later he founded Indian National Congress. He was not an advocate of India's freedom, on the contrary, he believed that British Indian fellowship was beneficial to India. He, however, was sympathetic to India's urge for progress and advancement. He was deeply pained to see millions of Indians living a wretched life under object poverty and illiteracy.

Mr. Hume was firmly of the opinion that the British Government was not adequately discharging its responsibility towards India. He felt the need of starting an organisation like the Congress which might ventilate the genuine feelings of the Indian public in a constitutional manner. The British Officers both in India and England approved of his plans, for they thought that such a peaceful organisation dominated by an Englishman, would divert the national forces from violent to non-violent channels.

Mr. Hume, whatever his motives, occupies an eminent place in the annals of the Congress. He was the first General Secretary of the organisation, which office he held till 1907. His 22-year association with the Congress establishes it beyond doubt that he was keenly interested in the uplift and advancement of the country. As a district officer too he had laboured hard to introduce many reforms in the Indian Administration. He also took up with great interest the cause of popular education, police reforms, the liquor traffic, the vernacular press, the juvenile reformatories and other domestic requirements. In 1879 he prepared a scheme for providing relief to the hungry mouths in the South. In short, nobody can deny that Mr. A.O. Hume awakened the soul of India from the age-long sleep of submission and fatalism.

DADABHAI NAOROJI (1825 - 1917)

Dadabhai Naoroji, the Grand Old Man of India, was born on September 4, 1825. He was quite a promising boy at school but for want of resources could not proceed to England for further studies. He started his career as a Professor of Mathematics in Elphinston College, Bombay. His social work went side by side with his teaching work. During his lifetime he associated himself with the starting of nearly 30 associations having political and social objectives. In 1885 he sailed for England as a Representative of M/s Cama and Co. After some time he became a partner of the firm and he settled down permanently in England. There he started East Indian Association and London Indian Society. Both these societies loudly dinned into the British ears the political demands of Indian people. In 1873 he furnished evidence on behalf of India before the Fawett Select Committee on Indian Finance. In 1874 he was appointed the Prime Minister (Dewan) of Baroda State. In 1885 he was nominated as the additional member of the Bombay Legislative Council. He had the rare distinction of presiding over the annual sessions of the Congress thrice—in 1886, 1893 and 1906. In 1892 he contested a British Parliamentary seat and became a member of the House of Commons. Dadabhai Naoroji thus served the nation for 61 years—40 years before the birth of the Congress and 21 years after it.

Dadabhai Naoroji

The partition of Bengal in 1905 caused much furore and unrest in the country. Extremism was on the increase. It was feared that there would be a tough contest for the Presidentship of 1906 session of the Congress between the Extremist group and the Moderates. Dada Bhai Naoroji commanded so much respect in both the camps that he was accepted by both of them unanimously. With Dada Bhai Naoroji in the chair, the Congress for the first time set before itself the goal of Dominion Status. It was a clear advance on its earlier demands which were confined to securing more responsible services for the Indians. In his Presidential address of 1906, he observed thus: "*Our faith and our future are in our hands. If we are true to ourselves and our country and make all the necessary sacrifice for our elevation and amelioration, I for one have not a shadow of doubt that in dealing with such justice-loving, fair-minded people as the British, we may rest assured that we shall not work in vain. It is this convinction which has supported me against all difficulties*". At Calcutta session he declared: *We do not ask favours. We want only justice. Instead of going into further divisions or details of our rights as British citizens, the whole matter can be comprised in one word—self-government or Swaraj, like that of the United Kingdom or the Colonies.*" Under his dynamic leadership began the second chapter of the Congress History. The Congress took a sharp turn from beggary to a firm demand for Swaraj.

Dadabhai Naoroji was essentially a moderate. He was a friend of the British Rule which he thought had a civilising impact on India. He was opposed to breaking up with the 'advanced humanitarian civilisation of Britain'. It was his belief that the Congress could surely achieve Dominion Status by constitutional means. Under his inspiring leadership, the Congress launched Swadeshi Movement and boycott of foreign goods. In his book "*Poverty and Un-British Rule in India*", speeches and articles he explained the causes of India's poverty. He wrote: "*It is at India's cost and blood that this British Empire has been formed and maintained up to this day. It is in consequence of the tremendous cost of these wars and because of the millions and millions you draw from us year by year that India is so completely exhausted and bled. You have brought India to this condition by the constant drain upon the wealth of that country.*"

Dadabhai Naoroji's contribution was many faceted. He built up the theory of the economic foundations of Indian nationalism. He pointed out how through various methods India was being exploited and robbed of its resources by British government. He elucidated this 'drain-theory' in his book—*Poverty and Un-British Rule in India.* This book presented graphically the appalling story of India's poverty. He wrote: "This drain consists of two elements—first that arising from the remittances by European Officials of their savings and for their expenditure in England, for their various wants both there and in India; and from Government expenditure in England and India. And the second was that arising from similar remittances by non-official Europeans. As the drain prevents India from making any capital; the British by bringing back the capital which they have drained from India itself, secure almost a monopoly of all trade and important industries, and thereby further exploit and drain India, the source of the evil being the official drain." He further pointed out that "England was eating India's resources at the rate of some £ 30,000,000 to £ 40,000,000 a year." He also referred to another sort of drain, in the form of experience, talent and skill. He said: "Beyond the position of deputy collectors or extra-commissioners or similar subordinate positions in the engineering, medical and all other services, all experience and knowledge of statesmanship, of administration or legislation, of high scientific or learned professions are drained away to England when the persons possessing them give up their service and retire to England."

Dadabhai Naoroji was a great patriot and devout political leader. He pleaded the cause of India quite boldly in British Parliament. He said in the House of Commons that the evils of foreign rule in India involved the triple loss of wealth, wisdom and work. In his presidential address at Calcutta Congress in 1906 he said that since India was an integral part of British Empire, the Indians were entitled to all those rights which were conferred on the British Citizens. He also insisted on the implementation of the promises made in Queen Victoria's Proclamation of 1858 and the provisions of the Act of 1833. He claimed three types of concessions to be given to Indians. The first was better and higher services and more effective Indian control on administration. Secondly, the Indians should be given an elected legislature as other self-governing Dominions had. Thirdly, financial relations between England and India should be fair and just. His conviction was that only fair means should be adopted to gain political ends. According to Gopal Krishna Gokhale: "If ever there is the divine in man, it is in Dadabhai Naoroji."

GOPAL KRISHNA GOKHALE (1866-1915)
(Political Philosopher of the Moderates)

Gopal Krishna Gokhale was born in 1866 in a poor Brahmin family. He was a true disciple of Justice Mahadev Gobind Ranade whom he acknowledged as his spiritual and political 'Guru'. He was in line with Dadabhai Naoroji and Sir Ferozeshah Mehta so far as his views were concerned. After his graduation in 1884, he set his heart on the service of his motherland. Guided by his missionary spirit, he joined the Deccan Education Society founded by Justice Mahadev Gobind Ranade. He started his career as a Professor of History and Economics at Fergusson College, Poona and retired as principal of the very college in 1902. He Presided over the Benares Congress in 1905. In 1897 he went to England to give evidence before the Welby Commission on behalf of the Deccan Education Society. This Commission was appointed to ascertain whether or not India was unreasonably encumbered with financial burdens which should be borne by England. In 1895 he became the Secretary of the Bombay Congress Committee. He pointed out the shortcomings in the Act of 1892 and told the Government in clear words that it was not going to pacify the Indians. In 1902 he was taken into Central Legislative Council where he delivered some of the finest speeches of the budget. In the Council he strove hard for the abolition of salt tax, introduction of compulsory primary education, inclusion of Indians in senior posts and reduction of Government expenditure.

Gopal Krishna Gokhale

At the time of Bengal Partition he condemned the government action and declared, "*Then all I can say is good-bye to all hope of co-operating in any way with the bureaucracy in the interests of the people.*" He gave full support to the boycott movement. In 1906 he was sent to England as Congress Envoy enlighten the British Public with the injured feeling of the Indians over the Bengal issue. His eloquence coupled with lucid presentation of facts won him a host of admirers there.

In 1905 Gopal Krishna Gokhale started '*Servants of India Society*' with the object of raising a band of self denying patriots. In the preamble to the Constitution of Society, Gopal Krishna Gokhale wrote thus: "A sufficient number of our countrymen must now come forward to devote themselves to the cause in the spirit in which religious work is undertaken. Public life must be spiritualised. Love of the country must so fill the heart that all else shall appear as of little moment by its side".

Gopal Krishna Gokhale had always a soft corner in his heart for the "starving, shrunken, shrivelled-up *Ryot* toiling and moiling from dawn to dark to earn his scanty meal, patient, resigned, for bearing beyond measure, entirely voiceless in the parliament of his rulers and he meekly prepared to bear whatever burdens God and man might be pleased to impose upon his back."

In 1912 he went to South Africa and helped Mahatma Gandhi in his movement against colour bar. The credit of persuading Mahatma Gandhi back to India to take part in Indian public life also goes to him. Mahatma Gandhi accepted him as his political 'Guru'. He also drafted a scheme of reforms which is called political Testament of Gopal krishna Gokhale and it was published after his death. He had his novel tests of ascertaining whether the Government of India was progressive or not. He judged the Government on the steps it took for the material and moral improvement of the Indians, for their education, sanitation and agriculture, for giving self governing institutions and lastly for admitting Indians in senior ranks of public services. He died on 15th February, 1915, when his reputation was at its zenith. All the leaders of India paid him lofty tributes. Bal Gangadhar Tilak described him as 'the Diamond of India, the Jewel of Maharashtra and the Prince of workers'. Lala Lajpat Rai found Gopal Krishna Gokhale's patriotism of the purest type.

Views of Gopal Krishna Gokhale. Gopal Krishna Gokhale belonged to the Moderate School of Indian life. He was indebted for the texture of his political views to his preceptor Mahadev Gobind Ranade. Like Dada Bhai Naoroji he was also of the view that constitutional agitation was the only way to secure constitutional reforms. The Congress clung to this creed for 35 years. He did not distrust the British and hence believed that as soon as Indians proved their capability to govern themselves, they would be given self-government by the British Parliament. British connection, he said, was in the interest of India. He nevertheless carried in his mind the glorious picture of future India. In his Budget speech in 1903 he said, "*The India of the future will, under Providence, not be an India of diminishing plenty, of empty prospect, or of justifiable discontent; but one of expanding industry, of awakened faculties, of increasing prosperity, and more widely distributed comfort and wealth. I have faith in the conscience and purpose of my own country, and I believe in the almost illimitable capacities of this...*"

Gopal Krishna Gokhale's position became awakward when the Extremists like Bal Gangadhar Tilak disagreed with him on many points and called him a 'faint-hearted moderate', and the British Government looked upon him as a seditionist in disguise' in view of his criticism of the Government in the Imperial Council. In fact, both the charges were unfounded. He was certainly not a revolutionary, nor was his design to incite the people to violence. All his efforts were directed towards accomplishing administrative reforms through petitions and constitutional and peaceful agitations. He was a leader of great courage and integrity. Bal Gangadhar Tilak's remark that he was a faint-hearted moderate was also unjust, for Gopal Krishna Gokhale had the knack of criticising the Government bitterly and boldly. In the words of Pt. Motilal Nehru: "Gopal Krishna Gokhale was the great apostle of self-government. He vehemently criticised the ruling bureaucracy for its gross irresponsibility and extreme callousness to public will in having effected the famous partition of Bengal. He made emphatic protests against the harshness and oppressiveness of the bureaucracy. Gopal Krishna Gokhale urged upon the bureaucracy not to be satisfied with having acted upon the maxims of 'efficiency' but so to govern India that Indians might be enabled to govern themselves according to the highest western standards. He lamented the growing destination of India under British rule. He also criticised the costly character of the administration of India by a foreign agency."

Gopal Krishna Gokhale was a great nation builder. If he refrained from preaching violence and extreme measures, it was because India was not strong enough to wrest freedom by force. He adopted peaceful methods to avoid unnecessary repression by the Government. He breathed the spirit of service and patriotism into young Indian hearts by this speeches and articles which were always critical of the British bureaucracy. Thus, he was neither weak nor fiery; he was a realist in politics or, we may say, a practical idealist.

Gopal Krishna Gokhale was an economist of a very high order. He made Himalayan efforts to improve the lot of the agriculturists and also to shorten the gap between low-paid and highly-paid groups. He demanded a radical change in the fiscal policy of the Government so as to offer more and better jobs to educated middle-class people. In his budget speeches, he urged the abolition of excise duty on cotton goods. In 1911 he vehemently opposed the seditious Meetings Act on the floor of the Imperial Legislative Council.

Gopal Krishna Gokhale's attitude to the British can be judged best by the following extract from his speech : "The Englishman who imagines that India can be governed much longer on the same lines as in the past, and the Indian who thinks that he must seek a destiny for his country outside this Empire, of which now, for better or worse, we are a part—both alike show an inadequate appreciation of the realities of the present situation." Gopal Krishna Gokhale stood for co-operation and reconciliation. He wanted decentralization of power and association of educated Indians with the actual work of administration. In fact, he was a pathfinder for Mahatma Gandhi. He paved the way of negotiation and moderation in politics for Mahatma Gandhi to walk upon. There can be no loftier tribute than that paid by Holyland. "He (Gokhale) was a great master of the possible, a constructive statesman of the first rank, a bringer together of the East and West in the common service of the needy; above all, an idealist, a foreseer, a prophet of new era of inter-racial goodwill and co-operation."

Estimate of Gopal Krishna Gokhale

According to Dr. V.H.Rutherford, "a diplomatist to his finger tips who knew how to play on the national lyre without offending the official ear." According to Bal Gangadhar Tilak, Gopal Krishna Gokhale was "*the diamond of India, the jewel of Maharashtra and the Prince of workers.*" According to Mahatma Gandhi, "Sir Ferozeshah Mehta seemed to me like the Himalayas unscalable; the Lokmanya Bal Gangadhar Tilak like the ocean one could not easily launch forth on the sea. But Gopal Krishna Gokhale was as the Ganges—it invited one to its bosom. In the sphere of politics, the place that Gopal Krishna Gokhale occupied in my heart during his life-time and occupies even now has been and is unique." According to Lala Lajpat Rai, "Gopal Krishna Gokhale was the noblest and best of Congress workers and his patriotism was the highest and of noblest type. According to Lord Morley, Gopal Krishna Gokhale had a politician's head and a sense of executive responsibility."

There are two different views about the role of Gopal Krishna Gokhale in the National Movement. While the Extremists in India dubbed him as a faint-hearted Moderate who was prepared to be a willing tool in the hands of the British Government, the reactionaries described him as a "seditionist in disguise." As a matter of fact he was neither a revolutionary nor a reactionary. He hated both the extremes. He was a constructive statesman who understood and fought for the rights and liberties of the people of India, but he was not ready to ignore or belittle the difficulties of the Government of India also. It has rightly been pointed out that Gopal Krishna Gokhale "Interpreted the popular aspirations to the Viceroy and the Government's difficulties to the Congress." It is notable that people disparaged his moderation and the government deprecated his extremism. His role was that of a unifier and reconciler. His view was that while both Britain and India stood to lose by mutual jealousies and hatred, a lot could be gained by good-will and healthy co-operation.

LOKMANYA BAL GANGADHAR TILAK (1856-1920)
(Political Philosopher of Extremism)

Lokmanya Bal Gangadhar Tilak was a born revolutionary. As a true Maratha, he drew inspiration from the thrilling and mighty exploits of Chhatrapati Shivaji. A burning rage against foreign domination, against all injustice and national wrongs flowed from his private talks and public discussions, from his books and articles. He was so to say a prophet hero of India's struggle for freedom.

Lokmanya Bal Gangadhar Tilak was born in 1856, incidentally the year of preparation for the great struggle of 1857. Like Abhimanyu, he had inborn skill and courage to fight. He got his law degree in 1879. In 1890 he started Poona New English School with a view to imparting inexpensive national education to young boys and girls. He was also the founders of Deccan Education Society and Fergusson College, Poona. In order to communicate to the public at large his religious and political views and also in order to awaken the latent love for the country in Indian youths, he brought out two papers—*Maratha* and *The Kesari*. In 1891 he opposed the enactment of the 'Age of Consent Bill' on the grounds that an alien Government had no right to meddle with our social and religious customs. He dreamt of a militant India which might not beg but snatch her freedom from the foreign hands. In order to organise and revitalise Hindu nation, he inaugurated Ganapati and Shivaji festivals. He also started *Akharas* and *lathi* clubs with the object of infusing spirit in Hindu youths.

In 1897 he entered the Bombay Legislative Council. There too he gave ample proof of his intellectual and moral courage by criticising the Government. The same year a terrible famine occurred in Maharashtra. Close on it heels came the raging plague. Thousands of people lost their lives. Lokmanya Bal Gangadhar Tilak opened a vigorous attack on the Government's callous and wilful indiference to the plight of the victims. He organised relief work and started 'No-Rent' campaign. This made him a suspect in the eyes of the Government. He was involved in Mr. Rand's murder case according to the British Government and sentenced to 18 months' rigorous imprisonment.

(Lal-Bal-Pal)

Lala Lajpat Rai **Lokmanya Bal Gangadhar Tilak** **Bipin Chandra Pal**

Lokmanya Bal Gangadhar Tilak's entry into the Congress was an event of great importance and consequence. It marked the beginning of a new era in Indian politics. The Congress got out of the confines of educated class and became a mass movement. Lokmanya Bal Gangadhar Tilak gave a sharp turn to the Congress technique of fighting for freedom. He saw the futility of petitions and beggary and hence encouraged aggressive activities. He had more faith in the cult of moral force. He gave voice to national urge when he said, "*Swaraj is our birthright and we shall have it.*" Lokmanya Bal Gangadhar Tilak was the pioneer and life force of the Extremist School in the Congress ranks. Unlike the Moderate (Gokhale and Ranade), who considered British rule as beneficial to India, Lokmanya Bal Gangadhar Tilak declared vibrantly that *it was positively harmful, a real course for India. He led the crusade against the use of foreign goods. He had no faith in British goodness. All means, he said, are justified to achieve a noble goal. He justified the tactics of Shivaji for planning the murder of Afzal Khan.* In short his was the policy of 'tit for tat'. *He wanted Home Rule and not merely reforms in the system of British Administration in India.* His heart was set on independence even if it was to be achieved at the cost of blood and life. It is for this reason that Lokmanya Bal Gangadhar Tilak has been called the *Father of Indian Unrest.* In one of his fiery speeches he said, "*The days of protests and prayers have gone. It is impossible to expect that our petitions will be heard unless backed by firm resolution ... unless backed by solid force. Look to the example of Ireland, Japan and Russia and follow their methods. Do not rely much upon the sympathy of the rulers." People strongly believed that Bal Gangadhar Tilak would be able to expel the British from Indian soil.*

Bal Gangadhar Tilak was a staunch Hindu but not fanatic or anti-Muslim. He rated Vedic Culture as far superior to Western Culture which had its roots in materialism. For this reason he always denounced the blind aping of the Western People. His conception of Hinduism is expressed in this extract: "The term Sanatan Dharma shows that our religion is as old as the history of the human race itself. Vedic Religion of the Aryans from a very early time. Hindu religion was the religion as a whole is made up of different parts co-related to each other as so many sons and daughters of one great religion ... Religion is an element in nationality."

Bal Gangadhar Tilak was a political genius, 'a prophet, a seer blest'. He was the first in many fields. He was the first powerful protagonist of Hindi. He declared that 'a common script is a part and parcel of a national movement; we must have a common language in the whole of India. If you want to draw a nation together, there is no force more powerful than a common language for all'. And Hindi written in Devanagri script was the only language which could serve the purpose. His creed was creed of defiance, of self-respect and national pride. In 1907, at Surat Session, the breach between the Moderates and Extremists became wider. Bal Gangadhar Tilak resigned his membership of the Congress. Bal Gangadhar Tilak's popularity and hold over the Indian masses alarmed the Government which took advantage of Surat-split and set about crushing the extremists. Bal Gangadhar Tilak was arrested and sent to Mandalay Jail for six years. In jail he completed his two classical monumental works—*Gita Rahasya* and *Arctic Home in the Vedas*. In 1916 he started Home Rule League but soon as a result of the efforts of Mrs. Annie Besant, he rejoined Congress.

Dr. Pattabhi Sitaramayya drawing a comparison of Bal Gangadhar Tilak and Gopal Krishna Gokhale observes: "Bal Gangadhar Tilak and Gopal Krishna Gokhale were both patriots of the first order. Both had made heavy sacrifices in life. But their temperaments were widely different from each other. Gopal Krishna Gokhale was a Moderate and Bal Gangadhar Tilak was an Extremist, if we may use the language in vogue at that time. Gopal Krishna Gokhale's aim was to improve the existing constitution, Bal Gangadhar Tilak's was to reconstruct it. Gopal Krishna Gokhale had necessarily to work with the bureaucracy; Bal Gangadhar Tilak had necessarily to fight it. Gopal Krishna Gokhale stood for co-operation wherever possible and oppositon wherever necessary, Bal Gangadhar Tilak inclined towards a policy of obstruction. Gopal Krishna Gokhale's primary concern was with the administration and its improvement; Tilak's supreme concern was the nation and its upbuilding. Gopal Krishna Gokhale's ideal was love and sacrifice. Bal Gangadhar Tilak's was service and suffering. Gopal Krishna Gokhale depended upon others' help; Bal Gangadhar Tilak upon self-help. Gopal Krishna Gokhale looked to the classes and the intelligentsia; Bal Gangadhar Tilak on the masses and the millions. Gopal Krishna Gokhale's arena was the council-chamber; Tilak's forum was the village mandap. Gokhale's medium of expression was English; Bal Gangadhar Tilak's was Marathi. Gopal Krishna Gokhale's objective was self-government for which the people had to fit themselves by answering the tests prescribed by the English; Bal Gangadhar Tilak's objective was Swaraj which is the birthright of every Indian and which he shall have without any hindrance from the foreigner. Gopal Krishna Gokhale was on a level with his age; Bal Gangadhar Tilak was in advance of his times". Bal Gangadhar Tilak was a prophet of aggressive nationalism whose roots were in the Hindu religion. He was in fact the uncrowned king of India, the idol of Indian youth and a thorn in the flesh of the British Government.

Swaraj, as he once wrote, was 'the foundation and not the height of India's prosperity'. By Swaraj he meant not the end of the British Rule but Dominion Status within the British Empire. He was thus modest and most reasonable in his demands. He was even prepared to let the British Government retain charge of India's external affairs. It can be gathered from his speeches that he was in favour of reorganisation of Indian Provinces on lingual basis and the Dominion Government to be formed on federal lines. At the end of First World War (1914 - 18), Bal Gangadhar Tilak sent his memorandum to Clemenceau, the President of the Peace Conference, on 21st March, 1919. In it he stated that India should be given the right of self-determination in order that she might also contribute to the maintenance of peace in the world. He further said that Montford Reforms were highly unsatisfactory. The Provincial Administration could not be democratic so long as the Central Government continued to be irresponsible and autocratic. He stated that the system of Dyarchy was unscientific and unworkable. He demanded the abolition of Indian Council. He was emphatic in his demand of offering senior military posts to Indians. Although Bal Gangadhar Tilak in his memorandum agreed to the British control over a few subjects under Swaraj, he in the heart of hearts always cherished the goal of full freedom. His restricted demands were dictated by his practical statemanship and realistic wisdom.

Bal Gangadhar Tilak was persecuted for writing inflammatory articles which contained the threat of mutiny and which preached in substance the gospel of 'bombs'. But in fact he was not in line with Russian Revolutionaries like Lenin and others. He, no doubt, justified violence if the motive behind it was good, but he never approved political murders, nor did he ever incite people to take to arms. He had faith in constitutional methods of protests and agitations. He felt that the situation in the country was not suitable for revolutionary activities. Since the country was unequipped for an armed revolt, he turned to the other means of passive resistance. He launched a vigorous campaign for national education. Swadeshi, and boycott of imported goods. He also advocated non-co-operation and non-payment of taxes in order to paralyse the Government. He was a thorough realist. He brought about a compromise between the Congress and Muslim League in 1916. So he was the author of Lucknow Pact. He started the Home Rule Movement. He also supported Non-co-operation and Khilafat Movement before his death.

Bal Gangadhar Tilak's appearance on the political horizon was, in fact, an event of great significance. He raised the slogan of Swaraj at a time when the people did not dare utter this word in public. His boldness nerved the timid hearts, his stress on religion and ancient Indian history restored the sagging pride of the people in their culture and heritage. He was undoubtedly the father of real political awakening in India.

Philosophy of defiance to the British Rule—Greatest contribution of Bal Gangadhar Tilak. The greatest contribution of Bal Gangadhar Tilak was that he taught the people how to defy the British Rule especially when the whole country had been totally crushed by the British Rulers in 1857 and the Moderates were always keen to placate them by their policies and programmes. They considered the British Raj as a divine blessing. They passed resolutions of loyalty to the throne and prayed for the safety and Prosperity of the British Empire. They reverted the programme of Swadeshi, Boycott and National Education in 1907 in order to please the British Rulers and framed a separate constitution after expelling Bal Gangadhar Tilak. When the bomb was throne on Lord Harding, then Gopal Krishna Gokhale assured him that his party would never oppose him. During the First

World War Mahatma Gandhi extended all possible help to the British Rulers. When Bal Gangadhar Tilak returned from Mandalay jail, then nobody in the Moderate group could stand against him. *He converted the Congress from the admires of the British Government into rebels against the British Empire. He was a thinker and fighter in one.* He dominated the Congress from 1916 till his death. *He was the father of non-co-operation because he always asked the people not to co-operate with the British Government. He was for complete independence as early as* 1897. He started Shivaji and Ganapati festivals with the same view. He delivered fiery speeches against the British rule and did not care for the consequences, though he suffered terribly. *He did not extend any co-operation to the British during First World War. On the other hand, he started Home Rule Movement against them to liberate the country from foreign clutches.*

Bal Gangadhar Tilak submits memorandum to the Paris Peace Conference. Bal Gangadhar Tilak's noble political career did not end with the Home Rule Movement. The First World War had ended on 11th November, 1918. The Allies had won the war and Germany and her allies (Turkey and Bulgaria etc.) had been badly defeated. As President Wilson of America was preaching the Right of Self determination for the subject nationalities, so Bal Gangadhar Tilak thought it fit to send a memorandum to the Paris Peace Conference also which opened on 12th January, 1919 under the Presidentship of French Prime Minister Mr. Clemenceau. Lloyd George, the British Prime Minister however, denied the right of Self-determination to the Indians.

Bal Gangadhar Tilak condemns the General Massacre of Jallianwala Bagh. Lokmanya Bal Gangadhar Tilak also visited the Jallianwala Bagh, Amritsar along with other top leaders of the Congress after tragedy and he severely condemned the tyrannies perpetrated over the innocent people of the Punjab particularly by General Dyer in Amristar, Captain Doveton in Kasur (near Lahore) and other military officers at Lahore and Gujranwala.

Bal Gangadhar Tilak and Mohammadans. Some people may wrongly think that Bal Gangadhar Tilak was deadly against the Mohammadans because he was the follower of Shivaji, justified the murder of Afzal Khan, encouraged the Hindus to celebrate the Ganpati festival and Shivaji birthday. Bal Gangadhar Tilak was a staunch Hindu but not anti-Mohammedan. He had to resort to the policy of defending and uniting the Hindus because the British Government was following policy of '*Divide and Rule*' since 1857 and encouraging Hindu-Muslim riots in order to retard the progress of nationalism. Such a riot was encouraged in 1893 by the British Government at Prabash Patam and Bombay, Later on such riots were encouraged by the British Government all over the country.

Mr. Muhammad Ali Jinnah, a Muslim Leader of that time, defended Lokmanya Bal Gangadhar Tilak as early as 1908. Lokmanya Bal Gangadhar Tilak was a firm believer in Hindu-Muslim unity, so he concluded Lucknow Pact in 1916 and thereby brought the Congress and the Muslim League nearer to each other. No Muslim, not even Maulana Mohammad Ali and Shaukat Ali, very prominent leaders of those times, ever doubted the sincerity of Lokmanya Bal Gangadhar Tilak. In other words, *he was the architect of HinduMuslim unity and cemented that unity by his foresight and wisdom.*

Bal Gangadhar Tilak and Non-co-operation Movement. Lokmanya Bal Gangadhar Tilak was laying seriously ill at Bombay in July, 1920. Mahatma Gandhi came to see him and asked if he would co-operate with the Non-co-operation Movement and Khilafat Movement which he was going to start in December 1920. Bal Gangadhar Tilak said about Non-co-operation to Mahatma Gandhi a few days before his Death: "I like the programme well enough, but I have my doubts as to the country being with us in the self-denying ordinances which Non-co-operation presents to people. I will do nothing and if you gain the popular ear, you will find in me an enthusiastic supporter." Lokmanya Bal Gangadhar Tilak, however, expired on 1st August, 1920 and could not see the fulfilment of the Non-co-operation Movement. He had always been a non-co-operator.

Estimate of Lokmanya Bal Gangadhar Tilak. Lokmanya Bal Gangadhar Tilak was one of the greatest figures in the political history of modern Asia. But he was also a profound scholar. By his monumental writings in the field of Vedic and Philosophic Researches, he had created a name and fame for himself in the literary and cultural annals of India. He will have permanent place not only in the political history of India but also in the history of the renaissance of the country. *The combination of scholarship and political leadership has given to Lokmanya Bal Gangadhar Tilak a unique place in the Indian History.* To the sober sense of keen political realism, he combined a vast intellectual idealism. It was unfortunate that due to the political servitude of India, Lokmanya Bal Gangadhar Tilak could not pursue his literary endeavours only in the enforced seclusion of political life. Lokmanya Bal Gangadhar Tilak had marvellous powers of intellectual creativism.[1]

According to Shri Raj Gopal, the writer of the biography of Bal Gangadhar Tilak rightly observes *"He (Tilak) had forestalled Gandhi in all the movements that Mahatma launched after Tilak's death, no rent campaign, boycott of Government service, prohibition, Swadeshi were all preached and practised by him. He talked of complete independence as back as* 1897. *Again, "His was the life divine and his countrymen elevated him not only to the position of Lokmanya but adored him as Tilak Bhagwan. In the encircling gloom, he appeared with a torch in his hand."* In 1908 *he was regarded another Shivaji and the people shouted, "Tilak Maharaj ki jai" and Chhatrapati Tilak Maharaj ki jai.*

According to Swami Shraddhanand, "Maharaj Tilak occupies an exalted position among the pioneers of political work, who were the first to preach the doctrine of political unity. Who other hero has suffered so much in the service of motherland as this illustrious person has done? Will not the soldiers constituting the army for the service of the motherland bow down before the mandate of this weather-beaten general?"

BIPIN CHANDRA PAL (1858-1932)

Bipin Chandra Pal, the great educationist, journalist and writer, was born in Sylhet district of Assam. He was a leader of the Extremist group. His ideas had great kinship with those of Lala Lajpat Rai and Balgangadhar Tilak. He began his career as a teacher but by virtue of his eloquence became a National Leader of all-India stature. On the issue of the Partition of Bengal, he led an agitation against the Government. He became one of the famous trio of the Congress History—Lal, Bal and Pal. He was clapped in jail several times because of his strident nationalism and strong views. He opposed the cult of begging and stood for complete swaraj. Maharshi Aurobindo once said with reference to Bipin Chandra Pal : "When I came I was not alone : one of the mightiest prophets of nationalism sat by my side. It was he (Pal) who then came out of the seclusion to which God had sent him, so that in the silence and solitude of his cell, he might hear the word that he had to say."

In 1911 he advanced the concept of an Imperial Federation, including Great Britain, Ireland, Egypt, India and other Dominions. The relation between Great Britain and the units was not to be that of the ruler and the slave but that of equals. For many years he had close association with the Congress, but he broke off from it because of differences with Mahatma Gandhi regarding the technique of Non-co-operation. The national awakening in India owes much to his eloquence and articles published in *New India* and *Vande Matram.*

MRS. ANNIE BESANT (1847-1933)

Mrs. Annie Besant was an Irish lady who came to India in 1893 as a Theosophist and made it her permanent home. She occupies an honoured place in the annals of Hindu Revivalism. She had profound faith in the superiority of Hindu Culture and Religion over Western Religions. She herself embraced Hinduism and set about popularising it. In the movement of Revitalisation and Revivalism of Hinduism, her name comes alongside Bal Gangadhar Tilak, Maharshi Aurobindo and Swami Dayanand Saraswati. She reminded the Hindus who were aping the West blindly, of the greatness

1. Dr. V.P. Verma, *Modern Indian Political Thought* (1961), p. 538.

of their spiritual and cultural heritage. She wrote several books on Hinduism and translated the *Gita* into English. She was one of the founders of Central Hindu College, Benaras, which later on took the shape and nomenclature of Benaras Hindu University. She was also a great advocate of *national education* and *swadeshi*.

Mrs. Annie Besant did not take any noteworthy part in the uproar against the partition of Bengal. She entered the political field in 1914 and started a weekly *The Commonweal* which later changed into a daily paper *New India* published from Madras. She founded Home Rule League in 1916. She claimed the support of Bal Gangadhar Tilak in her campaign. She demanded Home Rule for India. She was neither an Extremist nor a Moderate but followed the golden mean. "Her plan was to disentangle the National Extremists from the compromising alliance with the revolutionaries, to reconcile them to a position within the British Empire and to bring them with Moderates into line in a United Congress". She succeeded in bringing Lokmanya Bal Gangadhar Tilak and his associates who had resigned from the Congress after Surat split, back into the Congress in 1916. Probably the momentum gained by the Home Rule Movement compelled Mr. Montague Chalmsford in 1919 to promote gradual transfer of power from the British to Indian hands.

Her popularity as National Leader can be gauged from the fact that the Congress elected her to Preside over its Calcutta session in 1917. She described the Montford Schemes as disappointing and 'unworthy of England to offer and India to accept'. When Mahatma Gandhi launched the Non-co-operation Movement, she withdrew from the Congress and joined the liberals. In 1925, she sponsored the 'Commonwealth of India Bill' in the British Parliament through one of her friends. It was read in the House of Commons, but could not be carried through. Mrs. Annie Besant was a wonderful orator and writer of great charm and force. Her chief distinction was that she was a tireless worker for India's good.

PANDIT MADAN MOHAN MALAVIYA (1861-1946)

Pt. Madan Mohan Malaviya, the great oriental scholar, the founder of the Benaras Hindu University and the foremost political leader of his time, was a staunch Hindu Nationalist. He served the nation for more than six decades as an educationist, social reformer and political leader. He graduated in 1884 and came in contact with the Congress in 1886. Despite his frequent differences he retained his association with the Congress till his death. He was elected to the Provincial Legislative Council in 1902 and to the Imperial Legislative Council in 1910. In the Uttar Pradesh Legislative Council he made his mark as a speaker by the comments on the annual budget, Excise Bill and so on. In 1924 he again entered the Imperial Council as an independent Congressman and became the leader of the Nationalist Party in the Central Assembly in 1927. In 1929 when the Congress members resigned from the Assembly, he did not toe the party line because he happened to be an independent member. He, however, resigned a year later in 1930. Although he was not much agreeable to Non-co-operation and Civil Disobedience Movements, he took part in both as a true satyagrahi.

Pt. Madan Mohan Malaviya was keenly interested in the industrial advancement of India. As a result of his tireless efforts, Indian Industrial Conference was held at Benaras in 1905 and the meeting of Uttar Pradesh. Industrial Association was convened at Allahabad in 1907. He had a hand in starting the Prayag Sugar Company. In 1931 he sailed for England to participate in the Second Round Table Conference. Next year he Presided over the All India Unity Conference at Allahabad. In 1934 he, along with Mr. M.S. Aney, made emphatic protests against the Communal Award of Ramsay MacDonald.

Pt. Madan Mohan Malaviya was conservative and devout Hindu theist. He was a devotee of Lord Krishna whom he considered to be the incarnation of God. He followed the teachings of Gita to the letter. It was his conviction that sin and falsehood have to go down sooner or later against what is true and virtuous. He was also the founder of Sanatan Dharma Mahasabha. Although he was a staunch Hindu, he was far from being a fanatic. His religious outlook was rational and liberal. He was opposed to Hindu domination over other religious minorities. Needless to say that even Ali

Brothers (Maulana Muhammed Ali and Shaukat Ali) had a word of praise for him. He was prepared to accommodate the reasonable demands of Muslims.

Pt. Madan Mohan Malaviya had an elaborate political philosophy of his own. He had full faith in the constitutional agitations as a means to achieve the goal of Swaraj. He was frank in acknowledging that the growing national renaissance and political upsurge in India were the direct offshoot of Western Education. He was fully aware of the great political ferment going on in Asia after the Russo-Japanese war. He strove hard to press upon the British Government to march with the times and give India its due. He demanded Indianisation of key services and liberal representation of Indians in the Central and Provincial Executive Councils. Use of swadeshi, he said, was the surest cure of India's economic ills. In his Presidential address at Delhi Congress, he asserted India's right of self-determination and expressed hope that the British Government would be reasonable enough to grant it. He was opposed to any armed uprising or revolution in the country. He condemned the terrorists and revolutionaries on the basis of his concept of religion and *Ahimsa*. He gave the country a theory of nationalisation with cultural foundation. He wanted the religious and national education to go together in the mental make-up of Indian youths.

Pt. Madan Mohan Malaviya was an ardent nationalist with religious moorings. He was a Hindu but not a communalist. Twice did he preside over the Congress Sessions and thrice over the sessions of Hindu Mahasabha. Nobody ever doubted his secular outlook. He was a Congressite, but he never tolerated the Congress policy of appeasing the Muslims. When he found the swarajists hobnobbing with the Muslims at the cost of Hindu interests, he dissociated with them and along with Lala Lajpat Rai organised the Nationalist Party. He was sorely disappointed with the soft attitude of the Congress towards the Communal Award. He objected to showing undue favour to Muslims. He supported the Congress at the Round Table Conference, London, with dauntless courage and frankness. During the great upheaval of 1942, he was out of jail. He collected nearly one crore rupees towards Kasturba Fund.

Pt. Madan Mohan Malaviya started on a note of friendship with the British Government, but later on he was so much disillusioned that he became the foremost critic of the Government. He was a strong advocate of Hindi. He was a journalist of the fifst rank. For several years he edited papers like *Hindustan*, *Indian Union* and *Abhyudaya*. He had a hand in bringing out *Leader* an English daily from Allahabad. He was an embodiment of sacrifice and service. The fittest and the everlasting memorial of Pt. Madan Mohan Malaviya is the Banaras Hindu University itself.

LALA LAJPAT RAI (1865 - 1928)

Lala Lajpat Rai, popularly known as the 'Lion of the Punjab', was decidedly the greatest leader produced by the Punjab after Ranjit Singh. He was a powerful orator and an intrepid patriot of a very high order. He underwent the severest sufferings for his country's freedom. He was born on January 28, 1865, in the district of Ludhiana in Punjab. He graduated from the Government College, Lahore, and got a degree in Law in 1885. He started his practice at Hissar but soon shifted to Lahore. Arya Samaj was quite a powerful movement in the Punjab in those days. Lala Lajpat Rai threw his lot with it. He rendered valuable services to D.A.V. College, Lahore, and an orphanage in Ferozepore.

Lala Lajpat Rai joined the Congress formally in 1888 but his career as a fullfledged politician began in 1905 when he was sent along with Gopal Krishna Gokhale to England to protest against the Partition of Bengal. He spoke to the British public and tried to persuade the British Leaders to understand sympathetically the Indian sentiments but to no use. From there he made his first short trip to U.S.A. On his return to India he told his countrymen not to bank much upon the generosity of the arrogant white rulers but to fall back upon their own strength and resources in order to reach their goal.

Lala Lajpat Rai also like Lokmanya Bal Gangadhar Tilak and Bipin Chandra Pal was a leader of the Extremist School. He had not much faith in the 'go-slow' policy. By his written and spoken words he stirred the people out of their slumber. Lala Lajpat Rai was in a way a true socialist. He was opposed to capitalism and economic exploitation in watever form. He was the First President of the Indian Trade Union Congress in 1920. In 1907, he along with Sardar Ajit Singh led an agitation against Colonization Bill. The agitation was so forceful that it caused alarm to the British Imperialism. The Government arrested both Lala Lajpat Rai and Ajit Singh. Without trial they were sentenced to transportation for six months. Sardar Ajit Singh after his release went abroad and settled down there. Lala Lajpat Rai was given warm reception when he reached Lahore on November 18, 1907. At Surat Session of the Congress, Bal Gangadhar Tilak proposed the name of Lala Lajpat Rai for Presidentship but Gopal Krishna Gokhale in view of his radical views opposed his candidature. Lala Lajpat Rai quietly withdrew his name in order to avoid a conflict between the Moderates and the Extremists.

Lala Lajpat Rai from the Nationalist Party's platform supported the demand for Swaraj, Swadeshi, national education and boycott of foreign goods. In 1914 he created an Education Trust and laid the foundation of Radha Krishna High School, Jagraon. In 1914, he went to London again as a member of Congress Delegation. The war that broke out in Europe prevented his return to India till 1919. From England he went to the U.S.A. He spent six months in Japan also. Wherever he went, he carried on strong propaganda for India's Independence. In England he wrote his own famous books, *Young India* and *England's Debt to India*. He was allowed to sail back to India in 1919. He was profoundly shocked at the cold-blooded masscre of thousands of innocent people at Jallianwala Bagh, Amritsar. The ghastly police artocities filled him with rage and revolt. The Congress held a special session at Calcutta in 1920 to discuss the events of the Punjab. Lala Lajpat Rai occupied the chair. Although he differed with the Non-co-operation Resolution, he stood by it wholeheartedly after it was adopted by a majority vote. He was then arrested and imprisoned on December 3, 1922.

Soon after his release, he along with Motilal Nehru organised the Swaraj Party and entered the Central Legislature. He, however, resigned from the Swaraj Party with whose liberal attitude towards the unreasonable demands of the Muslims, he differed sharply. He joined hands with Pt. Madan Mohan Malaviya in forming the Nationalist Party. Lala Lajpat Rai had much in common with Pt. Madan Mohan Malaviya. Both were nationalists but staunch Hindus at the same time. Both were equally proud of Hindu culture and religion.

CHITTARANJAN DAS (1870-1925)

Deshbandhu Chittaranjan Das was one of the foremost leaders of the country's struggle for independence. He was an eminent barrister of Bengal. He attracted public attention in 1908 as a defence counsel of Sri Aurobindo Ghosh in Alipore Bomb Conspiracy case. He argued the case so nicely that the judges had to acquit Aurobindo Ghosh. He was a poet also with five famous collections of poems to his credit. He was associated with the publication of a Bengali Monthly '*Narayan*' and a paper '*Forward*'. In 1919 he led the opposition against the acceptance of Montford Reforms. In the beginning he was opposed to the programme of Non-co-operation of Mahatama Gandhi but ultimately changed his views and jumped into the Movement wholeheartedly. He gave up his practice forever in order to devote all his energies to national work. He was imprisoned in December, 1921, and released in July, 1922. By his powerful speeches he unleashed the mighty wave of nationalism in Bengal. He was, so to say, the dictator of Bengal with enormous following. People affectionately called him 'Deshbandhu'.

In 1923 Deshbandhu Chitranjan Das floated All India Swaraj Party, in cooperation with Pt. Motilal Nehru, Vithalbhai Patel, M.R. Jayakar and others. He put before the Congress the utility of entering the Councils. The Swaraj Party contested the elections to the Provincial Councils and Central Legislative Assembly witht the object of making the functioning of Dyarchy in the Provinces difficult.

Netaji Subhas Chandra Bose was the favourite disciple of Deshbandhu Chitranjan Das. At the time of the arrest of Netajee Subhas Chandra Bose in 1924, Chitranjan Das was the Mayor of Calcutta. He offered himself for arrest in order to save Subhas Chandra Bose, Chitranjan Das was inspired by the concept of a World Federation and a Parliament of Nations. His plan for the future of India was the formation of a federation with cultural autonomy guaranteed to the Provinces. He too believed in promoting the hearty co-operation of Hindus and Muslims in political struggle. He was greatly impressed by the economic revolution going on in Russia. Because of his ideological sympathies with trade unionism, he was sometimes regarded as a leftist in the Congress circles.

PT. MOTILAL NEHRU (1861-1931)

Pt. Motilal Nehru, the proud father of his illustrious son Pt. Jawaharlal Nehru was a leading advocate of Uttar Pradesh. His annual income from his practice ran into lakhs, and hence he lived a princely life. He came in contact with Congress, the premier organisation of India, in 1906. He was a Moderate in the beginning but the sufferings of the Punjab under Martial Law, the harrowing tale of Jallianwala Bagh Tragedy, the arrest of Annie Besant and the influence of his son Pt. Jawaharlal Nehru made him join the Extremist Group.

He was one of the members of the Congress Enquiry Committee, set up to report on the tragic incident of Jallianwala Bagh. Other members of this committee were Mahatma Gandhi, Chittaranjan Das, Fazlul Huq and Tyabji. Pt. Motilal Nehru presided over the Amritsar Session of the Congress in 1919. He courted arrest during the Non-co-operation Movement and suffered a jail term. After his release he organised the Swaraj Party with the co-operation of Chittaranjan Das. He was returned to the Central Legislative Assembly where he became the leader of the Swarajist Group. With the support of the Independents, he inflicted numerous defeats on the Government. He brought the Government policies under fire and made emphatic demand for self-government. In 1928 he took leading part in demonstrations against Simon Commission. Later on he headed the committee set up by the All Parties Conference to draw up a tentative constitution of free India. The draft prepared by the committee was called Nehru Report. Pt. Motilal Nehru had a leading hand in the preparation of this historic constitutional document. The Report suggested several compromise formulas to solve the communal and political problems of the country. He resigned his membership of the Assembly in 1930 and took part in the Civil Disobedience Movement started by Mahatma Gandhi. A little before his death when somebody asked him what his last wish was, Pt. Motilal Nehru murmured that he wished to die in free India. Alas, that could not be fulfilled.

SARDAR VALLABH BHAI PATEL (1875-1950)

Sardar Vallabh Bhai Patel was born on 21st October, 1875, in a village in Gujarat. He was a brilliant barrister of his time. Attracted by the personality and programme of Mahatma Gandhi, he entered into politics in 1918. He gave conclusive proof of his dynamic leadership in 1930 when he led Bardoli Satyagraha to a successful end. Mahatma Gandhi conferred on him the title of Sardar in appreciation of his hold on the masses. The Congress honoured him further by offering him Presidentship of the party in 1931. He organised the Congress election campaign in 1937. The formation of Congress Ministries in seven of the eleven Provinces brought him exceptional credit. He was elected chairman of the Parliamentary Board whose function was to supervise the working of the Ministries. His active participation in the 'Quit India Movement' 1942, landed him in jail for three years. After his release in 1945, he represented the Congress in the Interim Government. In 1946 he was elected the Deputy Prime Minister.

Sardar Vallabh Bhai Patel had a tough time when the Muslim League launched 'Direct Action' in some Provinces. The whole of the country was inflamed with communal hatred and lawlessness.

Sardar Vallabh Bhai Patel handled the situation quite tactfully. He was deadly opposed to the partition of the country. But when the unholy alliance between the Government and the Muslim League made the working of the coalition -government at the Centre nearly impossible. Sardar Vallabh Bhai Patel agreed to League demand for Pakistan. In the Cabinet of free India, he held the portfolios of Home and State. The way he restored law and order in the country and also secured the merger of hundreds of States without any bloodshed, speaks immensely of his constructive statemanship. The problem of Indian states was quite ticklish. The outgoing British Government had deliberately left the problem of the accession of the states in a mess. The rulers of 522 big and small states of India had begun to dream of declaring themselves independent sovereigns. Three cheers to Sardar Vallabh Bhai Patel who not only persuaded the states to join Indian Union but also replaced the autocratic structure of the states by democratic governments. In short, Sardar gave a big shock to the British who had hoped to see India split up into hundreds of small independent States. The 'Iron Man' as Sardar Vallabh Bhai Patel was called by his admirers used force also in the case of Hyderabad which tried to exist as a centre of anti-national and subversive activities in India. He was, in fact, a political genius, a top class statesman and a practical idealist. *His contribution to the consolidation of new India has been unique and always memorable.*

President of India on the contribution of Sardar Vallabh Bhai Patel

The President of India, Mr. Venkat Raman on 29th October 1990 said :

Sardar Vallabh Bhai Patel combined in him strength of steel and the purity of gold. Direct, totally honest and frank, the Late Sardar Vallabh Bhai Patel could be a commadant as well as combatant with equal efficiency. Incarcerated repeatedly, Sardar Vallabh Bhai Patel came to epitomise a stoic indifference to personal comfort and a monumental patience that was anchored in faith.

Sardar Vallabh Bhai Patel's role in the integration of the Indian states could never be adequately described in words. If Pt. Jawaharlal Nehru was regarded as an architect, *Sardar Vallabh Bhai Patel must be regarded as united India's engineer.*

Implicitly trusted by his mentor, respected by colleagues, venerated by the people, *Sardar Vallabhai Bhai, Patel is an all time reference point for India, a pillar of confidence and character.*"

MAULANA ABUL KALAM AZAD (1888-1958)

Life Sketch. Maulana Abul Kalam Azad was one of the few Muslims who threw their lot with the Congress and were inspired not by communal but national interests. He was born in Mecca on November 11, 1888 where his father had migrated after 1857. He was the descendant of Sheikh Jamalud-din, a profound scholar and an erudite doctor of divinity. He was the son of famous Arabic scholar Maulana Khair-ud-din and his mother was also the daughter of the Mufti of Medina and hence knew Arabic language only. He spent his childhood in Mecca and Medina where his father's house was a great centre of learning. He received his early education under his father's guidance and has also been to the world famous university of Al-Azar in Cairo. By the age of 14 he had covered the entire ground included in the original curriculum of the day and was actually put in charge of classes in various subjects. His parents were strictly orthodox and he had inherited orthodoxy from his parents. His father had migrated from Mecca and on the fervent pleadings of many devotees had settled finally at Calcutta in 1907. Several of his works were printed in Egypt and are still looked upon as a worthy contribution to theological discussion. He, however, died in 1908.

First Production. Maulana Abul Kalam Azad brought out his first production at the age of 15. This was a monthly literary magazine called the *LISANUL SIDQ* (THE VOICE OF TRUTH). It was greatly appreciated by the well-known poet of the age, Khawaja Altaf Hussain Hali. After some time Hali met Abul Kalam Azad and finding him only youth of 16 refused to believe that he was the editor. His incredulity over, he remained one of the warmest admirers of Abul Kalam for rest of his life. When he was only 14, the Maulana entered into correspondence with Maulana Shibli and also contributed some articles to the *MAKHAN* of Lahore. In 1904 he had occasion to meet Maulana Shibli in Bombay and Shibli spoke very highly of Abul Kalam's contribution but under the impression that he was speaking to Abul Kalam Azad's son. Nawab Moshinul Mulk always used to address Abul Kalam as young in years but old in learning. He also wrote a critical review of the *LIFE OF SIR SYED AHMAD KHAN* written by the great Urdu scholar and poet Khawaja Hussain Hali.

Other productions. His conscious political life, though a little older, can be definitely traced back to 1912 when he began to give expression to his mature thoughts in his journal *AL HILAL* which was the first of its kind in India and compared favorably at that time with the standard journals of the West in respect of form and substance. Maulana Abul Kalam Azad was convinced that a revolution in Muslim thought was urgently called for and *AL HILAL* was the medium through which he wanted to achieve his end. Like famous poet Iqbal he set most of the educated Mussalmans of India thinking about the fundamental and vital problems of life. The polularity which *AL HILAL* achieved within two or three months of its appearance was phenomenal. It became an organ of advanced political thought and national religious instructions, no less than a model of dignified and persuasive literature. Abul Kalam Azad initiated a vigorous campaign against Aligarh School of Thought in his journal and invited the Muslims to co-operate with the Congress in liberating the country from foreign domination.

Powerful influence. From the day of its appearance (1st June) in 1912 to the day it ceased publication in 1915 under the Defence of India Act, *AL HILAL* exercised a powerful influence among the Indian Mussalmans and upto this day neither in form nor in substance has it been surpassed, though many efforts have been made by several aspirants to reproduce its excellence. At first the Government snuffed it out of existence in 1915. Abul Kalam Azad's irrepressible genius, however, blossomed out in *AL BALAGH* which he brought out after the cessation of the *AL HILAL*. It had scarcely been in existence for a few months when in April, 1916, the Government of Bengal externed him from that province. The Punjab, Uttar Pradesh, Bombay and other Governments had already declared him an unwelcome guest and he was constrained to remove himself to Ranchi (Bihar) where he was interned for 5 months after his arrival there. Thousands of persons of high ranks pleaded for his release because he was the son of revered Khairuddin. He was released at the end of 1920. The First World War had already ended but he was the last detenu to be released.

Met Mahatma Gandhi in 1921, *elected president in* 1923 *and* 1940. He met Mahatma Gandhi in 1921. Since then he continued to be one of the staunchest suporters of the non-violent school of thought. He had held the high office of the President of the Muslim League which had changed into All India Khilafat Committee and in 1923, he definitely aligned himself with the old Swaraj party and was one of the Late. Chittaranjan Das and Pandit Motilal Nehru's effective collaborators. He was elected President of the Indian National Congress in 1923 and again on March 19, 1940 at Ramgarh (Bihar). He continued the President of the Indian National Congress till July 1946 when he handed over the Presidentship to Pt. Jawaharlal Nehru.

The Congress in its session at Ramgarh held on 19 and 20 March, 1940 Presided over by Maulana Abul Kalam Azad endorsed the emphatic protests made by the Working Committee and All India Congress Committee against the declaration of India "as a belligerent country without reference to the people of India" and reiterated that "*nothing short of complete independence can be accepted by the people of India.*"

Maulana Abul Kalam Azad's very famous Presidential Address at Ramgarh (Bihar) throwing some light on his political ideas. Maulana Abul Kalam Azad said in his Presidential address at Ramgarh session in March, 1940, "I repeat to-day what I have said throughout this entire period, *that the ninety million of Muslims of India have no other right course of action than the one to which I invited them in* 1912. I am a Musalman and am proud of that fact. Islam's splendid tradition of thirteen hundred years are my inheritance. I am unwilling to lose even the smallest part of my inheritance. The teaching and history of Islam, its arts and letters and civilisation are my wealth and my fortune. It is my duty to protect them. "*I am proud of being an Indian. I am a part of the indivisible unity, that is , Indian Natiionality.*"

Fusion of Hindu and Muslim Cultures. Maulana Abul Kalam Azad said, "This fusion was a notable even in history. Since then, destiny in her own hidden way began to fashion a new India in place of the old. We brought our treasures with us and India too was full of riches of her own precious heritage. We gave our wealth to her and she unlocked the doors of her own treasures to us. We gave her what she needed most, the most precious of gifts from Islam's treasury, *the message of democracy and human equality.* Eleven hundred years of common history have enriched India with our common achievements. Our languages, our poetry, our literature, our culture, our art, our dress, our manners and customs, the innumerable happenings of our daily life; everything bears the stamp of our joint endeavour. There is indeed no aspect of our life which has escaped this stamp. Our languages were different, but we grew to us a common language, our manners and customs were dissimilar but they acted and reacted on each other and this produced a new synthesis. Our old dress may be seen only in ancient pictures of bygone days; no one wears it today. This joint wealth is the heritage of our common nationality and we do not want to leave it and go back to the times when the joint life had not begun. *I am one of those who believe that revival may be a necessity in a religion but in social matters it is a denial of progress.*

Common Nationality. Maulana Abul Kalam Azad further said, "This thousand years of our joint life has moulded us into common nationality. This can not be done artificially. Nature does her fashioning through her hidden processes in the course of her centuries. The cast has new been moulded and destiny has set her seal upon it. *We have now become an Indian Nation, united and indivisible.* No fantasy or artificial scheming to separate and divide can break this unity. We must accept the logic of fact and history and engage ourselves in the fashioning of our future destiny. *Our success depends upon three factors; unity, discipline and full confidence in Mahatma Gandhi's leadership.* The glorious past record of our movement was due to his great leadership that we can look forward to a future of successful achievement."

His Works. Maulana Abul Kalam Azad's maturest thought, says Prof. Mujeeb "appears in the *Tarjuman-ul-Quran.* The Tarjuman is free from any tendency towards apologetics and from any attempt to read into the Quran what is really not there. This is because Maulana Azad's thought in fact does spring out of the Quran and from no other source and he had brought to the understanding of the Quran a rich and varied experience and an intensity of suffering along with the necessary knowledge. He has not written with an eve on the western or even the Indian reader. The Tarjuman is the product of deep personal convictions. It is perhaps, the first example of the constructive thinking enjoined on the Muslims."

Maulana Abul Kalam Azad's letters appeared in the book form as *Ghubar -i- Khatar.* It reveals the wealth of wit he possessed. He enriches the Urdu words with beautiful expressions and with Arabic and Persian metaphors. "It has been said of Lokmanya Bal Gangadhar Tilak", writes Dr. Rajendra Prasad "that if he had not been in the political movement *and devoted most exclusively to Vedic studies, he would have made even more invaluable contribution to learning than he actually did.*" Dr. P.N. Chopra believes "*the same is true of Maulana Abul Kalam Azad whose exclusive devotion to the study of Arabic and persian could have produced the same result.*"

His another famous work is '*India wins Freedom*' which is his autobiography and is a political work. Maulana Abul Kalam Azad expressed his views in Urdu Prof. Humayun Kabir had not the required command over Urdu but translated the same in English. The views expressed in it about partition and Cabinet Mission Plan especially are controversial. Maulana Abul Kalam Azad had wished that its 30 pages should not be opened for thirty years since Pt. Jawaharlal Nehru's relatives would be alive and the views expressed in them would hurt their feelings. In November, 1989 they were opened under Court's orders. He says that he made a Himalayan blunder in insisting with Mahatma Gandhi that not Sardar Vallabh Bhai Patel but only Jawaharlal Nehru should succeed him. He blames Pt. Jawaharlal Nehru for not implementing the Cabinet Mission Plan faithfully. Had Sardar Vallabh Bhai Patel been in his place, he would have faithfully implemented it. He says Pt. Jawaharlal Nehru gave a statement after taking over the Presidentship from him in July, 1946 that the Congress considered itself free to accept or not to accept the compulsory grouping of provinces. This was the greatest mistake of the Congress President because it enabled Pt. Jawaharlal Nehru Jinnah to retrace his footsteps, reject the Cabinet Mission Plan and launch Direct Action on 16th August of that year. *It ultimately resulted in the partition of the country and loss of the life and property of lakhs of people. Therefore he asserts that the statement of the Congress President was a great blunder because it changed the course of history.* This contention of Maulana Abul Kalam Azad was not accepted by Mahatma Gandhi even at that time, who was deadly against the partition of the country because Pt. Jawaharlal Nehru and Sardar Vallabh Bhai Patel had very bitter experience at the hands of the Muslim League in the Interim Government. Consequently, according to Mahatma Gandhi, the whole of the Congress Working Committee was ready to accept the partition of the country except a few leaders like Jaya Prakash Narain, Purshottam Dass Tandon and Khan Abdul Gaffar Khan. Even Maulana Abul Kalam Azad voted for the partition of the country when the Congress Working Committee met in July, 1947 to vote on the Mountbatten Plan.

Good Command over English Language and its Retention. It is wrongly believed that Maulana Abul Kalam Azad had very little knowledge of English. It is true that he always spoke in Urdu and even made official notings in Urdu. Many a time Dr. P.N. Chopra had seen him reading English novels.......His library contained works of some of the best known English authors, such as William Wordsworth, Willam Shakespeare, P.B. Shelly, Byron etc. His library too contained works of Tolstoy, Ruskin, Goethe, Marx, Hugo and many other philosophers and thinkers.

His views on the retention of English in our curricula were clear and explicit. He felt that "one hundred and fifty years of intimate contact has made English as a integral part of our educational system and this cannot be changed without injury to the cause of one of the major languages of the world and Indians can neglect the study only at the risk of loss to themselves." I am convinced that in future as well the standard of teaching English should be maintained at as high a level as possible, but the medium of instruction must from the very nature of the cause, be the mother tongue". He even tried to persuade the *Ulemas* in charge of Muslim religious education in *madarsas* to impart education with modern methods and technique and introduce English as a subject. His efforts did not meet with success as *Ulemas* were afraid that it would lead to Government interference in the independent affairs of a religious system of education.

Maulana Abul Kalam Azad also believed in the re-orientation of Islamic learning to meet the requirement of the modern age. He believed in changing with the changing times and not in sticking to old and outdate customs.

Career after independence. He became Education Minister in the Cabinet of Pt. Jawaharlal Nehru, which post he retained till his death. He was a member of Congress High Command after independence. He did a lot of praiseworthy work in the field of education. He remained the President of Jamait-ul-Ulma-Hind for several years. However he breathed his last on 22nd February, 1958 and was buried in old Delhi near Jama Masjid in Parade Ground. Rich tributes were paid to him from all sections of the people and different countries of the world especially from Iran. He will always be remembered for his selfless services.

Words of Wisdom from a Maker of Modern India (Azad). Maulana Abul Kalam Azad said : "Industries and agriculture, the social services and public utilities must be encouraged, modernised and rapidly extended in order to add to the wealth of the country and give it the capacity for self-growth, without dependence on others.

But all this must be done with the primary objective, and paramount duty of benefiting the masses of our people and raising their economic and spiritual level, removing unemployment and adding to the dignity of the individual."[1]

POLITICAL IDEAS OF MAULANA ABUL KALAM AZAD

The political ideas of Maulana Abul Kalam Azad can be summarised under the following heads:—

(1) Attitude towards Nationalism. Indian Nationalism as envisaged by Maulana Abul Kalam Azad was democratic and secular. Maulana Abul Kalam Azad's faith in Nationalism as Mahatma Gandhi described it "was as robust as his faith in Islam". Abul Kalam Azad's interpretation of Islam made a compromise with Nationalism. He was as devoted to his religion as was to the ideal of the liberation and independence of his country. Abul Kalam Azad made it clear that the prophet of Islam proclaimed the message of monotheism and announced his prohethood in the shape of messenger of God. The prophet tried to pray "O God I bear witness that all people are brothers to one another. Differences they might have created amongst themselves, but you have united them together, with a single bond of humanity." Thus, Islam fosters Nationalism avoiding communal and racial prejudices.

Every Indian Muslim, according to Abul Kalam Azad is a member of the Indian Nation and could not by virtue of the common bond of religion, separate himself from the larger Indian society and claim the status of independent nationhood. Religious to the core as he was, Abul Kalam Azad would not countenance nationalism based on religion, especially in the Indian context of multiplicity, as it would be a force for division, rather than unity in the wider sense. Even Gibb rejects that strict adherence to the teaching of Islam would lead to conflict with the secular character of the State. But Abul Kalam Azad felt that Muslim minority cannot and should not brand Indian Nationalism as un-Islamic for it embodies the broad vision of Islam. Nationalism in India was impossible of realisation without Hindu-Muslim Unity.

(2) Hindu-Muslim Unity. Abul Kalam Azad stressed unity so much that he considered it dearer than the freedom of the country itself. Abul Kalam Azad did not deny differences—so called religious and other differences–between the Hindus and Muslims. As Pt. Jawaharlal Nehru had observed,

"lesser men have sometimes found conflict in the rich variety of Indian life. He (Azad) was even big enough not only to see the essential unity behind all that diversity, but also to realise that only in this unity can be hope for India as a whole and for these great and varied currents of national life which course through her veins."

He therefore, asserted that "both the communities should have a common objective *i.e.* freedom of the country. The Muslims should join the Congress because because the Prophet did the same thing, when he had to overcome Abu Sufian."

(3) No Communal Approach. Abul Kalaam Azad, like Chittranjan Das, never adopted the communal approach for the solution of political and economic problems. He observed that in future constitution determined by Indian Representatives, the Hindus and Mohammadans, will have to think of the position and interest not as a Hindu or Musalman and so on, it will be nothing worth unless it reflects equality of opportunity and economic freedom for all". He therefore, wanted that a concerted effort should be made in this direction. Das's Pact of Bengal, for which Abul Kalam Azad had great admiration is an example in point. He was always optimistic and felt that the differences between the Hindus and the Mohammadans would never become so grave as to lead to mutual warfare and bloodshed. They are to be resolved in a spirit of compromise and toleration. In India, every kind of faith, every kind of culture, every mode of living was allowed to flourish and find out its salvation".

1. *National Herald*, February 22, 1977, p.45.

The question of Indian First or Muslim First was irrelevant for him. I am proud of being Indian, said he.

"Eleven hundred years of common history", said Abul Kalam Azad, "have enriched India with common achievements. Our languages, our literature, our culture, our art, our manners and customs, the innumerable happenings of our daily life, everything bears the stamp of our joint endeavour. There is indeed no aspect of life which had escaped this stamp. He, therefore, asserted that both the communities should have a common objective, freedom of the country.

(4) Attitude towards the Aligarh Movement of Sir Syed Ahmed Khan. Sir Syed Ahmed Khan's School of thought was prevalent amongst the educated Muslims since the foundation of Mohammadan Anglo-Oriental College in Aligarh which after his death in 1898 became Aligarh University. It taught the Muslims to learn English and Science, keep away from the Congress and be loyal to the British, so that they may get more services in the Government Department. Maulana Abul Kalam Azad had no doubt that "Sir Syed Ahmad Khan had done a great service to the Muslim community by impressing on the necessity of getting out of the narrow grooves of orthodox learning and theology and of profiting by Western Education and Sciences. But he also felt what few Muslims felt in those days that Sir Syed Ahmed khan had unconsciously made himself a tool of British Imperialism by stopping the Muslims from all political activities and by opposing the Congress. On the one hand he had hindcred the political regeneration of the whole country and on the other hand he had directed the footsteps of the Musalmans along ways that fostered in them a slavish mentality instead of self-respect, high mindedness and breadth of political outlook".

In 1908 when the Maulana Abul Kalam Azad was only twenty, his mind began to undergo rapid changes. One of these big changes was due to the political state of affairs in India. His Homeland was Bengal which was then seething with discontent due to the partition and full of new political awakening. He noticed that India was presenting to the world two kinds of contradictory pictures at one and same the time. On the one hand there were the Hindus, whose minds were fired with a new patriotism and dreaming dreams of freedom and no repression by government could stifle them. They were unflinchingly sacrificing their youthful lives on the altar of patriotism. On the other hand, the Muslims were against all political struggle and had become willing tools in the hands of government determined to crush the national movement. When young India was marching ahead under the banner of freedom from the British bondage, the slogan of the Muslims was loyalty to government. Muslim League had been formed in 1906 with the avowed aim to foster loyalty of the Muslims to the British throne. Nawab Mushtaq Hussain, Secretary of Aligarh College, who played a prominent role in organising the Muslim League, declared that the sword of Islam would be always ready in the service of the British Raj. The Maulana Abul Kalam Azad swore opposition to this policy from the very start. He started his journal *Al-Hilal* in 1912 for propagating this policy and its first issue came on 1st June, 1912. Even Maulana Muhammad Ali appreciated it. Maulana Abul Kalam Azad was also influenced and inspired by the teachings of Jamaluddin Afghani. An anti-imperialist by conviction, Jamaluddin Afghani could not reconcile himself with the Pro British attitude of Sir Syed Ahmed Khan. Besides, Sir Syed Ahmed Khan was concerned only with the problems of the Muslims in India, while Jamaluddin was free from such a narrow outlook. Maulana Shibli was also inclined towards the ideals of pan-Islamism. Thus Maulana Abul Kalam Azad's opposition to the local Aligarh Movement and the territorial nationalism was the natural outcome of the influence of Afghani and Shibli.

(5) Attitude towards Minorities. Maulana Abul Kalam Azad said in his Presidential address at Ramgarh Congress Session, "We could attach no greater importance to the minority problem (Muslims) than to make it the first condition for the attainment of our national goal. The Congress has always held this belief, no one can challenge this fact. It has always held to two basic principles in this connection, and step was taken deliberately with those in view.

(*i*) *Whatever constitution is adopted for India, there must be the fullest guarantees in it for the rights and interests of the minorities.*

(*ii*) "The minorities should judge for themselves what safeguards are necessary for the protection of their rights and interests. The majority should not decide this. Therefore, the decision in this connection must depend upon the consent of the minorities and not on majority vote ..... I venture to ask the world whether any more just and equitable course of action can be adopted than the one, suggested above ? If not. What is it?"

(6) Close to Gandhi. This approach of Maulana Abul Kalam Azad brought him very close to Mahatma Gandhi's line of thinking. But although Mahatma Gandhi was to become sole exponent and practitioner of non-co-operation, the idea did not orginate with him.

Maulana Abul Kalam Azad had already come to understand the usefulness of such a programme. "I had myself suggested a similar programme in some article in *AL HILAL*, said Maulana Abul Kalam Azad.

(7) On Mahatma Gandhi's Attitude towards Non-Violence. Maulana Abul Kalam Azad, unlike Mahatma Gandhi, regarded non-violence as a policy and not as a creed. He maintained that war is permissible to maintain freedom of religion and science. If tyranny can be eradicated by war, then war is justified. Maulana Abul Kalam Azad admitted. "*For me non-violence was a matter of policy, not of creed. My view was that Indians had the right to take the sword if they had no other alternative.*" Though Maulana Abul Kalam Azad adopted non-violence as a matter of policy only, he gave his sincere and unstinted support to Gandhi and became his close and trusted associate and a prominent leader of the National Congress. "Congress must place greater emphasis on the freedom of India than on non-violence as a creed," Maulana Abul Kalam Azad asserted.

(8) Attitude towards World War II. On the question of support to the British Government during the 2nd World War, Abul Kalam Azad wrote, "The issue was not one of pacifism but of India's freedom. He declared openly that Indian National Congress was not a pacifist organisation but one for achieving India's freedom. To my mind the issue raised by Mahatma Gandhi was irrelevant." Mahatma Gandhi was a convinced pacifist and the logic of facts would hardly persuade him to modify his position. He was opposed to the Cripps' proposals more on account of his aversion to war than his objection to the proposals as such. Maulana Abul Kalam Azad's mind was not certainly governed by such a consideration. *On many questions like settlement with the government, on the issue of boycotting the Prince of Wales at Calcutta, holding of the Round Table Conference, calling off the Non-co-operation Movement and support to Japanese vis-a-vis the British during the 2 nd World War. Maulana Abul Kalam Azad openly expressed disagreement with Mahatama Gandhi.*

(9) Maulana Abul Kalam Azad on war and Jehad. Maulana Abul Kalam Azad believed that Islam does not sanction war unless it becomes inevitable. War and Islam are contradictory and are poles apart. Islam has a message of peace for mankind. Islam preaches *Jehad*, not war as the means for the establishment of a permanent peace. He also quotes many verses from the Quran to prove that the essence of *Jehad* is patience, determination and sacrifice. The purpose of *Jehad*, when it implies warfare, is not the *accumulation of wealth or territorial expansionism but to oppose injustice, war and tyranny.* He knew too that consequences of war are not only cruel but disastrous. It had adverse effects on morality.

(10) Maulana Abul Kalam Azad and Khilafat. Maulana Abul Kalam Azad, no doubt, supported the Khilafat Movement. For him it was not entirely religious issue. *He said that it was a movement for the freedom of the country, which would inspire Muslims to fight against the alien rulers and unite them with their countrymen.* It had awakened an awareness of India's problems among the people of the country. Islam does not permit slavery. Faith in Islam and love of freedom are synonymous. Thus, the Khilafat Movement meant liberation of the country and establishment of the system of Shariat. Maulana Abul Kalam Azad considered the methods of the liberals ineffective. He observed, "I was of the opinion that these methods—begging, petitioning, waiting in deputation and so on-could not be of much avail. We had to try to find some means of exerting direct pressure. But most people fought shy of this line of thinking." Maulana Abul Kalam Azad, however, could not suggest hostility towards the British but drafted a plan of non-violent non-co-operation." It was characterised by conviction of unity, righteous action, patience, organisation and spirit of self - sacrifice for the cause of freedom.

(11) Maulana Abul Kalam Azad and Partition. Maulana Abul Kalam Azad was opposed to the partition of the country not only on political and Cultural but also on religious grounds. He held that the scheme of Pakistan is "harmful not only for India as a whole, but also for Muslims in particular and in fact, it creates more problems than it solves." It was, he felt, against the spirit of Islam, for it lays stress in division more than on unity and synthesis. The Prophet had also said, "God has made one whole world a mosque." Maulana Abul Kalam Azad argued that the Muslims are a minority of 90 million people who are in quality and quantity a sufficiently important element in questions of administration and policy.

ESTIMATE OF MAULANA ABUL KALAM AZAD

Views of Mahatma Gandhi

Mahatma Gandhi said about him, "I had the privilege of being associated with Maulana Abul Kalam Azad in national work since 1920. In the knowledge of Islam he is surpassed by no one. He is a profound Arabic Scholar. His *Nationalism is as robust* as his faith in Islam. That he is today the surpreme head of the Indian National Congress (President of Congress) had deep meaning which should not be lost sight of by every student of Indian politics."[1]

Views of Dr. Rajendra Prasad

Dr. Rajendra Prasad said about Maulana Abul Kalam Azad, "He held fast to Hindu-Muslim unity and never budged an inch, standing firmly by it like a rock in the midst of uncharitable criticism and worse from many of his co-religionists. He was a great scholar. His commentary on the Holy Koran is recognised as authoritative not only in this country, but also other countries. He was a great representative of Indian culture. He was elected Congress President in 1940 at a time when the Hindu-Muslims controversy was reaching a breaking point and a demand for separate independent State for Muslims was being formulated and expressed. He continued as President during the most momentous period of Indo-British relations when negotiations for transfer of power were carried on again and again between Congress through its president Maulana Abul Kalam Azad and the representatives of the British Government."

Views of Pandit Jawaharlal Nehru

Pt. Jawaharlal Nehru said, "Maulana Abul Kalam Azad was a peculiar and a very special representative in a high degree of that composite culture which has gradually grown in India. So, we mourn today the passing of a great man, a man of luminous intelligence and a mighty intellect with an amazing capacity to pierce through any problem to its core. He was a man of luminous mind and one of great captains and a general of our peaceful forces who have worked for the independence and progress and advancement of India, who have come and who have gone, leaving their message behind."

Views of Dr. Zakir Hussain

Dr. Zakir Hussain said, that "Maulana is no more with us. The pen which scattered pearls as well as hurled bolts is no more; the tongue that showered petals as well as emitted sparks, which consumed falsehood and illumined truth, is no more. The pen lies broken and the tongue is silenced. But the Maulana lives and we should follow his example."

Views of C. Rajagopalachari, former Governor-General of India

Mr. C. Rajagopalachari remained the Governor-General of Free India before the Republic was inaugurated on 26th January, 1950. He writes :

"If there is one man in India today to represent the keen understanding and synthetic ideologies

1. M.K. Gandhi, *Sevagram*, Wardha, May 18, 1940.

of the great Akbar who ruled our land four hundred years ago, it is Maulana Abul Kalam Azad. If even Akbar was disappointed by his fellow-Musalmans, why should we be surprised if Maulana Abul Kalam Azad receives no response from the organised Muslims of India today ? History and the thoughts of enlightened men and women will, however, not fail to appreciate the Maulana's services when passions have cooled and men's judgements are free .... His scientific outlook and extensive scholarship are a marvel to them who associate such characteristics with English university education."

Views of Sardar Vallabh Bhai Patel

Sardar Patel said about the Maulana Abul Kalam Azad

"There had not been a single occasion in these six years of great stress and strain when Maulana Azad failed to maintain the dignity and honour of the high office he holds. He never allowed the honour of the Congress to be sullied. Any one else in his position might not have been able to show the courage and determination with which he bore the responsibilities of this great office for long six years. The credit for bringing us to the present position in our struggle for our independence goes entirely to Maulana Azad. We asked the British to quit India in 1942. They have now told us that they are ready to quit. We are now discussing the ways and means of their quitting and how to make that quitting smooth and easy. Maulana Azad deserves all praise for this great achievement."

Views of late President, Fakhr-ud-din Ali Ahmad

He said on January 27, 1977 :

"Maulana Azad was a staunch patriot, an eminent statesman, a great humanist and a Muslim who stood for the best in Islam. Maulana Abul Kalam Azad was an embodiment of refinement and culture. He was an active representative of the synthesis of everything sacred to us in India.

Views of Mrs. Indira Gandhi

"Maulana Azad combined to himself the best of all thought processes and imbibed good things from the West, the Arabs and India's past. That is why he was a good and true representative of India. So long as we proceed on the path shown to us by him, we will progress on the right lines and our ideals will influence peoples of distant lands."[1]

So we can say that Maulana Abul Kalam Azad was one of the greatest scholars of Persian and Arabic, and Islam of his own times who spent his whole life for the Hindu-Muslim unity and independence of our country.

His life was a saga which would ever remain inspiration to our countrymen. "His greatest work is *Tarjuman-Quran* (a translation of Quran from Arabic to Urdu). His another famous political work is '*India Wins Freedom*' in which he has shown how India was able to win freedom from the British.

MAHATMA GANDHI (1869-1948)

Life-Sketch. Mohandas Karamchand Gandhi was born on 2nd October, 1869, at Porbunder in Kathiawar District of Gujarat. His father was the Dewan of Rajkot State. He went to England in 1887 where he qualified for the Bar. He returned to India and started his practice. In 1893 he went as the legal representative of an Indian firm to South Africa where he stayed for twenty years. There he fought relentlessly for racial equality. He himself had bitter experiences of colour-prejudice. He started satyagraha against apartheid or colour discrimination and achieved a good deal of success also. On the advice of Gopal Krishna Gokhale whom he accepted as his political 'guru', he returned to India in January, 1915. During the First World War he extended all-out help to the British Government in

1. *National Herald*, Feb. 22, 1977.

her war efforts. He fought against white tyranny on the peasants of Champaran in Bihar. He fought for the legitimate rights of the industrial labourers of Ahmedabad in 1918. He conducted Satyagraha successfully in Kheda in Gujarat and compelled the Government to exempt the peasants from paying land rent.

Mahatma Gandhi

Mahatma Gandhi in return of India's massive war help in the form of men, money and material demanded Swaraj. The British Government replied in the language of baton charge and bullets. India for all its sincere services got Rowlatt Bill. The reckless attitude of the Government shocked and disillusioned the entire populace of the country. The Muslims too were highly distressed with the British Government over the Khilafat issue. After defeating Turkey, the British Government deposed the Sultan who was looked upon as the spiritual head of the Muslim community. The Congress and the League in one voice protested against the British action. The Government opened fire to crush the agitation. The country witnessed the grim tragedy of Jallianwala Bagh. Mahatama Gandhi took up the cause of the Muslims and the Punjab wrongs and started Non-co-operation Movement in 1920. But when the Movement took a violent course, he suspended it abruptly in 1922. He was arrested on the charge of inciting the people against Government. He was released on grounds of ill-health. Mahatma Gandhi then decided to work for Hindu-Muslim Unity, *Charkha*, *Khadi*, and Harijan Uplift. In 1924 he was elected as the President of the Congress. He blessed the Swarajist Party to enter the Councils and continue India's fight for freedom through constitutional methods. He was called upon to organise demonstrations against Simon Commission. He started Civil Disobedience Movement in 1930. He also led a band of Congress Satyagrahis to the seashore in Dandi to break salt laws.

Mahatma Gandhi could not attend the First Round Table Conference in London because he was in jail. But as a result of Gandhi-Irwin Pact he agreed to attend the Second Round Table Conference as the sole representative of the Congress. He however, returned to India empty-handed because of communal discordance. The British Government once again used to repressive measures to crush the Congress and put Mahatma Gandhi and other Congress Leaders in jail. He observed a fast unto death against the Communal Award which was intended to separate the Harijans from the Hindus. He later evolved a compromise formula to keep the Harijans within the fold of Hinduism.

In 1939 Mahatma Gandhi came in conflict with Subhas Chandra Bose. The differences resulted in the exit of the latter. When the Second World War broke out in Europe, he refused to help the Government unless it made specific promises regarding India's future and also gave some immediate proof of its good intentions. In March, 1942, Japan's agressive designs and series of successes posed challenge to the security of India. The whole of South-East Asia came under its heels. The British Government sent Sir Stafford Cripps to negotiate with the Indian Leaders. Mahatma Gandhi rejected Cripps' proposals for they were unsatisfactory. In August, 1942, he issued the call of 'Quit India' to the British Element in India. He was arrested along with hundreds of his colleagues and followers. After his release in 1944, he started talks with Mohammad Ali Jinnah to resolve the constitutional and political deadlock but failed in his object.

The Muslim League after rejecting the Cabinet Mission proposals resorted to the extreme method of Direct Action. For this purpose it organised riots in several parts of the country to terrorise the Hindu Leaders to agree to Pakistan. Mahatma Gandhi led a spiritual mission to riot affected areas of Noakhali. He restored peace in Calcutta, Noakhali and Delhi.

It must be noted that the refugee leaders like Sir Gokal Chand Narang and Master Tara Singh (Akali Leader whose whole family was murdered in Rawalpindi) delivered very fiery speeches against the policies of Mahatma Gandhi as a result of which riots spread in Delhi. The Muslim Population of Delhi had enough arms and ammunition to resist the attacks of the refugees and particularly the sikhs, because the Muslim League had supplied them to it but ultimately they had to yield and the whole of Muslim Population was transferred to Purana Qila, Delhi, which Mahatma Gandhi visited at the instance of Mr. Nand Lal Mehta on September 13, 1947 but without informing Sardar Vallabh Bhai Patel, then Home Minister. Sardar Vallabh Bhai Patel later on severely rebuked Nand Lal Mehta for this lapse because it could involve the risk to Mahatma Gandhi's life.[1] Gandhi later on kept an indefinite fast to bring amity between the two communities. Sardar Vallabhbhai Patel objected to it because it involved the black mail of entire Hindu Community which was not at all responsible.

Mahatma Gandhi used his pressure on the Indian Government to pay ₹ 55 crores to Pakistan on account of the division of Defence stores. This he did at a time when Pakistan had been driving out Hindus from its territory and confiscating all their assets. The destitute millions who came to India as refugees held the Congress responsible for their untold sufferings. They also denounced Mahatma Gandhi for transferring ₹ 55 crores to Pakistan when she had appropriated their prosperity worth billions of rupees.

The growing frustration in the country found its expression in the form of the greatest political murder of the century. A fanatic Hindu Nathu Ram Godse fired at Mahatma Gandhi while he was attending a prayer meeting in Delhi. The most esteemed leader of the century died with 'Rama' on his lips. His death drowned every heart in profound grief. A complete strike for three days was observed by every section and community throughout the length and breadth of the country. His last rites were performed on Jamuna Bank at Rajghat where a befitting memorial has been raised to perpetuate his memory.

Mahatma Gandhi for his saintliness is placed alongside Buddha and Christ. He commanded worldwide recognitiion and regard. Even the United Nations Flag was lowered at his death. The period of Indian History from 1920 to 1948 was so much dominated by him that the Historians call it 'Gandhian Era'. The Nation owes much to this political saint for its emancipation. His name has been inscribed for ever in the hearts of his countrymen.

World Famous Scientist Einstein on Mahatma Gandhi

"A leader of his people unsupported by any outward authority, a politician whose success rests not upon craft nor mastery of technical devices but simply on the convincing power of his personality, a victorious fighter who has always scorned the use of force; a man of wisdom and humility armed with resolve and inflexible consistency, who has devoted all his strength to the uplifting of his people and betterment of their lot; a man who has confronted the brutality of Europe with the dignity of the simple human being and thus at all times risen superior.

Wherever, he walked a temple grew.

Generations to come, it may be, will scarce believe that such a one as this even in flesh and blood trod upon this earth."

1. *The Hindustan Times, A Gandhi Associte Reminiscences* Oct. 2, 1984.

POLITICAL VIEWS OF MAHATMA GANDHI

Mahatma Gandhi will always be remembered for his attempt to spiritualise politics or introduce purity into politics. He was not a philosopher like Shankaracharya or Kant. He did not preach any startling theory or ism. In his own words : 'So my patriotism is for me a stage on my journey to the land of eternal freedom and peace ...... for me there are no politics devoid of religion ..... Politics bereft of religion are a death-trap because they kill the soul.' Addressing some Congress Workers in 1936 he admitted that there was no such thing as Gandhism nor was he inclined to leave after him a sect of his followers. He never claimed to have originated any new 'ism'; he had merely tried to apply the eternal truths in his own way to everyday life and its problems. He also did not say that his opinions or the interpretation of truth was final and unchangeable. They were amenable to changes in new contexts. He had nothing new to teach to the world. His principles of truth and Ahimsa were as old as the hills of India. His effort had been only to make new experiments with truth and non-violence in a broader field. Mahatma Gandhi advised his admirers not to give the name of Gandhism to his philosophy for there was no innovation in it, nothing doctrinaire.

(a) Ahimsa and Satyagraha. Mahatma Gandhi was a religious man in the strictest sense of the word. His religion, however, was more broadbased and inclusive of all that was ethical and good in any religion of the world. Religion, according to him, was belief in the ordered moral goverance of the world. Humanism was the keynote of his outlook and behaviour. Politics and religion were for him two sides of the same coin. He gave religious basis to politics. Religion, he said, had driven him upto politics; and if he consented to dabble with politics, it was because there was no escape from it and he wanted to temper politics with religion. He said, "All religions are founded on the same moral laws. My ethical religion is made up of laws which bind men all over the world."

If truth is the ultimate reality and the highest ideal, it has to be safeguarded, not by brute force but Ahimsa. Non-violence, as Mahatma Gandhi meant, was the cult of love which alone promised a safe harbour to erring humanity. Ahimsa and Truth were inseparable, they anticipate each other. The weapon of Ahimsa and Truth could be handled not by a coward but a strong man only who could lift the sword but refrained from doing so on moral considerations. The true test of a votary of Ahimsa is when despite the strongest provocation to use force, he acts with reason in a non-violent way.

Mahatma Gandhi's noblest gift to mankind is 'Satyagraha' which literally means 'holding on to truth'. He used to call it spiritual force or the force of love. He made a distinction between passive resistance and satyagraha. *passive resistance may be a political weapan based on expediency; Satyagraha is a spiritual weapan. Passive resistance is weapan of weak; it is only a man who is morally and spiritually strong who can practise satyagraha. Passive resistance does not entirely ignore the possibility of violence ..., satyagraha will not tolerate violence in word or deed.*" So Mahatma Gandhi's satyagraha was not a negative act, it was a positive effort to correct the wrongdoer by the exercise of the purest soul force. There was no place for malice or ill-will against the opponent in the philosophy and technique of satyagraha. A true satyagrahi never tries to overpower the oponent to physical force or inflict physical injuries. This is the way to win his rival's mind and heart by his arguments and sacrifice. Satyagrahi is real *Karmayogi* who accepts no defeat. He fights for truth with full awareness of the ordeals on the way. He accepts death cheerfully as a gateway to heaven and welcomes imprisonment as a step towards freedom.

He believed that even armed aggression on one's country can be resisted with satyagraha. A Satyagrahi should prefer death to slavery. He should try to knock down the foreign rulers by holding back his co-operation and even by disobeying the laws of the Government. He claimed that the impact of Non-violent resistance was more formidable than all the warheads in the arsenal of the most well-equipped country. Even Hitler could be run down by the earnest application of Non-violent ways. A warring people become more desperate and cruel if resisted with force. They become milder when they find themselves face to face with an army of unarmed men, women and children who refuse to submit to the destructive power of arms. Mahatma Gandhi practised his principles in South Africa against racial hatred. His experiment was a resounding success. He recommended this weapon to Indians as an alternative to the cult of bombs which the terrorists were practising. In Champaran (Bihar), Ahmedabad and Kheda (Gujarat), the efficacy of satyagraha as a political weapon was conclusively proved. He clung to this belief firmly that howsoever heartless or imperialistic the British be, they were bound to respond to the wishes of non-violent satyagraphis of India.

(b) Conception of True Swaraj. The word Swaraj signified a government which truly represents the people of all classes and creeds, which is thoroughly democratic and in which there is no place for nepotism, corruption or abuse of power. Such a state, said Mahatama Gandhi was not an utopia. It could be realised by the people provided they were politically conscious, bold and literate. Mahatma Gandhi was against concentration of power. He preferred decentralisation of authority. He favoured the idea of vitalising the Panchayats and letting them work for the uplift of the villages. He wanted the process of delegation of powers to be reversed. The people, he said, should play vital role in the governance of the country. The governments should derive powers to the extent the people through their representative bodies might consent to give. The Centre should be invested with minimum of powers leaving maximum of sphere to be controlled by the Local Bodies and the Panchayats.

Mahatma Gandhi said, "*By Swaraj I mean the Government of India by the consent of the people as ascertained by the largest number of the adult population, male or female, native born or domiciled who have taken the trouble of having their names registered as voters. I hope to demonstrate that real Swaraj will come not by the acquisition of authority by a few but by the acquisition of the capacity by all to resist authority when abused. In other words, Swaraj is to be gained by educating the masses to a sense of their capacity to regulate and control authority.*"[1]

Mahatma Gandhi further says, "that by political independence I do not mean an imitation of the British House of Commons or the Soviet Rule of Russia or the Fascist Rule of Italy or the Nazi Rule of Germany. They have systems suited to their genius. We must have ours suited to us. What that can be more than I can tell. I have described it as *Ram Raj, i.e., sovereignty of the people based on pure moral authority.*"[2]

Mahatma Gandhi further said, "We have long been accustomed to think that power comes only through Legislative Assemblies. I have regarded this belief as a grave error brought about by inertia or hypnotism. A superficial study of British History has made us think that all power percolates to the people from parliaments. The truth is that power resides in the people and it is entrusted for the time being to those whom they choose their representatives. Parliaments have no power or even existence independent of the people. It has been my effort for the last twenty-one years to convince the people of this simple truth. Civil Disobedience is the store house of power. Imagine a whole people unwilling to conform to the laws of the legislature and prepared to suffer the consequences of non-compliance. They will bring the whole legislative and executive machinery to a standstill. The police and the military are of no use to coerce minorities, however, powerful they may be. But no police or military coercion can bend the resolute will of a people, out for suffering to the uttermost."[3]

Gandhi on Democracy

Mahatma Gandhi said:

"My notion of democracy is that under it the weakest should have the same opportunity as the strongest. That can never happen except through non-violence."

"Democracy must in essence mean the art and science of mobilising the entire physical, economic and spiritual resources of all the various sections of the people in the service of the common good of all."[4]

1. Mahatma Gandhi, *Young India*, dated 29-1-1925, pp. 40-41.
2. Mahatma Gandhi, *Young India*, dated 2-3-1922 p. 120.
3. Mahatma Gandhi, *Constructive Programme, Its Meaning and Place*, p. 5. Navjivan Press, Allahabad.
4. Mahatma Gandhi, *Harijan*, 27.5, 1939, p. 145.

"Swaraj can be maintained only where there is a morality of loyal and patriotic people to whom the good of the nation is paramount above all other considerations whatever including their personal profit. Swaraj means government by the many. Where the many are immoral or selfish, their government can spell anarchy and nothing else."[1]

"I hope .... to achieve the end by demonstrating that real Swaraj will come not by the acquisition of authority by a few but by the acquisition of the capacity by all to resist authority when it is abused. In other words, Swaraj is to be attained by educating the masses to sense of their capacity to regulate and control authority."[2]

Swaraj of my dreams is the poor man's Swaraj. 'The necessaries of life should be enjoyed by you in common with those enjoyed by the princes and the moneyed men. But that does not mean that you should have palaces like theirs. They are not necessary for happiness. You or I would be lost in them. But you ought to get all the ordinary amenities of life that a richman enjoys. I have not the slightest doubt that Swaraj is not the Puran Swaraj until these amenities are guaranteed to you under it."[3]

If Swaraj was not meant to civilize us and to purify and stabilise our civilization, it should be nothing worth.

Mahatma Gandhi on Communal Harmony

Mahatma Gandhi once said, "I shall work for an India, in which the poorest shall feel that it is their country .... an India in which there shall be no high or low classes of people, an India in which all communities shall live in perfect harmony.

The very essence of our civilization is that we give a permanent place to morality in all our affairs, public or private.[4]

True democracy cannot be worked by twenty men sitting at the Centre. It has to be worked from below by the people of every village[5].

Mahatma Gandhi on Socialism

Socialism was not born with the discovery of the misuse of capital by capitalists. As I have contended, socialism or even communism, is explicit in the first verse of *Ishopanshad.* Real socialism has been handed down to us by our ancestors who taught : "*All land belongs to Gopal*, where then is the boundary line? Man is the maker of that line and he can therefore unmake it." What is true is that when some reformers lost faith in the method of conversion, the technique of what is known as scientific socialism was born. I am engaged insolving the same that faces scientific socialism. It is true, however, that my approach is always and only through unadulterated nonviolence."

In the wake of the suspension of the Civil Disobedience Movement by Mahatma Gandhi in 1933, there emerged a "Socialist" group in the ranks of the Indian National Congress and at the First Congress Socialist Conference held at patna in 1934, the programme of the party was formulated. On the publication of this programme an attempt was made by some of the leaders of the party to ascertain Mahatma Gandhi's views on it.

I welcome the rise of the socialist Party in the Congress. But I can't say that I like the programme as it appears in the printed pamphlet. It seems to me to ignore conditions and I do not like the assumption underlying many of its propositions which go to show that there is necessarily antagonism between the classes and masses or between the labourers and the capitalists, such that they can never

1. Mahatma Gandhi, Young India, 28-7-1921.
2. Mahatma Gandhi, *Young India*, 29-1-1925 pp. 4-41.
3. Mahatma Gandhi, *Young India*, 26-3-1931, pp. 46-47.
4. Mahatma Gandhi, *Young India*, 23-1-1930, p. 26.
5. Mahatma Gandhi, *Harijan*, dated 18-1-1948 p. 519

work for mutual good. My own experience covering a fairly long period is to the contrary. What is necessary is that labourers or workers should know the rights and should also know how to assert them.

The progressive nationalisation of all the instruments of production, distribution and exchange is too sweeping to be admissible. Rabindra Nath Tagore is an instrument of marvellous production. I do not know that he will submit to be nationalised.

Abolition of the rule of the Indian Princes is an arrogance of power which does not belong to the party or which belongs as the power to abolish Portuguese and the French Authority in what is called Portuguese and French India. It may be unfortunate, but the dismemberment or India is a fact which may not be ignored. It is surely enough to concentrate upon what is called British India. It is large enough territory for any party to operate in and its successful operations in British India cannot but have their effects upon the other parts of India. On principle too I am not in favour of the abolition of the rule of the princes, but I believe in the reformation in consonance with the true spirit of democracy.

Some other questions were put to Mahatma Gandhi which are like this:

Q.1. Don't you recognise the conflict of interest between the possessing and the exploited classes resulting in a class struggle ?

Ans. Today there is conflict of interests between the capitalists and working people because the former dreams of profits of lakhs of rupees without giving anything to the worker. I would stop the capitalists from doing so. I have told them particularly in Ahmadabad, that they must regard the workers as partners. I say to them : You bring your capital into the concern, they bring their only capital–their persons." When the Ahmedabad Mill Owners came to me for a wage cut, I told them : "It is true you have a right to your interest but first you must guarantee the men's wages."

Q.2. But Socialists deny the right to draw interest.

Ans. But won't they reward brains ?

Q.3. Are you contemplating the perpetuation of private enterprise and free competition or planned economy by the State ?

Ans. I believe in private enterprise and also in planned production. If you have only state production, men will become moral and intellectual paupers. They will forget their responsibilities. *I would therefore allow the capitalists and zamindars to keep their factories and their land, but I would make consider themselves trustees of their property.*

Q.4. How will you do it ?

Ans. By Non-violence I would make them undergo a change of heart. It is possible to convert them.

Q.5. Will you adopt economic programme as a means of conversion ?

Ans. Yes, but it must be Non-violent.

Q.6. Do you think it is wrong to tell the workers that what they were really fighting is the system of imperialism and that so long as that system remains their condition cannot improve ?

Ans. Yet at present the workers should only be taught to impose their will on the mill owners. To bring in the Government also is to overprove your case. Whatever State there is even your own capitalist Government will support the Mill Owners. Even under this system I can teach labour to use its power and to claim partnership with capital. I would ask them to take possession of the Mills.

Q.7. What is your opinion about the socialist demand for the overthrow of the Indian Princes?

Ans. I do not agree with it. They should seek to make the Princes Constitutional Monarchs or leaders of the people ruling according to their wishes. To demand their overthrow is like asking for Socialism in Afghanistan.

Q.8. Should not the war be resisted by general strike of railwaymen, dockers, telegraphist and munition workers?

Ans. Yes, there should be a strike when war breaks out but we should not declare our intentions from now.

Gandhi on Economic Equality and Trusteeship

Mahatma Gandhi said, "My idea of society is that while we are born equal, meaning that we have a right to equal opportunity, all have not the same capacity. It is in the nature of things impossible. For instance, all cannot have the same height or colour or degree of intelligence, etc. therefore, in the nature of things, some will have ability to earn more and others less. People with talents will have more, and they will utilize their talents for this purpose. If they utilise their talents kindly, they will be performing the work of the State. Such people exist as trustees and no other terms. I would allow a man of intellect to earn more. I would not cramp his talent. But the bulk of his greater earnings must be used for the good of the State, just as the income of all earning sons of the father go to the family fund. They would have their earnings as trustees.

I want to bring about an equalisation of status. The working classes have all these centuries been isolated and relegated to a lower status.

They have been *shudras* and the word has been interpreted to mean an inferior status. I want to allow no differentiation between the son of a weaver, of an agriculturist and of a school-master.[1]

Mahatma Gandhi further observed : Economic equality is the master key to Non-violent independence. Working for economic equality means abolishing the eternal conflict between capital and labour. It means the levelling down of the few rich in whose hands is concentrated the bulk of the nation's wealth on the hand and a levelling up of the semi-starved naked missions on the other. A non-violent system of government is clearly an impossibility so long as the wide gulf between the rich and the hungry millions persists. The contrast between the palaces of New Delhi and the miserable hovels of the poor labouring class nearby cannot last one day in a free India in which the poor will enjoy the same power as the richest in the land. A violent and bloody revolution is a certainly one day unless there is a voluntary abdication of riches and the power that riches give and sharing them for the common good. I adhere to my doctrine of trusteeship in spite of the ridicule that has been poured upon it. It is true that it is difficult to reach. So is non-violence. But we made upon our mind in 1920 to negotiate that ascent.

Mahatma Gandhi's Communism

Mahatma Gandhi said, "Let no one try to justify the glaring differences between the classes and the masses, the princes and the pauper, by saying that the former need more. That will be idle sophistry and a trustee of my argument. The contrast between the rich and the poor today is a painful sight. The poor villagers are exploited by foreign government and also by their own countrymen ..... the city dwellers. They produce milk and their children have to go without it. It is disgraceful. Every one must have a balanced diet, a descent house to live in, facilities for the education of one's children and adequate medical relief. "That constituted his picture of economic equality. He did not want to taboo everything above and beyond the bare necessaries, but they must come after the essential needs of the poor are satisfied first.[2]

Q.1. What is the difference between your technique and that of the communists or socialists for realising the goal of economic equality.

Ans. The socialists and communists say they can do nothing to bring about economic equality

1. Mahatma Gandhi, *Harijan*, Dated 15-1-1933.
2. From the Article 'Mahatma Gandhi's Communism'; by Pyare Lal, *Harijan*, 31-3-1946.

today. They will just carry on propaganda in its favour and to that end they believe in generating and accentuating hatred. They say, "When they get control over the state, they will enforce equality. Under my plan the State will be there to carry out the will of the people, not to dictate to them or force them to do its will. I shall bring about economic equality through non-violence by converting the people to my point of view by harnessing the forces of love as against hatred. I will not wait till I have converted the whole society to my view but will straightaway make a beginning with myself. It goes without saying that I cannot hope to bring about economic equality of my conception If I am the owner of 50 motor cars or even ten bighas of land then I have to reduce myself to the level of the poorest of the poor. That is what I have been trying to do for the last fifty years or more, and as I claim to be foremost communist although I make use of car and other facilities offered to me by the rich. They have no hold on me and I can shed them at a moment's notice, if the interests of the masses demand it."[1]

Mahatma Gandhi had no doubt that "If India was to live an exemplary life of independence which would be the envy of the world, all the *bhangis*, doctors, lawyers, teachers, merchants and others would get the same wages for an honest day's work. Indian society may never reach the goal but it was the duty of every Indian to set his sail towards that goal and no other if India was to be a happy land.[2]

"Today there is gross economic inequality. The basis of socialism is economic equality. There can be no Rama Rajya in the present state of iniquitous inequalities in which a few roll in riches and the masses do not get enough to eat."[3]

Equal distribution : What India needs is not the concentration of capital in a few hands but its distribution so as to be within easy reach of the 7 $^1/_2$ lakhs of villages that make this continent 1900 miles long and 1500 miles broad.

"Now let us consider how equal distribution can be brought through non-violence. The first step towards it is for him who has made his ideal part of his being to bring about the necessary changes in his personal life. He would reduce his wants to a minimum, learning in mind the poverty of India. His earnings would be free from dishonesty. The desire for speculation would be renounced. His habitation would be in keeping with the new mode of life. There would be self-restraint exercised in every sphere of life. When he has done all that is possible in his own life, then only he will be in a position to reach this ideal among his associates and neighbours.

"Indeed at the root of the doctrine of equal distribution must lie that of the trusteeship of the wealth possessed by them. For according to the doctrine they may not possess a rupee more than their neighbours. How is this to be brought about ? Non-violently ? To do so we would naturally have to resort to violence.

This violent action can not benefit society. Society will be poorer, for it will lose the gifts of a man who knows how to accumulate wealth. Therefore the non-violent way is evidently superior. The rich man will be left in possession of his wealth, of which he will use what he reasonably requires for his personal needs and will act as a trustee for remainder to be used for the society. In this argument honesty on the part of trustee is assumed."

"As soon as a man looks upon himself as a servant of society, earns for its sake, spends for its benefit, then purity enters his earnings and there is *Ahimsa in his venture.* Moreover, if men's minds turn towards this way of life, there will come about a peaceful revolution in society and that without any bitterness."

Land to the tiller. If Indian society is to make real progress along peaceful lines, there must a definite recognition on the part of the moneyed class that the ryot possesses the same soul that they

1. From the Article 'Mahatma Gandhi's Communism'; by Pyare Lal, *Harijan*, 31-3-1946.
2. Mahatma Gandhi, *Harijan*, 16-3-1947.
3. Mahatma Gandhi, *Harijan*, 1-6-1947.

do, and that their wealth gives them no superiority over the poor. They must regard themselves, even as the Japanese nobles did as trustee holding their wealth for the good of their wards, the *ryot*. Then they would take no more than a reasonable amount as commission for their labours.

Mahatma Gandhi on Village Swaraj. My idea of village Swaraj is that it is complete republic independent of its neighbours for its own vital wants and yet interdependent for many others in which dependence is a necessity. Thus every village's first concern will be to grow its own food crops and cotton for its cloth. It should have reserve for its capital, recreation and play ground for adult, and children. Thus, if there is more land available, it will grow useful money crops thus excluding *ganja*, tobacoo, opium and the like. The village will maintain a village theatre, school and public hall. It will have its own waterworks ensuring clean water supply. This can be done through controlled wells or tanks. Education will be compulsory upto the final basic course. As far as possible every activity will be conducted on the co-operative basis.

There will be no castes such as we have today with their graded untouchability. Non-violence with its technique of satyagraha and non-co-operation will be the sanction of the village community.

Panchayats. The Government of the village will be conducted by the panchyat of five persons annually elected by the adult villagers, male and female, possessing minimum prescribed qualifications. They will have all the authority and jurisdiction required. Since there will be no system of punishment in the accepted sense, this panchyat will be the legislature, judiciary and executive combined to operate for its year of office. Any village can become such a republic today without much interference even from the present Government whose sole effective connection with them is the exaction of village revenue. Here there is a perfect democracy based upon individual freedom. The individual is the architect of his own government.

All Round Village Development. The villagers should develop such a high degree of skill that articles prepared by them should command ready market outside. When our villagers are fully developed, there will be no dearth in them of men with a high degree of skill and artistic talent...... Today the villages are duug heaps. Tomorrow they will be like tiny gardens of Eden where dwell high intelligent folks whom no one can deveive or exploit.

The construction of the villages along these lines should begin right now. The reconstruction of the villages should not be organised on a temporary but permanent basis. Craft, art, health and education should all be integrated into one scheme. Nai Talim is a beautiful blend of all the four and covers the whole education of the individual from the time of birth to the moment of death. Therefore, I would not divide village uplift work into water-tight compartments from the very beginning but undertake an activity which will combine all four instead of regarding crafts and industry as different from education.

Mahatma Gandhi on Charkha. The spinning wheel presents to me the hope of masses. The masses lost their freedom, such as it was with the loss of the *Charkha*. The *Charkha* supplemented the agriculture of the villagers and gave it dignity. It was the friend and solace of the widow. It kept the villagers away from idleness. For the Charkha included all the anterior and posterior industries-ginning, carding, warping, sizing, dyeing and weaving. These in their turn kept the village carpenters and the blacksmiths busy. The charkha enabled the seven hundred thousand villages to become self-contained. With the exit of the Charkha went the other village industries, such as the oil press. Nothing took the place of these industries. Therefore, the villages were drained of their varied occupations and their creative talent and what little wealth these brought them.

Hence, if the villagers are to come into their own, the most natural thing that suggests itself is the revival of the *Charkha* and all its means.

The Non-violent State

Many have shaken their heads as they have said, "But you can't teach Non-violence to the masses. It is only possible for individuals and that too in rare cases". That is in my opinion, a gross self-deception.

"If mankind was not habitually non-violent, it would have been destroyed ages ago. But in the duel between forces of violence and nonviolence, the latter has come out victorious in the end. The truth is that we have not had patience enough to wait and apply ourselves wholeheartedly to the spread of non-violence among the people as a means for political ends."[1]

To me political power is not an end but one of the means of enabling people to better their condition in every department of life. Political power means capacity to regulate national life through national representatives. If national life becomes so perfect as to become self-regulated, no representation becomes necessary. There is then a state of enlightened anarchy. In such a state every one is his ruler. He rules himself in such a manner that he is never a hindrance to his neighbour. In the ideal state, therefore, there is no political power because there is no state. But the ideal is never fully realised in life. Hence the classic statement of Thoreau that government is best which governs the least.[2]

Mahatma Gandhi said : "I look an increase in the power of the state with the greater fear, because although while apparently doing good by minimising exploitation, it does the greatest harm to mankind by destroying individuality which lies at the root of all progress.

"While I disapprove of an organisation based on force which a State is. Voluntary organisation there must be."[3]

"Centralisation is a system inconsistent with the non-violent structure of society."[4]

"It must be remembered that nowhere in the world does a State without government exist. If at all, it could ever come into being, it would be in India, for our is the only country where the attempt has at any rate been made. We have not been able to show that bravery to the degree which is necessary and for the attainment of which there is only one way. Those who have faith in the latter, have to demonstrate it. In order to do so, the fear of death has to be completely shed, just as we have shed the fear of prisons.[5]

Police force in a Non-violent state : "I suggest that if India is to evolve along non-violent lines, it will have to decentralise many things. Centralisation can not be sustained and defended without adequate force. Simple homes from which there is nothing to take away require no policing, the palaces of the rich must have strong guards to protect them against dacoity.

"So must huge factories. Rurally organised India will run less risk of foreign invasion than urbanised India, well equipped with military, naval and air forces."[6]

Government can not succeed in becoming entirely non-violent because it represented all the people. I do not today conceive of such a golden age. But I do believe in the possibility of a predominantly non-violent society and I a working for it.[7]

Even in a non-violent state a police force may be necessary. This I admit, is a sign of my imperfect Ahimsa. I have not the courage to declare that we can carry on without a police as I have in respect of an army. Of course, I can and do envisage a state where the police will not be necessary, but whether we shall succeed in realising it, the future alone will show.

1. Mahatama Gandhi, *Young India*, 2-4-1930.
2. Mahatma Gandhi, *Young India*, 2-7-1932
3. Mahatma Gandhi, *The Modern Review*, 1935, p. 412.
4. Mahatma Gandhi, *Harijan*, 18-1-1942.
5. Mahatma Gandhi, *Harijan*, 15-9-1946.
6. Mahatma Gandhi, *Harijan*, 30-12-1939.
7. Mahatma Gandhi, *Harijan*, 9-3-1940.

"The police of my conception will, however, be of a wholly different pattern from the present day force. Its ranks will be composed of believers in non-violence. They will be servants, not masters, of the people. The people will instinctively render them every help, and through mutual co-operation they will easily deal with the ever decreasing disturbaces. The police force will have some kind of arms, but they will be rarely used, if at all. In fact the policemen will be reformers. Their police work will be confined primarily to robbers and dacoits. Quarrels between labour and capital and strikes will be few and far between in a non-violent state, because the influence of the non-violent majority will be so great as to command the respect of the principal elements in a society. Similarly there will be no room for communal disturbances.[1]

Conception of an Ideal Society. Mahatma Gandhi was a great idealist. He always kept before him the distant vision of a classless and stateless society. In this respect his object appeared to be the same as that of the Anarchists and Marxists but the means that he suggested to reach that goal were quite different and novel. He did not approve violence or class war in any form. He proposed to end capitalism not by sending the capitalists to gallows but by promoting economic parity through cottage industries. He wanted the landlords to act not as masters but as trustees of the cultivable land. In case of their unwillingness to do so, they were to be deprived of their land in a peaceful way by the State. He advocated the doctrine that the land belonged to him who tilled it. He laid stress on sound and self-sufficient village economy. He wrote : "*At the same time I believe that some key industries are necessary .... I would have state ownership (of key industries) where a large number of people have to work together. But as I can conceive such a state only based on non-violence, I would not dispossess moneyed men by force but would invite their co-operation in the process of conversion to state ownership. There are no pariahs of society, whether they are millionaires or paupers*." But since he was practical idealist, he knew that the creation of an ideal state or ideal society was not an easy task till. man continued to be fallible and selfish. For this reason he did not elaborate his conception of an ideal society but he put accent on an ideal state which could with not much difficulty be realised.

Social conceptions of Mahatma Gandhi. Mahatma Gandhi was the pioneer champion of Basic Education. This, he considered, was the only way to make the poor students self-supporting. He also advocated for women education which he said, was a 'must' for social uplift and enlightenment. He was opposed to child marriage and social inequality. He permitted widow marriage. He stood for Hindi, Adult Education, Hindu-Muslim Unity and Religious Tolerence. He called himself a Hindu, but his definition of Hinduism was most liberal and enlightened. He called drinking the greatest bane of Indian People. He popularised charkha and Khadi because it promised employment to lakhs of jobless weavers. He made the use of Khadi compulsory for all Congressmen. He wanted jails to be converted from execution houses into reformatories. Mahatma Gandhi by his example oriented rather revolutionised the outlook of the people. His message to the masses included the creed of simplicity, courtesy and honesty. He was not much in favour of heavy industries because it led to the concentration of wealth in a few hands and loss of jobs for many.

Was Mahatma Gandhi a Practical Idealist ? Mahatma Gandhi was not a mere dreamer and idealist. He was a visionary, a prophet-politician who struck new paths for the downtrodden millions to go a long to their goal of freedom from want and political subjection. His philosophy was not completely divorced from realism. He believed in *Sarvodaya* 'which aims to replace the politics of power by the politics of co-operation'. The reigns of Ram and Ashoka were models before him. All that he taught in his writings, he practised in his life. The improvements he suggested in politics, society, character and state were all practicable ones. He proceeded with his eyes always fixed on the realities. He was, in fact, a citizen of the world. His teachings have been incorporated in the charter of U.N.O. The world is realising increasingly that its salvation lies in accepting the code of conduct laid down by Gandhiji. Without racial equality, political independence, tolerance and Ahimsa, the world will never enjoy a moment of peace. In Gandhi we come across a prophet and a patriot. He occupies the

1. Mahatma Gandhi, *Harijan*, 1-9-1940.

same place in Indian history as Washington in America or Mazzini in Italy. The ideals of Mahatma Gandhi are beacon lights for Indian Government. His ideas about Khadi, Charkha, Spiritualization of politics, abjuring force, cottage industries, international peace, religious amity or communal harmony, decentralisation, panchayati raj, social equality, rural uplift, simplicity and ideal society and state, good means to achieve good end, have found permanent place not only in the annals of our country but in the history of the world. He will always be remembered as a great seer, statesman, politician and a saint to the unity of mankind.

ESTIMATE OF MAHATMA GANDHI

Though many estimates of Mahatma Gandhi are available, yet the author has chosen to give only the views of Pt. Jawaharlal Nehru and Smt. Indira Gandhi because they seem to be the best.

Pt. Jawaharlal Nehru's Views. Mahatma Gandhi had pleaded for the adoption of the way of non-violence, of peaceful non-co-operation with all the eloquence and persuasive power which he so abundantly possessed .... He had instilled courage and manhood in his people and discipline and endurance, and the power of joyful sacrifice for a cause and with all his humility, pride. Courage is one sure foundation of character, he had said, "without courage, there is no morality, no religion, no love. "One cannot follow truth or love so long one is supposed to fear." With all his horror of violence, he had told us that "cowardice is a thing even more hateful than violence. And discipline is the pledge and guarantee that a man means business."

A man of the keenest intellect, of fine feeling and good taste, wide vision, very human and yet essentially the ascetic who has suppressed his passions and emotions, sublimated them and directed them in spiritual channels, a tremendous personality, drawing people to himself like a magnet and calling out fierce loyalties and attachments—all this so unlikely and beyond a peasant. In short *he was the spirit of India.*

Mrs. Indira Gandhi's Views : *"The idea of non-violence was not new but to forge it into an instrument of revolt, wielded by a whole nation, was indeed revolutionary.* Again, the idea of respecting the teachings and holy men of other religions was part of our tradition. But the Mahatma made secularism and linchpin of our political movement."[1]

Hillary Clinton's praise of Mahatma Gandhi : On 8th March, 1995 Hilary Clinton (wife of President Clinton) visited Sabarmati Ashram. She said that "the greatman had even in those days take about universal brotherhood and world peace. Mr. Gandhi's thinking crossed all boundaries and did not include Gujarat or India only but encompassed all mankind".

DR. RAJENDRA PRASAD (1884-1963)

Late Dr. Rajendra Prasad, the First President of Indian Republic, is counted amongst the few top-ranking leaders of Mòdern India. He was a true disciple of Mahatma Gandhi, the living example of Mahatma Gandhi's ideals of simple living and high thinking. He was a brilliant student of Calcutta University. He broke all previous records by his genius. He was offered a scholarship for higher studies in England but he refused to go on patriotic grounds. His practice at the bar also bore the stamp of his brilliance. But he gave up his lucrative practice to work with Mahatma Gandhi during Champaran Satyagraha. He went to jail several times in connection with Congress Movement. In 1946 he was unanimously elected President of the Constituent Assembly. He enriched it with his valuable suggestions in drafting the Constitution of free India. On January 26, 1950, when the New Constitution came into force, he was elected the First President of India. After the second general elections, he enjoyed another term of Presidentship. His timely and weighty advice on various important matters

1. Mrs. Indira Gandhi on 'Gandhiji's Legacy', *National Herald*, October 2, 1976, p. 1 & 2.

was greatly valued by the Prime Minister, Pt. Jawaharlal Nehru. He was a veteran politician, a reputed scholar, and a staunch patriot. He embodied in his life the spirit and cultural heritage of India. He wrote a large number of books—the most notable being *Divided India.* He retired on 12th May, 1962, after being in his exalted office for over 12 years. He went back to his Native State of Bihar where he made Sadaqat Ashram as his permanent home. Despite his long illness he was alive to all the crises and dangers confronting the nation. When the Chinese launched their massive attack along the Himalayan borders, he drew attention of the people to the peril from the north while addressing a meeting on 21st October, 1962, in Patna. He issued a clarion call to Indian youths to come forward and defend the country with all their main and might.

PT. JAWAHARLAL NEHRU (1889-1964)

Jawaharlal was born on 14th November, 1889, in the illustrious Nehru family of Allahabad. He inherited the temper, patriotic sentiments and brilliance of his father—Pt. Motilal Nehru. He got his early education at home and then studied at Harrow and Cambridge. His association with the Congress dates back to 1912 when he attended the Congress Session at Patna. Since then he attended all the Congress Session regularly. In 1914 he collected ₹ 55,000 at the call of Gopal Krishna Gokhale to help the Indians settled in Africa. He joined the Home Rule League established by, Lokmanaya Bal Gangadhar Tilak and Mrs. Annie Besant. He went to jail during the Non-Co-operation Movement. He had been in the vanguard of all youth and peasant movements. For two years he had been the Chairman of Allahabad Municipal Committee. For many years he held the office of the General Secretary of the Congress. In 1928 he took a bold stand against his own father who was the Author of Nehru Report. He was dissatisfied with the demand of Dominion Status instead of complete Swarajya. It was under Pt. Jawahar Lal Nehru's Presidentship in 1929 that the Congress adopted complete independence as its goal. In all the spent nearly 14 years in jail. Several times he was elected President of the Congress. Since 1946 when the Interim Government was formed at the Centre, he occupied the dignified office of the Prime Minister of India till his death.

Pt. Jawaharlal Nehru has made a significant contribution to the reconstruction of free India. He believed in socialism and as a result of his efforts the Congress at Avadi Session, adopted socialistic pattern of society in place of co-operative commonwealth as its goal. He was an ardent advocate of co-operative farming, Panchayati Raj, and International Peace. Being incharge of External Affairs he was the architect of India's foreign policy. He believed in non-alignment and neutrality, the principles of Panch Sheel formed the basis of his foreign policy. He was always a vehement critic of imperialism, capitalism, colonialisim and racism. He was also able to mobilise world opinion in favour of disarmament. He took leading part in the Bandung and Belgrade Conferences of Afro-Asian Nations. It has been his endeavour throughout to have cordial relations with all the countries of three continents. In pursuance of his policy he visited many countries and invited their dignitaries to India. The ruling passion of his life was to eradicate poverty and lead the country to economic prosperity and scientific advancement. He introduced Community Development Programme and three Five-Year Plans to secure this object. He hated provincialism and communalism. He had done yeoman's work in abolishing zamindari, introducing prohibition and removing untouchability. He was an idealist who had firm faith in universal religion, international ethics and cosmopolitan outlook. Besides being a fearless fighter for India's freedom, he was an astute politician and nation-builder. He undertook whirlwind tour of the country on the eve of general elections. His personality cast a spell on the voters and swung the balance in favour of the Congress. He might be called the soul of the party. He was truly an apostle of peace.

Pt. Jawaharlal Nehru extended exemplary support to U.N.O. on all occasions. He put Indian contingents at the disposal of U.N.O. for establishing peace in Korea, Indo-China, Egypt and Congo. He tolerated even the occupation of Tibet by Communist China and signed Panch Sheel so as to avoid conflict. China, however, showed her ingratitude and violated peace treaty by attacking India and occupying a large chunk of our territory on 20th October, 1962. Pt. Jawaharlal Nehru could not accept this aggression lying down. He called upon the nation to be prepared to defend her borders. At his call crores of rupees and maunds of gold poured into the Defence Fund. Thousands of young men joined the armed forces. On November 8, 1962 *addressing the members of Lok Sabha, he declared that "India was prepared to accept the challenge of aggressive China. Whatever be the cost, India was determined to push back the invaders."*

Pt. Jawaharlal Nehru believed in perfect communal harmony and the disturbances of January-March 26, 1964, greatly perturbed him. In a broadcast to the nation on March 26, 1964, Pt. Jawaharlal Nehru made an impassioned appeal to his countrymen to maintain communal harmony and warned that fear and bitterness caused by strife will be fatal to the nation. Pt. Jawaharlal Nehru further said in that broadcast, "This communal trouble is entirely opposed to our policy and to our future and I do appeal to you to fight it and to put an end to it. India is a country of many communities and unless we can live in harmony with each other, respecting each other's beliefs and habits we cannot build up a great and united nation. Ever since the distant past, it has been India's proud privilege to live in harmony with each other. That has been the basis of India's culture. Long ago, the Buddha taught us this lesson. From the days of Asoka, 2,300 years ago, this aspect of our thoughts has been repeatedly declared and practised. In our own days, Mahatma Gandhi laid great stress on it and indeed lost life because he laid great stress on communal goodwill and harmony. We have, therefore, a precious heritage to keep and we cannot allow ourselves to act contrary to it."

Dr. Radhakrishnan sheds light on the various aspects of Pt. Jawaharlal Nehru's Philosophy and Work

Prime Minister Pt. Jawaharlal Nehru died of heart attack on 27th May, 1964, a little before 2 p.m. While paying his tribute to the late Prime Minister Pt. Jawaharlal Nehru, President Radhakrishnan said the same day, "*Jawaharlal Nehru was one of the greatest figures of our generation, an outstanding statesman whose services to the cause of human freedom are unforgettable. As a fighter for freedom he was illustrious, as a maker of modern India his services were unparalleled. His life and work have had a profound influence on our mental make-up, social structure and intellectual development. As a man, Nehru combined a fine sensitivity of mind, a rare delicacy of feeling, with large and generous impulses. To the weak and the frustrated his heart went out in profound sympathy. He was an author of distinction.* Pt. Jawaharlal Nehru held the office of the Prime Minister of our country ever since the dawn of independence and in the long years of his premiership tried to put our country on a progressive, scientific, dynamic and non-communal basis. His steadfast loyalty to certain fundamental principles of liberalism gave direction to our thought and life. We can understand the endless suprises of his attitudes, all actions; and these fall into their place if we remember his faith in democracy and freedom. He used the existing social and political institutions and breathed into them a new spirit, a new vitality. *Pt. Jawaharlal Nehru was a great believer in world peace and the concept of one world community. No one had shown greater faith and allegiance to the charter of the United Nations than Pt. Jawaharlal Nehru.* He realised that in thermo-nuclear age, war would mean the extinction of all civilised values. That is why he was convinced that the true role of a statesman in this distracted world lay in the way of lessening tensions and conflicts and bringing about a climate of understanding and mutual accomodation, with a view to the settlement of international differences without resort to the horrors of war."

President Radhakrishnan continued, "Nehru had a love of liberty, not merely for his own people but for all people of the world. He, therefore expressed sympathy and support for all liberation movements in Africa, Asia and South America. *He believed in the liberty of all without distinction of class, creed or country.* His courage, wisdom and personality held this country together. It is these qualities which should be cherished, if we are to hold on. *Our toughts today go out to him as a great emancipator of human race, one who has given all his life and energy to the freeing of men's minds from political bondage, economic slavery, social oppression and cultural stagnation.*"

Other glowing tributes. Besides the Indian President, the U.N. Security Council, leaders and press all over the world, heads and representatives of foreign governments, the Indian and Foreign Parliaments and the public in India and abroad paid their glowing tributes to the memory of Pt. Jawahar Lal Nehru, a great humanist and crusader for peace. Soviet Premier Khruschev said, "It is not only the people of India who are bereaved on the death of their friend and wise leader, the fighter for the independence and national regeneration of India. All progressive people mourn the death of Prime Minister Pt. Jawaharlal Nehru, the man who till the last hour of his life gave all his strength, his mind of a statesman and experience to the service of the lofty ideals of humanism, peace and progress." Former U.S. President Dwight D. Eisenhower said, "No one has ever doubted the Indian leader's sincere devotion to universal peace." Dr. Heinrich Lubeke, the President of Federal Germany, said, "With the death of Mr. Jawaharlal Nehru India and the whole mankind have lost an eminent statesman who was held in high esteem throughout the world as leader in the struggle for peace and international understanding."

"Without the foresight and leadership of Pt. Jawaharlal Nehru, the Modern Commonwealth would not exist today," declared the Duke of Devonshire, Minister of State of Commonwealth Relations and for Colonies, when paying a tribute in London on Sunday, June 14, 1964, to the Indian leader. Pt. Jawaharlal Nehru believed above all else in humanities of the world, the Duke said. He was one of the very few men who became a legend in their own lifetime. That he had become one was the highest measure of respect any human being could achieve. Throughout the world, Pt. Jawaharlal Nehru evoked not only admiration but love. *He stood for what was best. He was a man who believed in peace.* "I have no doubt", said the Duke, "that his greatness will continue to grow in the centuries to come." The Duke then referred to the particular debt the Commonwealth owed to the Indian leader. "It was his foresight and leadership that from 1947 turned the small group of mainly Anglo-Saxon countries into the vast free association of nations which made up the Commonwealth today."

Pt. Jawaharlal Nehru's Gratitude to the People for their Affection. It was the wish of Pt. Jawaharlal Nehru who served the nation with his sweat and blood for nearly half a century that even his ashes be strewn in the fields of India so that they might mingle with the dust of his motherland and become part of it. In a will, which he wrote on June 21, 1954, Pt. Jawaharlal Nehru said that a part of his ashes be consigned to the Ganga at Allahabad but the major portion of them should be carried up in an aeroplane and scattered from the height over the field where the peasants of India toil, so that they might mingle with the dust and soil of India and become an indistinguishable part of it. Consequently, Pt. Jawaharlal Nehru's wish was carried out and his ashes were scattered over different parts of India by the planes of Indian Air Force.

Dr. Radhakrishnan's call to finish the incomplete task of Pt. Jawaharlal Nehru. President Dr. Radhakrishnan told the nation on May 26, 1965 on the occasion of first death anniversary of Pt. Jawaharlal Nehru that the best way to honour his memory was to get on with the work which he left unfinished—his work for peace, justice and freedom at home and abroad. Pt. Jawaharlal Nehru spent lavishly his rich, and varied gifts for the cause of human freedom. He was involved in the major events of his time national and international. He participated in them all while maintaining the highest standard of public conduct. Though he is no more with us, the qualities he possessed and the ideals he cherished remain with us."

Dr. Radhakrishnan further observed : "Nehru was a deeply spiritual man, though he did not uphold any particular form of religion. Nehru had a versatile, penetrating and gracious mind but this did not exclude a tender heart. He loved life and was a man of intense feeling. He never lacked compassion for others. Nehru was essentially a man of peace. He hated war not as an abstraction, but of what it did to man. He loathed the instincts of fear and hatred which caused wars, the suffering it inflicted and the destruction of values it resulted in"

President Dr. Radhakrishnan further remarked, "Nehru tried to apply ethical principles to potential problems. Under his guidance India took a leading part in the peace keeping operations of the United Nations—in Korea, Gaza and the Cango. He tried to prevent the division of the world into the two moving camps. He had a deep respect for Parliamentary institutions. The spread of scientific outlook and industrialisation of the country are due, to no small extent, to the influence of Nehru who strove to free the common people from shackles of poverty, disease and illiteracy and discrimination. Therefore, the best way to honour his memory is to get on with the work which he left unfinished, his work for peace, justice and freedom at home and abroad.

LAL BAHADUR SHASTRI (1904-1966)

Early Career. Lal Bahadur Shastri was born in 1904 on October 2 (thus sharing his birthday with Mahatma Gandhi) at Mughalsarai in Varanasi district of Uttar Pradesh. His father Sharda Prasad was a poor school teacher who, in later years, held a minor government post. Lal Bahadur Shastri was barely a year and half when his father died. The infant and his two sisters were brought up by his maternal grandfather who was materially little better off. He received his early education at an ordinary school of Varanasi. When Lal Bahadur was eleven years old, he first caught glimpse of Mahatma Gandhi who had come in 1915 to lay the foundation of the Banaras Hindu University. It made a deep impression on him. When Mahatma Gandhi gave a call in 1921 at the time of Non-Cooperation Movement to the youths of this country to leave their studies and help him in liberating the country, then Lal Bahadur Shastri who was only sixteen years old at that time and was about to appear in matriculation examination, gave up his studies for the time being and joined the National Movement. He courted arrest and remained in prison for some time. After his release from jail, in 1921, he joined the Kashi Vidya Peeth where he came under the liberal influence of Acharya Narendra Dev, Dr. Bhagwan Das and his son, Shri Prakash, Dr. Sampurnanand and Acharya Kriplani who were dedicated to Mahatma Gandhi's cause of disseminating the ideas of non-violent struggle against the alien rule for the attainment of Purna Swaraj. Lal Bahadur Shastri was a brilliant student and he passed with ease the Shastri Examination. Since then he began to be called Lal Bahadur Shastri.

Lal Bahadur Shastri came into contact with Lala Lajpat Rai in 1925 who was then organising his Servants of the People Society. He became its life member in 1926 and settled in Allahabad. After that he came into intimate contact with Pt. Jawaharlal Nehru. He did a laudable work for Harijan uplift, a cause which was the dearest to Mahatma Gandhi and Pt. Jawaharlal Nehru. In 1935 Lal Bahadur Shastri was elected the General Secretary of Uttar Pradesh Congress Committee. In 1937, he was elected a member of Uttar Pradesh Legislature. Here he worked incessantly for the welfare of the people. He forged an enduring association with Pt. Govind Ballabh Pant, who exercised tremendous influence on him. Pt. Gobind Vallabh Pant was the acknowledged leader of Uttar Pradesh at that time and Lal Bahadur Shastri worked with him in the Indian National Congress with a great zeal.

Lal Bahadur Shastri was picked up by Mahatma Gandhi in 1940 for individual Satyagraha. He was again elected as a member of Uttar Pradesh Legislative Assembly in 1941 and remained up till 1946. He courted imprisonment many a time for the liberation of his country and spent in all 9 years of his precious life in British prison. He even did not waste this time and wrote certain good books in Hindi, notably a biography of Madam Curie.

As a Road and Ttansport Minister and Home Minister of Uttar Pradesh. Chief Minister Govind Ballabh Pant of Uttar Pradesh appointed Lal Bahadur first as his Parliamentary Secretary and later as a full-fledged Minister and entrusted him the portfolio of Home and Transport. He reorganised and reformed Uttar Pradesh Police and introduced the Uttar Pradesh. Government Roadways service, a model nationalised system of inter-town road transportation that has since found followers among different State Governments.

As a Great Organiser and Railway Minister. In 1951, Pt. Jawaharlal Nehru asked Lal Bahadur Shastri to resign Uttar Pradesh Ministership and accept the post of the General Secretary of the Congress Party. Lal Bahadur Shastri did so at the bidding of Pt. Jawaharlal Nehru and organised the election campaign in 1952 for the Congress Party so well that it easily swept the polls. After this everybody was convinced about his talents as an organiser and administrator. In 1952 he was elected as a member of the Rajya Sabha and nominated Minister of Railways and Transport in the New Central Cabinet. *His tenure as Railway Minister came to an end in a dramatic manner because he resigned in 1956 as a result of a major Railway accident at Ariyalpur in South India. Though* he was not at all personally responsible for that Railway Accident, yet in order to establish good traditions about constitutional responsibility, he did so. Lal Bahadur Shastri made many reforms in the Railways and increased their capacity. In 1957 he again organised the Congress Machinery for Second General Election with great efficiency and greatly lightened the burden of Pt. Jawaharlal Nehru. In 1957, he was elected as member of the Lok Sabha. He was first appointed as a Minister of Transport and Communication but later on after the reshuffle of Cabinet, he was appointed as a Minister of Commerce and Industry. Lal Bahadur Shastri did a lot of work to promote cottage industries in the villages.

As Home Minister of India. On the death of Pt. Govind Ballabh Pant, Lal Bahadur Shastri took over the Ministry of Home Affairs on April 4, 1961. Till then he was known only as a good organiser of party and elections and impartial man for selecting Congress candidates but now fell the responsibility upon his shoulders of resolving the States' wranglings and solving many intricate and intractable problems. He performed his task admirably. In 1963 he was sent on a goodwill mission to Nepal because much misunderstanding had developed between the two countries up to that time. Lal Bahadur Shastri's mission was a great success and he cleared all misunderstanding. In August, 1963, Lal Bahadur Shastri once again resigned under Kamraj Plan to revitalise Congress but due to the illness of Pt. Jawaharlal Nehru he was again appointed as a Minister without Portfolio in order to solve his huge burden of office. After the death of Pt. Jawaharlal Nehru, the mantle of the nation's leadership fell on Lal Bahadur Shastri as he assumed office of Prime Minister on June 9, 1964.

As Prime Minister. Lal Bahadur Shastri had to face a difficult task after his assumption of the office of the Prime Minister. He had to take far-reaching decisions on the matter of planning, rising prices and food crisis. On all these matters his decisions were marked by pragmatism and flexibility. He took a difficult decision of allowing Sheikh Abdullah to go abroad ostensibly on a pilgrimage. Sheikh Abdullah misused this privilege and delivered such speeches which seemed to create much misunderstanding in Muslim countries about Kashmir. For this Lal Bahadur Shastri was much criticised by the opposition parties. Therefore, the government had to imprison Sheikh Abdullah again.

In order to raise food production, Lal Bahadur Shastri raised the slogan of *Jai Kisan.* He helped the agriculturist as he could do to raise production in order to meet food shortage and check the rising prices and save foreign exchange. He realised the persisting threat of invasion on the borders of the country, so he raised the slogan of *Jai Jawan.* He had to build up the heavy defences of the country because of the continuing hostility of China and Pakistan. He equipped the armed forces very well so that it may be able to defend the integrity and sovereignty of the country.

In the realm of foreign affairs Lal Bahadur Shastri continued to seek friendship with all countries of the world irrespective of their ideology or political systems. Lal Bahadur Shastri said, "We will steer clear of alignment with power blocs and pursue an independent policy. We adhere to the policy of non-alignment, co-existence, disarmament, anti-colonialism and antiraclism. But if the path of peace and negotiation is discarded and aggression is committed, we are duty bound to safeguard our freedom and to defend our frontiers. In such a situation we would consider no sacrifice too great. *Our responsibility for the preservation of our freedom is higher than any other responsibility. I want to make it clear that we have no desire whatsoever to take even an inch of any other country's territory.* In fact such an idea never occurs to our mind. At the same time we are determined that we will not allow any part of our territory to be annexed by force by any other country, no matter what its alignment and what its power."

Lal Bahadur Shastri went to many foreign countries like United Kingdom, Egypt, Canada, Burma, Belgrade and Russia. He impressed greatly all countries by his simplicity, warmth of friendship, sincerity, sagaciousness, foresight and clear grasp of international problems.

In the beginning of 1965, Pakistan started the violations of Kutch territory. After that Pakistan launched a full-scale attack of Kutch Territory and occupied with ease Kanjarkot on February 10, 1965, and Sardar Post on April 10, 1965, since there was no army of ours at Kutch border, but only police force. Pakistan occupied Biarbet and Point 84 on April 29, 1965. These were very anxious moments for Lal Bahadur Shastri and he immediately ordered the army to meet the challenge of Pakistani Aggression. Our army at once took the positions and checked the further advance of Pakistani Army. After this through the untiring efforts of Mr. Wilson, Prime Minister of Great Britain, a deadlock between India and Pakistan over Kutch was resolved and it was agreed that the matter would be ultimately decided by a Tribunal.

Pakistan was not content with this. She was training her armed personnel to infiltrate into Kashmir and overthrow the Government of Jammu and Kashmir by means of force even when she had concluded a pact about kutch. Ayub Khan, President of Pakistan, had concluded from the Kutch rehearsal that Indian Army was weak in comparison with the Pakistani Force. So, he sent infiltrators in large number to Kashmir in the 1st week of August, 1965. In the beginning of September 1965, Pakistani Forces launched a full-scale invasion on Kashmir Valley. After this Pakistan bombarded the airbase of Amristar. Under these circumstances Lal Bahadur Shastri had no alternative except to defend the country with full might. The army and air force were ordered to attack Western Pakistan's Military Bases. 'Our armed forces defeated Pakistani Army in the various tank battles and reached near Lahore and Sialkat, so the pride of Pakistan was shattered. Lal Bahadur Shastri emerged from this conflict a successful war leader. Through the noble efforts of Mr. U. Thant, Secretary-General of the United Nations, a cease-fire was agreed to between India and Pakistan.

Lal Bahadur Shastri reiterated, "that no pressure or attacks will deflect us from our firm resolve to maintain the sovereignty and territorial integrity of our country. If the Security Council does not identify the aggressor, and equates it with the party aggressed, chances of peace will fade out." He paid glowing tributes to the armed forces for its unparalleled heroism and great sacrifices.

Mr. Kosygin, Prime Minister of U.S.S.R., arranged a meeting between Lal Bahadur Shastri and President Ayub Khan at Tashkent in the first week of January, 1966 to restore normalcy between the relations of two countries. Through the ceaseless efforts of Mr. Kosygin an agreement was signed between the Indian Prime Minister Lal Bahadur Shastri and Pakistani President Ayub Khan. According to this agreement both India and Pakistan had to agree to renounce force for settling international disputes, surrender each other's gains of the war and restore pre-war boundaries. Both India and Pakistan had to return each other's captured goods, men and money and to restore diplomatic relations. Though it was obvious that India, being a victor, was in no way gainer by this agreement and she had to lose her strategic positions like Haji Pir pass, Tithwal, Kargil Post and others which she had occupied with very great difficulty and at a cost of tremendous sacrifice, yet it was a great courage on the part of Lal Bahadur Shastri to append his signature to this agreement.

Lal Bahadur Shastri's Death. Lal Bahadur Shastri died of heart attack at Tashkent (Russia) at 1.02 a.m. on January 11, 1966, less than nine and a half hours after signing of the Historic Tashkent Declaration. The whole world was deeply shocked at this international tragedy. President Dr. Radhakrishanan paid glowing tributes to Lal Bahadur Shastri and said that the highest honour of Bharat Ratna which he wanted to confer on him would now be given posthumously. In a broadcast to the nation on January 11, 1966, Dr. Radhakrishnan said that Lal Bahadur Shastri was a Determined Nationalist. At Tashkent he died pledging India and Pakistan to end their bitterness. A grateful nation is in deep mourning." Mr. Kosygin said, "It is a sad loss in which we all grieve with the Indian People. He was a great statesman, a great man with great wisdom and a man of great tact indeed. He did all he could do for peace and for Indo-Pakistan Friendship." Dr. Zakir Hussain, who was Vice-President at that time said, "Lal Bahadur Shastri was a man of peace and he laid down his life at the altar of peace." President Johnson said, "Our nation mourns the death of Prime Minister Lal Bahadur Shastri. As the leader of the world's largest democracy, he had already gained a special place in American hearts. His tragic loss after fruitful discussion at Tashkent, is a grievous blow to the hopes of mankind for peace and progress." Similar glowing tributes were received from all parts of the world.

KHAN ABDUL GAFFAR KHAN (1890-1988)

Khan Abdul Gaffar Khan, also known as Badshah Khan or Frontier Gandhi was born in 1890 at Hastanagar in Utmanzai village of Peshawar District. From the very beginning he spurned a life of affluence and ease and absolutely set out to awaken the Pathans whose backwardness was appalling.

So strong was his urge for the uplift of his people that he refused a king's commission in the British Army and threw away a chance to go to England for higher studies.

The Frontier Gandhi gained prominence when he led an agitation in the Frontier Provinces in 1919 against the Rowlatt Act which was enacted to restrict severely political activity in India.

Though he met Mahatma Gandhi and Pt. Jawaharlal Nehru for the first time at the Congress Meeting in Lucknow in 1929, he was attracted towards them nine years earlier, when he attended the Nagpur Congress in 1920. Since then he continued his struggle for the freedom of the country.

Gaffar Khan played a very prominent role in the Civil Disobedience Movement. He was released from Gujarat jail in 1931 in keeping with the Gandhi-Irwin Pact. In 1932 he was again arrested by Lord Willingdon for the no-rent campaign. The Governor-General also wanted to repress the Congress Movement but his effort was doomed to failure. In 1934 the Congress offered him the Presidentship of the party but he declined saying he was a born soldier and would die as one. Afterwards he played a notable role in the Quit India Movement.

Between 1920 and 1947, Gaffar Khan spent a total of 14 years in jail. He opposed the Muslim League and its communal politics throughout his career. He opposed the partition of the country tooth and nail but when the Congress in its helplessness, agreed to the partition of the country tooth and nail but when the Congress in its helplessness, agreed to the partition of the country owing to the dirty intrigues of the British Imperialists, and very serious communal riots were spread by the Muslim League, he told Mahatma Gandhi that the pathans have been thrown to wolves (Muslim Leaguers). However, Mahatma Gandhi bade him last farewell at the Delhi Railway Station in extremely sad mood.

Badshah Khan's sufferings continued even after independence because he opted for Pakistan where his home was situated. He spent 16 years of his precious life in the Pakistani jails because he stood for Pakhtoonistan. The condition of Pakistani jails was even more barbaric than the British jails. He was declared the prisoner of the year 1962 by 'Amnesty International' London. He attended the Congress Centenary Celebrations at Bombay in December 1985. He came for medical treatment twice to India. Lastly, he came for treatment in August, 1987. He was awarded the Bharat Ratna (the highest honour) on August 14, 1987 for the heroic role he played in the Indian Freedom Struggle and also in recognition of his relentless fight for independence, peace and non-violence.

The award was received by his son, Khan Abdul Wali Khan at a brief but glittering special investiture ceremony held at Darbar Hall of Rashtrapati Bhawan. The Frontier Gandhi was undergoing treatment at the All India Institute of Medical Sciences, New Delhi. The President R. Venkatraman handed over the award to Wali Khan amid applause from the distinguished gathering which included the then Prime Minister, Rajiv Gandhi, Mrs. Sonia Gandhi, the Speaker Mr. Balram Jakhar, the three service chiefs, members of the Union Council of Ministers, MPs and some members of the Khan family. Wali Khan afterwards said, "It showed that at least one part of the sub-continent was grateful to Badshah Khan."

Death and Homage. Khan Abdul Gaffar Khan had been flown to Peshawar on August 16, 1987 in an unconscious condition. He remained in coma till his death on January 20, 1988 in an unconscious condition. He remained in coma till his death on January 20, 1988 at 6-45 P.M. in Lady Reading Hospital, Peshawar. Khan Abdul Gaffar Khan was 98 years old, when he breathed his last. He was a stalwart of India's Freedom Struggle and personified Mahatma Gandhi's ideals. The then President R. Venkat Raman, in condolence message from Vijaywada said —

"Khan Abdul Gaffar Khan was one of the great leaders of out time. His long adventurous life symbolished the aspirations of the North-West Frontier for an identity. He was unswerving in his commitment to the cause of Pakhtoons and was as Gandhiji described him, their uncrowned king."

The then Vice-President, Shankar Dayal Sharma said, "The late leader epitomised humanist way of life. He presented the eternal human values of Mahatma Gandhi and the great generation which tought for freedom on the sub-continent. As a Khudai Khidmatgar, service of his fellowmen was the sole purpose of his endeavour throughout his life. Millions in India saw in him great kindness, simplicity, purity of purpose and powerful will. He was a friend of India who yearned to see the peace in the sub-continent.

The then Prime Minister, Rajiv Gandhi said in the death of Gaffar Khan, "The last of towering giants of our freedom struggle has gone."

"Khan Abdul Gaffar Khan was one of the tallest of Mahatma Gandhi's associates. He was respected and loved for his uncompromising integrity, courage and sacrifice. Rugged as the mountains where he was born, Badshah Khan became a byword for his steadfast devotion to non-violence. The transformation of fiery Pathans into Khudai Khidmatgars under his leadership is a great saga in the history of human spirit.

The Union Cabinet said in a resolution :

The death of Badshah Khan marks the end of an era. He was a titan of India's struggle for freedom. He belonged to that galaxy of eminent men—Jawaharlal Nehru, Vallabh Bhai Patel, Abul Kalam Azad, Rajendra Prasad, C. Rajgopalachari, Sarojini Naidu and many others who under the inspiring leadership of Mahatma Gandhi, led India to freedom. He participated in successive Satyagraha movements and spent many years in Jail.

"Like Mahatma Gandhi, Badshah Khan was an apostle of non-violence. Rightly was he known as 'FRONTIER GANDHI'. Thank to his leadership, the valiant pathans of the North-West-Frontier Province espoused non-violence. This achievement had few parallels in human history.

"Frontier Gandhi's life was a saga of peace, goodwill and good fellowship among our peoples."

In the end we can say that with monumental patience and perseverance, the Frontier Gandhi, as Khan Abdul Gaffar Khan came to be popularly known, spread the twin message of non-violence and Indian Nationalism among the people.

EXERCISES

Long Answer Type Questions

1. What do you know about Lokmanya Bal Gangadhar Tilak ? Discuss his contribution in Indian National Movement.
2. What do you you know about Gopal Krishna Gokhale? What is his contribution in Indian National Movement ?
3. Who was Sir Sayed Ahmad Khan ? Discuss his contribution in Indian National Movement.
4. What do you know about Annies Besent ? What is her Contribution in Indian National Movement?

5. What do you know about Lala Lajpat Rai ? Discuss his contribution In Indian National Movement.
6. What do you know about Bipin Chandra Pal ? What is his contribution in Indian National Movement ?
7. What do you know about B.R.Ambedkar ? Discuss his contribution in Indian National Movement.
8. What do you know about Sardar Vallabh Bhai Patel ? Discuss his contribution in Indian National Movement.
9. What do you know about Pt. Jawahar Lal Nehru ? Discuss his contribution in Indian National Movement.
10. Write a brief note on the life sketch of Mahatma Gandhi.
11. Discuss the contribution of Mahatma Gandhi in Indian National Movement.

Short Answer Type Questions

1. Write a brief note on Pt. Motilal Nehru.
2. Write a short note on khan Abdul Gaffar Khan.
3. Discuss the contribution of Mahatma Gandhi in Quit India Movement.
4. What was Satyagraha ? Discuss the contribution of Satyagraha in Indian National Movement.
5. What is meant by ahimsa ? Discuss the views of Mahatma Gandhi on Ahimsa.

APPENDIX

Heroic Struggle For Freedom In Assam

ASSAM AND FIRST INDIAN WAR OF INDEPENDENCE, 1857

In 1832, the British restored Purander Singh, the last independent Ahom King to the rulership of Upper Assam, as a tributary native prince because of the various rebellions in 1830, but the appetite of the imperialists was not statisfied and they deposed Purander Singh in 1838 and his territories were resumed by the British. The result was the lingering discontent in his royal house and amongst the upper classes who favoured his rule.

Maniram Dutt Dewan, an Assamese of distinguished personality had served the royal family in highly responsible position and also acted as an adviser to Purander Singh after his deposition and till his death in 1846. After that he served as an adviser to his son Kameswar Singh and grandson Kandarpeswar Singh. He was highlighted the evils of the British rule.

Repercussion of the revolt of 1857. It was on 6th May, 1857, only four days before the outbreak of the first armed struggle for freedom that Maniram Dewan had submitted to the Governor-General-in-Council a petition to restore young Kandarpeswar Singh for restoration to him at least a part of the ancient kingdom over which his forefathers ruled or to grant him a decent pension. When the news reached Maniram in Calcutta that Bahadur Shah had been proclaimed as the Emperor of Hindustan and all deposed princes were trying their level best to regain their possessions from the British Imperialists, he also organised an armed insurrection in Assam too for overthrowing the British and restoring the old native rule with Kandarpeswar Singh as the Raja of Assam. For that purpose the Kandarpeswar Singh, popularly known as Saring Raja made brisk preparations and the support of some jamadars of the British troops stationed at Dibrugarh and Golghat was obtained. Many leading men of the time including two Muslims Bhadur Gaonbura and Sheikh Formud Ali, actively joined the plot and others extended their sympathy. But unfortunately some of the letters of Maniram Dewan were intercepted by the District Officer of Sibsagar, Captain Charles Holroyd and the plot was foiled. It also seems that the scent of the plot had already been given by some members of the royal family whose support had been sought but did not support the revolt actually.

Martyrdom of Maniram Dewan and Peali Barua. To effect the arrest of Saring Raja, the District Officer of Sibsagar, Captain Charles Holroyd immediately called a contingent of British troops. The Raja's palace at Jorhat was attacked at night and he was arrested on September 7, 1857 and sent to Alipur Jail for detension. Maniram was also arrested at Calcutta and sent to Assam in a steamer on 31st December, 1857 after being detained in Alipur Jail. Many other patriots who took a leading part in organising the plot against the alien rule were arrested, notable amongst whom were Mahesh Chandra Barua alias Peali Barua, the Raja's right hand man and Madhu Mullik, a Bengali Musketeer sent by Maniram from Calcutta to help the Raja in his preparations. Caption Holroyd was appointed Special Commissioner under Act 14 of 1857 to try these conspiracy cases. *Maniram was tried on 23rd February*, 1858, *convicted of treason on inadequate grounds and publicly hanged on* 26 *of the same month at Jorhat with Peali Barua. Many others including Dantiram Barua, criminal sheristadar of Sibsagar, Madhu Mallik, Bahadur Gaonbura and Formud Ali, were given sentences of transportation or imprisonment.* The Saring Raja was not tried but kept in confinement first at Burdwan and later on at Gauhati. His whole property was seized by the British imperialists.

Disaffection in the local troops at Dibrugarh and Golghat amongst men of the First Assam Light Infantry and Local Artillery Corps was noticeable. Those men who were found implicated in the plot were court-martialled and sentenced to long terms of imprisonment. Thus, Assam played her prominent role in the first armed struggle for freedom. *It must never be forgotten that Maniram Dewan and Peali Barua became martyrs to the cause of freedom in Assam and their sacrifices did not go in vain because the later freedom fighters always took inspiration from their unparalleled martydom.*

ASSAM AFTER 1857

Between 1860 and 1900 there were agranian outbreaks in Assam, amongst whom the Phulagiri uprising of 1861, Manipur Rebellion and Rising of the Eastern Lushais, 1891, Assam Riots of 1893-94 were most famous. With the foundation of the Indian National Congress in 1885, there was a great national awakening throughout the country and Assam delegates also attended its sessions. After this there was a great cultural revival and many organisations wedded to the uplift of Assam came into existence. A new generation of Assamese literary men—Lakshminath Bezbarua, Chandra Kumar Agarwala, Padmanath Gohain Berua, Hem Chandra Goswami, Kamal Kanta Bhattacharya etc. renovated Assamese literature with the liberalism of the West and glorious traditions of Assam's past. Formation of national mind and rousing of political consciousness were the main achievements of some of these organisations. Modern journalism also took its shape in Assamese and English at this time and many newspapers began to be published.

After this *Assam Association* formed in 1903 by the educated gentry of Assam fought for the political rights of Assam and was able to achieve for it the status of Governor's Province instead of Chief Commissioner's Province given in 1874. Its ablest spokesman and President Nabin Chandra Bardoloi was able to get Assam included in the proposed MontaguChelmsford Reform Scheme in spite of the contrary recommendations of the Government of Assam.

Swadeshi Movement. Lord Curzon partitioned Bengal in 1905 and consequently the Swadeshi movement was started to get it annulled. Bipin Chandra Pal's stirring speeches before the Surma Valley Conference emitted burning flames of patriotism and their rays illumined the other valley too. The anti-partition movement succeeded in getting the partition of Bengal annulled in 1911, which was considered a settled fact by the British earlier. The Secretary of the Assam Association expressed satisfaction over the annulment of the partition and restoration of Assam the status quo because after the partition of Bengal, Assam had been tied up with East Bengal.

The Assam Students Conference in the 4th session held at Tejpur in 1919 under the Presidentship of Acharya P.C. Roy adopted a resolution sponsoring the use of Swadeshi in place of foreign goods. *In short, swadeshi Movement quickened the pace of nationalism.*

NON-CO-OPERATION MOVEMENT

The Montague-Chelmsford Reforms Scheme as embodied in the Government of India Act of 1919 failed to meet the aspirations of the people because India had helped Britain so much with men and money as no other country had helped. The British Government instead of giving Swaraj to India passed the repressive Rowlatt Act to curb the freedom of the Indians. When Mahatma Gandhi and other leaders of the Indian National Congress objected to the Rowlatt Act and gave a call *hartal*, then there was the massacre of Jallianwala Bagh. Therefore, the Indian National Congress in a special session held at Calcutta in September, 1920 under the Chairmanship of Lala Lajpat Rai decided to launch the great Non-Co-operation Movement. The Congress led by Mahatma Gandhi invented a new method of non-violent Non-Co-operation to wrest freedom from the British Imperialists. Nabin Chandra Bardoloi who attended the Nagpur Session of the Congress in December, 1920 from Assam supported the movement and he appealed to the people and the press to accept the Non-Co-operation. Later on the Assam Association was substituted by the Assam Provincial Congress Committee and all the politics of Assam became a part of All-India Movements.

Though Lokmanya Bal Gangadhar Tilak had first said that '*Swaraj is our birthright and we will have it*' and had accelerated the new spirit of nationalism generated by Swadeshi, yet it was Mahatma Gandhi who created mass awakening and presented a new method and technique of Satyagraha to fight the British Imperialists. The Father of Non-co-operation with an alien government was Lokmanya Bal Gangadhar Tilak when he got adopted the programme of Swadeshi and Boycott in the Congress Session held at Benaras in 1905. When Mahatma Gandhi started the Non-Co-operation Movement, then the history of freedom movement in India turned a new leaf because Mahatma Gandhi canalised the powerful currents of agitation engendered by the Punjab Atrocities and the Khilafat Movement in the great non-violent Non-Co-operation Movement of 1921. After this the Gandhi cap and Tricolour Flag of the Congress, with the emblem of the Charkha on it, became symbol of National Honour. Bankim Chandra's *Vandematram* song was sung as a National Anthem. All the peasants, labourers and the students played the most important role.

Non-co-operation Movement in Assam. In January, 1921, the students of Assam following the decision of the All-India students' Conference held at Nagpur in December, 1920 to participate in the Non-Co-operation Movement started a strong agitation for the boycot of schools and colleges. The contribution of the students for the success of Non-Co-operation Movement was noteworthy. Besides that the people adopted the programme of Swadeshi, boycott of foreign goods, law-courts and councils, propagation of Khaddar and picketing of liquor and opium shops was also adopted. Non-co-operation began to be preached from the press and platform and prominent leaders Nabin Chandra Bordoloi, Tarunram Phukan, Chandranath Sharma, Gopinath Bardoloi, Bishnuram Mehadi and many others addressed large gatherings at several places. The visit of Mahatma Gandhi along with Ali brothers in August, 1921 gave fillip to the movement throughout Assam. Mahatma Gandhi addressed mass meetings at Gauhati, Tejpur, Nowgong, Jorhat, Dibrugarh, Silchar, Sylhet and many other places. People burned large heaps of foreign cloth. Women adopted the programme of spinning on a large scale. Women led by Mrs. T.R. Phukan and his widowed sister Girija Debi, the wife of N.C. Bardoloi (Hemant Kumar Debi) and his widowed sister Dharmda Sundri Devi also contributed their mite to the success of the movement. A new awakening came amongst the women and they rose to the new responsibilities of winning freedom for the country when men had gone to the jails. Consequently, Mahatma Gandhi could not remain without admiring the unique contribution of the brave people of Assam to the Non-Co-operation Movement.

Repression. The British Government was quite apprehensive of large gatherings in the meetings, therefore it let loose the severest repression. The British authorities arrested a large number of political workers, leaders, peasants, students and others. They were beaten mercilessly. Meetings were dispersed by the police and the satyagrahis were lathicharged. All sorts of hardships had to be borne by all the political workers and leaders. There were no categories in jails those days and the political prisoners including the leaders had to suffer many indignities including their handcuffing. Ban was imposed on newspapers from printing the news of the repression. But the people withstood all the horrors fo the jail-life cheerfully because they had imbibed the lesson of non-violence preached by Mahatma Gandhi and did not consider any sacrifice too great for the cause of the freedom. Anyhow, the year 1921 gave Assam a definite place of distinction in the fight for freedom.

The Non-co-operation Movement also caused great awakening amongst the labourers of Assam, who were being badly exploited by the European tea-planters. So there were strikes in many tea-gardens in 1921 and there was mass exodus but the Government would not let them migrate easily. They were beaten mercilessly at Chandpur Railway station which evoked strong protests from the press. Even C.F.Andrews commented adversely against the British Government. Leaders of the Assam Congress, complained bitterly to the All India Congress about the severe repression that was still going on in Assam even after the suspension of the movement due to violence at Chauri-Chaura (Gorakhpur). Consequently, Dr. Rajendra Prasad and Pandit Madan Mohan Malviya visited Assam. Later on Rajaji (Shri Rajagopalacharia) also visited Assam and the repression was stopped.

Swaraj Party. After the Non-cooperation Movement, Swaraj Party in Assam did laudable work in Assam also which was led by T.R.Phukan in consultation with C.R. Das. Eight Swarajists returned to the Council of Assam. Joined by an equal number of Independents and sometimes even more, the Swarajist Members led by Moulvi Faiznur Ali, functioned with considerable effectiveness in criticising government actions, voting down unpopular measures and carrying through motions or resolutions of popular import. The Coalition Group succeeded in carrying a resolution to the effect that immediate steps be taken by the authorities concerned to establish full responsible government in Assam. A resolution was also carried for the formation of an Opium Enquiry Committee. The other achievement of the Group was the election of Gopendralal Das as the Deputy President of the Legislative Council. The motto of the Swarajists was to wrcek the Constitution from within and the party successfully carried out the policy of obstruction in the Council. Besides that 41st session of the Indian National Congress was held in December 1926 at Pandu near Gauhati. It was a great success as it roused national consciousness.

THE CIVIL DISOBEDIENCE MOVEMENT OF 1930-32

The Indian National Congress passed the resolution of complete independence on December 31, 1929 at Lahore under the Presidentship of Pandit Jawaharlal Nehru. It was also decided that January 26 was henceforth to be observed as Independence Day every year and a pledge was to be read by Congressmen to continue the fight against the British Government which had *"ruined India economically, politically, culturally and spiritually."* The Congress directed all its legislatures to resign their seats and prepare the country for Civil Disobedience Movement.

Assam was second to none in its sacrifices for the cause of the freedom of the country. So during 1930-32 Assam followed the pattern of All India Civil Disobedience Movement. Therefore, repressive laws and ordinances were defied, British goods were boycotted and salt laws were violated. Bishnu Ram Mehdi, President of the Assam Provincial Congress, led the movement fearlessly and he was ably assisted by Hem Chandra Barua, a genious of the Assam Congress and other leaders like N.C. Bardoloi, Omeo Kumar Das, Dr. Bhubaneshwar Barua, Siddhirath Sharma, Dibeshwar Sharma, Satradhikar Goswami of Gramur, Harendra Chandra Chowdhury, Rajendra Nath Barua, Lakshmi Dhar Sharma. Women too joined the movement in large number. Chandraprova Saikiani and Durgaprova Bora led the women organisation and picketted before the Cotton College at Gauhati. It is noteworthy that the students also played prominent part in the movement. The alien Government let loose the wheel of repression. All the leaders and workers, men and women both were lathi-charged and thrown into prison. Besides that their property was confiscated. But all these sufferings did not cool their enthusiasm. The people were ready to sacrifice everything for the cherished goal of freedom. The movement continued uptill 1934. After that Government of India enacted the Act of 1935.

EVENTS AFTER CIVIL DISOBEDIENCE MOVEMENT

The British had not given any thing substantial in the Government of India Act, 1935, but still the Congress decided to fight the elections according to this Act, which took place in February, 1937. The Congress won a huge majority in seven provinces out of eleven provinces. In Assam Syed Mohammad Saadulla, the leader of a Muslim Group formed the Ministry with the support of the European Group and other tribal and non-tribal members. The Congress Group was not even consulted by the Governor but the Saadulla Ministry was not popular and it had to face as many as eleven defeats through cut motions and resolutions in the first Budget Session that it faced. Mohammad Saadulla tendered his resignation on September 13, 1938. The resignation of Saadulla Ministry was accepted on 19-9-38 and after that Gopinath Bardoloi, the Leader of the Congress Party in the legislature formed the Ministry with the support of a number of independents and Muslim Members outside the Muslim League who had been dissatisfied with the working of the previous Ministry. The Congress Ministry adopted such alleviating measures as prohibition of opium, reduction of the landrevenue, restoration of lands confiscated by Government for failure to pay revenue due to poverty, restriction of immigration into Assam and safeguarding the interests of the indigenous population etc. But the most important Bill which the Ministry initiated was the Assam Agricultural Income Tax Bill which meant taxing the rich for the benefit of the poor. Therefore it was opposed tooth and nail by the European tea-planters of Assam but passed in spite of their opposition.

The Second World War and the Resignation of Congress Ministry. On 3rd September, 1939 Second World War broke out in Europe and Britain joined it. Lord Linlithgow, the Viceroy also declared that India had joined the War and did not even consult the representatives of Indian political parties. Consequently, the Indian National Congress objected to it and refused to be a party to Britain's imperialistic war ambitions and contribute to the war efforts unless India's demand for freedom was conceded at least in a substantial form. The British Government was not at all willing to concede this demand of the Congress. Therefore, the Congress Working Committee directed its ministries in the provinces to resign. By October-November, 1939 the Congress Ministries in eight provinces including the Coalition Ministry in Assam resigned their offices. Muhammad Ali Jinnah, then President of the Muslim League, taking advantage of this political situation, observed a Day of Deliverance and in March, 1940 advanced his demand for the partition of the country but the Congress without caring for it, advanced towards the goal of freedom steadily. The British Government was not at all willing to concede the demand of the Congress for the control of Defence during war time, though the Japanese had conquered the territory upto Burma and reached the gates of India.

QUIT INDIA MOVEMENT AND ASSAM

Ultimately, the Congress Working Committee decided that British must leave India to its fate. So, All India Congress Committee passed the famous '*Quit India Resolution*' on August 8, 1942. The British Government which had made huge preparations to meet the challenge of the Congress arrested all the leaders of the Congress next day. The Congress was declared as an illegal body and all its workers were arrested and offices sealed. When the people organised meetings and processions for the release of their beloved leaders, then there was firing by the police. In Bombay, Delhi and other cities of India the police fired several rounds.

Assam whih had passed through the ordeal in 1921 and 1930-32 did not lag behind other provinces in this historic battle. With '*do or die*' slogan given by Mahatma Gandhi, the people jumped into the fray unmindful of the British Government's atrocities and economic hardships due to the war which was at their gate. Muhammad Tayebullah, President Gopinath Bar-doloi, Siddhinath

Sharma, Fakhruddin Ali Ahmed, Bishnu Ram Mehdi, Deveshwar Sharma, Chief Whip of the Congress Party, Dr. Harkishan Das, Lila Barua etc. were arrested on 9th August (next day). Women and the students also participated in large number. The masses, left to themselves, initiated struggle of such a magnitude that, at least for a few months, the functioning of the normal government became extremely difficult. All sorts of brutalities were perpetrated by the police and the military who sometimes ran amuck in suppressing the popular revolt. People were savagely beaten, whipped, tortured, kicked and knocked down even in police lockups. At least one thousand people were the victims of such savagery. *Kushal Konwar and Kamala Viri were two of the top-ranking martyrs of this freedom struggle.* Imprisonment of hundreds of students for participatig in the '*Quit India Movement*' occupies a distinct place in the record of repression. Forced labour was also exacted from the villagers for safegurarding railway and telegraph lines. Levying of Punitive tax or collective fines was another method used extensively by the Government to repress the popular movement. According to the Congress estimates collective fines amounted to ₹ 3,86,911, out of which ₹ 2,13,815 were realised. Defence of India Rules were applied strictly and all sorts of freedom were curbed. Summing up the report on the atrocities of the 1942 Movement, Gopinath Bardoloi, former Chief Minister of Assam said :

"These deaths, injuries, humiliations and atrocities are the price of liberty, a price country is asked to pay for its desire to be free. Our people know that and therefore they are determined as never before to do or die. Untold miseries may be heaped on our people, but the caravan of India goes on to its destined goal—independence full and undiluted."

The Grouping Plan and Assam. The Cabinet's Mission's Plan to 'group' Assam with Bengal for creating a predominantly Muslim zone in Eastern India like the one proposed to be set up in western India was strongly opposed by the leaders and people of Assam alike because this had been done in order to create the essence of Pakistan. In this way separate cultural identity of Assam would have been lost for ever and Assam would have been permanently merged with Bengal because Jinnah would never have allowed Assam to opt out of Bengal. The whole Grouping was compulsory according to Cabinet Mission Plan. On July 16, 1946 the Assam Legislative Assembly adopted a resolution moved by Chief Minister Bardoloi himself expressing strong disapproval of the plan and directing the ten representatives of Assam to the Constituent Assembly not to sit in Group C with Bengal for devising the Constitution of Assam. Shri Gopinath Bardoloi met Mahatma Gandhi and convinced him of the genuineness of the cause of Assam. Thereafter, Pandit Jawaharlal Nehru, then President of Congress also strongly opposed the grouping of Provinces. Mohammad Ali Jinnah taking the advantage of Nehru's statement at once discarded the whole plan. Thus, Assam was saved from disaster.

ACHIEVEMENT OF FREEDOM

Lord Wavell was replaced by Lord Mountbatten in March 1947. The New Viceroy after studying the prevalent political situation soon became convinced that there was no alternative to Pakistan (partition of country) if India was to be given independence. According to Maulana Abul Kalam Azad, Sarder Vallabh Bhai Patel was the first top leader who nodded his assent to partition because he had the bitterest experience of the obstruction tactics of the League in the Interim Government. After this Pt. Jawaharlal Nehru and other leaders also agreed but Maulana Abul Kalam Azad and Khan Abdul Gaffar Khan did not agree to the partition upto the last. Mahatma Gandhi agreed to it when he saw no other alternative. Therefore, the Congress passed a resolution that Bengal and Punjab must be partitioned, and Assam should not be included in East Pakistan. Only one Muslim majority district of Assam, Sylhet opted for East Pakistan by means of referendum. Therefore, except for four thanas, Sylhet was transferred to East Pakistan and Mohammad Ali Jinnah got '*truncated and moth eaten Pakistan.*' After this India won freedom on August 15,1947. Thus, the unparalleled sacrifices and sufferings of millions of people of our country bore fruit and India at last achieved her cherished goal.

In the words of Rajaji (C. Rajgopalachari) Non-Co-operation blossomed forth into Independence. It is admitted on all hands that the unique character of the freedom struggle adopted by the Congress will inspire generations to come not only in this country but all the subject-nations of the world to fight against imperialism. India achieved freedom not by the policy of 'blood and iron' but by 'Truth and Non-violence' advocated by Mahatma Gandhi. There in no example in the whole history of the world so far when a subject people gets independence in this way. It will not be exaggeration to say that Mahatma Gandhi with his weapon Truth and Non-violence humbled the might of British imperialists who always boasted of having ultimately scored a crowning victory over the nasty forces of imperialism. When Mahatma Gandhi, Architect of India's freedom, was assassinated on January 30, 1948 at a prayer meeting in New Delhi, he became a martyr to the world peace.

PART – III

MODERN INDIAN CONSTITUTION

(GREATEST INSTRUMENT OF LEGAL POLITICAL SYSTEM)

1. Framing of the Constitution: ITS Basic Objectives and Philosophy
2. Sources of the Constitution
3. Salient Features of India's New Constitution
4. Nature of the Federal System
5. Fundamental Rights and Duties
6. Directive Principles of State Policy *(Positive Directions for State)*
7. The Union Executive *(The President)*
8. The Union Executive *(The Council of Ministers)*
9. Vice-President
10. Union Parliament
11. Reorganisation of States
12. The Role of Governor in State Politics
13. The State Council of Ministers and Chief Minister
14. Relations Between the Union and the States
15. Zonal Councils
16. Supreme Court
17. The State High Courts
18. Administration of Delhi and Other Union Territories
19. Social Justic and Weaker Sections
20. Amendments of the Indian Constitution
21. The Comptroller and Auditor-General and Attorney-General of India
22. Public Services (Bureaucracy) and Public Service Commission
23. Planning Commission and Five-Year Plans
24. Mid-Term Appraisal of the Eleventh Five-Year Plan
25. District Administration in India
26. Panchayati Raj or Local Self-Government
27. Pressure Groups *(Anonymous Empire)*

1

CHAPTER

Framing of the Constitution: Its Basic Objectives and Philosophy

THE FRAMING OF THE NEW CONSTITUTION AND THE PROBLEMS FACED BY THE CONSTITUENT ASSEMBLY

Constituent Assembly. The elections to the Constituent Assembly were held under the Cabinet Mission Plan in July, 1946. Out of 210 general seats, the Congress won 199 and the Muslim League captured 73 seats out of a total 78 Muslim seats. To the Constituent Assembly many top ranking Congress and Muslim League leaders, veteran statesmen, seasoned administrators and eminent jurists and public men drawn from all walks of life were elected. The Constituent Assembly was scheduled to meet on December 9, 1946, but the Muslim League boycotted it and it demanded a separate Constituent Assembly and the establishment of Pakistan. In the Mountbatten Plan, the demand for the establishment of Pakistan and a separate Constituent Assembly for her was conceded.

The Constituent Assembly of India, constituted on the pattern laid down in the Cabinet Mission Plan, met on 9th December, 1946, to accomplish the historic and the most arduous task of drafting a Constitution for free India. The Constitution-making body was not, in fact, a sovereign body. It had to draw up a Constitution within the framework of the Mission Plan. It had to keep in view and honour the obligations of the outgoing British Government towards the minorities and Indian States. The final draft also needed the approval of the British Government for the stamp of finality.

Last but not least baffling problem was that of the Princely States. The British Government declared that the paramountcy on the States would lapse after the transfer of power and that the States would be free to enter into a federal relationship with the Indian Government or remain outside as independent sovereign units. These States were also left free to negotiate with and join any foreign power. Our Constitution makers thus found themselves confronted with a critical problem. They had to devise means to persuade the States to join the Union of India. They had to forge their way across a multitude of problems. The position of the Indian National Congress was clear enough on the issue of Indian States. On July 15, 1947, the All-India Congress Committee categorically rejected the claim of some of the States and the Theory of Paramountcy. Speaking at this meeting, Jawaharlal Nehru said : "*The states have only two alternatives : they could join the Union of India either individually or in groups. There is no third way out of the situation—third way meaning independence or special relation to a foreign power.*" Coupland had aptly said, "*India could live if its Muslim limbs in the north-west and north-east were amputated but could it live without its heart?.*" The heart of India was its Princely States. The foremost concern of the Government of Independent India was to conserve the heart of India.

Immediately after the Mountbatten Plan to partition India and grant her Independence on August 15, 1947, was announced, the Interim Government decided to set up a State Ministry to deal with the problem of Indian States. Sardar Vallabhbhai Patel, the Deputy Prime Minister of India, was given the charge of it. Sardar Vallabhbhai Patel was very sagacious and wise man and by his convincing arguments, firmness and cajolery, he was able to persuade all the 562 Indian States with the exception of Hydrabad, Junagarh, Jammu and Kashmir to sign the Instrument of Accession and of surrendering their powers in the three fields of foreign relations, defence and communication, and maintaining unchanged all arrangements in other matters.

Problem of Junagarh. The Government of India was extremely concerned to preserve the unity of the rest of the country after partition and the White Paper announced that it "*could not view with equanimity and trifling with it.*"[1] The people of Junagarh revolted against the Nawab who was conspiring with Pakistan against India and forced him to flee to Karachi and the Muslim Dewan Shah Nawaz Bhutto was left with no alternative except to invite Government of India on 8th November, 1947, to take the administration. The Government of India took the administration of that State on 10th November, 1947. After this the Government of India held plebiscite on 20th February, 1948. The huge majority of the people of that State voted for India, as a result of which it became part of India on 20th February, 1948.

Problem of Hyderabad. The Nizam of Hyderabad was unwilling to accede to India and he was conspiring with Pakistan against India. As Hyderabad was geographically a part of India, so compelled by circumstances it had to sign a Standstill Agreement on 29th November, 1947. The Nizam of Hyderabad, however, was in no mood to abide by this agreement, so he violated it several times. Besides that, the Hyderabad radio declared in April 1948 that, "*If India attacks Hyderabad, thousands of Pathans will invade India.*"[2] The Muslim fanatics of Hyderabad, known as Razakars, wanted to establish Independent Muslim State with the help of Pakistan. They had threatened to destroy one and a half crore Hindus of Hyderabad if she was attacked by India. Kasim Razvi was their leader. While inaugurating the Arms Week on 31st March, 1948, he delivered a very fiery speech and instigated the Muslims of Hyderabad to march against India. He also said that five crores of Muslims of India would act as Fifth Columnists and help Hyderabad.[3] This statement was published in several newspapers of India on April 7, 1948. This could not be tolerated by Sardar Vallabhbhai Patel, the Iron Man of India. He called Laik Ali, the Prime Minister of Hyderabad in States Ministry, on April 16, 1948, and told him in plain words, "*You also know and I also know that Kasim Razvi has usurped whole power in Hyderabad. He has also declared that if Hyderabad was attacked by India, one and a half crore Hindu population would be totally destroyed. If this is so, the future of the Nizam and his dynasty will be at stake. I want to tell you this thing very plainly, so that you may not remain in the dark. The problem of Hyderabad will have to be tackled like the other States, we cannot agree that Hyderabad may remain as a separate independent State within the boundaries of India and may destroy the Union of India for which we have shed our blood.*"[4]

1. *White Paper on Indian States*, July 1948, p. 18
2. V.P. Menon, *The Story of the Integration of State*, p. 348 (September, 1956), Orient Longman Private Ltd., New Delhi.
3. *Ibid*, pp. 350-51.
4. Mr. Menon, *The Story of the Integration of States*, pp. 354-55.

Laik Ali did not care even for this warning. The Razakars began to attack trains in May 1948 which ran from Bombay to Madras via Hyderabad. Ten thousand Congressmen were thrown behind the bars and many Hindus were killed. Laik Ali also declared that the Nizam was ready to die as martyr with two lacs of Muslims but was not willing to accede to India. Nizam began to make huge purchases of arms from Pakistan. The Nizam also appealed tp the President of the U.S.A. and the U.N.O. against economic blockade of Hyderabad by India. All this had been done due to the instigation of Pakistan. The Government of India could not tolerate all these things and took police action against Hyderabad on September 13, 1948. The forces of Hyderabad surrendered on 17th September, 1948. After this Hyderabad acceded to India.

Problem of Kashmir. There was another problem, namely, that of Kashmir. Maharaja Hari Singh of Kashmir wanted to maintain his independence. He thought that if he acceded to India, his Muslim majority population would feel enraged and might revolt. If he acceded to Pakistan, he would soon be dethroned. Therefore, the best course would be to conclude standstill agreements both with India and Pakistan. On the other hand, Mahatma Gandhi and Pt. Jawaharlal Nehru tried their best to persuade Maharaja Hari Singh to accede to India before August 15, 1947, because he would not be able to maintain his independence in case of any aggression from Pakistan. Lord Mountbatten went up to this length that if Maharaja Hari Singh acceded even to Pakistan, India would not take it ill because he had the firm assurance of Sardar Vallabhbhai Patel in this regard, but Maharaja Hari Singh did not decide anything before Independence about accession.

The matters came to a head when Kashmir was attacked by 5,000 tribesmen coming from North-West Frontier Province of Pakistan on Octorber 22, 1947, at the instigation of Mohammed Ali Jinnah, the founder and Governor-General of Pakistan. The raiders occupied soon two places of Kashmir, Garhi and Domel, and reached Muzaffarabad (now the capital of Pakistan-occupied Kashmir). Muzaffarabad was a famous city of kashmir and here camped one battalion of Kashmiri forces consisting of Dogra Rajputs and the Muslims under the command of Lt.-Col. Narain Singh. The Muslims abandoned the battalion, joined the tribesmen, fired shots at Lt.-Col. Narain Singh and killed him. After this they occupied Baramula from where direct road to Srinagar lay. From Baramula, they advanced towards Uri. Brigadier Rajendra Singh was the overall incharge of armed forces of Kashmir. Upon hearing the advance of tribesmen, he marched towards Uri and in order to check their rapid advance at once blew up the bridge of Uri. He kept them engaged in heavy fighting for two days. Though he and all his soldiers were killed in action but he was able to save the rest of Kashmir valley and Jammu for India. *The unparalleled heroism shown by Brigadier Rajendra Singh and his men is to be written in golden letters because he was the true saviour of Kashmir.* The bravery shown by him has been compared with the Greek Heroes of the battle of Thermopali, who defended Greece against the marauding hordes of Iran in the ancient time. Therefore, when the system of awarding Mahavir Chakra for showing exemplary bravery was introduced in India, the first Mahavir Chakra was awarded to Brigadier Rajendra Singh after his death (to his wife).[1]

In the meanwhile the Maharaja of Kashmir, Hari Singh, left Srinagar and was able to manage to reach Jammu, the winter capital, where Dogra Rajputs were ready to shed their last drop of blood to defend Maharaja Hari Singh. The raiders continued to advance towards Srinagar and occupied Mahura Power House which supplied electricity to Srinagar, as a result of which the whole of Srinagar, the summer capital of Kashmir, plunged into darkness. The raiders were continuously advancing towards Srinagar because of ineffective resistance and had declared that they would celebrate Id there on 26th October (1947).

Maharaja Hari Singh had not slept for the last several days and, feeling with gravest anxiety that the whole of Kashmir valley would be lost to Pakistan, appealed to the Government of India on 24th

1. V.P. Menon, *The Story of the Integration of States*, pp. 396-97, Orient Longman Private Ltd., New Delhi.

October (1947) for most urgent help and sent his Prime Minister Mehar Chand Mahajan to Delhi for this purpose. He met Prime Minister Pt. Jawaharlal Nehru who placed the whole matter before the Cabinet. The Cabinet could not decide it because some members feared that it would involve India into direct war with Pakistan while Sardar Vallabhbhai Patel insisted for sending the forces into Kashmir at once. In order to get the guidance both Pt. Jawaharlal Nehru and Sardar Vallabhbhai Patel went to Mahatma Gandhi who said that *you ought to have sent the forces at once without wasting so much precious time. If Sheikh Abdullah and certain other people were killed in defending Kashmir valley, it would be an example for the whole of India.* After hearing the clear-cut advice of Mahatma Gandhi, Pandit Jawaharlal Nehru immediately sent V.P. Menon, Secretary in the States Ministry, to get the Instrument of Accession signed by Maharaja Hari Singh. Maharaja Hari Singh signed the Instrument of Accession on 25th October, 1947.

The letter of Accession read : "*With the conditions obtaining at present in my State and the great emergency of the situation as it exists, I have no option but to ask for help from the Indian Dominion. Naturally, they cannot send the help asked for by me without my State acceding to the Dominion of India, I have accordingly decided to do and to attach the Instrument of Accession for acceptance by your Government.*"[1] The Government of India accepted it.

After this the Government of India immediately sent the forces to Srinagar by air, as there was no road link of Jammu and Kashmir with the rest of India in those days except through Pakistan. The Indian forces occupied the position on October 27, and were able to repel the invaders and defend the rest of Kashmir Valley. Mohammad Ali Jinnah felt greatly annoyed over Indian action and ordered General Gracey, Acting Commander-in-chief, to send Pakistani forces at once. As General Auchinlauck was the Joint Commander-in-Chief of both India and Pakistan at that time, so, General Gracey told Mohammad Ali Jinnah that without obtaining permission from Auchinlauck, he could not comply with the order of Governor-General. After getting information from Gracey, Auchinlauck at once flew to Lahore and told Mohammad Ali Jinnah in plain words that if the forces of Pakistan entered Kashmir which had become part of India legally, then all the British Officers serving in Pakistani Army would resign. Therefore, Mohammad Ali Jinnah had to rescind his order. In this way, except the portion of Kashmir Valley occupied by the invaders under the orders of Mohammad Ali Jinnah, the rest of the Kashmir Valley remained with India.

OBJECTIVES RESOLUTION AND PHILOSOPHY OF THE CONSTITUTION

The Constituent Assembly elected Dr. Rajendra Prasad as its permanent Chairman on 11th December, 1946. In the first session of the Constituent Assembly Pandit Jawaharlal Nehru moved the Objectives Resolution and described it as a solemn pledge to the people "which they would redeem in the Constitution they would frame." *The fundamentals and philosophy of the Constitutional structure were laid by the Objectives Resolution.* It read :

(1) The Constituent Assembly declares its firm and solemn resolve to proclaim India as an Independent Sovereign Republic and to draw up for her future governance a Constitution;

(2) WHEREIN the territories that now comprise British India, the territories that now form the Indian States, and such other parts of India as are outside India and the States as well as other territories as are willing to be constituted into the independent sovereign India shall be a Union of them all;

(3) WHEREIN the said territories, whether with their present boundaries or with such others as may be determined by the Constituent Assembly and thereafter according to the law of the Constitution, shall possess and retain the status of autonomous units, together with residuary

1. Adapted from Pyare Lal, *Mahatma Gandhi, The Last Phase*, p. 494.

powers and functions of Government and administration, save and except such powers and functions as are vested in or assigned to the Union or resulting therefrom; and

(4) WHEREIN all power and authority of the Sovereign Independent India, its constituent parts and organs of government are derived from the people; and

(5) WHEREIN shall be guaranteed and secured to all the people of India justice, social, economic and political; equality of status, of opportunity, and before the law; freedom of thought, expression, belief, faith, worship, vocation, association and action subject to law and public morality; and

(6) WHEREIN adequate safeguards shall be provided for minorities, backward and tribal areas, and depressed and other backward classes; and

(7) WHEREBY shall be maintained the integrity of the territory of the Republic and its sovereign rights on land, sea and air according to justice and the law of civilised nations; and

(8) This ancient land attains its rightful and honoured place in the world and makes its full and willing contribution to the promotion of world peace and the welfare of mankind."[1]

The Objectives Resolution was adopted on January 22, 1947. These objectives were to be the fundamentals of the Constitution and guide the framers of the Constitution.

After the passage from the Constituent Assembly, it received the signature of Dr. Rajendra Prasad, President of the Constituent Assembly, on the same date and it was declared passed. The final session of the Constituent Assembly began on January 24, 1950. It unanimously elected Dr. Rajendra Prasad as the first President of India and decided to enforce the new Constitution from January 26, 1950 as on this historic date 20 years ago, our countrymen had taken the pledge under the leadership of Mahatma Gandhi to liberate themselves from foreign yoke. The pledge was redeemed on January 26, 1950, and India was proclaimed Sovereign Democratic Republic.

PREAMBLE AND PHILOSOPHY OF THE CONSTITUTION

Besides the objectives resolution the philosophy of the Constitution is further contained in the Preamble to the Constitution which runs as follows:

"WE, THE PEOPLE OF INDIA, having resolved to constitute India into a SOVEREIGN DEMOCRATIC REPUBLIC and to secure to all its citizens:

JUSTICE, social, economic and political;

LIBERTY of thought, expression, belief, faith and worship;

EQUALITY of status and opportunity; and promote among them all;

FRATERNITY assuring the dignity of the individual and the unity of the Nations;

IN OUR CONSTITUENT ASSEMBLY this twenty-sixth day of November, 1949, do HEREBY ADOPT, ENACT AND GIVE OURSELVES THIS CONSTITUTION."

The Preamble as amended by the 42nd Amendment

The 42nd Amendment came into force on 18th December, 1976. In the Preamble to the Constitution :

(*a*) for the words, "SOVEREIGN DEMOCRATIC REPUBLIC", the words "SOVEREIGN SOCIALIST SECULAR DEMOCRATIC REPUBLIC" shall be substituted; and

(*b*) for the words, "unity of the Nation", the words unity and integrity of the 'NATION" shall be substituted. So the Preamble as amended by the 42nd Amendment runs as follows:

"We, the PEOPLE OF INDIA, having solemnly resolved to constitute India into a SOVEREIGN SOCIALIST DEMOCRATIC SECULAR REPUBLIC and to secure all its citizens :

1. *Constituent Assembly Debates*, vol. 1, p. 57.

JUSTICE, social, economic and political; EQUALITY of status and opportunity; and promote among them all : FRATERNITY assuring the dignity of the individual and unity and integrity of the Nation;

In OUR CONSTITUENT ASSEMBLY this twenty-sixth day of November, 1949 do HEREBY ADOPT, ENACT AND GIVE OURSELVES THIS CONSTITUTION.

Sovereignty of the People. The Preamble to the Constitution begins with the words, "We the people of India having solemnly resolved to constitute India into a Sovereign Democratic Republic" and ends with the words, "in our Constituent Assembly this twenty-sixth day of November, 1949 do hereby adopt, enact and give to ourselves this Constitution." These words clearly prove that the people are ultimate source of all authority. Though there is no independent article as in the constitution of Ireland, declaring that all powers are derived from the people or vesting the sovereignty of the reserved powers in the people, as in the United States, yet our Constitution proves beyond doubt the sovereignty of the people. This fact was clearly emphasised in the famous case '*Gopalan vs. State of Madras*' in which Justice Patanjli Shastri observed, "There can be no doubt that the people of India in exercise of their sovereign will as expressed in the Preamble, adopted the democratic idea which assures to the citizens the dignity of the individual and other cherished human values as a means to the full evolution and expression of his personality, and in delegating to the Legislature, the Executive and the Judiciary their respective powers in the Constitution, reserved to themselves certain fundamental rights...."[1]

It may seem that the Constitution is sovereign as it is the Supreme Law of the Land.[2] However, the source of the Constitution is the people of India who have given to themselves this Constitution. The people of India have adopted and abided by the Constitution so far[3] and they will continue to be governed by this Constitution so long as they want to be governed by it. The fact that the Constitution has survived the vicissitudes of time (Emergencies, Internal and External) and many general elections have been held under it in the country, goes to prove beyond doubt that the people have generally liked it and have an abiding faith in it.

Union and States both the creation of the people. As the Indian Constitution derives its strength from the sovereignty of the people, therefore, states in India cannot claim that the Union of India is their creation and if they had not given powers to the Indian Union, it could not have come into existence. So no state in India can claim a right of secession from the Centre. Every state and the Union of India are the creatures of the Constitution. Therefore, the sovereignty of the people is all comprehensive and complete. This has been amply made clear by the Supreme Court in *Keshwanand Bharti v. State of Kerala*, (1973) case.[4] Therefore, the Parliament, and the Executive and the Judiciary all have to exercise their powers within the boundaries of the Constitution.

Establishment of Welfare State and Egalitarian Society. The main aim of the Constitution is to establish a Welfare State and Egalitarian Society projecting the aims and aspirations of the people of India who made unparalleled sacrifices for the attainment of the freedom of the country. Consequently, the Constituent Assembly constituted India into a Sovereign Democratic Republic in order to secure to its citizens justice, liberty, equality and fraternity. Therefore, the Constituent Assembly adopted the Preamble of the Constitution after the Draft Constitution was approved.[5]

Beaconlight to the Court. The Preamble serves another useful purpose. It serves as a beaconlight to the courts which are engaged in the most difficult task of interpreting the Constitution. Whenever any controversial constitutional law arises in the Courts, where the meaning is not clear, the judges

1. *Gopalan v. State of Madras*. (1950) S.C.R. 88 (198) ; *Union of India* v. *Madan Gopal* (1954) S.C.R. 541 (555)
2. See the views of Gajendragadkar, C.J. in Article 143 of the Constitution (1965) IS.C.R. 413, 446.
3. This was the position on February 25, 1991.
4. *Keshwanand Bharti* v. *State of Kerala* (1973) 4 S.C.C. 225.
5. Shiv Rao, *Framing of India's Constitution—A Study*, pp. 130-32; Constituent Assembly Debates, Vol. 10, pp. 423–42.

look to the Preamble in which the real intention of the framers of the Constitution is hidden. Some people contended that the Preamble was not a part of the Constitution but this opinion has changed now after the decision in *Keshwanand Bharti Case*.[1]

Establishment of Sovereign Democratic Secular Socialist Republic. The Preamble of the Constitution clearly declares that India is a sovereign State. The word Sovereign connotes that India does not recognize any outside authority. Its authority is absolute within its sphere. Indian Constitution is democratic because the real authority vests in the people. The Constitution declares India to be a Republic because besides being democratic, it is to have an elected Head. The Constitution provides for fair general elections after an interval of five years on the basis of adult franchise. The leader of the majority party in the Parliament is to act as Prime Minister and select a team of Ministers to form a Cabinet. The executive for all its act of commission and omission is responsible to the Parliament. The Constitution admits of no distinction based on blood, caste or creed. It guarantees fundamental rights to the people, to safeguard which there is an independent judiciary.

Former Chief Justice of the Supreme Court Mohammad Hidayatullah has aptly said that the "*Preamble resembles the declaration of independence of the United States of America, but is really more than a declaration. It is the soul of our Constitution and lays down the pattern of our political society which it states is Sovereign Democratic Republic. It contains a solemn resolve which nothing but a revolution can alter.*"

The amended Preamble lays special emphasis on Socialist and Secular character of our Republic. The Congress had passed a resolution at Bhubaneswar in January 1964 at the suggestion of Pt. Jawaharlal Nehru, the then Prime Minister of India. Since then the Congress Party set its goal as the establishment of socialism in India by parliamentary means.

42nd Amendment and 44th Amendment on Socialism. The Indian Constitution was amended by the 42nd Amendment (1976) and the word 'Socialist' State was inserted in the Preamble to ensure the goal of Indian polity. It is, however, to be noted that Indian type of socialism is quite different from the western type of socialism, which involves nationalisation of all means of production. Smt. Indira Gandhi explained :

> "*We have always said that we have our own brand of socialism. We will nationalise the sectors where we feel necessity. Just nationalisation is not our type of socialism.*"[2]

Therefore, the Indian Constitution does not abolish private property altogether but seeks to put it under restraints so that it may be used for public benefit. Instead of total nationalisation of all property and industry, India has followed a concept of mixed economy which aims at offering equal opportunities to all, and the abolition of vested interests.

But the obligation to pay compensation to the private owner for State Acquisition at market rates has been taken away by repealing Article 31 by the Constitution (44th Amendment) Act, 1978.

Secularism. The word '*Secular*' has been added to the Preamble of the Constitution by 42nd Amendment (1976) and retained by the 44th Amendment (1978). According to Venkataraman : "State is secular which is neither religious, nor irreligious, nor anti-religious but is wholly detached from religious dogmas and activities and thus neutral in religious matters." It means in other words that the State protects all religions equally and does not itself uphold any religion as the State religion. In our Constitution no state religion has been established as we find in Burma, Bangladesh, Pakistan, Iran and Saudi Arabia. This is a glowing achievement of our democracy. In our country to ensure equal protection to all religions liberty of belief, faith and worship has been guaranteed to all.

In India, no discrimination has been made since Independence for any political or administra-

1. *Keshwanand Bharti* v. *State of Kerala*, (1973) 4 S.C.C. 225, paras 94–98, p. 324 per Sikri, C.J.
2. The *Statesman*, 25. 10.1976, p.1, also 28.10.1976, p.1

tive office on the basis of caste, creed, religion or sex and equal opportunities are available to all the citizens of India. This was demonstrated well on the occasion of the election to the highest office in India when Dr. Zakir Husain and Fakhruddin Ali Ahmed were elected Presidents of India. Muhammadans have also enjoyed the office of Chief Minister, Governor, judges and Chief Justice of High Court and Supreme Court. Sikhs have also been given an honourable place. Giani Zail Singh has also remained President of India. So in India secularism prevails. There is no official religion in India as we find in some Muslim States of the world.

India's Commonwealth Membership and her Sovereign Status. The draft Constitution of India had declared India to be Independent Sovereign Democratic Republic. Later on the word 'Independent' was dropped because the word 'Sovereign' connotes the independence of a conutry. Prime Minister Pt. Jawaharlal Nehru informed the British Commonwealth countries of the impending decision of India to proclaim herself a republic and yet desirous of continuing the membership of the Commonwealth of Nations. Therefore, in order to consider the decision of India a Commonwealth Prime Ministers' Conference was called in April 1949. Pt. Jawaharlal Nehru emphasised the multi-racial and dynamic character of the British Commonwealth. At the suggestion of the Prime Minister Pt. Jawaharlal Nehru the word 'British' was dropped from the British Commonwealth of Nations and it remained only Commonwealth of Nations and a Republic like India was accommodated for the first time. Therefore, India continued her membership of the Commonwealth. This historic decision was embodied in the Declaration of the Conference released on April 27, 1949.

A Welfare State (Fundamental Rights, Equality and Liberty and Directive Principles of State Policy). The Constitution of India establishes a welfare State in India. For that purpose the Preamble clearly declares that social, economic and political justice will be established. Liberty of thought, expression, belief, faith and worship and equality of status and opportunity will be granted to the people. It strives to promote fraternity among all citizens assuring the dignity of the individual and unity of the nation. No welfare state in India can be established unless there is equality of status and opportunity and justice—social, economic and political. Therfore, various Articles of the Constitution give practical shape to the rights of Equality, Liberty and Fraternity. Directive Principles establish a welfare state.

Political Justice. In our country, political justice has been promised by the Preamble to the Constitution. In order to ensure political justice, Universal Adult Suffrage has been introduced in the country. This means that every person irrespective of wealth, education, sex, caste and religion has been allowed to participate in the political system of our country. After every five years the elections to the State Legislature and the Parliament are held and every adult has a right to exercise his right to vote at that time.

Economic Justice. The main aim enshrined in the Constitution is economic justice. No democracy can succeed without economic justice. Economic justice does not mean the deprivation of those persons of wealth who possess it but, on the other hand, it means that the national wealth should be increased and there must be an equitable distribution of the same. If the national wealth is concentrated in a fewer hands, *i.e.*, the capitalists, no economic justice can be achieved. Democratic Society or Welfare State or Economic Democracy can never be established without economic justice. Economic justice assured by the Preamble can hardly be achieved if the democracy envisaged by the Constitution were confined to a political democracy. In the words of Pandit Jawaharlal Nehru :

> "Democracy has been spoken of chiefly in the past as a political democracy, roughly represented by every person having a vote. But a vote by itself does not represent very much to a person who is down and out, to a person, let us say, who is starving or hungry. Political democracy, by itself, is not enough except that it may be used to obtain a gradually increasing measure of economic democracy, equality and the spread of good things of life to others and removal of gross inequalities."[1] Or as Dr. Radhakrishnan has put it—

1. Inaugural Address of Pandit Nehru at the Seminar on Parliamentary Democracy on 25-2-1956.

"Poor people who wander about, find no work, no wages and starve, whose lives are a continual round of sore affliction and pinching poverty, cannot be proud of the Constitution or its law."[1]

Social Justice or Social Democracy. The Preamble to the Constitution lays emphasis not only on political and economic justice but also social justice. Dr. Bhim Rao Ambedkar in his concluding speech in the Constituent Assembly said :

"Political democracy cannot last until there lies at the base of it social democracy. What does social democracy mean ? It means a way of life which recognises liberty, equality and fraternity which are not to be treated as separate items in a trinity. They form a union of trinity in the sense that to divorce one from the other is to defeat the very purpose of democracy. *Liberty cannot be divorced from equality, equality cannot be divorced from liberty. Nor can liberty and equality be divorced from fraternity.*"

Dignity of the Individual. The Preamble to the Constitution lays much emphasis upon the maintenance of the dignity of the individual. Only then the fraternity can be established. In order to enable the individual to maintain his dignity certain fundamental rights have been given to each individual. If these fundamental rights are violated either by any individual or state, then the individual has got right to seek a justice in the court. The framers of the Constitution fully realised that to maintain the dignity of the individual, it is not sufficient to make the fundamental rights justiciable unless he is free from economic wants and misery. Therefore, a number of Directive Principles have been included in Part IV of the Constitution, exhorting the State to shape its social and economic policies in such a manner that "all citizens, men and women equally, have the right to an adequate means of livelihood,"[2] "just and humane conditions of work" (Article 42) and a decent standard of life and full enjoyment of leisure and social and cultural opportunities (Article 43).

Promotion of International Peace. India took a very bold and magnanimous decision when it decided to continue as a member of the Commonwealth of Nations in spite of the manifold grievances under the imperialistic rule, powerful opposition at home, baffling international alignments and upsurge of racism in England. Similarly India has served United Nations to the best of her ability. So it speaks volumes about the sincerity of India to promote international peace. Article 51 specifically promotes it.

Thus the ideal of fraternity enshrined in the Indian Constitution is not limited to our country but reaches the loftier idea of universal brotherhood—which has been expressed in these memorable words of Pandit Jawaharlal Nehru :

"The only possible real object that we, in common with other nations, can have is the object of co-operating in building up some kind of world structure, call it one world, call it what you like."[3]

Thus, while India declares her sovereignty to manage her own affairs in no unmistakable terms, her sovereignty is not inconsistent with the concept of one world or universal brotherhood because the Indian Constitution does not support isolationism or Jingoism (Aggressive Nationalism).

Critical Evaluation of Preamble of the Constitution. About the Preamble Justice Bhagwati once said : "*What is, therefore, needed is that judiciary must not interpret any element of the Preamble that introduces a line of disconcerting incredibility which judicial review must constantly and scrupulously avoid.*"[4] In the case of Kerala Education Bill, 1957, the Supreme Court in 1958 held the view that "*where the enacting part is explicit and unambiguous, the Preamble cannot be resorted to control, to qualify or to restrict it but where the enacting part is ambiguous, the Preamble can be*

1. Speech of the Vice-President, Dr. Radhakrishnan, *Ibid*
2. *Article* 39 (*a*)
3. *Constituent Assembly Declaration*, dated 22-1-1947.
4. Seervai, H.M., *Constitutional Law of India*, p. 75.

referred to, to explain and to elucidate it." However, Sikri, Chief Justice in *Keshwanand Bharti vs. State of Kerala* held :

> "It seems to me that the preamble of our Constitution is of extreme importance and the Constitution should be read and interpreted in the light of the grand and noble vision expressed in the Preamble."[1]

The Preamble is not something superficial but very useful addition to the Constitution because it expresses the hopes, aspirations and wishes of the framers of the Constitution and throws ample light on their intentions. So it has to be invoked only where the main text of the Constitution is not clear and it cannot abridge any provision of the Constitution if it is unambiguous. It is also admitted on all hands that the Preamble is a part of the Constitution.

EXERCISES

Long Answer Type Questions:

1. What do you know about the problem of Junagarh ?
2. Write a note on the problem of Hyderabad.
3. Write a note on the problem of Kashmir.
4. Discuss the objectives resolution and philosophy of the Constitution.
5. What do you know about the Preamble of the Constitution ?

Short Answer Type Questions:

1. Write a critical evaluation of Preamble of the Constitution.
2. What is meant by Promotion of International Peace ?
3. What is meant by Social Justice ?
4. What is meant by Social Democracy ?
5. Discuss in brief the meaning of Economic Justice.
6. What is meant by Political Justice ?
7. Write a brief note on India's Commonwealth Membership and her sovereign status.
8. What is meant by 'Secularism'?
9. Write a brief note on 42nd Amendment and 44th Amendment of the Constitution.

Objective Type Questions:

Choose the correct answer

1. In which year the All-India Congress Committee categorically rejected the claim of some of the States and the theory of Paramountacy ?

   (*a*) 1947 (*b*) 1948

   (*c*) 1949 (*d*) 1950

2. Immediately after the Mountbatten Plan to partition India and grant her Independence on August 15, 1947, was announced, the Interim Government decided to set up a State Ministry to deal with the problem of Indian States. The Deputy Prime Minister of India was given the charge of it. Who was the Deputy Prime Minister ?

   (*a*) Pt. Jawaharlal Nehru (*b*) Sardar Vallabhbhai Patel

   (*c*) Pt. Motilal Nehru (*d*) Mahatma Gandhi.

1. AIR 1973 SC 1461 (1506).

3. In which year Junagarh became part of India ?
   (a) 1946 (b) 1947
   (c) 1948 (d) 1949
4. At the time of Independence of India; who was the Prime Minister of Hyderabad ?
   (a) Shabir Ali (b) Sayed Ahmad
   (c) Kasim Razvi (d) Laik Ali
5. Who was the leader of the Muslim fanatics of Hyderabad known as Razakars ?
   (a) Kasim Razvi (b) Laik Ali
   (c) Hashaat Ahmad (d) Mohammad Ali
6. What was the name of Maharaja of Kashmir ?
   (a) Rajendra Singh (b) Hari Singh
   (c) Narain Singh (d) Rameshwar Singh
7. In which year The Constituent Assembly elected its permanent Chairman ?
   (a) 1948 (b) 1947
   (c) 1946 (d) 1945
8. On which date the Objectives Resolution was adopted by the Constituent Assembly ?
   (a) January 19, 1947 (b) January 20, 1947
   (c) January 21, 1947 (d) January 22, 1947
9. The final session of the Constituent Assembly began on January 24, 1950. It unanimously elected the first President of India. Who was elected the first President of India ?
   (a) Dr. Rajendra Prasad (b) Pt. Jawaharlal Nehru
   (c) Pt. Motilal Nehru (d) Sardar Vallabhbhai Patel

ANSWERS

1. (a)	2. (b)	3. (c)	4. (d)	5. (a)
6. (b)	7. (c)	8. (d)	9. (a)	

CHAPTER 2

Sources of the Constitution

> *"While we want this Constitution to be as solid and permanent as we can make it, there is no permanence in Constitution. There should be a certain flexibility. If you make anything rigid and permanent, you stop the nation's growth, the growth of a living, vital, organic people ..... In any event, we could not make this Constitution as rigid that it cannot be adapted to changing conditions. When the world is in turmoil and we are passing through a very swift period of transition, what we may do today may be wholly incapable tomorrow."*[1] —***Pandit Jawaharlal Nehru***

Our Constitution is a very pious document. It is the Fundamental Law of the land. Therefore, it occupies a supreme and unique position in the country's political arrangements. All the laws of the land are to be consistent with the provisions of the Constitution. If any law conflicts with the Constitution, it can be decalred as null and void. Our Constitution is written and rigid, and a beautiful amalgam of the good features of the different Constitutions of the world.

DRAWN FROM DIFFERENT SOURCES

The Fathers of our Constitution were very wise and sagacious. They have prepared the best possible document for our country. For this purpose they have ransacked all the known constitutions of the world and most of its provisions are substantially borrowed from others. As Dr. Bhim Rao Ambedkar, the Chairman of the Drafting Committee, observed :

> "One likes to ask whether there can be anything new in a Constitution framed at this hour in the history of the world. More than hundred years have rolled by when the first written Constitution was drafted (U.S.A.). It has then been followed by many other countries reducing their Constitution to writing ...... Given these facts, all constitutions in their main provisions must look similar. The only new things, if there be any, in a Constitution framed so late in the day are the variations made to remove the faults and to accommodate it to the needs of the country."[2]

So, though our Constitution has been called a borrowed one by some people, yet the credit of its framers lies in this thing that they gathered the best features of other constitutions, avoided the faults which had been disclosed in their working and adapted those features to the requirements of our country. So if it is 'patchwork', it is a beautiful patchwork."[3]

1. *Constituent Assembly Debates*, dated 8.11. 1948, pp. 323-24.
2. *Constituent Assembly Debates*, Vol. VII, pp. 35-38.
3. VII CAD; 2, 242, XI C.A.D. 613, 616.

Its sources are being enumerated below :

(1) Government of India Acts. Before India attained Independence on August 15, 1947, she was being governed by the British Government. As the British Rule was a foreign rule, therefore, National Movements were launched by the Indians frequently in order to end imperialists' exploitation and gain independence. In order to assuage the feeling of the Indians on this point, the British Parliament enacted the various Acts from time to time, notable amongst them are Government of India Acts 1909, 1919 and 1935. The Indian Independence Act was passed by the British Parliament to enable India to achieve Independence and consequently it made certain temporary provisions. The lengthiest Act enacted by the British Parliament was the Government of India Act, 1935 which provided for the distribution of powers, federal structure of India, provincial autonomy, responsible form of Government, bicameral system at the Centre and in some states, discretionary and emergency powers of the Governors and Governor-general. The Indian Constitution adopted these provisions after modifying them to suit the needs of the changing time. So the Indian Constitution envisaged a strong Centre after the pattern of the Government of India Act, 1935 and provided for the federal system of Government, distribution of powers between the Centre and states, bicameral system of Central Legislature and some states, emergency powers of the President and special powers of the Governors. The Indian Constitution adapted the provisions of the Government of India Act, 1935 to suit the changed conditions after independence. Thus, the Lower House of Parliament known as Lok Sabha or House of People has been made stronger than the Upper House of Parliament known as Rajya Sabha or Council of States.

(2) British Parliamentary System. Since Indian leaders were well familiar with the working of the British Parliamentary Institutions, therefore, the Indian Constitution mainly adopted the British Constitutional System. India adopted the Parliamentary System of Government from England. The Indian Cabinet System also works on the same pattern as the British Cabinet.

Regarding Parliamentary Procedure, the passage of the Bills and the powers and position of the Speaker, we have followed more or less the British Model. Article 105 (3) of our Constitution goes to the extent of saying that unless legislated, our Parliamentary powers, privileges and immunities shall be the same as those enjoyed by the members of British House of Commons. These have not so far been codified and such powers, privileges and immunities of Members of Parliament in India are exactly the same as those enjoyed by Members of British House of Commons in England.

Cabinet Form of Government has been mainly borrowed from England. Our Constitution-framers adopted it because it suited Indian conditions and our leaders were well familiar with it. Just as in England the leader of the majority party in the House of Commons forms the Government, similarly in India also the leader of the majority party in the Lok Sabha or anyone who can command a majority in that House forms the Government. He is appointed as the Prime Minister and on his advice other Ministers are appointed by the President. The Indian Cabinet works on the same principles as its counterpart works in England. Just like England, our Prime Minister is the leader of the House and he remains in office so long as he enjoys the majority.

(3) Impact of other Constitutions. The intention of the Constitution-framers was not to enact an original Constitution but to give to our country such a Constitution which could embody the best features of all the Constitutions of democratic countries and at the same time, it might suit the prevailing conditions in India. During the last 150 years almost all the principles of the Constitution had been evolved. Consequently, they considered it useless to waste time in inventing new principles but devoted their whole energy in evolving such a constitution which may be quite workable under the prevailing conditions. Therefore, they did not shirk in adopting what was good in the British, American, Canadian and Irish Constitutions. At the same time they avoided those defects which had been disclosed in their working. For instance, Fundamental Rights were adopted from the U.S.A. and not from the U.S.S.R. They did not adopt all the Fundamental Rights enshrined in that Constitution blindly but adopted whatever suited the Indian conditions. For example, Right to keep arms was not granted. The Indian Constitution-framers added certain Fundamental Rights which were required in India. For instance, the Right of secession, Right to work, Right to rest and leisure have been granted in the U.S.S.R. but were not granted in India. Similarly, the U.S. system inspired them to provide for judicial review under which the courts could declare any law passed by the Legislature as unconstitutional or ultra vires if it conflicted with the Constitution.

It is again from the U.S. Constitution that we borrowed the concept of independence of judiciary so that it might be able to check the arbitrary encroachments of the Executive upon the Fundamental Rights and serve as a balance wheel between the Centre and the States. Therefore, in other words, it has to be custodian of the Fundamental Rights and has to uphold the supremacy of the Constitution by protecting the provisions contained in the Constitution. So any law which conflicts with any provision of the Constitution has to be declared null and void.

The distribution of powers between the Centre and States has been done mainly on the pattern of the Government of India Act, 1935, but in regard to the residuary powers, the Fathers of the Constitution neither followed the Government of India Act, 1935 nor the Australian or U.S. model but only Canadian Model *i.e.* they gave all the residuary powers to the Centre. Just like Canada, the Centre has been made strong. Therefore, many critics feel that India is over-centralised but it is not so. If the framers of the Constitution would not have made India strong, the unity of the country would have been torn asunder. Besides that, the Directive Principles of State Policy have been taken from the Irish Constitution.

(4) Debates in the Constituent Assembly. Another very useful source of the Constitution are the debates in the Constituent Assembly. The Constituent Assembly sat from 9th December 1946 to 26th November, 1949 when the present Constitution was adopted. It set up a Draft Constitution Committee[1] under the Chairmanship of Dr. Bhim Rao Ambedkar by a resolution on August 29, 1947, which submitted its report on February 21, 1948. It was here that every aspect of the Constitution was debated thoroughly and various alternatives and suggestions on the recommendations of different committees were discussed. These deliberations reveal the real purpose or aim of the Constitution-makers. Therefore, these debates form the original source for the study of Constitution. They serve as beaconlight to the court because whenever any controversial case regarding the interpretation of the Constitution arises, the judges look to these Constituent Assembly Debates to know the real intention of framers of the Constitution. So the judges of the Supreme Court and lawyers frequently refer to these Constituent Assembly Debates in different cases.

(5) Commentaries of the Critics. Various commentaries on the Indian Constitution have been written both by Indians as well as foreigners which bring to light deep insight in every clause of the Constitution. As these commentaries have been written by the different commentators giving their own view at many places, so they should be studied cautiously. Anyhow, one thing goes to their merit, that they throw ample light on the hidden aims of the Constitution-makers and thus clarify many concepts. These commentaries also help us in understanding minutest details of the Constitution because they have been written in a logical and convincing manner. Besides that, they focus our attention on the defects and drawbacks of our Constitution.

(6) System of Judicial Review. In India the judiciary has been made independent of the Executive and has also been made guardian of the Constitution. Therefore, it has to protect every clause of the Constitution. It can declare any law as null and void if it conflicts with the Constitution. The attitude of the Supreme Court is not rigid. It has not hesitated to review and amend its earlier decisions if in its opinion they were wrong and warranted any change, modification or amendment. For example, it

1. Other members of the *Draft Constitution Committee* were : (1) N. Gopalswami Ayyangar ; (2) Alladi Krishnaswami Ayyar ; (3) K.M. Munshi, (4) Saiyad Muhd. Saadullah ; (5) N. Madhava Rau ; (6) D.P. Khaitan ; and (7) Sir B.L. Mitter who could not attend the meetings after I[st] meeting and thus ceased to be a member.

changed its earlier decision given in *Shankri Prasad Case* (1951), *Sajjan Singh Case* (1965), *Golak Nath Case* (1967) and *A.K. Gopalan v. The State of Madras* (1951). The Supreme Court changed its earlier decision of Shankri Prasad and Sajjan Singh cases in 1967 when it decided Golak Nath Case. Golak Nath Case ruling was reversed by the Supreme Court on 24th April, 1973, when it decided Fundamental Rights case. Similarly, it reversed its earlier decision given in *A.K. Gopalan v. The State of Madras* after 22 years when it struck down Section 17A of the Maintenance of Internal Security Act on April 19, 1973. It has further revised the Fundamental Rights case in the Minerva Mill case. So the approach of court is flexible, dynamic and practical.

It will not be an exaggeration to say that the decisions of the Supreme Court have provided flesh and blood to the skeleton of the Constitution and made it workable. Its role is quite progressive and has awarded many decisions in favour of the labour class.

The decisions of the Supreme Court become precedents and are often quoted by lawyers in Lower Courts, High Courts and Supreme Court in order to strengthen the arguments of their own case. The judges are bound to be swayed by the earlier decisions of the Supreme Court unless there is some other constitutional and solid reason to give a different ruling. Therefore, the knowledge of the practical working of the Constitution can be gained only after deep study of the decisions of the Supreme Court.

(7) Constitutional Amendments. In India, we have got Parliamentary Form of Government which implies that the Cabinet (government) is responsible to Parliament which is supreme. One of the functions of the Government is to get such laws passed by the Parliament which are essentially required for the smooth running of the administration and are in the interest of the public as a whole. Therefore, the Government has to bring amendment to the Constitution whenever it is needed because the Constitution is not something static but a dynamic document which requires some change as the nation marches ahead. This was the approach of Pandit Jawaharlal Nehru who was one of the chief architects of our Constitution. Therefore, when the Congress Government at the Centre went ahead with the abolition of Zamindari System, the big landlords of U.P. and Bihar filed a petition against Zamindari Abolition in Allahabad and Patna High Courts respectively. Consequently, Pt. Jawaharlal Nehru, First Prime Minister of India, moved the 1st and 4th Amendments to the Constitution in order to carry on the Zamindari Abolition and take it out of the purview of courts. Later on the Government of India had to face many other difficulties, therefore, it had to move one amendment after another. It will not be surprising that though the framers of Indian Constitution had given the country best possible document, yet during a short span of 54 years,[1] 83 amendments[2] had been made in the Constitution while in U.S.A. from 1789 up till 25th February, 2000, only 26 amendments had been made. As there has been thorough discussion in the Parliament on these amendments and all the members of different political parties have expressed their independent views, therefore, for a student of Constitutional History (development) of India, these deliberations form an important source material which throws ample light on motives of those who piloted these amendments.

(8) Ordinances. Another source of the Constitution is ordinances. These ordinances are either issued by the President of India on the advice of the Central Government or the Governor on the advice of State Government to meet any emergency or peculiar situation when the State Legislature or Parliament is not in session. They enable the President or the Governor, as the case might be, to discharge his constitutional obligations. So it is very useful and essential to study the background of these ordinances especially when they deal with any constitutional problem or any aspect of the Constitution. As these ordinances meet with very difficult situation facing the nation, so it becomes all the more interesting to study these ordinances. Here it is worthwhile to remember that the ordinances have the same forces as the law of the land but they have to be placed before the Parliament

1. This is the position up to 25th February, 2004
2. *India 2004*

or the State Legislature as the case may be for approval within 6 weeks after the reassembly of State Legislature or Parliament. The importance of the ordinances can be realised from the fact that from 1956 onward more than 350 ordinances have been issued by the Central Government. This means in other words that approximately one ordinance has been issued after every month. This is very serious because it makes the Executive very powerful and it approaches the Parliament only to approve an action which has already been taken. Sometimes the ordinances are also issued to meet the situation arising out of any decision of the Supreme Court or the High Court declaring a particular law as null and void because it conflicts with the Constitution. So the study of these ordinances becomes very interesting and fruitful. When these ordinances are again challenged in the High Court or the Supreme Court, then in the course of discussion, several laws are interpreted, so these ordinances become important source of the Constitution.

IS THE CONSTITUTION A BAG OF BORROWING ?

Many critics have alleged that the Indian Constitution is a bag of borrowing but it is totally wrong. It is true that the framers of our Constitution did not hesitate in borrowing some good features of Constitutions of Great Britain, U.S.A., Canada and Ireland but they did not borrow anything blindly. They did not borrow anything from the Constitutions of the U.S.S.R., Australia and Switzerland. Whatever was good in the Constitutions of Great Britain, U.S.A. and certain other countries, they adopted it and whatever defects had been disclosed in their working, they avoided it. That was a positive and constructive approach and there is nothing to feel shy of it. Though they adopted the idea of Fundamental Rights and independent judiciary from the Constitution of the U.S.A. they adapted it to suit the Indian conditions. After all the Constituent Assembly worked hard for nearly three years to give the country best possible Constitution. If it had been only a bag of borrowing, the Constitution could be prepared at the most within six months. If the Constitution-framers took advantage of the long experience of other nations in constitutional matters, one must appreciate it. The beauty of the Indian Constitution lies in this thing that it has been nicely adjusted to the changed circumstances. Whatever has been adopted from other countries has been shown above. Now we have to show where the originality lies. The originality of the Indian Constitution lies in the following provisions:

(1) Strong federation and unique distribution of powers between the Centre and States. Every effort has been made to make the Centre as strong as possible; (2) Integrated judiciary; (3) Independent Election Commission; (4) Special provisions for the betterment of Scheduled Castes and Backward Classes; (5) Provision in the Constitution for Finance Commission, Language Commission and Public Service Commission; (6) Provision for All Indian Administrative Services; (7) Emergency Powers of the President which have been greatly modified by 44th Amendment to the Constitution. (Only the idea had been taken from the Government of India Act, 1935 but the powers envisaged are more or less original); (8) Universal Adult Franchise without reservation of seats for minorities and discarding of communal electorate; (9) Single Citizenship.

Besides that, whatever provisions have been adopted from other Constitutions, they have also been greatly modified to suit the Indian conditions.

Therefore, it is entirely wrong to say that the Indian Constitution is a bag of borrowing. Rather the truth is that it is the best possible Constitution which the framers could give and they produced it after great sweat and toil. So the posterity must feel the highest gratitude towards the Fathers of the Constitution. *In the end we agree with the verdict of Dr. Ambedkar that if the Constitution fails we should not blame the Constitution but say that man was vile.* So the success of the Constitution depends upon those persons who work it, especially the political parties.

EXERCISES

Long Answer Type Questions:

1. Discuss the sources of Indian Constitution.
2. Is the Constitution of India a bag of borrowing ? What is your opinion ? Write in brief.

Short Answer Type Questions:

1. Write a very brief note on Government of India Acts.
2. What do you know about British Parliamentary System ?
3. Discuss in brief the impact of other constitutions on Indian Constitution.
4. One very useful source of the Constitution are the debates in the Constituent Assembly. How? Discuss in brief.
5. Write a very brief note on System of Judicial Review.
6. Write a short note on Constitutional amendments.

Objective Type Questions:

Choose the correct answer

1. Which of the following most influenced the Constitution of India ?
   (*a*) Government of India Act, 1919 (*b*) Indian Independence Act, 1947
   (*c*) Government India Act, 1935 (*d*) All of the above.
2. The Dominion Status of India was established under
   (*a*) Government of India Act, 1919 (*b*) Government of India Act, 1935
   (*c*) Both (*a*) and (*b*) (*d*) Indian Independence Act, 1947
3. Why did the Constitution makers choose the Parliamentary Government of the British type as the form of Government both at the Union level and the State level in India?
   (1) Parliamentary system of Government was the only one dominant in the various politics of the world and it fitted well with the philosophy of mixed economy which the Government of India took immediately after independence.
   (2) People had a long experience of this system under the Government of India Acts, though the British were very slow in importing its features to the fullest length.
   (3) The makers of the Indian Constitution rejected the Presidential system of Government on the ground that under that system the Executive and the Legislatures are separate from and independent of each other, which is likely to cause conflicts between them, which the infant Indian democracy could ill afford to risk.
   (4) The leadership pattern that evolved out of the freedom struggle was not suitable to any but the Westminster form of Government

   Select the correct answer from the following :
   (*a*) (1) and (2) (*b*) (2) and (3)
   (*c*) (3) and (4) (*d*) (1), (2), (3) and (4).

ANSWERS

1. (*c*) 2. (*d*) 3. (*b*)

3

CHAPTER

Salient Features of India's New Constitution

> *"One likes to ask whether there can be anything new in the Constitution framed at this hour in the history of the world. More than three hundrerd years have rolled when the first written Constitution was drafted. It has been followed by many other countries reducing their Constitution to writing ...... Given these facts, all Constitutions in their main provisions must look similar. The only new things, if there be any, in a Constitution framed so late in the day are the variations made to remove the faults and to accommodate it to the needs of the country."*[1]
>
> **—Dr. Ambedkar**

The Constitution of India is remarkable. It has many outstanding features which will distinguish it from other Constitutions. It has been prepared after ransacking all the known constitutions of the world. Most of its provisions are substantially borrowed from constitutions of other countries.

So Indian Constitution may be said to be a 'borrowed' constitution, the credit of its framers lies in gathering the best features of each of the existing constitutions and in modifying them with a view to avoiding the faults that have been disclosed in their working and to adapting them to the existing conditions and needs of this country.

The following are some of its salient features:

(1) Written and Enacted Constitution. For a federal State a Written Constitution is a necessity because the powers between the Centre and the States have to be distributed and they are to be recorded in black and white in order to remove any chance of ambiguity and to make everything clear and precise. To base the arrangements which are inherent in a federal polity *"upon understandings and conventions"*, as Dicey said, *"would be certain to generate misunderstandings and disagreements."*[2] Moreover, the demand of a Constituent Assembly and the making of a constitution by that body postulates that it must be a written constitution. Besides that, there were many other reasons which compelled India to opt for a written Constitution, and that too for an elaborate and detailed document. We should not forget that at the time of Independence, India had inherited the Government of India Act, 1935, the lengthiest Act ever enacted by the British Parliament after much deliberation. Before partition, the British Parliament passed another Act, known as the Independence Act. This

1. *Constituent Assemblty Debates*, Vol. VII, pp. 35-38.
2. Dicey, A. V., *Law of the Constitution*, p. 142.

Act modified and supplemented the Government of India Act, 1935 to some extent. India continued to be governed by these two Acts till the New Constitution came into operation.

So our Constitution is a written and sacred document unlike the Constitution of England which is merely based on conventions and is an evolved one, ours has been painstakingly framed by the Constituent Assembly. The former is a flexible one, the latter is rigid, though less rigid than the American Constitution. The procedure for amending the Indian Constitution is not so intricate or devious as that of the U.S.A. It can be amended by a vote of two-third members of the Parliament present and voting and the absolute majority of total members of the House. Certain provisions relating to the units can be changed only when half members of the state legislature agree to it.

(2) It is the Lengthiest Constitution in the World. The Constitution of India, as *Sir Jennings* remarks, is a very comprehensive and detailed document. The Constitution makers could not help it in view of the complex political condition at the time of its drafting.

First reason of its inordinate length is that it specifies not only the structure and powers of the Central Government but also all the provisions relating to the Provinces, the Indian States, and Union Territories. Other Constitutions of the world are generally brief because they state clearly the scope of authority of either the Centre or the units only and leave the rest to be looked after by the other.

The *second reason* for the lengthy character is that it contains special provisions and safeguards for the Anglo-Indians, Scheduled Castes and Scheduled Tribes.

Thirdly, besides stating Fundamental Rights, it also incorporates the Directive Principles of State Policy which one finds in no other Constitution except that of Ireland.

Fourthly, the Indian Constitution lays down in details the nature of relationship between the Union and the units.

Fifthly, it contains the emergency powers of the President of India.

Sixthly, it details the composition and powers of not only the Supreme Court but also the High Courts.

Seventhly, it embodies the provisions relating to the constitution and functions of the Public Service Commission, Election Commission, Finance Commission and so on. According to Mr. Srinivasan : "*The new Constitution of India is like the Act of 1935, not merely a Constitution but also a detailed legal code dealing with all important aspects of the constitutional and administrative system of the country.*"

42nd Amendment has further increased the size of the Constitution. It added Part IV-A and Part XIV-A for the first time to the Constitution besides new Articles 31D, 39A, 43A, 48A, 313A, 139A, 144A, 226A, 228A, 257A. After this amendment number of Articles totalled 442 besides 12 Schedules. Besides this, Articles 103, 150, 192, and 226 were substituted by new Articles. 42nd Amendment amended the Preamble to the Constitution and Articles 31-C, 39, 55, 74, 77, 81, 83, 100, 102, 105, 118, 145, 166, 170, 172, 189, 191, 194, 208, 217, 225, 227, 311, 312, 330, 353, 356, 357, 358, 359, 366, 368, 371F.

All the amendments made since 42nd Amendment have further enlarged the size of the Constitution.

Some of these Articles have been repealed by later amendments. But still it can safely be concluded that Indian Constitution stays as the lengthiest document at present out of all the constitutions of the world.

Referring to the detailed nature of the Constitution, *Dr. Rajendra Prasad* observed :

> "Constitution has gone into great details regarding the distribution of powers and functions between the Union and the States in all aspects of their administrative and other activities. I do not wish to pass any judgement on this criticism and can only say that we cannot be too cautious about our future, particularly when we remember the history of the country extending over many centuries."

(3) It establishes a Parliamentary Form of Government. The Constitution of India both at the Centre and in the States establishes a Parliamentary Form of Government. The reasons for it are not difficult to trace. When we were being governed by the British, the educated Indians learned much about the British Parliamentary System, therefore, they began to demand the same for India. The Congress leaders had always couched their demands before Independence in terms of parliamentary democracy. The Commonwealth of India Bill and the Motilal Nehru Committee Report both proposed a Parliamentary Form of Government for India as did the Sapru Report in 1945. The Draft Constitution of Free India published by the groups of the Left, the Centre and Rights—those of Marxist, M.N. Roy, of the Socialist Party, and the Hindu Mahasabha, all envisaged a Parliamentary System of Government for the Constitution of India.

Pt. Jawaharlal Nehru speaking in the House of the People (Lok Sabha) on March 28, 1957 said :

"We chose it—let us give credit where credit is due—because we approved of its functioning in other countries, more especially in the United Kingdom."

Another reason for choosing it is that Parliamentary System is both responsible and responsive. There is both a daily and periodic assessment of the responsibility of government. Moreover, it can meet the crisis in social, economic and political sphere quickly because there is perfect harmony between the executive and legislative branch of the government, as the Cabinet is sure that the legislative wing of the government will support it. The system, therefore, secures swiftness in decision and vigour in action and enables the Government to press through such legislation as it thinks it is needed, and conduct both domestic and foreign policy with the confidence that its majority will support it against the attacks of the Opposition. The Ministers being in constant touch with the Opposition as well as in still closer contacts with the members of their own party can feel the pulse of the Legislature and through it the ebb and flow of public opinion. The Government under such a system cannot become arbitrary because it might lose the support of the majority in the Parliament in that case.

The third merit of this system is that it leaves no loophole for the emergence of a dictator. The Head of the State possesses only nominal powers while the real power resides in the Cabinet which too can remain in office till it enjoys the confidence of the popular House. Although the Government of India is headed by a President, it is different from the Presidential type of Government of the U.S.A. The President of America is the Chief Executive assisted in his functions by an advisory body. He is directly elected by the electoral college and is not responsible to the Legislature. The President of India is only a Constitutional Head with not much power to affect the working of the Cabinet. The principal merit of Parliamentary Government, according to Dr. Bhim Rao Ambedkar, '*lay in its ability to satisfy the essential test of democracy, a combination of stability and responsibility.*'

(4) It establishes a Federal Polity. The Constitution of India declares India a Union of States[1] but in fact a federal polity has been devised by dividing the country into States and allocating them functions as specified in the Constitution. There is a division of powers between the Centre and States which is the first criterion of every federal state. So for this purpose three lists of subjects have been provided in the Indian Constitution, Union List, State List and Concurrent List. The second criterion of the federation is the supremacy of the Constitution. For that purpose the Constitution must be written and rigid. So the Indian Constitution has been reduced to writing and made rigid. Thirdly, the criterion for the federation is that there must be a Supreme Court which should be empowered to decide the constitutional disputes between the Centre and the States arising out of the distribution of powers. In India the Supreme Court has been empowered to decide the disputes between the Centre and the States.

(5) A Unique Document Derived from Many Sources. The makers of the Indian Constitution proceeded with open mind to borrow freely what was best in other constitutions of the world. They suffered from no inhibitions. According to *Mr. O.P. Sharma*, "It is not the purpose of our constitution-makers to produce an original or unique constitution. What they wanted was a good and workable one". They modelled the Constitution on the pattern of English Constitution. Fundamental Rights and

1. Article I

the compositions of the Supreme Court speak of the influence of the American Constitution. Directive Principles have been borrowed in more or less the same form from the Irish Constitution. On the lines of the Canadian Constitution, the residuary powers have been given to the Union Government. Even the South African and Australian Constitutions have gone into the shaping of our Constitution. The power given to the President to suspend the Constitution in emergency smacks of the Weimar Constitution of Germany.

Besides the effect of foreign Constitutions, one that has influenced our Constitution most is the Act of 1935. According to *Sir Ivor Jennings*, "The Constitution derives directly from the Government of India Act, 1935 from which in fact many of its provisions are copied almost textually." For instance, Articles 352 and 358 relating to the Emergency Powers of the President are very much similar to Section 102 of the Act of 1935. Article 356 which provides for the declaration of Emergency in the country is a copy of Section 93 of the Act of 1935. The division of subjects into three separate lists also bears the stamp of the same Act. According to *Srinivasan*, "The borrowings of the New Constitution from the Act of 1935 are so considerable both in language and substance that it is a close copy of the Act of 1935 and its description as a palimpsest of the Act is not incorrect." According to *Dr. Punjabrao Deshmukh,* the Indian Constitution is essentially the Government of India Act with only adult franchise added. In fact, Mr. Punjabrao Deshmukh's remark is a little exaggerated. Our Constitution marks a great advantage on the Act in many respects.

(6) The Constitution has been supplemented by various amendments and practically recast by the 42nd, 43rd and 44th Amendments, 1976-1978. From time to time, the Constitution has been amended due to one reason or the other. Up till 25th February, 2004, 83 amendments to the Constitution had been made. It will not be out of point to emphasise that the Constitution had been practically recast by the 42nd Amendment Act, 1976 (as modified by the 43rd and 44th Amendment Acts, 1977-78)

(7) Fundamental Rights. Another novel feature of the Constitution is the inclusion of Fundamental Rights in it. Both in order to achieve the ends of democracy and for full flowering of man's personality, such rights have been granted to the people by the Constitution of Russia, America and France. The Fathers of our Constitution were inspired by the Fundamental Rights incorporated in the Constitutions of the U.S.A., the U.S.S.R. and France. They greatly appreciated the dictum of *Prof. Laski*, "A state is known by the rights it maintains." Some of the rights which have been extended to the people of India are: (1) Right to equality; (2) Right to freedom of speech; (3) Right to freedom of movement; (4)) Right to freedom of religion; (5) Right against exploitation; (6) Right to constitutional remedies and so on. According to *Mr. Srinivasan*, "The introduction of adult franchise and abolition of communal electorate are most progressive and radical features of the new Constitution." *Untouchability and forced labour are strictly prohibited. The law forbids the employment of boys below 14 in the factories. The Supreme Court acts as the guardian of the Constitution. All the Fundamental Rights are justiciable and constitutional remedies are provided for their enforcement.*

When the country was freed from the clutches of the imperialists, the framers of our Constitution deemed it their first and foremost duty to enshrine Fundamental Rights in the Constitution. Once the choice was made, the next step became inevitable that the judiciary must be made the custodian of Fundamental Rights. Though the Judicial Review has made the Constitution legalistic but there is no. body in India today who is aggrieved because the Supreme Court, each year, invalidates a dozen of statutes or a like number of administrative acts on the ground of violation of the Fundamental Rights.

At the same time, it must be admitted that since the inauguration of the Constitution, many amendments have been made which have taken out considerable area from the pale of judicial review, *e.g.*, by inserting Articles 31-A to 31-C; and by 1991 more than 188 Acts—Central and State—had been precluded from the judicial review on the ground of contravention of the Fundamental Rights, by enumerating them under the Ninth Schedule, whih relates to Article 31-B.

(7*a*) Fundamental Duties. For the first time Fundamental Duties have been added in the Indian Constitution according to the 42nd Amendment which became an Act on 18th December, 1976. For this purpose Part IV-A has been specially added. In Part IV-A a new Article 51A has been added which describes in detail the Fundamental Duties for the Indian people. This Article enjoins that it will be Fundamental Duty of the Indian People, (*a*) to abide by the Constitutiion, respect its ideals and institutions, the National Flag and the National Anthem; (*b*) to cherish and follow the noble ideas which inspired our national struggle for freedom; (*c*) to uphold and protect the sovereignty, unity and integrity of India; (*d*) to defend the country and render national service when called upon to do so; (*e*) to promote harmony amongst all sections of the people; (*f*) to value and preserve the rich heritage of our composite culture; (*g*) to safeguard public property and to abjure violence. All these duties are very important and must, necessarily, be performed by the Indian citizens in the interest of unity, integrity and progress of the country. So the Fundamental Rights have been checkmated by Fundamental Duties.

(8) Directive Principles of State Policy. The Constitution of India contains a list of Directive Principles of State Policy whose observance by the state is deemed essential for the welfare of the people. They direct the state to apply these principles in making law. They are not enforceable by court but have a moral force. These principles are in a way the ideals which the fathers of the Constitution directed the state to follow. Some of these ideas are the promotion of a welfare State, fair distribution of wealth, free and compulsory education for children up to the age of 14, adequate means of livelihood, help against unemployment, old age, sickness and disability, separation of judiary from the executive, organisation of panchayats and others. In the words of *G.N. Joshi*, "*They constitute a very comprehensive political, social and economic programme for democratic state.*"[1] The Directive Principles, as a critic points out, are a little more than a set of high flown aims and aspirations. The fathers of the Constitution hoped that a party intending to remain in power will not dare ignore these ideals because it has to meet the aspirations of the people.

(9) Secular State. Another bold feature of the Constitution is that it seeks to establish a secular State instead of a theocratic State. The term secular means, according to *Encyclopaedia Britannica*, non-spiritual, having no concern with religious or spiritual matters—anything which is distinct, opposed to, or not connected with religion of ecclesiastical things, temporal as opposed to spiritual or ecclesiastical."[2]

According to *Eric S. Waterhouse*, "Secularism is an ideology which provides a theory of life and conduct as against one provided by a religion."

The Forty-second Amendment (1976) has specially inserted the word 'Secular' in the Preamble. *Dr. B.R. Ambedkar* also said : "All that a secular state means is that this Parliament shall not be competent to impose any particular religion upon the rest of the people."

Religious equality in the Indian Constitution has been provided in Article 15 (I) and untouchability has been done away with by Article 17. In fact the cultural heritage of the minorities has been protected and there is absolutely no discrimination in matter of admission to educational and other institutions. Each religious community has been allowed to maintain its separate educational institutions. In recruitment to public services there is no discrimination on the grounds of religion, caste and creed. In his *Recovery of Faith*, Dr. Radhakrishnan said about India's secularism; "It tried to build up a fellowship of believers not by subordinating individual qualities to the group mind but by bringing them into harmony with each other."

"The whole idea of secularism, as enshrined in our Constitution, was very vividly explained by a member of the Constituent Assembly, Pandit Lakshmi Kant Maitra of West Bengal, who on 6 December, 1948 said thus: "*By secular State, as I understand it, is meant that the State is not going*

1. Joshi, G.N. : *Constitution of India*, p. 112.
2. *Encyclopaedia Britannica*, Vol. XX, p. 264.

to make any discrimination whatsoever on the ground of religion or community against any person professing any particular form of religious faith. This means in essence that no particular religion in the State will receive any State patronage whatsoever. The state is not going to establish patronage or endow any particular religion to the exclusion of or in preference to others; that no citizen in the state will have any preferential treatment, will be discriminated against simply on the ground that he professed a particular form of religion." By secular we mean non-recognition of any State religion. In the words of Mr. R Venkataraman. '*The State is neither religious nor anti-religious but is wholly detached from religious dogmas and activities and thus neutral in religious matters.*" *Mr. Rafsanjani* (President of Iran) lauded Indian secularism on 17th April, 1995 while inaugrating a three-day international conference on the teachings and writings of Caliph Ali, the first cousin of Prophet Mohammed. Mr. Rafsanjani said India had passed the litmus test for peaceful co-existence of people belonging to different religious faiths. He repeated the same sentiments after his visit to Imambara, Lucknow, when he said that secularism is the best way of holding different communities together.

(10) It Strengthens Our National Unity. The Indian Constitution is federal in form although Article I describes India as a Union of States. The framers of the Constitution were cautious enough not to see the word federation at any place. Federation comes into being when several independent states agree to form a union for the sake of administrative convenience. They join the federation of free will and withdraw if that right is not recognised. Indian Union is not a federation of that sort. The component units are neither independent nor have the power to secede from the Union. There is no double citizenship as we find in the U.S.A. The expression Union of States does not leave any scope for the secession of the states. The Constitution-makers had definitely in mind to ensure the political integrity of the country and to promote feeling of oneness. This they tried to achieve through making the Union Government more powerful than the Provincial Government and secondly by providing one national language, one flag, one national anthem, an integrated system of judiciary and All India Services.

(11) Universal Adult Franchise Without Communal Representation. The introduction of Universal Adult Suffrage (Article 326) without qualifications of any kind (sex, property or educational qualification) was the boldest step taken by the Constitution-makers having regard to the vast extent of the country and its population, with an overwhelming illiteracy. It will not be out of the point to emphasise that the suffrage in India is wider than that in England or the United States and India is the largest democracy on earth, because the population of our country is much more than these countries. Under the Government of India Act, 1919, only 3 per cent people of our country enjoyed the right to vote and under the Govenment of India Act 1935 only 14 per cent of the total population of the country secured franchise. The qualifications for the women were kept quite high and they, therefore, constituted only a negligible proportion of the total electorate. When the country won independence, the framers of our Constitution translated their dream into practice and adopted Universal Adult Franchise without communal representation. To ensure free and fair election an Independent Election Commission was set up (that commission was to be independent of the Executive but only under the control of Parliament).

It goes to the credit of the Election Commission and the Government of India that notwithstanding the vast illiterate population and a multitude of other difficulties, the bold experiment as envisaged by the Fathers of the Constitution has been a tremendous success till date.[1]

Pt. Jawaharlal Nehru and other freedom-fighters believed that the system of adult suffrage with direct election was the pillar of social revolution. Therefore, they provided direct elections to the Assemblies and House of People. So it is undisputable fact that adult suffrage is the acceptance of the fullest implication of democracy and it is the most striking feature of India's Constitution.

1. This is the position up to 25th February, 1991.

Adult suffrage has given power to the millions of people who had never exercised the right to vote during the British regime and who mainly depended on the whims of others to represent them and redress their grievances. The electorate has been widened by lowering the voting age from 21 to 18 by the 61st Constitution Amendment Act, 1988. Now they have suddenly realised that they are the makers and unmakers of the government at the time of election. This they have particularly realised after the 13 General Elections and the elections to state assemblies. Highlighting the implication of adult franchise, K.M. Panikkar said :

"Adult suffrage has social implications far beyond its political significance. Many social groups, previously unaware of their strength and barely touched by political changes that had taken place, suddenly realised that they were in a position to wield power."[1]

That, notwithstanding the outstanding difficulties, this bold experiment has been crowned with success will be evident from some of the figures relating to the first General Election held under the Constitution in 1952. Out of a total population of 356 million and an adult population of 180 million, the number of voters enrolled was 173 million and of these no less than 88 million, *i.e.*, over 50 per cent of the enrolled voters, actually exercised their franchise. The orderliness with which thirteen General Elections have been conducted speaks eloquently of the political attainment of the masses, though illiterate, of this vast sub-continent.

It is to be admitted that all the elections held so far reflect great deal of political awareness and maturity of the voters. But whereas this is the bright side of the picture, the dark side is also there. Adult franchise has led to mushroom growth of political parties and groups with local and regional roots. The local parties have promoted not only narrow loyalties and factionalism, but have abetted caste and class consciousness in the form that had not existed before. The national parties, too, in order to compete with them and catch votes also give their tickets to those persons who belong to a majority community in a particular constituency. Thus, caste and religion are brought into play by every political party irrespective of its label to secure more and more votes. Thus they fan the fire of cummunalism and casteism which are the bane of democracy.

(12) Integrated and Independent System of Judiciary. The framers of our Constitution deemed it necessary to safeguard it by providing independent judiciary. Therefore, the Supreme Court has been made the custodian of the Fundamental Rights and guardian of the Constitution. Consequently, it has been granted the power of Judicial Review and it can declare any law passed by the State Legislature or the Parliament or any ordinance issued by the Governor or the President as null and void if it contravenes any provision of the Constitution but the law or ordinance will be invalidated only to the extent that it conflicts with the Constitution. Besides this unlike U.S.A., our Supreme Court has been made the final court of appeal in all civil, criminal and constitutional cases. In order to make judicary independent of the executive, several measures have been adopted in the Constitution.

Firstly, according to Article 124, clause 2, of the Constitution the Judges of the Supreme Court are appointed by the President after consultation with the Chief Justice of India and such other judges of the Supreme Court and High Courts in the States as he may deem it necessary. Their election either by the Parliament or popular election has been avoided.

Secondly, the security of service has been granted to the judges of the Supreme Court. Article 124, clause 4, clearly lays down that a judge of the Supreme Court shall not be removed from his office except by an order of the President passed after an address by each House of Parliament supported by a majority of the total membership of that House present and voting has been presented to the President in the same session for such removal on the ground of proved misbehaviour or incapacity.

Thirdly, the qualifications have been laid down for the judges. So no inexperienced person can be appointed as a judge even by the President on the recommendations of the Prime Minister.

1. Panikkar, K. M., *Hindu Society at Crossroads*, pp. 63-64.

Fourthly, adequate salary has been give to judges and that salary is paid out of the Consolidated Fund of India. As their salary has been written in the Constitution itself, so it is a non-votable item and cannot be reduced by the Parliament at its sweet will where there is a transient majority of the Ruling Party. In order to keep them from the control of the Ruling Party, it has also been provided in the Constitution that their salaries will not be changed to their disadvantage. Similar provisions have been made in case of the judges of the High Courts. Both the courts have been given the right to recruit their own staff and have full control over it. It has also been provided that no discussion shall take place in the legislature of a State or in a House of Parliament with respect to the conduct of any judge, in the discharge of his duties. In the words of Shri *V.N. Shukla*, "Thus our Constitution has done everything to make the Supreme Court and the High Courts independent of the influence of the Executive. In our country there is integrated system of Judiciary because the Lower Courts are under the High Courts and High Courts are under the Supreme Court. There is also a uniformity in civil and criminal laws.

A judge of the Supreme Court gets a salary of ₹ 30,000 per mensem and the use of an official residence free of rent. The salary of the Chief Justice is ₹ 33,000.[1]

A judge of a High Court gets a salary of ₹ 26,000 per mensem while the Chief Justice gets ₹ 30,000 per mensem.

(13) Emergency Provisions. Another unique feature of the Constitution is that emergency provisions have been provided in the Constitution which enable the Executive to meet any emergency effectively. This emergency is of three types.

Firstly, there is a general emergency which can be declared when India is invaded by any other country or there is an imminent threat of the invasion or when India is involved in any war. According to the 44th Amendment of the Constitution, Emergency cannot be declared merely on the pretext of internal disturbance or the threat thereof. Emergency can be declared only when there is armed revolt.

Second type of emergency is constitutional Emergency. It can be declared on the report of a Governor when the constitutional machinery in any state breaks down or the Government cannot be carried according to the Constitution.

The **third** type of Emergency is the financial emergency. It can be declared only by the President when the financial stability or the credit of India or any part of India has been badly shaken.

During the emergency the Central Government becomes all-powerful. It has practically the effect of converting the federal structure of the Constitution into a unitary one. So the powers of the President are far-reaching. The general emergency in the country was proclaimed for the first time in the wake of the Chinese invasion on October 26, 1962. It was removed on January 10, 1968. So when Pakistan invaded India in September 1965, there was no need to proclaim fresh emergency as the emergency was still in operation.

After this general emergency was proclaimed on 3rd December 1971 when Pakistan invaded India again. This emergency lasted till March 22, 1977, when Mrs. Indira Gandhi was defeated and advised the Acting President, Mr. B. D. Jatti, to lift the emergency. After this the general emergency had not been proclaimed because there was no need of it.

The constitutional emergency has been declared many a time in various states. The financial emergency has not been declared so far.[2]

(14) Provision for One Official Language for the Entire Country. To cement the unity of the country, Hindi has been declared the official language of the entire country because it is the most spoken language over the greater part of India. Besides that it is understood over most of the parts

1. The salaries of Judges of the Supreme Court and the High Courts have been enhanced vide Act 18 of 1998, with effect from 1st January 1996.
2. This was the position as on 25th February, 1991.

of India. In the Eighth Schedule of the Constitution 15 regional languages have also been included. These are : Assamese, Bengali, Gujarati, Hindi, Kannada, Kashmiri, Malayalam, Marathi, Oriya, Punjabi, Sanskrit, Sindhi, Tamil, Telugu and Urdu. Sanskrit is the mother of all the languages of India and Hindi serves as a link language for the entire country. It was, however, provided in the Constitution that English shall continue to be used for all official purposes of the Union till 25 January, 1965. But later on it was felt that a complete changeover to Hindi was not practicable within the stipulated period. Hence the Offical Languages Act, 1963, as amended, lays down that English may continue to be used in addition to Hindi, for all official purposes of the Union for which it was being used immediately before 26 January 1965 and for the transaction of business in Parliament. It must be noted that all the Prime Ministers of India had to give assurance to the people of non-Hindi area that Hindi will not be imposed.

(15) Unique Blend of Rigidity and Flexibility. A constitution is called flexible if it can be amended by a simple majority vote of the Parliament. When a special procedure is required to be follwed for amendment, the Constitution is called rigid. Indian Constitution is neither flexible like that of Great Britain nor it is so rigid as that of the U.S.A. The framers of the Indian Constitution adopted the midway track so that it may neither become a handmaid of the ruling party nor fail in adapting itself to changing circumstances and needs of the country. It has several clauses which can be amended by a simple majority vote of the Parliament. The Parliament, for instance, can on the recommendation of the President establish a new state by making boundary adjustments, or change the name of any state or can abolish a state altogether. In short it can by an ordinary process of legislation after getting the opinion of the legislatures of the states concerned, redraw the map of India. Besides it, the Parliament can easily create a cadre of All India Services, applicable to all the states. In the same way it has amended the Constitution for the use of English in offices even beyond the deadline of 1965 by the Constitution.

Several other instances can also be cited to prove the flexible character of the Constitution. For example, Legislative Council can be created or abolished by the Parliament on the recommendation of the Legislative Assembly. An amendment in the provisions relating to the states, however, requires the sanction of at least half of the states concerned. In a state of Emergency, the federal structure of the Constitution can easily change into a unitary spirit. Besides it, if a state legislature by two-thirds majority agrees to transfer a state subject to the Union Parliament for legislation, the Parliament can make laws on that subject for one year.

EXERCISES

Long Answer Type Question:

1. What are the salient features of India's new Constitution ?

Short Answer Type Questions

1. What is meant by written and enacted Constitution ? Discuss in brief.
2. The Indian Constitution is the lengthiest constitution in the world. What are its causes ? Discuss in brief.
3. Indian Constitution establishes a Parliamentary form of Government. What is the meaning of this statement?
4. What is meant by Federal polity ? Does the Constitution of India establish a federal polity ?
5. How the Indian Constitution is a unique document ? Discuss in brief.
6. How the Constitution of India strengthens our national unity ?
7. What is meant by Universal Adult Franchise ?

Objective Type Questions:

1. At present how many Articles are there in the Indian Constitution ?
   (*a*) 442 (*b*) 443
   (*c*) 444 (*d*) 445
2. How many Schedules are there in the Indian Constitution ?
   (*a*) 11 (*b*) 12
   (*c*) 13 (*d*) 14
3. Which amendment of the Constitution have enlarged the size of the Indian Constitution ?
   (*a*) 40th (*b*) 41st
   (*c*) 42nd (*d*) 43rd
4. How many lists of subjects have been provided in the Indian Constitution ?
   (*a*) 6 (*b*) 5
   (*c*) 4 (*d*) 3

ANSWERS

1. (*a*) 2. (*b*) 3. (*c*) 4 (*d*)

4

CHAPTER

Nature of the Federal System

"The constitution of Union and States is a single frame from which neither (Provinces or States) can get out and within which they must work."[1] — *Dr. Ambedkar*

Ever since the framing of the Indian Constitution a controversy has existed among scholars whether the Indian Constitution can truly be described as federal or not, on the one hand, *Dr. B. R. Ambedkar*, the chairman of the Drafting committee, held that the constitution establishes a dual polity consisting of the Union at the centre and the States at the periphery, each endowed with sovereign powers to be exercised in the field assigned to them respectively by the constitution. On the other hand, *Dr. K. P. Mukerjee* says, "I have come to take the view that whatever might have been the position at the drafting stage or previous to that stage, the constitution that emerged out of the August deliberations of the Constituent Assembly of India in January 1950 is definitely unfederal or unitary constitution. Prof. K. C. Where says Indian Constitution establishes a "system of government which is almost quasi-federal almost devolutionary in character : a unitary state with subsidiary federal features rather than a federal State with unitary features". In view of the conflicting views expressed about the Federal Nature of the constitution it is desirable to examine what is a Federal constitution and how far the Indian Constitution possesses Federal features.

FEDERALISM IN INDIA

When India achieved independence, it was considered prudent not to introduce the Unitary Government but only the Federal Government which was widely welcomed by all shades of opinion. The Indian States also agreed to join the federation. *Article* 1 of the Indian Constitution describes India as a Union of States instead of Federation, though in India Federal Form of Government has been adopted. In his introductory note to the President of the Constituent Assembly, while submitting the Draft Constitution, Dr. Bhim Rao Ambedkar wrote, "It will be noticed that the Committee has used the term Union instead of Federation. Nothing much turns on the name, but the Committee has preferred to follow the language of the Preamble to the British North America Act, 1867 and considered that there are advantages in describing India as a Union although its constitution may be Federal in character."[2] The omission of the word Federation' is deliberate. Moving the Draft Constitution for

1. Dr. Ambedkar, *Constituent Assembly Debates*, Vol. VII, p. 34.
2. *Draft Constitution*, p. IV.

the consideration of the Constituent Assembly on November 4, 1948, he explained the significance of the use of expression "Union" instead of the expression "Federation." Dr. Bhim Rao Ambedkar said, "*It is true that South Africa which is a unitary state is described as a Union, but Canada which is a Federation is also called a Union. Thus, the description of India as Union, to usage. But what is important is that the use of the word 'Union' is deliberate. I do not know why the word Union was used in the Canadian Constitution. But I can tell you why the Drafting Committee has used it. The Drafting Committee wanted to make it clear that though India was to be Federation, the Federation was not the result of an agreement by the States to join in a Federation, and that the Federation not being the result of an agreement, no state has the right to secede from it. The Federation is a Union, because it is indestructible.*" Though the country and the people may be divided into different States for convenience of administration, the country is one integral whole, its people a single people living under a single imperium derived from a single source. The Americans had to wage a civil war to establish that the States have no right of secession and that their "federation was indestrucible". The Drafting Committee of the Constitution thought that it was better to make it clear at the outset rather than to leave it to "speculation or to dispute."[1] Thus the Indian Federation is not the result of an agreement amongst its various component units. The Indian Constitution is the creation of the representatives of people assembled in the Constituent Assembly. The States have no right to secede from the Centre and the Union is indestructible. Dr. Bhim Rao Ambedkar put it clearly, when he said that "*the Constitution of the Union and the States is a single frame from which neither can get out and within which they must work.*" *Prof. D.N. Banerjee* holds the opinion that the Indian Constitution is Federal in form with a unitary bias. *Mr. Durgadas Basu* also contends that it is neither wholly Federal nor wholly Unitary, it possesses the ingredients of both. Mr. K. C. Wheare, however, differs from this view. According to him, "India is a Unitary State with subsidiary Federal Features rather than a Federal State with Subsidiary Unitary Features."

The nature of our Constitution has thus given rise to a lot of controversy. The difficulty of any treatment of Federalism is that there is no agreed definition of a Federal State. The other difficulty is that it is habitual with scholars on the subject to start with the model of the United States of America because the Federation of that country is the oldest one (1787). Since then Federations have been formed in many countries of the world and many Federations will not be able to stand the test of Federalism except Switzerland and Australia but nothing would be achieved by excluding so many Federations of the world from the Federal contexts by accepting the U.S.A. as the model. Now-a-days Constitutions are classified as either Unitary or Federal but when a Constitution contains the features of both the systems, then the only alternative left before us is that we must study its features deeply and then to ascertain whether basically it is Federal or Unitary, though it may contain the subsidiary features of either variation. A liberal attitude towards the question of Federalism is, therefore, ineviatable particularly when most of the countries having Federal Constitutions are not strictly following the U.S. model as it does not suit their requirements. So many eminent scholars of the world on this subject have come round the view that whether a State is Federal or Unitary is one of degrees and the answer will depend upon "how many Federal Features it possesses." *Prof. W.T. Wagner*, who happens to be an American scholar, holds the same view.[2] Another American scholar '*Mr. Livingstone*' also observes that *Federation is more a 'functional' than an 'institutional' concept* and that any theory which asserts there are certain inflexible characteristics without a political system cannot ignore the fact "*that institutions are not the same things in different social and cultural environments.*"[3] Therefore, in order to come to any conclusion, it is essential to study first the various requirements of the federations and how far these are fulfilled by the Indian Federation.

1. Constituent Assembly Debates, Vol. VIII, p. 43.
2. Prof. W.T. Wagner, "*Federal States and their Judicary*" (Moulton & Co. 1969), p. 25.
3. Livingstone, *Federation and Constitutional Change*, 1956, pp. 6-7.

FEDERAL FEATURES OF THE INDIAN CONSTITUTION

The following are the main Federal Features of the Indian Constitution :

(1) Dual Polity. In a Federal System there are two governments, one is the Federal or National Government and another is the government of the component units or the states. The powers of each government are demarcated in the Constitution. Both exist according to their own constitutional rights. None can interfere in the allotted sphere of the other. On the other hand, in a Unitary State, there is only one government, namely, the Central or the National Government which can give the powers to the provincial or regional governments according to its sweet will or exigencies of the time. The remarkable features of the Unitary State is that the Regional or Provincial Governments do not exist of their own constitutional right. They solely depend on the mercy of the Centre and it can revoke any of their powers but this is not the case with the Federal Polity where both governments derive their authority from the Constitution. According to this test we have a Federal Government and not a Unitary one.

(2) Division of Powers. Another feature of the Federal Government is that it presupposes the existence of several independent States which agree to transfer some of the administrative powers to the Central body and part with some of their sovereignty. The political map of India at the time of transfer of power was such as did not advise the formation of a Unitary Government. The British Government instead of transferring its paramountcy over the Princely States to the Indian Union, declared it to have lapsed. The States were made free to join the Union on a Federal basis or remain independent. Thus, when the Constituent Assembly proceeded with the task of drafting a Constitution, it had the anxiety to devise a method that might secure the co-operation of the States, some of which were unwilling to compromise their freedom. There was no other alternative before the Constitution Makers except to draw up a Federal plan and persuade the rulers to surrender three subjects of Defence, External Affairs and Communications to Union care. On the model of other Federations of the world, the Indian Constitution also made a clear division of powers into three lists—the Union List, the State List and the Concurrent List. The subjects included in the Union or Federal List can be controlled by the Union Government alone. The State Legislature possesses the exclusive right to legislate on subjects included in the State List. On Concurrent subjects, the Legislatures of both the Union and the State enjoy Concurrent power to make laws.

Refuting the criticism of over-centralization in the Constituent Assembly, Dr. Bhim Rao Ambedkar said :

> "A serious complaint is made on the ground that there is too much centralization and that the states have been reduced to municipalities. It is clear that this view is only an exaggeration but is also founded on a misunderstanding of what exactly the Constitution contrives to do. As to the relations between the Centre and the State, it is necessary to bear in mind the fundamental principle on which it rests. The basic principle of federalism is that the legislative and executive authority is partitioned between the Centre and the States not by any law made by the Centre, but by the Constitution itself. This is what the Constitution does. The States in our Constitution are in no way dependent upon the Centre for their legislative and executive authority. The Centre and the State are co-equal in this matter..... The chief mark of Federalism lies in the partition of the legislative and executive authority between Centre and Units by the Constitution. There can be no mistake about it. It is, therefore, wrong to say that the States have been placed under the Centre."[1]

(3) Supremacy of Written and Rigid Constitution. Another Federal Feature of our Constitution is that it is written and rigid. It is unlike the British Constitution which is based only on practices and conventions and hence cannot be interpreted in a liberal and flexible manner. Both national and

1. *Constituent Assembly Debates*, Vol. VIII, p. 33.

regional governments derive their power from this supreme and sacred law of the land. There is no possibility of any confusion regarding the distribution.

(4) Special Position of the Judiciary. The third Federal Feature of our Constitution is the provision of a Supreme Court to act as the guardian of the Constitution. It interprets the controversial clauses and decides all constitutional disputes between the Central and the State Governments. It contains the Union and the States to the spheres allotted to them.

However, it may be added that the jurisdiction of the Supreme Court may be invoked not only by a person[1] who has been affected by a Union or State law which, according to him, has violated the constitutional distribution of powers but also by the Union and the States themselves by bringing a direct action against each other, before the Original Jurisdiction of the Supreme Court under Article 131[2]. It is because of these basic Federal Features that our Supreme Court has described the Constitution as 'Federal'.[3]

The points stated above bear testimony to the fact that Indian Constitution is Federal in form. But a Federal Government generally tends to be weak. The Fathers of the Indian Constitution as such tried to do their best to strengthen the hands of the National Government. They devised methods of intervention by the Centre in the affairs of the Provinces, which gave the Constitution a quasi-federal character. The centralisation of authority was essential in view of bitter lessons of history of medieval India. The slavery of India was in fact the result of multiplicity of petty independent States and our Constitution-makers were cautious enough not to repeat that mistake.

All Constitutions, as *Ivor Jennings* remarks, "are the heirs of the past as well as the testators of the future". The *Framers of the Constitution* were fully conscious of the centrifugal tendencies which were at work at the time of the partition and afterwards. The partition of the country and the keenness of main Indian States to declare their independence was shocking to them. Besides that, disruptive forces of caste, communalism and regionalism were at full play. There was war in Kashmir in October 1947, when Pakistan attached her. There was communist insurrection in Telangana and Razakar trouble in Hyderabad. Therefore, Nasiruddin Ahmed, a Member of the Constituent Assembly, declared, "There are forces of disintegration and disorder already visible everywhere."[4] Consequently, the Fathers of the Indian Constitution were anxious to strengthen the authority of the Centre in order to curb the disintegrating tendencies of casteism, communalism and regionalism. So while defending the emergency powers vested in the President, *T.T. Krishnamachari* observed, "*These Emergency Provisions have got to be tolerated that all our efforts to frame a Constitution may not ultimately be jeopardized.*" Thus the Constitution-makers were anxious to safeguard the unity and integrity of the country and for that purpose it was necessary to strengthen the authority of the Centre. Following Unitary elements were introduced in the federal polity of India in order to make a strong Centre.

NON-FEDERAL OR UNITARY FEATURES OF THE INDIAN CONSTITUTION

In addition to the above Federal Features, the Indian Constitution contains certain non-Federal or Unitary Features which have led the critics of the Indian Constitution to challenge its Federal character and charge that it is merely Federal in form but Unitary in spirit. At the outset it has to be admitted that the Framers of the Indian Constitution have deviated from the Traditional Federal system and incorporated a number of unitary Features. Some of the important Unitary Features of our Constitution are as under:

1. *Cf. Gujarat University* v. *Shri Krisna*, A.I.R. 1963 S.C. 703 (715-16) *Waverly Mills* v. *Rayman & Co.*, A.I.R. 1963 S.C. 90 (95).
2. *Cf. State of West Bengal* v. Union of India, A.I.R. 1963 S.C. 1241.
3. *Cf. Atiabari Tea Co.* v. State of Assam, (1961) I.S.C.R. 809 (860) ; *Automobile Transport* v. State of Rajasthan, A.I.R. 1962 S.C. 1406 (1416).
4. *Constituent Assembly Debates*, Vol. IX, p. 125.

1. Single Citizenship. That there is a definite swing towards Unitary System in the Indian Constitution is an established fact. In the Federal System of United States of America, there exists double citizenship—one of the Union and the other of the States. In India, as in Canada and Burma, there is only one set of citizenship. In respect of Fundamental Rights and Civil Rights all citizens are equal. The law guarantees equality of opportunity to every citizen, irrespective of his place of birth, race, caste, sex or religion. There is free movement of people from one Province to another without any problem of citizenship. Single citizenship curbs Provincialism and promotes the feeling of oneness in the country.

2. Distribution of Powers Favours the Centre. Whatever might have been the position at the drafting stage and impression taken by others, it is very clear for the final draft that the Constituent Assembly definitely meant to strengthen the hands of the Centre. The principle followed in the distribution of powers seems to be favourable to the Centre. The Union List contains 97 subjects of national importance. Though the power of the Centre and States to legislate on a Concurrent Subject is co-ordinate and equal, in case of dispute between the two, the Central law is to get the precedence. The Union Parliament also possesses the power to legislate, even on a State Subject under specified circumstances. The Residuary Powers that means powers on subjects not included in any of the three lists, have also been assigned not to the States but to the Union Government.

Here we have followed the Canadian model instead of the U.S. model.

3. Proclamation of Emergency. Federalism, generally, presupposes equality of status between two sets of government—the National and the Regional. The Constitution of India does not adhere to this principle rightly. It empowers the President according to Article 352 to declare emergency in the event of a threat to the security of India whether by war, aggression or an armed rebellion.[1] When a Proclamation of Emergency is in operation, the President can issue Directives to the State Governments and thus empower the Union Parliament to make laws for the whole or any part of India with respect to any matter mentioned in the State List. In that case the states can even be deprived of their autonomy leading to the concentration of powers in the Central Government as we find in a Unitary System.

The practical wisdom of this provision was demonstrated in the wake of Chinese Aggression (1962) and Pakistani Aggression (1965, 1971) when India was converted practically into a Unitary State and was able to pool all her resources to meet the challenge posed by the foreign aggression and could come out successfully, notwithstanding her Federal Structure.

According to Article 356, the President has been given powers to supersede the State Government and impose Central Rule if he is satisfied on the report of the Governor or otherwise that the State Government cannot be carried on according to the Constitution. This is called Constitutional Emergency. In that case either the State Legislature and the executive are dissolved or the Legislature is kept in animated suspension. Under such conditions the Governor of the State begins to govern the state as an agent of the President or in practice the nominee of the Ruling Party at the Centre. It is surprising that the Constitution-Makers did not vest in the President to assume to himself all such powers in case of breakdown of the constitutional machinery at the Centre. Hence K.M. Panikkar is justified in observing—

> "The Constitution itself has created a kind of paramountcy for the Centre by providing for the suspension of state government and the imposition of President's Rule under certain conditions such as the breakdown of the administration."

As the President can declare the Constitutional Emergency even without the report or advice of the Governor, so it is a coercive power available to the Centre to correct the erring states or the units of federation.

---

1. 44th Amendment (1978)

The third type of Emergency when the Constitution assumes a Unitary Form is during Financial Emergency. Article 360 provides that the President may proclaim a state of emergency when he is satisfied that the financial stability or credit of India is threatened. During the operation of this emergency the executive authority of Union extends to giving directions to the States to observe certain rules. Such directions may include a provision requiring the reduction of salaries of any class of persons in the state service, including the judges of the High Courts. The President may ask the States to reserve their Money Bills for his own consideration. In short the entire financial machinery of the States passes under the control of the Centre during the operation of the proclamation of emergency. Dr. Bhim Rao Ambedkar frankly admitted in the Constituent Assembly that "the Constitution has not been set in a tight mould of Federalism." It has been so designed as to work on a federal basis in times of peace and Unitary basis in times of war.

4. Extension of Union Parliament's Authority in Normal Times. Even in normal times the authority of the Union Parliament can be extended to the State List. If the Council of States by a majority vote admits that a subject hitherto included in a state list has become of national interest, the Parliament becomes authorised to enact laws on the subject for a period of one year.

5. No Right of the State to Secede. The component units in the Federation of the U.S.A., the U.S.S.R. and Switzerland have the right to draft separate Constitutions. In the U.S.S.R. the states also possess the right of self-determination which means that they can secede from the Federation if they like. The Indian Constitution, since it leans towards a Unitary System, does not give the states the right to frame separate Constitutions or break away with the Union.

6. Right of the Parliament to Tamper with the Territorial Integrity of the States. Another characteristic of Unitary System in our Constitution is that the Parliament is empowered to alter the boundaries and name of any State. It can also form a new State by cutting off territory from one or more than one state. A Bill proposing such a change can be introduced in the Parliament only after the President has ascertained the views of the State legislatures affected by alterations. The advice of the States is, however, not binding on the President. Availing itself of this provision, the Indian Parliament in 1956 went ahead with the reorganisation of the States and changed the political map of India.

From 1st November, 1966, the Punjab was bifurcated into two States, Punjab and Haryana. The Hindi-speaking areas of the Punjab were ceded to Haryana. District Kangra was merged with Himachal Pradesh and mainly Punjabi-speaking areas remained with the Punjab. Himachal Pradesh was previously a Union Territory, but on 25th January, 1971, Himachal Pradesh was given statehood. On the 20th January, 1972, North-East Frontier Agency (NEFA) was named Arunachal Pradesh and made a Union Territory. On 21st January, 1972, Mizoram consisting of the Mizo Hills of Assam was carved out separately and named Mizoram and made a Union Territory. According to the North-Eastern Areas (Reorganisation) Act, 1971, Manipur, Tripura and Meghalaya were given statehood. The then Prime Minister of India, Mrs. Indira Gandhi, inaugurated Meghalaya State and Union Territory of Arunachal Pradesh on January 20, 1972 and Union Territory of Mizoram and States of Manipur and Tripura on January 21, 1972. According to the 35th Amendment, Sikkim was made an Associate State of India from 1st March, 1975. Later on, according to the 36th Amendment it was made 22nd State of India from 26th April, 1975. Up to 15th November 2000 there were 28 states in India and 7 Union Territories. Goa became a State by virtue of Goa, Daman and Diu Reorganisation Act 1987, separating it from Daman and Diu with effect from 30.5.1987. A new State of Chhattisgarh was created by carving out its territory from that of the territories of the Madhya Pradesh by enacting the Madhya Pradesh Reorganisation Act 2000 (w.e.f 1-11-2000). The State of Uttaranchal came into being on 9-11-2000 by separating its territory out of the territories of Uttar Pradesh vide the Uttar Pradesh Reorganisation Act, 2000. By enacting the Bihar Reorganisation Act 2000, the State of Jharkhand was created on 15-11-2000 by carving its territory out of the territories of the Bihar state. Thus the political map of India had been redrawn completely. There is a possibility that some new states may be carved out in future out of the existing states or statehood may be conferred on some

Union territory. No such provision exists in U.S.A. where no territorial adjustment can be made without the approval of the states concerned.

7. Unequal State Representation in the Council of States. One of the essential features of Federation is the acceptance of equality of the component states without any consideration of their size or population. In the Federal Systems of United States of America, Switzerland and Australia, all the federating units have equal representation in the Upper House. In India, however, that federal principle has not been observed. The states are represented not uniformly but in proportion to their size and population.

8. Appointment of Governors by the President. Unlike the procedure followed in other federations, the State Governors in India are not elected, but appointed by the President. A Governor holds office during the pleasure of the President who can also remove him at will. It is expected of the Governor to keep the President duly informed of all the state affairs and also execute the directions issued by the President in emergency times. In this way the extent of the Central Authority covers the whole of Provincial Administration.

The Governor is expected to work as agent of the Central Government. The Central Government would naturally like to enforce its authority in the States with the help of the Governor. So long as the same party rules at the Centre and in the States, the chances of conflict are remote, but when the different political parties rule at the Centre and in the States, the conflicts often occur as happened after the 4th, 7th, 8th and 9th General Elections. During such times the Central Government uses the Governor to further its own ends and on the report of the Governor or otherwise, the Union Cabinet recommends to the President to impose his rule under Article 356. In this way, the State's Ministry is superseded and the Central Government can have its way. Article 356 of the present Indian Constitution resembles with Section 93 of the Government of India Act, 1935. The Sarkaria Commission has particularly recommended the cautious use of this Article but no Government has done it so far.[1]

9. Centre's right to give directions to the States and supersede them in cases of non-compliance. Article 356 lays down, "Where any State has failed to comply with, or to give effect to, any directions given in the exercise of the executive power of the Union under any of the provisions of this Constitution, it shall be lawful for the President to hold that a situation has arisen in which the government of the State cannot be carried on in accordance with the provisions of this Constitution. Under such conditions, the President can declare a Proclamation of Emergency under Article 356 and easily supersede the state concerned.

10. Governor's Powers to withhold the Bills passed by the State Legislature and reserve them for the assent of the President. Articles 200 and 201 empower the Governor to give his assent to any Bill passed by the State Legislature or withhold it or reserve it for the consideration of the President. Thus the Governors and the President exercise veto power and can delay the implementation of the Bills which they do not like. Article 200 further provides that the Governor shall not assent to but shall reserve for the Consideration of the President , any Bill which in the opinion of the Governor would, if it became law, so derogate from the powers of the High Court as to endanger the position which that Court is by this Constitution designed to fill. So under these pretexts the Governors and the President can bully the States Ministries of Opposition Parties and can have their way to some or great extent as the case might be and can get a Bill modified to suit their convenience.

11. Right of Parliament to enforce any treaty, agreement or convention. Article 253 lays down that, "Parliament has power to make any law for the whole or any part of the territory of India for implementing any treaty, agreement or convention with any other country or countries or any decision made at any international conference, association or other body." In Jammu and Kashmir State this provision cannot be applied without the consent of that state. While commenting on this

1. This was the position up to 20th October, 1990.

Article, Dr. Jennings observes, "The last phrase of Article 253, namely, any association or body is vague and the Union Parliament can acquire jurisdiction of any subject, as for example, even over university education, by the simple process of a decision of the Inter-University Board of India, which is an internatiional body because it contains representatives of universities in Burma and Ceylon.[1]

12. Power of Parliament to legislate for two or more States by consent and adoption of such legislation by any other State. As in India since the dawn of freedom up to March, 1988, Congress had been ruling at the Centre as well as in most States except for a brief spell of Janata Party Rule, therefore it had been easier for the Centre to persuade the States to agree to the legislation it wants to pass for them. The State Legislatures of Bombay, Madhya Pradesh, Orissa, Punjab, Uttar Pradesh, Rajasthan etc. allowed Parliament to levy estate duty on agricultural land situated in those States. Parliament accordingly passed the Estate Duty Act, 1953 and it applied to agricultural land situated in those states. Surrender of such powers, once made, is unconditional and irrevocable. Any such act can be repealed or modified only by the Parliament and not State Legislature. Therefore, after giving powers the States have to depend upon the sweet will of the Centre.

13. The Constitution ensures Uniformity in Basic Matters. Because of two sets of government under Federation—the national, there appear diversities in judiciary and legal disparities occur from State to State. According to Dr. Ambedkar, "Up to a certain point, this diversity does not matter. It may be welcomed as being an attempt to accommodate the powers of Government to local needs and circumstances. But this diversity, when it goes beyond a certain point, is capable of producing chaos in many Federal States." In order to avoid such confusions and diversities, the Indian Constitution makes clear-cut demarcation of administration of State Laws and Union Laws. There are State Services to administer State Laws and there are Union Services to execute and enforce Union Laws. But the Union can delegate any of its functions to state officers. Articles 256 and 257 lay down that it is the duty of the state to honour the Union laws and authority of the Union Executive. Besides this Central Authority over the States, the Constitution provides for All India Administrative Services, uniform civil and criminal codes, a Comptroller and Auditor-General to ensure uniformity in financial matters and an Election Commission to guarantee fair elections in the country.

IS INDIA A TRUE FEDERATION ?

What type of Federation should be made in India, exercised the minds of the Framers of the Constitution. The members of the Drafting Committee of the Constitution were in favour of making the Centre as strong as possible within the framework of federalism, because they were quite aware of the centrifugal forces in India since the dawn of her history. But some Members of the Constituent Assembly expressed their disappointment also with the Federal scheme envisaged in the Constitution. They contended that the Constitution provided for a strong Unitary Government and the States to the position of glorified district boards. For instance, Mr. P.T.Chacko said that "what the Constitution would establish was in the form of a federation.... in substance a Unitary Constitution."[2] *Mahboob Ali* and *N.G. Ranga* feared that "the emphasis on centralisation and the easy means with which the Central Government could convert the federal system into a unitary one might lead to totalitarianism and to the absolute negation of democracy."[3] *Shyamanandan Sahay* maintained that "the Constitution had created a kind of fedro-unitary system leaning heavily towards a unitary system and units would be perpetual wards of the Centre."[4] *Mr. B. M. Gupta* expressed the opinion that "India would be not a federal state, but a decentralised unitary State."[5] *Mr. K.M. Munshi* observed in 1953, "India is not

1. Jennings, *Some Characteristics of the Indian Constitution*, p. 66.
2. *Constituent Assembly Debates*, Vol. XI, p. 475.
3. *Ibid*, Vol. VII, pp. 296 and 350.
4. *Constituent Assembly Debates*, Vol. XI, p. 788.
5. *Ibid.*, p. 844

a federation, but a Union, and the Centre is not a federal Government, but a Government of plenary powers and social purpose."[1] *Mr. H.V. Pataskar*, former Governor of Madhya Pradesh, while addressing the State unit of the Indian Council of World Affairs, said, "To my mind our Constitution is not a federal one."[2] In his paper submitted to the All India Political Science Conference, entitled, *Is India a Federation ? Dr. Krishana P. Mukherjee* maintains, "I have come to take the view that whatever might have been the position at the drafting stage or deliberations of the Constituent Assembly of India in January, 1950, it is a definitely unfederal or unitary Constitution."[3] Dr. *K. C. Wheare*, the renowned authority of Federalism, says, "On the whole it seems evident that the Constituent Assembly intends the Union to be more centralised that was proposed by the Act of 1935, although in that case also there were methods of intervention permitted to the Centre in the affairs of the provinces which reminded one more of the Canadian conception of federation that of the United States one. The new Constitution goes further still. It establishes, indeed, a system of Government which is at most quasi-federal, almost devolutionary in character, a unitary state with subsidiary federal features rather than a federal State with subsidiary unitary features."[4] *Sir Ivor Jennings* and *Gledhill* also mainly agree with the conclusion of *Dr. K.C. Wheare. Professor Morris Jones* in *The Sunday Times* wrote that as a result of the Fourth General Elections "India comes of age as federal state in the full sense of the term and with all the difficulties that it entails. As the United States of America has learnt many times, this makes problems but also makes a step towards a pattern of policies that really fits her diversity."[5] After the 4th General Elections of 1967, Mid-term elections to the Lok Sabha were held in March 1971, and Legislative Assemblies in March, 1972, and the Ruling Congress Party won 352 seats in the Lok Sabha out of 518 elective seats and 1,926 seats out of 2,722 in the Legislative Assemblies. Therefore, the authority of the Centre has been further strengthened and the conflicts between the Centre and the States inherent in the federal structure have become less frequent.

On June 25, 1975, Internal Emergency was imposed on the country by the President, Mr. Fakhruddin Ali Ahmed, on the advice of the then Prime Minister Shrimati Indira Gandhi, who even did not care to take her Cabinet into confidence for such a drastic step. At that time the States were solely at the mercy of the Centre. In March, 1977, Elections to the Lok Sabha were held and Janata Party scored a resounding victory. It won 271 seats out of 539 seats, three seats were vacant at that time. The Congress lost heavily due to excesses in the Emergency period which lasted from June 25, 1975 to 22 March, 1977. The Congress was able to secure only 153 seats. Up till July, 1977 three vacant seats had been filled, out of them one more had been secured by the Janata Party and one seat had been shared by the Congress and one by Akali Party. Besides it, the Congress for Democracy had also merged with the Janata Party in May, 1977 with its 28 seats. Therefore, the strength of Janata Party had risen to 300 up to July, 1977 and it continued so till 1st May, 1978. So there was absolutely no fear of the breaking of the Indian Federation and the Centre continued to dominate the States because of the financial help it gave and various cogent reasons. After the 7th General Eelections, the Centre has been dominating the states.

Survival of the Indian Federation. At the same time there is no denying the fact that the States have frequently expressed their grievances against the domination of the Centre especially when some states are being ruled by a different party than at the Centre. The case of Karnataka is a point when President's Rule was proclaimed on 10th October, 1990.

The Centre has been dominating the States mostly due to financial reasons and the domination

1. *The Statesman*, New Delhi, August 14, 1953, p. 6.
2. *Hindustan Times*, New Delhi, December 24, 1964., p. 5.
3. *The Indian Journal of Political Science*, July-September, 1954, p. 177.
4. *Aspects of Indian Constitution*, p. 80
5. As reported in the *Hindustan Times*, New Delhi, March 25, 1967.

of one and the same party at the Centre as well as in most of the States. The Planning Commission which was not given such a place in the Constitution as Election Commission or the Public Service Commission finalises the plans of all the States and then it is approved in the National Development Council which consists of the Prime Minister, all the Chief Ministers and the Members of the Planning Commission. It decides how much financial help is to be given to the States.

During the Internal Emergency the Centre dominated the states completely. Even the Constitution was amended a good deal to give to the Centre a dominant position. According to the 42nd Amendment Act (1976), six subjects were transferred from the State List to the Concurrent List like education, forests, administration of justice, constitution and organisation of all courts except the Supreme Court and the High Courts, population control and family planning, weights and measures except establishment of standards. Besides that the Constitution 42nd Amendment Act inserted a new Article 257A empowering the Union Government to deploy any armed forces of the Union or any other force under the control of the Union for dealing with any grave situation of law and order in any State. Many persons regarded this provision as a silent transfer of federalism into virtual unitarianism. For instance, *K. Santhanam* described it as a paramountcy of the Centre in place of a strong Centre as visualised by the Founding Fathers.

The Janata Government, however, got enacted Forty-fourth Amendment Act, 1978 which removed many anomalies of the 42nd Amendment Act, 1976 because there was a strong reaction against over-centralism. The States had protested against the highly coercive power being vested in the Union which was not envisaged by the framers of the Constitution. Therefore, the Janata Government repealed Article 257A by getting passed 44th Amendment Bill by Parliament which later on became the 44th Amendment Act. It is worth noting that even the Congress Party, which had enacted this provision, did not object to its repeal in the Parliament but Entry 2A in the Union List, relating to the deployment of armed forces inserted by the 42nd Amendment Act, was retained.

Once Haryana, West Bengal, Andhra Pradesh and Karnataka demanded more rights for the States because the Opposition had come into power but the federation did not break down. Therefore, there is coexistence. There are two factors at interplay in India : (i) There is a division of powers between the Centre and States and under the federal scheme the States enjoy autonomy,within their allotted sphere. Some states are also demanding more and more autonomy, (ii) The Central Government and the saner people of India want to keep the Centre as strong as possible in the interests of the sovereignty and integrity of the country.

The interplay of the above two forces in the working of the federation in India has been acknowledged even by the Supreme Court the various provisions of the Constitution, *e.g.*, in explaining the significance of Article 301[1] thus —

> "The evolution of a federal structure of a quasi-federal structure necessarily involved, in the context of the conditions then prevailing, a distribution of powers and a basic part of our Constitution relates to that distribution with the three legislative lists in the Seventh Schedule. The Constitution itself says by Article 1 that India is a Union of States and in interpreting the Constitution, one must keep in view the essential structure of a federal or quasi-federal Constitution, namely, that *the units of the Union have also certain powers as has the Union itself*.... In evolving as an integrated policy on this subject our Constitution-makers seem to have kept in mind three main considerations .... first in the larger interest of India there must be free flow of trade, commerce and intercourse, both inter-state and intra-state; second, the *regional* interest must not be ignored altogether, and third, there must be a power of intervention by the Union in case of crisis to deal with particular problems that may arise in any part

1. *Automobile Transport* v *State of Rajasthan* A.I.R. 1962 S.C. 1406 (1415-16). In *Keshavanada* v. *Union of India*, A.I.R. 1973 S.C. 1461, some of the judges (paras, 302, 599, 1681) considered federalism to be one of the basic features of our Constitution.

of India .... Therefore, in interpreting the relevant articles in Part XIII, we must have regard to the *general scheme* of the Constitution of India with special reference to Part III. Part XII ... and their inter-relation to Part XIII *in the context of a federal or quasi-federal constitution* in which the States have certain powers including the power to raise revenues for their *purpose by taxation*."

Need for a strong Centre. The existence of a strong Centre is not inconsistent with the theory and practice of Federalism. Each country evolves its own pattern of Union-State relations in the light of its historical background and its political, economic and social conditions. But a strong Centre must not be so strong which may render the States hapless and helpless or in the words of Riker to overawe the constitutional governments.[1] But that is not the case. The States have survived of their own right. The strong Central bias of our federation has, however, been a boon to keep India together in spite of the separatist forces of communalism, linguism and scramble for power which are playing havoc, notwithstanding all the devices of Central control, even after three decades of the working of the Constitution. It is also to be admitted that the States are not working like the agents of Centre as some critics have alleged. If that would have been the case, the Assam and Punjab agitations could not be dragged for such a long time.

Indian Federation is a sure improvement on other federations of the world. It incorporates what is best in both the federal and unitary forms. The basic principles of Federalism are the distribution of powers between the Centre and the States, the supremacy of the Constitution and the establishment of a Supreme Court to uphold and interpret the Constitution. Judged in this light the Indian system conforms to federal principles. Critics allege that our Constitution tilts more towards unitary form by making the Centre strong. The autonomy of the States has been considerably restricted because of the overriding powers of the Centre. It is a partnership not among the equals but between a strong Centre and weak units. But this charge loses ground when we study the Constitution at work. The exceptional powers of the Centre are exercised only in emergency times, not normally. The framers of our Constitution intended to make the Constitution a living organism which may rise to the occasion and tackle the unusual situations with ease and firmness. The wide powers given to the Union Government are intended to face and overcome the constitutional crises and to check the separatist tendencies on the part of the States. The need of a strong Centre is being increasingly felt in every perfect freedom with regard to state subjects and the President possesses no constitutional right to declare a state of emergency. Still the Centre has on many occasions asserted its supremacy and tried to enforce its laws by sending armed federal forces to the states. The exeuse given for such interfeence was that the disturbance in the states was likely to prejudice the federal responsibility of ensuring inter-state trade and commerce and communications.

In every federation there is a growing tendency towards centralisation. *David Fallman* has correctly observed that the American Supreme Court "has snuffed out the heresy of dual federalism. The Court, by invoking the doctrine of Implied Powers, has assigned a vast sweep of authority to the Centre. In fact, the centralisation is the most significant aspect of the operative machinery not only of American Federalism, but also of the Australian, Canadian and Swiss Federalism." What courts, conventions, practices and usages have achieved in America, Canada, Australia and Switzerland, these have been enshrined in the express Constitutional provisions.[2]

DISTINCTION BETWEEN THE U.S. AND INDIAN FEDERATIONS (Comparison and Contrast)

India has not strictly adopted the United States of America pattern of Federation because the political conditions of India were different at that time. Secondly, the United States of America model

1. Riker William, H. *Federalism: Origin, Operation, Significance*, p. 86.
2. Constituent Assembly Debates, Vol. VII, pp. 335-36.

would not have suited India at all. It is also to be admitted that there are different variations of the federal system in the world. India had followed more or less Canadian system rather than the United States of America System of Federation. The following differences can be briefly summarised:

Position of the states in the Federation. 1. When the United States of America Federation was formed, they were independent states and they wanted to form the Union for certain common purpose. Therefore, they were ready to give only such powers to the Union as were necessary and they were most anxious to safeguard their rest of the rights. On the other hand, when the Indian Federation was formed, the provinces were not independent. The Indian States were made sovereign only in name on the lapse of British paramountcy and they were required either to join India or Pakistan. Except a few States, all other States joined India. First they were persuaded to adopt the whole Indian Constitution in the same way as the provinces. Then they were placed on the same footing and the difference between 'A' States (former provinces) and 'B' States (former Indian States) was ended. Therefore, the credit of the integration of states with the Indian Union goes to Sardar Vallabhbhai Pattel and Pt. Jawaharlal Nehru.

2. In the Constitution of U.S.A. the powers of the Union have been described which are very few and the rest of the powers have been reserved for the States. The Indian Constitution describes the powers of the Union and the States separately. There are three lists of distribution of powers in India, the Union List, the Concurrent List and the State List.

3. In the United States of America, the residuary powers are reserved to the States by the Constitution, while in India, the residuary powers are given to the Centre (Article 248) because we have followed here the Canadian System in vesting the residuary powers in the Union.

4. While the Constitution of the U.S.A. merely drew up the Constitution of the National Government and the States were left to draw up their own Constitutions in conformity with the Centre or to keep their original constitutions, the Constitution of India lays down elaborately the organisations of both the National (Central) Government and State Governments. In India, no State has been allowed to draw up its own constitution except the State of Jammu and Kashmir. Only that State has been awarded special status according to Article 370.

5. The American Federation has been described as indestructible consisting of indestructible States but this is not so in India, where the Parliament is empowered to reorganise the states or to alter their boundaries by a simple majority in the ordinary process of legislation [Article 4(2)]. Our Constitution does not require that the Parliament should obtain the *consent* of the state legislature before effecting the change in their boundaries; only the President of India has to 'ascertain' the views of the legislatures of the affected states to recommend a Bill for the Parliament. The President can also fix a time-limit within which the state has to express its views (Proviso to Article 3 as amended). If the state does not express its view, it will be presumed that the state has agreed to the proposals of the President or Parliament, as the case might be. Therefore, in 1956 according to the recommendations of the States Reorganisation Commission, an Act was made according to which the states were reorganised. Hyderabad State which was a premier state of India was eliminated from the political map of India and instead the Andhra State was formed *after taking parts of old Madras Presidency or Madras province*. Even after this several new states—Gujarat, Nagaland, Haryana, Meghalaya, Himachal Pradesh, Manipur, Tripura, Mizoram, Arunachal Pradesh and Goa—were formed. This could happen in India with ease because the states were destructible while in the U.S.A. the states are indestructible because their consent is required for the alteration of boundaries. In India only the Union is indestructible and the states cannot secede from the Centre at their will. According to 16th Amendment of the Constitution (1963), even the advocacy of secession will be totally illegal and it will not be covered by the freedom of expression. Our Constitution also differs in this respect fundamentally from the U.S.S.R. (Article 72 of the Constitution of 1977). The Australian Constitution also follows the pattern of U.S.A. and declares that the Commonwealth (Union) is "indissolvable" and that a popular referendum is required in the affected state to alter its boundaries.

6. In U.S.A. the theory of equality of states has been recognised because the federation is the result of agreement. Therefore in U.S.A., whether a state is big or small, it sends two representatives in the Senate. At present there are 50 states in the U.S.A., therefore, the strength of the Senate is 100. This principle of equality has not been recognised in India because the federation is not the result of agreement between the states. Therefore, in the Council of States, the states have been given representation on the basis of population. Consequently, big states dominate the small states in the Council of States in India. While Uttar Pradesh, the most populous State, has got 34 seats in the Council of States, Nagaland, Meghalaya, Manipur, Tripura and Sikkim have got one seat each in the Council of States.

Anybody who studies the Constitution of India impartially and acknowledges that there are various types of federations in the world, will have to admit that the Indian Constitution is federal but within the limits of federalism every effort has been made to make the Centre as strong as possible because the centrifugal forces are to be checked and the sovereignty and integrity of the country are to be defended. It will be readily admitted by all the same persons that only a very strong Centre can check the forces of communalism, casteism and separatism. While it is conceded that the state must enjoy autonomy within the allotted sphere, the Centre also has not to be weakened. Of course, the Constitution of our country harmonises the interests of both the Centre and the states in a beautiful way.

A spirit of co-operation will be visible in India after some time because the policy of confrontation with the Centre will not pay to the states. The Centre has already disallowed the new overdrafts to the states and converted previous overdrafts into loans. Under the above state circumstances, co-operative federalism is the only way which the Centre as well as states must adopt.

INDIAN FEDERATION COMPARED AND CONTRASTED WITH THE CANADIAN FEDERATION

As we have derived much from the Canadian Federalism, it is necessary to give it in detail so that we may learn where we have adopted some of its features and where we have avoided it. Canada consists of ten provinces which are termed as states in our country. The Canadian Constitution—the British North America Act, 1867 and certain subsequent amending Acts—present certain definite federal characteristics. *First*, it divides the powers between the Dominion and Provincial Governments by giving the latter exclusive legislative control over a list of enumerated subjects. The Dominion has exclusive legislative control over the rest, which for great clarity, as the British North America Act states have also been enumerated though not exhaustively. In other words, the subjects of the Provincial interest have been described in detail and given in the Provincial list and the subjects of national interest have been given in the Dominion (Central) list. The subjects of the provincial interest have been described in detail and the powers over the rest have been given to the central Government. Therefore, the residuary powers have been given to the Centre and efforts have been made to make the Centre as strong as possible. This was done because when the Constitution of Canada was framed, then a fierce civil war had swept the U.S.A. (There was a Civil War between the Northern and Southern states and President Abraham Lincoln had been assassinated) and the framers of the Canadian Constitution had learnt a lesson from the bitter Civil War raging U.S.A. Therefore to avoid the happening of U.S.A., they tried to strengthen the Centre. India has also followed the Canadian model to a great extent, because it gives residuary powers to the Centre and makes the Centre as strong as possible. The only difference is that the Indian Constitution, for clarity sake, describes the powers of the Centre and states in three lists.

Secondly, Governments of the Dominion (Centre) and the Provinces are distinct in personnel from each other and neither has the power to alter the Constitution so far as the distribution of subjects is concerned. The Constitution-changing power rested with the British Parliament at that time but recently it has been done away with. Finally, the Canadian Courts can declare Dominion or Provincial laws void on the ground that they transgress the jurisdiction assigned to the respective governments by the Constitution. This establishes the supremacy of the Constitution. India has also followed this pattern.

The majority of the delegates assembled at the Quebec Conference in 1867 had the abiding conviction that the first and foremost lesson which they had to learn from the Civil War raging U.S.A., was that they must strengthen the Centre to avoid such a happening in their own country. "The true principle of confederation", asserted *Sir John MacDonald*, "lay in giving to the Central Government all the principles and powers of sovereignty and that the subordinate or individual states should have no powers but those expressly bestowed on them. We should, thus, have a powerful Central Government, a powerful Central Legislature and a decentralised system of minor legislatures for local purposes."

At another occasion *Sir John MacDonald* confidently claimed that, "*Here we have adopted a different system. We have strengthened the Central Government. We have given the Central Legislature all the great subjects of legislation. We have thus avoided that great source of weakness which has been the cause of the disruption of the United States.*" Thus the framers of the Canadian Constitution tried to become wiser from the Civil War which had lent the Central Government of U.S.A. in greatest difficulty and avoid all possibilities to plague their own.

The Fathers of the Canadian Constitution departed from the U.S. Federal System in order to make the Centre as strong as possible. For this purpose they adopted the following measures:

(1) The provincial list contained subjects essentially of a local nature and such subjects as criminal law, marriage and divorce, were given in the Canadian Constitution to the Dominion.

(2) All the powers not expressly given to the Provinces were granted to the Dominion (Centre). On the other hand, the Constitution of the United States of America enumerated the powers of the Centre and gave the rest of powers to the states. This means in other words that the powers not given to the Centre were reserved for the states. The Tenth Amendment clearly stated that "the powers not delegated to the United States of America by the Constitution, nor prohibited by it to the states, are reserved to the states respectively, or the people." The Quebec Conference which drafted the Canadian Constitution decided to follow a different course which suited more the conditions prevalent in that country and reserved the residuary powers to the Centre. Therefore, instead of describing the powers of the Centre, they described powers of the Provinces only so that the powers of the Provinces may remain limited and the powers of the Centre may always grow. And in order to leave no vagueness for posterity, the Constitution of Canada after enumerating a long list of powers which were explicitly placed under the Dominion jurisdiction, Section 91 of the British North America Act empowered the National Parliament "to make laws for the peace, order and good government of Canada in relation to all matters not coming within the classes of subjects by this Act assigned exclusively to the legislatures of the Provinces." This is an all-embracing clause which enables the Dominion Parliament to make the laws even on subjects which are within competence of the Provinces on the plea that they affected the peace, order and good Government of Canada. India has followed the Canadian Model rather than the U.S. pattern to a great extent.

(3) The Dominion Government (Central Government) in Canada was given the power to disallow any law passed by a Provincial Legislature within a year of its passage. In India also the powers were given to the Central Government in a different form. Here those Bills which affected the Inter-State commerce or the powers of the High Court or any power of the Parliament, could be reserved for the President's Assent by the Governor.

(4) The Dominion Government possessed the power of appointing and removing the Lieutenant-Governor in each Province. This power has also been given to the President of India. The Dominion

Government can also instruct the Lieutenant-Governor to withhold his assent to Provincial Bills or reserve them for the consideration by this Governor-General. The Governor-General might refuse assent to such reserved Bills if he though fit. This power is also enjoyed by the President of India.

(5) All important judicial appointments in the Provinces were vested in the Dominion Government. This is also the case with India where all the judges and Chief Justices of the High Courts are appointed by the President of India.

(6) While in the United States equal representation to big and small states was given in the Senate, this is not the case in Canada. The Senate in Canada was not designed to protect provincial interests. So is the case with the Council of States where equal representation of big and small states is not given and they are not expected to protect provincial interests.

The Canadian Federation thus departed fundamentally from the U.S. Federation because its architects wanted to establish a very strong Centre. Speaking on the Quebec Resolution in Parliament of Canada on February 6, 1865, Sir John MacDonald said, "*We ...... strengthen the Central parliament and make the confederation one people and one government, instead of five peoples and five governments, with merely a point of authority connecting us to a limited and insufficient extent ... This is to be one United Province with the local Governments and Legislatures subordinate to the General Government and Legislature.*" Thus it was the definite intention of the constitution-makers to make the Provincial Governments in Canada subordinate to the Central Government and not co-ordiante with it. The British North America Act had empowered the Dominion Government to prevent the Provincial legislature from making laws upon its allotted subject, if the Dominion Government happened to disapprove the policy involved in such laws. The powers of disallowance and veto further rendered the Provinces helplessly dependent upon the Central Government. In *Disallowance and Reservation* (1938) the Supreme Court of Canada held that the Dominion Government's powers of disallowance and veto were unrestricted in laws and extended to all kinds of legislation, financial and ordinary. This is tantamount to placing the Provincial Governments entirely on the mercy of the Dominion Government. It should be noted clearly that the Indian Constitution does not contain any such clause because that would have been over-centralisation and would have converted the States into municipalities. So the Framers of Indian Constitution were not behind imitators. They have kept the true character of the federation intact.

All the above stated elements of the Canadian Constitution especially the powers of disallowance and reservation are unitary elements and Prof. K.C. Wheare, a renowned authority on Federalism, tersely puts it, "Could there be a more powerful weapon for centralising and unifying the governemnt than this?"[1] Secondly, he examines thoroughly this tough question whether Canada is a unitary or federal type of government. His conclusion is that in spite of these unitary elements, "*the federal principle is not completely ousted*" from the Canadian Constitution; it does find a place there and an important place "yet if we confer ourselves to the strict law of the Constitution," he adds, "it is hard to know whether we should call it a Federal Constitution with considerable unitary modifications, or a Federal Constitution with considerable federal modifications. It would be straining the Federal principle too far, I think, to describe it as Federal Constitution, without adding any qualifying phrase. For this reason I prefer to say that *Canada has a quasi-federal constitution*."

1. Wheare, K.C., *Federal Government*, p. 20.

EXERCISES

Long Answer Type Questions :

1. Discuss Federalism in India.
2. Discuss the Federal Features of the Indian Constitution.
3. What are the Non-Federal or Unitary Features of the Indian Constitution? Discuss in brief.
4. Is India a true Federation? What is your opinion ? Discuss in brief.
5. What is difference between the United States of America and Indian Federations ?
6. Compare and contrast Indian Federation with the Canadian Federation.

Short Answer Type Questions :

1. What is meant by dual polity? Discuss in brief the provision of dual polity in Indian Constitution.
2. Discuss division of powers in Indian Constitution.
3. Discuss special position of Judiciary in Indian Constitution.
4. What is meant by single citizenship ?
5. Distribution of powers in Indian Constitution favours the Centre. Do you agree with this statement? Discuss in very brief.
6. Write a very brief note on 'Provision of Proclamation of Emergency in Indian Constitution."
7. Write a very brief note on 'Survival of the Indian Federation.'
8. "There is need for a strong Centre." Do you agree with this statement ?

Objective Type Questions :

1. The founding fathers of the Indian Constitution have mainly been influenced by the provisions of:
   (*a*) American federation (*b*) Canadian federation
   (*c*) Australian federation (*d*) All of the above.
2. A renowned British authority on federalism has classified India as "a unitary state with subsidiary federal principles rather than a federal state with subsidiary unitary principles." He is :
   (*a*) Ivor Jennings (*b*) Harold Laski
   (*c*) K.C. Wheare (*d*) None of the above
3. Who among the following argues that India is a true federation, although, like all other federations, it has distinctive characteristics and it is misleading to refer to India as a quasi-federation ?
   (*a*) Charles Alexandrowicz (*b*) K.C. Wheare
   (*c*) M.V. Pylee (*d*) None of the above
4. Over the last few decades the Central government in almost all the federal systems around the world have developed their powers more and more intensively at the expense of the areas originally allotted to the regional governments. National governments, hence, have grown in importance in comparison to the regional governments and all this has given rise to a variety of federalism called unitarian federalism. Which of the following have proved to be the factors responsible for the rise of this phenomenon ?
   1. War politics
   2. Depression politics and welfare politics
   3. Techno-politics
   4. Grants-in-aid politics and party politics

   Select the correct answer from the following:
   (*a*) 1 and 2 (*b*) 2 and 3
   (*c*) 2, 3 and 4 (*d*) 1, 2, 3 and 4

5. A distinguished statesman and member of the Constituent Assembly held the view that the Constitution made India, "a quasi-federal union invested with several important features of a unitary government." He was :

(*a*) Jawaharlal Nehru (*b*) K.M. Munshi

(*c*) B.R. Ambedkar (*d*) None of the above

ANSWERS

1. (*d*) 2. (*c*) 3. (*a*) 4. (*d*) 5. (*b*)

5

CHAPTER

Fundamental Rights and Duties

> *"The objects of Fundamental Rights as far as I can gather from a reading of the Constitution was.... to provide certain standard of conduct, citizenship and fairplay."*
>
> *—Justice Sapru*

Ever since the enactment of the U.S. Constitution it has become customary for all democratic countries to incorporate a Chapter on Fundamental Rights in their Constitution. The Constitution of India also outlines the Fundamental Rights of its citizens in Part III of the Constitution, which are more 'elaborate and real' than those found in any other constitution. These rights are fundamental in the sense that they are paramount and superior to all laws, executive orders and judicial decisions. No branch of the government can abridge, curtail or violate them. A law or order is considered as void to the extent it is inconsistent with the fundamental rights enshrined in the constitution. Chief Justice Patanjali Shastri considers these rights as fundamental, because their insertion "in the fore-front of Constitution coupled with an express prohibition against Legislative interference with these rights and the provision of the constitutional sanction for the enforcement of such prohibition by means of judicial review.... is a clear and emphatic indication that these rights are to be paramount to ordinary State-made law."

Durga Das Basu defines Fundamental Rights in the process of drawing a distinction between the legal and Fundamental Rights. He says "A legal right is an interest which is protected by the law and is enforceable in the courts of law. While an ordinary legal right is protected and enforced by the ordinary law of the land, a Fundamental Right is one which is protected and guaranteed by the written constitution of the state. These are called 'Fundamental' because while ordinary rights may be changed by the Legislature in its ordinary process of legislation, a Fundamental Right, being guaranteed by the Constitution, cannot be altered by any process shorter than that required for amending the constitution itself. Nor can it be suspended or abridged except in the manner laid down in the Constitution itself."

According to Chief Justice Gajendragadkar "a Fundamental Right is a legally enforceable right governing the relations between the State and the individual. It has both negative and positive aspects. It must, as the words indicate, be fundamental. It does not mean a right of liberty permissible under the law; it also means a right of liberty in a positive sense which enables an individual to develop his personality and faculties and to live his life in his own interest and in the interest of the community as a whole".

Justice Bhagwati, highlighting the importance of the Fundamental Rights, observed in the *Maneka Gandhi* v. *Union of India* case, "These Fundamental Rights represent the basic values cherished by the people of this country (India) since the Vedic times and they are calculated to protect the dignity of the individual and create conditions in which every human being can develop his personality to fullest extent. They weave a pattern of guarantees on the basic structure of human rights and impose negative obligations on the State not to encroach on individual liberty in its various dimensions".

In simple words we can say that the rights enshrined in Part III of the Constitution are fundamental because they are most essential for the attainment by the individual of his full intellectual, moral and spiritual stature. Their inclusion in the Constitution serves as a reminder to the Government that the liberties assured to the people by the Constitution are to be respected. In the words of M.P. Sharma, "The statement of Fundamental Rights thus limits the range of State activity in appropriate direction in the interest of the liberty of the citizens."

Demand for Fundamental Rights in India. The demand for grant of fundamental liberties goes back to the mid-nineteenth century when the Indians under the leadership of Dadabhai Naoroji demanded certain basic considerations from the British Government. This demand gained greater momentum following the establishment of the Indian National Congress in 1885. In 1895 the Indian leaders pleaded for grant of freedom of speech, free state education, and insisted that the Indians should be imprisoned only by the competent authorities. In 1917 the Indian National Congress passed a formal resolution demanding right of equality before law, freedom of speech and freedom of press. But it was the Nehru Committee in its Report of 1928 which made a systematic demand for certain social, religious and cultural rights. It demanded that the Parliament should make "suitable laws for the maintenance of health and fitness for work of all citizens, securing a living wage for every worker, the protection of motherhood, welfare of children and the economic consequences of the old age, infirmity and unemployment". However, this demand did not evoke favourable response from the Simon Commission which paid a visit to India to review India's constitutional progress.

In 1931, the Indian National Congress at its Karachi Session prepared a document concerning Fundamental Rights and Duties, which became the forerunner of Part III of the Indian Constitution dealing with the Fundamental Rights. The Joint Parliamentary Committee on Indian Constitutional Reforms (1933-34) also did not approve of the inclusion of Fundamental Rights in the constitution. This aspiration of the people was ultimately fulfilled by the New Constitution of India which incorporated a chapter on Fundamental Rights in Part III of the Constitution.

NEED AND IMPORTANCE OF FUNDAMENTAL RIGHTS

Rights, according to *Laski*, "are those conditions of social life without which no man can seek to be himself at his best." The former Chief Justice *P.B. Gajendragadkar* defines a Fundamental Right as "a legally enforceable right governing the relations between the State and the individual. It has both a negative and positive aspect. It must, as the word indicates, be Fundamental. It does not only mean a right of liberty permissible under the law; it also means a right of liberty in a positive sense which enables an individual to develop his personality and his faculties and to live his life in his own interest and in the interest of the community as a whole."[1] Fundamental Rights have been rightly regarded as the soul of the Constitution.

According to *Justice Sapru*:

"The object of these Fundamental Rights, as far as I can gather from a reading of the Constitu-

1. Gajendragadkar, J. *The Constitution of India*, p. 24.

tion itself, was not merely to provide security and equality of citizenship to the people living in this land and thereby helping the process of nation-building, but also, and not less importantly, to provide certain standards of conduct, citizenship, justice and fairplay. In the background of the Indian Constitution, they were intended to make all citizens and persons appreciate that the paramount law of the land has swept away privileges and has laid down that there is to be perfect equality between one section of the community and another in the matter of all those rights which are essential for the material and moral perfection of man."

The Framers of Indian Constitution were especially influenced by Bill of Rights of the American Constitution, the Declaration of the Rights of Man in France, the Irish Constitution of 1935, the Post-War Constitutions of Japan and Burma and the Declaration of Human Rights by the United Nations. The Framers of Indian Constitution also wanted to remove untouchability because Raja Ram Mohan Roy, Swami Dayanand Saraswati and Mahatma Gandhi had launched a crusade against untouchability.

The Constitution of India contains an exhaustive list of Fundamental Rights. The theory of such elementary rights guaranteed to every individual gives a moral character to the state and puts a check on its absoluteness. *They prevent the government from becoming despotic.* They are above all other laws of land. The court ensures their observance by the State. There were two reasons for making them justiciable—the first to safeguard the individual from the encroachments of the Legislature when the ruling party sometimes gets intoxicated with power.

CONSTITUENT ASSEMBLY AND THE FUNDAMENTAL RIGHTS

The Constituent Assembly solemnly pledged itself to draw up for India's future governance a constitution wherein "*shall be guaranteed and secured to all the people of India, justice, social, economic and political, equality of status, of opportunity and before the law : freedom of thought, expression, belief, faith, worship, vocation, association and action, subject to law and public morality.*" Later on these were incorporated in Chapter III on Fundamental Rights.

FUNDAMENTAL RIGHTS AND THEIR ACTUAL WORKING: DECISIONS OF SUPREME COURT

Laws inconsistent with or in derogation of the Fundamental Rights (Article 13)

Clause 1 of Article 13 lays down that all laws in force in the territory of India immediately before the commencement of this Constitution, in so far as they are inconsistent with the provisions of this Part, shall, to the extent of such inconsistency, be void.

Clause 2 of Article 13 lays down that the State shall not make any law which takes away or abridges the rights conferred by this Part and any law made in contravention of this clause shall, to the extent of the contravention, be void.

Article 13 *in Practice.* While some rights are of general nature and are applicable to all the persons irrespective of the fact whether they are citizens or non-citizens, there are some rights also which apply to citizens only. The Supreme Court has laid down that a law inconsistent with a general Fundamental Right is ineffective for all persons but a law inconsistent with a Fundamental Right in the latter category is ineffective for citizens only and subsists for non-citizens who have no such fundamental right.[1]

The Fundamental Rights granted to the people of India by the Indian Constitution are : Right to Equality, Liberty, Freedom of Religion, Cultural and Educational right, Right against exploitation and Right to constitutional remedies.

1. *State of Gujarat* v. *Ambica Mills Ltd.*, AIR 1974 SC 1300 (1309)

1. Right to Equality (Article 14) : Decisions of the Supreme Court

Article 14 of the Constitution guarantees equality of all persons before law. Article 15 prohibits any discrimination on grounds of religion, race, caste, sex or place of birth as between citizens. It abolishes untouchability and ensures equality of opportunity in the matter of public employment. It says that no Indian citizen holding a post of trust and responsibility shall accept any gift or emoluments without the previous consent of the President. Also that no citizen shall be unreasonably prevented from using wells, tanks, bathing ghats, roads and public resorts maintained wholly or partly out of the state funds.

Article 14 guarantees to every person the right not to be denied equality before the law or the equal protection of laws. This phrase has been adopted from English Common Law. It is a declaration of equality of all persons within the territory of India. This means that there will be no privileged class or body of persons. Every person high or low, rich or poor will be subject to the jurisdiction of ordinary courts. No person will be regarded above the law. Every person can sue or be sued. *Prof. Dicey* in explaining the concept of legal equality, as operating in England, said, "With us every official, from the Prime Minister down to a constable or a collector of taxes, is under the same responsibility for every act done without any legal justification as any other citizen,"[1]

In *Satish Chandra* v. *Union of India*, the Supreme Court ruled that the guiding principle of Article 14 is that *all persons and things similarly circumstanced shall be treated alike both in privileges conferred and imposed.*[2] "*Jennings* remarks, '*Equality before the law' means that amongst equals, the law should be equal and should be equally administered and that the like should be treated alike.*"[3]

This leads us to the important question of legislative classifications or distinctions between persons and things made by law. Article 14 forbids class legislation, which is limited either in the objects to which it is directed or by the territory within which it is to operate. The Supreme Court in a number of cases[4] has upheld the view that Article 14 does rule out classification for purposes of legislation. The Supreme Court in *Kedar Nath* v. *State of West Bengal* explained this principle thus :

> "The equal protection of the laws guaranteed by Article 14 of the Constitution does not mean that all the laws must be general in character and universal in application and that the State is no longer to have the power of distinguishing and classifying persons or things for the purposes of legislation."

In the *State of Bombay* v. *Balsara*, the Supreme Court held:

> "If a law deals equally with members of a well-defined class, it is not obnoxious and it is not open to the charge of a denial of equal protection on the ground that it has no application to other persons". In the *Sakhwani* v. *State of Orissa* (1955), the Supreme Court ruled : "Legislation enacted for the achievement of a particular object or purpose need not be all-embracing. It is for the legislature to determine what categories it would embrace within the scope of legislation and nearly because certain categories which would stand on the same footing as those which are covered by the legislation are left out would not render legislation which has been enacted in any manner discriminatory and violative of Article 14." In the *Biswambhar* v. *State of Orissa* and *Ram Chand v. State of Orissa*, the Supreme Court held further that Article 14 did "not prevent the Legislature from introducing a reform gradually, that is to say, at first applying the legisla-

1. Dicey, *Law of the Constitution* (10th edition), p. 193.
2. *Satish Chandra* v. *Union of India*, AIR, 1953, SC, 250 at p. 252.
3. Jennings, *Law of the Constitution*, p. 94.
4. *Chiranji Lal* v. *Union of India*, AIR, 1251 SC 41 ; *Budhan Chowdhry* v. *State of Bihar* , AIR 1955 SC, 191; *Bidi Supply Co.* v. *Union of India*, AIR 1956 SC 479 ; *Kedar Nath* v. *State of West Bengal*, AIR 1953 SC 404 at 409 ; *Kathi Raning* v. *State of Saurashtra*, AIR 1952 SC 123 ; *State of West Bengal* v. *Anwar Ali*, AIR 1952, SC 75; *Ram Krishan* v. *Justice Tendolkar*, AR 1958 SC 530.

tion to some of the institutions or objects having common or particular areas only, according to the exigencies of situation."

In Bank Nationalisation Case, Dr. R.C. Cooper and *T.M. Gurbaxani* challenged the constitutional validity of the Banking Companies (Acquisition and Transfer of Undertakings) Ordinance, 1969 on the ground that it violated their Fundamental Rights guaranteed to them by Articles 14, 19 and 31 of the Constitution. The President had issued Ordinance nationalising 14 banks to implement the new policy of the then Prime Minister, Mrs. Indira Gandhi. The Supreme Court's 11 judges heard the case for many weeks and the Judgement was given on February 10, 1970. The majority judgement was written by Justice Shah and nine other judges concurred with him. The Supreme Court held that

> "Banking Companies (Acquisition and Transfer of Undertakings) Ordinance, 1969 and the Act which replaced it were unconstitutional as the Act was discriminatory and unauthorised. While the Act was within the competence of the Parliament, the Act was discriminatory against 14 banks named in the Act itself because while other Indian and foreign banks could carry on their business, these 14 banks could not do so without the control of the Government. Sections 4, 5 and 6 and Schedule II of the Act were bad as they could not be separated from the rest of the Act. Therefore, the whole Act should be declared void. This Act also violated the guarantee of the compensation under Article 31 (2) of the Indian Constitution. It was also held that 'the law providing for acquisition must either fix the amount of compensation or specify the principles on which and the manner in which the compensation was to be determined and given. The owner of the property must be given the value of his property if the same is acquired by the Government. The Supreme Court can decide whether the principles laid down by Parliament for determining compensation are valid or not.'[1]

The Government accepted this decision and amended it suitably and got passed by Parliament. As the objections pointed out by the Supreme Court had been fully met, therefore the Supreme Court did not declare the Bank Nationalisation Act or the Banking Companies (Acquisition and Transfer of Undertakings) Act as null and void again.

Prohibition on ground of Religion, Race , Caste, Sex or Place of Birth (Article 15)— Its Actual Working : Decisions of the Supreme Court

Article 15 prohibits discrimination on the basis of religion, race, caste, sex, place of birth or any of them. About the scope of this Article the Supreme Court has held that, "the Fudamental Right conferred by Article 15 (1) is conferred on a citizen as an individual and is a guarantee against his being subjected to discrimination in the matter of rights, privileges and immunities pertaining to him as a citizen generally."

The special provisions permitted by clause 4 of Article 15 are available to the backward classes, Scheduled Castes and the Scheduled Tribes. Backward classes are distinct from 'Scheduled Castes and Scheduled Tribes', although their backwardness may be as much as that of the Scheduled Castes and Scheduled Tribes. The State can determine that class of persons who constitute backward classes. The State can make special provision in favour of backward classes by an executive order and legislation in this connection is not needed. This is the decision of the Supreme Court in *M. R. Balaji* v. *State of Mysore*[2]. In making such orders, it may be kept in mind that Article 15 (4) authorises the making of special provisions for the advancement of the communities even if such provisions are inconsistent with the Fundamental Rights guaranteed under Article 29. The context therefore requires that executive action taken by the State may be based on an objective approach free from all extraneous pressure.[3]

1. AIR 1970, SC 56
2. *M.R. Balaji* v. *State of Mysore*, AIR, 1963 SC 640.
3. *Ibid.*

On July 26, 1958, the State of Mysore issued an order that all the communities excepting the Brahman community fell within the definitions of educationally and socially backward classes and Scheduled Castes and Tribes and 75 per cent of seats were reserved for them in educational institutions. After that Mysore Government again issued similar orders on May 14, 1959, July 22, 1959, June 9, 1960 and July 10, 1961. These orders, when challenged, were set aside. On July 31, 1962, the State of Mysore again issued orders to this effect which superseded all previous orders. This time Mysore Government divided the backward classes into two categories, backward classes and more backward classes and reserved 68% seats in the engineering, medical and other technical colleges. This order of the Mysore Government was challenged by 23 petitioners who alleged that if this order had not been issued and 68% seats would not have been reserved for the backward classes, they would have got admission. The petitioners further contended that the classification made under the order was irrational and the reservation of 68 per cent seats was a fraud on Article 15 (4) of the Constitution. The Supreme Court in the case of *M.R. Balaji* v. *State of Mysore* held that, "though the State was competent to reserve the seats for the backward classes, Scheduled Castes and Scheduled Tribes, yet it should be done within the reasonable limits. Reservation of seats has to be reconciled with the broader interests of the community as a whole. Thus Supreme Court set aside this order of Mysore Government holding to be unreasonable and subversive of the object of Article 15 (4). Speaking generally and in a broad way, a special provision should be less than 50 per cent. How much less than 50 per cent would depend upon the relevant circumstances in each case.

In *R.Jacob Mathew* v. *State of Kerala*[1] seats in the medical colleges of Kerala were reserved by a Government G.O. for (*a*) Ezhavas, Muslims and Latin Catholics on the ground that they belonged to socially and educationally backward classes, (*b*) in favour of children of registered medical practitioners, and (*c*) for outstanding sportsmen. The Court upheld the reservations in favour of Ezhavas, Muslims and Latin Catholics valid under Article 15 (4). Reservation in favour of outstanding sportsmen was also held valid on the ground that it was based on a valid classification under Article 14 but the Court struck down the reservation in favour of the children of medical practitioners on the ground that it was based on a classification which had no rational relation to the object to be secured[2]. It has also been decided that reservation of seats to the students of backward classes which is available under Article 29 (2) of the Constitution cannot be limited by reservations made under Article 15 (4). This means that if by merit the Backward Classes can secure more seats than already reserved for them under Article 15 (4), then they are free to get that advantage because the power conferred under Article 15 (4) of the Constitution can be exercised to advance the interest of the backward class persons and not to restrict them.[3]

Equality of Opportunity in Matters of Public Employment (Article 16)—Its Actual Working : Decisions of the Supreme Court ; carry forward rule was held null and void

Devdasan v. *Union of India.* The scope of clause 4 came for consideration in *Devdasan* v. *Union of India*[4] where the Supreme Court was called upon to pronounce upon the constitutionality of the "carry forward rule" framed by the Central Government to regulate appointment of persons belonging to backward classes in public services. By a resolution of September 13, 1950, the Government of India had vindicated its intention to reserve 12 $^1/_2$ per cent and 5 per cent of the total available vacancies in one year respectively for Scheduled Castes and Tribes candidates exclusively. It was further provided that if in any particular year the number of suitable candidates available was less than the number of reserved posts, the posts so in excess shall be treated as unreserved for that year but in the next year the number of posts which would have been otherwise reserved for such candidates in the normal course would be augmented by the number which had been converted into non-reserved

1. AIR 1964, Ker. 39.
2. *Raghuvramulu* v. *State of Andhra Pradesh.*
3. *Chamraja* v. *State of Mysore*, AIR 1967, Mysore 21.
4. AIR 1964, SC 1515 ; followed in *B.N. Tewari* v. *Union of India*, AIR 1965 SC 1430.

posts in the preceding year. This process of carrying over was to operate for a period of two years at one time. On the basis of reservation permitted by the "carry forward rule", out of 45 vacancies actually filled in 1961, 29 went to the members of the Scheduled Castes and Tribes. That came to about 64 per cent for reservation. The question for consideration was whether the "carry forward rule" was unconstitutional either because its operation would practically destroy the Fundamental Right guaranteed by Article 16(1) of the Constitution or because it was violative of the guarantee contained in Article 14 of the Constitution.

The Supreme Court by a majority of four to one held the rule of carrying forward ultra vires and invalid upon the ground that the power vested in the State Government under Article 16 (4) cannot be so exercised as to deny reasonable equality of opportunity in matters of public employment to members of the classes other than backward. The object of that provision, the majority thought, was to ensure that the backwardness of the backward classes did not unduly handicap their members from securing public employment and State, when it made reservations in favour of backward classes in matters of public employment. From this premise, it went further to hold that where the reservations were so excessive in character as to deny in practice a reasonable opportunity to other classes, it was a fraud upon the Constitution. Because in the instant case, the number of vacancies which came to be reserved by virtue of the 'carry forward rule' was nearly 68 per cent of the total vacancies which was *per se* unreasonable as held in an earlier case[1]. The rule was declared null and void.

In *Venkataraman* v. *State of Madras*[2], it was held that the communal order of the Madras Government which besides making reservation of posts for Harijans and backward Hindus as sanctioned by Article 16, clause 4 also made reservations of posts for other communities, *viz*. Muslims, Christians, non-Brahmin Hindus and Brahmins, was repugnant to the provisions of Article 16.

Abolition of Untouchability (Article 17)—Its Actual Working : Decision of the Supreme Court

Article 17 abolishes untouchability in any form or shape. It has been made an offence. This Article was further strengthened by the Untouchability (Offences) Act, 1955. It provided punishment for refusing admission to places of worship, restaurants, hotels, hospitals, and public wells.

The constitutionality of the Untouchability (Offences) Act, 1955 was challenged in *Banamali Das* v. *Panku Bhandari*. In this case Banamali lodged a complaint against Panku Bhandari on this ground that Panku Bhandari, a barber, refused to cut off his hair because he is a cobbler. He further contended that Panku Bhandari refused to cut off the hair of the other persons belonging to his community. Consequently, proceedings were instituted against Panku Bhandari. Panku Bhandari contended that Untouchability Offences Act was invalid because it placed unreasonable restrictions upon his profession as a barber. Besides that he contended that the Act was discriminatory in character. Calcutta High Court rejected the contention of Panku Bhandari. The Calcutta High Court observed thus, "All what the Untouchability Offences Act does is to prohibit him from discriminating between one Hindu and another in carrying out his duties as a barber. The Act compels him to serve all and really enlarge the scope of his services rather than restrict the same .... The citizens of India should not be subdivided but should form a united body and that is an end that is rightly sought for our law-making bodies. The makers of the Constitution have recognised it and have abolished untouchability and have also provided that there should be no discrimination only on the ground of caste or religion.... The Act does not discriminate but penalises and abolishes tendencies in Hindu society to discrimination...... It does not deny any person equality before the law. It tends to make all persons equal in society and before the law and it cannot possibly be argued that this Act denies any person equal protection of laws."

1. *M.R. Balaji* v. *State of Mysore*, AIR 1963 SC 649, where 68 per cent seats in educational institutions by the State under section were held invalid.
2. AIR 1951, SC 229.

Abolition of Titles (Article 18). The right to equality has been further strengthened and guaranteed by Articles 15, 16, 17, and 18. Article 18 provides the following : (1) No title,[1] not being a military or academic distinction, shall be conferred by the State. (2) No citizen of India shall accept any title from any foreign State. (3) No person who is not a citizen of India shall while he holds any office of profit or trust under the State, accept without the consent of the President any title from any foreign State. (4). No person holding any office of profit or trust under the state shall, without the consent of the President, accept any present, emolument or office or any kind from or under any foreign State. However, Military and Academic distinctions are exempted from the prohibition. Conferment of honours to military personnel which are not title under Article 18 are : (1) Param Vir Chakra; (2) Mahavir Chakra; (3) Vir Chakra and (4) Ashoka Chakra.

Conferment of honours to others are :

(1) Bharat Ratna; (2) Padma Vibhushan; and (3) Padma Shri.

It is curious that no penalty has been prescribed so far for violation of Article 18.[2] So it seems that this Article is mere directory.

2. Right to Freedom (Article 19)—Its Actual Working: Decision of the Supreme Court to decide reasonableness

Article 19 (1) of the Constitution grants to every citizen the right (a) to freedom of speech and expression, (*b*) to assemble peacefully and without arms, (*c*) to form associations or unions, (*d*) to move freely across the length and breadth of the country, (*e*) to reside or settle down in any part of India, (*f*) to own or dispose of property, and (*g*) to carry on any lawful trade or occupation.

The second part of Article 19 enumerates limitations on the various types of freedom given above. It underlines the fact that the rights can never be absolute. Consistent with this principle, the First Amendment Act adopted in 1951 laid down that the States shall be authorised to make any law restricting the exercise of the freedom of speech in the interest of the security of the state, friendly relations with foreign countries, public order, and decency and good conduct. The States have also been authorised to restrict the freedom of the Press in order to check slanderous articles and promotion of disaffection towards or contempt of court.

The right to move freely in the country is also subject to certain restrictions. The States possess the power to impose certain restrictions on the movement of an individual. How far such restrictions are reasonable or unreasonable is for the court to decide. The decision of the court is binding on the individual as well as the State. In *Chintamani* vs. *State of Madhya Pradesh*,[3] the Supreme Court observed thus:

> "The determination by the Legislature of what constitutes reasonable restriction is not final or conclusive. It is subject to supervision by this court. In the matter of Fundamental Rights, the Supreme Court watches and guards the right guaranteed by the Constitution and in exercising its functions it has the power to set aside an Act of the Legislature if it is in violation of the freedom guaranteed by the Constitution." The Constitution also laid down that no citizen shall be detained without trial under Preventive Detention Act.

Reasonableness of the Restriction and Objectives Concept; *Supreme Court's Decision.* The reasonableness of a restriction has to be determined in an objective manner and from the standpoint of the interests of general public and not from the point of view of the persons upon whom restrictions are imposed or upon abstract consideration. This was decided by the Supreme Court in *Hanif Qurreshi* v. *State of Bihar*.[4]

1. A title is an appellation given to a person or family as a sign of privilege or distinction or profession as the title of Lord. It is something that hangs to one's name as an addition.
2. This was the position as on March 5, 1991.
3. AIR 1951, SC 118.
4. *Hanif Qureshi* v. *State of Bihar*, A.I.R. 1958, SC 751.

Other Decisions of the Supreme Court : *State of Madras* v. *V.G. Row.* In the case, *State of Madras* v. *V.G. Row*[1] Chief Justice Patanjali observed :

> "It is important, ... to bear in mind that the test of reasonableness, wherever prescribed, should be applied to each individual statute impugned, and no abstract standard or general pattern of reasonableness can be laid down as applicable to all cases. The nature of the right alleged to have been infringed, the underlying purpose of the restrictions imposed, the extent and urgency of the evil sought to be remedied thereby, the disproportions of the imposition, the prevailing conditions at the time, should all enter into judicial verdict."

It was accordingly held that Section 15 (2) of the Criminal Law Amendment Act, 1908 as amended by the Criminal Law Amendment (Madras) Act, 1950 was ultra vires as the impugned provision imposed unreasonable restrictions on the freedom of association.

Brij Bhusan v. *State of Delhi*[2]. The Chief Commissioner of Delhi had passed an order under Section 7 (1) (*c*) of the East Punjab Public Safety Act requiring the printer, publisher and editor of '*Organizer*' (a weekly newspaper of Delhi) to submit for scrutiny in duplicate before publication all communal mattters and news and views about Pakistan including photographs and cartoons. The petitioners contended that the order of the Chief Commissioner infringed with their Fundamental Right of speech and expression granted to them under Article 19 (1) (*a*) of the Constitution. *Secondly*, they contended that the restrictions imposed upon them by the Order of the Chief Commissioner were unreasonable as they violated the spirit of Article 19 (2) of the Constitution. The Supreme Court accepted the petition. On behalf of the Supreme Court Justice Patanjli Shastri (as he then was) observed in the course of judgment that the imposition of pre-censorship on a journal is a restriction on the liberty of the press which is an essential part of the right to freedom of speech and expression. Consequently the Supreme Court quashed the order of the Chief Commissioner.

In Romesh Thapar v. *The State of Madras*,[3] the petitioner was Mr. Romesh Thapar. A journal namely 'Cross Road' was being published and printed in Bombay. The Madras Government banned its circulation in Madras. Mr. Thapar on behalf of the printers, publishers and editor of the '*Cross Road*' moved the Supreme Court and challenged the Madras Government on this ground that it was an infringement of his Fundamental Right of Freedom of Speech and Expression as guaranteed by Article 19 (1) of the Constitution. The Supreme Court held that the Constitution "has placed in a distinct category those offences against public order which aim at undermining the security of the State or overthrowing it and made their prevention the justification of legislative abridgment of the freedom of speech and expression, that is to say, nothing less than endangering the foundations of the State or threatening its overthrow could justify the curtailment of the freedom of speech and expression." Following the decision of the Supreme Court in *Romesh Thapar* v. *State of Madras*, many High Courts in India gave decisions to the effect that even incitement to individual murder or promoting disaffection amongst classes could not be restrained under the permissive limits set in Article 19 (2). The result was that an intolerable situation was created. This situation was remedied by the 1st Amendment Act of 1951.

1st Amendment, 1951

Objects, On May 12, 1951, about 16 months after the working of the Constitution, a Bill to amend the Constitution was introduced in Parliament. The main objects for amending the Constitution can best be explained from the objects and reasons attached to the Amending Bill.[4] The statement read, "During the last fifteen months of the working of the Constitution, certain difficulties have been brought to light by judicial decisions and pronouncements especially in regard to the Chapter on

1. *State of Madras* v. *V.G. Row*, AIR 1952, SC 196, SCR 597.
2. AIR 1950, SC 120, 1950, SCR 605.
3. AIR 1950, SC 124, 1950 SCR 594.
4. *Gazette of India*, 1951, Part II, Sec. 2, p. 357.

Fundamental Rights. The citizen's right to freedom of speech and expression guaranteed by Article 19 (*a*) has been held by some courts to be so comprehensive as not to render a person culpable even if he advocates murder and other crimes of violence. In other countries with written Constitutions, freedom of speech and press is not regarded as debarring the State from punishing or preventing abuse of this freedom. The citizen's right to practise any profession or to carry on any occupation, trade or business conferred by Article 19 (1) (*g*) is subject to reasonable restrictions, which the laws of the State may impose "in the interests of the general public. While the words cited are comprehensive enough to cover any scheme of nationalisation which the State may undertake, it is desirable to place the matter beyond doubt by a clarificatory addition to Article 19 (6)."

The Parliament passed the 1st Amendent Bill on June 2, 1951. The President assented to the Bill on June 18, 1951 and it became 1st Amendment of the Constitution. Article 19 (2) was amended. The State was allowed to impose reasonable restrictions on the freedom of the individual in the interests of the security of the State, friendly relations with foreign states, public order, decency or morality or in relation to contempt of court, defamation or incitement to an offence.

Sixteenth Amendment

Other Amendments are not relevant here, so the Sixteenth Amendment is being given here (other amendments have been given in Chapter XIV). It added that State could impose reasonable restrictions upon freedom of speech and expression of those individuals and organisations who want to propagate secession of any part from India at the time of election or afterwards.

3. Freedom of Religion (Article 25) and its Actual Working

Article 25 says that (*a*) all persons shall be entitled to freedom of conscience and the right to practise and propagate the religion freely; (*b*) the Sikhs shall be allowed to wear and carry kripans; (*c*) the Government shall be competent to make laws for social reforms and throwing open the Hindu religious instituions including those of the Sikhs, Buddhists, Jains, to all classes and sections of Hindus. Article 28 warns against imparting religious instructions in any educational institution wholly maintained out of state funds. The clause, however, does not apply to institutions established under any endowment or trust. Further that attendance in the classes held for religious instruction shall not be compulsory. Article 26 says that subject to public order, morality and health every religion or sect shall have the right to establish and run institutions for religious and charitable purposes and to own, acquire and administer such property. Article 27 prohibits raising funds through taxes in order to promote any religion. The above-mentioned rights guaranteed to the citizens, in fact, give a secular character to our state.

Decisions of the Supreme Court

(*a*) *Freedom of Conscience.* It was held in *Rati Lal* v. *State of Bombay*[1] that the term 'freedom of conscience' connotes a person's right to entertain beliefs and doctrines concerning matters which are regarded by him to be conducive to his spiritual well-being. It should be noted that freedom of conscience is the inner absolute freedom to mould his own relation with God in whatever manner he likes. A person has the right to believe in the principles of any religion he likes.

(*b*) *Right freely to profess and practise.* It was held in *Punjabrao* v. *D.P. Meshram*[2] that the term to profess a religion means right to declare freely and openly one's faith. A person may freely practise his own religion. It has been held by the Supreme Court in *Rati Lal* v. *State of Bombay*[3], that "Religious practices or performances of acts in pursuance of religious belief are much a part of religion as faith or belief in particular doctrines."

1. AIR 1954 SC 388. See also *Govindlalji* v. *State of Rajasthan*, AIR 1963 SC 1368.
2. AIR 1965 SC 1179.
3. AIR 1954 SC 388.

(c) Right to propagate. The Supreme Court in Rati Lal's case[1] held that the term 'to propagate religion' means to spread and publicise his religion for the edification of others. This term only indicates persuasion and exposition without any element of coercion. *It does not allow any conversion.*

In *Rev. Stanislaus* v. *State of M.P.*[2], the Supreme Court held as under: "What Article 25 (1) grants is not the right to convert another person to one's own religion, but to transmit or spread one's religion, by an exposition of its tenets. It has to be remembered that Article 25(1) guarantees 'freedom of conscience' to every citizen, and not merely to the followers of one particular religion, and that, in turn, postulates that there is no Fundamental Right to convert another person to one's own religion because if a person purposely undertakes the conversion of another person to his religion, as distinguished from his effort to transmit or spread the tenets of his religion, that would impinge on the 'freedom for conscience' guaranteed to all the citizens of the country alike.[3]

4. Cultural and Educational Rights (Article 29) and their actual working

Article 29 clause (1) of the Constitution allows all the Minorities in India to preserve and promote their language, script and culture. The Constitution permits all the Minorities, whether based on language or religion, to start and run their educational institutions and get financial aid without any discrimination from the State. No citizen, however, can be refused admission in any educational institution maintained or aided by the State.[4] Indian Constitution in this respect has close similarity with the Soviet Constitution which grants cultural and educational facilities to all the nationalities living in the State.

The words "on grounds only of religion, race, caste, language or any of them" were interpreted by the Supreme Court to mean that educational institution could impose restrictions or limitations other than those such as age, physical fitness, dissociation from subversive organisations and educational qualifications. Further, under clause (4) of Article 15, the State is entitled to reserve a minimum number of seats for members of the backward classes of citizens or for the Scheduled Castes and the Scheduled Tribes.

Decisions of Supreme Court about Article 29. Articles 15 (4) which was enacted into the Constitution by the Constitution (1st Amendment) Act 1951 is a proviso to Article 29 (2) and permits the State to make any special provision for the advancement of socially and educationally backward classes or for the Scheduled Castes and Scheduled Tribes. Thus it was held in *Chanchala* v. *State of Mysore*,[5] that the State is entitled to reserve a minimum number of seats for members of the Backward Classes, notwithstanding Article 29 (2). *However, the quantum of such reservations should not be so excessive as to be unreasonable.*

In *Deva Singh* v. *Kurukshetra University*[6], it was held that this Article does not take away the right of an institution to refuse admission or to expel a student on ground of indiscipline or the like, provided the discretion is not abused.

Right of Minorities to Establish and Manage Educational Institutions (Article 30)

In *D.A.V. College, Bhatinda* v. *State of Punjab*[7] the Supreme Court held that the right of minority to establish and administer educational institutions of their choice includes the right to have a choice of medium of instruction also. But if the University compulsorily affiliates colleges, run by

1. *Ibid.*
2. AIR 1977 SC 908.
3. *Ibid* at p. 911.
4. Article 29 (2).
5. AIR 1971 SC 1762. See also *State of A.P.* v. *Balram*, AIR 1972 SC 1375
6. AIR 1971 P. & H. 340 (345)
7. AIR 1971 SC 1731 : (1971) 2 SCC 261.

the Minorities and prescribes the medium of instruction and examination to be held in a language which is not their own, then it interferes with their Fundamental Right to conserve their script and administer their institutions.

However, in *D.A.V. College, Jullundur* v. *State of Punjab* [1], wherein Section 4 (2) of the Guru Nanak University, Amritsar, Act, 1969, which provided that the University shall make provisions for study and research on the life and teachings of Guru Nanak and their cultural and religious impact in the context of India and World Civilizations was challenged as violating Article 29 (1) and Article 30 (1), the Supreme Court held that this section did not offend the right of the petitioner either under Article 29 (1) or Article 30 (1). It was observed if the University makes provisions for an academic study and research of the life and teachings of any saint, it cannot be considered to require affiliated colleges to compulsorily study his life and teachings or to do research in them. The study and research on the life and teachings of Guru Nanak must be a study in relation to their culture and religious impact in the context of Indian and World Civilization which is mostly an academic and philosophical study.

5. Rights Against Exploitation

Indian Constitution recognises the dignity of the individual and protects him against any form of exploitation either by the state or by the privileged classes in the society. Article 23 prohibits all traffic in human beings and *begar* and other forms of forced labour. It declares that slavery or use of women for immoral or other purposes is a punishable offence. It also prohibits the employment of children below the age of 14 in any factory or mine. The state has, however, reserved to it right to secure compulsory service from the people for public purposes, *e.g.*, compulsory military training. The American Constitution contains a similar clause. It says, "Neither slavery nor involuntary servitude, except as punishment of crime whereof the party shall have been duly convicted, shall exist in United States." The right of Indian citizens against exploitation is of great significance. It has protected the people particularly women and children against being treated as cattle.

6. Right to Property before 44th Amendment, Deleted by 44th Amendment (1978)

Articles 31, 31A and 31B guaranteed the right of the individuals and trusts to own and administer their property. The Constitution also says that no person shall be deprived of his property except by a lawful authority. The state alone can compulsorily acquire any property for a public purpose but not without paying compensation. By invoking this right, the state succeeded in abolishing zamindari system in the country.

The question of determining the compensation is a ticklish one. In United States of America and Australia, the Constitution provides for payment of just compensation which is finally fixed not by the legislature but by the court. Article 31 read along with the First and Fourth Amendments of the Constitution lays down that the legislature alone shall finally fix the amount to be paid as compensation for any estate acquired by the state. The Act of the legislature relating to compensation cannot be challenged in a court of law on the ground that the compensation fixed in the law is not just or fair. The Congress adopted this amendment and declared the issue of compensation non-justiciable, after losing certain cases instituted by the zamindars who were affected by the Zamindari Abolition Act. The courts in certain states declared some of the provisions of the Zamindari Abolition Act as violation of the people's right to property. The Congress in power then proceeded with a constitutional amendment to save its face. *Right to property has been deleted by 44th Amendment and now it has been made only a legal right. This was done by Janata Government.*

7. Right to Constitutional Remedies

Article 32 provides for the enforcement of Fundamental Rights by the Supreme Court. It confers on the people the right to move the Supreme Court in case of encroachment on the Fundamental Rights by the State. In fact, Fundamental Rights would have been meaningless had there not been

1. AIR 1971 SC 1737 : (1971) 2 SCR 269.

legal sanction behind them and judicial remedies in case of their infringement. Such constitutional remedies have been described by Dr. Bhim Rao Ambedkar as the "heart and soul of the Constitution." The Soviet Constitution also mentions the Fundamental Rights but they are not enforceable by the Supreme Court. The result is that the ruling party grants them to the people to the extent it likes. In the unwritten Constitution of England, there is not any set of fundamental rights but these have been granted through prerogative writs. In America, there is no specific provision for the issue of writs. The fathers of their Constitution have, however, prohibited the suspension of *Habeas Corpus*. The Supreme Court of India possesses and exercises the right of judicial review for the protection and enjoyment of Fundamental Rights. It can issue writs in the nature of *Habeas Corpus*, *Mandamus*, *Prohibition*, *Quo warranto* and *Certiorari*.

The writ of *Habeas Corpus* literally means 'you may have the body'. The object of *Habeas Corpus* is that no person remains in detention without a valid reason and trial. The court by issuing this writ directs the arresting authority to produce the arrested person in court to enable it to decide whether the arrest or detention is lawful or not. If the court feels that the detention is not constitutionally valid, it issues the writ for the immediate release of the person under detention.

The word *mandamus* means '*we command*'. By issuing a writ of this nature, the court commands a public body or an official to perform a public duty.

Prohibition writ is issued by a superior court to an inferior court preventing it form dealing with a matter over which it has no jurisdiction.

The literal meaning of the word *certiorari* is "to be more fully informed of". It is issued by a superior court to a court inferior to it, requiring the latter to submit the record of a case pending before it. Such a writ is intended to prevent a court from dealing with a case which falls beyond its jurisdiction. It is more a preventive rather than a remedial measure.

The term *quo warranto* means 'by what authority'. It is in the nature of an injunction. It is issued to a person who acts in a capacity to which he is not entitled. It requires the person, who claims or usurps an office, to show on what grounds he has done so. The court then scrutinises the claim of that person in office and gives its ruling. It is issued only at the instance of the Union or a State Government.

CRITICISM OF FUNDAMENTAL RIGHTS

The chapter on Fundamental Rights in the Constitution has been the subject of criticism. Broadly classified, the critics are of three types. *Firstly*, there are those who think that the Constitution does not employ Fundamental Rights in reality but only an apology for them. According to them, many Fundamental Rights such as the right to work, education, etc., which ought to have found a place in the chapter have been ignored, *Secondly*, there are those who think that the spirit that pervades the whole chapter and much of its substance are taken away by the extraordinary provisions such as preventive detention, suspension of the right of constitutiional remedies, etc. These critics allege that what has been given by one hand has been taken away by the other. *Thirdly*, there are those who argue that even those rights that are attempted to be safeguarded are hedged in with so many exceptions, explanations and qualifications that it is difficult to understand what exactly is available to the individual by way of Fundamental Rights. One of these critics sarcatically suggested that the chapter on Fundamental Rights should be renamed as 'Limitations on Fundamental Rights' or 'Fundamental Rights and Limitations Theorem'?

(1) The list of Fundamental Rights included in Indian Constitution is not complete. It does not contain the right to work, right to leisure, right to free education and material security as given in the Soviet Constitution. The omissions are significant but the Constitution-makers could not help it in view of the circumstances prevailing at that time. They, however, made amends for it, by including them in the Directive Principles of State Policy.

(2) Prior to the 42nd Amendment the Indian Constitution did not contain Fundamental Duties, so the critics pointed out that the list of Fundamental Rights should also have contained Fundamental Duties just like the Soviet Constitution as the rights and duties are inseparable. We earn rights because of the duties that we perform. So in other words, rights are the fruits of duties. After the passage of 42nd Amendment in 1976, the critics have been silenced because it incorporates 10 Fundamental Duties as further enumerated in this Chapter.

(3) Another defect pointed out by the critics is that the Constitution has played a trick with the citizens. What it gives with one hand, it takes away with the other. Too many restrictions have been placed on the enjoyment of Fundamental Rights. Too many exceptions have rendered the rights sound hollow and meaningless. In emergency times the Constitution withdraws or suspends all the Fundamental Rights. Even in normal times the Preventive Detention Act takes away people's right to freedom.

(4) According to *Mr. Jennings*, the Indian Constitution is not as brief and clearly worded as the American Constitution. Unnecessary details could easily have been avoided by the framers of the Constitution.

(5) It is said that the emergency powers of the President to suspend the Fundamental Rights can lead to dictatorship. This charge, however, does not have sound legs. Other democratic constitutions of the world also have provisions relating to proclamation of emergency and suspension of Fundamental Rights. In America and England also the recourse to Rule of Law was greatly restricted during the two World Wars. Only if President of India during the operation of emergency does not misuse his powers, there can be no danger of our democracy transforming into a dictatorial regime. Moreover, the suspension of rights cannot continue for more than a fixed period unless approved and extended for another term by the Parliament.

(6) Lastly, the critics point out that the right of the legislature to decide finally the amount of compensation for the property acquired by the state is a serious cut in people's right to property. Since there is no constitutional remedy against a State Act regarding compensation, the people have been left at the mercy of the states and grave injustice may be done to them by the party in power.

Although it is admitted by everyone that rights cannot be absolute and that it is advisable to restrict them to a reasonable extent, it is also desirable that the court is made the guardian of those rights, to see that those rights are not flouted by the State Government in a whimsical way. *Chief Justice Abdul Karim Chagla* of the Bombay High Court made the following observation in the case entitled *Jeshingbai* vs. *Emperor*, "The Constitution has made the courts the custodians of Fundamental Rights of the citizens.....In deciding the question of the reasonableness of restriction, the court must look at the nature of the restriction, the manner in which it is imposed, its extent both territorial and temporal and if after considering all these the court comes to the conclusion that the restriction is unreasonable, then the court will not uphold it."

RESTRICTIONS UPON FUNDAMENTAL RIGHTS

As we have said already, unlimited rights are not possible under the present circumstances because certain anti-social elements in the society are always likely to misuse them. Nowhere these rights are absolute, though in most of the countries of the world these Fundamental Rights exist. For example, Great Britain is the home of democracy, but there also the absolute rights do not exist. In Great Britain many restrictions were imposed upon the Rule of Law during First World War (1914-18) and Second World War (1939-45). In the First World War 'Defence of the Realm Act' was passed and during the Second World War 'Emergency Powers (Defence) Act' was passed, according to which enormous powers of arrest and detention and making rules affecting the livelihood and property of the citizens were given to the executive agencies. In U.S.A. through the doctrine of Police Power the Supreme Court has recognised the inherent power of the State to impose such restrictions on Fundamental

Rights as may be deemed reasonable to protect the common good. In U.S.A. the governemnt cannot impose restriction upon the Fundamental Rights in the name of the security of State. The Constitution of India, on the other hand, empowers the government to impose restrictions upon the Fundamental Rights in the name of the security of state. Dr. Bhim Rao Ambedkar while introducing the Draft Constitution and supporting the restriction clauses, maintained, "What the Draft Constitution has done is, that instead of formulating Fundamental Rights in absolute terms and depending upon our Supreme Court to come to rescue of Parliament by inventing the doctrine of Police Power, it permits the state directly to impose limitations upon the Fundamental Rights."[1] It has been established in *Lakhinarayan* v. *Province of Bihar* (1949) and *Gopalan* v. *The State of Madras* that the courts cannot question the right of the Legislature to make the laws on the ground of restricting personal liberty if once it was proved that the Legislatures were competent to make those laws. In U.S.A. the Supreme Court can question the propriety of legislation and the courts are supreme against the legislatures but in India there is no judicial supremacy but only legislative supremacy, though the Constitution gives to the judiciary the powers to review legislature repugnant to the Fundamental Rights.

As previously stated, when the Constitution had worked for nearly 16 months, then certain difficulties arose about the abolition of Zamindari System. Allahabad and Patna High Courts issued injunctions against the abolition of Zamindari System. Therefore, Pt. Jawaharlal Nehru, the then Prime Minister of India, moved the First Amendment Bill, on May 12, 1951, in the Indian Parliament. The Parliament passed the Bill on June 2, 1951. The President assented to the Bill on June 8, 1951 and it became the First Amendment of the Constitution. The object of the Amendment can be gauged from the statement attached to it, which reads as follows :

> "During the last fifteen months of the working of the Constitution, certain difficulties have been brought to light by judicial decisions and pronouncements specially in regard to the chapter on Fundamental Rights. The citizen's right to freedom of speech and expression guaranteed by Article 19 (a) has been held by some courts to be so comprehensive as not to render a person culpable even if he advocates murder and other crimes of violence. In other countries with written constitutions freedom of speech and press is not regarded as debarring the State from punishing or preventing abuse of his freedom. The citizen's right to practise any profession or to carry on any occupation, trade or business conferred by Article 19 (1) (g) is subject to reasonable restriction which the laws of the State may impose in the interests of the general public."

Previously, the State could impose restrictions on the freedom of speech and expression if there was a case relating to libel, slander and defamation, contempt of court, violation of decency or morality and undermining the security of State. The freedom of speech could not be restricted for the purpose of public order or incitement to offence. *Now the amended Article* 19 *Clause* (2) *declares that the State will be able to impose reasonable restrictions on the exercise of the freedom of speech and expression in the interest of the security of the State, friendly relations with foreign States, public order, decency or morality or in relation to contempt of court, defamation or incitement to offence.* So with the inclusion of three more subjects (Public order, incitement to offence and friendly relations with foreign States), the scope of the freedom of speech and expression has been sufficiently lessened, yet this is heartening that the State can impose only reasonable restrictions on these Fundamental Rights. The Supreme Court would be the sole judge to decide whether the restrictions imposed upon the Fundamental Rights are reasonable or not. If in the opinion of Supreme Court, the restrictions are unreasonable, then it can declare them as unreasonable.

Restriction upon the Right to form Associations or Unions. Just like freedom of speech and expression, the right to form associations is also very important. The right has been recognised by Article 19 (1) (*c*). Clause 4 of Article 19 declares that nothing in sub-clause (*c*) of Article 19 (1) shall affect the operation of any existing law in so far as it imposes or prevents the State from making any

1. Constituent Assembly Debates, Vol VIII, p.41

law imposing, in the interest of public order or morality, reasonable restrictions on the exercise of the right conferred by the said clause.

So it is clear from the above clause that the restrictions imposed upon the right to form associations or unions must be reasonable and in the interest of public order and morality. In the *State of Madras* v. *V. G. Row*, Chief Justice Patanjli Shastri observed,

> "The right to form associations or unions has such wide and varied scope for its exercise and its curtailment is fraught with such potential reactions in the religious, political and economic field that the resting of authority in the executive government to impose restrictions on such right, without allowing the grounds of such imposition, both in their factual and legal aspects, to be fully tested in judicial inquiry, is a strong element which, in our opinion, must be taken into account in judging the reasonableness of the restriction imposed.....the formula of subjective satisfaction of the government or of its officers with an Advisory Board thrown in to review the material on which the government seeks to override a basic freedom guaranteed to the citizen, may be viewed as reasonable only in very exceptional circumstances and within the narrowest limits and cannot receive judicial approval as a general pattern of reasonable restrictions of Fundamental Rights."

Therefore, the Supreme Court held that Section 15 (2) of the Criminal Law Amendment Act, 1908 as amended by the Criminal Law Amendment (Madras) Act, 1950 was *ultra vires* as it imposed unreasonable restrictions on the freedom of association.

Supreme Court strikes down Section 17A of the Maintenance of Internal Security Act and Reverses the Decision of A.K. Gopalan v. State of Madras case

A seven-judge Constitution Bench of the Supreme Court struck down Section 17-A of the Maintenance of Internal Security Act as amended by the Defence of India Act, on April 19, 1973.

The impugned Section 17-A—a key section of the Act—enabled the Government of India and the State Governments to detain suspected persons for a period of 21 months without even a reference of the case to the Advisory Board as required in Article 22 (4) of the Constitution. Under Preventive Detention Law such detention without trial is possible only for a period of trhee months at the first instance.

The Supreme Court allowed the writ petition filed by Mr. Sambhu Nath Sarkar, a Government employee, held in detention in the Hooghly jail since January 29, 1972, by an order of the District Magistrate of Hooghly and directed on April 19, 1973, that he be released forthwith. In striking down Section 17-A of the Act, the Supreme Court reversed its own earlier judgment in the case of the Communist leader Mr., A.K. Gopalan. That judgment had held the field in constitutional law of India for the past 22 years. The Supreme Court held that authorising detention of a citizen without reference to the Advisory Board was bad law because it did not satisfy the requirement laid down in Clause (7) (A) of Article 22 of the Constitution. This unanimous judgment was pronounced by the Acting Chief Justice, Mr. J.M. Shelat.

The petitioner Shambhu Nath Sarkar was first prosecuted along with six other Government employees for alleged acts prejudicial to the maintenance of public order, but all of them were discharged by the magistrate on the basis of final police report. The petitioner was, however, detained under the impugned Act and lodged in Hooghly jail.

The petitioner's mother filed an application before the Calcutta High Court challenging the legality of the detention as having been made on vague and irrelevant grounds, but the application was dismissed. The petitioner then moved the Supreme Court. The Supreme Court heard the case for three days in November and December, 1972. But during the course of the arguments a new contention involving an issue decided upon by the Supreme Court in the A.K. Gopalan case in 1950 came up, and since this involved a review of the majority decision in this case, which held the field, it was decided that the case be referred to a larger Bench of seven Judges.

The contention on behalf of the petitioner was that Section 17A of the impugned Act, did not comply with the requirement of clause (7) of Article 22 of the Constitution in as much as enumeration of the subject on heads in Section 17A, except with respect to maintenance of essential supplies and services, would not mean prescribing the class or class of cases and circumstances as provided by clause (7).

In the present case while counsel for the petitioner canvassed for the reasoning given by the minority Bench in the Gopalan case, the Attorney-General, Mr. Niren De, who appeared on behalf of the Government of India, contended that the reasoning in the judgments of the majcrity Judges was to be accepted as being in consonance with Clauses (4) and (7) of Article 22.

The Supreme Court was of the view that since the matter involved the right of personal liberty, the fact that the decision in the Gopalan case held the field should not by itself be a deterrent against its reconsideration. While differing with the majority judgment in the A.K. Gopalan case, the court said : "With great respect to the distinguished Judges who formed majority in the Gopalan case, we are not able to concur with their view on the construction of clause 4 (B) and clause 7 (A) of Article 22. Section 17 of the Act, in our opinion, has failed to comply with the requirement of clause 7A of Article 22 and has, therefore, to be declared as being inconsistent with that clause.

Sixteenth Amendment of the Indian Constitution to check the secessionist activities

As previously stated, the Constitution (Sixteenth) Amendment Act was introduced in Parliament on January 21, 1963. The object of this Amendment Act was to amend Article 19 of the Constitution because the decisions of the Supreme Court made it clear that the Article in its present form was not sufficient to check the secessionist activities of any individual or organisation. It was made an Act on 5th October, 1963. This Act makes it binding on every one to uphold the sovereignty and integrity of India. No candidate now can form the secession from India as election issue. Even after his election, or nomination to any House of Parliament or State Legislature, he has to take an oath or affirmation to uphold the sovereignty of India.

Seventeenth Amendment of the Indian Constitution and historic judgment of the Supreme Court in Golak Nath's case

The Supreme Court declared Madras Land Reforms Act as *ultra vires* (null and void) in 1964, which fixed ceiling on landholdings. Therefore, the Government of India had to introduce the Bill for the Seventeenth Amendment of the Indian Constitution. The Bill was introduced in Parliament in May, 1964 before the death of Pt. Jawaharlal Nehru but was enacted on June 20, 1964, after the death of Pt. Jawaharlal Nehru. This amendment validated several tenancy acts of State in spite of the judgment of the Supreme Court to the contrary effect. It was contended again in the Supreme Court that Parliament was not competent to enact Seventeenth Amendment. *Chief Justice Subba Rao while delivering a majority decision of the Supreme Court in Golak Nath's case on February* 27, 1967, *held that the Fundamental Rights were beyond the reach of Parliament and none of the Fundamental Rights contained in Part III of the Constitution could be taken away or abridged by Parliament by amending the Constitution under Article* 368. The Supreme Court also held that the First, Fourth and Seventeenth Amendments which made laws valid against Fundamental Rights violated Article 13 (2) of the Constitution were void, and hence could not be enforced. As this historic judgment could create many legal difficulties about the past, so Chief Justice Subha Rao observed that this decision would apply to future, not to past. Justice Hidayatullah also concurred with Chief Justice Subba Rao. This means that the existing arrangements were valid but in future the Parliament would not be able to curtail the Fundamental Rights.

PARLIAMENTS RIGHT TO AMEND CONSTITUTION UPHELD. FUNDAMENTAL RIGHTS CAN BE ABRIDGED BUT NOT FRAMEWORK : DECISION ON GOLAK NATH CASE REVERSED, MAJORITY DECISION BY SUPREME COURT

The Supreme Court reversed on April 24, 1973, its 1967 Golak Nath Ruling and upheld Parliament's Right to amend the Constitution including the Fundamental Rights but not the basic structure of framework of the Constitution. This was the majority view of the Supreme Court summed up by nine out of the 13 Judges who heard the Fundamental Rights case.

The Court, thus, in the words of Mr. Justice S.N. Dwivedi, one of the 13 Judges of the Constitution Bench, shifted back to its original position, before the Golak Nath Case that Parliament is omnipotent. The Supreme Court's position in the Golak Nath Case of 1967, was that the Supreme Court is omnipotent.

The Supreme Court's stand on April 24, 1973, was summed up by the youngest Judge of the Bench, Mr. Y.V. Chandrachud : "Let us give to Parliament the freedom within the framework of the Constitution to ensure that the blessings of liberty will be shared by all." Declaring that if the State fails to create conditions in which the fundamental freedom could be enjoyed by all, the freedom of the few will be at the mercy of the many and then all freedoms will vanish.

Justice Y.V. Chandrachud sounded a note of caution to Parliament : *"if despite the large power now conceded to Parliament, the social objectives are going to be a dustbin of settlements, then woe be to those in whom the country has placed such massive faith."*

The Constitution Bench which heard the present case included two members of the majority in the 11-member Constitution Bench of 1967—Mr. S.M. Sikri, Chief Justice, and J.M. Shelat. Chief Justice S.M. Sikri ruled that Parliament could amend, but not abrogate the Fundamental Rights and upheld the 24th Constitution Amendment along with his 12 colleagues on the Bench saying the amendment met his test. Justice J.M. Shelat in the judgment he wrote with Justice A.N. Grover, said, the Golak Nath ruling had now become academic and that *the 24th Amendment was valid because in his view it did not add to the power originally conferred by the Constitution on Parliament.*

25th and 29th Amendments partly valid. Besides the 24th Amendment, 25th and 29th Amendments were challenged before the Supreme court by Swami Keshwanand Bharti, a Kerala Religious Head. The majority view, according to the sum-up, was that the 25th and 29th Amendments are partly valid. *The Court also held as invalid the new Article* 31 (*C*) *to the extent that no law made in furtherance of two of the Directive Principles of the Constitution could be declared void on the grounds that they were inconsistent with or abrogated or abridged the Fundamental Rights to equality before law, to freedom of speech and to property.*

The Directive Principles which, thus, override the three Fundamental Rights are the distribution of ownership and control of material resources of the community to subserve the common good and the prevention of the concentration of wealth and means of production to the common detriment.

Section 31 (C) of the 25th Amendment held invalid by the Supreme Court would have put out of judicial review the question whether laws declared by Parliament as furthering the two Directive Principles did in fact promote the objective. The majority did not touch the proviso to Article 31 (C) which brought under its purview only those laws of State Legislatures, which are reserved and receive the assent of the President.

Supreme Court also held the 29th Amendment, which seeks to protect two Kerala Land Reforms Acts of 1961 and 1969, as valid but said the two enactments should be further considered by the Constitution Bench.

According to the Chief Justice, the question to be determined is whether the two enactments merely abridge or totally abrogate the Fundamental Right to Property.

Also to be determined by the Constitution Bench in the light of today's ruling is the validity of the 26th Amendment which abolishes princely purses and privileges.

Beautiful Balance. The marathon Fundamental Rights case has ended at last. And it has ended in a judgment that will satisfy all reasonable men. Nine of the thirteen judges have, in their "majority view," upheld Constitutional Amendments 24 and 29 in their entirety and thus upheld Parliament's right to amend the Fundamental Rights. To that extent they have reversed the majority judgments in the Golak Nath Case. But they have invalidated the second part of Section 3 of the 25th Amendment, which gave Parliament and State Legislatures power to amend Fundamental Rights on mere insertion of a declaration that the same was necessary for giving effect to a directive principle.

Judge after Judge of the Supreme Court found this clause unconstitutional on more grounds than one. In the first place, it was pointed out, Article 368 did not empower the states on their own to amend the Constitution. Nor could Parliament destroy Fundamental Rights in the name of Directive Principles. As Chief Justice S.M. Sikri put it : "That expression amendment of this Constitution does not enable Parliament to abrogate or take away Fundamental Rights or to completely change the fundamental features of the Constitution, so as to destroy its identity." Chief Justice Sikri pointed out, Parliament "can amend or regulate or adjust them without destroying them." He added, "Within these limits, Parliament can amend every Article."

Note. See also further *Minerva Mill Case* in this chapter, delivered by the Supreme Court on 9th May, 1980 after emergency was over.

SOME OTHER CONSTITUTIONAL RESTRICTIONS ON FUNDAMENTAL RIGHTS

A. Suspension of Provisions of Article 19 during Emergencies

Although the Founding Fathers of the Indian Republic guaranteed to Indian citizens certain Fundamental Rights, they realised that there might be certain situations in life of the nation when it was not desirable to give absolute rights of freedom to the people, hence, they allowed the State to impose reasonable restrictions upon clauses 2 to 6 of Article 19 (dealing with the Right to Freedom). The Constitution allowed the State to impose more restrictions under Articles 358 and 359. The original Article 358 had provided that while the Emergency was in operation under Article 352 due to war, external aggression or internal disturbance, then the State became entitled to take any executive action or make any law for suspension of the Fundamental Rights. The Constitution (Forty-second) Amendment Act, 1976 added a new provision to Article 19 that if a proclamation was prevalent only in a particular part of India, then the State was also entitled to suspend the Fundamental Right to Freedom (clauses 2 to 6 of Article 19) in other parts of India where that Proclamation was not in operation. The Constitution (44th Amendment) Act, 1978 further provided that Article 19 could be suspended only if the Proclamation of Emergency under Article 352 was made due to a threat to the security of India or any part of the territory thereof by war or by external aggression. It did not apply to internal disturbance.

B. Suspension of other rights during Emergency

It is noteworthy that Fundamental Rights other than the Right to Freedom under Article 19 could also be suspended during the period of Emergency and provision for the same was originally made in the Constitution itself. The original Constitution, Article 359, provided that :

(1) Where a Proclamation of Emergency is in operation, the President may by order declare that the right to move any court for the enforcement of *such of the rights* conferred by Part III *as may be mentioned in the order* and all proceedings pending in any court for the enforcement of the rights so mentioned shall remain suspended *for the period during which the Proclamation is in force for such shorter period as may be specified in the order*.

(2) An order made as aforesaid may extend to the whole or any part of the territory of India.

(3) Every order made under clause (1) shall, as soon as may be after it is made, be laid before each House of Parliament.

Article 359 was further amended by the Constitution (Thirty-eighth) Amendment Act, 1975 and the Constitution (Forty-fourth Amendment) Act, 1978. The Thirty-eighth Amendment Act provided that while an order suspending such of the Fundamental Rights as might be mentioned in that order was in operation, the State shall become competent to make any law or take any executive action which the State would not be otherwise competent to do, and that any such law or executive action would become a nullity as soon as that order (that is the Presidential order) suspending the Fundamental Rights ceased to operate.

Article 359 as amended further by 44th Amendment Act, 1978 provides:

(1) Where a Proclamation of Emergency is in operation, the President *may* by order declare that the right to move any court for the enforcement of such of the rights conferred by Part III *except Articles* 20 *and* 21 as may be mentioned in the order and all proceedings pending in any court for the enforcement of the rights so mentioned shall remain suspended for the period during which the Proclamation is in force or for such shorter period as may be specified in the order. This amendment was passed during the Janata Party regime. It meant that the Right of Protection in respect of conviction for offences and the Right of Protection of life and personal liberty could not be curtailed during the period of Emergency.

C. Preventive Detention

Another restriction which has been imposed on the Fundamental Rights in the Constitution was through clauses (4), (5), (6) and (7) of Article 22 dealing with preventive detention. The question is what is meant by Preventive Detention. *Durga Das Basu* has defined it thus: "Preventive Detention means the detention of a person without trial in such circumstances that the evidence in possession of the authority is not sufficient to make a legal charge or to secure the conviction of the detenu by legal proof, but may still be sufficient to justify his detention. While the object of "*preventive detention*" is to punish a person for the offence he *has done*, and to *prevent him from doing* something which comes within entry 9 of List I and entry 3 of List III.[1] The objective of Preventive Detention is to prevent the individual not merely from acting in a particular way, but from achieving a particular object. No offence is proved nor any charge formulated and the justification is *suspicion* or reasonable probability and not criminal conviction which can only be warranted by legal evidence.

EROSION OF FUNDAMENTAL RIGHTS DURING INTERNAL EMERGENCY

A. Frequent Amendments of MISA (Maintenance of Internal Security Act)

The then President of India, Mr. Fakhruddin Ali Ahmed, declared Internal Emergency under Article 352 on the advice of the then Prime Minister Shrimati Indira Gandhi on the night of June 25, 1975 (as it was declared late at night, therefore, some writers have preferred to call it June 26, 1975 instead of June 25 but that makes no difference). The Central Government Authorities had felt much embarrassed after the decision of the Supreme Court upon the Fundamental Rights in 1973. Therefore, during the Internal Emergency the Central Government felt the need of amending the MISA (Maintenance of Internal Security Act) under which thousands of political workers and leaders of the Opposition including Jayaprakash Narain had been imprisoned. So real erosion of the Fundamental Rights particularly the rights granted under Articles 14, 19, 21 and 22 now started. Two days after the declaration of Internal Emergency the President late on the night of June 27 issued an order under Article 359 (1) of the Cosntitution, forbidding those detained under the proclamation of Emergency from moving the courts for relief during the period the Emergency would remain in force. The rights granted under Article 14 (Equality before law), Article 21 (Protection of life and personal liberty)

1. Entry 9 of Central Legislative List I deals with preventive detention for reasons connected with Defence, Foreign Affairs or the Security of India. Entry 3 of the Concurrent Legislative List deals with preventive detention for reasons connected with the security of a State, the maintenance of public order or the maintenance of supplies and services essential to the community.

and Article 22 (Protection against arrest and detention in certain cases) were suspended. It should be noted that this order extended to the whole of India except Jammu and Kashmir and was in addition to and not derogatory under clause (1) of Article 359 of the Constitution. Three days later the President further amended the MISA (Maintenance of Internal Security Act) by issuing an Ordinance. Previously it was necessary to provide to the detenu the reasons of his detention within a few days but now even this necessity was removed. It was sufficient if the detenu was given in writing after certain days that it was necessary detention to detain him for dealing with the Emergency. If the declaration to detain a person was issued by the authorities lower than the State Government, then it was to be reviewed within 15 days by the State Government. The ordinance also inserted a new provision in the MISA (Maintenance of Internal Security Act) whereby the amended provisions would have effect for one year and not more than one year if the emergency persisted. Another provision which was inserted in the MISA (Maintenance of Internal Security Act) was that even if an order had been earlier issued in favour of a person for his release, then another order could be issued for his detention. A person detained under MISA (Maintenance of Internal Security Act) could not be released either on bail or bail bond or otherwise.

Another Amendment of the MISA (Maintenance of Internal Security Act) was made by the Presidential Ordinance on July 16, 1975. Whereas the First Amendment of the MISA (Maintenance of Internal Security Act) had provided that detenu could not get any relief under the law of natural justice and no reasons were to be provided to him for his detention for a period of one year, the 2nd Amendment further stipulated that the detenu could not approach the courts for relief on the ground that no reasons had been provided to him for his detention or any contention that the detenu had not violated "rules of natural justice" or "national or common law". Another significant amendment to the MISA (Maintenance of Internal Security Act) was that the provisions of Sections 80 to 86 of the Criminal Procedure Code of 1973 were made applicable to the person against whom the detention order had been issued and who failed to surrender himself, had absconded or was concealing himself. According to this provision his property could be attached by making an appropriate report to a Metropolitan Magistrate or a Judicial Magistrate of the place where such a person ordinarily resided. Another provision was added that even the foreigners could be detained under MISA (Maintenance of Internal Security Act) for their subversive activities and they could not claim any right to personal liberty by virtue of natural law or common law if any.

In order to replace the above two Ordinances beyond courts, Union Home Minister introduced on 23rd July, 1975 a Bill, known as the Maintenance of Internal Security (Amendment) Bill, in the Lok Sabha. The statement of the objects and reasons of the Bill stated that consequent upon the promulgation of Emergency by the President on June 26, 1975, it became necessary for the government to arm itself with powers to take certain preventive measures in the interest of the security of the State which was being threatened by "internal disturbances." He said that an extraordinary situation had been created by certain political parties, organised groups and anti-social elements in the country, that their activities had injected violence into the public life, and they were trying to seize power through extra-constitutional methods. This Bill was passed by the Rajya Sabha on July 25, and by the Lok Sabha on July 29. Soon after, it received the President's assent and became the law of the land.

MISA (Maintenance of Internal Security Act) was amended for the third time. On October 17, 1975 the MISA (Maintenance of Internal Security Act) was amended for the third time again through a Presidential Ordinance. The Government of India had to issue this ordinance because the proceedings against the MISA (Maintenance of Internal Security Act) had been pending in certain cases in the Suprerme Court and the Court had insisted that the reasons for the detention might not be disclosed to the detenu but they should be disclosed at least to the court. So the new Ordinance made it clear that any person against whom a detention order was made would not be entitled to the communication of the grounds of detention or the relevant material. Such grounds or material would be "treated as confidential and shall be deemed to refer to matters of State." On June 16, 1976, the

President issued another Ordinance extending by one year the power of the Government to detain a person under the MISA (Maintenance of Internal Security Act) without giving him the grounds for his detention. The effect of this Ordinance was far-reaching. It made the detention of all the persons held under the MISA (Maintenance of Internal Security Act) legally valid up to 29 June, 1977. A Bill to replace this ordinance was also introduced in the Lok Sabha on 10 August, 1976 by the then Home Minister Brahmananda Reddy. It was named as the *Maintenance of Internal Security* (*Second Amendment*) Bill. It met with stiff resistance from the Opposition members who charged the police and the bureaucracy for misusing the provisions of MISA (Maintenance of Internal Security Act) but the Government was able to muster sufficient strength to get it passed by the Lok Sabha (House of People) and Rajya Sabha (Council of States) or both Houses of Parliament. The then President Mr. Fakhruddin Ali Ahmed, readily gave his assent to the Bill and thus it became an Act of the State.

B. Supreme Court Rules that Habeas Corpus Writs not Maintainable during Emergency

The last nail in the coffin of the Fundamental Rights was struck by the Supreme Court's judgment in the famous *habeas corpus* writ petition case. During the emergency some Opposition parties and Organisations had been banned and their workers had been arrested. So they filed petitions under *Habeas Corpus* under Article 226 of the Constitution and sought their release from jails. In a few cases, their petitions were upheld and the release of the affected detenu was ordered. A batch of 14 appeals involving in all 43 detenus, including four Opposition MPs held under the MISA (Maintenance of Internal Security Act), were filed before the Supreme Court in early December 1975. The Supreme Court delivered its judgment on 28 April, 1976. By a majority of four to one, it held as under :

1. In view of the Presidential Order dated June 27, 1975, no person had any *locus standi* (recognised position or right to appear in court) to move any writ petition under Article 226 before a High Court for *habeas corpus* or any other writ or order or direction to challenge the legality of an order of detention on the ground that the Order is not under, or in compliance with, the Act is illegal or is vitiated by mala fides factual or legal or is based on extraneous considerations.
2. Section 16 A (a) of the MISA (Maintenance of Internal Security Act) is constitutionally valid (This section prohibited the disclosure of the grounds of detention).
3. The appeals are accepted. Judgments of the High Court are set aside.
4. Petitions before the High Courts are now to be disposed of in accordance with the law laid down in these appeals.

Dissenting Historic Judgment of H.R. Khanna. Justice H.R. Khanna was the only judge of the Supreme Court who gave his dissenting judgment. He observed : "Unanimity which is merely formal and which is recorded at the expense of strong conflicting views is not desirable in a court of last resort." Justice H.R Khanna said that there was no provision in the Constitution of India which debarred the High Courts to issue writs of *habeas corpus* during the Emergency and that despite the existence of Presidential Order issued under Article 359 (1) of the Constitution a detenu could challenge his detention on the ground that either there was no law authorising his detention or that law had not been complied with. He also said that Article 21 was not the sole repository of the Right to Life and personal liberty, as had been contended by the Attorney-General. Even in the absence of Article 21, the State had no right to deprive a person of his life and personal liberty without the authority of law. "That is the essential postulate and basic assumption of the rule of law in every civilized society," he said. When the New Constitution of India was not enforced, then nobody could be deprived of his right to life and liberty without the authority of law and that in view of Article 372, those laws continued to be in force even after the Constitution came into force in 1950.

Justice H.R. Khanna maintained that the Presidential Order had suspended only the Fundamental Rights but not the other laws made by the legislature. These laws continued in force even during the Internal Emergency. The obligation and liabilities created by these statutes would remain unaffected. If the citizen of India could not get any relief during Emergency under any law, starting consequences would follow. Then the police and bureaucracy would be able to throw any person or a whole group or family of persons for reasons which had nothing to do with the security of the State or the maintenance of public order. This was a very bold judgment during Internal Emergency when terror was prevalent and nobody had the courage to say anything against the State. That is why this dissenting judgment has become historic and has immortalised the name of its deliverer (Justice H.R. Khanna) in the Legal History of India. His name deserves to be written in the letters of gold.

Keeping in view the majority decision of the Supreme Court the various High Courts dismissed the petitions filed under *Habeas Corpus* and the persons detained under MISA (Maintenance of Internal Security Act) continued to rot in jails.

JANATA GOVERNMENT RESTORES FUNDAMENTAL RIGHTS

The elections to the 6th Lok Sabha (House of People) were held from 16th to 18th March, 1977. Shrimati Indira Gandhi and her Congress Party was defeated at the polls and the Janata Party won a massive majority. Shrimati Indira Gandhi tendered her resignation to the Acting President B.D. Jatti on March 23, 1977 and recommended to him to lift the Internal Emergency. Morarji Desai, the Leader of Janata Party in the House of People, became the Prime Minister on March 24, 1977, and the Internal Emergency was revoked. After a few days the external emergency was also lifted on the recommendation of Prime Minister Morarji Desai. Consequently, all restrictions on the Fundamental Rights came to an end. After some time the Janata Governemnt moved a Bill in the Parliament to repeal the MISA (Maintenance of Internal Security Act). It was passed by the Lok Sabha on 20 July, 1978 and by the Rajya Sabha on 27 July, 1978. Thus all rights and freedoms of the Indian people curtailed under the "Draconian" measure were restored.

Later on the Janata Government sought to shield the Fundamental Rights from being amended by the Centre at the mere will of the Legislature, by the special majority prescribed by Article 368, by further providing that an Amendment of Fundamental Rights in Part III shall not be made unless, apart from the vote in the Legislature, it was approved by the people at a Referendum. This additional requirement was sought to be inserted in Article 368, by the Constitution 44th Amendment Bill, but the relevant clause of that Bill was defeated (voted down) by the Congress—Opposition in the Rajya Sabha. The Janata Proposal, in fact, sought to give constitutional support to the theory of 'basic structure' of the Constitution as propounded in Keshvananda Bharti's case. Till recently, the result was that Article 366 remained where it was after 42nd Amendment Act and that any Fundamental Right could be amended or repealed by the special majority in Parliament as provided in the original Article 368.

PRIMACY OF FUNDAMENTAL RIGHTS RE-ESTABLISHED

Supreme Court's Judgment in Minerva Mills Case after Emergency

In a momentous decision given on 9th May, 1980 (full text of the judgment appeared on 31-7-1980) the Supreme Court of India, in *Minerva Mills Ltd. and Others* v. *Union of India and Others*[1] struck down Section 55 of the Constitution (42nd Amendment) Act, 1976, which had placed unlimited powers on the Parliament of India to amend the Constitution. It was held as follows (as per Y.V. Chandrachud, Chief Justice) :

"These then are our reasons for the order which we passed on May 9, 1980, to the following effect.

1. AIR 1980 SC 1789.

Section 4 of the Constitution (42nd Amendment) Act is beyond the amending power of the Parliament and is void since it damages the basic or essential feature of the Constitution and destroys its basic structure by a total exclusion of challenge to any law on the ground that it is inconsistent with or takes away or abridges any of the rights conferred by Article 14 or Article 19 of the Constitution, if the law is for giving effect to the policy of the State towards securing all or any of the principles laid down in Part IV of the Constitution.

Section 55 of the Constitution (42nd Amendment) Act, 1976 is beyond the amending power of the Parliament and is void since it removes all limitations on the power of the Parliament to amend the Constitution and confers power upon it to amend the Constitution so as to damage or destroy its basic or essential features or its basic structure.

Justice P.N. Bhagwati who delivered a separate judgment held as follows :

"I would, therefore, declare Section 55 of the Constitution (Forty-second Amendment) Act, 1976 which inserted sub-sections (4) and (5) in Article 368 as unconstitutional and void on the ground that it damages the basic structure of the Constitution and goes beyond the amending power of Parliament. But so far as Section 4 of the Constitution (Forty-second Amendment) Act, 1976, is concerned, I hold that on the interpretation placed on the amended Article 31-C by me, does not contravene the Constitution and is within the amending power of Parliament and I would, therefore, declare the amended Article 31-C to be constitutional and valid."

The effect of the aforesaid decision now would be that the changes made by the Constitution (42nd Amendment) Act, 1976, would stand invalidated as those changes damaged the basic structure of the Constitution and violated the court's judgment in Keshvananda Bharti's case. *Mr. N.A. Palkhivala has remarked that his decision had rekindled the light of the Constitution of India. Hence the power of judicial review which was taken away by the Parliament has now been revived.*

FUNDAMENTAL DUTIES

There is an intimate co-relationship between the rights and duties. The Constitution of India granted certain Fundamental Rights to its citizens but failed to incorporate duties of the citizens which could remind them of their duty to observe certain basic norms of democratic conduct and democratic behaviour. This omission was rectified by the Forty-Second Amendment carried out in 1976 which added Article 51 A in Part IV of the Constitution dealing with the duties of the Indian citizens.

It is noted that the Indian Constitution is not the only constitution to incorporate duties of its citizens. The constitutions of several other countries like Italy, People's Republic of China, Albania, Czechoslovakia, the Netherlands, the Ex-U.S.S.R. also contain Fundamental Duties. A question may naturally arise as to why these duties were added to the Constitution after 26 years of inaguration of the constitution. The reasons were explained by H.R. Gokhale, the then Law Minister, thus: "... In post-independent India, particularly on the eve of emergency in June 1975, a section of the people showed no anxiety to fulfil their Fundamental obligations of respecting the established legal order.... the provision of chapter on Fundamental Duties would have a sobering effect on these restless spirits who have had a host of anti-national subversive and unconstitutional agitations in the past.

The Fundamental Duties are a novel feature of the Indian Constitution in recent times. Originally, the Constitution of India did not contain these duties. The Forty-second Constitution Amendment Act, 1976 has incorporated in Part IV A 'Ten Fundamental Duities'. in Article 51(A) of the Constitution of India. The Eighty-sixth Constitution Amendment Act, 2002 has added one more Fundamental Duty in Article 51(A) of the Constitution of India. As a result, there are now eleven Fundamental Duties of the citizens of India.

The following are the Eleven Fundamental Duties of every citizen of India :

"(*a*) to abide by the Constitution and respect its ideals and institutions, the National Flag and the National Anthem;

(*b*) to cherish and follow the noble ideals which inspired our national struggle for freedom;

(*c*) to uphold and protect the sovereignty, unity and integrity of India;

(*d*) to defend the country and render national service when called upon to do so;

(*e*) to promote harmony and the spirit of common brotherhood amongst all the people of India transcending religious, linguistic and regional or sectional diversities; to renounce practices derogatory to dignity of women;

(*f*) to value and preserve the rich heritage of our composite culture;

(*g*) to protect and improve the national environment including forests, lakes, rivers and wild life, and to have compassion for living creatures;

(*h*) to develop the scientific temper, humanism and the spirit of inquiry and reform;

(*i*) to safeguard public property and to abjure violence;

(*j*) to strive towards excellence in all spheres of individual and collective activity so that the nation constantly rises to higher levels of endeavour and achievement ; and

(*k*) to provide opportunities for education by the parent, the guardian, to his child, or a ward between the age of 6-14 years as the case may be."

An analysis of the above duties reveals that they are applicable only to citizens and not to the aliens. It is expected that a citizen of India, while enjoying fundamental rights, should also perform these duties. Although there is no provision in the Constitution for direct enforcement of any of these duties, yet the courts are guided by these duties while interpreting various laws. These duties have sanctity as these are included in the Directive Principles of State Policy. The incorporation of Fundamental Duties in the Constitution was an attempt to balance the individual's civil freedoms with his civic obligations. These rights cannot be judicially enforced.

Fundamental Duties had been inserted in the Constitution of the U.S.S.R. for the first time in the world in 1936. After that they were enshrined in the Constitution of China and other Communist countries of Eastern Europe whose constitutions were modelled more or less on the pattern of the U.S.S.R. The new Constitution of the U.S.S.R. which was adopted on 7th October, 1977, enlarges these duties further. So these duties are quite useful. Janata Party wanted to scrap the entire 42nd Amendment Act in 1977 after assumption of power on March 24, 1977, but could not do so because of the opposition of the Congress which continued to enjoy majority in the Rajya Sabha in 1977. Therefore, it was agreed between Prime Minister Morarji Desai and the Leader of the Opposition Mr. Yashwant Rao Chavan, in 1977 that the Fundamental Duties would be retained.

So Fundamental Duties exist now.

EXERCISES

Long Answer Type Questions :

1. What is meant by Fundamental Rights ?
2. Write a detailed note on classification of Fundamental Rights.
3. Write a note on suspension of Fundamental Rights.
4. Write a note on criticism of Fundamental Rights.
5. What is the position of Parliament on Fundamental Rights ?
6. Should Parliament be given the right to amend the Fundamental Rights ?
7. Write a note on Fundamental Duties.

Short Answer Type Questions:

1. Parliament should not have right to amend the Fundamental Rights. Do you agree with this statement? Write in brief.
2. What do you know about Fundamental Duties ?
3. Write a brief note on 'Parliament and the Fundamental Rights'.
4. What is Right to Constitutional Remedies ?
5. What is Cultural and Educational Rights ?
6. Write a note on 'Right to Freedom of Religion'.
7. What do you know about ' Right to Freedom' ?
8. What is meant by 'Right to Equality' ?
9. When were the Fundamental Duties incorporated in the Constitution ?

Objective Type Questions:

Choose the correct answer

1. The Fundamental Rights contained in the Constitution have been classified in how many categories?
   (*a*) Six (*b*) Seven
   (*c*) Eight (*d*) Nine
2. Which Articles of the Indian Constitution deal with the Right to Equality ?
   (*a*) Articles 13 to 18 (*b*) Articles 14 to 18
   (*c*) Articles 15 to 18 (*d*) Articles 16 to 18
3. Which Articles of the Indian Constitution deal with the Right to Freedom ?
   (*a*) Articles 17 to 20 (*b*) Articles 18 to 20
   (*c*) Articles 19 to 22 (*d*) Articles 20 to 24
4. Which Articles of the Indian Constitution are concerned with the Right against Exploitation ?
   (*a*) Articles 20 and 21 (*b*) Articles 21 and 22
   (*c*) Articles 22 and 23 (*d*) Articles 32 and 24
5. Which Articles of the Indian Constitution deal with the Freedom of Conscience and Religion ?
   (*a*) Articles 25 and 28 (*b*) Articles 26 and 28
   (*c*) Articles 28 and 29 (*d*) Articles 29 and 30
6. Which of the following is not included in the list of Fundamental Duties (Article 51A) in the Constitution?
   (*a*) To safeguard public property and to abjure violence.
   (*b*) Secularism
   (*c*) To uphold and protect the sovereiguty, unity and integrity of India.
   (*d*) To abide by the Constitution and respect its ideals.
7. Fundamental Duties were intrpduced in the Constitution by the
   (*a*) 40th Amendment (*b*) 42nd Amendment
   (*c*) 43rd Amendment (*d*) 44th Amendment

8. **The Fundamental Duties of the Indian citizens are enshrined in :**

(*a*) Part IV of the Constitution (*b*) Part IV A of the Constitution

(*c*) Part III A of the Constitution (*d*) In Schedule II A

9. **When were the Fundamental Duties incorporated in the Constitution ?**

(*a*) in 1975 (*b*) in 1976

(*c*) in 1977 (*d*) in 1979

10. **The idea of Fundamental Duties is derived from :**

(*a*) American Constitution (*b*) British Constitution

(*c*) Russian Constitution (*d*) None of these

ANSWERS

1. (*a*) 2. (*b*) 3. (*c*) 4. (*d*) 5. (*a*) 6. (*b*) 7. (*b*) 8. (*b*) 9. (*b*) 10. (*c*)

CHAPTER 6

Directive Principles of State Policy (Positive Directions for State)

Although the Directive Principles of State Policy confer no legal rights and create no legal remedies, they appear to be like an Instrument of Instructions, or general recommendations addressed to all authorities in the Union reminding them of the basic principles of the new social and economic order which the Constitution aims at building. These fundamental axioms of State Policy, though of no legal effect, have served as useful beacon-lights to courts. —*M.C. Setalvad*

The Directive Principles of State Policy which have been enshrined in Part IV of the Indian Constitution aim at realizing the high ideals of justice, equality and fraternity as outlined in the Preamble to the Indian Constitution. These are the ideals which are to inspire the State to work for the common good of the people and establish social and economic democracy in the country.

MEANING AND OBJECT OF DIRECTIVE PRINCIPLES

The phrase 'Directive Principles of State Policy' means the principles which the state should keep in mind while framing the laws and formulating policy. They impose certain obligations on the state to take positive action to promote the welfare of the people and establish economic democracy.

The framers of the Indian Constitution borrowed this feature from the Constitution of Irish Republic. The Charter of the United Nations and the Charter of Human Rights also inspired them a great deal in the drawing up of the list of Directive Principles. Above all, the ideas and thoughts of Mahatma Gandhi also influenced them.

Directive Principles of State Policy are contained in Part IV of the Indian Constitution. Article 37 says that the Directive Principles, although not enforceable by the Court, are nevertheless Fundamental in the governance of the country and it shall be the duty of the State to apply these principles in making laws. The Directive Principles are nothing but restatement of the ideals stated in the Preamble. They are intended to serve as instructions to Governments of the State and the Centre to act in a way so as to promote fraternity and equality and to guarantee justice and liberty to the people.

Views of Dr. Bhim Rao Ambedkar. Justifying the inclusion of these principles in the Indian Constitution, Dr.Bhim Rao Ambedkar observed :

"It is no use saying that the Directive Principles have no value. In my judgment the Directive Principles have a great value, for they lay down that our ideal is economic democracy. They are like the instruments of instructions which were issued to the Governor-General and Governors of the Colonies and to those of Indian by the British Government under the 1935 Act......The only difference is that they are instructions to legislature and the executive. Such a thing, to my mind, should be welcome. Where there is a grant of power in general terms for peace, order and good government, it is necessary that it should be accompanied by instructions regulating its exercise. Because we did not merely want a parliamentary form of government to be instituted through the various mechanisms provided in the Constitution, without any direction as to what our economic ideals, as to what our social order is to be, we deliberately included the Directive Principles in our Constitution." We owe a debt to Irish Constitution for inspiration to include these directions in our own. Such constitutional declarations of social and economic principles were once found in the Constitutions of Spain, Burma, Indonesia, Nepal and Thailand.

DISTINCTION BETWEEN DIRECTIVE PRINCIPLES AND FUNDAMENTAL RIGHTS

There is a great difference between the Directive Principles and Fundamental Rights. According to *Gledhill*, "Fundamental Rights are injunctions to prohibit the Government from doing certain things, the Directive Principles are affirmative instructions to the Governemnt to do certain things." Another point of difference between the two is that whereas Fundamental Rights have legal sanction behind, the Directive Principles have moral sanction only. The former are justiciable and enforceable by courts, the latter are not so.

Views of the Supreme Court. In the case of *State of Madras* v. *Champakam Dorairajan*, the Supreme Court observed thus : "These Directive Principles of State Policy which are expressly made unenforceable by a court cannot override the provisions in Part III which notwithstanding other provisions are expressly made enforceable by the appropriate writs, orders or directions under Article 32. The chapter on Fundamental Rights is sacrosanct and not liable to be adridged by any Legislative Act or Executive Order, except to the extent provided in the appropriate Articles in Part III. The Directive Principles of State Policy have to conform to and run subsidiary to the chapter on Fundamental Rights .... That is the correct way in which the provisions found in Part III and Part IV have to be understood. However, so long as there is no infringment of any Fundamental Rights, to the extent conferred by the Provisions in Part III, there can be no objection to the state acting in accordance with the Directive Principles set out in Part IV, but subject again to the Legislative and Executive powers and limitations conferred on the State under different provisions of the Constitution."

Views of Dr. K.C. Markandan. Therefore, whereas it is essential to implement the Directive Principles of State Policy in the national interest, it is equally important that as far as possible the Indian people should not be deprived of the Fundamental Rights because without them the personality of the individual cannot grow. The State should interfere in the Fundamental Rights only when they are misued. *K.C. Markandan* has remarked, while deliberating on the importance of the Directive Principles : "*Far from being a proclamation or promulgation of principles, the Directive Principles constitute a pledge by the framers of the Constitution to the people of India and a failure to implement them would constitute not only a breach of faith with the people but would also render a vital part of the Constitution practically a deal letter.*"[1]

1. Markandan, K.C., *Directive Principles in the Indian Constitution*, pp. 147-48.

CLASSIFICATION OF DIRECTIVE PRINCIPLES

The Directive Principles outlined from Articles 39 to 51 are amalgamation of Socialalistic, Gandhi- an and Liberal Principles and can be conveniently studied under the following heads :

***(a)* Principles which Help in the Establishment of a Welfare State or Socialist Principles.** Article 38 declares that the primary concern of the state shall be to promote the welfare of the people and create a social order in which justice—social, economic and political—shall be practised by all the national institutions.

The ideal of the welfare state is to be achieved by the State by (1) providing adequate means of livelihood; (2) distributing the ownership of material resources in a way that it does not lead to monopolisation; (3) reorganising the economic system in a way that it does not lead to centralisation of wealth in a few hands creating thereby acute poverty in another class which forms the bulk of the population; (4) securing equal pay for equal work for both men and women; (5) securing suitable employment for men, women and children so that their health is not undermined; (6) guarding the children and young men against exploitation and moral degradation; (7) taking effective steps to provide for work, education and public assistance in cases of unemployment, old age, sickness and disablement; (8) improving the conditions of work and providing material relief; (9) securing for all the workers reasonable leisure and cultural opportunities; (10) making arrangements within 10 years from the commencement of the Constitution for free and compulsory education for all children up to the age of 14; and (11) doing its best to raise the standard of living and to improve public health.

***(b)* Directive Principles which conform to the Gandhian Thought or Gandhian Principles.** The Directive Principles which intend to give a shape to Gandhian ideals are : *(a)* the State shall take steps to organise village panchayats and make them powerful enough to work as units of self-government; *(b)* it shall be the effort of the states to start and encourage cottage industries on an individual or co-operative basis in the villages; *(c)* the State shall work for the uplift of the Scheduled Castes and Scheduled Tribes by educating them and protecting their economic interests; *(d)* the States shall consider it their primary duty to stop the use of intoxicating drinks and drugs except for medical purpose; *(e)* it will be a part of duty of the state to improve the breeds of cattle and stop the slaughter of cows and calves; *(f)* the State shall also try to protect every monument and place of artistic and historic interest from destruction or disfigurement; and *(g)* the state shall take steps to separate the judiciary from the executive.

(c) Directive Principles which Promote International Peace. Article 51 of the Constitution enjoins upon the State to make efforts. *(a)* to secure international peace and security; *(b)* to maintain good and honourable relations between nations; *(c)* to foster respect to international law and treaty obligations; and *(d)* to encourage settlement of international disputes by arbitration and other peaceful means.

NEW DIRECTIVE PRINCIPLES ADDED BY 42ND AND 44TH AMENDMENTS

Pt. Jawaharlal Nehru had declared the '*Socialistic pattern of society and not socialism*' as the objective of Planning[1]. He observed :

> "Socialism to some people means two things : distribution which means cutting off the pockets of the people who have too much money and rationalisation. Both these are desirable objectives, but neither is by itself socialism.
>
> Any attempt to distribute by affecting the productive machinery is utterly wrong; to do so would be to weaken ourselves. The basis of socialism is greater wealth; there cannot be any socialism of poverty. Therefore, the process of equalisation has to be phased.

1. *Hindustan Standard*, Delhi, 17-5-1958. See also *Second Five-Year Plan*, p. 22.

Secondly, there is question of nationalisation. I think it is dangerous merely without being prepared to work it properly. To nationalise we have to select things. My idea of socialism is that *every individual in the State should have equal opportunity for progress.*"

However, in this context it has to be remembered that the governmental policy, at the Union level, had demonstrated a greater bias towards collectivism during the regime of his daughter Mrs. Indira Gandhi and many industries, trades and other means of production have been nationalised during the three decades since independence, either directly or through the agency of State-owned or State-controlled corporations, *e.g.*, banking, insurance, aviation, coal mines.

Changes brought about by 42nd Amendment Act, 1976. Mrs. Indira Gandhi during the Internal Emergency brought about 42nd Amendment of the Constitution. The Preamble was amended and the word '*Socialist*' was added. She said that her socialism did not indicate collectivism, but the offering of equal opportnities to all *through socio-economic reforms.* By bringing the 42nd Amendment she added 39A to enjoin the State to provide free legal aid to the poor and to take other suitable steps to ensure *equal justice* to all, which is offered by the Preamble. (*ii*) Article 43 A has been inserted to enable the workers to participate in the management of industries and profit-sharing. These Articles are produced below. This is a positive step in the advancement of socialism in the sense of *economic justice.*

(1) In Article 39 of the Constitution Clause (*f*) has been added which is as follows :

"that the children are given opportunities and facilities to develop in a healthy manner and in condition of freeedom and dignity and that childhood and youth are protected against exploitation and against moral and material abandoment."

(2) After Article 39 of the Constitution, the following article shall be inserted, namely :

"39A. The State shall secure that the operation of the legal system promotes justice, on a basis of equal opportunity, and shall, in particular, provide free legal aid, by suitable legislation or schemes or in any other way, to ensure that opportunities for securing justice are not denied to any citizen by reason of economic or other disabilities."

(3) After Article 43 of the Constitution, the following Article shall be inserted, namely :

"43A. The State shall take steps, by suitable legislation or in other way, to secure the participation of workers in the management of undertakings, establishments or other organisations engaged in any industry."

(4) After Article 48,of the Constitution, the following Article shall be inserted, namely :

"48A. The State shall endeavour to protect and improve the environment and to safeguard the forests and wild life of the country."

(5) According to 44th Amendment Act, 1978, "The State shall strive to promote the welfare of the people by securing a social order permeated by social, economic and political justice" Article 38(1) : to minimise inequality in income, status facilities and opportunities amongst individuals and groups.

N.B. It must be noted, however, that 42nd Amendment Act, 1976 enacted during Emergency had accorded primacy to the Directive Principles of State Policy in comparison with the Fundamental Rights.

Directive Principles of State Policy of a Glance

Directives in the Nature of Ideals of the State	Directives Shaping the Policy of the States	Non-justiciable Rights of Citizens
1. The state shall strive to promote the welfare of the people by securing a social order permeated by social, economic and political justice Article 38(i); to minimise inequality in income, status facilities and opportunities amongst individuals and groups (Article 38(2))[1]	1. To establish economic democracy and justice by securing certain economic rights (enumerated in the next column)	1. Right to adequate means of livelihood (Article 39 (a))
2. The state shall endeavour to secure just and human conditions of work, a living wage, a decent standard of living and social and cultural opportunities for all workers (Article 43).	2. To secure a uniform civil code for the citizens (Article 44)	2. Right of both sexes to equal pay for equal work (Article 39 (d).)
3. The state shall endeavour to raise the level of nutrition and standard of living and to improve public health (Article 47)	3. To provide free and compulsory primary education (Article 45)	3. Right against economic exploitation. (Article 39 (c) – (f)).
4. The state shall direct its policy towards securing equitable distribution of the material resources of the community and prevention of concentration of wealth and means of production. (Article 39 (b) – (c)).	4. To prohibit cosnumption of liquor and intoxicating drugs except for medical purpose. (Article 47)	4. Right of children and the young to be protected against exploitation and to opportunities for healthy development consonant with freedom and dignity (Article 39 (b)[2]
5. The state shall endeavour to promote international peace and amity. (Article 51)	5. To develop cottage industries. (Article 43)	5. Right to equal opportunity for justice and free legal aid. (Article 39 A)[3]
	6. To organise agriculture and animal husbandry on modern lines. (Article 48).	6. Right to work (Article 41)
	7. To prevent salaughter of useful cattle, *i.e.*, cows, calves and other milch and draught cattle (Article 48.	7. Right to public assistance in case of unemployment, old age, sickness and other cases of undeserved want (Article 41).
	8. To organise village panchayats as units of self-government. (Article 40).	8. Right to humane conditions of work and maternity relief. (Article 42)
	9. To promote educational and economic interests of weaker sections and to protect them from social injustice. (Article 46).	9. Right to a living wage and conditions of work ensuring decent standard of life for workers. (Article 43).
		10. Right of workers to participate in management of industries. (Article 43A)[4]
		11. Right of children to free and compulsory education (Article 46).

1. Added by the 44th Amendment Act 1978.
2. Provisions, 2, 3, and 4 added by the 42nd Amendment Act, 1976.

CRITICISM OF THE DIRECTIVE PRINCIPLES

According to Dr. K.C. Wheare, "the Directive Principles are little more than a manifesto of aims and aspirations, for they cannot be enforced in any court of law." Sri Nasiruddin, a member of the Constituent Assembly, called them no better than "New year's greetings". They are high sounding but smack of cheap publicity. It has become a fashion for every newly independent country to talk of establishing a welfare state or securing to all its citizens justice, liberty, equality and fraternity. At one place Dr. Jennings questions the reasonableness of inserting in the Constitution a collection of political principles, obviously derived from British experience in the 19th century and wrongly considered suitable for India in the middle of the 20th century. The ideas expressed in them will survive for a generation and some of them even for a longer period. The question whether they are suitable for the 21st century, when the Constitution might still be in operation, cannot be answered but it is quite probable that they will be entirely outmoded.

The severest charge directed against the Directive Principles is that they are in the nature of holy wishes having no legal sanction behind them. As no government is bound to implement them, they are just superfluous. Moreover, the economic principles stated in them are not eternal principles. The economic objectives and policies may have to be modified in future. The critics point out that the Directive Principles embody only a political philosophy rather than practical politics. They are meant to befool and overawe the ignorant and credulous people of India. High sounding but empty promises can have no appeal to any sensible person. In practice also some of the principles have not yielded satisfactory results. Prohibition, for instance, has proved a big flop, a costly failure. It has led to increase in crimes like bootlegging, illicit distillation and black marketing of imported wine.

IMPORTANCE AND UTILITY OF DIRECTIVE PRINCIPLES

There is no unamimity amongst scholars and Constitutional experts regarding the importance and utility of the Directive Principles. On the one hand critics describe them as 'pious wishes' devoid of all constitutional significance. On the other hand some scholars consider them as more important than the Fundamental Rights in so far as they provide the social and economic basis for democracy and aim at establishing a welfare state in the country. Some of the points of its importance and utility are as follows –

1. **Directive Principles as Moral Ideals.** The Directive Pricniples are not absolutely useless. They have their significance and utility even though they are 'old fashioned with a nineteenth century ring about them'. *Alan Gledhill* in his book "*The Republic of India*' observes thus :

   "*It would be superficial to discuss these precepts as good resolutions fit only for paving stones on the broad and primrose-strewn way. The lives of countless individuals have been shaped by moral precepts impinging upon their minds and it is not difficult to find instances of similar precepts directing the course of the history of nation.*" Such precepts appeal to the conscience of law makers and hence have a greater force than binding clause of the Constitutions.

2. **Directive Principles as the Basis of a Welfare State.** The Directive Principles are very significant in view of the fact that they lay the cornerstone of a welfare state. Dr. Bhim Rao Ambedkar also observed, "*The aim of Constitution, in short, is to establish a State which shall be a democracy not only in the political field where legislative authority is based on adult franchise and the executive in parliamentary field but also promote a welfare state where social and economic democracy prevails.*" That the pinciples are not enforceable in court is not a defect in the Constitution. It has its own advantages. The economic conditions and thoughts are ever changing. Had the principles been rigid, the ruling parties, not agreeing

to them, might have tried to change them by an amendment. Foreseeing this tendency the framers of the Constitution, instead of starting a clear-cut economic policy, stated only the broad outlines of a welfare state leaving the superstructure to be built by the ruling group. Dr. Bhim Rao Ambedkar made a similar observation in the Constituent Assembly. He said, "We have deliberately introduced in the language that we have used in the Directive Principles something which is not fixed or rigid. We have left enough room for the people of different ways of thinking, with regard to the reaching of the ideal of economic democracy to strive in their own way to persuade the electrorate that it is the best way of reaching economic democracy; the fullest opportunity to act in the way in which they want to act."

3. **Directive Principles as Beacon to the Courts.** Although the Directive Principles cannot be enforced by courts, yet they serve as ideals for the judges and influence their interpretation of laws. Since they are included in the Constitution and are accepted as guiding principles of state policy, they have both a sanctity and constitutional force. They are sure to affect indirectly the attitude of the judges at the time of interpreting the state laws. Former Chief Justice Kania also observed thus : "The Directive Principles represent not the temporary will of a majority in the legislature but the deliberate wisdom of a nation exercised while setting the paramount and permanent law of the country."

As the Directive Principles of State Policy are a part of the Constitution and they form the social, economic and political ideals of a nation, therefore, it is the sacred duty of the courts to protect them from the whims of different political parties, some of whom might like to ignore, mend or even end any provision. The Directive Principles impart a sort of continuity in our national policies.

When the government or executive of the day imposes certain restrictions upon the Fundamental Rights, the courts have to decide in the light of Directive Principles of State Policy whether the restrictions imposed upon the Fundamental Rights are reasonable or not, whether they are in the public interest or not. This point has been clearly explained in *Suraj Pal Singh* v. *Government of Uttar Pradesh*.

4. **Constitutional Importance of Directive Principles.** The liberal principles in Indian Constitution may seem strange and funny to the foreigners but they have a great significance for Indians. They form an essential background for all state action. Simply because they are not enforceable by court, they do not become meaningless. Any State policy in contravention of any of the Directive Principles will be considered as much unconstitutional as the violation of Fundamental Rights. No responsible government can dare go against the principles without creating unrest in the country. Mr. Alan Gledhill also remarks, "If the Indian Constitution becomes vested with the scope of sanctity essential to its durability, it will be difficult for any public figure to propose any important legislative measure without making an appeal either to the Fundamentla Rights or the Directive Principles. Measures will be attacked by the opposition as 'unconstitutional' in so far as they conflict with the Directive Principles."

5. **Mirror of Public Opinion.** The inclusion of Directive Principles in the Indian Constitution was not an act of frivolity or light-heartedness on the part of the Constituent Assembly. The principles reflect the will of the people whom the Assembly represented. According to *Raghavachariar* : "It may be objected that in as much as these Directive Principles create no right and impose no obligations, but are mere pious declarations with no legal sanction behind them, they are merely frivolous and futile and need not find a place in a sane and sober constitution. But it cannot be said that they are of no use at all even though they may not have binding force of law ...... Whoever may capture the governmental power, he will have to respect those Instruments of Instructions which are called Directive Principles. He cannot ignore them. He may not have to answer for the breach in court of law, but he will certainly have to answer for them before the electorate when the next election comes."

6. **Assertion of Noble Principles.** According to *M.C. Setalvad,* formerly Attorney-General of India, although the Directive Principles of State Policy "confer no legal remedies, they appear to be like an instrument of instructions or rights and create no legal general recommendations addressed to all authorities in the Union reminding them of the basic principles of the new social and economic order which the Constitution aims at building. The Directive Principles are but an amplification of the Preamble of the Indian Constitution which bases the authority of the Constitution of India on the solemn resolve of the people of India to secure to all its citizens justice in the social, economic and political fields, liberty in all spheres, equality of status and of opportunity, and the promotion among them all of fraternity assuring the dignity of the individual and unity of the Nation."
7. **Symbol of a Liberal Constitution.** *Prof. K.C. Wheare* remarks, "The Indian Constitution is a liberal constitution. There is something heroic these days in a people declaring publicly that they have established their government in order to secure to all its citizens justice, liberty, equality and fraternity. These words have an old-fashioned, nineteenth century ring about them, yet they need assertion in these days. If these declarations of liberal principles, strange as they may seem in a legal document to British eyes, help the Indian Constitution on its way and assist people in working their government, they are more than justified. This is biggest liberal experiment in the government of men by themselves has ever been tried."
8. **Real Sanction behind the Directive Principles.** The real sanction behind these Principles is the vigilant public opinion. Though these Directive Principles are not enforced by the courts like Fundamental Rights, yet the people will judge the performance of every political party in the light of the implementation of the Directive Principles. When a member of the Constituent Assembly moved an amendment which sought to make Directive Principles justiciable, another member observed, "There is no use of being carried away by sentiments. We must be practical. We cannot go on introducing various provisions here which any government, if it is indifferent to public opinion, can ignore. It is not a court that can enforce these provisions or rights. It is the public opinion that is behind a demand that can enforce these provisions. Once in four or five years elections will take place and then it is open to the electorate not to send the very persons who are indifferent to public opinion. This is the real sanction of any court of law."[1]

Though the public opinion is the main force behind the Directive Principles, yet the effectiveness of these principles shall really depend upon the political education of the Indian people. *Prof. Laski,* therefore, observes, "Musty parchment will doubtless give them greater sanctity; they will not ensure their realization. Therefore, we have to agree that the eternal vigilance is the price of liberty. If the people of India are always conscious of their welfare, then the government will always be careful to implement these principles."

Implementation of Directive Principles

Dissatisfaction has been expressed in certain sections of public and leaders of different political parties about the efforts made by the Government to implement the Directive Principles of State Policy. It is alleged that there has been no improvement in the general condition of the people since independence. This is on account of the failure of the government to implement the various Directive Principles of State Policy in right earnestness. However, this view is not acceptable to Prof. M.V. Paylee. He says that though India has not been able to become a 'welfare state' in spite of the various efforts of the Government during the past few years, but no impartial person can escape noticing the progress made in this direction in the country. He asserts that though the progress is not very fast it has not been very slow either. The adoption of Ten Five Year Plans by the Government is an ample proof that it wants to achieve quick and balanced economic development of the country with a view to raise the living standard of the people and assure them a rich and varied life.

1. *Constituent Assembly Debates,* Vol. VII, page 475.

Let us briefly review the steps taken by the Government to implement the various Directive Principles and the results they have yielded to form an idea about the implementation of the Directive Principles.

In the first place the Government has tried to ensure that "the ownership and control of the material resources of the community" are distributed with a view to subserve the common good. It has abolished the old institution of hereditary proprietors such as Zamindars, Jagirdars etc. and made the tillers of the soil the real owners of the land. Laws have also been enacted in various states to improve the conditions of the cultivators. To prevent concentration of landholdings in few hands, certain states have enacted laws fixing ceiling of the land which can be held by an individual owner. To implement the radical land reforms Zamindari Abolition Acts were passed and the Constitution was suitably amended.

Secondly, the Government has prevented concentration of economic resources in fewer hands by nationalising the Life Insurance as well as the key banking institutions in the country. It imposes heavy taxes on rich sections of the society in the nature of Income Tax, Wealth Tax, Succession Duties, etc. with a view to reduce the disparity between the rich and the poor. The finances thus raised are used for the welfare of the weaker sections of the society. The Government has sought to prevent the exploitation of the children as well as other weaker sections of society through enactment of numerous factory laws, fixation of minimum wages and assuring equal wages to women and men.

Thirdly, Panchayat Raj institutions have been set up throughout the country. A large number of laws have been enacted to implement the directive in Article 40 to organise village panchayats and endow them with powers of self-government. Almost 98 per cent of the rural population is covered by these institutions. At present there are over 2 million Panchayats in the country. The Panchayats have been vested with extensive powers of civil administration such as medical relief, maintenance of village roads, streets, tanks and wells, provision for primary education, sanitation etc. The Panchayats have also been vested with certain judicial powers.

Fourthly, the Central Government has set up several boards for the promotion of the cottage industries (Article 43). These Boards include the All India Khadi and Village Industries Board, Small scales Industries Board, Silk Board, All India Handicrafts Board, All India Handloom Board, the Coir Board, etc. Besides, the National Small Industries Corporation has been set with certain statutory functions and the Khadi and Village Industries Commission has been set up for the development of the Khadi and village Industries. The government extends every possible encouragement to the small industries by rendering financial assistance as well as giving preference to their products.

Fifthly, in the field of introducing compulsory primary education for children below the age of 14 years within the stipulated period of 10 years, the Government has not achieved much success. No doubt laws have been enacted in most of the states for compulsory education up to primary stage but the target laid down in the Constitution has not been achieved. In certain states however free education up to tenth standard has been introduced. Certain states also rendered assistance to people during sickness, old age, etc. though the progress in this regard is not uniform throughout the country. The various states have taken steps in this regard in accordance with their financial capacity.

Sixthly, the Government has tried to raise the living standard of the people, specially in the rural areas, the Government of India launched its Community Development Project in 1952. This programme which aims at better communications, better housing, improved sanitation, greater education facilities, etc. has been extended to almost 404 million people in 566 thousand villages. Later on Integrated Rural Development Programme (IRDP 1978-79), The Swaran Jayanti Programme, National Rural Employment Programme (NREP), Rural Landless Employment Guarantee Programme (RLEGP), Drought Prone Areas Programme (DPAP), Desert Development Programme (DDP) and some other schemes were launched.

Seventhly, the state has taken numerous steps to improve the condition of the weaker sections of society, particularly the members of the Scheduled Castes and Scheduled Tribes by extending them certain concessions and amenities so that they may be able to come on equal footing with the rest of the population.

Eighthly, the Government has taken numerous steps to introduce prohibition and check the consumption of intoxicating drinks and drugs. In the light of the recommendation of the Prohibition Enquiry Committee, the Planning Commission drew up a comprehensive plan for introduction of prohibition. However, states showed reluctance to implement the plan on account of the practical difficulties as well as the loss in revenue which followed as a result. Thus it can be said that the programme of prohibition has not uniformly been a success.

Ninthly, the State has taken every conceivable step to effect improvement in agriculture and animal husbandry. It has encouraged their development along scientific lines. Slaughter of calves and cows in some states also has been prohibited.

Tenthly, the Government has also achieved commendable success in effecting separation between the judiciary and the executive. In most of the states the judicial and the executive functions have been separated. In the states where they have not been separated so far, the matter is under active consideration of the government. Not only the judiciary and executive have been separated, a uniform civil code has also been made available. The enactment of Hindu Marriage Act, Hindu Succession Act etc. are some of the steps taken by the Government in this direction.

Finally, in the international sphere also the government has tried to promote just and honourable relations among nations and consistently worked for the promotion of international peace and security. The adoption of the principles of Panchsheel and Non-Alignment by India as guiding principles of its foreign policy is a clear proof that the Government has sincerely adhered to the principles enshrined in the Directive Principles. It is a matter of common knowledge that India has always expressed full faith in international law and international treaties and preferred settlement of disputes through peaceful methods like negotiations, arbitration etc. The valuable role played by India in promoting world peace and conducting of international relations on the basis of international law has been acknowledged in various quarters.

It is evident from the above analysis that the Government has made every possible effort to implement the Directive Principles of State Policy and has attaned appreciable amount of success in this regard. It is true that in certain respects the progress has not been that satisfactory but for this the Government is not to be entirely blamed. To a large extent the complexity of the problem and paucity of funds are to largely blame for these shortfalls. Further the objectives enshrined in the Directive Principles are so lofty and far reaching that it would be too much to expect their attainment within a short span of barely three decades. It is indeed commendable that the Government has so far accorded quite a high priority to the Directive Principles in its policy and its efforts have been quite encouraging and substantial in this regard.

EXERCISES

Long Answer Type Questions:

1. Discuss the meaning and objectives of Directive Principles.
2. Discuss the distinction between Directive Principles and Fundamental Rights.
3. Write a brief note on classification of Directive Principles.
4. Discuss new Directive Principles added by 42nd Amendment.
5. Discuss changes brought about by 42nd Amendment Act 1976 in Directive Principles.
6. Discuss the importance and utility of Directive Principles.
7. Write a brief note on implementation of Directive Principles.

Short Answer Type Questions:

1. What is real sanction behind the Directive Prinicples ?
2. What is Constitutional importance of Directive Principles ?
3. Write a brief note on 'Directive Principles' as the basis of a Welfare State.

Objective Type Questions:

Choose the correct answer

1. In which part of the Indian Constitution Directive Principles of State Policy are contained ?
   (*a*) In Part IV (*b*) In Part V
   (*c*) In Part VI (*d*) In part VII
2. From which country's Constitution the idea of Directive Principles of State Policy has been borrowed ?
   (*a*) England (*b*) Irish Free State
   (*c*) United States of America (*d*) Germany
3. To overcome the difficulties in the way of implementation of the Directive Principles certain Constitutional Amendments were carried out. In which year first such amendment was carried out ?
   (*a*) 1949 (*b*) 1950
   (*c*) 1951 (*d*) 1952
4. What is the main purpose of including Directive Principles of State Policy in the Indian Constitution?
   (a) to establish a welfare state.
   (b) to provide best opportunities of development
   (c) to check the arbitrary actions of the Government
   (d) to establish a secular state.
5. Which of the following is not a Directive Principle of State Policy?
   The State shall seeck to ensure :
   (a) equal pay for equal work by men and women.
   (b) equal right to an adequate means of livelihood.
   (c) abolition of untouchability.
   (d) just and human conditions of work.
6. What is the main difference between the Fundamental Rights and Directive Principles ?
   (a) Fundamental Rights are justiciable while Directive Principles are not.
   (b) Fundamental Rights are positive while Directive Principles are negative.
   (c) Directive Principles are given precedence over Fundamental Rights by courts in all cases.
   (d) None of the above.
7. Which of the following reflects a socialistic ideology ?
   (a) Prohibition. (b) Ban on cow slaughter.
   (c) The state being directed to strive for equal pay for equal work.
   (d) The state undertaking the organisation of Panchayats.
8. A socialistic ideology is reflected in the Directive Principle which calls for :
   (a) securing equitable distribution of material resources of the country to prevent concentration of weath.
   (b) promotion of cottage industries.
   (c) free and compulsory education for children up to 14 years of age.
   (d) all the above.

9. Which of the following describes the nature of the Directive Principles ?
   (a) They are positive instructions to do certain things.
   (b) They are negative instructions regarding certain things.
   (c) They are both negative and positive.
   (d) They are justiciable.
10. Regarding Directive Principles of State Policy it is not correct to say :
   (a) it is the duty of the state to apply these principles in making laws.
   (b) they are fundamental in governance of the country.
   (c) they impose a legal duty upon the state.
   (d) they are merely instructions or directives issued to the legistature and the executive of the country

ANSWERS

1. (*a*)	2. (*b*)	3. (*c*)	4. (*a*)	5. (*c*)	6. (*a*)
7. (*c*)	8. (*a*)	9. (*a*)	10. (*c*)		

7

CHAPTER

The Union Executive (The President)

> *There shall be a Council of Ministers with the Prime Minister at the head to aid and advise the President who shall, in the exercise of his functions, act in accordance with such advice.* —*Article 74 (as amended by 42nd Amendment)*

FORM OF THE UNION EXECUTIVE

The Constitution of India envisages a Parliamentary Governement in India. Although Article 53 of the Constitution says that the executive power of the Union shall be exercised by the President either directly or through officers subordinate to him, in practice, the President has to abide by the decisions of the Council of Ministers with the Prime Minister at the head. The Indian Constitution is a harmonious blend of the political system of the U.S.A. and the U.K. It is, however, noteworthy that although we have a Union President, ours is not a Presidential Form of Government. Whereas in the United States, the President is Head of the State as well as the Government, the Indian President is Head of the State only, the Head of the Government being the Prime Minister. The position of the Indian President is similar to the King of England who happens to be a constitutional head with nominal powers and who is bound to act upon the advice of popular Ministers. The Indian President is not much in picture in the actual working of the Government. Not he but the Prime Minister is cross-questioned at the bar of the legislature for the failure of government policies. The President merely represents the nation, he does not rule. The American system is based not on 'daily assessment' of policy but on a 'periodic assessment'. There is not much interdependence of the executive and legislative wings. The American Executive has no responsibility towards the American Congress. The Framers of Indian Constitution discarded the Presidental System fearing that it would create constitutional deadlocks. They preferred the parliamentary system of England, which ensures co-ordination between the executive and legislative departments.

METHOD OF ELECTION OF THE PRESIDENT

Article 54 of the Indian Constitution provides for the election of the President of India. The President is elected not directly by the people but by the members of an electoral college consisting of the elected members of both Houses of Parliament and the elected members of State Assemblies. Thus the nominated members in the Lower as well as the Upper House both at the Centre and in the

States do not possess voting rights in the election of the President. The method of his election is based on proportional representation by means of single transferable vote system. The system adopted for voting is secret ballot.

In order to secure uniformity in the scale of representation among the States themselves as well as parity between States as a whole and the Union, a unique method has been adopted to determine the number of votes to be cast by every member. The total population of each State is divided by the total number of elected members in the State Assembly. The quotient or the figure obtained is further divided by 1,000. The multiples of one thousand give the number of votes to be cast by each elected member of the State. If the remainder exceeds 500, then the number of votes is increased by one. For instance, the total population of the Punjab in 1971 was 13,551,060 and the number of elected members in the State Assembly was 117. The figure regarding the number of votes per member was obtained in the following manner :

$$\frac{13,551,060}{117} \times \frac{1}{1,000} = 116$$

Thus each member was allowed to cast 116 votes, worked out according to the formula given above, each elected member of the State Assemblies got 129 votes in Rajasthan, 58 in Delhi, 147 in Gujarat, 116 in Assam, 173 in Bihar, 175 in Maharashtra, 112 in Haryana, 149 in Orissa and so on. The total number of votes cast by the members of State Assembles in 2007's Presidential election was 549,474.

The method of determining the number of votes to be cast by each elected member of Parliament is to devide the total number of State votes by the strength of the Parliament. The formula is as given below :

$$\frac{\text{549,474 (votes cast by the members of State Legislatures)}}{\text{776 (combined strength of elected members in both Houses of the Parliament}}$$

The number obtained is 708.09. Each elected member of the Parliament was thus entitled to exercise 708 for the election of the President.

Note. Any candidate getting absolute majority of votes is elected.

Table 7.1 **13th Presidential Election (2007)**

Sl. No.	Name of State	Number of Assembly Seats (elective)	Population (1971 Census)	Value of vote of each MLA	Total value of votes for the State
1.	Andhra Pradesh	294	43502708	148	43512
2.	Arunachal Pradesh	60	467511	8	480
3.	Assam	126	14625152	116	14616
4.	Bihar	243	42126236	173	42039
5.	Chhattisgarh	90	11637494	129	11610
6.	Goa	40	795120	20	800
7.	Gujarat	182	26697475	147	26754
8.	Haryana	90	10036808	112	10080
9.	Himachal Pradesh	68	3460434	51	3468
10.	Jammu & Kashmir	87	6300000	72	6264
11.	Jharkhand	81	14227133	176	14256
12.	Karnataka	224	29299014	131	29344
13.	Kerala	140	21347375	152	21280
14.	Madhya Pradesh	230	30016625	131	30130
15.	Maharashtra	288	50412235	175	50400
16.	Manipur	60	1072753	18	1080

17.	Meghalaya	60	1011699	17	1020
18.	Mizoram	40	332390	8	320
19.	Nagaland	60	516449	9	540
20.	Orissa	147	21944615	149	21903
21.	Punjab	117	13551060	116	13572
22.	Rajasthan	200	25765806	129	25800
23.	Sikkim	32	209843	7	224
24.	Tamil Nadu	234	41199168	176	41184
25.	Tripura	60	1556342	26	1560
26.	Uttrakakhand	70	4491239	64	4480
27.	Uttar Pradesh	403	83849905	208	83824
28.	West Bengal	294	44312011	151	44394
29.	NCT of Delhi	70	4065698	58	4060
30.	Puducherry	30	471707	16	480
	Total	4120			549474

1. Total MPs = 776 (543 in Lok Sabha + 233 in Rajya Sabha)
2. Value of each MP's Vote = $\frac{549474}{776}$ =708.09 or 708
3. Total value of MPs' Votes = 776 × 708 = 549408
4. Total members in the electoral college = 4896 (4120 MLAs + 776 MPs)
5. Total votes in the electoral college = 1098882 (549474 MLAs + 549408 MPs)
6. Total votes polled = 969422
7. Total votes for Ms. Pratibha Patil = 638116
8. Total votes for B.S. Shekhawat = 331306

Table 7.2 **14th Presidential Election (1952-2012)**

Sl. No.	Election	Victorious Candidate	No. of Votes secured (%)	Main Rival Candidate	No. of Votes secured (%)
1.	1952	Dr. Rajendra Prasad	507400 (83.81)	K.T. Shah	92827 (15.3)
2.	1957	Dr. Rajendra Prasad	459698 (99.35)	N.N. Das	2000 (0.4)
3.	1962	Dr. S. Radhakrishnan	553067 (98.24)	Ch. Hari Ram	6341 (1.1)
4.	1967	Dr. Zakir Husain	471244 (56.23)	K. Subba Rao	363971 (43.4)
5.	1969	V. V. Giri	420077 (50.22)	N. Sanjeeva Reddy	405427 (48.5)
6.	1974	Fakhruddin Ali Ahmed	756587 (80.18)	Tridev Chaudhuri	189186 (19.3)
7.	1977	N. Sanjeeva Reddy		Unopposed	
8.	1982	Giani Zail Singh	754113 (72.73)	H. R. Khanna	282685 (??.??)
9.	1987	R. Venkataraman	740148 (72.29)	V. Krishna Ayyer	281559 (27.1)
10.	1992	Dr. Shankar Dayal Sharma	675564 (65.86)	George Swell	346485 (33.21)
11.	1997	K. R. Narayanan	956290 (94.97)	T. N. Sheshan	50451 (5.07)
12.	2002	Dr. A.P.J Abdul Kalam	922844 (89.58	Laxmi Sehgal	107366 (10.42)
13.	2007	Ms. Pratibha Patil	638116 (65.82)	B.S. Shekhawat	331306 (34.17)
14.	2012	Mr. Pranab Mukherjee	713763(69.31%)	Mr. P.A. Sangma	315987(30.69%)

Table 7.3 **VARIOUS PRESIDENTS OF INDIA**

	Name	Tenure
1.	Dr. Rajendra Prasad	26th January, 1950 – 13 May, 1962
2.	Dr. Sarvepalli Radhakrishnan	13th May, 1962 – 13 May, 1967

3.	Dr. Zakir Husain	13th May, 1967 – 3rd May, 1969 (died)
4.	Varahagiri Venkatgiri	3rd May, 1969 – 20th July, 1969 (Acting)
5.	Justice Mohammad Hidayatullah	20th July, 1969 – 24th August, 1969 (Acting)
6.	Varahagiri Venkatgiri	24th August, 1969 – 24th August, 1974
7.	Fakhruddin Ali Ahmad	24th August, 1974 – 11th February, 1977 (died)
8.	B.D. Jatti	11th February, 1977 – 25th July, 1977 (Acting)
9.	Neelam Sanjeeva Reddy	25th July, 1977 – 25th July, 1982
10.	Giani Zail Singh	25th July, 1982 – 25th July, 1987
11.	Mohammad Hidayatullah	6th October, 1982 – 31st October, 1982 (discharged the functions of the President)
12.	R. Venkatraman	25th July, 1987 – 25th July, 1992
13.	Dr. Shankar Dayal Sharma	25th July, 1992 – 25th July, 1997
14.	Dr. K.R. Narayanan	25th July, 1997 – 25th July, 2001
15.	Dr. A.P.J. Abdul Kalam	25th July, 2001 – 25th July 2007.
16.	Mrs. Pratibha Devisingh Patil	25th July 2007 – 27th July, 2012.
17.	Mr. Pranav Mukharjee	25th July 2012 – till date.

LEGISLATION REGARDING SUCCESSION OF THE PRESIDENT

The Lok Sabha passed on May 15, 1969, the 'President, Discharge of Functions' Bill. After its passage from Rajya Sabha and assent of the President, it became law. According to this law if any vacancy occurs in the office of the President and Vice-President simultaneously, then the Chief Justice of the Supreme Court will succeed to the office of the President. He will be followed by the next seniormost judge of the Supreme Court. On May 3, 1969, Dr. Zakir Husain died. He was succeeded by the then Vice-President, Shri V.V. Giri. But on 18th July 1969, Shri V.V. Giri gave up both the offices. Under these circumstances, Justice Hidayatullah who was the Chief Justice at that time became the Acting President. When V.V. Giri was elected as the President and assumed office on 24th August, 1969, then Justice Hidayatullah again assumed his own office, that is, of the Chief Justice.

OTHER MATTERS RELATING TO THE ELECTION OF THE PRESIDENT

It will not be out of place to mention that the candidate who secures equal to or more than the quota, is declared elected as the President. The quota is determined in the following way :

$$\frac{\text{Total number of votes polled} + 1}{\text{Number of candidates} + 1}$$

If at the first count, no candidate is able to secure absolute majority then the candidate securing the minimum votes is eliminated and his votes are transferred to the other candidates according to the second choice indicated on the ballot papers. This process of elimination and transfer goes on till a candidate is able to fulfil the quota. It is also possible that sometimes the third, fourth or fifth choice of the voters might be used to obtain the requisite number of votes. For the election to the Presidential Office, the names of the candidates can be proposed and seconded only by either the members of the State Legislative Assemblies or the Parliament. Nominations are then scrutinised and the valid names are published in the Gazette of India. The date of the election is fixed by the Election Commission. The election is held by secret ballot and in accordance with Proportional Representation and Single Transferable Vote System. All the disputes concerning the Presidential Election are heard and decided by the Supreme Court.

QUALIFICATIONS FOR THE OFFICE OF THE PRESIDENT

Article 58 lays down the following qualifications for eligibility for election as President : (a) He should be a citizen of India; (b) He should have completed the age of thirty-five years; (c) He should be qualified for election as a member of the House of the People (Lok Sabha). The Article further says that no person holding any office of profit under the Government of India or of the State or under any Local Authority or any other public authority can contest the election for President's Office. The President, the Governor of any State or a Cabinet Minister whether at the Centre or in the State are, however, not debarred from becoming a candidate. The election is supervised by the Chief Election Commissioner and all appeals arising out of President's Election are filed in the Supreme Court. The President cannot, besides holding his office, remain the member of Parliament or State Assembly. In case a Member of Parliament is elected as President, he is required to resign his seat in the Parliament.

Further, the nomination of a candidate for election to the office of President must be subscribed by at least 50 electors as proposers and 50 electors as seconders. Every candidate has to make a security deposit or of ₹ 15,000 in the Reserve Bank of India. The security deposit is liable to be forfeited in case the candidate fails to secure one-sixth of the votes polled. Before 1997, number of proposers and seconders was ten each and the amount of security deposit was ₹ 2,500. In 1997, they were increased to discourage the non-serious candidates.

TENURE OF THE PRESIDENT

The term of the office of the President of India shall be five years from the date on which he enters upon his office. The President shall, notwithstanding the expiration of his term, continue to hold office until his successor enters upon his office.[1] Article 57 declares, "A person who holds or who has held office as President shall, subject to the other provisions of this Constitution, be eligible for re-election to that office." Dr. Rajendra Prasad was re-elected to that august office in 1957 and he held that office up to May 12, 1962. He declined a third term. The Constitution of India is silent on that point. So Dr. Rajendra Prasad established a healthy convention that the President will not contest the election for the third term. Dr. Radhakrishnan even declined a second term.

The President may, by writing under his hand addressed to Vice-President, resign his office. The reasons of his resignation can be many. *Gledhill* writes that "the President may resign to resolve a conflict between himself and the Council of Ministers."[2] The resignation of the President shall be addressed to the Vice-President who shall communicate to the Speaker of the House of the People (Lok Sabha) forthwith. The President may, for violation of the Constitution, be removed from office by impeachment in the manner provided in *Article 61*. An election to fill a vacancy caused by the expiration of the term of office of President shall be completed before the expiration of term. An election to fill a vacancy in the office of President occurring by reason of his death, resignation or removal or otherwise shall be held as soon as possible after, and in no case later than, six months from the date of occurrence of the vacancy; and the person elected to fill the vacancy shall be entitled to hold office for the full term of five years from the date on which he enters upon his office.

Article 52 (1) clause (*b*) provides that the President can be removed from office by the Parliament by an impeachment for violating the Constitution. The phrase 'violation of the Constitution' is not properly defined in the Constitution. The American Constitution admits sedition, acceptance of bribe, misconduct and other crimes of a serious nature as amounting to violation of the Constitution. The Irish President can also be impeached on being proved guilty of some gross misconduct.

1. Article 56 (1) (*c*)
2. Gledhill, *Republic of India*, page 99

Method to Remove the President of India. *Article 61* of the Indian Constitution lays down the procedure for impeachment of the President. It says that charge against the President regarding violation of the Constitution can be made in either House of Parliament. The charge must come in the shape of a proposal contained in a resolution signed by at least one-fourth of the total members of that House and moved after giving at least fourteen days' advance notice. Such a resolution in order to be adopted finally must get the support of at least two-thirds majority of the total membership of the House in which it is moved. After that the other House shall investigate or cause to be investigated the charges. The President has the right to appear to be represented at such investigation. If the other House after investigation passes a resolution by the vote of two-thirds majority of the total membership of that House declaring that the charge is proved, the President is removed from the date on which resolution is passed. In America the power to initiate the impeachment proceedings lies with the Lower or the Responsible House which appoints a committee to investigate the charges. The findings of the House are then sent to the Senate for action. The Senate presided over by the Chief Justice of the Supreme Court hears the impeachment. If two-thirds majority of the senators present at the trial agree to the charges, the President is convicted and removed.

Increase in the salary and pension of the President. In 2008, the Parliament increased the salary of the President from ₹ 50,000 to ₹ 1.50 lakh per month and the pension ro 50 % of his salary per month. In addition, the former Presidents are entitled to furnished residence, phone facilities, car, medical treatment, travel facility, secretarial staff and office expenses up to ₹ 60,000 per annun. The spouse of a deceased President is also entitled to a family pension at the rate of 50% of pension of a retired President, furnished residence, phone facility, car, medical treatment, travel facility, secretarial staff and office expenses up to ₹ 12,000 per annum.

According to the Indian Constitution the President of India previously received a salary of ₹ 10,000 per month but the Parliament passed a Bill on 19th December 1985. According to this Act, salary of the President has been raised from ₹ 10,000 to 15,000 per month. His pension per year has also been increased from ₹ 15,000 to 30,000. The salary of the President was further raised when Lok Sabha on 31st May, 1990 passed a Bill seeking to raise the salary of the President from ₹ 15,000 to ₹ 20,000 and the pension of the ex-presidents to ₹ 10,000 per month.

The salary of the President was further raised by passing the President's Emoluments and Pension (Amendment) Act 1998, Parliament has raised the emoluments to ₹ 50,000 per month. The emoluments and allowances of the President shall not be diminished during his term of office (Article 59 (3).

The Amendment Act, 1998, referred to above also provides for the payment of an annual pension of ₹ 3,00,000 to a person who held office as President on the expiration of his term or on resignation, provided he is not re-elected to the office.

The pension of the President is income-tax free. The President is also entitled to spend ₹ 15,26,000 a year on travel, entertainment, discretionary grants, staff, household expenses and his own allowances. The emoluments and allowances of the President cannot be diminished during his term of office. The President shall be entitled without payment of rent to the use of his official residence and shall be also entitled to such emoluments, allowances and privileges as may be determined by Parliament by law and until provision in that behalf is so made, such emoluments, allowances and privileges as are specified in the Second Schedule.

Filling the Vacancy in the Office of the President. Article 62 of the Constitution says that the normal election to fill the vacancy caused by the expiration of one term of office of the President is to be completed before the term expires. If the vacancy occurs by reason of President's death, resignation or removal, another President has to be elected within six months. Till the new appointment is made, the Vice-President acts as President. In case of leave vacancy also, caused by the absence or illness of the President, the Vice-President discharges President's functions. During this period he does not act as Chairman of the Upper House and is entitled to all the powers, salary and allowances of the President.

Oath or Affirmation by the President. Every President and every person chosen to discharge the functions of President has to, before entering upon his office, take an oath administered by the Chief Justice of India. The wording of the oath is as follows :

> "I.....swear in the name of God that I will faithfully execute the office of President (or discharge the functions of the President) of India and will to the best of my ability preserve, protect and defend the Constitution and the law and that I will above myself to the service and well-being of the people of India."

POWERS OF THE PRESIDENT DURING PEACE TIME

The powers enjoyed and the functions performed by the President can be studied under the following heads : (a) Executive Powers (b) Legistative Powers (c) Financial Powers (d) Judicial Powers (e) Diplomatic Powers (f) Military Powers (g) Emergency Powers.

***(a)* Executive Powers of the President.** According to Article 52 of the Constitution, executive powers vested in the President are as under :

(1) He is the head of the Indian Republic. All executive functions are executed in the name of President.

(2) He appoints the Prime Minister and other Ministers. The convention has been established that the President invites the leader of the majority party in Lower House to choose other Ministers of his team.

(3) He appoints the Governors, the Chief Justice of India, the judges of the Supreme Court and the High Courts.

(4) He appoints the Chairman and members of the Union Public Service Commission and Inter-State Public Service Commission.

(5) He appoints the Chief Commissioners of Union Territories.

(6) He appoints the members of Finance Commission, Language Commission and Election Commission.

(7) He appoints the Ambassadors, other Diplomatic Representatives and Consuls in Indian Foreign Service.

(8) He appoints the Comptroller and Auditor-General of India.

(9) He is the Supreme Commander of Defence Forces.

(10) He appoints two representatives of the Anglo-Indian Community in the Lok Sabha and 12 members in Rajya Sabha from those having knowledge or practical experience of art, science, literature and social service.

(11) He represenus the Nation in International Affairs and receives the credentials of the Foreign Ambassadors posted in India.

All the officers of the Union are his officers and consequently his subordinates and he has a right to be informed of all the affairs of the Union. The President has also right to make rules for the convenient transaction of the business of the Government of India and for the allocation among Ministers of the said business. The President has got a right to be informed of all the decisions of the Council of Ministers relating to the administration of the affairs of the Union and proposals for legislation. He can get any other information regarding the administration of the affairs of the Union and proposals for legislation President so requires, he can legislation which he may call for. If the

President so requires, he can get submitted for the consideration of the Council of Ministers any matter on which a decision has been taken by a Minister but which has not been considered by the Council. The President of India appoints the Attorney-General of India. The President of India can appoint Inter-State Council, a commission to report on the administration of Scheduled Areas, special officer for Scheduled Castes and Scheduled Tribes and a Commission to investigate into conditions of backward classes.

Every Union Territory shall be administered by the President acting to such extent as he thinks fit, through an administrator to be appointed by him with such designation as he may specify. The President may appoint the Governor of a State as the Administrator of an adjoining Union territory and where a Governor is so appointed, he shall exercise his functions as such administrator independently of his Council of Ministers. The President of India may make regulations for the peace, progress and good government of the Union territory of *(a)* the Andaman and Nicobar Islands; *(b)* the Laccadive, Minicoy and Amindivi Islands; *(c)* Dadra and Nagar Haveli; *(d)* Daman and Diu; and *(e)* Pondicherry (Pudduchery).

Besides that the President of India has also got powers to make regulations for the administration of tribal areas mentioned in the Sixth Schedule of the Indian Constitution. The President of India has the power of making rules and regulations governing matters like the joint sitting of the two Houses of Parliament, appointment of officers and servants of the Supreme Court, recruitment of Union Services, etc. Approval of the President is also needed regarding the rules made by the Supreme Court governing its procedure, determination of forms accounts by the Auditor-General, etc.

It is, however, to be noted that in practice the President in the exercise of all his executive powers is guided by the advice of the Prime Minister.

(b) **Legislative Powers of the President.** The Parliament of India consists of the President and two Houses. He is a component part of the Union Parliament. In theory he possesses extensive Legislative Powers. Some of the Legislative Powers of the President are as under —

(1) He summons and prorogues the Parliament and can dissolve the Lok Sabha. The Constitution says that he must call the session of the Parliament within six months from the last sitting of the former session. He can, with the consent of the Prime Minister, dissolve only Lok Sabha and not the Upper House or Rajya Sabha which is a quasi-permanent House. If he is convinced that the Prime Minister's suggestion to dissolve Lok Sabha is mischievous, and that another stable Cabinet can be formed, he may even refuse to dissolve the Lower House.

(2) He inaugurates both Houses of the Parliament and gives in his inaugural speech brief outlines of State policy and programme. His speech too like that of the Queen in England is prepared by the Prime Minister of the country.

(3) If there is a conflict between the two Houses over a non-money Bill, he can call a joint sitting of both Houses to resolve the difference and deadlock.

(4) Every Bill passed by the Parliament is sent to him for approval. He cannot refuse to sign a Money Bill but as regards non-money Bills, he can return any of them to the Parliament for reconsideration. If the Parliament submits the Bill again, no matter in its original form or revised form, he is duty-bound to give his assent. In England also, the King in theory possesses the power of refusing a Bill to sign but in practice it has never been done. The question of his assent is only a formal affair and the assent is actually given by the commissioners appointed by the Crown. The American President can also veto a Bill and return it to the House in which it originated along with his objections. The veto falls if the Congress passes the Bill again by two-thirds majority in each House. If the Congress fails to obtain that majority, the veto stands.

(5) The President of India has the right to address and send messages to Parliament. He may address either House or both the Houses jointly. Such an address is essential on the commencement of the first session after general election.

(6) He can promulgate ordinance to meet any emergency. Such an ordinance is issued during the recess of the Parliament and has to be laid before both Houses as soon as they meet, for ratification. It ceases to operate, if not withdrawn earlier after the expiry of six weeks after the reassembly of the Parliament. Since the Parliament has necessarily to be summoned twice a year, the maximum period during which an ordinance can remain in force is six months and six weeks.

(c) **Military Powers of the President.** *Article 53 (2)* prescribes that the Supreme Command of the Defence Forces of the Union shall be vested in the President and the exercise thereof shall be regulated by law. According to *Article 246*, the Parliament had got the exclusive power to make laws with respect to any matter enumerated in the Union List. The Parliament of India can make laws in regard to the Defence of India and every part of it including preparation for defence and all such acts as may be conducive in times of war to its prosecution and after its termination to effective demobilisation. The Parliament can make any law in regard to Naval, Army and Air forces of the Union. The Parliament can make any law in regard to war and peace. In Great Britain declaration of war and peace is an executive function, but the President of India cannot declare war or employ forces of the country without the sanction of the Parliament or in anticipation of sanction of Parliament. In the U.S.A. the President is the Supreme Commander of the Armed Forces and there is no provision that the exercise of this power shall be regulated by law. In the U.S.A., though the power to declare war and peace belongs to the Congress, yet the President can create circumstances in which Congress finds no alternative except to declare war. For example, President McKinley despatched a battleship to Havana where it was blown and it helped to precipitate war with Spain. In 1918 President Wilson sent the U.S. troops to Russia to help Allied troops there who were fighting the Bolsheviks. The American President can assume emergency powers as the commander-in-chief, which was done during two World Wars but the Indian President cannot do so. Therefore, the President of India is only a figurehead in military matters and his position is quite different from the American President. In Great Britain the Parliament does not possess the power to declare war and it is done by a Royal Proclamation authorised by Order-in-Council as happened during the two World Wars.

(*d*) **Foreign Affairs and Diplomatic Powers.** The Parliament of India has Exclusive Legislative Powers to regulate foreign affairs, treaties, agreements and conventions with foreign countries or other matters concerning passports, visas, admission of foreigners into or expulsion from India. The President of India, thus, does not possess real power in this field but all diplomatic business is conducted in his name. Diplomatic Envoys and Consular Agents are accredited in his name. All International Treaties and Agreements are also conducted in his name but they are to be ratified by Parliament later on. All Ambassadors to this country present their credentials to him. In the U.S.A. the President possesses vast powers in this field, though the treaties concluded or negotiated by him require the subsequent approval of the Senate but he can also make executive agreements with foreign countries which are not subject to the approval of the Senate. In England foreign ambassadors are received by the Queen, though in the presence of a Minister. Treaties and international agreements are negotiated and concluded by the Crown. They are not made subject to the approval of the Parliament unless they involve some cessation of territory, payment of money or changes in the law of land which are to be approved by the Parliament. Besides that the tendency has grown recently that important treaties are generally placed before Parliament. In India the foreign affairs are conducted by the Prime Minister in the name of the President but important treaties are subsequently approved generally by the Parliament. The Parliament in India discusses foreign affairs while approving the grant for External Affairs Ministry.

(*e*) **Judicial Powers of the President of India.** According to *Article 72 (1)*, the President shall have power to grant pardons, reprieves, respites or remissions of punishment or to suspend, remit or commute the sentence of any person convicted of any offence—(*a*) in all cases where the punishment or sentence is by a Court Martial; (*b*) in all cases where the punishment or sentence is for an offence against any law relating to a matter to which the executive power of the Union extends; (*c*) in all cases where the sentence is a sentence of death. In India the President exercises this power on the advice of the Home Minister whereas in England the Queen does so on the advice of Home Secretary. In America, the President is empowered to grant pardon or remit the sentence in any case other than cases of impeachment, before as well as after the conviction. The Indian President can grant amnesty only after conviction and that too with parliamentary approval.

(*f*) **Financial Powers of the President.** The President is required to lay before the Lok Sabha the Budget and Supplementary Budget before Ist April of every year. From the Lok Sabha the Budget is sent to the Upper House. Besides the annual estimate of income and expenditure he also places before the Parliament the Report of the Comptroller and Auditor-General, and the Recommendations of the Finance Commission regarding the distribution of revenue from the various taxes between the Centre and the State. The President is also in charge of Contingent Fund from which he lends money to meet any unforeseen situation and expenditure. His sanction is also required before any legislation relating to money Bills, affecting taxation concerning the States, is introduced.

(*g*) **Miscellaneous Powers of the President.** The President also sees to it that the reports of the Language Commission, Public Services Commission and Election Commission are duly presented before the Parliament. He distributes portfolios among the Ministers. The Procedural rules made by the Supreme Court also need the approval of the President. He can obtain legal advice from the judges of the Supreme Court on any matter before him.

EMERGENCY POWERS OF THE PRESIDENT

Part XVIII of the Constitution arms the President with enormous emergency powers to deal with situation arising out of war, armed rebellion, breakdown of the Constitution or financial crisis. Three types of emergencies have been referred to in the Constitution.

Emergency arising out of war, External Aggression and armed rebellion (and not internal disturbances) or the threat thereof

Proclamation of Internal Emergency would be made only in the case of armed rebellion and not internal disturbances or the threat thereof. The 44th Amendment to the Indian Constitution says that a Proclamation of Emergency under Article 325 has virtually the effect of amending the Constitution by converting it for the duration into that of a unitary State and enabling the rights of the citizen to move the courts for the enforcement of fundamental rights—including the right to life and liberty—to be suspended. Adequate safeguards are, therefore, necessary to ensure that this power is properly exercised and is not abused.

It is, therefore, provided that a Proclamation of Emergency can be issued only when the security of India or any part of its territory is threatened by war or external aggression or by *armed rebellion*. Internal disturbance not amounting to armed rebellion would not be a ground for the issue of Proclamation.

Proclamation of Emergency to be made on the written advice of the Cabinet only. Further in order to ensure that a Proclamation of Emergency is issued only after due consideration, it is sought to be provided that an emergency can be proclaimed only on the basis of written advice tendered to the President by the Cabinet.

Proclamation of Emergency would have to be approved by the Parliament by the same majority which is necessary to amend the Constitution within one month instead of two as before the Amendment. 44th Amendment to the Indian Constitution says, "As a Proclamation of Emergency virtually has the effect of amending the Constitution, it is being provided that the Proclamation would have to be approved by the two Houses of Parliament by the same majority which is necessary to amend the Constitution and such approval would have to be given within a period of one month."

Article 352 clause 4 says that every such Proclamation issued under this Article shall be laid before each House of Parliament (not being a Proclamation revoking a previous Proclamation). When such a Proclamation is issued at a time when the House of the People has been dissolved or the dissolution of the House of the People takes place during the period of one month referred to in this clause, and if resolution approving the Proclamation has been passed by the Council of States, but no resolution with respect to such Proclamation has been passed by the House of People before the expiration of that period, the Proclamation shall cease to operate at the expiration of thirty days from the date on which the House of the People first sits after the reconstitution, unless before the expiration of said period of thirty days a resolution approving the Proclamation has been also passed by the House of the People.

Clause 5 of Article 352 further says that a Proclamation so approved shall, unless revoked, cease to operate on the expiration of a period of six months from the date of the passing of the second Proclamation under clause (4).

Provided that if and so often as a resolution approving the continuance in force of such a Proclamation is passed by both Houses of Parliament, the Proclamation shall, unless revoked, continue in force for a further period of six months from the date on which it would otherwise have ceased to operate under this clause.

Effect of the Proclamation of Emergency

Article 353 says, "While a Proclamation of Emergency is in operation, then (*a*) notwithstanding anything in this Constitution, the executive power of the Union shall extend to the giving direction to any State as to the manner in which the executive power thereof is to be exercised; (*b*) the power of Parliament to make laws with respect to any matter shall include power to make laws conferring powers and imposing duties, or authorising the conferring of powers and the imposition of duties, upon the Union or officers and authorities of the Union as respects that matter notwithstanding that is one which is not enumerated in the Union List.

Provided that where a Proclamation of Emergency is in operation only in any part of the territory of India —

(*i*) The Executive power of the Union to give direction under clause (a) and

(*ii*) The power of Proclamation to make laws under clause (b) shall also extend to any state other then a state in which or in any part of which the proclamation of Emergency is in operation if and in so far as the security of India or any part of the territory thereof is threatened by activities in or in relation to the part of the territory of India in which the Proclamation of Emergency is in operation.

Suspension of Provision of Article 19 during Emergencies. Article 358 as amended by 44th Constitution Amendment Act says that while a Proclamation of Emergency declaring that the security of India or any part of the territory thereof is threatened by war or by external aggression is in operation, nothing in Article 19 shall restrict the power of the State as defined in Part III to make any law or to take executive action which the State would for the provisions contained in that part be competent to make or to take, but any law so made shall, to the extent of the incompetency, cease to have effect so soon as the Proclamation ceases to operate, except as respects things done or omitted to be done before the law so ceases to have effect.

Suspension of the Enforcement of the Right Conferred by Part III during Emergencies. Article 359 of the Indian Constitution further says, "Where a Proclamation of Emergency is in operation, the President may by order declare that the rights to move any court for the enforcement of such of the rights conferred by Part III *except Articles 20 and 21* as may be mentioned in the order and all proceedings pending in any court for the enforcement of the rights so mentioned shall remain suspended for the period during which the Proclamation is in force or for such shorter period as may be specified in the order.

Declaration of Emergency due to Chinese Invasion. Such a Proclamation of Emergency was made by President Radhakrishnan on October 26, 1962, in the context of massive Chinese Aggression in N.E.F.A. and Ladakh. He also issued a Defence of India Ordinance on the same evening. The two measures invested the Union Government with extraordinary powers and strengthened its hands to meet squarely the threat to national security. By an order under his emergency powers, the President suspended the Fundamental Rights relating to personal liberty and free movement. This order took away the right of the people to know the reason of their detention and arrest, as well as their right to move a court of law in that connection. The detenus were deprived of their right of legal defence. In order to do justice to the persons under detention, the Union Government notified on November 17, 1962, its decision to appoint Special Tribunals to hear the cases and appeals arising out of emergency. An appeal against the judgements of such Tribunals could be taken to any High Court, if anybody was sentenced to 10 years imprisonment or more, death punishment or life imprisonment. This emergency ended on January 10, 1968.

Emergency due to Pakistani Invasion. When Pakistan attacked India in August-September, 1965, then the Emergency which had been proclaimed in the wake of Chinese Aggression was still in operation but when Pakistan again attacked India on 3rd December, 1971, then the previous emergency was no more, so the President of India declared emergency again on the same day after a few hours.

Emergency Due to Failure of Constitutional Machinery in the States

The Constitution requires the President to protect the States against foreign invasion as well as internal chaos.[1] It is President's duty to ensure that the Government of every State is carried on in a constitutional way. If on a report from any Governor or otherwise, he is satisfied that the constitutional machinery in that State cannot work, he is empowered to proclaim Emergency in that State.[2]

Effect of the Constitutional Emergency. In the event of breakdown of the Constitution in any State, the President has been empowered by Article 356 of the Constitution to assume to himself all or any of the functions of the Government of the State and all or any of the powers vested in or exercisable by the Governor or any body or authority in the State other than the Legislature of the State. He may declare that the powers of the Legislature shall be exercisable by or under the authority of Parliament or supervise the functioning of the State legislature. He may, if he feels the necessity, suspend any provision of the Constitution relating to any authority in the State. In no case, however, he is authorised to take upon himself the powers of the State High Court.

The President, at the request of the Parliament, can authorise any other authority in the State to make law for the State. He may even delegate all his executive functions to his nominee in the State. He himself or anybody duly appointed by him then can seek obedience from all the Union and State Officials.

1. Article 355 of Indian Constitution.
2. Article 356 of Indian Constitution.

The President can declare the breakdown of the Constitution in a State if the State Executive refuses to carry out the instructions of the Union Executive issued in accordance with the Constitution.[1] The procedure and duration of this type of emergency are the same as in other two types. Every Proclamation declaring the failure of constitutional machinery in States is also required to be presented before each House of the Parliament for approval. It ceases to operate at the expiry of two months unless extended by the Parliament for a further period.

Intention of the framers of the Constitution about Constitutional Emergency in the States. We have seen that the powers of the President to make over the governments of states are very wide and drastic. Mr. *Alladi Krishnaswami Ayyar*, a member of the Drafting Committee, supporting the provisions of this Article maintained that if the Constitution of a State was worked efficiently ensuring the proper functioning of a responsible Government, the Union would not and could not interfere. "Far from being an impediment to state autonomy, they were a bulwark in favour of state autonomy, because the primary obligation was cast upon the Union to see that the Constitution was maintained."

Dr. Bhim Rao Ambedkar, the Chairman of the Drafting Committee, while defending these provisions maintained that "there was no departure from the established principles and even in the U.S.A. there was an obligation on the National Government (Central Government) to defend the Republican form of Government of the State."

The importance of this power in the political system of India can hardly be overlooked in view of the fact that it has been used not less than 108 times during the first 50 years of the working of the Constitution (till March 2004).

The only change that the 44th Amendment Act, 1978 (sponsored by the Janata Government) has made in this Article, is to substitute clause (5) to limit the duration of a Proclamation made under Article 356 to a period of one year under a Proclamation of Emergency under Article 352 is in operation and the Election Commission certifies that it is not possible to hold elections to the Legislative Assembly of the State concerned, immediately, in which case, it may be extended up to three years, by successive resolutions for continuance being passed by both Houses of Parliament.

It is to be noted that the foregoing amendment has not specified any conditions or circumstances under which the power under Article 356 can be used. Hence, in the light of the Rajasthan decision (State of Rajasthan v. Union of India A. 1977 S.C. 1361) no legal challenge could be offered when Mrs. Indira Gandhi repeated the Janata experiment in February 1980, in the same nine states, on the same ground *viz.*, that the Janata Party, which was in power in those states, was routed in the Lok Sabha elections.

Table 2

PRESIDENT'S RULE IN STATES AND UNION TERRITORIES

Sl. No.	State/U.T.	No. of times President's rule imposed	Years of Imposition
1	2	3	4
1.	Andhra Pradesh	2	1954, 1973
2.	Arunachal Pradesh	1	1979
3.	Assam	4	1979, 1981, 1982, 1990
4.	Bihar	7	1968, 1969, 1972, 1977, 1980, 1995, 1999
5.	Goa	4	1966, 1979, 1990, 1999

1. In clause (1) of Article 356, reference to provisions of the Constitution shall, in relation to State of Jammu and Kashmir, be construed as including reference to provisions or provision of the Constitution of Jammu & Kashmir.

6.	Gujarat	5	1971, 1974, 1976, 1980, 1996
7.	Haryana	3	1967, 1977, 1991
8.	Himachal Pradesh	2	1977,1992
9.	Jammu and Kashmir	2	1986, 1990
10.	Karnataka	4.	1971, 1977, 1989, 1990
11.	Kerala	9	1956, 1956, 1959, 1964, 1965, 1970, 1979, 1981, 1982
12.	Madhya Pradesh	3	1977, 1980, 1992
13.	Maharashtra	1	1980
14.	Manipur	7	1972, 1973, 1977, 1979,,1981, 1992, 1994
15.	Meghalaya	1	1991
16.	Mizoram	3	1977, 1978, 1988
17.	Nagaland	3	1975, 1988, 1992
18.	Orissa	6	1961, 1971, 1973, 1976, 1977, 1980
19.	Patiala and East Punjab States Union (PEPSU)	1	1953
20.	Punjab	8	1951, 1966, 1968, 1971, 1977, 1980, 1983, 1987
21.	Rajasthan	4	1967, 1977, 1980, 1992
22.	Sikkim	2	1979, 1984
23.	Tamil Nadu	4	1976, 1980, 1988, 1991
24.	Tripura	3	1972, 1977, 1993
25.	Uttar Pradesh	9	1968, 1970, 1973, 1975, 1977, 1980, 1992, 1995, 1996
26.	West Bengal	4	1968, 1970, 1971, 1977
27.	Pondicherry (Puducherry)	6	1968, 1974, 1974, 1978, 1983, 1991
		115	

Financial Emergency

According to Article 360, if the President of India is satisfied that the financial stability or credit of India or any part of India has been badly shaken, the President may proclaim a financial emergency. In this case also the provisions relating to duration and other matters are the same as in other two types of emergencies. During the operation of emergency, the President is empowered to extend the authority of the Union Executive to the States. He may give directions to the State Governments as to the manner in which its economy has to be phased. The President is authorised to reduce salaries of any class of state officials, the judges of the Supreme Court and the High Courts. He may also require all the State Money Bills to be reserved for the consideration of the President. The provisions of Article 360 do not apply to Jammu and Kashmir State. Such emergency had not been declared up till March 2004.

CRITICISM OF THE EMERGENCY POWERS OF THE PRESIDENT

The Emergency Powers of the President have been severely criticised. *Prof. K. T. Shah* observed thus in the Constituent Assembly: "*Looking at all the provisions of this chapter particularly and scrutinising the powers that have been given in almost every Article, it seems to me, the name of liberty or democracy will remain only sham under the Constitution.*"

Mr. H.V. Kamath observed, "*I fear that by this single chapter we are seeking to lay the foundation of a totalitarian State, a police State, a State completely opposed to all the ideals and principles that we have held aloft during the last few decades, a State where the rights and liberties of millions of innocent men and women will be in continuous jeopardy, a State where if there be peace, it will be the peace of the grave and void of the desert.*"

According to *H.N.Kunzru*, the provisions of financial emergency were a serious threat to the financial autonomy of the States.

Defence of these Provisions. When these provisions were framed, abnormal circumstances prevailed in the country. For instance, war was going on in Kashmir because Pakistan had attacked it on 22nd October, 1947. There was an armed revolt in Telangana, inspired and sometimes led by the Communists. The problem of integration of the Indian States was an acute one, since the British had made them free by a declaration at the time of granting independence. Besides that there were disruptive forces within the country and foreign intrigues wanted to scuttle the newly won independence of the country. Therefore, the framers of the Constitution, through great champions of democracy, could not ignore these abnormal circumstances which were a threat to the integrity and independence of the country.

Dr. Bhim Rao Ambedkar, Chairman of the Drafting Committee of the Constitution, defended these provisions thus : "These overriding powers are not the normal features of the Constitution. Their use and operation are expressly confined to emergencies only." The second consideration is "Could we avoid giving overriding power to the Centre when an emergency has arisen ? Those who do not admit the justification for such overriding powers to the Centre even in an emergency, do not seem to have a clear idea of the problem which lies at the root of the matter."

"The solution of this problem depends upon one's answer to this question which is the crux of the problem. There can be no doubt that in the opinion of the vast majority of the people, the residual loyalty of the citizen in any emergency must lie to the Centre and not to the constituent States. For it is only the Centre which can work for a common purpose and for the general interests of the country as a whole. Herein lies the justification for giving to the Centre certain overriding powers to be used in any emergency... And after all what is the obligation imposed upon the constituent States by these emergency powers ? No more than this, that in an emergency, they should take into consideration alongside their own local interests the opinion and interests of the nation as a whole."

The view of Mr. *T.T. Krishnamachari*, a member of the Drafting Committee, was :

"These emergency provisions have got to be tolerated as a necessary evil and without these provisions it is well nigh possible that all our efforts to frame a Constitution may ultimately be jeopardised."

POSITION OF THE INDIAN PRESIDENT

Before 42nd Amendment. The position of the Indian President has been a subject of much discussion. Article 53(1) of the Constitution says that the Executive Power of the Union shall be vested in the President which he shall exercise through officers subordinate to him. Article 74 says that there shall be a Council of Ministers to aid and advise the President in the exercise of his functions. The next article lays down that the Prime Minister shall be appointed by the President and the other Ministers shall be appointed by him on the advice of the Prime Minister. The Ministers shall hold office during the pleasure of the President.

Real Intention of the Framers of the Constitution. According to Dr. Bhim Rao Ambedkar who was the Chairman of the Drafting Committee of the Constitution, "*The President occupies the same position as the King under the English Constitution...He is the Head of the Nation but does not rule the Nation. He will be generally bound by the advice of the Ministers. He can do nothing contrary to their advice, nor can do anything without their advice.*" A similar view was expressed by Dr. Rajendra Prasad as the President of Constituent Assembly in these words : "*Although there is no specific provision to accept the advice of his Ministers, it is hoped that the Convention under which in England, the King always acted on the advice of the Ministers, would be established in this country also and the President would become Constitutional President in all matters.*" Pt. Jawaharlal Nehru while moving the Report of the Committee on Principles of the Union Constitution told the Constituent Assembly, "We want to emphasize the ministerial character of the Government that power really resided in the Ministry and in the legislature and not in the President as such. At the same time we did not want the President just a mere figurehead like the French President. We did not give him any real power but we have made his position one of authority and dignity." He repeated the same point in a Press conference of 7th July, 1959. He said that he was pained to see the controversy regarding the constitutional position of the President going on in the papers. There is not a ghost of doubt that India had adopted a parliamentary system in which not the President but the Parliament rules the Nation.

The weak position of the President does not mean that his office is superfluous. He plays a vital role in the working of the Government. Being impartial and above party politics, he exerts or is likely to exert his influence on the decision of the Prime Minister. A capable President can certainly make his weight felt both by the executive and the legislative departments. Moreover, his tenure being fixed for five years as against the Governments likely to change hands at any time, the President does the vital job of calling the new Prime Mnister to form his Cabinet. *During the emergency in India caused by the Chinese invasion, President Radhakrishnan conducted himself in a noble and dignified way. He did not overdo his role, nor did he try to assert his authority. There has been no rivalry in India between the President and the Prime Minister. Both have acted in perfect co-operation. The conventions have proved stronger and more stable than any written word. Dr. Zakir Husain extended all co-operation to Smt. Indira Gandhi.* However, serious differences developed between the former President Giani Zail Singh and Prime MInister Rajiv Gandhi during the former's tenure of last few months especially in March, 1987.

On 25th July, 1987, Mr. Venkatraman assumed the office of the President. He had acted also on the advice of the Cabinet.

Position of the President after 42nd Amendment: The 42nd Constitutional Amendment Act of 1976 (enacted by the Indira Gandhi Government) made the President bound by the advice of the Council of Ministers headed by the Prime Minister[1]. The 44th Constitutional Amendment Act of 1978 (enacted by the Janata Party Government headed by Morarji Desai) authorised the President to require the Council of Ministers to reconsider such advice either generally or otherwise. However, he shall act in accordance with the advice tendered after such reconsideration. In other words, the President may return a matter once for reconsideration of his Ministers, but the reconsidered advice shall be binding.

In October 1997, the Cabinet recommended President K. R. Narayanan to impose President's Rule (under Article 356) in Uttar Pradesh. The President returned the matter for the reconsideration of the Cabinet, which then decided not to move ahead in the matter. Hence, the BJP-led governement under Kalyan Singh was saved. Again in September 1998, President K. R. Narayanan returned a

1. In the original Constitution, there was no such specific provision in Article 74.

recommendation of the Cabinet that sought the imposition of President's Rule in Bihar. After a couple of months, the Cabinet readvised the same. It was only then that President's Rule was imposed in Bihar, in Feburary 1999.

Though the President has no constitutional discretion, he has some situational discretion. In other words, the President can act on his discretion (That is, without the advice of the Ministers) under the following situations :

(*i*) Appointment of Prime Minister when no party has a clear majority in the Lok Sabha or when the Prime Minister in office dies suddenly and there is no obvious successor.

(*ii*) Dismissal of the Council of Ministers when it cannot prove the confidence of the Lok Sabha.

(*iii*) Dissolution of the Lok Sabha if the Council of Ministers has lost its majority.

The President is still a dignified Head of the State, his position is of great influence, though not of authority. What President V.V. Giri had said about the position of the President on August 18, 1974, just a few days before laying down his august office, still holds true about the position of the President. In an exclusive interview to Press Trust of India in his last week in office as Head of the State, Mr. V.V. Giri said, "Having contested successfully as an Independent, he had tried to maintain his position throughout his five-year term. That was why he believed not only Congressmen but also leaders of the Opposition parties had come to him so often to represent their views on matters of national concern and importance."

Emphasising the importance of the relationship between the President and the Prime Minister under the Indian system of Government, Mr. V.V. Giri said, "The President could play a useful role by exchanging views frankly and freely concerning the Government constantly—as I and the Prime Minister have done." Mr. V.V. Giri further said, "The concept of a President functioning in opposition to the Government will be a distortion of our Constitution." But, he added, the President could give advice.

> "We have deliberately adopted the Parliamentary system with responsible Government. The responsibility is exercised through the Council of Ministers which is continuously subject to control and constant criticism by Parliament. *I am clear in my mind that the President, while asserting his right to be informed, to be consulted and to warn, should not do anything which will result in any substraction from responsible Government.*"

President Venkataraman asked Mr. V.P. Singh to prove his majority on the floor of the House after the withdrawal of support by BJP. BJP withdrew its support on 23rd October, 1990 after the arrest of its President, Mr. L.K. Advani in Samastipur (Bihar). As a group of 86 MPs was supporting National Front Government, so after its withdrawal of support, National Front Government was reduced to minority, therefore the leader of the Front, Mr. V.P. Singh, was asked by the President, Mr. Venkataraman, next day to prove his majority in the Lok Sabha on 7th *November, 1990. Mr. V.P. Singh, however, failed to prove his majority on 7th November 1990. Hence the Government fell and Mr. Chandra Shekhar was installed next P.M. on 10th November, 1990 but he too resigned on 6th March 1991.* On 21st June, 1991, Shri P.V. Narasimha Rao was sworn in as Prime Minister.

The President is no longer a rubber stamp figure. The Office of the Head of the State assumes increasing importance as the next general elections may lead to a fractured Parliament, says *Neeraj Chowdhary*. The President in March, 1996 returned the two ordinances to curtail the campaign period and to provide reservation to Dalit Christians, has not only stirred a hornets nest in Raisina Hill but has turned the arc-lights on the role that Rashtrapati Bhavan might come to play in the months to come.

Dr. Shankar Dayal Sharma was on a sound wicket in returning the two ordinances on the grounds of propriety. There was no compelling reason for the Government to push it through, hours before the announcement of polls. The Opposition cannot be blamed for concluding that the government resorted to this method to gain an electoral advantage.

COMPARISON OF INDIAN PRESIDENT WITH AMERICAN PRESIDENT

The President of India has often been compared with his counterpart in America. The same designation creates confusion. There is, however, a world of difference between the two. American President is the real executive and is directly responsible to the people of his country. He appoints his Ministers who act as his assistants or secreataries. They had held office during his pleasure and owe responsibility to him alone and not to the American Congress. According to *Prof. Laski*, "the American President symbolises the whole nation in a way that admits of no competitor while he is in office. Alongside his, the voice of a cabinet officer is at best, a wishper, which may or may not be heard." He cannot be removed by a no-confidence motion or censure motion, or adjourment motion. In emergency times his powers become so extensive that he becomes virtually a dictator. He actually exercises the powers that the Constitution transfers to him.

The position of the President of India is not so strong and real as it appears to be on the reading of the Constitution. In practice he is only a figurehead, an ineffective angel who spreads his wings over the entire field of administration but does not direct the course of any department. Like a family god he sits on a gilded throne but fettered too strongly to the conventions to move from his seat. In theory he is to appoint the Prime Minister and distribute the departments to various Ministers. But in practice his choice is very much restricted, rather hard set. He cannot invite any one other than the leader of the majority group in the Parliament to form his Cabinet. In appointing the Ministers and allocating portfolios he is bound by the advice of the Prime Minister. Even during an emergency, he cannot act as an autocrat because the Parliament is there to impeach him for his unconstitutional actions. In short, he possesses a bold and dignified front, although he has been so much chained to conventions that he cannot act. His position is comparable more to the Queen of England than the President of America.

EXERCISES

Long Answer Type Questions:

1. Discuss the method of election of the President of India.
2. What are the powers of the President during peace time ? Discuss in brief.
3. Write a critical note on the emergency powers of the President. Discuss the effect of the Proclamation of Emergency.
4. What do you know about the Emergency due to failure of Constitutional Machinery in the States ?
5. What is the criticism of the emergency powers of the President ? Write in brief.
6. Discuss comparison of Indian President with American President.

Short Answer Type Questions:

1. Write a brief note on the form of the Union Executive.
2. Discuss the legislation regarding succession of the President.
3. What should be the qualifications for the office of the President ? Discuss in very brief.
4. Write a very brief note on the tenure of the President.
5. What is the method to remove the President of India ?
6. What do you know about the salary and pension of the President ?

Objective Type Questions :

Choose the correct answer

1. The President of India is elected by indirect election, that is, by an electoral college, in accordance with the system of proportional representation by means of the single transferable vote. Which among the following constitute the electoral college ?
   1. The elected members of both Houses of Parliament.
   2. The elected members of the Legislative Assemblies of the States
   3. The elected members of the local bodies of the district level
   4. The elected members of the Legislative Assemblies of Union Territories of Delhi and Pondicherry.

   (*a*) Only 1 (*b*) 1 and 2
   (*c*) 1, 2 and 4 (*d*) 2, 3 and 4
2. Indirect election to the office of the President is preferable over direct elections because :
   (*a*) Direct election by an electorate of several hundred millions would mean a tremendous loss of time, energy and money.
   (*b*) Under the system of responsible Government introduced by the Constitution, real power would vest in the ministry; so, it would be anomalous to elect the President directly by the people without giving him real powers.
   (*c*) Both (a) and (b)
   (*d*) Direct election of the President is more suitable under the Presidential system of government where the President is both *de jure* and de *facto* head of the state and government.
3. One of the qualifications that a person must have to be elected to the office of the President is that she or he must not hold any office of profit under the Government of India or the Government of any state or under any local or other authority subject to the control of any of the said Governments. Who among the following are not deemed as holding an office of profit ?
   (*a*) Sitting President or Vice-President of the Union
   (*b*) The Governor of any State.
   (*c*) A minister either for the Union or for any State
   (*d*) All of the above
4. In constituting the electoral college for the election to the office of the President, parity of representation is sought to be maintained between the States as a whole and the Union. This is done so that :
   (*a*) The votes of the states, in the electoral college shall, in the aggregate, be equal to that of the people of the country as a whole.
   (*b*) The President shall be a representative of the nation as well as a representative of the people in the different States.
   (*c*) Status of the States in the federal system could be maintained.
   (*d*) All of the above
5. Under which Article of the Constitution, the qualifications for election to the office of the President find mention ?
   (*a*) Article 55 (*b*) Article 56
   (*c*) Article 57 (*d*) Article 58
6. The President can be removed from the office only through the process of impeachment. The ground/grounds for impeachment specified under Article 61 (1) is/are :
   1. Violation of the Constitution
   2. Immoral conduct like illegal gratification, abusing the powers of the office of President
   3. Insolvency
   4. Mental instability

   Select the correct answer from the following :
   (*a*) Only 1 (*b*) 1 and 2
   (*c*) 1, 2 and 3 (*d*) 1, 2 and 4

7. Article 53 of the Constitution says that the executive power of the Union shall be vested in the President. The ambit of the executive power involves :
(*a*) Both the determination of the Policy as well as carrying it into execution.
(*b*) The maintenance of order, the promotion of social and economic welfare, the direction of foreign policy
(*c*) The carrying on or supervision of the general administration of the State
(*d*) All of the above

8. Who was the first Vice-President to be given the opportunity of acting as the President ?
(*a*) Dr. Radhakrishnan when Dr. Rajendra Prasad visited the Soviet Union
(*b*) V.V. Giri when Dr. Zakir Husain passed away
(*c*) Giani Zail Singh when Neelam Sanjeeva Reddy took ill.
(*d*) V.V. Giri when Fakhruddin Ali Ahmad paid a long visit to Soviet Union

9. Which of the following is not a qualification for election as President ?
(*a*) Citizenship of India
(*b*) Membership of Upper House of the Union Legislature
(*c*) Age of thirty-five
(*d*) Qualification for election as a member of the Lower House of the Union Legislature

10. President's office may terminate within the term of five years due to his resignation. President has to address the resignation to.
(*a*) Vice-President (*b*) Prime Minister
(*c*) Speaker of Lok Sabha (*d*) Any of the above

11. Which Article of the Constitution lays down that the President's term of office is five years though he is eligible for re-election ?
(*a*) Article 56 (*b*) Article 57
(*c*) Articles 56-57 (*d*) Article 58

12. If a member of either House of Parliament or of a House of the Legislature of any State is elected as President of India, she or he shall :
(*a*) Be able to hold the two posts simultaneously
(*b*) Be able to hold the two posts alternatively
(*c*) Be deemed to have vacated her or his seat in that House.
(*d*) None of the above

13. Which of the following Articles prescribes that the President shall not hold any other office of profit ?
(*a*) Article 56 (*b*) Article 57
(*c*) Article 59 (*d*) Article 60

14. Which of the following is not a manner in which a vacancy may arise in the office of the President?
(*a*) President's demise
(*b*) President's resignation
(*c*) President's long absence
(*d*) President's removal by impeachment

ANSWERS

1. (*c*) 2. (*c*) 3. (*d*) 4. (*d*) 5. (*d*) 6. (*a*) 7. (*d*) 8. (*a*) 9. (*b*)
10. (*a*) 11. (*c*) 12. (*c*) 13. (*c*) 14. (*c*)

8

CHAPTER

The Union Executive (The Council of Ministers)

> *"The Prime Minister is invested with formidable power and influence, and unless he be a genuine democrat by nature, he is very likely to become a dictator."* — *N.V. Gadgil*

The Constitution of India provides for a Parliamentary system of Government in which the President is only a nominal or constitutional ruler and the real executive authority of the Union is exercised by the Council of Ministers. Article 74 of the Constitution concerned with the Council of Ministers provides. "There shall be a Council of Ministers with the Prime Minister at the head to aid and advise the President, who shall, in the exercise of his functions, act in accordance with such advice." It may be noted that the original Constitution was absolutely silent on the point whether the President was bound by the advice of the Council of Ministers or not. However, generally the President acted on the advice of the Council of Ministers in keeping with the conventions of Parliamentary government. This convention was given a formal legal status by the Forty-Second Amendment, which made it obligatory for the President to act on the advice of the Council of Ministers.

COUNCIL OF MINISTERS

Formation of the Council of Ministers. The President of India is on paper the Head of the State but to all intents and purposes the real power to rule is vested in the Council of Ministers. Article 74(1) of the Constitution lays down that there shall be a Council of Ministers with Prime Minister as its head to aid and advise the President in the exercise of his functions. Thus the Union Cabinet consists of the Prime Minister and his colleagues. The Prime Minister is officially appointed by the President. Other members of the Cabinet are also appointed by the President but on the advice of the Prime Minister. The Ministers hold office during the pleasure of the President. They are collectively responsible to the Lok Sabha. Every Minister is administered an oath of secrecy before he joins the Cabinet.

The Ministers may be from either House of the Parliament. If a person does not happen to be the member of any House at the time of his inculsion in the Cabinet, he has to seek membership within six months or resign after that period. Every Minister is entitled to such salary and allowances as are fixed by the Parliament from time to time. The Ministers are immune from judicial probe for an advice they tender to the President on any issue.

It is, however, noteworthy that the President cannot act arbitrarily in the appointment of Prime Minister. According to conventions that have grown in India, he had to invite the leader of the majority group in the Lok Sabha. If no single political group commands absolute majority in the Lower House, the President is required to invite any person who claims to command a sizable majority in the House. He cannot disregard the advice of the Prime Minister in the appointment of Ministers.

The Council of Ministers and the Cabinet. The Constitution of India does at no place mention the word 'cabinet'. It provides only for the formation of a Council of Ministers headed by a Prime Minister. The Council of Ministers has three categories of Ministers; (1) the Ministers of Cabinet rank; (2) the Ministers of State; and (3) the Deputy Ministers.

A Cabinet Minister is the head of one or more departments. The Ministers meet jointly and frame the policies of the government. Ministers of State and Deputy Ministers do not have a share in the formation of State policies. They so attend the Cabinet meetings unless specially invited to do so. A Minister of State ranks lower than Cabinet Minister and higher than the Deputy Minister. The Ministers of State form second line of command. The function of the Deputy Minister is to assist the Cabinet Ministers in the affairs of their departments. The Parliamentary Secretaries do not belong to the rank of Ministers. They do not hold any portfolio or real executive power. They simply assist the Ministers in Parliamentary affairs. Hence it comes out that the Cabinet is only a sub-committee of the bigger body—the Council of Ministers.

Oath. Before entering upon their office the Prime Minister and other members of the Council of Ministers have to take an Oath of Office and Secrecy. The Oath of Office reads:

"I----- do $\dfrac{\text{do swear in the name of God}}{\text{solemnly affirm}}$ that I will bear true faith and allegiance to the Constitution of India as by law established, that I will uphold the sovereignty and integrity of India, that I will faithfully and conscientiously discharge my duties as a Minister for the Union and that I will do right to all manner of people in accordance with the Constitution and the law, without fear or favour, affection or ill will."

The oath of secrecy to be taken by a member of the Council of Ministers reads:

"I----- do $\dfrac{\text{do swear in the name of God}}{\text{solemnly affirm}}$ that I will not directly or indirectly communicate or reveal to any persons any matter which shall be brought under my consideration or shall become known to me as Minister for the Union except as may be required for the due discharge of my duties as such Minister."

Salary and Allowances. The salary and allowances of the members of the Council of Ministers have not been fixed by the Constitution and have been left to the Parliament. Article 75(6) lays down that "the salaries and allowances of Ministers shall be such as Parliament may from time to time by law determine and until Parliament so determines, shall be as specified in the Second Schedule. The salaries and allowances of Ministers were revised in 2008. Now each Minister is enitled to same salaries and allowances which are paid to the members of Parliament. This salary is ₹ 50,000 per month and sumptuary allowance of ₹ 2,000 to Cabinet Minister, ₹ 1000 to State Minister and ₹ 600 to Deputy Minister: They are also entitled to a constituency allowance at the rate to which the members of Parliament are entitled. In addition they receive a sumptuary allowance at a varying scale, according to this rant and a residence free of rent. The Ministers and members of their family accompanying them are entitled to travelling allowance in respect of not more than six return journeys performed during each year within India. The Ministers are exempted from liability to pay income tax on certain perquisites received by them, viz., rent-free and furnished residence (including maintenance thereof) provided to them.

Meetings of the Council of Ministers. The Council of Ministers does not hold frequent meetings. The real business is transacted by the Cabinet presided over by the Prime Minister, which holds its meetings at least once a week. In the meetings of the Cabinet only the Cabinet Ministers are present. The Ministers of State are permitted to attend its meetings only when the Cabinet is discussing a matter pertaining to that Ministry. Sometimes even the Chief Ministers of States and members of Planning Commission are also invited to attend the meetings of the Cabinet when their presence is felt desirable. In the absence of the Prime Minister (the meetings of the Cabinet are presided over by the Deputy Prime Minister, if there is one) or the seniormost Minister. Decisions at the Cabinet meetings are generally taken by consensus. In view of the secret nature of the proceedings of the Cabinet the decisions are generally not reduced to writing.

BASIC FEATURES OF THE WORKING OF COUNCIL OF MINISTERS IN INDIA OR PRINCIPLES ON WHICH CABINET WORKS

The system of ministerial responsibility has been borrowed from Great Britain. The Cabinet of India works on certain conventions and principles as follows:

1. President Acts only as Constitutional Head. The principal characteristic of a Parliamentary Government is that the Head of the State exercises only nominal powers. The administration of the country is run by the Head of the Government, that is, the Prime Minister. But Article 75(3) of the Constitution further lays down that the Council of Ministers is to be collectively responsible to the House of the People. The provision of responsibility to Parliament connotes that India has adopted Parliamentary Form of Government. The Prime Minister rules the country in the name of the President. According to Article 78 of the Constitution, all important decisions are actually taken by the Council of Ministers and they are communicated to the President by the Prime Minister. The President can only submit for the consideration of the Council of Ministers any matter of National Interest or any matter on which a decision has been taken by a Minister but not considered by the Council of Ministers.

The 42nd Amendment. Prime Minister Indira Gandhi's Government sought to put the question beyond political controversy by amending the Constitution itself. Article 74 (1) was thus substituted by the Constitution (42nd Amendment) Act, 1976.

> "(1) There shall be a Council of Ministers with the Prime Ministers at the head to aid and advise the President who *shall, in the exercise of his functions, act in accordance with such advice.*"

The 43rd and 44th Amendments. Through the Janata Government sought to wipe off the radical changes infused into Constitution by Mrs. Indira Gandhi's Government, it has *not* disturbed the foregoing amendment made in Article 74 (1). The only change made by the 44th Amendment Act over the 1976 provision is to add a Proviso which gives the President one chance to refer the advice given to the Council of Ministers back for a reconsideration; but if the Council of Ministers reaffirms their previous advice, the President shall be bound to act according to that advice. Article 74(1), as it stands after the 44th Amendment, 1978, stands thus:

> "(1) There shall be a Council of Ministers with the Prime Minister at the head to aid and advise the President who shall, in the exercise of his functions, act in accordance with such advice.
>
> *Provided* that the President may require the Council of Ministers to reconsider such advice, either generally or otherwise, and the President shall act in accordance with the advice tendered after such reconsideration."

2. Ministers Represent Majority Party of Parliament. Every Minister has to be a member of the Union Parliament either at the time of his appointment or within six months thereafter. Further the Ministers are collectively responsible to the Parliament. They attend the sittings of the Parliament and take part in its deliberations. The provision relating to Parliamentary Responsibility lays beyond doubt the foundation of a Parliamentary Government. The Ministers, as they are drawn from the majority party in the Lok Sabha, naturally enjoy the confidence of that group. Sometimes the Ministers are taken from the minority groups also. But as a team they command the confidence of the majority group.

3. Collective Responsibility of the Ministers to the Lok Sabha. Following the British Convention, the Ministers in India are collectively and not severally responsible to the Lok Sabha. While explaining the principle of collective responsibility in the Constituent Assembly, Dr. Bhim Rao Ambedkar said,

> "Obviously there can be no legal sanction for collective responsibility. The only sanction through which collective responsibility can be enforced is through the Prime Minister. In my judgement collective responsibility is enforced by the enforcement of two principles. One principle is that no person shall be nominated to the Cabinet except on the advice of the Prime Minister. Secondly, no person shall be retained as a member of the Cabinet if the Prime Minister says that he shall be dismissed. It is only when members of the Cabinet both in the matter of their appointment as well as in the matter of dismissal are placed under the Prime Minister that it would be possible to realise our ideal of collective responsibility. I do not see any other means or way of giving effect to that principle."[1]

Thus in practice every Minister is equally responsible for any lapse on the part of his colleague. A censure motion aganist one Minister amounts to no-confidence aganist the whole Ministry in which case all the Ministers including the Prime Minister have to go out of office. The Members of Parliament keep the Ministers under their thumb in other ways also. They ask questions and supplementary questions which have to be answered satisfactorily by the Minister concerned. By adopting adjournment motions or censure motions the President secures the obedience of the Ministers.

4. Principle of Secrecy. Every Minister before taking his office has to take an oath of secrecy. They are forbidden to divulge the secrets of the department to the public. They are absolutely free to express divergent views in the Cabinet meetings but once a decision is taken by a majority vote, each Minister has to honour it. They have to appear before the Public and Parliament as one strong team. The Cabinet Secretariat keeps a record of all Cabinet proceedings. The employees of the Secretariat are also warned not to leak out anything. Only the Prime Minister from time to time passes on Cabinet decisions to the Press. If a Minister intends to lay bare his differences with the Prime Minister before any House, he has to seek the consent of the Prime Minister.

5. Political Homogeneity. Usually all the Ministers belong to the same political party, naturally they try to work out the party's election manifesto. If the Prime Minister intends to form a coalition Ministry, then he arrives at an understanding with the leaders of other groups to work a common programme. If some Minister in a coalition Ministry does not agree to the majority decision, he relinquishes his office, as Dr. Shyama Prasad Mukherjee once did from Nehru Cabinet owing to his differences with the Prime Minister over the rehabilitation of Bengal refugees.

6. Leadership of the Prime Minister. Whereas in the English Constitution it is only a convention that the King will endorse the appointment of Ministers made by the Prime MInister, in Indian Constitution it is clearly written that the President will appoint the Ministers on the advice of the Prime Minister who will be the Head of the Council of Ministers. Thus the Indian Constitution acknowledges the leadership of his team of Ministers. The Prime Minister is the Chief of Union Cabinet. He occupies the chair in all the sittings of his Ministers. He advises the President regarding

1. *Constituent Assembly Debates,* Vol. VII, pp. 1159-60.

the allocation of portfolios to the Ministers. He can also dismiss any member of his team for being defiant. If a Minister refuses to resign; the Prime Minister tenders his own resignation and in the new Ministry he may drop out that defaulting Minister. Thus the Ministers are completely at the mercy of the Prime Minister. No Minister can take his case to the President without the previous permission of the Prime MInister. If a Minister loses the confidence of the Lok Sabha, the Prime Minister stands by his side and tenders his own resignation.

7. Right to dissolve the Lok Sabha. Another feature of the working of Council of Ministers is that it can request the President, through the Prime Minister, to dissolve the Lok Sabha even before the expiry of its normal term of five years and the President invariably accepts this advice. It is well known that in 1971 Prime Minister Mrs. Indira Gandhi advised the President to dissolve the Lok Sabha ahead of its schedule and sought fresh elections with a view to seek public mandate on her socio-economic programme. In the same way in 2004 Prime Minister Atal Behari Vajpayee also advised the President to dissolve the Lok Sabha ahead of its schedule and sought fresh elections with a view to seek public mandate on his achievements and victory in State Assembly elections. Thus the Council of Ministers in India operates along the well-established conventions of the British Parliamentany System.

FUNCTIONS OF THE COUNCIL OF MINISTERS

Constitutionally all the executive authority of the Union Government is vested in the President and the Council of Mmisters is there simply to aid and advise the President in the exercise of his functions.But in reality all these powers are exercised by the Council of Ministers on behalf of the President, who merely takes oath as a nominal or constitutional executive head of the union. The functions of the Council of Ministers are indeed extensive and can be studied under the following heads.

1. Framing or Determining the Policies. The Union Council of Ministers formulates the general policy of the country. It also shapes the foreign policy of the Government. All the important decisions are taken in the Council of Ministers' meetings. For instance, India's policy of non-alignment and the resistance to colonialism, imperalism, racism and military pacts has the support of all the Ministers. Policy-making is the most delicate and difficult task for any Parliament. If the Parliament refuses to endorse them, the Ministry is forced to resign or the Prime Minister having to get the verdict of the people in favour of his policies, requests the President to dissolve the House and hold fresh elections.

2. Running the Administration. The Council of Ministers forms the core of the government. It is the strongest administrative wing. Every Minister holds one or more portfolios and feels responsible for the good administration of his department. The Prime Minister co-ordinates the functioning of various departments. He promotes co-operation between various Ministers. A matter which concerns more than one department is discussed in the special meetings of the Council of Ministers.

3. Preparation of the Bills and Piloting them in Parliament. It is the function of the Ministers to prepare the draft of all important Bills and present it before the Parliament for approval. These are called official Bills and are given priority and preference over private Bills. A Bill moved by a private member has little chance of reaching the Statute Book unless supported by the ruling party. Besides moving and piloting the Bills, the Council of Ministers prepares a legislative programme or agenda for the new session of the Union Legislature. The Council of Ministers also prepares the text of President's inaugural address to be delivered on the first day of every year's new session. The Ministers also have to answer the questions and supplementary questions asked by the members of both the Houses. Since the Council of Ministers enjoys the backing of majority group in the House, it does not have to face much difficulty in getting all government measures approved by the House.

4. Budget. The Finance Minister with the co-operation of other Ministers prepares a budget for the next financial year. It is thoroughly discussed in the Council of Ministers before being presented in a final shape in the Lok Sabha. If the Parliament refuses to accept the Budget in its original form, the Council of Ministers is constrained to resign.

5. The Prime Minister generally consults his colleagues before taking any momentous decision. All commercial, political and military agreements have the approval of the majority in the Council of Ministers. The Prime Minister generally appoints all senior officers and ambassadors with the consent of his Ministers.

APPOINTMENT AND POWERS OF THE PRIME MINISTER

Under the Parliamentary System of Government adopted in India, though formally all the executive powers of the Union Government are vested in the President, in reality these powers are exercised by the Council of Ministers under the leadership of the Prime Minister. The office of the Prime Minister in India has a constitutional basis and is not based on conventions as in England. Article 74 (1) clearly mentions that there shall be a Council of Ministers *with the Prime Minister as the head* to aid and advise the President. The position of the Prime Minister has been made effective under the Forty-Second Amendment whcih provides that it shall be obligatory for the President to accept the advice of the Council of Ministers.

A bid was made to restore some of the lost prestige of the office of President by the Forty-Fourth Amendment, which authorised the President to refer back an issue for reconsideration of the Council of Ministers. However, even under the Forty-Fourth Amendment it was obligatory for the President to accept the advice of the Council of Ministers communicated to him after reconsideration. This enabled the Prime Minister to retain his pre-eminent position.

Appointment of Prime Minister of India: The Prime Minister is appointed by the President. However, it does not mean that the President is free to appoint anyone as the Prime Minister. He has to invite the leader of the majority party in the Lok Sabha to become the Prime Minister and under normal circumstances the appointment of Prime Minister by the President is just a constitutional formality. The President has hardly any discretion in the matter of the appointment of Prime Minister. However, if no single political party possesses a clear-cut majority in the Parliament or there is no acknowledged leader of the majority party, the President may have some discretion in the appointment of the Prime Minister. It may be noted that even under such circumstances, the President has to ensure that only such person should be appointed as Prime Minister who in his opinion shall be able to muster the support of the majority of the members of Lok Sabha and carry out the policies and programmes of his party. By convention the Prime Minister is generally taken from the Lok Sabha. So far all the Prime Ministers (with the exception of Smt. Indira Gandhi when she became Prime Minister for the first time in 1966 and was member of the Rajya Sabha) have been members of the Lok Sabha.

Term of Office. The Prime Minister holds office during the pleasure of the President, which seems to suggest that the President can remove him at any moment without assigning any reasons. In practice it is not so and the President cannot remove a Prime Minister so long as he enjoys the support of the majority of the members of the Lok Sabha. If the President in violation of this principle, dismisses the Prime Minister, it may not be possible for him to find out another person who may be able to secure the confidence of the Lok Sabha and form a stable government. Therefore, the term of the Prime Minister is automatically extended. Likewise if the Lok Sabha is dissolved earlier than its fixed term, the term of the Prime Minister is automatically cut short. In short, it can be said that the term of the office of the Prime Minister is co-terminus with that of Lok Sabha.

Oath. Before assuming his office the Prime Minister has to take oath of office and secrecy like the other members of the Council of Ministers. The oaths are administered to him by the President. In the oath of office he expresses faith and allegiance to the Constitution of India and undertakes to uphold the sovereignty and integrity of India and to conscientiously discharge his duties in accordance with the Constitution and the law; without fear or favour, affection or illwill. In the oath of secrecy he undertakes not to directly or indirectly communicate or reveal to any person or persons any matter which may be brought to his consideration or which may become known to him in his official capacity, except in so far he is required to do so for the discharge of his duties.

Salary and Allowances. The Prime Minister gets a monthly salary of ₹ 50,000 and other allowances which are paid to members of Parliament. He also receives constituency allowance at the same rate to which the MPs are entitled. At present the constituency allowance is ₹ 5 crore per annum. In addition the Prime Minister gets a sumptuary allowance of ₹ 3000 per month. Over and above he is entitled to free house, medical facilities and travelling allowances.

Powers and Functions of Prime Minister. The Prime Minister as the chief adviser of the President and the Chairman of the Council of Ministers enjoys very extensive functions and powers. The Constitution acknowledges the primary position of the Prime Minister in the Council of Ministers by specifically providing that "there shall be a Council of Ministers with the Prime Minister as its head" to aid and advise the President. Even if the Constitution had not specifically assigned a primary position to the Prime Minister, he would have assumed that position in actual practice. Emphasising this point Dr. B.R. Ambedkar told the Constituent Assembly, "There can be hardly any objection to giving statutory recognition to the position of the Prime Minister which is established for long by convention in England." It is a well-known fact that in Parliamentary system of government the Prime Minister is the centre of executive and imparts content and meaning to the policies to the government. The powers of the Prime Minister can be conveniently studied under the following heads :

1. In Relation to the Council of Ministers. As noted above, the Prime Minister occupies a pre-eminent position in relation to the Council of Ministers. The formation of the Council of Ministers starts with the appointment of the Prime Minister and the other members of the Council of Ministers are appointed by the President on the recommendation of the Prime Minister. Though technically the power to appoint the members of the Council of Ministers is vested by the Constitution in the President, but in actual practice he has hardly any say in the matter. It is the prerogative of the Prime Minister to prepare a list of the Ministers to be included in the Council of Ministers and the President merely appoints those Ministers. It is a different matter that the Prime Minister is also not completely free to include anyone in the list and has to keep various considerations into mind while formulating the list. For example, he has to ensure that various communities, interests, areas, etc. find due representation in it. Likewise he has to pick up all the Ministers from the two Houses of Parliament and accommodate most of the leading members of his party. The previous experience of the persons and their field of specialisation is also taken into account while preparing the list.

Once the Council of Ministers has been formulated, it is the prerogative of the Prime Minister to allocate the portfolios amongst the members. With a view to ensure that the administration is carried on efficiently the Prime Minister can also reshuffle the Council and re-allocate the portfolios. A Minister can stay in the Council of Ministers only as long as he enjoys the confidence of the Prime Minister. In case of differences the Prime Minister can ask a Minister to tender his resignation or ease him by reshuffling the Council of Ministers. In extreme cases the Prime Minister can even recommend the dismissal of a Minister to the President. It may be noted that the Prime Minister is likely to avoid such extreme action.

Emphasising the pre-eminent position of the Prime Minister in relation to his Council of Ministers, *Dr. B.R. Ambedkar* said that "nc person shall be nominated to the Cabinet except on the advice of the Prime Minister. Secondly, no person shall be retained as a member of the Cabinet if the Prime Minister says that he shall be dismissed. It is only when members of the Cabinet both in the matter of their appointment as well as in the matter of their dismissal are placed under the Prime Minister, that it would be possible to realise our ideal of collective responsibility".

The Prime Minister is the Chairman of the Council of Ministers and presides over its meetings. The agenda and the proceedings of the Council of Ministers are also largely determined and regulated by the Prime Minister. Though in the Council of Ministers all decisions are taken by consensus, it cannot be denied that the views of the Prime Minister have a decisive effect on the decisions of the Council of Ministers.

2. Co-ordination of Administration. As the leader of the Council of Ministers the Prime Minister is responsible for the general co-ordination of the work of various Ministers. He exercises general supervision on the working of the various Ministers and resolves the inter-departmental disputes. The Prime Minister with the assistance of the Cabinet Secretariat ensures that the policies and programmes of various departments do not clash with each other.

3. In Relation to the President. The Prime Minister is the chief channel of communication between the President and the Council of Ministers. It is a constitutional obligation of the Prime Minister to communicate all the decisions of the Council of Ministers to the President. Similarly, if the President so desires, the Prime Minister has to submit a matter for the consideration of the Council of Ministers, if a decision has been taken by an individual minister but no decision has been taken by the Council of Ministers as such. The Prime Minister is also duty-bound to supply such information to the President regarding proposals of legislation and administration of the Union, as the President may need. It is significant to note that no other member of the Council of Ministers is authorised to make any direct communication with the President unless he is so authorised.

The Prime Minister also assists the President in making all important appointments and shares his power of patronage. Some of the important appointments made by the President on the recommendation of the Prime Minister include the Chief Justice and Judges of the Supreme Court and the High Courts, Comptroller and Auditor-General, Attorney-General, Chief Election Commissioner, Chairman and members of the Union Public Service Commission, Governors, Chiefs of the Army, Navy and Air Force, Ambassadors and High Commissioners and other high officials. It may be noted that in reality all these appointments are made by the Prime Minister, although they are formally made in the name of the President.

4. In Relation to Parliament. The Prime Minister is also the chief link between the Parliament and the Council of Ministers. In fact he is appointed as Prime Minister because he is the leader of the majority party in the Lok Sabha and is responsible to the Parliament for all his actions along with other members of his Council of Ministers . As such he has to justify the policy and programme of the government on the floor of the Parliament. All important policy announcements in the Parliament are made by the Prime Minister. He also offers clarifications on matters pertaining to policy. He also comes to the rescue of other Ministers in the Parliament when they are in a tight corner and defends their actions in the Parliament. This is essential in view of the principle of 'collective responsibility' on which the Council of Ministers works. The sessions of the Parliament are summoned and prorogued by the President on the advice of the Prime Minister. The Prime Minister also reserves the right to advise the President about the dissolution of the Lok Sabha.

5. Conduct of International Relations. The Prime Minister also plays an important role in the conduct of India's international relations. Generally the Prime Minister keeps the portfolio of external affairs with him. Even if some other Minister is incharge of this department, he works in complete co-operation with the Prime Minister and keeps him posted with all the developments. The Prime Minister represents the country in the various international conferences. In short, the Prime Minister plays a vital role in the conduct of country's international relations.

6. Power of Patronage. The Prime Minister also enjoys great power of patronage. All important appointments are made by the President on the recommendation of the Prime Minister. The Prime Minister can elevate even the non-entities to the most important positions, specially the positions like Ministers, Governors, Chairmanship of various Commissions etc. which do not require any education or other qualifications. There are a number of instances when comparatively unknown persons were inducted into the Cabinet such as T.A. Pai, D.P. Dhar, T.N. Singh etc. and became national figures all of a sudden.

7. Leader of the Party. Finally, the Prime Minister is an important leader of the party and greatly influences its working and decisions. He keeps in constant touch with the other important members of his party to ensure the party solidarity and support, for he knows it too well that his existence in office depends on the support of his party. Often the Prime Minister also acts as the President of the Party. But at present Prime Minister and President of the party are separate. It is a well known fact that at times Prime Minister like Pt. Jawaharlal Nehru, Mrs. Indira Gandhi and Mr. Charan Singh were also the presidents of their political parties.

Position of the Prime Minister. A perusal of the powers of the Prime Minister clearly demonstrates that he enjoys tremendous power and influence both in the executive and the legislative sphere. As Chairman of the Council of Ministers he plays a decisive role in the formulation and implementation of the policy by the various ministers. The nominal or constitutional position of the President of India under the Indian political system further adds to the powers and prestige of the Prime Minister. In fact all the powers vested in the President by the Constitution are exercised by the Prime Minister. In this respect the position of the Prime Minister in Great Britain and all those epithets which are used for the British Prime Minister are applicable to him as well. Some of these epithets are *'primus inter pares'* (first amongst equals), 'steersman of the ship of the state', 'the moon among the lesser stars' and 'sun around which all other planets revolve'. In fact, the position of the Indian Prime Minister is superior to the position of the British Prime Minister in so far as his office enjoys a constitutional basis and is not a product of the conventions.

In view of the enormous powers vested in the Prime Minister of India, Prof.K.T. Shah observed in the Constituent Assembly: "The Constitution concentrates so much power and influence in hands of the Prime Minister that there is every danger to apprehend that the Prime Minister may become a dictator if he chooses to do so". To a large extent this view has been confirmed by the actual operation of the office of the Prime Minister. Nehru dominated the Cabinet like a 'gentle colossus'. About his position Prof. Palmer observed: "Nehru has been much more than Prime Minister of India, important as the role has been. He has been a leader of the Indian revolution which he interprets in economic and social as well as in political terms, the political heir of Gandhi, the leader of the dominant political organisation, a charismatic leader par excellence, the very symbol of New Delhi".

PRIME MINISTERS OF INDIA

1. Jawaharlal Nehru : India's first and arguably the best Prime Minister yet. Nehru was a statesman of the highest calibery. It accounts for both his achievements and his shortcomings.

Achievements :

1. Architect of Modern India through huge public sector industries and large infrastructure projects.
2. He was a pure democrat and secular. Any other person in his position may have misused the tremendous standing he had in his party and the country. No one would dare to accuse him of impropriety or nepotism.
3. Increased India's standing in the world by his work in the Non-aligned Movement, active support to peace efforts in Korea, China, etc. and by calling for global nuclear disarmament.

Shortcomings:

1. India's growth rate under him was not as good as it could have been.
2. Made historic mistakes in respect of Kashmir and China which resulted in India losing large parts of territory.

2. Lal Bahadur Shastri : Future generations in India might find it hard to believe that a man of such honesty and simplicity could have been in politics. However his reign was so short to have any great impact on the country.

Achievements:

Showed pragmatism and led India to victory in the 1965 war against Pakistan.

3. Indira Gandhi : India's most controversial Prime Minister. She was a woman of steel. What could have been the most productive and promising regime in India ended as the most controversial of all regimes.

Achievements :

1. Led India to a spectacular victory in the 1971 war against Pakistan which led to the creation of Bangladesh.
2. Dismantled the Third World mindset of India and improved India's relations with Soviet Union which helped India acquire defence hardware and improve nuclear and space cooperation.
3. Crushed militancy in Punjab (at least partially) by sending troops in Amristar.

Shortcomings:

1. Declared Emergency in 1975 which remains the darkest period in post-independence Indian History.
2. Reduced all Congressmen to sycophants (including the Indian President). Notorious for nepotism and undemocratic activities which allowed even fools like Sanjay and Rajfv Gandhi to call the shots in the government.
3. Promoted terrorism in East Pakistan and Sri Lanka.

4. Morarji Desai: India's first non-Congress Prime Minister. An influential politician from Western India who headed the Janata Party Government formed after the struggle against Emergency led by Jaya Prakash Narayan. Known more for his habit of drinking his own urine and his Feb 29 birthday than for his work in office.

5. Chaudhary Charan Singh: Very few people in India know that they even had a Prime Minister in the name of Chaudhary Charan Singh. A leader with an agricultural background from Uttar Pradesh he formed a puppet government, whom Indira Gandhi dispensed with soon after.

6. Rajiv Gandhi: A man who began his term as a promising young leader.

Achievements:

1. Tried some modernisation of the Defence Forces and the Indian industry. Introduced STD booths all over the country with the help of Sam Pitroda and India's ambitious Integrated Missile Development Programme was started during his term.
2. Encouraged many youngsters in politics like Rajesh Pilot, Rangarajan Kumaramangalam and Madhav Rao Sindhia (all now dead).

Shortcomings:

1. Messed up the Sri Lankan crisis with staggering consequences. 1,500 Indian soldiers dead. Indian soldiers indulged in large scale atrocities (rape, looting and killings) against the Tamils. Sri Lanka continues to burn till date.

2. Politicised the Ayodhya issue by allowing Shilanyas and by starting his 1989 election campaign from Ayodhya.
3. Bofors scandal involving his close associates and his massive cover-up of the case stands out as the most popular defence scandal in Indian History.
4. Reduced the massive 427-member strength of the Congress Party in 1984 (even Nehru did not have such numbers) to 180 seats in 1989.

7. V.P. Singh: A man of shrewd intelligence, he quickly turned the heat of Bofors on Rajiv Gandhi and captured power with his newly floated Janata Dal in 1989. A champion of caste politics, he implemented the Mandal Commission Recommendations (Reservations) which is certain to hurt India for several decades to come.

8. Chandra Shekhar : When he resigned his post of Prime Minister in 1991 everyone in the country heaved a sigh of relief !! (including himself !!). A product of the Lohia politics he went the same way as Choudhary Charan Singh, done in by Rajiv Gandhi.

9. P.V. Narasimha Rao: Only Prime Minister outside the Nehru-Gandhi family to have completed full five years in office. A man who believed that doing nothing is the best thing to do has in fact achieved more than many people would give him credit.

Achievements:

1. Along with his able Finance Minister Dr. Manmohan Singh, introduced economic reforms in India. The four years from 1993 to 1996 saw the highest growth rates in Indian history.
2. Successfully completed his term by political manoevring (He led a minority government of 240 MPs.)

Shortcomings:

1. Arguably the most corrupt of all Prime Ministers. He was sentenced to three years rigorous imprisonment by a lower court only to be acquitted in the Supreme Court. There are so many cases pending against him.
2. The economic reforms lost stream after the initial impetus. Did not do much in downsizing the government or disinvestment.

8. H. D. Deve Gowda: Virtually no one in India wanted or expected him to become Prime Minister, product of the great joke of Indian politics called the National Front, he was so unfit to be Prime Minister that criticising him would seem unfair.

9. I.K. Gujral: The man who gave the Gujral Doctrine of friendly relations with neighbouring countries, tried to improve relations with Pakistan. A good man with no political backing, he could not have made much impact and so he didn't.

10. Atal Bihari Vajpayee: The first truly non-Congress Prime Minister of India and the first to win two consecutive terms in office in 25 years. A man whose acceptance level among people is much greater than his party's acceptability.

Achievements:

1. Conducted India's second nuclear tests and declared India to be a nuclear weapon State.
2. Tried his level best to improve relations with Pakistan (Lahore and Agra) and when stabbed on the back by Pakistan, led India to victory in Kargil.
3. Carried forward the Second Generation Economic Reforms by increased disinvestment, privatisation and opening many sectors to foreign investments. (Insurance, telecom etc). India is showing signs of faster economic growth.

4. His pet project of linking the four metros in the Golden Quadrangular Highways Project is the only great effort made to improve the infrastructure in India in a long time.
5. On the personal front he is a legendary parliamentarian (Member of either House for 45 years) and statesman of the League of Nehru.

11. **Manmohan Singh:** A renowned economist, Manmohan Singh is also regarded as one of the "greatest statesmen in Asian History" Shown here with Indian delegation at the 33rd G8 summit, in Heiligendamm.

After the 2004 General Elections, the Indian National Congress ended the incumbent National Democratic Alliance (NDA) tenure by becoming the political party with the single largest number of seats in the Lok Sabha. It formed United Progressive Alliance (UPA) with allies and staked claim to form government. In a surprise move, Chairperson Sonia Gandhi declared Manmohan Singh, a technocrat, as the UPA candidate for the Prime Ministership. Despite the fact that Singh had never won a Lok Sabha seat, he "has enjoyed massive popular support, not least because he was seen by many as a clean politician untouched by the taint of corruption that has run through many Indian administrations." He took the oath as the Prime Minister of India on 22 May, 2004.

15th Lok Sabha

India held General Elections to the 15th Lok Sabha in five phases between 16 April, 2009 and 13 May 2009. The results of the election were announced on 16 May 2009. Strong showing in Andhra Pradesh, Rajasthan, Maharashtra, Tamil Nadu, Kerala, West Bengal and Uttar Pradesh helped the United Progressive Alliance (UPA) form the new government under the incumbent Manmohan Singh, who became the first Prime Minister since Jawaharlal Nehru in 1962 to win re-election after completing a full five-year term. The Congress and its allies were able to put together a comfortable majority with support from 322 members out of 543 members of the House. These included those of the UPA and the external support from the Bahujan Samaj Party (BSP), Samajwadi Party (SP), Janata Dal (Secular) (JD(S)), Rashtriva Janata Dal (RJD) and other minor parties. On 22 May, 2009, Manmohan Singh was sworn in as the Prime Minister during a ceremony held at Rashtrapati Bhavan. The 2009 Indian general election was the largest democratic election in the world held to date, with an eligible electorate of 714 million.

PUBLIC IMAGE

Manmohan Singh has always been perceived as a man of clean background. He is seen as a man of few words. *The Independent* described him as "one of the world's most revered leaders" and "a man of uncommon decency and grace," noting that he drives a Maruti 800, one of the humblest cars in the Indian market. Khushwant Singh iauded Singh as the best Prime Minister India has had, even rating him higher than Jawaharlal Nehru. He mentions an incident in his book *Absolute Khushwant: The Low-Down on Life, Death and Most Things In-between* where after losing the 1999 Lok Sabha Elections, Manmohan Singh immediately returned the ₹2 lakh (US $4.000) he had borrowed from the writer for hiring taxis. Terming him as the best example of integrity, Khushwant Singh stated, "When people talk of integrity, I say the best example is the man who occupies the country's highest office." His personal assets amount to five crore rupees (approx 1 million USD).

In 2010, *Newsweek* magazine recognized him as a world leader who is respected by other heads of state, describing him as "the leader other leaders love." The article quoted Mohamed ElBaradei, who remarked that Singh is "the model of what a political leader should be" Manmohan Singh's number is 18 on the 2010 *Forbes* list of the world's most powerful people. *Forbes* magazine described Singh as being "universally praised as India's best Prime Minister since Nehru".

His public image has been tarnished recently as he heads the government which is mired in some of the biggest corruption scandals in recent history. He is also accused of being a weak Prime Minister by several politicians and social activists.

Our Collective Failures

65 years have passed since Independence and we still have severe shortcomings in many fronts. We have listed some of them here. **Of course we have had some achievements but then no one considers them to be spectacular.**

1. India continues to be a developing country.
2. Indians are the most illiterate, most mal-nourished, most below poverty line and most without basic civil needs (Public health, drinking water, sanitation, better roads). All these based on the numbers rather than on the percentage of people.
3. India bleeds not being able to cope with the terrorists of all hues. (From Kashmir, North East to the petty Tamil terrorists).
4. India does not have good relations with any of its neighbours. We have not even solved boundary disputes with Bangladesh leave alone China and Pakistan.
5. India still has not developed into a mature democracy with people continuing to vote in the name of caste, religion and not to speak of the criminals in politics.

In conclusion it may be said that the position of the Indian Prime Minister does not entirely rest on the various powers bestowed by the Constitution. To a large extent it depends on his personality and prestige and the support he can muster within his party. Persons with magnetic personalities like Pt. Jawaharlal Nehru and Mrs. Indira Gandhi have enjoyed greater prestige in comparison to the other occupants of this offfice. Similarly, if the Prime Minister's party enjoys a clear-cut majority in Parliament and he has a hold on the party., he may assume dictatioral powers. Hence we can say that the position of the Prime Minister to a large extent depends on his personality and his hold on the party.

EXERCISES

Long Answer Type Questions:

1. Discuss Salient Features of Cabinet System.
2. Discuss the position of Prime Minister in the Council of Ministers.
3. Write a brief note on powers and functions of the Council of Ministers.

Short Answer Type Questions:

1. What do you know about the procedure of appointment of Ministers ?
2. What is meant by collective responsibility ?
3. What is difference between Council of Ministers and Cabinet ?
4. Write a brief note on ministerial responsibilities.
5. Write a brief note on Salient Features of India's Cabinet System.

Objective Type Questions:

Choose the correct answer

1. In which Article of the Indian Constitution is mentioned that there shall be a Council of Ministers with the Prime Minister as the head to aid and advise the President ?

   (*a*) Article 74 (1) (*b*) Article 75 (1)
   (*c*) Article 76 (1) (*d*) Article 77 (1)

2. By which Amendment the position of the Prime Minister has been made effective ?

   (*a*) 41st Amendment (*b*) 42nd Amendment
   (*c*) 43rd Amendment (*e*) 44th Amendment

3. By which Amendment a bid was made to restore some of the last prestige of the office of President ?

   (*a*) 42nd Amendment (*b*) 43rd Amendment
   (*c*) 44th Amendment (*d*) 45th Amendment

4. A main characteristic of the Cabinet system is :
   (*a*) inclusion of the President.
   (*b*) Leadership of the Prime Minister
   (*c*) Cabinet decision are not binding on all Ministers
   (*d*) all the above
5. How long is the tenure of the Prime Minister in India ?
   (*a*) 5 years.
   (*b*) So long as he is leader of the majority party in the Lok Sabha.
   (*c*) It depends on the President's direction
   (*d*) So long as he enjoys the confidence of the Lok Sabha.
6. Which of the following statements is not correct regarding the Prime Minister's position?
   (*a*) He presides over the meetings of Cabinet
   (*b*) He can remove any Minister who refuses to cooperate with him
   (*c*) He and his Ministers are responsible to the Lok Sabha
   (*d*) When the Prime Minister resigns, the seniormost minister in the Council of Ministers is appointed Prime Minister
7. The formation of the Council of Ministers starts with the appointment of :
   (*a*) the President (*b*) the Speaker
   (*c*) the Prime Minister (*d*) None of the above
8. The President can dismiss a member of the Council of Ministers :
   (*a*) on his own
   (*b*) on the recommendation of the Prime Minister
   (*c*) only under emergency conditions
   (*d*) with the consent of the Speaker
9. The meetings of the Council of Ministers are presided over by :
   (*a*) the President
   (*b*) the Vice-President
   (*c*) the Prime Minister
   (*d*) the members of the Council of Ministers by rotation
10. The Prime Minister is :
   (*a*) appointed by the President
   (*b*) appointed by the President on the recommendation of the Speaker of the Lok Sabha
   (*c*) elected by the Lok Sabha
   (*d*) elected by the Houses of Parliament
11. The office of the Prime Minister of India :
   (*a*) has a constitutional basis (*b*) has a statutory basis
   (*c*) has conventional basis (*d*) none of the above
12. The Prime Minister is :
   (*a*) the head of the state (*b*) head of the government
   (*c*) head of the Union Territories (*d*) None of the above

ANSWERS

1. (*a*)	2. (*b*)	3. (*c*)	4. (*b*)	5. (*d*)	6. (*d*)
7. (*c*)	8. (*b*)	9. (*b*)	10. (*a*)	11. (*a*)	12. (*b*)

Chapter 9

Vice-President

VICE-PRESIDENT

The Vice-President is the second highest office in the country. Its rank is next to the President in the official warrant of precedence. The form of this office is modelled on the lines of the American Vice-President.

ELECTION OF VICE-PRESIDENT

The Vice-President is elected not directly by the people but by the procedure of indirect election. He is elected by the members of an electoral college. This electoral college consists of the members of both Houses of Parliament. In this way this electoral college is totally different from the electoral college of the President in the following two respects:

1. The electoral college for Vice-President consists of both elected and nominated members of the Parliament, but in the case of President's election only elected members of the Parliament can participate in the election process.
2. In the election of Vice-President the members of the state legislative assemblies are not included but in the case of President's election the elected members of the state legislative assemblies are included.

   Explaining the reason for this difference, Dr. Ambedtar said "The President is the head of the State. His power extends both to the administration by the Centre as well as to the States. Consequently, it is compulsory that in his election, not only members of Parliament should play their role, but the members of the state legislatures should also have a role. But, when we come to the office of Vice-President, his normal functions are to preside over the Council of States or Rajya Sabja. It is only on a rare occasion that he may be called upon to assume the duties of the President. That being so, it does not seem necessary that the members of the state legislatures should also be included to take part in the election of the Vice-President".

But, the procedure of election is same in both the cases. Thus, the election of Vice-President is like that of the President's election. This election is held in accordance with the procedure of proportional representation by means of the single transferable vote system and the voting is by secret ballot.

Table 8.1 Elections of the Vive-Presidents (1952-2007)

Sl. No.	Election Year	Victorious Candidate	No. of Votes secured	Runner-up Candidate	No. of Votes secured
1.	1952	Dr. S. Radhakrishnan	—	Unopposed	—
2.	1957	Dr. S. Radhakrishnan	—	Unopposed	—
3.	1962	Dr. Zakir Husain	568	N. Samant Singh	14
4.	1967	V.V. Giri	486	Prof. Habib	192
5.	1969	G.S. Pathak	400	H.V. Kamath	156
6.	1974	B.D. Jatti	521	N.E. Horo	141
7.	1979	M. Hidayatullah	—	Unopposed	—
8.	1984	R. Venkataraman	508	B.C. Kambley	207
9.	1987	Dr. Shankar Dayal Sharma	—	Unopposed	—
10.	1992	K.R. Narayanan	700	Kaka Joginder Singh	01
11.	1997	Krishna Kant	441	Surjeet Singh Barnala	273
12.	2002	B.S. Shekhawat	454	Shushil Kumar Shinde	305
13.	2007	Mohd. Hamid Ansari	455	Najma Heptullah	222

Qualifications for the Post of Vice-President

To take part as a candidate for election as Vice-President, a person should fulfil the following qualifications:

1. He should be a citizen of India.
2. He should have completed 35 years of age.
3. He should be qualified for election as a member of the Rajya Sabha.
4. He should not hold any office of profit under the Union government or any state government or any local authority or any other public authority.

But, a sitting President or Vice-President of the Union, the Governor of any state and a minister for the Union or any state is not deemed to hold any office of profit and hence qualified for being a candidate for Vice-President.

The nomination of a candidate for election to the office of Vice-President must be supported by at least 20 electors as proposers and 20 electors as seconders. Every candidate has to make a security deposit of ₹ 15,000 in the Reserve Bank of India.

Oath

Before joining his office, the Vice-President has to make an oath. In his oath, the Vice-President swears:

1. to bear true faith and allegiance to the Constitution of India; and
2. to faithfully discharge the duties of his office.

The oath of office to the Vice-President is administered by the President or some person appointed in that behalf by him.

CONDITIONS OF OFFICE

According to Indian Constitution there are following two conditions of the Vice-President's office:

1. He should not be a member of either House of Parliament or a House of the State Legislature. If any such person is elected Vice-Presicent, he is deemed to have vacated his seat in that House on the date on which he joins his office as Vice-President.
2. He should not hold any other office of profit.

Term of Office

According to the Constitution, the Vice-President holds office for a period or term of five years from the date on which he Joins his office. In whatever manner he can resign from his office at any time by addressing his resignation letter to the President. He can also be removed from his office before completion of his term. There is no formal impeachment required for his removal. He can be removed from his post by only a resolution of the Rajya Sabha passed by an absolute majority (i.e., a majority of the total members of the House) and agreed to by the Lok Sabha. But, no such resolution can be moved unless at least 14 days' advance notice has been given. There is no ground mentioned in the Indian Constitution for his removal.

The Vice-President can hold office beyond his term of five years until his successor assumes charge. He is also eligible for re-election to that office. He may be elected for any number of terms.

Vacancy in the Vice-Presidents Office

A vacancy in the Vice-President's office can occur in any of the following conditions.

1. On the expiry of his term of five years.
2. In the condition of his resignation.
3. On his removal from the post
4. By his sudden death.
5. Otherwise, when he becomes disqualified to hold office or when his election is declared void.

When the vacancy is going to be caused by the expiration of the term of the sitting vice-president, an election to fill the post must be held before the expiration of the term.

If the office falls vacant by resignation, removal, death or otherwise, then election to fill the vacancy should be held as soon as possible after the occurrence of the vacancy. The newly-elected Vice-President remains in office for a full term of five years from the date he assumes charge of his office.

ELECTION DISPUTES ABOUT VICE-PRESIDENT

All disputes in connection with election of the Vice-President are inquired into and decided by the Supreme Court of India. The decision of the Supreme Court will be final. The election of a person as Vice-President cannot be challenged on the ground that the electoral college was incomplete. If the election of a person as Vice-President is declared void by the Supreme Court, acts done by him before the date of such declaration of the Supreme Court are not invalidated. They continue to remain in force.

POWERS AND FUNCTIONS OF VICE-PRESIDENT

The powers and functions of Vice-President are as follows:

1. According to the Constitution of India the Vice-President of India a the *ex-officio* Chairman of Rajya Sabha, so he acts as the *ex-officio* Chairman of Rajya Sabha. As an *ex-officio* Chairman of Rajya Sabha his powers and functions are same as those of the Speaker of Lok Sabha. In this respect, he resembles the Vice-President of America. The Vice-President of America also acts as the Chairman of the Senate—the Upper House of the American legislature.

2. The Vice-President of India acts as President also when a vacancy occurs in the office of the President due to his sudden resignation or removal from the post or death or otherwise. He can act as President only for a limited period of six months within which a new President has to be elected. Further, when the sitting President is unable to discharge his functions due to absence, illness or any other cause, the Vice-President discharges all his functions until the President resumes his office.

While acting as President the Vice-President does not perform the duties of the office of the Chairman of Rajya Sabha. During this period, those duties are performed by the Deputy Chairman of Rajya Sabha.

COMPARISON OF INDIAN AND AMERICAN VICE-PRESIDENTS

Though the form of the office of the Indian Vice-President is modelled on the lines of the American Vice-President but there is too much difference also. The American Vice-President succeeds to the presidency when it falls vacant, and remains President for the unexpired term of his predecessor. The Indian Vice-President, on the other hand, does not assume the office of the President when it falls vacant for the unexpired term. He merely serves as an acting President until the new President assumes charge.

From the above description it is clear that the Constitution has not assigned any important function to the Vice-President in that capacity. Therefore, some scholars of Political Science call him 'His Superfluous Highness'. Actually this office was created with a view to maintain the political continuity of the Indian State.

Emoluments

The Constitution has not fixed any emoluments for the Vice-President in that capacity. He draws his regular salary in his capacity as the *ex-officio* Chairman of the Rajya Sabha. On 11th September, 2008, the Parliament increased the salary of the Chairman of the Rajya Sabha to Rs 1,25,000 per month. In addition, he is entitled to daily allowance, free furnished residence, medical, travel and other facilities.

During any period when the Vice-President acts as President or discharges the functions of the President, he is not entitled to the salary or allowance payable to the Chairman of Rajya Sabha, but the salary and allowance of the President.

PRESIDENT VS. VICE-PRESIDENT

There are so many dissimilarities and similarities between President and Vice-Presidents of India. Some of them are as follows:

DISSIMILARITIES

President

1. The President is elected by an electoral college, consisting of elected members of Parliament and State Legislative Assemblies.
2. The candidate should have qualification for election as a member of the Lok Sabha.
3. Can be removed from office by impeachment in the manner prescribed in Article 61 of the Indian Constitution.
4. Responsible to run the executive action of the Union with the advice of Council of Ministers.
5. Salary drawn— ₹ 1,50,00 per month.
6. He could give his resignation to the Vice-President.

Vice-President

1. The Vice-President is elected by the members of the two Houses of Parliament, but members of State Legislative Assemblies do not participate in this election.
2. Should have the qualification for election as a member of the Rajya Sabha.
3. Can be removed by the Rajya Sabha through a resolution passed by 2/3rd majority of its members and likewise agreed to by the Lok Sabha.
4. No specific functions. The Vice-President is the ex-officio Chairman of the Rajya Sabha. His salary is 1,25,000 per months as ex-officio Chairman of the Rajya Sabha.

Similarities

1. Rest of the qualifications are same for candidates.
2. Both are elected through the system of proportional representation and by means of single transferable vote system.
3. The tenure is 5 years for both.
4. No specific functions. The Vice-President is the ex-officio Chairman of the Rajya Sabha. He discharges the functions of the office of President in case that post falls vacant.
5. Salary drawn is ₹ 1,25,000 per month as an ex-officio Chairman of the Rajya Sabha.
6. He could give his resignation to the President.

EXERCISES

Long Answer Type Questions:

1. Write a detailed note on Vice-President of India.
2. What is the procedure of election of Vice-President? Discuss in brief.

Short Answer Type Questions:

1. What are the qualifications for the post of Vice-President? Discuss in brief.
2. What do you know about the oath procedure and conditions of office of Vice-President of India?
3. What is the term of office of Vice-President ? Discuss in brief.
4. Write a short note on powers and functions of Vice-President.
5. What is the provision in Indian Constitution to settle the election disputes of Vice-President?

Objective Type Questions :

1. How is the Vice-President of India elected ?
   (*a*) By an electoral college consisting of the elected members of the Lok Sabha.
   (*b*) By an electoral college consisting of the elected members of both Houses of Parliament and the State Assemblies
   (*c*) By an electoral college consisting of the members of both Houses of Parliament
   (*d*) By the people directly
2. The Vice-President acts as the President of India when the President is:
   (*a*) unable to discharge his functions (*b*) ill
   (*c*) absent (*d*) all the three given cases
3. The Vice-President of India is:
   (a) Chairman (ex-officio) of the Lok Sabha

(*b*) Ex-officio Chairman of the Rajya Sabha
(*c*) Speaker of the Lok Sabha
(*d*) President of the Red Cross

4. When the Vice-President is acting as President he:
(*a*) will have all the powers and functions of both the President and Vice-President
(*b*) gets all the allowances and privileges of the President
(*c*) should continue to work as the Chairman of the Rajya Sabha
(*d*) All the above

5. During which one of the following situations does the Vice-President not discharge the functions of the President?
(*a*) When the President falls ill
(*b*) When the President vacates office
(*c*) When the President dies
(*d*) When the President has been suspended

6. The office of the Vice-President:
(*a*) has been created by the Constitution
(*b*) has been created by a Parliamentary law
(*c*) is an extra-constitutional provision
(*d*) None of the above

7. Which one of the following qualifications for the office of the Vice-President is incorrect?
(*a*) He must be a citizen of India
(*b*) He must be a member of the Rajya Sabha
(c) He must be over 35 years of age
(*d*) None of the above

8. The Vice-President is elected for a term of:
(*a*) 5 years (*b*) indefinite period (*c*) 6 years (*d*) 4 years

9. The Vice-President of India can be removed from his office before the expiry of his term:
(*a*) by the President
(*b*) by the Central Council of Ministers
(*c*) by the President on the recommendation of the Supreme Court of India
(*d*) by the Rajya Sabha through a resolution passed by two-thirds majority and agreed to by the Lok Sabha

10. The Vice-President of India holds office
(*a*) during the pleasure of the President
(*b*) for a term of four years
(*c*) for a term of five years
(*d*) for a term which is decided at the. time of his appointment by the Parliament

11. Regarding the re-election of the Vice-President our
(*a*) Constitution is absolutely silent
(*b*) Constitution places a clear ban
(*c*) Constitution prescribes re-election only once
(*d*) Constitution prescribes re-election for a maximum period of two terms

12. Which one of the following is not a function of the Vice-President as ex-officio Chairman of the Rajya Sabha?
    (*a*) He presides over the meetings of the Rajya Sabha and conducts its business
    (*b*) He protects the privileges of the members of the Rajya Sabha
    (*c*) He dissolves the Rajya Sabha
    (*d*) He acts as the spokesman of Rajya Sabha before the President and the Lok Sabha
13. On the death of the President the Vice-President succeeds him as President for
    (*a*) the remaining period of the term (*b*) a maximum period of six months
    (*c*) a maximum period of one year (*d*) a maximum period of three years
14. The monthly salary of the Vice-Presidenl of India as Vice-President is
    (*a*) ₹ 14,500 (*b*) ₹ 25,000 (*c*) ₹ 50,000 (*d*) ₹ 1,25,000
15. The Vice-Presidenl of India is:
    (*a*) a member of either House of Parliament (*b*) a member of Rajya Sabha
    (c) a separate wing of the Parliament (*d*) not a member of Parliament
16. When the Vice-President acts as President:
    (*a*) the Rajya Sabha has to elect another Chairman
    (*b*) the post of Chairman of Rajya Sabha must remain vacant
    (*c*) the Speaker of Lok Sabha presides over Rajya Sabha sitting
    (*d*) None of the above happens
17. Which of the following is/are correct?
    I. No formal impeachment is required for the removal of the Vice-President
    II. No functions are attached to the office of the Vice-President as such
    III. Dispute regarding election of Vice-President is referred to the Election Commission
    IV. If the election of a President or the Vice-President is declared void, acts done by him prior to the date of such decision shall be invalidated
    (*a*) I, II, III (*b*) I, III, and IV (*c*) I and II (*d*) All four

ANSWERS

1. (*c*) 2. (*d*) 3. (*b*) 4. (*b*) 5. (*d*) 6. (*a*) 7. (*b*) 8. (*a*) 9. (*d*)
10. (*c*) 11. (*a*) 12. (*c*) 13. (*b*) 14. (*d*) 15. (d) 16. (*a*) 17. (*c*)

10

CHAPTER

Union Parliament

The Federal Legislature in India is known as Parliament. It consists of the President and two Houses known respectively as the Council of States (Rajya Sabha) and the House of People (Lok Sabha). While the Rajya Sabha contains representatives of the states of the Indian Union, the Lok Sabha is a popular House and contains representatives of the people. The President of India is also an integral part of the Indian Parliament although he is not a member of either of the two Houses. However, he discharges numerous legislative functions and plays an important role in the working of the Parliament.

Indian Parliament Compared with the British Parliament. Union Parliament is often compered with the British Parliament but in fact there is a world of difference in their scope of powers. The British Parliament is a Sovereign Legislature whereas ours is not. *Dicey* said, "*Legally the British Parliament is so omnipotent that it can adjudge an infant of full age, it may attain a man of treason after death; it may legitimize an illegitimate child or if it sees fit, make a man judge in his own case.*" Compared with this unique and gigantic stature of the British Parliament, the Indian Parliament is a weak and small fry. Its powers are considerably limited by constitutional checks and Fundamental Rights guaranteed to the citizens. An Act by the British Parliament cannot be challenged in a court of law. No court can declare a British law as unconstitutional. The British Parliament enacts, revokes or amends its constitutional practices with utmost ease and facility. Such a thing is impossible in India where the Parliament has to uphold the sanctity of the Constitution which can be changed by a highly complicated procedure. The powers of the Union Parliament are further restricted by the judicial review of the Supreme Court. A Union Law if it violates the Constitution can be declared invalid and so it becomes inoperative.

The Bicameral Legislature is found in practice in England, France, Belgium, Austria, Canada, U.S.A., Japan, Germany, Australia and Russia also.

COUNCIL OF STATES

Composition. Rajya Sabha or the Council of States is the Upper House of the Union Parliament. The maximum strength of the House according to Constitution can at any time be 250; in 2004, its strength was 245. 238 members of the House were elected by the Legislative Assemblies of the States and Union Territories by the system of proportional representation. The remaining 12 were nominated by the President to represent literature, art, science and social service. The elected members represent the constituent units of the States. States are represented not uniformly but in proportion to their respective population. A different practice is observed in America where the States, be they big or small, are given equal representation in the Senate. There are 50 States and each sends two representatives to the Senate in U.S.A. In India some Union Territories have not been given representation.

Representation of States in Rajya Sabha (Council of States) (2004)

State	*Number of members*	*State*	*Number of members*
Andhra Pradesh	18	Uttar Pradesh	31
Assam	7	West Bengal	16
Bihar	16	Nagaland	1
Gujarat	11	Himachal Pradesh	3
Jammu & Kashmir	4	Meghalaya	1
Kerala	9	Manipur	1
Madhya Pradesh	11	Tripura	1
Tamil Nadu	18	Sikkim	1
Maharashtra	19	Mizoram	1
Karnataka	12	Arunachal Pradesh	1
Orissa	10	Goa	1
Punjab	7	Jharkhand	6
Haryana	5	Chhattisgarh	5
Rajasthan	10	Uttarakhand	3
		Union Territories	
		Delhi	3
		Pondicherry (Puducheri)	1
		Nominated by President	12
			245

Qualifications for Members. A candicate is eligible for election to the Rajya Sabha if he possesses the following qualifications:

(*a*) He is a citizen of India;

(*b*) He has completed 30 years of age; and

(*c*) He possesses such other qualifications as may be prescribed by Parliament. According to the Representation of the People Act, 1951, a candidate for election to the Rajya Sabha must be a parliamentry elector in the State from which he seeks election.

Rajya Sabha is a semi-permanent House. Its duration is six years. It is considered permanent because it cannot be dissolved by the President. Every member is elected for six years but one-third of its members retire after every two years.

Officials of Rajya Sabha. The Vice-President of India is ex-officio Chairman of this House. He draws a salary ₹ 1, 25,000/- plus other allowances per month. Rajya Sabha elects a Deputy Chairman also. Whenever a vacancy is created by death, resignation, removal by impeachment, or long illness in the office of the President, the Vice-President takes over the charge for a maximum period of six months. When he acts in the capacity of the President, he enjoys all the privileges of the latter's office.

When the Vice-President acts as President, he ceases to be the Chairman of Rajya Sabha. He can be removed by a resolution of Rajya Sabha, agreed upon by the Lok Sabha. He is not entitled to preside or exercise his vote when the issue of his removal is under discussion in the Rajya Sabha. The Deputy Chairman in that case occupies the chair and conducts the proceedings. The Vice-President during such a discussion has a right to speak and take part in the proceedings. A resolution for removal of the Chairman requires the support of two-third members of the House. The Deputy Chairman can also be removed by the same process. His removal does not require the assent of the Lok Sabha. No resolution regarding the removal of the Vice-President can be discussed in the House unless preceded by an advance notice of 14 days. Both the Chairman and Deputy Chairman are paid from the Consolidated Fund of India. The function of the Chairman is to conduct the proceedings of the House, to enforce discipline, to allow the members to speak and to declare the result after voting.

Quorum. No siting of the House can take place unless one-tenth of the total members of the House are present.

Privileges and Immunities of the Members. The Chairman and Deputy Chairman of the House enjoy the same privileges and immunities as are enjoyed by the members of Lok Sabha. A member of Rajya Sabha enjoys freedom of expression in the House. He cannot be tried in any court of law for any speech made by him on the floor of the House. Besides this immunity, he also cannot be arrested in any criminal case 40 days before the beginning of a session and 40 days after the last siting of the House.

Note. The relations between two Houses of Parliament have been described in the later pages.

LOK SABHA (HOUSE OF THE PEOPLE)

Composition. The Lower House of the Union Parliament is called the House of the People or the Lok Sabha. The strength of elected members of the 15th Lok Sabha is 545. Out of the total figure, 543 members are elected directly from the territorial constituencies in the States on the basis of adult franchise. Any person who has attained the age of 18 and is not otherwise disqualified by law is entitled to vote. The remaining two seats are filled by nominations by the President in order to give representation to the Anglo-Indians.

Reservation of Seats for the Scheduled Castes and Scheduled Tribes extended up to 2026 A.D.

109th Constitution Amendment Bill 2009 was passed by Rajya Sabha on 3rd August, 2009 and Lok Sabha on 4th August, 2009 and ratified by the legislatures of not less than one-half of the States, and assented to on 18th January, 2010.

The Bill is now known as the Constitution (Ninety-fifth Amendment) Act 2009.

Through this amendment in Article 334 of the Constitution, for the words "sixty years" the words "seventy years" shall be substituted.

This Article has sought to extend the reservation of seats for SCs and STs in the Lok Sabha and State Assembles by another 10 years. The time period of 60 years under Article 334 of the constitution was to lapse on January 25, 2010 and this Bill extends the reservation beyond January 25, 2010.

Qualifications for the Membership of Lok Sabha. The Constitution requires the following qualifications for becoming a member of the Lok Sabha:

(*a*) He is a citizen of India.

(*b*) He is not below 25 years of age.

(*c*) He possesses such other qualifications as may be prescribed for that purpose by the Parliament.

A person is disqualified from being elected to the Lok Sabha if (1) he holds any office of profit under the Union or a State Government; (2) he is of unsound mind and declared so by a competent court; (3) he is an insolvent; (4) he has acquired the citizenship of any foreign State; (5) he is otherwise disqualified according to any law of the land.

Tenure. The life of Lok Sabha is ordinarily five years which can be extended by a Parliamentary Act for one year at a time during the operation of a Proclamation of Emergency. The maximum period of extension in no case can exceed three years. The Lok Sabha can be dissolved even before the expiry of five years by the President at the request of the Prime Minister. Such an occasion as this arises when the Prime Minister loses the confidence of the Lok Sabha but hopes to retrieve his position after the mid-term general elections as happened with the 9th Lok Sabha.

Quorum. The quorum for any sitting of the Lok Sabha is one-tenth members of the total strength. Any decision taken in a meetting attended by less than fifty members is deemed to be illegal.

Privileges of the Members of the Lok Sabha. The members of the Lok Sabha enjoy certain privileges and immunites. They have absolute freedom of speech in the Lok Sabha and they cannot be tried in any court of law for any remark made by them on the floor of the House. They cannot be arrested in connection with any civil proceedings against them during the session and forty days before and after a session. The Speaker protects the members against any infringement of their privileges.

SPEAKER AND DEPUTY SPEAKER OF THE LOK SABHA

The Lok Sabha has two officers–the Speaker and the Deputy Speaker. They are elected by the members from amongst themselves. They act as the presiding officers. Normally the Prime Minister through an understanding with the leaders of the opposition parties secures unanimous election of both the officers. The Speaker generally hails from the ruling party, while the Deputy Speaker may be selected from the opposition benches if the ruling party agrees. This practice is in common with the British system but different from the practice in Amercia where the Speaker is seldom elected unopposed. The Speaker in a Parliamentary government occupies a unique position. He breaks away with his party temporarily in order to do justice to his office. He rises above party politics and becomes immune form party discipline.

Tenure and Method of Removal of Speaker and the Deputy Speaker. If a Speaker or a Deputy Speaker is unseated by the Supreme Court or because of any other reason ceases to be a member of Lok Sabha, he has to vacate his office. The Speaker can also resign at any time by addressing his resignation letter under his hand to the Deputy Speaker and *vice versa.* Both or either of them can be removed by a resolution of the House. However, a notice of 14 days is required to be given for moving such a resolution. If the Lok Sabha is dissolved, the Speaker does not vacate his office until the first meeting of the newly elected House. The Speaker or the Deputy Speaker, as the case may be, does not preside while a resolution for his removal is under consideration. In the absence of the Speaker his duties are performed by the Deputy Speaker and in the absence of both, such person occupies the chair as might be appointed by the President. While a resolution for the removal of the Speaker or Deputy Speaker is under discussion, both have the right to attend the sitting and vote also but if there is a tie, none can exercise his casting vote. The Speaker is entitled to a monthly salary of ₹ 1,25,000/- according to the Salaries and Allowances of Office of Parliament Act, 2008 as amended.

Powers and Functions of the Speaker : (1) The Speaker presides over the meetings of the Lok Sabha and conducts all its proceedings except when the resolution for his removal is under consideration; (2) He determines the order of business and prescribes the time limit for the speeches which are invariably addressed to him; (3) He maintains order and discipline in the House. He prevents the use of unparliamentary language in the House. If a person disregards or flouts his ruling, he can name him for suspension or ask him to leave the House or order his physical removal by the Marshal of the House; (4) If the House becomes unmanageable and the members unruly, he can suspend the business of the House; (5) He enforces the rules of conduct, counts the votes and declares the result ; (6) He gives his ruling whether a Bill is a Money Bill or not; (7) When a Bill is finally adopted by both the Houses, he puts his signature on it; (8) He gives his ruling whether a resolution or question is admissible or not; (9) During the joint sitting of both the Houses, he occupies the Chair; (10) He protects the members against infringement of their privileges; (11) Ordinarliy he does not vote but when the House is divided equally on any issue, he exercises casting vote; (12) He acts as the spokesman of the House; (13) He is authorised to decide whether an adjournment motion moved by a member is admissible or not; (14) He regulates the admission of visitors into the House. He can ask the visitors to leave the gallery if they prove noisy; (15) He gives his rulings–which are final—on the controversial points of procedure.

POSITION OF THE INDIAN SPEAKER AND HIS COMPARISON WITH THE SPEAKER OF ENGLAND AND U.S.A.

The Speaker of the House of Representatives occupies a position of great significance and prestige in U.S.A. He ranks seventh in the hierarchy of the county and is bracketed with the Chief Justice of the Supreme Court. The Indian Speaker occupies the same position as does the Speaker of the British House of Commons. *Mr. Bryce* remarks : "*From the moment the man occupies the chair of the Speaker in the House of Commons he is expected to shake off and leave behind all parties. Once invested with the wig and gown of office, he has no longer any political opinion and must administer exactly the same treatment to the political friends and opponents.*" Not only within the House, even outside he abstains from any political activity. He does not speak from the party platform nor attends the party meetings, so much so that he does not even canvass or campaign for his re-election. He remains impartial, a no-party man till he holds his office. The Speaker of the Amercian House of Representatives, however, does not give up his party affiliations. He remains attached with the majority group which votes him to that office. He exhibits his partisan spirit even in the discharge of his duties. Right or wrong, he sides with his party.

The position of the Indian Speaker is similar neither to that of the British Speaker who is completely divorced from politics nor to that of Amercian Speaker who remains an active party man. The Indian Speaker does break away from the party but simply ceases to take any active part in party activities. He feels the pulse of the whole House and tries to give adequate opportunities to the opposition benches for their points of view.

Mr. Purushottam Das Tandon, at one time the Speaker of U.P. Assembly, declared that the Speaker in India need not necessarily walk on the footprints of his British counterpart. He may act as a non-party man in the House and retain his party affiliations outside. Similar were the views of Mr. G.V. Mavalankar, the first Speaker of free India. He maintained, "*The Speaker in India is not today absolutely out of political arena as is the Speaker of the British House of Commons.... For the present the Speaker must continue to be a politician though with very extensive limitations of his activities. He may continue to be a member of his party but he should not take part in the affairs of the party, particularly in regard to matters which are likely to come before the House for discussion and decision. We have also considered it proper that he should not take side in public controversies in respect of matters likely to come before the House. In short, he should not identify with any propaganda or express any opinion which are likely to embarrass his position as the presiding authority or are likely to create an impression that the Speaker is a partisan.*" This is precisely the reason why the Indian Speaker does not command the same position as his British counterpart. On 18th December, 1954, a motion of no-confidence was moved in the Lok Sabha aganist Mr.G.V. Mavalankar. Although the motion was rejected by a voice vote, yet it clearly reflected on the position of Indian Speaker. Convention relating to upopposed re-election of the Speaker has also been established in India so far. Once Mr. Chetty had been defeated by a Congress candidate. This set a bad precedent for the future. During the third General Elections, the opposition parties put candidates aganist the Speaker, Mr. Ayyangar, and Deputy Speaker, Sardar Hukum Singh. Notwithstanding such unhealthy practices, the office of the Speaker is quite a dignified one. In the words of late Pt. Jawaharlal Nehru, " *The Speaker represents the dignity of the House and because the House represents the nation in a particular way, the Speaker becomes the symbol of the nation's liberty and freedom. Therefore, it is right that it should be an honoured position , a free position and should be occupied always by men of outstanding ability and impartiality.*"

Role of Indian Speaker. *Former Speaker tells Government of India to act firmly; concern over Bhindranwale's statement.* On 1st December 1983 a false despatch from a news agency created a crisis in the Punjab that a gurdwara had been burnt down in Churu (Rajasthan). Actualy there was no gurdwara in the village and the report was baseless. A minor fire outside a building had been wrongly described as a fire in a gurdwara. Sant Bhindranwale, while reacting to this report, threatened slaughter of the Hindus in Punjab. He gave this explosive statement at a Press conference on 1st December, 1983.

Members from all sections of the Lok Sabha on December 2, 1983, unequivocally condemned the staement of Sant Bhindranwale threatening the massacre of all Hindus in Punjab and bluntly told the government to either muster enough courage to arrest him for endangering national security or quit.[1]

The Sant's explosive statment roused the passions of members from several political parties who, in a rare show of solidarity, asked the government to shed its fears and act decisively.

Echoing the sentiments of the members, the then Speaker, Mr. Balram Jakhar, who hails from Punjab, told Home Minister Prakash Chandra Sethi that he should act firmly. "There is a serious danger to the country, you would have to do something," the Speaker said.

Mr. Balram Jakhar did some plain speaking when he told Mr. Prakash Chandra Sethi that this development was too serious to be ignored by anyone. "The more you are afraid, the more critical the situation will become. You have to face the situation," he told the Home Minister amidst thumping of desks.[2]

Not only that the Speaker does his routine work, he leads the Parliamentary delegations to foreign countries when the House is not in session. He highlights the achievements of our country there and brightens the image. So the Speaker plays a noble role in the parliamentary life of our country.

POWERS AND MUTUAL RELATIONS OF LOK SABHA AND RAJYA SABHA

Powers of Indian Parliament. The Parliament is not a sovereign body because sovereignty finally vests in the Constitution. The Constitution provides the irrevocable standards to which every Parliamentary Act must conform. Any Act in contravention of any provision of the Act is declared *ultra vires* by the Supreme Court. Moreover, the scope of law-making powers of the Parliament is further limited by the distribution of powers between the Union and the States. As a federal legislature it can legislate only on subjects mentioned in the Union List. It acquires authority to make law on a State subject only during the period of emergency or when the State legislature by a resolution supported by two-thirds majority of the House requests the Parliament to legislate on any State subjects. The Union Parliament possesses simultaneous right with the States to make laws on Concurrent subjects.

1. Balram Jakhar quoted in the *Indian Express*, Chandigargh, dated 3rd December, 1983, p.1, cols. 2-3.
2. *Ibid.*

The Parliament exercises a measure of control over the Council of Ministers and the Union Budget. It has also the right to amend the Constituion, impeach the President and remove the Judges of the Supreme Court and High Courts, Comptroller and Auditor-General and Chief Election Officer.

Relation between the two Houses on Money Bills. The powers of Lok Sabha and the Rajya Sabha over Money Bills are not equal. The Lok Sabha enjoys real supremacy over the Upper House because it controls the purse of the nation. It is definitely provided that a Money Bill will originate only in the Lok Sabha. Money Bill is presented before the House either by the Finance Minister or any other Minister in his absence. Money Bills generally relate to imposition, remission, alteration or regulation of any tax. After being passed by the Lok Sabha it is transmitted to Rajya Sabha for its recommendation. Such a Bill has to be returned to Lok Sabha within a period of 14 days along with recommendations. The Lok Sabha if it so desires accepts any or all the recommendations. It may even refuse to accept any. In either case the Bill is deemed to have been passed by both the Houses. The position and power of Rajya Sabha with regard to Money Bills is no better than that of the British House of Lords. The American Senate, however, is more powerful in this respect. It can make changes in the Bills sent to it by the House of Representatives.

Relation of Lok Sabha and Rajya Sabha Regarding Non-Money Bills. With regard to Ordinary Bill the powers of both the Houses are coordinate and equal. These can be presented in either House by any Member. In the case of a deadlock between the Houses, the President can call a joint meeting of both the Houses to resolve and iron out the differences. Such joint sittings are presided over by the Speaker of Lok Sabha. The Lok Sabha has definitely the advantage of its superior strength. It has the facility to impose its will on the Rajya Sabha. Thus in Non-Money Bills also, the position of Rajya Sabha is not so strong.

Control over the Executive. Lok Sabha in respect of control over the Executive is also more fortunate than the other House. The Council of Ministers owes collective responsibility to Lok Sabha and not to Rajya Sabha. This practice of tightening the hold of the People's House over the Executive is in vogue in West Germany, France, Sweden, Norway, Denmark and a few other countries. In England also, the members of the House of Lords can put questions and thus embarrass or corner the Ministers but have no power to dismiss a Minister. Removal of a Minister by censure or no-confidence motion is the prerogative of only the House of Commons. Similar is the case in India. Only Lok Sabha can entertian censure or no-confidence motions aganist the Government. It can also set up an enquiry committee to look into the charges of corruption in any department.

Other Functions and Powers of Lok Sabha and Rajya Sabha. Both the Houses of Parliament take part in the election of the President and Vice-President. Their powers to remove the President by impeachment are also equal. If the Rajya Sabha decides to remove its Chairman, who also happens to be the Vice-President of India, it has to seek the approval of the Lok Sabha. In the removal of the Judges of Supreme Court and High Courts and also in the removal of Chief Election Officer, Comptroller and Auditor General and Regional Election Commissioner, both Houses enjoy equal powers.

Utility of Rajya Sabha. It is evident from the aforesaid point that its vital function is to check and delay any hasty legislation by the Lower House. Prof. Jatindra Nath Ranjan remarks about our Rajya Sabha: *"It is not all too powerful a body like the U.S. Senate nor only a dilatory body like the British House of Lords and the French Council of Republics. Virtual veto power over legislation like that of the Japanese system has not been accepted in our Constitution. It is given only substantial revisory power, not equal powers over legislation.... It does not and should not require more than that because in democracy popular will ultimately prevails. The Council of States is not only the best constituted second Chamber in the world, it is also the most well-balanced in its power to fit in modern democracy and to serve the constitutional purpose which a second Chamber in democracy is required to perform in the best possible manner."*

Although the states are not represented uniformly in Rajya Sabha, yet no charge regarding any variation in the representation of any State in the Parliament of the division of subjects between the Union and States can be made without its approval. If in national interest Lok Sabha intends to legislate on any State subject, it can do so only with the approval of Rajya Sabha. Moreover, when the President dissolves Lok Sabha, Rajya Sabha being a permanent House does not break up. The President, then, has to seek the approval of Rajya Sabha regarding his order for the Proclamation of Emergency. Thus the second House justifies its existence and utility by revising the hasty legislation of Lok Sabha, by safeguarding the interests of the States and also by exercising its influence on the Proclamations of Emergency.

POWERS AND LIMITATIONS OF PARLIAMENT

Legislative Powers. The Union Parliament is certainly not a sovereign law-making body. It cannot amend the Constitution as easily as the British Parliament can do. Its function is merely to enact, change or invalidate ordinary law. Lok Sabha ordinarily is not authorised to touch State subjects except when Rajya Sabha by a two-thirds majority authorises it to do so by declaring that the matter has become of national importance and interest. The President can also confer upon it the right to legislate on State subjects during Emergency.

Every Bill passed by the Parliament is sent to the President for his assent. The President either gives his assent or withholds it or sends it back with his recommendations for reconsideration. A procedural deadlock may arise when the President does not return the Bill with his assent or dissent but simply sleeps over it . Ordinarily such a situation should not arise because such a step is not likely to serve any purpose. Such a situation so far has not arisen in India. The British Queen in theory possesses the power to refuse to sign a Bill but we know that such a right has never been exercised so far.

Control over the Finance. The Parliament has absolute control over the purse of the nation. No new tax can be levied or expenditure incurred without its consent. The Cabinet presents before it an estimated account of income and expenditure for the financial year on 31st March. The Parliament discusses it item by item and approves it . The limitations on its financial powers are that it has no right to vote on the Consolidated Fund of India and secondly, it cannot initiate a Money Bill or a demand for grant.

Executive Powers. The Parliament exercises fair measure of control over the day-to-day activities of the Council of Ministers. It commands the collective responsibility of the Ministers. By putting questions the Parliament keeps the Executive alert and clean. The members also discuss matters of urgent public importance by moving call-attention notices and adjournment motions. They sometimes censure the Government for its faults. In extreme cases they compel the Government to resign by expressing their want of confidence in the Executive.

Miscellaneous Powers. The Parliament can amend certain provisions of the Constitution by a specified majority without seeking the approval of the States. *It can remove the President or Vice-President and lastly its voice counts effectively with regard to emergency powers of the President.*

Limitations of its Powers. The Parliament of India as told above is *not a law-making body* as the British Parliament. In India, too, as in other federations of the world, the Constitution is supreme and inviolate. It is the highest law of the land. The Parliament's power to amend the Constitution is also not absolute. It has to consult the States in amending certain provisions. Secondly, if any Act passed by it conflicts with the Constitution, it can be declared *ultra vires* or unconstitutional by the Supreme Court. The power of the Supreme Court to conduct judicial review is also a great fetter on the power of the Parliament. Thirdly, no law passed by it can become an Act unless assented to by the President. Fourthly, the Parliament itself is brushed aside for a little period of two months during Emergency when the President assumes all the legislative and executive powers. Lastly, its powers over the financial matters are also considerably restricted. It can discuss but not vote the expenditure charged on the Consolidated Fund of India. A Money Bill cannot be moved even in the Lok Sabha by any private member. In fact the principle of sovereignty of Parliament does not harmonise with federal system.

PROCEDURE OF PASSING MONEY BILL (BUDGET)

The chief function of the Parliament is to make, revise or abrogate laws for the country. The Bills introduced in and passed by the Parliament are of two types–Money Bills and Non-Money or Ordinary Bills. A Money Bill is passed by a procedure quite distinct from that of an Ordinary Bill.

Meaning of Money Bills. It has already been stated that a Money Bill relates to imposition, abolition or remission of any tax. A Bill relating to addition or to withdrawal from the Consolidated or Contingency Fund is also called a Money Bill. In cases of doubt whether a Bill is or is not a Money Bill, the Speaker of Lok Sabha is empowered to give his ruling.

A Money Bill can originate only in the Lok Sabha or the House of People. The Constitution lays down that in the beginning of every financial year, an Annual Financial Statement or the Budget showing the estimated receipts and expenditures shall be laid before the Parliament. In order to prepare this statement the Finance Minister obtains the figures from other Ministers incharge of various portfolios. The Union Budget is presented in two parts–Railway Budget and the General Budget. The first is presented by the Minister for Railways. The General Budget is presented by the Finance Minister. The procedure of passing both types of budget is identical.

Although our system of considering the Budget has been borrowed from England, yet it is slight different. In England the Budget is considered in committees of the whole House of Commons. Such committees are presided over not by the Speaker of the House but by the Chairman of that committee. Budget in India is discussed by the whole House with the Speaker in the Chair. The Budget shows separately the expenditure charged on the Consolidated Fund of India and the sums required to meet other expenditure proposed to be made from the Consolidated Fund of India .

Expenditure Charged on the Consolidated Fund of India. The following expenditure comes under the charged account: (1) Emoluments and allowances of President and other expenditure relating to his office. (2) Salaries and allowances of the Chairman and Deputy Chairman of the Rajya Sabha and the Speaker and Deputy Speaker of the Lok Sabha. (3) Debt charges,for which the Government of India is liable, including interest, sinking fund charges and redemption charges, etc. (4) Salaries, allowances and pensions payable to or in respect of the Comptroller and Auditor-General of India. (5) Salaries, allowances and pensions of the Judges of the Supreme Court, the Federal Court of India. (6) Any sum required to satisfy any judgment, decree or award of any court or Arbitration Tribunal. (7) Any other expenditure declared by the Constitution or by Parliament to be so changed.

Items charged on the Consolidated Fund of India can be discussed but not voted upon in any House of the Parliament. No demand for grant under this head can be reduced or rejected.

Non-Charged Expenditure. The other expenditure proposed to be met from the Consolidated Fund is presented in form of demand for grants. This is called non-charged expenditure. The general discussion on these demands begins after the address to the Lok Sabha by the Finance Minister who in his speech discusses the financial position of the country and expounds the financial policy of the Government. The demands for grants are discussed thoroughly by the Parliament and submitted to vote.

The General Budget Debate. The budget speech by the Finance Minister is followed by discussions on the Budget as a whole. Neither the details of expenditure are discussed nor proposals for token cuts made. The general discussion which lasts for a couple of days provides an opportunity to the Opposition leaders to denounce the fiscal policy of the Government. According to *Mr. Morries Jones, "It is an occasion on which each House is able to express its mood and the Government may learn how a particular proposal will be received in the subsequent stages."* After general discussion is over, the Lok Sabha proceeds to the voting of demands. The House may assent to any demand.

refuse it or reduce it. The private members have no right to propose any new demand or any increase in expenditure on any head. The Executive has exclusive sway over the financial matters.

Appropriation Bill. When all the demands have been voted by the Lok Sabha, both the charged and non-charged expenditure are put together and incorporated in a Bill called the Annual Appropriation Bill. It is presented before and passed by the Lok Sabha in the same manner as any other Bill. Then it is certified by the Speaker as a Money Bill and sent to the Rajya Sabha for recommendation. The Rajya Sabha cannot reject or amend the Bill and has to send it back within 14 days. Lastly, the Bill receives the assent of the President to become an Act.

Finance Bill. A Finance Bill is presented along with the Budget. It relates to levying of new taxes or enhancing or reducing the existing taxes The House can pass, reject or reduce the estimate but has no right to increase it. The financial proposals become operative immediately after their presentation in Lok Sabha. A Finance Bill has to be passed or rejected before the end of April. If passed, it is sent to Rajya Sabha which has to return it within 14 days along with its recommendations which are in no case binding on the Lok Sabha. In any case the Bill is considered to have been passed by both the Houses, 14 days after its final stage in the Lok Sabha.

Assent of the President. Every Money Bill is submitted for the assent of the President who cannot withhold it. If the Budget is not passed before 1st April, the Paliament is authorised to sanction any grant in advance to meet the exprenses. This is known as vote on account. The Parliament also passes supplementary demands if it is convinced that the receipt from all the taxes is inadequate to meet the needs of the Government.

PROCEDURE FOR PASSING ORDINARY BILLS

All Bills other than Money are called Ordinary Bills. The procedure for passing Ordinary Bills is different from that adopted in the case of Money Bills.An Ordinary Bill, unlike Money Bill, need not be introduced first in the Lok Sabha. Moreover, it can be introduced even by private members. Ordinary Bills are of two types–Government Bills and private Member's Bills. Both undergo an identical procedure.

Emergence of Legislative Proposal. Most of the Ordinary Bills are moved by the Ministers. The Ministry concerned seeks the advice of experts, the Law Ministry and Attorney-General of India. After considering the legal and constitutional aspects of the proposed legislation, the Bill is moved in any House. Drafting of Bill is a technical job done by experts and approved by the Council of Ministers. Certain types of Bills require the previous permission of the President which is easily obtained. Every Ordinary Bill in order to become an Act passes through the following stages:

Introduction and First Reading. The draft of a proposed Ordinary Bill has to be sent to the Secretariat of the House in which it is to be presented. A month's notice is given to the Speaker regarding the introduction of the Bill. The Speaker or the Chairman, as the case may be, includes the Bills in the list of business and gives a date for its formal introduction. The pioneer to that Bill rises from his seat and requests the Chair to permit him to move the Bill whereupon the assent is given and the Bill is declared to have been moved. The introduction or first reading of the Bill is a mere formality and no discussion takes place at this stage. This convention has been broken on a few occasions. For instance, the Preventive Detention Amendment Act, moved on 23rd November, 1954, was opposed at the time of introduction on the ground that it was unconstitutional. In the past few years there have been such instances when a Government Bill was opposed on the ground that it was outside the competence of the House. In such cases the Chairman or the Speaker gives one opportunity each to the mover of the Bill and its opponents to explain their points of view. If any member raises a constitutional objection, the man in the chair allows a full debate at the time of first reading. After introduction, the Bill is published in the Gazette of India. The Speaker or the Chairman can allow the publication of Bill even before its first reading. In such a case the Bill does not have to pass through the Introduction stage.

Second Reading of the Bill. The second reading consists of consideration of the Bill. Generally, there is an interval of two days between the introduction and second reading. The mover of the Bill then adopts any of the three courses: (1) That the Bill may be taken into consideration by the House at once; (2) that it may be referred to a Select Committee; (3) that it may be circulated for eliciting public opinion. Only in exceptional cases is a Bill taken up for consideration at once. The members of the House are permitted to oppose the suggestion of the mover of the Bill. When the House decides to elicit public opinion, the Secretariat of the House requests the State Governments to publish that Bill in the State Gazette and invite opinions from local bodies and recognised associations. The gist of public opinion is then circulated amongst the members of the House. Then again a discussion takes place. The supporters of the Bill point out the merits of the Bill; the members opposing it attack the Bill. But it is to be noted that the Bill is discussed as a whole, not clause by clause.

Committee Stage. If the House accepts to refer the Bill to a Select Committee of the House, the mover suggests the names of persons who would constitute the committee. A time is also fixed for the submission of its report. The Speaker appoints the Chairman of the Committee from amongst its members. If the Deputy Speaker happens to be one of the members, he automatically becomes the Chairman. Generally, the strength of such a Select Committee varies between 20 and 30. The quorum for the sittings of a Select Committee is one-third of the total number. The committee makes a thorough scrutiny of the Bill and suggests some useful changes. A Minister, who is not a member of the committee, may, with the permission of the Chairman, address the Committee. The Chairman of the committee has a casting vote. He also signs the Report.

Report Stage. The Report of the committee is laid before the House either by the Chairman or some other members in his absence. The Bill along with the Report is then circulated among the members. At this stage the mover of the Bill either proposes that the Bill in the light of the Report may be considered by the House, or it may be submitted again for reconsideration either by the same committee or a different committee or that it may be circulated again for eliciting public opinion. If the House accepts the Bill as reported by the committee, the same is put to another reading. The Bill is then discussed thoroughly clause by clause. Amendments are moved and accepted or rejected. Report stage is the most important stage. Each amendment and each clause is submitted to the vote of the House. Every issue is decided by the majority vote of the persons present and voting.

Third Reading of the Bill. Third reading is the last stage of an Ordinary Bill in either House. Only commonplaces regarding the Bill are discussed at this stage. No amendment is accepted except that which aims at correcting some verbal flaw. The convention is that no Bill at this stage is ever rejected.

The Bill in the Other House. A Bill after being adopted by one House is sent to the other House. It has to undergo the same stages again. When the other House also passes the Bill in its original form, it is sent to the President for his assent. If the other House refuses to pass the Bill or suggests such amendments as do not find favour with the former House or does nor return the Bill within six months, a serious deadlock is created. In that case the President summons both the Houses to meet at a joint sitting for the purpose of voting on the Bill. The Speaker or in his absence the Deputy Speaker presides. The Bill is then put to the vote of the members of both the Houses. It is carried by the majority vote of the members present and voting.

Assent of the President. Every Bill in order to become an Act requires the assent of the President. The President may either give his assent, or return it for reconsideration with or without his suggestion for amendment. If the President gives his assent, the Bill becomes a law. If he sends back the Bill for consideration and if the Bill is passed by both the Houses again in an amended or origianl form, the President has to give his assent thereto. After the President's assent the Act is published in the Gazette of India.

PARLIAMENTARY COMMITTEES

As the Parliament is quite unwieldy body for the prompt and convenient transaction of vast business of Parliament and it cannot examine many complex and intricate issues dispassionately, so the Committee came into existence. The Committees assist the Parliament in its deliberations and do the preliminary work. Parliamentary committees are appointed or elected by the respective Houses on a motion made or are nominated by their presiding officers.

Broadly speaking, these committees are of two kinds–standing committees and *ad hoc* committees. The former are elected or appointed every year or periodically and their work goes on more or less on a continuous basis. The latter are appointed *ad hoc*, that is, as and when the need arises. They cease to exist as soon as they complete the work assigned to them.

Standing Committees

Among the standing committees, the three financial committees, *viz.*, Committee on Public Accounts, Estimates Committee and Committee on Public Undertakings, constitute a distinct class and between them keep a vigil over Government spending and performance.

1. *Public Accounts Committee.* The Public Accounts Committee consists of 15 members elected by the Lok Sabha and 7 associate members elected by the Rajya Sabha with no right to vote. A Minister is not eligible for election to this committee. It scrutinises the Appropriation Accounts of the Government of India and the report of the Comptroller and Auditor-General of India thereon. It ensures that public money is spent in accordance with Parliament's decision and calls attention to cases of waste, extravagance, loss or nugatory expenditure or lack of financial integrity in public services. The Committee is not concerned with questions of policy, but only with the execution of policy laid down by Parliament. Its life is one year. The Public Accounts Committee has pointed out the wasteful expenditure several times. As a matter of practice, since 1967, a member of opposition is being appointed as the Chairman of the Committee.

2. *The Estimates Committee.* It consists of 30 members elected by the Lok Sabha every year from amongst its members on the basis of proportional representation by means of a single transferable vote.The Chairman of the Committee is appointed by the Speaker from amongst its members but if the Deputy Speaker happens to be its member, he *ipso facto'* becomes the Chairman. In order to ensure continuity of the Committee, the members are re-elected year after year. It discharges the following functions: (*a*) It reports on 'what economies, improvements in organisation, efficiency or administrative reform, consistent with the policy underlying the estimates, may be effected. (*b*) It also examines whether the money is laid out within the limits of the policy implied in the estimates. (*c*) It suggests the form in which the estimate shall be presented to Parliament. (*d*) It suggests alternative policies in order to bring about efficiency and economy in administration.

These functions of the Estimates Committee make it amply clear that the Committee plays an important part not only in examining the financial estimates but also in suggesting the alternative policies to the Government so that efficiency and economy may be imparted to Government administration. Though the Committee has to discharge a very difficult task but it goes to its credit that it has handled these matters very efficiently. It has not only suggested economies in government expenditure but has also suggested valuable administrative reforms.

3. *The Committee on Public Undertakings.* This Committee consists of 22 members–15 from the Lok Sabha according to proportional representation and single transferable vote system and 7 from the Rajya Sabha in the same manner. Its Chairman is appointed by the Speaker. This Committee checks the accounts of public undertakings. It also examines their working and other financial matters and the reports of Comptroller and Auditor–General. One-fifth of the members of the Committee retire every year by rotation and new persons are elected in their place.

COMMITTEES OF LOK SABHA

Above three committees which are common to the Lok Sabha and Rajya Sabha have been mentioned . Now we describe the other committees of the Lok Sabha.

4. *Business Advisory Committee.* This committee is formed at the beginning of the Lok Sabha. It consists of 15 members and is presided over by the Speaker. The members are nominated by the Speaker. Since the House has to conduct a lot of business and the time at its disposal is comparatively very short, therefore, this Business Advisory Committee has to allocate time to every Bill keeping in view its importance. To avoid controversy, the leader of the House as well as Opposition leaders are also associated with it. Normally this Committee meets three or four times in session and makes recommendations regarding the plan of the House's work, which are generally accepted by the House. The work of this committee is becoming difficult day by day because the Opposition leaders unexpectedly raise many issues which consume sufficient time and consequently the time to the various Bills is reallocated.

5. *The Committee on Private Members Bill and Resolutions.* Besides the Ministers, many other members of Lok Sabha want to introduce the Bill. Therefore this Committee considers those bills and classifies them as important, less important, urgent or less urgent and allocates time for their discussion in the House. It also examines Constitution Amendment Bills and Resolution about which the House receives notice from Private Members.

This committee consists of 15 members who are nominated by the Speaker for one year.

6. *The Select Committee on Bills.* The number of the Select Committee is not fixed. Its strength increases or diminishes according to the necessity of the work of the House. The members of the Select Committee are appointed by the House. The Select Committee examines every Bill very minutely, collects all data relating to it and examines witnesses. After that it submits its report to the House and is dissolved when it is no longer needed.

7. *The Rules Committee.* The Rules Committee is nominated by the Speaker and Speaker is its chairman. The Rules Committee in both the Houses consists of 15 members nominated by the Speaker. It considers carefully the procedure of the House and conduct of its business and suggests changes whenever it becomes necessary. Besides that it considers the various rules and regulations of the House and suggests modifications in the old ones or suggests framing of the new ones in their place.

8. *The Committee on Privileges.* This is an important Committee and it consists of 15 members who are nominated by the Speaker and Deputy Speaker is its Chairman. It is constituted at the beginning of each Lok Sabha on its recommendation. To enable the members of the Parliament to discahrge their functions in the House or Committees fearlessly, they have been give certain privileges. For example, the members of the Parliament have been given complete freedom of speech and expression and no proceeding can be instituted against them in any court of law for anything said or the vote given in the House or in any Committee. Further, no remarks can be made by any person or agency regarding the Parliament or about the proceedings in the Parliament. Further, every Minister has to provide true information regarding the questions asked by the members. If these privileges are violated, the House can refer the matter to the Committee on Privileges. The committee can call the person or agency concerned and examine witnesses, if any, and then it recommends suitable actions against the persons concerned.

9. *The Committee on Petitions.* It consists of 15 members but no Minister can become its member. It examines the petitions on Bills and on matters of public interest and also entertains representations on central subjects. It also recommends remedial measures.

10. *The Committee on Subordinate Legislation.* The Committee on Subordinate Legislation came into existence on December 1, 1953. This committee consists of not more than 15members is each House, who are nominated by the Speaker or the Chairman as the case may be. Now-a-days the problem of legislation has become very complex and intricate. The Parliament neither has got sufficient time nor the technical knowledge to go into the details of every Bill. Therefore, it passes the skeleton or outlines of the Bill only and leaves the details to be filled by the Executive. The Executive or Cabinet makes detailed rules and regulations to supplement the Bill or fill its details. This rule-making power conferred on the Executive by the Parliament is known as *delegated legislation.* To ensure that his power is not misused by the Executive, *Committee on Subordinate Legislation* has been constituted which scrutinises whether the powers to make the rules and regulations, sub-rules and bye-laws conferred by the Constitution or delegated by Parliament are being properly exercised by the Government within the scope of such delegation.

11. *The Committee on Government Assurances.* It consists of 15 members who are nominated by the Speaker for one year. Ministers are not eligible to become its members. Various assurances are given by the Ministers on the floor of the House from time to time but sometimes they might not be implemented. The Committee on Government Assurances scrutinises whether the assurances given by the Minister have been fully implemented or not. If they have not been implemented, then it pursues them till they are implemented.

12. *The Committee on Absence from the Sittings of the House.* This Committee also consists of 15 members nominated by the Speaker for one year. This committee considers the leave applications of the members of Parliament who want to abstain from the sitting of the House and examines all such cases when the members might have been absent from the sitting of the House beyond sixty days. After asking from the member concerned it decides whether the absence of the member is to be condoned or his seat is to be declared vacant.

13. *Joint Committee on Salaries and Allowances of Members of Parliament.* It deals with salaries and allowances and frames rules in respect of matters like medical, housing, telephone, postal facilities etc.

14. *Joint Committee on Offices of Profit.* This Joint Committee consists of 15 members, on a Government motion moved in the Lok Sabha and concurred by the Rajya Sabha, 10 members are elected from the Lok Sabha and 5 from Rajya Sabha according to principles of proportional representation by means of single transferable vote. It examines the composition and character of the bordes and other bodies appointed by the Central or State governments in order to recommend which offices ought not to disqualify a person from being a member of either House of Parliament.

15. *House Committee.* It deals with residential accommodation, medical aid and other amenities to the members of Parliament.

Ad hoc Committee. Ad hoc Committees are constituted from time to time either by the Lok Sabha or by the Speaker to enquire into and report on specific subjects. For example, the Select or Joint Committees on Bills are appointed to consider a particular Bill and they are dissolved after their work is over. Another example of the Ad hoc Committee is the Railway Convention Committee.

Consultative Committees. The Consultative Committees are constituted for different departments and ministers. They provide a forum where the discussion on specific issues takes place between different ministries and the members of the Parliament . It is the policy of the government to consult the leaders of the Opposition on complicated national problems, so these Consultative Committees functiton according to the guidelines evolved by the Central Government.

How Committees Function?

Unless the Presiding Officer is himself the Chairman, he nominates from among the Members of a Committee a Chairman to conduct the proceedings of the Committee. Members take part in the discussion with the permission of the Chairman. Decisions are taken by a majority vote. A Committee may hear expert advice and call for papers and persons if it considers necessary for proper and expeditious disposal of its work. The conclusions of a Committee are embodied in a report which is presented to the House.

So important, indeed, is the work done by Committees that Hiren Mukherjee has suggested "reduction in Parliament's Ceremonial Session and increase in Committee work, drawing in more actively and consistently the service and talent of the members."

New Committee System in Parliament

On March, 29, 1993, the Lok Sabha took a historic decision, by an unanimous vote, to introduce the Standing Committee System in the Indian Parliamentary practice. The new committee system was inaugurated at a special function in Parliament House by the then Vice-President, Mr. K.R.Narayanan. The new system–recommended by the Rules Committee of the Parliament–envisages the formation of seventeen joint standing committees which are as follows : Committee on Commerce, Committee on Home Affairs, Committee on Human Resources Development, Committee on Industry, Committee on Environment, Forests, Electronics, Science and Technology, Committee on Transport and Tourism, Committee on Agriculture, Committee on Communications, Committee on Information and Broadcasting, Committee on Defence, Committee on Energy, Committee on External Affairs, Committee on Finance, Committee on Labour and welfare, Committee on Petroleum and Chemicals, Committee on Railways and Committee on Urban and Rural Development. Each Committee comprises 45 members — 30 from Lok Sabha and 15 from Rajya Sabha. Ministers are not eligible for the membership of the committees. The normal membership term of the Committee is one year. The chairpersons of the various committees are nominated by the Speaker in consultation with the Party Leaders. The main function of these committees is to examine and discuss in detail the budget proposals relating to the relevant ministers. They also scrutinise all other Bills (except highly technical ones) proposed to be moved in Parliament. Thus these Committees–which normally meet during the recess of Parliament–ensure a fuller examination and Parliamentary scrutiny of grants and bills. At the same time, by relieving the pressure on Parliament's time, they ensure fuller debate and discussion in the Houses on important measures and policy issues.

The merit of the new committee system is that Parliament is able to examine grants of departments in detail. At present Parliament only finds time to discuss the demands for about 7 or 8 ministers, and the rest are being guillotined, without detailed scrutiny of the financial allocations by Parliament. Under the new system, not only the annual grant of each ministry comes under detailed scrutiny by the standing committees, but their performance also is examined in detail.

EXERCISES

Long Answer Type Questions:

1. What do you know about Rajya Sabha or Council of States?
2. What do you know about Lok Sabha or House of the People?
3. Write a note on Speaker and Deputy Speaker of the Lok Sabha.
4. Discuss the position of Indian Speaker and discuss his comparison with the Speaker of United Kingdom and United States of America.
5. Discuss powers and mutual relations of Lok Sabha and Rajya Sabha.

6. Discuss the powers and limitations of Parliament .
7. Discuss the procedure of passing Money Bills in Parliament.
8. Discuss the procedure for passing Ordinary Bills.
9. Write a note on Parliamentary Committees.

Short Answer Type Questions :

1. Distinguish between Indian Parliament and the British Parliament.
2. Write a note on officials of Rajya Sabha.
3. What do you know about privileges of the Members of Lok Sabha ?
4. Write a very brief note on power and functions of Speaker.
5. Write a brief note on role of Indian Speaker.
6. Discuss relation between the two Houses on Money Bills.
7. Discuss relation of Lok Sabha and Rajya Sabha regarding Non-Money Bills.
8. What is meaning of Money Bills ?
9. Write a note on Standing Committees of Parliament.

Objective Type Questions :

Choose the correct answer

1. Parliament can assume legislative power with respect to a State subject only if:
   (*a*) President issues an ordinance to this effect
   (*b*) Lok Sabha passes a resolution to this effect
   (*c*) the Council of States passes a resolution to this effect supported by two-thirds of its members present and voting
   (*d*) All of the above
2. Which of the following acts, among other things, as an organ of information ?
   (*a*) Parliament
   (*b*) Ministry of Information and Broadcasting
   (*c*) Comptroller and Auditor-General
   (*d*) None of the above
3. Which of the following Articles lay down norms regarding making of laws by the legislature ?
   (*a*) Article 107 (*b*) Article 108
   (*c*) Article 245 (*d*) All of the above
4. Powers to authorise expenditures for the public services to specify the purposes to which that money shall be appreciated, to provide ways and means to raise the revenue required belong to :
   (*a*) Both Houses of the Parliament (*b*) Rajya Sabha
   (*c*) Lok Sabha (*d*) None of the above
5. Presidential power to dissolve the House of the People is laid down under Article
   (*a*) 56 (*b*) 61
   (*c*) 85 (*d*) 92
6. Which of the following terms represent termination of a session of the House of the People ?
   (*a*) Adjournment (*b*) Prorogation
   (*c*) Dissolution (*d*) None of the above

ANSWERS

1. (*c*) 2. (*a*) 3. (*b*) 4. (*a*) 5. (*c*) 6. (*b*).

11

CHAPTER

Reorganisation of States

> *"In the Government of such a vast country as India, it is but proper that the Head of each State should be a nominee of the Central Executive, so that the main lines of policy which the Centre may conceive, as conducive to the coherence and solidarity of the country as a whole may better be instilled into the government of each province through the Centre's representative."*
>
> — ***N.R. Raghavachariar***

INTEGRATION AND DEMOCRATISATION OF INDIAN STATES

Accession of Indian States to Indian Union. In July, 1947, States Ministry was set up in Delhi under the stewardship of Sardar Vallabhbhai Patel. Mr. V.P. Menon acted as Secretary of this important department. As a result of the combined efforts of Patel and Menon coupled with an appeal made by Lord Mountbatten to Indian Rulers on 15th August, 1947, all other States transferred the three vital subjects of external affairs, defence and transportation and communication to the Union. The States transferred the three vital subjects of external affairs, defence and transportation and communication to the Union. Junagarh was a small princely State in Kathiawad. This Hindu majority State was under a Muslim Nawab. With a lapse of paramountcy, the Nawab of Junagarh declared the accession of the State to Pakistan. The people of the State launched Satyagraha. The Indian forces also marched into the State. The Nawab fled to Pakistan in October, 1947. A plebiscite held in 1948 gave the verdict of the people in favour of Indian Union. The formalities of accession were completed and it became a part of Indian Union.

Accession of Hyderabad State. The Nizam of Hyderabad, encouraged by Pakistan agents, also refused to accede to India. The people of the State started agitation and became victim of Nizam's atrocities. The Nizam instigated a few communal organisations like Razakars to harass the Hindus. He began to dream of becoming a sovereign. He counted on the British support through the good offices of Pakistan. He appealed to American President and U.N.O. to guarantee the security of his State. The Razakar organisation under Qasim Rizvi established a reign of terror in the State. The Razakars even raided the neighbouring Indian territories. Union Government could not tolerate such lawlessness. It launched Police Action on 13th September. 1948, against Hyderabad. Five days later the Indian forces entered the State triumphantly. The Nizam submitted tamely to the language of force and agreed to join Union.

Accession of Kashmir. Another problem that confronted the newly-born Indian Union was that of Kashmir. Its borders touch both India and Pakistan. Both looked greedily at this Himalayan State. Mr. Mohammad Ali Jinnah was sorely annoyed at the British strategy which had deprived Pakistan of Kashmir. Maharaja committed another blunder by not signifying immediate accession to Indian Union. He had to pay by the nose for this mistake. Mr. Mohammad Ali Jinnah planned to grab Kashmir by force. On 22nd October, 1947, he deployed Pakistani Army for an attack on the green valley of Srinagar. Pakistani forces were accompanied by Afridi raiders. The ruthless raiders did not encounter much resistance from the State forces. They captured the Power House at Mahura which supplied electricity to Srinagar. Their next target was Srinagar itself. The Maharaja of Kashmir foresaw the gravity of the danger and implored the Government of India for immediate military help. He also signed the Instrument of Accession promptly. The Indian Government accepted to defend the valley on the condition that the future of Kashmir shall be decided by plebiscite. It is worth noting that Lord Mountbatten was reluctant to airlift Indian troops to Srinagar, but Mahatma Gandhi and Sardar Vallabhbhai Patel were strongly in favour of defending Srinagar against the raiders. The Indian forces went into action and recovered a considerable part of territory from the illegal occupation of Pakistan forces. Mr. Mohammad Ali Jinnah was so much enraged with the retreat of the raiders that he ordered the Commander-in-Chief of Pakistan to move regular troops into Kashmir. But by the timely mediation of Mr. Auchinlek, then incharge of the combined forces of India and Pakistan. Mohammad Ali Jinnah's order was cancelled. Mohammad Ali Jinnah, however, did not become inactive. He continued slandering India on various counts. The Indian Government, on the advice of Mountbatten, submitted the Kashmir issue for arbitration to the Security Council of U.N.O. Ceasefire was enforced on Ist January, 1949. The U.N.O. sent Mr. Graham and Mr Dixon to mediate but both failed to evolve a compromise formula. The U.N.O., then, directed Pakistan to withdraw its forces from the occupied Kashmir as a prelude to holding plebiscite. But because of non-compliance by Pakistan the issue remained hanging fire. Many times since the raid, the State of Kashmir has gone to polls and a responsible Government has been functioning in the State for all these years. The Constituent Assembly of Kashmir has also ratified the accession of Kashmir of Indian Union and State of Jammu and Kashmir has now become an integral part of the Union, although it enjoys a status distinct from other States of the Union.

Merger and Integration of States. The States had agreed to transfer external affairs, defence and transportation and communication to Union Government, but this was not sufficient. It was felt necessary that the States should recognise the Indian Constitution. Moreover, there was the need to make certain territorial adjustments. Thanks to the ingenuity of Sarder Vallabhbhai Patel who induced the States to accept the Indian Constitution and agree to the formation of bigger administrative units either by the merger of the States with the adjoining Provinces or by forming unions of several neighbouring States. Thus the Union of the States like Saurashtra, and Patiala and East Punjab States Union came into existence. Big States like Mysore, Hyderabad and Kashmir were left intact to become members of the Union separately. The States like Bhopal, Manipur and Tripura, which did not accept the proposal of merging themselves with the neighbouring Provinces were taken under direct control of the Union Government.

Thus four types of State came into existence after independence. (The new Constitution of India discontinued the use of the word Province and called the constituent units of the Union as States.) Part A States included former British Indian Provinces of Assam, Bihar, Bombay, Madhya Pradesh, Madras, Orissa, Uttar Pradesh, West Bengal and Punjab. Later on Andhra was also added to the list of Part A States. Part B States included Hyderabad, Jammu and Kashmir, Madhya Bharat, Mysore, Patiala and East Punjab States Union, Rajasthan, Saurashtra and Travancore-Cochin. Jammu and Kashmir, although included in Part B States, was placed on a special footing. Part C States included Ajmer, Bhopal, Coorg, Delhi, Himachal Pradesh, Kutch, Vindhya Pradesh, Manipur and Tripura. Anadaman and Nicobar Islands were placed in Part D States.

Importance of Integration. Thus a miracle was performed in India by welding of big and small, democratic and autocratic units into a compact Union. The integration of the States is, one should say, the greatest historical event of the country. This foiled the designs of the outgoing British rulers to leave the country in a state of mess. Sardar Vallabhbhai Patel, the master-builder, commented with justifiable pride: "The great ideal of geographical, political and economic unification of India, an ideal which for centuries remained a distant dream, after the advent of Indian independence, had been consummated by the policy of integration."[1] The staggering speed with which the great task of the political unification of India was completed, took even Nehru by surprise. He admitted in September, 1948, that he had never imagined that he would see a unified India so soon. Writing about the integration of States, Mr. Michael Brecher observes, "*The maguitude of the operations is brought into bold relief by the vital statistics, within a year an area of almost half a million square miles, with a population of almost ninety million, was incorporated into the Indian Union. It was a bloodless revolution without parallel in this century, comparable with the unification of Germany and Italy by Bismarck and Cavour respectively.*"[2]

Democratisation of the Administration of the States. Mere integration of the States was not enough. The greater task ahead was to install responsible Government in every State. Hence in order to enforce Indian Constitution in the States, the administration in the States was democratised. Part A States got full responsible Governments, each with an elected Legislature, a Cabinet and a Governor acting as constitutional head of the State. Part B States also got a democratic set-up under Rajpramukhs who acted as the agents of the President. Part C States also got a Territorial Council and a Cabinet each. But there the responsibility of the Cabinet to the Legislature was not complete. The Chief Commissioners interfered in the administration and remained overall incharge of the government of the State. Part D States did not get even the semblance of a responsible government. It was administered by a Chief Commissioner and had one representative in the Parliament. Thus the new political units of India came to have a simplified if not a uniform political structure. States in categories A and B stood in different relationship with the Central government but the difference was not sharply marked. They became the member units of the Union. The territories in Parts C and D, however, remained under the direct rule of the Centre. The people of the States heaved a sigh of relief on deliverance from the autocratic rule of the Princes. Pt. Jawaharlal Nehru rightly observed in September, 1948 : "*The historian who looks back will no doubt consider that one of the dominant phases of India's history today is this integration extemally but an inner integration, of States into India. What is more important is not this integration, that is, the growth of democratic institutions in the States.*"

STATES' REORGANISATION

Demand to reconstitute Provinces on the Linguistic Basis. The Political units that emerged after the integration of the States were of an *ad hoc* character. They needed some radical alteration. The units were widely dissimilar in area, population and economic viability but the gravest defect was that each was multilingual. There was a constant demand and agitation to redistribute the boundaries of the States on a more rational and scientific basis.

1. Mr. V.P. Menon—*The Story of the Integration of Indian States*, p.490.
2. Michael Brecher — *Nehru, a Political Biography*, p. 403.

Appointment of States Reorganisation Commission. The creation of Andhra Province on language basis touched off a spark which set the whole country ablaze with similar demands. The people became so insistent that Pt. Jawaharlal Nehru had to declare in December, 1953, that the Government was prepared to appoint a Commission to look into the demands of the people for unilingual Provinces. The States Reorganisation Commission was formed with Fazl Ali as Chairman and two other members—Sardar K.M. Panikkar and Pt. H.N. Kunzru. The Commission studied the mood of the people and submitted its report in October, 1955. The Commission took into consideration various other claims besides language and culture. It discarded the 'Homeland' concept. It was guided by the administrative, financial and national considerations too.

The Commission in its Report suggested the abolition of distinction between Parts 'A', 'B' and 'C' States and recommended that they be given equal status in the federal polity. The Commission also recommended the abolition of the office of Rajpramukhs. It also rejected the demands for a separate Punjabi Suba. Haryana Province, Jharkhand and Maru Pradesh. It did not accept the demand of separation of Maharashtra from Gujarat. It proposed the retention of Punjab and Bombay as bilingual Provinces. It also recommended the formation of 16 States and three centrally administered territories as against the existing 27 States. The States which were to disappear were those of Travancore-Cochin, Mysore, Kutch, Saurashtra, Coorg, Madhya Bharat, Bhopal, Vindhya Pradesh, P.E.P.S.U., Himachal Pradesh, Ajmer and Tripura. It suggested the reorganisation of Union territory into Punjab (including Himachal Pradesh), Uttar Pradesh, Bihar, Bengal, Assam, Orissa, Andhra, Madras, Karnataka, Kerala, Hyderabad, Bombay, Vidarbha, Madhya Pradesh, Rajasthan, Jammu and Kashmir. Besides 16 States there were to be three centrally administered territories—Delhi, Manipur and Andaman and Nicobar.

States Reorganisation Act, July, 1956. The Commission's Report was received with mixed feeling. There was a good deal of agitation against its proposals. The Opposition parties capitalised the situation to discredict the Congress. They also fanned the feeling of discontent and linguism. Bombay turned into a great trouble spot. The Maharashtrians pressed their demand for a separate State of Marathi-speaking people. The Gujaratis demanded Maha Gujarat. Both communities resorted to violence and lawlessness. Mr. C.D. Deshmukh, failing to prevail upon the Congress High Command to accept Maharashtra, resigned from the Cabinet. In July, 1956, the Parliament passed the States Reorganisation Act with slight modification in the Commission's recommendations. Under this Act the Union territory was divided into 14 units : (1) Jammu and Kashmir; (2) Punjab; (3) Uttar Pradesh; (4) Bihar; (5) Bengal; (6) Assam; (7) Orissa; (8) Andhra; (9) Madras; (10) Kerala; (11) Mysore; (12) Bombay; (13) Madhya Pradesh; (14) Rajasthan. Besides these, the Act created five Union territories – Delhi, Manipur, Tripura, Andaman and Nicobar, Laccadive and Minicoy Islands. The States were further grouped into five zones : Northern, Eastern, Western, Southern and Central. Each of these zones was given a Zonal Council to discuss matters of common interests.

Creation of other States. Even after the reorganisation of States according to the Act of 1956, demand coupled with strong agitation continued for separate States of Maharashtra and Gujarat, Punjab and Haryana etc. and in some other parts of the country. Therefore the new states of Maharashtra and Gujarat were created by the Bombay Reorganisation Act, 1960. French Government agreed to transfer its possessions in India, Pondicherry, Yenam, Mahi and Chander Nagar and the deed for that purpose was signed by the Government of France and India on 28th May, 1956 in New Delhi.[1] While Pondicherry was made a Union territory and responsible government was introduced in it with an Assembly of 30 seats, other territories were merged with the adjoined provinces or states. The Portuguese territories of Goa. Diu and Daman were liberated on 20th December, 1961 and were formally incorporated into the Union on 12th March, 1962. First of all they were made a Union territory

1. See *India 1957*, p.471

but later on Goa was made a separate state. Nagaland was made a separate state on 1st December, 1963. Punjab was bifurcated into two states, Punjab consisting of Punjabi area and Haryana consisting of Hindi area with effect from 1st November, 1966.

Himachal Pradesh was granted statehood on 25th January, 1971. Meghalaya was carved out of Assam and given statehood on 20th January, 1972. Manipur and Tripura were conferred statehood on 21st January, 1972. All the three states were formally inaugurated by Mrs. Indira Gandhi and 27th Amendment to the Indian Constitution was made to this effect. According to the 36th Amendment (May, 1975) Sikkim was conferred statehood. After that Mizoram, Arunachal Pradesh and Goa were given statehood and necessary Amendments were made in the Indian Constitution to that effect.

Administration of States

On 30th January 1997, there were following states in India: (1) Punjab; (2) Rajasthan; (3) Uttar Pradesh; (4) West Bengal; (5) Andhra Pradesh; (6) Assam; (7) Bihar; (8) Jammu and Kashmir; (9) Kerala; (10) Madhya Pradesh; (11) Tamil Nadu; (12) Maharashtra; (13) Karnataka; (14) Orissa; (15) Gujarat; (16) Nagaland; (17) Haryana; (18) Himachal Pradesh; (19) Tripura; (20) Manipur; (21) Meghalaya; (22) Sikkim; (23) Mizoram; (24) Arunachal Pradesh; (25) Goa; and (26) Delhi.

The administration of these states is run by the Governor or Lt. Governer with the help of Council of Ministers which is responsible to the Legislative Assembly. The Council of Ministers is in turn helped by many administrative officials (Secretaries. Joint Secretaries, Deputy Secretaries, Under Secretaries, Section Officers) and clerks. Each Minister holds one or more than one portfolio. Ministers are the heads of the departments and Secretaries assist them. Ministers formulate policies and the Secretaries implement them with the help of other officials and clerks under them.

Administration of Union Territories

On 30th January 1997, there were following Union Territories; (1) Chandigarh (2) Andaman and Nicobar Islands; (3) Lakshadweep and Minicoy Island; (4) Pondicherry (Now Pudduchery), (5) Diu and Daman; (6) Dadra and Nagar Haveli.

The administration of the Union Territories is run either by the Lt. Governor of the Chief Commissioner who is nominated by the President of India. The President makes all these appointments on the recommendation of the Prime Minister. All the Union Territories are directly under the Home Ministry of the Government of India. In Delhi, there is a ministry to help the Lt. Governor of Delhi in running the administration smoothly. In Pondicherry, Goa, and Mizoram each there is a Legislative Assembly and the Council of Ministers. The Council of Ministers aid and advise the Lt. Governor in the discharge of administrative duties.

Chhattisgarh as the Twenty-sixth State

On November 1, 2000, a new state to be known as the state of Chhattisgarh comprising the following territories of the existing state of Madhya Pradesh came into existence :

Bastar, Bilaspur, Dantewara, Dhamtari, Durg, Champa, Jashpur, Kanker, Kawardha, Korba, Koriya, Mahasamund, Raigarh, Raipur, Rajnandgaon and Sarguja districts. The state has been assigned 5 seats in the Rajya Sabha and 11 seats in the Lok Sabha. The state shall have a 90-member Legislative Assembly. There shall be separate High Court for the state.

Chhattisgarh became a reality without anyone rearly wanting it. Chhattisgarh did not even experience a mass movement. The BJP adopted the demand because it thought that after the 1998 Assembly elections it would be in a majority in the Chhattisgarh region; the Congress played along because it was afraid of losing its hold over the region.

Uttarakhand as the Twenty-seventh State

On November 9, 2000, a new state to be known as Uttarakhand comprising the following territories of the existing state of Uttar Pradesh came into existence :

Pauri Garhwal, Tehri Garhwal, Uttarkashi, Chamoli, Dehradun, Nainital, Almora, Pithoragarh, Udham Singh Nagar, Bageswar, Champawat, Rudraprayag and Hardwar districts.

The state has been assigned 3 seats in the Rajya Sabha and 5 seats in the Lok Sabha. The state shall have a 70-member Legislative Assembly.

There shall be a separate High Court for the State of Uttarakhand.

Jharkhand as the Twenty-eighth State

On November 15, 2000, a new state to be known as Jharkhand comprising the following territories of the existing state of Bihar came into existence :

Bokaro, Chatra, Dhanbad, Dumka, Garwa, Giridih, Gumla, Hazaribagh, Kodarma, Lohardagga, Pakur, Palamu, Ranchi, Sahibganj, Godda, Deoghar, Singhbhum (East), Singhbhum (West).

The newly created state is allotted 6 seats in the Rajya Sabha and 14 seats in the Lok Sabha. The number of seats in the legislative Assembly of Jharkhand shall be 81. There shall be a separate High Court for the State of Jharkhand.

The tribals in the region always had good reason to be resentful of the 'outsider' who invariably became the symbol of economic exploitation.

This failure to rectify elements of economic injustice and exploitation gave a cutting edge to the idea of a separate political entity of the tribals, who would presumably be able to run the collective affairs differently and better than the Patna-based rulers.

Separate Statehood Demands in other parts of India

Demands for separate statehood were made in several parts of the country. The people of Telangana raised voices throughout the 1960's that they should be separated from Andhra Pradesh and a new State of Mysore demanded separation from the Karnataka Districts. The Hilly Region of Kumaon and Tehri-Garhwal in Uttarakhand aspired for a state of their own. In West Bengal, the Gorkhaland National Liberation Front (GNLF) has demanded, occasionally by violent means, a separate State of Gorkhaland in Darjeeling District.

The Bodo agitation is led by the Assam Bodo Students Union (ABSU), which is demanding a separate state and has resorted to widescale violence and a series of crippling bandhs to pursue their demand.

The Buddhists of Ladakh had been carrying on an agitation, which at times turned violent, in support of their demand for grant of Union Territory status since the existing set-up in the State of Jammu and Kashmir had not provided them fair and just treatment.

On the basis of the recommendations of the Committee on Reorganisation of Delhi set-up, the Constitution (Sixty-ninth) Amendment Act, 1991 and the Government of National Capital Territory of Delhi Act, 1991 have been enacted for establishment of a Legislative Assembly and a Council of Ministers for the National Capital Territory of Delhi.

Although the number of states has increased from fourteen in 1956 to twenty-eight in 2000, many of them are still quite large sized—larger, indeed, then many sovereign states in the world. The formation of new states cannot be ruled out, but the argument for smaller, more administratively viable states is countered by concern that the smaller state may be more easily dominated by vested interests. The creation of more and more states meant more Governors, more Chief Ministers, more

Ministers and more MLAs and these were what the politicians in India cared for. The narrow and sectarian instincts of the ignorant masses were at times stirred up by the professional politicians to serve their own narrow ends, sometimes in the name of language and very often in the name of their region or state.

As of 2011 census India has a total population of 1,210,193,422 people in 35 States and Union Territories. Among them 62,37,24,248 are men and 58,64,69,174 are women. Uttar Pradesh tops the state-wise population table with 19,95,81,477 (16.49%) people.

Next top four States with highest population according to 2011 census are:

1. Maharashtra has second highest population with 11, 23, 72, 972 (9.29%) people.
2. Bihar the third highest populated state in India with 10, 38, 04, 637 (8.58%) population.
3. West Bengal stands fourth with 9, 13, 47, 736 (7.55%) population.
4. Andhra Pradesh is at number five with 8, 46, 65, 533 (7%) population.

Five least populated states in India as of 2011 census are:

1. Sikkim the lowest populated state in India has a population of 6,07,688 (0.05%).
2. Mijoram second lowest state with a population of 10, 91, 014 (0.09%).
3. Arunachal Pradesh has a population of 13, 82, 611 people and ranks third on lowest-populated states list.
4. Goa ranks fourth with 14,5737,23 (0.12%) people.
5. Nagaland fifth lowest populated state in India with 19,80,602 (0.16%) people.

For Union Territories NCT of New Delhi, the highest populated Union Territory, has a population of 1,67,53,235 people. Lakshadweep, the lowest populated Union Territory, has a population of 64,429 people.

STATEWISE POPULATION OF INDIA AS PER 2011 CENSUS

State/ UT Code	India/State/Union Territory #	Population	Males	Females	Per cent
	India	1210193422	623724248	586469174	100.00
1.	Jammu & Kashmir	12548926	6665561	5883365	1.04
2.	Himachal Pradesh	6856509	3473892	3382617	0.57
3.	Punjab	27704236	14634819	13069417	2.29
4.	Uttarakhand	10116752	5154178	4962574	0.84
5.	Haryana	25353081	13505130	11847951	2.09
6.	Rajasthan	68621012	35620086	33000926	5.67
7.	Uttar Pradesh	199581477	104596415	94985062	16.49
8.	Bihar	103804637	54185347	49619290	8.58
9.	Sikkim	607688	321661	286027	0.05
10.	Arunachal Pradesh	1382611	720232	662379	0.11
11.	Nagaland	1980602	1025707	954895	0.16
12.	Manipur	2721756	1369764	1351992	0.22
13.	Mizoram	1091014	552339	538675	0.09

14.	Tripura	3671032	1871867	1799165	0.30
15.	Meghalaya	2964007	1492668	1471339	0.24
16.	Assom (Assam)	31169272	15954927	15214345	2.58
17.	West Bengal	91347736	46927389	44420347	7.55
18.	Jharkhand	32966238	16931688	16034550	2.72
19.	Orissa	41947358	21201678	20745680	3.47
20.	Chhattisgarh	25540196	12827915	12712281	2.11
21.	Madhya Pradesh	72597565	37612920	34984645	6.00
22.	Gujarat	60383628	31482282	28901346	4.99
23.	Maharashtra	112372972	58361397	54011575	9.29
24.	Andhra Pradesh	84665533	42509881	42155652	7.00
25.	Karnataka	61130704	31057742	30072962	5.05
26.	Goa	1457723	740711	717012	0.12
27.	Kerala	33387677	16021290	17366387	2.76
28.	Tamil Nadu	72138958	36158871	35980087	5.96
		Union Territories			
1.	Chandigarh	1054686	580282	474404	0.09
2.	NCT of Delhi	16753235	8976410	7776825	1.38
3.	Daman and Diu	242911	150100	92811	0.02
4.	Dadra and Nagar Haveli	342853	193178	149675	0.03
5.	Lakshadweep	64428	33106	31323	0.01
6.	Puducherry	1244464	610485	633979	0.10
7.	Andman and Nicobar Islands	379944	202330	177614	0.03

EXERCISES

Long Answer Type Questions

1. Write a detailed note on Integration and Democratisation of Indian States.
2. What do you know about the reorganisation of Indian States?

Short Answer Type Questions

1. What is the importance of Integration ?
2. Write a brief note on 'Separate Statehood' demands in other parts of India.

Objective Type Questions

1. According to the census of 2011 which State is on the top of population?

   (*a*) Uttar Pradesh (*b*) Maharashtra

   (c) Bihar (*d*) West Bengal

2. Which State has second highest population according to the census of 2011?

(a) Bihar (b) Maharashtra

(c) West Bengal (d) Andhra Pradesh

3. Which State is the lowest populated State in India?

(a) Goa (b) Nagaland

(c) Sikkim (d) Mizoram

4. Telangana is situated in which State of India?

(a) Maharashtra (b) Tamil Nadu

(c) Kerala (d) Andhra Pradesh

5. The demand of Gorkhaland is related from which State?

(a) West Bengal (b) Nagaland

(c) Goa (d) Tamil Nadu

ANSWERS

1. (a) 2. (b) 3. (c) 4. (d) 5. (a)

CHAPTER 12

The Role of Governor in State Politics

"The functions of the Governor shall be to lubricate the machine of the Government, to see that its wheels are going on well by reason not of his interference, but of friendly co-operation."
—Dr. P.K. Sen

The Constitution of India has adopted a Parliamentary system of Government at the Centre as well as in the states. At the state level, executive authority is vested in the Governor, who enjoys a position analogous to the President at the Centre. Article 154 of the Constitution vests all the executive powers of the State in the Governor, which are exercised by him either directly or through officers subordinate to him in accordance with the Constitution. It may be noted that the Governor of State, like the President of India, is only a constitutional head and the real powers are exercised by the Council of Ministries headed by the Chief Minister.

Appointment. The Governor of a State is appointed by the President for a period of five years. He holds his office at the pleasure of the President. A Governor may be removed by the President in mid-term or may resign at any time he likes. A person becomes eligible for the Governor's office only if he is a citizen of India and has crossed 35 years of age. After his appointment he cannot remain the member of any House, nor can he hold any office of profit.

Salary and Allowances. A Governor, or Rajyapal as he is called, is entitled to a monthly salary of Rs. 1,10,000 plus various allowances and privileges as are specified in the Governor's (Emoluments, Allowances and Privileges) Act, 1982 as amended in 2006. He is entitled to the use of his official residence. His emoluments once fixed cannot be reduced during his term of office.

Executive Powers. The executive power of the State is vested in the Governor as the executive power of Union vests in the President. He exercises his executive power either directly, or through his subordinates. All executive actions of the State are executed in the name of the Governor. His executive power extends to all those subjects on which the State Legislature is empowred to make laws. The Constitution says that he will appoint a Council of Ministries headed by a Chief Minister. In the appointment of the Minister, he is guided by the advice of the Chief Minister. The Ministers hold office during the pleasure of the Governor. He also appoints the Advocate General, the Chairman and the members of the State Public Service Commission. He also nominates representatives of the Anglo-Indian community in the State Assembly. He can secure from the Chief Minister any information relating to the executive and legislative affairs of the State. He himself decides which matter should be decided in his discretion. His decision is final and cannot be questioned in any court of law.

Legislative Powers. The legislative powers of the Governor are identical with those of the President. He is part of the State Legislature. He has the right to summon, prorogue or dissolve the Legislative Assembly. He can call a joint sitting of both the Houses. He can address either or both the Houses assembled together. He may send messages to the Legislature and request the consideration of some topic for a new Legislation. No Bill passed by the Legislature can become a law without his assent. He may give his assent in which case the Bill receives the validity of law. He may, if he likes, withhold his assent or send it back to the House for reconsideration with or without his message, or reserve it for the consideration of the President. He, however, cannot withhold his assent if the Bill returned by him for reconsideration is passed and presented before him by the Legislature again. He delivers the inaugural address to the House. He has the power of making ordinances during the recess of the Legislature to meet some emergency. A Governor's Ordinance ceases to operate six weeks after the reassembly of the Legislature if not disapproved earlier by the State Legislature.

Financial Powers. The Governors of States are vested with enormous financial powers. No Money Bill can be introduced in the State Assembly except with his permission. He is also responsible for getting the Annual Budget prepared and laid before the House or Houses of the Legislature. No demand for grant from the State revenue can be made by any Minister except with his consent.

Judicial Powers. The judicial powers of the Governor include the appointment and promotion of the District Judges. He is also consulted in the appointment of the Judges of High Court by the President. He has the power to pardon, commute and remit sentence of any person convicted by a State Court. He cannot be sued in any court of law during his term of office.

Position of the Governor. The position of the Governor is not exactly the same as that of the President of India. The President of India is only a Constitutional Head. He is required to act generally on the advice of the Council of Ministers.

Even in the light of the Governor's powers given above, it should not be concluded that the Governor can at any stage become a dictator. In normal time he has to abide by the recommendations of his Ministers who remain for all their actions answerable to the State Legislature. In times of Proclamation of Emergency, he has to execute the orders of the President *i.e.* the Central Government. Our opinion is also confirmed by the observations, regarding the power of the Governor under the new Constitution, made by a special Bench of the Calcutta High Court in the case of Sunil Kumar Bose and others *vs.* the Chief Secretary to the Government of West Bengal (1950):

"The Governor under the present Constitution cannot act except in accordance with the advice of his Ministers. Under the Government of India Act, 1935, the position was different. The Governor could do certain acts in his discretion, that is, without asking for the advice of any Minister, he could do certain acts in his individual capacity, that is, only after consulting his Ministers but he was not bound when acting in his individual capacity to follow the advice of his Ministers. Under the present Consitution, the power to act in his discretion or in his individual capacity has been taken away and the Governor, therefore, must act on the advice of his Ministers. This is the constitutional position as explained to us by the Advocate-General and we accept his view."

An Ex-Governor, Dr. Gopal Singh, speaks on the position and practical useful role of the Governor. Dr. Gopal Singh has been one of the leading intellectuals and statesmen of his age. He has written many good books. He has been an M.P., ambassador and Chairman of the Minorities Commission.

He has been Lt. Governor of Goa and later on its Governor when it attained statehood. He was the Governor of Nagaland when he resigned his office at the bidding of the President in mid-January, 1990 along with others when the National Front Government requested the President to ask the Governors appointed in the Congress regime to quit. Even after the President asked all Governors to quit, he was persuaded by the Foreign Minister I.K. Gujral and Prime Minister, Mr. V.P. Singh, not to quit but he was offered the Governorship of Arunachal Pradesh in addition to it. But he declined the offer. Just a few days before his death, he gave an exclusive interview to the *Hindustan Times* dated 12th August, 1990 in which he expressed his view about the useful practical role of the Governor. He says: "The Supreme Court has adjudicated, a Governor is neither an agent of the Central Government nor its employee nor subservient to the Central Government."

"He is the head of a particular State, his word carries weight, therefore, with the Central Government and also with the State Government.

"If the Governor is not biased or hostile, his advice (even reprimind) is always accepted gracefully by everyone, not excluding the Opposition. Particularly, he can be guardian angel for the weak and the oppressed and also engage himself through voluntary agencies, like the Red Cross for their welfare. His address to various organisations in defence of peace and harmony against sectarianism and provincialism and for the unity of the nation could create an atmosphere of stability in the State. But it all depends on the particular individual; how much respect and moral authority he commands, due to his many qualities of head and heart.

"If a Governor keeps a fair equation with a democratically elected Government and also with the Opposition (equally democratically thrown up), so as to not only look but also act impartially, by and large, it only brings credit to the incumbents as well as the appointing authority. It makes the stability in the state, and infuses democratic morality in the general environment.

"Whenever a crisis occurred during my tenure as Governor, I used my powers of intellectual persuasion and moral authority to resolve the issue.

"Only once during my four and a half years of tenure as Lt. Governor and later Governor in Goa was firing resorted to, in which one young person lost his life. This was the height of the language agitation. I refused to budge, however, and insisted on the question being resolved only on the floor of the Assembly and not on the streets. This was ultimately agreed to by everyone. Goa had political stability and communal harmony all throughout. During my time it was connected by air not only with the rest of India but also with the Western Europe and the Middle East. Its tourist traffic more than doubled, from four lakhs to nearly one million. I built a new university for Goa."

Lastly, he says, " The Governors are sometimes obliged to play politics not on their own, but the worthies at the Centre is thus very obvious. If he does not, he becomes a *persona non grata*. But although those who want to keep their conscience and adhere also to the constitutional norms, may suffer a setback in their own careers, they are a salt of the earth and ultimately their actions and judgements become the norms of the democratic behaviour in the days to come."

Governor not agent of Centre—Views of Dr. P.C. Alexander. The outgoing Governor of Tamil Nadu, Dr. P.C. Alexander, looking back at his 28 months of Governorship of the state as the most satisfying period in his career, made it plain on May 23, 1990 that *"A Governor was not an agent of the Centre in state"*. While expressing his gratitude to Mr. Karunanidhi, Chief Minister and others for their unreserved support, he said that *"A Governor does not have to take instructions from the Centre."* He stated that "Just as the President took oath to work for the interests and welfare of the people of the country, the Governor took the oath to do work for the welfare of people of the state."

Dr. Alexander also said that "The Governor and the Chief Minister worked for the same cause and that he represented the executive powers of the state for promoting the interests and welfare of the people and not to function merely like a watchdog of the Centre."

Governor not the Central Agent, says former Governor (Mr. Bhishma Narain Singh) after their resignations on the advice of the President. On the advice of the Prime Minister, Mr. Vishwa Nath Pratap Singh, the President of India Mr. Ramaswami Venkataraman asked all the Governors and Lt. Governors to resign on January 15, 1990 and consequently all the Governors resigned. Their resignations were accepted till 1st February, 1990.

"A State Governor is not an agent of the Centre but an independent constitutional office which serves as a vital link between the Centre and the States." This view was expressed on 9th February, 1990 at New Delhi by Mr. Bhishma Narain Singh, former Governor of Assam and Meghalaya who had steered the State through the turbulent days of the agitation.

Mr. Bhisma Narain Singh felt that he should have a secure tenure of five years in accordance with Article 156 (3) of the Constitution and asking them to resign *en masse* was not setting a healthy precedent. He said the Governor was a creature of the Constitution and he or she was the head of the State. The Governor's duties and functions had been laid down in the Constitution itself (Part VI, Chapter II). This issue of the role of Governor was examined by a committee of Governors set up by the President in 1970 and by the Sarkaria Commission on Centre-State relations too. *Besides, there was the judicial pronouncement by the Supreme Court by a full bench headed by Chief Justice Y.V. Chandrachud in 1978 in Dr. Raghukul Tilak's case (then Governor of Rajasthan).*

In no case, Mr. Bhisma Narain Singh said quoting these reports and judgments, was the Governor subservient or subordinate to the Government of India and he or she was not amenable to any direction by the Union Government.

Asked in this connection what was the difference between the roles the President on the one hand and the State Governors on the other hand had to play, Mr. Bhisma Narain Singh said : "Both offices are those of heads of state. Both offices have more moral than executive authority. Both functionaries are friends, philosophers and guides to their Governments. Excepting in the case of the appointment of Prime Minister, the President functions on the advice of the Council of Ministries. The Governors have greater discretionary powers and some have special responsibilities."

He does not find anything wrong in former governors joining politics. He cites the example of Mr. C. Rajagopalacharya who had taken over as the Chief Minister of (the then) Madras state even after remaining the Governor-General of India. This had only enhanced the prestige of the office he held later and the senior statesman was quite conscious of this impartiality and non-political role while he had held exalted office of the Governor-General. Mr. Bhisma Narain Singh, however, said that a Governor should not indulge in or get associated with politics.

On being asked what should be the role of Governors in determining the majority support a prospective Chief Minister in the newly elected State Assembly enjoyed, Mr. Singh said that *this should be tested, as far as possible, on the floor of the House only.* However, it was also true that an Assembly could not be summoned without a Chief Minister being in office. The Governor, therefore, had to depend on some other evidence too, in order to decide upon this issue and appoint a Chief Minister, he said.

He added: "I firmly believe on two points in this connection. First, there should not be no head count or a parade of supporters before the Governor, and, secondly, in the event of a clear majority, not being apparent, *the Chief Minister must be asked to establish his support in the House within as short a time as is reasonably possible.*"

Conclusion

Thus we come to the conclusion that although the Governor is a constitutional head, yet he wields tremendous influence and can have a permanent impact on the administration by rendering useful service in every walk of life by his intellect, capacity and long experience. Thus the office of the Governor is not superfluous as has been alleged by several persons but is of great utility.

CHANGED ROLE OF GOVERNORS AFTER INDEPENDENCE

Mr. Dharam Vir, who had been Governor of the Punjab, West Bengal and Karnataka, had expressed his views about the changed role of the Governors in some interviews and articles. He said on October 10, 1969, "In the early period after independence, when there was one party stable Government all over the country, the responsibilities of the Governor were merely those of a constitutional head. But in the present, when political loyalties are shifting fast and when multi-party Governments and Governments different politically from that operating at the Centre are functioning, his responsibilities have greatly increased."[1] Dharam Vir has said, "It is the responsibility of the Governor to see that the Government of the State is run in accordance with the letter as well as with the spirit of the Constitution. When political complexions of political parties change on account of shifting loyalties, it becomes very necessary that the Governor should be very vigilant in order to ensure that the government is run by a party or collection of parties, which have the majority in their favour. He has to ensure that by taking shelter behind certain consitutional lacuna a minority government does not continue to function indefinitely. He has also to exercise considerable discretion at the time of the formation of a Government. If there are multi-party groups coming together this discretion has to be exercised very carefully to ensure that the group or the party which wants to form the Government is really in a majority and can form a stable Government."[2]

What the Government should do if the Ministry loses majority?—Mr. Dharam Vir again expressed his views about the changed role of the Governors in his Article[3] on December 21, 1972. He writes, "Under Article 174 (1) not more than six months shall intervene between the last sitting of the Legislature in one session and the date appointed for the first sitting in the next session. If the Chief Minister taking advantage of this provision in the Constitution attempts to prolong the life of his Ministry, even after seemingly losing majority support, what should the Governor do in the interests of the spirit of the Constitution and the traditions of parliamentary democracy? Should he be a helpless spectator of the violation of democratic practices or should he after giving sufficient time to the Chief Minister to advise him to call the Legislature, dismiss the Ministry and call the leader of new majority to form the Government? While raising these questions it must be remembered that normally the matter of a Government enjoying or losing majority support should be settled on floor of the House and not elsewhere. A Governor who tries to settle this ticklish question at his discretion in this matter should do so only in very extreme circumstances and only in the true interest of the Constitution and democratic practices. In fact, it would really be desirable to get this lacuna in the Consitution remedied. Instead of subjecting the Governor to the necessity of exercising his discretion in this matter, *he should under certain circumstances be enabled to summon the Legislature at his discretion, regardless of the advice of the Chief Minister, to settle the question of majority support.*[4]

Governor's position in advising President's Rule. There comes the uncertain and tricky period when the Ministry in the State becomes unstable. At this juncture the Governor becomes the true custodian of the Constitution. He must act in a completely unbiased and objective manner in the true spirit of the Constitution and parliamentary democractic practices. It is a difficult task but it is to perform only such tasks that people are raised to such exalted positions. There comes a stage when the Governor finds that a situation has arisen in the state under which the Government of the State cannot be carried on in accordance with the provision of the Constitution.

When the President takes over the administration of the State under Article 356, the Ministry ceases to be and the Governor is required to administer the State on behalf of the President. He,

1. "Interview with Dharam Vir", *The Hindustan Times*, New Delhi, October 11, 1969.
2. *Ibid*
3. See the Article of Dharam Vir, about the 'Changed Role of Governors' in *The Motherland*, New Delhi, dated December 22, 1972, p. 5 columns, 3-6.
4. *Ibid.*

in fact, becomes the Governor and Ministry rolled into one and his work, functions and duties get increased considerably.[1]

Governor's duty to safeguard the interests of the State during President's Rule. Another matter which is very important during the President's rule is that of safeguarding the interests of the states. When a Ministry is in office, it is the guardian of the interests of the State *vis-a-vis* the Centre and other States. During the President's rule, however, there is no Ministry. What is the duty of the Governor during this period when he is not only the Head of the State, but also is the *de facto* Ministry? If he feels that in some matters the State is being unfairly treated, is it his duty to speak out or should he keep quiet on the plea that ultimately it is really the President's concern and, at the most, he should be satisfied with bringing matters to the notice of the President? Here again the oath of office of the Governor comes into operation. According to the oath a Governor undertakes to devote himself to the service and well-being of the people entrusted to his charge to the best of his ability."[2] In the face of this oath a Governor worthy of his salt cannot and should not keep quiet if he genuinely feels that the interests of the State entrusted to his charge are jeopardised. It would not be enough to shift his responsibility by merely drawing the attention of the President to the matter. He has a constitutional duty, particularly in the absence of a Ministry, to discharge, and if need be, he must speak out even at the risk of incurring the displeasure of the powers-that-be at the Centre.[3]

CONTROVERSY REGARDING THE ROLE OF GOVERNORS

Controversy regarding the role of the Governor of Bihar

After the 4th General Elections S.V.D. (Sanyukt Vidhayak Dal) Government was formed under the leadership of Mr. Mahamaya Prasad Sinha, but due to defections, the S.V.D. lost majority. The Governor did not recommend the President's Rule and gave an opportunity to the Congress to form the Government. Mr. Bhola Nath Paswan formed the Congress Government, but it also could not last long due to defections. So the Governor of Bihar recommended the President's Rule to the Centre. Opposition parties criticised this action of the Governor as they had been denied the opportunity to form the alternative Government.

Controversy regarding the role of the Governor of Bengal

In Bengal after the 4th General Elections S.V.D. (Sanyukt Vidhayak Dal) Government was formed under the leadership of Mr. Ajoy Mookerjee. Except the Congress, nearly all other parties participated in the Government. Due to internal quarrels and bickerings among the various constituents of S.V.D. and the encouragement given by the Congress to the defectors, Mr. Ajoy Mookerjee's Government lost majority. After that Mr. Prafulla Chandra Ghosh formed the Congress Government. That Government also did not last long and ultimately Mr. Dharam Vir, the Governor of West Bengal, recommended the President's Rule. When Mr. Ajoy Mookerjee was removed from Chief Ministership by the Governor, then his action was severely criticised by S.V.D. In February, 1968, the President's Rule was imposed on Bengal. In February, 1969, mid-term elections were held and again Sanyukt Vidhayak Dal Government was formed under the leadership of Mr. Ajoy Mookerjee.

Governor Dharam Vir created history in the West Bengal Legislature on March 6, 1969, by refusing to read from the address given to him by the United Front Cabinet-portions which were derogatory to him and the Central Government. *These paragraphs had described the dismissal of the previous United Front Ministry on November 21, 1967, as constitutional, accused the Central Government of acclaiming this anti-democractic act and referred to the results of the mid-term poll as a decisive warning that the democratic rights of the people could not be trifled with by unprincipled tampering with the Constitution.* The two Houses of the West Bengal Legislature had assembled for the inaugu-

1. *Ibid.*
2. *Ibid*
3. *Ibid*

ration of the budget session in an atmosphere surcharged with emotion. After an exchange of letters between him and the Chief Minister, Mr. Ajoy Mookerjee, over the text of speech–the Governor had pleaded in vain with the Cabinet to delete the objectionable portions–Mr. Dharam Vir made it clear long before the joint session that he would not read the portions he had objected to. Inaugurating the budget session, Mr. Dharam Vir said : "The present state of affairs in which the States have an ever-increasing multiplicity of responsibilities to discharge with virtually inelastic resources and powers and the Centre commands the bulk of resources and constitutional powers, while being comparatively remote and isolated from the people, is frankly intolerable. The new Government will therefore try to do its utmost to bring about this overdue readjustment of power between the Centre and States."[1]

Mr. Dharam Vir did not read the paragraphs to which he had objected. The then Bengal Chief Minister, Mr. Ajoy Mookerjee, criticised this step of the Governor and termed it as unconstitutional. Mr. Bhupesh Gupta (Communist) criticised this step of the Governor in Rajya Sabha. In Lok Sabha Communist leader Mr. S.A. Dange, Jana Sangh leader Atal Bihari Vajpayee, Marxist leader Nambiar and N.G. Ranga criticised this act of the Governor on March 6, 1969. Swatantra Party leader, N.G. Ranga, said, "Here is a Governor who goes against the Constitution and the Centre allows him."[2] The Cabinet of Bengal demanded the recall of Governor Dharam Vir. United Front Cabinet headed by Mr. Ajoy Mookerjee demanded the Governor of its choice. On March 22, 1969, Chief Minister Ajoy Mookerjee and Deputy Chief Minister Jyoti Basu told Prime Minister Indira Gandhi on the same day (March 22, 1969) on the telephone that the responsibility for the appointment of the person suggested by her as the new Governor of West Bengal will entirely rest with the Central Government.

They said any new Governor sent to the State without prior consultation with the State Government would be your choice, not ours.[3] Centre rejected the Bengal United Front list for governorships.[4] Dharam Vir, however, insisted on his transfer and he asked for leave. He left West Bengal on March 28, 1969.

Controversy regarding the role of the Governor of M.P.

In M.P. the Congress Ministry was formed under the leadership of Mr. Dwarka Prasad Mishra after the 4th General Elections, but in July, 1967, Mr. Govind Narain Singh with 20 Congress Legislators defected to the Opposition. Therefore, the Congress Ministry fell. Mr. Govind Narain Singh, thereupon, formed Sanyukt Vidhayak Dal with the help of the Opposition parties and Ministry was installed into office under his leadership. The various constituents of Sanyukt Vidhayak Dal could not pull on together due to ideological and other reasons; consequently Mr. Govind Narain Singh tendered his resignation on March 10, 1969. After that Mr. K.C. Reddy, Governor of M.P., invited S.V.D. leader Raja Naresh Chandra Singh of Sarangarh to form the Ministry. The action of the Governor was criticised on the ground that he did not invite Raja Naresh Chandra immediately to form the Government as was insisted by the outgoing Chief Minister Govind Narain Singh. Govind Narain Singh wanted that the respective claims of strength of S.V.D. and the Congress should be tested on the floor of the House, but the Governor refused to invite Raja Naresh Chandra Singh to form the Ministry before the meeting of Legislative Assembly. Thereupon, Mr. Govind Narain Singh advised the Governor to prorogue the Assembly which the Governor did. The Opposition leaders criticised this action of the Governor, Mr. K.C. Reddy, in Lok Sabha on March 12, 1969. After a week Govind Narain Singh and his 19 other supporters left S.V.D. and rejoined the Congress. Therefore the S.V.D. lost majority and on 19th March, 1969 Chief Minister Raja Naresh Chandra Singh submitted his resignation to the Governor. He also recommended to the Governor the dissolution of the Assembly because of defections and instability that had been created. Governor K.C. Reddy informed caretaker

1. *Hindustan Times*, New Delhi, dated March 7, 1969, p. 1, columns 1-3, and p.2, columns 3-5.
2. *Ibid*
3. *Hindustan Times*, New Delhi, dated March 23, 1969.
4. *Hindustan Times*, New Delhi, dated March 22, 1969, p.1, columns 1-3.

Chief Minister Raja Naresh Chandra Singh on March 21, 1969, that he was not accepting his advice to dissolve the Assembly. A press communique issued from Raj Bhawan on that day that "after carefully examining all aspects of the issue, the Governor has decided to reject the advice of the Chief Minister, that is, dissolution of the Assembly." The communique added that necessary steps will be taken for forming an alternative Government. "Till such a time a Government is duly constituted, the Governor has requested the Chief Minister to carry on."[1] Rajmata Vijaya Raje Sindhia, Jan Sangh Secretary Kushabhau Thakre and SSP leader S.P. Chanpuria criticised the Governor's decision and described it as partisan.[2] The Rajmata said it was obvious that Mr. Reddy had been influenced by party interests. She said that defections could not lead to the establishment of a stable Government, and remarked she will have to "pull out thorn with thorn."[3] The Congress M.P.s. from Madhya Pradesh also felt sore at the re-admission of 20 defectors (Govind Narain Singh and others).[4]

Controversy regarding the role of the Governor in U.P. in 1970, a very famous case

The Governor asked for the opinion of the Attorney-General, Mr. Niren De, in this connection. According to the opinion received from the Attorney-General, the Governor, Mr. Gopal Reddy, decided that Chaudhary Charan Singh first of all should tender his resignation because after the withdrawal of support of the Congress (I) he had been reduced to a minority. The Governor also refused to dismiss 27 Ministers of Congress (I). The Governor also told Mr. Charan Singh that the session of the Legislative Assembly could be called before October 6, 1970, only on the advice of the Council of Ministers but as there was no Council of Ministers, so the session of the Legislative Assembly could not be called earlier. He also told Chaudhary Charan Singh that if he had got the support of Jana Sangh, Congress (Organisation) and Swatantra then, first of all he should resign, and when he was called upon to form a new Government, then he should do so with the help of other parties, whose support he claimed, but Chaudhary Charan Singh refused to tender his resignation from the Chief Ministership. Consequently, Mr. Gopal Reddy, the Governor of U.P., sent a report to the President that the party position in the State was very fluid due to claims and counter-claims of the various parties to form the Government, therefore, he was of the opinion that no stable Government could be formed in the State. He further said in his report, "It is not in public interest to allow this uncertainty to remain, therefore, I recommend the Legislative Assembly should be suspended." He also recommended that the President should take over the administration of U.P. in accordance with Article 356 of the Constitution. The President, Mr. V.V. Giri, had gone to Russia at that time on a State visit. In his absence the Prime Minister deliberated over this report in her Council of Ministers and showed agreement with the report of the Governor. The Prime Minister sent a courier to Russia to get the signature of the President for proclamining Presidential rule in U.P. The President, Mr. V.V. Giri, signed this proclamation on October 2, 1970. In this way President's Rule was imposed on U.P. and the Government of Chaudhary Charan Singh came to an end.

Criticism. This action of the Governor of U.P. was criticised by the leaders of the various Opposition parties and constitutional experts on following grounds:

First, when the session of the Legislative Assembly was scheduled to be held on 6th October, 1970, then it was improper for the Governor to recommend the President's Rule. He should have given an opportunity to the former Chief Minister Charan Singh to prove his strength in the Assembly, especially when he was ready to call the Legislative Assembly even earlier on September 30, or October 1, 1970.

1. *Ibid.*
2. *Ibid.*
3. *Ibid.*
4. *Hindustan Times*, New Delhi, dated 22 March, 1969, p. 1, column 1.

Secondly, when before this in a similar situation in the Punjab, Jana Sangh had left the coalition of Akali Party, then the Punjab Governor, Mr. D.C. Pavate, had not asked Chief Minister Prakash Singh Badal to resign, but he had allowed Chief Minister Badal to prove his majority in the Legislative Assembly.

Thirdly, previous to this happening in Uttar Pradesh, it had been decided in various conferences of the Governors and Speakers of the Legislative Assemblies that the Governor himself would not decide whether the Chief Minister commanded the majority or not, rather he will allow the Chief Minister to test his strength on the floor of the House.

Fourthly, when the President had been on a State visit of U.S.S.R. and he was not in the know of full facts of U.P.'s fluid political position, then he should not have acted like a rubber stamp on the report of the Governor and decision of the Central Cabinet.

Fifthly, when due to the split in the Congress Party in 1969, Indira Gandhi's Government had been reduced to minority, then the President had not asked her to resign first and then form the Government with the help of other parties.

As this case of U.P. is most important for the functioning of democratic system in our country, so some opinions of the constitutional experts are being given below:

Former Attorney-General, Mr. S.V. Setalvad, was of the view that it was highly improper for the Governor to have asked the Chief Minister to resign when the Assembly was to meet in a few days. It should have been left to the Assembly to decide as to whether he had the majority support or not. The imposition of President's Rule, he asserted, could not be justified. It was an extraordinary development to put the State under Central rule, when the Assembly was scheduled to meet within a week.[1]

Former Solicitor-General, Mr. S.V. Gupta, did not consider it necessary that Mr. Charan Singh should have resigned following withdrawal of support by coalition partner, the Congress (I). Mr. Charan Singh was entitled to continue as Chief Minister though his party might be in a minority as at one time the Prime Minister did at the Centre. He should be required to establish majority in the Assembly at the earliest opportunity.[2]

According to Dr. L.N. Singhvi, "When an Assembly is in session or has been summoned to meet shortly, it is not for the Governor to determine whether or not a Chief Minister enjoys majority support. It is constitutional imperative for him to keep detached from party controversy and not get involved over the question of majority as far as he can avoid it and get it decided by the Legislature as early as possible."[3]

Chaudhary Charan Singh sought the opinion of the Advocate-General of U.P., Mr. K.L. Mishra, on this constitutional point. The Advocate-General expressed his opinion in these words: The opinion of the Attorney-General on Governor's role was not based upon any provisions of the Constitution or any authority, but a "vague and uncertain criterion" on what the Governor called "the Principles of Parliamentary democracy." Mr. Mishra further said in a reply to the letter of Mr. Charan Singh, "The Attorney-General has said, in his opinion, that a Chief Minister will have no right to advise the Governor to dismiss some Ministries of the Coalition Ministry. I frankly concede that I have not been able to understand this portion of opinion. It is a settled propostion in Great Britain and in other countries having parliamentary democracy that the continuance of a Minister is completely and irrevocably in the hands of the Chief Minister. It is also settled that the pleasure of the Governor in the matter of tenure of the Minister is really the pleasure of the Chief Minister. I can only say that I am not aware of a single instance in the constitutional history of any parliamentary democracy

1. *Hindustan Times*, New Delhi, dated October 1, 1970. p.1, column 5.
2. *Ibid*
3. *Ibid*

within the last 100 years where the advice of a Chief Minister about the termination of the office of a Minister has not been accepted."[1]

The former Chief Justice of India, Mr. K. Subba Rao, criticised that imposition of President's Rule in U.P. on 4th October, 1970 at Bangalore as indefensible from legal, practical and Parliamentary democratic conventional point of view. Talking to newsmen Mr. Rao said that the President's order could be challenged in High Court on the ground that the conditions envisaged in the Consitution for such an action were not satisfied by a reasonable mind. Mr. Rao said, the constitutional provision had clearly laid down that the President should satisfy himself that the Government of a State could not be carried on in accordance with the provisions of the Constitution before imposing the President's Rule. This meant that the President should satisfy himself and not the Central Ministry that a situation had arisen to impose President's Rule."[2]

Mr. Morarji Desai who had been the member of undivided Congress Working Committee and Finance Minister of India and later on became the Prime Minister of India, said on October 7, 1970, "Chaudhary Charan Singh's dismissal by the Governor when only three days had been left in the meeting of the Legislative Assembly, was wholly improper. In a similar situation in the Punjab President's Rule had not been imposed because it suited the Central Government. Instead of amending the Constitution it is proper to punish the erring Governor."[3] Mr. S. Nijalingappa, the then President of the Congress (Organisation), said that the imposition of President's Rule in U.P. was politically wrong, objectionable and undemocratic. We do not know where are we being taken in this way?[4] Mr. Atal Behari Vajpayee, the then President of Jana Sangh, said, that it was dark day for democracy. The opinion of the majority of the legislators of U.P. Speakers' Conferences, Administrative Reforms Commission and National Press have been violated only in order to please the Prime Minister.[5]

Controversy regarding the role of the Governor of Orissa in 1973

After the mid-term elections New Congress secured 51 seats out of the 140 total seats of the House. Swatantra Party got 37 seats, Congress (Organisation) one seat, Communists 4 seats, Marxists 2 seats. P.S.P. (Praja Samajvadi Party) 4 seats, Independents 4, other parties 37 seats. In the mid-term election, the Congress emerged as the largest single party, but failed to secure a majority. A Swatantra-Utkal Congress-Jharkhand coalition Ministry headed by Mr. Bishwanath Das was sworn in after the mid-term elections. This ministry resigned on June 9, 1962 after the Utkal Congress decided to merge with the New Congress, paving the way for the formation of Satpathy Ministry on June 14, 1972.

The Orissa Ministry headed by Mrs. Nandini Satpathy resigned on March 1, 1973, following defections from the ruling party, among the defectors being the Deputy Chief Minister, Mr. Nilamony Routray, who announced he had rejoined Utkal Congress which had separated itself again from the Congress. Mrs. Nandini Satpathy who had been asked by the Governor to continue as Chief Minister till alternative arrangements were made also recommended the dissolution of the Assembly. The Utkali Congress leader, Mr. Biju Patnaik, who was also the leader of the new Pragati Party, Opposition in the State Assembly, called on the Governor, B.D. Jatti, within hours of Mrs. Satpathy's resignation early on March 1, 1973 and staked his claim to form a Government. *Mr. Patnaik who claimed the support of 78 members in the 140-seat House, later in the evening led his supporters to Raj Bhawan in a parade before the Governor to give physical backing to his claim.*

In spite of this, the State Governor, Mr. B.D. Jatti, recommended the President's Rule and dissolution of State Assembly. In making this recommendation the Governor accepted the advice of

1. *Hindustan Times*, New Delhi, dated September 30, 1970. p.1. column 1.
2. *Hindustan Times*, New Delhi, October 5, 1970, p.5, cols 5-7
3. *Hindustan Times*, dated October 8, 1970, p. 5, cols 5-7.
4. *Hindustan Times*, New Delhi, dated October 3, 1970, p. 12, cols. 1-4.
5. *Ibid.*

the Chief Minister to dissolve the Assembly, so that her party could seek a fresh mandate from the poeple for its progressive policies.[1] The Governor's report is understood to have rejected the claim of the Opposition Pragati Legislature Party, headed by Biju Patnaik, to form an alternative Government on the ground that it could not provide a stable Government in the prevailing political situation in the State.[2] Mr. Biju Patnaik warned the Centre against imposition of the President's Rule in the State and reiterated that he should be invited by the Governor, as the leader of the single majority party in the Assembly, immediately to assist in the formation of an alternative Government. He said that the Pragati Legislature Party had a clear majority support in the Assembly to establish a stable Government. Strongly opposing the reported suggestion made by the Congress President Shankar Dayal Sharma for a spell of President's Rule in Orrisa to be followed by mid-term poll, Mr. Patnaik said, "It would be a mistake if the Delhi 'badshahs, (kings) manoeuvre to subvert established democratic practices and conventions and get President's Rule in the State."[3] He further said that "the people of the State would not tolerate President's Rule which is undemocratic and will assert their democratic right."[4]

On March 3, 1973, the President, Mr. V.V. Giri issued a proclamation under Article 356 of the Constitution dissolving the Orissa Assembly and imposing Central rule in the State. In this way Orissa came under the Central rule for the second time. It had come under President's Rule for the first time in January, 1971.

The Opposition reacted fiercely to the imposition of President's Rule in Orrisa. "It is a fraud on the Constitution"; "It is a butchery of democracy"; "It is an authoritative measure" were some of the epithets used by them to describe the Central action in Orissa.[5] The strongest condemnation came from Mr. Piloo Mody, the President of Swatantra Party and also M.P., who said, on March 3, 1973 that with the imposition of the Central rule the "vultures of power" had once again made a mockery of democracy just because the Congress (Indicate) *i.e.*, Congress of Indira Gandhi was thrown out of power.[6] "The present situation in Orissa Legislature", Mr. Piloo Mody added, "was exactly the same as it was eight-and-half months ago. It was through a series of defections that the Congress (Indicate) had converted a hopeless minority into a majority and captured power. That was the right time to dissolve the Assembly. Today when the *status quo ante* has been resorted, it can truly be construed that the Congress will stoop to any level to perpetuate its own power."[7] Commenting on the Governor's report that went in favour of the outgoing Chief Minister Nandini Satpathy, Mr. Mody said, "that the entire institution of Governors had been disgraced by this service compliance with Central pressure."[8]

Speaking at Meerut on 3rd March, 1973 at Dev Nagri Degree College, Shri Atal Behari Vajpayee, former Jana Sangh President and later on Foreign Minister, said, "Orissa Governor B.D. Jatti, strengthened the hands of Central Government by unconstitutionally recommending President's Rule in the State. The Ruling Party at the Centre wanted to rule in every state and could not brook any Opposition Party coming to power in the States."[9]

Manipur placed under Central Rule, Advice of the Governor not accepted regarding the suspension of the Assembly

On March 28, 1973, President V.V. Giri took over the administration of Manipur but dissolved the Assembly instead of keeping it under suspension as had been recommended by Governor B.K.

1. *The Tribune*, Chandigarh, dated March 3, 1973, p.1, columns 7-8.
2. *Ibid.*, p. 12, column 4.
3. *The Tribune*, March, 3, 1973, p. 12, columns 4-5.
4. *Ibid.*
5. The Motherland, New. Delhi, dated March 4, 1973, p. 1, column 3.
6. *Ibid.*
7. *The Motherland*, New Delhi, dated March 4, 1973, p. 1, columns 3-6.
8. *Ibid.*
9. *Ibid.*

Nehru. The proclamation under Article 356 of the Constitution was issued by Mr. Giri soon after a meeting of the Union Cabinet took the decision on the morning of March 28, 1973. *This is for the first occasion the President has disagreed with a Governor's recommendation regarding takeover of a State administration. All along the convention had been to accept the Governor's suggestion regarding imposition of President's rule or dissolution or suspension of the Assembly.*[1]

Controversy over the Sacking of Tamil Nadu Governor in 1980

The Tamil Nadu Governor, Mr. Prabhudas Patwari, was removed by the President under Article 156 on October 26, 1980. A Rashtrapati Bhawan Communique said on the night of October 25 that Mr. Patwari shall cease to hold office as Governor of Tamil Nadu with immediate effect. Mr. Prabhudas Patwari, a close associate of the former Prime Minister, Mr. Morarji Desai, had figured in the Baroda dynamite case, which had been initiated during the previous Indira Gandhi government and dropped by Janata Government. He became Governor of Tamil Nadu on March 24, 1977.

The removal of Mr. Prabhudas Patwari is the first instance of this kind since the Constitution came into force. In recent months Mr. Patwari incurred the wrath of some political parties, in particular the Congress (I) and the Dravida Munetra Kazhagam, who have been making allegations that he was aligning too much with the ruling All India D.M.K.

Criticism by Janata Party leaders. Former Prime Minister Morarji Desai and Janata Party President Chandra Shekhar described the ouster of Mr. Prabhudas Patwari from the governorship of Tamil Nadu as the most improper step while giving a Press statement in Bombay on October 27, 1980. Mr. Desai said no government had the right to change governors whose appointment was non-political. We did not change governors.[2] Stating that he was not surprised with the swift and unprecedented move, Mr. Desai said the pressure on Mr. Patwari to resign had been increasing for a long time. All that I can say is that he was very popular in Tamil Nadu and he might have been removed due to this.[3]

Janata Party President, Mr. Chandra Shekhar, while reacting sharply to Mr. Patwari's removal said, "the action which was in extreme indignity to democratic behaviour was expected of this government."[4] He further said that some people do not learn anything from their experiences.[5]

Controversy regarding the Role of Haryana Governor in 1982

Elections to the Haryana Assembly were held in May 1982. Out of 90 seats, the result of 89 seats had been declared in Haryana by 22 May, 1982. In Hissar the election to one seat had been postponed due to violence. The Congress (I) could secure 36 seats out of 89 seats, while the Lok Dal could secure 32 seats and Bharatiya Janata Party only 5 seats. The Bharatiya Janta Party extended its support to the Lok Dal. Therefore the Lok Dal leader Devi Lal claimed that he had the support of 5 members of BJP, 3 members of Congress (J), 12 Independents and one Janata member, so he should be invited to form the government. Governor G.D. Tapase asked Devi Lal to present all his supporters on 24th May, 1982 so that his claim to command majority may be verified. Before Devi Lal could do so, Mr. Tapase swore Mr. Bhajan Lal as Chief Minister of Haryana on the evening of 23rd May, 1982. This enraged Devi Lal too much and he brought all his followers to Raj Bhawan. He met the Governor and caught him by the chin or manhandled him. The Governor called his military aide and got cleared the Raj Bhawan of all the Opposition MLAs. A sharp controversy arose about the role of Governor and Devi Lal's conduct manhandling him (the Governor) which was unprecedented.

1. *The Tribune*, Chandigarh, dated March 29, 1973, p.1, columns 6-7.
2. Mr. Desai's statement as reported in the *Hindustan Times*, New Delhi, dated October 29, 1980, p.8, col. 6.
3. *Ibid.*
4. *Ibid.*
5. *Ibid.*

Fresh Controversy about the role of Governor, Opposition demand recall of Kashmir Governor

Leaders of the 19 Opposition parties in a rare unanimity called on President Zail Singh on July 12, 1984 and requested him to immediately recall the present Governor of Jammu and Kashmir and dismiss the defector Government of the State and order dissolution of the State Assembly followed by fresh elections.

In a memorandum submitted to the President by Lok Dal President Charan Singh on behalf of these parties, they expressed the hope that the President being the head of the State and the custodian of the Constitution would take immediate action on the request "so that the democratic structure, unity and integrity of our great country may flourish and prevail."

The Jammu and Kashmir Governor had removed Farooq Abdullah from Chief Ministership on 2nd July, 1984 as he had lost majority in the House followed by defections and the majority had backed Mr. G.M. Shah, son-in-law of late Sheikh Abdullah. So Mr. G.M. Shah was installed as new Chief Minister by him.

The memorandum said that the meeting of the 19 parties yesterday (July 11, 1984) had come to the conclusion that the action of the Governor of Jammu and Kashmir in dismissing Dr. Abdullah's Ministry was "unwarranted and against all democratic norms, propriety, and conventions and a deliberate subversion of the verdict of the electorate of Jammu and Kashmir."[1]

Later on addressing a Press Conference at Andhra Pradesh Bhawan, at which leaders of all the 19 Opposition parties were present, Mr. N.T. Rama Rao (then Chief Minister of Andhra) and Jyoti Basu (Chief Minister of Bengal) said that the President told them that he would study the memorandum and the constitutional aspects of the questions raised in it.

Controversy about the conduct of the Governor of Andhra Pradesh

The Governor of Andhra, Mr.. Ram Lal, dismissed the ministry of Mr. N.T.Rama Rao on August 16, 1984 because there had been a split in the Telugu Desham Party. The dismissed Chief Minister Rama Rao wanted to prove his majority before the Legislature within two days but the Governor did not give him so much time and installed Bhaskar Rao as Chief Minister instead. He gave Mr. Bhaskar Rao one month's time to prove his majority on the floor of the House.

There was a strong reaction against this move of the Governor in the Opposition circles, Rama Rao and his party Telugu Desham criticised the action of the Governor strongly. Opposition leaders especially Shri Atal Behari Vajpayee (then President of B.J.P.) condemned the action of the Governor by saying that it was the murder of democracy. The leaders of the eleven opposition parties termed the action of the Governor as immoral and unconstitutional. The entire opposition also organised two days' Bandh (complete strike) in whole of Andhra. Charan Singh, Chandra Shekhar and Sharad Pawar in a joint statement issued in Bombay on August 16, 1984 termed the action of the Governor as wholly unconstitutional and tantamount to increasing the corrupt methods. The leaders of 14 opposition parties also jointly submitted the memorandum against the Governor to the President on August 21, 1984 under the leadership of Ch.Charan Singh. President Giani Zail Singh told the opposition leaders that he would do whatever was possible in the constitutional limits.

Resignation of Ram Lal. Due to his strong denunciation in the press and by opposition parties, Ram Lal (Governor of Andhra) was asked by Mrs. Indira Gandhi to tender his resignation which he did on August 24, 1984. After this the President appointed Mr. S.D. Sharma as the new Governor of Andhra. Mr Bhaskar Rao had been given the time of one month (up to September 20, 1984) to prove his majority on the floor of the House. As Mr. Bhaskar Rao failed to prove his majority up to

1. *Hindustan Times*, New Delhi, July 13, 1984

the fixed time, so he had to resign and Mr. N.T. Rama Rao was again installed as Chief Minister. This was again a victory of democracy.

Office of the Governor has been subverted by the Centre, says the Karnataka Government

The Karnataka Government on Tuesday, September 22, 1983 said : "The constitutional position of the office of the Governor has been subverted to serve the interests of the ruling party at the Centre. The independence of the Governors has been destroyed and they were not being allowed to follow established conventions in regard to the appointment of a Chief Minister and the dissolution of a Legislature."

A White Paper on "*The office of the Governor : Constitutional position and political perversion*," placed on the table of the Assembly by Chief Minister, Ram Krishna Hegde said, "Governors have not only lent their services to keep the opposition parties out of office but also to help the Congress Party resolve its internal feuds."[1]

The second part lists case studies of deviations from the constitutional position at the instigation of the rulign party at the Centre. It mentions cases of Governors who have dabbled in politics while being in office from the days of Mr. A.P. Jain in Kerala in 1966 to the latest case of Mr. J.J. Talyerkahan in Sikkim.

It shows how Governors have applied double standards in regard to the appointment of Chief Ministers and dissolutions of Legislatures, depending upon whether the Congress Party stood to gain or lose by their decision. Among the cases covered in this regard are that of Dr. Sampurnanand of Rajasthan in 1967, Dr. B. Gopal Reddy of Uttar Pradesh in 1970 and Mr. G.D. Tapase of Haryana in May 1982.

The White Paper said that it was universally accepted that Article 356 on imposition of President's Rule has been abused. Quoting the statement of Dr. Ambedkar that "the position of the Government is exactly the same as the position of the President," the document said that this clear constitutional position has been subverted by destroying the Governor's independence and suborning his impartiality. Such action to use Governors to serve the interests of the ruling party at the Centre has undermined the norms of democracy and federal principle and violated autonomy of states.

Views of Dharam Vir, former Governor, to reform the office of the Governor

Mr. Dharam Vir, a former Governor, has suggested the removal of certain lacunae in the Constitution "which came in the way of effective functioning of Governors."

Speaking on *Role of Governor* in New Delhi on October 22, 1983, he said the law should be amended to empower the Governor to summon the Legislature by himself to decide the "limited question" whether the ruling party had lost its majority?

He suggested that when the ruling party was said to have lost its majority in the House, the Governor should go to the Assembly to check its veracity.

Mr. Dharam Vir, who served as Governor in a number of States, also suggested that Governor should remain in office for his full five-year term and the procedure for his removal should be the same as prescribed for a judge.

Controversy regarding Kashmir Governor Shri Jagmohan during the rule of National Front Government

Farooq Abdullah has been in conflict with Jagmohan, Governor of Kashmir at the time of Mr. Rajiv Gandhi. Therefore when he was appointed for the 2nd time by the Janata Dal Government on 18th January, 1990, he (Farooq Abdullah) resigned. After that Governor's rule was proclaimed for

1. *Indian Express*, Chandigarh, September 23, 1983, p. 7, cools. 4-5.

six months. After the expiry of the Governor's rule, President' Rule was proclaimed for six months and extended later on. In Kashmir the President's Rule continued till Farooq Abdullah was elected again and was sworn on 9th October 1996, as Chief Minister.

Controversy regarding the conduct of Governor Chenna Reddy — Jaya plea against Chenna order fails : The Madras High Court on Thursday (27th April, 1995) dismissed the writ petition from Tamil Nadu Chief Minister J. Lalitha to quash the order of Governor Dr. M. Chenna Reddy granting permission to the Janata Party President Dr. Subramanium Swami to launch proceedings against her on corruption charges. The High Court ruling evoked strong action from the opposition in the State Assembly. Mr. S.R. Balasubramanium demanded the resignation of the Chief Minister.

Lessons from Jaya-Chenna clash, Governor should be appointed in consultation with C.M., says Soli J. Sorabjee, an eminent legal brain.

The head-on clash between constitutional functionaries in Tamil Nadu is a sordid blot on the functioning of our Constitution.

Under our constitutional scheme, the Governor is a formal constitutional head who in the discharge of his functions, except a few matters in which he can act in his individual discretion, is required to act on the aid and advice of the Ministry headed by the Chief Minister. Nonetheless, he is not a mere decorative emblem and has an important role to play. B.G. Kher put the matter in the proper perspective in the Constituent Assembly when he said, *"I do not agree with the comment that he is a mere figurehead. A Governor can do a great deal of good if he is a good Governor, similarly he can do a great deal of mischief."*

The efficacy of the Governor's role as a "sagacious counsellor" would much depend on the respect commanded by him. He should not only be scrupulously fair but be manifestly seen and known to be fair to all sides. Therefore the selection of a right person as Governor is vital.

In Alladi's view the Governor should be a person of "undoubted ability and position in public life who at the same time has not been mixed up in provincial party struggle and the factions". **Munshi (K.M.)** and **Krishnamachari** were emphatic that the person selected as Governor should be able to "hold the scales impartially as between the various factors in the politics of the state. **Nehru's (J.L.)** ideal was to have "eminent people to have not taken too great a part in politics".

The manner in which Governors exercise their functions has significant impact on the Union-State relations and naturally the States have an important stake in the Governor's appointments and should be consulted. According to Nehru (J.L.) *The Governor "must be acceptable to the Government of the Province"*.

Although there was no requirement in the draft constitution for consultation, the founding fathers believed that there would be a convention of the Government of India consulting the provincial Cabinet in the selection "of the Governor and that the Cabinet at the Centre would also be guided by the advice of the provincial Cabinet". This belief has been sadly belied. The recommendations of ARC and Sarkaria Commission have not been implemented as yet.[1] The painful fact is that in many cases, the Governors are fostered upon States.[2]

Note.

Justice Fatima Devi has been appointed New Governor after the death of Chenna Reddy.[3]

Controversy about the role of the Governor of Karnataka at the time of National Front Government–Blow to the institution of Governor

Whatever be the political compulsions on the part of National Front Government to impose President's Rule in Karnataka under Article 356 of the Constitution, the Front has once again dealt a serious blow to the institution of Governor, for the second time this year[4]

1. This was the position on 1st Feb., 1997.
2. See *The Indian Express*,
3. See the *Indian Express* dated 25th January, 1997 p-1, col. 1.
4. See *Hindustan Times*, New Delhi, dated 12th October, 1990, p.1.

The first was the directive to the State Governors *en masse* to tender their resignations early in 1990 when the theory that the Governors were agents of the Centre was propounded by the authors of this act which had gone against the spirit of the Constitution and federal character of the country's polity.[1]

For one thing, Governor Bhanu Pratap Singh does appear to have committed an act of impropriety by holding a press conference when the Chief Minister was still in the saddle. Normally the Governors do not hold press conferences when they are constitutional heads. However, they might become necessary for a Governor who runs the Government of a state where President's Rule has been imposed, just as Virendra Verma or his predecessor in Punjab S.S. Ray have been addressing, However, a state governor holding Press Conference is just not the thing done. Secondly, without taking recourse to two options, he had to deal with the situation created by the long illness of Mr. Virendra Patil, he straightaway recommended President's Rule. One of these options was to discreetly suggest to Mr. Patil, after the Congress Legislature Party demonstrated its massive show of strength at the Raj Bhawan to relinquish office either he himself or the Secretary to the Governor, a very high ranking officer, could have conveyed his message to Mr. Patil when more than 140 of the 180-odd Congress MLAs clearly demonstrated their loss of faith in the Chief Minister's leadership. The other option left before him was to ask Mr. Patil in case he had not heeded the advice of the Governor to prove his majority in the Assembly within a specified time-limit. Upon Mr. Patil's failure to do so, the Governor would have had no option but to have called the leader of the larger party in the state Assembly—in this case the Congress-I—to form a Government.[2]

Mr. Bhanu Pratap Singh, Governor, could also have avoided making any comments on the propriety or otherwise of holding the meeting of Congress-I Legislature Party for electing a new leader. His comments on this score declaring the proposed meeting as illegal before it was held, also smacks of rank partisanship on the part of constitutional figurehead.The *Hindustan Times* also contended that many precedents (past cases) quoted by the National Front Government in support of the action of the Governor are quite different from the present case.

DISMISSAL OF NAGALAND GOVERNOR M.M. THOMAS

President R. Venkataraman removed the Nagaland Governor, Mr. M.M. Thomas, from office on April 11, 1992. Earlier on March 28, Mr. Thomas had dissolved the Nagaland Assembly on the advice of the then Chief Minister, Mr. Vamuzo, at the end of the Budget session. While doing so, Mr. Thomas had asked the Ministry headed by Mr. Vamuzo to continue as the caretaker Government.

The Governor's decision to dissolve the State Assembly, without consulting the Centre, as well as the Union Government's subsequent move to bring the State under President's Rule were both subjects of controversy in Parliament.

Addressing a Press conference in New Delhi, Mr. Thomas said in dissolving the Nagaland Assembly and ordering fresh elections, he had fully acted within the constitutional authority and responsibility of the Governor. He asserted that a Governor had the authority to take decisions on certain matters of the state without prior consultation with the President or the Home Ministry. He said that in the absence of any solid constitutional ground for dismissing him, the Centre was making imaginary charges like shielding corrupt officials and abetting conversion activities of Christian missionaries 'friendly to a super power'.

The question is whether the Centre has observed constitutional propriety in dismissing a head of state? When a Governor is to be removed from office, the nation should be told unambiguously why he deserves such a harsh punishment.

1. See *Hindustan Times*, New Delhi, dated 12th October, 1990, p.1.
2. *Ibid.*

R. Venkataraman observes in his book *My Presidential Years*, "The relations between the Governor and the Central Government have not been defined anywhere. Whether the Governor should consult the Union Home Ministry on a matter of this kind is not clear."

UTTAR PRADESH GOVERNOR ROMESH BHANDARI'S QUESTIONABLE ACTIONS

India Today observes about the role of Uttar Pradesh Govenor : "Uttar Pradesh Governor Romesh Bhandari is to the constitution what a reckless bus driver is to pedestrians. Both have scant respect for rules."

In September 1996 Mr. Romesh Bhandari did not follow the example set by Dr. Shankar Dayal Sharma in Delhi the previous May, and call upon the BJP, the largest single party, to form a Government but 'suspended' the Legislature instead. It facilitated rule by proxy from Delhi, through Raj Bhawan, Lucknow. The period of President's Rule saw the administration of U.P. sink to new depths. The number of murders and dacoities multiplied. When the Home Minister Indrajit Gupta visited U.P. in December, he was moved to expostulate that U.P. was in a state of anarchy. Mr. Gupta's statement not only put the cat among the pigeons, but exposed the extent to which the Governor, Mr. Romesh Bhandari, had compromised the integrity of his position.

When former Chief Minister Mayawati strode into Raj Bhawan on October 19, 1997, to inform Bhandari that the 67-member BSP was withdrawing support to Kalyan Singh Ministry, it seemed Uttar Pradesh was in for another spell of President's Rule. A jubilant Mulayam Singh Yadav asked Prime Minister Inder Kumar Gujral to sack Kalyan Ministry instantly. Gujral and Home Minister Indrajit Gupta, however, insisted on playing by the book. They told Bhandari to ask Kalyan to seek a vote of confidence "as soon as possible". Bhandari put Kalyan on 36 hours' notice.

The shortness of the time he gave Kalyan Singh to face the House, the detailed instructions he sent to the Speaker on how to conduct the vote, and the despatch of observers to monitor the vote were all without precedent. They gave rise to a strong suspicion that Bhandari was playing to a pre-written script. This was confirmed when in the face of a clear majority for Kalyan Singh in the Vidhan Sabha, he wrote to the President recommending the imposition of President's Rule. In refusing to blindly accept the Union Cabinet's recommendation that Central rule be imposed in Uttar Pradesh, the President did more than merely save a legitimate State Government.

Governor Romesh Bhandari's questionable action in February 1998 ushers in a return of the horse-trading culture in the State's politics. On February 21, 1998 at 2 p.m. Mayawati led her partymen, Loktantrik Congress Party (LCP) MLAs—partners in the Kalyan-led coalition and an assortment of Congress, SP, BKKP and Janata Dal (Raja Ram Group) legislators to Raj Bhawan. They informed Governor Romesh Bhandari that the LCP's Jagdambika Pal, Transport Minister in Kalyan's Cabinet, was their leader and commanded a majority in the Assembly.

The trusting Bhandari took them at face value. By 5 p.m. Kalyan had rushed to Lucknow from Gorakhpur (275 km away) preparing for the next day's Lok Sabha election and tried to convince the Governor that he could prove his majority. However, at 10.16 p.m. Bhandari swore in Jagdambika Pal as the new Chief Minister amid thunderous cheers from non-BJP legislators.

The battle was over; but the war had only just begun. At about the moment Pal was taking his oath, N.K. Singh Gaur, one of Kalyan's ministers, was petitioning the Allahabad High Court while Justice N.K. Saith reversed the Governor's order dismissing the BJP government, Justice Birendra Dixit reserved his decision. A day and a half later, at 3 p.m. on February 23, Dixit concurred with Saith and sought to reinstate Kalyan. Two hours later, Kalyan was back in the State Secretariat in Lucknow. Pal remained seated in the Chief Minister's chair despite being taunted as a "trespasser". He moved the Supreme Court which asked for the Assembly to be convened for a "composite floor test." That, of course, took place on February 26. MLAs were effectively asked to choose between Kalyan and Pal, seated on either side of the Speaker. In the end Kalyan won. He needed 213 votes to prove his superiority in the 425-member House, he got 12 more than that. It was a nine-hour process, as the MLAs voted under the gaze of 16 video cameras. Less than a week after, the reins of administration were back in Kalyan's hands.

The political drama in U.P. had brought to the fore the openly defiant unconstitutional role played by U.P. Governor Romesh Bhandari and the enigmatic role of caretaker Prime Minister I.K. Gujral. The President wrote to the Prime Minister virtually accusing Bhandari of insubordination for dismissing Kalyan against Rashtrapati Bhawan's wishes. All the President did was to ask the Prime Minister to 'advise' him on the conduct of Uttar Pradesh's Governor.

Thus, one of the foremost problems plaguing Uttar Pradesh is the politicisation of the Governor's offices.

ROLE OF GOVERNOR S.S. BHANDARI (SEPTEMBER 1998)

In September 1998, S.S. Bhandari, the Governor of Bihar, recommended for the imposition of the President's Rule in the state. According to the Governor, "The Bihar Government symbolises the most malignant and uncouth levels of functioning in Indian politics." However, President K.R. Narayanan repeated history by returning a Union Cabinet resolution seeking the imposition of President's Rule in Bihar and the suspension of the Assembly. After mulling over and discussing the subject for nearly 80 hours, the President, in a lengthy note, asked the Government to reconsider its decision. He saw no evidence of a constitutional breakdown in Bihar. Thereafter the Union Cabinet, under the pressure of regional allies, withheld its recommendation and did not press it once again.

The President listed three grounds on which he felt the Central contention on Bihar was unacceptable. In his three-page noting to the Prime Minister, he discounted the Centre's position on worsening law and order situation. He observed that law and order situation in some other States was also grave and prone to mafia influence. Bihar is not an exception as regards law and order as it has been projected by the Governor. Secondly, the Sarkaria Commission Report has also opposed dismissal of a majority Government in any State. The President referred to the report which mentioned that "the situation of maladministration in a State where a duly constituted ministry enjoying majority support in the Assembly is in office, imposition of President's Rule will be extraneous to the purpose for which the power under Article 356 is conferred." Thirdly, the President assessed that the Union Government did not give any warning to the "errant State Government" which has also been mentioned in the Sarkaria Report. In the Bommai case the Supreme Court said that the Centre must "warn an errant State in specific terms."

At one level Governor S.S. Bhandari was right. Despite the President's disbelief, there is something rotten about the State of Bihar. Where else would a State Government be confronted with a multiplicity of scams involving misappropriation of nearly Rs. 2,870 crore of public funds? Where else would a bankrupt Government look on with brazen unconcern at some 1,200 strictures of judicial contempt and 2,186 pending contempt cases ? And where else would a government claim normalcy with extremist groups running parallel administraton in nine districts? All this amounts to subversion of the Constitution.

T.N. Governor Fathima Bibi Resigns Before Recall

On July 1, 2001, giving in to the collective mood within the NDA to assert the Centre's authority *vis-a-vis* an unheeding Tamil Nadu Government, the Union Cabinet recommended to the President, Mr. K.R. Narayanan, that he withdraw his pleasure from the Tamil Nadu Governor, Ms. Fathima Bibi. As the Cabinet saw it, the Governor failed to live up to the constitutional obligations of her office in the wake of the unprecedented arrest of the former Chief Minister, Mr. Karunanidhi, and two Union Ministers, Mr. Murasoli Maran and Mr. T.R. Baalu in Chennai on June 30, 2001.

Rather than let the Centre invoke Article 156(1), the Governor sent in her resignation to the President, who forwarded it to the Prime Minister.

The Governor's failure to send a report earlier was deemed as "a clear defiance" of the Centre's authority. The Governor's report itself came after the Centre virtually issued a kind of demarche to Ms. Fathima Bibi to send a report by nine of July 1st. And the Cabinet found the Governor's report totally unacceptable. As the Union Law Minister, Mr. Arun Jaitley, told reporters, the Cabinet found that the Governor had failed to make an independent assessment of the situation and was merely content to forward the State Government's views. According to a Cabinet-Minister, the Governor's two and a half page report was, more or less, "comma for comma, full stop for rull stop" reproduction of the reports sent by the Tamil Nadu Chief Secretary. This, according to Mr. Jaitley, constituted a default on the part of the Governor.

Moreover, the Cabinet found that the Governor's report was silent on "the constitutional impropriety" of the state police going to a Union Minister's residence and assaulting him when there was no case against him.

As far as the Centre is concerned, the Governor was expected to exercise independent judgement; instead, she merely chose to endorse the views and assessment of the State Government.

RECOMMENDATIONS OF THE ARC

The Administrative Reforms Commission in its report on Centre-State relations pointed out that the office of the Governor has ceased to be merely ritualistic and ceremonial. The Governor has to face situation in which he has to take decision in view of his oath of his office to preserve, protect and defend the Constitution and the law. The ARC report insisted that the Governor must be impartial and must have a sense of fair play. He must have firm faith in the constitutional set-up and the democratic institutions. The specific recommendations made by the ARC are as follows:

(*i*) A person to be appointed as a Governor should be one who has had a long experience in public life and administration and can be trusted to rise above party prejudices and predilections.

(*ii*) He should not be eligible for further appointment as a Governor after the completion of his term. Judges, on retirement, should not be appointed as Governors.

(*iii*) The convention of consulting the Chief Minister before appointing a Governor is a healthy one and may continue.

(*iv*) He must act according to his own judgment and discretion in making his reports to the President and also in regard to the reservation of Bills for the consideration of the President.

(*v*) When the Governor has reason to believe that the Ministry has ceased to command a majority in the Assembly, he should come to a final conclusion on this question by summoning the Assembly and ascertaining its verdict on the support enjoyed by the Ministry.

(*vi*) When a question arises as to whether the Council of Ministers enjoys the confidence of the majority in the Assembly, and the Chief Minister does not advise the Governor to summon the Assembly, the Governor may, if he thinks fit, *sou motu* summon the Assembly for the purpose of obtaining its verdict on the question.

Studying the operational aspect of the office of the Governor during 1950-2004 we find that it was the involvement of the Governors in active politics of the State which made the office subject to considerable public criticism. Throughout the fifties and early sixties, there were definite signs of this tendency, but after 1967 some of the Governors dangerously overstepped their jurisdiction which resulted in public demands for their removal. The manner in which the power of appointing and dismissing the Council of Ministers, summoning, proroguing and dissolving the Assembly, and also of recommending the imposition of President's Rule has been used in a sad commentary on the role of some of the Governors. The Governors in some of the States by using their powers purely for partisan and personal ends, not only deprived the office of its dignity, but also brought disrepute to it.

EXERCISES

Long Answer Type Questions :

1. Discuss the power of the Governor.
2. Write a note on the position of Governors.
3. Write an essay on changed role of Governors after independence.
4. Write a detailed note on the controversies regarding the role of Governors in different states.

Short Answer Type Questions :

1. What are the Executive powers of Governor ?
2. What are the legislative powers of Governor ?
3. Write a brief note on financial powers and judicial powers of Governor.
4. What a Governor's position in advising President's Rule.
5. "Governor is responsible to safeguard the interests of the State during President's Rule." Do you agree with this statement ?

Objective Type Questions :

Choose the correct answer

1. The executive power of the State is vested in the Governor and all executive action of the State has to be taken in the name of the Governor. Governor's position in a state is akin to President's position in the Union. Though, normally there shall be one Governor for each state, however under which Article it is possible to appoint the same person as the Governor for two or more states ?

   (*a*) Articles 56 and 61 (*b*) Article 153
   (*c*) Article 261 (*d*) None of the above

2. Which Article of the Constitution discusses removal of the Governor ?

   (*a*) Article 155 (*b*) Article 156
   (*c*) Article 157 (*d*) Article 158

3. The Governor can dismiss a Council of Ministers only when the Legislative Assembly has expressed its want of confidence in the Council, either by a direct vote of no confidence or conserve or by defeating an important measure or the like, and the Governor does not think fit to dissolve the Assembly. The Governor cannot do so at his pleasure on his subjective estimate of the strength of the Chief Minister in the Assembly at any point of time. In which case the Supreme Court has buttressed up this position by observing that wherever a doubt arises whether a Ministry has lost the confidence of the House, the only way of testing is on the floor of the House ?

   (*a*) S.R. Bommai v. Union of India, 1994
   (*b*) Shamsher v. State of Punjab, 1974
   (*c*) Rajnarain v. Bhajanlal
   (*d*) None of the above

4. Which of the following Articles of the Constitution provides for a Governor for each state?

   (*a*) Article 92 (*b*) Article 143
   (*c*) Article 84 (*d*) Article 261

5. The Executive of the State is headed by :
   (*a*) The Governor (*b*) The Chief Minister
   (*c*) The State Cabinet (*d*) The State Legislative Council
6. The Governor of the State is appointed by:
   (*a*) the President on the recommendation of the Chief Minister of the State
   (*b*) the President and the Central Council of Ministers
   (*c*) the President
   (*d*) tbe Prime Minister
7. A Governor can issue an ordinance
   (*a*) whenever he likes
   (*b*) whenever the Chief Minister advises him
   (*c*) whenever the State Legislature is not in session and the Governor is satisfied that immediate action is needed
   (*d*) when the Union Government tells him to do so
8. The Governor of a State is responsible for his acts to:
   (*a*) the State Legislature (*b*) State Legislative Assembly
   (*c*) the President (*d*) the Prime Minister
9. The ordinances promulgated by the Governor are subject to the approval of the
   (*a*) President (*b*) State Legislature
   (*c*) Vice-President (*d*) Prime Minister
10. Under which of the following circumstances can President's Rule be imposed in a State?
   (*a*) If no stable government can be formed
   (*b*) If the Cabinet has lost majority and no other ministry commanding a majority in the Assembly can be formed at once
   (*c*) If the State Government does not obey the directives given by the Union Government
   (*d*) In all the above cases
11. The normal term of a Governor's office is
   (*a*) 3 years (*b*) 5 years
   (*c*) 6 years (*d*) dependent on the tenure of the State Legislators
12. If the Governor of a State dies, who becomes the acting Governor ?
   (*a*) Anyone appointed by the President of India (*b*) The Chief Justice of the State
   (*c*) The Chief Secretary (*d*) The Chief Minister
13. Which one of the following legislative powers of the Governor has been wrongly listed?
   (*a*) He summons or prorogues either House of Stale Legislature
   (*b*) He addresses either or both the Houses at the commencement of the new session after each General Election
   (*c*) He dissolves both the Houses in case of difference over the enactment of law
   (*d*) He sends messages to the State Legislature on a Bill pending before it
14. When a Governor reserves a Bill passed by the State Legislature:
   (*a*) he may be impeached (*b*) he sends it to the President
   (*c*) he may keep the Bill pending indefinitely (*d*) he may give assent to the Bill later
15. The Governor is generally taken from:
   (*a*) the State (*b*) outside the Slate
   (*c*) the same zone (*d*) the majority party

ANSWERS

1. (*b*)	2. (*b*)	3. (*a*)	4. (*b*)	5. (*a*)	6. (*c*)	7. (*c*)	8. (*c*)
9. (*b*)	10. (*d*)	11. (*b*)	12. (*b*)	13. (*c*)	14. (*b*)	15. (*b*)	

13

CHAPTER

The State Council of Ministers and Chief Minister

"The Governor would have no function to discharge by himself and would have no power to override the ministry in any matter. But he would have the duty to advise the ministry, not as the representative of any particular party but of the people as a whole..."

—*B.R. Ambedkar*

COUNCIL OF MINISTERS

The Constitution provides for a Council of Ministers in each State on the pattern of the Union Council of Ministers. Article 163(1) of the Constitution provides: "There shall be a Council of Ministers with the Chief Minister at the head to aid and advise the Governor in the exercise of his functions, except in so far as he is by or under Constitution required to exercise his functions or any of them in his discretion". The Constitution does not specify the strength of the Council of Ministers and leaves it entirely to the discretion of the Chief Minister. The formation of the Council of Ministers starts with the appointment of the Chief Minister. The Governor of the State is free to appoint any-one as Chief Minister who in his opinion enjoys the confidence of the Legislative Assembly and is likely to provide a stable government. However, in actual practice he has to invite the leader of the majority party in the State Legislature to become the Chief Minister. The other members of the Council of Ministers are appointed by the Governor on the advice of the Chief Minister.

Qualifications. The Constitution does not lay down any qualifications for the members of the Council of Ministers except that he must be a member of either of the two Houses of the State Legislature. A non-member can also be appointed as a Minister but he must get a seat in either of the two Houses within six months from the date of his appointment, otherwise he shall cease to be a minister. Thus it is implied that the members of the Council of Ministers must possess the qualifications prescribed for the members of the State Legislature.

Oath. Each member of the Council of Ministers has to subscribe to the oath of office and secrecy before entering upon his office. The oath of office runs like this:

"I.A.B., do $\frac{\text{swear in the name of God}}{\text{solemnly affirm}}$ that I will have true faith and allegiance to the Constitution of India as by law established, that I will uphold the sovereignty and integrity of India, that I will faithfully and conscientiously discharge my duties as a Minister for the State of .... (name of the

State) and that I will do right to all manner of people in accordance with the Constitution and the law without fear or favour, affection or ill will". In the oath of secrecy the members undertake not to communicate or reveal to any person or persons any matter which is brought to their consideration or becomes known to them as Minister for the State, except as may be required for due discharge of their duties.

Term. The members of the Council of Ministers hold office during the pleasure of the Governor. This seems to suggest that the members of the Council of Ministers stay in office at the pleasure of the Governor and he can remove them from office at will. This is, however, not true. The Council of Ministers stays in office as long as it enjoys the confidence of the majority of the members of the State Legislature. As the Council of Ministers works on the principle of collective responsibility, a vote of no confidence against any member of the Council may lead to the resignation of the entire body. In case of the death or resignation of the Chief Minister the Council of Ministers is dissolved and a fresh ministry is formed. Usually the seniormost member of the outgoing Council of Ministers is requested to continue as the caretaker Chief Minister, till a regular appointment is made. The individual members of the Council of Ministers can also relinquish their office by tendering voluntary resignation.

Salary and Allowances. The salary and allowances of the members of the Council of Ministers are determined by the Legislature of the State from time to time. These expenses are charged to the Consolidated Fund of State and are not subject to the vote of the State Legislature.

Powers and Functions. The Constitution is absolutely silent about the powers and functions of the Council of Ministers. The only provision of the Constitution which deals with the powers of the Council of Ministers states: "There shall be a Council of Ministers with the Chief Ministers at the head to aid and advise the Governor in the exercise of his functions, except so far as he is by or under this Constitution required to exercise his functions or any of them in his discretion". [Article 163(1)]. This provision suggests that the Council of Ministers is there simply to aid and advise the Governor in the exercise of his functions. But in reality the Council of Ministers is the real executive of the State. Though the entire administration of the State is carried on in the name of the Governor, in reality the powers are exercised by the Council of Ministers. The Governor cannot afford to go against the advice of the Council of Ministers in normal times. But under certain circumstances, he has certain discretionary powers which he can exercise without the advice of the Council of Ministers. It is noteworthy that these occasions are rather very limited. For the sake of convenience the powers of the Council of Ministers may be studied under the following heads.

1. Executive Powers. In the executive field the Council of Ministers is the highest authority of the State and is responsible for running the administration of the State in accordance with provisions of the Constitution. It not only formulates the policy of the government but also tries to give a practical shape to that policy. It may be noted that while important policy decisions are collectively taken by the Council of Ministers, in the less important matters the individual ministers take policy decisions. Once a policy has been accepted by the Council of Ministers all the members are expected to justify it on the floor of the State Legislature as well as outside. Within the Department it is the duty of the Ministers to ensure proper implementation of the policy. With a view to ensure that the various departments do not pull in different directions and there is cohesion in the policy pursued by different ministers, the Council of Ministers brings about the necessary co-ordination in their policies. In short, the Council of Ministers is not only concerned with the formulation of the policy of the Government but is also responsible for giving it a practical shape.

2. Legislative Powers. The members of the Council of Ministers are intimately connected with the State Legislature and as such play an important role in determining its legislative programme. The business and time-table of the State Legislature is decided by the Council of Ministers. Almost 90 per cent of the bills are introduced in the Legislature by members of the Council of Ministers. These bills are easily passed by the State Legislature because the Council of Ministers enjoys the backing of the majority of the members. Even the bills introduced by the ordinary members of the State Legislature stand no chance of passage unless they enjoy the support of the Council of Ministers.

3. Financial Powers. The Council of Ministers also enjoys extensive financial powers. It is the responsibility of the Council of Ministers to formulate the budget proposals for the year and present the same to the State Legislative Assembly for approval. Though the Legislative Assembly reserves the right to refuse, reduce or reject the demands presented by the Council of Ministers, in reality this never happens. Generally the demands presented by the Council of Ministers are approved by the State Legislature without any change. Only those changes are effected in these demands which are acceptable to the Ministers. The responsibility for formulating the proposals for taxation etc. also rests with the Council of Ministers. The State Legislature does not enjoy any power to propose new taxes, etc.

4. Formulation of Plans. The Council of Ministers plays a vital role in the preparation of the Five-Year Plans for proper utilisation of the resources and energies of the State. After the plan has been prepared by the Council of Ministers it is submitted to the Planning Commission for approval and sanction. After it is scrutinised and approved by the central authorities, it is the duty of the Council of Ministers to help in implementing the plans.

It is thus evident that the Council of Ministers enjoys very extensive executive, legislative, financial and other powers. It would not be wrong to describe it as the driving force behind the machinery of the State.

Relations of Council of Ministers with Governor— Constitutionally speaking, a Minister holds office during the pleasure of the Governor. This provision, however, does not imply that the Governor has a free hand in dismissing any Minister. This position of supremacy of the Governor is, however, not so real as on paper. Theoretically, he enjoys enormous powers but actually he does not exercise them. The administration of the State is in fact run by the Chief Minister and his team. A Governor cannot remove any Minister till the latter enjoys the confidence of the Legislature. With the formation of responsible Ministries in the state, the Governors have been divested of their power to act in discretion or individual judgment. He has become a rubber stamp to endorse the decisions taken by the Ministers. He wields no power because he owes no responsibility to the Legislature. If he disagrees with a Minister on any issue, he can, at best, request the Council of Ministers to reconsider that matter. Although the entire administration of the State is run in the name of the Governor, he cannot be held responsible for any act of the State executive or legislature. All said and done, the Governor is not certainly a white elephant or a 'good for nothing' fellow. Besides ornamental, a really capable Governor can influence the administrative field.

A Governor does not ordinarily ignore the advice of the Ministers. Only during the Proclamation of Emergency he is not bound by the decision of the Ministry, then he looks to the President for directions. During a state of breakdown of constitutional machine, once again the Governor is empowered to dissolve the Legislative Assembly and act as the nominee of the President. In dealing with the tribal areas of Assam, Nagaland and Arunachal Pradesh, the Governor is not bound by the Council of Ministers.

Relations of the Council of Ministers with the Legislature—The Council of Ministers is irrevocably related to the State Legislature. One may say that it is but an administrative or executive wing of the Legislature. The Constitution requires that all the Ministers should be the members of either House of State Legislature. Thus all the Ministers are selected from the members of one or both the Houses. The captain of the team of Ministers also happens to be the leader of majority group in the Assembly. The Ministry as such has to be faithful and obedient to the parent body. The Constitution clearly lays down that the Council of Ministers shall be collectively responsible to the Legislature. It means that a Ministry can remain in office till it commands the confidence of the Lower House. Lack of confidence in one Minister tantamount to a vote of no-confidence aganist the Ministry as a whole. If one member is defeated on any issue in the House, the whole Ministry has to go out. The members of the Legislature exercise their control over the Government by putting questions and by criticising its failings. They can indicate their want of confidence by proposing a token cut in the State Budget or by throwing out a Bill moved by any Minister. The Legislature has full control over the state purse. No expenditure can be incurred by the Cabinet except with approval of the Legislature. The Council of Ministers, too, has weapon to subdue the Legislature. The Chief Minister, on being defeated on any issue, can recommend the dissolution of the Legislatures and holding of fresh elections. The power of the Legislature to dislodge the Ministry by a censure motion and Chief Minister's power to recommend the dissolution of the Assembly pave the way for healthy co-operation of the Executive and the Legislature.

THE CHIEF MINISTER

The Chief Minister of a State enjoys a position analogous to the Prime Minister at the Centre and exercises the real executive authority of the State. He is appointed by the Governor of the State. The power of the Governor with regard to the appointment of the Chief Minister varies according to the political complexion of the Legislative Assembly. If a single political party enjoys a clear-cut majority in the Legislative Assembly the Governor has hardly any discretion in the matter of the appointment of the Chief Minister. He has to invite the leader of that party to become the Chief Minister and appoint other ministers of the council on his advice. This is also the case if a coalition of political parties contest the election and secure a clear majority in the Legislative Assembly and elect a common leader. In 1967 E.M.S. Namboodiripad was appointed Chief Minister because he was unanimously elected as the leader of the Coalition. Likewise in West Bengal Ajoy Mukerji was appointed Chief Minister by the Governor because he was unanimously elected as leader of the alliance. The Governor can have some discretion with regard to the appointment of the Chief Minister if no single political party is able to secure a clear-cut majority in the Assembly or if there is an alliance of the various political parties which are not quite well-knit. Under the circumstances the Governor is free to appoint anyone as Chief Minister who in his opinion would be in a position to provide a stable ministry. The Governor can also seek the advice of the Advocate-General of the State with regard to the appointment of the chief minister. The Governor of Bihar sought the advice of the Advocate-General of Bihar while making the appointment of B.P. Mandal as Chief Minister. In case the Governor is satisfied that a stable government cannot be formed in the state on account of no single political party having a clear-cut majority in the Legislature, he can recommend to the President that the State be placed under Centre's rule.

Qualifications. The Constitution does not prescribe any qualifications for the office of the Chief Minister, although it is expected that he must be a member of the Legislative Assembly. It may be noted that there is no constitutional bar to the appointment of outsiders as Chief Ministers. On a number of occasions persons have been appointed as Chief Ministers even though they were not members of the State Legislature. There have been instances where the leaders defeated at the polls were appointed Chief Ministers. The case of Morarji Desai who was appointed Chief Minister of Bombay even though he was defeated at the polls, is an instance. Similarly C.B. Gupta was made the Chief Minister of Uttar Pradesh even though he was twice defeated at the polls. Likewise there have been a number of cases where a person was appointed as Chief Minister even though he was not a member of the State Legislature. The appointment of Prakash Singh Badal as Chief Minister of Punjab in 1977 and appointment of A.R. Antulay and Jagan Nath Pahadia as Chief Ministers of Gujarat and Rajasthan in 1980 can be quoted as instances. However, such persons on appointment as Chief Ministers must become the members of the State Legislature within six months, otherwise they cease to be Chief Ministers.

Term. There is no fixed term for the Chief Minister. Constitutionally he stays in office during the pleasure of the Governor but in actual practice he stays in office as long as his party enjoys majority support in the State Legislature. Under normal circumstances the term of the Chief

Minister is little over five years because he stays in office till after the general elections of the State Legislature, which are generally held after every five years. The term of the Chief Minister is automatically extended if the life of the State Legislature is extended. His term can be cut short by his resignation, death or removal from party leadership.

Powers of the Chief Minister. As the real executive head of the state administration the Chief Minister enjoys very extensive powers. His powers may be studied under the following heads:

1. In relation to Council of Ministers. The Chief Minister enjoys central position in the Council of Ministers and is vital to its formation as well as life. The formation of the Council of Ministers starts with the appointment of the Chief Minister. The other members of the Council of Ministers are appointed by the Governor on the advice of the Chief Minister. However, in actual practice the Chief Minister while forming the Council of Ministers has to take into account a number of practical considerations. He has to ensure that adequate representation is provided to various groups, sections and interests to make the Council of Ministers broad-based. The Chief Minister heading a Coalition ministry is faced with all the more constraints and has to ensure that the various components of the coalition are adequately represented so that he may extend full support to the ministry in the State Legislature. A minister stays in the Council only as long as he enjoys the confidence of the Chief Minister. A minister who has lost the confidence of the Chief Minister can be asked to tender his resignation. However, if a minister is reluctant to comply with the desire of the Chief Minister he can be dropped from the Ministry through reshuffling of the Cabinet. In extreme cases the Chief Minister can even seek the dismissal of the minister through the Governor.

The size of the Council of Ministers is determined by the Chief Minister. Though generally it is accepted that the strength of the Council of Ministers should not exceed one-tenth of the total membership of the Legislative Assembly, yet this convention is not strictly adhered to. The general tendency is that the Chief Ministers prefer to have larger Councils of Ministers to make is broad-based. Even the allocation of portfolios and removal of the ministers is the prerogative of the Chief Minister. Generally the Chief Minister assigns important portfolios to senior members of his party and personal confidants. Often the wishes and preferences of the ministers are also given due weightage. In coalition ministers the allocation of portfolios is generally decided by mutual discussions among the leaders of the coalition parties.

The Chief Minister presides over meetings of the Council of Ministers and approves its agenda. No item can be discussed without his approval. He also greatly influences the deliberations and decisions of the Council. He brings about necessary co-ordination in the working of the various departments and resolves all the differences between two or more ministers. In fact it is his duty to ensure that the Council of Ministers works as a team and do not criticise each other and can face the State Legislature collectively.

The Central position of the Chief Minister in the Council of Ministers is further evident from the fact that his resignation as Chief Minister automatically leads to the dissolution of the Council of Ministers. While tendering resignation he can suggest to the Governor the name of a person who can form the ministry or even advise him to disslove the Legislative Assembly. It is, however, up to the Governor to accept his advice or not.

2. In relation to Governor. The Chief Minister is the chief link of communication between the Governor and the Council of Ministers. It is his duty to communicate to the Governor of the State all the decisions of the Council of Ministers relating to the administration of the affairs of the State and proposals for legislation. If the Governor so requires, the Chief Minister has to submit for the consideration of the Council of Ministers any matter on which a decision has been taken by a Minister but which has not been considered by the Council. He is also duty-bound to supply to the Governor information on such matter relating to the administration of the State or proposals for legislation as the Governor may call for. The power of making all major appointments in the State government vested by the Constitution in the Governor, is actually exercised by the Chief Minister. The Governor makes all important appointments in the state in consultation with the Chief Minister. Thus, the appointment of the judges of the High Courts, State Advocate General, members of the State Public Service Commission etc. is made in consultation with the Chief Minister. In the matters of postings and transfers also the Chief Minister has a decisive say.

3. In relation to Legislature. The Chief Minister of a state has very close relations with the Legislature. As the leader of the majority party he exercises profound influence on its working. The agenda of the Legislative Assembly (as well as the Legislative Council if there are two Houses) is determined by the Speaker in consultation with the Chief Minister. The Chief Minister also plays a vital role in the deliberations and discussions of the House. He makes all important policy announcements on the floor of the House and defends the policies of his government. He reserves the right to intervene in the debate of the House and defend the policies of other members of the Council of Ministers. In fact, the House always looks up to the Chief Minister for all important policy announcements. The Chief Minister also reserves the right to recommend to the Governor the dissolution of the Legislative Assembly even before the expiry of its term. However, the Governor is not bound by the advice of the Chief Minister.

Position of the Chief Minister. The foregoing discussion makes it amply clear that the Chief Minister of a State enjoys very extensive powers and occupies an important position in the state administration. However, the Chief Minister's real position depends on the position of his party in the state legislature, the backing of the central leadership and his own personality. If the Chief Minister's party has a clear-cut majority in the State Legislature and he is their undisputed leader, he shall hold dominant position. For example, Chief Ministers like Pratap Singh Kairon. G.B. Pant, B.C.Roy, Sheikh Abdullah, etc. were more powerful Chief Ministers than others because of their complete hold on the party members. On the other hand if the Chief Minister is dependent on other ministers for the majority supprot in the State Legislature his position becomes somewhat weak if the legislators of his party are divided and a section is hostile to the Chief Minister.

The position of the Chief Minister is also dependent on the factor whether his own party is also in control at the Centre or not. The position of a Chief Minister belonging to a party which does not control power at the Centre is rather weak and shaky. The Governor of the State, who acts as the representative of the Centre, is likely to create all sorts of problems for him and thus render his effective working difficult. On the other hand if his own party is in control of power at the Centre, the Governor will offer him full co-operation and the Chief Minister shall be able to dominate within reasonable limits.

The position of a Chief Minister heading a coalition ministry is comparatively weak. Most of his energy is wasted in keeping the various partners united and preventing cracks in the government. He cannot take decision by himself and has to follow the directions of the Co-ordination Committee with regard to the management of the government. The experience of the coalition government which emerged in various states after the Fourth General Election of 1967 shows that the Chief Ministers heading the coalition governments cannot play an effective role. Similarly, the Chief Ministers appointed at the behest of the Central leadership cannot be so assertive. Being the nominee of the Party High Command or the Prime Minister they owe complete allegiance to them and are reluctant to show any initiative or assert their authority. Such Chief Ministers stay in office as long as the High Command desires them to be there and are willing to faithfully carry out its directives. The Chief Ministers like Mir Qasim in Jammu and Kashmir, Abdul Gafoor in Bihar, Ghanshyam Oza in Gujarat, T. Anjiah in Andhra Pradesh etc. who were imposed by the Central leadership virtually acted as tools of the Centre and could never assert themselves.

Finally, the position of the Chief Minister also depends on his own personality. Persons with dominating personalities like Sheikh Abdullah, Bansi Lal, Pratap Singh Kairon, B.C.Roy, G.B.

Pant, etc. have been more effective Chief Minisers than others like Abdual Gafoor, Ghanshyam Oza, Chiman Bhai Patel, T.Anjiah etc.

In conclusion it can be said that the position of the Chief Minister in various states is not identical. It depends on a number of factors like the position of the party in the state legislature, the hold of the Chief Minister on the party members, his relations with the Central leadership and his own personality.

ADVOCATE-GENERAL

Besides appointing the Ministers, the Governor also appoints an Advocate-General from amongst those who are qualified to become the judge of any High Court. The function of the Advocate-General is to tender legal advice to the Government of the State on such matters as may be referred to him from time to time by the Governor. He is appointed by the Governor and gets such emoluments as may be fixed by the Governor. He enjoys all those privileges which are enjoyed by a member of the State Legislature except that he cannot vote on any issue.

STATE LEGISLATURE

Unicameral and Bicameral System–Out of all the states in the Union, some have two chambers, *i.e.* bicmaeral legislature, while others have only one House or unicamerl legislature. Uttar Pradesh, Bihar, Karnataka, Jammu and Kashmir, Maharashtra, Andhra and Tamil Nadu each have two Houses of Legislature. In Tamil Nadu the resolution has been passed by the House but the Council of States has not enacted any law so far[1]. The states which have only one House each are Haryana, Rajasthan Assam, Orissa, Gujarat, Kerala, Nagaland, Punjab, Madhya Pradesh, Chhattisgarh, West Bengal, Manipur, Tripura, Himachal Pradesh, Meghalaya, Jharkhand, Uttarakhand, Sikkim, Arunachal Pradesh, Mizoram and Goa.The variation in regard to the number of Houses in the state was the doing of each state itself. The states which signified their willingness to have two Houses were allowed by the constituent Assembly to create the Upper House.

There has been a good deal of controversy over the issue of a second chamber. Many arguments have been advanced both for and aganist the Upper Chamber. The champions of the Upper House justify it on the ground that it puts a healthy check on hasty legislation by the Lower House. Those who side with unicameral system argue that it is silly to apprehend hastiness in the adoption of a Bill in one House. Every Bill undergoes the stage of three readings, deliberations by a Select Committee and consideration of the Governor. The Upper House serves no useful purpose, it simply drains the purse of the State unnecessarily. If the second chamber simply approves every Bill sent to it by the Lower House, it may be called superfluous. If it disagrees with the Lower House, it is considered as mischievous.

Right of the Parliament to create or abolish the Legislative Council—Article 169 of the Constitution empowers the Parliament to abolish or create Legislative Council in a state if the Legislative Assembly of that state by an absolute majority of the total strength of the House and two-thirds members present and voting requests the Parliament to create or abolish a second chamber. A Union law to this effect does not amount to an amendment in the Constitution.

LEGISLATIVE ASSEMBLY

Composition– The strength of State Assemblies varies from state to state. The members of this House are elected directly by the people on the basis of adult franchise. The number of members in each state is determined in the ratio of one representative for every 75,000 or somewhat more of the population. The strength of various State Assemblies is as follows:[2] Punjab-117; Rajasthan-200; Uttar

1. This was the position on June 2012
2. This was the position on June 2012

Pradesh-403; West Bengal-295; Andhra Pradesh-294; Assam-126; Bihar-243; Jammu and Kashmir-75; Kerala-140; Madhya Pradesh-230; Tamil Nadu-235; Maharashtra-288; Karnataka-224; Orissa-147; Gujarat-182; Nagaland-60; Haryana-90; Himachal Pradesh-68; Manipur-60; Meghalaya-60; Tripura-60; and Sikkim-32; Arunachal Pradesh-60; Mizoram-40; Nagaland-60; Goa-40; Jharkhand-81; Uttarakhand-70; Chhattisgarh-90.

Adult Franchise-The members of the State Assemblies are elected on the basis of universal suffrage which means that every adult citizen of eighteen and above has the right to vote provided he is not disqualified on grounds of unsoundness of mind, crime or corrupt practices. Only the registered citizens of India are entitled to the right of vote. The new Constitution of India has abolished communal electorate and recommended joint electorate. There is no provision for the reservation of seats for any community except the Scheduled Castes and Scheduled Tribes for a period of thirty years from the day of enforcement of the Constitution. The Governors have, however, been empowered to nominate as many representatives of Anglo-Indian community as they deem proper if this community fails to get adequate representation through elections in the State Assembly. A few seats are reserved for the autonomous district of Assam in the Legislative Assembly of that State.

Qualifications for members.— The eligibility of a person for the membership of the Assembly depends on the fulfilment of following qualifications:—

(*i*) He is a citizen of India;

(*ii*) He has completed the age of 25 years; and

(*iii*) He possesses such other qualifications as are prescribed by law.

A person becomes disqualified for election to the Assembly if he is of unsound mind, insolvent or holding an office to profit under the State.

Tenure. The term of Legislative Assembly is five years. It may be dissolved earlier by the Governor on the recommendation of the Chief Minister. Its duration may be extended also during the Proclamation of Emergency. Such an extension is never for more than a period of one year and in no case can extend beyond six months after the withdrawal of Emergency.

Privileges of the Members of State Assemblies—The members of a State Assembly enjoy the same privileges and immunities as the members of they Parliament. The have freedom of speech in the House and they cannot be tried in any court in respect of anything said by them on the floor of the House. They are entitled to receive such salaries and allowances as are fixed by the Legislature of the State.

Speaker and Deputy Speaker of Legislative Assembly

Every State Assembly elects two officers called the Speaker and the Deputy Speaker. The Speaker acts as the presiding officer of the House. His functions are similar to those of the Speaker of the Lok Sabha. He conducts and supervises the proceedings of the House, maintains order and prevents the use of unparliamentary language. Normally he does not vote, but has a casting in the event of a tie in the House. He is impartial and just. He allows the members to address the House. He is custodian of the rights of members to address the House.

A Speaker is generally the unanimous choice of the House. The Chief Minister in consultation with the opposition leaders selects a person who is agreeable to all the groups in the House. In England the Speaker soon after his election to this august office becomes a non-party man. In our country the Speaker continues to be the member of his party outside the House, but he does not remain an active party worker and he does not favour his party in the House. He takes exile from politics.

The Speaker occupies an office of dignity. He maintains order and decorum. He may even name a member and ask him to withdraw from the House for violation of any rule of the House. He decides finally whether a Bill is Money Bill or not. In the absence of the Speaker, his chair is occupied by the Deputy Speaker. If the Assembly is dissolved in mid-term, the Speaker does not vacate his office until immediately before the first meeting of the new Assembly. He does not remain in chair when a resolution to remove him is being considered in the House. In the same way the Deputy Speaker does not preside when a resolution for his removal is under consideration of the House.Both have, however, the right to be present in the House and to vote in the first instance. Each, then, votes like an ordinary member and hence no longer possesses a casting vote.

If the Speaker or a Deputy Speaker loses his seat in the House, he has to vacate his office also. Either of them can resign at any time. When the Speaker resigns, he addresses his letter of resignation to the Deputy Speaker, and if the person resigning happens to be Deputy Speaker, he addresses to the Speaker. A resolution to remove the Speaker or the Deputy Speaker can be moved only after 14 days advance notice of the intention to move such a resolution.

Quorum—The Quorum for a legal sitting of the House is ten members or one-tenth of the total members of the House whichever is more. Hence when the number of persons present at a sitting falls below quorum, the sitting is postponed.

Sessions—The Governor of the State summons the State Legislature to meet at such time and places as he thinks fit. But the Constitution requires that not more than six months intervene between the last sitting of the first session and the first sitting of the next session. The Governor who calls the sitting of the Legislature can discontinue or suspend it also.

POWERS OF LEGISLATIVE ASSEMBLY

The functions of the Legislative Assembly are legislative, financial and relating to control over administration.

The State Legislature has the power to make laws on all the subjects included in the State List. Besides 66 State subjects, it possesses the right to deal with Concurrent subjects. If a State law on a concurrent topic does not agree to a corresponding Union law, it becomes invalid.

Ordinary Bills—The powers of the State Assembly far exceed the powers of the Legislative Council. The second chamber cannot impose its decisions on the Assembly. An ordinary Bill after being passed by the Assembly is sent to the Council for its approval. The Council, then, has three courses open before it. It may (*i*) reject the Bill; (*ii*) not consider the Bill for three months; (*iii*) send it back with such recommendations as may not be agreed to by the Assembly. After this, if the Assembly sends the Bill again to the Council with or without incorporating its recommendations, the Council can delay its approval for a month more. At the end of one month, whatever the attitude of the Council, the Bill is deemed to have been passed by both the Houses. The Bill is then sent to the Governor for his assent. The Governor either gives his assent or sends it back for reconsideration. When the Assembly presents the Bill again before the Governor whether in changed form on not, the Governor has to put his signature.

Financial Powers—The Legislative Assembly is virtually in full control of the finances of the State. Its control over the State Budget is also complete. Money Bills can originate only in this House. The other House can only delay the enactment of a Money Bill by a period of 14 days. The Lower House votes upon all the heads of expenditure mentioned in the Budget except those which are charged upon the Consolidated Fund of the States. All demands for grants and supplementary grants are laid before this House for sanction. No new taxes in the States can be levied without its approval. It can reject or reduce any demand but not increase it.

Control over the Executive—The control of the Legislative Assembly over the Council of Ministers is real and complete. The Ministers are drawn from majority party in the Assembly. Constitution holds them collectively responsible to the legislature. The term responsibility implies that the Ministry can remain in office during the pleasure of the Assembly. It can make its influence felt by accepting adjournment motions, censure motions, a cut in the Minister's salary or by rejecting a Government Bill. By expressing its lack of confidence, it can obtain the resignation of the Ministry. The Council of Ministers has only one weapon to use against the Assembly. It can recommend the dissolution of the House leading to fresh elections.

LEGISLATIVE COUNCIL

Legislative Council is the Upper House of the State Legislature. The States which had a Upper House on 1st September, 1993 are Bihar, Uttar Pradesh, Maharashtra, Jammu and Kashmir, Karnataka, Andhra Pradesh. No Legislative Councils existed on 25th May, 1995 in Rajasthan, Haryana, Assam, Madhya Pradesh, Kerala, Orissa, Gujarat, Nagaland, Punjab, West Bengal, Manipur, Tripura, Himachal Pradesh, Meghalaya, Sikkim, Arunachal Pradesh, Mizoram and Goa.

Composition.– The Constitution says that the Legislative Council of any state shall have not less than 40 members and not more than one-third of the total membership of that state's Assembly.However, there is one exception to this clause also. The present strength of the Legislative Councils of various states is U.P.-99; Andhra-90; Bihar-75; Jammu and Kashmir-36;[1] Maharashtra-78; Karnataka-63; and Tamil Nadu-63.

Rajya Sabha passes resolution for the creation of Legislative Councils in Andhra Pradesh and Tamil Nadu. The Rajya Sabha passed a resolution on 28th May, 1990 for the creation of Legislative Councils in Andhra Pradesh and Tamil Nadu.

The composition of Legislative Councils in the states is as follows: (*i*) one-twelfth members to be elected by the University graduates of not less than 3 years' standing; (*ii*) one-twelfth members to be elected by teachers of at least three years' standing in educational institutions not lower in standard than secondary schools; (*iii*) one-third to be elected by local bodies like Zila Parishads and Municipalities; (*iv*) one-third to be elected by the members of the Legislature Assembly from amongst persons who are members of the Assembly; and (*v*) the remainder one-sixth to be nominated by the Governor from amongst persons who have distinguished themselves in field of literature, science, art, cooperative movement, and social services. The elections to the Council are held in accordance with the system of proportional representation by means of single transferable vote.

Qualifications of the Members. The qualifications laid down for a person seeking election to the Legislative Council are: (*i*) he must be a citizen of India, (*ii*) he must have completed 30 years of age; (*iii*) he must possess such other qualifications as may be prescribed by the State Legislature.

Besides this, he should not otherwise be disqualified under the Representation of the People Act, 1961 as amended up to 1st April, 1991.

Tenure. The Legislative Council is a permanent House. It cannot be dissolved by the Governor. At first, one-third of its members are elected for two years, another one-third for four years and the remaining one-third for six years. After the first elections, one-third of its total members retire every second year. The seats thus falling vacant are filled by new elections. Every member as such remains a member of this House for a period of six years.

Quorum. The quorum for legal sitting of this House is ten members or one-tenth of the total membership of this House, whichever is more.

The members of this House can resign their seats whenever they like. Absence of a person from the sittings of the Council for a continuous period of 60 days without any notice, entitles the House

1. The Legislative Council of Jammu and Kashmir has 36 members vide Section 50 of the Constitution of Jammu and Kashmir.

to declare his seat vacant. No person can remain a member of both the Houses of State Legislature. If a person is elected to both the Houses, he has to resign from one House.

Disqualifications for Membership– A person becomes disqualified from being chosen as a member of the Legislative Council: (*i*) if he holds any office of profit under the Government of India or Government of any State; (*ii*) if he is of unsound mind; (*iii*) if he is an undischarged insolvent; (*iv*) if he is not a citizen of India; (*v*) if he has acquired the citizenship of a foreign State.

Privileges of the Members– The members of Legislative Council enjoy the same privileges and immunities as the members of the Assembly. They cannot be arrested during the session and 40 days before and after the session. They cannot be tried in any court for any speech delivered by them in the House. Their salary and allowances are fixed by the House.

Sessions and officers of the Council– The Constitution requires at least two sessions of the Council in one year. The Governor decides the time and place for the sitting of the Council. The Council elects a Chairman and a Deputy Chairman to act as presiding officers. Their salaries and allowances are paid out of the Consolidated Fund of the State. According to convention, a Chairman soon after his election to this office ceases to be the active member of his party. He has to be impartial and just. It is expected of him to be prejudiced against the opposition benches.

The Chairman or the Deputy Chairman can resign at will. If their election to the Council is set aside, they have to vacate the office. Either of them can be removed from office by a resolution of the House provided that 14 days' notice has been given regarding the intention to move such a resolution. When a resolution for removal is under consideration, the person concerned cannot be in the chair. The Chairman and in his absence the Deputy Chairman presides over the meetings and conducts business. He maintains decorum and discipline. He can name a person for removal from the House for violation of any rule of the House. He does not vote except when there is a tie, in which case he exercises his casting vote.

Powers of the Legislative Council.-The second chamber in every country is less powerful than the Lower House. It does not possess any effective control over financial matters. No Money Bill can be introduced in the House. It cannot refuse to give its approval to a Money Bill sent to it by the State Assembly. It can only delay its enactment by 14 days. Even if it does not agree to the provisions of the Money Bill, the Bill is deemed to have been passed by it at the end of fourteen days.

Even in regard to ordinary Bills, the real power vests in the Assembly. It can at the most keep in abeyance the enactment of a Bill sent to it by Lower House for four months. Its control over the State executive is also quite nominal. The Council of Ministers is collectively responsible not to the Council but to the Assembly. The Council has no constitutional right to dislodge the ministry by a vote of no-confidence. The utmost that the members of this House can do is to ask questions from the Ministers and criticise the governmental actions.

The position of the Legislative Council *vis-a-vis* the Assembly can be judged from the fact that its very existence is at the mercy of the latter. The State Assembly can by a resolution passed by two-thirds majority of the members present and voting, and absolute majority of the total strength request the Union Parliament to abolish or create a second chamber. The Councils are merely advisory bodies. They are not only second chambers but in fact secondary chambers. They are even worse off than the British House of Lords which gets a period of one month for discussion over Money Bill.

LIMITATIONS OF THE POWERS OF STATE LEGISLATURE

As stated earlier, the State Legislature possesses and exercises wide legislative powers on all matters included in the State List and Concurrent List. But it is to be noted that they are not sovereign bodies. They have no right to amend the Constitution which the Union Parliament alone can do. Secondly, a State law on a Concurrent subject becomes inoperative and invalid to the extent it is repugnant to a Union law on the same subjects. The third limitation on its powers is that it cannot in any case legislate on a Union subject whereas the Union Parliament can under specified circumstances bring a State subject under its control. The right of the State Legislature to make laws on State subjects is not absolute or exclusive. It is deprived of its legislative functions during the period Proclamation of Emergency lasts. Whenever the President is convinced that a grave threat to peace and security of India exists, he can authorize the Union Parliament to make laws even on State subjects. The President can also, on the basis of a report from the Governor, declare that the constitutional machinery in the State has failed. In that case he can suspend the State Legislature and direct the Governor to act as his agent and rule the State. The power of the State Legislature is further restricted by Article 304 which says that no Bill which seeks to impose restrictions on the freedom of trade, commerce or intercourse within or out of that State, shall be introduced without the previous sanction of the President. The Parliament can also pass laws on a subject which is declared by the Council of States as of national importance. The Governor also can reserve certain Bills for the consideration of the President of India. Even in normal times the Parliament can pass laws on a State subject when the legislatures of two or more States request it to do so.

PROCEDURE OF MONEY BILLS IN STATE LEGISLATURE

Articles 196 to 201 cover the rules regarding procedure of law-making in the States. Bills may be put in two categories–Money Bills and Ordinary Bills. A Bill is deemed to be a Money Bill if it concerns imposition, abolition, remission, alteration or regulation of any tax, or the borrowing of money or the payment of money into or the withdrawal of money from the Consolidated Fund of the State. A Money Bill can originate only in the Legislative Assembly which controls the pursestrings of the State. Ordinary Bills can be first moved in either House. The Legislative Assembly alone can propose a reduction in any Money Bill although it cannot increase the amount of expenditure. A Money Bill or a Financial Bill is presented before the House either by the Finance Minister or any other Minister in his absence. No ordinary member can bring any such Bill in the House. Budget or the Annual Financial Statement is also a Money Bill. It is presented before 1st of April every year. It is divided into two parts–sums charged on the Consolidated Fund of the State and the demands for grants. The expenditure charged on the Consolidated Funds includes the emoluments and allowances of the Governor, the salaries and allowances of the Speaker and the Deputy Speaker of the Assemblies and the Chairman and Deputy Chairman of the Council; the salaries and allowances of the Judges of the High Court, and the interest, sinking fund charges and other debt charges of the State. Expenditure under the first head can be discussed but not put to vote. The demands for grants are made with the sanction of the Governor. Every demand is discussed thoroughly and put to vote. The members can either reject a demand for grant completely or propose a reduction in it. After the grants have been sanctioned by the Assembly, it is consolidated in the form of Annual Appropriation Bill and then is passed into a statute. Then there are Finance Bills which aim at imposing new taxes to raise revenues. The Finance Bill is presented along with the Annual Budget and has to be passed before the end of April. Every Money and Finance Bill after being passed by the Assembly is sent to the Legislative Council. Fourteen days' time is given to the Council to discuss the Bill and then return it with recommendations to the Assembly. It is at the option of the Assembly to accept or reject the recommendations of the Council. In both cases, the Bill is deemed to have been passed by both the Houses and is presented before the Governor for his assent. The Governor cannot withhold his assent on Money Bills. After Governor's signature the Bill becomes an Act.

ORDINARY BILLS

Ordinary Bills are also of two types: Private Member's Bills and Government Bills. Ordinary Bills do not deal with money matters. An Ordinary Bill does not necessarily come from a Minister.

Any member can introduce an ordinary Bill. A Bill moved by a Minister is called a Government Bill whereas a Bill moved by an ordinary member is called a Private Member's Bill. Every such Bill has to pass through the following stages:

Introduction and First Reading. For introducing a Government Bill an advance notice of one month is not required in the case of Private Member's Bill. The first reading of the Bill covers the introduction of the Bill in either House and its publication in the State Gazette. The notice to a motion for leave to introduce has to be accompained by a required number of copies of the draft and a statement of its objects and reasons. The member wishing to introduce the Bill reads out its title. If the Bill is opposed at the time of introduction, the Speaker may allow the member to make an explanatory statement after which the votes are taken. When the House has given its approval, the Bill is published in the Gazette. A Government Bill can be discussed at any time after its publication in the Gazette; a Private Member's Bill is put to first reading on a fixed date. The first reading at this stage is complete.

Second Reading. The second reading of the Bill is further divided into two stages. The mover of the Bill may choose any of the three courses: (*i*) he may request for the consideration of the Bill immediately or at some future date; (*ii*) he may suggest that the Bill be referred to a Select Committee; or (*iii*) he may recommend that the Bill be circulated for the purpose of eliciting public opinion. A Bill is rarely taken up for consideration at once unless it is very urgent or absolutely non-controversial. The mover at this stage explains his point of view and gives such material information regarding the Bills as may be necessary. The opposition members oppose the Bill. The discussion at this state, however, centres round the principles of the Bill. Neither is the Bill discussed in details nor any amendment made.

Select Committee Stage. After being approved by the House, the Bill enters Committee Stage. The Select Committee consists of 20 to 30 members of that House, named by the mover of the Bill. The Speaker appoints one of its members to act as Committee's Chairman. The Bill is thoroughly examined and even modified by the Committee. The report of the Committee along with the Bill is published in the State Gazette.

Report Stage. The Report of the Committee along with the Bill is circulated among the members of the House. It is discussed clause by clause and submitted to vote. At this stage the member in charge of the Bill can also make a request that Bill be recommitted to the Select Committee to make some additioal provisions in it. The Report stage of the Bill is thus the most crucial stage of the Bill.

Third Reading. The third reading of the Bill is only a formal affair. A motion is moved that the Bill be passed. At this stage no vital amendments can be made except verbal ones. The discussion confines to whether the Bill should be passed or rejected as a whole.

After one House has passed the Bill, it is sent to the other House if there is any. If there is no second chamber it is sent straightaway to the Governor for his assent. If there is a Legislative Council, the Bill passes through the same three stages there as in the former House. The second House can reject the Bill or send it back with its recommendations. It may even sleep over the Bill for three months. If the Legislative Assembly passes the Bill again with or without changes, the Council cannot reject it again. Even if it rejects it, the Bill is deemed to have been passed by both the Houses after a month.

A Bill after being adopted by both the Houses is presented before the Governor for his signature or assent. The Governor either gives his assent or reserves it for consideration of the President or returns the Bill to the Legislature for reconsideration. If the Legislature passes the Bill again whether in an amended or original form, the Governor has to give his assent after which the Bill goes into the Statute Book.

EXERCISES

Long Answer Type Questions :

1. Write a detailed note on 'The State Council of Ministers'.
2. Write a note on Chief Minister of State.
3. Write a note on State Legislature.
4. Write a note on Legislative Assembly.
5. What are the powers of Legislative Assembly ?
6. What do you know about Speaker and Deputy Speaker of Legislative Assembly ?
7. Write a brief note on Legislative Council.
8. Discuss the limitations of the powers of State Legislature.
9. Discuss the procedure of Money Bills and Ordinary Bills in State Legislature.

Short Answer Type Questions:

1. What are the executive powers of State Council of Ministers ?
2. What are the legislative powers of State Council of Ministers ?
3. What are the financial powers of State Council of Ministers.
4. Discuss the relation of Council of Ministers with Governor.
5. Discuss the relation of Council of Ministers with the Legislature.
6. What are the powers of the Chief Minister in relation to Council of Ministers ?
7. What are the powers of the Chief Minister in relation to Governor ?
8. What are the powers of the Chief Minister in relation to Legislature ?
9. Write a brief note on the position of Chief Minister.
10. Write a short note on Advocate-General.
11. What is Unicameral and Bicameral system ?
12. What are the powers of Legislative Assembly ?

Objective Type Questions:

Choose the correct answer

1. The States having Bicameral Legislatures are.
   (*a*) Bihar, Rajasthan, Uttar Pradesh, Orissa and Jammu and Kashmir
   (*b*) Bihar, Maharashtra, Karnataka, Uttar Pradesh and Jammu and Kashmir
   (*c*) Rajasthan, Assam, Madhya Pradesh, Uttar Pradesh, Bihar, West Bengal
   (*d*) Tamil Nadu, Punjab, Kerala, Bihar, Jammu and Kashmir
2. Which Article of the Constitution provides the procedure for the abolition of the Second Chamber of the Legislature (Legislative Council) in a State where it exists as well as for the creation of such a chamber in a State where there is none at present ?
   (*a*) Article 139 (*b*) Article 231
   (*c*) Article 169 (*d*) None of the above
3. Which of the following are necessarily the part of every State Legislature in India ?
   (*a*) Governor
   (*b*) Governor and Legislative Assembly
   (*c*) Legislative Assembly and Legislative Council
   (*d*) Governor and Legislative Council

4. What is the procedure presented in the Constitution for the creation or abolition, of the Legislative Council in a State ?
   (*a*) A Presidential ordinance on the request of the State Council of Ministers made through the Governor of the State.
   (*b*) An Act of Parliament on the recommendation of the President passed by an absolute majority of the members of both Houses present and voting.
   (*c*) A resolution of the Legislative Assembly of the State concerned passed by a special majority, that is, a majority of the total membership of the Assembly not being less than two-thirds of the members actually present and voting, followed by an Act of Parliament.
   (*d*) An Act of Parliament on the recommendations of the Speaker of the Legislative Assembly of the State concerned passed by a simple majority in a joint sitting.
5. Of the total number of members of the Legislative Council in State what is the proportion of members nominated by the Governor of the State ?
   (*a*) One-fourth (*b*) One-fifth
   (*c*) One-sixth (*d*) One-seventh

ANSWERS

1. (*b*) 2. (*c*) 3. (*b*) 4. (*c*) 5. (*c*)

CHAPTER 14

Relations between the Union and the States

"The States are as sovereign in the field which is left to them by the Constitution as the Centre in the field which is assigned to it."[1] —*Dr. Ambedkar*

According to V.N. Shukla : "The distribution of legislative powers between the Centre and the Units is an essential feature of a Constitution based on the federal model. Every Federal Constitution, thus, established a dual polity, the Central polity and the subsidiary sovereign polities. The Constitution of the U.S.A. makes the division by enumerating specifically powers of the Federal Government and assigning all the residuary powers to the component States. In Canada, the American system was reversed; the residuary powers were to belong to the Federal Legislature and not to the Provincial Legislature. The present Constitution of India, in making the distribution of Legislative powers between the Union and the States adopts the method followed in the Government of India Act 1935".

Legislative Relations between the Union and the States

The Constitution of India provides for a Federal System of Government. One salient feature of the Federation is the division of powers between the Union and the Units. The second trait of a federation is the supremacy of a Constitution which is both written and rigid. The third characteristic is the setting up of a Supreme Court which interprets the Constitution and acts as its guardian The Indian Constitution possesses all the three ingredients of a Federal Government.

The Constitution of India divides the subjects into three lists—the Union List, the State List and the Concurrent List. The Union List contains 99 topics including Defence, External Affairs, Currency and Coinage, Post and Telegraph, Communication, Railways, Insurance and Establishment of Standard of Weights and Measures, War and Peace, Citizenship, Banking, Naturalisation and Aliens, Inter-State Trade, Telephone, Wireless, Broadcasting and commerce and foreign loans. The Union Parliament enjoys the exclusive right to make laws on the Union subjects.

1. *Constituent Assembly Debates*, Vol. VIII, p. 22.

The Concurrent List contains 52 subjects, *e.g.*, Power, Lunatic Asylums. Civil Procedure, Criminal Laws, Economic and Social Planning Marriage and Divorce, Education, vital statistics including registration of births and deaths, Newspapers, Books and Printing Presses, Legal, Medical and other professions, Trust and Trustees, Factories, Price Control and Adulteration of Foodstuffs and other Goods. Both the Union Parliament and State Legislatures possess simultaneous rights to frame laws on Concurrent topics. But the Constitution lays down that if Union law on a Concurrent topic conflicts with a State Act on the same topic, the former shall have precedence.

The State List contains 61 subjects which are of regional importance. The State List includes Police, Local Self-Government, Agriculture, Jail, Land Revenue and so on. Although the State Legislatures are fully empowered to enact on State subjects, its right is not exclusive or absolute. It is subject to certain limitations imposed by the Constitution. The Union Parliament can also make laws on State subjects in the following cases:

(1) When according to Article 356 the President on the basis of a report from the State Governor declares Constitutional Emergency in that State and empowers the Parliament to make laws for that State;

(2) The Parliament under Article 253 can make laws for the whole of India to implement any treaty or agreement with any other country;

(3) Under Article 250, the Parliament, during the period the Procalmation of Emergency remains in operation, can legislate for the whole of India;

(4) When according to Article 252 the Legislatures of two more States request the Parliament to make laws on any State subject, the Parliament can do so;

(5) If the Council of States or Rajya Sabha declares by a resolution supported by two-thirds members of the total strength that a particular subject has become of national interest, the Parliament can encroach upon the State sphere with regard to that subject.

The powers conferred by Article 253 on the Union of the India are far reaching and very comprehensive. This Article lays down clearly that the Parliament has power to make any law for the whole or any part of the territory of India for implementing any treaty, agreement or convention with any other country or countries or any decision made at any international conference, association or other body.[1] *So the Union Parliament for the above purpose can legislate not only on the Union List and Concurrent List but also on the State List without any limitation. The States cannot challenge the law of the Parliament in the Supreme Court on this ground that it touches or affects any subject contained in the State List. Such sweeping powers have not been given in a democratic country like Canada. In Attorney-General of Canada v. Attorney-General of Ontario, the Privy Council held that "in a federal State where legislative authority is limited by a constitutional document or is divided up between different legislatures in accordance with the classes of subject matter submitted for legislation...the obligation imposed by treaty may have to be performed if at all, by several legislatures and the executive have the task of obtaining the legislative assent not of the Parliament to whom they stand in no direct relation. The question is not how the obligation is formed, that is, the function of the executive but how is the obligation to be performed and that depends upon the authority of the competent legislature or legislatures."*

Article 254 (1) provides, "If any provision of a law made by the legislature of a State is repugnant to any provision of a law made by Parliament which Parliament is competent to enact or to any provision of any existing law with respect to one of the matters enumerated in the Concurrent List, then, subject to the provisions of clause (2) of Article 254, the law made by Parliament whether

1. In its application of Jammu and Kashmir State to Article 253, the following proviso shall be added: "Provided that after the commencement of the Constitution (Application to Jammu and Kashmir) Order, 1954, no decision affecting the disposition of the State of Jammu and Kashmir shall be made by the Government of India without the consent of the Government of that State."

passed before or after the law made by the Legislature of such state, or as the case may be, the existing law shall prevail and the law made by the Legislature of the State shall, to the extent of the repugnancy, be void.

Article 254 Clause (2) provides, "Where a law made by the Legislature of a State with respect to one of the matters enumerated in the Concurrent List contains any provision repugnant to the provision of an earlier law made by Parliament or an existing law with respect to that matter, then, the law so made by the Legislature of such State shall, if it has been reserved for the consideration of the President and has received his assent, prevail in that State:

Provided that nothing in this clause shall prevent Parliament from enacting at any time any law adding to, amending, varying or repealing the law so made by the Legislature of the State."

According to Article 255, no Act of Parliament or of the Legislature of a State and no provision in any such Act shall be invalid by reason only that some recommendation or previous sanction required by this Constitution was not given, if assent to the Act was given :

(*a*) where the recommendation required was that of the Governor, either by the Governor or by the President;

(*b*) where the recommendation or previous sanction required was that of the President, by the President.[1]

Residuary Powers. The Indian Constitution, unlike the practice in America, gives residuary powers not to the States but to the Central Government. The residuary powers of the Union Government extended to all the subjects not included in any of the three lists. In this respect India has adopted the model of Canada where also the Centre has been armed with residuary powers. Thus it becomes evident that the makers of Indian Constitution were guided by the principle of making the Centre stronger than the State Governments.

Administrative Relations between the Union and the States

Indian Federation is of a highly integrated nature with a bias towards unitary system. The Constitution is so devised as to make the Central Executive stronger than the State Governments. The Union Government exerts its influence over the State Governments in the following ways :

1. *Appointment of the Governor*. The State Governor is appointed by the President not with the consent of the State Legislature but on the advice of the Prime Minister. The Governor, although a titular head, acts as the agent of the Union Government. In certain circumstances he is also empowred to act in his discretion.

2. *Directions to the State Governments*. According to Article 256, "The executive power of every State shall be so exercised as to ensure compliance with the laws made by Parliament and any existing laws which apply in the State, and the executive power of the Union shall extend to the giving of such directions to a State as may appear to the Government of India to be necessary for that purpose."

The Centre has given directions to the State on various occasions. When the Internal Emergency was declared, then the directions were given to the States by the Centre that the workers and leaders of the Non-CPI Opposition parties should be arrested immediately and put under MISA, if possible. After the complete rout of the Congress in March 1977 elections the Janata Party came into power at the Centre. It issued instructions to the States to protect Harijans, and to implement the programme of prohibition and take steps to check the soaring prices and to ensure effective law and order to the people. The Annual Report of the Home Ministry for 1977-78 stated that in pursuance of Article 46 of the Constitution special care was being taken to promote the educational and economic interests of the weaker sections. Offences against the members of the Scheduled Castes and Tribes such as

1. Article 225 is not applicable to Jammu & Kashmir State.

murder, rape, arson etc. come within the definition of "Public order" which is a State subject according to the Seventh Schedule of the Constitution. However, the Centre has been making requests and suggestions to the State Governments to ensure prompt and effective action in all cases of offences. The suggestions include holding Collectors and Suprintendents of Police directly responsible for not taking prompt and effective action.

In the areas prone to offences against the Scheduled Castes and Scheduled Tribes, special police guards should be set up to take prompt action against the offenders and to prevent recurrence of such offences.

3. *Executive Power of the Union not to be hampered by the exercise of State Executive Power.* According to Article 257 (1) the executive power of every State shall be so exercised as not to impede or prejudice the exercise of the executive power of the Union and the executive power of the Union shall extend to the giving of such direction to a State as may appear to the Government of India to be necessary for that purpose.

4. *Right of the Centre to give direction to States regarding the maintenance of means of communication.* Article 257, clause 2, provides that the executive power of the Union shall also extend to the giving of directions to a State as to construction and maintenance of means of communication declared in the direction to be of national or military importance :

Provided that nothing in this clause shall be taken as restricting the power of Parliament to declare highways or waterways to be national highways or national waterways or the power of the Union with respect to the highways or water ways so declared or the power of the Union to construct and maintain means of communications as part of its functions with respect to naval, military and air force work.

Clause 3 of Article 257 provides that the executive power of the Union shall also extend to giving directions to State as to the measures to be taken for the protection of railways within the State.

5. *Power of the Union to confer powers, etc., on State in certain cases.* Article 258 (1) provides that notwithstanding anything in this Constitution, the President may, with the consent of the Government of a State, entrust either conditionally or unconditionally to that Government or to its officers functions in relation to any matter to which the executive power of the Union extends. Article 258 (2) provides that "A law made by Parliament which applies in any State may, notwithstanding that it relates to a matter with respect to which the Legislature of the State has no power to make laws, confer powers and impose duties or authorise the conferring of powers and the imposition of duties, upon the State or officers and authorities thereof."

Clause 3 of Article 258 provides, "Where by virtue of this Article powers and duties have been conferred or imposed upon a State or officers or authorities thereof, there shall be paid by the Government of India such sum as may be agreed or in default of agreement, as may be determined by an arbitration appointed by the Chief Justice of India, in respect of any extra costs of administration incurred by the State in connection with the exercise of those powers and duties."

6. *Power of the States to entrust functions to the Union.* Notwithstanding anything in this Constitution, the Governor of a State may, with the consent of the Government of India, entrust either conditionally or unconditionally to that Government or to its officers functions in relation to any matter to which the executive power of the State extends.

7. *Jurisdiction of the Union in relation to territories outside India.* Article 260 provides, "The Government of India may by agreement with the Government of any territory not being part of the territory of India undertake any executive, legislative or judicial functions vested in the Government of such territory, but every such agreement shall be subjected to, and governed by, any law relating to the exercise of foreign jurisdiction for the time being in force."

8. *Public acts, records and judicial proceedings.* Article 261 (1) provides, "Full faith and credit shall be given throughout the territory of India to public acts, records and judicial proceedings of

the Union and of every State." Article 262 (2) provides that the manner in which and the conditions under which the acts, records and proceedings referred to in clause (1) shall be proved and the effect thereof determine shall be as provided by law made by Parliament. Clause 3 of Article 261 provides that final judgments or orders delivered or passed by Civil Courts in any part of the territory of India shall be capable of execution anywhere within that territory according to law.

9. *Adjudication of Disputes relating to waters of inter-State rivers or river valleys.* Parliament may by law provide for the adjudication of any dispute or complaint with respect to the use, distribution or control of the waters of, or in, any inter-state river or river valley. Article 262, clause 2 provides that notwithstanding anything in this Constitution, Parliament may by law provide that neither the Supreme Court nor any other Court shall exercise jurisdiction in respect of any such dispute or complaint as referred to in clause 1 of Article 262.

10. *Provisions with respect to an Inter-State Council.* Article 263 of the Indian Constitution provides that if at any time it appears to the President that the public interests would be served by the establishment of a Council charged with the duty of:

(*a*) inquiring into and advising upon disputes which may have arisen between States;

(*b*) investigating and discussing subjects in which some or all of the States or the Union and one or more of the States have a common interest; or

(*c*) making recommendations upon any such subject and in particular, recommendations for the better co-ordination of policy and action with respect to that subject,

it shall be lawful for the President by order to establish such a Council, and to define the nature of the duties to be performed by it and its organisation and procedure.

11. The Judges of the State High Courts are appointed, transferred or removed by the Union Government. The elections in the State are supervised by the Election Commission appointed by the President. The control of the Auditor-General of India extends to financial accounts of all the States.

Financial Relation between the Union and the States

The political autonomy of the constituent units of a federation cannot be deemed complete unless they enjoy financial autonomy but such a thing hardly exists in any federation of the world. The essence of a federation is the distribution of functions but no State can function independently if it does not have specified financial resources. The distribution of the sources of revenue between the Centre and the States is as follows:

1. *Taxes levied by the Union but collected and wholly retained by the States.* Stamp duties in respect of Bills of Exchange, cheques, promissory notes, letters of credit, policies of insurance, transfer of shares and excise on medicine and toilet preparation containing alcohol.
2. *Taxes levied and collected by the Union but whose proceeds are given over to the States.* Duties in respect of succession to property other than agricultural land, estate duty on property, terminal taxes on goods and passengers, taxes on railway fares and freights, taxes on the sale or purchase of newspapers and advertisements published therein and so on.
3. *Taxes levied and collected by the Union but whose proceeds are shared between the Union and the States.* Income tax is the only item which comes under this head. The ratio in which the proceeds from this tax are shared between the Union and the States is decided by the President after considering the report of the Finance Commission.
4. Taxes which are levied and collected by the Government of India but whose proceeds may be distributed among the States in accordance with such principles as may be formulated by a Union law. Under this head come Union duties of excise other than those on medical and toilet preparations.

Grants-in-aid. Besides the distribution of sources of revenue, the Constitution also makes provision for certain *grants-in-aid* of the States from the Union fund. The Union levies and collects the proceeds on export duty on jute and jute products. Out of the receipts, a grant-in-aid is given to the States of Assam, Bihar, Orissa, and West Bengal. The Parliament is also empowered to other financial assistance to the states from the Consolidated Fund of India. Apart from it, the Parliament, in discharge of its duty towards the Scheduled Castes and Scheduled Tribes, can finance any State scheme for the welfare of those tribes and Scheduled Castes.

Control of the Centre over the borrowing powers of the States. The borrowing power of the State Government is also subeject to limitations imposed by the Union Government. A State can borrow only within India and cannot raise a new loan without the consent of the Union Government. The Comptroller and Auditor-General of India also, with the approval of the President, can prescribe the pattern in which the States have to maintain their accounts.

Finance Commissions and Their Recommendations

The Finance Commission of India came into existence in 1951. It was established under *Article 280* of the Indian Constitution by the President of India. It was formed to define the financial relations between the Centre and the States. The Finance Commission Act of 1951 states the terms of qualification, appointment and disqualification, the term, eligibility and powers of the Finance Commission. As per the Constitution, the commission is appointed every five years and^consists of a chairman and four other members. Since the institution of the First Finance Commission, stark changes have occurred in the Indian economy causing changes in the macroeconomic scenario. This has led to major changes in the Finance Commission's recommendations over the years. Till date. Thirteen Finance Commissions have submitted their reports.

History: Genesis of the Finance Commission

The Indian State, like ail other federations, is also ridden by the problems of Vertical and Horizontal Imbalances. Vertical Imbalances result because states are assigned responsibilities and in the process of fulfilling those, they incur expenditures disproportionate to their sources of revenue. This is because the states are able to gauge the needs and concerns of their people more effectively, and hence, are more efficient in addressing them. Factors like historical backgrounds, differences in resource endowments etc. lead to widening Horizontal Imbalances. The Constitution of India, in recognition of these two problems, has made several provisions to bridge the gap of finances between the Centre and the States. These include various Articles in the Constitution like *Article 268.* which facilitates levy of duties by the Centre but equips the states to collect and retain the same. Similarly, there are *Articles 269, 270, 275. 282 and 293* all of which specify ways and means of sharing resources between Union and States. Apart from the above-mentioned provisions, the Indian Constitution provides an institutional framework to facilitate Centre-State transfers. This body is the *Finance Commission.* which came into existence in 1951, under *Article 280* of the Indian Constitution, which states:

1. The President will constitute a Finance Commission within two years from the commencement of the Constitution and thereafter and at the end of every fifth year or earlier, as deemed necessary by him/her, which shall include a Chairman and four other members.
2. Parliament may by law determine the requisite qualifications for appointment as members of the Commission and the procedure of selection.
3. The Commission is constituted to make recommendations to the President about the distribution of the net proceeds of taxes between the Union and States and also the allocation of the same amongst the States themselves. It is also under the ambit of the Finance Commission to define the financial relations between the Union and the States. They also deal with devolution of non-plan revenue resources.

Functions

Functions of the Finance Commission can be explicitly stated as:

1. Distribution of net proceeds of taxes between the Centre and the States, to be divided as per their respective contributions to the taxes.
2. Determine factors governing Grants-in-Aid to the states and the magnitude of the same.
3. Work with the State Finance Commissions and suggest measures to augment the Consolidated Fund of the States so as to provide additional resources to Panchayats and Municipalities in the state.

The Finance Commission (Miscellaneous Provisions) Act, 1951

With the objective of giving a structured format to the Finance Commission of India and to bring it at par with world standards, the Finance Commission (Miscellaneous Provisions) Act, 1951 was passed. It lays down rules regarding qualification and disqualification of members of the Commission, their appointment, term, eligibility and powers.

- **Qualifications of the Members**

The Chairman of the Finance Commission is selected from among people who have had the experience of public affairs. The other four members are selected from people who:

1. are, or have been, or are qualified, as judges of High Court, or
2. have knowledge of Government finances or accounts, or
3. have had experience in administration and financial expertise; or
4. have special knowledge of economics

- **Procedure and Powers of the Commission**

The Commission has the power to determine their own procedure and:

1. has all powers of the civil court as per the Code of Civil Procedure. 1908;
2. can summon and enforce the attendance of any witness or ask any person to deliver information or produce a document, which it deems relevant;
3. can ask for the production of any public record or document from any court or office; and
4. shall be deemed to be a civil court for purposes of Sections 480 and 482 of the Code of Criminal Procedure. 1898

- **Disqualification from being a Member of the Commission**

A member may be disqualified if:

1. he is mentally unsound;
2. he is an undischarged insolvent;
3. he has been convicted of an immoral offence; and
4. his financial and other interests are such that it hinders smooth functioning of the Commission.

- **Terms of Office of Members and Eligibility for Reappointment**

Every member will be in office for the time period as specified in the order of the President, but is eligible for reappointment provided he has. by means of a letter addressed to the President, resigned his office.

- **Salaries and Allowances of the Members**

The members of the Commission shall provide full-time or part-time service to the Commission, as the President specifies in his order. The members shall be paid Salaries and Allowances as per the provisions made by the Central Government. So far, 13 Finance Commissions have submitted their recommendations. More or less, all of them have been accepted by the Union Government.

Finance Commissions appointed so far

So far 13 Finance Commissions have been appointed which are as follows:

Finance Commissions Appointed

Finance Commission	Year of Establishment	Chairman	Operational Duration
First	1951	K..C Neogy	1952-57
Second	1956	K.Santhanam	1957-62
Third	1960	A.K.. Chanda	1962-66
Fourth	1964	P.V. Rajamannar	1966-69
Fifth	1968	Mahavccr Tyagi	1969-74
Sixth	1972	K. Brahmananda Reddy	1974-79
Seventh	1977	J.M. Shelat	1979-84
Eighth	1983	Y. B. Chavan	1984-89
Ninth	1987	N.K.P. Salve	1989-95
Tenth	1992	K.C. Pant	1995-2000
Eleventh	1998	A.M.Khusro	2000-2005
Twelfth	2003	C.Rangarajan	2005-2010
Thirteenth	2007	Vijay I Kelkar	2010-2015

Finance Commissions, their Terms of Reference and Recommendations

- **First Finance Commission**

The First Finance Commission was appointed by the President on November 20. 1951. which was chaired by Mr. K.C. Neogy. Other members of the commission included Mr. V.P. Menon. Mr R. Kaushalendra Rao, Dr. B K Madan and Mr. M.U. Rangachari. After Mr. V,P. Menon's resignation on February 18, 1952. Mr. V.I.,. Mehta was appointed as a member. The commission was asked to make recommendations regarding:

1. Allocations of income tax and Union Excise Duties and tax sharing.
2. Amounts payable as Grants-in-Aid to the States in need of assistance under the 'substantive portion of Clause I of Article275'.
3. Grants-in-Aid to certain States in lieu of their share of export duty on jute and jute products according to Article 273.
4. Continuation or adjustment of the terms of agreement with Part B States under Article 278 (I) or under Article 306.

Recommendations

- The share of States in the proceeds of income tax was to be 55 per cent.
- The First Commission recommended that shares of States in the Union excise duties be 40 per cent of the proceeds of the tax on three commodities, 25 per cent of the proceeds of the tax on eight commodities and 20 per cent of the proceeds of the tax on 35 commodities, respectively.

- As far as Horizontal Distribution is concerned, overwhelming weightagc is given to population (80%). Only residual weightage of 20% given to contribution.
- No recommendations regarding grants for meeting capital requirements of the state were made by the Commission.
- The Commission provided Grants-in- Aid (under Article 273) to only four states, namely. Assam Bihar, Orissa and West Bengal. However. Grants were provided to many states under Substantive Portion of Article 275 (I) and under the head of Primary education grants.

All recommendations made by the Commission were accepted by the Union Government.

- **Second Finance Commission**

The Second Finance Commission was constituted by President Rajendra Prasad on June 1, 1956. The Commission was chaired by Shri K. Sanlhanam and consisted of Shri Ujjal Singh, Shri L.S. Misra (Retired Chief Justice, Hyderabad), Shri M.V. Rangachari and Dr. B.N. Ganguli, as its other members.

The Commission was asked to make the following recommendations:

1. Grants-in-Aid to certain States, in need of assistance under Article 275 having regard to the requirements of Second Five Year Plan and the efforts made by those states to raise additional revenue.
2. Allocation of Estate Duty and Tax on Railway Passenger Fares proposed to be levied by the Railway Passenger Fares Bill, 1957, introduced in the I.ok Sabha on 15th May, 1957.
3. Grants-in-Aid to the States of Assam, Bihar. Orissa and West Bengal, to compensate for their share of the export duty on jute and jute products as per Article 273.
4. The principles which should govern the distribution under Article 269 of the net proceeds of estate duty in respect of property other than agricultural land, levied by the Government of India in the States within which such duty is leviable.
5. Revisions, if any. of the rates of interest on loans made by the Centre to the States between August 15, 1947 and March 31. 1956 and their terms of repayment. The phenomenal growth of the Union loans to the States justified such adjustments.
6. Apportionments of the net proceeds of the additional Excise Duties proposed to be levied in view of States' Sales Taxes on the mill made textiles, sugar and tobacco, and the amounts which should be assured to the States as the income now derived by them from the levy on these commodities and the States Sales Tax (which is to be replaced by the additional duty of excise).

With regard to the distribution of Income Tax, the Commission made the following recommendations:

- Despite the receding contribution by the Income Tax to the devolution of revenue to the States, the Commission recommended an increase in the per cent of the net proceeds to the States from 55 to 60, and the share of the Union Territories should be 1 per cent.
- It was recommended that the distribution of the share of Income tax among the States should be 10 per cent on the basis of collection and 90 per cent on the basis of population, thereby giving greater importance to population than it was earlier.

As far as the allocation to the States from the Union duties of excise on matches, tobacco, vegetable products, tea, coffee, sugar, paper and vegetable non-essential oils was concerned, the Commission considered that it should be 25 per cent.

The table below summarizes what each State was to expect in each of the five years starting from April 1. 1957 under the Second Finance Commission's recommendations:

States	Share of Taxes	Grants under Article 273	Grants under Article 275	TOTAL
Andhra Pradesh	8.50	–	4.00	12.50
Assam	2.75	0.45	4.05	7.25
Bihar	10.00	0.43	3.80	14.23
Bombay	14.75	–	–	14.75
Kerala	3.75	–	1.75	5.50
Madhya Pradesh	7.00	–	3.00	10.00
Madras	8.25	–	–	8.25
Mysore	5.50	–	6.00	11.50
Orissa	4.00	0.09	3.35	7.44
Punjab	4.25	–	2.25	6.50
Rajasthan	4.25	–	2.50	6.75

- **The Third Finance Commission**

The Third Finance Commission was appointed in the year 1960, for the period 1960-64. by the President and was chaired by Shri A.K. Chanda and its members were :- Shri Govinda Menon, Shri Dwijendra Nath Roy, Prof. M.V. Mathur. Shri G.R. Kamat. Member Secretary. The Commission was asked to make recommendations to the President with regard to the following:- I) On account of Tax Sharing between the Centre and the States and allocation of Income Tax and Central Excise Duties 2) Under Article 275, Grants-in-Aid to States in need of assistance, other than the sums specified in the provisos to Clause of Article 275 a) with regard to the requirements of Third Five Year Plan b) Secondly, with regard to the efforts to be made by those states to raise additional revenue amount 3) Allocation of duties, namely, additional excise duty and estate duty 4) The manner of distribution of Ad hoc Grants in lieu of tax on Railway Passenger Fares. With regard to the TOR the following were the recommendations made by the FC: The Finance Commission recommended the formulation of an independent commission to assess the tax potential of each state, to review its tax structure and to recommend rates under different heads of the levies of the State List :- Income Tax. With regard to the divisible pool of income tax among the states the FC adopted the criterion of the first FC that 80% be distributed on the basis of population and 20% on the basis of collection. The recommended percentage share of the states in divisible pool of the Income Tax: Maharashtra- 13.41, Bihar-9.33. Punjab - 4.49. Uttar Pradesh - 14.12, Kerala -3.55 Union Excise Duty. With regard to the distribution of the proceeds of UED the FC decided to cover all commodities on the existing list. It recommended that 20% of the net proceeds of UED on all commodities on which such duties were collected and the yield of which exceeded Rs. 50 lakhs in 1960-61 should be allocated to the state. The share of each state in the distribution of UED was determined by the Commission on the basis of population and it rejected consumption as the basis of distribution due to two major reasons—(a) Reliable data on consumption wasn't available, (b) As it would have given advantage to the more urbanised and financially stronger states. Percentage share of the 20%) of proceeds of the UED for certain major states were:- Maharashtra - 5.73. Bihar -11.56. Punjab - 6.71. Uttar Pradesh - 10.68, Kerala - 5.46 Additional Duties of Excise The GOI in consultation with the state governments .decided that an AED be levied on mill-made textiles, sugar tobacco, rayon among others and the net proceeds of which should be distributed among them subject to the income derived by each state being assured to it. The Commission rejected this contention as the rales of sales taxes had been revised by them since then.

The Commission distributed the guaranteed amount of Rs. 32.54 crores among the States and the remaining amount was distributed, first, on the basis of the percentage increase in the collection of sales tax in each state since 1957- 58 when AED were imposed and then on the basis of the population. The Act imposing a lax on the railway passenger fares was repealed after the Third Finance Commission had been constituted. Hence the Commission was asked to make recommendations on the principle on which the ad hoc grant should be distributed among the states. The Commission adopted the principle of compensation based on which the grants should be distributed.

- **The Fourth Finance Commission of India**

The Fourth Finance Commission was constituted on May 18. 1964. under the chairmanship of Dr. P.V. Rajamannar. Other members of the Commission included:

Shri Mohan Lal Gautam, Shri D.G. Karve, Prof. Bhabatosh Datla, Shri P.C. Mathew. Member Secretary.

The Commission suggested in its report that there should be greater co-ordination between the Centre and the States in common financial interests for which it recommended the establishment of a permanent organization in the Ministry of Finance

Recommendations

Tax sharing and allocation of Income-tax and Union Excise Duties.

Grants-in -aid to States in need of assistance, having regard to:

The revenue resources of States for Five Years ending with 1970-71 on the basis of the levels of taxation likely to be reached at the end of 1965-66; Creation of a fund out of Estate Duty proceeds over a specified limit, for repayment of State's debt to the Centre: and scope for economy with efficiency in States', administrative expenditure.

The changes to be made in the principles governing the distribution amongst the States of the grant to be made available to the States in lieu of taxes on railway fares;

To study the combined incidence of Sales Tax and Union Excise Duties on the production, consumption or export of products, the duties on which are shareable with the State.

The changes to be made in the principles governing the distribution of the net proceeds in any financial year of the additional excise duties levied on commodities, namely- cotton fabrics, silk fabrics, woollen fabrics, sugar and tobacco- in replacement in the States' tax formerly levied by the state governments.

- **The Fifth Finance Commission of India**

The Fifth Finance Commission was constituted by the President of India on March 15, 1968. The Terms of Reference of the Fifth Finance Commission were wider than those of the earlier ones. Apart from the matters referred to in the earlier Commissions, this Commission was required to:

Examine the desirability or otherwise of maintaining the existing arrangements in regard to additional excise duties levied in lieu of Sales Tax and the scope for extension of such arrangements to other items;

To inquire into the unauthorized overdrafts of the States and recommend the procedure for avoiding such overdrafts;

Examine the scope for raising revenue from taxes and duties mentioned in Article 269. the scope for States in raising additional revenue from their sources as well as their scope for better fiscal management and economy in expenditure, and make a comprehensive study of the States' expenditure on various subjects;

Grants-in-aid recommended under Article 275 (1) are to be for purposes 'other than the requirements of the Five Year Plan', and while making its recommendations, the Commission was called upon to have regard to "the resources of the Central Government and the demands thereon" on account of expenditure on civil administration, defence, debt servicing, etc.

The Commission was asked for the first time to indicate the basis of its findings and make available relevant information. Since then these were made clear in the Terms of Reference of every successive Finance Commission.

- **The Sixth Finance Commission of India**

The Sixth Finance Commission was incorporated in the year 1973 consisting of Shri K. Brahmananda Reddy as the chairman and the following four other Members, namely:

Mr. Justice Syed Sadat Abal Masud

Dr. B.S. Minhas

Dr. I.S. Gulati

Shri G. Ramachandran. Member Secretary

Recommendations

The States demanded the inclusion of corporation tax into the divisible income tax and 1005 allocation of the net proceeds to them. The Commission expressed that such inclusion was constitutionally forbidden but it can be reviewed by National Development Council.

States' share was increased from 75 % to 80 % due to the decrease in the divisible pool as the arrears of the advance tax collection had been cleared.

In view of the increasing integration of the national economy and for eliminating the regional imbalances, the contribution factor was kept at 10% in the distribution of share amongst the states. The distribution *inter se* the states should be on the basis of fixed percentages.

Out of the net proceeds of the income tax, 1.79 % should be allocated to the Union Territories.

- **The Seventh Finance Commission of India**

The Seventh Finance Commission was incorporated in the year 1978 consisting of Shri J.M. Shelat as the chairman and the following four other Members, namely:

Dr. Raj Krishna, Dr. C.H. Hanumantha Rao, Shri H.N. Ray, Shri V.B. Eswaran, Member Secretary.

Recommendations

The share of the states in the net proceeds should be raised to 85% excepting the share of the Union Territories which would be 2.19%> of net proceeds.

The *inter se* distribution between the states should include 10% contribution factor and rest 90% would be on basis of population. The 10% allotment would be based on the State-wise net assessments.

- **The Eighth Finance Commission of India**

The Eighth Finance Commission was constituted by the President of India on April 28. 1984 under the chairmanship of Shri Y.B. Chavan. The Commission also consisted of the following members:

Mr Justice Sabya Sachi Mukherjee, Dr. C.H. Hanumantha Rao, Shri G.C. Raveja, Shri A.R. Shirali, Mr Justice T.P.S. Chawla, Shri N.V. Krishnan, Secretary.

It was asked to make recommendations on:

The distribution of net proceeds of taxes between the Union and the States which are to be or may be divided between them under Chapter I of Part XII of the Constitution and allocation between the states of the respective shares of the same. The principles which govern the grants-in-aid of the revenues of the states out of the Consolidated Fund of India and the amount to be paid to the needy States which seek assistance by way of grants-in-aid of their revenues under Article 275 of the Constitution for purposes other than those specified in the provisions to clause (i) of that Article.

The Commission is to examine the possibility of increasing revenue from the taxes and duties mentioned in Article 269 of the Constitution but which are not levied at present. It will probe into the scope for enhancing revenue from the duties mentioned in Article 268. Making an assessment of the non-plan capital gap of the states on a uniform and comparable basis for the 5 years ending with 1988-89 also comes under its agenda. It will review the policy and arrangement in regard to the financing of relief expenditure by the States affected by natural calamities and make appropriate suggestions. The Commission shall make its report by October 31,1986, on each of the matters aforesaid.

The major objective of the Eighth Finance Commission was to reduce inter-state disparities through their scheme of devolution.

Recommendations

Sharing of Income Tax. To retain the share of the States in the proceeds of the income tax at 85% level. Withdrawal of surcharge on income tax from the financial year 1985-86 is also recommended.

Union Excise Duties. Recommended its increase from 40% to 45%. It made a beginning by using one unified formula to distribute the net yield from Union Excise Duties and 90% share of the income tax.

Additional Excise Duties. The distribution from the net yield firm additional duties of the excise was made 50% on the basis of the share of each state in the average state domestic products of all the states for the years from 1976-77 to 1978-79 and 50% on the basis of the population figures as given in 1971 census.

Grants in lieu of tax on railway passenger fare. It has boldly defended the case of the state government in regard to their claim on the tax on railway fare. The compensatory grant which replaced the tax was increased to ₹ 95 crores.

Grants-in-Aid. They have been made more flexible. The Commission has provided for an annual growth of 5% in respect of the amount of grants payable in nature of the forecast period commencing from 1984-85 The recommendation to write off a substantial portion of loan amounting to ₹ 2285.39 crores is an appropriate step towards strengthening the state finances.

- **The Ninth Finance Commission of India**

The Ninth Finance Commission was set up in June 1987 under the chairmanship of Mr. N.K.P Salve along with the following members:

Mr. Justice Abdus Sattar Qureshi, Dr. Raja .J. Chelliah, Shri l.al Thanhawla, Shri Mahesh Prasad, Shri S. Venkitaramanan, Shri R. Kcishing, Shri K.V.R. Nair

Terms of Reference

The Commission has been asked to adopt a normative approach in assessing the receipts and the expenditures on the revenue account not only of the States but also of the Centre with due regard to the special problems of each state and the special requirement of the Centre. Generating surpluses on revenue account of both the States and the Centre for capital investment should also be considered. Changes in the principles that govern the distribution between the Union and the States and also the states *inter se* of the net proceeds of central taxes are to be made.

The Commission will also make recommendations regarding the principles which should govern the grants-in-aid of the revenue of the state out of the Consolidated Fund of India. It is to assess the debt position of the states as on March 31.1989, and suggest corrective measures. In regard to the financing of the relief expenditure by the states affected by natural calamities the Commission is to examine the feasibility of establishing a National Insurance Fund to which the state governments may contribute a percentage of their revenue receipts. The government's decision to accept all the major recommendations of this Commission which would bring substantial benefits to the States during the Eighth Five Year Plan period (especially in relation to debt relief) shows the upper hand enjoyed by this body.

Recommendations

Income Tax. 85% of the divisible pool of the income tax to be assigned to the states and out of the net distributable proceeds a sum equal to 1.437% should be deemed to represent the proceeds attributable to the Union territories.

Relief Funds. The existing arrangements to be replaced by a new order under which the states will have greater autonomy and accountability. A calamity relief fund to be constituted for each state to which contribution is to be made in the ratio 75:25 (Centre: State).

Debt Relief. The Commission recommended that the RB1 may work out a formula for amortisation of the states' market borrowings. From 1990-91 the direct central loans for states' plans should have a maturity period of 20 years with 50% of the loans enjoying a grace period of 5 years. The loans given to the federating states for drought relief during 1986-89 as outstanding on March 31. 1989 are to be waived. The state plan loans advance to the states during the 1984-89 period and outstanding on March 31. 1990 should be consolidated, rescheduled to 15 years in the case of all the states.

- **The Tenth Finance Commission of India**

The Tenth Finance Commission was incorporated in the year 1995 consisting of Shri Krishna Chandra Pant as the Chairman and the following four other members, namely:

Dr. Debi Prosad Pal, Member of Parliament, Shri B.P.R. Vithal, Dr. C. Rangarajan, Shri M.C. Gupta, Member Secretary.

Recommendations

The share of the Union Territories would not be determined on the grounds used lor state share but it would be decided on the basis of population solely. The percentage would be 0.927% for the years 1995-2000. The proceeds from the 'penalties' and "interest recovered' under the miscellaneous receipts should be included in the divisible income tax pool as recommended by the Ninth Commission with effect from I April 1995. The share of the net proceeds would be 77.5 % for five years. The Commission dropped the collection factor as the criterion for distribution The distribution of the net proceeds among states would be as follows:

§ 20% on the basis of population of 1971

§ 60 % on the basis of distance of per capita income

§ 5 % on the basis of area adjusted

$ 5 % on the basis of infrastructure index

§ 10 % on the basis of tax effort

- **The Eleventh Finance Commission of India**

The Eleventh Finance Commission was appointed by the President on July 3, 1998 for the period 2000-05. It was chaired by : Prof. A.M. Khusro and its members were Shri N.C Jain, Shri J.C Jetly, Dr. Amaresh Bagchi, Shri T.N. Srivastava. The Commission was asked to make recommendations to the President with regard to the following: (*a*) With regard to Chapter I of Part XII of the Constitution, the distribution between the Centre and the States of the net proceeds of taxes and the allocation between the States of the shares of these proceeds (*b*) The principles governing the grants-in-aid of the revenues of the States out of the Consolidated Fund of India and with regard to Article 275, the sums to be paid to the States which arc in need of assistance by way of grants-in-aid of their revenues for purposes other than those specified in the provisos to clause (I) of that Article; (*c*) With regard to the recommendations made by the Finance Commission of the State, the measures needed to augment the Consolidated Fund of a State to supplement the resources of the Panchayats and Municipalities in the State (*d*) Suggestions for a restructuring of the public finances so as to restore budgetary balance and maintain macro-economic stability.

With regard to the TOR the following were the recommendations made by the FC: (*a*) The total share of the States in the net proceeds of central taxes and duties would be 29.5 per cent for the next five years (*b*)With regard to the revenue deficit grants to States, a lump sum amount of ₹ 11.000 crore in the Central Budget 2000-01. (*c*) Grants. For the five years commencing from April 1, 2000. ₹ 4.972.63 crore be given for upgradation of standards of administration and specific grants to certain States for special problems. For the five years commencing from April 1,2000. ₹ 10,000 crore for local bodies, to be directed for maintenance of civic services, ₹ 1600 crore per annum is for rural local bodies and ₹ 400 crore per annum is for urban local bodies. (*d*) With reference to the Grants-in-Aid under Article 275 (I) of the Constitution, which amounts to a total of ₹ 35,359 crore for the period 2000-2005 to be provided to such States (15 States) which will have deficit non-plan revenue account even after the devolution of central tax revenues, equal to the amount of deficits assessed during the period 2000-2005. (*e*) With regard to the Calamity Relief Funds in States with an aggregate size of Rs. 11007.59 crore during 2000-05. The tax devolution from the Centre to the Slate should not exceed 37.5 per cent of total Centre's revenues. This should be inclusive of the Central taxes/duties to States and grants-in-aid to States. The FC recommended that each State be given a share as specified. The net proceeds of all shareable Union taxes and duties except the expenditure tax and service tax. Data for percentage share for certain states is : Bihar-14.597. Maharashtra-4.632. Kerala-3.057. Uttar Pradesh-19.798. Punjab-1.147.

- **The Twelfth Finance Commission of India**

The Twelfth Finance Commission was appointed on I November 2002 to make recommendations on the distribution of net proceeds of sharable taxes between Union and States. The Commission was headed by veteran economist of India. C. Rangarajan. The Commission submitted its report on 30 November 2004 and covered the period from.2005-10.

Major Recommendations of 12th Finance Commission

(*a*) **Macro-economic stability**

The total Fiscal Deficit for Centre and States to be reduced to 3% of GDP and the total tax-GDP ratio of both Centre and States to be increased to 17.6% of GDP in 2009-10. The revenue deficit for the Centre and States combined to be reduced to 0% by 2008.

(*b*) **Distribution of Union Tax**

The total share of states in the total sharable central taxes to be fixed at 30.5% and the share of states will come down to 29.5% if the states levy sales tax on sugar, textiles and tobacco.

(*c*) **Grants to Local Bodies**

The total grant that will have to be given to the states for panchayati raj institutions and local urban bodies for the period of 2005-09 will be ₹ 20,000 crores and ₹ 5,000 crores respectively.

(*d*) **Calamity Relief Fund**

The calamity relief fund scheme will continue as it was in the previous plans with Centre and States contributing in the ratio of 75: 25. The size of fund will be ₹ 21,333 crore for the period of 2005-10.

(*e*) **Grant-in-aid to the States**

For the period of 2005-10, the total non-plan revenue deficit grant of ₹ 56856 crores is recommended to 15 states and the total grant of ₹ 10172 crores is recommended for 8 educationally backward states. A grant of ₹ 15,000 crores is recommended for building roads and bridges which is in addition to the normal expenditure of the states while the grants that is recommended to the states for maintenance of public buildings, forests, heritage conservation and specific needs of states is ₹ 500 crore., ₹ 100 crore, ₹ 625 crore and ₹ 7100 crore.

Terms of Reference

The Commission shall make recommendations on the following matters:

(1) The distribution of net proceed of taxes between Union and States which arc to be divided under Chapter 1 Part XII of the Constitution.

(2) The policies required to increase the consolidated fund of states on the basis of recommendation made by the Finance Commission of states to supplement the resources of municipalities and panchayats in the state.

In making the recommendation, the Commission shall have its regard, among other considerations, to :

(1) The resources of the Union government and State government for five years starting from I April 2005 on the basis of the total tax and non-tax that it will likely to receive by the end of 2003-04.

(2) The demand of the resources by the Central government, in particular the need of expenditure on civil administration, internal security, defence, debt servicing and other committed expenditure and liabilities.

- **Major Recommendations of 13th Finance Commission**

1. The share of states in the net proceeds of the shareable Central taxes should be 32%. This is 1.5% higher than the recommendation of the 12th Finance Commission.
2. Revenue deficit to be progressively reduced and eliminated. followed by revenue surplus by 2013-14.
3. Fiscal deficit to be reduced lo 3% of the GDP by 2014-15.
4. A target of 68% of GDP for the combined debt of Centre and States.
5. The Medium Term Fiscal Plan (MTFP) should be reformed and made the statement of commitment rather then a statement of intent.
6. FRBM Act needs to be amended to mention the nature of shocks which shall require targets relaxation.
7. Both Centre and States should conclude 'Grand Bargain' lo implement the model Goods and Services Act (GST). To incentivise the states, the Commission recommended a sanction of the grant of ₹ 50,000 crore.
8. Initiatives to reduce the number of Centrally Sponsored Schemes (CSS) and to restore the predominance of formula-based plan grants.
9. States need to address the problem of losses in the power sector in time-bound manner.

Demand for More Financial Power by States : Before closing this Chapter, it should be pointed out that there is a growing demand from some of the States for greater financial powers, by amending the Constitution, if necessary, which was stoutly resisted by Prime Minister Desai. There are two relevant considerations on this issue:

(*i*) The steps taken by Pakistan to make nuclear bombs together with the equivocal conduct of China leave no room for complacence in the matter of defence. Hence, the Union cannot yield to any weakening of its resources that would prejudice the defence potential of the country.

(*ii*) On the other hand, the welfare activities of the States involving huge expenditure, natural calamities, etc., which could not be fully envisaged in 1950, call for a revision of the financial provisions of the Constitution.

The entire subject of Centre-State Relations has been reviewed by the Sarkaria Commission. Its Report is under consideration by the Government.

42ND AMENDMENT TO ESTABLISH THE PREDOMINANCE OF THE CENTRE

Changes in the State List. The 42nd Constitution Amendment Act was passed by the Parliament and assented to by the President in 1976, which clearly established the predominance of the Centre over the States. It made far-reaching changes in the Constitution and altered its original federal character by transferring certain items like education, weights and measures, forests, protection of wild life and administration of justice (excluding Supreme Court and High Court) from the State List to the Concurrent List. Taxes on advertisements by broadcasting or telecasting media were also excluded from the purview of entry 55 of the State List.

Deployment of Central Forces in States without their Permission. Seventh Schedule to the Indian Constitution was amended. Besides that new Article 257A was inserted to empower the Union to send any armed force or other force of the Union for dealing with any grave situation of law and order in any State. Such force shall act in accordance with the directions of the Central Government and shall not be subject to the control of State Government. Provision has also been made accordingly in Article 257 A, clause (3) to empower Parliament to define the powers, functions and liabilities of the members of such force.

Supremacy of Parliament was established beyond any shadow of doubt and the courts were deprived of the power to declare any Constitutional amendment as void. According to 42nd Amendment Act, 1976, supremacy of the Parliament was established beyond any shadow of doubt by clipping the powers of the Courts. It was laid down that no Constitutional amendment could be challenged in the courts on any grounds whatsoever.

Emergency. Article 352 was suitably amended in that respect and empowered the President to declare the Emergency in respect of the whole of India or such part of the territory thereof as may be specified.

During the Emergency all the States had to toe the lines of the Central Government and none dared to defy it.

PRIME MINISTER ANNOUNCES SARKARIA COMMISSION TO REVIEW CENTRE-STATE RELATIONS

Prime Minister Mrs. Indira Gandhi announced on March 24, 1983 in Parliament the appointment of a Commission under the chairmanship of Justice Ranjit Singh Sarkaria, retired judge of the Supreme Court, to review the existing arrangements between the Centre and States. It was set up to examine all spheres of Centre-State relations and recommend appropriate changes. The long awaited terms of reference of the Commission, notified on June 17, 1983, said that review could cover "*the working of the existing arrangements between the Union and the States in regard to powers, functions and responsibilities in all spheres.*" A general statement notable for brevity, outlined the Commission's task. The earlier idea of listing constitutional provisions and specific points was given up because it was felt that it would restrict the scope of work.

SARKARIA COMMISSION'S REPORT ON CENTRE-STATE RELATIONS

The Sarkaria Commission headed by the retired judge of the Supreme Court, Mr. Ranjit Singh Sarkaria, had been appointed by the late Prime Minister, Indira Gandhi to go into the whole question and suggest suitable ways and means to harmonise the Centre-State relations. Later on two more members were added to it. The commission laboured hard for more than four years. Though it submitted its report some time earlier but it was made public only on 30th January, 1988. It gave the following suggestions:

Amendment of Article 356 : The opposition parties had been insisting on the repealing of Article 356 because in their opinion the Centre had misused it totally. The Sarkaria Commission did not agree to its repeal but at the same time had suggested amendment to Article 356 to prevent arbitrary imposition of the President's Rule in the States. The Commission has not only suggested that the material and the grounds justifying the imposition of President's Rule to be incorporated in the Presidential proclamation but has also ruled that dissolution of the State Assembly in such cases should be resorted to only after the Parliament had approved the Presidential proclamation.

Inter-State Council : The proposed Inter-State Council to be set up under Article 253 of the Constitution should be called Inter-Government Council. It will consist of a general body comprising the Prime Minister as Chairman and all Chief Ministers and all Union Cabinet Ministers as members. A smaller standing committee should consist of the Prime Minister as chairman and six Chief Ministers, one from each zone, elected annually and six Union Cabinet Ministers, to be nominated by the Prime Minister as members.

The general body will meet at least twice a year and the standing committee at least four times. The Council will evolve guidelines for identification and selection of issues to be brought before it and will make sure that only such matters of national importance relating to subjects of common interest are brought before it as would fall within the ambit of Article 263.

Selection of Governor : On the selection of Governor, the Commission has recommended that it is desirable that a politician from the ruling party at the Centre is not appointed as Governor of a State which is being run by some other party or a combination of other parties.

A Governor should be eminent in some walk of life, should be from outside the state, should be a detached figure not too intimately connected with the local politics of the State and a person who has not taken active part in politics generally and particularly in the recent past. Persons belonging to minority groups should continue to be given a chance as hitherto.

Consultation with the Chief Minister regarding appointment of Governor to be mandatory. The Commission had recommended that the requirement of consultation with the Chief Minister on the appointment of a person as Governor of the State should be prescribed in the Constitution itself.

Inter-State River Water Dispute : On the question of inter-state river water disputes, the Commission says that once an application under section 3 of the Inter-State River Disputes Act is received from a State, it should be mandatory on the Union Government to constitute a tribunal within one year. The Act may be suitably amended for this purpose and also to empower the Union Government to appoint a tribunal *suo moto*, if necessary, when it is satisfied that such a dispute exists in fact. The Act should also be amended to ensure that the award of a tribunal becomes effective within five years from the date of its constitution. The tribunal's award should have the same force and sanction behind it as an order or decree of the Supreme Court to make it really binding.

Union Territories' Matters : As regards Union Territories all matters which need to be sorted out between the Centre and the Union Territory with a legislature may be discussed by a standing committee for the Union Territory as members.

Appointment of Judges and their Transfers : On the matter of appointment of High Court judges an amendment of Article 217 has been suggested. This will provide for the President in consultation with the Chief Justice of India, making rules to ensure that the vacancies of High Court judges are promptly filled in with a time schedule.

As a matter of healthy practice, the Chief Justice of India should be consulted before formulating an opinion in his individual judgment as to the proposed transfer of a judge from one High Court to another.

Emergency Provisions : Examining the relevant provisions of the Constitution regarding emergency powers and the President's Rule (Articles 352, 355, and 356), the Commission has expressed the view that these provisions were made with the object of ensuring the integrity of the nation and were not conceived as a grant of overriding powers to the Union.

Role of All India Services : The Commission has found the institution of All India Services to be as necessary today as when the Constitution was framed. On the role of the All India Services, which have shown themselves capable of discharging the roles that the framers of the Constitution envisaged for them, it has observed that any move to disband these services or to permit a State Government to opt out of the scheme must be regarded as retrograde and harmful to the larger interests of the country. Such a step was sure to encourage parochial tendencies and undermine the integrity, cohesion, efficiency and co-ordination in administration of the country as a whole.

The All India Services should be further strengthened. This could be achieved through well-planned improvements in selection, training, deployment, development and promotion policies and methods. The present accent of generalism should yield place to greater specialization in one or more areas of public administration.

Reference of the State Bills to the Centre for assent : On the subject of the Governor's powers to refer State Bills to the Centre for assent, the commission had made detailed suggestions for the guidance of the Centre and the States including the observance of a time frame for dealing with the Bills. As a matter of convention, assent should not be withheld merely on policy differences in matters relating to Concurrent List on the ground that the Union is contemplating a comprehensive law. The Commission has further suggested that reasons for withholding assent should be communicated to the States.

Grants to States : The Commission had suggested that grants should be given to the states in lieu of railway passenger fare tax as recommended by the Finance Commission. It has suggested review of royalty rates of minerals etc. once every two years as against the practice of reviewing it every four years.

It has also made suggestions in regard to overdraft by States, modernisation of the Treasury system and making available foreign exchange to the States. The Commission has suggested that the Centre should give its consent to the States for borrowing from banks etc. for periods less than one year. The system of tax-free municipal bonds should be introduced. In regard to assistance for natural calamities, it has been suggested that States should be left with discretion to make some adjustment in the use of relief funds and strict penalties should be imposed for diversion and misappropriation of funds.

The Commission has suggested setting up of an expert body to recommend desirable directions or reforms in taxation and resource mobilisation of the Union and States. It has also suggested the preparation of a comprehensive paper on the subject of Government's subsidies and the setting up of an official committee to evolve steps for coordination of economic policies and to ensure a consensus on financial matters.

The Finance Commission's important role has been affirmed and detailed suggestions have been made for its effective functioning. The Commission has suggested that the terms of reference should be drawn up after informal consultation with the States and there should be no delay in the implementation of its recommendations.

INTER-STATE COUNCIL SET UP TO SETTLE DISPUTES

The President issued a notification on June 24, 1990 formally constituting an Inter-State Council headed by the Prime Minister as recommended by the Sarkaria Commission on Centre-State relations.

Besides the Prime Minister, six Cabinet Ministers to be nominated and all Chief Ministers of States and Union territories will constitute the Council, set up as forum for dialogue to ensure better co-ordination between the Centre and States.

Article 263, under which the Inter-State Council has been set up, states that if at any time it appears to the President that the public interests would be served by the establishment of council charged with the duty of;

(*A*) Inquiring into and advising upon disputes which may have arisen between states.

(*B*) Investigating and discussing subjects in which some or all the states or the Union and one or more of the states have a common interest; or

(*C*) Making recommendations upon any such subject and in particular, recommendations for the better co-ordination of policy and action with respect to that subject.

It shall be lawful for the President by order to establish such a council and to define the nature of the duties to be performed by it and its organisation and procedure.

SUGGESTIONS FOR SMOOTH CENTRE-STATE RELATIONSHIP

After the Fourth General Elections the issue of Centre-State relationship became a subject of serious public concern in India and constitutional experts began to suggest ways and means of avoiding a confrontation between the two. Various suggestions were made: (*i*) The powers and duties of the President and Governors in regard to the suspension of a State government in case of the breakdown of constitutional machinery needed fuller investigation. (*ii*) The Planning Commission should be made an independent and autonomous body. (*iii*) The Finance Commission should be a permanent body. (*iv*) A person to be appointed as a Governor should be one who has had a long experience in public life and administration and can be trusted to rise above party prejudices and predilections. He should not be eligible for further appointment as a Governor after the completion of his term. (*v*) The convention of consulting the Chief Minister before appointing a Governor is a healthy one and may continue. (*vi*) When the Governor has reason to believe that the ministry has ceased to command a majority in the Assembly, he should come to a final conclusion on this question by summoning the Assembly and ascertaining its verdict on the support enjoyed by the ministry. (*vii*) Before issue of directions to a State under Article 256, the Centre should explore the possibilities of setling points of conflict by all other available means. Former Chief Justice K. Subba Rao observed that since different parties held power in different States the emphasis hereafter should be more on co-operation than on control, more on patriotism than on authoritarianism, more on healthy competition in common interests than on regimentation, more on objective appraisals of the State problems than on a partisan approach. M. Hidayatullah stated that the Constitution will be put to severe strain unless the States are given a free rein on legislative, administrative and financial matters.

The suggestions which Professor Rasheeduddin Khan has mentioned to revamp Centre-State relations are far more radical than the recommendations of the Sarkaria Commission. For instance, he is in favour of deleting Articles 356 and 357 (emergency provisions, giving right to the Centre to dissolve a State Assembly and impose Presidents' Rule), whereas the Sarkaria Commission has only suggested that proclamation of emergency provisions (Article 356) should be done sparingly and only in extreme cases. Again, whereas the Commission has suggested the bifurcation of residuary powers between the Union List and the Concurrent List, Mr. Khan has highlighted the view that residuary powers should remain with the States only.

In fact, the factors responsible for the tension in Centre-State relations are politically motivated. In the first instance, the Constitution has provided for a federal system of government with an exceptionally strong Centre. This has naturally made the States apprehensive and suspicious of the policies of the Central Government. Secondly, the partisan attitude adopted by the Central Government towards various states has also been responsible for tension between the Centre and States. Thirdly, the difference in the ideology of the party in power at the Centre and the party in power at the State level has also been responsible for tension in the Centre-State relations. The negative role which some of the political parties have played has also been responsible for strained relations. These political

parties deliberately raised certain disputes and saw to it that they were not amicably settled, so that they could continue to lead the agitation and make selfish gains.

The best way to avoid Centre-State conflict is for the Centre to show imagination, understanding and a spirit of accommodation, and that it should grant the States adequate finance without discrimination.

The present-day situation is that co-operative federalism in India having lost its support base in the Congress system is in search of a new anchorage amidst pressures of democracy, national development, regional growth and state autonomy.

EXERCISES

Long Answer Type Questions:

1. Discuss in brief the legislative relations between the Union and the States.
2. Write a brief note on administrative relations between the Union and the States.
3. Discuss the financial relations between the Union and the States.
4. Write a note on recommendations of 12th and 13th Finance Commissions about the distribution of revenue between the Centre and States.
5. What do you know about Sarkaria Commission? Discuss its report on Centre-State relations.
6. What will be your suggestions for smooth Centre-State relations?

Short Answer Type Questions:

1. The Constitution of India divides the subjects into three lists—the Union List, the State List and the Concurrent List. What is meant by Union List? How many subjects there are in Union List?
2. What do you know about State List?
3. What is meant by Concurrent List?
4. In which conditions the Union Parliament can also make laws on state subjects?
5. What was the aim of 42nd Amendment in respect of Centre-State relations?

Objective Type Questions :

Choose the correct answer

1. Which of the following indicates non-interference of the Centre in the prescribed domain of the States?
   (*a*) Regional autonomy (*b*) State autonomy
   (*c*) Commercial autonomy (*d*) None of the above
2. In 1966-67, which of the following parties demanded that "this newly created Punjab state be accorded the same status and powers which are given to the state of Jammu and Kashmir under the Indian Constitution of 1950" ?
   (*a*) Congress (*b*) Akali Dal
   (*c*) D. M. K. (*d*) C. P. I. (M)
3. Consider the following statements regarding Sarkaria Commission:
   1. The Governor of a State should be appointed with the concurrence of the Chief Minister.
   2. Article 356 should be used very sparingly, in extreme cases as a measure of last resort
   3. Before issuing directions to a State under Articles 256 and 257, the Union should explore the possibilities of setling points of conflict by all other available means

4. Before deploying Union armed and other forces in a State in aid of the civil power, it is desirable that the State Government should be consulted

Which of the above were the recommendations of the Commission to improve Centre-State relations?

(*a*) 1 and 2 (*b*) 2 and 4

(*c*) 2 and 3 (*d*) 1, 2, 3 and 4

5. Which of the following arguments is in favour of State autonomy?

(*a*) Autonomy is not independence of the states and the autonomy is demanded under the Indian federal structure and therefore there is no danger for disintegration.

(*b*) State autonomy is essential for the establishment of a true and genuine federal policy

(*c*) Autonomy will inculcate the responsibilities among the States.

(*d*) All of the above

ANSWERS

1. (*b*) 2. (*b*) 3. (*d*) 4. (*d*)

15

CHAPTER

Zonal Councils

Birth of the Zonal Councils. The publication of the Report of the States Reorganisation Commission in 1995 was followed by a wave of agitation and hooliganism in various parts of the country. The interested parties made a capital of the situation to malign the Government. They encouraged the silly demand for unilingual States. In order to pacify the regional demands, Pt. Jawaharlal Nehru in a speech in Lok Sabha expressed his plan of grouping the States into four or five zones and setting up a Zonal Council in each zone to develop the habit of co-operative thinking. He said, "The more I thought of the organisation of the States, the more I have been attracted to something which I used to reject previously....that is, whatever final decision Parliament arrives at in regard to the States, we shall still have what I would call Zonal Councils, that is, a group of three, four or five States as the case may be, should have common council...Let us see how it develops. Let the Centre be associated with it for dealing with economic problems as well as the multitude of border problems and other problems that might arise." This idea got a ready response from the Parliament which adopted a Bill in this regard in 1956. The Act sought to divide the country into five zones, each having its own Council. The five Zonal Councils are :

1. North Zone comprises the States of Haryana, Punjab, Rajasthan, Jammu and Kashmir, Delhi and Himachal Pradesh.
2. The Eastern Zone includes Bihar, Jharkhand, West Bengal, Orissa, Assam, Manipur, Tripura, Meghalaya, Nagaland, Mizoram and Arunachal Pradesh.
3. The Central Zone includes the States of Uttar Pradesh, Uttaranchal, Madhya Pradesh and Chhattisgarh.
4. The Western Zone consists of States of Gujarat, Maharashtra and Karnataka.
5. Southern Zone consisted of Andhra, Tamil Nadu and Kerala.

Composition of the Zonal Council. Each Zonal Council consists of (*a*) a Union Minister nominated by the President ; (*b*) the Chief Ministers of all the States grouped in that Zone ; (*c*) two other Ministers of each State ; (*d*) two representatives of the Union Territories, if any, nominated by the President. The Union Minister in each Zonal Council acts as its chairman. Each Council has a set of advisers. There are Deputy Commissioners and Chief Secretaries one from each State in the Zone. Besides the advisers from the States there is one nominee of the

Planning Commission of India. The advisers are permitted to sit in the Council meetings but have no right to vote. The Chief Ministers act as Deputy Chairman of the Council one by one for a year each. The decisions at the Council are taken by majority vote. In the event of equal division of votes, the Chairman exercises his casting vote.

Functions of the Zonal Councils. The Zonal Council acts as an advisory body and discusses such matters as are of common interest of the constituent units. The subjects on which it can make recommendations to the States are : (1) Social Planning ; (2) Economic Planning ; (3) Inter-State Transport ; (4) Border Disputes ; (5) Any matter concerning minorities.

Main Objectives of the Zonal Councils. The riots that followed the publication of the States Reorganisation Commission's Report drew the attention of the political leaders to the disintegration tendencies in the country. It was a bad omen. Every sensible person realised the importance of emotional integration to put down separatist tendencies. The creation of zones and Zonal Councils was the offshoot of this growing realisation. Pt. Pant rightly remarked that "no region could prosper unless the security and unity of India were completely ensured and generated for today, for tomorrow and ever." At the inaugural meeting of Northern Zonal Council, he summed up the main objectives of the Zonal Scheme as follows: (*a*) to achieve an emotional integration of the country; (*b*) to help in arresting the growth of acute State consciousness, regionalism, linguism and particular trends; (*c*) to help in removing the after-effects of separation in some cases so that the processes of reorganisation, integration and economic advancement may coalesce and synchronise ; (*d*) to enable the Centre and States to co-operate and exchange ideas and experiences in order that uniform policies for the common good of the community are evolved and the ideal of a socialistic society is achieved; (*e*) to co-operate with each other in the successful and speedy execution of major development projects ; and (*f*) to secure some kind of political equilibrium between different regions in the country.

Utility of the Zonal Councils. The Zonal scheme has been received with mixed feelings. It has been on trial for a sufficiently long period and it has a record of creditable service. Some critics, however, fear that it is too idealistic a scheme. They apprehend that in course of time it will become so powerful a body as to reduce the participating State governments to non-entities. It may also weaken the Centre by enlarging its scope of functions. But such fears are unfounded, rather exaggerated. Actual working of the scheme has yielded encouraging results. It has promoted co-operative approach to economic and other border disputes between the participating States. No State singly can claim self-sufficiency in material and mineral resources for economic development. Combined effort of the contiguous State serves a very useful purpose. Bhakra project is a boon to both Punjab and Himachal Pradesh. The economy of the Punjab is also tied up with that of Kashmir. The utility of Zonal Scheme can be gauged from the fact that Rajasthan Canal is a joint project of Punjab and Rajasthan. Chambal Valley project, which is nearing completion, is also a product of the joint efforts of Madhyal Pradesh and Rajasthan. Similarly there were many common projects in many states. Nobody can deny that the Zonal Scheme has marked the beginning of an epoch of co-operation and emotional integration.

Meeting of the Zonal Councils have been held from time to time. In these Councils decisions to solve dacoit problem, improve the law and order situation, develop the natural resources and common projects have been taken. There have been food zones also consisting of more than one state, therefore, the co-operation has been achieved through these councils. Various common views have been harnessed by the joint efforts of Zonal Councils and electricity created by joint endeavour. Zonal Councils have also played a great part in the improvement of agriculture and irrigation, combating the danger of floods and fighting the evils of drought and famine. *A co-ordination in regard to development schemes and implementation of Five-Year Plans has been achieved through the Zonal Councils.*

Praiseworthy work of Eastern Zonal Council. The Eastern Zonal Council has done a remarkable work regarding the development schemes and co-ordination of Five-Year Plan of seven different states (Assam, Nagaland, Mizoram, Arunachal Pradesh, Manipur, Tripura and Meghalaya). They are called seven sisters.

EXERCISES

Long Answer Type Questions:

1. Write in detail a note on Zonal Councils.
2. Discuss in brief the objectives and utility of Zonal Councils.

Short Answer Type Questions:

1. Discuss in brief the birth of Zonal Councils.
2. Write the names of five Zonal Councils.
3. Discuss in brief the composition of Zonal Councils.
4. Discuss the main objectives and functions of Zonal Councils.
5. Discuss in brief the utility of Zonal Councils.

Objective Type Questions :

Choose the correct answer

1. In which year was the Report of the States Reorganisation Commission published ?
   (*a*) 1955 (*b*) 1956
   (*c*) 1957 (*d*) 1958
2. Who expressed his plan in a speech in Lok Sabha about the setting up of Zonal Councils ?
   (*a*) Lal Bahadur Shastri (*b*) Pt. Jawaharlal Nehru.
   (*c*) Pt. Gobind Vallabh Pant (*d*) Rajeev Gandhi
3. In which year the idea of Zonal Council got a ready response from the Parliament ?
   (*a*) 1954 (*b*) 1955
   (*c*) 1956 (*d*) 1957
4. How many Zonal Councils are there in India ?
   (*a*) Two (*b*) Three
   (*c*) Four (*d*) Five

ANSWERS

1. (*a*) 2. (*b*) 3. (*c*) 4. (*d*)

CHAPTER 16

Supreme Court

"There is no better test of the excellence of a Government than the efficiency of its judicial system for nothing more greatly touches the welfare and security of the citizen, than his knowledge that he can rely on the certain, prompt and impartial administration of justice."

— *Bryce*

IMPORTANCE OF JUDICIARY

The three wings of any Government are : the Executive, the Legislature, and the Judiciary. The Legislature makes laws for the country; the executive enforces those laws and administers the country; the law courts punish the law-breakers and act as the guardian angel of the Constitution. The judiciary guarantees fairness and justice, and protects the individual from the despotism of the Government. It is difficult to imagine a civilised State without an efficient judicial system. Law saves the society from becoming anarchic or lawless. In the absence of an impartial judiciary the citizens are as much exposed to danger from the public servants as from the outlaws. The Constitution of free India envisages a federal government for the country. The Supreme Court has been invested with the important task of settling disputes between the Union and the States and interpreting the ambiguous clauses of the Constitution. Another duty of the Supreme Court is to prevent State's encroachment on the Fundamental Rights of the citizens.

Under the Act of 1935, for the first time an all India Court was set up. The name of this 'All India Court' was 'Federal Court of India'. With the coming into force of the Indian Constitution, the Federal Court of India was substituted by the Supreme Court.

Composition : strength of judges raised. The Supreme Court at presents consists of the Chief Justice and 25 other judges. In 1950, when the Court was imaugurated with the New Constitution in had only 8 Judges. Parliament was, however, authorised to change the member of its judges. On account of the increase in its workload the strength of the Supreme Court judges has been raised from time to time. In 1956 the Parliament passed the Supreme Court Number of Judges Act, which raised the total strength to 11. In 1960, the Supreme Court Number of Judges Amendment Act was passed further raising the strength of the Court judges to 14 including the Chief Justice. Its strength was further increased to 18 in 1977. The Parliament again passed the Bill in May, 1985 to increase the number of judges in the Supreme Court from 18 to 26 including the Chief Justice. The then Union Law Minister, Mr. Asoke Sen, had earlier indicated that the strength would go up to 30. Now the number of judges in the Supreme Court is 30, according to Act 11 of 2009. The decision is in the context of the heavy backlog that has accumulated in the court over the years.

The Union Parliament is authorised to reduce or increase the number of Judges.[1] The President appoints the judges of Supreme Court in consultation with such judges of the Supreme Court and High Court as he may deem proper to consult. Besides that, in the appointment of judges of the Supreme Court, he also consults the Chief Justice of India.

Appointment

The Constitution provides that a Judge of the Supreme Court will be appointed by the President in consultation with such of the Judges of the Supreme Court and of the High Court in the States as the President may deem necessary for the purpose. In the case of appointment of a Judge other than the Chief Justice, the Chief Justice of India must be consulted. In practice, the appointment of the Chief Justice of India as well as of the other Judges of the Supreme Court is recommended by the Home Ministry and after the matter has been examined by the Appointments Committee of the Indian Cabinet and the decision received the blessings of the Prime Minister, it is formalised by the Indian President.

For nearly two decades now, the judiciary has been embroiled in the controversy over who should appoint or transfer judges. The issue seemed settled in 1993 when a nine-judge Bench of the Supreme Court said that the Chief Justice of India (CJI) held the key in all such matters. The judgement still left a patch of grey area on whether the CJI could override his senior 'brothers' or was merely the first among equals.

Former CJI M.M. Punchhi, who retired in October 1998, resolutely defended the first view, bringing appointments to the Supreme Court and the High Courts to a standstill. However, in October 1998, yet another nine-judge Bench of the Apex Court headed by Justice S.P. Bhurucha, finally overturned the retired CJI's interpretation. The Bench has ordered that the collegium for appointment to the Supreme Court should comprise the CJI and four seniormost judges of the court. Thus the judgement makes the Chief Justice of India one among other judges in appointing colleagues.

Former President K.R. Narayanan put a note on a file recommending that Scheduled Caste and Scheduled Tribe candidates be duly considered for appointment as judges of the Supreme Court. It is for the first time in the history of the Republic that a President has chosen to put his suggestion on record. Though the President has no constitutional power to suggest any changes in the selection process, his active intervention is bound to lead to an unseemly confrontation with the judiciary.

Seniority rule in the appointment of Chief Justice. The seniormost judge in the Supreme Court was elected to the most important judicial office of the country, *i.e.*, the Chief Justice and this practice was followed since the inception of the Constitution up to April 24, 1973. On April 24, 1973 the Supreme Court gave the decision in the Fundamental Rights case. In this case Justices J.M. Shelat, K.S. Hegde and A.N. Grover held that the Basic Structure of the Constitution could not be changed by the Parliament and that power is not inherent in Article 368. According to them, the following were the Basic elements of the Constitution : (1) The supremancy of the Constitution; (2) The Republican and Democratic form of Government and sovereignty of the country; (3) Secular and federal structure of the Constitution; (4) Demarcation of power between the Legislature, the Executive and the Judiciary; (5) The dignity of the Individual secured by the various freedoms and basic rights in Part III and the mandate to build a Welfare State contained in Part IV and the unity and integrity of the nation.

The Government did not like the decision of these judges. When Chief Justice Sikri retired the next day, *i.e.* on April 25, 1973, then these three judges were superseded and Mr. Ajit Nath Ray

1. Article 124 (1)

was appointed as the Chief Justice. Consequently these three judges resigned and there were loud protests from the All-India Bar Association, State Bar Associations, Opposition leaders, former chief justices and other prominent persons.

When Mr. Ajit Nath Ray retired on January 28, 1977, then there was another suppression by the Government. Mr. H.R. Khanna was superseded because the Government did not like his dissenting judgment in Habeas Corpus Case given on April 28, 1976. After superseding Mr. H.R. Khanna the Government appointed Mr. M.H. Beg as the Chief Justice of India on January 29, 1977. (At that time Mrs. Indira Gandhi headed the Goverment and on her advice the President made the appointment of Chief Justice Ajit Nath Ray as well as M.H. Beg). Mr. M.H. Beg retired on 17th February, 1978, Janata Government headed by Mr. Morarji Desai, had been formed on March 24, 1977. Therefore when Mr. M.H. Beg retired, then again the question arose who should be appointed the Chief Justice of India. The seniormost judge was Yashwant Vishnu Chandrachud. Though the Government did not like his decision in the Habeas Corpus Case, yet in order to follow strictly the policy of noninterference in the highest judicial office of the land, the Government recommended to the President that Mr. Chandrachud may be appointed as the Chief Justice and the President appointed him as the Chief Justice of India on 18th Feburary, 1978. This was also the wish of Loknayak. Jaya Prakash Narain and the public at large. So the Janata Government rendered an unparalleled service to the country by restoring the seniority rule in the appointment of Chief Justice. This will go a long way in making judiciary independent and fearless. After this there has not been any supersession and seniority rule is being strictly followed.

Qualifications of Judges. According to Article 124 (3) a person for appointment as a judge of the Supreme Court requires qualifications as follows :

(*a*) He is a citizen of India;

(*b*) He has been a judge of one or more High Courts for five successive years; or

(*c*) He has been an advocate of one or more High Courts for ten successive years; or

(*d*) He is in the opinion of the President an eminent jurist.

Salary of the judges raised. A Judge of the Supreme Court gets a salary of Rs. 90,000 per mensem. The salary of the Chief Justice is ₹ 1,00,000. Every judge is entitled without payment of rent to the use of furnished residence. The salaries of judges are charged on the Consolidated Fund of India and hence are outside the purview of the Parliament. Neither the privileges and allowances of a judge, nor his rights in respect of leave of absence and pension can be changed to his disadvantage after his appointment according to Article 125 (2). If a judge before entering upon his new office is receiving a pension in respect of his previous service under the Government of India, his salary is reduced by the amount of his pension. The salaries of the Judges may be reduced by a law of Parliament during a grave financial emergency proclaimed by the President.

Tenure of Judges. According to Article 124 every judge of the Supreme Court holds office till the age of 65. After attaining that age, he retires and receives pension as fixed by Union law. He cannot be removed arbitrarily by any authority. He is not subject to the whim or caprice of any agency. The Constitution provides that a judge can be removed by an order of the President on the basis of an address passed in both the Houses of Parliament and supported by a majority of not less than two-thirds members present and voting and an absolute majority of total members of each House.[1] The grounds on which a resolution for the removal of a judge can be moved are unsoundness of mind, proved misbehaviour and incapacity to discharge his functions. The Constitution guarantees to the Judges' security of service and emolument with the intention of keeping them beyond the influence of Executive or Legislature. The motive of the Constitution-makers had been to ensure the independence of judiciary so that the judges remain impartial and incorruptible.

1. Article 124 (4)

Restriction on Practice. Article 124 (7) provides, "No person who has held office as a judge of the Supreme Court shall plead or act in any court or before any authority within the territory of India."

Appointment of acting Chief Justice. When the office of Chief Justice of India is vacant or when the Chief Justice is by reason of absence or otherwise unable to perform the duties to his office shall be performed by such one of the other judges of the court as the President may appoint for the purpose. Our Constitution provides for the appointment of ad hoc judges. According to Article 127, if at any time the session of the Supreme Court cannot be held or continued for want of a quorum, the Chief Justice, with the prior consent of the President, may make such appointments. An ex-Judge of the Supreme Court may also be requested by the Chief Justice to act as Judge of the Supreme Court.

Supreme Court to be a court record. According to Article 129 of the Constitution the Supreme Court shall be a court of record and shall have all the powers of such a court including the power to punish for the court would be kept and can be called as an evidence in any subsequent case. Secondly, the court can punish anybody who imputes any bad motive to the judge. In *Vinayak Shamrao v. Moreshwar Ganesh*, Justice Bose observed, "That is the whole point of a court of record. All its judgments are preserved and not merely those which are specially approved or favoured. Why ? Because they operate as precedents and may be sent for and studied and followed as occasion requires."

Immunity of Judges and contempt proceedings. No discussion regarding the conduct or decisions of a judge can take place in the Parliament in order to ensure the independence of the judges. No bad motive of any kind can be imputed to any judge nor can his decisions be criticized in public or Parliament. The Supreme Court can start contempt proceedings against anyone who indulges in malicious propaganda against the judges or whose criticism is *mala fide*. In the contempt proceedings against the Editor, Printer and Publisher of *The Times of India*, the Supreme Court held, "No objection could have been taken to the article (editorial), but had it merely preached to courts of law the sermon of divine detachment. *But when it proceeded to attribute important motive to the judges, it not only transgressed the limits of fair and bona fide criticism, but had a clear tendency to affect the dignity and prestige of this court.* The article in question was thus a gross contempt of court. It is obvious that if an impression is created in the minds of the public that the judges in the highest court of the land act on extraneous considerations in deciding the cases, the confidence of the whole community in the administration of justice is bound to be undermined and no greater mischief than that can possibly be imagined. It was for this reason that the rule was issued against respondents."[1]

The Supreme Court can also start contempt proceedings against anyone who tries to influence the judges or prejudice their minds in any way. In *Dixit v. State of U.P.*, the Supreme Court held, "that the object of writing this paragraph and particularly of publishing it at the time it was actually done was quite clear to affect the minds of the judges and detract them, from the strict performance of their duties. The offending passage and the time and place of its publication certainly tended to hinder or obstruct the due administration of justice and was a contempt of court.[2]

Seat of the Supreme Court. Article 130 of the Constitution says that the Supreme Court shall sit in Delhi or any other place as the Chief Justice may decide from time to time with the approval of the President.

POWERS OF THE SUPREME COURT

The Constitution of India gives both original and appellate jurisdiction to Supreme Court. By original jurisdiction we mean that the court can hear and entertain suits directly from the parties in dispute. Under appellate jurisdiction the court entertains appeal against a decision by any other court of India. Besides these, the Court has other miscellaneous duties, namely, the interpretation of any clause of the Constitution and rendering legal advice to the Union Government.

1. S.C.R. 1953, 215.
2. A.I.R. 1954, S.C. 743.

Original jurisdiction of the Supreme Court. The Supreme Court hears directly any dispute (a) between the Government of India and one or more States, (b) between the Government of India and any State or States on one side and one or more other States on the other or (c) between two or more States[1]. Such a dispute should, however, involve some question of law or fact on which the existence or extent of a legal right depends. The treaties concluded between the Centre and the Princely States are excluded from court's original jurisdiction[2]. The court does not directly entertain suits in which the citizens or public servants are directly involved. It should, however, be noted that the Supreme Court of India, unlike the American Supreme Court, has no original jurisdiction over cases involving ambassadors and public Ministers or treaties. Those cases in which individuals are involved, they cannot also be brought before the Supreme Court directly. Such cases must begin in lower courts and an appeal can lie to the Supreme Court only if any question of law is involved or interpretation of the Constitution arises or the High Court certifies that such cases are fit to be heard by the Supreme Court.

Disputes relating to Waters. According to Article 262 clause (1) Parliament may by law provide for the adjudication of any dispute or complaint with respect to the use, distribution or control of the waters of or in any inter-State river or river valley.

Article 262 clause (2) further provides that notwithstanding anything in this Constitution, Parliament may by law provide that neither the Supreme Court nor any other court shall exercise jurisdiction in respect of any disputes or complaint as is referred to in clause (1).

As a Guardian of the Constitution : Directives of the Supreme Court. The principal function of the Supreme Court is to act as the guardian of the Constitution, particularly the Fundamental Rights guaranteed to the citizens. The Court comes in if the Government ever attempts to encroach upon any Fundamental Right. The Supreme Court has concurrent rights with the High Court to issue directions in the form of writs for the enforcement of Fundamental Rights. The writ may be of any of the following types—*mandamus,* writ of prohibition, *quo warranto* and *certiorari*. If a citizen is wrongly confined by the State, the Court can issue writ of *habeas corpus* for his release.

It is also within the jurisdiction of the Supreme Court to sit in judgment on the doings of the Execution and Union laws. If it is convinced that some law or act is contrary to spirit of the Constitution, it can declare that void or illegal. The Supreme Court of India, as its counterpart in America, also possesses the power of reviewing its own judgements. The Constitution requires all disputes arising out of the interpretation of any Article of the Constitution to be considered by a bench of at least five judges. If the judges do not arrive at a unanimous conclusion, the issue is decided by majority opinion whereas the judges who disagree with the majority opinion write their dissenting note separately. .

Though the High Court and Supreme Court prossess the Concurrent jurisdiction of issuing writs, yet the right to move the Supreme Court by appropriate proceedings for enforcement of the rights conferred by Part III is guaranteed. In *Romesh Thaper vs. State of Madras* the Supreme Court held that "Article 32 of the Constitution does not merely confer powers on the Supreme Court as Article 226 does on High Court to issue writs for the enforcement of Fundamental Rights or for other purpose as part of its general jurisdiction. Article 32 provides a guaranteed remedy for the enforcement of those rights and this remedial right is itself made a Fundamental Right by being included in the chapter on Fundamental Rights in the Constitution. The Supreme Court as such constituted is the protector and guarantor of Fundamental Rights, and it cannot consistently, with the responsibility so laid upon it, refuse to entertain applications seeking protection against infringement of such rights. A citizen can resort directly for such relief to the Supreme Court without first resorting to the High Court under Article 226 of the Constitution."

The Supreme Court can also decide any dispute relating to the election of the President or Vice-President.

1. Article 131
2. Instituted by the Constitution (Fifteenth Amendment) Act, 1963, S.3.

Changes made by the 43rd Amendment to the Constitution

According to 43rd Amendment Act, Article 131A has been omitted and sub-section (2) has been changed. According to Article 131A inserted by 42nd Amendment exclusive jurisdiction had been conferred upon the Supreme Court in regard to questions of Central Laws. The High Courts had been debarred to judge the constitutional validity of the Central Laws, they could judge only the constitutional validity of the State Laws. Now the 43rd Amendment has again conferred powers upon the High Courts to judge the constitutional validity of the Central Laws.

Changes made in the jurisdiction of the Supreme Court by 44th Amendment to the Constitution

Appellate jurisdiction of Supreme Court in appeals from High Courts in certain cases. (1) Article 132 lays down that an appeal shall lie to the Supreme Court in appeals from any judgment, decree or final order of a High Court in the territory of India whether in a civil, criminal or other proceeding (if High Court certifies under Article 134-A[1] that the case involves a substantial question of law as to interpretation of this Constitution).

Where such a certificate is given, any party in the case may appeal to the Supreme Court on the ground that any such question as aforesaid has been wrongly decided.

Appellate jurisdiction of Supreme Court in appeals from High Courts in regard to civil matters.

1. According to Article 133 an appeal shall lie to the Supreme Court from any judgment, decree on final order in a civil proceeding of a High Court in the territory of India [if the High Court certifies under Article 134A.][2]

   (*a*) that the case involves a substantial question of law of general importance; and

   (*b*) that in the opinion of the High Court the said question needs to be decided by the Supreme Court.

2. Notwithstanding anything in Article 132, any party appealing to the Court under clause (1) may urge as one of the grounds in such appeal that a substantial question of law as to the interpretation of this Constitution has been wrongly decided.

3. Notwithstanding anything in this Article (132), no appeal shall, unless Parliament by law otherwise provides, lie to the Supreme Court from the judgment, decree or final order of one judge of a High Court.

Appellate jurisdiction of Supreme Court in regard to criminal matters.

1. Article 134 lays down that an appeal shall lie to the Supreme Court from any judgment, final order or sentence in a criminal proceeding of a High Court in the territory of India if the High Court

   (*a*) has on appeal reversed an order of acquittal of an accused person and sentenced him to death; or

   (*b*) has withdrawn for trial before itself from any Court subordinate to its authority and has in such trial convicted the accused person and sentenced him to death; or

---

1. Substituted by Constitution (Forty-Fourth Amendment) Act, 1978.
2. Substituted by Constitution (Forty-Fourth Amdndment) Act, 1978.

Note: In a concurrent finding of fact given by the two courts below, it is the practice of the Supreme Court not to interfere in the absence of any extraordinary or special reasons, (Ratnam Chettiar *v*. S.M. Kuppaswami Chettiar, A.I.R. 1976 S.C.I.)

(*c*) Certifies under Article 134][1] that the case is a fit one for appeal to the Supreme Court:

Provided that an appeal under sub-clause (c) shall lie subject to such provisions as may be made in that behalf under clause (1) of Article 145 and to such conditions as the High Court may establish or require.

2. Parliament may by laws confer on the Supreme Court any further powers to entertain and hear appeals from any judgment, final order to sentence in criminal proceeding of a High Court in the territory of India subject to such conditions and limitations as may be specified in such law.

Special leave to appeal by the Supreme Court. (1) Article 136 lays down that notwithstanding anything in the chapter, the Supreme Court may, in its discretion, grant special leave to appeal from any judgment, decree, determination, sentence or order in any case or matter passed or made by any court or tribunal in the territory of India.

(2) Nothing in clause (1) shall apply to any judgment, determination, sentence or order passed or made by any court or tribunal constituted by or under any law relating to the Armed Forces.

Certificate of Appeal to the Supreme Court as instituted by 44th Amendment to the Constitution. Article 134A institution specially by 44th Amendment Act 1978 lays down that every High Court passing or making a judgment, decree, final order or sentence, referred to in clause (1) of Article 133 or clause (1) of Article 134

(*a*) may, if it deems fit so to do, on its own motion; and (*b*) shall, if an oral application is made, by or on behalf of the party aggrieved, immediately after the passing or making of such judgment, decree, final order or sentence, determine, as soon as may after such passing or making the question whether a certificate of the nature referred to in clause (1) of Article 132, or clause (1) of Article 133 or as the case may be, sub-clause (*c*) of clause (1) of Article 134 may be given in respect of that case.

Advisory jurisdiction of the Supreme Court. Article 143 (1) provides: "If at any time it appears to the President that a question of law or fact has arisen or is likely to arise which is of such a nature and of such public importance that it is expedient to obtain the opinion of the Supreme Court upon it, he may refer the question to that court for consideration and the court may, after such hearing as it thinks fit, report to the President its opinion thereon." Besides that the President can refer any dispute of the above kind for the opinion of the Supreme Court. The Supreme Court will report its opinion to the President after hearing such a case.

Enlargement of the Jurisdiction of the Supreme Court. The jurisdiction of the Supreme Court may also be enlarged with respect to any matter in the Union List by a Paliamentary law. The Parliament may confer on the Court the power to issue directions, orders or writs for any other purpose in addition to the enforcement of Fundamental Rights. It may also invest the Court with additional powers, not consistent with the Constitution, in order to enable it to discharge its duties more effectively (Article 138).

Review of Judgment or Orders by the Supreme Court. Subject to the provisions of any law made by Parliament or any rules made under Article 145, the Supreme Court shall have power to review any judgment pronounced or order made by it (Article 137). On a level with the Higher Courts in other countries, the Supreme Court of India is also not bound by its own decisions and orders for ever. It possesses the right to review its judgments. An application for review has to be filed with the Registrar of the Supreme Court within thirty days from the pronouncement of its judgments. The applicant is required to state grounds for review and a certificate by the counsel that it is supported

1. Substituted by Constitution (Forty-Fourth Amendment) Act, 1978.

Note: It is held that a new case on facts neither admitted nor established cannot be allowed to be sent up in appeal by special leave. Pratap Narain Singh Dev *v.* Shriniwas Sabata, A.I.R. 1976 S.C. 222.

by proper grounds. The Supreme Court has reviewed its own two famous cases *Gopalan* v. *The State of Madras* and *Golak Nath* v. *The State of Punjab* and reversed its earlier decisions.

Enforcement of its Decrees and Orders. Article 141 says that the decisions of the Supreme Court are binding on all courts in India. The Supreme Court can pass such decrees or issue such orders as are necessary to meet the ends of justice with regard to any case pending before it. Such a decree or order is enforceable throughout the country. It is imperative for all the authorities, civil and judicial, to assist and aid the court in the execution of its order. (Article 143).

THE ROLE OF THE SUPREME COURT AND ITS COMPARISON WITH THE SUPREME COURT OF U.S.A.

As Guardian of the Constitution. The Constitution of a country is a sacred document, and the supreme law of that country. The laws of the land, however, become meaningless if there is no paramount authority to enforce it. The Court of a country does the duty of checking both the citizens and the Government from desecrating or abusing the Constitution. This very idea had been emphasised by Chief Justice Marshall of the U.S.A. in the famous case of *Marbury* v. *Madison*. The learned Judge observed. "The powers of the Legislature are defined and that these limits may not be mistaken or forgotten, the Constitution is written......The Constitution is either superior, a paramount law, unchangeable by ordinary means nor it is on a level with ordinary Legislative Acts and like other Acts, is alterable. When the legislature shall please to alter it.......if the latter part of the people to limit a power, in its own illimitable......It is emphatically the province and duty of the judicial department to say what the law is......if, then courts are to regard the Constitution and the Constitution is superior to any ordinary Act of the Legislature, the Constitution and not such ordinary Act must govern the case to which they both apply."

The Constitution of U.S.A. does not specifically confer upon the Supreme Court of that country the right of interpreting the Constitution and sit in judgment on the constitutionality or otherwise of any State or Federal Act. The Court, however, derives its power from two important provisions. Article VI holds the Constitution supreme and Article III extends the federal jurisdiction to "all cases, in law and equity arising under this constitution." It was in the context of the above-mentioned provisions that Chief Justice Marshall had established the right of the Federal Court to declare any Act unconstitutional whether passed by the Federal or State Government if it violated the Constitution. Although the Indian Constitution does not empower the Supreme Court to bring the Union and State Acts under judicial review, it, at the same time, does not restrict the right of the court to judge the constitutionality or otherwise of any Act passed by any Legislative authority in the country. The federal character of the Constitution clearly limits the scope of Authority of the Union and the States. The exercise of authority beyond that scope, naturally, amounts to violation of the Constitution. The Supreme Court, as such, is the only competent authority to decide whether the Constitutional limitations have been observed or not. The Supreme Court is also empowered to ensure the enjoyment of Fundamental Rights by the citizens. No doubt the Parliament and the State Legislatures are competent in certain circumstances to restrict the Fundamental Rights but then the court interferes again to declare how far the restrictions are just or unjust.

In the words of Shri Alladi Krishnaswami Aiyar, the Supreme Court of India *"has more powers than any other Supreme Court in any part of the world."* A comparison of the Supreme Courts of India and America shows that if the former has wider jurisdiction with regard to appeals from lower Courts, the latter has an advantage over the former with regard to original jurisdiction which extends in addition to the settlement of disputes between the units of the federation, to all cases relating to ambassadors, Consuls, Ministers, Treaties, Naval Forces and maritime matters. On the appellate side, the Indian Supreme Court enjoys wider powers than its American counterpart which does not deal with appeals in civil and criminal cases, except the constitutional ones. Unlike the practice in

India, an appeal in civil and criminal cases cannot be taken to the Supreme Court of America from the highest courts of the States. The Indian Supreme Court has advisory functions also which the American Supreme Court does not have. Above all the Indian Supreme Court is a Court of record. Its decision cannot be called in question in any Court or by any authority. Its orders are enforceable throughout India. The judgments pronounced by it are preserved and referred to in all the inferior Courts. The American Supreme Court is deprived of these privileges.

Another point of difference between the two Supreme Courts of India and America is that whereas the latter recognizes judicial supremacy, the former gives importance to Legislative supremacy. Both can declare a law void if it goes against the spirit of the Constitution. The American Supreme Court is, in addition to it, also empowered to declare an Act unconstitutional if it fails to satisfy requirements of the "due process of law" means standards of natural justice. Thus the American court examines a federal law on two counts—whether it is consistent with the Constitution and secondly whether it is reasonable and just. There is under the Indian Constitution no "due process of law" clause and no doctrine of judicial supremacy. The 'due process' clause in the Constitution of the United States and the doctrine of "judicial supremacy" have made the American Supreme Court the arbiter of social policy in the United States, a kind of super legislature which justifies the claim of Chief Justice Hughes correctly that "we are under a Constitution but the Constitution is what the judges say it is." The Supreme Court of India does not consider at all whether a law is reasonable or not. It examines it in the light of the Constitution. It submits blindly to a constitutional law duly passed by a competent authority.

In the famous case *Gopalan* vs. *State of Madras*, 1950, the Supreme Court judge, Shri S.R. Das. observed, "Instead of judicial supremacy we have the doctrine of legislative supremacy, subject to Constitutional limitations. Though the Supreme Court will nullify an act which is in clear contravention of a Constitutional limitation, it will not assume the role of suppressing or correcting the law passed by the legislature under any theory of Natural Rights of Justice, ideals of the Constitution.... It will not question the reason or reasonableness of any law except where the Constitution itself has expressly authorised the court to exercise the power. In India, the position of the judiciary is somewhere between the courts in India and the United States." In short, the Indian Supreme Court is not the conscience-keeper of the Legislature. It can protect a citizen against the excesses of the Executive but not against the despotism of the Legislature.

Though the Supreme Court has revised its decision of Gopalan v. *The State of Madras, still the Supreme Court has frankly conceded the Legislative supremacy of Parliament in its Fundamental Rights case decision delivered on April 24, 1973.* However, the Supreme Court has restored the power of judicial review in the famous case *Minerva Mills Ltd.* vs. *the Union of India* (1980) after striking down section 55 of the 42 Amendment Act (1976).

INDEPENDENCE OF JUDICIARY

An independent judiciary alone can shield the citizen against the excess of the Executive or Legislature. The following measures have been employed in India to ensure that the judges work freely and impartially :

(1) The Constitution guarantees to the judges security of service and salaries. They cannot be removed except by a prescribed process and no other grounds except proved misbehaviour and incapacity. (2) The post of the judge is not a sort of political prize to be given to favourites by the party in power. The judges are appointed by the President who in making appointments is guided not by party consideration but merits and capability of the persons concerned. (3) The salaries and allowances of the judges are charged upon the Consolidated Fund of India, which means that the emoluments of judge cannot be altered to his disadvantage after his appointment. A judge's salary cannot be reduced except by amending the Constitution to that effect or by the President during Emergency. (4) The

post of a Supreme Court Judge is not an elective post. The judges are appointed by the President and not elected by an electoral college as is the case in America and Switzerland. The tenure of service of judges of Indian Supreme Court and High Court is fairly long. The retirement age of a Supreme Court judge is 65 and of a High Court judge 62.[1] Long period of service enables the judges in India to work independently. (5) Every judge before entering upon his office is administred an oath to have faith in the Constitution and to perform his duties to the best of his ability, knowledge and judgment without fear, favour, affection or ill will. (6) Another provision to protect the Supreme Court judges against corruptibility is that no judge after retirement is permitted to practise in any court of law. A High Court judge is, however, allowed to practise, after retirement, in any court except the one in which he had acted as a judge.[2] The motive behind imposing such a restriction is that the acting judges may while trying a case not be influenced by their ex-colleague, appearing before them as a counsel.

SUPREME COURT AND ITS IMPORTANT CONSTITUTIONAL DECISIONS (JUDICIAL REVIEW)

The report on the working of the Supreme Court of India has been quite heartening. The judges have all along been acting with dignity and impartiality. They have inspired trust and faith in the ideals of justice. They have never failed to uphold justice fearlessly whenever they were called upon to defend the Constitution or hold inquiries. They have not hesitated in opposing strictures against corrupt officials, even the Chief Ministers of the States when they found them guilty. The court undertook to make judicial inquiries into charges against Mundra into Jabalpore riots and disturbances created by Akalis in Amritsar and Ludhiana. Thus the Supreme Court has lived up to the expectations of the people. It has been the repository of justice and human rights, an ever vigilant guardian of the Constitution and conscience-keeper of the Government.

Conflict of Jurisdiction Between U.P. Assembly and Allahabad High Court

In March, 1964, a conflict of jurisdiction arose between the U.P. Legislature and Allahabad High Court. The conflict of jurisdiction arose out of judges' orders on March 19, 1964, releasing on bail Keshav Singh, a socialist worker of Gorakhpur who was undergoing seven days' imprisonment in Lucknow jail under orders of the House for contempt of the House. The U.P. Assembly then passed a resolution on March 21, 1964, summoning Mr. B. Solomon, an advocate of Keshav Singh, to appear before the Bar of the House under custody to answer the charge of contempt of the House. The U.P. Assembly also issued warrants against two judges of the High Court, namely, Justice N.U.Beg and Justice G.D.Sehgal, who had ordered the release of Mr. Keshav Singh. The Allahabad High Court stayed the order of the U.P. Assembly. Then the U.P. Assembly withdrew its warrants against Justice N.U. Beg and Justice G.D. Sehgal and Mr. Solomon and gave a chance to explain their conduct before the Bar of the House. A full Bench of the Allahabad High Court also stayed the new resolution of U.P. Assembly on March 27, 1964. So a head-on clash occurred between U.P. Assembly and Allahabad High Court.

The President of India in order to solve the question of conflict of jurisdiction between the Allahabad High Court and the U.P. Assembly referred the whole issue to the Supreme Court under Article 143 of the Constitution. The Supreme Court gave its verdict in favour of the Allahabad High Court.

Supreme Court as a Guarantor and Protector of the Fundamental Rights — Golak Nath Case

In *Golok Nath* v *State of Pubjab*, the Supreme Court led by Chief Justice Subba Rao (up to 11th April, 1967) declared by a majority of 6 to 5 that "the Parliament will have no power in future,

1. Article 217.
2. Article 220.

i.e., from the date of this decision (27th February, 1967) to amend any of the provisions of Part III of Constitution so as to take away or abridge the Fundamental Rights enshrined therein. Any further inroad into these rights as they exist today will be illegal and unconstitutional unless it complies with Part III in general and Article 13 (2) in particular."

Chief Justice Subba Rao, in that case, further observed, "Shankri Prasad's case (1951) and Sajjan Singh's case (1965). conceded the power of amendment to Parliament over Part III on an erroneous view of Article 13 (2) and to that extent they are not good laws."

The Chief Justice, Shri Subba Rao, further declared in that case, "The Fundamental Rights are given a transcendental position under our Constitution and are kept beyond the reach of Parliament. At the same time Parts III and IV constituted an integrated scheme forming a self-contained code. The scheme is made so elastic that all the Directive Principles of State Policy can reasonably be enforced without taking away or abridging the Fundamental Rights."

Former Chief Justice Subba Rao has written in an Article,[1] *The beginning of the end of the Rule of Law in the country* that the criticism of some people, that this historic decision of the Supreme Court put obstacles in the path of the socio-economic reforms is unfounded. He argues, "The Supreme Court held on the application of the doctrine of prospective over-ruling that all the amendments made by the Parliament up to the date of judgment (27th February, 1967) were and would continue to be valid. With the result, all the agrarian reforms already made were sustained and the Parliament continued to have the power to introduce further agrarian reforms under the cover of amendments already made. Right to property is not the only right. There are other Fundemental Rights also like the right of equality, right to freedoms, right against explanation, right to freedom of religion and right to constitutional remedies. It is, therefore, clear that under the judgment of the Supreme Court the State is particularly free to bring in all socio-economic reforms it chooses and what is really produced are the other rights which are so essential for the development of human personality." He further says, "During a short period of 18 years the Constitution was amended as many as 21 times either to over-ride the decisions of the Supreme Court or to anticipate them in regard to cases pending before it later on. A critical analysis of these amendments discloses that by a continuous process of amendment, a totalitarian slant has been introduced in our Constitution. While the original Constitution declared that the promised social order should be reached by the rule of law without suppressing the freedoms of the people, the amendments enable that Parliament to pursue an authoritarian path. A brief survey of the amendments discloses the deep inroads made by them in the Constitution on the anvil. By this proposed amendment, the Parliament proposes to amend Article 368 conferring power on the Parliament by special majority to take away or abridge the Fundamental Rights of the people. Any power conferred on the Parliament would be in fact a power conferred on the executive. Therefore, if the amendment is carried, it will give every opportunity to a future despot to suppress the freedoms of the people. That apart, as the amendment will be in the teeth of the Supreme Court judgment, it may turn out to be the beginning of the end of the rule of law in our country."[2]

Now, this Golak Nath case decision of 1967 has been revised by the Supreme Court in Fundamental Rights case decision delivered on April 24, 1973.

Deciding the Constitutional Conflict between the Speaker of the Punjab Assembly and Governor

On March 7, 1968, the Speaker of the Punjab Assembly, Mr. Joginder Singh Mann, adjourned the Punjab Assembly for two months while the Appropriation Bill was under consideration. Later the Governor prorogued the House and issued an ordinance directing the House to transact the Financial business without any adjournment. Former Finance Minister Mr. Baldev Prakash and Mr.

1. See former Chief Justice Subba Rao's article on "*The beginning of the end of the Rule of Law in the country*" in *Organiser*, Delhi, dated October 19, 1968.
2. Former Chief Justice Subba Rao's article in the *Organiser*, Delhi dated Oct 19, 1986.

Satya Pal Dang, M.L.A., challenged the validity of the subsequent proceeding of the House as well as the Governor's Ordinance in the High Court. They contended that the Governor could not issue an Ordinance when the House was in session: A special Bench of the High Court of Punjab and Haryana unanimously held that the two Appropriation Acts passed after the Governor resummoned the House, were unconstitutional and void.

The Punjab Government appealed to the Supreme Court and obtained stay of operation of the High Court's judgment. Referring to the Speaker's ruling that the adjourned House could only be convened by him, the Supreme Court in its judgment said it was based on a wrong assumption.

Chief Justice Hidayatullah of the Supreme Court, who delivered the verdict of the Constitution Bench which heard the appeal, said that the Speaker of the Punjab Assembly had reduced the House to a state of inaction by adjourning it for two months. Even if the most liberal view of the action contrary to law and injunction of the Constitution that law made under Article 209 is to prevail over the Rules of Procedure of the House.

On the question whether certification of Money Bills by the Deputy Speaker was valid, he said that the Speaker's certificate was not mandatory under the Constitution. He added, "If the Constitution saw the necessity of a Deputy Speaker to act as the Speaker, it stands to reason that it could never have reposed a power of mere certification absolutely in the Speaker and Speaker alone. The Legislature could not be allowed to hibernate for two months, while financial business languished and constitutional democracy and machinery itself were wrecked."

"If by adopting the present course, parliamentary Government could be restored, there was neither an error of judgment nor a *mala fide* exercise of power by the Governor. There was nothing colourable about it. It was intended to achieve a definite purpose by using Governor's constitutional power. We are therefore quite clear that the action of the prorogation cannot be questioned," the Chief Justice added. This judgment was delivered by Chief Justice Mr. Hidayatullah on July 30, 1968.

Nationalisation of 14 Banks Held Invalid by the Supreme Court

On July 9, 1969 the President of India issued an ordinance nationalising 14 major commercial banks with deposits of not less than ₹ 50 crores each. The banks which were nationalised were the following:

(1) Central Bank; (2) Bank of India; (3) Punjab National Bank; (4) Bank of Baroda; (5) United Commercial Bank; (6) Canara Bank; (7) United Bank; (8) Dena Bank; (9) Syndicate Bank; (10) Union Bank; (11) Allahabad Bank; (12) Indian Bank; (13) Bank of Maharashtra; (14) Indian Overseas Bank.

A Bill to replace this ordinance, *viz.*, the Banking Companies (Acquisition and Transfer of Undertaking) Bill, 1969 was passed by the Lok Sabha on August 4, 1969 and by the Rajya Sabha on August 8, 1969. The President gave his assent on August 9, 1969. On February 10, 1970, the Supreme Court by a majority of 10–1 declared the Banking Companies (Acquisition and Transfer of Undertakings) Act, 1969, under which 14 top commercial banks in the country had been nationalised, to be invalid and unconstitutional.

The Supreme Court further held that the impunged Act is discriminatory and that the action taken or deemed to be taken in exercise of the power under the Act was authorised. In substance the majority has held :

(*a*) The Act is within the Legislative competence of Parliament; but

(*b*) It makes hostile discrimination against the named banks in that it prohibits the named banks from carrying on banking business. Whereas other banks—Indian and foreign—are permitted to carry on banking business, and even now banks may be formed which may engage in banking business;

(c) It, in reality, restricts the named banks from carrying on business; other than banking as defined in Section 5(b) of the Banking Regulation Act, 1949.

(d) That the Act violates the guarantee of compensation under Article 31 (2).

14 Major Banks Renationalised after Removing the Objections of the Supreme Court

Mr. V.V. Giri, President of India, promulgated on February 14, 1970 an Ordinance renationalising 14 major Indian Banks, the nationalisation of which was set aside by the Supreme Court on February 10, 1970. The renationalisation takes effect from July 19, 1969, the day when these banks were first nationalised under the Banking Companies (Acquisition and Transfer of Undertakings) Act. The Ordinance thus removed the vacuum created by the Supreme Court verdict on February 10, 1970 invalidating the bank nationalisation law. It restored *status quo ante* as on July 19, 1969. Unlike the invalidated Banking Companies (Acquisition and Transfer of Undertakings) Act the Ordinance has specified the exact amount to be paid by the Central Government as compensation for the takeover.

The invalidated Act had left determination of the quantum of compensation to agreements. In case of failure to reach agreements a tribunal was to decide it. The compensation scheme now provides that the amount will be payable in cash or in Central Government securities, according to the option of the recipient company.

The Banking Companies (Aquisition and Transfer of Undertakings) Bill, to replace the ordinance promulgated on 14th February, 1970, was passed by the Lok Sabha on 24th March, 1970, and the Rajya Sabha on 26th March, 1970. The Bill received the President's assent on 31st March, 1970.

Decision of the Supreme Court over the Petition against the Presidential Election

The Supreme Court delivered its judgment on September 14, 1970 in the election petition against Mr. V.V. Giri. The petition had been filed by Mr. Abdul Ghani Dar, Mr. Shriram Reddy and 13 others against the election of President V.V. Giri. The Supreme Court held that the distribution of a pamphlet against Mr. Sanjeeva Reddy, during the Presidential Election on August 29, 1969 constituted "undue influence", but it had not been proved that the result of the election had been materially affected.

The judges held that the conclusion they had been led to reach by the evidence was that "it did some effect but the vast majority of the electors were able to throw off the pamphlet and vote according to the mandate of their party". There was no landslide against Mr. Sanjiva Reddy, they voted. The judges further held—the allegation had not been proved that Mr. Fakhruddin Ali Ahmad and Mr. Yunus Saleem (Central Ministers) had warned Muslim voters that the fate of their community would be in danger if Mr. Sanjiva Reddy was selected. Allegation also had not been proved that Mrs. Indira Gandhi and other Ministers had misused their position to further the prospect of Mr. V.V. Giri.

Central Council of Ministers Mandatory even after the dissolution of House of People (Lok Sabha) and Prime Minister can continue in office after the dissolution of Lok Sabha

The Supreme Court delivered its detailed judgment on March 17, 1971 on the appeal of Mr. U.N.R. Rao, a Madras Advocate, challenging Mrs. Indira Gandhi's continuance as the Prime Minister after the dissolution of the Lok Sabha on December 27, 1970. Mr. U.N.R. Rao filed the appeal against the judgment of the Madras High Court dismissing his petition for a writ of *quo warranto* against Mrs. Indira Gandhi and praying to declare that the respondent had no constitutional authority to hold office of and to function as the Prime Minister of India.

Their Lordships observed : "Is there anything in the Constitution and in particular in Article 75 (3), which renders her carrying on as Prime Minister contrary to the Constitution ?" They referred to the oath which the President has to take and also dealt at length with the Council of Ministers.

"Article 74 (1) is mandatory. It says, 'There shall be a Council of Ministers with the Prime Minister at the head to aid and advise the President in the exercise of his functions.' We are unable to agree with the appellant that in the context the word 'shall' should be read as 'may'. Article 52 is mandatory. In other words, 'There shall be a President of India.' So is Article 74 (1). The Constituent Assembly did not choose the Presidential System of Government. Under Article 75(2) the Ministers hold office during the pleasure of the President. The President has not said that it is his pleasure that the respondent shall not hold office.

"Article 74 (1) is mandatory and, theretore, the President cannot exercise the executive power without the aid and advice of the Council of Ministers. We must harmonise the Provisions of Article 75(3) with Article 74 (1) and 75 (2). Article 75 (3) brings into existence what is usually called Responsible Government. But in the context, this clause only applies when the House of People does not stand dissolved or prorogued. The view we have taken is in accordance with conventions followed not only in the United Kingdom (Great Britian) but in other countries following similar system of responsible Government." With these remarks their Lordships dismissed the appeal.[1]

The Supreme Court also dismissed another appeal on identical lines, questioning the continuance in office of the Tamil Nadu Chief Minister, Mr. M. Karunanidhi.

Supreme Court Strikes Down Section 17A of the Maintenance of Internal Security Act, April 19, 1973 and reverses its own earlier decision of A.K. Gopalan v. The State of Madras

As has been stated earlier in detail in the 'Fundamental Rights' Chapter, the Supreme Court struck down Section 17-A of Maintenance of Internal Security Act as amended by the Defence of India Act. The impugned Section 17-A—a key section of the Act—enabled the Government of India and the State Governments to detain suspected persons for a period of 21 months without even a reference of the case to the Advisory Board as required in Article 22 (4) of the Constitution.

The Supreme Court allowed the writ petition filed by Mr. Shambhu Nath Sarkar, a Government employee held in detention in the Hoogly jail since January 29, 1972 by an order of the District Magistrate of Hooghly and directed that he be released forthwith.

In striking down Section 17-A of the Maintenance of Internal Security Act, the Supreme Court reversed its own earlier judgment in the case of the Communist leader, *Mr. A.K. Gopalan* v. *The State of Madras*. The judgment in that case had held the field in Constitutional Law of India for the past 22 years. The Supreme Court held that authorising detention of a citizen without reference to the Advisory Board was bad law, because it did not satisfy the requirement laid down in Clause (7) (A) of Article 22 of the Constitution. The unanimous judgment was pronounced by the Acting Chief Justice, Mr. J.M. Shelat.

Parliament's Right to Amend Constitution upheld, Fundamental Rights can be abridged, but not framework, Golak Nath Case Ruling reversed, Majority decision by Supreme Court on April 24, 1973

The Supreme Court upheld the Parliament's right to amend the Constitution including Fundamental Rights but not the basic structure or framework of the Constitution. This was the majority view of the Court as summed up by nine of the 13 judges who heard the Fundamental Rights case. The Supreme Court, however, said Parliament's Constitution amending power did not mean that it can alter the basic structure of the Constitution.

1. *The Mother land,* New Delhi dated March 18, 1971, p. 1, columns 5-6.

The declaration by Parliament that a particular law was to give effect to such a principle and provision that such a law should not be called in question, before a court was, however, made subject to judicial review.

The Supreme Court remitted for further disposal by the Constitution Bench the petitions challenging the 26th Constitution Amendment abolishing privy purses and privileges and the two Kerala Land Reform Acts protected by the 29th Amendment.

The majority decision of the 13-member Constitution Bench would reverse the stand taken by the Court in 1967 in the Golak Nath case. That too was a majority decision but of 11-judge Constitution Bench.

Chief Justice Sikri ruled that Parliament can amend, but not abrogate the Fundamental Rights and upheld the 24th Constitution Amendment along with his 12 colleagues on the Bench, saying the amendment met his test.

Besides the 24th, 25th and 29th Constitution Amendments were challenged before the Court by Swami Keshwanand Bharti, a Kerala Religious Head. The majority view of the judges, according to the sum-up, was that 25th Constitution Amendment is partly valid. The portions held valid include the provision that Parliament can by law fix an "amount"—rather than "compensation"— to be paid for property acquired or requisitioned for a public purpose.

While generally upholding the new Article 31(C) introduced in the Constitution by means of the 25th Amendment and saving from challenging in courts of law, all laws giving effect to the Directive Principles of State Policy specified in Clause B distribution of ownership and control of material resources of the community to subserve the common good and the prevention of the centralisation of wealth and means of production to the common detriment of Article 31, the Court by a majority of 9 to 4 held the second part of Article invalid.

Supreme Court upholds bar on Habeas Corpus petitions of Detenus held under MISA during Emergency

The Supreme Court gave its famous decision about Habeas Corpus Petitions of detenus held under MISA during internal emergency on April 28, 1976. The Supreme Court ruled that no detenu held under the Maintenence of Internal Security Act (MISA) can move a court and seek release as long as the enforcement of Fundamental Rights remains suspended during emergency. By a four to one majority verdict, the five-judge constitution Bench of the court also ruled that the Presidential order of June 27, 1975 under Article 359(1) of the Constitution took away the *locus standi* of detenus to move any writ petition under Article 226 before a High Court for habeas corpus or any other writ or order or direction to challenge the legality of the order of detention on the ground that the order is not under or in compliance with the Act or is illegal or is invalidated by mala fides, factual or legal or is based on extraneous considerations.

The majority verdict as handed down by the Chief Justice, Mr. A.N. Ray, and three other judges on the bench, Mr. M.H. Beg, Mr. Justice Y.V. Chandrachud and Mr. Justice P.N. Bhagwati, held that habeas corpus petitions by MISA detenus are not maintainable in High Courts. Mr. Justice H.R. Khanna was the only judge on the bench who directed a dissenting judgment. He held that in spite of the existence of the presidential order a detenu can challenge his detention on the ground that either there was no law authorising his detention or that the law has not been complied with.

Dissenting judgment by Mr. H.R. Khanna. Mr. Justice H.R. Khanna delivered a dissenting judgment in this case on April 28, 1976. "The Constitution does not confer any power or any authority to suspend the power of the High Courts to issue writs of habeas corpus during the emergency. Mr. Justice H.R. Khanna held in this dissenting judgment in the habeas corpus case. Article 226 of the Constitution under which the High Courts can issue writs, was an integral part of the Constitution and the same could not be suspended by putting a particular interpretation on the presidential order issued under Article 359 (1), Mr. Justice H.R. Justice Khanna held. The question of construction of the Presidential order, issued on June 27, 1975 suspending the enforcement of Fundamental Rights conferred by Articles 14, 19, 21 and 22 arose in view of the arguments raised by the Attorney-General, Mr. Niren De, that since the June 27 (1975) order was a blanket order, the Supreme Court decision in the Makhan Singh's case will not apply.

In the Makhan Singh's case, the court had held in 1964 that if a detenu challenged his detention on the ground that it violated some statutory provisions, the challenge could not be barred because of the Presidential order under Article 359 (1).

"The startling consequences", according to Mr. Justice Khanna, "were that if any official, even a head constable of police, capriciously or maliciously, arrests a person and detains him indefinitely without the authority of law, the aggrieved preson would not be able to seek any relief from the courts against such detention during emergency."

"It would also not be necessary for Legislaure to enact any law on the subject. Even in the absence of any law, *any official would be able to throw behind the bars any person or a whole group or family of persons for reasons which have nothing to do with the security of state or maintenance of public order.*"

He said thus the position would be that "*so far as the Government officers were concerned, they would not be governed by any law, they would not be answerable to any court and they would be wielding more or less despotic powers in matters relating to the life and personal liberty of citizens.*"

Mr. Justice H.R. Khanna held that Article 21 cannot be considered the sole repository of the life and personal liberty. He observed that even in the absence of Article 21, the State had no power to deprive a citizen of his life or personal liberty without the authority of law and in view of Article 372, such laws continued to be in force even after the Constitution came into force in 1950.

Mr. Justice H.R. Khanna said in a long series of judgments, the Supreme Court had held in the past that rule of law, according to which the executive could not take away any action prejudicial to the truths and individual without the authority of law, prevailed in India. There was no reason to depart from those decisions, he added.

His dissenting decision deserves to be written in letters of gold because everybody was extremely afraid of Governemt in times of emergency.

Death penalty upheld by Supreme Court

By a majority of 4 to 1, the Supreme Court in its decision given on May 9, 1980, upheld the constitutionality of the death sentence as an alternative to the punishment of life imprisonment prescribed by the Indian Penal Code (IPC) for the offence of murder. Four of the majority judges of the Court, Chief Justice, Mr. Y.V. Chandrachud, Mr. Justice R.S. Sarkaria, Mr. Justice A.C. Gupta and Mr. Justice N.L. Untwalia also upheld the constitutionality of Section 354 (3) of the Criminal Procedure Code, 1973 by which the normal punishment of murder is the life imprisonment and a judge while amending the sentence of death has to state "Special reasons" for such a sentence.

Delivering the majority judgment Mr. Justice R.S. Sarkaria on behalf of himself and other judges declared that Section 302, I.P.C. (Indian Penal Code) could not be tested on the grounds of reasonableness and public interest enshrined in Article 19 (1) for two reasons. First, penal laws do not deal with the subject-matter of rights enshrined in Article 19 (1), especially penal law dealing with vicious or pernicious crimes. Secondly, the death sentence prescribed for murder had no direct or indirect effect on the seven freedoms guarnateed to citizens in Article 19. R.C. Cooper case (Bank Nationalisation decision) and Mrs. Maneka Gandhi's decision by Supreme Court have not annulled the test of "direct and indrect effect" laid down by Chief Justice Mr. Kania and Justice Fazal Ali in

A.K. Gopalan's decisions before Article 19 could be applied to discover the constitutionality of an impugned law.

Hanging not cruel or unusual. Their Lordships further held that various provisions of the Constitution clearly showed that the founding fathers of the Constitution were aware of the existence of death penalty in the Indian Penal Code as an alternative to life imprisonment. In view of Articles 72, 161 and 134 it could not be said that death penalty in Section 302 either *per se* or because of its execution by hanging constituted an unreasonable, cruel or unusual punishment, which violated Article 21. Articles 21 itself recognised the right of the State to deprive a person of his life or personal liberty in accordance with procedure established by valid law.

PROGRESSIVE ROLE OF SUPREME COURT

1. Land Ceiling Laws held valid by Supreme Court

A five-judge Bench of the Supreme Court on May 9, 1980, dismissed all the petitions challenging the constitutionality of the Maharashtra, Andhra Pradesh, Haryana, Uttar Pradesh and West Bengal Agricultural Land Ceiling Acts. Chief Justice Mr. Y.V. Chandrachud, Mr. Justice P.N. Bhagwati, Mr. Justice Krishna Iyer, Mr. Justice V.D. Tulzapurkar and Mr. Justice A.P. Sen also upheld the constitutionality of Article 31-A of the constitution protecting agrarian reforms from any attack on the ground of violation of fundamental rights.

Article 31-B as it existed at the time of the Keshwananda Bharti judgment on April 24, 1973, and Article 31-C as it stood prior to the 42nd Amendment, 1976.

Article 31 states that no law would be void on the ground of its inconsistency with or abridgement of the constitutional right to equality, the right to seven freedoms guaranteed by Article 19 and the right to compensation for compulsory acquisition of property guranteed by Article 31. However, such law must be for the acqusition of any estate, the takeover of the management of any property in public interest for a limited period, the amalgamation of two or more corporations in the public interest and the extinction or modification of mining lease or of directors or managers of corporations.

Article 31-B protects all laws put in 9th Schedule of the Constitution from being attacked on the ground of violation of Fundamental Rights. The Keshwananda Bharti judgement had declared by a majority that Parliament could not amend the Constitution in a way so as to damage its basic structure or essential features. Their Lordships have held that all laws put into the 9th Schedule after the judgment was delivered on April 24, 1973, would be open to challenge on the ground that they destroy the basic structure or essential features of the Constitution. Such laws would be protected only to the extent that they are covered by Article 31-A or by Article 31-C as it stood prior to its amendment by the 42nd Constitutional Amendment.

2. Land Laws strengthen basic structure : View of the Court

The Supreme Court held on November 15, 1980 that the Constitutional Amendment incorporated for the extinguishment or modification of rights in lands held or let for purposes of agriculture or purposes-ancillary thereto strengthen rather weaken or destroy the basic structure of the Constitution. The judges held, "It seems to us ironical indeed that the laws providing for agricultural ceiling should be stigmatised as destroying the guaranatee of equality in matter of agricultural holdings, a Constutition Bench of the Court said in its judgment giving reasons for upholding the agricultural land ceiling laws enacted by various State Governments.

On the validity of the Constitution First Amendment which incorporated Articles 31-A and 31-B in the Constitution with retrospective effect from the date when the Constitution came into force protecting all the laws to bring about land reforms from questioning in a court of law, the court said it was aimed at removing social and economic disparities in the agricultural sector.

The court said it was impossible for any Government, however expertly advised, socially oriented and prudently managed, to remove every economic disparity without causing some hardship or injustice to a class of persons who also are entitled to equal treatment under the law.

3. A Judicial Victory for Workers

Workers' right to be heard in the Winding up Proceeding of the Company held by the Supreme Court. In a major judgment supporting the workers, the Supreme Court held that the workers are entitled to be heard in the winding up proceedings of a company.

"It is only the shareholders who supplied capital who are interested in the enterprise which is being run by a company but the workers who supply labour are also equally if not more interested because what is produced by the enterprise is the result of labour as well as the capital." Mr. Justice P.N. Bhagwati, who wrote the main judgment on December 11, 1982, said.

Justice Bhagwati stated that the workers have a right to be heard in such a vital manner like the winding up of a company. This was part of natural justice, he said.

Moreover, the concept of a company had undergone radical transformation in last few days. The traditional view that a company is the property of the shareholders is now an exploded myth. The judge pointed out that the new social values have emerged and now the State is an active participant in the socio-economic life of the citizen.

The new theory of corporate responsibility and the socialistic goals enshrined in the Directive Principles of State Policy of the Constitution have pushed into the background the 19th century *laissez faire* doctrine.

The workers have a special place in socialistic pattern of society. "They are no vendors of toil—a marketable commodity to be purchased by capital," the judges observed. The majority view held that the workers could not be turned away at the very threshold. The workers may have suggestions to make for restructuring the company or for the transfer of the undertaking as a running business. They themselves may offer to run after forming a society.

"It is true that shareholders bring capital but capital is not enough. There is another important factor of production and that is labour," Mr. Justice P.N. Bhagwati added.

"Capital is only one of the factors of production and it cannot confer on the owner exclusive domain over all other factors. While the owner invests only a part of his money in the company and bears only limited financial risk and otherwise contributes nothing to production, the workers contribute a major share of the product. The workers invest their sweat and toil, in fact their life itself," Justice Bhagwati said in his judgement.

Coalmines' takeover was upheld by Supreme Court. The Supreme Court held takeover of coalmines by the Government as legal on 14th December, 1982 as there were unsatisfactory conditions of work there for the workers. The private owners of the coalmines challenged the order of the Government in the Supreme Court. The Supreme Court held it valid.

4. Supreme Court directs Haryana to free bonded labourers

In a landmark judgment the Supreme Court on December 16, 1983 directed the Central Government and State of Haryana to free and rehbilitate all bonded labourers and ensure that the minimum wages were paid to those employed at the stone quarries and stone crushers in Faridabad district and other parts of the state. The Court directed the Haryna Government to formulate within three months a rehabilitation programme for the bonded labourers, whose identification would be undertaken by the District Magistrate.

Inspecting officers should make surprise visits to the quarries and the State Government should provide immediate medical and legal assistance to the labourers, the Court said.

A list of 21 significant directions for the benefit of the labourers at the quarters was given to the Central Government and the State of Haryana by Mr. Justice P.N. Bhagwati in his judgment.

Supreme Court Justifies Death for Bride Burning

Rarest of rare crimes identified. The Supreme Court held on July 21, 1983 that in case of 'bride-burning' and what are known as 'dowry-deaths', death penalty is justified.

A Divison Bench consisting of Mr. Justice Murtaza Fazil Ali, Mr. Justice A. Varadarajan and Mr. Justice M.P. Thakkar, stated in a Judgment that due to the anti-social and "socially abhorrent" nature of the crime, these murders belonged to the "rarest of rare" class which deserved capital sentence.

The court made these statements while confirming the death sentence on three men accused of killing 17 people in quick succession in August 17 in five villages in Punjab.

Among the other crimes which deserve death penalty, according to the judges, was murder committed to remarry for the sake of extracting dowry once again or to marry another woman on account of infatuation.

Three years ago, a Constitution Bench of the Supreme Court headed by Chief Justice had upheld the validity of capital sentence in the "rarest of rare" cases. But which crimes belonging to this category had not been defined. The present judgment attempts to describe such crimes.

The Supreme Court classified the circumstances which demanded death panalty from five angles.

Firstly, when the murder is committed in an extremely brutal manner so as to arouse intense and extreme indignation in the community. For instance, when the house of victim is set aflame to roast him alive or when the body is cut into pieces or when the victim is subjected to inhuman torture.

Secondly, when the murder is committed for a motive which evinces total depravity and meanness. For instance, when a hired assassin commits murder for the sake of money or reward murder committed to inherit property or a murder committed in the course for betrayal of the morherland.

In the third category the bride-burning case has been listed because it is "socially abhorrent". Also included in this category is the instance of a murder of a Harijan or a member of a minority community which arouses social wrath.

Fourthly, when the crime is enormous in proportion like multiple murders.

Fifthly, when the victim is an innocent child, a helpless woman, or a public figure generally loved and respected—whose murder is committed for political or similar reasons other than personal reasons.

5. Warrants issued by the Supreme Court in the Sudha Goel bride burning case

The Supreme Court on February 22, 1984 ordered bailable warrants to be issued against the three accused in the controversial Sudha Goel bride burning case.

While granting special leave to the Indian Federation of Women Lawyers, 12 Women Organisations and the Delhi Administration to appeal against the November 3, 1983 judgment of the Delhi High Court, the Supreme Court, however, rejected the plea of directing non-bailable warrants against the three persons.

The High Court had acquitted Sudha's mother-in-law, Mrs. Shakuntala Devi, brother-in-law Mr. Subhash Chand and husband, Mr. Laxman Kumar, on charges of burning her with kerosene on December 1, 1980, while reversing the verdict of Additional Sessions Judge, Mr. S.M. Aggarwal.

In his judgment delivered on May 27, 1983, Mr. S.M. Aggarwal had convicted and imposed death sentence on the three accused.

Sudha Goel died as a result of third-degree burn injuries at 6-10 a.m. on December 2, 1980 in a Delhi hospital while she was in an advanced stage of pregnency.

Mr. Aggarwal had sentenced the three with double murder—that of Sudha and her unborn child. Sudha, he held, was burnt to death 10 months after her marriage for not complying with her in-laws' dowry demands of a scooter, a refrigerator and ₹ 10,000 in cash.

6. Judiciary — Arm of Socio-Economic Revolution

Mr. Justice P.N. Bhagwati of the Supreme Court on August 13, 1983 said the judiciary should be functionally involved in the process of achieving the goal of socio-economic justice. As an arm of socio-economic revolution, the judiciary should ensure the impelmentation of justice to make law meaningful, he said while inaugurating an international workshop at Surajkund (near Delhi) on the "*Role of the Judiciary in Rural Societies*."

He said the Judiciary should be independent in every respect. It should be free from executive pressure, prejudices and fear of power circles.

Mr. Justice P.N. Bhagwati said the workshop could examine what role the judiciary could play in eliminating the tension prevailing among enthnic minorities of various countries and in protecting their socio-economic rights.

Mr. Enrique Fernando, Chief Justice of Philippines, who presided, said the judiciary had a crucial role in the promotion of socio-economic drives and the time had come for immediate action.[1]

LANDMARK JUDGMENTS OF SUPREME COURT

SUPREME COURT SETS TIME-FRAME FOR CHILDERN'S TRIAL

In a significant ruling which will benefit hundreds of children held in jails without trial, the Supreme Court on Wednesday, August 13, 1986, set a time-frame for the trial of young offenders.

According to the order, which covers childern younger than 16 years, the Supreme Court said those accused of offences punishable with less than seven years' imprisonment must be acquitted or convicted within nine months of the filing of the complaint.

It this rule is not followed, the whole prosecution would be liable to be quashed, the order said.

"We would regard a period of three months from the date of filing of the complaint or lodging of the first information report as the maximum time permissible for investigation and a period of six months from the filing of the charge-sheet as a reasonable period within which the trial of the child must be completed", said the judgment written by Chief Justice, Mr. P.N. Bhagwati, and Justice Rangnath Mishra.

This is the first time the Supreme Court has laid down a deadline for criminal trials. In death sentence cases, the Supreme Court has laid down that if the execution is not carried out within two years, the condemned person is entitled to a remission in the penalty.

JUDGMENT AGAINST MODIS ABOUT POLLUTION

The Supreme Court judgment, ordering the *prosecution of chairman and eight directors of the Modi Industries Limited "for discharging highly noxious and polluted trade efluents from the Modi distillerry into the Kali river sets an important precedent on the question of liability for pollution.* The UP Pollution Control Board had sought to prosecute the Modi industries for discharging untreated effluent into the Kali river. Although its plea, upheld by the chief judicial magistrate of Ghaziabad, was however, subsequently overturned by the Allahabad High Court, where the Industrial house went on appeal claiming that only the distillery unit should be prosecuted and not the industrial group.

1. See *Indian Express*, dated August 14, 1983, p.4, col. 6.

The Supreme Court, however, categorically stated that "every person who at time of the commission of offence was in charge of and responsible to the company for the conduct of business of the company, as well as the company, shall be deemed to be guilty of the offence and shall be liable to be proceeded against.and punished accordingly." The import of this judgment is that the parent company in such instance cannot escape responsibility for the actions of one of its units or subsidiaries. But the judgment has also focussed on the shabby working of the UP Pollution Control Board which delayed prosecution through "sheer negligence" in the manner in which it drafted the order against the industry, thereby providing it a technical loophole.

The judgment has also focussed on the fact that the owners of distilleries, mostly big industrial houses as in UP or part of a strong political lobby, as in Maharashtra, have escaped prosecution over the years despite discharging their untreated spentwash either into rivers and streams or into unlined lagoons from which the effluents seep into the underground aquifers, polluting surrounding wells and rendering good agricultural land fallow as in more than a dozen locations in Maharashtra alone. The Modi judgment leaves the Maharashtra Pollution Control Board with no execuse for delaying action against the State's errant distilleries.

SUPREME COURT JUDGMENT ABOUT POLLUTION CONTROL—CLOSURE OF THIRTY TANNERIES

Perhaps the only language a section of industry will heed with regard to pollution control is the kind spoken by the Supreme Court on September 22, 1987. In a precedent setting judgment in response to a public interest writ petition, the Supreme Court ordered the closure of 30 tanneries in Kanpur discharging untreated industrial waste into the Ganga. It has given another cluster of tanneries six months to instal primary effluent treatment plants or face closure. Mr. Justice E.S. Venkatramiah and Mr. Justice K.N. Singh have been quite unequivocal in their 35-page judgment where they stated, "Just like an industry which cannot pay minimum wages to its workers cannot be allowed to exist, a tannery which cannot set up a primary treatment plant cannot be permitted to continue to be in existence for the adverse effect on the public at large."

SUPREME COURT ORDERS QUIT NOTICE ON CAPITAL'S 9000 HAZARDOUS INDUSTRIES

The Supreme Court directed the Central Pollution Control Board on March 24, 1995 to issue notice to 9,038 hazardous, noxious, water and air polluting and other industires in the capital for shifting them elsewhere in the National Capital Region area which forms the part of Uttar Pradesh, Rajasthan and Haryana states. Issuing notices to the Union Urban Development Secretary and the Chief Secretaries of the three aforesaid states for identifying areas in NCR for relocating these industries, the Divison Bench of Mr. Justice Kuldip Singh and Mr. Justice S. Sagffier Ahmed asked the Board to issue individual and public notices to these industries. Prominent industries have been identified in this respect.

The Supreme Court shut down many polluting industries near the Taj Mahal, Agra. On the same date it directed Haryana and U.P. Governments to provide to Delhi 26,000 cubic metre water under the Jamuna agreement during summer season.

BHOPAL GAS LEAK COMPENSATION IS SETTLED BY THE SUPREME COURT

The Bhopal gas tragedy case was settled in the Supreme Court for $ 470 million on 14th February, 1989 between the Union Carbide Corporation (UCC) of the U.S., majority shareholder in the Union Carbide of India plant at Bhopal, and the Union Government, representing the victims of the world's largest industrial disaster. Creating internal judicial history, in terms of a parent of a multinational subsidiary agreeing to pay for the disaster caused by the leak of gas by the subsidiary's plant in Bhopal on the night of December 2, 1984. A five-judge Bench of the Supreme Court directed that the sum be paid on or before March 31, 1989, to the Union Government. The Union Government had claimed that over 2000 people had died and about five and a half lakh left disabled by gas leak.

Chief Justice R.S. Pathak, Mr. Justice E.S. Venkatramaiah, Mr. R.N. Mishra, Mr. M.N. Venkatachaliah and Mr. N.D. Ojha held it "*just equitable and reasonable, particularly in view of the enormity of the tragedy and the pressing relief for the victims*," that the matter be settled for this sum. They passed the order after Mr. Fali S. Nariman, counsel for UCC, and Mr. Parasaran responded affirmatively to Chief Justice Pathak's query as to whether an order should be passed "now" subsequent to their agreement to the terms proposed by the Chief Justice on behalf of the Bench. The Chief Justice ordered that in terms of this full and final settlement of all claims, rights and liablilities, all civil proceeding relating to the tragedy stand concluded after being transferred to this court. Also all criminal proceedings, whatever pending in relation to this tragedy, shall stand quashed.

The previous Congress Government has accepted this settlement but did not give anything to the Bhopal gas tragedy victims even after a lapse of five years though it was the biggest chemical disaster of the world. The National Front Government has decided to give ₹ 200 per mensem to the victims.[1]

Hawkers' Fundamental Rights to earn their living. In a significant and far-reaching decision the Supreme Court held on 2nd September, 1989 that the hawkers had a fundamental right to earn their living on the footpaths and sidepaths while roaming but did not possess the right to claim fixed places from the authorities.

SUPREME COURT RULING ON INHERITANCE

Hindu widows' right absolute. In the case Jagannathan Pillai *v.* Kujiapodam Pillai and others, the Supreme Court held on April 21, 1987 that a Hindu widow who had limited ownership in an inherited property before the Hindu Succession Act of 1956 was entitled to regain full ownership if the property had been retransferred to her after the Act.

The ruling has revolved the differences between the decisions of two sets of High Courts. the Orissa and Andhra Pradesh High Courts, while interpreting Section 14(1) of the Hindu Succession Act, had proclaimed that Hindu widow could only be a "limited owner" of such property in case of re-transfer.

The High Courts of Madras, Punjab, Bombay and Gujarat had taken the contrary view that she would become an "absolute owner" of such property in the same situation.

Dismissing an appeal by Jagannathan Pillai against a High Court verdict, Mr. Justice M.P. Thakkar and Mr. Justice B.C. Roy said the Supreme Court had to "remove the unaesthetic wrinkles from the face of law" to ensure that Hindu widow had the same rights under the same law all over the country.

The judgment underlined that Section 14(1) of the Act had abolished the concept of limited ownership in respect of Hindu woman. She would now be a full owner.

The court further clarified that there was nothing in the Act to indicate that a Hindu woman should have been in actual physical possession or in constructive possession of any property on the day the Act came into force.

The court pointed out that according to Section 4 of the Act, any text, rule or interpretation of the Hindu law or customs or usage as part of that law in force immediately before the commoncement of the Act "shall cease to have effect with respect to any matter for which provision is made in the Act". Therefore, the intentions of the legislature are clear, the judgment said.

1. See *Hindustan Times*, Delhi, dated 6th March, 1990.

In his appeal, Jagannathan Pillai had challenged a widow, Kujiapodam Pillai's right to become an absolute owner of a property that had been alienated by her before the Act, but which she re-acquired after the Act came into force.

Supreme Court Bans Children from Work in Circus

The Supreme Court on April 18, 2011 banned the employment of children in circuses and directed the government to rescue children employed in the sector and formulate a rehabilitation programme for then.

A Bench headed by Justices Dalveer Bhandari said that in order to protect the fundamental rights of children, it was imperative that the Government issued a notification prohibiting employing children in the sector,

The court also directed the Government to conduct raids to rescue children working in circuses and formulate a proper rehabilitation programme for them.

The court passed the order on a petition filed by NGO Bachpan Bachao Andolan seeking direction to the Government for rescue and rehabilitation of children below 14 years of age working in circuses.

EXERCISES

Long Answer Type Questions:

1. Describe the composition and power of Supreme Court.
2. Describe the jurisdiction of Supreme Court and what arrangements have been made in the Constitution for the independence of Supreme Court.
3. What is the place of Supreme Court in the Constitution of India ? Describe its functions.
4. Describe the composition and powers of Indian Supreme Court. Why it is called the protector of Constitution ?
5. Describe the organisation and functions of Supreme Court. What is the importance of Supreme Court in Indian Constitution ?
6. Discuss the role of Supreme Court as guardian of the Constitution.
7. Write a brief note on important constitutional decisions of the Supreme Court.
8. What changes have been made by the 43rd Amendment in the jurisdiction of Supreme Court.

Short Answer Type Questions:

1. Write a brief note on 'Immunity of Judges and contempt proceedings.
2. Write a brief note on original jurisdiction of the Supreme Court.
3. Discuss Supreme Court as a guardian of the Constitution.
4. What is Supreme Court's judgment about pollution control ?
5. Discuss in brief the appointment procedure of Chief Justice and a Judge of the Supreme Court.
6. Discuss Supreme Court to be a court record.
7. Discuss in brief the tenure of Judges of Supreme Court.
8. Write a brief note on qualifications and salary of Chief Justice and Judges.
9. What changes are made by the 43rd Amendment to the Constitution in jurisdiction of Supreme Court ?
10. What changes are made in the jurisdiction of the Supreme Court by 44th Amendment to the Constitution ?

Objective Type Questions:

Choose the correct answer

1. Under Article 143 of the Constitution, the President of India may seek the advice of the Supreme Court on any question of law or fact of public importance under the Supreme Court's:
   (*a*) Original Jurisdiction.
   (*b*) Appellate Jurisdiction .
   (*c*) Advisory Jurisdiction .
   (*d*) None of the above.
2. Choose the wrong statement.
   (*a*) The judgments of the Supreme Court are declared in open court.
   (*b*) The advice given by the Supreme Court is binding on the President.
   (*c*) The advice given by the Supreme Court is not binding on the President.
   (*d*) All the authorities, civil and judicial, in the territory of India are bound to act in aid of the Supreme Court.
3. The Supreme Court of India has specifically been given the power in its discretion to grant special to appeal from any judgment, decree, leave determination, sentence or order in any cause or matter passed or made by any court or tribunal in the territory of India under :
   (*a*) Article 142
   (*b*) Article 133
   (*c*) Article 135
   (*d*) Article 136
4. The salaries of the Judges of the Supreme Court are charged upon the ;
   (*a*) Consolidated Fund of India and are not votable in the Parliament
   (*b*) Contingency Fund of India and are not votable in the Parliament
   (*c*) Contingency Fund of India and are votable in the Parliament
   (*d*) Consolidated Fund of India and are votable in the Parliament
5. The phrase 'procedure established by the law' means that the judges in India :
   (*a*) cannot question the fairness or validity of a law, provided it is within the limit of the Constitution
   (*b*) can declare a law invalid simply because in their opinion the law is not due or is unjust
   (*c*) can question the fairness or validity of an undue law even if it is within the limits of the Constitution
   (*d*) none of the above

ANSWERS

1. (*c*) **2.** (*b*) **3.** (*d*) **4.** (*a*) **5.** (*a*)

17

CHAPTER

The State High Courts

> *"The Indian Federation, though a dual polity, has no dual judiciary at all. The High Courts and Supreme Court from one single integrated judiciary having jurisdiction and providing remedies in all cases under the constitutional law, the civil or the criminal law. This is done to eliminate all diversities in a remedial procedure".* — **B.R. Ambedkar**

The High Court stands at the apex of the State's judicial administration, even though they form a part of the single integrated judicial system headed by the Supreme Court of India. Under the Constitution every State has a High Court which operated within the territorial jurisdiction of the State. However, the Parliament can set up common High Court for two or more States.

The Central Government has constituted three new High Courts for North-Eastern State, with these the number of High Court in India has now gone up from 21 to 24. Tripura, Manipur and Meghalaya.

At present there are 24 High Courts in India. The names, the States and the jurisdiction of these High Courts are given in the following table:

S. No.	*Name of High Court*	*Seat*	*Territorial jurisdiction*
1.	Allahabad High Court[1]	Allahabad	Uttar Pradesh
2.	Andhra Pradesh High Court	Hyderabad	Andhra Pradesh
3.	Gauhati High Court[3]	Shillong	States of Arunachal Pradesh, Assam, Mizoram and Nagaland
4.	Mumbai High Court	Bombay	Maharashtra, Goa, Union Territories of Dadra and Nagar Haveli, and Daman and Diu
5.	Kolkata High Court	Calcutta	West Bengal and Union Territories of Andaman and Nicobar Islands
6.	Delhi High Court[2]	Delhi	Union Territory of Delhi
7.	Gujarat High Court	Ahmedabad	Gujarat
8.	Himachal Pradesh High Court	Simla	Himachal Pradesh

9.	Jammu and Kashmir High Court	Srinagar	Jammu and Kashmir
10.	Kerala High Court[5]	Ernakulam	Kerala and Union Territory of Lakshadweep
11.	Madhya Pradesh High Court[7]	Bhopal	Madhya Pradesh
12.	Tamil Nadu High Court	Madras	Tamil Nadu and Union Territory of Pondicherry
13.	Karnataka[4]	Bangalore	Karnataka
14.	Orissa	Bhubaneswar	Orissa
15.	Patna High Court	Patna	Bihar
16.	Punjab and Haryana High Court[8]	Chandigarh	Punjab, Haryana and Union Territory of Chandigarh
17.	Rajasthan High Court	Jaipur	Rajasthan
18.	Sikkim High Court	Gangtok	Sikkim
19.	Jharkhand High Court	Ranchi	Jharkhand
20.	Chhattisgarh High Court	Bilaspur	Chhattisgarh
21.	Uttarakhand High Court	Nainital	Uttarakhand
22.	Manipur High Court	Imphal	Manipur
23.	Tripura High Court	Agartala	Tripura
24.	Meghalaya High Court	Shillong	Meghalaya

1. Originally known established at Agra. Shifted to Allahabad in 1875.
2. Lahore High Court established in 1919-03 -21. Jurisdiction covered undivided Punjab and Delhi. In 1947-08-11 a separate High Court of Punjab was created with its seat at Simla under the Indian Independence Act, 1947 which had jurisdiction over Punjab, Delhi and present Himachal Pradesh and Haryana. In 1966 after the reorganisation of the State of Punjab, the High Court was designated as the High Court of Punjab and Haryana. The Delhi High Court was established on 1966-10-31 with its seat at Simla.
3. Originally known as the High Court of Assam and Nagaland, renamed as Gauhati High Court in 1971 by the North East Areas (Reorganisation) Act, 1971.
4. Srinagar is the summer capital, Jammu is the winter capital.
5. Originally known as Mysore High Court, renamed as Karnataka High Court in 1974.
6. The High Court of Travancore-Cochin was inaugurated at Ernakulam on 7 July 1949. The state of Kerala was formed by the States Reorganisation Act, 1956.

   That Act abolished the Travancore-Cochin High Court and created the Kerala High Court. The Act also extended the jurisdiction of the Kerala High Court to Lakshadweep.
7. Under the Government of India Act, 1935 by Letters Patent dated 2-1-1936 a . High Court was established at Nagpur for the Central Provinces. After the reorganization of States, this High Court was shifted to Jabalpur in 1956.
8. Originally known as Punjab High Court, renamed as Punjab & Haryana High Court in 1966.

Composition. The Constitution says that there shall be a High Court for each State.[1] Every High Court shall consist of one Chief Justice and such other judges as the President may from time deem

1. Article 214.

it necessary to appoint.[1] Since the number of the Judges of the State High Courts has not been fixed by the Constitution, it varies from court to court. The Chief Justice of the High Court is appointed by the President in consultation with the Chief Justice of India and Governor of the State. In appointing other judges of the High Court, the President, besides consulting the Chief Justice of India and the State Governor, also consults the Chief Justice of the High Court.[2]

Qualifications and Tenure of Judges. The qualifications for appointment as a judge of a High Court are that (1) he must be a citizen of India; and (2) he has for at least 10 years held a judical office or has for at least 10 years been an advocate of a High Court in any State.[3]

The retirement age of a court judge was previously 60 years but now it is 62 years, according to Article 217 (clause 1) (Fifteenth Amendment). A judge after his retirement is entitled to pension and other benefits. A High Court judge may also resign voluntarily or may be removed from office. But no judge can be removed except by an order of the President. The Judges have been guaranteed security of service so that they may not play into the hands of the executive. The Constitution says that a judge can be removed by the President only after receiving an address to this effect from the Parliament. Such an address needs support of the absolute majority of total members of each House and two-thirds of the members present and voting. He can be removed only on the ground of proved misbehaviour or incapacity to perform his functions.[4]

Salary of the Chief Justice and judges. The Chief Justice of a High Court in a State draws a salary of ₹ 90,000 per month and the other judges get ₹ 80,000 per month apart from various other allowances.

Their salaries cannot be varied by any authorities except the President during Proclamation of Financial Emergency. The Constitution forbids any change in the privileges, allowances, and rights in respect of leave of absence or pension, to the disadvantages of any judge after his appointment.

Oath. Every judge before entering upon his office shall make and subscribe before the Governor or some person appointed by him an oath in the prescribed form.

Powers and Jurisdiction of High Court

High Court is the highest court of appeal both in civil and criminal cases. It has both appellate and original jurisdiction. It is also a court of record. Its functions include both judicial and administrative.

Original jurisdiction of the High Court. Subject to the provisions of the Constitution and to the provision of any law of the appropriate Legislature made by virtue of powers conferred on that Legislature by this Constitution, the jurisdiction of, and the law administered in any existing High Court, and the respective powers of the judges thereof in relation to the administration of justice in the Court, including any power to make rules of court and to regulate the sittings of the Court and of members thereof sitting alone or in division Courts, shall be the same as immediately before the commencement of this Constitution.[5]

So the High Courts enjoy and exercise nearly the same powers with a few modifications only, as they did before the commencement of the present Constitution. Formerly, the High Courts of Bombay, Calcutta and Madras had both original and appellate jurisdictions. They could hear civil cases involving an amount exceeding Rs. 2,000. They had original jurisdiction in regard to criminal cases referred to them by Presidency Magistrates. The new Constitution has not withdrawn their rights. Every High Court has original jurisdiction in regard to admiralty, will, divorce, marriage

1. Article 216.
2. Article 217.
3. Article 217, Clause 2 (a and b).
4. See Article 217 and Article 124 (clause 14).
5. Article 225 of Indian Constitution.

laws, and fall outside their pale of influence.[1] According to Article 225 the present Constitution has extended their original jurisdiction to revenue cases also. Besides possessing the right to issue writ of *habeas corpus*, High Courts have now been empowered to issue *mandamus*, writ of prohibition, *quo warranto* and *certiorari* in order to protect the Fundamental Rights of the people.[2]

Changes introduced by the 43rd Amendment Act of the Constitution (1977). The amendment has repealed Articles 226A and 228A according to which the High Courts could not consider the constitutional validity of any Central Law and had no jurisdiction to declare any Central law as invalid. Now with the introduction of 43rd Amendment, this right of the High Courts has been restored. Now they can consider the constitutional validity of any Central law and declare it as invalid if it conflicts with the Constitution.

Changes introducted by the 44th Amendment Act (1978) in the jurisdiction of the High Court. 42nd Amendment had banned the High Courts from hearing the revenue cases. Now after the passage of 44th Amendment Act of 1978, the High Courts have been empowered again to hear the revenue cases. Secondly, the right of the High Courts to issue the writs had been restricted by the 42nd Amendment only to the enforcement of the Fundamental Rights but with the passage of this Amendment, the High Courts can issue the writs for other purposes also as before the passage of 42nd Amendment.

Appellate Jurisdiction. High Courts, as stated earlier also, is the highest court of appeal in any State. It entertains appeals against the judgments of the subordinate courts. If a Sessions Judge awards death sentence, an appeal lies to High Court. On the civil side it entertains appeals involving an amount exceeding Rs. 5,000. It also hears cases relating to patent and designs, succession, land acquisition, insolvency and guardianship.

As a Court of Record. The judgments of the High Courts are considered authoritative and they serve as case laws. They are published and cited by pleaders in the lower courts. The High Court can punish any person or body for the contempt of court.

A High Court has the right of superintendence over all other courts subordinate to it. It may call for returns, make and issue general rules and prescribe forms for regulating the practices and proceedings of lower courts. Its power of superintendence over inferior courts is both judicial and administrative. A High Court, in the exercise of extraordinary jurisdiction, can remove and try any suit falling within the jurisdiction. It can make rules relating to the appointment, demotion, promotion and leave of absence for the officers of the district court and other subordinate courts. It can declare any act of the State unconstitutional and hence void if it does not agree to the provision of the Constitution.

Transfer of certain cases to High Court. Article 228 provides: "If the High Court is satisfied that a case pending in a court subordinate to it involves a substantial question of law as to the interpretation of this question the determination of which is necessary for the disposal of the case, it shall withdraw the case and may:

(*a*) either dispose of the case itself or (*b*) determine the said question of law and return the case to the court from which the case has been so withdrawn together with a copy of its judgment on such question and the said court shall on receipt thereof proceed to dispose of the case in conformity with such judgment.

Establishment of a common High Court for two or more States. Article 231 Clause 1 provides, "Parliament may by law establish a common High Court for two or more States or for two or more States and a Union Territory."

1. Article 227 (4).
2. Article 226.

Power of Appointment : According to Article 229, the Chief Justice of the High Court is empowered to appoint officers and servants of the Court. The Governor may in this respect require the Court to consult the Public Service Commission of the State. He also consults the High Court in the appointment, posting, and promotion of district judges and along with the State Public Service Commission in appointing person to the judicial service of the State. The Chief Justice is also authorised to regulate the conditions of service of the staff subject to any law made by the State Legislature in this respect. The power of the Chief Justice to appoint any member of the staff of the High Court also includes his power to dismiss any such member from the service of the court. The powers of posting and promotions and grant of leave to persons belonging to the judicial service is also vested in the High Court. The Constitution also provides for charging all the administrative expenses of the High Court on the Consolidated Funds of the State.

Parliament has passed the Administrative Tribunals Act, 1985, implementing Article 323A, under which the Centre has set up Central Administrative Tribunals with respect to service under Union. As a result, all courts of law including the High Court shall cease to have any jurisdiction to entertain any litigation relating to the recruitment and other service matters relating to persons appointed to the public services of the Union, whether in its original or appellate jurisdiction. The Supreme Court has, however, been spared its special leave jurisdiction of appeals from these Tribunals, under Article 136 of the Constitution.

Position of High Courts : High Courts of India have been given full freedom and independence in imparting justice to the people and ensure that Executive and Legislature shall in no way interfere in the day-to-day life of the people. As a Court of Record the High Court has the power to punish those who are adjudged as guilty of contempt of court. All its decisions are binding and cannot be questioned in any Lower Court. As the Judiciary has a vital role in the working of the Constitution and in the maintenance of the balance between authority and liberty and as a safeguard against the abuse of power by the Executive, its independence is secured by permanence of tenure and the conditions of service of the judges. It will be noted that the salaries of the Judges and of the staff of the High Court are charged on the Consolidated Fund of the State.

The working of the State High Courts for more than five decades has brought to the fore certain inherent defects which deserve our attention :

Firstly, the process of justice is very costly and an average man cannot afford to bear the expenses of court fees, lawyer's fee and other miscellaneous expenses. The administration of justice is also quite dilatory. A person taking the case to the Court has to wait for many years before he can expect a verdict.

Secondly, the rules of procedure followed in the Court are so complicated and complex that only a lawyer or a highly experienced litigant can understand them.

Thirdly, though the Constitution has provided for the appointment of the judges of the High Court on merit basis, in fact the appointments are not always made on merit. M.C. Setalvad, Chairman of the Law Commission, observed in 1954 that "appointments in the past had not been satisfactory because of executive interference with the recommendation made by the Chief Justice of the State." "If the state ministry continues to have a powerful voice in the matter, in my opinion, in ten years' time or so, when the last of the judges appointed under the old system will have disappeared, the independence of the judiciary will disappear and High Courts will be filled with judges who owe their appointments to politicians."

Fourthly, the Constitution prohibits judges of the High Court to hold office under the Government after their retirement and there have been a number of instances where the High Court judges have been appointed as Governors, ambassadors, ministers and vice-chancellors.

Fifthly, the salaries offered to the High Court Judges are not lucrative enough to attract those lawyers who are having good practice. There are innumerable instances where the invitations to become judges of the High Courts have been declined by many prominent lawyers.

Sixthly, the work of almost all the High Courts has been running in arrears. On December 31, 2000 the number of cases pending in the various High Courts was 3.4 million. What is worse, there seems to be no possibility of the arrears getting reduced.

On May 24, 1949, Pandit Jawaharlal Nehru stated in the Constituent Assembly that our judges should be 'first rate' men of 'the highest integrity' who could 'stand up against the executive Government and whoever may come in their way.' But his standards are no longer in vogue. Judges who stand up against the executive are sought to be transferred to other states with the ostensible purpose of furthering 'national integration'. Thus : "In reality, the policy of transfer of judges is calculated to accomplish disintegration of Judicial independence rather than national integration." Dealing with the case of *Sankal Chand Sheth* who was transferred during the Emergency. J. Chandrachud remarks : "There are numerous other ways of achieving national integration more effectively than by transferring High Court judges from one High Court to another .... Considering the great inconvenience, hardship and possibly a slur which a transfer from one High Court to another involves, the better view would be to leave the Judges untouched and take other measures to achieve that purpose."

On 18th March, 1981, the Law Minister issued a circular addressed to the Chief Ministers of different states in which he requested them to obtain from all the additional judges of the High Court in the State their consent to be appointed as permanent judges in any other High Court in the country and the consent of those persons who have been, or in the future are to be, proposed for appointment as judges. The letter also carried a request to obtain from the Additional Judges and the proposed appointees names of three High Courts in the order of preference to which they would like to be appointed as judges or permanent judges as the case may be. It was added that the written consent and preferences of the Additional Judges and the proposed appointees should be sent to the Law Minister within a fortnight of the receipt of the letter. In '*Judges Transfer Case*' the validity of the circular letter of the Union Law Ministers was challenged. A Seven-Judge Bench of the Court by 4-3 majority held that the circular letter was valid and it did not affect the independence of the Judiciary. According to Arun Shourie : "In the transfer of Judges case on general principles, the Supreme Court has waxed eloquent but on specific it has given the Government enough to pummell the Judiciary into obedience."

During the Emergency the transfer of 16 Judges took place. The record showed that none of them was transferred for the ostensible purpose that is of 'national integration' and there was already prepared a list of 40 other judges who were to be transferred later. In January 1976, the refusal to extend the term of U.R. Lalit, the Additional Judge of Bombay High Court, who had granted bail to some students during the Emergency; and in February 1976 the refusal to continue R.N. Aggarwal, the Additional Judge of the Delhi High Court, who had ordered Kuldip Nayar to be released from Preventive Detention. O.N. Vohra, an Additional Judge in the Delhi High Court, was being reverted back to the local courts because he had indicted Sanjay Gandhi and his associates in the *Kissa Kursi Ka* case. S.N. Kumar, another Additional Judge in Delhi, was being thrown out as his wife, once a Municipal Councillor from the Congress Party, was said to have developed links with the opposition. In 1980 five High Courts had only acting Chief Justices, who remained unconfirmed. The shocking new practice of appointment of Additional Judges for only a few months at a time leaving Additional Judges guessing till the last moment whether their term would be extended or not, with the result that some of them had to be re-sworn just a few hours or minutes before their term was due to expire.

Commenting on the judgment in the *Judges case*, Arun Shourie comments : "The one, who is the largest litigant in the country, indeed the principal violator of laws today—the executive has been given a near absolute right to determine who will hear us there.....this new judgment affect the Judiciary itself."

Previously, in almost all instances a person was first appointed as an Additional Judge for two years. When a vacancy occurred in the High Court for the post of a permanent Judge, the seniormost Additional Judge was almost invariably elevated to fill that post. If no vacancy were available when the two-year term of an Additional Judge came to an end, he was almost invariably reappointed as an Additional Judge and just as invariably every Additional Judge became a permanent Judge. No Additional Judge ever needed to fear that he may lose his job after two years because the Government did not, for instance, like his judgments. But now when his (Additional Judge) term comes to an end his suitability is to be assessed all over again and there are to be restrictions on the criteria the Central Government may use to decide whether or not the man should be reappointed an Additional Judge, be made a permanent Judge, or dropped.

In short, in case High Courts were to function impartially, it was essential that service conditions of Additional Judges in these Courts should be radically improved.

In the historic judgment in *S.C. Advocate-on-record vs. Union of India*, delivered on October 7, 1993 the Supreme Court has overruled 'The Judges Transfer case' and held that in case of transfer of Judges of High Courts the opinion of the Chief Justice of India has not the primacy, but is determinative in the matter. It was also held that the consent of the transferred Judge/Chief Justice of a High Court is not required for either the fresh or any subsequently transfer from one High Court to another. Any transfer made on the recommendation of the Chief Justice of India is not deemed to be punitive, and such transfer is not justiciable on any ground.

In a landmark judgment in November 1998 in view of a Presidential reference, the Apex Court has allowed for the judicial review of transfer of High Court judges when it lacks adequate consultation between the Chief Justice of India and the Chief Justice of the High Court where the candidate was posted, on the one hand and the Chief Justice of the High Court of his new posting on the other. The inter High Court transfers have offen been arbitrary and generated acrimony.

Recommendations of the Sarkaria Commission: There are two major problems in the area of appointment and transfer of Judges of High Courts. *First*, there have been endemic delays in filling up vacancies of Judges in the High Courts and this is one of the major factors contributing to the accumulation of arrears of cases in these courts. The second is that transfer of Judges against their consent from one High Court to another has demoralising effect on the higher Judiciary, and compromises their capacity to administer justice without fear or favour.

While delays in the appointment of Judges continue, the arrears in the High Courts are piling up at an alarming rate. As on January 1, 1987, in the High Courts, out of a total strength of 440 sanctioned posts (409 permanent and 31 additional posts), as many as 57 posts consisting of 40 permanent and 17 Additional Judges were vacant. It was stated in the Lok Sabha that posts of 25 permanent and 65 Additional High Court Judges are to be created. If these figures are added to the existing vacancies, there would be a shortfall of 65 permanent and 82 Additional Judges in all the High Courts in the country.

The Union Government is of the view that the main reason of the delay in filling up the posts of judges in High Courts is the unusually long time taken by the Chief Ministers to send their recommendations (in consultation with the concerned Governors) to the Government of India on proposals received by them from the Chief Justice of the High Courts. One State Government has, however, pointed out that the names sent by them, unanimously approved by the Chief Justice, the Governor and the Chief Minister, were not approved for over two years. The Report of the Estimates Committee clearly shows that inordinate delays, sometimes extending to four years, in filling vacancies of Judges have taken place. This is a matter of serious concern. Therefore, Sarkaria Commission recommends for insertion in Article 217, a clause on these lines :

> "The President may, after consultation with the Chief Justice of India, make rules for giving effect to the provisions of clause (i) of the Article, and in order to ensure that vacancies in the posts of Judges in the High Courts are promptly filled in, these rules may prescribe a time-schedule within which the various functionaries having consultative role in the appointment of Judges under this Article, shall complete their part of the process."

About the issue relating to the transfer of Judges from one High Court to another, the Union Government is of the view that recommendations of the Law Commission of having a convention according to which one-third Judges in each High Court should be from outside has been accepted and this decision is to be implemented gradually either by making initial appointments from outside the state or by effecting transfers.

The Supreme Court has held that Article 222 cannot be construed to mean that for transfer of a Judge to another High Court, it is necessary to obtain his consent as a matter of constitutional obligation. Even so, the Court significantly suggested:

"By healthy convention normally the consent of the Judge concerned should be taken, not so much as constitutional necessity, but as a matter of courtesy....."

The Commission on Centre-State relations recommends: (i) The healthy convention that as a principle High Court Judges are not transferred excepting with their consent should continue to be observed; (ii) the advice given by the Chief Justice of India regarding a proposal to transfer a Judge, after taking into account the latter's reaction and the difficulties, if any, should, as a rule of prudence, be invariably accepted by the President and seldom departed from.

ORGANISATION OF SUBORDINATE OR DISTRICT COURTS

Panchayats. Article 40 of the Constitution says that it shall be one of the Directive Principles of State Policy to take steps to organise village panchayats and endow them to function as units of self-government.

Judicial Functions of the Panchayats. The Panchayats are empowered by law to hear criminal cases arising out of vulgar songs, exchange of hot words leading to physical injuries, cruelty to animals or obstruction in a public passage. Some of the Panchayats have also been empowered to hear and try cases relating to insult of a public servant, unlawful confiscation of property, spreading of infectious diseases, theft involving a small amount, etc. In the Punjab ordinary Panchayats can impose fine up to Rs. 100. A few of them invested with enhanced powers can fine up to Rs. 200. They can also sentence a convict to a short-term imprisonment or let off a person after warning or induce the parties in dispute to settle by compromise. The decision of the Panchayat court in a criminal case can be cancelled or changed by the Deputy Commissioner. A village Panchayat can try a civil case involving not more than Rs. 200. A civil judge can change the award given by the Panchayat. There is no place for pleaders in Panchayat scheme. A Deputy Commissioner can send a case back to the Panchayat for reconsideration. The State Government has the right to dissolve a Panchayat if it does not function satisfactorily. The Director of the Panchayats can remove any member of a Panchayat.

High Court's Control over the Subordinate Courts

Article 235 provides, "The control over district courts and courts subordinate thereto including the posting and promotion of, and the grant of leave to, persons belonging to the post of a district judge shall be vested in the High Court but nothing in this article shall be construed as taking away from any such person any right of appeal which he may have under the law regulating the conditions of his service as authorising the High Court to deal with him otherwise than in accordance with the conditions of the service prescribed under such law."[1]

Three types of Subordinate Courts are found in every State : (1) Criminal Courts; (2) Civil Courts, and (3) Revenue Courts.

Criminal Courts

The Indian Penal Code and the Code of Criminal Procedure apply uniformly to all the courts in India. The highest judicial authority in every district is a Sessions Court presided over by a Sessions Judge. At the lowest rung of the State judiciary is the Panchayat which generally tries minor

1. Articles 234 and 235 shall not apply to Jammu and Kashmir State.

civil and criminal cases. It can impose fines. Its decisions are non-appealable. Above the Panchayat is the court of Third Class Magistrate who hears minor cases and can award punishment up to one month and a fine not exceeding ₹ 50. The Magistrate of the Second Class can pass sentence up to six months and impose fines up to ₹ 200. The Magistrates of the Third and Second Class have only original jurisdiction and cannot entertain appeals. The next in seniority is the Magistrate, First Class who hears appeals against the decisions of lower courts. He can award legal punishment up to two years and fine not exceeding ₹ 1,000.

Besides the three classes of Magistrates, there are in every district an Additional District Magistrate or Judicial Officer and a Sub-Divisional Magistrate. In the districts of the Punjab, Haryana, Rajasthan and U.P. most of the judicial powers of the Deputy Commissioner have been given to aforementioned magistrates. Additional District Magistrates and Sub-Divisional Magistrates have been invested with all the powers mentioned under Section 30. They can hear and try all cases excepting those which merit capital punishment.

Appeals from the magistrates of the Second and Third Classes lie to the District Magistrate whereas appeals from the Magistrate of First Class lie to Sessions Court. The Sessions Judge hears cases relating to serious offences, *e.g.*, murder and dacoities. He sits either with a jury or with assessors. He can pass any legal sentence but death sentences passed by him is subject to confirmation by the High Court. All sentences are appealable except sentences of imprisonment not exceeding one month passed by a Sessions Court, District Magistrate or 1st Class Magistrate.

Civil Courts

The lowest courts in a district on the civil side are Small Causes Courts which have been established in big towns to dispose of civil cases speedily. They hear cases involving amounts not exceeding the limit fixed by the States. Its decisions are, ordinarily, not appealable. Any legal error can, however, be rectified in revision. Above the Small Causes Court are the Sub-Judges of the Second, Third and Fourth Class. A Sub-Judge of Fourth Class can hear cases relating to amounts not exceeding Rs. 1,000. A Sub-Judge of Class III can hear cases involving ₹ 5,000 and Class II up to Rs. 10,000 Then there is a Senior Sub-Judge in every district who can entertain cases involving any amount. All these judges have only original jurisdiction. Appeal from these judges can be taken to District Judge. The Sessions Judge of the District also acts as a District Judge. He has original as well as appellate jurisdiction. He hears appeals from all courts subordinate to him. He has wide powers under special Acts such as the Succession Act, the Guardian and Wards Act, the Provincial Insolvency Act, and Divorce Act. The District Judge is also the guardian of Trusts. He superintends the work of all the inferior civil courts. An appeal against him lies to the High Court.

Revenue Courts

There are Revenue Courts in every district to hear revenue cases. The juniormost officer is Tehsildar who holds a court. Appeals from his court lie to the Collector and then to the Commissioner. An appeal against the decision of the Collector may be taken to Board of Revenue of Finance Commissioner.

Separation of Executive and Judiciary at the District Level

Article 50 of the Constitution advises the States to separate the judiciary from the executive in the public services of the State. Several States have acted upon this advice. This division has been enforced in the States of Andhra, Gujarat, Kerala, Tamil Nadu, Maharashtra, Karnataka, West Bengal, Bhopal in Madhya Pradesh, Vindhya Pradesh, Haryana, Punjab, U.P. and Bihar. The Deputy Commissioner of every district in the aforesaid States has been relieved of his judicial functions. His judicial functions have been entrusted to Additional District Magistrate or the Judicial Officer. Both have been brought directly under the High Court. The principle of separation will, it is hoped, be given effect to in other States also before long.

DEFECTS OF OUR JUDICIAL SYSTEM

Our Judicial system suffers from serious defects. The more important ones are as follows :

(1) Highly expensive— The judicial system of our country is highly expensive. It is beyond the means of poor people. Hence the common people are not able to derive benefit from our judicial system. Besides the legal expenses in the court, there are certain illegal expenses which the clients have to meet. No serious efforts have so far been made to protect the clients from these illegal expenses. This is the burning problem of the time and needs to be tackled urgently.

(2) Delay in justice— Another serious defect of our judicial system is that the justice can be achieved only after a long delay. Sometimes people file the cases in the youth and are not able to get justice even up to their old age. As compared to the number of cases that come before the court the number of court is far less. It has been rightly remarked, 'Justice delayed is justice denied." It is, therefore, necessary for the Government to give urgent and serious consideration to this problem.

(3) Favouritism and corruption— Corruption, bribery, favouritism etc.. are rampant in the courts. There are certain courts where no work can be got done without giving bribes to officials there. What is still more deplorable is the fact that the transactions of giving and taking of bribe go on in the court in the presence and knowledge of the president officers of the courts. However, it is heartening to note that the judges of the Supreme Court of India and the High Court of States are almost free from any sort of favouritism and corruption.

(4) Defective System of appointment of High Court Judges— Constitutionally, the Chief Justice of High Court is appointed by the President, after consultation with the Chief Justice of India and the Governor of the State concerned and the other Judges are appointed by the President after consultation with the Chief Justice of the High Court concerned. But the position is somewhat different in actual practice. As a matter of fact, in practice, Judges of a High Court are often appointed on the initiative of the Chief Justice of that High Court. He recommends some name to the Chief Minister who, after consulting the Governor, forwards it to the Home Minister, who, after consulting the Chief Justice of India, recommends it to the President, who formally makes the appointment. As regards the appointment of the Chief Justice of a High Court, the Chief Minister of the State concerned takes the initiative and after consultation with the Governor, forwards his recommendation to the Home Minister, who, after consulting the Chief Justice of India, advises the President. If the Governor is obliged to act on the advice of the Chief Minister, the Chief Justice of the High Court will owe appointment to the Chief Minister who is a rank politician. That, of course, is most deplorable. Thus, we see that although the provisions of Constitution clearly seek the Judiciary free from the influence of the Executive yet in actual practice there is always some, though of course indirect, influence of the Executive over the Judiciary.

EXERCISES

Long Answer Type Questions:

1. Give a brief account of the organisation, powers and functions of High Courts of Indian States.
2. Discuss powers and jurisdiction of High Courts of Indian States.
3. Discuss the position of High Court.
4. What do you know about the recommendation of the Sarkaria Commission about High Courts?
5. Write an essay on organisation of subordinate or district courts.

6. Give a brief account of the judicial system of Indian States.
7. What are the main defects of Judicial System in India ?

Short Answer Type Questions:

1. What do you know about the composition of High Courts in Indian States ?
2. Write a brief note on Original Jurisdiction of the High Court.
3. What changes were introduced by the 44th Amendment Act in the jurisdiction of the High Courts in Indian States ?
4. Write a brief note on 'Power of appointment' of High Courts in Indian States.
5. Write a note on Judicial functions of the panchayats.
6. What do you know about High Court's control over the subordinate courts ?
7. Write a brief note on 'Criminal Courts'.
8. Write a brief note on 'Civil Courts'.

Objective Type Questions:

Choose the correct answer

1. How many High Courts are there in India?
   (*a*) 21 (*b*) 19
   (*c*) 20 (*d*) 18
2. In which Article of the Constitution the provision of High Court is discussed?
   (*a*) Article 213 (*b*) Article 214
   (*c*) Article 215 (*d*) Article 216
3. What is the salary of Chief Justice of a High Court?
   (*a*) ₹ 28,000 (*b*) ₹ 29,000
   (*c*) ₹ 90,000 (*d*) ₹ 31,000
4. What is the salary of a judge of High Court?
   (*a*) ₹ 23,000 (*b*) ₹ 24,000
   (*c*) ₹ 25,000 (*d*) ₹ 80,000

ANSWERS

1. (*a*) 2. (*b*) 3. (*c*) 4. (*d*)

18

CHAPTER

Administration of Delhi and Other Union Territories

There were seven Union Territories on 1st February, 2004, namely (i) Chandigarh, (ii) Andaman and Nicobar Islands, (iii) Lakshadweep, Minicoy and Amindivi Islands, (iv) Daman and Diu, (v) Dadra and Nagar Haveli, (vi) Pondicherry and (vii) National Capital Territory of Delhi. Previously Himachal Pradesh was Union territory, but was conferred statehood on 25th January, 1971. Similarly Manipur and Tripura were Union territories previously but they were made full-fledged States with effect from January 21, 1972.

Mizoram was given statehood according to 53rd Amendment Act 1986. Arunachal Pradesh was given governance of each Union Territory with such designation as may be specified. The administrators of some Union Territories are called Lt. Governors and some are called Chief Commissioners.

In Chandigarh, Andaman, Nicobar, Minicoy, Dadra, Nagar Haveli, Diu and Daman, there was no responsible form of government up to 1st June, 1991. Therefore, the administration of these territories was run by the Administrator, who was known as the Chief Commissioner and who was appointed by the President of India. The Chief Commissioner was responsible to the Home Minister who on behalf of the President looked to the administration of these territories.

The Bill to confer statehood to Delhi was passed on 21st December, 1991. Elections to Delhi Legislative Assembly were held on 6th November, 1993. BJP won the elections and Mr. Madan Lal Khurana became the Chief Minister, but Delhi had not been given full statehood. There is some control of the Centre. Later on Mr. Sahib Singh Verma became the Chief Minister of Delhi.

PARLIAMENT PASSES DELHI BILL

Absolute Powers for Lt.-Governor

The State Assembly Bill for Delhi was introduced in Parliament on December 17, 1991. The Lt.-Governor, a Central Government nominee, enjoyed absolute powers and the people's representative *i.e.* Chief Minister enjoyed little powers as was evident in the Bill itself.

There is very little mention of the Chief Minister in the entire Bill which underlines the Lt. Governor's domination of the Assembly as he solely has the right to address the Legislative Assembly "and for that purpose require the attendance of members". It is also upon the Lt. Governor to inform the Assembly of the causes of its summons.

The Lt. Governor also holds the powers to pay salaries to the members of the Assembly. "Members of the Legislative Assembly shall be entitled to receive such salaries and allowances as may from time to time be determined by the Legislative Assembly by law and until provision in this behalf is so made, such salaries and allowances as the Lt. Governor may, with the approval of the President, by order determine."

A financial Bill or amendment cannot be introduced in the Legislative Assembly "except on the recommendation of the Lt. Governor and prohibits the appropriation of money out of the consolidated fund of the capital and "declaring any expenditure to be charged on the consolidated fund or increasing the amount of any such expenditure.

The Lt. Governor has absolute powers to give assent to Bills. "When a Bill has been passed by the Legislative Assembly, it shall be presented to the Lt. Governor and the Lt. Governor shall declare that he withholds assent."

According to the Bill, laws made by Parliament shall prevail over those made by the Assembly. The Bill makes it clear that no demand for a grant shall be made "except on the recommendations of the Lt. Governor".

The Bill provides vast discretionary powers to the Lt. Governor. It applies in cases "which fall outside the purview of the powers conferred on the Legislative Assembly but in respect of which powers or functions are entrusted or delegated to him by the President."

The Bill on a new Assembly set-up for Delhi is remarkably silent on the status of local governing bodies like the Delhi Development Authority (DDA), Delhi Milk Scheme (DMS), New Delhi Municipal Corporation (NDMC) and Delhi Transport Authority (DTC) and others.

The main opposition parties like the BJP and the Janata Dal have been critical of multiplicity of authorities in the capital by all indications present in the Bill, the real powers to run these bodies would be vested with the Central Government. The Assembly has little power to legislate on its own steam.[1]

BJP extracts assurance from the Home Minister. The way for the passage of the Bills (National Capital Region Bill and 74th Amendment Bill) was cleared by meetings between the Government and opposition leaders during 18th and 19th December, 1991. The Government is understood to have agreed to fix the duration of imposing of President's Rule in Delhi after the dissolution of the Assembly to a maximum three years. Originally it was proposed to impose President's Rule for an indefinite period.

According to reliable sources, the Government has also agreed to give members of the Delhi Assembly the right to become part of the electoral college for the purpose of election of the President. For this purpose a legislation is expected to be introduced in the next session of Parliament. As BJP wanted full statehood for Delhi, so it agreed to give half-hearted support.

Lok Sabha passes Bill on new set-up for Delhi Constitution Amendment (Home Minister's defence)

Lok Sabha passed the National Capital Region Bill and 74th Amendment to the Constitution for that purpose. The Lok Sabha passed the first Bill with an amendment incorporating the word 'Delhi' by 349 votes and three absentions.

1. *Indian Express*, New Delhi dated December 18,1991, p.4, columns 2-5

The Delhi Bill based on the report of the Balkrishan Committee on the adminstrative set-up of Delhi provides for a 70-member assembly and a seven-member Council of Ministers. The powers to legislate on matters of public order, police and law will be vested with the Central Government. While moving the Delhi Bill for adoption, Mr. S.B. Chavan (Home Minister) warned members, particularly the BJP, that it would not be possible to grant full statehood to Delhi. Urging that a healthy convention be established, and that the seven-member Council of Ministers work in harmony with the Government-appointed. Lieutenant Governor. Mr. Chavan said the President of India would be the final authority in case of any conflict between the two.

The Home Minister also agreed with Mr. Advani that a suitable Legislation would be introduced later on, to enable the members of Delhi and Pondicherry Legislative Assemblies to be part of the electoral college that votes for the President. Lok Sabha passed both the Bills on 20th December, 1991 and Rajya Sabha the next day. After that the President gave his assent. Consequently, it became an Act.

Genesis of Union Territories. As stated earlier, in the original Constitution of 1949, States were divided into three categories and included in Parts A, B and C of the First Schedule of the Constitution.

Part C States were 10 in number, namely,—Ajmer, Bhopal, Bilaspur, Coorg, Delhi, Himachal Pradesh, Kutch, Manipur, Tripura and Vindhya Pradesh. Of these, Himachal Pradesh, Bhopal, Bilaspur, Kutch, Manipur, Tripura and Vindhya Pradesh had been formed by the integration of some of the smaller Indian States. The remaining States of Ajmer, Coorg and Delhi were Chief Commissioner's Provinces under the Government of India Acts, 1919 and 1935, and were thus administered by the Centre even before the Constitution.

The special feature of these Part C States was that they were adminstered by the President through a Chief Commissioner or a Lieutenant Governor, acting as his agent. Parliament had legislative power relating to *any* subject as regards the Part C States, but the Constitution empowered Parliament to create a Legislature as well as a Council of Advisers or Ministers for a Part C State. In exercise of this power, Parliament enacted the Government of Part C States, 1951, by which a Council of Advisers or Ministers was set up in each Part C State, to advise the Chief Commissioner, under the overall control of the President, and also a Legislative Assembly to function as the Legislature of the State, without derogation to the plenary powers of Parliament.

In place of these Part C States, the Constitution (7th Amendment) Act, 1956 substituted the category of 'Union Territories' which are also similarly administered by the Union. As a result of the reorganisation of the States by the States Reorganisation Act, 1956, the Part C States of Ajmer, Bhopál, Coorg, Kutch, and Vindhya Pradesh were merged into other adjoining States.

Union Territories: The list of Union Territories, accordingly, included the remaining Part C States of Delhi, Himachal Pradesh (which included Bilaspur), Manipur and Tripura. To these were added the Andaman and Nicobar Islands and the Laccadive and Amindivi Islands. Under the original Constitution, the Andaman and Nicobar Islands were included in Part D of the First Schedule. The Laccadive, Minicoy and Amindivi Islands (renamed *'Lakshadweep'* in 1973), on the other hand, were included in the territory of the State of Madras. The States Reorganisation Act and the Constitution (7th Amendment) Act, 1956 abolished Part D of the First Schedule and constituted it a separate Union Territory.

By the Constitution (Tenth, Twelfth, Fourteenth and Twenty-seventh) Amendment Acts, some others were added to the list of Union Territories.

Since some of the erstwhile Union Territories (Himachal Pradesh, Manipur, Tripura, Mizoram, Arunachal Pradesh[1] and Goa) have been lifted up into category of 'States', the number of Union Territories is, at the end of 2003, seven.

Though all these Union Territories belong to one category, there are some differences in the actual system of administration as between the several Union Territories owing to the provisions of the Constitution as well as of Acts of Parliament which have been made in pursuance of the Constitutional provisions.

Administrator: Article 239(1) provides that save as otherwise provided by Parliament by law, every Union Territory shall be administered by the President acting, to such extent as he thinks fit, through an Administrator to be appointed by him with such designation as he may specify. Instead of appointing an Administrator from outside, the President may appoint the Governor of a State as the Administrator of an adjoining Union Territory; and where a Governor is so appointed, he shall exercise his functions as such Administrator independently of his Council of Ministers [*Art.*239(2)].

All the Union Territories are thus adminstered by an Administrator as the agent of the President and not by a Governor acting as the Head of a State.

Provision for Legislative Assembly and Council of Ministers: In 1962, however, Art.239A (amended by the 37th Amendment, 1974) was introduced in the Constitution, to empower Parliament to create a Legislature or Council of Ministers or both for some of the Union Territories. By virtue of this power, Parliament enacted the Government of Union Territories Act, 1963, providing for a Legislative Assembly as well as a Council of Ministers to advise the Administrator, in these Union Territories. Pondicherry alone is now left in this category, all other Union Territories have become States.

On 1-2-1992, Arts. 239AA and 239AB (inserted by Constitution 69th Amendment) came into force. To supplement these provisions the Government of National Capital Territory of Delhi Act, 1991 was enacted. Delhi has from 1993 a Legislative Assembly and a Council of Ministers. The Government of Delhi has all the legislative powers in the State List excepting entries 1 (Public order), 2 (Police) and 18 (Land)

Legislative Power: Parliament has exclusive legislative power over a Union Territory, including matters which are enumerated in the State List [*Art.* 246(4)]. But so far as the two groups of Island Territories– Dadra and Nagar Haveli and Daman and Diu, Pondicherry– are concerned, the President has got a legislative power, namely, to make regulations for peace, progress and good government of these Territories. This power of the President overrides the legislative power of Parliament in as much as a regulation made by the President as regards these Territories may repeal or amend any Act of Parliament which is for the time being applicable to the Union Territory [*Art.* 240(2)]. But the President's power to make regulations shall remain suspended while the Legislature is functioning in any of these States– to be revived as soon as such Legislature is dissolved or suspended.

High Courts for Union Territories: Parliament may by law constitute a High Court for a Union Territory or declare any court in any such Territory to be a High Court for all or any of the purposes of this Constitution [*Art.* 241]. Until such legislation is made the existing High Courts relating to such territories shall continue to exercise their jurisdiction. In the result, the Punjab and Haryana High Court acts as the High Court of Chandigarh; the *Lakshadweep* is under the jurisdiction of the Kerala High Court; the Calcutta High Court has got jurisdiction over the Andaman and Nicobar Islands [*vide* TableXVI], the Madras High Court has jurisdiction over Pondicherry; the Bombay High Court over Dadra and Nagar Haveli; and the Gauhati High Court (Assam) over Mizoram and Arunachal Pradesh. The Territory of Goa, Daman and Diu had a Judicial Commissioner but recently the jurisdiction of the Bombay High Court has been extended to this Territory. Delhi has a separate High Court of its own since 1966.

Acquired Territories: There are no separate provisions in the Constitution relating to the administration of Acquired Territories but the provisions relating to Union Territories will extend by virtue of then definition of 'Union territory' [*Art.* 366(30)], as including "any other territory comprised within the territory of India but not specified in that Schedule". Thus, the Territory of Pondicherry, Karaikal, Yanam and Mahe, was being administered by the President of India through a Chief Commissioner until it was made a Union Territory, in 1962. Parliament has plenary power of legislation regarding such territory as in the case of the Union Territories [*Art.* 246(4)].

EXERCISES

Long Answer Type Questions:

1. Write a note on Delhi Bill.
2. Discuss in brief the administration procedure of Union Territories.

Short Answer Type Questions:

1. Write the names of Union Territories of India.
2. Write a note on genesis of Union Territories.
3. Discuss the provisions for Legislative Assembly and Council of Ministers in Union Territories.
4. Discuss the Legislative Powers of Parliament over a Union Territory.
5. Discuss the provision of High Courts for Union Territories.
6. What is meant by Acquired Territories ?

ObjectiveType Questions:

Choose the correct answer

1. How many Union Territories are there in India?
   (*a*) 7 (*b*) 8
   (*c*) 9 (*d*) 10
2. In which year the State Assembly Bill for Delhi was introduced in Parliament ?
   (*a*) 1990 (*b*) 1991
   (*c*) 1992 (*d*) 1993
3. On which report Delhi Bill is based ?
   (*a*) Sarkaria Report
   (*b*) Nehru Report
   (*c*) Balkrishan Committee Report
   (*d*) None of the above

ANSWERS

1. (*a*) 2. (*b*) 3. (*c*)

19

CHAPTER

Social Justice and Weaker Sections

Provisions for Scheduled Castes and Scheduled Tribes

While framing the Constitution, the Fathers of our Constitution laid down special provisions for the protection of minorities. Scheduled Castes and Scheduled Tribes (weaker sections of the community) in order to impart social and economic justice to them. Though *Article 15* provides that the state shall not discriminate against any citizen on grounds only of religion, race, caste, sex, place of birth or any of them, yet at the same time it also lays down that nothing shall prevent the State from making any special provision for the advancement of any socially and educationally backward classes of citizens or for the Scheduled Castes and the Scheduled Tribes. *Article 46* provides that the State shall promote with special care the educational and economic interests of the weaker sections of the people and in particular, of the Scheduled Castes and the Scheduled Tribes and shall protect them from social injustice and all forms of exploitation.

Reservations regarding Scheduled Castes and Scheduled Tribes

In addition to the above, Part XVI of the Constitution makes special provisions relating to certain classes. Article 330 as amended by the Constitution (Fifty-first Amendment) Act 1985 lays down that the seats shall be reserved in the Lok Sabha for Scheduled Castes and Scheduled Tribes in every state except the Scheduled Tribes in the autonomous districts of Assam.

Similarly, Article 332 has been amended. Previously the seats were not reserved for the Scheduled Castes and Scheduled Tribes in the tribal areas of Assam, Nagaland and Meghalaya. Now the seats will be reserved for Scheduled Castes and Scheduled Tribes in Legislative Assembly of every State.

Article 334 as amended by the Forty-fifth Amendment of the Constitution in 1980 provides that the provisions of the Constitution relating to the reservation of seats for the Scheduled Castes and Scheduled Tribes in the House of the People and in the Legislative Assemblies of the States and the representation of the Anglo-Indian community in the House of the People and in the Legislative Assemblies of the States by nomination, shall cease to have effect on the expiration of a period of 40 years from the commencement of the Constitution on January 26, 1950.

Article 335 lays down that the claims of the members of the Scheduled Castes and Scheduled Tribes shall be taken into consideration, consistently with the maintenance of efficiency of administration, in the making of appointments to services and posts in connection with the affairs of Union or of a State.

Article 338 provides for a Special Officer for the Scheduled Castes and Scheduled Tribes, who will be appointed by the President. It shall be the duty of the Special Officer to investigate all matters relating to the safeguards provided for the Scheduled Castes and Scheduled Tribes under the Constitution and report to the President safeguards at such intervals as the President may direct and the President shall cause such reports to be laid before each House of Parliament. In this Article, references to the Scheduled Castes and Scheduled Tribes shall be construed as including references to such other backward classes as the President may by order specify and also to the Anglo-Indian Community.

Provisions regarding Anglo-Indian Community

Article 331 provides that the President, if he is of opinion that the Anglo-Indian Community is not adequately represented in the House of the People, nominate not more than two members of that community to the House of People.

Article 337 makes special provision with respect to educational grants for the benefit of Anglo-Indian Community. After 30 years from 25.1.1980, such grants, to the extent to which they are special concession to the Anglo-Indian Community, shall cease. No educational institution shall be entitled to receive any grant under this Article unless at least 40 per cent of annual admission therein are made available to members of communities other than the Anglo-Indian Community In *State of Bombay v. Bombay Education Society,*[1] an order of the State Government which prevented the Anglo-Indian Schools to admit students of other communities was held unconstitutional on the ground that it prevented the Anglo-Indian Schools from performing the constitutional obligation of admitting at least 40 per cent students of other communities.

Commission regarding Scheduled Castes and Tribes : Article 339 lays down that the President at any time shall at the expiration of 10 years from the commencement of the Constitution, by order appoint a Commission to report on the administration of the Scheduled Areas and the welfare of the Scheduled Tribes in the States. The order may define the composition, powers and procedure of the commission and may contain such incidential or ancillary provisions as the President may consider necessary or desirable. The executive power of the Union shall extend to the giving of directions to a State as to the drawing up and execution of schemes specified in the direction to be essential for the welfare of the Scheduled Tribes in the State.

Commission regarding Backward Classes. Article 340 deals with the appointment of a Commission to investigate the conditions of backward classes. It lays down that the President may by order appoint a Commission consisting of such persons as he thinks fit to investigate the conditions of socially and educationally backward classes within the territory of India and the difficulties under which they labour and to make recommendations as to the steps that should be taken by the Union or State to remove such difficulties and to improve their condition and as to the grants that should be made for the purpose by the Union or any State and conditions subject to which grants should be made, and the order appointing such Commission shall define the procedure to be followed by the Commission. The Commission shall investigate the matters referred to it and present to the President a report setting out the facts as found by it and making such recommendations as it thinks proper. The President shall cause a copy of the report so presented together with a memorandum explaining the action taken thereon to be laid before each House of Parliament.

1. *AIR* 1954 *SC* (1955) *ISCR* 568

Linguistic Minorities

Certain provisions have been made in the Constitution to safeguard the interests of the linguistic minorities. A linguistic minority is a class of people whose mother tongue is different from the majority in the State or a part of the State.

Article 347 provides that on a demand being made in that behalf, the President may, if he is satisfied that a substantial proportion of the population of the State desires the use of any language spoken by them to be recognised by that State, direct that such language shall be officially recognised throughout that State or any part thereof for such purpose as he may specify.

Article 350A provides that it shall be the endeavour of every State and of every authority within the State to provide adequate facilities for instruction in the mother tongue at the primary stage of education to children belonging to linguistic minority groups. The President may issue such directions to any State as he considers necessary or proper for securing the provision of such facilities.

Article 350B provides for the appointment of a Special Officer for linguistic minorities by the President. It shall be the duty of that officer to investigate all matters relating to the safeguards provided for linguistic minorities under the Constitution and report to the President upon those matters at such intervals as the President may direct. The President shall cause all such reports to be laid before each House of Parliament and sent to the Governments of the States concerned.

EXERCISES

Long Answer Type Question:

1. What are the provisions in the Constitutions for Scheduled Castes and Scheduled Tribes?

Short Answer Type Questions:

1. Discuss the provisions regarding Anglo-Indian Community.
2. Write a note regarding commissions for Scheduled Castes and Scheduled Tribes.
3. Write a brief note on commission regarding Backward Classes.
4. Write a note on Linguistic Minorities.

Objective Type Questions:

Choose the correct answer

1. Which part of the Constitution makes special provisions relating to certain classes ?
   (*a*) Part XVI (*b*) Part XVII
   (*c*) Part XVIII (*d*) Part XIX
2. Which amendment is related to Article 330 of the Constitution ?
   (*a*) Fiftieth (*b*) Fifty-first
   (*c*) Fifty-second (*d*) Fifty-third

ANSWERS

1. (*a*) 2. (*b*)

20

CHAPTER

Amendments of The Indian Constitution

A Constitution is a dynamic document. It should grow with a growing nation and should suit the changing needs and circumstances of a growing and changing people. Sometimes under the impact of new powerful social and economic forces, the pattern of government will require major changes. If the Constitution stands as a stumbling block to such desirable changes, it may, under extreme pressure, be destroyed. A Constitution, as such, cannot have any claim to permanence; nor should it, because it has been adopted and has been working ever since, claim absolute sanctity. Mulford has rightly said: "An unamendable constitution is the worst tyranny of time or rather the very tyranny of time."

Herman Finer defined constitution as the process of amendment, for in his view, to amend is to deconstitute or reconstitute. W. Munro has rightly observed: "... it is impossible to conceive of an unamendable constitution as anything but a contradiction in terms."

A Constitution is a fundamental document of the land. It is a document which defines the position and power of the three organs of the State—the Executive, the Legislature and the Judiciary. It also defines the powers of the Executive and the Legislature as against the citizens. In fact, the purpose of a Constitution is not merely to create the organs of the state but also to limit their authority, because if no limitation is imposed upon the authority of the organs, there will be tyranny and oppression. Naturally, such a fundamental document as a constitution should not undergo too frequent and easy changes, as that would undermine the confidence of the citizens in the abiding nature of the Constitution. Jawaharlal Nehru has rightly said, "... The constitution cannot and should not be changed frequently. Obviously also, it can and must be changed when the situation requires it to be changed." A Constitution to be living must be growing; must be adaptable; must be flexible, must be changeable. Indeed, any amendment of the constitution should be justified by compelling reasons and circumstances.

AMENDMENT PROCEDURE OF THE CONSTITUTION

Like other written constitutions, the Indian Constitution also contains provisions for its own amendment. In the Constituent Assembly two views were expressed about the amendment process. Certain members like K.T. Shah, K.M. Munshi, Sir Alladi Krishnaswami Ayyar etc. insisted on adoption of rigid method of amendment of constitution to prevent its frequent amendment. On the other hand members like H.V. Kamath, Jawaharlal Nehru, Mahavir Tyagi etc. favoured a flexible constitution which should be capable to change according to changing socio-economic and political needs of the community. They argued that a rigid constitution would stand in the way of gradual innovation and come in conflict with the will of the people. After due deliberations the Assembly decided to adopt a procedure of amendment which is a mixture of rigidity and flexibility. But in contrast to the practice in other Federal Constitutions of the world, the process of amending the Constitution of India is much simpler. The framers of the Indian Constitution deliberately avoided the rigidity of the U.S. Constitution because they shared the views of Macaulay that the Constitution should be flexible so that it can change with the call of the time. A rigid constitution, they felt, would fail to mould itself according to the needs of the time and would not only bring about its own destruction but also result in revolution. Accordingly they adopted a procedure of amendment which is rather flexible. Justifying the amendment provisions of the Constitution Pandit Jawaharlal Nehru said: "While we want this Constitution to be as solid and permanent as we can make it, there is no permanence in a Constitution. There should be certain flexibility. If you make any constitution rigid and permanent you stop the nation's growth, the growth of a living, vital, organic people."

The amendment process of the Indian Constitution has been outlined in Article 368 of the Constitution, which is neither as rigid as the process of amendment in U.S.A. nor as flexible as in Britain. Further, unlike U.S.A. there is no single procedure for the amendment of the Constitution, instead there are three different methods for the amendment of various provisions of the Constitution. Firstly, certain provisions of the Constitution can be amended by simple majority of the two Houses of the Indian Parliament without the approval of the states. Some of the important provisions which can be amended through this process include creation of new states, reconstitution of exsisting states, qualifications of Indian citizenship, creation or abolition of upper chambers in states, provisions regarding the administration of Scheduled Area and Scheduled Tribes, etc.

Secondly, there are certain provisions which can be amended by the Parliament by two-thirds majority and also require the approval of majority of the states. The provisions which can be amended through this process include election of President, the executive powers of the Union, executive powers of states, High Courts for Union Territories, the Union Judiciary, the High Courts in the States, Legislative relations between the Union and the States, the representation of States in Parliament, provisions concerning amendment of the Constitution, etc.

The remaining portions of the Constitution can be amended by two-thirds majority of the members present in each House of Parliament. But this majority must also constitute a majority of the total membership in each House of Parliament.

After amendment has gone through relevant procedure it is submitted to the President for his assent. The Prersident's assent is merely a formality and he cannot refuse it. It may be observed that before the enactment of the Twenty-fourth Amendment in 1971 the President had some discretion in this regard, but he was denied the same by the Twenty-fourth Amendment. However, there is no time limit within which the President has to accord his assent. As a rersult the President can keep it pending for sometime. It is noteworthy that in United States the constitutional amendments do not require presidential assent.

A look at the above provisions regarding amendment of Constitution shows that the consent of the States is required only with regard to those provisions of the Constitution which affect the federal character or powers of the states. Secondly, all amendments can be initiated in the Union Parliament alone and the states do not possess any initiative in this regard. Their approval is sought only after the amendment has been adopted by the two Houses of Parliament by two-thirds majority of its members present and voting. Thus the amendment procedure in India is a strange mixture of flexibility and rigidity.

Defects in the Amendment Procedure. The amendment procedure under the Indian Constitution has met with severe criticism at the hands of critics. The chief charges levelled against it are as follows:

Firstly, unlike U.S.A., there is no provision for Constitutional Conventions for initiating the amendments. All amendments to the Constitution can be proposed by the Parliament alone. The states have a share in the amendment of the Constitution only with regard to those provisions which require ratification by majority of the state legislatures.

Secondly, the states do not possess any power to initiate amendments to the Constitution. They can only propose to the Central Government to initiate measures with regard to the establishment or abolition of the Upper Houses in the states.

Thirdly, majority of the provisions of the Constitution can be amended by the Parliament single-handed, either by two-thirds majority or by simple majority. Only very few provisions can be amended with the approval of the state legislatures. But no time-limit has been prescribed by the Constitution for this approval by the states. An effort has been made to overcome this defect through the enactment of a law under which the President can fix the time-limit wihin which the states have to convey their approval.

Fourthly, the Constitution is also silent on the point whether a proposal regarding amendment can be withdrawn or not. Similarly, it is silent on the issue whether the states can withdraw their approval after according the same. Likewise, the Constitution is not clear as to what would happen if the two Houses do not agree on a particular amendment or if the President refused to accord his approval to the amendment.

Finally, the provisions concerning amendment are too sketchy, that there is always a possibility of the same being challenged before the courts. Often the government is not clear on the need of amendment to the Constitution. For example, the Government did not consider a constitutional amendment necessary to abolish the privileges and privy purses of the Indian Princes and sought to achieve the same through an Ordinance of the President. But subsequently when the Ordinance was held *ultra vires* by the Court the Government went ahead with the Twenty-sixth Amendment. At this stage another doubt arose in the mind of the Government whether it was essential to seek the approval of the state legislatures or not. Ultimately, the Government decided to seek the approval of the state governments so that the Supreme Court may not knock down the amendment on this regard.

Despite the above shortcomings and defects in the amendment procedure, it cannot be denied that the process has proved to be very simple and easy. This is borne out by the fact that during the thirty six years of its existence the Constitution has been amended forty-six times. So many amendments could be possible because for most of the time the Congress enjoyed a clear-cut majority at the Centre as well as in majority of the states. Commenting on the amendment procedure in India Prof. Jennings says, "What makes the Indian Constitution so rigid is that in addition to somewhat complicated process of amendment, it is so detailed and covers so vast a field of law that the problem of Constitutional validity must often arise." He further asserts, "What the Cionstituent Assembly has done is to produce a long and complicated document which cannot easily be amended. It is quite obvious that there are clauses which do not need to be constitutionally protected. An example taken at random is Article 224 which empowers a retired Judge to sit in a High Court. Is this provision of such constitutional importance that it needs to be constitutionally protected and be incapable of amendment except with the approval of the two-thirds of the members of each House sitting and voting in the Union Parliament." Prof. K.C. Wheare has admired the variety of amendment procedures contained in the Indian Constitution. He says: "This variety in the amending process is wise but rarely found."

PARLIAMENT'S POWER TO AMEND CONSTITUTION AS MODIFIED OR INCREASED BY 24TH AMENDMENT

The Amendment Act (1971) enabled the Parliament to amend the Fundamental Rights Article (13) and Article (368) the procedure to amend the Constitution in order to remove all doubts about the competence of the Parliament to amend the fundamental rights. This situation arose out of the decision of the Supreme Court in Golak Nath Case; according to which the Parliament had no right to amend the Fundamental Rights whatever may be the excuse of the Government.

SUPREME COURT UPHOLDS AMENDMENT OF ARTICLE 368

The Supreme Court has held the validity of 24th Amendment of the Constitution which has suitably amended Article 368 as laid down above. The Supreme Court in its judgment delivered on April 24, 1973 on the Fundamental Rights case upheld the Parliament's right to amend the Constitution including the Fundamental Rights but not the basic structure or framework of the Constitution. This was the majority view of the Court as summed up by 9 of the 13 judges who heard the Fundamental Rights case. The Supreme Court, however, said, Parliament's Constitution amending power did not mean that it can alter the basic structure of the Constitution.

VARIOUS AMENDMENTS TO THE CONSTITUTION

The Constitution (First Amendment) Act, 1951. An Act to amend the Constitution of India (18th June, 1951). This amendment amended Article 15 (prohibition of discrimination on grounds of religion, race, caste, sex or place or birth) and 19 (protection of certain rights regarding freedom of speech etc.)

This amendment has permitted reasonable restrictions to be imposed by law on the exercise of the right of freedom of speech and expression and the right to practise any profession or to carry on any trade or business as contained in Article 19 of the Constitution. These restrictions relate to public order, friendly relations with foreign states or incitement to any offence in relation to the right of freedom of speech and to the prescribing of professional or technical qualification necessary for practising or carrying on any occupation, trade or business or carrying on by the State or by a corporation owned or controlled by the State, of any trade, business, industry or service, whether to the exclusion complete or partial of citizens or otherwise.

The amendment also inserted two new Articles, 31A and 31B, and Ninth Schedule to give protection from challenge to land reforms laws.

The Constitution (Second Amendment) Act, 1952. An Act to amend the Constitution of India (1st May, 1953).

It amended Article 81 with a view to readjust the scale of representation in the Lok Sabha (House of People) necessitated by the completion of the 1951 census.

The Constitution (Third Amendment) Act, 1954. An Act to amend the Constitution of India. This amendment substituted entry 33 of the List III (Concurrent List) of the Seventh Schedule by a new one including foodstuffs, cattle for fodder, raw cotton and jute as additional items whose production and supply can be controlled by the Central Government if found expedient in the public interest.

The Constitution (Fourth Amendment) Act, 1955. An Act to amend the Constitution of India (27th April, 1955). The Amendment provides that when the State compulsorily acquires private property for a public purpose, the scale of compensation prescribed by the authorising legislation could not be called in question in a court. Another clause excludes the temporary taking over of a property by the State, either in public interest or to secure its better management, from the compensation clause. The amendment also operates as a saving clause for State monopolies. Seven new entries were also added to the 9th Schedule.

The Constitution (Fifth Amendment) Act, 1955. An Act further to amend the Constitution of India (24th December, 1955). Be it enacted by Parliament in the Sixth Year of the Republic of India.

The amendment made a change in Article 3 so as to empower the President to specify a time-limit for the State Legislatures to convey their views of the proposed Central laws affecting the area, boundaries etc. of their States.

The Constitution (Sixth Amendment) Act, 1956. An Act further to amend the Constitution of India (11th September, 1956). This amendment made some changes in Articles 269 and 286 relating to taxes on sale and purchase of goods in the course of inter-state trade and commerce. A new entry 92A was added to the Union List of the Seventh Schedule to the Constitution.

The Constitution (Seventh Amendment) Act, 1956. An Act further to amend the Constitution of India. (19th October, 1956). This Amendment Act purported to give effect to the recommendations of the States Reorganisation Commission and the necessary consequential changes. Broadly, then existing States and territories were changed to have a two-fold clarification of States and Union territories. The Amendment Act also provided for composition of the House of the People, re-adjustment after every census, provisions regarding the establishment of new High Courts, High Court Judges etc.

The Constitution (Eighth Amendment) Act, 1959. An Act further to amend the Constitution of India (5th January, 1960). According to the 8th Amendment, Article 334 was amended and the duration of representation of the Anglo-Indian Community in the House of People and the Legislative Assemblies of States was extended from ten to twenty years from the commencement of the Constitution.

The Constitution (Ninth Amendment) Act, 1960. (28th December, 1960). This Act further to amend the Constitution of India was made to give effect to the transfer of certain territories to Pakistan in pursuance of the agreements entered into between the Governments of India and Pakistan on 10th September, 1958, 23rd October, 1959 and 11th January 1960. First Schedule to the Constitution of India was amended and half of territory of Berubari Union No. 12 (West Bengal) was given to East Pakistan.

The Constitution (Tenth Amendment) Act, 1961. An Act further to amend the Constitution of India (16th August, 1961). Article 204 and the First Schedule to the Constitution were amended so as to include in India the freed territories of Dadra and Nagar Haveli from the Portuguese possession. This amendment shall be deemed to have come into force on the 11th day of August, 1961.

The Constitution (Eleventh Amendment) Act, 1962. An Act further to amend the Constitution of India (19th December, 1961). Previously it was essential according to Article 66 that the two Houses of Parliament should assemble together for vote to elect the Vice-President, but then Article 66 was amended and it did not remain obligatory for the two Houses together and they could vote to elect the Vice-President separately.

Besides that Article 71 was amended and in it clause 3 was inserted. It was laid down that the election of a person as President or Vice-President shall not be called in question on the ground of the existence of any vacancy for whatever reason among the members of the electoral college electing him.

The Constitution (Twelfth Amendment) Act, 1962. (27th March, 1962). This Act shall be deemed to have come into force on the 20th day of December, 1961.

Goa, Diu and Daman were freed from the Portuguese domination on 20th December, 1961. Article 240 and the First Schedule was amended to include Goa, Diu and Daman in India.

The Constitution (Thirteenth Amendment) Act, 1962. An Act further to amend the Constitution of India (28th December, 1962). In December 1962 the Constitution of India was amended for the thirteenth time to confer statehood on Nagaland. Nagaland was previously part of Assam State. Nagaland was made the 16th State of India.

The Constitution (Fourteenth Amendment) Act, 1962. (28th December, 1962). This amendment was made on 28th December, 1962. According to it Article 81 was amended and the Union territories were given a representation of 25 instead of 20 in the Lok Sabha.

Before 16th August, 1962, the French colonies in India comprised Pondicherry, Karikal, Mahe and Yanam. The French Parliament on 16th August, 1962 ratified the treaty which the French Government had made with the Government of India some years earlier regarding the transfer of its colonies to the Government of India. The First Schedule of the Indian Constitution was amended and all the territories included in the French colonies (Pondicherry, Karikal, Mahe and Yanam) were given the name of Pondicherry and included legally in India.

A new Article 239-A was inserted for the creation of local legislature or Council of Minister or both for certain Union territories of Himachal Pradesh, Manipur, Tripura, Goa, Daman and Diu, and Pondicherry.

The Constitution (Fifteenth Amendment) Act, 1963. This amendment was provided for the increase in the age of retirement of High Court Judges and for the provision of compensatory allowance to Judges who are transferred from one High Court to another. The Act also provided for the appointment of retired judges to act as Judges of the High Court. Article 226 was also enlarged to empower the High Courts to issue directions, orders or writs to any Government authority, etc. If the cause of action for the exercise of such power arose in the territories wherein the High Court exercises jurisdiction notwithstanding that the seat of such Government authority is not within these territories. The Act also provided for the exercise of the powers of the Service Commissions, in their absence, by one of their Members.

The Constitution (Sixteenth Amendment) Act, 1963. (5th October, 1963). According to this amendment, Article 19, Article 84, Article 173 and Third Schedule of the Indian Constitution were amended and it was expressly provided that the candidates contesting elections to the State Legislature or Parliament will have to take an oath to uphold the sovereignty and integrity of India and they will not make any propaganda for the cession of any territory from India during the elections or afterwards.

The Constitution (Seventeenth Amendment) Act, 1964). An Act to further amend the Constitution of India (20th June, 1964). Article 31A was further amended to prohibit the acquisition of land under personal cultivation unless the market value of the land is paid as compensation and the definition of "estate" as contained in that Article had also been enlarged with retrospective effect. The Ninth Schedule was also amended to include 44 more Acts.

The Constitution (Eighteenth Amendment) Act, 1966. An act to further amend the Constitution of India. (27th August, 1966). Article 3 was amended by this Act to specify that the expression "State" will include a Union Territory also and to make it clear that the power to form a new State under this Article includes a power to form a new State or Union territory by uniting a part of a State or Union territory to another State or Union territory.

The Constitution (Nineteenth Amendment) Act, 1966. An Act further to amend the Constitution of India [11th December, 1966]. Article 324 was amended. Previously the Election Commission had been empowered to hear all the election appeals concerning State Legislatures and Parliament. According to this amendment this jurisdiction was taken from the Election Commission and was vested in the High Courts.

Constitution (Twentieth Amendment) Act, 1966. It validated the appointment, posting, promotion or transfer of a judge as district judge if such appointment was illegal or void. All the judgments delivered by such judges were held legal in spite of the fact that such appointments were not made according to the provisions of Article 233 or Article 235.

The Constitution (Twenty-first Amendment) Act, 1967. An Act further to amend the Constitution of India. [10th April, 1967]. This Act was made in the 18th year of the Republic of India. The Eighth Schedule of the Constitution of India was amended and Sindhi language was included in it.

The Constitution (Twenty-Second Amendment) Act, 1969. The Twenty-second Amendment to the Indian Constitution was passed by Lok Sabha on April 15, 1969. The main aim of this amendment was to create an Autonomous State, namely, Meghalaya within the State of Assam. This step had been taken by the Government of India in order to solve the Naga problem. Autonomous Meghalaya State was formed out of the Garo hills and Jowai territory of Assam. This autonomous state was given the right to make laws for education, health, agriculture, communication, medical amenities, co-operation, cottage industries, land and mines, administration of justice and tribal welfare. On matters of common interest, *i.e.*, highways, irrigation projects, flood control, drainage, electricity, water transport, etc., the Assam Legislature would have a final right to make laws. Meghalaya and Assam will have a common Governor, High Court and State Public Service Commission. It was given assent by the President of India on 25th September, 1969.

The Constitution (Twenty-Third Amendment) Act, 1969. This amendment was passed by the Lok Sabha on December 9, 1969, unanimously. By this amendment the reservation of seats for the Scheduled Castes, Scheduled Tribes and Anglo-Indians in the State Legislatures, Parliament and Services was extended from 26th January, 1970 to 25th January, 1980. It was given assent by the President on 23rd January, 1970.

The Constitution (Twenty-Fourth Amendment) Act, 1971. An Act to further amend the Constitution of India. (As introduced in Lok Sabha on 28th July 1971). This amendment was passed in the context of a situation that emerged with the verdict in Golaknath's case by the Supreme Court. Accordingly, this Act amended Article 13 and Article 368 to remove all doubts regarding the power of Parliament to amend the Constitution including the Fundamental Rights. It received the assent of the President on 20th April, 1972.

The Constitution (Twenty-Fifth) Amendment Act, 1971. This amendment further amended Article 31 in the wake of the Bank Nationalisation case. The word 'amount' was substituted in the place of 'compensation' in the light of the judicial interpretation of the word 'compensation' meaning "adequate compensation".

The Constitution (Twenty-Sixth Amendment) Act, 1971. By this amendment, the privy purses and privileges of the former rulers of Indian States were abolished. This amendment was passed as a result of the Supreme Court's decision in Madhav Rao's case. The President gave his assent to the Bill on 28th December, 1971 and from 1st January, 1972 the privy purses of the rulers of the Indian States were abolished.

The Constitution (Twenty-Seventh Amendment) Act, 1971. This amendment Act was passed to provide for certain matters necessitated by reorganisation of the North-Eastern States. A new Article 239B was inserted which enabled the promulgation of ordinances by the Administrators of certain Union territories.

The Constitution (Twenty-Eighth Amendment) Act, 1972. This amendment deleted Article 314 of the Constitution which gave protection to the ICS officers' conditions of service and privileges.

The Constitution (Twenty-Ninth Amendment) Act, 1972. It was enacted in the twenty-third year of the Republic of India. It received the President's assent on 9th June, 1972. According to it, the Kerala Land Reforms (Amendment) Act, 1969 (Kerala Act 35 of 1969) and Kerala Land Reforms (Amendment) Act 1971 (Kerala Act 25 of 1971) were included in the Ninth Schedule to the Constitution so that they may not be challenged in any court of law.

The Constitution (Thirtieth Amendment) Act, 1972. An Act further to amend the Constitution of India (22nd February, 1973). Previously the appeal from the High Court to the Supreme Court lay if the amount in the case involved was ₹ 20,000 or more but the purpose of this amendment was to further curtail the number of appeals to the Supreme Court. Therefore, Article 133 was amended and it was laid down that an appeal to the Supreme Court could be filed in the civil proceedings on a certificate issued by the High Court that the case involved a substantial question of law of general importance and that in the opinion of the High Court, the question needed to be decided by the Supreme Court. It received the assent of the President on 22nd February, 1973.

The Constitution (Thirty-First Amendment) Act, 1973. It was enacted in the twenty-fourth year of the Republic of India and received the assent of the President on 17th October, 1973. This Act amends Article 81 of the Constitution and thereby raises the upper limit for the representation of the States in the House of the People from 500 members to 525 members and reduces the upper limit for the representation of the Union territories from 25 to 20 members in the House of People or Lok Sabha.

The Constitution (Thirty-Second Amendment) Act, 1973. It was enacted by Parliament in the twenty-fourth year of the Republic of India and received the assent of the President on 3rd May, 1974. It amends Article 371 and inserts new Articles 371D and 371E. This Act confers the necessary constitutional authority for giving effect to the Six-Point Formula in respect of the State of Andhra Pradesh in so far as it relates to the provision of equitable opportunities for people of different areas of the State of Andhra Pradesh in the matter of admission to educational institutions, and public employment and constitution of an Administrative Tribunal with jurisdiction to deal certain disputes and grievances relating to public services. It also seeks to empower Parliament to legislate for establishing a Central University in the State.

The Constitution (Thirty-Third Amendment) Act, 1974. It was enacted by Parliament in the twenty-fifth year of the Republic of India. It received the assent of the President on 19th May, 1974. Articles 101 (3) and 190 (3) of the Constitution permit a member of either House of Parliament or a member of a House of the Legislature of a State to resign his seat by writing under his hand addressed to the presiding officer of the House of which he is a member. The amendment of Article 101 and Article 190 would enable the presiding officer not to accept such resignation if he, after making such inquiry as he thinks fit, is satisfied that the resignation is not voluntary or genuine.

The Constitution (Thirty-Fourth Amendment) Act, 1974. It was enacted by Parliament in the Twenty-fifth year of the Republic of India. It received the assent of the President on 17th September, 1974. This Act amends the Ninth Schedule of the Constitution to include therein the revised 20 land ceiling acts of different States, so that no court may be able to question their validity. These laws have been enacted in broad conformity with the guide-lines formulated on the basis of the suggestions made by the Chief Ministers' Conference. These laws were included in the 9th Scheduled so that they may not be questioned in any court as being inconsistent with the provisions of part III relating to Fundamental Rights.

The Constitution (Thirty-Fifth Amendment) Act, 1974. It was enacted by the Parliament in the Twenty-fifth year of the Republic of India. However, it received the assent of the President on 22nd February,1975. Under this Act, Sikkim was associated with the Union of India on the terms and conditions set out in the Tenth Schedule of the Constitution.

The Constitution (Thirty-Sixth Amendment) Act, 1975. It was enacted by the Parliament in the Twenty-sixth year of the Republic of India and received the assent of the President on 16th May, 1975. Under this Act, the First Schedule to the Constitution was amended to include Sikkim as a full-fledged state within the Union of India. The Assembly for Sikkim formed as a result of elections held in April 1974 is to be deemed to be first Legislative Assembly of the new State of Sikkim. Besides making provision for the election of a representative of the State of Sikkim in the existing Lok Sabha by the members of the Legislative Assembly of Sikkim, certain special provisions with respect to that State like the special responsibility of the Government of India and extension of laws to that State have been provided for. The Governor of Sikkim shall have special responsibility for peace and for an equitable arrangement for ensuring the social and economic advancement of different sections of the population of Sikkim.

The Constitution (Thirty-Seventh Amendment) Act, 1975. It was enacted by Parliament in the Twenty-sixth year of the Republic of India. It received the assent of the President of India on 3rd May, 1975. Articles 239A and 240 were amended to provide for Arunachal Pradesh a legislature and Council of Ministers. Previous to this amendment there was no responsible Government in Arunachal Pradesh. It was directly administered by an administrator who was appointed by the President of India.

The Constitution (Thirty-Eighth Amendment) Act, 1975. According to this amendment the *satisfaction* of the President and Governor shall be final and conclusive and shall not be questioned in any court on any ground.

"The power conferred on the Presided by Article 352 shall include the power to issue different Proclamations on different grounds, being war or external aggression or internal disturbance or imminent danger of war or external aggression or internal disturbance.

The Constitution (Thirty-Ninth Amendment) Act, 1975. It placed the election of the President, Vice-President, Prime Minister and the Speaker beyond judicial scrutiny. By this Act, disputes relating to the election of the President, Vice-President, Prime Minister and the Speaker are to be determined by such authority as may be determined by Parliamentary law. When a person has been appointed Prime Minister or chosen as a Speaker during the pendency of an election such petition shall abate.

Certain central zamindari abolition enactments were also included in the Ninth Schedule by this Act (86 Acts had already been included in the Ninth Scheduled and 38 more Acts were included). It received the assent of the President on 10th August, 1975.

The Constitution (Fortieth Amendment) Act, 1976. This was enacted by Parliament in the Twenty-seventh year of the Republic of India. It received the assent of the President on 27th May, 1976. According to this amendment it was decided that all lands, minerals and other things of value underlying the ocean within the territorial waters, or continental shelf or the exclusive economic zone of India shall vest in the Union and be held for the purposes of the Union. All other resources of the exclusive economic zone of India shall vest in the Union and be held for the purposes of the Union. 64 more Acts were included in the Ninth Schedule, thus making the impressive grand total of 188 which stand outside the purview of the Court or are excluded from the judicial scrutiny and thus cannot be challenged in any court.

The Constitution (Fourty-First Amendment) Act, 1976. This Act was made by the Parliament in the twenty-seventh year of the Republic of India and received the assent of the President on7th September, 1976. According to it *the age of retirement of member of a State Public Service Commission or Joint Commission was raised from sixty years to sixty-two years.*

The Constitution (Forty-Second Amendment) Act, 1976. This Act made for-reaching changes in the Constitution of the country. It was passed by Parliament on November 2, 1976 and after having been ratified by half of the State Assemblies received presidential assent on December 18,1976. The Amending Act is a comprehensive piece of legislation touching many fundamental questions. As it was the lengthiest amendment, so the main features of this Amending Act are being given here :

(1) *Preamable.* The Preamble to the Constitution was altered for the first time from 'sovereign democratic republic' to 'sovereign socialist secular democratic republic' and 'unity of the nation' into 'unity and integrity of the nation.'

(2) *Precedence of Directive Principles over Fundamental Rights.* The Directive Principles were given preponderance over the Fundamental Rights for the first time wherever they came into conflict with each other because many vested interests have misused the fundamental rights to further their own ends at the cost of Directive Principles of State Policy. In this way the social progress was hampered.

(3) *Prohibition of anti-national activities.* It has laid down that the anti-national activities would be strictly prohibited in the name to Fundamental Rights. Prohibition of anti-national activities would take precedence over Fundamental Rights.

(4) *Fundamental Duties.* Certain Fundamental Duties were prescribed for the first time in the Constitution and their non-observance was made punishable under law of the land. No court would question the validity of such actions.

Note. Fundamental Duties have been given in chapter V of the Indian Constitution in detail.

(5) *No change in the Lok Sabha and Assembly seats till 2001.* Number of seats in the Lok Sabha and State Assemblies which were fixed on the census of 1971, were to remain frozen till 2001 A.D.

(6) *Increase in the duration of Lok Sabha and State Assemblies.* The duration of Lok Sabha and State Assemblies is increased from 5 to 6 years.

(7) *Quorum.* The quorum for the Lok Sabha and State Assemblies will no longer be a constitutional necessity.

(8) *Right and privileges of members.* The rights and privileges of members and committees of each House of Parliament are to be decided by each House from time to time.

(9) *Constitution Validity of State laws not to be considered by the Supreme Court.* A new Article 32A has been inserted in the Constition which lays down that "notwithstanding anything in Article 32, the Supreme Court shall not consider the Constitutional validity of any State law in any proceedings under that Article unless the constitutional validity of any Central law is also in issue in such proceedings."

(10) *Other Provisions relating to the Supreme Court and High Courts.* No constitutional amendment, can be challenged in any court of law.

The Central and State laws are clearly defined and the jurisdiction of the Supreme Court and the High Courts are sharply divided for deciding the constitutionality of laws.

No Central or State law can hereafter be declared unconstitutional except by a two-thirds majority of a Constitution bench composed of a minimum of seven judges.

The High Courts cannot probe into the constitutionality of any Central law and can declare a State law invalid only through a two-thirds majority of a Constitution bench with at least five judges on it.

The Supreme Court is to hear all cases which either in the opinion of the High Court or the Attorney-General of India requires determination of the constitutionality of any Central law or of both Central or State laws.

While the High Courts are to continue to have powers to enforce fundamental rights, their jurisdiction is to be restricted to cases involving substantial injury to citizens becuase of the contravention of the statute or substantial failure of justice.

Even in such extreme cases, the citizen must satisfy the court that he has no other remedy :

(11) *Tribunal.* Part XIVA has been inserted in the constitution to provide for the tribunals for the adjudication or trial by administrative tribunals of disputes and complaints with respect to recruitment and conditions of service of persons appointed to public services and posts in connection with the affairs of the Union or of any State or of any local or other authority within the territory of India or under the control of the Government of India or of any corporation owned or controlled by the Government. *The courts are to have no jurisdiction over government servants' disputes which are to be disposed of by administrative tribunals.* The Supreme Court, can, however,grant special leave for appeal from those tribunals.

Government servants can make representation before disciplinary proceedings are instituted but they lose their right to make a second representation before the penalty is imposed.

Provision is also being made to constitute tribunals to decide tax, import-export labour, land reforms, urban ceiling, elecltion and civil supplies disputes.

(12) *The President to be bound by the advice of the Cabinet.* Article 74 clause (1) of the Constitution has been amended. The amended clause lays down :—

"There shall be a Council of Ministers with the Prime Minister at the head to aid and advise the President who shall, in the exercise of his functions, act in accordance with such advice."

(13) *Sending Army to States.* Seventh Schedule to the Indian Constitution has been amended. Besides that a new Article 257A has been inserted to empower the Union to send any armed force or other force of the Union for dealing with any grave situation of law and order in any State. Such force shall act in accordance with the directions of the Central Government and shall not be subject to the control of the State Government. Provision has also been made accordingly in Article 257A clause (3) to empower parliament to define the powers, functions and liabilities of the members of such force.

(14) *Emergency.* Article 352 has been amended and the President has been empowered to declare the Emergency in respect of the whole of India or of *such part of the territory there of* as may be specified in the Proclamation. Previous to it the Emergency could be declared only as regards the whole of India and not any part of it. So the Amendment enables the President to rerstrict the Emergency in respect to any part of the country. Previously under the Article 356, a proclamation approved by Parliament ceased to operate after a period of six months unless revoked earlier — and could be renewed for a period of six months at a time but in no case beyond a total period of 3 years. The period of six months has now been enlarged to one year under the amended Article 356 clause (4).

(15) *Some new entries made in the Concurrent List.* Some new subjects have added in the Concurrent List. Following new entries have been made :

(*i*) *11A.* "Administration of Justice; constitution and organisation of all courts, except the Supreme Court and the High Courts".

(*ii*) *17A*, "Forests."

17*B*, "Protection of wild animals and birds"

(*iii*) *20A.* "Population control and family planning."

(*iv*) For entry 25 the following entry shall be substituted, namely :—

"25. Education, including technical education, medical education and universities, subject to the provisions of entries 63,64,65 and 66 of List; vocational and technical training of labour."

(*v*) *33A.* "Weights and measures except establishment of standards."

The Constitution (Forty-Third Amendment) Act, 1977. This Bill was introduced in the Lok Sabha or the House of People on December 1, 1977 after consenus between the Government and the Opposition when Janata Party Government had come into existence. It was passed by the Lok Sabha on December 20, 1977 and Rajya Sabha (Council of States) on December, 23, 1977. It recieved the assent of the President on April 13, 1978.

Objects, reasons. The Statement of objects and reasons on the Bill says : The Constitution (42nd Amendment) Act, 1976, inserted various Articles in the Constitution to curtail both directly and indirectly the jurisdiction of the Supreme Court and the High Courts to review the constitutionality of laws. Article 32A barred the Supreme Court from considering the constitutional validity of any State law in proceedings for the enforcement of fundamental rights unless the constitutional validity of any Central law was also in issue in such proceedings. Article 131A gave to the Supreme Court exsclusive jurisdiction to decide the constitutional validity of a Central law and thus deprived the High Courts of their jurisdiction in respect of the same. Article 144A provided that the minimum number of judges of the Supreme Court who shall sit for the purpose of determining the constitutional validity of any Central law or State law shall be seven and required a special majority of two-thirds for the invalidation of such law. Article 226A barred the High Courts from deciding the validity of any Central law and Article 228A requires that there should be a bench of at least five judges for determining the constitutional validity of any State law and prescribed a special majority for a judgement invalidating such a law.

"It is considered that Articles 32A, 131A and 228A cause hardship to persons living in distant parts in India. Further Article 32A would lead to multiplicity of proceedings as cases relating to the validity of a State law which could be disposed of by the Supreme Court itself have to be heard first by the High Court. The minimum number of judges in every case wherein constitutional validity of a law is involved, however, unsubstantial the challenge might be, results valuable judicial time being lost in hearing and rejecting submissions that have no substance. The Supreme Court has in *M/s. Misrilal Jain* vs. *The State of Orissa and others* (A.I.R. 1977 Sc 1686) expressed the hope that Article 144A would engage the prompt attention of Parliament and would be amended so as to leave to the court itself the duty to decide how large a bench should decide any particular case. In fact a number of cases have been held up in the Supreme Court and High Courts as a result of the aforementioned Articles.

The Act, therefore, omitted Articles 32A, 131A, 114A, 226A, 228A. It also made special provisions to enable the Supreme Court and High Courts to deal with pending cases in the same manner as if the said Articles had been omitted with effect from 1st February, 1977 viz., the date on which those Articles were brought into force. Necessary consequential amendments to Articles 145, 228, and 336 have also been made in this Act.

Article 31D confers a special power on Parliament to enact certain laws in respect of anti-national activities. It is considered that these powers of Parliament to make laws for dealing with anti-national activities and antinational associations are of a sweeping nature and are capable of abuse. *It is, therefore, proposed to omit Article 31D.*

This Act has achieved the above objects and obnoxious Articles have been either omitted or amended.

The Constitution (Forty-Fourth Amendment) Act, 1978. Law Minister Mr. Shanti Bhushan pointed out, *only after an amendment was approved by Parliament by two-thirds majority and if it was felt that it violated the basic structure, then a reference would be made to the people through a referendum.*

Objects. According to the Statement of objects and reasons, recent experience has shown that the fundamental rights, including those of life and liberty, granted by the Constitution, are capable of being taken away by a transient majority. It is,therefore, necessary to provide safeguards against the recurrence of such a contingency in future and to ensure to the people themselves an effective voice in determining the form of government under which they are to live. This is one of the primary objects of this Bill.

Following are the *provisions* of the Bill :

(1) *Basic structure not to be changed, provision of referendum.* It is, therefore, proposed to provide that certain change in the Constitution which would have the effect of impairing its secular or democratic character, abridging or taking away fundamental rights prejudicing or impending free and fair elections on the basis of adult suffrage and compromising the independence of judiciary, can be made only if they are approved by the people of India by a majority of votes at a referendum in which at least 51 per cent of the electorate participate. *Article 368 is being amended to ensure this.*

(2) *Right to property is to be deleted from the list of Fundamental Rights and be made only legal right.* In view of the special position to be given to Fundamental Rights, the Right of Property which has been the issue for more than one amendment of the Constitution, would cease to be a fundamental

right and become only a legal right. Necessary amendments for this purpose are being made to Article 19, and Article 31 is being deleted.

It would, however, by ensured that the removal of property from the list of fundamental rights would not affect the right of minorities to establish and administer educational institutions of their choice.

Similarly, the right of persons holding land for personal cultivation and within the ceiling limit to receive compensation at the market value would not be affected.

Property, while ceasing to be Fundamental Right, would, however, be given express recognition as a legal right, provision being made that no person shall be deprived of his property save in accordance with the provision of law.

(3) *Proclamation of Internal Emergency would be made only in case of armed rebellion and not internal disturbance or the threat thereof.* A Proclamation of Emergency under Article 352 has virtually the effect of amending the Constitution by converting it for the duration into that of a unitary State and enabling the rights of the citizen to move the courts for enforcement of fundamental rights—including the right to life and liberty—to be suspended. Adequate safeguards are, therefore, necessary to ensure that this power is properly exercised and is not abused.

It is, therefore, proposed that a Proclamation of Emergency can be issued only when the security of India or any part of its territory is threatened by war or external aggression or by *armed rebellion*. Internal disturbance not amounting to armed rebellion would not be a ground for the issue of a proclamation.

(4) *Proclamation of Emergency to be made on the written advice of the Cabinet only.* Further in order to ensure that a Proclamation of Emergency is issued only after due consideration, it is sought to be provided that an emergency can be proclaimed only on the basis of written advice tendered to President by the Cabinet.

(5) *Proclamation of Emergency would have to be approved by the Parliament by same majority which is necessary to amend the Constitution within one month instead of two as at present (before the Amendment).* In addition, as a Proclamation of Emergency vertually has the effect of amending the Constitution, it is being provided that Proclamation would have to be approved by the two Houses of parliament by the same *majority which is necessary to amend the Constitution and such approval would have to be given within a period of one month.* Any such proclamation would be in force only for a period of six months and can be continued only by further resolution passed by the same majority. The Proclamation would cease to be in operation if a resolution disapproving the continuance of the proclamation is passed by Lok Sabha. Ten per cent or more of the members of Lok Sabha can requisition a special meeting for considering a resolution for disapproving the proclamation.

(6) *The citizen would not be deprived of the right to move the court for enforcement of his right to life and liberty.* As a further check against the misuse of the emergency provisions and to put the right of life and liberty on a square footing, it would be provided that the power to suspend the right to move the court for the enforcement of a fundamental right cannot be exercised in respect of the fundamental right to life and liberty.

(7) *Detention cannot be more than two months without the Authority of the Advisory Board.* The right to liberty is further strengthened by the provision that a law for preventive detention cannot authorise in any case, detention for a longer period than two months, unless an Advisory Board has reported that there is sufficient cause for such detention.

(8) *Chairman of Advisory Board will consist of a judge.* An additional safeguard would be provided by the requirement that the chairman of an Advisory Board shall be serving judge of the appropriate High Court and that the Board shall be constituted in accordance with the recommendations of the Chief Justice of that High Court.

(9) *Guarantee for the freedom of the Press.* During the internal Emergency, the freedom of the Press had been totally destroyed and it was made to dance with the tune of the Ruling Party. It was used to boost the image of Mrs. Indira Gandhi and Sanjay Gandhi. Therefore, a special provision is being made guranteeing the right of the media to report freely and without censorship the proceeding in Parliament and State Legislatures.

(10) *President's Rule in the States to be for shorter duration.* The provision with regard to the breakdown of the constitutional machinery in the States is being amended so as to provide that a proclamation issued under Article 356 would be in force only for period of six month in the first instance and that it cannot exceed one year ordinarily (according to 42nd Amendment the President's rule can be for one year and it can be extended by the Parliament for a three-year term)

However, if proclamation of emergency is in operation and the Election Commission certifies that the extension of the President's rule beyond a period of one year is necessary on account of difficulties in holding elections to the Legislative Assembly of the State concerned, the period of operation of the proclamation can be extended beyond one year. This is subject to the existing limit of three years.

(11) *Appeals to the Supreme Court.* With a view to avoiding delays, it is proposed to amend Articles 132, 133 and 134 and insert a new Article 134A to provide that a High Court should consider the question of granting a certificate for appeal to Supreme Court immediately after the delivery of the judgement, decree, final order or sentence conferred on the basis of an oral application by a party or if the High Court deems fit to do so, on its own motion. Cases of special leave to appeal by Supreme Court will be left to be regulated exclusively by Article 136.

Changes made in the 44th Constitution Amendment Bill by the Rajya Sabha. The Rajya Sabha amended the 44th Constitution Amending Bill on August 31, 1978 as follows :

There was a majority of the Congress in Rajya Sabha, hence some changes were made.

(1) Education and forest to remain the Concurrent List.

(2) The referendum provision for changes in the basic structure to go.

(3) Move to define secularism and socialisms turned down.

(4) Provision for setting up of administrative tribunals under the Constitution 42nd Amendment Act remains.

(5) Supremacy of Directive Principles vis-a-vis Fundamental Rights accorded by the Constitution 42nd Amendment Act continues.

Lastly, the Rajya Sabha has ratained the 42nd Amendment provision which had empowered the Central Government to deploy armed forces or any other forces under the control of the Union of India in the aid of civil power in the States.

Lok Sabha passes the 44th Amendment Bill again as amended by the Rajya Sabha. The Government of India accepted all the amendments made by Rajya Sabha. Therefore, on its insistence the Lok Sabha passed all the amendments on 7th December, 1978. There were 357 votes in favour, one against the Bill and 36 abstained.

Assent of the President. After its passage, the Bill was sent to the States for approval. After some time the States passed it. On April 30, 1979 the President gave his assent to this Bill. After receiving the President's assent, it became the 44th Amendment to the Indian Constitution.

The Constitution (Forty-Fifth Amendment) Act, 1980. Mrs. Indira Gandhi had been returned to power on 14th January 1980 after winning elections of 7th Lok Sabha. The Lok Sabha with rare unanimity passed the 45th Constitutional Amendment Bill on 24 January, 1980 extending the reservation of seats in the Lok Sabha and the State Assemblies for the Scheduled Castes and Tribes and representation of Anglo-Indians by nomination for another ten years upto 25th January, 1990. After a brief discussion all the 423 members present in the House voted for the Bill piloted by the Home Minister Zail Singh. There are 78 members of the Scheduled Castes and 39 members belonging to the Scheduled Tribes and two nominated members of the Lok Sabha, while there are 546 members of the Scheduled Castes and 291 members of the Scheduled Tribes in the Legislative Assesmblies of the States.

The Rajya Sabha passed this Bill on January 25, 1980 unanimously. The President gave his assent to the Bill on April 14,1980. So in this way the reservation for the Scheduled Castes and Scheduled Tribes was extended upto 25th January, 1990.

The Constitution (Forty-Sixth Amendment) Act, 1983. The Constitution 46th Amendment Bill received assent of the President on 12th February, 1983 and came into force from Feb. 13, 1983.

The amendment carried out through the Act, enabled government to plug loopholes and overcome deficiencies in the administration of sales tax laws by the states. The measure was passed by Parliament following complaints from state governments about large-scale avoidance of Central sales tax leviable on inter- state sale of goods through the device of consignment transfers. They also reported leakage of sales tax revenue in higher purchase transactions, work contracts, supply of food-stuffs etc. by hotels in view of the restricted interpretation of the term "sale" by courts.

The Constitution (Forty-Seventh Amendment) Act, 1984.[1] This Act was enacted in the Thirty-fifth year of the Republic of India. According to it 14 Land Reform Acts of various states were included in the Ninth Schedule to give them protection against the proceedings in the court because in the past several affected parties (landlords) have challenged them in the court of law and certain laws were declared as null and void in the past. Previously, (before 26th August, 1984) 188 such Land Reform Acts of various states of India had been included. Now according to the amendment made in the Constitution of India on 14th August, 1984, 14 more Land Reforms Acts have been included, so the strength of such Acts has now arisen to 202.

This Act received the assent of the President on August 26, 1984.

The Constitution (Forty-Eighth Amendment) Act, 1984. This Act was enacted in the Thirty-fifth year of the Republic of India.

Statement of Object and Reasons. The Proclamation issued by the President under Article 356 of the Constitution on 6th day of October, 1983 with respect to the State of Punjab cannot be continued in force more than one year unless the special conditions mentioned in clause (5) of Article 356 of the Constitution are satisfied. Although the Legislative Assembly is in suspended animation and a popular government cannot be installed, having regard to the prevailing situation in the State, the continuance of the Proclamation beyond 5th October, 1984 may be necessary. To facilitate the adoption of a resolution by the two Houses of Parliament approving the continuance in farce of the Proclamation beyond 5th October, 1984, it is necessary to amend Article 356 of the Constitution. It is, therefore, proposed to amend clause (5) of Article 356 so as to make the said Proclamation upto a period of two years from the date of its issue.

This Act received the assent of the President on August 26, 1984.

The Constitution (Forty-Ninth Amendment) Act, 1984. This Act was enacted by Parliament in the Thirty-fifth year of the Republic of India as follows :

Statement of objects and Reasons. The Tripura Legislative Assembly passed a resolution on the 19th March, 1982 and again on 11th February, 1983, urging the Government of India to apply the provisions of the Sixth Schedule to the Constitution to the tribal areas of the State of Tripura. (Previously, they were being applied to Assam, Meghalaya and Mizoram only). The State Government

1. This Act was published in the Gazette of India, extra, Part II, Section I, dated 26th August, 1984 P.1 - 2

of Tripura, therefore, recommended amendment of the Constitution for the purpose. Though under the Tripura Tribal Areas Autonomous District Council Act, 1979, an Autonomous District Council had been functioning in the State, it was considered necessary to give it Constitutional sanctity with a view to meet the aspirations of the tribal populations. The Council is expected to ensure rapid development of tribal areas and self governance by the tribals.

Consequently, the Parliament and State Legislature of Tripura got the right to frame laws regarding the District Tribal areas and the Council.

This Act received the assent of the President on 11th September, 1984.

The Constitution (Fiftieth Amendment) Act, 1984. This Act was enacted by Parliament in Thirty-fifth year of the Republic of India as follows :

By Article 33 of the Constitution, Parliament has been empowered to enact laws determining to what extent any of the Fundamental rights shall in their application to the members of the Armed Forces or the Forces charged with the maintenance of public order be restricted or abrogated so as to ensure the proper discharge of their duties and the maintenance of discipline among them. Article 33 has been amended to achieve those objects. It received the President's assent on 11th September, 1984.

The Constitution (Fifty-First Amendment) Act, 1984. It was enacted by Parliament in the thirty-fifth year of the Republic of India as follows :

Article 330 has been amended. Previously the seats for the Scheduled Castes and Scheduled Tribes had been reserved in the Lok Sabha for every state (except the Scheduled Tribes (1) in the tribal areas of Assam; (2) in Nagaland; (3) in Meghalaya; (4) in Arunachal Pradesh; and in Mizoram) and the Scheduled Tribes in the autonomous districts of Assam. Now the words in the bracket have been dropped and the word *except* has been added regarding the Scheduled Tribes in the autonomous districts of Assam. *This means in other words that the seats shall be reserved in the Lok Sabha for Scheduled Castes and Scheduled Tribes in every state except the Scheduled Tribes in the autonomous districts of Assam.*

Similarly Article 332 has been amended. Previsouly the seats were not reserved for the Scheduled Castes and Scheduled Tribes in the tribal areas of Assam, Nagaland and Meghalaya. Now the seats will reserved for Scheduled Castes and Scheduled Tribes in the Legislative Assembly of every State. The President gave his assent to this Bill on 29th April, 1985.

The Constitution (Fifty-Second Amendment) Act, 1985 to check defections. This Act was enacted in the Thirty-sixth year of the Republic of India as follows :

1. *Prefactory Note, Statement of Objects and Reasons.* The evil of political defections had been a matter of national concern. If it was not combated, it was likely to undermine the very foundations of our democracy and the principles which sustaind it. With this object, an assurance was given in the Address by the President to Parliament that the Government intended to introduce in the current session of Parliament as anti-defective Bill. This Bill is meant for outlawing defections and fulfilling the above assurance.
2. The Bill seeks to amend the Constitution to provide that elected member of Parliament or a State Legislature, who has been elected as a candidate set up by a political party and a nominated member of Parliament or a State Legislature who is a member of a political party at the time he takes his seat or who becomes a member of a politicial party within six months after he takes his seat would be disqualified on the ground of defection if he voluntarily relinquishes his membership of such political party or votes or abstains from voting in such House contrary to any direction of such party or is expelled from such party. An independent member of Parliament or a State Legislature shall also be disqualified if he joins any political party after his election. A nominated member of the Parliament or a State Legislature who is not member of a political party at the time of his nomination and

who has not become a member of any political party before the expiry of six months from the date on which he takes his seat shall be disqualified if he joins any political party after the expiry of the said period of six months. The Bill also makes a suitable provision with respect to splits in and mergers of political parties. A special provision has been created for a presiding officer of a House to severe his connection with his political party. *The question as to whether a member of a House of Parliament or State Legislature has become subject to the proposed disqualification will be determined by the Presiding Officer of the House,* where the question is with reference to the presiding officer himself, it will be decided by a member of the House elected by the House in that behalf.

3. The Bill sees to achieve above objects and amends Articles 101, 102, 190,191 and adds Tenth Schedule for that purpose.

Disqualification on ground of Defection. (1) A member of a House belonging to any political party shall be disqualified for being a member of the House —

(*a*) if he has voluntarily given up his membership of such political party; or

(*b*) if he votes or abstains from voting in such House contrary to any direction issued by the political party to which he belongs or by any person or authority authorised by it in this behalf, without obtaining, in neither case, the prior permission of such political party, person or authority,and such voting or absention has not been condoned by such political party, person or authority within fifteen days from the date of such voting or abstention.

(2) *Disqualification on ground of defection not to apply in case of split.* Where a member of a House makes claim that he and any other members of his Legislature party constitute the group representing a faction which has arisen as a result of a split in his original political party and such group consists of not less than one-third of the members of such Legislature Party :

(*a*) he shall not be disqualified on the ground :

(*i*) that he has voluntarily given up his membership of his original political party; or

(*ii*) that he has voted or abstained from voting in such House contrary to any direction issued by such party or by any person or authority authorised by it in that behalf without obtaining the prior permission of such party, person or authority within fifteen days from the date of such voting or abstention; and

(*b*) from the time of such split, such faction shall be deemed to be the political party to which he belongs for the purposes of original political party.

(3) *Disqualification on ground of defection not to apply in case of merger.* A member of a House shall not be disqualified where his original party merges with another political party and he claims that he and any other members of his original political party :

(*a*) have become members of such other political party or as the case may be, of a new political party formed by such merger;

(*b*) have not accepted the merger and opted to function as a separate group, and from the time of such merger, such other political party or new political party or group, as the case may be, shall be deemed to be the political party to which he belongs.

(*c*) The merger of the original political party or a member of a House shall be deemed to have taken place if, and only if, not less than two-thirds of the members of the legislature party concerned have agreed to such merger.

(4) *Exemption.* Not with standing anything contained in theTenth Schedule, a person who has been elected to the office of the Speaker or the Deputy Speaker of the House of the people or the

Deputy Chairman of the Legislative Council of a State or the Speaker or the Deputy Speaker of the Legislative Assembly of a State, shall not be disqualified under this Schedule :

(*a*) if he by reason of his election to such office, voluntarily gives up the membership of the political party to which he belonged immediately before such election and does not, so long as he continues to hold such office thereafter, rejoins the political party or becomes a member of another political party; or

(*b*) if he, having given up by reason of his election to such office his membership of the political party to which he belonged immediately before such election, rejoins such political party after he ceases to hold such office.

6. *Decision on Question as to disqualification on ground of defection.* (1) If any question arised as to whether a member of a House has become subject to disqualification under this Schedule, the question shall be referred for the decision of the Chairman or as the case may be, the Speaker of such House and his decision shall be final :

Provided that where the question which has arisen is as to whether the Chairman or the Speaker of a House has become subject to such disqualification the question shall be referred for the decision of such member of the House as the House may elect in this behalf and his decision shall be final.

The Constitutional (Fifty- third Amendment) Acts, 1986— Mizoram State Created. The Lok Sabha on Tuesday, August 5, 1986 passed the Constitution (53rd) Amendment Bill and the State of Mizoram Bill, seeking to give effect to the Mizoram accord reached between the Central Government and the MNF leader, Mr. Laldenga. The State of Mizoram Bill provides for the grant of statehood to the Union Territory of Mizoram, thus making it the23rd State of Union, the Constitution Amendment Bill was passed by a majority of 308 to two. Bhartiya Janata Party members opposed the Bill.

The Constitution (Fifty-fourth Amendment) Act, 1986—Salary of Judges raised.

The salary of the Chief Justice of the Supreme Court has been raised to Rs. 10000/- and other judges to Rs. 9000/- per mensum. The salary of the Chief Justice of the High Court has been raised to Rs. 9000/- from Rs. 4000 per mensum. The salary of the judges of the High Court has been raised from Rs. 3500 to Rs. 8000 per mensum. After being passed by Parliament and receiving the assent of the President, it became 'The Constitution (54th Amendment) Act.'

The Constitution (Fifty-fifth Amendment) Act, 1986—(Arunachal Pradesh given Statehood) The Lok Sabha (House of People) passed a Bill on December 8, 1986 providing for the establishment of the state of Arunachal Pradesh and also the Constitution (55th Amendment) Bill, 1986 at the end of a four hour debate during which members from both sides vehemently opposed the special powers proposed to be given to the Governor of the new north-eastern state.

The Bill was also passed by Rajya Sabha next day (9th December, 1986). So according to it Arunachal Pradesh has been granted statehood. It had become the 24th state of the Indian Union.

The Constitution (Fifty-sixth Amendment) Act, 1987. Home Minister Buta Singh moved a Bill called the Constitution (Fifth-Sixth Amendment Bill, 1987 in the Lok Sabha on February 27, 1987. The measure is sought to be given effect to by two Articles, one providing for an amendment to the heading to part XXII of the Constitution and the other by inserting a new clause in Article 39 of the Constitution.

Instead of the heading "Short Title Commencement and Repeals in part XXII, new heading will be : Short Title, Commencement, Authoritative Text in Hindi and Repeals."

The new Article 394A says :

(1) The President shall cause to be published under his authority :

(*a*) the translation of the Constitution in Hindi language signed by members of the Constituent Assembly, with such modifications as may be necessary to bring it in confirmity with the language, style, technology adopted in the authoritative texts of Central Acts in the Hindi language, and incorporation there in all the amendments of this Constitution made before such publication : and

(*b*) the translation of this Constitution and of every amendment thereof published under clause (1) shall be constructed to have the same meaning as the original thereof and if any difficulty arises in so contruing any part of such translation, the President shall cause the same to be revised suitably.

(2) The translation of this Constitution and of every amendment thereof published under this Article shall deemed to be, for all purposes, the authoritative text in the Hindi language."

Objects and Reasons :

In a statement of objects and reasons, the Home Minister said the Constitution of India was adopted by the Constituent Assembly in English. A Hindi translation of the Constitution, signed by the members of the Constitutent Assembly was also published in 1950 under the authority of the President of the constituent Assembly in accordance with a resolution adopted by the Assembly.

There had been, Mr. Buta Singh said, general demand for the publication of an authoritative text of the Constitution in Hindi, *incorporating all the subsequent amendments.* It was also imperative to have an authoritative text of Constitution for facilities to use in the legal process.

Any version of the Constitution should not only conform to the Hindi translation published by the Constituent Assembly, but should be in confirmity with the language, style and terminology adopted in the authoritative texts of Central Acts in Hindi. It was, therefore, proposed, the Home Minister said, to amend the Constitution so as to empower the President of India to publish under his authority the translation of Constitution in Hindi signed by the members of the Constituent Assembly with such modifications as might be necessary to bring it in conformity with the language, style and terminology adopted in the authoritative texts of the Central Acts in the Hindi language. The President would also be authorised to publish the translation in Hindi of every amendment of the Constitution made in English.

The Bill moved by him sought to achieve these objectives, Mr. Buta Singh said.

The Constitution (57th Amendment), Act 1987 (Statehood for Goa). A two piece legislation to grant statehood to Goa and to create a new Union Territory comprising Daman and Diu was introduced in the Lok Sabha on May 8, 1987 by the Union Home Minister, Mr. Buta singh. The Constitution (57th Amendment) Bill, 1987 seeks to make a special provision in the Constitution for the setting up of a new state of Goa. The Bill introduced, with a view to satisfy the desire and aspirations of the people of the Union territory of Goa, propose setting up of a Legislative Assembly of the new State of Goa with 40 members. There shall be a common High Court for the States of Maharashtra and Goa,and for the Union Territory of Dadra and Nagar Haveli and Diu, to be called as the High Court of Maharashtra and Goa. It was passed by the Lok Sabha on May 11, 1987 and Rajya Sabha next day. After that it received the assent of the President.

The Constitution (58th Amendment) Act, 1987. *Reservation of seats for Scheduled Tribes of Mizoram, Nagaland, Meghalaya and Arunachal Pradesh in the Lok Sabha and Assemblies.* The 58th Amendment to the Constitution of India was passed by the Lok Sabha on August 28, 1987 and by the Rajya Sabha on August 31. The measure was wholly non-controversial and was passed without any opposition. It provides for the reservation of seats for Scheduled Tribes of Mizoram, Nagaland, Meghalaya and Arunachal Pradesh in the Lok Sabha and the respective Legislative Assemblies.

The Constitution (51st Amendment) Act, 1984 was enacted to provide for reservation of seats in the House of the People for the Scheduled Tribes in Nagaland, Meghalaya, Mizoram and Arunachal Pradesh and also for the reservation of seats for Scheduled Tribes in the Legislative Assemblies of Nagaland and Meghalaya by suitably amending Articles 330 and 332. Even though these States are predominently tribal areas, the underlying objective of the aforsaid Act was to ensure that the members of the Scheduled Tribes in these areas do not fail to secure a minimum representation becuase of their inability to compete with the advanced sections of the people.

The Constitution (51st Amendment) Act, though formally enforced, cannot be fully implemented unless parallel action is taken to determine the seats which are to be reserved for Scheduled Tribes in these areas. The number of seats reserved for Scheduled Castes and Scheduled Tribes in the Legislative Assembly of any State under Article 332 of Constitution will have to be determined having regard to the provisions of Article 323 (3) of the Constitution. The new section 9A proposed to be introduced in the Representation of People Act, 1950 by clause (2) of the Bill empowers the Election Commission to determine, having regard to the provisions of the Constitution and section 9 (1) (d) of the Delimitation Act, 1972, the Assembly Constituencies in the States of Meghalaya, Mizoram and Nagaland which shall be reserved for the Scheduled Tribes. Such determination with regard to Assembly constituencies in the State of Arunachal Pradesh will be done by the Election Commission under the powers given to it by section 14 of the State of Arunachal Pradesh Act, 1986.

59th Constitutional Amendment Act, 1988

The highly controversial 59th Constitutional Amendment, designed to empower the Central Government to impose Emergency in Punjab when deemed necessary, was passed by both Houses of Parliament in the last week of March. It was first introduced in the Rajya Sabha and passed by it on 15th March, 1988. Later on it was passed by the Lok Sabha on 23rd March, 1988. The two-thirds majority required for passing a constitutional amendment was ensured by the Government in each House.

The main provisions of the measures are : (a) It gives power to the Government to extend President's rule in Punjab, when necessary, up to three years. Earlier the period of such role was restricted to two years. (b) The Central can impose Emergency in Punjab on grounds of internal disturbances. (c) In effect, the amendment deprives the citizens of the right to the security of personal life and liberty guaranteed by Article 21 of the Constitution. Under the measures, this Article can be suspended by the President.

Emergency Bill becomes Law : President R. Venkatraman, on March 30, 1988 gave his assent to the controversial 59th Constitution Amendment Bill empowering the Government to impose emergency in Punjab. He explained that he had no discretion under the Constitution to refuse assent to a Constitutional amendment Bill.

Sixtieth Amendment to the Indian Constitution, December 1988. It empowers the State Governments to increase the ceiling of professional tax from Rs. 250 to Rs. 2500 per person per year. The Lok Sabha passed it on 30th November, 1988. After that it was passed by the Rajya Sabha. The President has given his assent.

Sixty-first Amendment to the Indian Constitution 1988. A controversial proposal seeking to transfer the subject of sports from the jurisdiction of the States List to the Concurrent List in the Seventh Schedule, incorporated in the 61st Amendment to the Constitution was introduced in winter session of the Parliament in 1988. It has been done in implement effectively the national policy of sports. It was aslo necessary to bring descipline and order in the management. After being passed by the parliament and receiving the assent of the President, it became Constitutional Amendment Act.

Sixty-second Amendment, 1988 and election reforms. This Bill seeks to lower the age of the voters in India from 21 to 18. It was introduced in the Parliament by the law-minister Shri Shankranand on 13th December, 1988 in the Lok Sabha. It was termed historic and revolutionary by the then Prime Minister, Mr. Rajiv Gandhi. It was passed by the Parliament at the close of the winter session in December 1988. Referring to the major step in enfranchising the young men in the Age group 18 to 21, Mr. Rajiv Gandhi expressed full faith in youth and expressed hope that they would full participate in the political process. The youthful voters in the country were estimated at 50 million.

The second part of the Bill related to election-reforms. It seeks to amend Representation of the people (Amendment) Act. Its notable features are :

(*a*) All political parties will have to get themselves registered. They will have to show their deep and abiding faith in the ideals of secularism, socialism and democracy enshrined in the Constitution. Mr. Rajiv Gandhi, then Prime Minister of India said that those parties which did not believe in those ideals did not deserve to be registered.

(*b*) After the new measure comes into force, any party that has been deemed to be communal will be debarred from election contests unless it throws its membership opens to other communities. But the Prime Minister has made it clear that there would be no forcing of secularism on any party. The Union Government is trying to 'push' secularism through the electoral process and through persuation.The concept obviously is that by strengthening secularism the Government would be reinforcing democracy in the country.

(*c*) The measure increases the number of offences which would entail disqualification for convicts from contesting elections. For the first time any one who has been convicted for violation of foreign exchange laws and regulations (FERA) for smuggling or adulteration will not be permitted to contest an election. Under an amendment, the House, offences committed under the Religious Institutions (Prevention of Misuse) Act, 1988 also will disqualify the persons from contesting elections.

(*d*) Provision has been made for introduction of electronic voting machines in the sensitive constituencies, to be determined by the Election Commission,to start with. The factors to be kept in mind are the law and order position and interests of the weaker sections.

(*e*) The measure makes booth capturing, which has been growing menace in recent elections as a conginsable offence with deterrent punishment. The Union Government hopes that the new legislation would provide protection to the weaker sections when they turned out for voting. Feudal elements had tried to prevent *Dalits*, women and other weaker sections from exercising their voting right. By making booth capaturing cognisable offence and declaring it a corrupt practice, the hands of the weaker sections had been strengthened.

Though the Bill aims at some electoral reforms, yet many electoral reforms need the attention of the government in a most urgent way : (1) Misuse of official machinery; (2) Use of balck money supplied by profiteers, black marketeers, smugglers and anti-social elements; (3) Use of money-power and muscle power in the election; (4) Declaration of bonanza on the eve of election which is a malpractice.

RESERVATION BILL GETS APPROVAL, FIRST GIFT OF NATIONAL FRONT GOVERNMENT

Parliament on December 26, 1989 extended by ten years the reservation for the Scheduled Castes and Scheduled Tribes after the Lok Sabha unanimously adopted the 62nd Amendment to the Constitution passed by the Rajya Sabha last week, this being the first legislation piloted by the National Front Government.

Labour Minister Ram Bilas Paswan, who piloted the Bill, said the Government would consider a numbner of related issues, including the demand for the reservation in Rajya Sabha and the State Legislative Councils. He said the Bill was limited in scope and had nothing to do with the reservation of jobs in the Government for which a there was no time limit and did not need extension.

63rd Amendment (1989). *Fifty-Ninth Constitution Amendment Repeated, Second Gift of National Front Government.* Parliament on December 29, 1989 passed the Bill repealing the 59th Constitution Amendment which empowered the Government to impose the emergency in the Punjab. While the Bill was passed by the Lok Sabha after a brief debate, in the Rajya Sabha it was passed without any discussion with all the140 members present voting in its favour. Mr. Muhammad Mufti Sayeed, Home Minister, moved the Bill in the Lok Sabha and piloted it in the Rajya Sabha as well. The Congress-I leader and former Prime Minister had pleged his support to Mr. V.P. Singh, the Prime Minister who said that such a Bill should not remain on the Statute Book any longer as it had taken the right to life from the people of Punjab.

Note. After this the numberings of the Constitution amendments has been done again. 60th, 61st and 62nd Constitution amendments have been numbered as 59th, 60th and 61st. So the Reservation Bill about Scheduled Castes and Tribes has been termed as 62nd amendment.

64th Amendment, April 1990. It was passed during the regime of National Front Government. The Lok Sabha passed it on 5th April 1990 and Rajya Sabha on 10th April, 1990. The President has no veto on the Constitution Amendment Bill. It extended President's rule for another six months in the Punjab with effect from 11th May, 1990.

65th Amendment, 1990. It was given statutory status to the Comission for Scheduled Castes and Scheduled Tribes consisting of a Chairperson, Vice-Chairperson and other members to be appointed by the President. The Commission has given wide powers to inquire into all cases relating to the atrocities committed on Scheduled Castes and Scheduled Tribes.

66th Amendment Bill, 1990. The Lok Sabha passed on May 30, 1990 the 66th Constitution Amendment Bill with overwhelming support becuase the Congress Party had agreed to support the Bill. The Rajya Sabha passed it on 1st May, 1990. The 66th Amendment Bill seeks to bring all the land reform Acts in the 9th Schedule, so that they may not be challenged in any court of law. 66th Amendment enabled N.F. Government to include 55 land reform Bills in the 9th Schedule. Before it 202 land reform Bills had been included in the 9th Schedule. Thus we have now 257 land reform Bills in the 9th Schedule of the Indian Constitution which cannot be challenged in any court of law.

The Sixty-Seventh Amendment of 1990: It has provided that in respect of the State of Punjab the proclamation imposing President's rule shall remain in force for not more than four years.

The Sixty-Eighth Amendment of 1991 : It has provided that in respect of the State of Punjab the proclamation imposing President's rule shall remain in force for not more than five years.

The Sixty-Ninth Amendment of 1991 : It provides that the Union Territory of Delhi shall be called the National Capital Territory of Delhi to be administered by the Lieutenant-Governor. It shall have Legislative Assembly and the seats of the Assembly shall be filled by members chosen by direct election from the territorial constituencies in the National Capital Territory and shall also have a Council of Ministers consisting of not more than ten per cent of the total number of members in the Assembly with the Chief Minister as its head.

The Constitution (Seventieth) Amendment of 1992 : It provides that in Articles 54 and 55, "State" shall include the National Capital Territory of Delhi and the Union Territory of Pondicherry. Delhi and Pondicherry shall have a right to vote in the Presidential election.

The Constitution (Seventy-First) Amendment of 1992 : It provides that Konkani, Manipuri and Nepali languages shall be included in the Eighth Schedule.

The Constitution (Seventy-Second) Amendment Act, 1992[1] **:** It amended Article 332 of the Constitution. It provides that the number of seats in the Legislative Assembly of the State of Tripura, the seats which shall be reserved for the Scheduled Tribes in the Legislative Assembly shall be, such number of seats as bears to the total number of seats, a proportion not less than the number, as on the date of coming into force of the Constitution (Seventy-second) Amendment Act, 1992 of members belonging to the Scheduled Tribes in the Legislative Assembly in existence on the said date bears to the total number of seats in that Assembly.

The Constitution (73rd & 74th) Amendment Acts, 1993 : Panchayati Raj-A challenging task for the political parties— The Narasimha Rao Government was put into power after the General Election of 1991, to push forward the legislation seeking to amend the Constitution to incorporate local government including Panchayati Raj endowing it with the power, resources and independence in functioning. As the amendment bill needed ratification by the requisite number of State legislatures, this formality took sometime to complete. *In May, 1993 the Constitution (Seventy-third Amendment) Bill, 1991 was notified by the Central Government and as such has become a part of the Constitution of India. The constitutionalisation of local government including Panchayati Raj and urban government is perhaps the single most outstanding event of its kind since the commencement of the Republic.*

Panchayati Raj is a four-tiered structural arrangement comprising gram sabha, village panchayat and bodies at the intermediate (block) and district levels. The gram sabha consisting of all voters of a village is the only example of direct democracy in India. It is now an integral part of the panchayati raj structure. An exception is made in the case of States with less than 20 lakh population : these need not have the intermediate-level body. Seats in all such bodies are filled up by direct election from territorial constituencies. The Constitution provides for reservation of seats for Scheduled Castes, Scheduled Tribes and women.

A special concern, one may note, is shown for women. *A minimum of one third seats in a panchayat body is reserved for women, and while providing for reservation for Scheduled Castes and Tribes, a further reservation for at least one-third of the total quota is made form them. Furthermore, reservation for the office of chair persons of panchayat bodies has been made for these three categories.*

The term of the panchayat is five years. In the event of a body being dissolved, a fresh election is mandatory within six months, and the re-elected body is to exist for the remainder of the term. The advocates of President's rule should take a lesson from such an arrangement at the local level.

The Constitution provides for two independent authorities, one to conduct free and fair election to panchayati raj bodies, and the other to devolve adequate funds to make them financially viable.

The proposed one-member State Election Commission is to enjoy the status and independence of the High Court. A Finance Commission is set up every five years to determine the devaluation of finances on the panchayati raj bodies.

The Constitutional amendment specifies twenty-nine functions for the panchayati raj bodies including agriculture, land reform, animal husbandary, minor irrigation, housing, roads, rural electrification etc. All these functions are of local interest, import or impact.

The Constitution (Seventy-third Amendment) Act, 1992 is sensitive to the historical fact that local government including panchayati raj falls within the sphere of the State government and thus takes every care not to bind its hand in any way. The Act is a skeleton legislation leaving maximum, initiative and discretion with the State government. Decisions on many important matters are left to the State legislature. For instance, the legislature of a State may, by law, provide for the representation of elected MPs and MLAs in the panchayati raj bodies. *In the real sense, therefore, the State Govern-*

1. Published in the Gazette of India,, Extraordinary. Part II, Section I, dated 4. 12.92

ment holds the key to the energisation of the panchayati raj institution. What specific powers and functions are to develop on the latter are to be defined by it.

Major Milestone : *The passage of Panchayati Raj and Nagarpalika Bills in the Lok Sabha is a major milestone in the process of local self-government.* Although the Bills are far from perfect and cannot by themselves ensure good government and fair representation, they provide an opporunity for local people to decide matters for themselves in a democratic fashion rather than be at the mercy of local elites or bureaucrats and politicians in distant state capitals. *Most importantly, by making elections to village panchayats and municipalities mandatory every five years, the new legislation will guarantee the right of local self-government bodies to exist independent of the whims and political colour of the State Government.*

The second significant feature of the legislation, after the provision for regular elections, is that local bodies be made financially solvent. Decentralised decision-making is meaningless without the wherewithal to carry out local programmes. But while the Bills provide for the devolution of resources to local bodies and also empower them to raise some resources of their own, the process of sharing resources between the Central Government, State Governments and local bodies is likely to be long drawn out and contentious. Therefore, the sooner State Finance Commissions begin the task of allocating adequate resources to Panchayati Raj institutions, the better.

A third critical factor for the success of local bodies is representation of the weaker sections in them. The reservation of seats for women and members of the Scheduled Castes and Tribes is envisaged but experience shows that this could amount to no more than token representation and that real power will continue to be exercised by the existing elites through a process of cornering seats and co-opting other members of panchayats.

The Constitution (Seventy-fifth Amendment) Act, 1993

It has amended Article 323-B and added a new clause (h) providing for establishment of tribunals for rent control cases.

The Constitution (Seventy-sixth Amendment) Act, 1994

This Amendment Act raises the reservation quota of government jobs and seats for admission in the educational institutions in favour of socially and educationally backward classes to 69 per cent in Tamil Nadu. Further, the Amendment Act has been included in the Ninth Schedule of the Constitution to exempt it from the purview of judicial scrutiny.

The Constitution (Seventy-seventh Amendment) Act, 1995

This amendment has added a new clause (4-a) to Article 16 of the Constitution which empowers the State to make any provisions for reservation in promotions in government jobs in favour of SCs and STs, if it is of opinion that they are inadequately represented in the services under the State. This has been done to nullify the effect of the Supreme Court Judgement in the Mandal Commission Case (*Indra Sawhney vs. Union of India*) in which the Court has held that reservation in promotions cannot be made.

The Constitution (Seventy-eighth Amendment) Act, 1995

This amendment has aamended the Ninth Schedule of the Constitution and inserted 27 Land Reform Act of various States in the Ninth Schedule. After this the total number of Acts included in the Ninth Schedule has gone upto 284. Now these acts cannot be challenged in the courts on the plea for the violation of Fundamental Rights.

The Constitution (Seventy-ninth Amendment) Act, 1999

By this Act the Government has extended the reservations of seats for the Scheduled Castes and the Scheduled Tribes as well as for the Anglo-Indians in the House of the People and in the Legislative Assemblies of the States for another ten years.

The Constitution (Eightieth Amendment) Act, 2000

Based on the recommendations of the Tenth Finance Commission, an alternative scheme for sharing taxes between the Union and the States has been enacted by the Constitution (Eightieth Amendment) Act, 2000. Under the new scheme of devolution of revenue between Union and the States, 26 per cent out of gross proceeds of Union taxes and duties is to be assigned to the States in lieu of their existing share in the income-tax, excise duties, special excise duties and grants in lieu of tax on railway passenger fares.

The Constitution (Eighty-first Amendment) Act, 2000

By this amendment the unfilled vacancies of a year which reserved for the Scheduled Castes and the Scheduled Tribes for being filled up in that year in accordance with any provision for reservations made under Article 16 of the Constitution, shall be considered as a separate class of vacancies to be filled up in any succeeding year or years, and such class of vacancies shall not be considered together with the vacancies of the year in which they were filled up for determining the ceiling of fifty per cent reservation against total number of vacancies of that year.

The Constitution (Eighty-second Amendment) Act, 2000

The amendment provides that nothing in Article 335 shall prevent the State from making any provision in favour of the members of the Scheduled Castes and the Scheduled Tribes for relaxation in qualifying marks in any examination or lowering the standards of evaluation for reservation in matters of promotion to any class or classes of services or posts in connection with affairs of the Union or of a State.

The Constitution (Eighty-third Amendment) Act, 2000

The Act amended Article 243M of the Constitution to provide that no reservation in Panchayats need be made in favour of the Scheduled Castes in Arunachal Pradesh wholly inhabited by tribal population.

The Constitution (eighty-fourth amendment) Act, 2000 related to creating of new States of Jharkhand , Chhattisgarh and Uttaranchal.

The Constitution (eighty-fifth amendment) Act, 2001 Provides for consequential seniority in the case of promotion by virtue of rule of reservation for the Government servants belonging to SC/STs. It also provides retrospective effect from June 17, 1995.

Till October 2003, 93 amendments were made to the Constitution of India. However, all of them have not been gazetted. A few important gazetted amendments are :

The Constitution 89th Amendments Act 2003 : It provides for Constitution of a National Commission for Scheduled Tribes. (Earlier, there was a combined National Commission for both SC/STs).

The Constitution 90th Amendments (2003) : It provides that the representation of the Scheduled Tribes and non-Scheduled Tribes in the constituencies included in the Bodoland Territorial Area District (BTAD) as existing prior to the Constitution of BTAD, shall be maintained for the purpose of elections to Legislative Assembly of the State of Assam.

The parliamentary system of government, both at the Centre and in the States in India is based on adult franchise whereby all citizens of India who are not less than 18 years of age and are not disqualified under the Constitution or any law made by the appropriate legislature on certain grounds like non-residence, unsoundness of mind, crime, illegal or corrupt practices, have the right to be registered as voters in any election to the Lok Sabha and Legislative Assemblies of the States.

The Constitution (Ninety-first Amendment) Act, 2003 – In Article 75 of the Constitution, after clause (1), the following clauses shall be inserted, namely :

"(1 A) The total number of Ministers, including the Prime Minister, in the Council of Ministers shall not exceed fifteen per cent of the total number of members of the House of the People.

(1 B) A member of either House of Parliament belonging to any political party who is disqualified for being a member of that House under paragraph 2 of the Tenth Schedule shall also be disqualified to be appointed as a Minister under clause (1) for duration of the period commencing : from the date of his disqualification till the date on which the term of his office as such member would expire or where he contests any election to either House of Parliament before the expiry of such period, till the date on which he is declared elected, whichever is earlier".

The Constitution (Ninety-second Amendment) Act, 2003—In the Eighth Schedule to the Constitution,—(*a*) existing entry 3 shall be re-numbered as entry 5, and before entry 5 as so renumbered, the following entries shall be inserted, namely:

"3. *Bodo;*

4. *Dogri*".

(*b*) existing entries 4 to 7 shall respectively be re-numbered as entries 6 to 9;

(*c*) existing entry 8 shall be re-numbered as entry 11 and before entry 11 as so renumbered, the following entry shall be inserted, namely:

"10. *Maithili*".

(*d*) existing entries 9 to 14 shall respectively be re-numbered as entries 12 to 17;

(*e*) existing entry 15 shall be re-numbered as entry 19 and before entry 19 as so re-numbered, the following entry shall be inserted, namely :

"18. *Santhali*".

(*f*) existing entries 16 to 18 shall respectively be re-numbered as entries 20 to 22.

The Constitution (Ninety-third Amendment) Act, 2006 Greater access to higher education, including professional education, is of great importance to a large number of students belonging to the Scheduled Castes, the Scheduled Tribes and other socially and educationally backward classes of citizens. The reservation of seats for the Scheduled Castes, the Scheduled Tribes and the Other Backward Classes of citizens in admission to educational institutions is derived from the provisions of clause (4) of Aarticle 15 of the Constitution. At present, the number of seats available in aided or State maintained institutions, particularly in respect of professional education, is limited, in comparison to those in private unaided institutions.

Clause (i) of Article 30 of the Constitution provides the right to all minorities to establish and administer educational institutions of their choice. It is essential that the rights available to minorities are protected in regard to institutions established and administered by them. Accordingly, institutions declared by the State to be minority institutions under clause (1) of Article 30 are excluded from the operation of this enactment.

To promote the educational advancement of the socially and educationally backward classes of citizens, i.e., the Other Backward Classes or of the Scheduled Castes and the Scheduled Tribes in matters of admission of students belonging to these categories in unaided educational institutions, other than the minority educational institutions referred to in clause (1) of Article 30, the provisions of Article 15 were amplified. The new clause (5) of said Article 15 shall enable the Parliament as well as the State Legislatures to make appropriate laws for the above mentioned purpose.

EXERCISES

Long Answer Type Questions:

1. Discuss in brief the amendments procedure of the Constitution.
2. What are the defects in the amendments procedure of the Constitution?
3. Write a brief note on various amendments to the Constitution.
4. Write a brief note on 42nd Amendment to the constitution. What is its importance in politics of India?

Short Answer Type Questions:

1. Write a short note on 43rd Amendment Act to the Constitution.
2. Write a brief note on 44th Amendment Act to the Constitution.

Objective Type Questions:

Choose the correct answer

1. In which year 42nd Amendment Act passed ?
   (*a*) 1976 (*b*) 1977
   (*c*) 1978 (*d*) 1979
2. In which Article of the Constitution the Amendment Process of the Indian Constitution has been outlined ?
   (*a*) 367 (*b*) 368
   (*c*) 369 (*d*) 370
3. Which Amendment Act enabled the Parliament to amend the Fundamental Rights ?
   (*a*) Amendment Act 1969 (*b*) Amendment Act 1970
   (*c*) Amendment Act 1971 (*d*) Amendment Act 1972
4. In which year the First Amendment Act of Constitution was passed ?
   (*a*) 1954 (*b*) 1953
   (*c*) 1952 (*d*) 1951

ANSWERS

1. (*a*) **2.** (*b*) **3.** (*c*) **4.** (*d*)

21

CHAPTER

The Comptroller and Auditor-General and Attorney-General of India

The Comptroller and Auditor-General of India is the most important post under the Constitution of India. It is the guardian of the public purse and it is his duty to see that not a farthing is spent out of the Consolidated Fund of India or of a State without the authority of the appropriate Legislature.

APPOINTMENT AND CONDITIONS OF SERVICES OF THE COMPTROLLER AND AUDITOR-GENERAL

Article 148 (Clause 1) of the Indian Constitution lays down that there shall be Comptroller and Auditor-General of India who shall be appointed by the President by a warrant under his hand and seal and shall only be removed from office in like manner and on the like grounds as Judge of the Supreme Court. Article 148 (Clause 2) lays down that any person appointed to the Comptroller and Auditor-General of India, shall, before he enters upon his office, make and subscribe before the President or some person appointed in that behalf by him, an oath or affirmation according to the form set out for the purpose in the Third Schedule of Indian Constitution. In the Third Schedule of the Constitution, following oath has been given for the Comptroller and Auditor-General of India:

"I, A.B., having been appointed Comptroller and Auditor-General of India $\dfrac{\text{do swear in the name of God}}{\text{solemnly affirm}}$ that I will bear ture faith and allegiance to the Constitution of India as by law established, that I will duly and faithfully and to the best of my ability, knowledge and judgment perform the duties of my office without fear or favour, affection or ill-will and that I will uphold the Constitution and the laws."

The Comptroller and Auditor-General of India's salary shall be equal to that of a judge of the Supreme Court which is now Rs. 90,000 per month. On retirement, he shall be eligible to an annual pension. The salary and other conditions of service of the Comptroller and Auditor-General shall be regulated by the rules applicable to a member of the I.A.S. holding a rank of secretary to. the Government of India.

Article 148 (Clause 4) lays down that the Comptroller and Auditor-General shall not be eligible for further office either under the Government of India or under the Governemnt of any State after he has ceased to hold his office. Clause 5 of Article 148 further lays down that subject to the provisions of the Constitution and of any law made by Parliament, the conditions of service of persons serving in the Indian Audit and Accounts Department and the administrative powers of the Comptroller and Auditor-Genreal shall be such as may be prescribed by rules made by the President after consulation with the Comptroller and Auditor-General. Clause 6 of Article 148 lays down that the administrative expenses of the Office of the Comptroller and Auditor-General, including all salaries, allowances and pensions payable to or in respect of persons serving in that office, shall be charged upon the Consolidated fund of India.

DUTIES AND POWERS OF THE COMPTROLLER AND AUDITOR-GENERAL

Article 149 of the Indian Constitution prescribes the duties of the Comptroller and Auditor-General in the following words: "The Comptroller and Auditor-General shall perform such duties and exercise such powers in relation to the accounts of the Union and of the States and of any other authority or body as may be prescribed by or under any law made by Parliament and until provision in that behalf is so made, shall perform such duties and exercise such powers in relation to the accounts of the Union and of the States as were conferred on or exercisable by the Auditor-General of India immediately before the commencement of this Constitution in relation to the accounts of the Union and States shall be kept in such form as respectively. Article 150 of the Indian Constitution further says that the accounts of the Union and States shall be kept in such form as the Comptroller and Auditor-General of India may, with the approval of the President, prescribe.

Audit Report. Article 151 Clause (1) says that the reports of the Comptroller and Auditor-General of India relating to the accounts of the Union shall be submitted to the President who shall cause them to be laid before each House of Parliament. Clause (2) of the Article 151 further lays down that the reports of the Comptroller and Auditor-General of India relating to the accounts of a State shall be submitted to the Governor of the State who shall cause them to be before the legislature of the State.

HEADQUARTERS ORGANIZATIONS

The Headquarters office of the Comptroller and Auditor-General is under the immediate supervision of the Comptroller and Auditor-General of India. It is located in New Delhi.

ORGANISATION OF INDIAN AUDIT AND ACCOUNTS DEPARTMENT AS A WHOLE

Besides the Headquartes Organistation, the Indian Audit and Accounts Department is divided into four Classes, namely:

1. The Civil Audit and Accounts Offices.
2. The Post and Telegraphs (Audit and Account) offices.
3. The Railway Audit Offices.
4. The Defence Services Test Audit Offices.

In addition,the Comptroller and Auditor-General has under him two offices abroad:

1. Director of Audit, Indian Accounts, London.
2. Audit Officer, Indian Accounts, Washington.

The Director of Audit, Indian Accounts, in London audits all the expenditure from Indian revenues in countries on the European Constinent and the U.K. Audit Officer, Indian Accounts, Washington, audits all the expenditure met from the Indian revenues in both Amercias (North as well as South Amercia). This office has been working in Washington from the beginning of December 1951.

As the Government sponsored,owned and controlled commercial undertakings are coming into existence the Commercial Wing of the Audit Department has been reorganised by setting up a separate office of the Director of Commercial Audit with effect from October 1, 1955 with Headquarters in New Delhi. Some regional offices have also been established. Many subordinate offices are working under the Audit Department.

Independence of Comptroller and Auditor-General. The Constitution of India provides the following safeguards to ensure the independence of the Comptroller and Auditor-General of India. First, though the Comptroller and Auditor-General is appointed by the President he cannot be removed by him on his own. The President can issue orders for the removal of the Comptroller and Auditor-General only if both the Houses of Parliament pass a resolution to this effect and recommended the removal of the Comptroller and Auditor-General of India. Such a resolution must be passed by two-thirds majority of the members present and voting, which must also be the majority of the total membership of each House.

1. Secondly, the salary and emoluments of the Comptroller and Auditor-General of India are chargeable on the Consolidated Fund of India and are not subjected to the vote of the parliament. Further, the salary, service conditions pensions etc. of the Comptroller and Auditor-General cannot be changed to his disadvantage during his term of office.
2. The Comptroller and Auditor-General has been debarred from holding any office of profit under the Union or the State Government after his retirement.
3. Fourthly, the Comptroller and Auditor-General has direct access to the Parliament and no Minister can represent him.
4. Finally, the Comptroller and Auditor-General has full administrative control over all the officers and staff serving in the audit Department. Though the service conditions of the employees of the Comptroller and Auditor-General are formulated by the President, he does so only in consultation with the Comptroller and Auditor-General.

THE ATTORNEY GENERAL OF INDIA

The Attorney General of India is the Chief Legal Adviser to the Government of India, who renders necessary legal assistance to the Government.

Appointment. Article 76 (1) lays down that the President shall appoint a person who is to be appointed a Judge of the Supreme Court to be Attorney-General for India. This means that the qualifications for the post of the Attorney-General are the same as those for the Supreme Court Judge. Article 124 (Clause 2) provides that, "A person shall not be qualified for appointment as a judge of the Supreme Court unless he is a citizen of India and-

(*a*) has been for at least five years a Judge of a High Court or of two or such courts in sucession; or

(*b*) has been for at least ten years an advocate of a High Court or of two or more such Courts in succession; or

(*c*) is in the opinion of the President a distinguished jurist.

Therefore the Attorney-General of India must possess these qualifications.

Tenure. Article 76 (4) lays down that the Attorney-General shall hold office during the pleasure of the President, and shall receive such remuneration as the President may determine and the President has determined that the Attorney-General shall be paid a monthly retainer of Rs.5000.

Duties or Functions. Article 76, clause 2, provides, "It shall be the duty of the Attorney-General to give advice to the Government of India upon such legal matters, and to perform such other duties of a legal character, as may from time to time referred or assigned to him by the President, and to discharge the functions conferred on him by or under this Constituion or any other law for the time being in force." But he is not a whole time counsel for the Government nor a Government Servant.

Article 76, clause 3, provides that in the performance of his duties the Attorney-General shall have the right of audience in all courts in the territory of India.

EXERCISES

Long Answer Type Questions:

1. Write a note on 'Comptroller and Auditor-General of India'.
2. Write a note on 'The Attorney-General of India'.

Short Answer Type Questions:

1. Discuss the procedure of appointment of Comptroller and Auditor-General of India.
2. What are the duties and powers of Comptroller and Auditor-General of India ?
3. What do you know about the organisation of Indian Audit and Accounts Department ?
4. Write a brief note on 'Independence of Comptroller and Auditor-Genreal of India'.
5. What do you know about the functions of Attorney-Genreal of India ?

Objective Type Questions :

Choose the correct answer

1. Which Article of the Constitution lays down that there shall be Comptroller and Auditor-General of India ?
   (*a*) 148 (Clause 1) (*b*) 148 (Clause 2)
   (*c*) 149 (*d*) 150
2. In which Schedule of the Constitution oath proforma has been given for the comptroller and Auditor- General of India ?
   (*a*) Second Schedule (*b*) Third Schedule
   (*c*) Fourth Schedule (*d*) None of the above
3. What is the Salary of the Comptroller and Auditor-General of India ?
   (*a*) 26,000 (*b*) 27,000
   (*c*) 30,000 (*d*) 50,000
4. Which Article of the Constitution prescribes the duties of the Comptroller and Auditor-General of India ?
   (*a*) Article 146 (*b*) Article 147
   (*c*) Article 148 (*d*) Article 149
5. Which Article of the Constitution lays down that the President of India shall appoint a Attorney -General of India ?
   (*a*) 76(1) (*b*) 77
   (*c*) 78 (*d*) 79

ANSWERS

1. (*a*) 2. (*b*) 3. (*c*) 4. (*d*) 5. (*a*)

22

CHAPTER

Public Services (Bureaucracy) and Public Service Commission

IMPORTANCE OF OUR PUBLIC SERVICES AND THEIR COMPARISON WITH THE BRITISH CIVIL SERVICES

No Government, particularly a democartic one, can function smoothly without the help of competent and permanent officials who serve as 'permanent brain trust' in every department. The Ministers remain mobile. They come and go frequently. Moreover the Ministers are amateurs in the art of administration. The continuity of the administrative machinery. The Ministers have no alternative except to depend on the civil servants for their expert advice. The members of the Parliament frame laws and act according to the dictates of the Constitution. The Ministers lay down the policies but the efficient enforcement of laws and execution of policies depend on the civil servants. Nobody cares much for the political theories and principles so far as the administraive machinery works satisfactorily. Hence the essence of a good government is efficient administration. Pope had rightly remarked:

For forms of Government, let fools contest.
Whatever is best administered is best.

The position of the parliamentary secretaries is not the same as that of the permanent secretaries. The former happen to be political figures and hence go out with change in the ministry. The permanent secretaries belong to the civil service cadre and so remain unaffected by the political changes. They have no political affiliations. They are expected to obey and be faithful to whichever party comes to power. They lend their services to the Ministers in preparing the draft of the Bills, to be presented by the Ministers concerned in the Parliament. In formulating the policies also, the Ministers seek the advice of their subordinate staff although they are in no way bound to accept their advice. The permanent secretaries remain in the background, the Ministers alone have to face and reply the volley of questions in the Parliament.

ALL INDIA SERVICES AND STATE SERVICES

Public services in India may be put into two categories-All India Services and the State Services.

Services in Pre-independence Days. During British rule, Indian Civil Service was the backbone of the administration. All-India Services then included Indian Medical Service, Indian Police Service, Indian Forest Service and Irrigation Branch of the Service of Engineers. These services were directly under the charge of the Secretary of State for India. The recruitment to the Civil Service of India was made through competitive examinations,held simultaneously in India and Engaland. Appointments to lower services were usually made by the Governor-General partly through competitive examinations and partly by nominations. At the time of India's Independence, the members occupying superior posts were given the option either to retire or to continue in office under the existing rules and regulations. Most of the European officials preferred retirement.Those who agreed to serve in free India were assured of the existing facilities in regard to leave, pension and salary.

Classification of Services after Independence. After independence, the Indian Civil Service was renamed All-India Administrative Service. All the appointments to civil services are now made in the name of the President by the Union Public Service Commission. The All-India Services include, besides the I.A.S., some other cadres also, *e.g.* Central Services, Indian Foreign Service. Indian Audit and Accounts Service, Military Accounts Service, Indian Customs and Excise Service, Income Tax Officers Service, Central Engineering Services, Both Class I and II. The Union Public Service Commission conducts examination for making appointment to the services of the Union. Any graduate who satisfies the age-conditions can take the competitive examination. The tests include both written test and personality test or interview, as we call it.

Training of services. The probationers of the Indian Administrative Service and the Indian Police Service are trained at the National Academy of Administration, Mussoorie, and the Central Police Training College, Abu, respectively. Among the principle subjects taught to the I.A.S.Officers are Indian History and Constitution, Elements of criminal, and civil law. The Theory and Dractice of Public Administration and the Language of the State to which the trainees are allotted. Probationers of the Indian Foreign Service are taught Asian History, International Law, Economic Geography and International Trade as additional subjects.

The principle subjects for the course of training at the Central Police Training College, Abu, are : Indian Criminal Law, Constitution of India, Police Procedure and Administration, Medical Jurisprudence, Drill, Weapon Training, Wireless Training, Fire Service and so on.

The National Academy of Administration also conducts fresher course for Central and State Government officers with 10 to 15 years' service. A new feature of the training of programme, both for the I.A.S. and I.P.S. is an educational and cultural tour to army and police training institutions, development project areas and community development blocks.

Their Appointment and Security of Service. The services are the backbone of any Government. The welfare of the masses depends on he honesty and efficiency of civil servants. In recognition of this fact, our constitution lays down clear-cut rules regarding the recuitment, tenure and termination of services of the public servants. The appointment for the civil services are made by a selection board duly constituted by the Government. The Constitution provides special provisions for the Public Services of India. It says that member of the Civil Services of the Union or of an All-India Service or Civil Service of a State cannot be dismissed or removed. Further, no member or the superior service can be removed until he has been given reasonable opportunity to refute and explain the charges levelled aganist him.

The State service too are put under two heads-Superior State Services and Subordinate State Services. The Superior Services have two wings-Executive Branch and Judicial Branch. The Civil Judges and Deputy Collectors are drawn from State Services. For recruiting personal to Subordinate Services, the State has a Subordinate Services Selection Board. The appointments to Superior State posts are made by State Public Service Commission consituted on the model of the Union Commission. The Commission conducts written and oral test and then submits the list of deserving candidates to the State Government for appointments. The recommendation of the Commission carry weight and are, as a rule, accepted.

Central Secretariat Service. The Central Secretariat Service for manning posts in the Central Secretariat, was created in 1950. The service was originally organised into four grades, viz., Grade I (Under Secretary), Grade II (Superintendent), Grade III (Assistant Superintendent) and Grade IV (Assistant). Later on Grade II and III were merged into a single grade of Section Officer. Half the number of vacancies in this grade are made entirely by selection on the basis of merit at the competitive examinations and the remaining half by promotion from the grade of Assistants. Half the number of vacancies in the grade of Assistants is filled by direct recruitment and remaining half by promotion from the grade of Upper Division Clerks. Appointments from the grade of Section Officer Grade I (Under Secretary) are made entirely by selection on the basis of merit.

Industrial Management Pool. In order to man the industries and projects being run in public sector, the Government of India constituted in November, 1957, an Industrial Managemnt Pool. The Scheme is under the administrative control of the Union Ministry of Home Affairs. Ministers that have agreed to participate in the scheme are of Steel, Mines and Fuel, Transport and Communications and Commerce and Industry. The doors are open for any other Ministry running industrial undertaking to join scheme.

BUREAUCRACY AND ITS SIGNIFICANT ROLE IN IMPLEMENTING THE POLICIES OF THE GOVERNMENT

The term bureaucracy is derived from 'bureau' which means an of office or post. H.J. Laski says, "*Bureaucracy is term applied to a system of government, the control of which is so complete in the hands of the officials that power jeopardises the liberties of the ordinary citizen.*" But it could not be appropriate to use bureaucracy in the bad sense so far as India is concerned because it has played a noble role in implementing the progressive policies of the government. Prof. Fredrick Austin Ogg correctly observes,

> "The work of the government would never be done if there were only the Secretaries of State (Ministers) and other heads of departments, the Presidents of the Boards, Parliamentry Under-Secretaries, junior lords and civil lords-in other words the ministers to do it. These people cannot be expected to collect taxes, audit accounts, inspect factories, take censuses, to say nothing of keeping accounts, delivering mail and carrying messages. Such manifold task falls, rather to the body of officials and employees known as the permanent civil servants...It is this great body of men and women that transfers law into action from one end of the country to the other and brings the national government into the daily contact with the rank and file on the country-less in the public eye than the ministry, this army of functionaries is not a bit less necessary to the realisation of purpose for which government exists.[1]

Difference between British Bureaucracy and Indian civil Service or Bureaucracy. No doubt we have adpoted the British Parliamentary system of government as our model but the working of the Indian Civil Service differs widely from the British Civil Service. Regarding the role of the British Bureaucracy Prof. Ramsay Muir writes, "*In our system the power of bureaucracy is the cloak of ministerial repsonsibility and cabinet dictator-ship has thriven and grown until like Frankenstein's monster, it sometimes seems likely to devour its creator..it has become the most vital and potent element in your system of government.*" He further says, "*The power of this bureaucracy, the permanent Civil Service, is to be found not only in administration, but also in legislation and finance; it not only administers, the law, it largely shapes them; it not only spends the proceeds of taxation, it largely decides how much is to be raised and how.*"

1. Fredrick Austin Ogg : *English Government and Politics*, p. 202

In England and civil servants exercise the power of delegated legislation besides implementing the policies of the government of the day. They run the administration and prepare the draft of the various bills according to the directions of the Ministers. The delegated legislation means that the Parliament does not go into the details of every Bill due to lack of time and technical skill and passed only the skeleton laws. It leaves the details to be filled by the government. The Ministers do not find sufficient time to do the needful and leave to the Civil Service to work out its details. The bureaucracy or Civil Service frames various rules and regulations to fill the details of the Bills. The Ministers generally ditto the various rules and regulations, the drafts of the Bills, and various administrative measures adopted by the civil servants because they have no time to scrutinise the details of every thing. They have full confidence in the civil servants. They only see that their main directions are followed by the civil servants. In this way the civil servants exercise a lot of influence not only in the field of administration but also in legislation and finance.

While it is also true about India but even then the civil servants have not turned bureaucrats because the Ministers hear the grievances of the people directly and order the civil servants to act accordingly. Secondly, India has beocme a wealfare state since independence and the civil servants are busy in implementing various development schemes and thousands of projects. The rule of the Indian civil service has been highlighted by various eminent persons in India which is as follows:

Role of the Civil Services. Mr.R.K.Ramdhyani, writing on the role of civil servants, says,"The civil servant has thus the dual role of being the executive for the policy of a party and of being its interpreter; he is also in a good measure a maker of policy on its behalf. It is mainly in executing the policy of the party the conflict may arise, it can only be seondary in making new or subsidiary policy. A civil servant exercising his democratic right to vote, may have even cast his vote against the party which has come into power. He is now called upon to implement the policy of the party and very clearly he is duty bound to do so, as he is not a ruler by himself but a public servant. It is his duty, threfore, to try to understand the policy of the party which has the mandate of the people and to implement it in the most faithful way. If he did not do so he would not be true to the democratic form of Government which requires that for the time being the rule of the majority has to be accepted by the minority."[1] The Prime Minister, Shri Jawaharal Nehru, reminded his audience consisting of civil servants at Kurnool on December 9, 1995 the exact purpose of the services. "The services", he explained, "as their name implies are supposed to serve, obviously. Serve whom ?-society, the people, the country. Why I say this, because the test always has to be how far the services, whether as a whole or any individual member of them, are serving the larger cause that society has, that the nation has."[2] Therefore the civil servant should possess initiative, spirit of selfless service, political neutrality, habit of obedience and discipline. He must be loyal and efficient.

Mr.Morarji Desai on the role of the Civil Service, the Administrators to be the servants and not master of the people. On February 26, 1978, speaking to a group of about 80 Indian Administrative Service probationers, Mr.Morarji Desai said, "the administrators should not depend on hearsay and not accept anything without proof. *Administrators in a democartic country like India should learn to be servants of the people and not behave as they were masters.* They should be fair, fearless and act according to what they thought was proper. They should also see to it that work before them was disposed of quickly.

PUBLIC SERVICE COMMISSION

The Union Public Service Commission, constituted under Article 315 (1) of the Constitution of India, is an independent authority. Its Chairman and all other members are appointed by the President.

1. *Hindustsan Times* ,New Delhi, May 10, 1957.
2. Published in the *Indian Journal of Public Administration*, October-December 1955, p. 289.

The Constitution provides that nearly one-half of the members must be men having served at least for 10 years either under the Government of India or the Government of a State.

According to Article 316, Chairman and other members of a State Public Service Commission are appointed by the Governor of the State. Two or more States are constitutionally allowed to have joint State Public Service Commission, of course, with the approval of the Parliament. The personal of a Joint Public Service Commission are appointed by the President. The strength of State Public Service Commission varies from State to State.

Condition of Service. According to Article316 (2) a member of a Public Service Commission shall hold office for a term of six years from the date on which he enters upon his office or until he attains, in the case of the Union Commission, the age of sixty-five years and in the case of a State Commission or a Joint Commission, the age of sixty-two years (according to 41st amendment), *whichever is earlier*:

Provided that—

(*a*) a member of a Public Service Commission may by writing under his hand addressed, in a case of the Union Commission or a Joint Commission, to the President, and in the case of a State Commission to the Governor of a State, resign his office;

(*b*) a member of a Public Service Commission may be removed from his office in the manner provided in clause (1) or clause (3) of Article 317.

Besides that Article 316 (3) provides that a person who holds office as a member of a Public Service Commission shall, on the expiration of his term of office, be ineligible for reappointment to that office.

Removal and Suspension of a member of Public Service Commission. Subject to the provisions of Clause (3) the Chairman or any other member of a Public Service Commission shall only be removed from his office by order of the President on the ground of misbehavior after the Supreme Court, on reference being made to it by the President, has on inquiry held in accordance with the procedure prescribed in that behalf under Article 145, reported that the Chairman or such other member, as the case may be, ought on any such ground to be removed.

According to Article 317 (2) the President, in the case of the Union Commission or a Joint Commission, and the Governor in the case of State Commission, may suspend from office the Chairman or any other member of the Commission in respect of whom a reference has been made to the Supreme Court under Clause 1 of Article 317 until the President has passed orders on receipt of the report of the Supreme Court on such reference.

According to Article 317 (3), not withstanding anything in Clause (1) of Article 317 the President may by order remove from office the Chairman or any other member of a Public Service Commission if the Chairman or such other member as the case may be

(*a*) is adjudged an insolvent; or

(*b*) engages during his term of office in any paid employment outside the duties of his office; or

(*c*) is, in the opinion of the President, unfit to continue in office by reason of infirmity of mind or body.

According to Article 317 (4) if the Chairman or any other member of Public Service Commission is or becomes in any way concerned or interested in any contract or agreement made on or on behalf of the Government of India or the Government of a State or participates in any way in the profit thereof or in any benefit or emolument arising there from otherwise than as a member and in common with the other members of an incorporated company, he shall, for the purposes of Clause (1), be deemed to be guilty of misbehavior.

Power to make regulations as to the conditions of service of members and staff of the Commission. Article 318 provides that in the case of the Union Commission or a Joint Commission, the President and in the case of a State Commission, the Governor of the State may by regulations—

(*a*) determine the number of members of the Commission and their conditions of service; and

(*b*) make provision with respect to the number of members of staff of the Commission and their conditions of service;

Provided that the conditions of service of a member of a Public Service Commission shall not be varied to his disadvantage after his appointment.

Functions of Public Service Commissions. Article 320 of the Indian Constitution prescribes the functions of the Public Service Commissions. According to Clause 1 of Article320, it shall be the duty of the Union and the State Public Commissions to conduct examinations for appointments to services of the Union and the services of the State respectively. Clause 2 of Article 320 provides it shall be the duty of the Union Service Commission if requested by any two or more states so to do, to assist these states in framing and operating schemes of joint requirement for any services for which candidates special qualifications are required.

Clause 3 of Article 320 provides, "The Union Public Service Commission or the State Public Service Commission as the case may be, shall be consulted—

(1) on all matters relating to methods of recruitment to civil services and for civil posts.;

(2) on the principles to be followed in making appointments to civil services and posts and in making promotions and transfers from one service and to another and on the suitability of candidates for such appointments, promotions or transfers;

(3) on all disciplinary matters affecting a person serving under the Government of India or the Government of a State in a civil capacity, including memorials or petitions relating to such matters;

(4) on any claim by or in respect of a person who is serving or has served under the Government of India or the Government of a State or under the Crown in India or under the Government of an Indian State, in a civil capacity, that any costs incurred by him in defending legal proceeding instituted against him in respect of acts done or purporting to be done in the execution of his duty should be paid out of the Consolidated Fund of India or, as the case may be, out of Consolidated Fund of the State;

(5) on any claim for the award of a pension in respect of injuries sustained by a person while serving under the Government of India or the Government of a State or under the Crown in India or under the Government of an Indian State, in a civil capacity, and any question as to the amount of any such award.

It shall be the duty of a Public Service Commission to advise on any matter so referred to them and on any other matter which the President or, as the case may be, the Governor of State, may refer to them :

Provided that the President as respect the all-India services and also as a respect to other services and posts in connection with the affairs of the Union and the Governor as respect other services and posts in connection with the affairs of a State, may make regulations specifying the matters in which either generally or in any particular circumstances, it shall not be necessary for a Public Service to be consulted.

Matters in which the Public Service Commission need not be consulted. Under Article 320 (e) the President and Governor have been authorised to make regulations in which the Union or State Public Service Commission needs to be consulted.

The President made in 1958 the Union Public Service Commission (Exemption from Consultation) Regulations. These regulations provide that it shall not be necessary to consult the Union Public

Service Commission in regard to any of the matters mentioned in Article 320 in the case of the following services and posts :

(1) Posts in respect of which the authority to appoint is specially conferred on the President by the Constitution.

(2) Posts of Chairmen or members of any Board, Tribunal, Commission, Committee or other similar authority created by or under the provisions of a statute.

(3) Posts of Chairmen or members of any Board, Tribunal, Commission, Committee or other similar body appointed by or under the authority of a resolution of either House of Parliament or by a resolution of Government for the purpose conducting any investigation or enquiry into or advising Government on specified matters.

(4) Posts of Head of Diplomatic, Consular and other similar Indian Mission in countries abroad (*e.g.*, Ambassadors, High Commissioners, Ministers, Commissioners, Consulate-Genreal, Representatives Agents).

(5) Posts on the Personal staff attached to holders of posts mentioned in items 1 to 4 above.

(6) Posts in the Secretariat of the Lok Sabha and Rajya Sabha.

(7) All technician and administrative posts in or under the Atomic Energy Commission.

(8) Judicial Commissioners and Additional Commissioners, District Judges and Additional District Judges in Union Territories.

(9) Subordinate Judges and Munsiffs in the former Union Territories of Manipur, Himachal Pradesh.

(10) All class III and class IV services and posts, save as otherwise expressly provided in the relevant rules or orders governing recruitment thereto.

(11) Any service or post concerned with the administration of the North-East Frontier Agency (now Arunachal Pradesh).

It is also provided that it shall not be necessary to consult the Commission in regard to the election for appointment to a post included in All-India Service of any officer who is already a member of an All-India Service, to a post included in the Central Service, Class I, of any other officer in the Armed Forces of the Union or any officer who is already a member of an All-India Service or Central Service Calss I, to a Central Service Class II, or to a post included in a Central Service Class II, of any officer who is already a member of a Central Service Class II, or a Central Service Class III, or of any officer in the Armed Forces of the Union and to a tenure post included in a Central Service Class I, or Central Service Class II, or an officer of a State Service.

It has also been provided in the regulations that is shall not be necessary to consult the Commission on regard to the selection for a temporary or officiating appointment to a post ,if the person appointed is not likely to hold the post for a period of more than one year and it is necessary, in the public interest, to make the appointment immediately and reference to the Commissions will cause undue delay. However, such an appointment shall be reported to the Commission as soon as it is made. If the appointment continues beyond a period of six months, a fresh estimate as to the period for which the person appointed is likely to hold the post, shall be made and reported to the Commission. If the estimate indicates that the person appointed is likely to hold the post for a period of more than one year from the date of appointment, the Commission shall immediately be consulted in regard to the filling of the post :

According to the Regulations laid down by President, it shall not be necessary to consult the Commission in regard to the making of any order in any disciplinary case other than an original order by the President, imposing the penalty or censure, withholding of increments or promotion, recovery from pay of the whole or part of any pecuniary loss caused to the Government by negligence or breach of orders, reduction to a lower service, grade or post or to a lower time-scale, or to a lower stage in time-scale, compulsory retirement and dismissal from service. It shall not be necessary to consult the Commission in regard to the making of any order other than an order by the President on an appeal against an order imposing any of the above mentioned penalties made by a subordinate authority or an order by the President over-ruling or modifying after consideration of any petition or memorial or other wise, an order imposing any of the above-mentioned penalties made by the President or by a subordinate authority. It shall not be necessary to consult the Commission in regard to any disciplinary matter affecting a person belonging to a Defence Service Civilian). It shall not be necessary to consult the Commission in regard to any order made under the Central Civil Service (Safeguarding of National Security) Rules, 1953 of the Railway Service (Safeguarding of National Security) Rules, 1954.

Power to extend functions of Public Service Commissions. Article 321 provides, "An Act made by Parliament or , as the case may be, the Legislature of a State may provide for the exercise of additional functions by the Union Public Service Commission or the State Public Service Commission as respects the services of local authority or other body corporate constituted by law or of any public institution."

Utility of Public Service Commissions. Mr. S.P. Bapat remarks that "consultation with the Commission is not overlooked, that the advice of the Commission is as a rule accepted and that the Government are free in cases where they consider the matter of sufficient importance, to follow their own judgment provided they are prepared to justify their action before the Legislature." The Commissions have undoubtedly justified their existence. They have placed checks on the misuse of executive authority and thus curbed the evils of nepotism and corruption in regard to appointments. Their working has proved for certain that merit of the candidate is the first and fore most consideration. Anybody possessing the requisite qualification and merit now stands fair chance or being selected even for the superiormost services.

At present the salary of chairman of Union Public Service Commission is ₹ 90,000 per month and the salary of member of Union Public Service Commission is 80,000 per month. The salary of Sate Public Service Commission's chairman is 80,000 per month and the salary of members of State Public Service Commission is 70,000 per month.

EXERCISES

Long Answer Type Questions :

1. What is the importance of Public Services in India ? Discuss their comparison with the British Civil Services.
2. Discuss All India Services and State Services in India.
3. What is Bureaucracy ? Discuss its Significant role in implementing the policies of the Government.
4. What do you know about Union Public Service Commission? Discuss its functions also.

Short Answer Type Questions :

1. What was the condition of Civil Services during British Rule ?
2. Discuss the classification of Indian Civil Services after Independence.
3. What is difference between British Bureaucracy and Indian Bureaucracy ?
4. What are the functions of Union Public Service Commission ?

Objective Type Questions :

Choose the correct answer

1. What was the backbone of the administration during British Rule ?
   (*a*) Indian Civil Services (*b*) Indian Administrative Services
   (*c*) Indian Foreign Services (*d*) None of the above.
2. What was the name of 'Indian Civil Services' after independence ?
   (*a*) Indian Government Services (*b*) Indian Administrative Services
   (*c*) Indian Foreign Services (*d*) None of the above
3. At which place The National Academy of Administration is situated ?
   (*a*) Dehradoon (*b*) Agra
   (*c*) Mussoorie (*d*) Kolkata
4. At which place The Central Police Training College is situated ?
   (*a*) Agra (*b*) Delhi
   (*c*) Gwalior (*d*) Abu
5. The administrative machinery of the government is run by
   (*a*) Elected representatives (*b*) Ministers
   (*c*) Civil servants (*d*) People of India
6. An independent constitutional agency to recruit civil servants is known as :
   (*a*) Staff Selection Board (*b*) Election Commission
   (*c*) Planning Commission (*d*) Public Service Commission
7. An independent agency for recruitment of civil servants is required because :
   (*a*) it maintains the merit system and neutrality in civil services.
   (*b*) it protects the rights of the people.
   (*c*) it serves the aspiration of the Ministers.
   (*d*) it is an appointing authority of the civil servants.
8. Public Service Commission is a
   (*a*) constitutional body
   (*b*) statutory body
   (*c*) body set up by an executive decision
   (*d*) none of these
9. Public Service Commission works as
   (*a*) a recruiting agency
   (*b*) an appointing authority
   (*c*) an advisory body on all government appointments
   (*d*) none of these
10. The chairman and the members of the UPSC can be removed from their post by the
    (*a*) Council of Ministers (*b*) President
    (*c*) Prime Minister (*d*) Supreme Court

11. It is the duty of the President of India to place the annual report of UPSC before :
    (*a*) Supreme Court of India
    (*b*) Parliament
    (*c*) Comptroller and Auditor-General of India
    (*d*) Council of Ministers
12. Under Article 321 of the Indian Constitution additional functions to the Union Public Service Commission can be assigned by the:
    (*a*) President (*b*) Prime Minister
    (*c*) Parliament (*d*) Supreme Court
13. The age limit up to which a member of state PSC may hold his post is :
    (*a*) 60 years (*b*) 62 years
    (*c*) 63 years (*d*) 64 years.
14. The tenure of a member of SPSC is:
    (*a*) 4 years (*b*) 5 years
    (*c*) 6 years (*d*) 7 years
15. The chairman of the Joint Public Service Commission is appointed by the :
    (*a*) President (*b*) Governor
    (*c*) Prime Minister (*d*) Supreme Court

ANSWERS

1. (*a*)	**2.** (*b*)	**3.** (*c*)	**4.** (*d*)	**5.** (*c*)	**6.** (*d*)	**7.** (*a*)	**8.** (*a*)
9. (*a*)	**10.** (*a*)	**11.** (*b*)	**12.** (*b*)	**13.** (*c*)	**14.** (*b*)	**15.** (*c*)	

23

CHAPTER

Planning Commission and Five-Year Plans

A Planning Commission was set up in March 1950, under the chairmanship of Prime Minister Pt. Jawaharlal Nehru, to prepare a Plan for the most effective and balanced utilisation of the country's resources.

OBJECTIVES OF PLANNING

The central objective of planning was defined as initiating "a process of development which will raise living standards and open out to the people new opportunities for a richer and more varied life." Economic planning has to be viewed as "an integral part of faculties and the building up of an institutional framework adequate to the needs and aspirations of the people."

Another objective is to ensure that the economy can, after a period of ten years or so, reduce substantially dependence on assistance from abroad. This aslo postulates a steady and sizable increase in exports through appropriate policies and measures.

FUNCTIONS OF THE PLANNING COMMISSION

The Planning Commission was to discharge the following functions according to its terms of reference :

(1) To assess the material, capital and human rèsources of the country, including the technical personnel and to investigate the possibilities of augmenting such of these resource as are found to be deficient in relation to the nation's requirements.

(2) To formulate a Plan for the most effective and balanced utilisation of the country's resources.

(3) To define the stages of the Plan and propose the allocation of resources on the determination of priorities.

(4) To indicate the factors which are tending to retard economic development and to determine the conditions which in view of the current social and political situation should be established for the success of the Plan.

(5) To suggest machinery for securing the successful implementation of each of the Plan.

(6) To appraise from time to time the programme achieved in the execution of each stage of the Plan and to recommend the adjustments of policy and measures that such appraisal might show to be necessary.

(7) To make interim or ancillary recommendations for the discharge of the duties assigned to it; or an examination of specific problems referred to it for advice by the Central or State Governments.

ORGANISATION OF THE PLANNING COMMISSION

There is no formal order of Government of India prescribing either the number or qualifications essential for the members of the Planning Commission. The Government of India pays due regard to the academic distinctions and brilliant career of a person while appointing him as a member of the Planning Commission. They are not appointed for fixed term. The number of members of the Planning Commission is not fixed and changes from time to time. It consists of Chairman, Deputy Chairman, and a few eminent educationists, scientists, economists, experts in other affairs. The Prime Minister is the Chairman and Planning Minister is the Deputy Chairman. The Planning Minister is naturally its very active member. Besides that Home Minister, Defence Minister, Finance Minister, and some top economists are also its members. The following are generally the portfolios which are distributed amongst the members:

(1) General Planning and Social Services.

(2) Finance.

(3) Industries.

(4) Education and Health.

(5) International Trade and Development.

(6) Irrigation and Power.

(7) Social Labour.

(8) Agriculture.

(9) Administration and Transport.

(10) Natural Resources.

The Planning Commission is a collective body. It is only an advisory body. This means that its recommendations are not binding. However, the Government tries its best to give concrete shape to most of its recommendations. At the State level also there is a Planning Commission and co-ordination is achieved through National Development Council. The Planning Commission tries to enlist public co-operation for the Plan. Besides that it directs and supervises the Community Projects also. For all the activities of the Planning Commission, the Minister of Planning is responsible to the Parliament.

The Planning Commission has got one Secretariat which at present consists of one Secretary, six Joint Secretaries, three Deputy Secretaries, five Under-Secretaries, three Officers on Special Duty and sixteen Section Officers. The number of these officers is not fixed and it increases or decreases according to the requirements of the Government. Besides that there is one organisation named the Programme Evaluation Organisation working along with the Planning Commission.

There are three main parts of the Planning Commission —

(*i*) Programme Adviser.

(*ii*) General Secretariat.

(*iii*) Technical Divisions.

Now we deal with the functions of each :

(i) *Programme Adviser.* The possess the status of Additional Secretaries to the Government. They pay great attention to the finances, public co-operation and administration, connected with the implementation of the Plan and advise the Planning Commission accordingly. They assist the Planning Commission regarding the field study, progress and implementation of the various schemes and projects of the Plan.

(ii) *General Secretariat.* It consists of the following branches : Administration Branches (General Branch, Administration Branch, O. & M. Section and Accounts Branch); (*b*) General Co-ordination Branch; (*c*) Plan Co-ordination Branch; (*d*) Information and Publicity Branch (headed by the Director of Information).

(iii) *Technical Divisions.* The Technical Divisions study every aspect of the whole Plan detail and decide which schemes and projects should be incorporated in Plan. They are also responsible for research regarding various technical matters of the Plan. Besides that these Divisions are also responsible for the pursuance and completion of various projects and schemes of the Plan and preparation of the reports about the progress of the Plan.

Technical Divisions comprise of the following Divisions and Sections:

1. Economic, Finance and Resources Division.
2. Education Division.
3. Food and Agriculture Division.
4. Health Division.
5. Housing Division.
6. Industry and Mineral Division (including public enterprises unit).
7. Irrigation and Power Division (Natural Resources).
8. Labour Reforms Division.
9. Programmes Administration Division.
10. Perspective Planning Division.
11. Public Co-operation Division.
12. Resources and Scientific Research Division.
13. Statistics and Survey Division.
14. Social Welfare Division.
15. Transport and Communications Division.
16. Village and Small Industries Division.
17. Management and Development Administration Division.

Now a brief description of work of each Division and Section is given, so as to give some idea of the Planning Commission's working :

1. *Economic, Finance and Resources Division.* This division is concerned with the overall aspects of Planning and assessment of resources. So far as overall aspects of Planning are concerned, the Division scrutinises the size, objectives, priorities and broad economic policy of each Plan. The Division also tries to assess all the available resources (domestic as well as foreign) for the financing of the Plan. When the Plan comes into operation, then it looks to the progress of the Plan periodically. This division also examines the various suggestions for the improvement of the Plan received from different sources.

2. *Education Division.* It deals with the physical, general, technical rural and women's education and advises the Planning Commission accordingly. Besides that it is concerned with the National Cadet Corps, Social Service Camps, Student and Youth Camps, Development of Hindi and other regional languages, Central Assistance to State for educational purpose, establishment of mere libraries, scholarships, cultural activities National Academies, archaeology, museums and national theatres, school feeding and school health programmes.
3. *Food and Agricultural Division.* This Division of the Planning Commission is concerned with increasing production, Grow More Food Schemes, Community Development and Extension Service. While formulating a Plan, this Division also deals with such matters as agricultural labour,agricultural marketing, soil conservation, development of warehouses, fisheries, and forests, animal husbandry and dairying, co-operation and agricultural credit. It also organises special studies on such important topics as the methods of accelerating agricultural production.
4. *Health Division.* This Division undertakes all work connected with the health. It collects various satistical datas relating to health, so as to be able to guide the Planning Commission and the Government in this direction properly. It carefully examined the report and advice of the various consultative bodies and panels regarding health.
5. *Housing Division.* This Division is responsible for house, town and country planning. It keeps intimate contact with the Ministers of Works, Housing and Supply, Community Development, Home Affairs Labour etc.
6. *Industrial and Mineral Division.* It studies various schemes for the development of heavy and cottage industries and utilisation of minerals. It maintains intimate contact with the Ministries of Commerce, Industry, Steel, Mines, Fuel and other technical organisations.
7. *Irrigation and Power Division (Natural Resources Division).* This Division studies the various methods of improving irrigation facilities and creating more electricity in the country. It also considers the various schemes of flood control. Various multipurpose projects are also closely studied by it and after careful deliberation it gives its own suggestions. It remains in touch with many technical experts and some specialised agencies.
8. *Labour and Employment Division.* All problems relating to labour and employment are closely studied by this Division. It gives its various useful suggestions for harmonising labour-capital relations, resolving various conflicts and improving conditions of labour and removing unemployment. This Division remains in constant touch with the Ministry of Labour and Employment for this purpose.
9. *Land Reforms Division.* This Division makes a specialised study of the problems concerning the tenure, management, distribution and cultivation of land. As the State Governments are launching land reforms with a view to ameliorate the conditions of the peasants, therefore, they submit those proposals to the Division for opinion before enforcement. This Division carefully examines those proposals and gives its advice accordingly.When the States implement these proposals and difficulties arise,then this Division after carefully suggests various steps to make necessary adjustments. For this purpose it maintains close contact with the Central Committee of Land Reforms and assists it in every way. It also keeps a contact with the Ministry of Food and Agriculture for this purpose.
10. *Programmes of Administration Division.* This Division co-ordinates the Plans of the Centre and States. It prepares periodical reports about the progress of the Plan.
11. *Perspective Planning Division.* This Division studies the prospects of long-term development of agriculture, power resources, increases in employment and basic industries in the context of rapid industrialization.

12. *Public Co-operation Division.* This Division deliberates over the methods how to get best co-operation of the people in implementing the plans. Its proposals are given concrete shape by the Central and State Government.

13. *Resources and Scientific Research Division.* This Division undertakes scientific and industrial research for the development purposes. It keeps itself informed of all the researches in this fields taking place in India and abroad. This section also keeps a contact with various scientific centres, laboratories, universities or other organisations doing research in these fields.

14. *Statistics and Surveys Division.* This Division prepares periodical report about the progress of the Plan. It collects the essential data about the progress and implementation of the Plans through States' Statistical Bureaus and Centre's Statistical agencies. Therefore, it provides all the statistics about the Plan to the Planning Commission.

15. *Social Welfare Section.* This section studies the various measures which should be adopted in the Plan and by the Government for the benefit of the Harijans, backward classes and tribes. Therefore, it remains in constant touch with the Central Social Welfare Board, States' Social Welfare Department, Ministries of Community Development, Home Affairs and Education and a host of other agencies spread throughout the length and breadth of the country for the welfare of the backward classes and tribes.

16. *Transport and Communication Division.* This Division of the Planning Commission makes a special study of the porblems of transport and communication and suggests measures for their development to the Planning Commission and the Government.

17. *Village and Small Industries Division.* This section of the Planning Commission studies carefully the problems facing small-scale and village industries (Coir Industries, Village Industries, Silk and Sericulture,Normal Khadi and Ambar Khadi, Small-scale Industries including Industrial Estates, Handloom and Powerloom and suggests measures for their development.

18. *Management and Development Administration Division.* It looks to the problems of management and Development of administration and gives its opinion to the Government.

ADVISORY BODIES TO THE PLANNING COMMISSION

Following Advisory Bodies are functioning in the Planning Commission :

(*i*) National Development Council.

(*ii*) Committee on Plan Projects.

(*iii*) Advisory Committee on Irrigation and Power Projects.

(*iv*) Co-ordination Committee for Public Co-operation.

Now a brief description of each of the above bodies is given :

(*i*) *National Development Council of India.* The National Development Council was created by the Government of India vide their Resolution dated 6th August, 1952. The resolution defines its function as follows :

"To strengthen and mobilise the efforts and resources of the nation in support of the Plans; to promote common economic policies in all vital spheres; and to ensure the balanced and rapid development of all parts of the country; on the recommendation of the Planning Commission, the Government of India have decided to set up a National Development Council."

Functions of the National Development Council. The functions of the National Development Council are as follows :

(1) To review the working of the National Plan from time to time;

(2) To consider important questions of social and economic policy affecting national development;

(3) To recommend measures for the achievement of the aims and targets, set out in National Plan. For that purpose it tries to enlist the best co-operation of the people and improve the efficiency of the administration. It sees that special attention is paid to the fullest development of backward regions and communities. With the maximum co-operation of the people and voluntary agencies, it tries its best to build up sources for national development.

Composition of the National Development Council. Paragraph 3, which defines the composition of the National Development Council, runs as follows :

"The National Development Council, which will make its recommendations to the Central and State Governments, will be composed of the Prime Minister of India, the Chief Minister of all States and Members of the Planning Commission." The Prime Minister of India is its Chairman and the Secretary of the Planning Commission act as its Secretary. Besides that those Union Ministers whose subjects figure for discussion in the National Council are also invited. The Minister-in-charge of various subjects prepare papers for the discussion of the Council. The Planning Commission also sometimes prepares the papers for the discussion in the Council in consultation with various Ministers.

Role of the National Development Council. The National Development Council is playing a vital role in economy of our country. Though it is an advisory body to advise the Centre as well as the States, yet its decisions bear the stamp of certainty and carry conviction to the people, since Prime Minister presides over its meetings and all the members of the Planning Commission and the Chief Ministers of States are present. It provides a good forum to the Chief Ministers to discuss the Plan in all its aspects, and finalise it. The Central Government in this way ensures the co-operation of the States before getting it approved by the Parliament. After that the approval of the Parliament also comes rather sooner than later. When the time of the implementation of Plan comes, the States extend their full support to the Centre. In this way, with the hearty co-operation of all, it becomes easier for the Centre to implement it and achieve the targets. When the Plan is approved by the National Development Council, and the Parliament, it becomes a national Plan and the heartiest co-operation of the péople is always forthcoming.

(ii) Committee on Plan Projects. The Committee on Plan Projects was set up in September 1956. The Home Minister is its Chairman and Finance Minister and Planning Minister are its members. Besides that the Prime Minister, in the capacity of the Chairman of the National Development Council, nominates two Chief Ministers as members of the Committee.The Central Ministers concerned with the Projects are co-opted members.

After giving the organisation of the Committee, the functions of the committee are also given :

The Committee investigates and inspects various projects with the help of eminent persons, specialists and technical experts. Besides that it considers various methods to impart efficiency to various projects and avoid waste. It is also responsible for the execution and audit of various projects. It carries out any other work assigned to it by the National Development Council.

(iii) Advisory Committee on Irrigation and Power Projects. The organisation of the Committee is as follows :

Its Chairman is the State Minister for planning and one representative each is taken in this Committee from the Ministries of Finance, Irrigation and power, Central Water and Power Commission, Central Board of Irrigation and Power.

The main function of the Committee is to scrutinise thoroughly the various schemes prepared by the Central or State Government regarding Power and Irrigation. It examines whether the estimates are complete and technically accurate or not. Besides that it also verifies whether benefits expected and financial forecasts are based on hard facts or not.

(iv) *Co-ordination Committee for Public Co-operation.* This Committee was set up in 1952 with a view to secure maximum co-operation of the people for achieving the targets of the Five-Year Plans. Therefore, it gives various suggestions to the Planning Commission for this purpose. The Chairman and Deputy Chairman of the Planning Commission are also its Chairman and Deputy Chairman respectively. Besides that it consists of many eminent persons from all walks of life and leaders of various groups. With the help of these persons, it tries to achieve maximum co-operation of the people in the formulation and implementation of the Plans.

Other Consultative Committees

Besides the above-mentioned Committee, there are also some other Committees whose role is also purely advisory. For example, there is an *Informal Consultative committee of Members of Parliament and a Research Programmes Committee.* The Government or the Planning Commission consults this Committee of the Parliament whenever there is a need to do so. Research Programmes Committee consists of the Deputy Chairman to the Planning Commission who is also the Chairman of this committee and certain scientists. Its main function is to undertake or encourage research on economic, social, administrative and political aspects of development.

Panel. The Planning Commission has instituted a number of Panels to secure the opinions of experts. For example, there are panels of Economists, Scientists and Educationists. There are also panels for Land Reforms, Housing, Health and Regional Planning. These panels give very valuable advice on different matters.

EVALUATION OF PLANNING COMMISSION

There has been a severe criticism of the Planning Commission. Mr.D.R. Gadgil and C. Rajgopalachari strongly asserted that Planning Commission had failed and continued to fail since it had lost advisory character and became an official body and policy-making agency as the Prime Minister was its Chairman and some Cabinet Ministers were associated with it. They felt that the Prime Minister should no longer be its Chairman, Ministers should not be its members and it should consist of some specialists and experts who should give their independent opinion or judgment on every issue. It is felt that in the presence of the Prime Minister, specialists and technical experts cannot express themselves freely. Some technical expert or an eminent economist should preside over its meetings. Similarly, Estimates Committee of the Parliament (1957-58) which examined the working of the Planning Commission, stated that "there is a feeling that the Planning Commission is not only advisory body but it was an additional authority to reckon with as it decided every programme of work and the decisions were to be carried out by all." It has, therefore, been suggested that in order to give it an independent advisory status, Cabinet Ministers, who are incharge of functional Ministries should not be members of the Planning Commission. Secondly, it has been said that the Planning Commission should have a separate Secretary and the Cabinet Secretary should not hold that office. Thirdly, it has also been said that here is too much centralisation in the planning and corresponding Planning Commission should be established at State-level. Economy should be decentralised and planning should start from below. Fourthly, it has been said that the functions of the Planning Commission and the Ministries are overlapping. On the other hand, there are some enthusiastic supporters of the present structure of the Planning Commission who decry the above criticism and call it ill-conceived.

In spite of all this criticism let us look to the whole thing in a sober way and not be led away by mere criticism. It is better to study the views of some foreigners like Mr.John Lewis and Mr.A.H. Hansen who have studied the whole thing in a dispassionate way.Mr. John P. Lewis has expressed his views in his book *The Quiet Crisis in India.* He says that "Planning must be in the last resort a political process and, therefore, the Planning Commission should be charged with performing a number of quasi-political functions also. It has to play an overall advisory role in its relations with Central Ministers and State Governments." Prof. Lewis is not against this thing that Prime Minister should be the Chairman of the Planning Commission. Similarly, Mr. A.H. Hansen hails "the constitutional set-up of the Planning Commission, criticises the Estimates Committee of 1957-58 for its suggestion to consider whether it is necessary for the Prime Minister and Cabinet Ministers to be its members and he even recommends for other under-developed countries to follow India's model in this respect." After examining the various arguments we feel that if the Prime Minister does not preside over the meetings of the Planning Commission and the Ministers are not associated with it, then the Planning will not be real and effective. After all the Prime Minister and the other Ministers have to run the Government and Planning is ultimately their responsibility. If they are not intimately associated with the Planning Commission, then they may accept or may not accept any suggestion of the Planning Commission. In this way the recommendations of the Planning Commission will not be weighty, but when the Prime Minister, himself, is present and other Ministers are associated with it, then there is a good exchange of views between the Ministers and specialists (economists and experts). In this way something which is good and final emerges. If the Prime Minister and other Minsters are not members of the Planning Commission, then the Planning Commission will plan in a vacuum because sometimes the specialists and experts are not quite aware of the needs of the peasants, labourers and common, men, since they do not come in touch with them. Therefore, in an under-developed country like India, it is better to have a Planning Commission just as we have at present in order to give economic planning a maximum political impetus for achieving success. When we admit that the Prime Minister should be associated with it, naturally he should be its Chairman. In the presence of Prime Minister, if anybody else presides, then naturally it does not look nice. The argument that in the presence of the Prime Minister specialists, economists and technical experts cannot express their views freely is not tenable. They have got full freedom to express their views and their independent views are not only tolerated but they are most welcomed, heeded and acted upon. The Ministers are not experts and they have to depend upon the views of the experts. After all there is no rivalry between the two sides and the entire work is carried on in a harmonious way.

Secondly, regarding the criticism that the Cabinet Secretary should not be a secretary of the Planning Commission, we can say that there is some force in it. Though the Cabinet Secretary is very influential, yet he is overburdened with work, so it will be better if the Planning Commission has got an independent whole-time Secretary.

Thirdly, it is said that there should be decentralisation of the Planning Commission and of Indian economy. States should have separate Planning Commission like China and planning should start from below. We do not agree with this view. The reason being that there is already a federal structure in our country, so naturally there is a division of powers and decentralised economy. Besides that the Planning Commission consults the State necessarily while formulating a plan. The States have got Planning Departments which consult the Deputy Commissioners in regard to the Plan because the Deputy Commissioner or District Officers or Collectors are also the Chief Development Officers of the Districts, and they preside over the Development Committees of the District. The District Development Committee consists of various Development Offices of the District. The Block Development Officers consult the Panchayats, while formulating a plan for the development of the block. The District Development Officer integrates the development plan of all the blocks of his District. After that he submits it to the Planning Department of the State which integrates the development plan of all the Districts of the State. So in this way every Planning Department of the State submits its development plan to the Planning Commission which in turn co-ordinates or reshapes all the development plans of the States in the light of various suggestions received from the States.

Fourthly, it has been said that the functions of the Planning Commission and Ministers are overlapping. Though we admit that if there is some duplication that must be avoided but at same time it is also ture that in regard to those subjects which seem common between the two, the Planning Commission makes a specialised study while the Ministers run the administration of those subjects. The Planning Commission is an advisory body and not the administrative department of the Government. Therefore, the functions are quite separate.

Achievements of the Planning Commission. Every impartial observer will admit that the Planning Commission has rendered a most commendable service to the nation. It has formulated Ten 'Five-Year Plans' uptill now. The results of all these Plans are most encouraging. Foundations of a sound and progressive economy have been laid. Production and national income are constantly rising, poverty and illiteracy are continuously diminishing and India is marching ahead with full speed. The Planning Commission has rendered a yeoman service by providing the Governrment with expert technical advice on many matters and saving the time and energy of the Government. So in the ultimate analysis we can say that it has served the nation is every way and if there is any shortcoming in its organisation or deficiency in work, that must be removed.

OUTLAY AND INVESTMENT IN ALL THE SIX PLANS

The public sector outlay as planned in the First, Second and Third Plans was Rs. 2, 378 crore, Rs. 4,600 crore, and Rs. 7,500 crore while the actual expenditure was Rs. 1, 960 crore,Rs. 4, 672 crore and Rs. 8,577 crore respectively. The investment by the private sector in the First, Second and Third Plans was Rs. 1,800 crores, Rs.3,100 crores and Rs. 4,190 crores respectively. The total public sector outlay during the three Annual Plans was Rs. 6,665 crores. The Fourth Plan outlay envisaged originally was Rs. 24,822 crore, consisting of the public sector outlay of Rs. 15,902 crores. The actual public sector expenditure during the Fourth Plan was estimated at Rs. 15,779 crores. The Fifth Plan envisaged public sector outaly of Rs. 39,322 crores and expected private investment was Rs. 27,049 crore. The actual expenditure of the public sector during the Fifth Plan was 39, 426 crores. With recording of investment priorities, the Plan for 1979-80 envisaged a public sector outlay of Rs. 12,601 crore against which the actual expenditure was Rs. 12,176 crores. The 1980-81 Plan was fixed at Rs. 15,109 crores against which the actual expenditure is estimated at Rs.15,023 crores. The Annual Plan for 1981-82 has a public sector outlay of Rs. 17,417 crores against which, the actual expenditure is estimated at Rs. 18,373 crores. For 1982-83, public sector plan outlay of Rs. 20,934 crores has been fixed.

Achievements of all the Plans

Growth rate in national income. During the First Plan, owing largely to increase in agricultural production the national income went up by 18 per cent as against the target of 12 per cent. The increase in the Second Plan was 20 per cent as against the target of 25 per cent. In the Third Plan, national income (revised series) at 1960-61 prices rose by 20 per cent in the first four years but declined by 5.7 per cent in the last year. During the three Annual Plans (1966-67 to 1968-69) there was modest increase in the national income. In the initial years of the Fourth Plan, the growth rate in national income and per capita income was quite satisfactory. In the latter part of the Plan, there was slackening in the growth rate. As against the projected overall rate of 5.7 per cent per annum during the Fourth Plan, the realised rate of growth is estimated at 3.3 per cent during 1969-74. The growth rate in the national income achieved during the Fifth Plan is estimated at 5.2 per cent as against the target of 4.4 per cent. The growth rate in national income at 1970-71 prices was 8.1 per cent in 1980-81 and 5 per cent in 1981-82.

Agricultural Production. The index of agricultural production with triennium ending 1969-70 as base rose from 71.9 at the end of the First Plan to 86.7 at the end of the Second Plan. During the Third Plan, the performance of agriculture was not quite satisfactory. Widespread droughts in 1965-67 slowed down the rate of growth and led to increased imports of food grains and other items. The index of agricultural production receded to 80.8 in 1965-66 and 80.7 in 1966-67. Subsequent years, however, recorded substantial improvements, and the index number reached 98.9 in 1967-68, further increasing steadily to 112.4 in 1973-74. The next year, 1974-75 was again a bad one for agriculture when the index declined to 108.8. This was followed by considerable improvement in 1975-76 when the index reached 124.8. In 1976-77, the index registered a decline of 8.4 points and stood at 116.4 but again shot up to 132.7 in 1977-78 and 137.8 in 1978-79. The year 1979-80, again a bad year due to drought and flood in many states, witnessed a fall by 20.7 points and the index number of agricultural production stood at 117.1. The index stood at 134.9 in 1980-81. Agricultural production increased by 5.5 per cent during 1981-82. During 1982-83, kharif production was adversely affected due to monsoon which was inadequate in coverage and uneven in its timings with the result that overall agricultural production during 1982-83 is estimated to be around 12.5-12.8 crore tonnes compared to 13.3 crore tonnes in 1981-82 and 12.96 crore tonnes in 1980-81.

Increase in Net Irrigation Area. The net irrigation area increased from 2.08 crore hectares in 1950-51 to 2.27 crore hectares at the end of the First Plan, 2.46 crore hectares at the end of the Second Plan, 2.63 crore hectares at the end of the Third Plan and 2.90 crore hectares in 1968-69. By the end of the Fourth Plan, the net irrigated area was 3.25 crore hectares and by 1978-79 the figure is estimated at 3.66 crore hectares. The gross area under irrigation increased from 5.42 crore hectares in 1980-81 to 6.62 crore hectares in 1981-82.

Powers development during the Plans. Power development during the last three decades has been significant. Successive plans with large outlay on power development have added substantial generating capacity and a basic transmission and distribution system has been developed. The power systems have developed from the rudimentary stage of isolated generating stations to the stage of fairly well planned integrated systems in most of the states and emergence of regional and inter-regional grids. The total installed generating capacity which was only 2,300 mw in 1950 increased to over 31,184 mw by the end of March 1980 and in addition about 1,823 mw was commissioned during 1980-81. The additional capacity in 1981-82 was 2,175 mw. Under rural electrification programme, a total of 2.94 lakh villages had been electrified out of a total of 5.76 lakh villages by the end of March, 1982. The number of irrigation pump sets in operation by March 1981 was 43.30 lakh and by March 1982, another 3.2 lakh pump sets were added in the country. Extension and electrification of *bastees* for scheduled castes and scheduled tribes is being accorded increasing priority.

Rapid growth in Industrial Production. Large investment in the industrial and mineral sectors, particularly from the begining of the Second Plan, have brought about a significant transformation in the industrial scene. There was a rapid and almost continuous growth in industrial production during the first three Plan periods. Industrial production which increased at an average rate of 7 per cent in the first decade of planning (1950-51 to 1960-61) recorded an increase of around 9 per cent per annum during the next four years, *i.e.,* 1961-62 to 1964-65. The performance since then, however, has been uneven and substantially below the earlier achievements and projected expectations. The growth declined to 5.3 per cent in 1965-66, was almost stagnant in the subsequent two years witnessed a sprut to 7.4 per cent in 1969-70 and hovered around 3 to 4 per cent over the next five years. A significant improvement took place in 1976-77 when the index of industrial production showed a growth rate of around 9.5 per cent. In 1979-80, there was a decline in industrial growth to the extent of 1.4 per cent. There was, however, recovery in 1980-81 when the index recorded an increase of 4 per cent. In 1981-82 industrial production increased by 8.6 per cent.

Educational Growth. The educational system has recorded, over the years, a phenomenal growth. At the end of 1976-77 the number of educational institutions increased to 6.51 lakh from 2.31 lakh in 195051, the corresponding increase in enrolment was 2.73 crores to 9.97 crores. Enrolment at the elementary stage (class I to VIII) in 1979-80 was 10.85 crores. The gross enrolment rate in class I-V and VI-VIII in 1978-79 was 83.6 and 40.2 respectively. In the Sixth Plan, it was proposed to enrol additional 1.17 crore children in class IV and 63 lakhs in class VI-VIII. The enrolment in class I-V and VI-VIII in 1984-85 is expected to be 8.37 crores and 2.58 crores respectively, which would be 95 per cent and 50 per cent of the population in the corresponding age groups. In addition to the enrolment in full time formal schools, about 80 lakh children at the elementary stage would be enrolled in non-formal/part-time classes during the Sixth Plan.

Seventh Plan (1985-1990) (Planned Development)

Growth Rate. The Seventh Five-Year Plan (1985-1990) envisaged an aggregate outlay of Rs. 3,48,148 crores with a public sector outlay of Rs. 1,80,000 crores and private sector outlay of Rs.168,148 crores. It seeks to achieve an overall growth rate 5 per cent for the economy during the five years (1985-90), with the growth rate of agriculture fixed at 4 per cent and that of industry at 8 per cent. The plan envisaged a total investment of Rs. 3,22,366 crores. Ninety four per cent of the total investment would be financed from domestic fund with a "tremendous" effort at resource mobilization.

A significant change expected by the Planning Commission in the Seventh Plan was a fall in the share of agriculture from.37 per cent at present, to 25.5 per cent by the beginning of the next decade. In the same period the share of industry would go up from 24 per cent to 35.5 per cent.

Poverty ratio would decline. The poverty ratio is expected to decline from 36.9 per cent in 1984-85 to 25.8 per cent in 1989-90. The number of people below poverty line will come down from 272.2 million to 210.8 million. The Plan had been formulated as a part of the longer term strategy which sought virtually eliminate poverty, illiteracy and achieve near full employment by the year 2000 A.D.

Food Front. Continued self-sufficiency in food and expansion of national system of food security had been given high priority. Special efforts were launched to increase the production of oil seeds, pulses, vegetables and horticulture to meet the shortages. Special efforts were made to increase the production of rice in the eastern sector through effective utilisation of irrigation and other potentials.

Increasing the Production. While the aim of self-sufficiency in food was continued, special efforts were launched to increase the production of oilseeds, pulses, vegetables and horticulture to meet the shortage. Special efforts were made to increase the production of rice in the eastern sector through effective utilisation of irrigation and other potentials.

Industry. In the field of industry, the emphasis was on modernisation and introduction of high technology with a view to reduce the cost, so that this sector becomes competitive.

Development. A vastly expended housing programme, growth of industry which utilised the finance to be made available by financial institutions were all expected to contribute in providing greater employment opportunities. Both in the field of industry and agriculture, the emphasis was on improvement of infrastructure and investment aimed at modernisation. It was hoped that the shortages in power, transport and coal would not arise in the undertaking of enhanced activities envisaged in the plan. It was for this reason that the allocation for energy had been raised to 31 per cent of the total public sector outlay.

Another thrust area in the plan was human resource development. For this purpose not only the existing programmes in education, health, science and technology have expanded but new initiatives undertaken and some innovations introduced.

Power and Rural Development. Dr. Manmohan Singh, then Deputy Chairman of the Planning Commission said power (electricity) would get a higher priority with 31 per cent of the outlay being spent on it, with rural development schemes under different heads getting 40 per cent. This he said, aimed at reducing the regional disparities as agricultural production was the major factor responsible for these disparities.

Employment Opportunities. The Plan also assured reasonable growth in employment opportunities which was expected to be faster than the growth of the labour force. The aim was to increase employment by 40 million standard persons against an increase in the labour force of 39 million standard persons. The other notable achievements of the Plan were to eliminate poverty and illiteracy and to satisfy the basic needs of food, clothing, shelter and health care for all.

Drinking Water for problem village. Dr. Manmohan Singh also assured the NDC that safe drinking water would be supplied to all problem villages by the end of the Plan period. Similarly, health care would expand and immunisation programme would be strengthened.

Deficit financing. Deficit financing would be to the tune of Rs. 14,000 crores and net borrowings Rs. 30,562 crores. As much as 94 per cent of the total investment would be financed from domestic fund, which necessitated "tremendous effort" at resource mobilisation.

Savings. The ratio of savings will go up from 23.3 per cent of gross domestic products (GDP) to 24.5 per cent by 1989-90 and the rate of gross investment will rise from 24.5 per cent of GDP in 1984-85 to 25.9 per cent.

Eighth Five Year Plan

The Seventh Five-Year Plan ended on March 31, 1990. In the normal course the Eighth Plan should have begun on April 1, 1990. However, due to some unavoidable circumstances including the changes in party in power at the Centre, the Plan document could not be finalised. It was only when the Government under P.V. Narasimha Rao assumed office that the Plan was finalised and implemented with effect from April 1, 1992. The duration of the Eighth Plan is thus from April 1, 1992 to March 31, 1997.

Objectives of the Eighth Plan : The Eighth Plan sought to give priority to the following set of six objectives :

(*i*) Generation of adequate employment to achieve near full employment level by the turn of the century;

(*ii*) Containment of population growth through active people's cooperation and an effective scheme of incentives and disincentives;

(*iii*) Universalisation of elementary education and complete eradication of illiteracy among the people of the age group of 15 to 35 years;

(*iv*) Provision of safe drinking water and primary health care facilities, including immunisation to the entire population and complete elimination of scaveanging;

(*v*) Growth and diversification of agriculture to achieve self-sufficiency in food and generate surpluses for exports; and

(*vi*) Strengthening the infrastructure (energy, transport, communication, irrigation) in order to support growth process on a sustainable basis.

The Eighth Plan was to concentrate on these objectives keeping in view the need for (a) continuous reliance on domestic resources for financing investment, (b) increasing the technical capabilities for the development of science and technology, (c) modernisation and competitive efficiency so that the Indian economy could keep pace with and take advantage of the global developments.

Growth Rate : The Eighth Plan aimed at achieving a growth rate of 5.6 per cent per annum in Gross Domestic Product (GDP) over the five-year period 1992-97. This growth traget had been set against the backdrop of 5.8 per cent GDP growth rate achieved during the Seventh Plan period 1985-90. In view of this encouraging performance of Seventh Plan, some people advocated for a 6 per cent growth target. But due to resource crunch that the public sector was facing, the growth target was fixed at 5.6 per cent.

Public Sector Outlay of Major Heads of Development with Eighth Plan 1992-97

(Rs. *crore at 1991-92 prices)*

	Heads of Development	*Outlay*	*Per cent of the total outlay*
1.	Agriculture and allied activities, irrigation and flood control	54992.50	12.67
2.	Rural Development	34425.36	7.93
3.	.Special Area Programmes	6750.16	1.55
4.	Energy	115561.09	26.62
5.	Industry and Minerals	46921.75	10.81
6.	Transport	55925.57	12.88
7.	Communications	25109.98	5.78
8.	Science and Technology	4131.71	0.95
9.	Ecology and Environment	4909.98	1.13
10.	General Economic and General Services	6360.00	1.47
11.	Social Services	79011.90	18.20
	Grand Total	434100.00	100.00

Eighth Plan Outlay and Investment : The Eighth Plan envisaged a total outlay of Rs.7,98,000 crores in both public and private sectors taken together of which public sector outlay was Rs. 4,34,100 crores. This means that the share of public sector in total Plan outlay under the Eighth Plan was 45.2 per cent as against 52.9 per cent in the Sixth and 47.8 per cent in the Seventh Plan. Of the total public sector outlay of Rs. 4,34,100 crores, Rs. 3,61,000 crores was public sector investment and Rs. 73,100 crores current outlay i.e. outlay of recurring and non-investment nature.

The sectoral distribution of public sector outlay is given in the following table. As is evident from the table, the energy sector received the largest share in the outlay followed by the transport sector. Taken together, these two sectors accounted for about 40 per cent of the public sector outlay in the Eighth Plan. Share of agriculture had been put at about 12.7 per cent, which combined with about 8 per cent share of rural development claims over one-fifth of the public sector outlay. In fact, the share of outlay for rural development in the Eighth Plan was larger than any other preceding Plan and thus signified the emphasis of rural development and poverty alleviation that the Plan sought to place on it in the context of overall development of the economy. Industry sector was allocated around 11 per cent of the total public sector outlay.

SECTORAL DEVELOPMENT PROFILE

Agriculture : The Eighth Plan for agricultural development aimed at generating surplus for exports in foodgrains and attaining self-sufficiency in respect of pulses and oilseeds. The agricultural sector was expected to grow at an average annual rate of a little more than 4 per cent in terms of gross value of output and 3 per cent in terms of value added.

In order to attain the desired growth in agriculture special efforts were made for enhancing the productivity and reducing the instability of production. Since about two-thirds of the area was still unirrigated and largely rainfed, greater stress was laid on dry land farming. Efforts were made to spread the benefits of the Green Revolution to other parts of the country, particularly to the eastern regions which have adequate rainfall and fertile soil. Investment was made in the expansion of irrigation potential and improve efficiency of irrigation system to reduce water wastage.

Industry and Minerals : The output in mining and manufacturing sector during the Eighth Plan period was expected to grow at an annual rate of 8 per cent. The private sector was expected to play an increasing role in industrial activities during the Eighth Plan. The series of reforms introduced by the Government in the industrial sector were intended to deregulate or unshackle the industry and enable it to take decisions on its own without the need for government approval. It was then believed that the private sector had come of age and needed independence in decision making to meet the needs of the dynamic market. The role of the public sector, on the other hand, was sought to be limited. The new industrial Policy of July 1991 brought down the areas reserved for the public sector from 29 to 8 industries and now the public sector would concentrate on basic and core sector alone. The Policy laid great reliance on competitiveness to improve efficiency and hence sought greater share for the private sector.

Employment : The Eighth Plan aimed at reducing unemployment to negligible levels within the next ten years. The labour force was projected to increase by about 35 million during 1992-97 and by another 36 million during 1997-2002. In view of the backlog of unemployed persons numbering around 23 million, the total number of persons requiring employment was estimated at 58 million during 1992-97 and 94 million during 1997-2002. This called for an employment growth rate of 4 per cent per annum over the ten years period, if employment to all was to be provided by the end of the Eighth Plan. The Eighth Plan, therefore, had set a target of 2.6 to 2.8 per cent per annum growth in employment, which, if achieved, would have reduced unemployment to negligible levels by 2002 A.D. The Plan focussed not only on the creation of new jobs but also on augmenting productivity and income in the existing jobs because it was realised that larger and efficient use of available human resources was the most effective way of poverty alleviation, reduction of inequalities and for high pace of economic growth. It, however,was able to achieve actual employment growth of only 2 per cent.

Ninth Five-Year Plan

The broad objectives of 9th Plan (1997-2002), arising from the Common Minimum Programme (CMP) of U.F. Government and the Chief Ministers' Conference on basic minimum services are : (i) priority to agriculture and rural development to generate adequate productive employment and cradication of poverty (ii) accelerating growth rate with stable prices (iii) ensuring food and nutritional security for all especially vulnerable sections of society (iv) providing minimum services of safe drinking water, primary health care, universal primary education, shelter etc. (v) checking growth of population (vi) ensuring environmental sustain-ability of development process (vii) empowerment of women and socially-disadvantaged groups such as SC/ST/OBCs and Minorities (viii) promoting and developing people's participatory institutions like Panchayati Raj institutions, cooperatives and self-help groups (ix) strengthening efforts to build self-reliance. The over-all approach thus envisaged was "growth with social justice and equality". The Plan envisages a gross tentative investment of Rs.2190,000 crores — Public sectors Rs. 759,000 crores (10% of GDP), Private corporate Rs. 683,000 (8.9%), Household Rs. 748,000 crores (9.7%).

Draft Ninth Plan Document : The Draft 9th Plan document released on March 1, 1998 by the then Deputy Chairman, Planning Commission, Prof. Dandavate, attempted to strike an ideological balance of vigorously pursuing economic reforms and simultaneously fulfilling the socialistic agenda of a welfare state. The 1500-page document envisaged a 7% growth rate in GDP annually [industry to grow by 9.3% (as against 4.5%),exports by 14.5% (10.3%), agriculture 4.5% (– 2%), full literacy by 2005 AD, creation of 44.36 crore jobs, reduction of poverty ratio to 18% with total poverty alleviation, expected to be achieved by the end of 11th Plan] and a zero monetised deficit.

In order to achieve an annual growth rate of 7% in GDP, an investment rate of 28.3% and domestic savings rate of 26.2% was recommended.

While aiming at zero monetised deficit, the plan envisaged support from budgetary resources worth Rs. 374,000 crores. Rs. 33,319 crores through borrowings and net inflow of Rs. 60,018 crores from abroad. The rest was to be mobilised by the States through tax revenues as well as borrowings.

Simultaneously, the fiscal deficit was sought to be brought down from the projected 5% in 1997-98 to 3.5% of GDP by 2002.

However, it was conceded that allocations worth another Rs. 70,000 crores were needed to fully meet the basic requirements like safe drinking water, universalisation of primary education, health care and nutritional security.

Priority was accorded to infrastucture (with an allocation of 40%), followed by energy and social services (25.4%), agriculture (including irrigation and rural development —19.4%) transport (14.2%): The Ninth Five-Year Plan achieved a GDP growth of 5.5% against a target of 6.5%.

Tenth Five-Year Plan

Every Five-Year Plan is conceived on the bedrock of high expectations and on the conviction of avoiding past mistakes and implementing new ideas in order to build a more prosperous India. The Plan has taken on a fresh look in the light of the different innovations introduced during the Vajpayee regime, especially in the areas of information technology, bio technology, infrastructure, tourism, etc.

The Plan was approved on October 5, 2002 at a full meeting of the Planning Commission presided over by Prime Minister, Mr. Atal Bihari Vajpayee who is also the Chairman of the Planning Commission.

Our overall performance has been improving from Plan to Plan. For instance GDP growth in the post-liberalisation period has improved from an average of about 5.7% in the 1980 to an average of about 6.5% in the Eighth and Ninth Plan periods, making India one of the ten fastest growing economies. The percentage of population below poverty line has, also, declined, even though it may not be to the extent the planners had planned. Population growth has declerated below 2% for the first time in four decades. Literacy has increased from 52% in 1991 to 65% in 2001. Sectors such as software services, entertainment and IT-enabled services have emerged as new sources of strength creating confidence about India's potential to be competitive in the world economy.

The Tenth Plan is all geared to take up the challenges left over by the previous Plans. For a vast country like India with a rising population, constraints on utilisation of resources and frequent natural calamities, development work, however well planned, may not be that smooth sailing. A prolonged drought, unprecedented floods and a warlike situation on the border, a hike in international oil prices, global recession, the economic fallout of September 11-all could throw our plan targets out or order. Still India has been able to stand its ground. And a strong nation can ill-afford to run away from the host of its burning problems. The problems are too many and the people hope that the present Plan would try to alleviate them to the maximum extent possible. For instance, the incidence of unemployment on Current Daily Status is relatively high at about 7%. More than half of the children of 1-5 years age in rural areas are undernourished while the infant mortality rate has stagnated at 72 per 1000 for the last several years. As many as 60 per cent of rural households and about 20 per cent of urban households do not have a power connection.Only 60 per cent of urban households have taps within their homes, and far fewer have latrines inside the house. Deterioration in urban environment, proliferation of slums and a steady rise in air and water pollution in the cities have impaired the quality of life in urban India. Things are no better in the vast countryside. There is both land and forest degradation. Overexploitation of groundwater threatens not only the sustainability of farming but sources of supply of potable water as well.

Against this background, the Tenth Plan provides an opportunity to build upon the gains of the past and address the weaknesses that have emerged. The era of liberalisation has made the country take a hard look at the role of the Government. Gone are the days when the Government tended to take on too many responsibilities, imposing severe strains on its limited financial and administrative capabilities and also stifling individual initiative. Over the years the private sector has come into its own, growing strong, dynamic and innovative. Public sector organisations have lost their punch and it is just matter of time before private sector plays a predominant role in the industrial scene of the country. This does not mean that the government has no role to play; it does have a role, but a totally different one.In social sectors and infrastructure development, government has to come in, though in a modified way. Here too, in sectors like telecommunications, power, ports, etc. the private sector can play a much larger role provided an appropriate policy framework is in place. Here the role of the government needs to change to facilitate such investment as much as possible while still remaining a public service provider for quite some time. In all these areas, the role of government in creating and maintaining a modern regulatory system for ensuring a fair deal for consumers, transparency and accountability, and a level playing field is also extremely important.

Traditionally, the level of per capita income has been regarded as a summary indicator of the economic well-being of the country and growth targets have therefore focused on growth in per capita income or per capita GDP. The Prime Minister has directed the Planning Commission to examine the feasibility of doubling per capita income in the next ten years. With population expected to grow at about 1.6% per annum, this target requires the rate of growth of GDP to be around 8.7% over the Tenth and Eleventh Plan periods.

It has been found that a mere rise in GDP does not take us anywhere. The ultimate aim is the quality of human life and provision of minimum needs. The inevitable question arises : Are the people getting enough food and do they have easy access to basic social services like education, health, drinking water and basic sanitation ? The concept of real development includes the expansion of economic and social opportunities for all individuals and groups, reductions in disparities, and greater participation in decision-making. In addition to the 8% growth traget, the Plan has set forth the following major objectives :

- Reduction of poverty ratio by 5 percentage points by 2007 and by 15 percentage points by 2012;
- Providing gainful high quality employment to the addition to the labour force over the Tenth Plan period;
- All children to be enrolled in schools by 2003;
- All childern to complete 5 years of schooling by 2007;
- Reduction in gender gaps in literacy and wage rates by at least 50% by 2007;
- Reduction in decadal rate of population growth between 2001 and 2011 to 16.2%;
- Increase in Literacy Rate to 75% within the Plan period;
- Reduction of infant mortality rate (IMR) to 45 per 1000 live births by 2007 and to 28 by 2010;
- Reduction of Maternal mortality ratio (MMR) to 2 per 1000 live births by 2007 and to 1 by 2012;
- Increase in forest and tree cover to 25% by 2007 and 33% by 2012;
- All villages to have sustained access to potable drinking water within the Plan period;
- Cleaning of major polluted rivers by 2007 and other notified stretches by 2012.

The Plans have traditionally focused on setting national targets, but it has been found that there is a variation in the performance of different States. The Tenth Plan focuses on ways and means of correcting the regional imbalance.

Census 2001 has shown that India's population is 102.7 crore—which is 1.5 crore more than the projections for 2001 made by the Technical Committee on Population Projection. Currently, eight States, with poor health and demographic indices, constitute 44.7 per cent of India's population. Special efforts have to be made during the Tenth Plan to enable these States to fully achieve their potential. The human and economic development of the country would, to a large extent, depend upon the success of these efforts.

The Plan lays great emphasis on agriculture since growth in this sector is likely to lead to the widest dissemination of benefits, especially to the rural poor including agricultural labour. Also, since the majority of women workers are engaged in agriculture, investments in this sector have enormous implications for gender equality. Incidentally, the first generation of reforms concentrated on reforms in the industrial economy and reforms in the agricultural sector were neglected. And this trend would change in the Tenth Plan.

The growth strategy of the Tenth Plan will seek to ensure the rapid growth of those sectors which are most likely to create high quality employment opportunities. Particular attention will be paid to the policy environment influencing a wide range of economic activities which have a large employment potential. These include such sectors as construction, real estate and housing, transport, SSI, modern retailing, entertainment, IT-enabled services and a range of other new services,which need to be promoted through supportive services.

The Plan admits that growth as such may bypass certain vulnerable groups like women who are at present covered by such programmes as "social safety nets". These programmes may be modified where necessary. In pursuance of the Ninth Plan objective of empowering women as agents of socio-economic change and development,the National Policy on Empowerment of Women was adopted in April 2001. On this basis, a National Plan of Action (NPA) is being formulated to ensure the requisite access of women to information, resources and services. The Tenth Plan will focus on the effective implementation of NPA.

The Plan has also focused on the welfare and development of other vulnerable sections of society like the scheduled castes, scheduled tribes and other backward classes.

The ultimate idea of planning is to bring all sections of society to the mainstream of socio-economic development and this is exactly what the Tenth Plan seeks to secure.

TENTH FIVE YEAR PLAN PERFORMANCE

Tenth Five Year Plan, started from 2002-03 onwards, reflected the priorities of the Indian Government in the direction of promoting overall development including welfare.

Based on the availability of resources, the outlay for Tenth Plan was approved for Rs. 46,614 crores. However, the ultimate actual plan allocation for the Tenth Plan worked out to Rs. 69,511 crores, with an increase of nearly 49% of the approved outlay. Actual expenditure up to December, 2006 is 78%. Year-wise plan outlay and expenditure are as under:

Table 1

Year-wise Outlay and Expenditure during 10th Plan

Year	Outlay (Rs. Crs.)	% Increase	Expr. (Rs. Crs.)	% Increase	%of Expenditure
2002-03	10100	20.55	8315	4.34	82
2003-04	10970	8.61	10759	29.39	98
2004-05	12790	16.59	11457	6.49	90
2005-06	15651	22.36	13439	17.30	86
2006-07 Nov. '06	20000	27.79	10026	—	50
Total	69511	19.18	52395	—	78

Planning Commission fixed a growth target of 6.8% for Tenth Plan and the average growth up to the end of 2005-06 worked out to 6.72%. The GSDP growth rate for the first four years of 9th Five Year Plan was reported at 6.01% and for five years the growth rate was 5.78%. The absolute growth of GSDP during the 1st four years of the 10th Plan over that of 9th Plan worked out to 6.01%. The growth recorded during the 10th Plan can be termed as significant as it is the result of revival of economic growth after the initial setback.

Tenth Plan performance year-wise is summarized as follows:

- 2002-03: Outlay for the year was ₹ 10100 crores and the actual expenditure was ₹ 8315 crores, constituting 82.33%. There is an increase of 20.55% in the outlay over that of previous year. The plan was focusing on infrastructure sectors *viz* Energy, Irrigation and Transport with an allocation of 60.62% of the budgeted outlay.
- 2003-04: Approved outlay for the year was ₹ 10970 crores, with an increase of 8.61% over the previous year and the expenditure incurred during the period was ₹ 10759 crores, which is 98% of the approved budget. Priority areas were Social Services sector with 26.45% followed by Irrigation, Energy and Transport sectors together accounting for 53.37%.
- 2004-05: An amount of ₹ 12790 crores was the plan outlay which is 16.59%. more than the preceding year. Actual expenditure incurred was ₹11457 crores, which is 90% of the plan budget. Irrigation and Energy sectors were again given the priority, which together account. for about 49 per cent of the total plan budget. Social Services sector is provided with 27.33 per cent.
- 2005-06: Allocation was ₹15651 crores, which is 22.36% more than that of 2004-05. Expenditure incurred during the plan period was ₹ 13439 crores and the percentage of expenditure is 86%. Irrigation sector consecutively got priority, accounting for 40.57% followed by Energy sector with 14.01 per cent.
- 2006-07: The plan outlay for 2006-07 was approved for ₹ 20000 crores, with an increase of 27.79% over the budgeted outlay for 2005-06. The expenditure incurred up to December 2006 is Rs. 10026 crores. Irrigation sector with an outlay of ₹10041 crores got more than 50% of the total plan outlay followed by Housing, Rural Development and Transport sectors.

Overall increase in the plan outlay for Tenth Plan over that of Ninth Plan (₹ 29944 crores) is 232%.

EXERCISES

Long Answer Type Questions:

1. What are the objective of Planning in India ? Discuss the functions of Planning Commission.
2. What do you know about the organisation of the Planning Commission ?
3. Write a note on 'advisory bodies to the Planning Commission'.
4. Write a note on 'Evaluation of Planning Commission'.

Short Answer Type Questions:

1. Write a short note on performances of Tenth Five-Year Plan.
2. Write a note on Ninth Five-Year Plan.
3. Write a note on Eighth Five-Year Plan.
4. Write a note on Seventh Five-Year Plan.
5. What were the objectives of Eighth Five-Year Plan ?

Objective Type Questions:

Choose the correct answer

1. In which year Planning Commission was set up ?

   (*a*) 1950 (*b*) 1951

   (*c*) 1952 (*d*) 1953.

2. In which year The National Development Council was created by the Government of India ?
(a) 1951 (b) 1952
(c) 1953 (d) 1954
3. In which year The Committee on Plan Projects was set up ?
(a) 1954 (b) 1955
(c) 1956 (d) 1957
4. In which year The Coordination Committee for Public Cooperation was set up ?
(a) 1955 (b) 1954
(c) 1953 (d) 1952
5. In which year Tenth Five Year Plan started?
(a) 2002-03 (b) 2003-04
(c) 2004-05 (d) 2005-06
6. How much outlay was approved for Eleventh Plan?
(a) ₹47614 crores (b) ₹46614 crores
(c) ₹45614 crores (d) ₹44614 crores
7. What was the ultimate actual plan allocation for the Tenth Plan?
(a) ₹67511 crores (b) ₹68511 crores
(c) ₹69,511 crores (d) ₹70511 crores
8. What was actual expenditure up to December 2006 of Tenth Five Year Plan?
(a) 75% (b) 76%
(c) 77% (d) 78%
9. How much growth target was fixed by Planning Commission for Tenth Five Year Plan?
(a) 6.8% (b) 7.8%
(c) 8.8% (d) 9.8%
10. What was the average growth up to the end of 2005-06 of Tenth Five Year Plan?
(a) 6.71% (b) 6.72%
(c) 6.73% (d) 6.74%

ANSWERS

1. (a) 2. (b) 3. (c) 4. (d) 5. (a) 6. (b) 7. (c) 8. (d)
9. (a) 10. (b)

24

CHAPTER

Mid-Term Appraisal of the Eleventh Five Year Plan

The Eleventh Plan (2007-08 to 2011-12) sought to build on the gains achieved in the Tenth Plan and shift the economy to a path of faster and more inclusive growth. Inclusiveness, a critical element in the strategy, was to be achieved by ensuring that growth was broad-based and was combined with programmes aimed at overcoming deficiencies in critical areas, which affect large numbers of the vulnerable sections of our population, particularly the Scheduled Castes (SCs), Scheduled Tribes (STs), the Other Backward Classes (OBCs), women, and the minorities. The Plan sought to deal with these deficiencies through programmes aimed at providing access to health, education, and other essential services and programmes of livelihood support.

The Mid-Term Appraisal (MTA) reviews the experience in the first three years of the Plan and seeks to identify areas where corrective steps may be needed. This chapter presents a broad overview of the findings of the MTA.

AGGREGATE AND SECTORAL GROWTH

The Eleventh Five Year Plan aimed at an average growth rate of 9 per cent per annum, beginning with 8.5 per cent growth in the first year and accelerating this to reach 10 per cent in the last year. The economy exceeded expectations in the first year of the Eleventh Five Year Plan (2007-08) with a growth rate of over 9 per cent but the momentum was interrupted in 2008-09 because of the global financial crisis.

As in other countries, the government responded to the global recession by introducing fiscal stimulus and monetary accommodation which continued into 2009-10 when the economy was further hit by a severe drought. The growth rate in 2008-09 declined to 6.7 per cent but rebounded to 7.4 per cent in 2009-10, despite the fact that agriculture showed negligible growth at 0.2 per cent. The drought also led to an increase in inflationary pressure, especially in food prices, which were also affected by high international commodity prices, as well as some of the food prices that were high. Bringing inflation under control has thus become a priority.

RESILIENCE OF THE ECONOMY

The relatively modest slowdown in the face of an exceptionally sharp contraction in output in the industrialized world has established the resilience of the Indian economy in terms of its ability to manage a downturn despite greater openness. While the advanced economies saw their growth decline from a trend rate of 2.0 to 2.5 per cent to (-) 2.0 to (-) 3.0 per cent, growth in India declined by only about 2 percentage points. Since this reduction applied to an underlying growth rate that was much higher, the outcome was a GDP growth rate that remained relatively robust. China and other East and South-East Asian countries have also had a similar experience.

There are several reasons for the superior performance on the growth front. Some of them are as follows:

First, India's financial system was not exposed to the 'toxic' assets which affected the financial system in most industrialized countries. This was the result of a traditionally conservative approach to bank regulations and of a conscious government decision to adopt a cautious approach in liberalizing capital flows, especially short-term debt, combined with building up ample foreign exchange reserves. If the financial system had suffered a severe shock, the disruptive effects of the crisis on the real . economy would have been much greater.

Second, although the economy is much more open now than it was in the past, it still is much less dependent on exports as a demand side driver of growth than some other countries. The growth in demand which supported rapid growth in GDP was predominantly domestic demand, particularly domestic investment, which increased rapidly in the pre-crisis years.

Third, the underlying macro-fundamentals were strong. The level of private savings has been high and fiscal consolidation in previous years had improved public savings performance. *As* a result, the domestic savings rate had increased to 36.4 per cent of GDP in 2007-08 and then declined to 32.5 per cent in 2008-09 because of the adverse effect of the crisis on tax revenues coupled with the fiscal stimulus. However, the private savings rate was more or less unchanged. Gross investment declined from 37.7 per cent in 2007-08 to 34.9 per cent in 2008-09 and is expected to recover to 36.2 per cent in 2009-10. Gross fixed capital formation remained at about 33 per cent through these years.

PROSPECTS FOR THE ELEVENTH FIVE YEAR PLAN

Growth prospects in the remaining two years of the Eleventh Five Year Plan period depend to some extent on the global economic prospects which remain uncertain at present. However, if the industrialized countries show positive annual growth of 2.3 per cent in 2010, and 2.4 per cent in 2011, as is currently thought likely, it is possible to envisage India's growth rate increasing to around 8.5 per cent in 2010-11, with a further increase to 9 per cent in 2011-12.

Projecting a return to 9 per cent growth may appear optimistic since growth at this rate in the past has only been achieved in years when the industrialized countries grew at close to 3 per cent per year. However, India's macroeconomic fundamentals suggest that 9 per cent growth can be achieved despite slower growth in industrialized countries provided supportive policies are put in place.

MACROECONOMIC FUNDAMENTALS

The high rates of domestic savings and investment are important strengths of the economy that will help ensure an early return to high growth. Equally important is the considerable entrepreneurial and managerial capacity in the private sector. Private corporate investment was particularly buoyant in the years before the crisis and confidence levels remain high. This should help ensure an early return to higher growth.

Slower growth in world trade will, however, be a problem area in the coming years. Exports, which grew at an annual rate of 25 per cent (in US$) from 2003-04 to 2007-08, are likely to grow at a much slower rate. Export growth decelerated to 13.7 per cent in 2008-09 and (-) 4.7 per cent in 2009-10, and an early return to very rapid growth is unlikely. Weaker export demand will have to be offset by some other source of domestic demand to sustain high rates of GDP growth. This should ideally be through increased investment in infrastructure, using a combination of public and private investment and Public-Private Partnerships (PPPs). Enhanced investment in infrastructure will not only provide the demand needed to replace export demand in the short term, it will also ease a critical supply constraint on growth over the medium term.

A strategy of raising investment in the face of lower export growth implies a somewhat larger balance of payments deficit, especially since oil prices are unlikely to drift downwards. However, the increase in the current account deficit in the next two years is likely to be modest, at approximately 2.5 per cent or at most 3 per cent of GDP. A deficit of this order could be financed relatively easily through long-term capital flows including foreign direct investment (FDI).

Despite the crisis, FDI flows (which exclude FII inflows) have held up well and the estimated FDI inflow in 2009-10 was over US$ 31 billion. India's prospects for attracting FDI in the years ahead are very good if it continues to be seen as a dynamic economy and the overall macroeconomic environment remains positive and economic policies are seen to be investor friendly.

An important area of concern in this context is the size of the combined fiscal deficit of the Centre and the States, which increased from 6.3 per cent of GDP in 2006-07, to about 10 per cent in 2008-09, and remained around the same in 2009-10. A higher fiscal deficit was an inevitable consequence of the stimulus strategy, but it is also necessary to signal a return to fiscal prudence. This signal has been given in the Budget for 2010-11, which shows the central fiscal deficit declining from 7.8 per cent of GDP in 2008-09 to 6.9 per cent in 2009-10, and further to 5.5 per cent in 2010-11, with further decline projected in subsequent years. Adherence to this time path will contribute to creating investor confidence and help bring inflationary pressures under control.

If the economy achieves 8.5 per cent growth in 2010-11, and accelerates to 9 per cent in the last year of the Eleventh Five Year Plan, the average rate of growth "in the Plan period could be a little over 8 per cent. Although this is below the original Eleventh Five Year Plan target of an average of 9 per cent growth it would be better than the 7.8 per cent attained in the Tenth Five Year Plan period. To achieve this outcome in an otherwise highly unfavourable external environment would be a major achievement. More importantly, the economy would be well-positioned for transition to a growth rate higher than 9 per cent in the Twelfth Plan period.

GROWTH IN THE STATES

The pattern of Gross State Domestic Product (GSDP) growth across states in recent years has some interesting positive features. Such data as are . available (up to 2008-09) suggest that all the states have experienced some acceleration in growth and even the states in the lowest quartile have experienced significant acceleration. This pattern is also reflected in the performance in agriculture across states.

The median growth rate of GSDP in the states was 7.6 per cent in the Tenth Five Year Plan and 8 per cent in the first year of the Eleventh Five Year Plan. In states for which data is available for 2008-09 the median growth rate dropped to 6.4 per cent on account of the slowdown caused by the global crisis.

The distribution of growth across states appears to have improved in favour of the slower growing states. The median growth rate for the lowest quartile of the states (ranked by descending order of growth rates) did not exceed 4.9 per cent in the Seventh, Eighth, and Ninth Five Year Plans. It rose to 6.3 per cent in the Tenth Five Year Plan and remained at that level in 2007-08 suggesting that all states have benefited by the improved growth climate. Although growth rates continue to differ across states, the variation has tended to decline.

PROSPECTS FOR AGRICULTURE

An important sectoral target of the Eleventh Five Year Plan was to raise the rate of growth of GDP in agriculture from about 2.5 per cent in the Tenth Five Year Plan to 4 per cent during the Eleventh Five Year Plan period. Higher agricultural growth was expected to contribute directly to overall GDP growth and even more so to inclusiveness. Since more than half of the labour force still derives its income from agriculture, faster agricultural growth is perhaps the most effective instrument for reducing rural poverty. It would mean raising farm incomes for landowning farmers and wage income for landless labourers.

It is difficult to judge growth performance in agriculture based on short periods because of the volatility to which agriculture is subjected. The average growth rate of agriculture in the first two years of the Eleventh Five Year Plan was 3.2 per cent, which was better than that of the Tenth Five Year Plan, but the drought in 2009-10 reduced the average for the first three years to a little over 2 per cent. In case of a normal monsoon across the country in 2010, a substantial rebound can be expected. As pointed out above, achieving the target of 4 per cent growth in agriculture would require an average growth of 7 per cent per annum in the next two years. This may be difficult but with normal weather conditions there is a good chance of agricultural growth averaging 3.0 to 3.5 per cent over the Eleventh Five Year Plan period. If this happens, agriculture would at least have overcome the prolonged deceleration which occurred between 1996 and 2003 and returned to the earlier high growth path from which a transition to 4 per cent could be attempted in the Twelfth Five Year Plan.

As discussed in detail above, there are several positive developments in agriculture:

- Total public and private investment in agriculture as a percentage of agricultural GDP has improved from 14.1 per cent in 2004-05 to 19.5 per cent in 2008-09 according to the new national accounts series.
- The write-off of farm debts in 2006 gave many farmers the opportunity to start afresh and the flow of agricultural credit has expanded considerably in the Eleventh Five Year Plan period with the Kisan Vikas Card experiment proving to be very successful.
- Programmes such as the Rashtriya Krishi Vikas Yojana (RKVY), the National Horticulture Mission, and the National Food Security Mission are doing well.
- Minimum support prices have been raised to give farmers greater incentives to produce food grains.
- Investment in irrigation is being expanded significantly and the Accelerated Irrigation Benefit Programme (AIBP) has stepped up allocations in support of State Government efforts.
- The Mahatma Gandhi National Rural Employment Guarantee (MGNREG) programme, which is focussed on schemes that improve water conservation, together with enhanced efforts at watershed management, holds out the hope of greatly improving access to water in rainfed areas.
- Improved rural road connectivity through the implementation of the Pradhan Mantri Gram Sadak Yojana (PMGSY), has given farmers improved access to markets supporting faster growth in farm incomes.

None of this should detract from the fact that a great deal more needs to be done in the remaining years of the Eleventh Five Year Plan. A detailed agenda for action is spelt out in covering improved access to water, improving the supply of good quality seeds, replenishing soil nutrients, improving agricultural research and extension, reforms in land tenancy, and improving agricultural marketing, which is particularly important for perishable produce. Most of these lie in the domain of state governments.

THE MANUFACTURING SECTOR

The Eleventh Five Year Plan had noted that the high growth of the economy in recent years had not been accompanied by rapid growth in manufacturing as happened in other fast developing economies. The Plan called for double digit growth in manufacturing and emphasized that this was essential if we wanted to shift substantial numbers of the labour force out of agriculture into the formal sector. Performance in this dimension in the first three years of the Eleventh Five Year Plan has been below expectations.

Manufacturing grew at an average 9.3 per cent during the Tenth Plan, and reached 10.3 per cent during the first year of the Eleventh Five Year Plan, but thereafter it was hit by the global slowdown in 2008-09, causing the rate of growth in the sector to decline to 3.2 per cent. It recovered to 10.8 per cent in 2009-10 and our objective should be to maintain the growth of manufacturing at double digit levels in the last two years of the Eleventh Five Year Plan.

Several institutional and policy reforms are needed to achieve this objective. Improved power supply is particularly important since shortages of power or poor quality of power supply have an adverse effect on the competitiveness of manufacturing. The Micro, Small, and Medium Enterprise (MSME) sector needs special attention because it creates more jobs than large companies do. It is also an important seed bed for entrepreneurship and innovation. Credit is, however, a key constraint for this sector and this calls for continued deepening and strengthening of the financial sector as well as the mechanisms for expanding access to equity financing. 'Clustering' is an effective way of providing small units with infrastructure support and should be encouraged.

Manufacturing units in India are also burdened by a plethora of regulations, including many at the state level, resulting in low scores on indices of the ease of doing business. There is an urgent need to review these regulations in individual states. The need for greater flexibility of labour laws also has to be addressed if labour-intensive manufacturing is to be encouraged.

The fear that any change in labour laws which increase flexibility would necessarily be anti-labour is misplaced and must be overcome. In fact, more flexibility, broadly in line with what exists in other countries, would help increase the demand for labour and expand the size of the labour force in the organized sector. This would be in the interest of unorganized workers who would be absorbed in the organized sector in larger numbers thereby increasing the worker base and their bargaining power in this sector.

Rapid industrialization also requires release of land for industrial projects and infrastructure and this has become more difficult over time. The existing land acquisition laws are widely seen to be inequitable and unfair to those from whom land is acquired, especially since acquisition is sometimes used to benefit projects being developed by the private sector. The Government had introduced bills to modernize land acquisition and rehabilitation laws but the bills lapsed with the dissolution sector. The Government of the Lok Sabha prior to the 2009 elections. They need to be reintroduced at an early date. The Supreme Court of India released so many judgements for the betterment of farmers and in the direction of modernizing land acquisition and rehabilitation laws in 2010-2011.

INCLUSIVENESS AND THE ELEVENTH FIVE YEAR PLAN

The Eleventh Five Year Plan viewed inclusiveness as multi-dimensional objective and listed 27 monitorable targets. Of these, two were: (*a*) growth of GDP and (*b*) the growth of agricultural GDP. There were also 25 other parameters relating to poverty reduction, employment, education, health services, child nutrition, gender balance, access to basic infrastructural services, and environmental sustainability. The MTA provides an assessment of progress made in this area, together with suggestions about the corrective steps needed in the major programmes.

POVERTY REDUCTION

The Eleventh Five Year Plan target was to reduce the percentage of poverty by 10 percentage points over the Plan period, or 2 percentage points per year, which is more than twice the pace observed in the past. It is not possible to measure progress against this target at this stage because no official estimates of poverty are available after 2004-05. The next estimate of poverty will be for 2009-10, based on the NSS survey currently being conducted in the field, data from which will become available only in 2012.

An issue that has attracted considerable attention is whether the poverty lines used in the official estimates, which were fixed in 1973-74 and have been updated for inflation since, need to be revisited in view of the many changes that have taken place in our economy. A High Level Committee under Professor Suresh Tendulkar was appointed in December 2005 to consider this issue.

Although the Report of the Committee has been submitted and the Committee has recommended that the urban poverty line need not be changed, but the rural poverty line should be raised to reflect the basket of commodities that can be purchased at the urban poverty line after allowing for the difference in urban and rural prices. The Tendulkar Committee has recomputed poverty lines for individual states for 2004-05 on this basis.

The revised poverty lines recommended by the Tendulkar Committee have been accepted by the Planning Commission for 2004-05. They indicate no change in urban poverty estimates, but the rural poverty line has been revised upwards significantly and as a consequence the percentage of the population below the poverty line in rural areas is higher than it was in the earlier estimates. The percentages of the population in poverty in rural and urban areas using official estimates as well as estimates of the Tendulkar Committee are given in Table 11.1.

TABLE 11.1

Estimates of Population in Poverty
(Percentage below the Poverty Line)

	Official Estimates			Tendulkar Committee		
	Urban	Rural	Total	Urban	Rural	Total
1993-94	32.4	37.3	36.0	31.8	50.1	45.3
2004-05	25.7	28.3	27.5	25.7	41.8	37.2

The Tendulkar Committee has specifically pointed out that the upward revision in the percentage of rural poverty in 2004-05, resulting from the application of a new rural poverty line should not be interpreted as implying that the extent of poverty has increased over time. To assess the underlying time trend using the new method of computing poverty lines, we should compare poverty estimates in 2004-05 with those for 1993-94, using the new methodology for both years. These estimates, as reported by the Committee, are presented in Table 11.1. They clearly show that whether we use the old method or the new the percentage of the population below the poverty line has declined by about the same magnitude.

The findings of the Tendulkar Committee, therefore, endorse the earlier Planning Commission assessment that the growth process witnessed in India led to a reduction in poverty between 1993-94 and 2004-05, though the reduction was less than what might have been expected. However, this change tells us nothing about what has happened to poverty after 2004-05. With GDP growth having accelerated after 2004-05 and its distribution across states being somewhat better, with some improvement in performance in agriculture, and with the introduction of programmes, such as the Mahatma Gandhi National Rural Employment Guarantee (MGNREG) and Bharat Nirman, there is reason to expect that there will be a significant reduction in poverty over the Eleventh Five Year Plan period as a whole. However, this can only be verified much later when the total data for the Eleventh Five Year Plan period become available.

An important programme contributing to poverty reduction in rural areas is Mahatma Gandhi National Rural Employment Guarantee (MGNREG) which began in the first year of the Eleventh Five Year Plan and was quickly expanded to cover the entire country. This programme is expected to generate about three times the volume of employment generated by the rural wage employment programmes that were in place before it was introduced in 2009-10. There is evidence that implementation of the Mahatma Gandhi National Rural Employment Guarantee (MGNREG) programme has reduced distress migration and improved the bargaining power of agriculture labour leading to higher wages.

However, it must be emphasized that while the Mahatma Gandhi National Rural Employment Guarantee (MGNREG) programme provides much-needed minimal employment security, it is not a substitute for a long-term solution to rural poverty. That requires shifting significant numbers of the labour force out of low productivity employment in the agricultural sector to higher productivity employment in the non-agricultural sector, such as in labour-intensive manufacturing and the organized sector in general.

ACCESS TO EDUCATION

The Eleventh Five Year Plan recognized that higher growth rates would require a large expansion in both the quantity and quality of formal education and skill development. It also recognized that for growth to be inclusive, access to quality education must be broadened so that all sections of the population could benefit from the new and more productive employment opportunities generated by faster growth. There is substantial progress in these areas.

ELEMENTARY SCHOOLING

The Sarva Shiksha Abhiyan (SSA), in combination with the Mid-Day Meal (MDM) scheme, has succeeded in achieving near universal enrolment in primary schools. The number of rural habitations with at least one primary school increased from 87 per cent in 2002 to 99 per cent in 2008 and those with upper primary schools within a radius of 3 km from 78 per cent to 92 per cent in the same period. Enrolment has increased for both boys and girls with a welcome narrowing of the gender gap. Similarly, the disparity between SCs/STs and the general population in this area has narrowed, though it has not been entirely eliminated.

While enrolments are impressive, dropout rates remain high with as many as 43 per cent of the children dropping out before completing elementary school. The quality of schooling is also a matter of concern. The Annual Status of Education Report (ASER) 2010, which reports learning achievements based on a survey conducted in 2009, shows that as many as 38 per cent of the children in Class V could not read a text meant for Class II and 37 per cent could not do a simple division. In this regard, the percentages have not changed significantly from the past.

Several steps are necessary to improve the quality of teaching and a number of initiatives have been taken:

- The Pupil-Teacher Ratio in primary schools has improved from 45:1 in 2006-07 to 33:1 in 2008-09.
- The Right of Children to Free and Compulsory Education Act, which became effective from 1 April 2010, provides a framework for universalizing elementary education and also lays down standards which all schools must meet.
- The Thirteenth Finance Commission has provided additional grants to the states to meet their share of the expenditure on education and the Central Government has increased its allocation.

- Efforts are being made to improve teacher's training.

The responsibility for improving the quality of education lies with the state governments. Lacunae in systems of governance make it difficult to enforce teacher accountability. This problem is sought to be tackled by making schools responsible to the elected Panchayati Raj Institutions (PRIs) and some steps have been taken in this direction. However, the effectiveness of these oversight mechanisms is often limited in practice because Panchayati Raj Institutions (PRIs) do not have effective administrative control over teachers in most states, in large part because teachers belong to state cadres and appointments are highly politicized. More effective devolution and empowerment of Panchayati Raj Institutions (PRIs) combined with better system of school inspections, is needed if the quality of teaching is to be improved.

SECONDARY EDUCATION

As the flow of children completing elementary school increases, attention will have to be focussed on the development of adequate infrastructure to absorb them into secondary and higher secondary schools. The primary responsibility for developing schools lies with the state governments, but the Eleventh Five Year Plan recognizes that the Centre has to play a supporting role as it does in the case of SSA.

A number of steps have been taken to assist the states to fulfil their responsibilities in this area. These include expanding and increasing the number of Jawaharlal Nehru Navodaya Vidyalayas and Kendriya Vidyalayas, and launching the Rashtriya Madhyamik Shiksha Abhiyan. The Plan also envisaged a new initiative in the form of a scheme for establishing 6,000 model schools through central assistance. Of these, 2,500 schools will be established through the PPP mode. Implementation of these programmes needs to be accelerated to ensure that the last two years of the Eleventh Five Year Plan give us a good start.

HIGHER AND TECHNICAL EDUCATION

The Eleventh Five Year Plan set a target of raising the Gross Enrolment Ratio (GER) for higher education from around 10 per cent at the start of the Plan to 15 cent by 2015. The importance of these targets is underscored by the fact that countries in East Asia that were behind India in higher education have now moved ahead.

Several new initiatives have been launched to meet the set targets. Capacity in the existing Central Government institutes of higher education, such as central universities, the Indian Institutes of Technology (IITs), Indian Institutes of Management (IIMs), the All India Institute of Medical Sciences (AIIMS), and the Postgraduate Institute of Medical Education and Research, Chandigarh, were expanded by 54 per cent to accommodate reservation for OBCs. The Central Government has also taken steps to establish 8 new IITs, 8 new IIMs, 10 NITs, 20 IIITs, and 3 IISERs. The Central Government has also set up 16 new central universities. In addition, it is also proposed to set up 14 'innovation' universities, the legislative framework for which is being worked out. These initiatives represent a massive expansion of Central Government Institutions of higher education.

The Central Government has also decided to undertake a comprehensive reform of the regulatory structure governing higher education along the lines recommended by the National Knowledge Commission and the Yashpal Committee. The objective is to give universities greater freedom and flexibility, while also enforcing standards. It is expected that there will be an expansion of properly regulated private universities in parallel with the expansion of public universities set up by the Centre and the States. It is also proposed to permit reputed foreign education providers to enter the higher education sector. Availability of quality human resources for teaching and research to meet the demands of proposed expansion in higher education is a major constraint and calls for advance planning. These initiatives, including the new regulatory framework, should be in place by the end of the Eleventh Five Year Plan, so that the stage is set for a transformation in higher education in the remaining years of the Eleventh Five Year Plan and it continues to take effect during the Twelfth Five Year Plan period.

SKILL DEVELOPMENT

The formulation of a National Policy on Skill Development and the setting up of the PM's National Council on Skill Development reflect the importance the government attaches to skill development. A number of initiatives have been taken to strengthen skill development. As on 1 January 2007 there were 5,114 ITIs/ITES in the country with a seating capacity of 7.42 lakh. Three years later, there was an impressive increase in the number of such institutions to 7,984 ITIs/ITES—an increase of 56 per cent; the seating capacity had increased to 11.07 lakh. In the Union Budget of 2007-08, a scheme for upgrading 1,396 government ITIs into Centres of Excellence (CoEs) through PPP was announced. About 900 ITIs have been taken up under this programme. Of these, 815 have already been approved and are in various stages of implementation. Another 500 ITIs are to be upgraded with the help of the World Bank. Under the Modular Employable Skills Scheme, 1,103 specially designed short-term modules have been introduced to train school dropouts and informal sector workers.

The Skill Development Corporation, which was set up as a vehicle to provide financial support to skill development initiatives emanating from the private sector, has become operational and has sanctioned assistance to several projects.

HEALTH SERVICES

Access to good quality health services is another critical element of the inclusiveness strategy. The deficiencies in this area are well known. The Eleventh Five Year Plan had noted that while total expenditure on health in India as a percentage of GDP was comparable to that in the other developing countries, there was disproportionate reliance on private medical services which many can ill-afford. Total public expenditure on health in India (Centre and States combined), was below 1 per cent of GDP at the start of the Eleventh Five Year Plan. It is felt that this needs to be increased to about 2 to 3 per cent of GDP.

The greatest deficiency of medical services is in the rural areas, where a large part of the population simply does not have access to functioning health centres with minimum medical facilities and essential drugs. The Eleventh Five Year Plan sought to address this problem through the National Rural Health Mission (NRHM), which aimed at creating the necessary physical infrastructure of sub-centres, Primary Health Centres (PHCs), and Community Health Centres (CHCs) linked by district hospitals. An innovation in this programme was the reliance on locally recruited young women as Accredited Social Health Activists (ASHAs), who could serve as a link between the community and the public health service delivery system.[1]

The National Rural Health Mission (NRHM) has now been in operation for five years, which is not a long enough time to judge the impact on health outcomes. The Mission has made progress in expanding the physical infrastructure for health, and also making flexible resources available at PHCs and sub-centres. It has also successfully appointed 7.5 lakh ASHAs though their training is behind schedule. Availability of doctors and technicians, in particular specialists, to support the health infrastructure in rural areas also remains a major challenge. Some states have successfully recruited

1. ASHAs receive basic training and also allowed to adminsiter some basic drugs for common maladies. An important function of ASHAs is to encourage pregnant women to go in for institutional deliveries for which both the women and the ASHA receive an incentive payment under the Janani Suraksha Yojana.

health personnel on contracts, but a satisfactory solution can only come from a large expansion in trained human resources in the health sector. This calls for a substantial expansion of capacity in medical and nursing colleges.

An important new initiative in the area of curative healthcare was the launch of the Rashtriya Swasthya Bima Yojana (RSBY) under which state governments provide health insurance for the below poverty line (BPL) population for in-patient treatment in approved public or private sector hospitals. The Central Government pays 75 per cent of the premium and the state governments pay the rest. A key element of the Rashtriya Swasthya Bima Yojana (RSBY) is that the patient can choose from alternative providers of health services and there is no cash transaction. As many as 1.25 crore smart cards have already been issued covering a population of more than 6 crore. When fully operational, the scheme will provide hospitalization cover to over 30 crore people.

The primary healthcare needs of the urban poor also need to be addressed. Both rural and urban health initiatives may need to be combined under an integrated National Health Mission. Public Health Specialists need to be integrated with the health system at all levels. It is also important to consider a paradigm shift from viewing the government as a 'provider of health services' to one of 'financing healthcare while providing choice in health services' through innovative public-private Health Insurance Schemes which enable the poor to choose among alternative health service providers.

The effort to expand the government's role in healthcare has thus far raised the total public expenditure on health only marginally from 0.96 per cent of GDP in 2005-06 to 1.09 per cent in 2009-10. This increase has occurred primarily because of an increase in the Central Government health expenditure, with state government expenditure increasing very little. The target of increasing public sector expenditure on "health to between 2 and 3 per cent of GDP obviously calls for much stronger efforts by the Central Government and even more so by the state governments in the years ahead.

OTHER INCLUSIVENESS PROGRAMMES

The Eleventh Five Year Plan contains a number of other programmes aimed at promoting inclusiveness. Some such critical programmes are:

- The Integrated Child Development Services (ICDS) focusing on pre-school education and supplementary feeding;
- The Accelerated Rural Drinking Water Supply Programme, which aims at covering all unserved villages with a safe source of drinking water;
- The Total Sanitation Programme, which aims at providing individual household latrines to combat the widespread practice of open defecation;
- The Indira Awas Yojana (IAY), which provides assistance for construction of houses to those among the BPL population who do not have housing;
- The Rajiv Gandhi Grameen Vidyutikaran Yojana (RGGVY), which aims at electrifying all unelectrified villages and providing free connections to BPL households; and
- The National Social Old Age Pension, which provides pensions to the BPL population above the age of 65 years.

The total allocation to these programmes, which essentially aim at inclusiveness, is budgeted at Rs 40,490 crore for 2010-11.

The performance of each of these programmes is discussed in detail in the relevant chapter of the MTA. The overall picture shows progress in many areas, but it also reveals deficiencies in the implementation of individual programmes which need to be addressed. Progress in reducing malnutrition among children has been particularly slow despite long years of effort. It is now recognized that malnutrition cannot be dealt with by a single instrument such as the ICDS. It needs action on multiple fronts, including raising the income levels of families, age at the first pregnancy and the nutritional status of pregnant women, availability of clean drinking water, state of sanitation, and knowledge of feeding practices especially promoting exclusive breast feeding for the first six months. There are programmes that are directed to each of these ends, but their effectiveness needs to be improved.

SOCIAL JUSTICE

Inclusive growth implies delivering social justice to all, particularly disadvantaged groups such as SCs, STs, OBCs, minorities, persons with disabilities, senior citizens, and other marginalized groups. One aspect of social justice is that all programmes that provide generalized access to essential services, such as health, education, clean drinking water, and sanitation, should be implemented in a way that ensures that disadvantaged groups get full access to these services. Another aspect of social justice is the promotion of schemes specifically targeted at these groups. The Eleventh Five Year Plan contains several such programmes.

Scholarships for SCs and STs have been greatly expanded. Schemes of post-matric scholarships for 'SCs, STs, and OBCs are implemented with the aim of promoting higher education among these disadvantaged groups. The Rajiv Gandhi National Fellowships scheme for SCs and STs is being implemented through the University Grants Commission (UGC) to encourage these groups to take up university education. Students from these groups are also encouraged to pursue higher studies, including those that lead to award of M Phil and PhD degrees.

The scheme of pre-matric scholarships for children of those engaged in unclean occupations was revised in terms of the norms, value of scholarships, and by enhancing central assistance from 50 per cent to 100 per cent. This will improve the state of education among those children thereby giving them better livelihood opportunities.

A comprehensive and focused development programme was implemented for the development of 75 Partieularly Vulnerable Tribal Groups (PVTGs). The government also enacted the Scheduled Tribes and the Other Forest Dwellers (Recognition of Forest Rights) Act in 2006 and framed the rules in 2007 with the objective of recognizing and vesting forest rights of forest land to persons who have been inhabiting these places for generations.

In pursuance of the Prime Minister's New 15-Point Programme for the minorities, the government introduced three new scholarship schemes: pre, post, and merit-cum-means based to promote education among minorities. A Multi-Sectoral Development Programme has also been launched in 90 districts identified on the basis of the minority population percentage above the age of 25 years, combined with backwardness criteria of the particular district.

The concept of a District Scheduled Castes Sub-Plan and Scheduled Tribes Sub-Plan was introduced to ensure that an adequate share of the Plan expenditure went to the benefit of SCs. The Mid Term Appraisal (MTA) reveals Chat the manner in which these sub-plans have been implemented, both in central ministries and the states, has not been satisfactory. The Planning Commission is reviewing experience in this area to see how the SC/ST sub-plan implementation can be improved. New guidelines will be developed taking into account the practical difficulties in the existing guidelines, so that the sub-plans can be implemented more effectively in the future.

BACKWARD REGIONS

An aspect of inclusive development that has received growing attention in recent years is the problem of backward districts, or of backward regions within states. The relative levels of development of a state as a whole are taken into account in determining the state's share in tax revenues. This aspect is also reflected in the Gadgil-Mukherjee formula, which determines the share of normal central assistance. It is, however, felt that these mechanisms do not take care of the special problems of backward regions within states.

The Backward Regions Grant Fund (BRGF), covering 250 districts in the country, was introduced in August 2006 to address this problem. Each district receives an amount depending upon its total population size and area. The allocation is untied, but its availability is conditioned upon the preparation of a District Development Plan which is expected to take a comprehensive view of the development constraints affecting the district. The Backword Regions Grant Fund (BRGF) can be used to fill gaps after faking account of resources available through other schemes. As in other local area programmes, it has taken time to prepare District Development Plans but these have since been prepared for most of the districts. The Backword Regions Grant Fund (BRGF) also includes a special additional allocation for the eight districts constituting the original Kalahandi, Bolangir, Koraput (KBK) group in Orissa and a special allocation for Bihar.

A Special Bundelkhand Drought Mitigation Package of Rs 7,266 crore comprising Rs 3,506 crore for six districts of Uttar Pradesh and Rs 3,760 crore for seven districts of Madhya Pradesh, has also been approved recently to be implemented over three years. Additional Central Plan Assistance of Rs 3,450 crore will be provided to the governments of Uttar Pradesh and Madhya Pradesh over a period of three years from 2009-10 to 2011-12. This is over and above the resources pooled from various ongoing schemes of different departments.

Neglect of Balanced Regional Development, including the development of tribal areas, can lead to serious consequences, such as the growth of left wing extremism, which is evident in many districts in the country. Successful development in these areas is the only viable solution to the underlying discontent which extremism can feed upon. This calls for an innovative approach, especially efforts to improve governance and people's participation. Implementation of Panchayat Extension to Scheduled Areas (PESA) Act is absolutely essential but progress has been slow. States and the Central Government will have to pay special attention to the challenges that this poses in terms of evolving an effective development strategy and creating credible systems of governance in those areas.

INFRASTRUCTURE DEVELOPMENT

Weaknesses in infrastructure, particularly in the energy and transport sectors, are perhaps the most important constraints in the growth of the economy in the medium term. Recognizing the importance of infrastructure development, the Eleventh Five Year Plan had estimated that the investment needed over the Plan period was about US$ 500 billion, compared to a likely 'business as usual' projection of US$ 300 billion. This investment was to be achieved through a combination of public investment and private initiative, including through PPP. Public investment was to be directed at areas which were not expected to attract private investment, whereas the scope for PPP was to be exploited wherever feasible.

Experience over the first three years shows that there has been a commendable increase in the total investment in infrastructure. The total level of investment in infrastructure is likely to come close to the Eleventh Five Year Plan target. The experience has been varied across sectors with some performing much better than expected and some sectors experiencing shortfalls. In general, private investment in infrastructure has done better than expected while public investment has fallen short. The government should give top priority to continuing the infrastructure investment thrust in the remaining years of the Plan.

TELECOMMUNICATIONS

The Plan target for 600 million telephone connections by the end of the Plan period is likely to be reached by the end of the third year itself and the target for doubling rural connections from 100 million to 200 million is also likely to be met by the end of the fourth year. This expansion is being led by a very dynamic private sector in the mobile telephone segment. It is taking place in an environment of strong competition which ensures that telecommunication charges in India are among the lowest in the world.

The introduction of 3G services, which promise further expansion of capacity in this sector, was delayed because of difficulty in getting the spectrum vacated. These problems have now been overcome. Auction of the 3G spectrum has been largely completed in the first quarter of 2010-11. Broadband connectivity, an area that needs special attention, has also been expanding but progress has been modest.

ELECTRIC POWER

Power shortages and its unreliable quality have been major weaknesses of our economy and supply continues to lag behind demand. However, compared with the Tenth Plan, there has been an improvement in the pace of addition of new generation capacity.

The capacity added in the first three years will be only about 20,000 MW, but a large number of projects are currently under construction and are expected to be completed in the remaining two years. As a result, the expected addition of capacity in the Eleventh Five Year Plan period will range between 62,000 and 64,000 MW. This is short of the Plan target of 78,000 MW, but it is three times the capacity added during the entire Tenth Five Year Plan period.

The capacity added by the private sector is actually running ahead of the target, whereas both the central and state sector performance will be below target. There is obviously considerable room for improving project management in the public sector.

Availability of coal for thermal plants will be an important constraint in electricity generation in the years ahead. Import requirements for coal by the end of the Eleventh Five Year Plan will be higher than originally targeted, but the scale is manageable. The real problem is likely to arise in the Twelfth Five Year Plan as coal imports are likely to increase from 81 million tonnes at the end of Eleventh Five Year Plan to 230 million tonnes at the end of the Twelfth Five Year Plan. Advance action is necessary to develop the capacity for handling coal imports of this scale.

The distribution segment of the electricity sector is clearly a weak link. Transmission and Distribution (T&D) losses are falling, but much more slowly than targeted. The system continues to suffer huge losses which are estimated to be over Rs 40,000 crore for 2009-10. The scale of losses in the distribution segment is simply unsustainable and determined action is needed to reverse this trend. However, performance in this area depends entirely on the states. It is important to redouble efforts to contain losses in the last two years of the Eleventh Five Year Plan to improve the financial viability of the distribution segment. The recently restructured Accelerated Power 'Development Programme (APDP), which provides central assistance to the states to support efforts to improve distribution efficiency, needs to be closely monitored.

Private sector involvement in distribution could help improve efficiencies, but very few states have taken initiatives in this area. The experience of privatization in Delhi is that it has resulted in significant reduction in losses. The recent experiment in Bhiwandi (Maharashtra), franchising part of the distribution system to a private company, has been highly successful in reducing T&D losses. A similar franchise has been awarded to a private sector company for distribution in Agra. The franchisee route is a viable option where states are reluctant to privatize. Experiments along these lines should be encouraged through appropriately structured concession agreements.

HIGHWAYS AND ROAD DEVELOPMENT

The Eleventh Five Year Plan envisaged an ambitious National Highway Development Programme (NHDP) aimed at upgrading and expanding the national highways in phases. It also envisaged accelerated development of rural roads through the Pradhan Mantri Gram Sadak Yojana (PMGSY).

Implementation of National Highway Development Programme (NHDP) is behind schedule but it has improved more recently. In the first two years of the Plan, road construction contracts on the build-operate-transfer (BOT) basis were awarded for only 1,800 km. This was partly due to the financial crisis that adversely affected the appetite of private investors. However, the situation improved in the third year and build-operate transfer (BOT) contracts are expected to increase to 5,000 km in 2009-10. The pace is expected to pick up further in the remaining years of the Eleventh Five Year Plan. The Ministry of Road Transport and Highways (MORTH) has set a target of completing 7,000 km per year and is building up a project portfolio to achieve this.

Construction of rural roads under PMGSY is satisfactory. The programme was re-phased to achieve time-bound targets of rural connectivity under the overall umbrella of Bharat Nirman initiated in 2005-06. It aimed at providing all-weather road connectivity to all habitations of more than 1,000 population in the plains and more than 500 in hilly or tribal areas by 2009. Although there has been some slippage, about 84 per cent of the target has been met and the remaining 16 per cent will be completed by the end of 2010-11. The resulting improvement in rural road connectivity is a major achievement, which has already contributed to improved market linkages for farmers as well as improved access to health and educational services for the rural population.

RAILWAYS

Railways has steadily expanded its freight and passenger business, but steady expansion is no longer enough. A radically new and more ambitious approach is needed. A long-term vision for modernizing and restructuring the Railways has been spelt out in the Indian Railways' Vision Document presented to Parliament. The vision involves substantial expansion in line capacity and rolling stock and technological modernization, including the introduction of high speed trains and upgrading locomotive production.

Realizing this vision will require a large investment programme and financing it will present a major challenge. The Railways has thus far mobilized much less by way of internal resource generation than was projected in the Eleventh Five Year Plan. Rather, the Railways has relied on budgetary resources more than originally envisaged. Given the other demands on budgetary resources, financing for the modernization and expansion of the Railways cannot come from the Budget. It has to be mobilized through greater internal resource generation and through PPP. Improved internal resource generation in turn requires a rebalancing of fares to reduce the extent of present subsidy on passenger fares which has now reached approximately Rs 19,000 crore.

The Railways has steadily lost freight to road transport and a reversal of this decline in share must be an important element of any transition to a more fuel efficient and lower carbon development strategy. Two Dedicated Freight Corridors, one from Kolkata to Ludhiana and the other from Delhi to Mumbai, are being implemented. Special efforts will be needed to monitor their implementation to ensure that these projects are completed on target by 2016.

The changes required in Railway planning and management to realize the long-term vision are far-reaching and can only be implemented over two Plan periods. Nevertheless, substantive progress must be made in the remaining period of the Eleventh Five Year Plan.

AIRPORTS

Faster GDP growth in recent years had brought about a rapid growth in air traffic. This was built into the Eleventh Five Year Plan projections for the requirement of airport infrastructure. This was temporarily interrupted because of the global slowdown in 2008-09, but it can be expected to recover as GDP growth accelerates. Airport development and modernization must therefore remain a critical part of the infrastructure agenda.

The Eleventh Five Year Plan has seen substantial initiatives in this area, including the commissioning of two new private airports in Hyderabad and Bangalore, expansion of Delhi and Mumbai airports by private investors on a PPP basis, development of Chennai and Kolkata airports through the Airports Authority of India (AAI), and expansion and modernization of 35 non-metro airports by the AAI. In addition, new airports are being constructed in the North-East to ensure that each state capital has a functioning civil airport.

Work on the Delhi and Mumbai airports is expected to be completed on schedule. Work on 9 of the 35 non-metro airports plus 13 other airports has been completed and work on the remaining non-metro airports is expected to be completed within the Eleventh Five Year Plan period. Restructuring of AAI, including separation of Air Traffic Control into a separate corporate entity to be wholly owned by the AAI, should be expedited.

PORTS

Efficient ports are critical for the global competitiveness of an open economy but progress in capacity building of ports has lagged significantly behind target. Against an expected addition of 88 million tonnes to port handling capacity in the Eleventh Five Year Plan for major and minor ports put together, the actual achievement is likely to be only about 55 per cent of the target.

Capacity expansion has been much faster in the non-major ports, where many state governments have adopted a strategy of developing new ports entirely through the private sector. The Central Government policy does not encourage privatization of entire ports, but it does envisage private sector participation in the development of individual berths/terminals. Unfortunately, progress in inviting bids for such capacity expansion projects in the first three years of the Plan was disappointing. A determined effort must be made in the last two years, with well-defined annual targets, to achieve the best outcomes possible.

URBAN INFRASTRUCTURE

Urbanization in India has been relatively slow in the past, but is now expected to accelerate. The urban population share may reach 50 per cent in 25 years adding 300 to 400 million people to the existing population of about 350 million in urban areas. Since the present urban population is seriously underserved in terms of infrastructure, such as water supply, sewerage, solid waste disposal, and urban transport, the task of making up existing deficiencies and providing for the required expansion presents a huge challenge for the future.

A start in addressing these challenges was made in the form of the Jawaharlal Nehru National Urban Renewal Mission (JNNURM) that was launched in 2005 to cover the period through to the end of the Eleventh Five Year Plan. Central assistance under this scheme is linked to the preparation of a Comprehensive Development Plan (CDP) for cities and to the implementation of reforms, some of which are mandatory, such as reforms in municipal accounting, rent control laws and e-governance for transparency. Some others, such as repeal of the Urban Land Ceiling Act, introduction of property title certification system, and encouraging PPPs are optional.

The, Mid Term Appraisal (MTA) reveals that after a slow start, the programme has gathered pace. As of September 2009, 2,523 projects had been approved with Rs. 52,687 crore of central assistance already committed, with a matching commitment of Rs. 44,334 crore from the states. The total investment in essential urban services triggered by JNNURM is therefore close to Rs. 1,00,000 crore to be implemented over the remaining two years of the Eleventh Five Year Plan. This is clearly an impressive beginning for the first major national initiative aimed at developing urban infrastructure.

FINANCING THE ELEVENTH FIVE YEAR PLAN

The Eleventh Five Year Plan programmes for creating social and economic infrastructure to meet the requirements of rapid and inclusive growth implied a significant increase in Plan expenditure. Total plan expenditure of the Centre and the States combined was expected to increase from an average of 9.5 per cent of GDP in the Tenth Five Year Plan to 13.5 per cent of GDP in the Eleventh Five Year Plan. This increase was to be financed primarily through an increase in the balance from current revenues in the budgets of the Centre and the States and from improved internal resource generation in the public sector.

Three years of the Plan have been completed and the central budget estimates for 2010-11 are known. Based on available data, and making some assumptions about 2011-12, it is possible to say that in the case of the Centre, the realization of Plan expenditure is likely to be between 95 and 100 per cent of the Eleventh Five Year Plan target. In the case of the states it will be lower, but much better than in the Tenth Five Year Plan.

The main weakness in performance is that the financing of Plan expenditure departs significantly from the pattern originally envisaged. The increase of 4 percentage points of GDP in the Eleventh Five Year Plan compared with the Tenth Five Year Plan was to be achieved, primarily through higher balance of current revenues and greater internal resource mobilization. This objective could not be met partly because the economic slowdown meant a lower growth in revenues, some of which was itself due to tax reduction measures introduced as part of the stimulus.

The result has been a much larger volume of borrowing than was envisaged in the Eleventh Five Year Plan to support desired levels of Plan expenditure. This is reflected in the fact that the combined deficit of the Centre and the States, which was to have been contained at 6 per cent of GDP by 2009-10 was actually around 10 per cent of GDP and only a gradual reduction will be possible over the next few years. The slippage in containing the fiscal deficit can be defended as a temporary response to the global slowdown, and is in line with what has been done by most other countries. However, with the global economy stabilizing and hopefully resuming growth, there is concern everywhere on the need to get back to a fiscally prudent position.

The pattern of fiscal consolidation envisaged in the Centre for the remainder of the Eleventh Five Year Plan has been outlined in the 2010-11 Budget, which projects a fiscal deficit of 5.5 per cent of GDP for 2010-11 falling to 4.8 per cent in 2011-12. The projected compression in the fiscal deficit will pose financing challenge to find the resources needed for Plan expenditure.

Three factors are critical in this context. These factors are as follows:

First, it is essential to keep control over non-plan expenditure, most notably subsidies. The major Central Government subsidies in the system at present are on food, petroleum products, and fertilizers. The main subsidies at the state level are due to power sector losses and losses on irrigation. While there is a role for targeted subsidies to help the poor meet their essential requirements, the present system of subsidies has evolved in an ad hoc manner and the extent of the total subsidy is much larger than any benefit that reaches the genuinely deserving. Several of the subsidies are also dysfunctional leading to wasteful use of scarce resources. It is necessary to review the system comprehensively to ensure that subsidies are efficiently designed to reach the target group and the resources saved from this restructuring could be devoted to meet essential plan requirements in health and education.

Second, it will be necessary to adopt an aggressive programme of disinvestment in Public Sector Undertakings (PSUs). Even if the government share of equity must not go below 51 per cent, there is very substantial scope for disinvestment to mobilize resources for Plan expenditure through the budget.

Third, the scope for PPP needs to be vigorously explored wherever possible in a manner consistent with the overall development objectives. The past few years have shown that investments through PPP are possible and both the Centre and the States have taken a number of initiatives in this area. These initiatives need to be expanded keeping in mind the need for transparency and competition in awarding concessions.

GOVERNANCE

Poor governance is often at the heart of poor outcomes from government policies and programmes. Poor governance includes a wide range of failings like: (i) inability to ensure law and order, which is an essential requirement for investment an economic expansion, (ii) lack of efficiency in executing government programmes to achieve end results, and (iii) lack of an environment in which business both in the private and public sector can be conducted efficiently with minimum transaction costs. Inevitably each of these weaknesses is linked to corruption in the sense of being caused by corruption and giving rise to it.

SIMPLIFYING PROCEDURES AND TRANSPARENCY

There is no magic wand to resolve these problems. Each one has to be taken up at the relevant level and addressed on a sustained basis. The easiest steps are those aimed at making procedures less cumbersome and more transparent. There is considerable scope for such simplification of procedures at both the central and state government levels. Implementation of the recommendations of the Second Administrative Reforms Commission should receive priority. The states should be encouraged to take similar action.

The Right to Information Act is a critical building block to increase transparency and shed light on the functioning of the government.

EMPOWERING PRIs AND URBAN LOCAL BODIES

A more difficult governance challenge relates to creating a system which can efficiently deliver critical services like health services, education and skill development services, anganwadi centres, and sanitation and drinking water, which are the focus of a great deal of the government's efforts today. These services are all delivered at the local level and hence the importance of effective governance at that level. Empowerment of Panchayati Raj Institutions (PRIs) to and Urban Local Bodies (ULBs) combined with an effective participation of the people can create points of monitoring and intervention. Progress in empowering Panchayati Raj Institutions (PRIs) to perform the functions entrusted to them has been far below expectations. While most states have transferred the necessary functions, there has been very limited transfer of functionaries who in most cases remain departmental employees sent to Panchayati Raj Institutions (PRIs) on deputation. Progress in transferring finances has been even less. The situation varies across states, but except for a few cases, empowerment of Panchayati Raj Institutions (PRIs) is much below what is needed.

Along with empowerment there is need to build capacity of the people's representatives to perform the monitoring and oversight functions they are supposed to perform.

In the absence of effective participation and in situations where empowerment is weak, the effectiveness of programmes in the field will be low and the scope for leakages and corruption will be correspondingly high. This is especially true in the case of tribal districts many of which are affected by left wing extremism.

MONITORING AND EVALUATION

We also need much better systems of monitoring and evaluation of programmes with a view to generating MIS feedback and creating a base for auditing. At present, many programmes in the. social sectors as well as other programmes aimed at inclusiveness are funded as Centrally Sponsored Schemes (CSSs). These schemes involve substantial disbursements by the Centre to the states or to state-level implementing agencies. However, reliable information within an acceptable time on whether the money transferred from the Centre has actually been spent by the implementing agency at the state level is difficult to obtain. This problem is being addressed by an improved expenditure tracking system which is being developed by the Controller General of Accounts in consultation with the Planning Commission. Once operationalized, this would help monitor actual expenditure on Plan schemes and also strengthen audit.

There is also need for much stronger *ex-post* evaluation to ascertain whether the expenditure on a programme is delivering the outcomes intended. Centrally Sponsored Schemes (CSSs) today account for more than half of the Central Plan Budget. While there are approximately 150 such schemes, the largest 25 account for 93 per cent of the total Centrally Sponsored Schemes (CSS) expenditure. These large schemes must be subjected to systematic and scientific *ex-post* evaluation to determine whether expenditures incurred have actually had the impact intended on outcomes. To undertake such evaluation, it has been decided to establish an independent evaluation organization linked to but distinct from the Planning Commission.

SOME FUTURE CHALLENGES

The Mid Term Appraisal (MTA) has also thrown up some issues, the importance of which was not fully recognized at the time that the Eleventh Five Year Plan was drafted. Addressing these issues goes beyond making mid-course corrections. It calls for an in-depth review of our policies in these areas and may require restructuring of policies which can be fully achieved only in the Twelfth Plan.

INTEGRATED ENERGY POLICY

At the time that the Eleventh Five Year Plan was finalized, the Planning Commission had received the report of an Expert Group on Integrated Energy Policy but the report was still under consideration. Since then, the recommendations of the group have been considered inter-ministerially and an Integrated Energy Policy based on the recommendations of the Group was approved by the Cabinet in 2009.

The policy draws attention to a number of issues in the energy sector relating to energy pricing, regulatory structures, and issues related to energy production and energy security. Since the responsibility for energy policy is fragmented among several different ministries dealing with individual energy sub-sectors (for example, electric power, coal, petroleum and natural gas, and renewable energy), the policy in different sectors has not been based on common principles. For example, the pricing policy differs across different sources of energy, with no clear relationship with world prices. Policies related to energy production also differ, for example, between coal which is nationalized, and petroleum and natural gas which are not. The tax subsidy structure also varies across different energy sources.

The Integrated Energy Policy outlines a large number of policy changes needed for rationalizing energy policies across different energy groups. Many of these changes, though approved by the Cabinet, have yet to be implemented. A determined effort should be made to complete implementation of this agenda in the remaining two years of the Eleventh Five Year Plan so that the economy enters the Twelfth Five Year Plane period in a much stronger position on the energy front.

MANAGEMENT OF WATER

Management of scarce water resources poses a major challenge. The total annually usable water resources available in the country is fixed and depends upon total precipitation after allowing for the minimum flow in the rivers which must be maintained. Calculations suggest that the total demand given the present population and production structure is already close to the available usable water resources. Since demand is bound to rise as population expands and growth of GDP generates higher demand from agriculture and industry, we could face a water crisis if the problem is not addressed holistically, recognizing the limited options for expanding supply and the consequent need for managing demand and increasing water use efficiency.

Unfortunately, the problem is currently handled by different departments operating in silos. The traditional approach on the supply side has been building dams to store water, with very little focus on ensuring optimal use to maximize productivity of this scarce resource. As a result, head-end canal users adopt far more water-intensive cropping patterns than are optimal, leaving very little water for tail-end farmers. The tendency to grow water-intensive crops is unavoidable as long as canal water is severely underpriced. In this situation, there is need for a statutory mechanism to enforce equitable distribution over the entire command area as has been done in Maharashtra, where the Water Regulatory Authority is empowered to enforce equitable distribution with active involvement of stakeholders through water users associations which collect water charges and are also responsible for its maintenance.

Management of groundwater resources also poses serious problems. Groundwater is a common property resource, but the law as it stands allows a farmer to extract any amount of water from a borewell dug on his own land, even though such withdrawal affects the water table. Free or very cheap power for agriculture compounds the problem leading to overdrawal of water beyond the annual recharge of the aquifer. This is evident in states, such as Punjab and Haryana and in the hard rock regions in Southern India. This 'water mining' has resulted in steadily falling water tables and a serious increase in water pollution.

The usual response of limiting the boring of new wells is ineffective since it only confers a monopoly on existing well owners, allowing them to sell water to others at premium prices. Efforts must be made to obtain collective agreements to limit the use of groundwater to sustainable levels through participatory processes. A cess on the use of power for agriculture in all areas where groundwater is under stress, with the proceeds earmarked for water conservation in the same watershed, is well worth considering.

The problem of pollution of rivers and water bodies has reached alarming proportions. The 'polluter pays' principle is widely asserted in our policies but is not enforced in practice. Our cities and industries dump large quantities of untreated sewage and untreated industrial effluent in the rivers. We need much stricter monitoring and enforcement to ensure that untreated waste is not dumped into the rivers, with strict penalties for violation. In principle, these penalties would have to be applied to government agencies also, such as those responsible for sewage disposal. There is also need for much stronger regulation to ensure recycling of industrial water.

Since the total supply of water is limited, a large part of the solution to water scarcity problems lies in the management of demand. The greatest scope is clearly in agriculture, which uses 80 per cent of the water. More scientific cultivation practices (for example, the SRI system of rice cultivation) and the use of sprinkler and drip irrigation can cut water use to less than half. However, with canal water and electric power seriously underpriced, farmers have little incentive to use alternative technologies which involve an extra cost.

Managing the water crisis clearly requires action on multiple fronts. We have to increase usable supply through means, such as construction of large storages, harvesting of rainwater wherever possible, recharging groundwater through afforestation, and watershed management programmes. We also have to act on the demand side, encouraging less water-intensive production patterns and managing demand by encouraging recycling. These objectives have to be pursued through a combination of regulatory control, rational pricing, and increased people's awareness and participation. These different instruments have different costs associated with them and an optimal strategy for bridging the water gap must identify least cost solutions for doing so. These vary according to hydro-geological conditions, which are area specific. The optimal mix may therefore vary from place to place.

Tackling all these problems requires coordinated action by different ministries and also intensive consultation with state governments. The Planning Commission is working on preparing an Integrated Water Management Policy which can identify key policy issues. This must be done before the Twelfth Plan begins.

CLIMATE CHANGE

Climate change has emerged as an area of concern worldwide. Changes in rainfall and temperature, which may occur, have the potential of generating serious adverse consequences in most parts of the world including India.

An ideal response to climate change has to be anchored in a globally agreed cooperative framework which ensures a fair distribution of the burden of mitigation and adaptation between different groups of countries. India is actively engaged in the ongoing international negotiations to achieve a satisfactory and fair outcome. However, pending the evolution of a global consensus it is also necessary to take national steps to combat climate change. Accordingly, a National Action Plan for Climate Change has been announced which lays down initiatives that the government will take in both mitigation and adaptation.

As far as mitigation is concerned our objective must be to increase energy efficiency and reduce the intensity of emissions consistent with our basic goal of increasing our per capita income to improve the living standards of our people. India has one of the lowest levels of per capita use of energy among large developing countries and we will certainly need an increase in total energy use to sustain rapid growth. However, it should be our endeavour to increase energy efficiency as much as possible, and also shift to non-fossil fuel energy.

The government has indicated, that emissions intensity per unit of GDP could fall by 20 per cent by 2020. Several steps have been taken to achieve this outcome. We are committed to expanding base of nuclear power generation with the National Solar Mission, which has an ambitious programme of adding 20,000 MW of solar power over the next two decades. State electricity regulators have laid down that distributing companies must purchase 5 per cent of the electricity from renewable sources thus introducing an implicit cross subsidy to support green energy. The introduction of a cess on coal to fund green technology development in the Budget for 2010-11 is an important initiative for financing clean energy technologies.

Much of the agenda in the Integrated Energy Policy serves the basic objective of improving energy efficiency and reducing dependence on fossil fuel energy. Similarly, our programmes of watershed conservation help reduce net CO_2 emissions. Programmes of watershed management and water conservation are precisely the programmes we need to strengthen in order to deal with the challenges of adaptation.

All these initiatives will have to be strengthened in the remaining period of the Eleventh Five Year Plan and more thoroughly mainstreamed in the Twelfth Five Year Plan to constitute a credible national response to climate change. The Planning Commission has set up an Expert Group on Low Carbon Development under the chairmanship of Dr Kirit Parikh to outline the scope of action we can consider to pursue a low carbon development strategy without compromising our basic development goals. The report of the group will be an important input into the Twelfth Five Year Plan.

SCIENCE AND TECHNOLOGY

Science and Technology (S&T) has a critical role to play as the economy moves to a higher and sustainable growth path. We must be open to absorbing technology from wherever it is available; economic maturity and industrial depth also require the building up of high quality indigenous capability which is globally competitive. The Mid Term Appraisal (MTA) indicates that the S&T effort in the various scientific departments and laboratories is proceeding broadly as envisaged in the Eleventh Five Year Plan, though there are cases where implementation has been slow, notably in meteorology. The government laboratories and scientific institutions have a major role to play in developing our technological capability and deserve full support.

Research and development cannot however be left only to government efforts. Much greater investment in this area is needed by the corporate sector, including both public sector and private sector corporations. There is need for a much larger S&T input in a wide range of fields, including agriculture, water management, medicine, clean energy, and transport, and looking ahead, to bringing about a more environmentally sustainable development strategy. Technological capacity in all these areas needs to be accelerated based on our own efforts as well as through global partnerships between Indian and foreign research institutions.

INNOVATION

To achieve growth that is both inclusive and sustainable within the constraint of limited resources it is necessary to promote innovations on a wide scale. Innovations are needed in products and services which reduce costs, economize on energy, and serve the needs of the common man m an affordable manner. Innovations are also needed in processes and delivery mechanisms, especially in government delivery mechanisms which need to be redesigned so that they can deliver outcomes commensurate with the considerable resources they now absorb.

To some extent, openness and competition combined with a strong technical scientific base spurs innovation and these aspects of policy must be maintained. However, the government can also play a proactive role in creating an environment that supports innovation. India needs to stimulate its entire innovation eco-system—the formal scientific-industrial system, as well as its large informal ecosystem—to develop solutions for the country's agenda of inclusive and sustainable growth. Government purchase policies in certain areas are an instrument that can promote innovation consistent with efficiency and cost minimization. Financial institutions are another important element promoting innovations by providing capital through various stages of product development.

12TH PLAN (2012-17): VARIOUS TARGETS AS SHOWN IN APPROACH PAPER

Tha Approach Paper of 12th Five Year Plan (2012-17) has been approved by National Development Council. The coming plan, like the previous 11th Plan repeats 9 per cent per annum average growth target. According to the Planning Commission, the 9 per cent target requires a significant acceleration in growth in agriculture, electricity, gas, water supply and also manufacturing. Agricultural growth has always been an important component for inclusiveness in India, and recent experience suggests that high GDP growth without such agricultural growth is likely to lead to accelerating inflation in the country, which would jeopardise the larger growth process. However, even if such agricultural growth is achieved, it is unlikely that the agricultural sector will absorb additional workers. Thus, the main responsibility for providing additional jobs to the growing labour force will rest on manufacturing and construction and on the services sectors. The target set for the mining sector, mainly reflecting additional production of coal and natural gas, is also very demanding, but is necessary to meet the primary energy requirements without resorting to excessive imports. As shown in the table below, taking the growth rate to 9.5 per cent would require much faster growth in the manufacturing, as well as in electricity, gas and water supply sectors. The feasibility of achieving such large acceleration in key sectoral performance needs to be considered carefully before the growth targets for the Twelfth Plan are fixed. This is particularly true for the energy sector where supply constraints could be severe.

Sectors	Target set for 9% GDP Growth
Agriculture, Forestry and Fishing	4.0
Mining and Quarrying	8.0
Manufacturing	9.8
Elect. Gas and Water Supply	8.5
Construction	10.0
Transport, Communication and Storage and Tourism	11.0
Financing, Insurance, Real Estate and Business Services	10.0
Community, Social and Personal Services	8.0
Total GDP	**9.0**
Industry	9.6
Service	10.0

EXERCISES

Long Answer Type Questions:

1. Write an essay in brief on aggregate and sectoral growth in Mid-Term Appraisal of Eleventh Five Year Plan.
2. What are the reasons for the superior performance on the growth front in Eleventh Five Year Plan ? Discuss in brief.
3. Discuss prospects for agriculture in Eleventh Five Year Plan.
4. What are positive developments in agriculture according to Mid-Term Appraisal of in Eleventh Five Year Plan ?
5. Write a note on Poverty Reduction in Eleventh Five Year Plan.
6. What is assessment about education in Mid-Term Appraisal of Eleventh Five Year Plan ?
7. What is the position of Health Services in Mid-Term Appraisal of Eleventh Five Year Plan ?
8. Write an essay on infrastructure development in Eleventh Five Year Plan according to Mid-Term Appraisal of Plan.
9. Write a note on financing the Eleventh Plan according to Mid-Term Appraisal of Eleventh Five Year Plan.
10. What are the future challengers for Eleventh Five Year Plan ? Write in brief.

Short Answer Type Questions:

1. Write a short note on resilience of the economy in Mid-Term Appraisal of Eleventh Five Year Plan.
2. What were Macro-Economic Fundamentals for Eleventh Five Year Plan according to Mid-Term Appraisal of Eleventh Five Year Plan ? Write in brief.
3. Write a brief note on 'Growth in the States' during Mid-Term Appraisal of Eleventh Five Year Plan.

4. Write a brief note on condition of the Manfacturing sector in Mid-Term Appraisal of Eleventh Five Year Plan.

5. Write a brief note on 'Inclusiveness and the Eleventh Plan' of the basis of Mid-Term Appraisal of Eleventh Five Year Plan.

6. Write a short note on 'Skill Development' under Eleventh Five Year Plan according to Mid-Term Appraisal of the Plan.

7. Write a short note on 'Other Inclusiveness Programmers' of Eleventh Five Year Plan.

8. Write a short note on 'Social Justice' under Eleventh Five Year Plan.

9. Write a brief note on 'Bckward Regions' under Eleventh Five Year Plan.

10. Write a short note on draft of 12th Five Year Plan.

Multiple Choice Type Objective Questions:

1. What was the period of Eleventh Five Year Plan?

(*a*) 2007-08 to 2011-12 (*b*) 2008-09 to 2012-13

(*c*) 2006-07 to 2010-11 (*d*) 2005-06 to 2009-10

2. The Eleventh Five Year Plan aimed at an average growth rate of-

(*a*) 8 per cent per annum (*b*) 9 per cent per annum

(*c*) 10 per cent per annum (*d*) None of the above

3. According to Mid-Term Appraisal of Eleventh Five Year Plan what was the growth rate in the first year of Eleventh Five Year Plan ?

(*a*) 6.5 per cent (*b*) 7.5 per cent

(*c*) 8.5 per cent (*d*) 9.5 per cent

4. Why the momentum was interrupted in 2008-09 during Eleventh Five Year Plan ?

(*a*) Due to disturbance in Central Cabinat

(*b*) Due to laziness of Planning Commission

(*c*) Due to weak economic condition

(*d*) Due to Global Financial Crisis.

5. What was the estimated FDI inflow in 2009-10?

(*a*) over US$ 31 billion (*b*) over US$ 30 billion

(*c*) over US$ 29 billion (*d*) over US$ 28 billion

6. What was the median growth rate of Gross State Domestic Product (GSDP) in the States in the first year of Eleventh Five Year Plan?

(*a*) 7.6 per cent (*b*) 8 per cent

(*c*) 6 per cent (*d*) 5 per cent

7. In which sector of the Eleventh Plan was to raise the rate of growth of G.D.P. ?

(*a*) In the sector of Health (*b*) In the sector of Education

(*c*) In the sector of Agriculture (*d*) In the sector of Infrastructure

8. What is the period of 12th Five Year Pan?

(*a*) 2011-16 (*b*) 2010-15

(*c*) 2009-14 (*d*) 2012-17

9. In 12th Plan what target is fixed per annum for average growth rate?

(*a*) 9 per cent (*b*) 10 per cent

(*c*) 8 per cent (*d*) 7 per cent

10. What target is for Agriculture, Forestry and Fishing in 12th Five Year Plan?

(*a*) 5.0 per cent (*b*) 4.0 per cent

(*c*) 3.0 per cent (*d*) 2.0 per cent

ANSWERS

1. (*a*)	2. (*b*)	3. (*c*)	4. (*d*)	5. (*a*)
6. (*b*)	7. (*c*)	8. (*d*)	9. (*a*)	10. (*b*)

25

CHAPTER

District Administration in India

Importance of the District. District is the most important unit of the State Administration because it is the pivot of the administration of the whole State. From the revenue, law and order and development point of view the district is the principal unit of the administration. All offices—Revenue Administration, Civil and Criminal Justice, Education, Public Health, Medical, Treasury, Police, Jails, Public Works, Excise and Taxation, Co-operation, Irrigation, Agriculture, Electricity, Civil Supply and Food—are concentrated at the District Headquarters. The size, number and population of the Districts are not fixed. They vary of course considerably. Even in one State there are variations.

THE DISTRICT OFFICER AND HIS CHANGING ROLE

Recruitment of the District Officer. The officer-in-charge of the District administration is called the District Officer. In the Punjab he is called the Deputy Commissioner but in other States he is known as Collector. Formerly (during the British times) he used to be a member of the Indian Civil Service but now he generally belongs to the Indian Administrative Service because after the dawn of independence the name of the Indian Civil Service was changed to Indian Administrative Service. Sometimes senior and distinguished members of the Provincial Civil Service are also promoted to fill up the post. The District Officer resides at the District Headquarters but he frequently goes on the tour of different places of his District. In this way he can keep himself in touch with the people and happenings of his District.

Functions or Duties of the District Officer. The District Officer has to perform multifarious duties in every State of India which may be classified as under :

1. *As a Collector.* The District Officer as a Collector is the head of the revenue administration of his District and is responsible for the collection and recovery of the land revenue and other cesses and duties of the Government. All officers of the revenue department of the District—Revenue Assistants. Tehsildars, Naib Tehsildars, Kanungos, Lambardars and

Patwaris —work under his direction, supervision and control. The District Officer administers the revenue laws and sees that the land revenue records and agricultural statistics of District are properly maintained. He is responsible for implementation of the land reforms in his District and grants loans to the agriculturist. If famine,, floods, scarcity of fodder for the animals, invasion of locusts, earthquake or any other natural calamity occurs, then he provides relief to the affected persons. The District Officer manages the Government lands, property and the estates placed under the management of the Court of Wards or under the direct management of the Government. He acquires or requisitions for public purposes land and buildings. He administers the stamp laws also.

2. *As a District Magistrate.* Previously he exercised the powers of First Class Magistrate but now there has been a separation of Executive and Judiciary in most of the States following the Directive Principles of State Policy enshrined in the Constitution of India, therefore the Collector does not take up criminal cases. The powers of deciding criminal cases now vest in the additional District Magistrate or Judicial Officers ; the District Magistrate (Collector) only exercises general supervision over the criminal administration of his District. The District Magistrate is responsible for the maintenance of law and order and the Superintendent of Police directly assists him for that purpose. Though the Superintendent of Police is directly under the Deputy Inspector-General of Police in departmental matters, yet in the matters of law and order he is required to give all possible help to the Deputy Commissioner. In order that the Superintendent of Police may fully co-operate with the Deputy Commissioner, it has been provided in Rajasthan and some other States that the character roll of the Superintendent of Police will be initiated by the District Magistrate. The District Magistrate inspects some Police Stations and the Station House Officers are transferred with his consultation.

The District Magistrate controls the Jails of his own District and he inspects them from time to time. He is responsible for the proper administration of criminal laws in his District. He grants licences or arms, explosives, petroleum, cinemas etc. He issues domicile certificates. When anybody needs a certificate to prove that he is a political sufferer or belongs to a scheduled caste or backward class, he has to get that certificate from the Deputy Commissioner or District Magistrate. Similarly, when any Indian wants to go abroad and applies for passport or visa, then the Government of India grants the passport and visa only with the consent or recommendation of the District Magistrate of the District to which the applicant belongs. The District Magistrate also supervises the activities of foreigners in his District and can recommend the extension of their visas. During the election times, he is responsible for conducting the elections and he extends all help to the election officers. Besides that he appoints a panel of lawyers in consultation with the District Judge.

3. *As a District Officer.* As a District Officer, the Collector or Deputy Commissioner, he looks after the general interests of the Government and he is the principal agency of the State Government in the District. He coordinates all the activities of other Government offices in the District and is responsible for the proper implementation of all the Government rules, regulations and orders. He is the general incharge of the treasury and carries out its work according to Government rules. He hears the public grievances and tries his best to redress these grievances. He acts as a link between the Government and the people and tries to place the Government's view before the people. In this way he harmonises the relations between the two.

The Deputy Commissioner (the District Officer) controls and supervises all the cases which are initiated by the Government against private citizens for the violation of the laws or those cases which are brought against the Government by the private citizens for the redress of any legal wrong done by the Government officials or any legal claim. He also trains the junior, officers in administrative work and procedures and dealings with the public.

The District Officer has some functions regarding Municipal Committees. He supervises their working and recommends various measures to the Government. The State Government can suspend the working of any Municipal Committee and appoint an administrator on the recommendations of the Deputy Commissioner. The Deputy Commissioner can suspend any resolution of the Municipal Committee if it is found contrary to the public interest. The Divisional Commissioner can make any change in the budget of the Municipal Committee on the recommendation of the District Officer. He is generally the ex-officio Chairman of the Urban Improvement Trust of his District. Besides that he makes proper arrangements for the proper distribution and allotment of controlled or essential commodities and supplies, through the District Food and Supplies Officer.

4. *As a District Development Officer*. Before independence the District Officer had not to do any development work but with the dawn of independence this work has become his main responsibility. The District Officer is now the presiding officer of the Development Committee of his District. He carries on all the development work of his District and all the Block Development Officers are under him in this respect. *So he is responsible for the implementation of Five-Year Plans, 20-Point Programme and Panchayati Raj*. He draws the development plan of his District with the help of other development officers. He maintains a close contact with the people and their representatives at his headquarters and during the tours. The Public Relations Department or the Publicity Department also works under his care and the District Public Relations Officer remains in close touch with him in order to popularise the various schemes launched by the Government.

Position of the Deputy Commissioner (the Collector) or District Officer in the changed circumstances. The District Officer or Collector occupies a unique position in his District. During the British days he was called the *Sarkar* and *Mai Bap* of the people. The Deputy Commissioner in the British times was expected to maintain the authority of State (law and order) and prevent the spread of revolutionary activities and crimes. Thus he was the most important pillar of British imperialism and he had a combination of judicial and executive authority in him to discharge his functions well. The Deputy Commissioners were before independence considered main instruments to check the freedom movements, punish freedom fighters and maintain peace at all costs. Since independence all this has changed. The Deputy Commissioner is no longer the officer of the people but the servant of the people. Though the Deputy Commissioner is required to maintain law and order as before, yet he is no longer expected to crush freedom-lovers. He is to punish only the criminals and violators of law. All the judicial powers which the District Officer enjoyed as the First Class Magistrate has been taken from him and conferred upon the Additional District Magistrate or Munsif Magistrate or the Judicial Officer but as the Chief Executive Officer of the District, he still enjoys all those powers which are necessary to maintain law and order. *While commenting upon the position of the Deputy Commissioner in the per-independence days, Sir William Hunter had said, "The District Officer is the fiscal officer charged with collection of Land Revenue, is also a revenue and criminal judge both of first instance and appeal... Police, Jails, Education, Municipalities, Roads, Sanitation, Dispensaries, Local Taxation and the Imperial revenues of district are to him matter of daily concern. He is expected to make himself acquainted with every phase of the social life of the natives and with each natural aspect of the country. He should be a lowyer, an accountant, a financier and a ready writer of State papers. He ought also to possess no mean knowledge of agriculture, political economy and engineering."* These remarks of Sir William Hunter are still true with this exception that the Deputy Commissioner or the Collector no longer enjoys the powers of the First Class Magistrate which were once enjoyed by him in per-independence days. The reason being that the framers of the new Indian Constitution thought it a violation of justice, hence they laid down in the Directive Principles of State Policy that the State shall strive to separate Executive and Judiciary on the District level. Following this directive of the Constitution most of the States have enacted laws accordingly. Though the Collector no longer enjoys the powers of the First Class Magistrate, yet his authority, dignity and prestige have not suffered in any way. Since independence numerous laws have been enacted which have conferred many new powers on him and enhanced his prestige. In regard to the Municipalities, Jails, Police, Revenue, Law and Order, Development work, Loans, he still wields tremendous authority and at the time of floods, famine or any other natural calamity the people still look to him for support. Though he is no longer the Chairman of the Zila Parishad and in most of the States of India, Zila Parishads have their own elected Chairman, still the Zila Parishads looks to him for guidance and support on many matters because the Deputy Commissioner is the principal representative of the State Government in the District and all help by the State Government to the Zila Parishad is rendered through him and generally on his recommendation. He is also required to submit monthly and annual reports to the State Government regarding the development work and the achievement or failure of the Panchayati Raj. He is still the main co-ordinator among the various departments of the District and provides technical assistence or other types of the help in case of need. Therefore, it will be true to admit that all the strings of District administration are gathered together in his hands.

Besides the numerous functions of the District Officer mentioned above, he looks to the proper representation of Scheduled Castes and backward classes in the various appointments made by the Government officials in the District. He is in charge of the Games and Sports of his District. He is also the ceremonial head of his District, as all the Government functions are celebrated through him and he hoists national flag on the Republic Day at the District Headquarters. *In the war and emergency, his role is unique because he gives all possible help to the Government in the recruitment, collection of funds for national defence, organisation of civil defence, mobilising the efforts of the people of his District and keeping their morale high for resisting the invader, and checking the espionage of the enemy or reporting about the activities of the enemy to the Government.* When the troops pass through his territory, then he extends all facilities to them. So we can say that the Deputy Commissioner enjoys a wide range of powers and occupies a position of great dignity in his District and he is truly the eyes, the ears, the mouth and hands of the State Government.

It was once thought after independence that the M.L.As and M.Ps would seriously jeoardise his position and mar his popularity because they are the representatives of the people but these apprehensions have not come true and Collector or the Deputy Commissioner continues to enjoy all powers and prestige as before and his authority or prestige has not suffered or received any setback in any way. Rather he has developed harmonious relations with these representatives of the public. The District Officer is still the real head of his District and the people look to *him* for every governmental work. Therefore, we can say that though he is not held in awe like his counterpart of British time, but still he is greatly respected and admired. As the nation is passing through economic crisis and the development work is increasing with a fast speed, so it is expected that the responsibilities, work and consequently the powers of the District Officer or the Deputy Commissioner will increase more and more with the passage of time and he will continue to occupy a key position in the District administration.

DISTRICT ADMINISTRATION

The powers and changing role of the District Officer has been amply explained. Now we proceed to the working of District administration as a whole.

Definition of District Administration. Before we discuss the District administration, it is rather essential to define the term, the District administration. Mr. S.S. Khera has explained meaning of District administration in the following words :

> "District administration includes all the agencies of Government, the individual officials and functionaries, public servants, including a public servant who is a Government servant and equally one who is not. For the term public servant includes many who are not Government servants as such. It comprehends all institutions for the management of public affairs in the District ; all the bodies corporate such as the Panchayats of different kinds, the Gram Sabhas, the Nyaya

Panchayats (which are courts of law), the Panchayat Samitis, the Zila Parishads, Municipal Committees and Local Bodies of every kind. It includes all advisory bodies associated with the administration as well as individuals serving in such a way as assessors and jurors do in the trial of cases. There may be an advisory committee, for instance, to advise the District Magistrate in the issuing of arms licences' in the District or any advisory committee for the selection of Honorary Magistrates and indeed for many other purposes."[1]

The definition of the District administration of Mr. S.S. Khera is quite comprehensive and it covers in details various aspects of the District administration. It lays great emphasis upon the Panchayati Raj. Now we take up various aspects of the District administration.

Various Departments of the District

There are various departments working at the District level, prominent among them being Police, Jails, Health and Medical, Education, Public Works Department, Civil Supplies, Judicial Organisation, Irrigation, Agriculture, Industries, Revenue Department, etc. Now we deal with them one by one.

1. *Police.* The Head of the Police organisation in the District is called the IG (Inspector General of Police). His main responsibility is to maintain law and order and prevention and detection of crimes and prosecution of offenders. He is assisted in this respect by a number of other Police officials, namely, Superintendent of Police, Deputy Superintendent of Police, Inspectors, Sub-Inspectors, Assistant Sub-Inspectors and Head Constables. The Superintendent of Police is under the Deputy Inspector-General of Police in departmental matters but in matters affecting law and order he is directly under the Deputy Commissioner. To keep the control of the Deputy Commissioner or the District Officer effective over the Superintendent of Police, the annual police administration report prepared by the Superintendent of Police is submitted through the District Officer to the State Government. The District Officer closely examines that report and makes his own suggestions or comments. The District Officer can inspect the Police Stations.The character roll or the Superintendent of Police is initiated by the District Officer in Rajasthan and elsewhere. Besides that there is a close collaboration between the Police and the District Officer regarding criminal intelligence work. Whenever any Magistrate accompanies a procession and the Police wants to fire or use force in case of any disturbance, it has to seek the approval of the Magistrate in duty before doing so.
2. *Jails.* The District Jails are under the General control of the District Officer, though for routine purposes there is a Superintendent or Deputy Superintendent of Jails in-charge of the District Jail. Superintendent or Deputy Superintendent of Jail is under the Inspector-General of Prisons, though he closely collaborates with the District Officer in other matters. Previously Civil Surgeon or the District Medical Officer used to be in-charge of the District Jail but the practice has been given up now. Civil Surgeon or the District Medical Officer may examine the food, etc., given to the prisoners and he may give his report to the Superintendent of Jail or the District Officer who may make any change in the food accordingly.
3. *Health and Medical Departments.* The Health and Medical Departments are two separate Departments in the District, though both of them are ultimately under the Health Minister of the State. The Health Department is Directly under the District Health Officer who in departmental routine work is directly under the District Health Officer who in departmental routine work is directly under the Director of Health. The Medical Department is under the District Medical Officer who in departmental matters and routine work is directly under the Inspector-General of Hospitals. Both the Director of Health and Inspector-General of Hospitals are under the Health Minister of the State. The Health Department and Medical

1. S.S. Khera, *District Administration in India*, p.5.

Department work in close collaboration with the District Officer. In case of an epidemic like plauge, malaria, cholera, etc., it becomes the responsibility of all these officers to adopt control measures. Similarly, whenever there is mismanagement of anything in the departments and cause unrest in the public then the District Officer becomes specially concerned. The District Officer sees that these departments work smoothly in the public interest. The District Officer is also the in-charge of post-mortem of the dead bodies which are brought before it by the Police. The District Medical Officer after doing postmortem submits its report and the Government or the Police case against the murders proceeds before the Magistrate on that basis. Similarly, the Health Department has to check the adulteration in foodstuffs and the District Officer is directly concerned with it. Therefore, these departments maintain close contact in common matters.

4. *Education Department.* The District Officer is directly interested in the spread of literacy and general welfare of his District. Therefore, the Adult Education Centres and the public libraries are established by mutual consultation of D.C. and D.E.O. The District Officer also sees that there is no grave unrest or large-scale agitation in the schools and colleges of his District and if there is any serious threat to law and order, then he deliberates upon the measures in consultation with the District Education Officer and other Educational authorities of his District to maintain peace. The District Education Officer exercises supervision upon the schools of his district and in purely departmental work, he is directly under the Minister of Education of his State.
5. *Public Works Department.* The District Executive Engineer is incharge of the Public Works Department. This department is divided into three main branches—Roads and Buildings, Electricity and Irrigation. Each branch has a separate Executive Engineer. All these branches work in close co-operation with Deputy Commissioner because he is directly interested in the construction of roads, Government buildings, and extending the facilities of electricity and irrigation, particularly in rural areas.
6. *Civil Supplies Department.* The District Supplies Officer is incharges of this Department. He allots quotas of cement and other controlled commodities to the people. If the Government decides rationing of any commodity, then this department undertakes the same, as this department is responsible for the proper distribution of the Government controlled commodities to the people. The District Officer sees that there is no grave unrest amongst the people and the department works without any let or hindrance.
7. *Judicial Organisation.* Judicial Organisation of the District is headed by the District and Sessions Judge. He exercises original jurisdiction in murder cases committed to his court by a First Class Magistrate. He enjoys appellate jurisdiction in both civil and criminal cases. Appeals are made to him against the decisions of the First Class Magistrate in criminal cases and Senior Sub-Judge in civil cases. District and Sessions Judge can award a death sentence but that needs confirmation by the High Court. He works under the control of the High Court. His appointment, posting and transfer is made by the Governor in consultation with the High Court according to Article 233 of the Indian Constitution. Both the District Judge and District Officer work in close co-operation as both of them are interested in the smooth working of the Lower Courts (District Courts).
8. *Irrigation, Agriculture and Industries*. As has already been stated, Irrigation Department is under a separate Executive Engineer. He looks after the entire irrigation work of his District and provides irrigation facilities to the agriculturists and realises the dues from them. The Agricultural Department is under the Extra Assistant Director of Agriculture. He maintains agricultural farms on which some research work and new experiments regarding agriculture

are conducted. Besides that he tries to disseminate knowledge of improved seeds. Whenever there is any locust invasion or the cultivation suffers in any way, he takes up the rescue work of his District with him staff.

The Industries Department has a separate Officer at the District level. Regarding big industries this officer only sees that all those conditions are fulfilled by the industrialists which are laid down in the various Factories Acts. The Industries Department also ensures that the minimum wages to the workers are given and in case of accident or death, the workers are given proper compensation by the industrialists. Regarding small-scale industries, there is a departmental organisation in the State and there are some local officials at the District level. The District establishment looks to their smooth working, general prosperity and progress. Besides that the Zila Parishads, Panchayat Samities and Panchayats also look to the advancement of the industries.

9. *Revenue Department, Sub-Divisional Officers and Tehsildars*. For revenue purposes a District is divided into a number of subdivisions tehsils or taluqas. The Collector is the chief of Revenue Department of the District. He is further assisted by the Sub-Divisional Officers, Tehsildars, Naib Tehsildars, Kanungo, Patwaries, etc. Important Tehsils in the Punjab and some other States have been made sub-divisions and the additional powers of the First Class Magistrate have been conferred on the Sub-Divisional Officers. So now in Punjab they are called Sub-Divisional Magistrates who enjoy both the powers to hear revenue and criminal cases. In some States as in Uttar Pradesh, Sub-Divisional Officers are called Deputy Collectors or Revenue Divisional Officers as in Kerala and Tamil Nadu or an Assistant Collector as in Maharashtra and Gujarat. The Sub-Divisional Officer is in-charge of a Sub-Division, which is a particular portion of the District as discussed earlier. The Tehsildar is in-charge of Tehsil which does not enjoy the status of Sub-Division. The Tehsildar is also called by different names. Though in the northern States of India, he is generally called Tehsildar but in Gujarat and Maharashtra he is called Mamlatdar and in Orissa, at least in one District, he is called the Taluqa Officer. Naib Tehsildar is also called the Deputy Tehsildar in some States of India.

In the village, Patwari is the pivot of the Revenue administration. He is called by different names in different parts of the country. In Punjab he is called Patwari, while in U.P., he has been given more recently the designation of *Lekhpal* (writer), while in Bihar he is called *Karamchari*, in Gujarat, Maharashtra, Madhya Pradesh and Karnataka he is called the Patel. In Orissa, the Patwari is called the village Munsif or Judge of Uttar Pradesh. Kanungo is also an important revenue official above the Patwaris. He is also called by different names in different parts of the country. He is called so (Kanungo) in Punjab and Uttar Pradesh but in other parts of India he is called a Circle Officer or a Revenue Inspector or a dependent Deputy Tehsildar. All the records concerning the District revenue, land acquisition and reforms, sale purchase or division of land and fields are maintained by this Department. The Patwari maintains the record of various village holdings which shows not only all the changes regarding their sale, purchase and division but also their size, the nature of the soil and the crop grown on it.

We have dealt with the various departments' working in the District. The Post Office and Railways, though, are important departments but all are outside the scope of District administration and are a reponsibility of the Central Government.

Role of the District Officer in regard to the various departments of the District. Some Departments have very close relationship with the District Officers, while others have a very distant relationship. As the District Officer, he is the head of the District administration as a whole, so various departments have to work in harmony under his general supervision only. Various departments work without any let or hindrance on his part and whenever any such furore arises in any Department which might disturb the public sector or peace, then the District Officer becomes deeply concerned.

Sometimes it also happens that the smooth working of the various departments is hindered due to the lack co-ordination, in that case the District Officer imparts a unity of approach. Again sometimes various officers come to the Deputy Commissioner with some difficulties which can only be removed by him (the Deputy Commissioner). Therefore, the Deputy Commissioner or the District Officer, by playing a leading part in the District administration, by becoming the accelerator, is a mediator and co-ordinator between offices and officers.

He has to pay his special attention to the implementation of the Five-Year Plans and all the development schemes of his district.

N.B. The Panchayati Raj, though an important part of the District administration, requires a seperate treatment. Therefore, it will be dealt with in the next chapter.

EXERCISES

Long Answer Type Questions :

1. What do you know about District Officer ? What are its duties ?
2. Discuss the position of District Officer in the changed circumstances.
3. Define District Administration. What do you know about various departments of the District ?

Short Answer Type Questions:

1. What is importance of District ?
2. What is the duty of District Officer as a Collector ?
3. What are the duties of a Collector as a District Megistrate ?
4. What are the duties of Deputy Commissioner ?
5. What are the duties of a District Officer as a District Development Officer ?
6. Define District Administration.

Objective Type Questions:

Choose the correct answer

1. The District Officer as a Collector is the head of
   (*a*) Revenue Department (*b*) Police Department
   (*c*) Development Department (*d*) None of the above
2. As a District Megistrate the duty of collector is
   (*a*) To punish Criminals (*b*) To maintains Law and Order
   (*c*) To Supervise Police Department (*d*) None of the above.

ANSWERS

1. (*a*) 2. (*b*)

26

CHAPTER

Panchayati Raj or Local Self-Government

> *"Local institutions constitute the strength of free nations. A nation may establish a system of free governments but without municipal institutions, it cannot have the spirit of liberty"*
>
> **—De Tocqueville**

Necessity and Importance of Local Self-Government

Leacock has said, "The distinction between local and Central Governments lies partly in their relative constitutional positions and partly the nature of public services performed." Local self-governing institutions may be called the cradle for democracy. They provide the best training in good citizenship. They are primary schools for the future parliamentarians and national leaders. In the complicated political structure of today, the three vital organs of the Government remain burdened with duties of different types. Local problems demand on the spot enquiry and quick solutions. This demand is met best by the local institutions. Besides relieving the pressure on the Government, the local bodies serve some other useful purposes. They bring about awakening in the people of the locality and arouse their active interest in problems which concern them vitally. They moreover, make the citizens feel actively associated with the administrative machinery of their country.

Local institutions have very deep roots in Indian soil. History tells us that every Indian village in olden times had a village panchayat which used to function as an autonomous body, The panchayats were largely free from State interference. They were mainly concerned with administrative and judicial work. Their working was so efficient that every village community was a sort of small republic. Sir Charles Metcalf goes to the extent of saying, "They (village communities) seem to last where nothing else lasts. Dynasties tumble down, revolution succeeds revolution. Hindu, Pathan, Moghul, Maratha, Sikh and English—all are masters in turn but the village communities remain the same." The village communities by their unwillingness to change have been in the past preserves of Indian culture and Indian way of life. Above all the local self-governing institutions as a rule are more efficient and economic. The councillors or corporators know well that any waste of money means loss and disadvantage to the tax-payers. They as such work more judiciously and sincerely.

The distribution of powers between the Centre, the State and local bodies is not based on any rigid principles. It is difficult to define their respective scopes. Gilchrist similarly observes : "It can be described but not defined, for a definition requires limits and local government and Central Government cannot always be clearly demarcated. As a rule, subjects that concern the whole country, *viz.*, defence, external affairs, currency, inter-State commerce and customs are administered by the Centre. Education, jail and revenue are managed by the State Governments. Subjects like primary education, sanitation, drainage, street light and registration of births and deaths are handled by the local bodies.

DEVELOPMENT OF LOCAL BODIES

Development of Local Institution during the British Times. Steps were taken during the Viceroyalty of Lord Ripon who has been rightly called the Father of Local Self-Government in India. He directed the Provincial Governments to maintain and extend a network of local boards in every district and also that the boards should have independent sources of income. He suggested that the local bodies have limited jurisdiction and the official element in them was not to exceed one-third of the whole. He allowed the boards to elect their chairmen also. His scheme thus was a landmark in the growth of municipal institutions in India. Some of Lord Ripon's suggestions were approved by the Crown and thus the beginning of a major and real experiment in local self-government was made in India. Ripon's scheme and policy, however, was not carried out by his successors. The progress in this direction became slow. The local bodies could not deliver the goods because they continued to be under too much control of the Government. Secondly, their sources of income were inadequate. Lastly, the elective element continued to be weak and ineffective.

Montford Reforms were proposed to remove the above-said evils in the municipal system. It was expected that under the dyarchical system of Government, the machinery would be set in order. The Department of Local Self-Government, no doubt, was transferred into the hands of an Indian Minister but the Minister incharge could not do much on account of lack of funds. They key portfolio of Finance continued to be under the charge of an Executive Councillor who had no sympathy for nation-building schemes.

Things improved under the Act of 1935 which granted autonomy to the Provinces. The popular Minister who looked after the department of Local Self-Government did not have handicap of funds. But two years after entering upon office, the Congress ministries submitted their resignation. The system of local administration thus drifted along without any radical change till the advent of independence in 1947.

Progress of Local Bodies after Independence

The Constitution of free India contains specific provisions for the progress of local bodies. The State Government went ahead with Panchayati Raj Acts. The Panchayats were formed in every village, with adequate powers to deal with local affairs. Most of the district boards have been dissolved and their functions have now been entrusted to Zila Parishads or Panchayats.

One of the directive principles of the Constitution of India is that the State shall take steps to organise village Panchayats and endow them with such power and authority as may be necessary to enable them to work as units of self-government. In pursuance of this directive, nearly all the States rushed through a legislation and now nearly whole of the country today has been covered with Panchayats. This number has been increasing steadily. These bodies are endowed with power and responsibilities for the development of the areas they represent. The Panchayats send representatives to the Block Samitis. The Block Samitis have a Chief Executive Officer as their Development Officer. All other Panchayats have Tehsildar as their executive chief. The Panchayat Samitis are fully empowered to make budget and formulate schemes for village development. They are assured of getting all sort of technical or administrative help from the State.

PHILOSOPHY AND OBJECTIVES OF PANCHAYATI RAJ

Recommendations of the Balwant Rai Mehta Committee Report. On 12th January, 1958, the National Development Council endorsed the recommendations made by the *Balwant Rai Mehta Committee* on Democratic Decentralisation. The Central Council in 1959 took stock of the action taken by the States to implement the decision of the National Development Council and recommended that :

"While the broad pattern and the fundamentals may be uniform, there should not be any rigidity in the pattern. In fact, the country is so large and Panchayati Raj (Democratic Decentralisation) is so complex a subject with far-reaching consequences, that there is the fullest scope of trying out various patterns and alternatives. What is most important is the genuine transfer of power to the people. If this is ensured, form and pattern may necessarily vary according to conditions prevailing in different states."

This recommendation has largely determined the policy of the Government of India in the matter. Accordingly there has been no insistence on the States to follow a given or prescribed pattern. Only certain fundamentals or basic principles of Panchayati Raj have been emphasised. The important ones are:

(*a*) It should be a three-tier structure of local self-governing bodies from the village to the District, the bodies originally linked up.

(*b*) There should be genuine transfer of power and responsibility to them.

(*c*) Adequate resources should be transferred to the new bodies to enable them to discharge these responsibilities.

(*d*) All development programmes at these levels should be channelled through these bodies.

(*e*) The system evolved should be such as will facilitate further devolution and dispersal of power and responsibilities in the future.

States have evolved patterns of Panchayati Raj suitable to local conditions in the light of these principles. Panchayati Raj has revolutionised administration and called for new codes of administrative relationship and behaviour. Each State stands to benefit from the experience of other and can add, alter or change its own system in order to improve its working. The entire approach is pragmatic as Panchayati Raj is a growing concept and there is no finality or rigidity about the pattern or system evolved at any time.

Panchayati Raj is a culmination of the recognition given by our Constitution to the role of Panchayats. One of its Directive Principles enjoins that the State shall take steps to orgainse village Panchayats and endow them with such powers and authority as may be necessary to enable them to function as units of self-government. The devolution of powers is an implementation of a Directive.

Panchayati Raj aims to make democracy real by bringing the millions into functioning of democracy. It is a system of grass roots democracy which seeks to link the individual family in the remotest village with the Central Government. The basic unit of self-government is the family. The family has been guaranteed certain fundamental rights which cannot be interfered with by the State. But there are certain spheres of activity which can only be executed by several families collectively. These activities will obviously have to be left to an organisation called the village Panchayat. It is essential to build up the Panchayat as a dynamic organisation which can look after all the facets of life of the village community. It has to draw its strength and sanction from the village people as a whole, simultaneously working in close co-operation with self-governing bodies at higher levels in an organic setup.

Shri Jayaprakash Narain observed, *"Panchayati Raj institutions should act as the units of self-government at the village, Block and District levels. In acting as the units of self-government, they will undertake responsibilities which they can discharge within the framework of their resources and requirements. It would mean that what the Panchayat cannot undertake will be accomplished by the Samiti and what the Samiti cannot do by itself will be transferred to the next higher unit. It should be stated that in a few years' time these institutions should be enabled to flourish and function on their own as governments at their respective levels."*

The Panchayats must constitute a strong base for a three-tier structure of self-governing institutions located at block and district levels. Responsibilities and activities which fall beyond its scope will be surrendered by the Panchayat to the next higher body which is called the Panchayat Samiti. While the Samiti will look after these activities it will also try to use the Panchayat as its agent for some of its numerous tasks.

The Panchayat Samiti will be linked to the next higher body at the District level known as Zila Parishad. The latter will guide the former in technical and administrative matters and engage in activities which only a district organisation can discharge effectively. This process of assuming responsibilities with the requisite authority within its own sphere and surrendering those which involve inter-unit co-operation are the main features of the Panchayati Raj system. In other words, as one steps down these three tiers, the co-ordination and policy-making functions decrease correspondingly to the executive responsibilities which increase at the village level, the Panchayat becomes mostly as an executive body.

It will be seen that by this pattern Panchayati Raj will bring about a complete link-up of the millions in this country from the Gram Sabha to the Lok Sabha. It seeks to bring to the individual family the highest guidance available from Parliament downwards. People will be free to handle matters within specified sphere without interference from others. This freedom to think, plan and work will draw out the latent initiative and ability in every individual for the growth and welfare of the family and the community. Panchayati Raj is thus a way of life and involves a new approach to Government.

Implementation of Panchayati Raj. Panchayati Raj was first introduced in Rajasthan in October 1959 and after it has also been introduced in all states with the exception of Meghalaya, Nagaland and Mizoram. It had also not been introduced in Lakshdweep, but after the efforts are being made in that direction and soon it will follow the model of other States. Kerala and Jammu and Kashmir have also taken steps to introduce the Panchayati Raj.

Though there are a little variations in the pattern of Panchayati Raj of different States, yet everywhere in India three-tier system has been followed except Delhi, where in the absence of Zila Parishads, Circle Panchayats have been introduced in between the Block Panchayat Samiti and the Gaon Sabha, but before we describe it, it is necessary to give some idea of the Gram Sabha which is a bigger body than the Panchayat and a real repository of the sovereign will be the people of the villages.

GRAM SABHA AND PANCHAYATS

The lowest ladder of the Panchayati Raj is Gram Sabha. It is generally known as Gram Sabha except in Assam, U.P. and Delhi where it is known as Gaon Sabha, in the Bihar where it is known as Panchayat and in Orissa where it is known as Pali Sabha. Gram Sabha is the General body of the village Panchayat and consists of all the eligible voters in the jurisdiction of the Gram Panchayat which extend over a village or a group of villages. It functions through its executive, generally known as Gram Panchayat except in Assam, U.P. and Delhi, where it is known as Gaon Panchayat, in Gujarat where it is known as Gram or Nagar Panchayat, in Tamil Nadu where it is known as Village or Town Panchayat, in Kerala and Karnataka where it is known as Panchayat and in Bihar where it is known as the Executive Committee of Panchayat. The Gram Sabha is recognised as a statutory body in all the States except Jammu and Kashmir, Kerala, Tamil Nadu, Karnataka and Rajasthan, the Panchayat Acts provide for the meetings of all the adult residents of the Panchayat area. In Tamil Nadu and Kerala there is no provision for Gram Sabha.

In Andhra Pradesh, Assam, Bihar, Gujarat, Madhya Pradesh, Maharashtra, Orissa, Punjab, Uttar Pradesh and West Bengal there is the provision of at least two meetings in a year. In Jammu and Kashmir there is a provision of at least one meeting in a year. In Karnataka and Rajasthan the number of the meetings has been prescribed by the Panchayat Acts. The Gram Sabha hear the annual statements of occupants, audit report of the preceding year and decide the programme of work for the ensuing year, the taxation proposals and any other specific schemes of a development nature involving community service, voluntary labour, ect.

GRAM PANCHAYATS

Composition of the Gram Panchayats. The Gram Panchayat is the executive of the Gram Sabha and is elected by the latter (Gram Sabha). The size of the Panchayat varies considerably from State to State. The number of the members of the Panchayat is being shown against each State: Andhra Pradesh (6—16); Assam (11—15); Bihar (9); Gujarat (9—15); Jammu and Kashmir (7—11); Kerala (7—15); Madhya Pradesh (5—15); Tamil Nadu (Madras) (5—15); Maharashtra (7—15); Karnataka (11—19); Orissa (11—15); Punjab (5—11); Haryana (5—9); Rajasthan (6—16); Uttar Pradesh (16—31); West Bengal (9—15); Andaman and Nicobar Islands (9—15); Delhi (4—11); Himachal Pradesh (7—15).

Duration. The term of the Panchayat is three years in Assam, Rajasthan, Delhi and Himachal Pradesh; While in Gujarat, Jammu and Kashmir, Maharashtra, Karnataka, Orissa, West Bengal, Andaman and Nicobar Islands, it is four years. In Punjab, Haryana, Andhra Pradesh, Kerala, Madhya Pradesh, Tamil Nadu, Uttar Pradesh the term or duration of the Panchayats is five years, while in Bihar the term of Tritiya Varga (third class or category) Gram Panchayats is three years, that of Dwitiya Varga Panchayats (second class) is four years and Pratham Varga (first class) Panchayat is five years.

Mode of Election of the Panches and Sarpanches. The Panches or the members of the Panchayat are elected by the Gram Sabha by secret ballot in all States except U.P., Assam, Jammu and Kashmir, and Himachal Pradesh where they are elected by show of hands. The Governments of Assam and U.P. have, however, decided to hold the next elections by secret ballot. The Sarpanches are elected by Gaon Sabha or Gram Sabha (directly by voters) in Assam, Bihar, Punjab, Haryana, Rajasthan, Uttar Pradesh and Himachal Pradesh while in Andhra Pradesh, Gujarat, Jammu and Kashmir, Kerala, Madhya Pradesh, Tamil Nadu, Maharashtra, Karnataka, Orissa, West Bengal, Andaman and Nicobar islands and Delhi, they are elected by the Panches. There is no Up-Surpanches (Deputy Sarpanches) in Punjab but in Assam and Himachal Pradesh they are elected by Gaon Sabha, while in Andhra Pradesh, Bihar, Gujarat, Jammu and Kashmir, Kerala, Madhya Pradesh, Tamil Nadu, Maharashtra, Karnataka, Orissa, Rajasthan, Uttar Pradesh, West Bengal, Andaman and Nicobar Islands and Delhi, they are elected by the Panches.

Number and Coverage of the Village Panchayats. There were 2,50,000 Panchayats in India covering more than 96 per cent of the villages.

Up to 2011, the institution of the village Panchayats covered all the States excepting Meghalaya, Nagaland and Mizoram. The institution of village Panchayat existed in all Union Territories except Lakshdweep. Slowly and gradually entire India will be covered by the these Panchayats.

Functions of Panchayats. The functions of the Village Panchayats may be classified under three categories :

(*i*) Civic Amenities.

(*ii*) Social Welfare Activities.

(*iii*) Development Work.

Sanitation, public health, street lighting, maintenance of village roads and schools, supply of drinking water, etc., come under the civic functions of the Panchayats and are considered obligatory functions of the Panchayats. Other functions of the Panchayats are optional. Social Welfare activities include maintenance of burning and burial ground, keeping the statistics of births and deaths, establishment of child welfare and maternity centres, control of cattle-pounds, propagation of family planning and promotion of agriculture. When the Panchayats do some development work, then they act as the agent of the Panchayat Samiti. The development activities of the Panchayat include the construction of roads, public buildings, wells, tanks schools, Panchayat houses, establishment of akharas (wrestling grounds), libraries, reading rooms, promotion of co-operative societies and cottage industries, looking after minor irrigation works, organising collective farms, etc.

Resources. The Gram Panchayats in all the States have been authorised to levy certain taxes, though there are considerable variations from State to State. The main sources of income of the Panchayats are : a tax on property, profession tax, a tax on animals and vehicles, cess on land revenue or rent. These taxes are generally compulsory. Panchayats are also empowered to levy some other taxes and fees like octroi, tax on shops, fees for the use of rest houses, drainage fee, light rate, water rate, etc., where such services are provided by the Gram Panchayats. The Panchayats also derive income from their property, investments, certain undertakings and public contributions. The resources of the Panchayats are further augmented by the grant received from the State Government.

Anchal Panchayat in West Bengal. Before we mention the Panchayat Samiti, it is essential to describe the Anchal Panchayats in West Bengal. Anchal Panchayats are constituted for a group of Panchayats. The Anchal Panchayats members are elected by the Panches of the constituent Gram Panchayats but no person can be a member of both these bodies.

The main functions of the Anchal Panchayats are: (i) Maintenance and control of *dafedars* and *chowkidars* for watch and ward, and law and other purposes; (ii) Management of State Government's properties; (iii) Supervision over Nyaya (Law) Panchayats; (iv) Such other duties as may be assigned by the State Government.

The Anchal Panchayat can levy taxes like vehicle tax, house tax, profession tax, property tax, etc.

NYAYA PANCHAYATS

Nyaya Panchayats have been constituted in Andhra Pradesh, Assam, Bihar, Gujarat, Jammu and Kashmir, Kerala, Madhya Pradesh, Maharashtra, Karnataka, Orissa, Rajasthan, U.P., West Bengal, Delhi and Himachal Pradesh but no Nyaya Panchayats had been constituted in Nagaland and Meghalaya upto 12 May, 1984. The term, jurisdiction and mode of election of the Nyaya Panchayats vary considerably from State to State. The term of Nyaya Panchayat is three years in Andhra Pradesh, Assam, Kerala, Orissa, Rajasthan, Delhi and Himachal Pradesh, it is four years in Gujarat, Jammu and Kashmir, Maharashtra and West Bengal, while it is five years in Madhya Pradesh and Uttar Pradesh. In Bihar the term of Tritiya Varga (Third Class) Nyaya Panchayats is three and of Dwitiya Varga Panchayats is four years, while for Prathama Varga Panchayat (First Class Nyaya Panchayat) the term is five years. The strength of the members of the Nyaya Panchayats also differs from State to State. The Head of Nyaya Panchayat is called Sarpanch in Bihar, U.P., Delhi and Himachal Pradesh. In Assam, Gujarat, Jammu and Kashmir, Kerala, Maharashtra and Rajasthan, he is called Chairman, while in Madhya Pradesh, West Bengal and Andhra Pradesh, he is called Pradhan, Pradhan Vicharak and Nyaya Adhyaksha respectively. The Head of the Nyaya Panchayat is elected by Gaon Sabha in Assam, Bihar, Maharashtra, while in Andhra Pradesh, Jammu and Kashmir, Madhya Pradesh, Orissa, Rajasthan and Uttar Pradesh, he is elected by Nyaya Panches. In West Bengal he is elected by members of Anchal Panchayat. In Kerala he is appointed by the State Government.

The State Governments divide a District into a number of circles. Each circle consists of some villages and for each circle a Nyaya Panchayat is constituted. The State Government decides how many members of the Nyaya Panchayat are to be appointed and in what manner they are to be appointed. The Nyaya Panchayats possess jurisdiction to hear some petty civil and criminal cases. They can impose the fine but cannot award a sentence of imprisonment. Generally there are no appeals against the decision of the Panchayats but in certain special cases the Sub-Divisional Magistrates and Sub-Judges or Munsifs have been empowered by the various Panchayat Acts of State Governments to hear appeals. In those cases they are empowered to set aside the decision of the Nyaya Panchayats. The Nyaya Panchayats have rendered a valuable service to the villagers. They have brought agreement in most cases amongst the contending parties and thus prevented their waste of money in suits. They have harmonised village life by preventing perpetual enmity, which otherwise litigation would have generated. The lawyers cannot appear before these Panchayats.

PANCHAYAT SAMITIS

Above the Panchayats and below the Zila Parishads is the body known as Panchayat Samiti in the States of Andhra Pradesh, Bihar, Maharashtra, Orissa, Punjab and Rajasthan. In U.P., it is called Kshetra Samiti, in Tamil Nadu as the Panchayat Union Council, in West Bengal as the Anchalik Parishad and in Assam as the Anchalik Panchayat. This body is at the block level in all States except Gujarat, Maharashtra and Karnataka. The Taluka Level body is known in Gujarat as the Taluka Panchayat and in Karnataka as the Taluka Development Board.

Similarly, the President of the Samiti is known as the 'President' in Andhra Pradesh, Assam, Gujarat, Madhya Pradesh, Karnataka and the West Bengal, while he is called Chairman in Maharashtra, Tamil Nadu, Orissa and Punjab. In Rajasthan, the President of the Samiti is designated as the Pradhan, while in Bihar and Uttar Pradesh he is known as the Pramukh.

Composition of the Panchayat Samitis. There are some variations from State to State regarding the constitution of Panchayat Samitis. However, the Panchayat Samiti generally consists of the Sarpanches of the Panchayats within the Samiti's jurisdiction or of members elected indirectly by the Panches or of directly elected members. Besides, special representation is provided to the weaker sections like women, scheduled castes and scheduled tribes. In Andhra Pradesh, Bihar, Gujarat, Orissa, Rajasthan and Uttar Pradesh, the President of the Gram Sabha are ex-officio members of the Panchayat Samiti. In addition, in Orissa, each Gram Panchayat also elects a person—other than a Panch—to the Panchayat Samiti. In Assam, the Gram Sabha directly elects its representatives to the Panchayat Samiti. In Karnataka the Taluka is divided into Constituencies and from each constituency two or three members are directly elected to the Taluka Development Board. In Tamil Nadu, the Panches of each Gram Panchayat elect one representative from among themselves to sit on the Samiti. In Madhya Pradesh, Maharashtra and Punjab, however, all the Panches within the block, or within some specified portions thereof, constitute an electoral college to elect the representatives of the Panchayats that should sit on the Panchayat Samiti. Beides, in Maharashtra and Uttar Pradesh, the local members of the Zila Parishad who are directly elected from the constituencies within the block are also members of the Panchayat Samiti. In West Bengal all the Pradhans of Anchal Panchayats are members of Anchalik Parishad. A prescribed number of women and persons from the scheduled castes and tribes are coopted as members of the Samiti in all States.

Functions of the Panchayat Samitis. The Panchayat Samitis look to the development work in all the States. They prepare the plans for the development work and when they are finalised by the Government, they are responsible for their implementation. They are also responsible for the execution of the Community Development programme. The Samitis take steps for the advancement of health, primary education, sanitation and communication within their area. They exercise supervision over the working of the Panchayats and can scrutinise their budgets and offer suggestions in Andhra Pradesh, Bihar and Gujarat, while in Assam, Orissa, Rajasthan and Maharashtra, the Samitis sanction the budget of the Gram Panchayats.

Finances of the Panchayat Samitis. The Panchayat Samitis receive that amount which is allotted by the State Governor for the development work within their areas. The finances of the Panchayat Samiti consist essentially of the funds drawn from the Block Budget. They can levy certain taxes and receive some share of the land revenue and grant from the Government.

Functioning of the Panchayat Samitis. The Panchayat Samitis function through many standing committees which look after their finances, development work, social welfare work, etc. The Presidents of the Panchayat Samitis are generally ex-officio members of all the important committees. The Block Development Officer acts as the Chief Executive Officer of the Block Samitis. Under him are various Extension Officers, Village Level Workers, etc. Block Development Officer and his staff look to the implementation of the Community Development and other work assigned by the Panchayat Samiti. The Panchayat Samitis exercise administrative control over him and his staff.

Panchayati Raj Institutions in the States. A three-tier system exists in Karnataka and Tamil Nadu but instead of Zila Parishads, they have the District Development Councils which are advisory bodies with no executive powers. Laws have been enacted to set up elected Zila Parishads in Karnataka, Assam, Haryana, Manipur and Orissa. Delhi and Pondicherry have a two-tier system while in the remaining States and Union Territories a one-tier system is operative.[1]

ZILA PARISHADS

Zila Parishad is the third and the highest tier at the District level. In Tamil Nadu, however, for the purpose of constituting the district level body, 12 Revenue Districts have been delimited into 21 Development Districts. The District level body is known as the District Panchayat in Gujarat, District Development Council in Tamil Nadu, while it is known as Zila Parishad in Andhra Pradesh, Maharashtra, Punjab, Rajasthan, Uttar Pradesh and West Bengal.

Constitution of the Zila Parishad. The Zila Parishad generally consists of the representatives of the Panchayat Samiti and some representatives of the weaker sections. Besides M.Ps, M.L.As and M.L.Cs—with or without voting rights—and directly elected members are also on the Zila Parishads in some States. For example, in West Bengal the M.L.As and M.L.Cs exercise voting rights but in other States of India they do not exercise the right to vote. Except in Jammu and Kashmir, Kerala, West Bengal, and Tamil Nadu, special representation to scheduled castes and scheduled tribes has been given in all the States. Special representation has also been given to women in all the States of India except Tamil Nadu, Kerala, Jammu and Kashmir. The Presidents of the Panchayat Samitis are ex-officio members of the Zila Parishads in all the States. In Uttar Pradesh, Maharashtra and Gujarat some members of the Zila Parishad are directly elected. In West Bengal, the Zila Parishad has two representatives of Adhyakshas of Gram Panchayats of each subdivision. The Chairman of the Zila Parishad is elected by the members of the Panchayat Samiti. In the States of Gujarat, Punjab and Uttar Pradesh, the Panchayat Samitis elect a representative to sit on the Zila Parishad.

Functions of the Zila Parishad. The functions and powers of Zila Parishad vary considerably from State to State. In Tamil Nadu, the Zila Parishad is a co-ordinating body which exercises a general supervision over the working of Panchayat Samitis and advises the Government on the implementation of the development schemes. In Andhra Pradesh Zila Parishads approve budgets of Panchayat Samitis and distribute funds among Panchayat Samitis or Blocks, co-ordinate plan and supervise activities of the Samiti, advise Government on development activities, etc., establish and maintain secondary, vocational and industrial schools. In Maharashtra, Zila Parishad is the strongest body and it looks to the educational needs of backward classes including grant of scholarships, maintenance of hostels, etc. It implements programmes for economic development and programmes for welfare of backward classes. It is also responsible for the following: (1) Establishment, maintenance and inspection of primary, basic and secondary schools, dispensaries and hospitals, primary health centres and

1. *Competition Success Year Book*, 1991, p. 681

maternity and child welfare centres; (2) construction and maintenance of roads, parks, lights, railways and tramways and telephone lines; (3) water supply and drainage, minor irrigation works; promotion of local industries and local arts, promotion and execution of co-operatives; (4) rural broadcasting, community development works, rural housing, village uplift; (5) maintenance of poor houses, etc.

In Uttar Pradesh the Zila Parishad is responsible for the following functions: (1) Classification of fairs, festivals, roads, etc. (2) General supervision of Gaon Panchayats and Kshetra Samitis. (3) Construction and maintenance of public roads, bridges, human and veterinary hospitals, schools above primary stage and up to junior high schools, library, ect. (4) Water supply, preparation of district plans and review and co-ordination of Kshetra Samiti Plans. (5) Distribution of *ad hoc* grants allocated by the Government or other bodies.

We have given above examples of some States. In rest of the States more or less similar functions are discharged by the Zila Parishads. In brief, we can say that the Zila Parishads look to the development work of the District, co-ordinate and supervise the activities of the Panchayat Samitis and Panchayats; establish and maintain or expand secondary, technical and industrial schools; provide relief in times of scarcity; establish markets, schools, libraries, dispensaries, primary health centres; construct and maintain roads and buildings. In Jammu and Kashmir and Kerala the Zila Parishads have not been established as yet but it is expected that they will be established very shortly.

Finances of Zila Parishads. The finances of the Zila Parishads consists of the grants received from the Government and share in the land cess and local taxes. The Zila Parishads get those funds which are allotted by the Government for development purposes. The Zila Parishads in some States have been allowed to levy certain taxes or enhance the taxes already levied by the Panchayat Samitis and Panchayats subject to a certain limit.

Note. See 73rd & 74th Amendments (given assent in May, 1993) in Chapter 15 for statutory changes in Panchayats and urban bodies.

EXERCISES

Long Answer Type Questions:

1. Discuss the necessity of Local Self-Government. Discuss its importance also.
2. Discuss in brief the condition of Local Institutions during British Rule. Discuss also the progress of Local Bodies after independence.
3. Discuss the philosophy and objectives of Panchayati Raj.

Short Answer Type Questions:

1. Write a note on Gram Sabha and Panchayats.
2. What is Gram Panchayat? Discuss its composition and functions also.
3. What do you know about Nyaya Panchayats ?
4. Write a note on Panchayat Samiti.
5. What are the functions of Panchayat Samitis?
6. Discuss Zila Parishad.

Objective Type Questions:

Choose the correct answer

1. Who was the father of Local Self-Government in India during British Rule ?
   (*a*) Lord Ripon (*b*) Lord Mountbettan
   (*c*) Lord Linlithgo (*d*) Lord Dalhausie

2. In which year the National Development Council endorsed the recommendations made by the Balwant Rai Mehta Committee on Democratic Decentralization ?
   (*a*) 1957 (*b*) 1958
   (*c*) 1959 (*d*) 1960
3. In which year The Central Council look stock of the action taken by the States to implement the decision of the National Development Council ?
   (*a*) 1957 (*b*) 1958
   (*c*) 1959 (*d*) 1960
4. In which State Panchayati Raj was first introduced ?
   (*a*) Madhya Pradesh (*b*) Andhra Pradesh
   (*c*) Uttar Pradesh (*d*) Rajasthan
5. Which is the lowest ladder of the Panchayati Raj
   (*a*) Gram Sabha (*b*) Nyaya Panchayat
   (*c*) Gram Samiti (*d*) Zila Parishad

ANSWERS

1. (*a*) 2. (*b*) 3. (*c*) 4. (*d*) 5. (*a*)

27

CHAPTER

Pressure Groups (Anonymous Empire)

"Groups like structures in society are multifunctional. Patterns of group identity, mobilisation and politicisation have a significant impact on the patterning of cleavages within the society, but they may also serve as critical agents of social integration and as channels of communication between the individual and the State. Perhaps the primary function of the groups, however, is to serve as mechanism for the articulation of demands and the processing of group claims for the political system. —*Stanley A. Kochaneck*

Difference between Party and Pressure Group. Leacock says, "By a political party we mean more or less organised group of citizens who act together as political unit. They share or profess to share the same opinions on public questions and by exercising their voting power towards a common end, seek to obtain control of Government." On the other hand, a Pressure Group consists of those people who without gaining formal control of the government try to influence the behaviour of the Ministers, legislators (M.Ps and M.L.As) and government officers through various means in order to achieve their specific ends.

Significance of Pressure Groups. The study of pressure groups has become extermely important ever since Arthur Bentlay wrote in *The Process Government* (1908) and David B. Truman made a significant improvement on it in his book *The Government Process* (1936). However, V.O. Key Jr. in his book *Politics, Parties and Pressure groups*(1954) made a monumental contribution in this direction. Since then many writers have been attracted towards this important field of study. Prof. S.E. Finer has called these pressure groups as 'anonymous empire'. Thorsten Sellin and Richard D. Lambert have 'termed these pressure groups as 'unofficial government' and D.D. Mckean have designated them as unofficial government. These pressure groups are especially active in democratic systems because there they can influence Ministers, legislators and administrators easily while it is not so in communist countries. Therefore, vast literature has appeared on this subject in the United States, Britain, France and Italy. Their techniques to influence the government are especially studied now-a-days. Myron Weiner in this regard points out, that "*Choice of techniques employed by individuals or groups to influence public policy and administration is determined not only by the structure of the political system but also by the attitudes within and outside the government*".

Like western democracies, these pressure groups are also active in India, therefore, foreign writers like Myron Weiner and Stanely A. Kochnek and many Indian writers have been doing strenuous efforts to study carefully the techniques and role of these pressure groups.

TYPES OF PRESSURE GROUPS IN INDIA

Pressure groups in India can be broadly classified as under:

1. Business Groups

Business groups in India exercise tremendous pressure on the policies of the government, legislators and administrators. Federation of India Chambers of Commerce and Industry maintains its office in New Delhi and acts as a lobbying agency. Besides that individual industrial houses like Delhi Cloth Mills, Birlas, Tatas, the Dalmias, the Singhanias and the Thapars, etc., also exercise substantial influence upon the government by various means. They give donations to political parties and make contributions to various public funds. They also set up remunerative jobs in industrial firms and oblige the political leaders and administrators by employing their men there. They also give big donations to charitable institutions and construct dharamshalas and temples and invite ministers to preside over the religious functions. They invite the Ministers to inaugurate various industrial plants. So they influence the policies of the government and the laws by various means.

Besides the Federation of Indian Chambers of Commerce and Industry, other pressure groups in the business are (1) All-India Manufacturers'Organisation, (2) Associated Chambers of Commerce.

2. Trade Unions or Labour Organisations

In the Trade Unions which exercise a lot of influence upon the Government and act as a pressure group to protect the interests of the labour class are: (1) All India Trade Union Congress; (2) Indian National Trade Union Congress; (3) Hind Mazdoor Sabha; (4) United Trade Union Congress; (5) Hind Mazdoor Parishad.

These labour organisations are mainly attached to various political parties. For instance All India Trade Union Congress is attached to Communist Party of India. Indian National Trade Union Congress (INTUC) is attached to the Congress. Hind Mazdoor Sabha is attached to Socialists. United Trade Union Congress is attached to CPM (Communist Party of India, Marxist). Hind Mazdoor Parishad was formerly attached to Jana Sangh. Now it is attached to Bharatiya Janata Party (BJP). Trade Unions mainly struggle for the improvement in working conditions and hours, protection against automation or retrenchment, and a share in the management, etc.

It is deplorable that the labour is so much divided in India. It cuts at the root of the unity of the labour movement. Therefore, Crough rightly observes, "*For many Indian trade unionists and observers of Indian trade unionism, its worst feature is its divisions into four main federations and numerous, unaffiliated local units. This feeling is reflected in the almost universal tendency found in the official pronouncements of trade unions to advocate some sort of reunification of the trade union movement. A by-product of this is the equally universal tendency to denounce political 'unionism' and to put the blame for disunity on the interference of political parties in the other three federations.*"

3. Agrarian or Peasant Organisations

Like the business and the labour farmers and peasants have also organised themselves into unions to protect their interests. The history of the agrarian movement in India dates back to the pre-independence period. The credit goes to Sardar Vallabhbhai Patel for organising the peasants under umbrella of the Indian National Congress. Sardar Vallabhbhai Patel was himself a peasant and he frequently said that his only culture was agriculture. So All India Kisan Congress was founded by him and he was elected its first president.

The Indian National Congress adopted the following agrarian resolution in 1936 at its Lucknow session:

"The most important and urgent problem of the country is the appalling poverty, unemployment, and indebtedness of the peasantry due fundamentally to antiquated and repressive land tenure and revenue systems and intensified in recent years by the great slump in prices or agricultural produce. The final solution of this problem invariably involves the removal of British recognition by the State of its study to provide work for the unemployed rural masses."

After some times the name of All India Kisan Congress was changed and it became All India Kisan Sabha.

In the post-independence period several agrarian Organisations came into being. The names of such organisations are: (1) Hind Kisan Panchayat controlled by the Socialists and united Kisan Sabha controlled by the Marxists of the country. Other peasant organisations are Jharkhand Party in Bihar and Peasant Party in Maharashtra.

The most important event in the history of agrarian movement took place when Shri Raj Narain founded the All India Kisan sammelan (Farmers' conference) on the birth day of his mentor Choudhry Charan Singh on December 23, 1978. The policies and programmes of the All-India Kisan Sammelan are given in a Declaration on the State of Economy and charter or demands. It was announced on the Kisan Day (December 23) in 1978 that its main demands were the following:

"(1) demand for parity in prices in order to make the terms of trade more favourable to the farmers without delay; (2) increase in the income of the farmers and the establishment of a Kisan Bank to supply them credit on a lower rate of interest; (3) fight for economic democracy in the Gandhian tradition; (4) abolition of all unnecessary control and restrictions; (5) diversion of public funds for the development of irrigation and agriculture including bridges, roads, cold storages, tube-wells, warehouses, etc. (6) revision of import-export policy in the interest of production and sale of industrial goods; (7) reservation of at least 50 per cent of additional generation of electricity for utilisation in rural areas; (8) availability of fertilisers at a lower price; (9) allocation of at least 20 per cent of inevitable resoures for irrigation purposes; (10) opening of agricultural polytechnics in every district; (11) exemption of holdings below 1.25 hectares form land revenue; (12) establishment of a planning board in each district; (13) reduction of Central excise duties on farm machinery like tractors and motors; (14) decentralisation of powers so as to make panchayati raj a more effective system; (15) due representation to farmers in various committees empowered to take decisions affecting rural areas; (16) provision of an effective machinery to hold buffer-stocks; (17) immediate implementation of all land reforms schemes, etc. Besides announcing the charter of demands the leaders of Kisan Sammelan at the grand Kisan Rally asked the then Janata Government to implement all promises given in its Election manifesto towards rural reconstruction and also issued a strong threat of direct action in case nothing was done in the desired direction.[1]

4. Religious and Cultural Organisations

In this category the following religious and cultural organisations fall (1) Anglo-Indian and Christian Associations; (2) Catholic Bishops Association; (3) Jamat-e-Islami; (4) Arya Samaj; (5) Majlis-e-Ithad-ul-Musalmeen; (6) Rashtriya Swayam Sweak Sangh; (7) Republican Party; (8) Akali Dal.

Amongst all these religious and cultural organisations from the point of view of pressure groups, Akali Dal is most powerful because at the same time it is political organisation and started the agitation on August 4, 1982 to get its religious-cum-political demands accepted. That movement turned violent later on and resulted in the killings of some hundred people and huge loss to industries. It engaged greater attention of the Government of India during 1983 and 1984. A detailed narrative of these demands has been given in the last chapter. Every above mentioned cultural and religious organisation is doing its best to protect the interests of its community. R.S.S. is another effective organisation of the Hindus. It preserves Hindu interests.

1 *The Times of India*, New Delhi, December 29, 1988.

5. Caste Organisations

Among the caste organisations following organisations fall : (1) Scheduled Castes Federation; (2) Vannijakul Khatriya Sangam; (3) Gujrat Kshatriya Sabha; (4) Dravida Munnetra Kazhagam; Anna-DMK; (5) Republican Party. These organisations protect the interests or their castes through various means. Anna-DMK (Anna Dravida Mennetra Kazhagam has been a ruling party in Tamil Nadu and wields considerable influence amongst the opposition parties.

6. Tribal Organisations

Among the Tribal organisations following organisations are included; (1) Jharkhand (Hul) in Bihar; (2) All India Jharkhand in Bihar and Orissa; (3) Naga National Convention; (4) Tribal Sangh of Assam; (5) Tribal League of Assam; (6) United Mizo Federal Organisation; (7) Khasi-Jaintia Rurla Organisation (Assam); (8) Khasi-Jaintia National Federated State Conference; (9) Garo National Conference; (10) Eastern India Tribal Union; (11) Mizo National Front. They protect the interests of their tribes through various means.

7. Linguistic Groups

In this category fall Andhra Mahasabha, Tamil sangh and Hindi Sahitya Sammelan. While Andhra Mahasabha works for the promotion of Telugu language, Tamil Sangh works for safeguarding the interests of Tamil language, Hindi Sahitya Sammelan works zealously to protect the interests of Hindi throughout India and sees that Hindi is promoted by the Central Government in the offices as a national language.

8. Students and Youth Organisations

In this category fall the following organisations: (1) National Students Union of India; (2) Students Federation; (3) Akhil Bharatiya Vidyarthi Parishad; (4) Progressive Students Organisation; (5) Socialist Students Organisation; (6) Samajvadi Yuvjana Sabha; (7) Yuva Janata; (8) Gana Sangram parishad; (9) All Assam Students Union.

Most of these student-organisations have leanings towards one or another party. These organisations promote and protect the interests of the students. Gana Sangram Parishad and All Assam Students Union continued their agitations for a long time to check the influx of refugees from Bangla Desh into Assam because there was every likelihood that the people of Assam would be reduced to minority in their own land.

9. Organisations representing the Gandhian heritage

In this category fall various organisations like Gandhian Institute of Studies, Varanasi, Gandhi Peace Foundation, Delhi, Gandhi Smarak Nidhi, New Delhi, etc. They were run by the disciples of Gandhiji in order to protect his cherished heritage. Acharya Vinoba Bhava and Shri Jaya Prakash Narian worked for the long time to preserve the precious heritage of Gandhiji, Various Gandhian Organisations wielded considerable influence upon the government and got liberal grants in the past to run these organisations because the Congress has been at the helm of affairs of the country since independence except for a brief spell of Janata rule. Even the Janata Government was wedded to the policies of Gandhiji. After that Janata Dal remained in power.

Techniques of the Pressure Groups

The Pressure Groups in India are not so strong as in U.S.A. but amongst all the Pressure Groups which we have in our country, business pressure groups are the strongest. They maintain their offices in New Delhi and try to influence the Ministers, M.Ps. and administrators by various means. The most potent method in their hands is the big donations to the political parties. Secondly, they give remunerative jobs to the relatives and friends of those VIPs who exercise tremendous influence upon the government to get their own newspapers and praise or criticise the policies of the government as it suits them. So by controlling the newspaper industry, they exercise tremendous pressure upon the government policies.

EXERCISES

Long Answer Type Questions:

1. What is difference between Political Party and Pressure Group? Discuss significance of Pressure Group.
2. Discuss the types of Pressure Groups in India.

Short Answer Type Questions:

1. Discuss business pressure groups.
2. Discuss Trade Unions or Labour organisations as Pressure groups.
3. Discuss Agrarian or Peasant organisation as pressure group.
4. Write a short note on Religious, Cultural and caste organisation in the role of Pressure Groups.
5. Write a short note on Tribal organisations, Linguistic Groups, Student and youth organisations in the role of Pressure Groups.
6. Discuss the techniques of Pressure Groups.

Objective Type Questions :

Choose the correct answer

1. The study of Pressure Groups has become extermely important ever since Arthur Beutlay wrote is his book "The Process Government. In which year this book published ?

   (*a*) 1908 (*b*) 1909
   (*c*) 1910 (*d*) 1911

2. David B. Truman made a significant improvement on it is his book 'The Government Process'. In which year this book Published ?

   (*a*) 1935 (*b*) 1936
   (*c*) 1937 (*d*) 1938

3. V.O. Key Jr. is his book 'Politics, Parties and Pressure Groups made significant contribution to clear the importance of Pressure Groups. In which year this book published ?

   (*a*) 1952 (*b*) 1953
   (*c*) 1954 (*d*) 1955

4. Which author has called these Pressure Groups as 'anonymous empire' ?

   (*a*) D.D. Mckeau (*b*) Thorsten Sellin
   (*c*) Richard D Lambert (*d*) Prof S.E. Finer

ANSWERS

1. (*a*) 2. (*b*) 3. (*c*) 4. (*d*)

CHAPTER 28

Article 370 of the Constitution of India (Special Provisions for Jammu and Kashmir)

The constitution of India provides for uniform rule over the whole country. But certain regions of the country are governed by special provisions. These provisions ensure the protection of cultured identities, customs, economic and political interests of the original inhabitants of these areas. One of them is Jammu and Kashmir, Jammu and Kashmir is a constituent state of Indian Union, but its constitutional position and its relation with the Central Government, somewhat differ from that of other State and the same enjoys special autonomy which is enstrined in part xxi under article 370 of the constitution of India, according to which, no law enacted by the Parliament of India, except for those in the field of defence, communication and foreign policy, will be extendable in Jammu and Kashmir unless it is ratified by the State legislature of Jammu and Kashmir, Subsequently, jurisdiction of the Supreme Court of India over Jammu and Kashmir has been extended.

The State was acceded to Dominion of India by Maharaja Hari Singh, who was the ruler of the state in 1947 at the time when India was itself burning in the flames communal riots. Jammu and Kashmir is also the only Indian State that has its own flag and constitution, and Indian from other states cannot purchase land or property in the state. Designed by the then ruling National Conference, the flag of Jammu and Kashmir features a plough on a red background symbolizing labour substituted the Maharaja's State Flag.

The internal position of the Jammu and Kashmir was also not far better than India communal disturbances and hunger for power in the subcontinent were provocating the religious feelings of community in order to fulfil their long awaited desire to assume political supremacy. The division of the sub-continent on the basis of religion was creating hindrances in achieving the very objective of "Independence".

HISTORICAL BACKGROUND

There are some constitutional changes that took place in the state of Jammu and Kashmir. The letter dated October 27, 1947, the Governor General, the Maharaja of Jammu and Kashmir, Hari Singh, offered to accede the Dominion of India. On March 5, 1948 the Maharaja issued a proclamation forming a responsible government of the Council of Ministers headed by the Prime Minister which was to take steps to constitute a National Assembly bases on adult franchise to frame a constitution for the state. On November 25, 1949, Yuvraj Karan Singh, to whom the power was entrusted by the Maharaja, issued a proclamation directing that the constitution of India to be adopted by the constituent Assembly of the State insofar as it was applicable in Jammu and Kashmir in order to govern the relationship of the state and the contemplated union of India. The Constitution of India was adopted on November 26, 1949, and on the same day some of its provisions came into force and the remaining provisions came into force on January 26, 1950. In October 1947, the accession was made by the ruler in favour of India in consideration of certain commitments made by Pt. Jawahar Lal Nehru the then Prime Minister of India. It was in the pursuance of those commitments that Article 370 was incorporated in the Constitution of India. Article 370 of the constitution of India dealt with the relationship of the State of Jammu and Kashmir with the union of India. On January 26, 1950 the constitution which was applicable to Jammu and Kashmir order, 1950 was made by the President of India. On April 20, 1951, the Maharaja issued a proclamation in pursuance of which the Constituent Assembly of the State submitted the interim report recommended that—

(*a*) The form of the future constitution of Jammu and Kashmir shall be wholly democratic.

(*b*) The institution of hereditary rulership shall be terminated.

(*c*) The office of the Head of the state shall be elective.

RECOMMENDATIONS ADOPTED BY THE CONSTITUENT ASSEMBLY

The Constituent Assembly of the State by a resolution adopted these recommendations. The relevant part of the resolution is as follows :

(1) (*i*) That the Head of the State shall be the person recognised by the President of the Union the recommendations of the Legislative Assembly of the State :

(*ii*) He shall hold office during the pleasure of the President ;

(*iii*) He may, by writing under his hand addressed to the President resign his office;

(iv) Subject to the foregoing provisions, the Head of the State shall hold office for a term of five years from the date he Centers upon his office ;

Provided that he shall, notwithstanding the expiration of his term, continue to hold office until his successors enters upon his office;

(2) That the recommendations of the Legislative Assembly of the State in respect of the recognition of the Head of the State specified in sub-para (1) of paragraph 1, shall be made by elections.

(3) That the Head of the State shall be designated as the Sadar-i-Riyasat.

On May 14, 1954, in exercise of the power conferred by Article 370 (1) of the Constitution of India, the President, with the concurrence of the government of the State, made the Constitution of (Application to Jammu and Kashmir) Order, 1954. It superseded the earlier Order of 1950, and extended the application of various provisions of the Constitution of India to the State. One such provision was Article 368 but a proviso was added to the effect that **"no State of Jammu and Kashmir unless applied by order of the President under clause (1) of Article 370"**. On November 17, 1956, the Jammu and Kashmir Constitution was adopted. Some sections of the Constitution came into force on January 26, 1957.

The State of Jammu and Kashmir is a part of Indian Territory and is included in the List of States in the First Schedule of the Constitution.

How Special Position of Jammu and Kashmir is Different from Other States?

The position of this State differs from other States in the following respects :

Gist of Special Provisions	
• **Legal Power of the Parliament.**	• The legislative authority dealing of the Union Parliament in respect of this state is limited to those matters in the Union List and Concurrent List which are declared by the President, in consultation with the government of the State, to conform the term of the Instrument of Accession.
• **Separate Constitution.**	• The only State in India i.e. Jammu and Kashmir has a separate Constitution which was adopted on November 17, 1956 and came into force on 26th January, 1957.
• **Provisions Related to Emergency.**	• The power does not vest with the Union to declare Financial Emergency in the State. The Union can declare emergency in the State only in case of War or External Aggression. No proclamation of emergency made on the grounds of internal disturbance or imminent danger thereof shall have effect in relation to the state unless the following situations arises : It is made at the request or with the concurrence of the government of the state; or where it has not been so made, it is applied subsequently by the President to that state at the request or with the concurrence of the government of that state.
• **Fundamental Rights, Directive Principles of State Policy and Fundamental Duties.**	• Article 19 (1) (f) and Article 31 (2) of the Constitution are still applicable to Jammu and Kashmir. • Supplementary to above, Directive Principles of State Policy and Fundamental Duties are also not applicable to Jammu and Kashmir.
• **High Court of Jammu and Kashmir.**	• The High Court of J & K has very limited powers as compared to other High Courts within India. • It can't declare any law unconstitutional. Unlike High Courts in other states, under Article 226 of the Constitution, it can't issue writs except for enforcement of Fundamental Rights.

• **Official Languages.**	• The official language for communication between one state and another; or between a state and the Union. • The official language of the Union; • The language of the proceedings in the Supreme Court; • Urdu is the official language of Jammu and Kashmir but use of English is permitted for official purposes unless the state legislature provides otherwise.
• **Preventive Detention Laws.**	• The power of legislation regarding preventive detention laws vests in the State Legislature alone and not in the Parliament.
• **Other provisions of the Constitution of India**	• The other provisions of the Constitution of India shall apply to Jammu and Kashmir as the President may by order specify.

Power of the President under Article 370

Article 370 clearly States that due to the special position given to State of Jammu and Kashmir, the President is given the power to apply the provisions of the Constitution to that State subject to such exceptions and modifications as the President may by order specify. The President has power to say by order that certain provisions of the Constitution will be accepted from application to the State of Jammu and Kashmir and on such order being made those provisions would not apply to that state. Besides this power of making exceptions, the President is also given power to apply the provisions of the Constitution with such modifications as he thinks fit. The meaing of the word 'modification' used in article 370 (1) must be given the widest effect, including making racial modifications.

How can we Amend Article 370 when the Constituent Assembly of Jammu and Kashmir no longer Exists ?

According to the provision enshrined under Article 370 (3) of the Constitution of India, consent of the Constituent Assembly of the State Legislature are required to amend Article 370. This issue has been raised at par. Various Constitutional Experts and Jurists are silent on this aspect. Some of them say it an be amended by an amendment Act under Article 368 of the Constitution of India and the amendment Extended under Article 370 (1), but the proper answer is yet to come. In reality, this is the actual Status of Article 370 which is still a very debatable and mooted question and remains unanswered.

Judicial Approach

Now, let us see the vital role played by the judiciary in the light of the following decided cases which are related to Article 370 of the Constitution of India.

In the case of Sampat Prakash v. State of J & K : The main issue which was raised by the petitioner was based on the fact that Article 35 (C) of Jammu and Kashmir Constitution (Application to Jammu and Kashmir) Order, 1954, had given protection any law relating to preventive detention in Jammu and Kashmir against invalidity on the ground of infringement of any one of the fundamental rights guranteed by part III of the Constitution for a period of five years only. Subsequently this period was extended to ten years and later to fifteen years by the Presidential order dated 1959 and

1964. These extensions were challenged by the petitioner on the ground that the orders making such modifications could not be validly passed by the President under Article 370 (1). Article 370 could only have been intended to remain effective until the constitution of the states was framed and thereafter it must be held to become ineffective that any modification made by the President subsequent to the enforcement of the constitution would be without any authority of law. The above argument was rejected by the Supreme Court and held Article 370 should be held to be continuing in force because the situation had existed when this article was incorporated in the constitution had materially altered, and the purpose of introducing this article was to empower the President to exercise his discretion in applying Indian Constitution and a reference was also made that Article 368 is of no consequence in the State of J & K unless applied by the President under Article 370 (1).

In the case of Mohd. Damnoo v. State of J & K : The petitioner challenged the validity of his detention under the J & K preventive Detention (Amendment) Act, 1967, on the ground that the Act is invalid as it has not been asserted to by the Sardar-i-Riyasat of the State. On November 16, 1952, the President had made an order substituting another Explanation for the existing one in clause (1) of Article 370, as "For the purpose of this article, the Government of the State means the person for this time being recognised by the President on the recommendation of the Legislative Assembly of the State as the Sardar-i-Riyasat of J & K, acting on the advice of Council of Ministers of the State for the time being in office." According to the counset on behalf of the petitioner, neither the State Assembly nor the President were competent to impair the functioning of the Sardar-i-Riyasat of the State unless the Constitution of India was amended under Article 368 and 370 (3) or a fresh Constituent Assembly was Convened to amend the Explanation. The above argument was not accepted by the Supreme Court and the Court explained the following feature of Article 370 (1) (*b*) and (*d*) is the necessity of the concurrence of the State Government. Article 370 (1) merely recognised a constitutional position in the State. It was contended Article 370 (1) (*b*) and (*d*) places no limitation on the farming or amendment of the constitution of J & K. Basically, it was pointed out that the change in the designation and the mode of appointment of the Head of the State, the Constitutional position in the State remains basically the same and the Governor is the successor to the Sardar-i-Riyasat and can validly exercise his powers as Head of the State.

Conclusions

With the passage of time, **The constitution (Application to Jammu and Kashmir) order, 1954** was promulgated by the President of India in consultation with the Government of J & K, regulating the constitutional status of the State; and apart from it several Central laws got extended to the J & K State and even the nomenclature of Sadar-i-Riyasat and Prime Minister were changed to Governor and Chief Minister on March 30, 1965.

The state of Jammu and Kashmir which is a constituent unit of the Union of India, shall, in its relation with the Union, continue to be governed by Article 370 of the Constitution of India.

Despite of continuous efforts by various political parties. Article 370 of the Indian Constitution could neither be made permanent nor abolished, so it continues to be as such in the Indian Constitution with J & K having its own Constitution and State flag and resulting into non-application and non-extension of Central laws without approval of the State Legislature.

EXERCISES

Long Answer Type Questions:

1. What is article 370 of Indian Constitution ? What are its provisions ? Discuss in detail.
2. How special position of Jammu and Kashmir is different from other States ? Discuss in brief.

Short Answer Type Questions:

1. What is historical background of article 370 ? Discuss in brief.
2. Discuss in brief the recommendations adopted by the Constituent Assembly of Jammu and Kashmir.
3. What are the powers of President under article 370 ? Discuss in brief ?
4. How can we amend article 370 when the constituent assembly of Jammu and Kashmir no longer exists.
5. What are the judicial approach on article 370 ?

Multiple Choice Type Objective Questions :

1. Article 370 is related from which state :
   (*a*) Jammu and Kashmir (*b*) Tripura
   (*c*) Meghalaya (*d*) Nagaland
2. Who was the ruler of Jammu and Kashmir in 1940.
   (*a*) Karan Singh (*b*) Maharaj Hari Singh
   (*c*) Ram Ratan Singh (*d*) None of these
3. At present what position is of Jammu and Kashmir ?
   (*a*) Not integral part of India (*b*) Totally free from India
   (*c*) Integral Part of India (*d*) None of these

ANSWERS

1. (*a*) 2. (*b*) 3. (*c*)

Appendix – 1

Karnataka Legislative Assembly election, 2013

A Legislative Assembly election was held on 5 May 2013 for 223 out of all 224 assembly constituencies in Karnataka, India. The Indian National Congress emerged as the majority party winning 121 seats defeating the incumbent Bharatiya Janata Party which won only 40 seats. The Janata Dal (Secular) and Karnataka Janata Paksha won 40 seats and 6 seats respectively. Congress won the Periyapatna assembly polls held later, taking the total number of MLAs of ruling side of 122 in the 224-member assembly.

Background

In 2008, the Bharatiya Janata Party emerged victorious winning 110 seats. Although the party fell short of a clear majority, it was able to form the government with the support of 6 independents. This was the first time the BJP came to power on its own in Karnataka and in any south Indian state.

Election

The election was held in a single phase on 5 may 2013 for 223 out of total 224 seats. A voter turnout of 70.23 was recorded. 50,446 polling stations were set up for the 4.18 crore voters in Karnataka. Election in the constituency of Periyapatna had been adjourned due to the death of the BJP candidate, Sannamogegowda, a day before polls.

Following the defeat, Chief Minister Jagdish Shettar submitted his resignation on 8 May. Governor H.R. Bhardwaj later appointed INC legislative leader Siddaramaiah as the next Chief Minister.

Votes were counted on 8 May.

Summary of results of the Karnataka Legislative Assembly Election, 2013.

Political Party	Flag	Candi-dates	Seats Won	Net Change in seats	% of Seats	% of Votes	Change in % of vote
Congress		223	122	▲43	54.26	36.6	▼1.8
BJP		222	40	▼72	17.93	20.1	▼13.9
JD(S)		222	40	▲12	17.93	20	▲1.1
KJP		203	6	▲6	2.69	9.8	▲9.8
BRS Congress		175	4	▲4	1.79	2.7	▲2.7
Samajwadi Party		27	1	▲1	0.45	0.3	▼0.6
Karnataka Makkala Paksha		7	1	▲1	0.44	0.2	▲0.2
Sarvodaya Karnataka Paksha		6	1	▲1	0.44	0.3	▼0.1
Independent		1217	9	▲3	4.03	7.4	▲0.5
		Total	**223**	**Turnout**	**70.23%**	**Voters**	**4,36,00,000**

Appendix – 2

In 2012 Assembly elections were held in seven states. The tenure of the assemblies of Goa, Gujarat, Himachal Pradesh, Manipur, Punjab, Uttar Pradesh and Uttarakhand expired during the year. In the first rounds of elections, Manipur and Punjab resulted in an incumbent government victory; while in UP and Goa there was a heavy anti-incumbency wave and Uttaranchal resulted in an hung assembly, which resulted in coalition government.

Punjab

The Punjab assembly election was held on 30 January 2012. Shiromani Akali Dal-BJP combine emerged victorious as the alliance bagged 68 seats in a 117-member assembly. Shiromani Akali Dal chief Parkash Singh Badal became the chief minister of the State.

Shiromani Akali Dal & BJP	–	68
Congress Alliance	–	46
Other	–	3

Uttarakhand

Uttarakhand witnessed a hung house as none of the party got the majority. While the Congress pocketed 32 seats, the BJP finished at 31. Congress, however, formed the government with support of 4 BSP MLAs. Vijay Bahuguna was appointed as the chief minister of the hilly state.

BJP	–	31
Congress	–	32
Other	–	7

Gujarat

The 2012 Gujarat assembly election was held in the Gujarat in two phases 13 through till 17 December, 2012. As per the results, Chief Minister Narendra Modi led BJP was chosen by people of Gujarat giving it a majority with 115 seats. The BJP has been in power in Gujrat since 1995.

BJP	–	115
Congress	–	61
Other	–	6

Uttar Pradesh

UP assembly election was held in Uttar Pradesh, from 8 February through till 3 March, 2012. Samajwadi Party had won more than 80 seats. The incumbent CM Mayawati's Bahujan Samaj Party was defeated by Samajwadi Party. Akhilesh Yadav, son of SP leader Mulayam Singh Yadav, was sworn in as the 33rd Chief Minister of UP.

SP	–	224
BSP	–	80
BJP	–	47
Congress	–	28
Other	–	24

Goa

The Goa assembly election result were announced on 6 March, 2012. BJP defeated the incumbent Congress government in Goa. The election was won by the BJP–Maharashtrawadi Gomantak alliance, which won 24 seats in the 40–seat assembly. BJP leader Manohar Parrikar was sworn in as Chief Minister of Goa.

BJP Alliance	–	24
Congress	–	9
Other	–	7

Manipur

Chief Minister Okram Ibobi Singh brought the Congress back to power in Manipur for a third consecutive time, winning a simple majority in the 60-member Assembly. The ruling party has won all the 42 constituencies.

Congress	–	42
TMP	–	7
Other	–	11

Himachal Pradesh

The Himachal Pradesh legislative assembly election results were declared on December 20, 2012. Congress defeated BJP and won outright majority by bagging 36 of the 68 assembly seats. Congress leader Virbhadra Singh was sworn in as state's chief minister for a record sixth term.

Congress	–	36
BJP	–	26
Other	–	6

Appendix – 3

INDIAN PARLIAMENT COMPLETES 60 YEARS OF ITS EXISTENCE

On May 13, 2012, the Indian Parliament completed 60 years of its existence. To commemorate the occassion a special sitting of both houses was organised. India bacame a republic on 26 January, 1950 but the first general elections were held in 1952. Constituted on April 17, 1952, the Lok Sabha held its first session a month starting May 13.

President Pratibha Patil (now former) addressed the joint sitting of the two houses of the parliament. She congratulated the MPs and the people on upholding the glory and dignity of the Parliament.

On this occassion parliamentarians vowed to uphold and maintain the dignity of the August house and make it an effective instrument of change and strengthen the democratic values and principles.

Members of both the houses also resolved to enhance the accountability of Government towards people through Parliament oversight and rededicate themselves in the sacred task of nation building and also said that more has to be accomplished.

Parliament is Supreme

Cutting across the party lines, MPs made it very clear that supermacy of Parliament must be preserved, holding that laws are made by it and not by mobs. This was a veiled reference to civil society campaign against parliamentarians during the course of Lok Pal movement.

Parliament Building : A Brief History

Indian Parliament was designed by two famous architects — Sir Edwin Lutyens and Sir Herber Baker, who were also responsible for the planning and construction of New Delhi. The Duke of Cannaught laid the foundation stone of Parliament House on 12th February 1921. The construction of the building took six years and the opening ceremony was performed on the 18th January 1927 by the then Governor-General of India, Lord Irwin. The cost of construction for the building was ₹ 83 Lakhs.

Interesting Facts About Lok-Sabha

Education

— The percentage of MPs without secondary education has decreased from 23 per cent in 1952 to 3 per cent in 2009.

— The Percentage of graduates has increased from 58 per cent in 1952 to 79 per cent in 2009.

— The percentage of postgraduates has increased from 18 to 29 per cent.

Women

— There are 11 per cent of women MPs in 15th Lok Sabha. In comparison only 5 per cent of MPs in the 1st Lok Sabha were women.

— The percentage is still lower in comparison to other countries. In Sweden it is 45 per cent, Argentina it is 37 per cent.

No. of days

— Lok Sabha met for an average of 127 days in the 1950s and Rajya Sabha for 93 days. This has decreased to 73 days for both houses in 2011.

No. of bills passed

— The first Lok Sabha passed an average of 72 bills each year. This has decreased to 40 bills a year in the 15th Lok Sabha.

— Parliament passed 118 bills in 1976. This was the highest number of bills passed by Parliament in a single year.

— The lowest number of bills was passed in 2004. In this year, only 18 bills were passed.

INDEX

PART - I

PART - II

PART-III